baseness = bad

yet base → supports all else

BIOLOGICAL SCIENCE

A Molecular Approach

BSCS Blue Version
Seventh Edition
BSCS

Pikes Peak Research Park
5415 Mark Dabling Blvd.
Colorado Springs, CO 80918-3842

Revision Team:
Katherine A. Winternitz, BSCS, Revision Coordinator
William J. Cairney, BSCS, Revision Coordinator
Edward Drexler, Pius XI High School, Milwaukee, WI
Lynda B. Micikas, BSCS
Jean P. Milani, BSCS
George Nassis, Ward's Natural Science Establishment, Inc.
Ken Rainis, Ward's Natural Science Establishment, Inc.
Richard D. Storey, The Colorado College
Douglas Swartzendruber, University of Colorado, Colorado Springs
Martha Taylor, Cornell University
Richard R. Tolman, Brigham Young University

 D.C. Heath and Company
HEATH **Lexington, Massachusetts   Toronto**

Biological Science: A Molecular Approach

BSCS Blue Version, Seventh Edition

The *BSCS Blue Version* program includes the following components:
Pupil's Edition
Teacher's Annotated Edition
Study Guide, Pupil's Edition
Study Guide, Teacher's Annotated Edition
Teacher's Resource Book
Computer Test Bank
Computer Test Bank, Teacher's Guide
Overhead Transparencies with Concept Maps

D.C. Heath Staff
Executive Editor: Ceanne P. Tzimopoulos
Supervising Editor: Rosemary E. Previte
Editorial Development: Anne Renwick Boy, Kathryn A. Goldner, Leslie Williams Marsh
Design Manager: Lisa Fowler
Designer: Prentice Crosier
Production Coordinator: Donna Lee Porter
Laboratory Safety Consultants: Jack A. Gerlovich, Ph.D., Jay A. Young, Ph.D.
Readability Testing: J & F, Incorporated

BSCS Production Staff	**Artists**	**BSCS Administrative Staff**
Terri J. Johnston	Janet Chatlin Girard	Timothy Goldsmith, Chair, Board of Directors
Linda K. Ward	Carl J. Bandy	Joseph D. McInerney, Director
	Bill Border	Rodger W. Bybee, Associate Director
	Kathy M. Foraker	Larry Satkowiak, Chief Financial Officer
	Lewis Keller	
	Marjorie C. Leggitt	
	David J. Roberts	
	Roy Udo	

Cover Design: Caroline Bowden

Cover Photo: False-color scanning tunneling micrograph (STM) of DNA. A sample of uncoated, double-stranded DNA was dissolved in a salt solution and deposited on graphite prior to being imaged in air by the STM. An STM image is formed by scanning a fine point just above the specimen surface and electronically recording the height of the point as it moves. The main feature of this image is a right-handed, double-stranded DNA molecule (a DNA duplex), which appears as the row of orange/yellow peaks at center-left. These peaks correspond to the ridges of the DNA double-helix. Magnification × 1 600 000 at 6 × 7 size.

Cover Photo Credit: Lawrence Livermore Laboratory/Photo Researchers, Inc.

Back Cover Inset Photos (top to bottom): Science Source/Photo Researchers, Inc.; Ken Eward/Science Source/Photo Researchers, Inc.; Irving Geis/Science Source/Photo Researchers, Inc.; Ken Eward/Science Source/Photo Researchers, Inc.

Published simultaneously in Canada
Printed in the United States of America
International Standard Book Number: 0-669-31600-8
2 3 4 5 6 7 8 9 10-RRD-99 98 97 96

FOREWORD

All around us, life on Earth is engaged in an ancient and delicate dance of interdependence, and although we humans are only recent partners in this performance, we are deeply involved. We are involved biologically, because all life is related. We are involved intellectually, because evolution has blessed us with mental capacities that allow us to probe the complexity of life in ever-greater detail and—today—to manipulate living systems in ways that were mere science fiction when you were in elementary school. And we are involved emotionally, because biology engages the human spirit at very basic levels. We not only *know* that we are part of the living world, we *feel* it—in our love of pets and zoos, in the pleasure we feel while in our gardens, in our fascination with the primates that are our closest cousins.

These days, it is virtually impossible to avoid exposure to the implications of modern biology. Television news programs announce the discovery of a gene that is associated with breast cancer; newspapers report on the use of DNA analysis in criminal cases, popular magazines discuss the most recent discoveries about human evolution, and rock stars warn about over-population, starvation, and threats to tropical rain forests. Although such issues may appear unrelated at first glance, they actually illustrate a rather small number of major principles that are common to all living systems. These principles help to inform our study of biology, and they provide the foundation for this book:

- evolution: patterns and products of change
- interaction and interdependence
- genetic continuity and reproduction
- growth, development, and differentiation
- energy, matter, and organization
- maintenance of a dynamic equilibrium
- science, technology, and society

BSCS Blue Version approaches these seven principles largely from the perspective of molecular biology and focuses on minute structures such as cells and genes, as well as on the processes related to them. It would be a mistake, however, to assume that one can understand life on earth only by studying its smallest parts, because all of these parts and their processes ultimately exert their effects in whole organisms, which in turn interact with their external environments. This book will introduce you to the nature of some of those interactions as well. Equally as important, BSCS Blue Version will introduce you to the nature of science. It will require you to use the intellectual tools of inquiry that are common to all of science, which is a unique and powerful system for asking questions about the natural world.

As you work with your fellow students and your teacher to improve your understanding of biology, you will encounter a variety of intellectual challenges (and maybe even some frustration) about the intricacies of life on earth. But we hope you also will find that the rewards of your study are great. For as you uncover some of the mysteries of living systems, you likely will develop an increased sense of wonder and respect for life's stunning complexity, yet elegant simplicity.

If we have done our job well, this book will leave you with an improved understanding of the myriad steps in life's dance of interdependence. In addition, you will have acquired the insights necessary to make informed decisions about personal and societal issues that have their roots in biology, and the skills necessary to debate those issues—sometimes passionately, but always mindful of reason and civility.

We hope you, your fellow students, and your teacher will let us know whether we have accomplished our goals. We welcome your feedback, and we welcome you to the seventh edition of BSCS Blue Version.

BSCS Blue Version Revision Team
Katherine A. Winternitz and William J. Cairney, Coordinators

CONTENTS

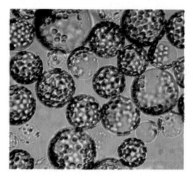

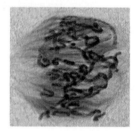

**Unit 3
Genetic Continuity**

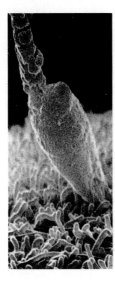

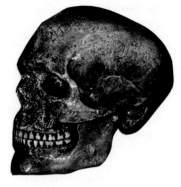

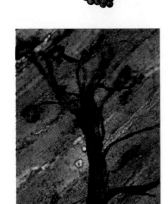

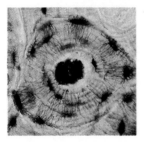

Unit 6
Organisms and Their
Environment

Chapter 25: Animal Interactions 555

Chapter 26: Interrelationships 575

Biological
Challenges

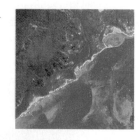

Laboratory Investigations

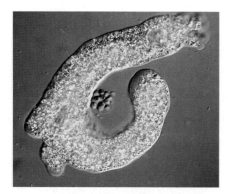

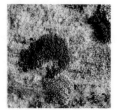

APPENDICES

ACKNOWLEDGMENTS

Contributors
Barbara Andrews, Colorado Springs, CO
Richard Benz, Wickliffe High School, Wickliffe, OH
Edward Drexler, Pius XI High School, Milwaukee, WI
Scott Greenhalgh, Tempe High School, Tempe, AZ
Barbara Grosz, Pine Crest School, Ft. Lauderdale, FL
Gerald Joyce, The Scripts Research Institute, LaJolla, CA
Barbara Littlewood, Madison, WI
Joseph D. McInerney, BSCS, Colorado Springs, CO
Lynn Margulis, University of Massachusetts, Amherst, MA
Donald Mason, Colorado Springs, CO
Barry Mitchell, Brigham Young University, Provo, UT
George Nassis, Ward's Natural Science Establishment, Rochester, NY
Gordon Peterson, San Marino High School, San Marino, CA
Carl Pierce, The Don and Sybil Harrington Cancer Center, Amarillo, TX
Kenneth G. Rainis, Ward's Natural Science Establishment, Rochester, NY
Dorion Sagan, Science Writers, Boston, MA
John Settlage, Quincy High School, Quincy, IL
Carol Leth Stone, Science Writer, Alameda, CA
Dennis Travis, Bloomfield Hills Lahser High School, Bloomfield Hills, MI
Patricia L. Waller, Tower Hill School, Wilmington, DE

Reviewers of the Seventh and Previous Editions
Steve Almond, Halliburton Services, Oxnard, CA; Aimee Bakken, University of Washington, Seattle, WA; Bob Barela, Bishop Manogue High School, Reno, NV; Warren Bennett, Hampton High School, Hampton, VA; Richard Benz, Wickliffe High School, Wickliffe, OH; Mary Ann Braus, Chadwick School, Palos Verdes Peninsula, CA; Lornie Bullerwell, Dedham High School, Dedham, MA; Jack Carter, The Colorado College, Colorado Springs, CO; Ron Clarno, Sunset High School, Beaverton, OR; Donna Coffman, Colorado Springs, CO; Wilma M. Giol de Rivera, Colegio San Ignacio de Loyola, Puerto Rico; Steve DeGusta, J.F. Kennedy High School, Sacramento, CA; Kevin de Queiroz, University of California, Berkeley, CA; James Enderson, The Colorado College, Colorado Springs, CO; Raymond G. Edwards, Tamaqua Area High School, Tamaqua, PA; Frank Fitch, Ben May Institute, Chicago, IL; Al Fruscione, Lexington High School, Lexington, MA; Suzanne S. Galando, Mt. Pleasant Area Senior High School, Mt. Pleasant, PA; Lotte, R. Geller, Roeper, The School for Gifted Children, Bloomfield Hills, MI; JoAnne Gray, Corliss High School, Chicago, IL; Barbara Grosz, Pine Crest School, Ft. Lauderdale, FL; Edward A.J. Hall, Catonsville High School, Catonsville, MD; Robert C. Heck, Moniteau High School, West Sunbury, PA; Bobbie S. Hinson, Providence Day School, Charlotte, NC; Michael Hoffman, The Colorado College, Colorado Springs, CO; Dick Howick, Belmont High School, Belmont, MA; Marlene H. Jacoby, Charlotte Country Day School, Charlotte, NC; Duane Jeffery, Brigham Young University, Provo, UT; Marian S. Johnson, River Dell Regional Schools, Oradell, NJ; Eric E. Julien, Turlock High School, Turlock, CA; Robert Jurmain, San Jose State University, San Jose, CA; John C. Kay, Iolani School, Honolulu, HI; Donald W. Lamb, Manning High School, Manning, IA; Barbara Lester, M.A., Ransom Everglades School, Coconut Grove, FL; Stephen R. Lilley, J.E.B. Stuart High School, Falls Church, VA; Daniel R. Lipinski, Bishop Eustace Preparatory School, Pensauken, NJ; Lynn Margulis, University of Massachusetts, Amherst, MA; Robert Martin, Colorado State University, Fort Collins, CO; Robert T. Mills, P.S.B.G.M., Montreal, Quebec, Canada; Janice Morrison, Hathaway Brown School,

Shaker Heights, OH; Jeff Murray, University of Iowa Hospitals, Iowa City, IA; Joseph D. Novak, Cornell University, Ithaca, NY; Larry Ochs, The Norwich Free Academy, Norwich, CT; Gordon Peterson, San Marino High School, San Marino, CA; Annette Prioli-Lee, St. Bernard High School, Playa Del Ray, CA; Robert L. Ragley, Beachwood High School, Beachwood, OH; Ken Rainis, Wards Natural Science Establishment, Rochester, NY; R. Ward Rhees, Brigham Young University, Provo, UT; John A. Rhodes, Avery Coonley School, Downers Grove, IL; Ailene Rogers, National Cathedral School, Mt. St. Albans, Washington, DC; Parker Small, University of Florida, Gainesville, FL; William G. Smith, Moorestown Friends School, Moorestown, NJ; Richard D. Storey, The Colorado College, Colorado Springs, CO; Douglas Swartzendruber, University of Colorado, Colorado Springs, CO; Jean Paul Thibault, Cape Elizabeth High School, Cape Elizabeth, ME; Kent VanDeGraaff, Brigham Young University, Provo, UT; Alex Vargo, The Colorado College, Colorado Springs, CO; William H. Wagstaff, Mead Senior High School, Spokane, WA; Bruce Wallace, Virginia Tech, Blacksburg, VA

BIOLOGICAL SCIENCE

A Molecular Approach

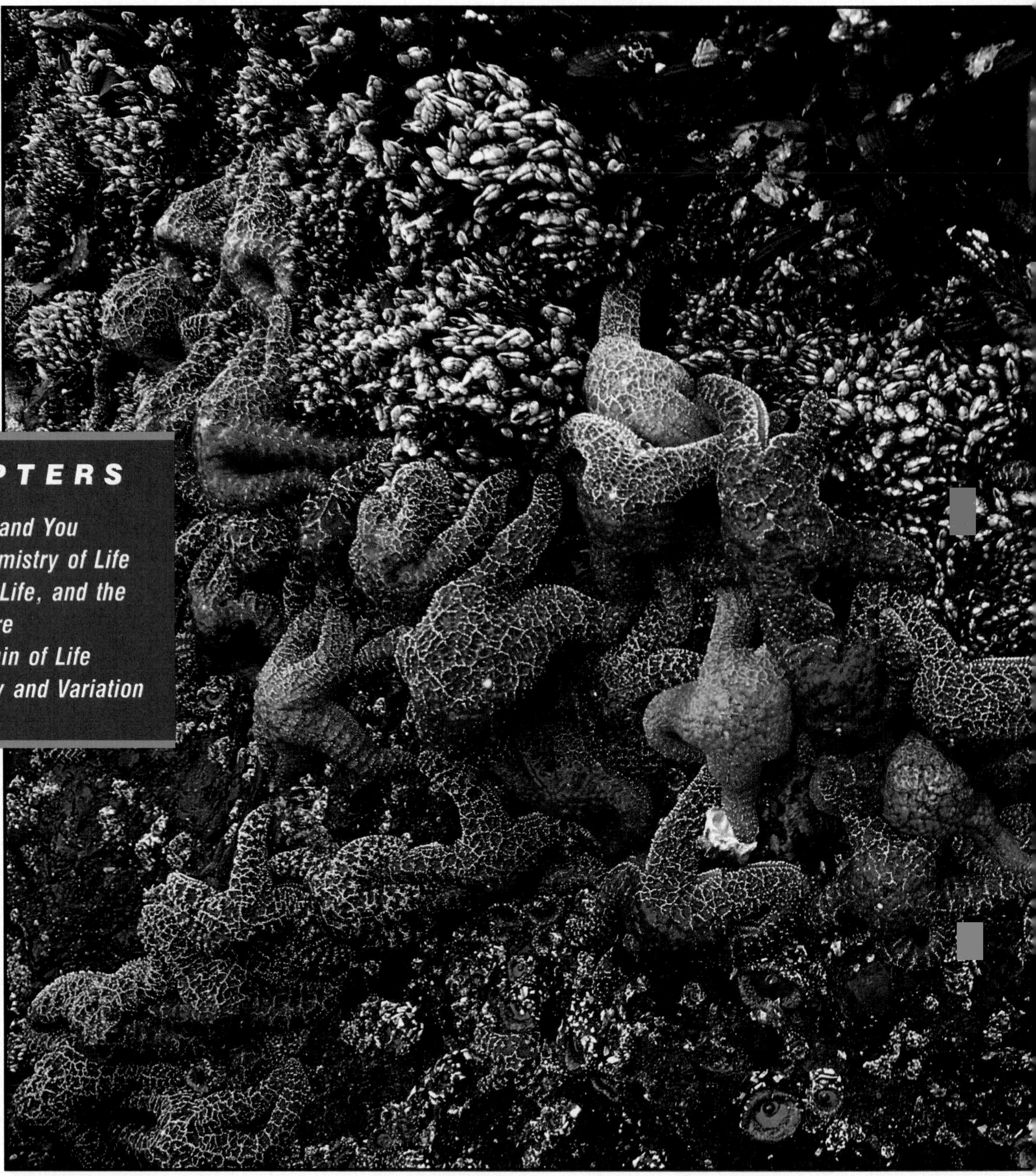

CHAPTERS

Unity and Diversity

*T*he sea stars you see here are but one of the many types of living things in tidal pools. Throughout the entire world, there is an overwhelming number and diversity of living things. Biologists have described nearly 3 million types of organisms, and more are discovered each year. Why are there so many types of living things? In what ways are all living things related?

*H*ow many different types
of living things do you see?

*W*hat conditions must each
of these organisms be able to tolerate
to live in a tide pool?

CONTENTS

Biology and You

*T*he twentieth century has been a time of great change. In 1900, nuclear energy was unknown, no vitamin had been identified, no hormones discovered, and no antibiotics developed. Because the biological actions of molecules and atoms were undiscovered, little could be done to determine the causes of diseases and birth defects. Similarly, the significance of environmental changes—such as water pollution and the dumping of hazardous waste—on the living world was not well understood.

When your parents took biology in high school, genetic engineering and other modern techniques were little more than science fiction. Now, human insulin is manufactured by genetically modified bacteria, and other bacteria have been used experimentally to protect crop plants from freezing. Physicians can transplant organs into children and adults with some degree of success and assist infertile couples in conceiving children. Prenatal diagnosis can identify many possible birth defects before a child is born. Sometimes doctors can even perform corrective surgery on unborn children. Where did this knowledge come from? How was it developed? What will the science of the twenty-first century be like?

This chapter introduces biology, the study of life. Biology is much more than merely the study of plants and animals. It unites scientific methods with technology to search for answers to fundamental questions—questions about what is happening all around us in the living world.

*I*n this technique, plant cells are placed in a container with minerals, water, and hormones to stimulate growth and development.

*H*ow might the use of this technique affect your life?

◆ *Plant tissue culture.*

The New Biology

1.1 Biology in Your World

Today, it is virtually impossible to open a newspaper or magazine without seeing something related to biology. Every day there are television programs that deal with some aspect of biology. Genetic engineering, AIDS, nutrition, pollution, and physical fitness are but a few of the topics that are frequently discussed (Figure 1.1). There also are many topics that affect your life every day. How does weight training work? Why do muscles become sore after a workout? How does the stress of coping with school-work, home life, social life, a job, and such extracurricular activities as sports or student government affect you physically and emotionally? What can you do to alleviate that stress and its effects? How does diet affect performance in sports and academics? Are there certain foods or vitamins that can help you perform better or that should be avoided?

Answers to many such questions lie at the levels of cells and molecules and their interactions. These topics are the focus of this book. Your life in the future will be affected by the science of molecular biology. Genetic engineering, which involves the modification of DNA in living cells, can be used to relieve disease, correct some genetic disorders, and improve crops. How can you prepare yourself for this new world?

The new biology confronts you with questions and choices people once had never imagined. Who will resolve the ethical and moral issues that stem from new technologies? How will you respond to the biological challenges of the twenty-first century—your century? Without an understanding of how living systems function and how they are interrelated, it is impossible to make intelligent decisions about issues that affect your life and the lives of those around you. This book will help you acquire a basic knowledge of biology, which, in turn, will enable you to understand biological issues and make informed judgments in the future.

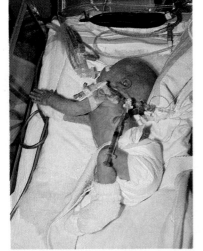

FIGURE 1.1 We are bombarded daily with information related to biology, such as new techniques for the care of premature infants, the benefits of staying in shape, and the hazards of water pollution.

1.2 AIDS—A Serious Global Problem

AIDS (Acquired Immune Deficiency Syndrome) is caused by a virus that infects a type of cell in the immune system, which normally helps fight infection. As the virus destroys these cells, the immune response gradually is destroyed as well. Infections that would be minor in a healthy person can be fatal in a person with AIDS. Because an immune system weakened by the virus provides the opportunity for these infections, they are called "opportunistic infections."

The virus responsible for AIDS was identified in 1983 and later named *H*uman *I*mmunodeficiency *V*irus, or HIV (Figure 1.2). Although HIV primarily affects certain cells of the immune system, it also can affect other types of cells, especially in the brain. The genetic material of the virus is copied inside infected cells and is then incorporated into the cells' own genetic material. Thus, infected cells lose their ability to function normally and become "factories," producing more HIV. When an infected cell bursts, many new viruses, each capable of infecting other cells, are released. Many infected cells, however, do not burst. They simply merge with nearby uninfected cells to form a large mass. The virus, therefore, may pass directly from one cell to another. This mode of spreading between cells worries researchers, because it means that drugs or vaccines that are effective in the blood or other body fluids, but that cannot enter the cells themselves, will not prevent the spread of infection.

Because HIV affects the body at the cellular and molecular levels, biologists must use their knowledge of genetics and the functions of molecules and cells within the immune system to develop treatments for AIDS. One of the first drugs used to treat people with AIDS was AZT. AZT apparently interferes with the reproduction of HIV inside affected cells. Later, a drug known as pentamidine was found useful in preventing a unique type of pneumonia called PCP, a common cause of death in people with AIDS. Eventually, almost all (if not all) HIV-infected individuals develop an infection that physicians cannot treat, and they die.

The more important issue for the future, therefore, is to develop a vaccine that would prevent infection from occurring. Although many scientists are working on the development of an HIV vaccine, they have yet to succeed. One approach uses the technique of genetic engineering to insert parts of the genetic material from HIV into the genetic material of another (but harmless) virus called *Vaccinia*. The modified *Vaccinia* might then be injected into the body, triggering an immune reaction against the HIV proteins, which were made by the HIV genetic material in the *Vaccinia*. Then, if the vaccinated individual is exposed to HIV, the immune system should recognize the virus and destroy it before it can cause harm.

One characteristic of HIV that causes the greatest difficulty in developing a vaccine is that its genetic material mutates, or changes, rapidly. Therefore, a vaccine that is effective against one strain, or form, of HIV may not be effective against another strain. The virus evolves so rapidly that different strains develop within the course of infection in a person.

Safety trials of at least a dozen different vaccines already are underway worldwide. Many scientists are hopeful that an HIV vaccine will be developed by the turn of the century, but other scientists are doubtful.

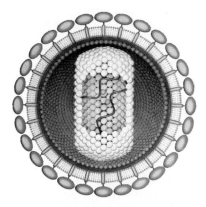

FIGURE 1.2 A drawing of the virus that causes AIDS. About 0.0001 of a millimeter in diameter, it is covered by a two-layer membrane (blue) studded with proteins (green). Other proteins (brown and ivory) compose the core.

CONNECTIONS

Science and society are inseparable. AIDS is a societal problem that science must help solve, and society must decide how to educate people about AIDS prevention.

FIGURE 1.3 Ideas of what constitutes "normal" height can vary for many reasons. A professional basketball player 6 feet 11 inches tall is considered "normal," while a player 5 feet 7 inches tall is considered short.

Try Investigation 1A, Analyzing Ethical Issues.

1.3 Growth Hormone—New Solution, New Problem

What do you consider "short" (Figure 1.3)? Is a person short if *he* is 5 feet 2 inches (about 157 centimeters) tall? If *she* is 5 feet 2 inches tall? If there were a way to make each of us as tall as we wanted to be, would that be a wise or a foolish use of biological knowledge?

Such a possibility exists with treatment for a disorder called growth hormone deficiency. Human growth hormone (GH), a protein that controls growth, is made by a small gland in the brain called the pituitary (pih TYOO ih ter ee). Most people produce the proper amount of growth hormone to attain a height within the "normal" range. Children with growth hormone deficiency, however, do not produce enough GH and cannot reach a height in the normal range unless they are given extra hormone. However, for children who are short as a result of heredity, growth hormone treatment has not been proven to increase their final adult height. Because the deficiency involves the interaction of molecules and occurs in cells, the search for solutions must begin there.

In the past, children with the deficiency were treated with GH taken from the brains of people who had died. Because many pituitary glands are needed to obtain even small amounts of GH, the procedure was expensive. More recently, this procedure was found to be dangerous because some of the pituitary glands contained a deadly virus that was transmitted to the children along with the hormone.

Genetic engineering now enables biologists to use bacteria to produce GH. Human DNA, the genetic material, is inserted into bacteria, which thereby acquire the ability to manufacture the exact sequence of the molecule found in the human hormone. New generations of bacteria can make an almost limitless supply of GH.

The genetically engineered GH is good news for children with growth hormone deficiency, but its ready availability has raised some troubling questions. For example, should GH be prescribed for teenagers who do not have growth deficiency but who wish to add a few inches of height to gain an advantage in athletics? GH can have some serious side effects. If doctors do not make the hormone available, the aspiring athletes may be able to obtain it on the "black market" and use it without supervision. What should doctors do in this situation?

This dilemma is an example of the types of issues raised by new technologies. An understanding of genetics and the fact that all organisms share the same genetic material—DNA—has produced startling breakthroughs for health and medicine. The technologies may improve our ability to fight disease, solve environmental problems, and increase life expectancy, but they also create new, often difficult choices for society.

CHECK AND CHALLENGE

1. Why is knowledge of biology important today?
2. How do technology and biology affect each other?
3. Why is a knowledge of cells and molecules important in understanding problems like AIDS and growth hormone deficiency?
4. How are moral and ethical issues involved in modern biology?

Biological Challenges

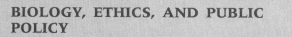

BIOLOGY, ETHICS, AND PUBLIC POLICY

Although there is much we do not know, an improved understanding of biology and an ability to manipulate some basic life processes raise many new and troubling issues. For example, medical technology now allows health care professionals to save many severely handicapped infants who might have died had they been born only 15 years ago. Should attempts be made to save such babies? Should fetuses found to have a genetic disorder or a birth defect be aborted? On whom shall we test new vaccines developed to combat AIDS, especially if some small risk exists that the vaccine will cause AIDS? Technology now allows us to identify certain genes that cause disease and to test individuals for those genes. Is it beneficial to patients to diagnose a disease for which there is no known treatment, such as Huntington's disease?

These issues involve a mixture of science and values that falls into the realm of ethics—the study of right and wrong actions. When the study of ethics is applied to biological issues it is called bioethics, and many colleges and universities now train people in this field. People who study bioethics work in settings ranging from hospitals to government research institutions.

Because the analysis of bioethical issues involves values, you might think that such analyses are not very rigorous. Sound ethical analysis, however, is like sound science: It is a process of critical thinking that proceeds from a basis of facts and requires well-founded support for all statements. Ethical analysis requires thinking through a position very carefully and expecting careful analysis from others. It also requires that we respect the views of others, whether or not we agree with them. Eventually, we must decide which views will be incorporated into laws and actions.

Science can be very helpful in telling us what we *can* do and in predicting the effects of each alterna-

FIGURE A   In 1994, researchers discovered the location of a gene that is responsible for some cases of breast cancer. Once a test to identify carriers is available, should these young women be tested, even though there is no cure for breast cancer yet?

tive. Science, however, cannot tell us what we *should* do. Although evidence might point toward one alternative, the final decision often is a matter of values. Those values are often represented in public policy—laws and regulations that govern how science is applied.

Public policy should be based on sound ethical judgments, but that is not always enough to make policies workable. A policy may be ethically sound, but if most people do not agree with it or if it cannot be enforced, it probably will not work. Many of the issues in this book are so new that there is no national policy to govern them, and there still is sharp ethical disagreement about many of them. Each person has a responsibility to understand and contribute to debates about the ethical and policy aspects of advances in science and technology. The first step is understanding the basic science. This book will help you do that. The second step is to analyze bioethical issues. Investigation 1A is a model that will help with the second step.

The Methods of Science _____

1.4 Solving Problems

Everyone makes decisions every day. What clothes should you wear? Should you go out tonight or stay home and study? Most of the decisions people make are based on what they *feel* will be the best solution. Feelings and judgments of how others feel toward you play a major role in how you choose to resolve your day-to-day problems.

True problem solving, however, goes beyond feelings. To solve a problem, you must look beyond how you feel and combine information that you already know with new observations. Then, based on your knowledge of the situation, you can evaluate the problem and formulate the best plan to solve it.

Imagine that it's Saturday and you are to meet your friends at the mall at 12:00. You've been busy all morning and suddenly you notice it is 11:45. You race to get ready and then jump in the car. What route probably is the fastest? You know where the mall is and you choose the best route based upon what you know about the distance, the amount of traffic on the roads at that time, and the number of stop lights you are likely to encounter. If a lot of other drivers are using the same route, it might be faster to use an alternate route where the traffic is much lighter. In essence, you make observations and combine those observations with your best guesses. You arrive at a possible solution of how to get to the mall quickly. If you are late, next time you may try another route, because you know the first does not work well. Eventually, through trial and error, you find the fastest route.

In science, problem solving is based on the interpretation of **data**, which is information gained through observation, measurement, or experimentation. For example, you could time how long it takes to get from your home to the mall. You could take every possible route twice—once in heavy traffic, and once with light traffic. You could then interpret the results and determine which route is fastest. If you really wanted to be sure, you could run several more trials. If one route was consistently faster than others, you would have solved the problem—what is the fastest route from your home to the mall—by using scientific methods.

Scientific problem solving is used to address numerous questions people have about issues that affect their lives. The questions may range from the common, "Is salt really bad for you?" to the more imaginative, "Are there really aliens from outer space?" Using scientific methods in problem solving can help you determine what is reasonable and what is not. It can help you evaluate claims made by others about products or events. It can help explain how organisms function and how they interact in the environment.

The easiest way for you to become familiar with how these methods work is to use them yourself (as you frequently will in this course) and to see how other people use them. One good example is the topic of evolution. Evolution is considered one of the major unifying themes of biology. How widely does evolution apply, and how does it occur? What data

Try Investigation 1B, Scientific Observation.

Try Investigation 1C, The Compound Microscope.

*S*cience as inquiry—the understanding that all is not known and that concepts must be revised and restructured as new data become available—pervades all scientific methods.

provide evidence for evolution? In the following sections you will see how scientific methods were used to develop a theory that explains how organisms change through time.

1.5   A Mechanism for Evolution—Science at Work

The world is filled with beautiful and intriguing organisms. It also contains a record of equally amazing extinct forms of life. Observe the pictures of organisms in Figure 1.4. Which organisms are similar and in what ways? Which organisms are different and in what ways? More important, how did these diverse forms arise?

By the beginning of the nineteenth century, biologists had observed that living organisms were different from the fossil organisms found in rocks. These observers developed a theory—evolution—that the organisms of the past had given rise to the organisms of the present, and that organisms had changed through time. A **theory** explains current observations and predicts new observations—in this case, observations about how organisms change through time. The theory of evolution, for example,

a

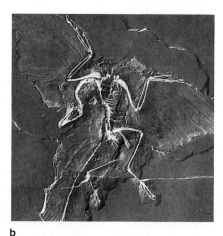

b

FIGURE 1.4 What are the similarities between Canada geese, *Branta canadensis* (a) and the fossil *Archaeopteryx* (b)? How are they different? Another example of animals that look alike and yet are dissimilar is the mountain lion (c) and the extinct saber-toothed cat (d).

c

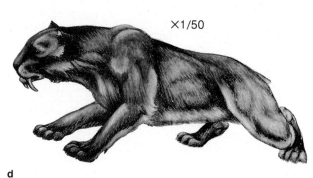

×1/50

d

predicts that there should be observable differences between modern organisms and fossils found in rocks, as well as observable similarities. Evidence from thousands of observations of modern and fossilized organisms from all over the world supports the theory of evolution.

How could evolution have occurred? A French biologist, Jean Baptiste Lamarck (1744–1829), was one of the first to propose that organisms were not fixed in form but could change through time. He proposed a well-developed theory to explain how organisms evolve. The basis for Lamarck's theory was his reasoning that a change in the environment produces a *need* for change in animals. This idea, coupled with observations of the great diversity of organisms in nature, led Lamarck to two major assumptions. Lamarck's first assumption was that if an animal uses one part of its body frequently, that part will become stronger and more well-developed. Conversely, if an animal uses some part of its body infrequently, that part will slowly weaken, become smaller, and may disappear. Furthermore, Lamarck assumed that these *acquired characteristics* would be passed on to the offspring in that changed form.

This theory of evolution may seem reasonable, and one portion is valid: Parts of an animal do change as a result of use or disuse. Theories, however, sometimes are evaluated through a series of **hypotheses**—questions that are testable through experimentation or observation. One hypothesis based on the theory of evolution could be stated as follows: Ancient organisms have given rise to modern organisms by evolution. Predictions that follow from hypotheses can be stated in an *If . . . then* format. One prediction based on this hypothesis could be stated as follows: *If* ancient organisms have given rise to modern organisms, *then* modern organisms should differ from ancient organisms in some ways, yet they also should retain certain similarities.

FIGURE 1.5 Acquired characteristics are not inherited as Lamarck thought. Even though this adult Doberman has had its tail and ears cropped, you can see that its offspring still was born with long ears and tail.

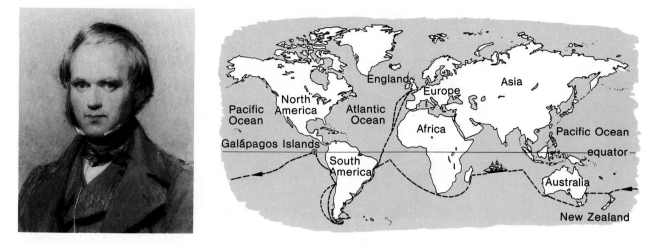

FIGURE 1.6 Young Charles Darwin *(left)* sailed around the world on the *Beagle*. The route taken *(right)* included a stop in South America and the Galapagos Islands. During the trip, Darwin found evidence that would later support the theory of evolution by natural selection.

Consider a testable prediction based on Lamarck's theory of evolution through inheritance of acquired characteristics: *If* the ears and tails of Doberman Pinschers are cropped, *then* the offspring in successive generations will have cropped ears and tails. This experiment has been done thousands of times, but Doberman Pinscher puppies are still born with long ears and long tails (Figure 1.5). Consider a similar prediction involving humans: *If* a male and a female increase the size of their muscles through weight training, *then* their children will be born with large muscles. Again, we know from observations that this is not the case. Both predictions must be rejected.

Lamarck's theory does not do a very good job of explaining or predicting observations about the changes of organisms through time (at least, not based on the tests described). Extensive experimentation for more than 100 years has failed to show that acquired characteristics will be inherited.

Another person who developed a theory to explain evolution was the British naturalist Charles Darwin, who lived from 1809 to 1882. Many things influenced Darwin during his life. One was his experience as a naturalist on the five-year voyage of the *Beagle* (Figure 1.6) during which he observed unique and diverse organisms from around the world. Another influence was a book written by Darwin's friend, the geologist Charles Lyell (1797–1875). Lyell set forth the hypothesis that natural forces existing in the past were the same as those that exist today. He stated that those forces have apparently produced changes on Earth in the past, and he predicted that the same forces would continue to produce changes in the future.

Darwin raised the following questions: If Earth has had a long history of change, what was it like before? Could it have supported the diversity of life it has now? What other forms of life might have lived before now? Darwin reviewed existing data and made numerous observations around the world as he formulated his answers to these questions.

FIGURE 1.7 How are the red and blue arrow poison frog, *Dendrobates pumilis (left)*, and the flounder, *Paralichthys lethostigma (right)* well adapted?

1.6 The Theory of Natural Selection

On the basis of his extensive research, Darwin published a book in 1859 titled *The Origin of Species by Means of Natural Selection*. Darwin's theory stated that new forms of life are produced by means of **natural selection**, the survival and reproduction of organisms that are best suited to their environment (Figure 1.7). Natural selection occurs because some members of a population or species have characteristics that enable them to survive and to reproduce more offspring than others. (A species is a group of similar organisms capable of reproducing with one another—see Figure 1.8.) Their characteristics become more common in succeeding generations

FIGURE 1.8 Even though two animals may look alike, they are not necessarily closely related. The mountain lion, *Felis concolor (left)*, and the leopard, *Panthera pardus (right)*, are classified in different groups, even though they closely resemble one another.

FIGURE 1.9 A population of ladybird beetles (X2). How many differences can you see within this population? What is the range in number of spots present? What important characteristic of populations does this illustrate? What is responsible for these differences?

because characteristics of organisms that are most successful at survival and reproduction stand the best chance of being perpetuated. These characteristics, which increase the chances that an organism will survive and reproduce in its particular environment, are called **adaptations**.

Like Lamarck, Darwin based his theory on several major observations. He noticed that, given no interference, the number of organisms in any species or population tends to increase from generation to generation. Thus, each generation of organisms tends to be larger in number than the previous one. Darwin also observed that although populations have this tendency to increase in numbers, the actual number of organisms in a particular population remains about the same. (See **Appendix 1A**, Ideas Behind Natural Selection.)

These observations led Darwin to develop a hypothesis. *If* more offspring are produced by each generation than by the one before it and *if* the number of individuals in a species remains relatively constant each generation, *then* it must follow that there is competition for food, water, light, and other environmental factors. Some organisms survive this competition, others do not.

Darwin also observed that naturally occurring **variations**, or small differences (Figure 1.9), occur within the members of all species. On the basis of these observations, Darwin concluded that some variations would help members of a species survive in a particular environment (Figure 1.10), whereas other variations would not be helpful. His theory proposes that natural selection tends to eliminate those organisms with variations that are not advantageous.

FIGURE 1.10 Notice the large ears and long legs on this jackrabbit. How are these features adaptations to hot environments?

Darwin's theory suggests a number of predictions. For example, *if* organisms with favorable variations are most likely to survive and reproduce, *then* those organisms with unfavorable variations would be less successful at reproduction and would, therefore, die out. Because variations can be inherited, the favorable variations—adaptations—would accumulate through time. Further, *if* organisms with those favorable variations become so different from members of the original species in shape, biochemistry, and especially reproductive systems, *then* a new species may have evolved (Figure 1.11).

Extensive field work and experimentation have supported Darwin's theory of natural selection as a mechanism for evolution. For example, scientists studying fossils predicted that they would find fossils that represented intermediate forms between living organisms and fossils discovered in the older layers of Earth. This prediction has been confirmed in an overwhelming number of cases by scientists all over the world. The data include intermediate forms between many species within the kingdoms of living things that form the basis of the system for classifying organisms.

Lamarck and Darwin proposed different theories to explain the same observation: Organisms change through time. Darwin's theory has prevailed because it explains existing observations and predicts future observations. The theory of evolution through natural selection provides an explanation for the evolution of species and the diversity of organisms on Earth (see Chapter 5). The theory also explains the similarities between

FIGURE 1.11 (a) Cotton bollworms (*Heliothis zea*) and (b) tobacco budworms (*Heliothis virescens*) are destructive agricultural pests that once were the same species. Differences evolved in the structure of their sex organs, however, that now prevent mating between the two groups. (X2)

a

b

humans and other animals that allow scientists to apply some conclusions from animal research to humans.

The theory of evolution by natural selection shows how theories and hypotheses are related. A hypothesis is a testable statement about an observation. A theory is a model that explains a great many current observations and predicts the outcomes of future observations. Theories that serve as models in science—evolution theory, atomic theory, the germ theory of disease, for example—have been supported repeatedly by data resulting from testable hypotheses. In addition, virtually no opposing data have yet been found, further strengthening these theories. Any theory, however, no matter how well established, can be changed or even discarded if new experiments and observations do not support the model. All theories mentioned here have been modified as new research has been done, and undoubtedly these theories will be modified in the future. This continuous modification is another example of the way science works.

CHECK AND CHALLENGE _____

1. Describe the nature of scientific methods.

2. What is a hypothesis and how does it differ from a theory? Give a concrete example of each.

3. Describe the theory of evolution by means of natural selection.

4. Describe how natural selection operates on species.

5. How did Lamarck's theory and Darwin's theory differ?

Science as a Way of Knowing _____

1.7   Scientific Perspectives

There are many different and often valid ways to look at the world and to explain natural phenomena. For example, history, religion, art, philosophy, literature, astronomy, and sociology all provide ways for people to examine the world we live in, and they all contribute to today's body of knowledge.

Science is one way of explaining the natural world, and the characteristics of science serve as a basis for establishing what qualifies as science. Several characteristics generally define science. First, science is based on the results of observations and controlled experiments. Second, the results of these observations and experiments must be (at least in principle) repeatable and verifiable by other scientists. Third, the findings of science must be refutable. In other words, if a hypothesis has been accepted by many scientists and later another explanation becomes better supported by evidence, there must be a way to disprove the original hypothesis. The same principle holds true for theories. Fourth, science is based on the assumption that the natural world can be investigated and explained in terms we can understand. Science is also committed to the idea that our explanations will change or become modified through time as new knowledge is acquired. Methods of explaining natural phenomena that do not meet these standards do not qualify as science.

Science is a human enterprise and can be influenced in some ways by personal biases and by politics. Consider the great astronomers Copernicus

FOCUS ON *A View of Nature*

Many disciplines other than science have examined the concept of evolution and the interactions between humans and other animals. For example, the poet Carl Sandburg wrote:

*T*here is a wolf in me . . . fangs pointed for tearing gashes . . . a red tongue for raw meat . . . and the hot lapping of blood — I keep this wolf because the wilderness gave it to me and the wilderness will not let it go.

*T*here is a fish in me . . . I know I came from salt-blue water-gates . . . I scurried with shoals of herring . . . I blew waterspouts with porpoises . . . before land was . . . before the water went down . . . before Noah . . . before the first chapter of Genesis.

*T*here is an eagle in me and a mockingbird . . . and the eagle flies among the Rocky Mountains of my dreams and fights among the Sierra crags of what I want . . . and the mockingbird warbles in the early afternoon before the dew is gone, warbles in the underbrush of my Chattanoogas of hope, gushes over the blue Ozark foothills of my wishes—And I got the eagle and the mockingbird from the wilderness.

O, I got a zoo, I got a menagerie, inside my ribs, under my bony head, under my red-valve heart — I got something else: it is a man-child heart, a woman-child heart: it is a father and mother and lover: it came from God-Knows-Where: it is going God-Knows-Where — For I am the keeper of the zoo: I say yes and no: I sing and kill and work: I am a pal of the world: I came from the wilderness.

Notice the relationships that Sandburg felt among himself, other animals, and the wilderness. Sandburg was a poet; his observations about nature, expressed by the words of his poem, are valid, though different from those of a scientist. His poetry conveys a metaphorical message, and the exact meaning of his words must be interpreted by each individual. Science, on the other hand, is more literal. In science, words are chosen to convey as precise and unambiguous a meaning as possible.

and Galileo. Copernicus (Figure 1.12) developed a theory that Earth is one of several planets revolving around the sun. Galileo observed moons revolving around the planet Jupiter. Their conclusions about the solar system were judged wrong because they contradicted religious authority—the church of that day and the prevailing interpretation of the scriptures. The scriptures were interpreted to say that the sun moved around Earth, and the Church held to the ancient belief that Earth is the center of the universe. Both scientists were chastised by the Church. Galileo was forced to publish a statement saying that his work was incorrect, and he was then sentenced to live out his life under house arrest.

Because of its very nature, science cannot be legislated or dictated. The Church's decision that the scientists were wrong was not based on the validity of their findings. No matter what Galileo signed, it did not change the fact that Earth is not the center of the solar system. Rejecting science does not change the science—it merely prevents people from learning and understanding how things really are.

1.8 Pseudoscience

Pseudoscience means, literally, false science. Some investigators claim their research is scientific, yet if the research does not meet the criteria of science, discussed in Section 1.6, it must be classified as pseudoscience. The following example clearly illustrates the far-reaching consequences of confusing science and pseudoscience.

In 1981, the state of Arkansas enacted a law requiring science teachers to devote equal time in class to teaching evolution and creationism, or "creation science." Creationism, as defined by the originators of the law, involves the literal interpretation of the creation of all living things in six 24-hour days by a supreme being, as in the first chapter of Genesis in the Old Testament. This definition requires a "young" Earth, about 10 000 years old, and excludes creation accounts other than interpretations of the account in Genesis. The law was contested, and the Federal District Court in Little Rock, Arkansas, ruled against it. The court reasoned that to require the teaching of creationism in public schools would establish the teaching of a particular type of religion, thus violating the "establishment clause" of the United States Constitution's first amendment, which requires separation of church and state. In a similar case in 1987, the United States Supreme Court ruled unconstitutional a Louisiana law requiring the teaching of creationism whenever evolution theory was taught in science classrooms, a so-called balanced treatment.

"Creation science" is not science because its working assumptions cannot be examined by scientific methods. The word *creation* is associated with religion and a supreme being. It is, therefore, a matter of faith—not of scientific investigation. Furthermore, some creationists resist modifying their model even when observations fail to support it. These characteristics do not exclude creationism from a place in the school curriculum. Rather, they strongly suggest that creationism should be taught as a religious belief and not as a scientific theory.

FIGURE 1.12 In the sixteenth century, Copernicus claimed that the sun was at the center of the universe—not Earth, as was believed. Earth revolves around the sun, not vice versa. Although he "proved" this was so, Copernicus died without his ideas being accepted.

The theory of evolution by natural selection does not address the question of the existence of a supreme being. Some people believe that Charles Darwin must have been an atheist to propose his theory. The following quote from the last paragraph of his book, *The Origin of Species* (second and subsequent editions), may serve as Darwin's own response to the issue.

> It is interesting to contemplate a tangled bank, clothed with many plants of many kinds, with birds singing in the bushes, with various insects flitting about, and with worms crawling through the damp earth, and to reflect that these elaborately constructed forms, so different from each other, and dependent upon each other in so complex a manner, have all been produced by laws acting around us . . . . There is grandeur in this view of life, with its several powers, having been originally breathed by the Creator into a few forms or into one; and that, whilst this planet has gone cycling on according to the fixed law of gravity, from so simple a beginning endless forms most beautiful and most wonderful have been, and are being evolved (Figure 1.13).

Yet Darwin also recognized that the question of a deity is a personal religious decision and that deities cannot be investigated by scientific methods and, therefore, are outside the realm of what qualifies as science. Many other examples of pseudoscience exist: astrology, ''miracle cures'' for diseases such as cancer and arthritis, and some dieting programs and health practices. A great deal of time, effort, and money can be saved by learning to evaluate pseudoscientific claims carefully.

FIGURE 1.13   The tropical rain forest is home to a majority of the plant and animal species on Earth. Among some of the inhabitants are the orangutans, *Pongo pygmaeus*, large primates somewhat closely related to humans.

1.9   Your Role as a Biologist

Science is a method of answering questions and explaining natural phenomena. You have already encountered a few of the many questions biologists ask when they study living things. Throughout the year, you will be asked to answer such questions as: To what environment is this organism adapted? What is being released into my environment that could be hazardous to my health and that of my friends and family? How does a change in DNA affect the proteins of an organism?

As you deal with biological issues in this course, and throughout your life, ask at least five basic questions:

1. What is the question? Identify the critical question and find out what it really means before you attempt to answer it.

2. What are the data and how were they obtained? Determine what the facts are before you attempt to make a decision. Learn to separate data from opinions. Be sure that the data were gathered in a scientific manner and can be validated.

3. What do the data mean? Determine if the data support the arguments that are being offered on several sides of an issue. Again, it is important to separate facts from opinions.

4. Who is reporting the data? Not all people are reliable sources for data. Determine the credentials of persons who claim to be ''experts'' on an issue. Is this person reporting as a scientist or as a person with personal interests? Learn to question everyone but especially those who do not have the background to know the relevant data and understand the scientific aspects of problems you will be investigating. Most important, remember that even experts can make mistakes.

5. How complete is the present state of our knowledge? Is our knowledge about a subject changing, as in the case of AIDS, or is our knowledge apparently quite complete, as in the case of smallpox?

These five questions also can help you connect new information to what you already know. Such connections can increase your understanding of basic concepts in biology and other areas. Establishing these connections can help you detect errors in logic or content—a crucial ability when you must make important decisions. Your own ethics, feelings, and values affect how you learn and will enter into every decision you make. As you study biology this year, you will be able to examine closely your positions on some controversial issues. As you do so, you will be developing skills that will serve you for the rest of your life—and in many areas, not just in the study of biology.

Try Investigation 1D, Developing Concept Maps.

CHECK AND CHALLENGE

1. Describe the characteristics of science.
2. What is pseudoscience, and how does it differ from science?
3. Why is creationism considered pseudoscience?

Summary

Knowledge of biology increases every day and presents everyone with new choices. An understanding of biology at the cellular and molecular level is crucial if we are to make educated and informed decisions about biological issues that affect us individually and as a society. These issues include AIDS and the appropriate uses of human growth hormone, now easily available through the techniques of genetic engineering. By using scientific methods, you can discover new ways to examine life around you. Darwin used scientific methods to develop the theory of evolution by means of natural selection. He made observations and assumptions and developed a theory to explain them. His theory has withstood years of testing and serves as a model for explaining and predicting observations in biology.

Science is one of many different and often valid ways to look at the world. The characteristics of science determine what qualifies as science. Science is based on the assumption that the natural world can be investigated and explained. Pseudoscience is false science. One example of pseudoscience is creationism because it is largely a matter of faith and its assumptions cannot be investigated or rejected by the methods of science.

Science is a means of answering questions. Learning to analyze the nature of a question, to interpret data, and to assess the reliability of a source will help you evaluate new information. Developing connections between new knowledge and what you already know can help you detect errors in logic and the content of new material. With increased knowledge, you are more prepared to cope with the moral and ethical issues raised as a result of the growth of scientific knowledge.

Key Concepts

Make a list of the major concepts you have learned in this chapter. Group the terms so related ideas are together.

Reviewing Ideas

1. Explain the relationships among technology, biology, and ethics.

2. Give some examples of how biology affects your life.

3. How does an understanding of cells and molecules relate to a cure for AIDS?

4. How are hypotheses, observations, and experiments used in science?

5. What are the principles behind the theory of evolution by means of natural selection?

6. How did Darwin use the methods of science to develop his theory?

7. Why was Lamarck's hypothesis invalid? On what assumptions was his theory based?

8. Compare and contrast a hypothesis and a theory.

9. What is the relationship between natural selection and the environment?

10. What are the characteristics of science, and how does it differ from pseudoscience?

11. What type of questions should you ask when considering biological issues, and why?

Using Concepts

1. Imagine you are going to investigate the origin of Earth. How would you go about it? What would have to be done? What problems would you encounter?

2. Some animals, such as the arctic fox and the ptarmigan (a bird), change the color of their fur or feathers from summer to winter. Relate this to natural selection.

3. Darwin stated that a struggle for existence—for adequate food, space, water, and so on—occurs in all species. Is this true for the human species as well? Give concrete examples to substantiate your answer.

4. Why does biological research require good observational skills?

5. Observe and prepare a list of the objects in your classroom. Based on your observations, develop a hypothesis about the uses of that room.

6. Identify several acquired characteristics that you think are not inherited. Verify your list by consulting genetics textbooks.

7. Observe your classmates. What variations can you identify among them?

8. Identify several moral or ethical questions that occurred to you while reading this chapter.

9. Imagine a long-legged wolf and a short-legged wolf. Relate the length of their legs to their ability to catch enough rabbits to feed their offspring. Would one wolf be more successful than the other in providing enough food for its offspring to survive? Would it be advantageous to have long legs?

10. Explain the basis for the rejection of Lamarck's theory of evolution and the acceptance of Darwin's theory.

Extensions

1. Choose a topic of interest and define a problem or question you have about that topic. State the problem or question as a hypothesis. Now, design a test for the hypothesis. What experiment(s) will you do? What methods will you follow?

2. Draw a sketch that illustrates natural selection in progress. Be sure to show some environmental conditions that might favor the adaptations you depict.

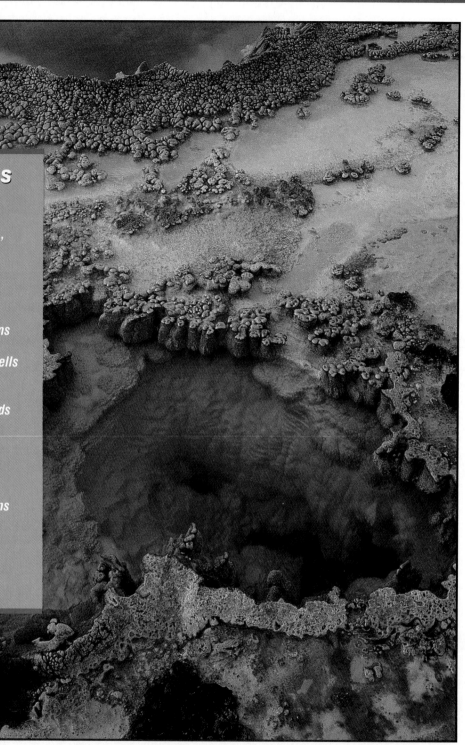

CONTENTS

The Chemistry of Life

*A*t one time, studying the form and function of intact organisms was the accepted route to understanding evolution and the place each organism fills in the scheme of life on Earth. As knowledge increased, biologists began to recognize that organisms are composed of chemicals and that an understanding of life requires an understanding of chemistry. Biochemistry—the chemistry of living organisms—is centrally important in research to solve some of today's biological questions. Information about causes and cures of cancer, AIDS, and mental illness is being found in the biochemistry of human cells. Evolutionary relationships are being more clearly defined through comparisons of biological structures in different organisms.

This chapter presents some principles of general chemistry and of biochemistry that are important for an understanding of how living cells function. Symbols and models are introduced to represent molecules and other structures that are too small to see with the unaided eye.

General Chemistry

2.1 Atoms, Molecules, and Compounds

◆ *A hot spring in the Lower Geyser Basin of Yellowstone National Park.*

Water is abundant on Earth today—as a gas, as a liquid, and as a solid. The physical state of water depends on temperature. If the temperature is high enough, water is a gas. If the temperature is low enough, water freezes and forms ice. Although the forms of water may vary, its *chemical* composition remains the same. Water has some unusual physical and chemical properties that have had a powerful effect on the evolution of life. A close look at the chemistry of water can provide information about the chemical nature of matter and about the function of biological organisms.

Suppose you found a way to subdivide a drop of water into smaller and smaller droplets until you could not even see them under a microscope. No matter how small the water droplet, it would still be made of identical units called molecules. Molecules of water are the smallest units into which water can be subdivided (or broken down into) and still have the essential chemical properties of water.

When an electric current flows through water under proper conditions, a remarkable change occurs: water becomes two gases. One is the lightest gas, hydrogen, which burns with a very hot flame in air. The other gas is oxygen. Any burning object thrust into oxygen will continue to burn with a more brilliant flame. Thus, under certain conditions, water molecules can break down into two different substances, hydrogen and oxygen. Neither substance has the appearance or any other property of water.

If molecules can break down, what are the particles of which molecules are made? This question brings up the most important of all chemical theories, the atomic theory. In 1805, the British teacher and chemist John Dalton finished a long series of experiments and measurements that indicated every substance is made of minute particles. Dalton believed these particles could not be broken into smaller particles, so he named them atoms (from the Greek word *atomos* meaning indivisible). He stated several principles to describe an atom's chemical behavior. New data have changed the atomic theory since Dalton's time, but this theory is still basic to an understanding of chemistry and biology.

Molecules are made of atoms that have been chemically combined. Molecules may be made from more than one kind of atom (as in water), or from atoms of the same type. For example, hydrogen gas consists of hydro-

FOCUS ON *Molecular Models*

What is a model of a molecule? In a sense, a molecular model has some things in common with models of planes, ships, and automobiles that you can purchase in a hobby shop. A model of a ship, for example, is an approximation of the real object, except that the model is much smaller. The model makes it easier to understand how a ship is built and how it operates, but it is not the real thing.

In the same way, a molecular model gives an idea of its molecular structure. Unlike the ship model, however, we do not know what the molecule actually looks like. It is impossible to observe the structure of a molecule directly, because a molecule is too small for the eye to see, even with a microscope. Molecular models

are constructed from laboratory data such as X-ray diffraction. As more is learned about a molecule, the model is changed and improved to be consistent with new information. In this way, a model can serve as a learning tool and be used in developing new hypotheses. The symbol H_2O represents a molecule of water. H and O are printed symbols used to illustrate hydrogen and oxygen in water, and H_2O is a printed model of a molecule of water. (In one drop of water there are about a billion trillion molecules of H_2O.)

The figures and symbols shown in this chapter are models that make it easier to visualize and understand the structure and the function of elements and molecules.

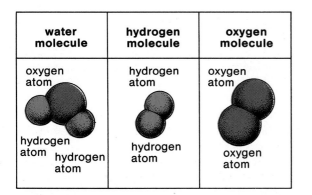

FIGURE 2.1 Molecules of water, hydrogen, and oxygen are made from the combinations of atoms as shown in these models.

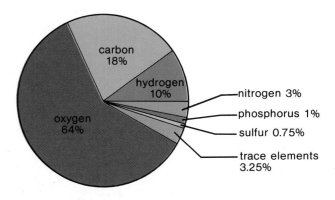

FIGURE 2.2 Elements present in the human body

gen atoms that exist in combination with each other. A molecule of hydrogen has two hydrogen atoms (see Figure 2.1). The same arrangement is true of an oxygen molecule, which has two oxygen atoms. (Oxygen also forms molecules of *ozone* that contain three atoms of oxygen.)

A substance that cannot be chemically broken down into simpler substances is called an element. More than 100 different elements are known today. A substance that can be chemically broken down into elements is called a compound. A compound (such as water) always contains two or more different types of atoms. Elements can combine chemically in many ways to form the millions of compounds that give Earth its variety of materials.

Chemists have given each element a symbol of letters from the element's name. H stands for hydrogen, O for oxygen, C for carbon, and N for nitrogen. Iron, however, is Fe, derived from the word *ferrum*, reflecting that some symbols come from an element's Latin or Greek name. (See **Appendix 2A,** The Periodic Table of the Elements.)

Despite all the variety of materials, organisms are made of a limited number of compounds, of which water is the most abundant. About 97 percent of the compounds present in organisms contain only six elements—carbon, hydrogen, oxygen, nitrogen, phosphorus, and sulfur. The remaining 3 percent contain small amounts of other elements. The basic six elements are essential to *every* organism. Some 20 others are essential, too, but only in smaller amounts (Figure 2.2).

The number of atoms of each element in a molecule is shown by the number, called a subscript, *following* the symbol for the element (the number "one" is always understood and not written). For example, the formula for carbon dioxide, CO_2, means that a molecule of this gas contains one carbon atom and two oxygen atoms. A molecule of ammonia, written as NH_3, contains one nitrogen atom and three hydrogen atoms. Finally, a molecule of methane is written as CH_4. The formula tells what elements are in each molecule and how many atoms of each element the molecule contains.

CONNECTIONS

*T*he presence of the same six elements in all living organisms is an example of unity of pattern and diversity of type.

2.2 The Composition of Atoms

Atoms are built of many smaller particles. The particles of atoms that are basic to an understanding of biology are electrons, protons, and neutrons. The electron carries a negative charge. A proton has a positive charge, and a neutron has no charge.

Protons and neutrons remain in the center, or nucleus, of the atom. The electrons, however, seem to be everywhere at once *except* in the nucleus. The rapidly moving electrons form a negatively charged "cloud" around the nucleus. Electrons are distributed throughout the cloud based on differing levels of energy. Electrons near the nucleus have less energy than those farther from the nucleus.

The simplest of all atoms is hydrogen. A hydrogen nucleus has a single proton, no neutron, and a single electron that moves about the nucleus (Figure 2.3a). Atoms of other elements are more complex than the hydrogen atom. For example, an atom of carbon (Figure 2.3b) has six protons and six neutrons in its nucleus, and six electrons outside the nucleus. The number of neutrons may vary, but six protons in an atom always signify carbon. Similarly, nitrogen has seven protons and seven electrons, and oxygen has eight protons and eight electrons (Figure 2.3c,d).

In any atom, the number of protons and electrons is equal. Thus, the charges are balanced, and the atom itself has no overall electric charge. However, the atoms of most elements can undergo chemical change by having one or more electrons added, removed, or shared with other atoms.

Only electrons in the outer energy levels of the atoms pictured in Figure 2.3 are involved when the atoms react during a chemical change. Many elements have atoms with electrons in more than two energy levels, but again, only the outermost electrons normally interact during chemical changes. The outer electrons provide a reliable indicator of the chemical

FIGURE 2.3 Simplified models of hydrogen (a), carbon (b), nitrogen (c), and oxygen (d). Red circles represent protons, gray circles represent neutrons. The models show electrons as a cloud of negative charge around the nucleus. The number of electrons in the outer level determines chemical activity.

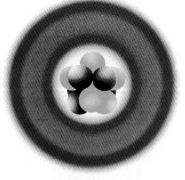
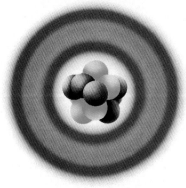
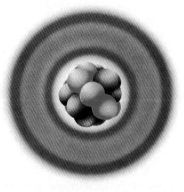

a. hydrogen atom
(1 proton)

b. carbon atom
(6 protons, 6 neutrons)

c. nitrogen atom
(7 protons, 7 neutrons)

d. oxygen atom
(8 protons, 8 neutrons)

activity of an atom, but the structure of the entire atom also influences chemical reactions.

Atoms of different elements differ in their number of protons, neutrons, and electrons. Atoms of the same element can differ only in their numbers of neutrons; they always have the same number of protons and electrons and the same chemical behavior. Atoms of the same element that differ in their number of neutrons are called isotopes (EYE suh tohps). For example, 99 percent of oxygen atoms are like the one pictured in Figure 2.3. This atom is called the oxygen-16 isotope, named for the sum of its protons and neutrons. Oxygen-17 and oxygen-18 also exist, with 9 and 10 neutrons, respectively. Some isotopes have unstable atomic nuclei from which radiation energy escapes. Such radioisotopes are useful in biological research because they can help to determine some of the chemical reactions organisms carry out. (See **Appendix 2B,** Radioisotopes and Research in Biology.)

Reactions in Living Cells

2.3 Chemical Reactions

When two or more atoms react to form compounds, chemical bonds are formed by the attraction, sharing, or transfer of outer electrons from one atom to the other. Such bonds between atoms can be broken, the atoms rearranged, and new bonds formed. A chemical reaction involves the making and breaking of chemical bonds. Chemical reactions are always occurring in living organisms. Living organisms are sometimes compared to chemical factories, but the number and complexity of chemical reactions that occur in living organisms are vastly greater than in any factory.

In chemical reactions, substances interact and form new bonds and new substances. These events are important in a cell for two reasons. First, chemical reactions are the only way to form new molecules that the cell requires for such things as growth and tissue maintenance (Chapter 3). Second, the making and breaking of bonds involves changes in energy. As a result of chemical reactions in a cell, energy may be stored, used to do work, or released.

Chemical reactions can be represented as short statements called chemical equations. For example, the decomposition of water can be represented by the following equation:

$$2H_2O \xrightarrow{\text{electric energy}} 2H_2 + O_2$$

2 molecules of water   2 molecules of hydrogen   1 molecule of oxygen

Why is it necessary to use two molecules of water in the equation? Remember that hydrogen and oxygen molecules each consist of two atoms. A single molecule of water does not yield enough oxygen atoms to make an oxygen molecule, but two molecules of water do. The equation is

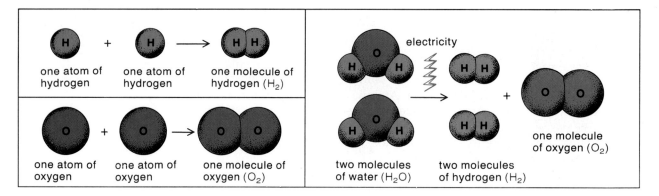

FIGURE 2.4 Models of chemical reactions. In the decomposition of water, twice as many hydrogen molecules as oxygen molecules are produced.

written to reflect this fact. Notice that the number of molecules is shown by a numeral *preceding* the formula for the molecule. Figure 2.4 shows models that represent chemical reactions.

When molecules collide they may or may not react, depending on the energy and orientation of the molecules. **Activation energy** is the energy needed to get a chemical reaction started. Sometimes an outside source of extra energy is necessary to initiate a reaction. For example, hydrogen (H_2) and oxygen (O_2) gases can be mixed without reacting until a lighted match, a spark, or ultraviolet light adds energy. This relatively small amount of energy causes some hydrogen molecules and oxygen molecules to react to form water and produce heat, which continues to activate the remaining molecules of hydrogen and oxygen. The reaction is often experienced as an explosion. The product, water, has less energy than the hydrogen and oxygen gases had separately in the mixture. The difference in energy is accounted for mainly in the amounts of light and heat emitted as the hydrogen and oxygen combine.

2.4   Chemical Bonds

When atoms interact, they can form several types of chemical bonds. One type forms when electrons are transferred from one atom to another. This type of chemical bond occurs in many substances, including table salt, also known as sodium chloride (NaCl). As the latter name suggests, table salt is made of two elements, sodium (Na) and chlorine (Cl). When atoms of these two elements react, an electron passes from a sodium atom to a chlorine atom (Figure 2.5). The resulting sodium atom is positively charged, for it has one less electron than protons. It becomes a sodium **ion,** written as Na^+. The chlorine atom is negatively charged, for it has one more electron than protons. It becomes a chloride ion, written as Cl^-. Note the change in name from chlorine to chloride.

As these examples suggest, an *ion* can be defined as an atom or a group of atoms that has acquired a positive or negative charge as a result of gaining or losing one or more electrons. By this definition molecules as well as atoms can become ions by gaining or losing electrons.

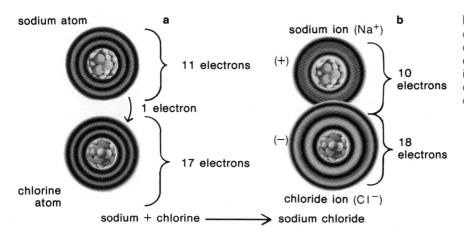

FIGURE 2.5 Sodium and chlorine can react to form the salt sodium chloride (NaCl). By losing one electron, sodium becomes a positive ion, and by gaining one electron, chlorine becomes a negative ion, chloride.

Table salt consists of positively charged sodium ions and negatively charged chloride ions, each strongly attracted to the other. The attraction between oppositely charged ions forms an **ionic bond** (Figure 2.5).

In a second type of chemical bond, two atoms share one or more pairs of electrons. The diagrams in Figure 2.6 show examples of electron-sharing or **covalent** (koh VAY lent) **bonds.** Two atoms of hydrogen join to form a molecule of hydrogen gas (H_2) by sharing a pair of electrons. In a molecule of water, each of the two hydrogen atoms shares a pair of electrons with the same oxygen atom.

The chemical behavior of water indicates that the atoms do not share the electrons equally. The larger oxygen atom attracts the electrons more strongly than the smaller hydrogen atoms do. If the electrons of a bond are not shared equally, the bond is called a polar covalent bond. In contrast, the electrons in a molecule of hydrogen gas are shared equally, and the resulting covalent bond is said to be nonpolar.

The unequal sharing of electrons in a water molecule gives the oxygen atom a slight negative charge and each hydrogen atom a slight positive charge (Figure 2.7). Such a molecule is known as a polar molecule. The

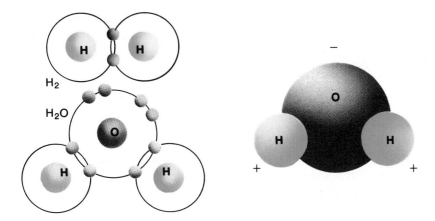

FIGURE 2.6 *(far left)* Covalent bonds form when two atoms share a pair of electrons. Only electrons in the outer energy levels are shown here.

FIGURE 2.7 *(left)* The polar nature of water. Oxygen atom attracts electrons more strongly than hydrogen, giving the oxygen a slight negative charge and each hydrogen a slight positive charge. The net charge of the molecule is zero.

FOCUS ON *Structural Formulas*

Structural formulas are models that show both the numbers and arrangement of atoms in molecules. In writing structural formulas of compounds, a covalent bond is indicated by a line. For example, the structural formula for hydrogen gas is written H—H. (Sometimes two atoms share two pairs of electrons between them, forming a double bond that is shown by a double line (=), as in O=C=O, carbon dioxide. When three pairs of electrons are shared by two atoms, they form a triple bond that is represented by three lines (≡).) Figure A shows several methods of representing molecules. Note that the molecular formula tells you only the number of atoms of each kind present in the molecule, whereas the structural formula indicates how the atoms are bonded. The space-filling and ball-and-stick models provide a picture of the spatial arrangement of the atoms.

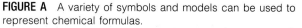

name/molecular formula	structural formula	models	
		space-filling	ball-and-stick
hydrogen/H_2	H—H		
water/H_2O	H—O—H		
ammonia/NH_3	H—N—H | H		
methane/CH_4	H | H—C—H | H		

FIGURE A A variety of symbols and models can be used to represent chemical formulas.

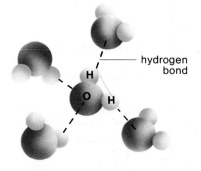

hydrogen bond

FIGURE 2.8 A hydrogen bond is a weak attraction between a slightly positive hydrogen atom in one polar molecule and a slightly negative atom in another.

polar nature of water is biologically significant. Most cells and tissues contain large amounts of water—up to 95 percent in some, with an average of 70 to 80 percent water throughout all organisms. Molecules must dissolve in water in order to move easily in and between living cells. Polar molecules, such as sugar, and ions, such as Na^+, dissolve in water because of the electrical attraction between them and the water molecules. Nonpolar molecules, such as simple fats and oils, do not dissolve in water.

Polar molecules may form still another type of chemical bond. An attraction can occur between a slightly positive hydrogen atom in a molecule and a nearby slightly negative atom of another molecule (or of the same molecule if it is large enough). This type of attraction is called a **hydrogen bond** (Figure 2.8). In compounds found in organisms, hydrogen bonds usually involve hydrogen bonded to oxygen or nitrogen. Hydrogen bonds provide the attractive force between water molecules (Figure 2.8) and are essential in maintaining the three-dimensional shape of large, complex molecules such as proteins and DNA.

2.5 Ions and Living Cells

When table salt dissolves in water, the ionic bonds are broken. Na^+ and Cl^- ions separate, or dissociate, but remain as ions in solution. The positive sodium ion is attracted to the slightly negative end of water, and the negative chloride ion is attracted to the slightly positive end.

When a nonionic compound, such as water, is converted to ions, the process is called ionization. The ionization of water is a vital reaction in

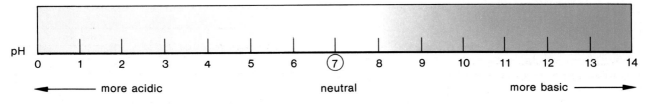

FIGURE 2.9 The pH scale is used to denote the acidity and alkalinity of solutions.

living cells. When a water molecule separates, one of its H—O bonds breaks. The result is a positively charged hydrogen ion (H^+) and a negatively charged hydroxide ion (OH^-). The hydrogen ion—a proton— quickly combines with a water molecule to form a hydronium ion (H_3O^+). It still is convenient, however, to refer to the number of hydrogen ions (H^+) in a solution, even though what really is meant is the concentration of hydronium ions (H_3O^+).

Only about one in every 10 million water molecules ionizes, yet all life processes depend on this tiny amount of ionization. Indeed, living cells must maintain their internal levels of H^+ and OH^- ions within narrow limits because even small changes greatly influence important reactions.

The level of H^+ and OH^- ions in solution is described by a range of numbers known as the **pH scale** (Figure 2.9). The scale runs from 0 to 14. A solution that has the same number of H^+ and OH^- ions is neutral and has a pH of 7. Pure water has a pH of 7. A solution having more H^+ than OH^- is acidic and has a pH less than 7 (low pH). A solution that has more OH^- than H^+ ions is basic (or alkaline) and has a pH greater than 7 (high pH). Thus, a solution with a pH of 2 is highly acidic, and a solution with a pH of 10 is highly basic. Figure 2.10 shows the pH of several common substances.

The pH scale is important in biology because one regulator of every reaction in a living system is the pH of the solution in which that reaction occurs. As a result, organisms vary in their response to the pH of their environment. For example, certain fungi and bacteria can grow in acidic solutions but not in basic ones. On the other hand, some marine organisms have become so adapted to the slightly basic pH (7.8–8.6) of seawater that they cannot live in less basic solutions. The pH of normal urine is about 6, but human blood must remain near pH 7.4. Death nearly always results if the blood pH falls to and stays at 6.8 or rises to and stays at 8.0. Failed kidney function is most often the reason a person cannot maintain normal blood pH.

Try Investigation 2A, Organisms and pH.

FIGURE 2.10 The pH of several common substances

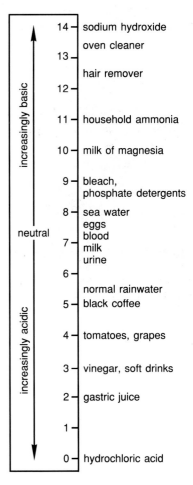

CHECK AND CHALLENGE

1. What is the relationship between atoms and elements?
2. What are the particles of an atom and how do they interact?
3. How are chemical reactions important in cells?
4. Distinguish among the various types of chemical bonds.
5. How is the ionization of water important to living organisms?
6. In what ways are polar molecules important to cells?

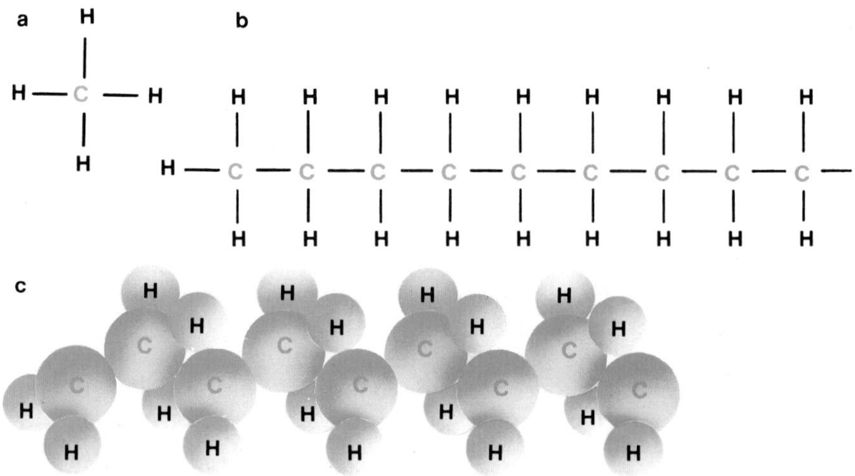

FIGURE 2.11 Structural formulas show how carbon atoms link with other atoms. In each formula, a short line indicates a covalent bond: (a) shows a complete molecule; (b) is part of the carbon skeleton of a molecule; (c) a view of (b) that indicates the three-dimensional structure of molecules. Other atoms, such as oxygen or nitrogen, can be attached to the carbon skeleton instead of hydrogen.

Biochemistry

2.6 Organic Compounds and Life

CONNECTIONS

The structure–function concept is critical in understanding the relationship between chemistry and biology. Biological function depends on chemical structure. Biological molecules do what they do because of their unique chemical structures.

Many chemical compounds besides water are needed for life to exist. The most important are organic compounds—compounds in which the carbon atoms are combined with hydrogen and usually oxygen. Organic compounds frequently also contain nitrogen, sulfur, or phosphorus. A few carbon compounds have never been included with organic compounds: carbon dioxide (CO_2), carbon monoxide (CO), and carbonic acid (H_2CO_3).

The name "organic" was coined long ago when it was thought these compounds could be formed only by living cells. Since then millions of different organic compounds have been synthesized in the laboratory. There is no longer any reason to call these compounds "organic," but the name is so well established that it is still widely used to describe nearly all carbon compounds, essential for life or not.

Carbon can combine in long chains that form the backbone of large complex molecules, or macromolecules. The backbone of carbon atoms is called the carbon skeleton (Figure 2.11). Other atoms and molecules can attach to the carbon skeleton, giving each macromolecule a particular structure and, therefore, a particular function. The following sections of the chapter discuss the characteristics of the four most important classes of macromolecules—carbohydrates, lipids, proteins, and nucleic acids.

2.7 Carbohydrates

Try Investigation 2B, Compounds of Living Things.

All known types of living cells contain **carbohydrates** (*carbo* for carbon, *hydrate* for water). In addition to carbon atoms, carbohydrates contain hydrogen and oxygen atoms in the same two-to-one ratio as water. The simplest carbohydrates are single sugars called monosaccharides

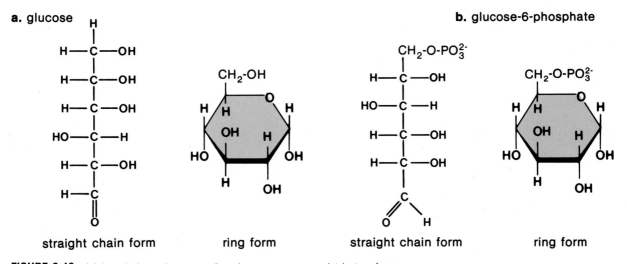

FIGURE 2.12 (a) In solution, glucose, a 6-carbon sugar, can exist in two forms: a straight chain and a ring form. The ring form, in which 5 carbon atoms and an oxygen atom form a closed ring, is by far the most abundant. (b) The two forms of glucose-6-phosphate

(MON oh SAK uh rydz). Most organisms readily use the monosaccharide glucose (which is also referred to as blood sugar) as a source of energy. In Figure 2.12a, the structural formulas of two forms of glucose are shown. Monosaccharides may contain from three to seven carbon atoms in their carbon skeletons.

Biologically important sugars often have a phosphate group attached to the carbon skeleton and are called sugar phosphates. The phosphate group, which is composed of an atom of phosphorus and three atoms of oxygen, often is shown as Ⓟ when attached to a carbon skeleton (see Figure 2.25 on page 39).

Two monosaccharides may bond together to form a double sugar, or disaccharide (DY SAK uh ryd), represented in Figure 2.13a on the next page. The most familiar of all disaccharides is sucrose, commonly called table sugar. Sucrose contains glucose and another monosaccharide, fructose. Lactose, or milk sugar, is a disaccharide formed of glucose and the monosaccharide galactose. Maltose, or malt sugar, is a common disaccharide made of two glucose molecules.

Several glucose molecules may bond together to build complex carbohydrates called polysaccharides (POL ee SAK uh rydz), represented in Figure 2.13b. Starch and cellulose are the complex carbohydrates commonly formed by plants. Starch is an energy-storage and carbon-reserve compound in many plants and is an important food source for humans, as discussed in Chapter 18. The rigid walls surrounding plant cells contain cellulose, an important part of wood and cotton fibers, and other polysaccharides. The human liver and muscles store carbohydrates in the form of glycogen (GLY ko jen), also called animal starch. Molecules of starch, cellulose, and glycogen consist of thousands of glucose units and have no fixed size.

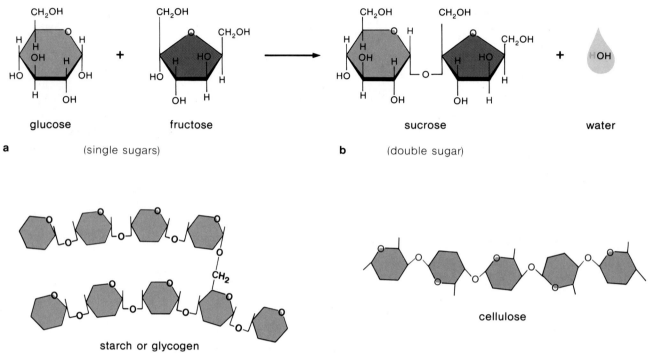

glucose   fructose   sucrose   water

a   (single sugars)   **b**   (double sugar)

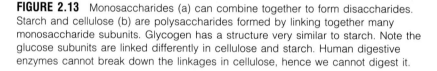

cellulose

starch or glycogen

c   (polysaccharides)

FIGURE 2.13 Monosaccharides (a) can combine together to form disaccharides. Starch and cellulose (b) are polysaccharides formed by linking together many monosaccharide subunits. Glycogen has a structure very similar to starch. Note the glucose subunits are linked differently in cellulose and starch. Human digestive enzymes cannot break down the linkages in cellulose, hence we cannot digest it.

2.8 Lipids

Lipids (LIP idz), or fats and oils, are macromolecules that have two primary functions: the long-term storage of energy and carbon and the building of structural parts of cell membranes. Lipids generally do not dissolve in water, because they are nonpolar. Like carbohydrates, lipids contain carbon, hydrogen, and oxygen, but not in a fixed ratio. Building blocks of lipids, called fatty acids and glycerol, make up the simple fats most common in our diets and bodies. Three fatty acid molecules and one glycerol molecule join to form a simple fat, or triglyceride (try GLIS uh ryd), as shown in Figure 2.14.

The biologically important properties of simple fats depend on their fatty acids, which may be either alike or different. For example, the fats in meat are different from the oils in vegetables because the fatty acids are different. The properties of fatty acids, in turn, depend on the length of their carbon chains and the type of bonds between the carbons. Common fatty acids have a total of 16 or 18 carbon atoms. Fatty acids in which single bonds join the carbon atoms are saturated fatty acids. Unsaturated fatty acids are fatty acids in which double bonds join some of the carbon atoms. Figure 2.14 shows both types of fatty acids. Unsaturated fats (fats containing unsaturated fatty acids) tend to be oily liquids at room temperature.

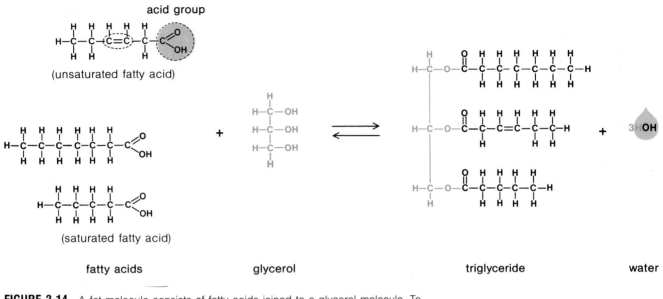

(unsaturated fatty acid)

(saturated fatty acid)

fatty acids

glycerol

triglyceride

water

FIGURE 2.14 A fat molecule consists of fatty acids joined to a glycerol molecule. To form a fat, one molecule of glycerol combines with three molecules of fatty acids. The fatty acids in one fat may be alike or different. Examine the diagram. What is a by-product of this reaction?

Olive oil, corn oil, and sunflower oil are unsaturated. Saturated fats, such as butter and lard, usually are solid at room temperature. Chapter 18 discusses the important roles of saturated and unsaturated fats in the diet.

Two other lipids important in cells are phospholipids and cholesterol (koh LES ter ol), illustrated in Figure 2.15. Phospholipids form when two fatty acids combine with a phosphate group. Together with proteins, phospholipids form cellular membranes, discussed in Section 6.5. Cholesterol is part of the membrane structure of animal cells and is important in nutrition. Cells in the human body manufacture many essential substances, such as sex hormones, from cholesterol.

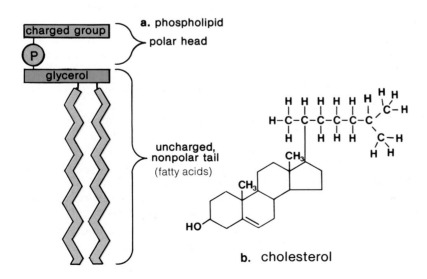

a. phospholipid

b. cholesterol

FIGURE 2.15 Glycerol joins with two fatty acids and a phosphate group to form a phospholipid (a). When phospholipids form membranes, the polar head associates with water on the membrane surface, and the nonpolar tail faces the interior of the membrane, away from water. See Figure 6.15 for more detail about the molecular structure of membranes. Cholesterol (b) has a fused four-ring structure with additional side groups. Cholesterol is important in membrane structure, and the sex hormones are derived from it.

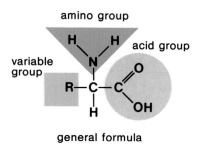

amino group

variable
group

acid group

R—C—C

general formula

FIGURE 2.16 Amino acids (except for proline) have a central carbon atom bonded to a hydrogen atom, an amino group, an acid group, and an R-group. The R-group is any of 20 different arrangements of C, H, O, N, and S atoms, depending on, and giving unique structure to, each amino acid.

2.9 Proteins

Every living cell contains from several hundred to several thousand different macromolecules known as **proteins** (PROH teens). Proteins are structural components of cells as well as messengers and receptors of messages between cells. They play an important role in defense against disease (Chapter 20). Skin, hair, muscles, and parts of the skeleton are made of proteins. Their most essential role, however, is as **enzymes,** specialized molecules that facilitate the many reactions occurring in cells.

Cells make proteins by linking building blocks called **amino** (uh MEE no) **acids.** Amino acids contain carbon, hydrogen, oxygen, and nitrogen atoms; two also contain sulfur atoms. Figure 2.16 shows the general structural formula for an amino acid. Amino acids all have a central carbon atom to which is attached a hydrogen atom, an amino group ($—NH_2$), an acid group ($—COOH$), and a variable group, symbolized by R, which may be one of 20 different atoms or groups of atoms. Observe in Figure 2.17a that in the amino acid glycine (GLY seen) R is an H atom, and in alanine (AL a neen) R is a $—CH_3$ group.

Any two amino acid molecules may combine when a chemical bond forms between the acid group of one molecule and the amino group of the other (Figure 2.17a). Covalent bonds of this sort, formed between amino

FIGURE 2.17 A peptide bond forms when the acid group ($—COOH$) of one amino acid joins to the amino group ($—NH_2$) of another amino acid (a). The acid group loses an atom of hydrogen and an atom of oxygen. The amino group loses an atom of hydrogen. These atoms combine to form a water molecule. More peptide bonds can form in the same way, joining a chain of amino acids to form a polypeptide (b).

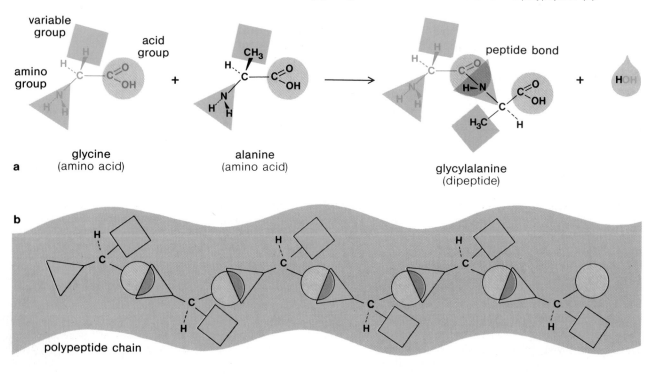

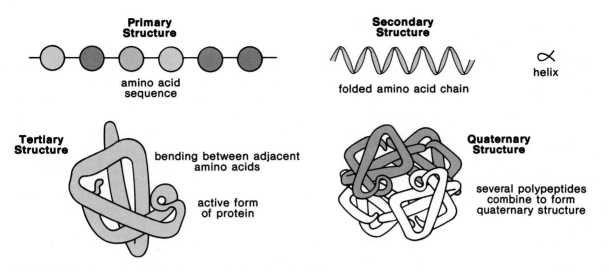

FIGURE 2.18 Stages in the development of a functional protein

acids, are called **peptide bonds**. Additional peptide bonds may form, resulting in a long chain of amino acids, or **polypeptide** (Figure 2.17b). Longer polypeptide chains form proteins; a protein molecule may contain from about 50 to 3000 amino acid units. The type, number, and sequence of its amino acids distinguishes a particular protein from all others. Each type of amino acid may occur in many places in a protein's chain. The sequence of amino acids in the chain forms the *primary* structure of a protein. In most proteins, the chain twists, forming a *secondary* structure and then folds back on itself, forming a *tertiary* structure, which usually is globular, or spherical, in form. Figure 2.18 shows diagrams of these structures. The tertiary structure determines the three-dimensional shape, or architecture, of the protein, which in turn determines its function. Each individual protein has a unique shape, which helps to give it a specific function. A few proteins become active only when two or more tertiary forms combine to form a complex quaternary structure (Figure 2.18).

2.10 Enzymes and Chemical Reactions

Chemical reactions in most organisms take place within a fairly narrow range of temperatures. Those temperatures are not high enough to supply the activation energy (Section 2.3) needed to start a reaction. Unlike the example at the end of Section 2.3, cells obviously cannot use a lighted match or an electric spark to provide activation energy. How do organisms carry out the thousands of chemical reactions needed for survival? All living cells contain specialized proteins called enzymes that lower the activation energy required to make a reaction proceed (Figure 2.19 on the next page). In that way, enzymes greatly speed up chemical reactions that would otherwise occur too slowly to sustain life. The reactions do not

Try Investigation 2C, Chemical Reactions and Cells.

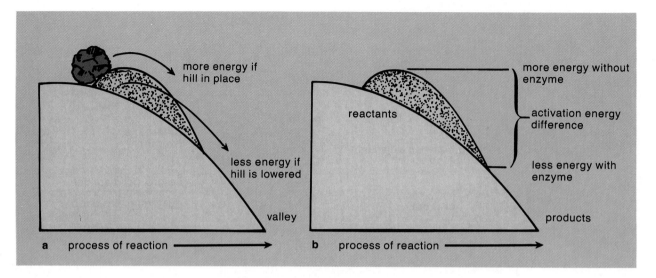

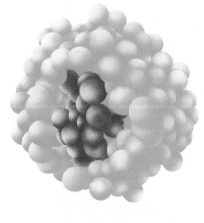

FIGURE 2.19 In (a), the hill is a barrier that prevents the rock from rolling down to the valley. Energy can be expended to push the rock over the hill or to lower the hill. The hill represents the activation energy required to start a reaction. In (b), an enzyme lowers the activation energy requirement, making it possible for the reaction to proceed.

consume the enzymes, which are thus reusable. Chemicals that lower activation energies are called catalysts. Enzymes are catalysts in living organisms and are highly specific for the reactions they catalyze.

The specific reaction catalyzed by an enzyme depends on a small area of its tertiary structure called the active site (Figure 2.20). This is a unique region of the enzyme where specific binding and associations with molecules can occur. Thus, the active site can attract and hold only specific molecules. An enzyme and the molecules on which it acts—the substrates—may fit together the way a lock fits around a key (Figure 2.21). Current evidence, however, indicates that an enzyme may change shape slightly when it interacts with the substrate, much as a leather glove changes shape somewhat to fit the hand it covers (Figure 2.22). Each enzyme can catalyze only one or a few specific chemical reactions because only a few molecules are sufficiently alike in structure and shape to fit the active site.

To act as a catalyst, an enzyme must *temporarily* take part in a chemical reaction. The reacting molecules (reactants) combine with the active site of an enzyme, forming an enzyme-substrate complex. By bringing the reacting molecules together, the enzyme lowers the activation energy so that chemical changes can be completed rapidly. One of the characteristics of enzymes is that they greatly speed up reactions that otherwise would take place very slowly. Once the reactions occur, the newly formed molecules break away, leaving the enzymes the same as they were before the reactions. Thousands of different chemical reactions occur in cells, and thousands of different enzymes are present. Several thousand enzyme-catalyzed reactions may occur every minute in each of your cells.

An important characteristic of reactions catalyzed by enzymes is that they are often reversible. With the aid of enzymes, two reacting molecules

FIGURE 2.20 A space-filling model of the tertiary structure of an enzyme, showing the active site deep in the molecule.

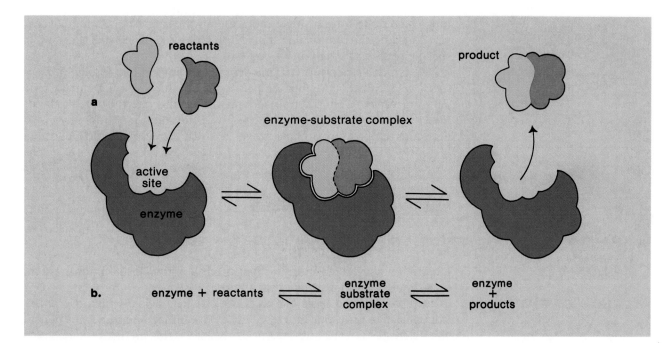

FIGURE 2.21 The lock-and-key hypothesis of enzyme action (a). The reactant fits in the enzyme the way a key fits in a lock. The enzyme takes part in the reaction but is only temporarily changed. It emerges again in its original form. The equation for the reaction is shown in (b). Note the reaction is reversible, and both the reactant and the product can be substrates for the enzyme.

FIGURE 2.22 The induced-fit hypothesis of enzyme action. (a) The substrates (reactants) bind to the enzyme at the active site of the enzyme (in red). (b) On binding, the enzyme changes shape to fit and hold the substrates. (c) The product of the reaction forms and the enzyme is recycled. The same enzyme can also catalyze the reverse reaction, a capacity of fundamental importance in biology.

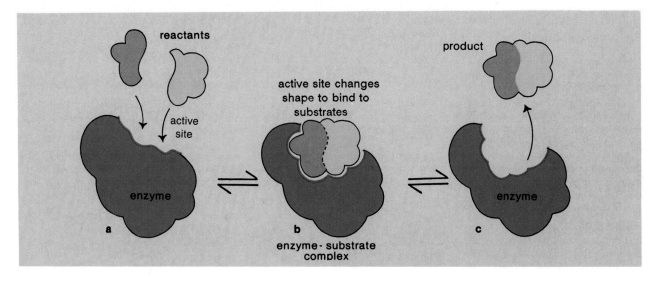

may combine to form a single molecule, or the single molecule may convert back into the two smaller molecules. Thus, an enzyme can speed up its specific reaction in *both* directions.

Two other aspects of enzyme activity are important to cells. Enzyme reactions are faster at higher temperatures, but only within a narrow temperature range. Above certain temperatures, the enzymes break down. Enzyme activity also varies with the pH of the solution. Thus, there is an optimum temperature and pH range at which enzymes are most effective.

Genetic Coding in Cells

2.11   Nucleic Acids

Experimental evidence indicates that **nucleic** (noo KLEE ik) **acids** are the macromolecules that dictate the amino acid sequence of proteins, which, in turn, control the basic life processes. Nucleic acids, which are passed from parent to offspring, also store information that determines the genetic characteristics of cells and organisms. Nucleic acids are thus the chemical link between generations, dating back to the beginning of life on Earth. How can one type of molecule play such a dominant role in all living things? The answer lies in the structure of the molecules.

Nucleic acids are made of relatively simple units called **nucleotides** (NOO klee oh tydz) connected to form long chains. Each nucleotide consists of three parts. One part is a pentose (5-carbon sugar), which may be either ribose (RY bohs), or deoxyribose (dee OK sih RY bohs). Compare their structural formulas in Figure 2.23. What differences can you see? Attached to the sugar is the second part, a phosphate group (Ⓟ). The third part of a nucleotide is a nitrogen base, which is a single or double ringlike structure of carbon, hydrogen, and nitrogen (Figure 2.24).

Nucleic acids that contain ribose in their nucleotides are called ribonucleic (RY boh noo KLEE ic) acids, or **RNA**. Nucleotides containing deoxyribose form deoxyribonucleic (dee OK sih RY boh noo KLEE ic) acids, or **DNA**. In DNA, each of the four different nucleotides contains a deoxyri-

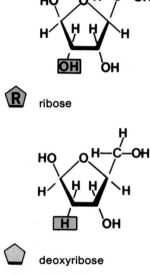

ribose

deoxyribose

FIGURE 2.23 Ribose and deoxyribose form ring structures with four carbon atoms joined by an oxygen. The blue boxes highlight the difference between the two sugars. Ribose has a hydroxyl group (—OH), whereas deoxyribose has only a hydrogen atom at the same carbon. Compared to ribose, deoxyribose is missing one oxygen atom; *deoxy* in the name means "minus oxygen."

FIGURE 2.24 Four nitrogen bases that occur in nucleotides. Note that cytosine and thymine have a single ring structure; adenine and guanine a double ring.

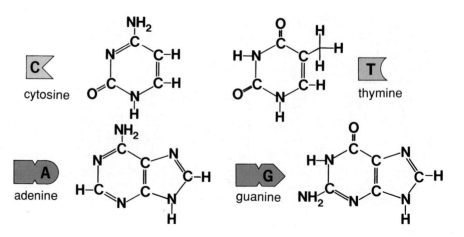

cytosine

thymine

adenine

guanine

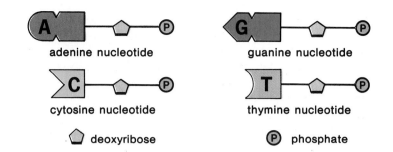

FIGURE 2.25 Symbols represent adenine, guanine, cytosine, and thymine in these diagrams of nucleotides. Each nucleotide contains one of the bases, one sugar, and one phosphate group. The sugar is deoxyribose, making these the four nucleotides of DNA.

bose, a phosphate group, and one of the four bases shown in Figure 2.24—adenine, thymine, guanine, or cytosine. The possible DNA nucleotides that can form from these bases are illustrated in Figure 2.25.

2.12 The Double Helix

In a short scientific paper published in 1953, James Watson and Francis Crick (Figure 2.26) proposed a model for the structure of the DNA molecule that is still accepted with some modification today. They founded their model on the principle of specific pairing of the nucleotides, shown in Figure 2.27 on the next page. Hydrogen bonds form only between the

a

b

c

d

FIGURE 2.26 In 1953, James D. Watson (a) and Francis H.C. Crick (b) proposed a model for the DNA molecule based partly on the X-ray diffraction studies of Rosalind Franklin (c) and M.H.F. Wilkins (d). Watson, Crick, and Wilkins shared the Nobel prize in 1962.

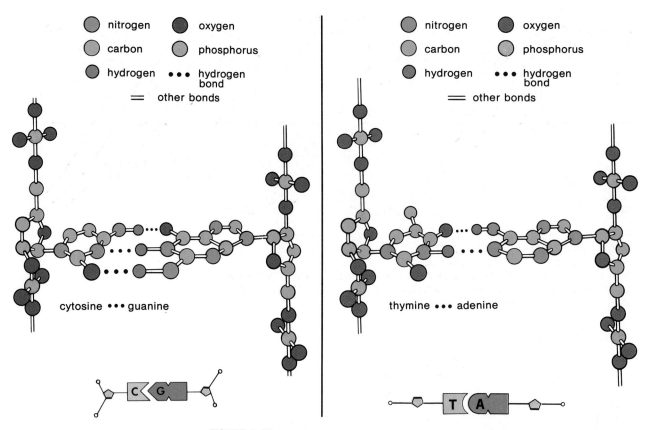

FIGURE 2.27 A diagram showing the pairing of two nitrogen bases. Hydrogen bonds connect cytosine to guanine and adenine to thymine.

nucleotide bases of adenine (A) and thymine (T) or cytosine (C) and guanine (G). X-ray diffraction photographs taken by Rosalind Franklin in the laboratory of Maurice Wilkins suggested to Watson and Crick that DNA molecules have a double-helix structure.

The DNA molecule is composed of two long chains of nucleotides. The nucleotides of each chain are connected between their deoxyribose sugars by phosphate groups (Ⓟ). The two chains run next to each other but, chemically speaking, in opposite directions. Between chains, the nucleotides are connected through their nitrogen bases to form a long double-stranded molecule. Because of the specific pairing between bases, the two strands are a complement of each other. The two strands intertwine, forming a double helix that winds around a central axis like a spiral straircase (Figure 2.28).

DNA forms the **genes,** units of genetic information that pass from parent to offspring. The structure of DNA explains how DNA functions as the molecule of genetic information. Those functions are summarized in the concept map in Figure 2.29. Many of the concepts in this map are the topics of later chapters and will take time to understand. To help you link the concepts, refer back to Figure 2.29 as you study those chapters.

CONNECTIONS

The universality of DNA as the genetic material is evidence of a common evolutionary origin for life.

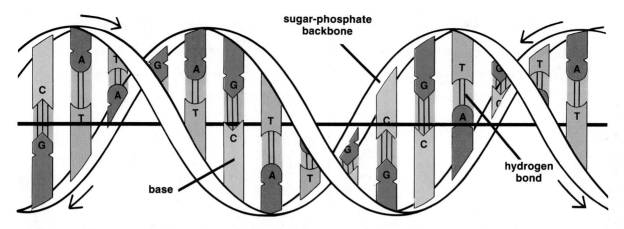

FIGURE 2.28 The structure of DNA. Alternating sugar and phosphate molecules connect each chain of nucleotides. Two chains are held together by specific pairing of the bases—A to T and G to C—and coiled around a central axis to form a double helix. The axis is shown to help visualize the correct twisting. The two strands run in opposite directions, and there are 10 nucleotides per turn of the helix. Only a small portion of a DNA molecule is shown.

FIGURE 2.29 Functions of DNA

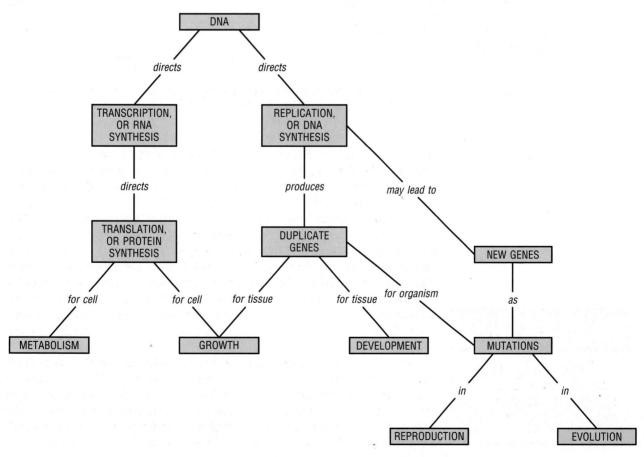

THE SCANNING TUNNELING MICROSCOPE

Although the electron microscope is useful for observing the overall features of a sample, it cannot reveal the surface structures because electrons from the electron source penetrate too deeply. The scanning tunneling microscope, however, uses only electrons already in the sample, rather than an external source. A characteristic of all materials is that some electrons leave the surface and form an electron cloud around the material. The scanning tunneling microscope uses this electron cloud as the source of radiation.

To scan the surface of a sample, the tip of the microscope (a needle) is pushed toward the sample until the electron clouds of the tip and the sample touch. Then electricity is applied between the tip and the sample, causing electrons to flow through a narrow channel in the electron clouds. This electron flow is called the tunneling current. The tunneling current is extremely sensitive to the distance between the microscope tip and the surface of the sample and allows precise measurements of the ver-

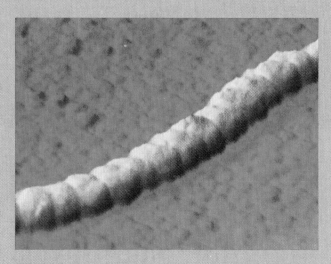

FIGURE C   The scanning tunneling microscope reveals the surface features of DNA, magnified 3.8 million times.

tical surface features of the sample. A feedback mechanism maintains the tip at a constant height as it sweeps across the sample surface, following the contours of the surface atoms. The motion of the tip is read and processed by a computer and then displayed on a screen. A three-dimensional image of the surface is obtained by sweeping the tip in parallel lines (see Figure B). To achieve high-resolution images of surface structures, the microscope must be shielded from even the smallest of vibrations, such as a footstep or sound.

In addition to revealing the atomic topography of a surface, the scanning tunneling microscope reveals atomic composition. Investigators probing the structure of DNA also have generated images depicting the helical twists and turns of a strand of DNA. Because scanning tunneling microscopes can operate equally well with samples in air or liquid, the DNA was observed under normal atmospheric conditions. (In an electron microscope, samples must be observed in a vacuum.) Researchers currently have achieved even higher degrees of resolution than that shown in Figure C.

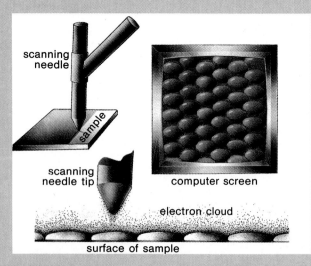

scanning needle

sample

scanning needle tip

computer screen

electron cloud

surface of sample

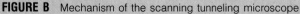

FIGURE B   Mechanism of the scanning tunneling microscope

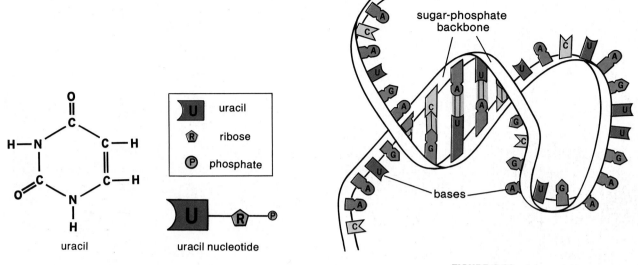

uracil

uracil nucleotide

sugar-phosphate backbone

bases

FIGURE 2.30 *(above left)* A uracil nucleotide is found in RNA in place of a thymine nucleotide.

FIGURE 2.31 *(above right)* A single- and double-stranded model of an RNA molecule. Most of the molecule is single stranded, but the shaded region shows base pairing to form a double-stranded region. Note the four bases in RNA.

2.13 RNA

RNA contains the sugar ribose instead of deoxyribose, and rarely contains the base thymine. A similar compound, uracil (YUR uh sil), shown in Figure 2.30, almost always replaces the thymine. The other three bases, adenine, guanine, and cytosine, are the same in RNA and DNA.

In RNA, just as in DNA, the nucleotides are arranged in long chains. RNA, however, occurs as single strands, which may be highly folded. The folds are held together by the same kind of base pairing as in DNA (Figure 2.31). There are three types of RNA in cells, each of which performs a different role in the synthesis of proteins (Chapter 10).

The number and arrangement of the nucleotides can vary in RNA as they do in DNA. The different arrangements of nucleotides in a nucleic acid provide the key to how these molecules may account for the diversity of organisms living on Earth.

CHECK AND CHALLENGE

1. Describe how the respective smaller building-block molecules combine to form each of the four types of macromolecules.
2. What is the relationship between the primary and tertiary structure of a protein?
3. How do enzymes work as catalysts to help reactions proceed at accelerated rates?
4. What is the active site of an enzyme?
5. Describe the structure of a nucleotide.
6. How do the chemical structures of ribose and deoxyribose differ?
7. What determines which nitrogen bases form pairs in DNA?

Summary

Cells are chemical factories. They carry out their biological functions through chemical reactions. Elements are materials that cannot break down into substances with new or different properties. They are the basic structural components of matter. Atoms containing a characteristic number of positively charged protons, negatively charged electrons, and neutral neutrons make up all elements. Ions are atoms or groups of atoms that have gained or lost electrons; ions have a positive or negative charge. Chemical bonds hold atoms together to form molecules. When atoms share electrons, the molecules are held together by covalent bonds. The attraction of two oppositely charged ions is an ionic bond.

In chemical reactions, molecules interact and form different substances. Those interactions are accompanied by energy changes that drive the reactions living cells use for growth, reproduction, and all other functions. Organic catalysts called enzymes help carry out most reactions in living cells, reactions that would otherwise not occur at adequate rates.

Organisms contain four major types of macromolecules. Carbohydrates store and transfer energy in cells and contribute to cell structure. Lipids store energy and form a major part of membranes. Proteins act as enzymes and form such tissues as muscle and blood. The nucleic acids DNA and RNA store, transfer, and direct the expression of genetic information. Chemical compounds have biological activity because of their specific chemical structures. Chemical structure dictates biological function.

Key Concepts

Below is the beginning of a concept map. Use the concepts that follow to build a more complete map. Add as many other concepts from the chapter as you can. Include appropriate linking words.

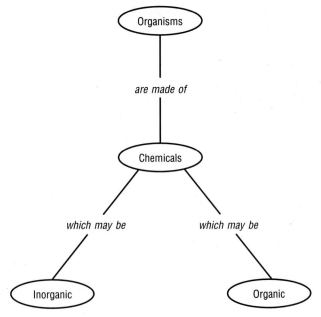

Energy, Life, and the Biosphere

*B*iology is the study of life, but what is life? What do we mean when we say an object is living? Although no definition of life is completely satisfactory, biologists agree that the ability to absorb and convert energy is a basic characteristic of life. Thus, the energy required for the growth and organized maintenance of individual cells, entire organisms, and even communities is a fundamental topic in biology. The study of the energy flow and energy transformations among living systems is called bioenergetics. This chapter examines the characteristics of living things and introduces the underlying topic of bioenergetics.

---

*H*ow does the bear's fishing for salmon demonstrate the relationship between life, energy, and the biosphere?

◆ *A brown bear sow,* Ursus arctos, *fishing for salmon with cubs.*

Organisms and Energy

3.1 Characteristics of Organisms

If you were a member of an astronaut team sent to another planet, how could you tell whether objects on that planet were alive? You could gather clues and match them to your prior notions of what constitutes life. To answer the question with confidence you need to consider what characteristics living things have in common.

Take a few minutes to list several characteristics of living things that would help separate them from nonliving objects. Compare your list with those of your classmates. Notice the characteristics everyone included. Did you disagree on any? Investigation 3A provides additional information to help separate living things and nonliving things.

Movement and growth are two characteristics you may have included in your list, yet both living and nonliving things can move and grow. What makes living things different from nonliving things?

To help answer this question, consider not only *what* something does but also *how* it does it. Clouds move because they are carried by an external energy source, the wind. Clouds do not move on their own. Living things move by obtaining energy and transforming it into motion.

Table 3.1 lists characteristics generally found in living organisms (although not all organisms possess these characteristics to the same degree). Later chapters in this book consider these characteristics in detail. As you read these chapters during the year, you may wish to refer back to the list. Compare the list with the one you developed. How are the two lists alike? How are they different?

TABLE 3.1
Characteristics of Organisms

- Take in and convert materials and energy from the environment; give off by-products, or wastes
- Have a higher degree of chemical organization compared to nonliving objects (see Figure 3.1)
- Have complex structural organization that is responsible for their appearance and activities
- Contain coded instructions for maintaining their organization and activities
- Sense and react to changes in their environment
- Grow and develop during some part of their lives
- Reproduce others like themselves
- Communicate with other similar organisms
- Move under their own ability

FIGURE 3.1 The arrangement of crystals in a granite rock (a) shows less organization than the highly ordered structure of a corn stem, *Zea mays* (b), seen in cross section.

a

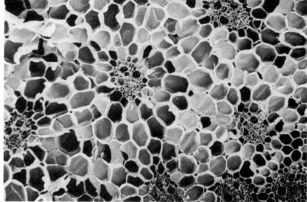

b

Biological Challenges

IDENTIFICATION OF LIFE

In the summer of 1976, two United States space-crafts, *Viking I* and *II*, arrived at Mars. The primary purpose behind the missions was to determine if life existed on that planet. Although no one imagined that Mars harbored higher forms of life, almost everyone agreed that microscopic forms might be present.

Three microbiology experiments were designed to determine if there was any detectable life on Mars, particularly in the soil (Figure A). The soil on Earth is a vast biological community inhabited by bacteria, yeasts, and molds. Besides being abundant, these organisms are very hardy and are the last survivors in extreme environments.

Accordingly, each *Viking* lander carried instruments for three experiments designed to detect the chemical activities of soil microorganisms. The experiments were similar in that they exposed small samples of the Martian surface material to substances of various kinds and then monitored the fate of those substances. The assumptions were that if microorganisms are present in the Martian soil, they must take in food and give off waste gases; or they must take in gases from the atmosphere and convert them to useful substances.

In one experiment, Martian soil and a nutrient broth were mixed together. If microorganisms were present, waste gases should be produced, much as they are in a bowl of soup left out on a kitchen table. Indeed, complex changes were observed in the levels of various gases, but the responses varied greatly.

In another experiment, five simple chemicals were supplied. The carbon atoms in these chemicals were radioactively tagged so their fate could be followed. If Martian microorganisms "ate" any of the supplied chemicals and released the carbon atoms in a gas, the change could be detected. This experiment seemed to give a positive indication of life on Mars.

On the whole, the microbiological experiments pointed in a positive direction. When Martian soil was mixed with an organic nutrient, something in the soil chemically broke down the nutrient—

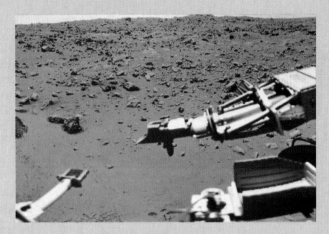

FIGURE A The mechanical arm of the *Viking* lander dug into the floor of the crater Chryse in the search for life on Mars.

almost like digestion. When gases from Earth were introduced into the Martian soil sample, the gases chemically combined with the soil—almost as if microorganisms synthesized organic material from the gases.

Is there life on Mars? The situation is complex. The biggest drawback of these experiments is the lack of controls. How can you control for something you do not know about? Moreover, it is impossible to repeat the experiments on Earth, because there is no way to exactly duplicate Martian conditions on Earth.

Although the experiments point toward the possibility of life on Mars, there are too many unknown factors. How do we know that these results are not the product of complex chemical reactions we do not understand? Perhaps there is an inorganic component of Martian soil that can break down nutrients by itself. Perhaps there is some special inorganic catalyst in the soil that is capable of converting gases into organic molecules.

We may never know for certain whether life, as we understand it, exists on Mars. All we can do is refine the experiments, account for as many variables as possible, develop better controls, and wait for future Martian probes so more tests can be run.

3.2 Energy and Nutrients

The need for energy is a fundamental characteristic of living things. Energy is the capacity to do work or to cause change. The energy living organisms use to do work is called **free energy.** Examples of free energy are the energy plants use for growing and producing food or the energy you use for exercise and thinking. Free energy becomes available in an organism when energy stored in one form changes to another form during chemical reactions. Organisms store energy in the organic molecules from which the organisms are made. Such energy is known as **chemical energy**, and the portion of this chemical energy available to do work is free energy.

Living cells need a constant source of free energy for chemical and mechanical work and for transport. Chemical work includes constructing and breaking down large complex molecules, such as proteins and nucleic acids, in chemical reactions. Organizing these molecules into the larger structural components of cells, such as in muscle and skin, is also chemical work. Transport work involves the movement and concentration of the raw materials, or **nutrients**, needed to make complex molecules and to increase cellular organization during growth. Mechanical work includes movement, such as muscle contractions that enable you to kick a ball.

How do organisms obtain energy and nutrients? Some organisms, known as heterotrophs (HET eh roh trohfs; *hetero* = other, *troph* = feed), obtain energy and nutrients from other organisms, either living or dead. Animals, fungi (mushrooms and molds), and most bacteria are heterotrophs. Other organisms are capable of producing their own food. They obtain energy and nutrients from nonliving sources such as the sun, soil, and the air. These organisms are autotrophs (AWT oh trohfs; *auto* = self). Autotrophs include plants, certain bacteria, and other organisms that capture energy from the sun and use it to synthesize organic compounds from inorganic materials absorbed from their surroundings.

The process by which most autotrophs capture energy from sunlight and use it to synthesize organic compounds from carbon dioxide and water

Try Investigation 3B, Food Energy.

FOCUS ON *KCALS*

The unit of measure for energy traditionally has been the calorie: the amount of heat required to raise the temperature of one gram of water from 15°C to 16°C. The unit of measure for food energy is the kilocalorie (kcal; also called the large Calorie), which is 1000 calories. In the international system, the *joule* (J) is now the unit assigned to energy, but the kcal still is a common measure of energy flow in living systems. One kilocalorie is equivalent to 4.18 kilojoules (kJ).

The minimum energy available from a specific food can be measured by completely burning the food in a calorimeter. A calorimeter is a chamber designed to record energy changes while preventing energy exchange with the outside environment. For example, if one gram of sugar is burned in a calorimeter, 4 kcals of heat are produced. The mass of a teaspoon of sugar is about 5 grams, so a teaspoon of sugar in your diet provides 20 kcals, or about 84 kJ, of food energy. You use some of that energy for chemical and physical work and some for heat to maintain your body temperature.

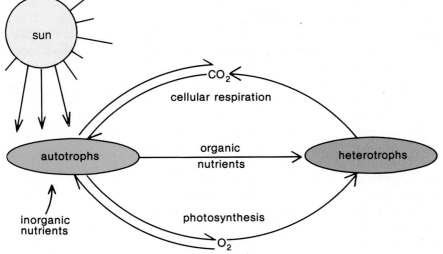

FIGURE 3.2 The relationship between autotrophs and heterotrophs

is **photosynthesis**, explained in Chapter 7. Some of the energy captured in photosynthesis is stored as chemical energy in the organic compounds and later serves as the source of free energy for cellular work. Autotrophs also use the organic compounds made during photosynthesis as building blocks for maintenance, growth, and reproduction. Only autotrophs are capable of photosynthesis.

Heterotrophs consume autotrophs and other heterotrophs as food that supplies the energy and organic nutrients needed for their own maintenance, growth, and reproduction (Figure 3.2). You are a heterotroph and must eat to obtain the nutrients and energy you need to grow and develop.

Both autotrophs and heterotrophs carry out chemical reactions that convert the chemical energy stored in organic compounds to free energy that is available to do work. These reactions occur as a series of many steps that ultimately involve oxygen in most organisms. Together, the reactions are known as **cellular respiration** and are the subject of Chapter 8.

3.3 Energy and Ecosystems

The need for energy and nutrients links organisms in many complex ways. Autotrophs, which produce food other organisms use, are the **producers** in a community of living organisms, such as a forest or an ocean. Heterotrophs eat plants and other organisms for food; they are the **consumers**. For example, the trees in a forest or the seaweeds in an ocean capture energy from the sun to make their own food from nutrients in the air, soil, and water. In turn, animals eat the plants, or they eat animals that have eaten plants. The plants are producers, and the animals are consumers. Bacteria, fungi, and other heterotrophs that break down and use dead plants and animals for food are **decomposers**.

In a system of living organisms, the energy and nutrient links among producers, consumers, and decomposers form a **food web** (Figure 3.3 on page 52). In a food web, energy and nutrients flow from the environment through the producers to the consumers and finally to the decomposers. Decomposers complete the breakdown of organic nutrients and return inorganic nutrients to the soil or water, where they are available for reuse.

The organisms in a food web grow and reproduce in a complex, non-living environment made of **abiotic factors**, such as the soil, minerals, water, and weather. The organisms of a food web make up the **biotic**, or

FIGURE 3.3 A food web

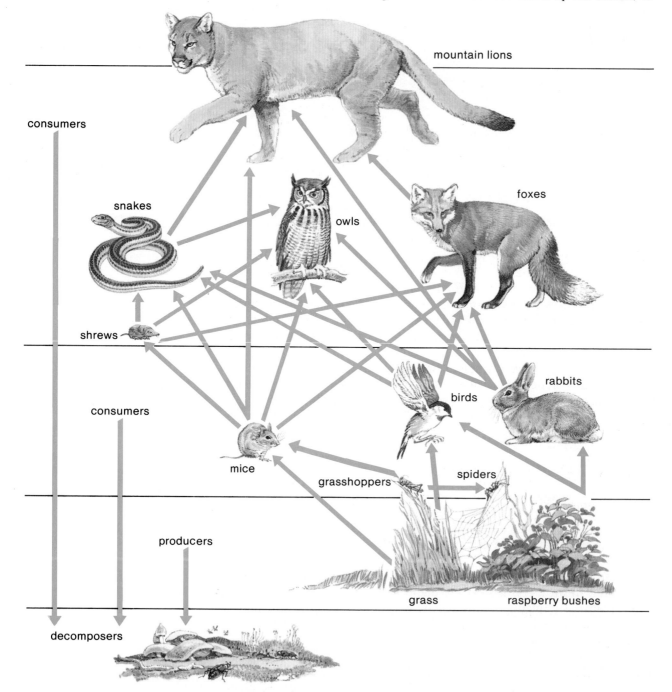

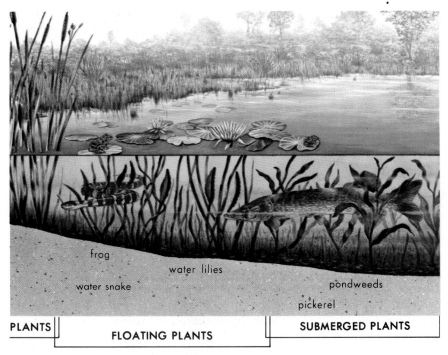

PLANTS   FLOATING PLANTS   SUBMERGED PLANTS

frog
water lilies
water snake
pondweeds
pickerel

FIGURE 3.4   Abiotic and biotic factors interact to form an ecosystem such as this pond. How many habitats can you identify?

CONNECTIONS

The flow of energy and cycling of nutrients in the biosphere are examples of the interaction of organisms and their environment.

living, **factors**. The interaction of the biotic and abiotic components of a particular place make up an **ecosystem** (Figure 3.4), such as a forest, a pond, or a prairie. Within each ecosystem are many **habitats**, places where particular organisms live. For example, in a pond, some organisms are bottom dwellers and others live along the shore; these are different habitats. All ecosystems combine to make up the **biosphere** called Earth. The biosphere contains many distinct ecosystems such as coral reefs, deserts, marshes, and oak-hickory forests. Chapter 26 explains how energy flows through ecosystems and how nutrients cycle among them.

CHECK AND CHALLENGE

1. Automobiles use energy from gasoline to move. Is an automobile alive? Cite evidence to support your answer.

2. What is the relationship between energy and nutrients in an organism?

3. Distinguish between heterotrophs and autotrophs and give examples of each.

4. What is the difference between the two basic components of an ecosystem?

5. Describe the relationship of producers, consumers, and decomposers in an ecosystem.

FIGURE 3.5 During burning, chemical reactions change some of the chemical energy stored in the log into heat energy that disperses into the surroundings. Some of the log's energy remains in the compounds that make up the ash.

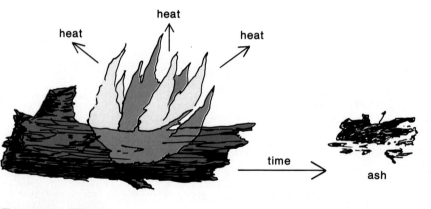

Energy Flow

3.4 Energy Conversions

Energy flow and energy conversions within ecosystems are described by physical principles called the laws of bioenergetics. The first law of bioenergetics states that energy in living things cannot be created or destroyed, but it can be changed in form. On a broader scale, the first law is called the law of conservation of energy. This law states that the *total* energy of the universe is constant but is found in many forms, such as a log, an electric current, sunlight, a carbohydrate, or an ecosystem.

The chemical energy in a log is stored in its molecules. When a log burns, chemical reactions occur that change most of its energy to heat, which is released into the surroundings (Figure 3.5). A small amount of the log's chemical energy remains in the ash after it burns. The heat can warm a room, but eventually it spreads out into the surroundings, where it is no longer available to do work. The first law tells us that before, during, and after the burning, the *total* energy of the universe is the same. More precisely, the *total* energy of the log (a system) plus its surroundings (all of the universe except the log) has remained the same. Energy has neither been created nor destroyed, just changed in form and in location.

FIGURE 3.6 A wolf consumes a rabbit, a source of energy and nutrients.

What does the first law of bioenergetics mean for cells and organisms? Living things cannot create their own energy, but must obtain it from an outside source. For most autotrophs, the source of energy is the sun; for heterotrophs, it is the chemical energy in food. Organisms then convert the energy they obtain into free energy, which allows them to do work for their own survival. For example, in an ecosystem, a wolf consumes a rabbit as food—a source of energy and nutrients (Figure 3.6). The wolf digests the food to simple compounds—such as glucose, fatty acids, and amino acids. In the wolf's cells, these compounds undergo further chemical changes accompanied by a release of free energy, which is used for cellular work such as muscle contraction, growth, and tissue repair.

Like the log, the wolf releases some energy as heat (Figure 3.7). In the wolf, however, the conversion of chemical energy also results in the release of free energy to do work in the living cells of the animal. That difference is a major distinction between living and nonliving things.

FOCUS ON *Bioenergetics—Primary Concepts*

The task of biologists who study bioenergetics is to analyze and explain energy exchanges in living systems. What is a system? Simply stated, a system is whatever you are studying. A biological system is the specified collection of living matter in which energy changes occur. The system can be a log or a single chemical reaction in a cell, such as the breakdown of sucrose to glucose and fructose. A system can be a series of chemical reactions leading to the synthesis of a complex organic molecule, such as a protein. In a larger context, an entire organism, a group of organisms, an ecosystem, or even the biosphere can be a system. All the other things, living and nonliving, around the system are known as the surroundings. The surroundings of a chemical reaction are everything apart from the reaction. The surroundings of an ecosystem, such as a forest, are everything outside that ecosystem. Thus, the system plus its surroundings equals the universe (Figure B).

When biologists study bioenergetics, they compare the initial energy content of the system to the final energy content after a process occurs. For example, the energy in a log can be compared to the energy in the ashes after the

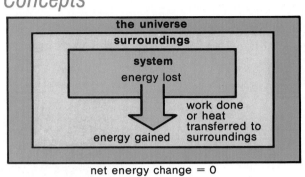

FIGURE B A system and its surroundings

process of burning has occurred. The energy in a seed can be compared to the energy in a tree following the process of growth. In the first example, energy in the system decreases as the log burns. In the second example, energy in the system increases as the tree grows. Energy is released from the system to the surroundings in the first example, whereas energy is absorbed by the system from the surroundings in the second example, but the total energy of the universe remains the same. Remember these concepts as you read about bioenergetics in this chapter.

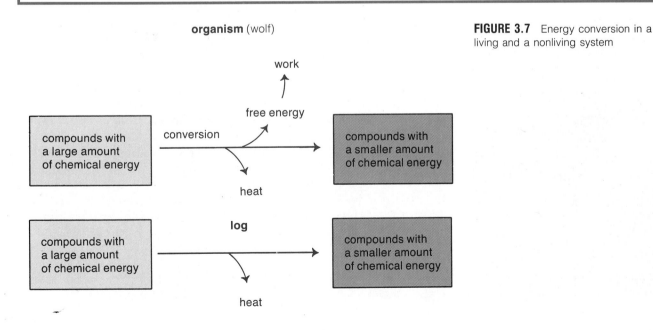

FIGURE 3.7 Energy conversion in a living and a nonliving system

FIGURE 3.8 The tendency toward increasing disorder of a system and its surroundings.

From *Living in the Environment, Third Edition,* by G. Tyler Miller, Jr. © 1982 by Wadsworth, Inc. Used by permission.

3.5 Energy and Entropy

Note that in the wolf, not all the energy derived from food is useful. As with the log, energy is released to the surroundings as heat and is no longer available to do work. In these examples, as in all energy conversions, energy tends to spread out into the surroundings. Thus, after each energy conversion, the free energy in a system is *slightly less than* before. The second law of bioenergetics states that natural processes tend to proceed in a way that increases the disorder, or entropy (EN troh pee), in a system (Figure 3.8). This statement means that the system becomes increasingly disordered as its free energy is released. In the example of the log, the process of burning releases energy as heat from the ordered chemicals in the log. The chemicals in the ashes are less ordered and contain less free energy than the chemicals in the log. Free energy decreases and entropy increases in the system as the log burns.

What does the second law of bioenergetics mean for living systems? One of the characteristics of life described in Section 3.1 is complex organization. Organisms are constructed and maintained in an orderly way and

FIGURE 3.9 As an organism grows, order and organization increase. Compare the size and complexity of the embryo in the center of the seed with the mature tree.

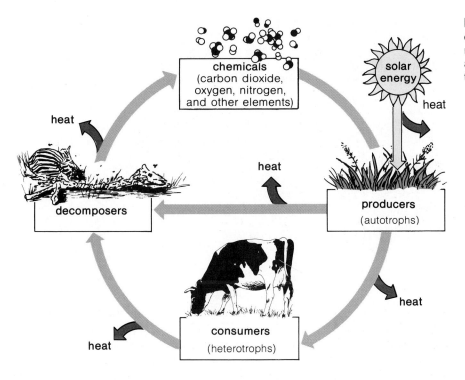

must stay that way to remain alive and grow. For example, a pine seed contains stored energy and nutrients and a tiny immature plantlet called an embryo (Figure 3.9). After the seed germinates, the embryo grows and develops into a seedling, then a sapling, and finally a mature pine tree made of leaves, branches, stems, cones, bark, and roots. The mature pine tree is much more complex and organized than the embryo. Free energy was required for the embryo to grow into the organized tree. The source of this energy was sunlight, harnessed through photosynthesis.

A key to maintaining organization in all living systems is energy. In most ecosystems, energy flows from the sun to producers to consumers to decomposers. Producers, however, do not use all the light energy they absorb in photosynthesis. (Photosynthesis, like all chemical reactions, is not 100 percent efficient.) Some of the light energy is converted into heat, which is released into the surroundings. Consumers convert part of the chemical energy from their food into free energy, which they use to do work. The remainder of the chemical energy becomes heat that is released into the surroundings. (Organisms cannot use the energy of heat to do work because it is too disordered.)

Thus, as energy flows through food webs, it eventually is released into the surroundings in the form of heat (Figure 3.10). As a result, there is only a one-way flow of energy from the surroundings into food webs. The second law of bioenergetics states that all systems, including living ones, tend to become more disorganized. Living systems overcome that tendency toward entropy by constantly obtaining energy from their surroundings.

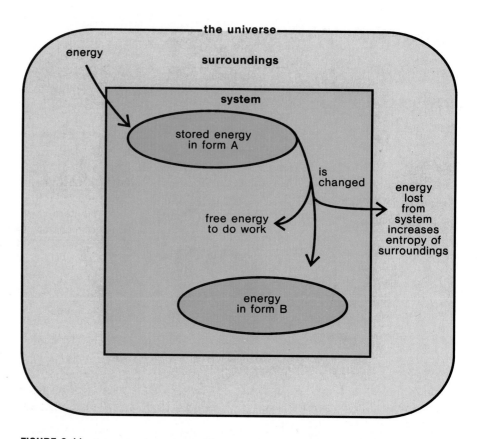

FIGURE 3.11   As energy is converted from one form to another in a system, some free energy is made available to do work and some is released as heat to the surroundings. With time and with each conversion, energy decreases and entropy increases in the system. The total energy of the universe, however, remains constant.

Thus, organisms stay organized and can function and grow only by increasing the entropy of their surroundings. The total energy of the universe remains the same (first law of bioenergetics). It is, however, randomly dispersed as heat—an unusable form of energy for organisms—which increases the entropy of the universe (second law) (Figure 3.11).

CHECK AND CHALLENGE

1. How do the laws of bioenergetics apply to living systems?
2. How do living things maintain a high degree of organization in spite of the universal tendency toward entropy?
3. What will happen to a system as entropy increases?
4. What is chemical energy? What are some activities in cells that could make energy available for cell work?
5. How are free energy and entropy related?

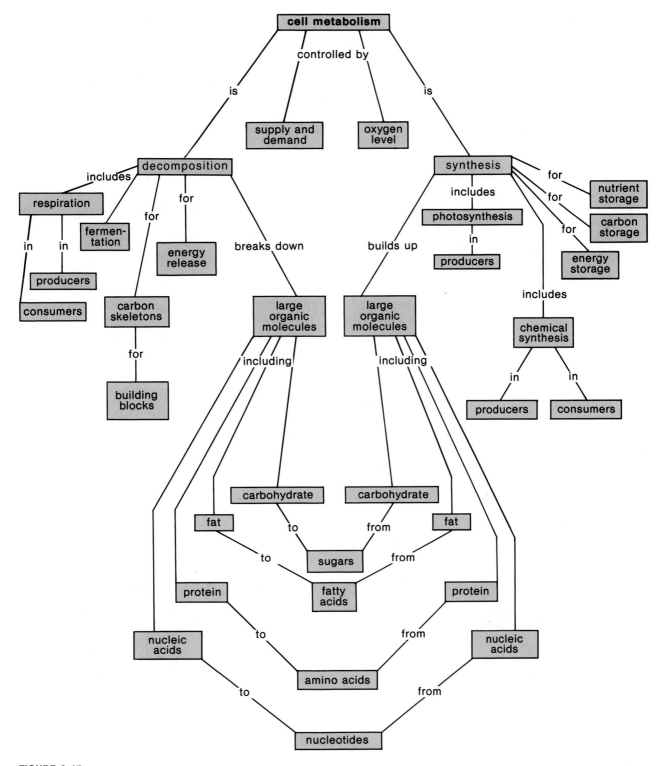

FIGURE 3.15 A concept map for cell metabolism. The map shows that synthesis includes biosynthesis reactions and stores energy, whereas decomposition includes degradation reactions and releases energy. Note how synthesis and decomposition are linked by simple molecules, which are the building blocks of macromolecules.

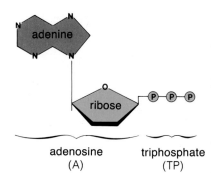

adenosine   triphosphate
(A)   (TP)

FIGURE 3.16 Where is the energy stored in ATP?

3.7   Energy Transfer and ATP

The free energy that is released during decomposition drives the reactions of biosynthesis. The linking of the two types of reactions usually is made possible by the energy carrier **ATP**, adenosine triphosphate. ATP connects many energy-conversion reactions during metabolism and has been called the "energy-currency" of living cells.

To see why ATP has been compared to money, imagine foreign tourists who arrive in New York City with only foreign currency. It would be difficult for the tourists to pay for dinner, a newspaper, or a theater ticket with their money. Now suppose the tourists change their foreign money into dollars. They would pay a fee for the exchange, but they would be able to use the money for their purchases. In a similar manner, a cell carries out chemical reactions that exchange the chemical energy of various organic compounds (foods) for the chemical energy of ATP. Then ATP pays most of the energy "debts" inside a cell. The "fee" is the energy lost as heat during the conversion.

ATP is a nucleotide consisting of adenine and ribose joined to a chain of three phosphate groups (Figure 3.16). The overall structure of ATP allows it to serve as an efficient and useful energy-transfer molecule in cells. Usually when an ATP molecule is involved in a chemical reaction, the bond between the second and third phosphate groups breaks and free energy is released. In organisms, cells lose some of the chemical energy from ATP breakdown as heat, but they use the remaining free energy to do work. (In a test tube, all of the breakdown energy would appear as heat.)

In many reactions, the third phosphate group is transferred to another molecule, along with some of the energy previously stored in the ATP. The

FIGURE 3.17 In synthesis, ATP is used to make glucose-6-phosphate, an energized form of glucose, or blood sugar. Glucose-6-phosphate then can be added to lengthen a chain of glycogen by one glucose molecule. Glycogen is a useful storage form of glucose. (P_i is inorganic phosphate.)

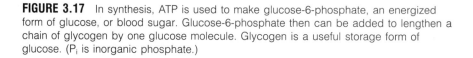

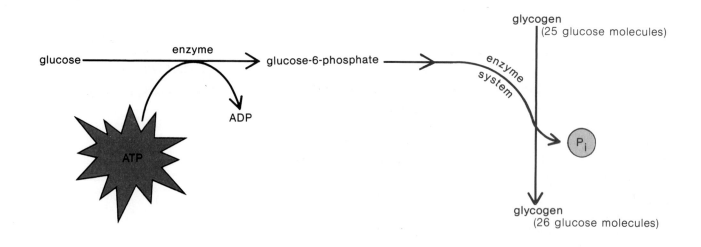

molecule that accepts the phosphate group from ATP gains free energy and is activated; it then can react usefully with other molecules in the cell. Figure 3.17 shows how the biosynthesis of glycogen from glucose uses ATP to form an activated intermediate compound, glucose-6-phosphate. Cells can use energy stored in the ATP molecule to supply áctivation energy or to drive energy-requiring reactions that bring about cellular growth and reproduction.

ATP is continually being synthesized and broken down in cells. This synthesis and breakdown forms a cycle, as illustrated in Figure 3.18. When a molecule of ATP gives up one phosphate group, it becomes **ADP**, adenosine diphosphate (Figure 3.18). To form a molecule of ATP again, ADP must combine with one phosphate group. The linking of a phosphate group to ADP requires free energy from the chemical breakdown of organic compounds within the cell. ATP thus acts as an energy carrier, a go-between for those reactions in the cell that release energy and those reactions that consume energy. GTP (guanosine triphosphate) and UTP (uridine triphosphate) also are energy carriers in cells, but ATP is used much more often.

Cells need energy not only to fuel biosynthesis but also to remove wastes and take in nutrients. ATP supplies much of the energy for this transport work. In addition, cells use the energy in ATP to maintain the internal ion concentrations necessary for their activities. Energy in ATP also is used to move or to cause movement, as in muscular activity and the movement of single cells from place to place. During cell division, cells change shape as offspring cells form. Energy carried by ATP also can provide the power for this mechanical work.

ATP is the principal energy currency of living cells today and was probably an energy carrier of the primitive heterotrophs. The free energy released during ATP breakdown enables a person to walk, a fish to swim, a bud to open into a flower, and a yeast cell to divide. The use of ATP as an energy carrier in all known living cells—from primitive heterotrophs to cells of humans and plants—is strong evidence for the unity of life on Earth.

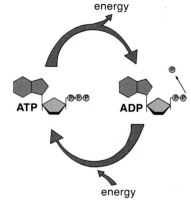

FIGURE 3.18 The ADP–ATP cycle. ATP molecules are continually rebuilt from ADP molecules, phosphates, and chemical energy.

*T*he use of ATP as an energy carrier in all organisms is evidence of a common evolutionary origin.

CHECK AND CHALLENGE

1. What are the components and functions of metabolism?

2. What are the connections between synthesis and decomposition? How are they similar? How are they different?

3. Give an example of a reaction in which synthesis and decomposition are linked. Why are such reactions important?

4. Explain why ATP is referred to as the "energy-currency" of the cell.

5. Describe several specific ways in which cells use the energy that is supplied by ATP.

Summary

All organisms require energy, which nearly always originates with the sun. Organisms use free energy to grow, move, reproduce, maintain internal order, carry out chemical reactions, take in nutrients, remove wastes, communicate, and respond to changes in the environment.

Biotic and abiotic components together make up an ecosystem. Producers, consumers, and decomposers are the biotic components of an ecosystem. The environment is the abiotic component, and includes air, soil, water, and weather. Energy flows in one direction from the sun to producers and then through a series of consumers in the form of food. Living things cannot recycle energy because their activities convert it to a form (heat) they cannot use to do work. Thus living things require a continual input of energy to carry out their activities.

The laws of bioenergetics allow us to predict the flow of energy in organisms and ecosystems. The first law states that it is not possible to create or destroy energy but that it is possible to change its form. For example, chemical energy in a log changes to heat energy as the log burns. The second law states that the universe, and all systems that make up the universe, naturally proceed to a state of disorder, or entropy, at minimum energy. Organisms, as systems in the universe, fall into this category. Organisms, however, must maintain and even increase a highly ordered state to stay alive. Maintenance of that highly ordered state requires a continual input of energy. Producers obtain energy from the sun, and consumers obtain energy by eating the producers and other consumers. Decomposers obtain energy through the decay of dead producers and consumers.

Metabolism is the sum of all chemical reactions and interactions in living systems. Synthesis includes all the biosynthesis reactions in an organism and requires energy to make complex molecules from simple ones. Cell growth and maintenance involve synthesis reactions. Decomposition includes all the

degradation reactions. Complex, energy-storing compounds change to simpler molecules, providing free energy to do the work of a cell.

ATP is the main energy currency of the cell. It is the linking molecule between synthesis and decomposition. Among other things, the breakdown of ATP powers the mechanical work of an organism and the synthesis reactions of cells.

Key Concepts

On the next page is the beginning of a concept map about living things. Use the concepts below to build a more complete map. Add as many other concepts from the chapter as you can. Include appropriate linking words for all concepts.

biotic factors	entropy
abiotic factors	free energy
producers	chemical energy
consumers	chemical reactions
decomposers	synthesis
autotrophs	decomposition
heterotrophs	ATP

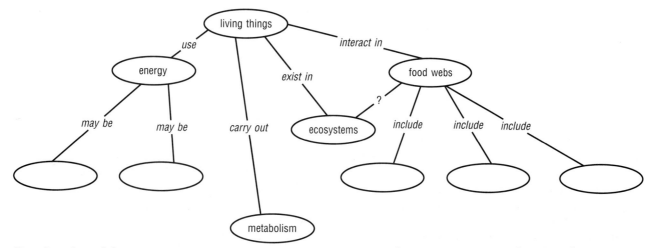

Reviewing Ideas

1. What is meant by "free energy" in organisms?

2. How do organisms use chemical energy to do work?

3. Discuss the functions and give examples of the living components of an ecosystem.

4. How are the biotic and abiotic components of an ecosystem related?

5. In your own words, state the first and second laws of bioenergetics.

6. Why is ATP the "currency" of metabolism?

7. How is ATP used as an energy carrier? Give an example.

Using Concepts

1. What would happen to ecosystems if there were no decomposers?

2. Figure 3.8 gives an example of entropy and the second law of bioenergetics. Think of another example and construct a model to illustrate it.

3. Organisms lose heat to their environment during metabolism. If this loss did not happen, would organisms still need an input of energy to survive? Explain.

4. You are part of a scientific team assigned to sample material brought back to Earth from Mars. What tests would you run on the samples to determine whether they contain life? Explain how you would run the tests and what information each test would provide.

5. Develop a concept map showing the structure and function of ecosystems.

6. How could you determine experimentally the number of kilocalories in a quarter-pound-hamburger meal?

7. The first law of bioenergetics states that energy cannot be destroyed. What eventually happens to the energy from the sun after it has passed through an ecosystem?

8. When ATP breaks down, ADP forms. Does ADP contain energy? Explain. How could you answer this question in the laboratory?

9. How can one chemical reaction in a cell be both a synthesis and a decomposition reaction?

Synthesis

1. How are chemical reactions, chemical bonds, and energy related?

2. How does ATP as a universal energy currency relate to the theory of evolution by natural selection?

Extensions

1. Describe how the first and second laws of bioenergetics might be used to explain the presence of some type of pollution (for example, smog, garbage, industrial waste) in your area.

2. Show in a cartoon the role of ATP in a cell.

CONTENTS

The Origin of Life

*O*f all the questions investigated by science, none evokes as much emotion and public debate as the question of how life on Earth originated. Why is the question so difficult to answer? First, there are no witnesses who can actually describe what happened. Second, there is no direct evidence to investigate. The rocks of Earth contain a testimony of those events, but the language in which the testimony is written is difficult to decode. Scientists in many different disciplines are engaged in a search for answers to the question of life's origins. Time, money, and effort may eventually yield answers, but those answers will not be easy to obtain. We will continue to try to decode the records held in the rocks of Earth and hope that new data or new interpretations of old evidence will lead to answers.

*W*hat are some of the characteristics of volcanic eruptions?

*H*ow are these characteristics reminiscent of conditions on early Earth?

◆ *East Rift zone eruption of Kilauea in Hawaii.*

Origin of the Universe

4.1 The Big Bang

Many science-fiction books and movies have stories that include the use of time machines, but do such machines really exist? The answer is a qualified yes, because they are time machines only at night; they serve other functions during the day. What are these time machines? They are your eyes. As you look out into space on a dark night, you are actually looking back in time (Figure 4.1 on the next page). You can look even farther into space (and farther back in time) by using a telescope. Light from the stars is traveling toward Earth at a speed of approximately 300 000 km per second. Some of the stars you can see in the night sky may no longer exist; they may have burned out or exploded thousands or millions of years ago. You still see their light because it takes a long time to reach Earth. For example, in February 1987, astronomers observed an exploding star that

FIGURE 4.1 The astronomer looking out into space through the telescope is also looking back in time. Photographed at the Black Forest Observatory, Colorado Springs, Colorado.

was 170 000 (1.7×10^5) light years away (Figure 4.2). The explosion actually occurred 170 000 (1.7×10^5) light years ago but was only recently visible on Earth because the light took that long to get here. The farther away you look into space, the farther back in time you see.

The interpretation of data from telescopic explorations deep into space indicates that the universe is expanding. The stars and galaxies were much closer to each other in the past than they are at the present, and they are currently moving rapidly away from each other. Why? Evidence indicates that about 15 billion years ago, all the matter in the universe was concentrated in one huge superdense mass that exploded. That explosion, called the Big Bang, hurled matter and energy into space. Gravity caused some of the matter to come together to form galaxies and stars (Figure 4.3). Gravity may also pull matter into orbit around the stars. The clumps of matter around our own star, the sun, became planets. Some planets were large enough and had enough gravity to attract matter that became moons or satellites.

FIGURE 4.2 This supernova, photographed April 15, 1987, is a star that exploded 1.7×10^5 years ago. It was first sighted by observers in South America.

FIGURE 4.3 A spiral galaxy in the constellation Hydra. The galaxy is 10 million light years away and has a diameter of 30 000 light years.

FOCUS ON *Light Years*

Distances in space are so great that we cannot measure them in kilometers—the numbers would be too large to comprehend. Instead, we measure distances in units called light years. A light year is the distance light travels in one year. One light year can be calculated in kilometers in the following way: 300 000 km per second × 60 seconds per minute × 60 minutes per hour × 24 hours per day × 365 days per year, or 9 500 000 000 000 (9.5×10^{12}) km.

This distance is roughly equivalent to 100 000 round trips between Earth and the sun.

The closest star to Earth is Alpha Centauri, 4.4 light years, or 41 800 000 000 000 (4.18×10^{13}) km, away. As you can see from these numbers, it is simpler to use light years instead of kilometers for distances in space, especially for stars and galaxies that are billions of light years from Earth.

Precambrian						Paleozoic				Mesozoic			Cenozoic		Era
millions of years ago					580			245							
4600	3700	3500	2000	1400		500	430	395		225	135	66	38	7	
origin of earth	oldest earth rocks	oldest stromatolites and prokaryotic microfossils	significant levels of O$_2$ in the atmosphere	oldest eukaryotic fossils		first vertebrates appear	first land plants appear	first amphibians and insects appear		mammal-like reptiles appear	flowering plants appear	dinosaurs become extinct	origin of modern mammals	ape-like ancestors of humans appear	event
			abundant stromatolites		→										

FIGURE 4.4 Geological time scale relating several major biological events to the history of Earth

The best current estimate is that Earth formed approximately 4.6 billion years ago. Moon rocks and meteorites, respectively 4.6 and 4.5 billion years old, indirectly confirm that estimate. As illustrated in Figure 4.4, geologists have worked out a chronology of Earth's history based on evidence in its rocks. (**Appendix 4A**, Radiometric Dating Methods, describes how scientists calculate the age of materials.) Evidence indicates that the moon formed at about the same time as Earth. Meteorites are thought to be remnants of material from the formation of our solar system. Figure 4.5 compares the 4.6 billion years of Earth's history to a time scale of a calendar year.

FIGURE 4.5 Moving clockwise, in this calendar 4.6 billion years of the earth's history are compressed into one year. Each day on the calendar is equal to almost 13 million years on earth.

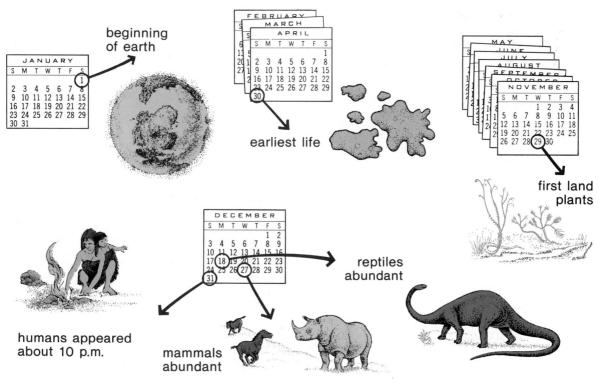

beginning of earth

earliest life

first land plants

reptiles abundant

humans appeared about 10 p.m.

mammals abundant

4.2 Early Earth

Evidence indicates that Earth's interior is hot. Miners encounter higher temperatures as they descend deep into mine shafts. Volcanoes and hot springs are further evidence of a hot interior (Figure 4.6). The hot lava and water originate far under Earth's surface where temperatures are much higher than at the surface. Radioactive elements such as uranium, thorium, and potassium are a possible source of heat for the core because they give off tremendous amounts of heat as they slowly decay. The entire planet was probably hot when it first formed. As the outer crust cooled, gases escaping from within the planet formed a primitive atmosphere.

The composition of the early atmosphere has been the topic of much experimentation. Data indicate the atmosphere originated within Earth itself and consisted mainly of gases such as nitrogen (N_2), carbon dioxide (CO_2), water vapor (H_2O), and hydrogen (H_2), with only small amounts of carbon monoxide (CO). Earlier hypotheses included ammonia (NH_3) and methane (CH_4), but most scientists now agree that ammonia could only have been present in small concentrations. Because the sun rapidly converts it to nitrogen and hydrogen, ammonia would have to have been continually resupplied to the atmosphere from the surface.

Evidence indicates that oxygen gas (O_2) probably was not present in the early atmosphere but was bound in compounds such as water and carbon dioxide. Thus it would not have been available for organisms to use. Atmospheric oxygen is a product of photosynthesis, and significant amounts did not appear until after photosynthesis evolved. At first, the oxygen released by photosynthesis would have combined with other elements, such as iron, and would not have remained as free oxygen gas in the atmosphere. Oxygen-containing compounds such as iron oxides are present only in small quantities in the oldest rocks and did not become abundant until much later in Earth's history (see Figure 4.4).

FIGURE 4.6 Eruption of the volcano Kilauea in Hawaii

CHECK AND CHALLENGE _____

1. Describe how you are using a time machine as you look at the stars on a clear night.

2. What was the Big Bang?

3. What data support the conclusion that Earth has a hot core?

4. What gases were probably present in Earth's early atmosphere?

5. Explain why free oxygen gas probably was not present in the early atmosphere of Earth.

Evolution of Life on Earth _____

4.3 The Beginnings of Life

The surface of Earth 4.6 billion years ago had an environment that would have been hostile to modern life. Tremendous amounts of energy, in the form of ultraviolet radiation from the sun, poured onto the surface of Earth. Ultraviolet radiation is particularly harmful to DNA, the molecule that stores genetic information in all living organisms. Today, a layer of ozone (O_3) in the atmosphere (Figure 4.7) protects life from ultraviolet

FIGURE 4.7 The Earth's atmosphere. Ozone in the stratosphere absorbs most of the ultraviolet radiation from the sun. Early Earth did not have this protection.

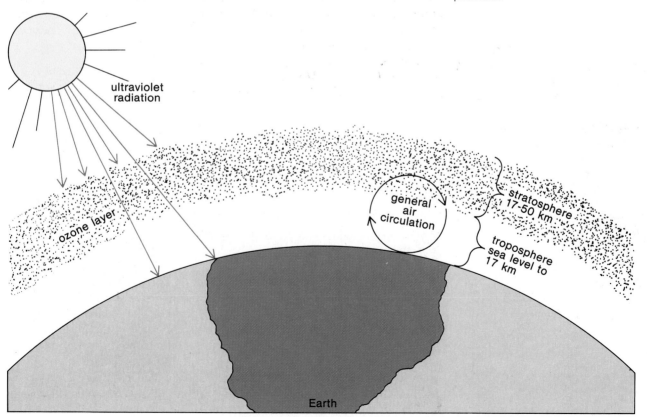

radiation, but Earth at first had no such protection. The ozone layer originated by the action of ultraviolet radiation on oxygen gas in the atmosphere.

Also abundant was energy from radioactivity, lightning, cosmic rays, and heat from volcanic eruptions. Any one of those sources could have provided energy for the complex chemical reactions that led to the first living organisms.

The surface of the young Earth was too chaotic, temperature variations too extreme, oxygen too scarce, and radiation too intense for life to survive in its present form. How, then, could life have originated on Earth? Prevalent ideas include the following:

1. Life originated by unknown means on Earth. The earliest life may have been made of inorganic matter, such as clays, and was thus very different from organisms that now exist. Because no traces remain of those early organisms, which evolved into living forms made of organic compounds, their detection is extremely difficult.

2. Life originated by unknown means (outside Earth) on some other planet of another star in the universe and was transported to Earth through space.

3. Life was created by a supernatural force or deity. This idea is common to many religions, but does not have a scientific basis.

4. Life evolved from nonliving matter (chemicals) by interaction with the natural geological and astronomical environment. Life forms are chemical systems with self-maintaining properties and are capable of undergoing biological evolution (see page 75). These characteristics resulted from complex chemical changes through time, or chemical evolution.

The fourth idea, which can be stated in the form of a hypothesis, is the most suited to investigation through the use of scientific methods. Some of the experiments designed to test that hypothesis are described in the following sections. All of these ideas about the origin of life have advocates and critics. The idea that a supernatural force or deity created life is not within the realm of science. (In other words, it can neither be confirmed nor rejected through the use of the scientific process.) Therefore, this idea is not part of scientific debates about the origin of life. The dynamic, spirited exchange of ideas in research on the origin of life is another example of the investigative nature of science.

4.4 Chemical Evolution

In the 1920s, the Soviet scientist Alexander Oparin and the British scientist J.B.S. Haldane independently developed the first extensive hypothesis about how life may have originated. Oparin and Haldane based their hypothesis on the idea that the atmosphere consisted of methane, ammonia, hydrogen, and water vapor. According to their hypothesis, the energy sources described in Section 4.3 acted on the atmosphere to produce organic compounds that accumulated in the oceans until the oceans reached the consistency of a hot dilute soup. Figure 4.8 shows how such

1. primitive atmosphere

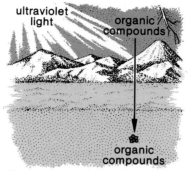

2. organic compound formation

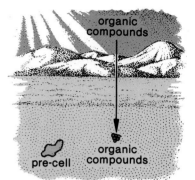

3. pre-cell formation

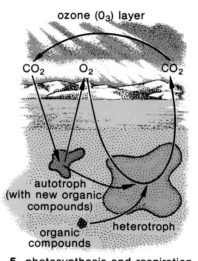

4. anaerobic processes

5. photosynthesis and respiration

FIGURE 4.8   The heterotroph hypothesis assumes that life processes developed gradually. The first organisms were heterotrophs that lived on the organic compounds in the oceans. Autotrophs evolved later, and photosynthesis resulted in the oxygen-rich atmosphere of today.

chemical evolution might have occurred. Oparin and Haldane hypothesized that life evolved by further chemical reactions and transformations in that complex organic soup. The details of how life actually evolved differed in the writings of the two men, but both thought the first life forms were heterotrophs (Section 3.2) that fed on the organic compounds provided by chemical evolution. That idea is the basis of the **heterotroph hypothesis** for the first life form on Earth.

What organic compounds were formed before the emergence of life? Harold Urey and Stanley Miller worked on this problem in the 1950s at the University of Chicago. In laboratory experiments they simulated the conditions that might have existed on Earth 4.6 billion years ago. Miller built and sterilized an airtight apparatus like the one shown in Figure 4.9 (page 74). In the apparatus, methane, hydrogen, and ammonia gases circulated past a high-energy electrical spark. A container of boiling water connected to the apparatus supplied heat and water vapor. As the water vapor circulated, it cooled and condensed as "rain." Thus Miller created some of the conditions (gases, alternating light and dark, heat, rain, and flashes of lightning) that may have been present in the early atmosphere.

FIGURE 4.9 A drawing of Miller's apparatus, in which conditions thought to exist in the primitive atmosphere were reproduced in the laboratory. What was Miller trying to find out?

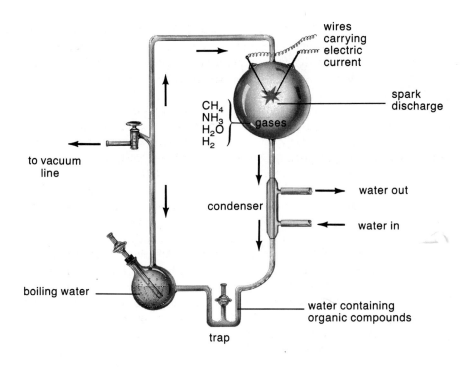

While circulating the gases for a week, Miller examined the liquid in the apparatus. There were two visible differences from the original setup. First, there was a small mass of black tar in one part of the apparatus. Second, the liquid condensed from the boiling water, colorless at the start of the experiment, had turned red. Chemical tests showed that the liquid contained many compounds, most unidentifiable, not present when the experiment began. The atoms of some of the gas molecules had recombined to form new and more complex molecules.

When Miller and Urey analyzed the liquid, they found a variety of organic compounds including some amino acids. That was an exciting discovery, because amino acids are the building blocks of proteins (Chapter 2). No known form of life on Earth exists without proteins.

Based on the new hypotheses that only low amounts of methane and ammonia were present in the atmosphere, Miller and others have repeated his experiment using only carbon dioxide, water, nitrogen, and hydrogen. As long as oxygen is absent and certain critical ratios of hydrogen and carbon dioxide are maintained, simple amino acids, such as glycine, are produced. After those latest experiments, Miller noted that if the origin of life requires amino acids more complex than glycine, at least a little methane must be present in the atmosphere.

Perhaps some amino acids arrived on Earth by means of objects from space. Evidence from meteorites indicates that organic compounds do originate in space. In 1970, at the Ames Research Center in California, Cyril Ponnamperuma and others found amino acids and other organic compounds in a meteorite that fell to Earth near Murchison, Australia, in September 1969 (Figure 4.10). Of the seven amino acids found, two do not occur in organisms on Earth. These amino acids certainly were synthesized in the absence of terrestrial life somewhere in space. Since 1970, examination of many other meteorites has revealed organic compounds that originated in space.

In 1986, several spacecraft with sophisticated instruments were sent to fly through the tail of comet Halley (Figure 4.11) when it passed near Earth. The instruments detected several organic compounds, including formaldehyde. The presence of formaldehyde is interesting because it is needed for the formation of ribose, the sugar in RNA.

Geologic evidence indicates that Earth grew very hot after it first formed. As the planet cooled, much of the water vapor present in the atmosphere condensed and formed ever-expanding oceans. At first glance, it is difficult to think of life originating from a hot, smelly chemical soup, yet there is considerable evidence to support this idea. The ideas and hypotheses presented here indicate that chemical evolution could have occurred under the conditions presumed to have been present on early Earth. Simple organic compounds could have formed on early Earth, or they could have been transported here from somewhere in space. Some of the small organic molecules could have combined to form more complex compounds such as small proteins or nucleic acids. Still, the difference between these early compounds and the proteins and nucleic acids of even the simplest organisms is enormous. What were the first life forms like, and how might they have evolved?

FIGURE 4.10   Meteorites, such as this one found lodged in an aspen tree in Colorado, show that organic compounds can form in space as well as on Earth. Photographed at the Black Forest Observatory, Colorado Springs, Colorado

FIGURE 4.11   Comet Halley, seen on April 29, 1986

CONNECTIONS

The concept of evolution is central to the heterotroph hypothesis, which suggests that the first life forms fed on organic compounds in the ocean. Eventually, those compounds would have become scarce, and natural selection would have favored life forms able to use other sources of energy, such as inorganic compounds or light.

4.5 Biological Evolution

Chapter 3 discusses the characteristics of living organisms, but what is life? There is no single agreed upon definition of "life." However, the Exobiology Program within NASA, which studies and searches for extraterrestrial organisms, has adopted the following working definition: *"Life" is a self-sustained chemical system that is capable of undergoing Darwinian, or biological, evolution.* Thus, the origin of life coincides with the origin of biological evolution. Biological evolution consists of three processes: self-reproduction, mutation (genetic change) that can be inherited, and natural selection. To be considered alive, a substance must be able to reproduce itself, be subject to mutations that can be passed onto its offspring, and be subject to natural selection.

How could these abilities have developed? Scientists have two general ideas about that question. One idea suggests that the first life forms were cell-like structures enclosed in a membrane. The second idea suggests the first life forms were "naked" organic molecules or inorganic crystals (with no membrane or membranelike structure) that could self-replicate.

If the first life forms were cell-like structures, how could they have come to be? In 1924, the Russian biologist A.I. Oparin proposed a model for precell droplets he called coacervates (koh AS er vayts). The name is derived from a Latin word meaning "heaped" or "clustered." Coacervates are clusters of proteins or proteinlike substances held together in small droplets within a surrounding liquid. When proteins dissolve in water, parts of each protein molecule may ionize, or develop a charge. A layer of water molecules then forms around the charged protein molecule. A cluster of protein molecules surrounded by a water layer constitutes a complex coacervate (Figure 4.12).

In the early 1980s Carl Woese, at the University of Illinois, also proposed a model for the formation of the first cells. Woese hypothesized that life began on Earth before the planet was fully formed. The atmosphere contained a high level of carbon dioxide that produced a tremendous warming "greenhouse effect" (Figure 4.13). Conditions on Earth were similar to those that exist on Venus. For example, the dense atmosphere on

Try Investigation 4A, Coacervates.

FIGURE 4.12 This drawing shows how a complex coacervate is formed when a water layer surrounds a cluster of protein molecules.

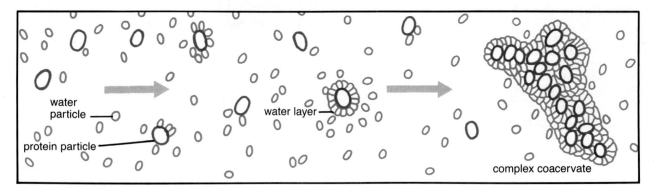

water particle

water layer

protein particle

complex coacervate

FOCUS ON *The Greenhouse Effect*

Research suggests that Earth has always had a moderate climate because the carbon dioxide in its atmosphere produces a greenhouse effect. The greenhouse effect occurs when carbon dioxide allows the warming rays of the sun in but absorbs heat that rises from the surface and reflects it back to Earth. A cycling mechanism acts to regulate carbon dioxide levels in response to changes in Earth's surface temperature. As the surface cools, carbon dioxide levels rise, and as the surface warms, carbon dioxide levels decline.

The cycle begins when carbon dioxide in the atmosphere dissolves in rainwater and forms carbonic acid (H_2CO_3), a weak acid. The acidic rain erodes rocks, releasing calcium and bicarbonate ions (HCO_3^-) into groundwater that ultimately reaches the ocean. There the ions are incorporated into the calcium carbonate ($CaCO_3$) shells of marine organisms. When the organisms die, their shells settle to the bottom of the ocean. Over millennia, spreading of the sea floor carries these sediments to the edge of continents where the materials slide under the landmasses and turn toward Earth's interior. Pressure and rising temperature cause the calcium carbonate to react with quartz, forming rocks and releasing carbon dioxide. The gas reenters the atmosphere by way of midocean ridges or volcanic eruptions.

Normally, the cycle is balanced. However, human activities, such as the burning of fossil fuels and the clearing of forests, are increasing the amount of carbon dioxide in the atmosphere. The increase speeds up global warming because of the increased greenhouse effect.

FIGURE 4.13 Greenhouse effect. CO_2 in the atmosphere allows visible light to reach Earth but prevents radiation of heat back to space, increasing the surface temperature.

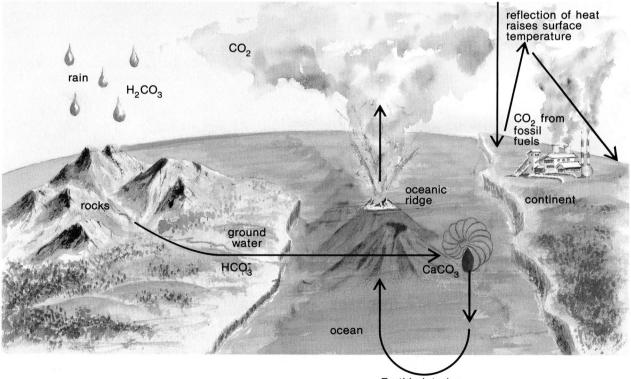

FIGURE 4.14 Repeating structures in kaolinite clays. The first chemical systems to self-replicate may have been clays. Minerals in the clay may have formed a crystalline pattern that served as a blueprint for assembling more minerals into layers of similar patterns.

Venus is mostly carbon dioxide, which acts like the roof of a greenhouse, preventing heat from escaping. Meteorites that hit primitive Earth provided large quantities of dust that were spread by the wind. Woese hypothesized that water vapor condensed around the dust particles, forming droplets. Each droplet, warmed by the atmosphere, then acted as a primitive cell in which chemical reactions occurred that allowed life to begin.

As research continues, the models of proteinlike clusters of molecules for the first life forms are being revised considerably. In 1982, Thomas Cech and his colleagues discovered that RNA can code hereditary instructions and catalyze chemical reactions. This discovery may indicate that RNA or DNA was present along with proteinlike materials in the first precells.

In 1985, A.G. Cairns-Smith, of the University of Glasgow, Scotland, proposed the second idea—that the first life forms were self-replicating "naked" organic molecules or inorganic crystals. He suggests that clays might have formed the first self-replicating systems. Minerals dissolved in clay could have crystallized to form layers with a definite, repeating structure (Figure 4.14). Such layered clays could have acted as "crystal genes" able to store and transmit information. Cairns-Smith argues that this structure could encode messages, somewhat in the way that DNA molecules encode messages. Furthermore, clay surfaces attract organic molecules such as RNA, which may have helped shape the clay crystals or, instead, received information from them. At some point, organic molecules took over the message-encoding function of the clay crystals. Those inorganic crystals thus represented an intermediate step in the path toward an organic molecule that could store genetic information.

4.6 Proteins, DNA, and RNA Life Forms

Other possibilities for the first life forms include proteins, DNA, and RNA. Could the first life form have been a protein? Many proteins function as enzymes in the synthesis of other chemical substances. Proteins also can store information because they are produced when information is passed from DNA to RNA in modern cells. Amino acids, which can form under conditions similar to those that may have existed in Earth's early atmosphere, may have joined to form proteins, but proteins apparently cannot replicate themselves without the help of RNA. If there is a method of protein self-replication, it remains undiscovered.

Could DNA or RNA have been the first life form? Short strands of RNA can self-replicate, and RNA stores information, directs the synthesis of proteins, and has limited ability as a catalyst. In certain viruses, such as the virus that causes AIDS, RNA also directs the synthesis of DNA (see Figure A on page 85). Some of the precursor molecules of RNA are common ingredients in meteorites and comets and may have been present in the primitive oceans. For example, formaldehyde is a precursor of the nitrogen base adenine. Adenine and ribose both are components of RNA, as well as of other organic molecules such as ATP.

A few scientists maintain that because the first life form was a functioning system, it is unlikely that it could have been made of only protein, only nucleic acids, or only clays. Perhaps instead the "naked" first life form was similar to a virus. Viruses have either DNA or RNA contained in a central core surrounded by a protein coat (Figure 4.15). They form crystals

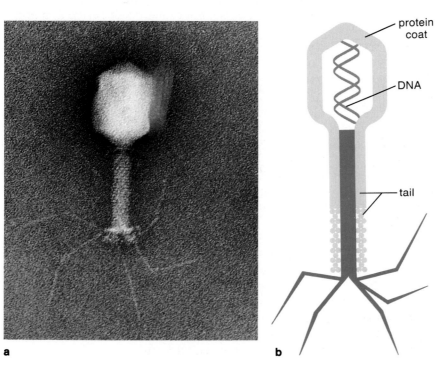

a

b

FIGURE 4.15 Viruses are made of DNA with a protein coat. (a) Electron micrograph of a virus, X190 000; (b) diagram of the same type of virus

FOCUS ON *RNA as a Catalyst*

For decades scientists thought that only proteins had catalytic ability in cells. That concept was deeply rooted in biology and chemistry. In the early 1980s, however, biologists learned that RNA serves as the catalyst in a chemical reaction that occurs in small unicellular organisms called protozoa. Later RNA was found to serve as a catalyst for the same reaction in other cells. In this reaction, RNA is cut and rejoined (see Chapter 10).

More than the startling realization that we can no longer think of enzymes only as proteins, this discovery serves to remind us that biology is an experimental science. It is a process of discovery, not a body of facts (see Chapter 1). The concepts, ideas, and hypotheses given in this and other textbooks are examples of knowledge that can change. The discovery that RNA is a catalyst in cells reminds us that science is a constantly evolving attempt to understand how nature works.

FIGURE 4.16 This single crystal of polio virus, magnified 600 times, appears hollow because the crystal is transparent. This crystal contains about 200 million viruses.

(Figure 4.16) and can reproduce only within living cells. Although sometimes their changes may benefit the cells they invade, viruses can disrupt normal cell function and cause permanent damage to invaded cells.

Viruses are so intimately connected to their host cells that they probably are relatively recent—as recent as their hosts—in origin. Until more data become available, their evolutionary significance remains obscure.

All the ideas about the origin of life and nature of the first life forms have proponents and opponents. With time, more experiments, or further exploration of other planets in our solar system, additional information may be revealed.

CHECK AND CHALLENGE

1. Which of the ideas about the origin of life on Earth can be stated as hypotheses and investigated by the methods of science? Why? Which cannot be? Why not?

2. What energy sources were most likely to have contributed to the origin of life on Earth? Why?

3. Describe the "hot soup" in which some scientists hypothesize life may have originated.

4. What is the evidence for the synthesis of organic chemicals in space? How might they have arrived on Earth?

5. What is the meaning of the heterotroph hypothesis?

6. Compare the basic ideas about the first life form.

7. Why do some researchers suggest the first life forms may have been based on RNA?

The Record of the Rocks

4.7   Microfossils and Prokaryotes

The oldest microfossils, or fossil microorganisms, known were discovered in 1993 in northwestern Australia by an American scientist, Dr. J.B. Schopf of the University of California at Los Angeles. The fossils represent 11 distinct types of microorganisms and are more than 1.3 billion years older than any other comparable group of fossils found.

The fossils are of single-celled organisms forming minute filaments (Figure 4.17). Their wormlike shapes resemble those of certain modern bacteria capable of photosynthesis. Because of their similarity to modern microorganisms, scientists hypothesize that they already may have developed photosynthesis to obtain energy.

The microscopic fossils were embedded in mineral grains, which were encased in a type of rock that formed almost 3.485 billion years ago. The grains in which they were found are almost certainly older than the rock encasing them, but scientists have been unable to determine just how old. The fossil microorganisms prove that life was thriving and diversified at that time. The existence of these microfossils dramatically shortens the time available for life to have evolved naturally on Earth, and could focus more attention on the hypothesis that life originated elsewhere in the universe and somehow reached Earth.

The Australian fossils were found associated with domelike structures called stromatolites (stroh MAT uh lyts; *stroma* = bed, *lithos* = rock). The domes, about 30 cm high by 1.5 m across, are constructed of many wafer-thin layers of rock (see Figure 4.18). At Hamelin Pool, an extremely salty arm of Shark Bay, Australia, lime-secreting bacteria today produce stromatolites similar in structure to the fossilized ones. Microfossils associated

FIGURE 4.17   A 3.485 billion-year-old prokaryote fossil in stromatolite from western Australia

FIGURE 4.18   (a) These fossil stromatolites from western Australia are about 3.5 billion years old. Note the layered structure, which is characteristic of stromatolites. (b) Modern living stromatolites in Shark Bay, Australia, built by cyanobacteria

a

b

with stromatolites are found at Gunflint Lake in western Canada and around the shores of ancient Lake Bonneville in Utah.

Geologists have determined that the oldest rocks on Earth, in Greenland, are about 3.8 billion years old. Rocks older than those in Greenland have melted, eroded, or otherwise changed until they are no longer recognizable. Thus, there is no direct evidence left of the appearance of the first life forms. The earliest fossils are interpreted to be **prokaryotes** (pro KAIR ee ohts), organisms that lack a membrane enclosing their DNA. The first organisms were probably less organized than modern prokaryotes. Their genetic information may have been scattered in pieces, rather than organized in discrete structures. (Chapters 9 and 10 discuss the organization, storage, and replication of genetic material in modern organisms.)

As indicated in Section 4.4, the first organisms probably were heterotrophs. Because the early atmosphere lacked free oxygen gas (Section 4.2), those organisms also were anaerobic (an eh ROH bik; *an* = without, *aer* = air, *bios* = life). Carl Woese suggests the first organisms may have been methanogens (meth AN uh jenz)—anaerobic bacteria that obtain energy by combining carbon dioxide and hydrogen to produce methane gas (Figure 4.19). Methanogens and other related bacteria exist now in conditions not unlike those hypothesized for early Earth. Some live near hydrothermal vents deep in the ocean where temperatures are much higher than the boiling point of water. Other bacteria that Woese classifies as relatives of methanogens have been found in acidic environments, such as residues from mining (mine tailings), and in conditions with extremely high salt concentrations, such as the Dead Sea and Great Salt Lake.

Some of the 3.485 billion-year-old fossils appear very similar to certain modern autotrophic bacteria. If the microfossils were, in fact, autotrophs, then photosynthesis is a very old process, and oxygen gas has been accumulating in the environment for at least 3.485 billion years. Although the levels of oxygen gas in the atmosphere probably were not significant until

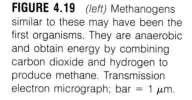

FIGURE 4.19 *(left)* Methanogens similar to these may have been the first organisms. They are anaerobic and obtain energy by combining carbon dioxide and hydrogen to produce methane. Transmission electron micrograph; bar = 1 µm.

FIGURE 4.20 *(right)* A eukaryote fossil 1.4 billion years old

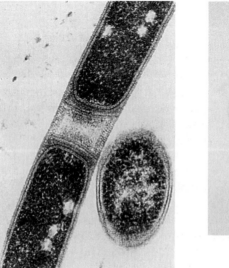

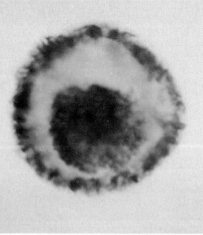

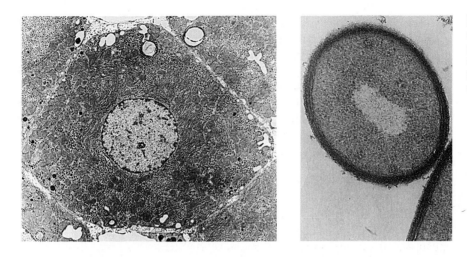

FIGURE 4.21 Electron micrographs of eukaryotic *(left)* and prokaryotic *(right)* cells. Notice the membrane-enclosed organelles and generally more complex structure of the eukaryotic cell.

about 2 billion years ago, the presence of oxygen gas nevertheless had profound implications for living organisms. Because oxygen reacts readily with organic molecules, it would have been toxic to most early organisms. As the concentration of oxygen increased, many species of organisms probably became extinct. Others remained in environments in which oxygen continued to be largely absent, such as sediments at the bottom of ponds and lakes. Still others evolved ways to use oxygen to produce large amounts of ATP from their food sources.

4.8   Eukaryotes

Prokaryotes probably were the only organisms on Earth for more than 2 billion years. The first microfossils that may have been **eukaryotes** (yoo KAIR ee ohts) are about 1.4 billion years old (Figure 4.20). Cells of eukaryotes have at least one membrane-enclosed structure, the nucleus, containing their DNA. The DNA of eukaryotes is usually organized into several distinct bodies (chromosomes) within the nucleus. Compare the prokaryotic and eukaryotic cells in Figure 4.21.

Besides a nucleus, eukaryotic cells also contain other membrane-enclosed structures, or **organelles** (or guh NELS), which prokaryotes lack. Each organelle has a specific function or functions. Two major organelles appear to have similar evolutionary origins. They are the **mitochondria** (my toh KON dree uh), in which oxygen is used to synthesize ATP during cellular respiration (Chapter 3), and the **plastids** (PLAS tids), in which light is used to synthesize ATP during photosynthesis.

Lynn Margulis, of University of Massachusetts, Amherst, hypothesizes that both mitochondria and plastids originated as free-living prokaryotes (Figure 4.22 on page 84). Many prokaryotes use oxygen to produce ATP; others carry out photosynthesis. Margulis proposes that such specialized prokaryotes may have formed close associations with larger anaerobic prokaryotes. Instead of being digested, the smaller prokaryotic cells continued their specialized activities in the host cell. The resulting increase in energy yield would have been beneficial to the host cell. Those prokaryotes

FIGURE 4.22 Mitchondria and chloroplasts may have originated as free-living cells.

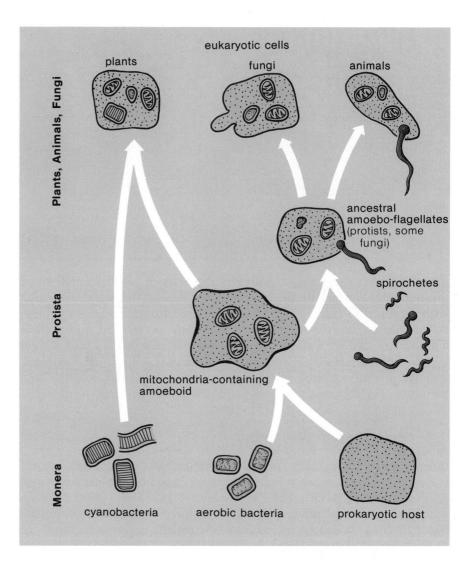

that used oxygen to produce ATP could have been the ancestors of mitochondria in eukaryotic cells. Photosynthetic prokaryotes could have been the ancestors of plastids. A large body of evidence supports this widely accepted hypothesis.

CHECK AND CHALLENGE

1. What is the evidence that the oldest fossils were autotrophs?
2. What characteristics make methanogens and related bacteria good candidates for the first organisms?
3. How might mitochondria and plastids have originated?
4. What characteristics distinguish prokaryotes and eukaryotes?

Biological Challenges

AN RNA WORLD

(Adapted with permission from Gerald F. Joyce, "The RNA World: Life Before DNA and Protein" in *Extraterrestrials: Where Are They?*, (B. Zuckerman, ed., Cambridge University Press.)

All known organisms on Earth today and in the past share the same type of genetic material based on DNA and protein. This biological system is too complicated to have arisen spontaneously. Some scientists suggest that DNA and protein-based life was preceded by RNA life in a period called the "RNA world."

For something to be "alive," it must be able to self-replicate (produce copies of itself), undergo and pass on mutations, and be subject to natural selection. How does RNA fit these requirements? Like proteins, RNA can have complex functions. For example, RNA can both carry genetic instructions and act as an enzyme, and it can produce copies of itself that sometimes include mutational errors. RNA also is subject to natural selection—the variant copies that are best able to cope with problems imposed by the environment are selected to begin the next round of copying, mutation, and selection.

What is the evidence that an RNA-based life form existed on Earth prior to DNA and protein-based life? First, there are a number of viruses that use RNA, rather than DNA, as their genetic material, such as HIV, the virus that causes AIDS. The existence of RNA viruses demonstrates that RNA-based genetic systems can exist. Second, in a purely chemical system, an RNA molecule can be made to copy itself. Although, the copying process does not allow for mutations, this fact demonstrates that RNA can carry genetic information that can be copied. Third, the discovery that RNA can function as an enzyme shows that RNA is a functional molecule as well as a genetic molecule—it can provide the chemical basis for Darwinian evolution.

What remnants of prior RNA-based life form can we see in the succeeding DNA and protein-based life form? Genetically, RNA is involved in almost every-

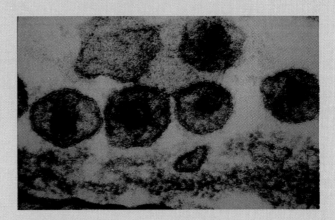

FIGURE A A TEM of Type D retrovirus (X142 500), which causes slow infections of the brain, suppression of the immune system, and some tumors.

thing, especially the central, most primitive aspects of cell function. RNA is a messenger, carrying genetic instructions from DNA to the protein-synthesizing machinery. RNA is also part of that machinery—it draws in the protein subunits and helps join the subunits to form mature proteins. RNA also is involved in editing and splicing genetic information, to arrange the genetic instructions properly prior to translation. Replication of DNA requires RNA. When DNA is copied, the process is initiated by the production of a partial RNA copy.

RNA also is involved in functional processes of the cell. Nearly all the protein enzymes for the fundamental aspects of metabolism rely on co-enzymes. Besides assisting proteins in carrying out biochemical reactions, co-enzymes play a crucial role in how the reactions take place. Almost all of the known co-enzymes contain components of RNA.

When might the RNA world have existed? To carry out its functions, RNA must dissolve in water. Thus, the newly formed Earth must have cooled to the point that water was available. RNA-based life may have existed between this time—4.0 billion years ago—and the appearance of DNA and protein-based life forms in the geologic and fossil record.

Summary

The Big Bang occurred about 15 billion years ago. Since then, all the stars and galaxies have been moving away from each other as the universe expands. Planets, including Earth, formed around the sun about 4.6 billion years ago. Gases escaping from within the planet formed a primitive atmosphere. Scientists hypothesize that chemical evolution, driven by a variety of energy sources, led to the origin of life on Earth. The first living thing may have been "naked": a mineral crystal or an organic compound, such as RNA, DNA, or protein. It may have been a cell-like structure similar to a coacervate. The exact conditions of Earth and its atmosphere during that time are not known, but experiments have shown that the origin of a carbon-based chemical system leading to cells some 4 billion years ago could have occurred.

The first life forms were probably heterotrophs that lived on organic compounds in Earth's oceans. The oldest fossils appear to be prokaryotes similar to modern bacteria. Photosynthesis probably evolved very early, but significant levels of oxygen did not accumulate in the atmosphere until about 2 billion years ago. The first fossils interpreted to be the remains of eukaryotes have been dated at about 1.4 billion years old. Eukaryotes became abundant in aquatic environments by 750 million years ago.

There are more questions than data relating to the origin of life on Earth. Creative thinking and additional research may one day yield more definitive information.

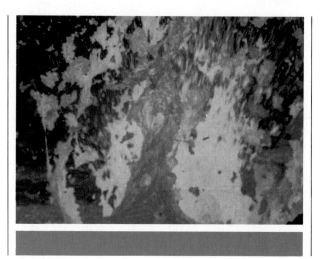

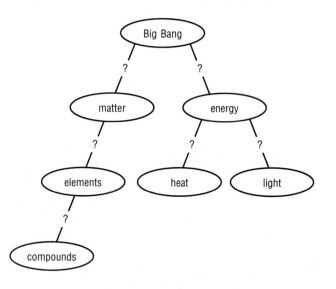

Key Concepts

Copy the concept map that follows and fill in the missing linking words. Use the concepts listed and other concepts from the chapter to expand the map.

chemical evolution	photosynthesis
Darwinian evolution	prokaryote
first life form	eukaryote
heterotroph	

Reviewing Ideas

1. Explain how the Big Bang may have started an expanding universe.

2. How can a telescope be used as a "time machine"?

3. Explain how the ages of meteorites help determine the age of Earth.

4. What is the evidence that free oxygen gas was not present in the primitive atmosphere?

5. Explain the limitations of science in investigating some of the ideas about the origin of life.

6. Explain why there was no ozone layer on Earth when life first originated.

7. Describe the events in chemical evolution that might have led to the first life form.

8. What properties of a mineral crystal make it a possible candidate for the first life form?

9. Why would a "naked" organic molecule be a less-likely candidate for the first life form than an organism with a membrane?

10. Why has no one found fossils older than 3.485 billion years?

11. Describe the results obtained by Miller in his experiments with and without methane and ammonia. What is the significance of the difference?

Using Concepts

1. Describe how Miller's experiment either supported or refuted the Oparin-Haldane chemical-evolution hypothesis.

2. Explain why the identification of formaldehyde in the tail of comet Halley is important to the hypothesis of chemical evolution for the origin of life.

3. Explain why RNA is a more likely candidate than DNA for the first life form.

4. Compare the suggested conditions of early Earth with the present conditions on Venus and Mars.

5. Explain why the first life form was more likely to be a prokaryote than a eukaryote.

6. Which radioactive dating method(s) would be most helpful in dating the oldest rocks on Earth?

Synthesis

1. Describe the differences between Darwinian evolution, as described in Chapter 1, and chemical evolution.

2. A characteristic of living things is their need for energy. How was that need met for the earliest organisms, and in what way did that need drive the evolution of early life forms?

3. Use the discussion in Chapter 1 about pseudo-science to explain why the third idea in Section 4.3 cannot be investigated scientifically. In addition, list several hypotheses that you might investigate to test the validity of the fourth idea.

Extensions

1. Describe possible interactions between early life forms and the materials in the seas around them.

2. Write a story about a scientist trying to decode the fossil record coded in the rocks.

3. Write a story or poem describing the Big Bang from an eyewitness's viewpoint.

4. Make a drawing that shows how you think primitive Earth appeared as it was cooling down from its molten state.

5. If intelligent life existed on a planet around a star in another galaxy, describe the problems you would have in trying to communicate with the extraterrestrials by radio signals. Assume the technology exists to send and receive signals.

CONTENTS

Diversity and Variation

We share this planet with an incredible number of different types of living things. There are more than 3 million named types of organisms. This incredible diversity—a basic characteristic of life on Earth—is referred to as **biodiversity.** Some of these living things resemble each other, but most organisms do not. Dogs do not look like cats, and cats do not look like humans. Even organisms from the same group, for example Siamese and Persian cats, can show a great deal of variation.

To deal with the overwhelming diversity among organisms, we need some method of putting them in order in a logical and meaningful way. Many different systems of classification are possible. Flowering plants, for example, could be classified according to the color of their flowers: all yellow-flowered plants in one group, all blue-flowered plants in a second group, all red-flowered plants in a third, and so on. This type of system is useful, but it also has limitations, because the type of information it conveys about an organism is superficial. For example, it does not recognize such factors as the numbers and variations of the parts of flowers. The classification system used most widely today considers how organisms are related, and groups them on the basis of their evolutionary history, in so far as it is known. This chapter discusses how classification systems bring order to the diversity of life and how they make the study of diverse life forms more understandable.

How many different organisms can you identify?

What important biological phenomenon is illustrated?

◆ *A coral reef in the Caribbean.*

Bringing Order to Diversity _____

5.1 The Species Concept

From very early times, humans have tried to group organisms in ways that would reflect relationships and help distinguish one organism from another. (See **Appendix 5A**, Early Classification Schemes.) The science that grew out of these efforts is called **taxonomy** (tak SAHN uh mee).

The grouping used in most biological classification is the **species** (SPEE sheez). A biological species is, in general, a group of closely related organisms capable of breeding, or mating, in nature to produce fertile offspring with each other, but not with members of other groups. The potential ability to breed unites members of a species. For example, a housewife in California has little probability of having offspring with an Australian aborigine, but if the two should mate they could produce children who would grow into fertile adults.

Members of a species may look very different from each other and still belong to the same group. For example, not all dogs look alike. There are recognizable breeds, such as collies and beagles, yet there are a great number of intermediate mongrels because different breeds can mate and produce fertile offspring. Those offspring can also mate, and they can produce young that are even more varied than their parents. Even extremely different breeds such as Great Danes and Pekingese form part of a related group because they can mate with other intermediate breeds.

Such genetic differences between related individuals within a species are known as variations (Figure 5.1). Variations are the raw material of evolution. They provide additional genetic information on which natural selection can act, resulting in the evolution of new species (Chapter 16).

The variations in a population include individual variation, geographic variation, and variation in form, or polymorphism. Polymorphism occurs when two or more distinct forms, or morphs, coexist in a population. The

FIGURE 5.1 Five breeds of dogs. Beginning with the Great Dane, breeds are represented by every other dog. Mongrel offspring are intermediate between the breeds. What types of variations can you see?

great dane   collie

pekingese   beagle   terrier

FIGURE 5.2 Geographic variations in the human species. Originally, climatic factors such as temperature, humidity, latitude, and altitude contributed to human variation. Today many of the barriers separating human populations have disintegrated, and many distinctive geographic variations are disappearing. There are, however, a few variations that remain, such as height and body form.

light and dark forms of the peppered moths in England are an example (see Figure 16.6). The physical difference between males and females of the same species is another example of polymorphism.

Geographic variation occurs when a species occupies a large geographic range that includes distinct local environments. Populations in those local environments often exhibit unique physical characteristics. Geographic variation accounts for many of the differences in the human species (Figure 5.2).

Individual variation occurs in populations of all sexually reproducing organisms and is less obvious than geographic variation. We are very aware of the variations within the human population; we are less sensitive to individuality in populations of other animals and plants because the variations may be very subtle (Figure 5.3).

FIGURE 5.3 (a) Variation within a human population and (b) variation within a sheep population. In which population are the variations more pronounced?

a

b

a b

FIGURE 5.4 (a) Domestic dog, *Canis familiaris*, and (b) coyote, *Canis latrans*. Though related, the two species are behaviorally isolated and rarely interbreed.

Sometimes individuals from two different species may interbreed on a limited basis. If the two groups fail to interbreed enough to produce a significant number of intermediate individuals, however, they remain separate species. An example is domestic dogs and coyotes (Figure 5.4). Behavioral differences in the care and feeding of the young have successfully limited the number of individuals in the intermediate population. Because there are so few hybrid offspring, and the few that exist are so scattered, there is little likelihood that two members of the intermediate population will meet each other and mate.

FIGURE 5.5 (a) The grizzly bear, *Ursus arctos horribilis*, and (b) the polar bear, *Ursus maritimus*, remain distinct species. Why?

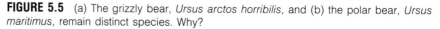

a b

A species, then, is a population of individuals that breed and produce fertile offspring *under natural conditions* (as opposed to unnatural conditions such as captivity). A species is maintained in three basic ways: (1) potential mates do not meet, (2) potential mates meet but do not breed, and (3) potential mates meet and breed, but do not produce fertile or viable offspring. An example of the first case is provided by the grizzly bear and the polar bear (Figure 5.5). Although these two species have reproduced together in captivity, no hybrids have been discovered in the wild. There is a very simple reason: grizzly bears live in forests and eat fish, berries, and small animals; polar bears live on snowfields and ice floes and depend on seals for food. The two species of bears do not come in contact with one another in the wild and so remain separate.

Organisms that share the same habitat provide examples of the second case, where potential mates meet but do not breed. Clearly, a Colorado blue spruce cannot breed with a Colorado blue columbine growing in its shade (Figure 5.6). Similarly, a giraffe and an ostrich cannot mate even though they may come in contact with one another.

The dog and coyote example illustrates the third case, in which potential mates meet and breed but with poor results. In addition, sometimes the offspring of two species may be sterile, or incapable of reproducing. The mule, a cross between a horse and a donkey, is almost always sterile.

There are certain limitations to the biological species concept. First, it does not apply to organisms that do not reproduce sexually, because there is no way to test the interbreeding criteria. Second, even in species that reproduce sexually, isolation may be only partial. Frequently, populations are found that are in an intermediate stage of differentiation between subspecies, which can interbreed, and species, which cannot. Third, the biological species concept does not accommodate the slow and usually unmeasurable changes that occur in a species through time.

FIGURE 5.6   (a) The Colorado blue spruce, *Picea pungens*, and (b) Colorado blue columbine, *Aquilegia caerulea*, do not crossbreed, even though the two share the same habitat.

a   b

FOCUS ON *Species*

Horses and donkeys are known for producing hybrid offspring called mules. Technically, a mule is a cross between a male donkey and a female horse. Normally, mules are sterile because they are a hybrid of two species. Sometimes strange things happen, however. In 1984, a mule named Krause gave birth to a colt. Geneticists from the San Diego Zoo determined the number of chromosomes of both the mule and the new colt. (Chromosomes are structures in cells that carry genetic material.) The tests showed that Krause and her offspring were mules. Horses have 64 chromosomes, donkeys 62, and mules 63. Krause did not stop there, however; in 1987, she gave birth to another colt. Researchers hope that

Krause and Chester, the father donkey, will continue to reproduce. Instances such as these illustrate the difficulty in defining a species.

FIGURE A The mule Krause with her two colts

5.2 Classification and Structural Similarities

What characteristics are most helpful in classifying organisms? If you look at the organisms in Figure 5.7, you will note they are all red but have little else in common. Specialists in taxonomy use a number of characteristics to classify organisms, including structure, function, biochemistry, behavior, genetic systems, and evolutionary histories, among others. The more consistent a characteristic is, the more valuable it is for determining classification. For example, within a species, structures such as skeletons (in ani-

FIGURE 5.7 One similarity among these organisms is obvious—their color. How else are they alike?

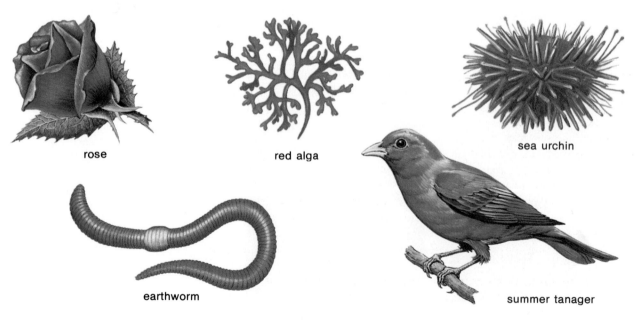

rose

red alga

sea urchin

earthworm

summer tanager

☐ humerus ■ ulna ☐ radius ☐ carpals ■ metacarpals and phalanges

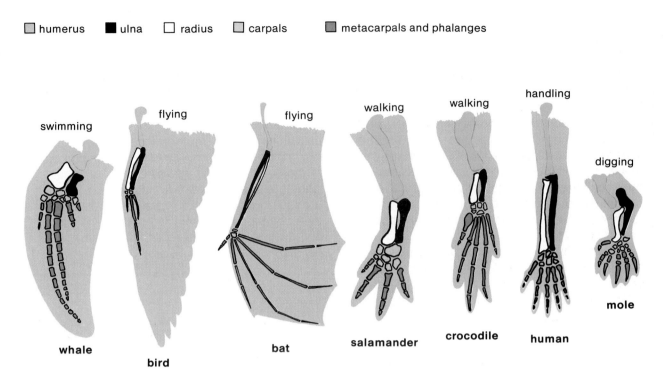

FIGURE 5.8 Bones of the forelimbs of seven vertebrates. Follow the color key to similarities; they indicate that these animals once had a common ancestor. Also check the structure of each forelimb for its adaptations to the animal's way of life.

mals) and the reproductive parts of flowers are less variable characteristics than are size and color. Anatomical structure thus provides a useful and consistent basis for classifying organisms.

Similarities of structure that indicate *related evolutionary ancestry*, not merely shared physical characteristics, are the principal criteria used for classification. These structural similarities are called **homologies** (hoh MOL uh jees; singular, homology). For example, as Figure 5.8 shows, the flipper of a whale, the wing of a bat, and the arm of a human have many similarities in their bone and muscle structure. The limbs have the same relationship to the body, and they develop the same way in the young. In addition, fish, amphibians, reptiles, and birds share this same limb pattern with mammals.

Two factors make anatomical characteristics particularly important. The first is that a taxonomist can observe those characteristics in preserved specimens or geologic records, and those observations are easily verified. In addition, anatomical evidence in the form of fossils is all we are ever likely to have for species that are no longer alive. Extinct organisms may be the ancestors of living organisms. Thus, knowledge of past organisms can help us determine the relationships of living ones.

Chemical homologies, such as similarities in blood or chemicals in cells, also indicate close evolutionary relationships. Comparisons between different organisms of nucleotide sequences in DNA or RNA, or of amino acid sequences in proteins, are particularly revealing.

FOCUS ON *Protein Similarities*

Cytochrome *c* is a protein that plays an important role in respiration in animal and plant cells. The differences in cytochrome *c* between species results from differences in the amino acid sequence. The more closely two species are related in their evolutionary history, the fewer amino acid differences there will be between their comparable proteins. By comparing the amino acid sequences of cytochrome *c* from different species, one can determine how closely the species are related.

An interesting finding in protein studies is that some positions in a particular type of protein molecule are occupied by the same amino acid in every species analyzed. Termed invariant, these amino acids may be part of the protein's active site or play a role in maintaining the protein molecule's tertiary structure. Changing one of those amino acids would result in a protein with an altered function. An individual with such a protein would be at a reproductive disadvantage compared to other members of the population. Hence, natural selection would act against variations in the invariant amino acids.

5.3 Classification Hierarchies

Based on homologies, organisms from different species are grouped into larger and more general categories (Figure 5.9). Species with many similar characteristics are grouped into the same **genus**. For example, domestic dogs, coyotes, and wolves all belong to different species, but they are similar in many ways. Therefore, taxonomists group them in the genus, *Canis*.

Similar genera (plural of genus) are grouped in the same **family**. The fox, genus *Vulpes*, belongs with *Canis* in the family Canidae. At the same time, the dog family is related to a number of other families (for example, the cat, bear, raccoon, weasel, otter, and hyena families). All of these ani-

FIGURE 5.9 The classification of 12 animals

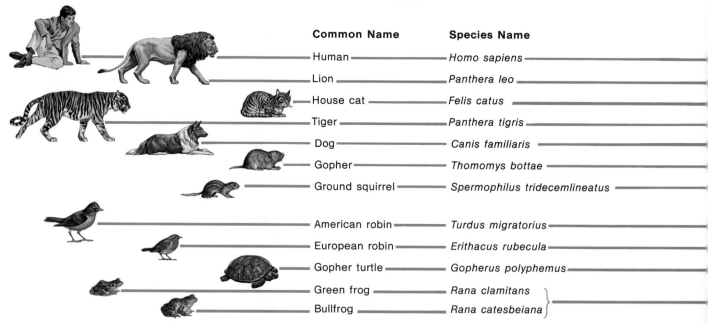

Common Name	Species Name
Human	*Homo sapiens*
Lion	*Panthera leo*
House cat	*Felis catus*
Tiger	*Panthera tigris*
Dog	*Canis familiaris*
Gopher	*Thomomys bottae*
Ground squirrel	*Spermophilus tridecemlineatus*
American robin	*Turdus migratorius*
European robin	*Erithacus rubecula*
Gopher turtle	*Gopherus polyphemus*
Green frog	*Rana clamitans*
Bullfrog	*Rana catesbeiana*

FIGURE 5.10 Some animals in the order Carnivora. Which two look most alike? Which two look most different? In what way?

bear
× 1/56

wolf
× 1/42

coyote
× 1/47

× 1/28
fox

weasel
× 1/16

mals have a distinctive anatomy and way of life that characterizes them as flesh eaters. They are grouped in the **order** Carnivora (Figure 5.10).

Cats, wolves, and raccoons have many differences, but they still share many likenesses. Certainly they have more in common with each other than with rabbits. Rabbits are placed in a different order, Lagomorpha. Rabbits (along with rats, horses, pigs, and animals from other orders) share some characteristics with members of the order Carnivora. Those similarities are the basis for putting the orders together in the next larger grouping—at the **class** level—Mammalia.

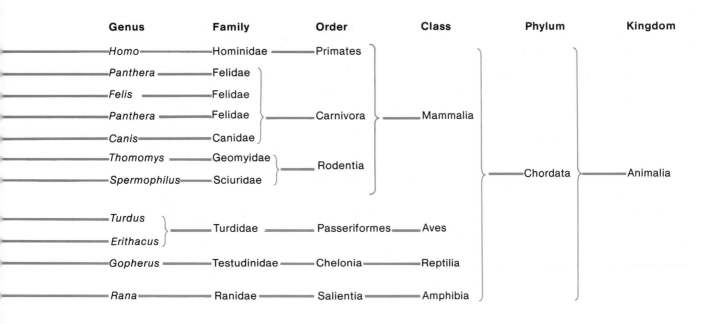

Genus	Family	Order	Class	Phylum	Kingdom
Homo	Hominidae	Primates			
Panthera	Felidae				
Felis	Felidae				
Panthera	Felidae	Carnivora	Mammalia		
Canis	Canidae				
Thomomys	Geomyidae	Rodentia			
Spermophilus	Sciuridae			Chordata	Animalia
Turdus	Turdidae	Passeriformes	Aves		
Erithacus					
Gopherus	Testudinidae	Chelonia	Reptilia		
Rana	Ranidae	Salientia	Amphibia		

Continuing with this method of grouping, taxonomists place the classes containing birds, snakes, fish, and frogs with the Mammalia into the **phylum** (FY lum) Chordata. Botanists, people who study plants, do not consistently use the term *phylum*. Instead, they group organisms at this level into **divisions**. Most botanists prefer to use the term *division* because the term *phylum* implies a knowledge of ancestries that is often lacking for the major plant groups.

Finally, the chordates, snails, butterflies, and thousands of other organisms are grouped in the **kingdom** Animalia. That kingdom contains all the living things you think of as animals.

As you go from species to kingdom, the organisms that are grouped together share fewer characteristics at each succeeding level. At the species level, individuals are so alike they can interbreed. Organisms at the kingdom level share only a few common characteristics. How many common characteristics can you name for the animals whose classifications are shown in Figure 5.9 on pages 96 and 97?

Scientists use binomial nomenclature, or a two-word naming system, to name each species. This system was first devised by Carolus Linnaeus. (See **Appendix 5A**, Early Classification Schemes.) The first word in each name is the genus name, and the second word is the descriptive, or species, name that refers to that particular group of organisms. Together these two

FIGURE 5.11 Two species of mice, (a) *Peromyscus leucopus* and (b) *Peromyscus truei*. What differences can you see?

FIGURE 5.12 (a) The ponderosa pine, *Pinus ponderosa* and (b) the loblolly pine, *Pinus taeda* are not members of the same species even though they look very similar.

a

b

a

b

words are called the **scientific name**. The genus name is always capitalized but the descriptive name is not. The entire scientific name appears in italics in print or underlined when handwritten. For example, the white-footed mouse is *Peromyscus leucopus,* and the piñon mouse is *Peromyscus truei.* Both of them are mice, but each is a different species (Figure 5.11). In addition, there are still other species of mice within the genus *Peromyscus.* Another example of different species sharing the genus name is the ponderosa pine (*Pinus ponderosa*) and the loblolly pine (*Pinus taeda)* shown in Figure 5.12.

Why use a latinized binomial system? First, a classification system has to be understood internationally while remaining unaffected by the inevitable changes that occur in spoken languages. For this reason, Latin or latinized names are used rather than names from a particular modern language. (See Figure 5.13.) The following lines from a textbook used in Yugoslavia refer to a species of bacteria you may be able to identify, even though you do not know the language:

> Te besede se slisijo, kot da bi bile bakterije reaggirale po Lamarckovi teoriji. (Poglavje 3-2). Naslednji opis eksperimenta, pri katerem so uporabili bakterijo *Staphylococcus aureus*, vam bo pokazal, ali je ta proces res lamarckovski ali ne.

FIGURE 5.13 A short section on poisonous mushrooms from a Chinese BSCS biology book. Note the scientific name.

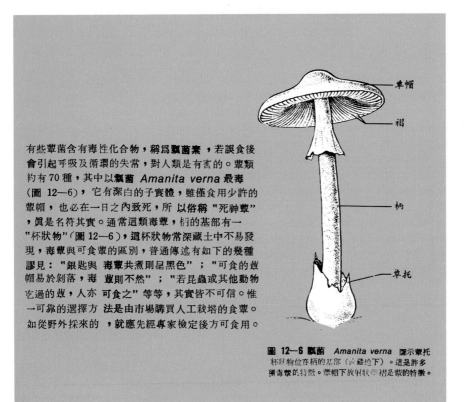

有些蕈菌含有毒性化合物，稱爲飄菌素，若誤食後會引起呼吸及循環的失常，對人類是有害的。蕈類約有70種，其中以飄菌 *Amanita verna* 最毒（圖 12—6），它有潔白的子實體，雖僅食用少許的蕈帽，也必在一日之內致死，所 以俗稱 "死神蕈" ，眞是名符其實。通常這類毒蕈，柄的基部有一 "杯狀物" (圖 12—6)，這杯狀物常深藏土中不易發現，毒蕈與可食蕈的區別，普通傳述有如下的幾種謬見："銀匙與 毒蕈共煮則呈黑色"； "可食的蕈帽易於剝落，毒 蕈則不然"； "若昆蟲或其他動物吃過的蕈，人亦 可食之" 等等，其實皆不可信。惟一可靠的選擇方 法是由市場購買人工栽培的食蕈。如從野外探來的 ，就應先經專家檢定後方可食用。

草帽

褶

柄

草托

圖 12—6 飄菌 *Amanita verna* 圖示蕈托杯狀物位在柄的基部 (或藏地下)。這是許多種毒蕈的特徵。蕈帽下放射狀的褶是蕈的特徵。

A second reason for using the binomial system is that it is precise. Common names are regional and imprecise. For example, if people from different parts of North America are discussing a gopher, they may not be talking about the same species at all. In California, a gopher is a small burrowing rodent with the scientific name *Thomomys bottae*. In Florida, a gopher is a type of tortoise whose scientific name is *Gopherus polyphemus*. Imagine how difficult it is for people who use the same common name for different organisms to communicate without confusion. The use of scientific names avoids this problem.

CHECK AND CHALLENGE

1. What condition is necessary for organisms to be considered members of the same species?
2. What is binomial nomenclature and what function does it serve?
3. Give two examples of how the number of characteristics shared by members of a classification level changes as you proceed from species to kingdom.
4. Define homologies and explain their importance in classification.
5. Explain how species maintain their distinctness.

The Kingdoms of Organisms

5.4   Cell Structure

As you move through the classification system from species to kingdoms, each successive category contains more types of organisms. The more types of organisms there are within a category, the less similarity and fewer homologies among them. Cell structure, however, provides a basic homology that biologists use to separate all organisms into two major groups, the prokaryotes (bacteria) and eukaryotes you read about in Chapter 4.

The differences between these two groups are profound. Prokaryotic cells are distinguished mainly by the lack of membrane-enclosed structures. Thus, they do not have a nucleus, nor organelles such as mitochondria. The cell walls of prokaryotes are usually rigid and are formed from proteinlike chains. The genetic material of prokaryotes consists of a single circular thread of DNA, though some prokaryotes have additional small rings of DNA called plasmids (PLAZ midz).

Eukaryotic cells generally are larger than those of prokaryotes and are distinguished by a membrane-enclosed nucleus. Various other membrane-enclosed organelles are also present, and the cellular material often appears to move, or stream, within the cell. If there are cell walls, they are usually composed of cellulose or another polysaccharide, chitin (KYT in). The DNA of eukaryotes is organized into chromosomes within the nucleus. Chromosomes are made up of thousands of genes, the units of genetic information that contain the hereditary instructions. Eukaryotic cells do not have plasmids.

Plasmids are tools for the genetic engineer, who can insert into them DNA from a variety of organisms. Bacteria that receive foreign DNA in the form of plasmids treat the DNA as their own. This is possible because all organisms share the same genetic material—DNA. Such sharing is an example of genetic continuity even between species.

FOCUS ON *Bacteria*

Bacteria are small in size but present in enormous numbers. A spoonful of garden soil may contain 10 billion bacteria, and the number in your mouth is greater than the number of humans who have ever lived. Bacteria play important roles in the biosphere. They are primarily responsible for the cycling of gases such as nitrogen, oxygen, carbon dioxide, hydrogen, and ammonia, among many others. They are essential to all food webs because of their role as decomposers—they break down complex organic compounds into inorganic materials used by plants. They also do the reverse, transforming inorganic materials into complex organic compounds. Bacteria serve as food for other microorganisms too. Although some bacteria cause diseases that affect plants, humans, and other animals, the vast majority are beneficial. For example, bacteria living in our intestines produce essential vitamins that we absorb and use.

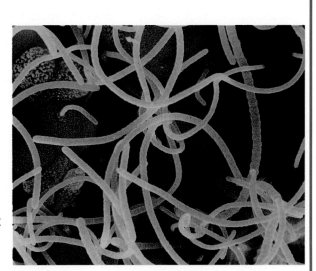

FIGURE B Bacteria in the human digestive tract break down materials humans cannot digest and release vitamins in the process. Scanning electron micrograph, X4225.

5.5 Five Kingdoms

If, indeed, organisms at the kingdom level have very little in common, then what criteria can be used to group them into kingdoms? Biologists consider several questions. Is the organism a prokaryote or a eukaryote? Is it an autotroph or a heterotroph (Chapter 3)? Does the organism reproduce asexually or sexually? **Asexual reproduction** requires only one parent, and the offspring is a duplicate of the parent. **Sexual reproduction** requires two parents, and the organism develops from a fertilized egg. Finally, what is the general structure and function of the organism? None of these questions, however, resolves all the problems of classification, and the systems continually change with new knowledge. Today, most biologists favor the five-kingdom classification system (Figure 5.14).

All prokaryotes presently are grouped in one kingdom called the **Monera** (moh NEHR uh), although some taxonomists call this kingdom Prokaryotae. Prokaryotes display a greater variety of chemical and functional patterns than do eukaryotes. They are classified into one of two basic groups, **eubacteria** (true bacteria) or **archaebacteria** (AR kee bak TIR ee uh; ancient bacteria). Like plants and some other green eukaryotes, many prokaryotes produce food through photosynthesis, but the prokaryotes use a wider variety of substances as raw materials. Other prokaryotes use energy obtained from chemicals rather than light to produce food, and many prokaryotes are heterotrophs. Prokaryotes generally are unicellular, or one-celled, though multicellular, or many-celled, forms exist as well. Reproduction is accomplished largely through cell division, which is asexual. Figure 5.15 on page 104 shows examples of prokaryotes.

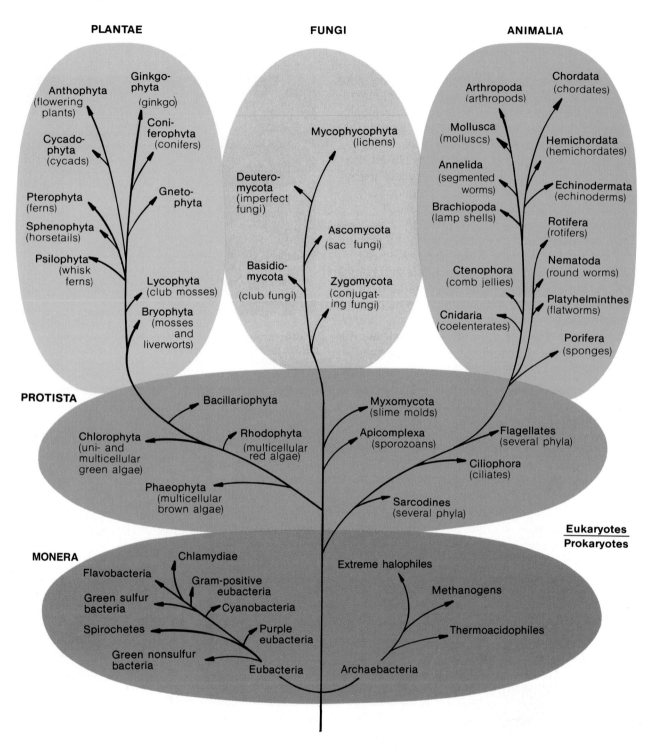

PLANTAE

FUNGI

ANIMALIA

Anthophyta (flowering plants)

Ginkgo-phyta (ginkgo)

Coni-ferophyta (conifers)

Cycado-phyta (cycads)

Gneto-phyta

Pterophyta (ferns)

Sphenophyta (horsetails)

Psilophyta (whisk ferns)

Lycophyta (club mosses)

Bryophyta (mosses and liverworts)

Mycophycophyta (lichens)

Deutero-mycota (imperfect fungi)

Ascomycota (sac fungi)

Basidio-mycota (club fungi)

Zygomycota (conjugat-ing fungi)

Arthropoda (arthropods)

Chordata (chordates)

Mollusca (molluscs)

Hemichordata (hemichordates)

Annelida (segmented worms)

Echinodermata (echinoderms)

Brachiopoda (lamp shells)

Rotifera (rotifers)

Ctenophora (comb jellies)

Nematoda (round worms)

Platyhelminthes (flatworms)

Cnidaria (coelenterates)

Porifera (sponges)

PROTISTA

Bacillariophyta

Myxomycota (slime molds)

Chlorophyta (uni- and multicellular green algae)

Rhodophyta (multicellular red algae)

Apicomplexa (sporozoans)

Flagellates (several phyla)

Ciliophora (ciliates)

Phaeophyta (multicellular brown algae)

Sarcodines (several phyla)

<u>Eukaryotes</u>
<u>Prokaryotes</u>

MONERA

Chlamydiae

Extreme halophiles

Flavobacteria

Gram-positive eubacteria

Methanogens

Green sulfur bacteria

Cyanobacteria

Spirochetes

Thermoacidophiles

Purple eubacteria

Green nonsulfur bacteria

Eubacteria

Archaebacteria

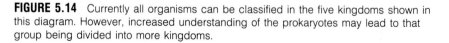

FIGURE 5.14 Currently all organisms can be classified in the five kingdoms shown in this diagram. However, increased understanding of the prokaryotes may lead to that group being divided into more kingdoms.

ARCHAEBACTERIA
AND CLASSIFICATION

Although they share some characteristics with other prokaryotes, archaebacteria differ in basic ways from all other forms of life. Many scientists believe the early atmosphere of Earth was rich in carbon dioxide and hydrogen, and that extreme conditions such as hot acid springs and salt ponds may have existed. Because archaebacteria are adapted to such conditions, some scientists think that they were among the first organisms on Earth.

There are three distinct types of archaebacteria. One type, the thermoacidophiles, lives in hot acid environments in which temperatures average 70° to 90°C and the pH of the water may be 2 or less. These environments include hot sulphur springs, such as the one shown on page 20. Another type, the extreme halophiles, requires a high concentration of salt to survive and lives in salty environments such as the Great Salt Lake. The third type, the methanogens, are the most widely distributed of the archaebacteria and live only in anaerobic conditions. Commonly occurring in stagnant water, sewage treatment plants, the ocean bottom, hot springs, and the digestive tracts of animals, these organisms produce methane gas from hydrogen and carbon dioxide.

Currently, the archaebacteria are classified in the kingdom Monera, along with other bacteria. Some biologists propose that they be placed in a separate kingdom, Archaebacteria, as they believe these organisms are as different from other prokaryotes as they are from eukaryotes. However, other biologists do not consider the differences significant enough to justify a sixth kingdom. They also are concerned that if the classification system becomes too subdivided,

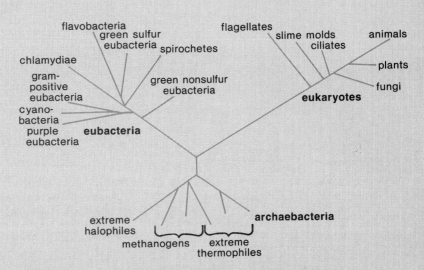

FIGURE C The relationship of the archaebacteria, eubacteria, and eukaryotes, based on RNA sequence data

it will no longer be useful in helping us learn about life on Earth.

Still other scientists propose a genetically based "superkingdom" classification that consists of archaebacteria, eubacteria, and eukaryotes. All organisms have a type of RNA called rRNA (ribosomal RNA), and the study of an organism's rRNA can reveal its evolutionary history. The sequence of amino acid bases within rRNA changes little through time. By comparing the rRNA of different organisms, scientists can estimate the relationship of the organisms to each other. If the sequence of rRNA bases is very similar, the organisms are considered to be closely related. The greater the differences in the sequence, the less closely related the organisms are thought to be. Figure C shows the relationship among archaebacteria, eubacteria, and the eukaryotes based on rRNA analysis. Some scientists argue that the differences between archaebacteria and eubacteria are sufficient to warrant placing them in separate superkingdoms (Archaebacteria and Eubacteria), but that all eukaryotes are similar enough to be placed in a third superkingdom, Eukarya.

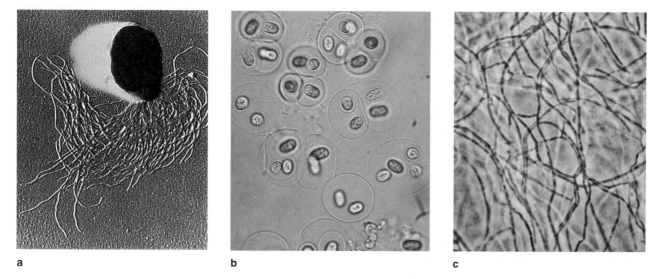

a   b   c

FIGURE 5.15 Examples of Monera. (a) *Pyrococcus furiosus* can grow at temperatures up to 103°C. (b) *Gloeocapsa*, a photosynthetic bacterium, is abundant in aquatic ecosystems. (c) Decomposer bacteria in the soil break down complex organic compounds into inorganic materials used by plants. Some, such as the ones shown here, also produce antibiotics.

FIGURE 5.16 Members of the kingdom Plantae: (a) moss, *Polytrichium,* (b) ferns, *Cystopteris fragilis,* (c) Douglas fir, *Pseudotsuga menziesii,* a conifer, and (d) sand lily, *Leucocrinium montanum.*

a

b

c

d

Currently, the eukaryotes are divided into four kingdoms. Most of the autotrophic, multicellular eukaryotes that produce their own food through photosynthesis (Chapter 7) belong to the kingdom **Plantae** (PLAN tee). Plants have cellulose-containing cell walls and store food as starch; their cells contain chloroplasts. Mosses, ferns, conifers, and flowering plants all belong to this kingdom (Figure 5.16). The bulk of the world's food and much of its oxygen are derived from plants.

Heterotrophic, multicellular eukaryotes are placed in the kingdom **Animalia** (an uh MAYL yuh). They range in size from microscopic organisms to giant whales and are the most diverse in form of the members of all five kingdoms. Members of the kingdom Animalia include **vertebrates**—animals with a spinal column, or backbone, such as birds, frogs, snakes, and humans; and **invertebrates**—animals lacking a backbone, such as sponges, worms, and insects. Some familiar examples are shown in Figure 5.17. Most members of this kingdom are motile, or capable of locomotion, and have senses and nervous systems.

Try Investigation 5B, Structural Characteristics of Animals.

FIGURE 5.17 Four members of the kingdom Animalia: (a) sea star, (b) monarch butterfly, (c) canary rockfish, *Sebastes pinnager*, and (d) giraffe, *Giraffa camelopardalis.*

a

b

c

d

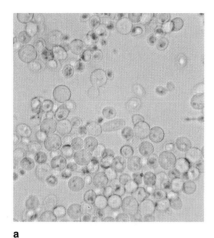

a b c

FIGURE 5.18 Examples of the kingdom Fungi: (a) yeast, *Saccharomyces*, (b) mushroom, *Stropharia squamosa*, and (c) rust, *Uredinales*.

Organisms of the kingdom **Fungi** (FUN jy) are heterotrophs that absorb small molecules from their surroundings through their outer walls. Most fungi are multicellular (yeast is an exception) and have chitinous cell walls. Many are decomposers and play an important role in breaking down organic material. Fungi vary in size and include yeasts, molds, bracket fungi, and mushrooms (Figure 5.18).

All the eukaryotes not included in the three kingdoms already described are grouped in the kingdom **Protista** (pro TIST uh). Many protists are microscopic and unicellular, but others, such as kelp, are multicel-

FOCUS ON *Lichens*

Lichens often resemble mosses or other simple plants, but lichens are not plants at all. Technically, they are not even individual organisms. Lichens, like the ones shown here, are actually fungi and algae that live together in a close association. The nature of the relationship is debated. The algae definitely provide the fungi with food, but it is not known whether the algae receive any benefits other than protection by the fungi. Furthermore, the fungi actually kill some of the algae. For this reason, some biologists who study lichens argue that the relationship is really parasitic, that is, one organism makes its living directly at the expense of another. However, the merging of the fungi and algae is so complete that lichens actually are given binomial species names as if they were a single organism.

FIGURE D Lichens colonizing a rock, X1

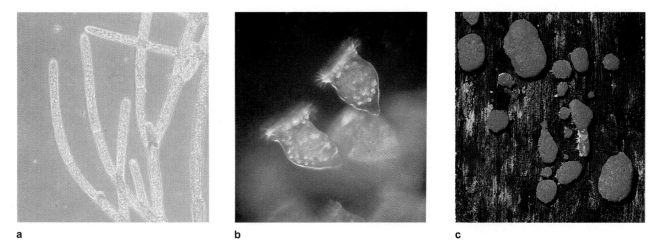

a   b   c

FIGURE 5.19 Examples of Protista: (a) filamentous alga, *Cladophora*, (b) protozoa, *Vorticella campanula* (X125), and (c) red raspberry slime mold, *Tubifera ferruginosa* (X1).

lular organisms that may reach 10 meters or more in length. There is great variation in cellular organization, method of reproduction, and life-style within this group. Protists may be producers, consumers, or decomposers. Some protists switch from one form of nutrition to another, depending on conditions. The kingdom includes algae (plantlike protists), protozoa (animallike protists), slime molds (funguslike protists), and other organisms (Figure 5.19).

5.6 Classification and Change

Keep in mind that *taxonomic classification is not fixed.* Classification schemes depend on the interpretation of evidence, and there is no total agreement among biologists as to which organisms fit where. The more information we obtain, the more complex the relationships of organisms appear to be. As a result, there are many classification schemes. New knowledge often requires changes in the way organisms are grouped. That is especially true at the kingdom level.

At one time it seemed that organisms could be classified into two kingdoms—plants and animals. As improved microscopes increased the knowledge and understanding of microscopic organisms, it became evident that many of these microorganisms did not fit well into either of the two kingdoms. As a result, additional kingdoms were suggested.

After electron microscopes made clear the profound differences in cell structure between the prokaryotes and the eukaryotes, taxonomists added the kingdom Monera for the prokaryotes. Because the fungi share few characteristics with any of the other groups, a separate kingdom was proposed for them. Recently, the kingdom Archaebacteria was proposed for certain bacteria with distinct differences from other Monerans. Figure 5.20 (page 108) shows the classification of an organism from each of the five generally accepted kingdoms.

The five-kingdom system of classification presented here is not accepted by all biologists. Some people place multicellular algae with the

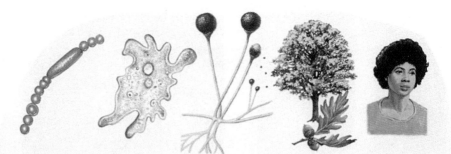

	Anabaena cyanobacteria	Amoeba	Rhizopus bread mold	Quercus alba white oak	Homo sapiens human
kingdom	Prokaryotae	Protista	Fungi	Plantae	Animalia
phylum/division	Cyanobacteria	Sarcodina	Zygomycota	Anthophyta	Chordata
class	Eubacteria	Lobosa	Phycomycetes	Dicotyledoneae	Mammalia
order	Oscillatoriales	Amoebina	Mucorales	Fagales	Primates
family	Nostocaceae	Amoebidae	Mucoraceae	Fagaceae	Hominidae
genus	*Anabaena*	*Amoeba*	*Rhizopus*	*Quercus*	*Homo*
species	*circinalis*	*proteus*	*stolonifer*	*alba*	*sapiens*

FIGURE 5.20 Classification of an organism from each kingdom.

plants and heterotrophic protists in the animal kingdom. Further studies of bacteria may require the formation of still other kingdoms.

Classification systems also reflect the purposes of the person performing the classification. Grouping organisms as producers, consumers, or decomposers may work quite well for people studying ecology (Chapter 26) but would not work well for biologists studying the anatomy of most organisms.

Classification systems are products of our knowledge of the living world. Species, genera, families, orders, classes, and kingdoms do not exist in nature; only individual organisms exist. Classification systems are simply a way for us to think more clearly about the great diversity that surrounds us. The changing systems of classification reflect how science works—it is open to modification on the basis of new data. The Brief Survey of Organisms that follows the Chapter Highlights shows but a few examples of the diversity of life.

CONNECTIONS

Changes in classification systems reflect the changes groups of organisms undergo as they evolve.

CHECK AND CHALLENGE

1. Describe the difference that separates prokaryotes and eukaryotes.
2. List characteristics used to separate organisms into kingdoms.
3. Describe the characteristics of each kingdom and give an example of an organism from each.
4. List factors that result in changes in classification systems.

Biological Challenges

CLASSIFICATION OF THE GIANT PANDA

Giant pandas live in the high alpine bamboo forests in western China and are one of the most widely recognized and cherished animal species. From an evolutionary point of view, however, the species is also one of the most puzzling. For almost 120 years biologists have disagreed about the taxonomic classification of the panda. Some have placed the panda in the bear family; others with the red panda in the raccoon family.

Giant pandas look like bears yet have many traits that are not at all bearlike. They are largely vegetarian, eating mostly bamboo. The panda has a large, massive head with flattened teeth and jaws well developed for grinding (Figure E). The panda is the only species aside from the apes known to have a thumb that can grasp objects.

In addition, giant pandas are unlike bears for reasons not directly related to diet. Alpine bears usually hibernate; giant pandas do not. Pandas do not sound like bears either. Instead of a growl or roar, pandas bleat like sheep. On a cellular level, biologists have discovered that the number and type of giant panda chromosomes (21 pairs) is much more like the red panda's (22 pairs) than the bear's (37 pairs).

Through new techniques allowing the detailed study of homologies in DNA and chromosomes, a new classification expressing the evolutionary relationships of bears, raccoons, and pandas was developed. These techniques are based on the molecular clock hypothesis. According to this hypothesis, populations and their genetic material became isolated from one another. Because of this isolation, differences appeared in the populations through time. Such differences arise from mutations in the population's DNA that are passed from generation to generation. These mutations may occur in portions of the DNA that code for particular amino acids, or in noncoding portions of the DNA that have no apparent effect on the composition of an organism.

In either case, the rate of accumulation of mutations can be measured, and the extent to which the DNA of the two species differs is a good indication of their relationship. On the basis of this information, the approximate point when two species diverged from a common ancestor can be determined.

The giant panda is now classified in the bear family, Ursidae. Within that family, pandas are distinctive enough to be placed in a subfamily. The red panda is still classified in the Procyonidae, or raccoon family, also in a subfamily. The molecular relationships suggest that the raccoon and bear families diverged from a common ancestor between 35 and 40 million years ago.

FIGURE E Giant panda, *Ailuropoda melanoleuca*

C H A P T E R Highlights

Summary

Classification systems provide an organized approach to the study of the great diversity of organisms that exists in the biosphere. Taxonomists have devised a system that names organisms and indicates diversity among groups and variation within groups. The variations within groups are the result of genetic changes that have been maintained by natural selection, and are the raw material of evolution. The latinized system is generally accepted worldwide, and through the use of binomial nomenclature, biologists from different parts of the world can understand one another when discussing a particular organism. Classification systems may be based on numerous characteristics, but the most important ones are structural and biochemical homologies. Currently all organisms are classified in five kingdoms—Monera, Protista, Fungi, Plantae, and Animalia, but further study of bacteria indicates that the system may need to be revised. Classification systems are always in a state of change. Their current status reflects the best information available and the purpose of the person who does the classification.

Key Concepts

Use the following pairs of terms to develop a concept map. Include appropriate linking words and add as many other concepts as you can.

classification systems—change

genus—species

eukaryote—prokaryote

diversity—variation

Reviewing Ideas

1. Define species. What are the problems associated with defining distinct species?
2. Give examples of the chemical and structural relationships that indicate related ancestry.

3. How do eukaryotes and prokaryotes differ?
4. Compare and contrast variation and diversity.

Using Concepts

1. What characteristics distinguish Protista from the other kingdoms?
2. Lichens are a close association of fungi and algae, but whether the relationship is mutually beneficial, and to what extent, is not known. How would you go about determining that? State the problem as a hypothesis.
3. Explain how advances in technology can influence classification systems.

Synthesis

Can homologies suggest that many species evolved from a few species? Defend your answer through examples.

Extension

Design an imaginary organism that has characteristics that would classify it in one of the five kingdoms. You may either sketch the organism or write about it, but you should do so in detail.

A Brief Survey of Organisms

The variety of organisms seems almost endless. They vary from those that carry out all of the functions of life within a single cell (unicellular) to highly-specialized collections of trillions of cells (multicellular). Some are autotrophic — they can make their own food from energy and materials in the environment. Others require ready-made food — they are heterotrophic. Some move about in their environment; they are said to be motile. Others are fixed to one spot; they are said to be sessile. The great variety of size, shape, color, and way of life of organisms is evident in the examples in this survey. All living organisms presently are classified in five major kingdoms: Monera, Protista, Fungi, Plantae, and Animalia. Each kingdom is divided into smaller groups called phyla (singular phylum) or divisions (for plants). In turn, phyla and divisions are divided into smaller groupings. Where possible, common names are given for the illustrated organisms as well as a size indication. Scientific names are used for the organisms that have no common names. Major characteristics are listed for each group. Consult specialized reference works for more complete and detailed information on a specific group of organisms.

Kingdom Monera: prokaryotes; lack membrane-enclosed organelles; circular DNA without protein; plasmids usually present; unicellular, chains, colonies, or branched filaments; heterotrophic or autotrophic; many anaerobic; reproduction by fission; exchange of genetic material in some species; more than 5000 species described; two major groups

---

archaebacteria: biochemically unique; may represent the first organisms; adapted to extreme conditions; methanogens, thermoacidophiles, extreme halophiles

eubacteria: three major groups based on characteristics of cell wall; includes cyanobacteria, anaerobic phototrophic bacteria, chemoautotrophic bacteria, spirochetes, enteric bacteria, fermenting bacteria, aerobic nitrogen fixers, actinobacteria

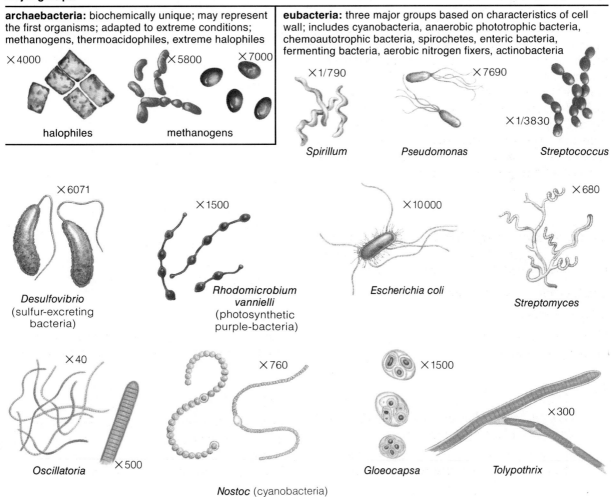

×4000

×5800   ×7000

halophiles   methanogens

×1/790   *Spirillum*

×7690   *Pseudomonas*

×1/3830   *Streptococcus*

×6071   *Desulfovibrio* (sulfur-excreting bacteria)

×1500   *Rhodomicrobium vannielli* (photosynthetic purple-bacteria)

×10000   *Escherichia coli*

×680   *Streptomyces*

×40   ×500   *Oscillatoria*

×760   *Nostoc* (cyanobacteria)

×1500   *Gloeocapsa*

×300   *Tolypothrix*

112

Kingdom Protista: eukaryotes; have membrane-enclosed nuclei and organelles; DNA organized into chromosomes complexed with protein; unicellular to multicellular; autotrophic or heterotrophic; reproduction asexual or sexual; 27 phyla; more than 100 000 species

flagellates (several phyla): locomotion by flagella; unicellular or colonial; heterotrophic, autotrophic, or both; about 2000 species

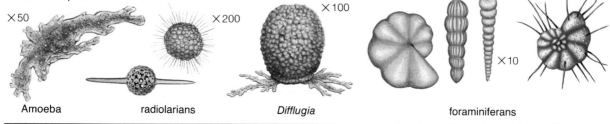

×40

Gonyaulax

×270

Phacus

×1000

Trypanosoma

×500

Peranema

×1400

Euglena

×100

Noctiluca

sarcodines (several phyla): locomotion by pseudopods; unicellular, many with intricate skeletal structures; heterotrophic; about 8000 species

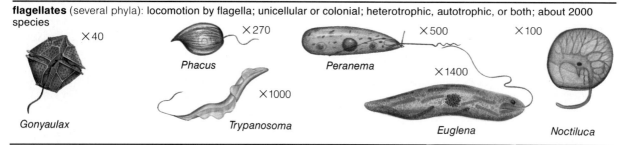

×50

Amoeba

×200

radiolarians

×100

Difflugia

×10

foraminiferans

sporozoans (Phylum Apicomplexa): usually nonmotile; heterotrophic; parasites with complex life cycles; about 2000 species

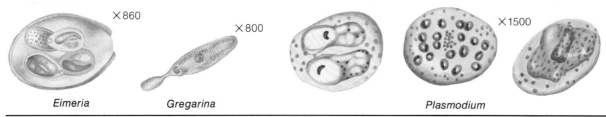

×860

Eimeria

×800

Gregarina

×1500

Plasmodium

ciliates (Phylum Ciliophora): locomotion by cilia; unicellular; heterotrophic; contain macro- and micronuclei; about 5000 species

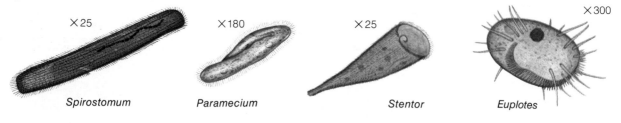

×25

Spirostomum

×180

Paramecium

×25

Stentor

×300

Euplotes

slime molds (Phylum Myxomycota): amoebalike colonies; heterotrophic; sexual reproduction by spores; about 450 species

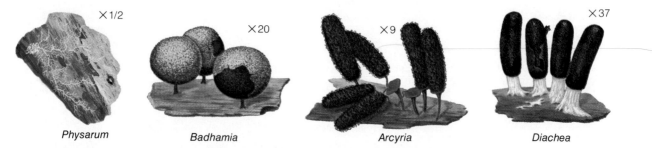

×1/2

Physarum

×20

Badhamia

×9

Arcyria

×37

Diachea

Protista *(continued)*

diatoms (Phylum Bacillariophyta): unicellular, colonial, or multicellular; autotrophic; food stored as oil; two-part shells of silica; about 10 000 species

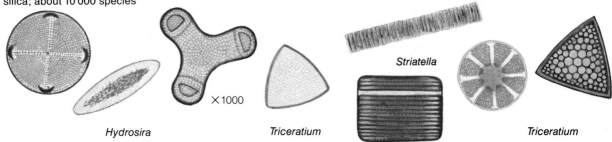

Striatella

×1000

Hydrosira   *Triceratium*   *Triceratium*

brown algae (Phylum Phaeophyta): multicellular, macroscopic (up to 100 m); marine; autotrophic; about 1500 species

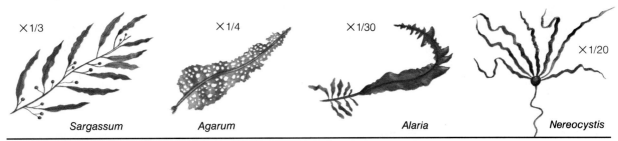

×1/3   ×1/4   ×1/30   ×1/20

Sargassum   *Agarum*   *Alaria*   *Nereocystis*

red algae (Phylum Rhodophyta): multicellular, macroscopic; marine, nonmotile gametes; autotrophic; source of agar; about 4000 species

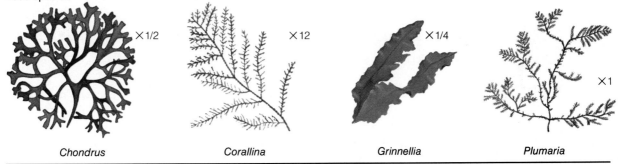

×1/2   ×12   ×1/4   ×1

Chondrus   *Corallina*   *Grinnellia*   *Plumaria*

green algae (Phylum Chlorophyta): unicellular, colonial, or multicellular; autotrophic; asexual and sexual reproduction; probably ancestral to plants; about 7000 species

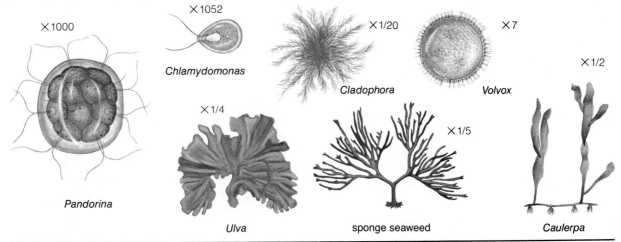

×1000   ×1052   ×1/20   ×7   ×1/2

Chlamydomonas   *Cladophora*   *Volvox*

×1/4   ×1/5

Pandorina   *Ulva*   sponge seaweed   *Caulerpa*

Kingdom Fungi: eukaryotic; nonmotile; heterotrophic (saprotrophic); many parasitic; important decomposers; sources of antibiotics; used in production of cheese, beer, and wine; reproduction by spores; 5 phyla; more than 100 000 species

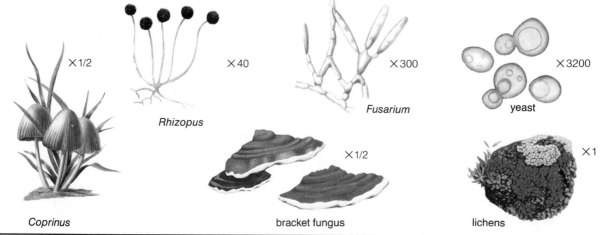

×1/2

×40

Rhizopus

×300

Fusarium

×3200

yeast

×1/2

×1

Coprinus

bracket fungus

lichens

Kingdom Plantae: eukaryotic multicellular; autotrophic; cellulose-containing cell walls; chloroplasts containing chlorophylla *a* and *b*; reproduction vegetative or sexual, with alternation of generations; 9 divisions; more than 500 000 species

mosses and liverworts (Division Bryophyta): small; nonvascular; moist habitats; haploid gametophyte dominant; about 24 000 species

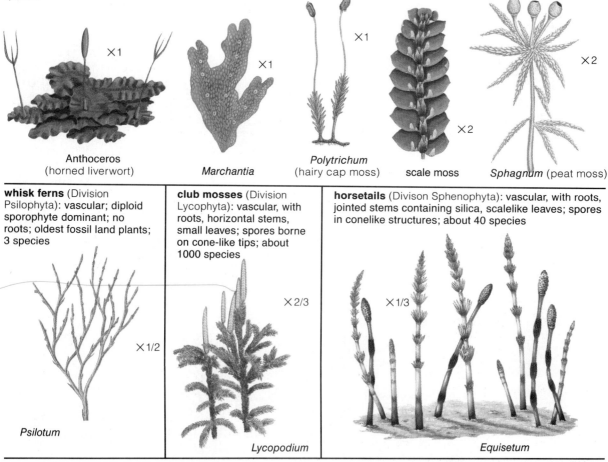

×1

Anthoceros
(horned liverwort)

×1

Marchantia

×1

Polytrichum
(hairy cap moss)

×2

scale moss

×2

Sphagnum (peat moss)

whisk ferns (Division Psilophyta): vascular; diploid sporophyte dominant; no roots; oldest fossil land plants; 3 species

club mosses (Division Lycophyta): vascular, with roots, horizontal stems, small leaves; spores borne on cone-like tips; about 1000 species

horsetails (Divison Sphenophyta): vascular, with roots, jointed stems containing silica, scalelike leaves; spores in conelike structures; about 40 species

×1/2

×2/3

×1/3

Psilotum

Lycopodium

Equisetum

Plantae *(continued)*

ferns (Division Pterophyta): vascular, with roots, horizontal underground stem, compound leaves; gametophytes independent; about 12 000 species

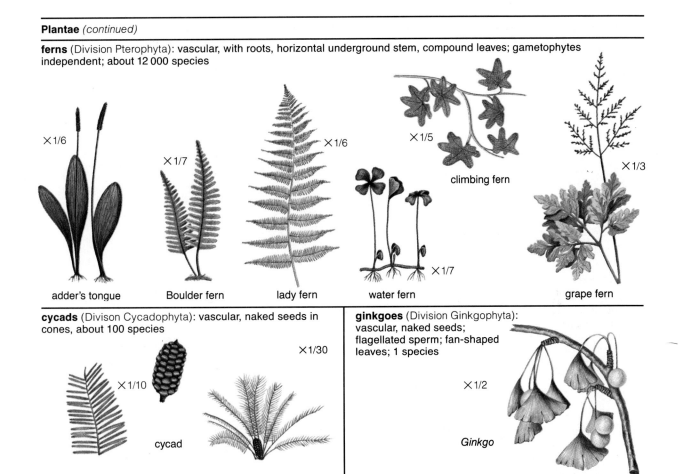

×1/6
adder's tongue

×1/7
Boulder fern

×1/6
lady fern

×1/7
water fern

×1/5
climbing fern

×1/3
grape fern

cycads (Divison Cycadophyta): vascular, naked seeds in cones, about 100 species

×1/10

×1/30

cycad

ginkgoes (Division Ginkgophyta): vascular, naked seeds; flagellated sperm; fan-shaped leaves; 1 species

×1/2

Ginkgo

conifers (Division Coniferophyta): vascular; naked seeds in cones; needle-shaped leaves; many evergreen; about 700 species

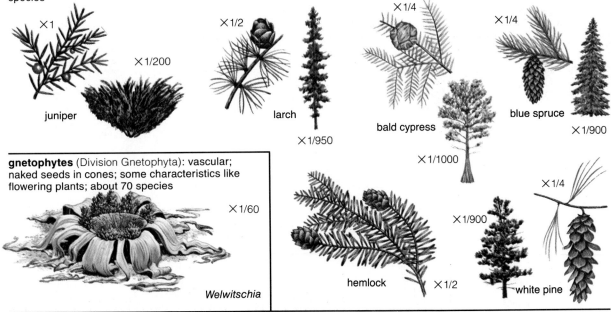

×1
×1/200
juniper

×1/2
larch
×1/950

×1/4
bald cypress
×1/1000

×1/4
blue spruce
×1/900

gnetophytes (Division Gnetophyta): vascular; naked seeds in cones; some characteristics like flowering plants; about 70 species

×1/60

Welwitschia

hemlock
×1/2

×1/900

×1/4
white pine

Plantae *(continued)*

flowering plants (Division Anthophyta): vascular; seeds enclosed in fruit; sperm in pollen tube; gametophyte reduced, inside sporophyte; about 230 000 species

monocots (Class Monocotyledonae): flower parts in threes; parallel-veined leaves; embryo with one cotyledon

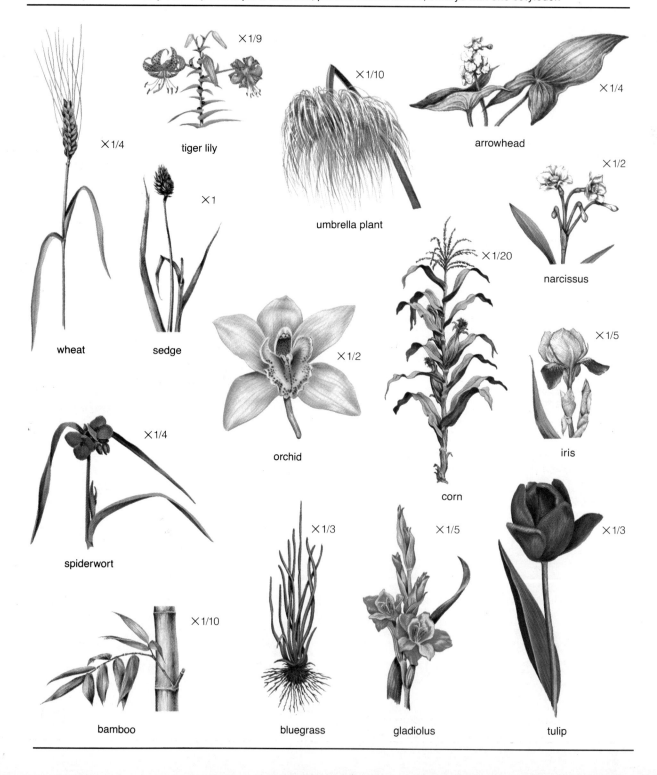

×1/9

tiger lily

×1/10

arrowhead ×1/4

×1/4

×1/2

narcissus

×1

umbrella plant

wheat   sedge

×1/20

×1/5

orchid ×1/2

iris

×1/4

corn

spiderwort

×1/10

bamboo   bluegrass ×1/3   gladiolus ×1/5   tulip ×1/3

Plantae *(continued)*

dicots (Class Dicotyledonae): flower parts in fours or fives; net-veined leaves; embryo with two cotyledons

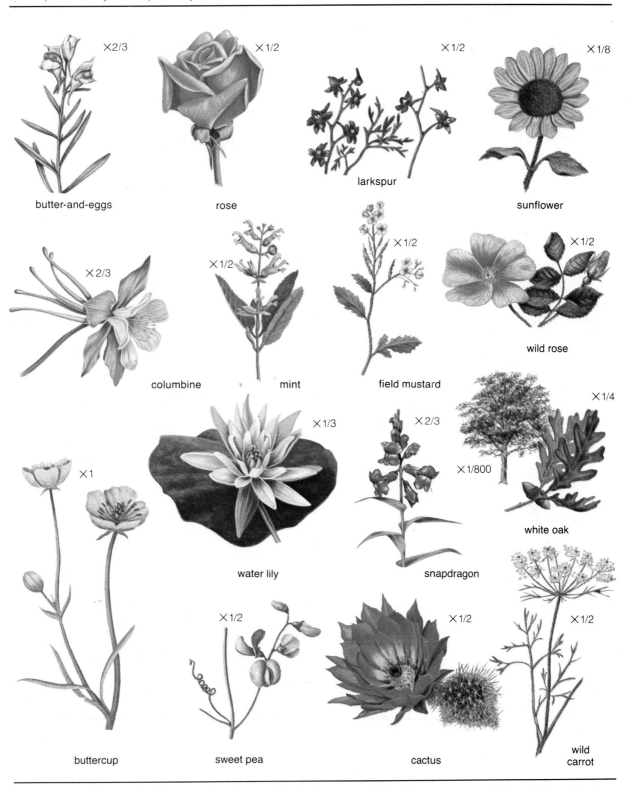

×2/3

butter-and-eggs

×1/2

rose

×1/2

larkspur

×1/8

sunflower

×2/3

columbine

×1/2

mint

×1/2

field mustard

×1/2

wild rose

×1/3

water lily

×2/3

snapdragon

×1/800 ×1/4

white oak

×1

buttercup

×1/2

sweet pea

×1/2

cactus

×1/2

wild carrot

Kingdom Animalia: eukaryotic; multicellular; heterotrophic; most motile at some stages; reproduction mainly sexual; 33 phyla; more than 1 million species

sponges (Phylum Porifera): sessile; two cell layers; body with pores; asexual and sexual reproduction; about 10 000 species

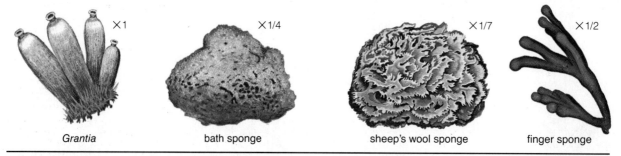

×1

Grantia

×1/4

bath sponge

×1/7

sheep's wool sponge

×1/2

finger sponge

stinging tentacled animals (Phylum Cnidaria): motile stages; radially symmetrical; two cell layers; mouth surrounded by stinging tentacles; saclike gut; nerve network; asexual and sexual reproduction; about 9700 species

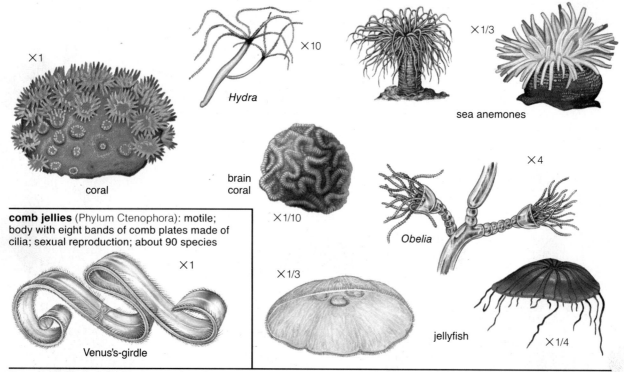

×1

×10

Hydra

×1/3

sea anemones

coral

brain
coral

×1/10

×4

Obelia

comb jellies (Phylum Ctenophora): motile; body with eight bands of comb plates made of cilia; sexual reproduction; about 90 species

×1

Venus's-girdle

×1/3

jellyfish

×1/4

flatworms (Phylum Platyhelminthes): motile, bilaterally symmetrical; three cell layers; head; gut with one opening; many parasitic; asexual and sexual reproduction; about 15 000 species

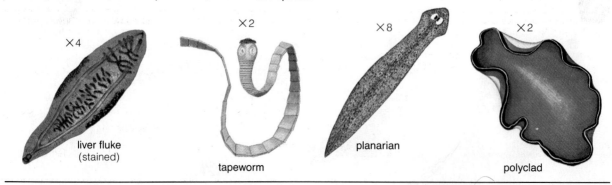

×4

liver fluke
(stained)

×2

tapeworm

×8

planarian

×2

polyclad

Animalia *(continued)*

roundworms (Phylum Nematoda): motile, bilaterally symmetrical; slender, cylindrical body; gut with two openings; many parasitic; more than 80 000 species

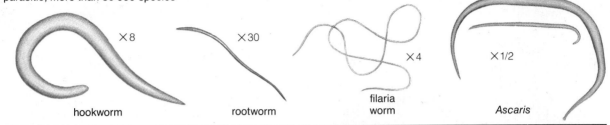

hookworm   ×8   rootworm   ×30   ×4   filaria worm   ×1/2   *Ascaris*

rotifers (Phylum Rotifera): mostly motile; bilaterally symmetrical; cilia form a wheel around mouth; asexual and sexual reproductive stages; about 2000 species

lamp shells (Phylum Brachiopoda): attached or burrowing; bilaterally symmetrical; dorsal-ventral shells enclosing tentacle-bearing arms; open circulatory system; about 335 species

×28

rotifers

×1

Lingula (lamp shells)

mollusks (Phylum Mollusca): sessile or motile; bilaterally symmetrical or asymmetrical; soft-bodied, usually with shell; true body cavity; well-developed digestive, circulatory, and nervous systems; sexual reproduction; about 110 000 species

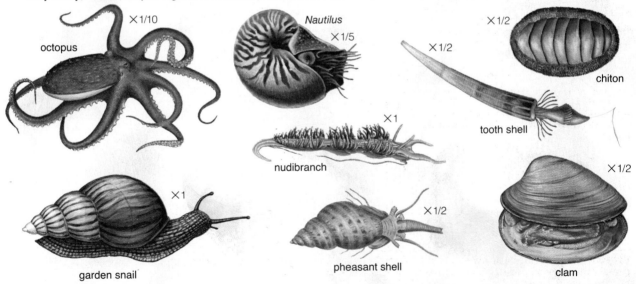

×1/10   octopus

Nautilus   ×1/5

×1/2

×1/2   chiton

×1   nudibranch

tooth shell

×1   garden snail

×1/2   pheasant shell

×1/2   clam

segmented worms (Phylum Annelida): motile, bilaterally symmetrical; body internally and externally segmented; asexual and sexual reproduction; about 8700 species

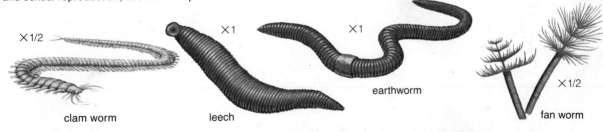

×1/2   clam worm

×1   leech

×1   earthworm

×1/2   fan worm

Animalia *(continued)*

arthropods (Phylum Arthropoda): motile, bilaterally symmetrical; segmented body fused to two or three parts; jointed appendages; exoskeleton; sexual reproduction; about 800 000 described species

crustaceans (Class Crustacea): two body parts; two pairs of antennae; mostly aquatic; gas exchange through gills

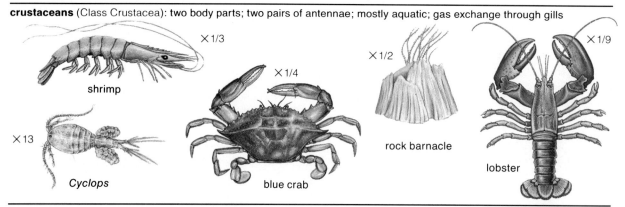

×1/3 shrimp

×13 *Cyclops*

×1/4 blue crab

×1/2 rock barnacle

×1/9 lobster

insects (Class Insecta): three body parts; one pair of antennae; three pairs of legs; generally one or two pairs of wings; gas exchange through trachea; perhaps 10 million species

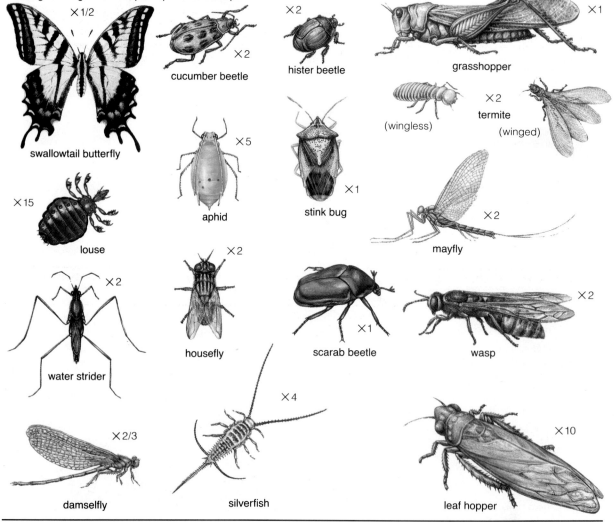

×1/2 swallowtail butterfly

×2 cucumber beetle

×2 hister beetle

×1 grasshopper

termite (wingless) ×2 (winged)

×5 aphid

×1 stink bug

×2 mayfly

×15 louse

×2 water strider

×2 housefly

×1 scarab beetle

×2 wasp

×2/3 damselfly

×4 silverfish

×10 leaf hopper

Animalia *(continued)*

arachnids (Class Arachnida): two body parts; no wings, no antennae; four pairs of legs; gas exchange through trachea, lungs, or gill books

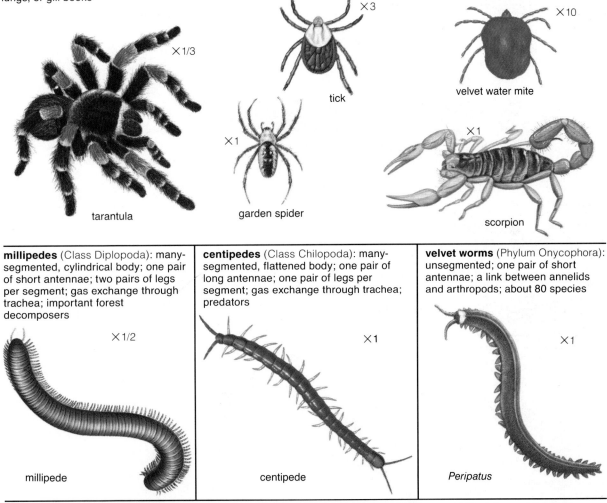

×1/3

×3

tick

×10

velvet water mite

×1

garden spider

×1

scorpion

tarantula

---

millipedes (Class Diplopoda): many-segmented, cylindrical body; one pair of short antennae; two pairs of legs per segment; gas exchange through trachea; important forest decomposers

×1/2

millipede

centipedes (Class Chilopoda): many-segmented, flattened body; one pair of long antennae; one pair of legs per segment; gas exchange through trachea; predators

×1

centipede

velvet worms (Phylum Onycophora): unsegmented; one pair of short antennae; a link between annelids and arthropods; about 80 species

×1

Peripatus

---

echinoderms (Phylum Echinodermata): no head or brain; unsegmented; adults radially symmetrical; larvae bilaterally symmetrical and chordatelike; tube feet serve for feeding, locomotion, and gas exchange; about 6000 species

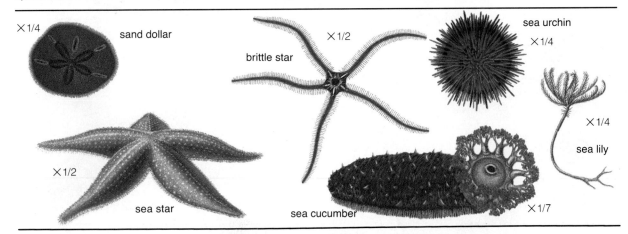

×1/4

sand dollar

×1/2

brittle star

sea urchin

×1/4

×1/4

sea lily

×1/2

sea star

sea cucumber

×1/7

Animalia *(continued)*

chordates (Phylum Chordata): segmented; bilaterally symmetrical; hollow dorsal nerve tube; stiff notochord that may be replaced during development; pharyngeal gill slits; about 45 000 species

acorn worms (Phylum Hemichordata): unsegmented; bilaterally symmetrical; dorsal nerve cord and pharyngeal gill slits; about 65 species

tunicates (Subphylum Urochordata): adults nonmotile; notochord disappears during development; no brain

lancelets (Subphylum Cephalochordata): notochord and nerve cord extend the length of body and persist in adults; no brain

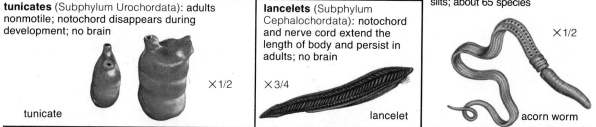

×1/2

tunicate

×3/4

lancelet

×1/2

acorn worm

vertebrates (Subphylum Vertebrata): notochord replaced by a backbone of vertebrae during development; brain protected by cartilage or bone; usually with paired appendages

jawless fishes (Class Agnatha): cartilaginous skeleton; no true jaws or paired appendages; two-chambered heart; gas exchange through gills

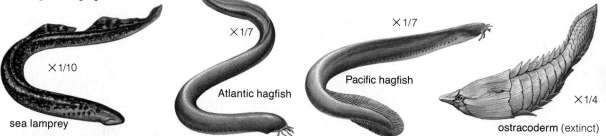

×1/10

sea lamprey

×1/7

Atlantic hagfish

×1/7

Pacific hagfish

×1/4

ostracoderm (extinct)

cartilaginous fishes (Class Chondrichthyes): cartilaginous skeleton; gill slits visible; jaws, paired fins; two-chambered heart; gas exchange through gills

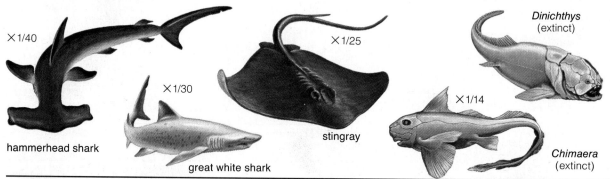

×1/40

hammerhead shark

×1/30

great white shark

×1/25

stingray

×1/14

Dinichthys (extinct)

Chimaera (extinct)

bony fishes (Class Osteichthyes): bony skeleton; gill slits covered; jaws; paired fins; scales; two-chambered heart; gas exchange through gills

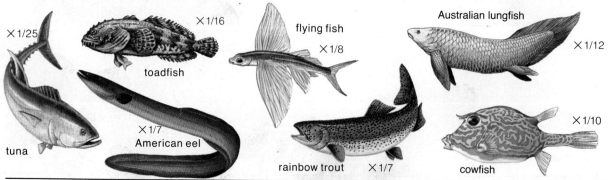

×1/25

tuna

×1/16

toadfish

flying fish
×1/8

Australian lungfish
×1/12

×1/7

American eel

rainbow trout   ×1/7

×1/10

cowfish

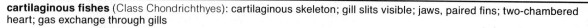

Animalia *(continued)*

amphibians (Class Amphibia): bony skeleton; moist, glandular skin; most with two pairs of limbs; three-chambered heart; gas exchange through skin or lungs in adult; through gills in larvae

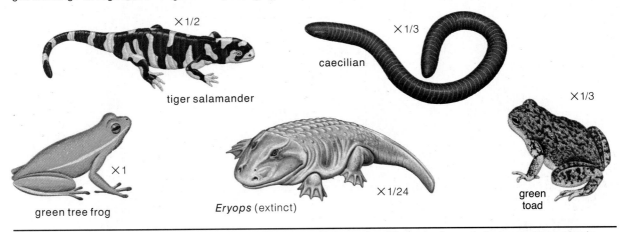

× 1/2

tiger salamander

× 1/3

caecilian

× 1

green tree frog

Eryops (extinct)   × 1/24

× 1/3

green toad

reptiles (Class Reptilia): bony skeleton; dry, scaly skin; most with two pairs of limbs; leathery-shelled eggs; incompletely divided four-chambered heart; gas exchange through lungs

× 1/2

six-lined race runner

× 1/4

box turtle

× 1/40

alligator

corn snake   × 1/6

Pteranodon (extinct)   × 1/120

× 1/10

rattlesnake

× 1/5

Gila monster

chameleon

× 1/3

Triceratops   (extinct)   × 1/115

Brontosaurus (extinct)   × 1/120

Animalia *(continued)*

birds (Class Aves): bony skeleton; scales modified as feathers; no teeth; forelimbs modified as wings; hard-shelled eggs; four-chambered heart; endothermic; gas exchange through lungs

×1/80
ostrich

×1/7
mourning dove

×1/27
brown pelican

×1/5
robin

×1/3
lazuli bunting

×1/8
quetzal

×1/12
kiwi

×1/3
broad-tailed hummingbird

×1/6
tree sparrow

×1/16
red jungle fowl

×1/36
albatross

×1/14
turkey vulture

×1/7
yellow-headed parrot

×1/16
barred owl

×1/8
grebe

×1/24
king penguin

×1/25
flamingo

×1/20
Hesperornis (extinct)

heath hen
×1/14

×1/14
ring-necked pheasant

Animalia (continued)

mammals (Class Mammalia): bony skeleton; scales modified as hairs; mammary glands in females secrete milk, four-chambered heart; endothermic; gas exchange through lungs

×1/40
rhinoceros

×1/25
aardvark

×1/15
koala

×1/60
horse

×1/35
red kangaroo

×1/5
long-eared bat

×1/13
armadillo

×1/22
baboon

×1/32
cougar

×1/80
elephant

×1/80
manatee

×1/8
platypus

×1/30
seal

×1/14
cottontail rabbit

×1/20
porcupine

×1/36
human

×1/40
gorilla

×1/450
blue whale

×1/10
pika

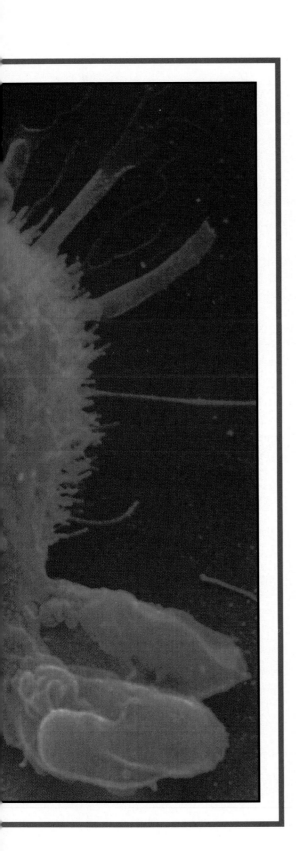

Structure and Function of Cells

*C*ells are the basic units of life. All life begins as a single cell, and many organisms exist only as individual cells. Most organisms are composed of many cells—often trillions of them—such as the human macrophage (an immune system cell) shown here magnified 9000 times.

Just as a car is made of many parts, a cell is composed of many structures. The parts of a car work together so that it can function. Similarly, each part of a cell is necessary for the cell to function properly. How are cells organized to perform the work they do? What are the complex processes that operate in cells?

---

*W*hat role do macrophages play in the immune system? (The root macro means large; phage means one that eats.)

---

*H*ow do they move?

CONTENTS

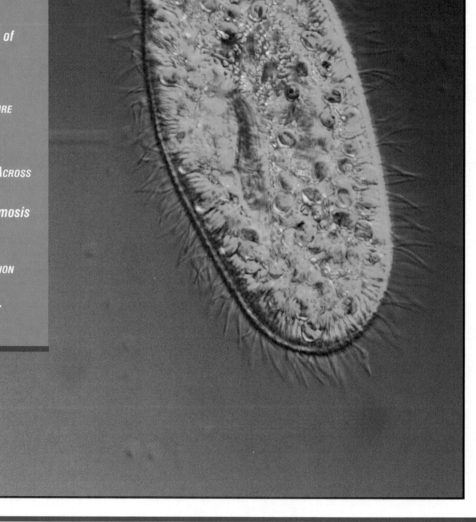

Organization of Cells

Cells and their workings are so complex that we are still learning about some of the things that make them work. Compared to all the processes that occur inside cells, there is still much to be discovered about how cells are made and how they function. Nonetheless, the miniature world of cells holds the answers to most of the major health problems that face the world. Heart disease, cancer, some forms of mental illness, and AIDS are all diseases of cells. The problem of hunger is directly related to the cellular limits of photosynthesis and food production in plants.

People say there are two great areas remaining for human discovery—the cell and the universe. One is tiny and the other is huge; both stretch the limits of the imagination. Researchers who study either cells or stars encounter similar problems. They would like to be able to touch, sample, and directly observe their individual parts, but even with improved technology, much remains impossible. The parts that make up the cell are too small, and stars are too large. Both, in different ways, remain too far away to study completely. In spite of the difficulties, however, new discoveries occur continuously. Biologists are making enormous progress toward unlocking the mysteries of the cell. In this chapter you will learn what research has revealed about the cell so far.

◆ *A single-celled organism,* Paramecium bursaria, *magnified 100 times.*

The Basic Unit of Life _____

6.1 Cell Study and Technology

You are composed of trillions of tiny, highly active compartments called cells. Plants and other animals also are made of cells. In nature, there are many billions of single-celled organisms such as bacteria, yeasts, protozoa, and algae. Whether single-celled or multicelled, they all are organisms and are composed of cells—the basic units of life. Figure 6.1 shows a few of the great variety of cell types that make up organisms.

The idea that cells are the basic units of life began to take shape in the

FIGURE 6.1 All organisms are made of cells. (a) Unicellular (single-celled) green alga, (b) cross-section of a young maple stem, (c) cells from the lining of the cat stomach, (d) cells from the lining of the human cheek.

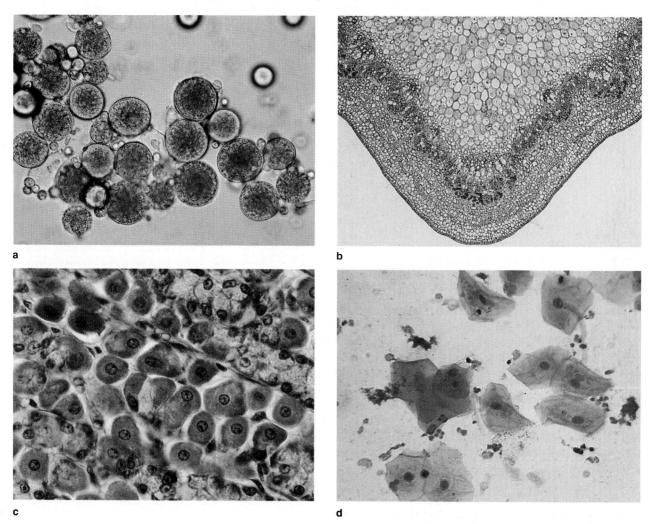

a

b

c

d

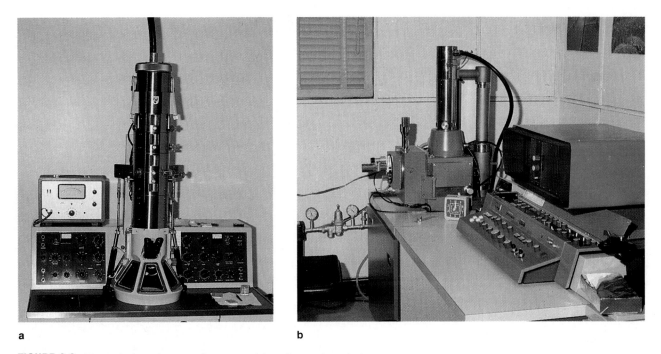

FIGURE 6.2   Transmission electron microscope (a) and scanning electron microscope (b).

1800s and early 1900s, as numerous biologists contributed data and ideas to formulate the **cell theory** (see Biological Challenges on page 133), which can be stated in two parts:

1. Cells, or products made by cells, are the units of structure and function in organisms.

2. All cells come from preexisting cells.

Once the cell theory was established, scientists began to study cell structure and function in detail. The cell was just a tiny blob of jelly to early workers, who had no idea of its complexity and detail. Progress depended on the technology of improved microscopes, better techniques to prepare cells for observation, and studies of cell function. Even modern light microscopes cannot uncover all the detailed wonders of the cell—its structures are too small to see without the electron microscope, which was developed in the 1930s. (See **Appendix 6A**, Preparing Cells for Study.)

Electron microscopes (Figure 6.2) reveal very tiny cell parts and even some organic molecules down to 0.5 nanometers (nm)—a magnification of more than a million times. (How does that compare to the magnification of the microscope you use in biology class?) The major drawback of the electron microscope is that cells are killed by the steps needed to prepare them for examination. Therefore, the movements and reactions that occur in living cells remain largely invisible. In addition, the preparation of cells for the electron microscope can damage cell structure, so the structures seen may differ from those actually present in a living cell.

CONNECTIONS

*T*he cell theory reinforces the concepts of genetic continuity and a common evolutionary origin for life.

Cells differ in size but average 10 to 20 micrometers (μm) in diameter. In many cells, the nuclei are one-half to one-fourth the size of the cell (5 to 10 μm); other nuclei may be only 1 μm. Figure 6.3 shows the relative sizes of cells and cell parts as compared to the units of measurement biologists use to study cells. Because of the small size of cells, models and diagrams, such as those in this chapter, are used to represent the current ideas about cell structure and function. (See Focus On Models, Chapter 2.)

FIGURE 6.3 A comparison of sizes. Note that most cells are too small to be seen with the naked eye.

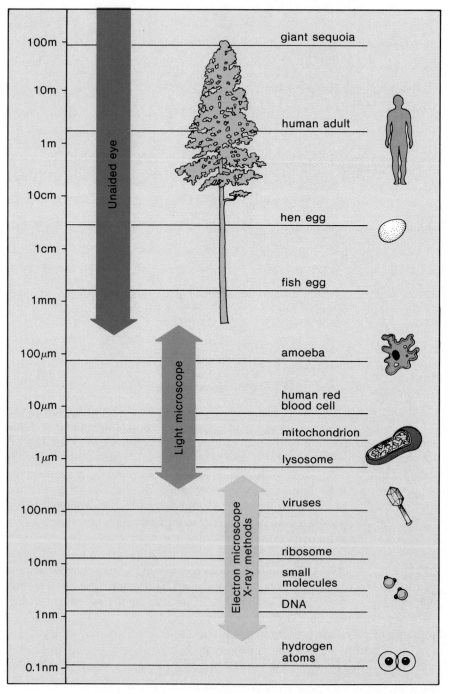

THE CELL THEORY

In the seventeenth century, Robert Hooke used his microscope (Figure A) to examine shreds of cork. Magnified many times under the microscope, these cork shreds revealed an inner structure—little box-like units that appeared to be quite empty; Hooke could see right through them. He called these structures cells.

In 1839, Theodor Schwann examined animal tissues. Careful study showed that small bits of animal material seem to be self-contained. Often these bits looked like fluid-filled sacs, and in the middle was what appeared to be a nucleus (Figure A). Schwann realized that the cell question was incorrectly based on the boxlike cell structure of plants instead of what was inside the cell. M.J. Schleiden, a botanist, and Schwann advanced the idea that both plants and animals are made of cells that contain nuclei and cell fluid.

Anton van Leeuwenhoek observed microscopic organisms, or microorganisms, 30 years after Hooke discovered cells. Water from ponds, rain barrels, and the river at Delft, Holland, revealed a wealth of tiny creatures. Soon after Leeuwenhoek published his paper, there were many microbiologists looking for living organisms in soil, spoiled food, and other places.

Eventually, the structure of microorganisms was compared to the structures of both plants and animals. In smaller microorganisms, no internal cell structure could be discerned. Instead, they appeared to be about the size of one cell from a larger organism. The idea quickly took hold that they were unicellular. Nuclei were discovered in many of these microorganisms. Some plasma membranes were identified, as well as cytoplasm and vacuoles. A large group of scientists advanced the idea that the cell is the basic unit of life—either a complete organism or part of a multicellular organism.

A physician and biologist, Rudolph Virchow, added another hypothesis to the growing body of information about cells. Discoveries of cells in an increasing number of organisms suggested to Virchow that their wide occurrence is no coincidence.

Numerous biologists had observed cells dividing and producing more cells. Similarly, many microbiologists had observed microorganisms dividing, thus producing more microorganisms. Virchow saw in these events a principle—cells producing more cells through time. Virchow stated the hypothesis simply—"All cells come from cells." It meant that investigations of the cell theory were extended into the past to the ancestors of living cells.

Today, new technologies make possible extremely detailed studies of cell structure and function. New hypotheses about cell evolution are being investigated. Still, the cell theory remains one of the unifying themes of biology.

FIGURE A *left:* One of Robert Hooke's microscopes; *right:* The microscopic structure of small parts of animals as seen by Schwann—(top) six cells from a fish, oval cell from the nervous system of a frog, long cell from the muscle of an unborn pig, spindle-shaped cell, also from an unborn pig.

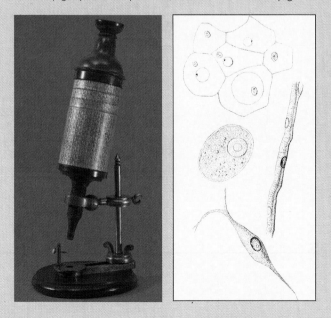

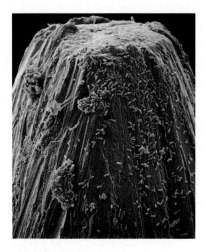

FIGURE 6.4 Prokaryotes are extremely small. Many prokaryotes are visible in this scanning electron micrograph of the point of a pin magnified 383 times.

6.2 Two Basic Types of Cells

Living cells can be separated into two groups, prokaryotes and eukaryotes, based on their distinctive cellular structure. This grouping is fundamental to the modern classification scheme in biology and to an understanding of the evolution of cells and organisms. Prokaryotes—the bacteria—are thought to represent the simplest type of living cell, yet they are everywhere—in the soil, the air, and the water, and in or on every organism, including humans. Some prokaryotes inhabit extreme environments, such as salt flats, hot springs such as those in Yellowstone National Park, and thermal vents located deep in the ocean floor. The smallest prokaryotes are only about 0.3 μm in diameter; others are 1 to 5 μm across. Up to 35 000 could fit side by side on the head of an ordinary thumbtack, and even the point of a pin can hold hundreds. (See Figure 6.4.)

Eukaryotic cells are larger (10 to 50 μm), more complex, and more specialized than prokaryotes. Plants, animals, and other multicellular organisms are composed of eukaryotic cells (Chapter 5). Eukaryotic cells are more successful than prokaryotes in achieving a high level of organization and are the building units of the dominant creatures on Earth. Figure 6.5 compares a prokaryotic and a eukaryotic cell. You will learn about the structures shown in the diagram as you read this chapter.

Recall from Chapters 4 and 5 that prokaryotic cells lack an organized, membrane-enclosed nucleus as well as other membrane-enclosed organelles such as mitochondria and chloroplasts. Table 6.1 compares structural

FIGURE 6.5 A prokaryotic cell (top) compared with a eukaryotic cell (bottom). Note the greater structural complexity of the eukaryotic cell (an amoeba) and the presence of many membrane-enclosed organelles.

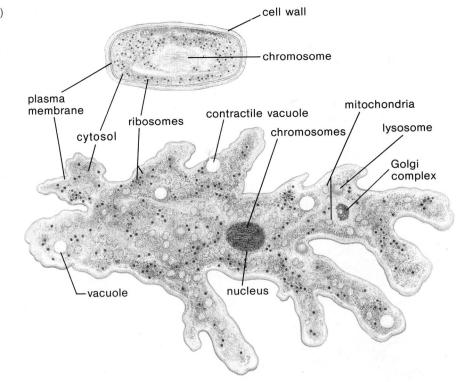

TABLE 6.1 Some Differences between Prokaryotic and Eukaryotic Cells	
Eukaryotes Have	**Prokaryotes Have**
• nucleus	• no nucleus
• membrane-enclosed organelles	• no membrane-enclosed organelles
• chromosomes in pairs	• single chromosome
• streaming in the cytoplasm	• no streaming in the cytoplasm
• cell division by mitosis	• cell division without mitosis
• complex flagella	• simple flagella
• larger ribosomes	• smaller ribosomes
• cytoskeleton	• no known cytoskeleton
• cellulose in cell walls	• no cellulose in cell walls
• DNA bound to histone proteins	• DNA bound to other proteins

and chemical features of eukaryotic and prokaryotic cells. Many of the differences listed in Table 6.1 include structures and features unfamiliar to you. Refer to the table as these features are explained.

6.3   Prokaryotic Cell Structure

The prokaryotes belong to the kingdom Monera—the bacteria. They are one-celled organisms in most cases but can associate together in clusters and chains to form multicellular structures. Prokaryotic cells have a rigid cell wall made of lipids, carbohydrates, and protein, but no cellulose. Figure 6.6 is a diagram of the structures of a prokaryote. Just inside the cell wall is a **plasma membrane** that encloses the cell. The mesosome (MEZ oh sohm) is an infolding of the plasma membrane that may aid in movement of particles out of the bacterium (secretion) and in copying the chromosome before division. Prokaryotes have one chromosome made of a

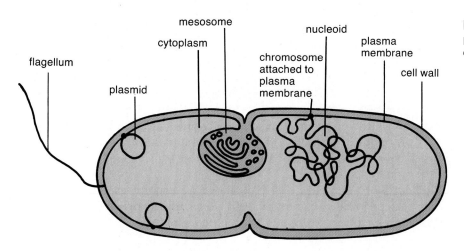

FIGURE 6.6 The structure of a prokaryotic cell, as revealed in electron micrographs.

continuous, circular molecule of double-stranded DNA. Because there is only one chromosome, the genes are not present in pairs as they are in eukaryotes. The chromosome is attached to the plasma membrane and located in an area of the cell known as the **nucleoid** (NOO klee oyd). In addition, bacteria usually contain one or more smaller circular DNA molecules called plasmids. These ''extra-chromosomal'' elements consist of a few genes and are also attached to the plasma membrane.

Prokaryotes exhibit great diversity in their metabolism. Many of their metabolic processes are similar to those of eukaryotes, but others are unique. For example, numerous reactions essential to the cycling of nutrients in the biosphere are carried out only by bacteria. Prokaryotes are major decomposers in most ecosystems (Chapter 3); many are photosynthetic; still others are the source of antibiotics. Although some bacteria can cause human diseases such as strep throat, rheumatic fever, and skin infections, most are beneficial. They help digest your food, provide you with certain vitamins, and are used in manufacturing foods such as cheese and yogurt and life-saving drugs.

CHECK AND CHALLENGE _____

1. What is the cell theory?
2. In what ways does an understanding of cells depend on technology?
3. In centimeters, how long is your pencil? Your textbook? How does their size compare to that of a bacterium? Of a eukaryotic cell?
4. What characteristics distinguish prokaryotic cells?
5. What is one disadvantage of using stains to examine living cells?

Eukaryotic Cell Structure _____

6.4 Organelles

Try Investigation 6A, Cell Structure

A key feature of eukaryotic cells is the structural division of the cell into smaller functional parts called organelles. Any part of the eukaryotic cell that has its own structure and function can be considered an organelle. Thousands of chemical reactions occur continuously and simultaneously in eukaryotic cells. Many of those reactions are not compatible, yet they proceed without difficulty because they are separated from each other in organelles. For example, the genes, which are made of nuclear material, are separated from the rest of the cell components. This separation allows copying of DNA to occur more efficiently and without interference from other processes in the cell. Thus, compartmentation increases functional efficiency by isolating specific processes and permitting a division of labor within the eukaryotic cell.

Figure 6.10 on pages 138–139 shows the major organelles and structures present in most eukaryotic cells. Refer to this figure and locate the organelles as you read the descriptions that follow.

A plasma membrane (Figure 6.10a) encloses the contents of both eukaryotic cells and prokaryotic cells. This structure is described in detail in Section 6.6. Surrounding and protecting the plasma membrane of plant cells is a rigid structure, the **cell wall** (Figure 6.10f). The wall provides support because it is composed of stiff fibers of cellulose and other complex carbohydrates (Figure 6.7). Animal cells lack a rigid cell wall, the most consistent difference between plant and animal cells.

Within the plasma membrane, but outside the nucleus, is the cellular material, or **cytoplasm**. A more specific term, **cytosol** (SYT oh sol), sometimes is used to describe the protein-rich, semifluid material in the cell that surrounds and bathes the organelles (Figure 6.10j). The cytoplasm includes the cytosol and the organelles.

The most conspicuous organelle in a cell generally is its genetic control center, the **nucleus** (Figures 6.10b and 6.8). The nucleus is enclosed by two membranes that form the nuclear envelope, and it contains the chromosomes made of DNA and protein.

A system of membranes forming tubes and channels, the **endoplasmic reticulum** (en doh PLAZ mik   reh TIK yoo lum), or **ER**, (Figures 6.10h and 6.9), connects organelles in the cell. In electron micrographs, the ER resembles wrapping paper folded back on itself running through the cell. Attached to the ER are small bodies called **ribosomes**, in which proteins are synthesized. The proteins may undergo final assembly in the membranous **Golgi** (GOHL jee) **apparatus** (Figure 6.10i).

FIGURE 6.7 Overlapping layers of cellulose fibers and other materials give rigidity to the plant cell wall.

FIGURE 6.8 Transmission electron micrograph of a mouse liver cell nucleus, X4900. Note the double membrane that makes up the nuclear envelope. The large dark round body is the nucleolus.

FIGURE 6.9 Rough endoplasmic reticulum in a liver cell. Transmission electron micrograph, X40 800.

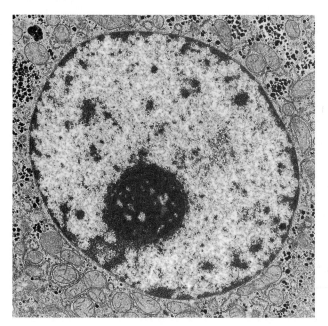

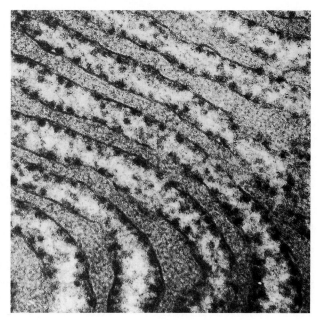

a. Plasma membrane. 0.004-0.005 μm thick; 2 lipid layers; surface and embedded proteins with attached carbohydrates. Semifluid cell boundary; controls passage of materials into and out of cell.

b. Nucleus. 5-10 μm; control center of cell; contains most of cell's genetic information in DNA, which condenses to form chromosomes during mitosis. Nuclear envelope with pores, formed of 2 membranes. Contains one or more **nucleoli,** sites of synthesis and assembly of rRNA and tRNA.

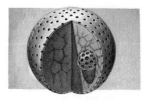

c. Cytoskeleton. Network of proteins of hollow microtubules 0.0025 μm thick, solid, flexible microfilaments 0.0005 μm thick, and connecting intermediate filaments 0.001 μm thick. Provides shape, internal organization, and movement.

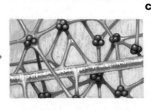

d. Lysosome. 0.25-0.5 μm site of intracellular digestion; formed by budding from Golgi apparatus; fuses with vesicles containing food particles ingested by cell.

e. Centrioles. 0.15 μm diameter by 0.5 μm long; tubular structures formed of microtubules; occur in pairs during interphase; duplicate prior to mitosis and form organizing centers for mitotic spindles in protist and animal cells.

FIGURE 6.10 Generalized animal (*left*) and plant (*right*) cells, with enlargements of the major organelles. Some of the terms used here are not explained in this chapter. They are defined in later chapters. Colors are artificial.

f. Cell wall. 0.1-10 μm thick; formed by living plant cells; made of cellulose fibers embedded in a matrix of polysaccharides; provides rigidity to plant cells and allows for development of turgor pressure.

g. Mitochondrion. 2-10 μm long by 0.5-1 μm thick; enclosed in double membrane; inner membrane much folded; most reactions of cellular respiration occur in mitochondrion; contains small amounts of DNA and RNA; may be several hundred per cell.

h. Endoplasmic reticulum (ER). 0.005 μm diameter; tubular membrane system that compartmentalizes the cytosol; plays a central role in biosynthesis reactions. Rough ER is studded with **ribosomes,** the site of protein synthesis; smooth ER lacks ribosomes.

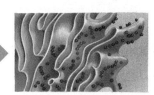

i. Golgi apparatus. 1 μm diameter; system of flattened sacs that modifies, sorts, and packages macromolecules in vesicles for secretion or for delivery to other organelles.

j. Cytosol. semi-fluid material surrounding organelles; contains enzymes that catalyze cellular reactions.

k. Chloroplast. 5 μm long by 0.5-1 μm thick; enclosed by double membrane; third membrane system forms thylakoids in which light-absorbing pigments are embedded. All reactions of photosynthesis occur in chloroplasts.

l. Vacuole. Variable size; large vesicle enclosed in single membrane; may occupy more than 50% of volume in plant cells; contains water and digestive enzymes; stores nutrients and waste products.

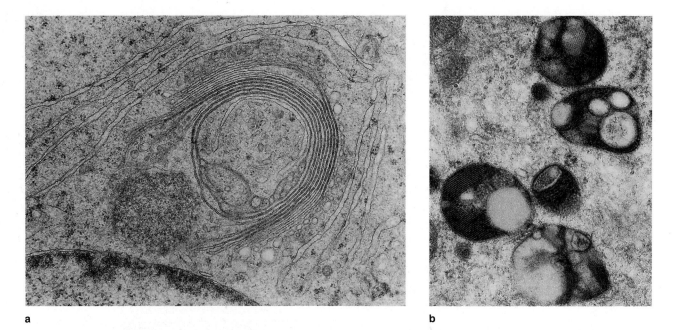

a   b

FIGURE 6.11   (a) Transmission electron micrograph of a Golgi apparatus, X9240. Note the endoplasmic reticulum at the top of the micrograph and the vesicles to the right of the Golgi apparatus. (b) Transmission electron micrograph of lysosomes from a mouse kidney cell, X9306.

In the Golgi apparatus, proteins are packaged in spherical membrane-enclosed **vesicles** that appear to pinch off. The vesicles can become containers that carry substances out of the cell. Together the ER, Golgi apparatus, and vesicles form an interconnected system (Figure 6.11a). Other proteins made in this system become part of membranes of the cell or end up inside various organelles. The structure of the system facilitates its function as a "highway" that directs proteins to target points inside the cell and to the plasma membrane for passage out of the cell.

Lysosomes, shown in Figure 6.10d and 6.11b, are special vesicles in animal cells. They contain enzymes that digest or disassemble old macromolecules for recycling of materials. Lysosomes may also leave the cell and destroy bacteria and foreign particles. For example, lysozyme, an enzyme found in lysosomes of tear duct cells, protects the eyes from bacterial infection by breaking down bacterial cell walls. The **vacuoles** present in most plant cells (Figure 6.10l) appear to be vesicles that enlarge as the cells age. Vacuoles contain water, organic acids, enzymes (probably similar in activity to those in lysosomes), salts, and pigments that give plants such as beets their characteristic color.

Chloroplasts (Figure 6.10k) and mitochondria (Figure 6.10g) are double-membrane organelles involved in energy reactions in the cell. Chloroplasts are the structures in which photosynthesis occurs in plants and autotrophic protists. Mitochondria are the major sites of ATP synthesis in most cells and have been called the powerhouses of the cell. These structures are described in detail in Chapters 7 and 8. **Centrioles** (Figures 6.10e and 6.12) are tubular structures in animal cells that play an important role in cell reproduction.

FIGURE 6.12   Cross section of a centriole, X138 600. The nine triplet microtubules that form the centriole show clearly in this transmission electron micrograph.

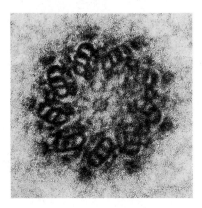

Flagella (fluh JEL uh) are long, whiplike extensions of the cell surface. They are made of tubular protein structures called microtubules (Figures 6.10c and 6.13). **Cilia** (SIL ee uh) are short flagella, usually present in greater numbers. Flagella and cilia provide locomotion by whipping in an oarlike motion against the fluid surrounding a cell. Cilia also may serve to move material along a cell or tissue. Cells in the human bronchi and bronchioles are lined with cilia that move mucus and foreign particles out of the lungs.

The **cytoskeleton** is a very fine network of protein scaffolding that provides shape, internal organization, and movement for the cell. The protein scaffolding is made up of hollow microtubules (25 nm thick), solid but flexible strands called microfilaments (5nm thick), and connecting intermediate filaments (10nm). Organelles may be held in place by the cytoskeleton, which may also enable a cell to change shape.

FIGURE 6.13 *Trichonympha* (a), a protist covered with hundreds of flagella that provide locomotion. In cross section (b), flagella consist of doublet microtubules in a 9 + 2 arrangement. A diagrammatic cross section of a flagellum is shown in (c).

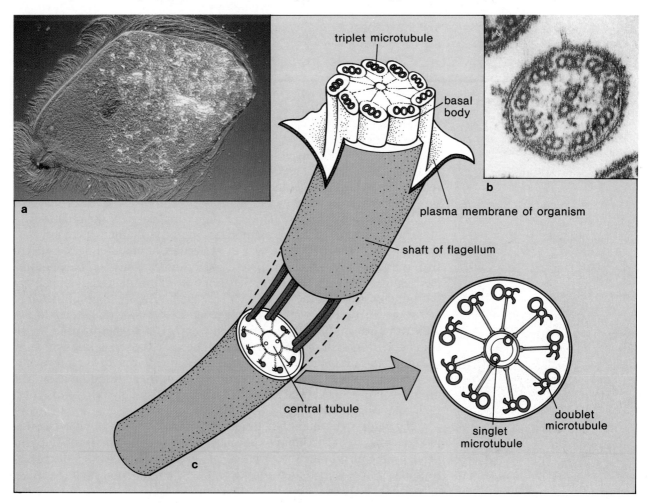

FOCUS ON *The Cytoskeleton*

The ability of eukaryotic cells to assume different shapes and to carry out coordinated and directed movements depends on the cytoskeleton (Figure B), a complex network of protein filaments that extends throughout the cytoplasm. The cytoskeleton is directly responsible for the movement or "crawling" of cells, muscle contraction, and the changes in shape of developing vertebrate embryos. The cytoskeleton also provides the mechanism for actively moving organelles from one place to another in the cytoplasm. Apparently absent in prokaryotes, the cytoskeleton may have been a crucial factor in the development of eukaryotic cells.

Because the cytoskeleton is composed of proteins, it is responsible for the gelatinlike consistency of the cytosol. Some researchers maintain that the cytoskeleton is part of the cytosol. Other researchers believe that the cytoskeleton itself is an organelle.

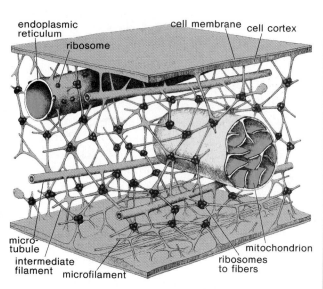

FIGURE B   The cytoskeleton is a network of proteins in the cytoplasm that facilitates movement and helps the cell maintain its shape.

FIGURE 6.14   Cross section of the plasma membrane (yellow) of a human red blood cell, X62 200.

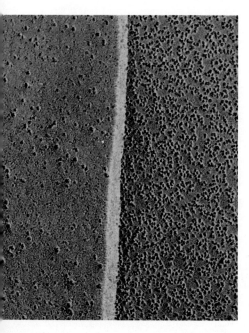

6.5   Membranes

Membranes are thin layers of proteins and lipids responsible for many functions essential to life. For example, the cell is packaged in the plasma membrane, which defines and separates the cell from the external environment and regulates the flow of molecules into and out of the cell (Figure 6.14). Organelles also may be formed and organized by membranes.

The lipids that compose membranes are phospholipids (Section 2.8), which form a bilayer (two rows) of molecules oriented end to end. The hydrophobic (*hydro* = water; *phobic* = fearing) tails of the phospholipids (see Figure 2.15) face each other in the middle of the membrane, much like the buttered sides of the bread in a sandwich. The hydrophilic (*philic* = loving) heads face the watery environment on each side of the membrane. This structure is the most stable arrangement of lipids possible in the watery environment of the cell. Cholesterol is often present in membranes of animal cells. Proteins are embedded in the membrane or are attached to its inner or outer surface. Sugars are often attached to the lipids and to proteins on the outer surface, forming glycolipids and glycoproteins. These molecules apparently play a role in cell-to-cell recognition.

The lipids and proteins are fluid, not rigid, and float around each other like ice cubes in a punch bowl. Because of the location and position of the proteins, the membrane is asymmetrical—the outside is shaped differently from the inside. Membranes of different cells and organelles may contain

outside

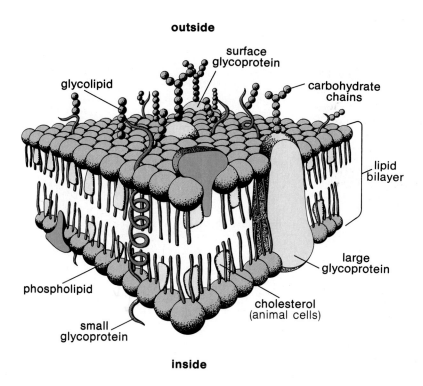

surface
glycoprotein

glycolipid

carbohydrate
chains

lipid
bilayer

large
glycoprotein

phospholipid

cholesterol
(animal cells)

small
glycoprotein

inside

FIGURE 6.15 The fluid-mosaic model of a membrane's structure. The bilayer of phospholipids provides fluidity. Proteins extending through the bilayer or embedded in its inner or outer surface are responsible for its asymmetry. Carbohydrate chains may be attached to both lipids and proteins.

different amounts and types of lipids and proteins, but the basic structure and organization appears to be similar for all membranes.

The structure of membranes (Figure 6.15) allows them to perform many functions in the cell. For example, the proteins involved in ATP synthesis are situated in the inner membrane of chloroplasts and mitochondria in a way that enables them to convert efficiently either light energy (photosynthesis) or chemical energy (respiration) to ATP. Glycoproteins on the outer surface of membranes act as antennae to receive chemical messages from other cells. Proteins are synthesized at ribosomes attached along membranes of the ER. Membranes also regulate the movement of materials in and out of cells and organelles, as described in the next sections.

CHECK AND CHALLENGE

1. What is the advantage of compartmentation in eukaryotic cells?
2. Briefly describe the functions of each of the following: nucleus, mitochondrion, chloroplast, ribosome, and vacuole.
3. Are membranes of each organelle similar or different? Explain.
4. Describe the cytoskeleton. What is its function?

FIGURE 6.16 Diffusion is the movement of molecules from an area of high concentration to an area of low concentration until the concentration is the same throughout. In (a), a crystal of potassium permanganate was dropped into a glass of water. The molecules diffuse through the water (b) until they are evenly distributed throughout (c).

a   b   c

Try Investigation 6B, Cells and the Movement of Materials.

FIGURE 6.17 A diagram of osmosis. When water concentration is higher *inside* the cell (a), water moves out of the cell, and the cell shrinks. When water concentration is higher *outside* the cell (b), water moves into the cell, and the cell swells. Does this diagram help you understand why supermarkets spray their produce with fresh water?

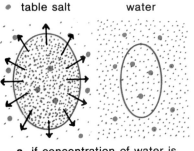

a. if concentration of water is higher inside the cell, water diffuses out of the cell

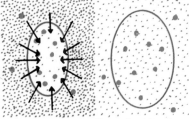

b. if concentration of water is higher outside the cell, water diffuses into the cell

Transfer of Materials Across Membranes _____

6.6 Diffusion and Osmosis

As explained in Chapter 4, primitive heterotroph cells probably obtained their nourishment from the organic compounds in the surrounding primitive ocean. Before they could be used, the compounds had to pass from the ocean water into the cells. How do organic and other compounds enter living cells? To answer that question you must first understand how molecules move from one place to another.

If a drop of perfume evaporates in one corner of a room, the scent soon permeates the entire room. Similarly, a lump of sugar dropped in a glass of water eventually sweetens all the water in the glass, even if it is not stirred. Both cases are examples of **diffusion**, the movement of molecules from an area of greater concentration into areas of lesser concentration until the concentration is the same everywhere (Figure 6.16). Diffusion is a spontaneous process that results in a random distribution of molecules and thus in an increase in the entropy of a system. (See Section 3.5.)

How does diffusion occur? The molecules in a gas or a liquid are in constant motion. Moving molecules continually collide, and the higher the concentration of molecules, the greater the number of collisions. These collisions cause the molecules to change direction and to spread out until they eventually become uniformly distributed. If there is a difference in concentration across a distance, the measure of this difference is called the **concentration gradient**. Because molecules diffuse from regions of higher concentration to regions of lower concentration, they are described as moving down their concentration gradient. Diffusion is responsible for the movement of substances, such as gases and some cellular wastes, into and out of cells.

Water may constantly pass into and out of cells through their plasma membranes. This apparently uninterrupted diffusion of water through the membranes of cells is called **osmosis** (os MOH sis). Like other substances, water diffuses down its concentration gradient (Figure 6.17). For example, suppose a living cell is placed in a solution that has a concentration of water lower than that inside the cell. Water diffuses out of the cell (from higher to lower concentration), and the cell shrinks (Figure 6.17a).

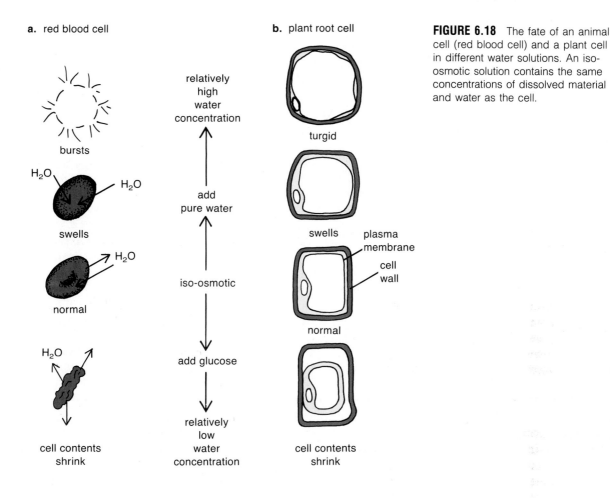

a. red blood cell

bursts

H$_2$O   H$_2$O

swells

H$_2$O

normal

H$_2$O

cell contents
shrink

relatively
high
water
concentration

add
pure water

iso-osmotic

add glucose

relatively
low
water
concentration

b. plant root cell

turgid

swells

plasma
membrane

cell
wall

normal

cell contents
shrink

FIGURE 6.18 The fate of an animal cell (red blood cell) and a plant cell in different water solutions. An iso-osmotic solution contains the same concentrations of dissolved material and water as the cell.

On the other hand, if the concentration of water molecules is greater outside a cell, water diffuses inward, and the cell swells (Figure 6.17b). When an animal cell is placed in pure water, osmosis usually causes it to burst. A plant cell swells a little but does not burst because of the rigid cell wall. Figure 6.18 shows how animal and plant cells react to changes in water concentrations as a result of osmosis. Without a cell wall what would be the fate of cells in the roots of a plant when it is watered?

6.7 Other Transport Mechanisms

If osmosis and diffusion were the only processes of materials exchange, many substances needed by cells would soon become evenly distributed throughout the cells and their surroundings. Yet organisms must establish and maintain concentrations of materials inside their cells that may differ from concentrations resulting from diffusion. In addition, many substances cannot pass through plasma membranes by diffusion.

Membranes are selectively permeable—they regulate the movement of most molecules into and out of cells and organelles. Selective permeability depends on the barrier formed by the lipid bilayer and on the specific proteins in the membrane. The nonpolar phospholipid tails of the lipid bilayer tend to repel charged particles but allow lipid soluble molecules to diffuse easily. Small molecules that are electrically neutral, such as water, oxygen, and carbon dioxide, readily diffuse across the lipid bilayer of plasma membranes. The plasma membrane also is permeable to specific ions and certain polar molecules of moderate size, such as sugars. These molecules, however, do not diffuse across the lipid bilayer but must pass through specific transport proteins in the membrane. The plasma membrane is generally impermeable to large molecules such as proteins, which can enter cells by other mechanisms.

Transport proteins play either a passive role or an active role in moving substances across a membrane (Figure 6.19). In **passive transport**, substances move down their concentration gradient through the appropriate transport proteins. In **active transport**, substances move through trans-

FIGURE 6.19 In passive transport (a), substances move through membrane proteins down their concentration gradient. Active transport (b) requires the use of ATP energy as well as membrane proteins. Active transport can move substances against their concentration gradient as well as with their concentration gradient.

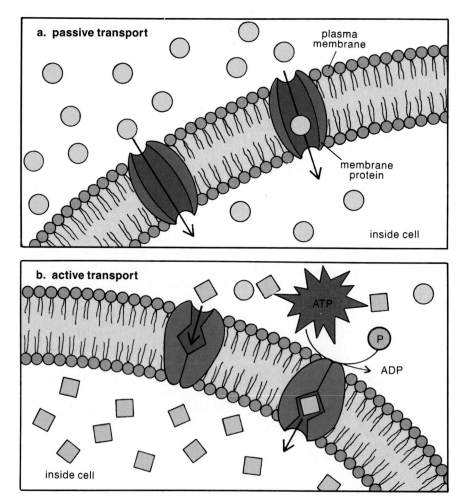

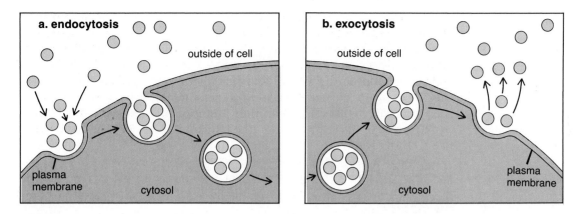

FIGURE 6.20 The transport of masses of material (larger molecules) into a cell (endocytosis) and out of a cell (exocytosis). These processes require energy.

port proteins, but *against* their concentration gradient (from a lower to a higher concentration). Cells use free energy, usually supplied by ATP, for active transport.

Transport proteins are of two general types. One type forms channels through which specific ions can diffuse. The other type acts as a carrier that binds to the molecule to be transported and physically moves it across the membrane. During transport, the carrier generally changes shape. If the carrier moves the molecules *down* their concentration gradient (in the same direction as diffusion), the passive transport process is known as facilitated diffusion. In active transport, the carriers require energy supplied by ATP to move the molecules. Figure 6.19 illustrates a model of these transport proteins.

Many necessary substances could not enter or leave cells (or organelles) without active transport. For example, the concentration of nutrient ions, such as nitrate (NO_3^-) or potassium (K^+), is often greater inside the roots of a plant than in the surrounding soil. Yet plants require a constant input of these ions. Active transport by the root cells moves ("pumps") the ions into the roots, despite the higher concentration inside the roots than in the soil. (The ions also may diffuse out of the root cells, but the rate of active transport is greater than the rate of diffusion.) In this way, plants can grow in an environment of relatively dilute soil nutrients. Such "pumping" of select ions and molecules through a membrane to an area with an already higher concentration of the same ions or molecules is essential to cell metabolism and growth.

In another transport mechanism, the membrane may fold inward, forming a tiny "pocket" that fills with fluid and particles from the cell's surroundings (Figure 6.20a). The membrane then closes over the pocket and releases it into the cell. The bubblelike result is a new vesicle containing fluid and particles that were once outside. In this manner, large molecules and particles can be incorporated into the cell. This activity can occur in reverse to expel materials from the cell as shown in Figure 6.20b.

In summary, living cells constantly exchange materials with their surroundings. Water moves freely through and among cells by osmosis. Most other molecules move through membranes by active and passive transport. These activities are selective processes regulated by transport proteins in the membranes. Active transport moves materials against their concentration gradients and requires energy. Passive transport, on the other hand, moves materials down their gradients rather than against them, and thus does not require energy. This energy requirement is the primary difference between active and passive transport. Diffusion and transport are essential to life and are made possible by the structure of the membranes.

CHECK AND CHALLENGE

1. What is a concentration gradient? How does it affect diffusion?
2. Explain the differences between active and passive transport. Why is each important to a cell or organelle?
3. In what way is a plasma membrane selective?
4. Would you expect osmosis and diffusion to stop when substances are evenly distributed? Explain.
5. What type of evidence demonstrates that active transport occurs?
6. How do membranes regulate the movement of molecules in and out of the cell?

Multicellular Organization

6.8   Cooperation

When one-celled organisms divide, some new cells may remain together in a cluster (Figure 6.21). However, a cluster of cells is not necessarily a multicellular organism. Each cell has an individual life and may break away from the cluster at some point.

Among multicellular organisms, the cells are more closely related. For example, the protist *Volvox*, found in many ponds during the spring and early summer, is a colony shaped like a hollow ball, as illustrated in Figure 6.22a. Inside the colony may be other developing colonies. Each colony has several hundred to tens of thousands of cells.

The cells of *Volvox* resemble the one-celled organism *Chlamydomonas* (Figure 6.22b). Each cell has a nucleus, two flagella, contractile vacuoles, an eyespot, and a cup-shaped chloroplast. A gelatinlike layer surrounds each cell and separates it from its neighbors. Under the microscope a *Volvox* colony looks like a gelatinous sphere with cells embedded in it (Figure 6.22c).

If you observe *Volvox* under high magnification, you can see delicate strands connecting the cells. You also can see that certain cells are larger than the rest. The colony appears to have a front end and a back end. As flagella move the *Volvox* through the water, the larger cells are usually at the back.

FIGURE 6.21 Though bacteria like these exist in clusters, chains, and as isolated cells, every bacterium is still an individual organism.

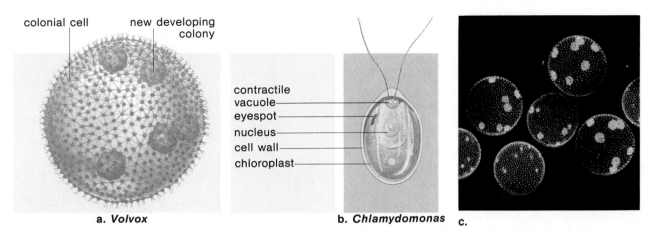

colonial cell   new developing colony

contractile vacuole
eyespot
nucleus
cell wall
chloroplast

a. Volvox   **b. Chlamydomonas**   c.

FIGURE 6.22 Individual cells of a *Volvox* colony (a) are similar in appearance to the unicellular protist *Chlamydomonas* (b). *Volvox* colonies as seen through the light microscope, X53 (c).

Volvox moves in a coordinated way. If the flagella of each individual cell of a *Volvox* colony were to move at random, only irregular motion of the colony would result. Instead the colony spins on its front-to-rear axis as it moves through the water. All the cells of a colony have to move their flagella in the same pattern to achieve this motion. Thus, the cells are organized into a working unit as the colony moves.

Volvox is useful for investigating the functions of cells in simple multicellular organisms. If a *Volvox* cell is punctured, the cell dies, but the rest of the colony continues to live. Damage to, or removal of, cells can test whether those cells carried on any essential function for the whole organism. For example, only a few cells in the colony are capable of producing the offspring colonies. Different-sized cells in the colony may have different functions as well.

6.9 Division of Labor

Many different types of cells exist in multicellular organisms more complex than *Volvox*. All cells must carry on some basic activities of life, but each type of cell often takes on a special job as well. For example, one type of cell, a gland cell, is efficient at making certain types of chemicals. Another, a nerve cell, is efficient in conducting electrical nerve impulses, enabling the organism to respond to its internal and external environments. Still another type of cell, a muscle cell, is efficient in movement. Even the cells that form an organism's outer covering, or **epidermis**, may be specialized. The drawing of a *Hydra* in Figure 6.23b shows cells with such specializations.

Hydra is a small, threadlike freshwater animal with a ring of tentacles at one end (Figure 6.23a). The animal's cells show small differences in appearance, along with differences in specialization. In later chapters and in your laboratory work, you will see that cells of larger organisms are

Eukaryotic cells show a unity of type and a diversity of specialized subtype. The basic cellular "design" is modified for the diverse, specialized cells that function cooperatively in a multicellular organism.

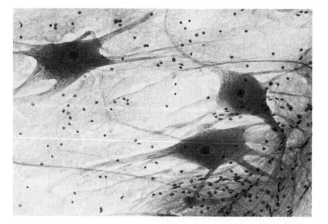

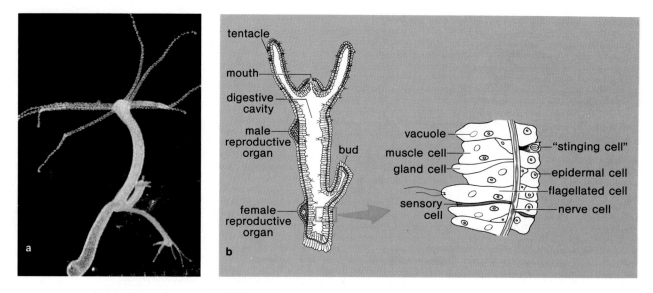

FIGURE 6.23 (a) A *Hydra* viewed under low magnification X15. (b) A drawing of a section through a *Hydra* and an enlarged view of some of the specialized cells in its body wall. The bud is the beginning of a new *Hydra*.

much more distinctive in appearance. For example, nerve and muscle cells are very long and thin (Figure 6.24), and human red blood cells are shaped like flattened spheres.

In multicellular organisms, a group of cells with the same specialization usually works together. Each specialized group of cells is called a **tissue**. The cell that is labeled *epidermal cell* in Figure 6.23b is part of a tissue and has similar cells on either side of it. They form the covering, or epidermal, tissue of the *Hydra*, along with stinging cells and sensory cells.

Most animals and plants have many types of tissues. Different tissues may be organized into **organs** (eyes, hearts, and stomachs, for example).

FIGURE 6.24 Specialized cells of a multicellular organism; (a) nerve cells, X124, (b) muscle cells, X288.

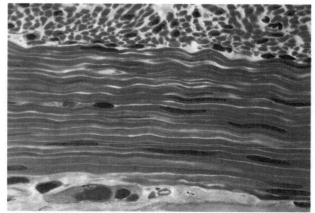

FOCUS ON *Junctions and the Extracellular Matrix*

Cells in direct contact with each other often are connected at specialized regions of their plasma membranes called junctions. Several types of junctions are present in animal cells. Some hold cells together; others provide channels for communication between cells. In tight junctions (a), specific proteins in the plasma membranes of adjacent cells make direct contact, so the plasma membranes are fused, preventing transport of substances through the spaces between the cells. Cytoplasmic materials and protein filaments form desmosomes (b), which act like rivets that hold cells together but still permit the passage of substances through the spaces between the cells. Gap junctions (c) are channels formed by doughnut-shaped proteins embedded in the plasma membranes of adjacent cells. They allow small water-soluble molecules to pass directly from the cytoplasm of one cell to the next. Junctions are particularly important in epithelial tissue, which consists of cells tightly connected into sheets that cover the body and line many internal cavities.

In plants, the cell walls are perforated by channels called plasmodesmata (d), through which continuous strands of cytoplasm connect adjacent cells. Plasma membranes line the channels, and water-soluble materials can pass freely from cell to cell throughout the plant.

The cells of most multicellular organisms are at least partially surrounded by a solution of macromolecules called the extracellular matrix (e). These protein and carbohydrate molecules are secreted into the space outside cells (extracellular space) and form a meshwork, or matrix, that holds cells together and allows them to migrate and interact with neighbor cells. In vertebrate animals, the matrix may regulate the behavior of cells in contact with it. The matrix is currently the subject of considerable research.

FIGURE C Examples of junctions in animal cells.

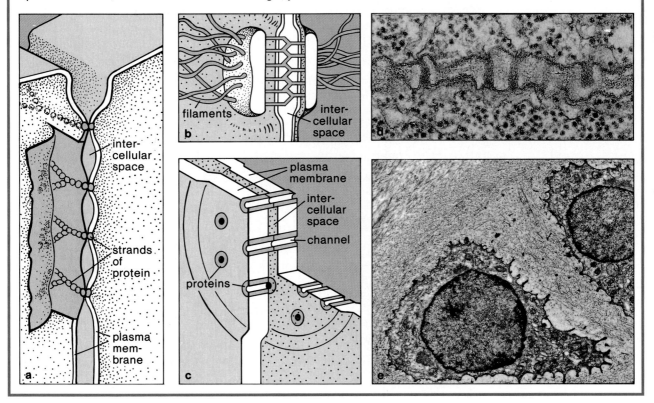

Organs may be incorporated into **systems** of organs. For example, a circulatory system usually includes a heart, blood vessels, and blood. No matter how specialized the structures in an organism become, they are made from the same building blocks—cells and cell products.

6.10 Systems

Try Investigation 6C, Diffusion and Cell Size.

In most multicellular organisms, cells are small compared to the size of the entire organism. (See **Appendix 6B**, Constraints on Cell Size.) The inner cells cannot obtain materials directly from the outside environment nor pass their wastes directly to the outside environment. Specialized systems handle deliveries between the environment and the cells (Figure 6.25). In animals, a circulatory system is needed to transport materials. In fact, in most animals more than one system is involved in this transport of materials through the organism's body.

Most multicellular plants also have some system of transport. A tree's leaves admit air and can absorb water from the air (although much more water usually is lost than absorbed). Most of the water and minerals come from the soil. A transport system takes water and minerals from where they are absorbed in the roots to where they are needed in the leaves. Another transport system carries food produced in the leaves by photosynthesis to other parts of the tree. Both systems extend throughout the tree.

In general, specialized systems account for most of the complexity of multicellular organisms. Most of the systems, in turn, are necessary for these three reasons:

1. a division of labor occurs among cells;
2. many individual cells cannot work together without regulation and coordination;
3. the majority of the cells are not in direct contact with the outside environment.

The different systems in an organism unite all its parts into a smoothly functioning whole.

FIGURE 6.25 Two diagrams of cells in a multicellular organism. Cells that are not in direct contact with the organism's external environment are shown in color on the left. To obtain food and get rid of waste as efficiently as outer cells, these inner cells require a system for deliveries as shown on the right.

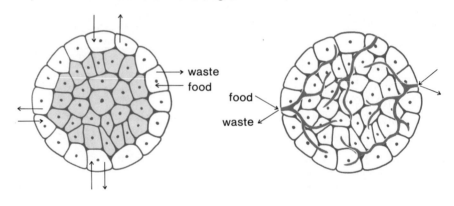

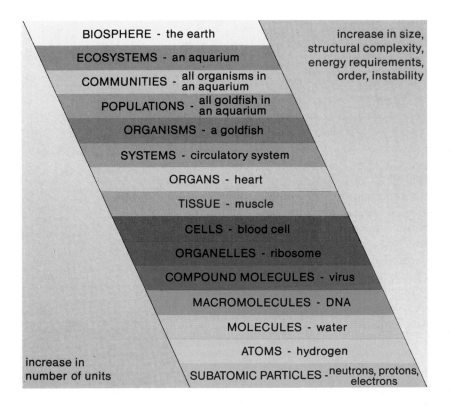

BIOSPHERE - the earth

ECOSYSTEMS - an aquarium

COMMUNITIES - all organisms in an aquarium

POPULATIONS - all goldfish in an aquarium

ORGANISMS - a goldfish

SYSTEMS - circulatory system

ORGANS - heart

TISSUE - muscle

CELLS - blood cell

ORGANELLES - ribosome

COMPOUND MOLECULES - virus

MACROMOLECULES - DNA

MOLECULES - water

ATOMS - hydrogen

SUBATOMIC PARTICLES - neutrons, protons, electrons

increase in size, structural complexity, energy requirements, order, instability

increase in number of units

FIGURE 6.26   Matter in the biosphere is characterized by increasing levels of organization and complexity. Each higher level of order requires a greater input of free energy for its maintenance than the level below it. Where would you draw a line to distinguish between life and non-life?

In many organisms, added specializations have developed even within their specialized systems. For example, cells whose jobs involve transport occur in the circulatory system. Some of the cells in the circulatory system play no part in transport but instead have other specialized tasks such as protecting the body from infection. Thus, continuing specialization has led to development of many different types of cells. Specialized systems, in turn, have contributed enormously to the diversity and complexity of multicellular organisms. Figure 6.26 summarizes the increasing complexity of organization of matter from subatomic particles to the biosphere. Cells, the basic unit of life, are about midway on this continuum of organization. They also are the lowest level of organization that truly can be considered living. Functions of cells, as well as those of the higher levels of organization, are considered in the remaining chapters of this book.

CHECK AND CHALLENGE

1. Give three reasons why specialized systems are necessary in large multicellular organisms.
2. Arrange these terms in increasing order of complexity: cells, organ systems, organs, tissues, organisms.
3. Can a single cell form a system or a tissue? Explain.
4. What structural and functional characteristics limit the size of cells?
5. How are cells organized together in higher organisms? What are the advantages of that organization?

Summary

Prokaryotic and eukaryotic cells differ primarily in basic structural ways. Prokaryotic cells are smaller and less specialized than eukaryotic cells, but the most distinguishing characteristic is the presence of a membrane-enclosed nucleus in eukaryotes. In addition, eukaryotes are generally organized into organelles, cellular units of structure and function that increase efficiency. Organelles include mitochondria, chloroplasts, ribosomes, vacuoles, endoplasmic reticulum, and other compartments with specific functions in the eukaryotic cell.

Membranes are essential to all cells. They are composed of lipid and protein molecules in a fluid, asymmetric structure that regulates the movement of substances in and out of the cell or organelle. Substances may move by simple diffusion or be transported by membrane proteins. Passive transport selectively moves molecules to regions of lower concentration. Active transport moves molecules into regions of higher concentration and therefore requires energy.

Cells may exist alone as unicellular organisms. In fungi, plants, and animals, cells may be clustered and form multicellular organisms. Tissues, organs, and systems become more complex in larger multicellular organisms. In fact, most of the complexity of multicellular organisms results from their specialized systems.

Key Concepts

Use the following concepts to develop a concept map for a eukaryotic cell. Include appropriate linking words and add as many other concepts from the chapter as you can.

structure	active transport
function	unicellular organism
organelles	multicellular organism
diffusion	division of labor
osmosis	

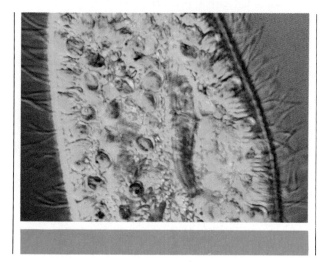

Reviewing Ideas

1. Compare the differences and similarities of prokaryotic and eukaryotic cells.

2. How do the walls of plant and bacterial cells differ? How are they similar?

3. Why does a cell exchange materials with its environment?

4. How are diffusion and osmosis related?

5. How does active transport differ from diffusion in terms of (a) cell energy? (b) changing the distribution or concentration of materials?

6. Define *unicellular, colonial,* and *multicellular.*

7. What difficulties are encountered in studying living cells of multicellular organisms?

8. What differences are likely to exist between unicellular organisms and cells of larger organisms?

9. What cell part specializes in packaging certain materials? Give an example of how the plasma membrane also can package materials.

Using Concepts

1. Why is it important for cells to package some of their products?

2. How does the environment of cells differ for a unicellular and a multicellular organism?

3. Explain one way in which the plasma membrane of a cell is unlike an artificial membrane or plastic bag.

4. A cell uses materials as it needs them. How does this influence the direction of diffusion?

5. The motion of molecules in diffusion is random: The molecules move in all directions, colliding with other molecules. Based on this information, how can diffusion occur in "one" direction?

6. Prokaryotes have no clearly defined cell nuclei. What other evidence could you look for in trying to determine whether they are cells?

7. Some biologists once wondered whether the ER (endoplasmic reticulum) was formed only after death by the process used to fix cells for study. Why might they have asked such a question?

8. In what ways are fluidity and asymmetry important in membranes?

9. If cells are the units of structure and function in organisms, why would tissues and organs be needed?

10. Choose one of the differences between prokaryotic and eukaryotic cells from Table 6.1. Explain how the difference improves the efficiency of eukaryotic cells.

Synthesis

1. How do the laws of bioenergetics help explain diffusion?

2. How are the characteristics of the biological macromolecules important in the structure and function of cells?

3. How does the development of multicellularity demonstrate evolution through natural selection?

Extensions

You are a scientist studying the movement of compound Z into the cells of an animal. You do not know whether the compound is moved by active or passive transport. Design an experiment to answer this question and predict the results.

CONTENTS

Photosynthesis: Harvesting Light Energy

*T*he process of photosynthesis can be compared to a "living bridge"—connecting the sun and the organisms on Earth by providing the energy needed for life. Green plants and other photosynthetic organisms harvest solar energy and use it to combine molecules of carbon dioxide into complex, energy-rich organic compounds. Without photosynthesis, life as we know it would not exist. In a sense, green plants are the "supermarket" that feeds the world. This chapter discusses why photosynthesis is important to living creatures and how the processes of photosynthesis evolve and function in different ecosystems.

*W*hat gives fall leaves their colors?

*W*hat other factor can affect the intensity of the colors?

Organisms and Photosynthesis

7.1   Importance of Photosynthesis

Photosynthesis uses the energy of sunlight to convert carbon dioxide to sugars. In most instances, it is the process that supplies usable chemical energy for life on Earth. In addition, almost all organisms ultimately rely on photosynthesis for the carbon building blocks of their cells and tissues. Photosynthesis also supplies the oxygen that most organisms require. Thus, plants and photosynthetic bacteria and protists are producers (autotrophs), and heterotrophic animals that eat the autotrophs are consumers (Chapter 3).

Photosynthesis is the fundamental system for capturing energy that sustains farming and ranching. Farmers depend on photosynthesis to grow the grains, vegetables, and fruits they supply to supermarkets. Ranchers feed the grains and vegetables to their livestock, and humans eat the meat. We even rely on the products of ancient photosynthesis—petroleum and coal—to power automobiles, run factories, and heat our homes. Eons ago,

◆ *Large-toothed aspen leaves,* Populus grandidentata *on a carpet of hairy cap moss,* Polytrichium *sp., in Gulf Hagas, Maine.*

green plants and the consumer animals that fed on them died and partially decayed to form the oil and coal deposits we utilize today. We wear clothing made from cotton, wool, or petroleum products, and we build houses and schools from wood and wood products. These are just a few of the many ways we depend on photosynthesis for food, clothing, and shelter. Photosynthesis is vital to our survival.

7.2 Origin of Photosynthetic Organisms

The heterotroph hypothesis (Section 4.4) suggests that the earliest organisms were heterotrophs that fed on a "soup" of organic molecules in the primitive ocean. As these first heterotrophs consumed the available amino acids, proteins, fats, and sugars, the nutrient soup became depleted and could no longer support a growing population of heterotrophs. Organic compounds probably continued to be made by energy from ultraviolet radiation and lightning but not fast enough to feed the increasing numbers of heterotrophs; food would have become scarce.

How might some organisms have adapted to the food shortage and managed to survive whereas other organisms did not? Organisms that could use an alternate source of energy would have had a great advantage. Consider that the Earth was (and continues to be) flooded with solar energy that actually consists of different forms of radiation. Figure 7.1 illustrates the relationship among these forms, which are distinguished from each other by their different wavelengths. Ultraviolet radiation is destruc-

FIGURE 7.1 Radiations from the sun form a continuous series. The range of radiations that organisms can detect with their eyes—visible light—is roughly the same range plants use. Shorter wavelengths (blue light) contain more energy than longer wavelengths (red light). Leaves are green because chlorophyll absorbs red and blue wavelengths, but little green.

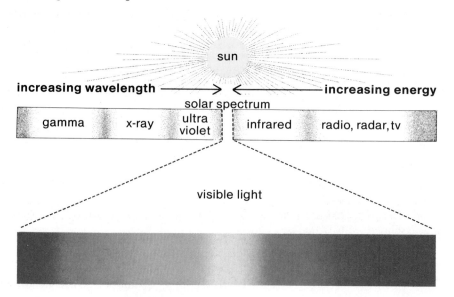

tive to life, but visible light is energy-rich and less destructive. Thus, as organic compounds became increasingly rare, an already-present ability to use visible light as an alternate source of energy might have enabled such organisms and their descendants to survive.

The first organisms able to use visible light probably would have acted partly like heterotrophs, taking in existing organic compounds, and partly like autotrophs, making other organic compounds with the energy from visible light. Certain bacteria living today show exactly those properties. Other bacteria are true autotrophs, using the energy of visible light to make *all* of their essential organic compounds from carbon dioxide and about 15 other raw materials. According to the hypothesis described in Section 4.8, primitive photosynthetic bacteria might have been incorporated as components of eukaryotic cells and eventually evolved into the chloroplasts of modern plant cells. Thus, modern photosynthetic organisms might have evolved from prehistoric bacteria.

7.3 Leaf Structure

To appreciate the functioning pathways of photosynthesis, it is useful to understand the structure of leaves and chloroplasts. The leaf is a food-supply factory, and the leaf structure of higher plants is adapted to maximize light absorption and carbon dioxide diffusion (Figure 7.2). A network of veins acts like a plumbing system that supplies water and minerals to the leaf and that carries the products of photosynthesis away to other parts of

Try Investigation 7A, Leaf Structure and Stomates.

FIGURE 7.2 Diagram of a leaf in cross section as it might appear under a microscope. The leaf structure provides maximum efficiency of photosynthesis. The arrows show the movement of carbon dioxide, oxygen, and water into or out of the leaf.

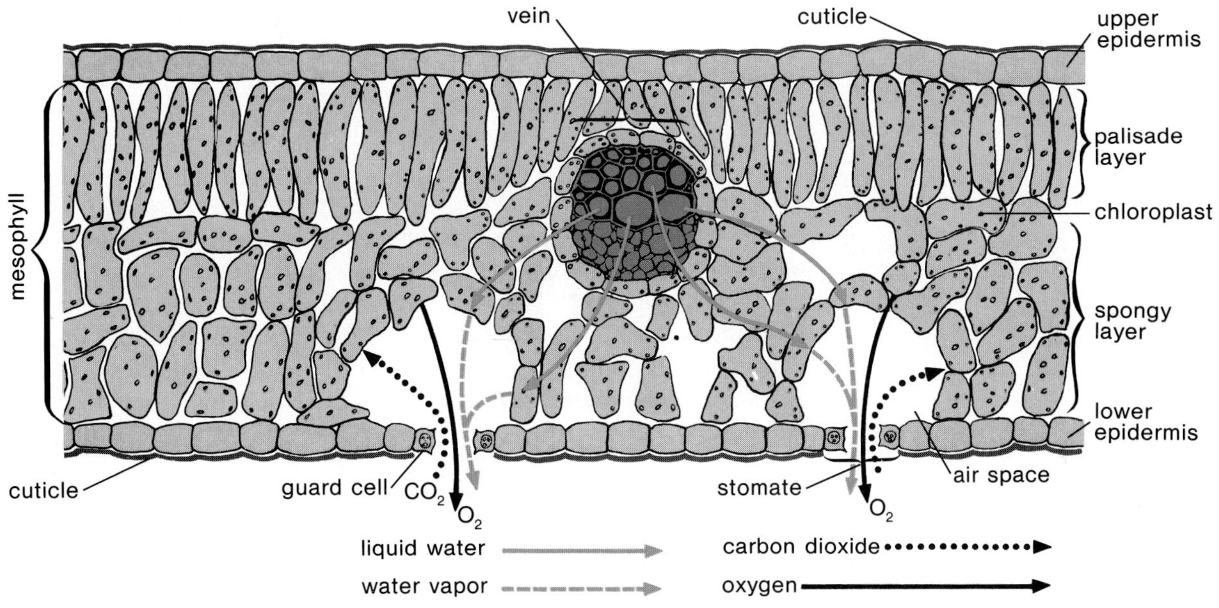

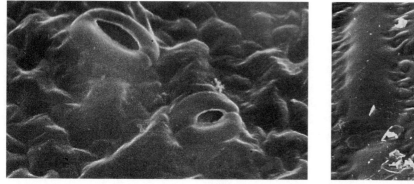

a   b

FIGURE 7.3 Stomates are minute pores in the epidermis, seen here in these scanning electron micrographs. A pair of guard cells controls opening and closing. When the guard cells swell with water, the stomates open (a). Stomates close when guard cells lose water (b).

CONNECTIONS

The leaf is an excellent example of the relationship between structure and function.

the plant. Surrounding the veins in the middle of most leaves is a photosynthetic tissue known as the **mesophyll** (MEZ oh fil). Mesophyll cells are loaded with chloroplasts. Air spaces in the mesophyll act as reservoirs for carbon dioxide and water vapor. The epidermis, a single layer of cells, covers the upper and lower surfaces of the leaf. Epidermal cells often secrete a waxy substance that forms a water-repellent covering called the **cuticle**.

Gases move into and out of the leaf by diffusion through **stomates** (STOH mayts), minute pores in the epidermis. Each stomate is surrounded by a pair of specialized guard cells. When guard cells swell with water, the stomates open (Figure 7.3), and carbon dioxide diffuses into the air spaces and chloroplasts of the mesophyll cells.

When the stomates are open, oxygen and water vapor diffuse out of the leaf. Evaporation of water from the leaf, or **transpiration** (trans pih RAY shun), is the major source of water loss from plants. The problem is that stomates must open for carbon dioxide to diffuse into the leaf, but the plant loses water in the process. Perhaps you have seen house plants or garden vegetables wilt in the heat of a summer day. That effect occurs if the rate of transpiration from the leaves is greater than the rate of water absorbed by the roots, or in other words, when water loss exceeds water gain. Consequently, the plant wilts and may even die.

Guard cells open and close the stomates in response to environmental conditions. Stomates usually are open during the day and closed during the night. If water supply to the roots (and therefore the leaves) is low, however, or the daytime air temperature is extremely high, the stomates may close during the day, thus preventing excessive transpiration. The rate of photosynthesis usually is proportional to carbon dioxide concentration, as discussed in Section 7.8. When the stomates are closed, the carbon dioxide in the leaf is quickly depleted. Little or no carbon dioxide diffuses into the leaf, and photosynthesis slows accordingly. (See **Appendix 7A,** The Mechanisms of Stomate Opening).

7.4 Chloroplast Structure

Try Investigation 7B, Photosynthesis.

Figure 7.4 is an electron micrograph of a chloroplast from a corn plant leaf (*Zea mays*). An outer membrane regulates the flow of materials into and out of each chloroplast. The internal membrane system of this organelle consists of flattened sacs, or thylakoids (THY luh koids), which increase membrane surface area. Many of the thylakoids are stacked, forming structures called grana (GRAY nuh; singular: granum). The grana are oriented in a way that allows maximum absorption of sunlight. Chloroplast membranes have the same basic structure as other cellular membranes (Section 6.6). In addition, light-absorbing pigments and enzymes are embedded in the thylakoids. Surrounding the thylakoids is the stroma (STROH muh), which contains other enzymes as well as DNA, RNA, and ribosomes. Chloroplasts can make several organelle proteins under the direction of their own genes. The DNA in chloroplasts is similar to bacterial DNA and thus is evidence for the bacterial origin of chloroplasts.

Photosynthesis depends on the green pigment **chlorophyll** (KLOR uh fil), which is present in two forms, *a* and *b*, compared in Figure 7.5. In

FIGURE 7.5 The structure of chlorophyll *a*. Chlorophyll *b* differs only in having a —CHO group in place of the circled CH₃.

FIGURE 7.4 Electron micrograph of a chloroplast in a leaf of corn, *Zea mays*, X24 000. The darker areas are stacks of thylakoids called grana; the drawing shows the structure of a granum enlarged still more. Photosynthetic pigments and electron carriers are embedded in the thylakoid membranes; DNA, RNA, ribosomes, and Calvin cycle enzymes are in the stroma.

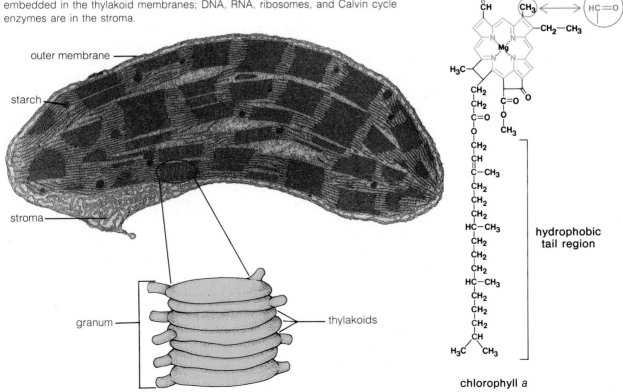

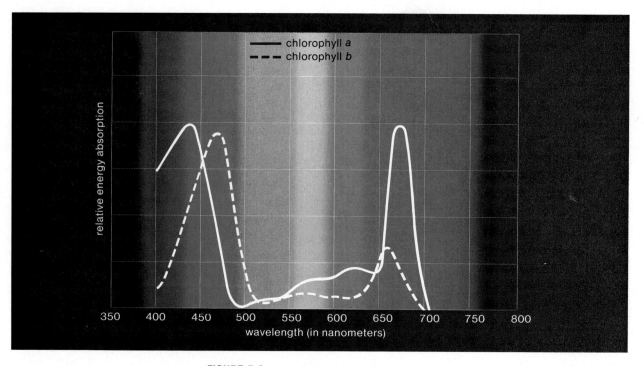

FIGURE 7.6 Absorption spectra for chlorophylls *a* and *b*. What wavelengths do these chlorophylls absorb most? Least?

chloroplasts, chlorophylls *a* and *b* absorb light in the violet/blue and orange/red regions and reflect light in the green region (Figure 7.6). Green plants contain other, accessory pigments that work with the chlorophylls to absorb additional wavelengths of light. Their absorbed light energy is transferred to a special type of chlorophyll *a* for use in photosynthesis. Some of the accessory pigments are responsible for fall coloration of leaves and become more visible as the chlorophyll content declines (Figure 7.7).

FIGURE 7.7 The fall coloration of leaves is due to the presence of accessory pigments.

CHECK AND CHALLENGE

1. How is photosynthesis essential to life on Earth?
2. If the first organisms were heterotrophs, what conditions might have favored the evolution of photosynthetic autotrophs?
3. Why are photosynthetic organisms called producers in an ecosystem?
4. How does the arrangement of structures in the leaf increase the efficiency of photosynthesis?
5. How are stomates and transpiration related?
6. How do the membranes of the chloroplasts differ from other membranes in the cell?

THE SECRET OF VEGETATION

People have long realized that they and all other animals grow and develop by eating plants or by eating other animals that feed on plants. What is the "food" that plants eat? The keenest observers of plants could find no sign that plants ever consumed any food. The lack of food intake, they reasoned, explains why plants excrete no waste products.

How could plants develop and increase in size? In the seventeenth century, a physician named Jean Baptiste van Helmont announced an astonishing conclusion reached not by observing plants in nature but by performing what had never been done before: a quantitative scientific experiment on plant growth. In van Helmont's own words:

> I took an earthenware pot, placed in it 200 lb of earth dried in an oven, soaked this with water, and planted in it a willow shoot weighing about 5 lb. After five years had passed, the tree grown therefrom weighed 169 lb. and about 3 oz. But the earthenware pot was constantly wet only with rain or (when necessary) distilled water . . . and, to prevent dust flying around from mixing with the earth, the rim of the pot was kept covered with an iron plate coated with tin and pierced with many holes . . . Finally, I again dried the earth of the pot, and it was found to be the same 200 lb minus 2 oz. Therefore, 164 lb of wood, bark, and root *had arisen from the water alone.*

Van Helmont performed a beautifully simple experiment and tried to measure carefully, but he did not take into account the air or consider the missing two ounces of soil very important. This small soil loss gave a hint of what is now known to be an uptake of soil minerals by plant roots. Second, and most important, neither van Helmont nor anyone else for another 100 years had any reason to suspect that the "food" that made plants grow and develop was being silently and efficiently manufactured in the leaves by a mysterious chemical process that required carbon dioxide and sunlight.

In 1772, Joseph Priestley discovered that green plants affect air. In one experiment, he noted that when a burning candle is covered with a jar, its flame is quickly extinguished. However, when a sprig of mint is placed in the jar for a few days, and then the candle is covered, the candle burns for a short time.

By 1804, it had been demonstrated that plants must be exposed to light for results such as Priestley's to occur. It had also been demonstrated that plants release oxygen and absorb carbon dioxide. Nicolas de Saussure showed that the increase in plant weight after exposure to sunlight is greater than the weight of carbon dioxide taken in. Therefore, he concluded that plant growth results from the intake of both carbon dioxide and water.

Julius Robert Mayer brought these concepts into focus in 1845. He recognized the essential steps in photosynthesis—the absorption of light energy and its transformation into chemical energy, which is then stored in compounds. These compounds account for more than 90 percent of all plant substance.

FIGURE A van Helmont's experiment

willow tree 5 lbs
soil 200 lbs

willow tree 169 lbs 3 oz
soil 200 lbs-2 oz

The Process of Photosynthesis _____

7.5 An Overview

Three major steps in the energy conversion process occur in photosynthesis: (1) absorption of light energy, (2) conversion of light energy into chemical energy, and (3) storage of chemical energy in sugars. The reactions by which these events occur may be categorized in two distinct but interdependent groups, summarized in Figure 7.8. In the **light reactions**, pigment molecules in the thylakoids absorb light and convert it to chemical energy carried by short-lived energy-rich molecules. These molecules are then used to make 3-carbon sugars from carbon dioxide in a series of reactions known as the **Calvin cycle**. In that cycle, chemical energy is stored in the sugars, and the carbon-containing products are incorporated into the plant for future growth.

The following equation summarizes the reactions of photosynthesis.

$$3CO_2 \; + \; 3H_2O \; \xrightarrow[\text{chlorophyll}]{\text{light energy}} \; C_3H_6O_3 \; + \; 3O_2$$

$$\text{carbon} \quad \text{water} \qquad\qquad \text{3-carbon} \quad \text{oxygen}$$
$$\text{dioxide} \qquad\qquad\qquad\qquad \text{sugar} \qquad \text{gas}$$

This equation indicates only the major raw materials and two of the products of photosynthesis. The many chemical steps and other substances involved in photosynthesis are explained more fully in Sections 7.6 through 7.8. As you read the details that follow, you will find it helpful to keep a mental picture of the overall process as it has been described to this point. Remember that the products of the light reactions are used subsequently in the Calvin cycle. The two groups of reactions together accomplish the changes summarized by the above equation.

FIGURE 7.8 An overview of photosynthesis

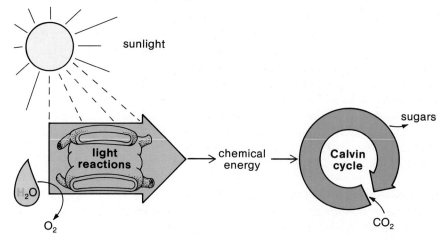

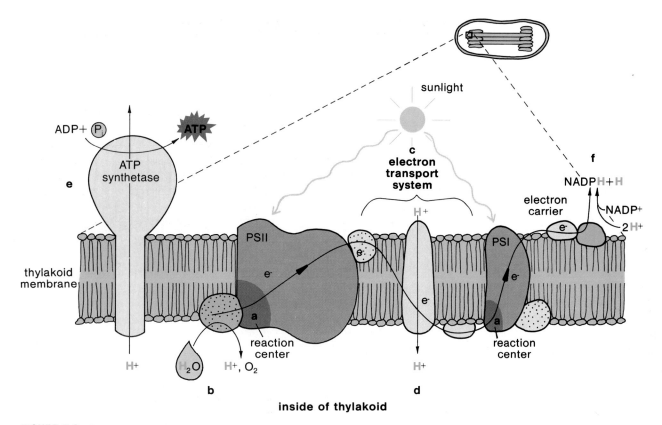

FIGURE 7.9 The light reactions of photosynthesis take place in the thylakoid of a chloroplast. Light is absorbed by pigment molecules in each photosystem (PSI and PSII) and transferred to the reaction center, which loses energy-rich electrons (a). Water is split, freeing electrons, protons, and oxygen (b). As electrons flow along an electron transport system (c), protons are transported to the inside of the thylakoid (d). ATP forms as protons are transported back to the outside via the membrane enzyme ATP synthetase (e). The electrons and protons finally join with the hydrogen carrier NADP$^+$ (f).

7.6 The Light Reactions

The light reactions of photosynthesis convert visible light into the chemical energy that powers sugar production. In these reactions, chlorophyll and other pigments in the thylakoid absorb light energy, water molecules are split into hydrogen and oxygen—releasing oxygen gas to the atmosphere, and light energy is stored as chemical energy. These events are diagrammed in Figure 7.9. Refer to the diagram as you read.

The molecules involved in the light reactions are embedded in the thylakoid membranes and organized in a way that ensures their efficient operation. Two structurally distinct groups of pigments, photosystems (PS) I and II, work best in harmony to absorb light energy. Specific protein molecules in the membrane that serve as electron carriers form an electron transport system between the two photosystems. Some of the electron carriers are mobile, and they move through the membrane as they transport electrons to the next carrier in the system.

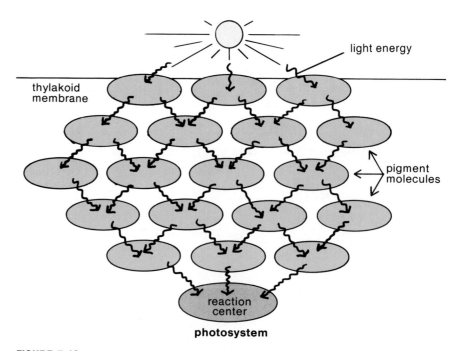

FIGURE 7.10 Each photosystem consists of several hundred molecules of chlorophyll and other pigments that absorb light energy and transfer it to a special chlorophyll *a* molecule, the reaction center. The reaction center is the only pigment molecule that can participate directly in electron flow in the light reactions.

The chlorophylls and other pigments in each photosystem act together to absorb, concentrate, and transfer light energy to a special chlorophyll *a* molecule called the reaction center (Figure 7.10). Each special chlorophyll *a* molecule is associated with particular proteins and other membrane components; it is thus made special by its chemical environment.

The absorption of light energy sets up a flow of electrons. In each photosystem, the reaction center loses energy-rich electrons, which are captured by electron carriers. The electrons lost by photosystem I are replaced by electrons lost from photosystem II. Electrons lost by photosystem II are replaced by electrons removed from water. As a result, water is separated into protons, electrons, and oxygen: $H_2O \rightarrow 2H^+ + 2e^- + \frac{1}{2}O_2$. (Recall from Chapter 2 that a hydrogen atom consists of a single proton in the nucleus and a single electron. Thus, a hydrogen ion, H^+, is a single proton.)

At the end of the electron flow, the electrons, along with protons from water, combine with a hydrogen carrier, **NADP$^+$**—nicotinamide adenine dinucleotide phosphate (nik uh TEE nuh myd AD uh neen DY NOO klee oh tyd FOS fayt). The resulting molecule, NADPH, transports the protons and electrons needed for the Calvin cycle and other biosynthetic reactions in the chloroplast.

As electrons flow from carrier to carrier along the electron transport system, some of the energy they originally captured from the sun powers the active transport of protons across the thylakoid membrane. A relatively high concentration of protons accumulates inside the thylakoid, a situation that cannot be maintained. As a result, protons diffuse down a steep concentration gradient, passing through an enzyme complex in the membrane. The complex, **ATP synthetase**, uses energy from the diffusion of protons to synthesize ATP from ADP + P$_i$. **Appendix 7B,** ATP Synthesis in Chloroplasts and Mitochondria, explains how the movement of electrons and protons results in ATP synthesis.

In summary, you can think of the energy from light as causing the electrons from water to flow in the chloroplast. The flow powers the synthesis of ATP and NADPH, which contain chemical energy, not light energy. Thus, photosynthesis converts light energy into chemical energy. In essence, plants use light energy to make ATP and NADPH, which they later use to make sugars from carbon dioxide. ATP and NADPH, along with oxygen gas, are the products of the light reactions of photosynthesis.

Why does photosynthesis not stop with the synthesis of ATP and NADPH? There are two reasons. First, ATP and NADPH are not particularly stable compounds; a plant can neither efficiently store them for later consumption nor transport them to other tissues that require energy. Second, a plant cannot directly use ATP and NADPH as carbon skeletons (Chapter 2) for cell growth. Instead, the ATP and NADPH are used in the Calvin cycle to convert carbon dioxide into stable, easily transported sugars that contain energy and carbon skeletons for building cells and tissues.

FOCUS ON *Organelles and Pathways*

Sometimes it is confusing to think about cycles, pathways, and molecules of metabolism in cells and organelles. Remember that the diagrams in the text are models based on the best available experimental data about cellular processes. Even most electron microscopes cannot reveal individual molecules, such as PGAL, or enzymes that make up the pathways of the Calvin cycle. Models help us understand how cells and organelles work, but there are no arrows, labels, or enclosing boxes in the actual organelle or cell. (There are, however, transport channels, preferred directions of reactions, and compartments within cells.)

Pathways and cycles are made of multiple copies of the enzymes and molecules. The enzymes may have an orderly attachment to a membrane, making the pathway or cycle more efficient. For example, the enzymes and electron-carrying proteins of the light reactions are embedded in sequence in the individual thyla-koids. Calvin-cycle enzymes in the stroma may be attached to the surface of the chloroplast membranes. The sugar molecules of the Calvin cycle are probably dispersed evenly about the chloroplast. You can think of the millions of copies of these molecules as existing in "pools." Individual molecules such as PGAL leave the pool, and the cell uses them in metabolism.

Photosystems I and II occur at many places along the thylakoids and make millions of molecules of ATP and NADPH. Because there are numerous copies of each Calvin-cycle enzyme, many molecules of carbon dioxide can be converted into sugar in the chloroplast stroma at the same time. Likewise, the activities of photosynthesis occur simultaneously in the thousands of chloroplasts in a single leaf. Do not let diagrams and models mislead you. They provide a way to represent and study biochemical cycles but do not mirror natural processes. Evolutionary forces, not models, determine these processes.

7.7 The Calvin Cycle

The reactions of the Calvin cycle are not powered directly by the absorption of light energy, but by the products of the light reactions. Figure 7.11 summarizes the enzyme-catalyzed steps of the Calvin cycle as they occur in the stroma of a chloroplast. Follow these steps as you read the description.

At (a), the beginning of the cycle, a molecule of carbon dioxide combines with the 5-carbon sugar RuBP, ribulose bisphosphate (RY byoo lohs BIS fos fayt). This reaction is known as carbon dioxide fixation. The resulting short-lived 6-carbon molecule immediately splits into two molecules of the 3-carbon acid PGA, phosphoglyceric (fos foh gly SER ik) acid. At (b), two enzymatic steps use one molecule each of ATP and NADPH from the light reactions to convert each molecule of PGA to the 3-carbon sugar phosphate PGAL, phosphoglyceraldehyde (fos foh glis uh RAL deh hyd). As the Calvin cycle continues (c), PGAL undergoes a series of reactions that form several 4-, 5-, and 6-carbon sugar phosphates. The final step uses an ATP molecule from the light reactions to regenerate RuBP from a 5-carbon sugar phosphate, thus completing the cycle. Three turns of the cycle, each turn incorporating one molecule of carbon dioxide, result in the formation of six molecules of PGAL. Of these, five molecules are required to regenerate RuBP, and one is available for use by the plant in biosynthesis, respiration, and other metabolic processes.

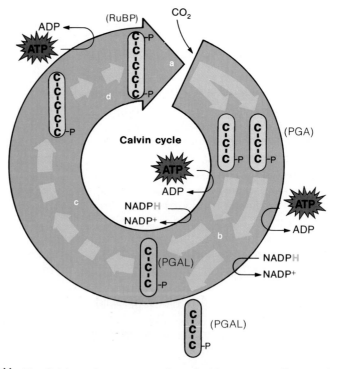

FIGURE 7.11 The Calvin cycle converts carbon dioxide to sugars. Enzymes in the stroma of the chloroplast catalyze each step of the cycle. Rubisco, the enzyme at (a), catalyzes carbon dioxide fixation. The reactions require ATP and NADPH from the light reactions. ADP and NADP$^+$ return to the light reactions.

An enzyme called rubisco (roo BIS koh), catalyzes the reaction that initially incorporates (fixes) carbon dioxide into the cycle (Figure 7.11a). Carbon dioxide is first fixed into the 3-carbon acid PGA. Plants that use the Calvin cycle exclusively to fix carbon dioxide are called C_3 plants.

The Calvin cycle is directly dependent on ATP and NADPH from the light reactions of photosynthesis. In addition, light activates rubisco and several other enzymes of the cycle that are inactive in the dark. For these reasons and also because sufficient carbon dioxide is unavailable while the stomates are closed, the Calvin cycle cannot operate in the dark.

7.8 Products of the Calvin Cycle

Most textbooks state that glucose ($C_6H_{12}O_6$) is the product of photosynthesis. In fact, plant cells contain very little, if any, pure glucose, the 6-carbon sugar present in human blood. Instead, sugar phosphates such as PGAL are removed from the Calvin cycle for use in other cellular functions, as shown in Figure 7.12. From these sugar phosphates, plants can synthesize the other compounds they need.

Sucrose made in the cytosol and starch made in the chloroplast may be correctly regarded as the end products of photosynthesis. Sucrose can be

Try Investigation 7C, Rates of Photosynthesis.

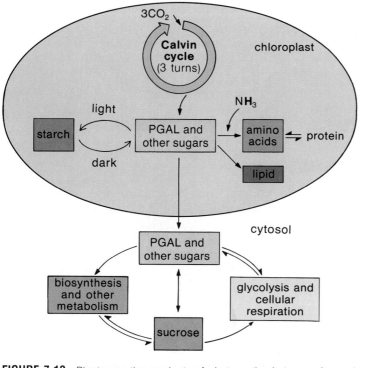

FIGURE 7.12 Plants use the products of photosynthesis to supply energy and carbon skeletons for biosynthesis and other cell work. Sucrose and starch are considered the end-products of photosynthesis.

used in leaf metabolism or be exported from the leaf through the veins to supply energy and carbon skeletons for growth and development in other parts of the plant. In this way, sucrose in plants serves a role similar to that of glucose in animals (Chapter 8). In the chloroplast, starch may accumulate in the light and then be broken down in the dark to supply the plant with energy and carbon skeletons when photosynthesis is shut down at night.

Plants, like all living organisms, require food for growth and development. PGAL and other sugar phosphates from the Calvin cycle are food for the plant. They can be used to supply energy and carbon skeletons for metabolism in the leaf and entire plant, as shown in Figure 7.12. (Chapter 8 discusses how these processes occur.) Some of the sugar phosphates are made into lipids and others into amino acids and then protein. This activity can happen right in the chloroplast. Humans and other animals consume plants, thus using the materials from photosynthesis for building proteins and as a source of sugars and energy.

CHECK AND CHALLENGE

1. How is light used in photosynthesis?

2. Describe the roles of photosystems I and II.

3. What are the products of the light reactions, and how are they used?

4. Why does the Calvin cycle not operate at night?

5. What are the products of the Calvin cycle, and how are they used?

6. What is the role of rubisco?

Photosynthesis and the Environment

7.9   Rate of Photosynthesis

Environmental conditions profoundly affect photosynthesis and, therefore, productivity in an ecosystem or in agriculture. An understanding of environmental influences can help humans make more efficient use of Earth's resources as well as protect them. When considering environmental effects on any metabolic system it is necessary to think in terms of the **rate**, or activity per unit of time, of some process in the system. For example, you can measure photosynthesis by the amount of oxygen released or carbon dioxide consumed. Suppose a lab team reports that the activity of photosynthesis in a bean plant was 25 cm^3 of carbon dioxide consumed. Was it 25 cm^3 per second, per hour, or per day? These are very different rates with very different photosynthetic efficiencies for the bean plant. The value expressed without the unit of time is meaningless. By expressing cell functions in terms of a rate, you answer the question: How fast did the process occur?

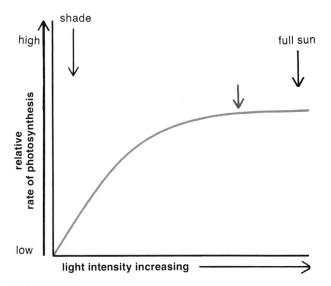

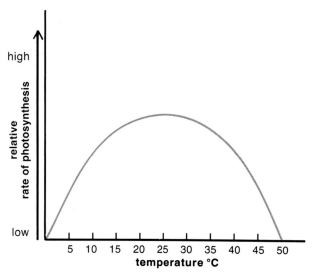

FIGURE 7.13 As light intensity increases, the rate of photosynthesis increases, but only up to a point called the light saturation point (indicated by the arrow). Data are generalized to show trends in C_3 plants.

FIGURE 7.14 As temperature increases, the rate of photosynthesis also increases up to a point where the rate levels off and then declines. Data are generalized to show trends in C_3 plants, showing optimum temperatures between 20°C and 30°C.

Four environmental factors that directly affect the rate of photosynthesis have been studied extensively. They are light intensity, temperature, and the concentrations of carbon dioxide and oxygen. Some of the findings of these studies are described here.

You might expect an increase in light intensity to increase the rate of photosynthesis. Is that always the case? Study the graph in Figure 7.13. What happens to the rate of photosynthesis as light intensity increases? Note that before the light reaches the intensity of full sunlight, the rate of photosynthesis levels off. Where the leveling off occurs, the light reactions are saturated with light energy and are proceeding as fast as possible, so a further increase in light intensity will not result in an increased rate of photosynthetic activity.

From these data, consider the fate of a pine tree growing under a maple tree in a forest. Studies in northeastern North America have shown that certain species of trees, such as pine, require more light when young than broad-leafed trees such as maple, beech, and oak. In the shaded understory of pine forests, the light intensity is too low to sustain the necessary rate of photosynthesis in the pine seedlings. Thus, broad-leafed trees, rather than pine, regenerate and eventually take over the forest as the pine die off. That, in turn, determines the type of animals found in the forest (Chapter 26). This situation is an example of how a cellular adaptation can influence an entire ecosystem.

Temperature also affects photosynthesis, but in a way different from light intensity. Study the graph in Figure 7.14 and explain the shape of the curve. Look carefully at each axis of the graph so you know what data points make the curve. Develop a hypothesis to explain the changes in the rate of photosynthesis as the temperature increases.

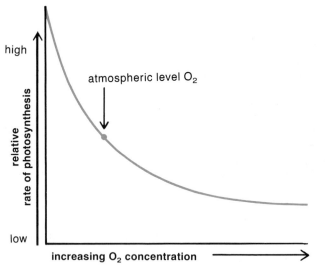

FIGURE 7.15 Increasing concentrations of oxygen inhibit the rate of photosynthesis in C_3 plants at atmospheric levels of carbon dioxide (0.035%).

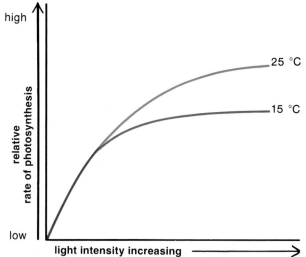

FIGURE 7.16 At high light intensity, the rate of photosynthesis is less at 15°C than at 25°C. Thus, temperature becomes a limiting factor as light intensity increases.

CONNECTIONS

The effects of environmental conditions on photosynthesis and the adaptations of plants that enable them to thrive in unfavorable conditions are examples of the interactions between organisms and the environment and between natural selection and evolution.

The concentrations of carbon dioxide and oxygen around a plant influence the rate of photosynthesis, but in opposite ways. An increase of carbon dioxide concentration increases the rate of photosynthesis to a maximum point, after which the rate levels off. A curve showing the effect of increasing carbon dioxide levels on photosynthesis would be very similar in shape to one for light intensity in Figure 7.13. Figure 7.15 shows the effect of oxygen on photosynthesis by a C_3 plant. Normal atmospheric concentrations of oxygen (about 20 percent) may inhibit photosynthesis by as much as 40 percent in some plants.

Because these four environmental factors—temperature, light, carbon dioxide, and oxygen—interact, their combined effects must be considered. Any one of the factors may be at an optimum level when another is far below optimum. The overall effect is a lower rate of photosynthesis. This effect is the principle of **limiting factors**, illustrated in Figure 7.16. Note that in maximum light, a lowered temperature will cause a slower rate of photosynthesis. Thus, for example, rose plants cultivated in a greenhouse will not grow at the maximum rate, even in full sunlight, if the greenhouse is cold. In a forest, limiting factors include light, water, temperature, and nutrients. Cactus plants do not grow in forests because they require large amounts of light and small amounts of water, as well as the extremes of temperature common to deserts. In the oceans, the most important limiting factor may be light needed by the producers for photosynthesis. Depth (pressure) and temperature also are important. For example, in the vent communities, chemosynthetic organisms (producers) can live because the water temperature is warm enough, despite the depth (pressure) and lack of light for photosynthesis.

7.10 Photorespiration and Photosynthesis

The effect of oxygen on the rate of photosynthesis bears closer examination. Recall from Section 7.7 that the enzyme rubisco is needed to incorporate carbon dioxide into the Calvin cycle. The structure and activity of this enzyme explains how oxygen can inhibit the process. Rubisco can bind to either oxygen or carbon dioxide. When carbon dioxide binds to rubisco and combines with RuBP, two molecules of PGA form. The binding of oxygen to rubisco, on the other hand, produces one molecule of PGA and one molecule of the 2-carbon acid glycolate, as shown in Figure 7.17. Glycolate is transported out of the chloroplast and undergoes a series of reactions that lead to the release of carbon dioxide. This overall process is called **photorespiration** because it requires RuBP from the Calvin cycle, which can function only in the light, and because the pickup of oxygen and the subsequent release of carbon dioxide resembles cellular respiration (Chapter 8).

When rubisco binds oxygen in the chloroplast, no new carbon dioxide is fixed, and RuBP (containing previously fixed carbon dioxide) is converted to carbon dioxide. As a result, the overall rate of photosynthesis slows. Each chloroplast contains thousands of rubisco and RuBP molecules, so both photorespiration and photosynthesis occur simultaneously

FIGURE 7.17 Photorespiration is the light-dependent uptake of oxygen and release of carbon dioxide in plants. It occurs simultaneously with photosynthesis and results in the loss of previously fixed carbon dioxide. The enzyme rubisco, which can react with either carbon dioxide or oxygen, is involved in both processes.

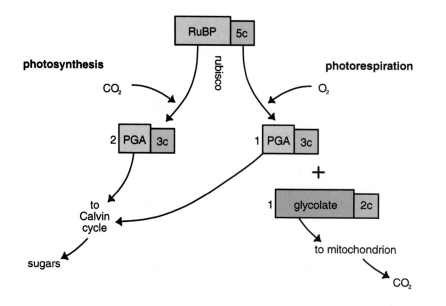

FIGURE 7.18 The relationship between the relative levels of carbon dioxide and oxygen and the relative rates of photosynthesis and photorespiration

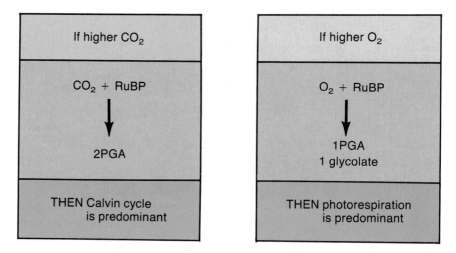

in a plant. Relatively high levels of carbon dioxide favor photosynthesis. Relatively high levels of oxygen favor photorespiration (Figure 7.18).

Photorespiration interferes with the successful performance of the Calvin cycle by preventing carbon dioxide fixation and removing RuBP. In fact, photorespiration is counterproductive to photosynthesis because it results in the release of previously fixed carbon dioxide, which otherwise would remain in organic form in the plant. Thus, photorespiration is considered an undesirable characteristic of plants, and any obvious advantage of the process remains unknown.

7.11 Special Adaptations

Hot, dry weather leads to high transpiration rates, causing many plants to lose valuable water through the stomates. Many plants avoid excessive water loss by keeping their stomates partially closed much of the time. When stomates are closed, however, carbon dioxide levels in the leaves may drop so low that photorespiration is favored over photosynthesis.

Some plants such as sugarcane, corn, and crabgrass have adapted to hot, dry environments and have evolved a specialization known as C_4

FOCUS ON *The Evolution of Photorespiration*

Why would such a questionable, even damaging, process as photorespiration have evolved in green plants? Metabolic processes tend to evolve to be just as good as they need to be, rather than to be perfect. Evolution favors workable systems that develop from already existing systems. Perfection, or even an optimum solution, is seldom achieved. Photosynthesis is an example of an adequate—but not optimum—process.

When the Calvin cycle evolved there was little oxygen in the air, and the binding of oxygen by rubisco was not a problem. After millions of years of photosynthesis, oxygen levels built up in the atmosphere and the binding of oxygen by rubisco became the photorespiration problem of today. Perhaps photorespiration is mere "evolutionary baggage," but its cost may be high because reduced plant growth reduces food production.

photosynthesis, so-called because carbon dioxide is first incorporated in a 4-carbon acid. C_4 plants have two systems of carbon dioxide fixation that involve specialized leaf anatomy. Surrounding each vein is a layer of tightly packed cells, the **bundle sheath** (Figure 7.19). Mesophyll cells, which are in contact with the air spaces in the leaf, surround the bundle sheath.

The two systems each involve a different enzyme pathway for carbon dioxide fixation. In the mesophyll cells, the first system fixes carbon dioxide by combining it with a 3-carbon acid. The resulting 4-carbon acid is rearranged and then transported to the bundle-sheath cells, as shown in Figure 7.20. The second system operates in the bundle-sheath cells where carbon dioxide is released from the 4-carbon acid and refixed by rubisco, forming PGA by way of the Calvin cycle (Section 7.7).

The system in the mesophyll cells provides an efficient pipeline that delivers carbon dioxide to the bundle-sheath cells. As a result, the concentration of carbon dioxide is higher in the bundle-sheath cells than in the atmosphere, a state that favors photosynthesis and inhibits photorespiration. Even at high temperatures, which increase the rate of photorespiration faster than the rate of photosynthesis, the high concentration of carbon dioxide around rubisco in C_4 plants overcomes photorespiration. Thus, C_4 plants can function at maximum efficiency in conditions of high temperature while keeping stomates closed to avoid excessive water loss.

By contrast, high temperatures may inhibit photosynthesis in C_3 plants by as much as 40 or 50 percent. In general, C_4 plants grow more rapidly than C_3 plants, especially in warm climates where C_4 plants evolve. Many C_4 plants can be about twice as efficient as C_3 plants in converting light

CONNECTIONS

C_4 photosynthesis is an adaptation in certain plants to a hot, dry environment. It is an example of evolution through natural selection.

FIGURE 7.19 Specialized leaf anatomy in a C_4 plant. Notice the tightly packed layers of cells—bundle sheath cells and mesophyll cells—that surround the vein.

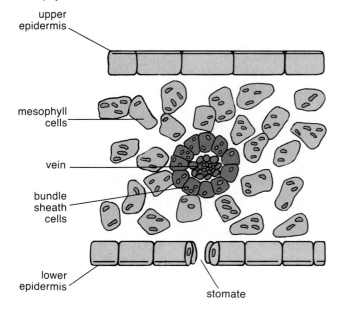

FIGURE 7.20 In C_4 photosynthesis, carbon dioxide is first fixed into a 4-carbon acid in the outside mesophyll cells. The 4-carbon acid is then transported inside to the bundle-sheath cells, where carbon dioxide is released to the Calvin cycle and refixed by rubisco.

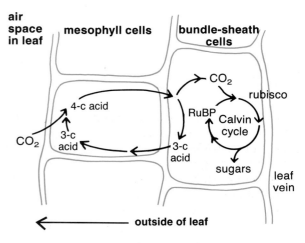

FOCUS ON *Biotechnology*

One goal of biotechnology is to produce more efficient food crops to feed the world. The production of C_3 crop plants in which oxygen does not inhibit rubisco is the subject of two areas of genetic engineering research. First, if we can discover the gene for the enzyme rubisco, we might be able to change the part of the enzyme inhibited by oxygen. If the genetically engineered enzyme would still fix carbon dioxide and initiate the Calvin cycle, then we might greatly enhance photosynthesis and crop productivity.

Second, plant physiologists would like to incorporate the genes for the C_4 system into C_3 plants. If we could genetically engineer critical C_3 crops, such as soybeans, wheat, and rice, to photosynthesize as C_4 plants, food production might be increased, especially in hot, dry regions of the world. These are not trivial challenges. The problems associated with altering photosynthesis via genetic engineering are enormous, even with the present-day technology to study and manipulate genes.

FIGURE 7.21 The jade plant *(Crassula)* is an example of a CAM plant.

energy to sugars. Most of our important food crops, such as soybeans, wheat, and rice, are C_3 plants. Photorespiration, by counteracting photosynthesis in C_3 plants, may be a major factor limiting plant growth and world food production today.

Another specialization for photosynthesis was first discovered in desert plants such as cactus, jade (Figure 7.21), and snake plants. Called **CAM**, for crassulacean (kras yoo LAY see un) acid metabolism, it is an important adaptation in arid-land ecosystems. CAM plants, in contrast to C_3 and C_4 plants, can open their stomates at night and incorporate carbon dioxide into organic acids in the cell vacuoles. During the day, with high temperature and low humidity, the stomates close, preventing transpiration that could kill the plant. The organic acids release carbon dioxide that diffuses to the chloroplasts and feeds a normal Calvin cycle powered by the light reactions of photosynthesis. The CAM system probably evolved in plants that grow in conditions of extreme heat and very little rain. CAM photosynthesis, however, is not very efficient, and although desert plants that use this system can survive intense heat, they usually grow very slowly.

7.12 The Largest Chemical Process on Earth

The greenhouse effect is a science-and-society issue. Science and technology can alleviate some of the problems, but there are many implications for society, such as rising sea levels and loss of species diversity.

How long has photosynthesis existed on Earth? Evidence of photosynthesis exists in rocks 3.5 billion years old (Section 4.7). Embedded in those rocks are fossil cells that resemble modern cyanobacteria and probably were the first photosynthetic organisms that produced oxygen. Today, aquatic and land plants carry out most photosynthesis, producing oxygen in enormous amounts. Each year plants use as much as 140 billion metric tons of carbon dioxide and 110 billion metric tons of water to produce more than 90 billion metric tons each of organic matter and oxygen gas.

Because photosynthesis is today the largest single biochemical process on Earth, any disruption of that process may have dramatic effects. The carbon dioxide content of the atmosphere recently reached the highest level recorded in history. The increase is due primarily to the release of large amounts of carbon dioxide from burning fossil fuels and the destruc-

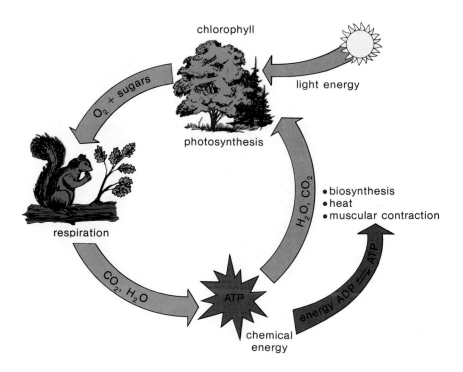

FIGURE 7.22 Summary of the energy relationships in the biosphere

tion of rain forest plants, which absorb CO_2 through photosynthesis. Many biologists think that if the carbon dioxide level continues to rise, the resulting greenhouse effect (see Focus On the Greenhouse Effect, Chapter 4) will heat up the Earth's climates. Although increased levels of carbon dioxide could increase Earth's photosynthesis, it may be vital to the future of life on Earth to preserve the balance of oxygen and carbon dioxide levels in the atmosphere.

Photosynthesis supplies oxygen gas to Earth's atmosphere and food to Earth's organisms. Most of the organisms use oxygen and give off carbon dioxide. Plants use the carbon dioxide again in photosynthesis, completing the cycle. Those relationships are shown in Figure 7.22.

CHECK AND CHALLENGE

1. State in general terms the influence of increasing light intensity on the rate of photosynthesis.

2. Why is metabolic activity most accurately expressed as a rate?

3. How does oxygen concentration affect the rate of photosynthesis?

4. Describe the process of photorespiration. What is its effect on the rate of photosynthesis?

5. Describe the location and function of the two systems of carbon dioxide fixation in C_4 plants.

6. Which enzyme in photosynthesis is inhibited by oxygen? Construct a graph that shows the effect of oxygen on C_3 and C_4 plant photosynthesis.

7. What is unique about CAM photosynthesis?

CHAPTER Highlights

Summary

Photosynthesis, the most abundant chemical process on Earth, transforms sunlight into the chemical energy that supports life on the planet. It also releases the oxygen that supports respiration by plants and animals.

The cellular processes of photosynthesis include the production of ATP and NADPH by the combined actions of photosystems I and II of the light reactions. NADPH and ATP are used to fix carbon dioxide into sugars during the Calvin, or C_3, cycle. Plants and animals use the sugars for energy and the manufacture of cellular components. In eukaryotes, photosynthesis occurs in, and depends on, the structure of the chloroplast.

The four environmental factors that directly influence the rate of photosynthesis in plants are light intensity, temperature, and the concentrations of carbon dioxide and oxygen. An increase of light intensity and carbon dioxide concentration tends to increase the rate of photosynthesis up to the point of saturation. After this, further increases do not stimulate the rate of photosynthesis. Increasing temperatures affect photosynthesis in the same way, except that high temperatures usually cause a decline in the rate of reactions. High concentrations of oxygen inhibit the rate of photosynthesis by fueling photorespiration. In nature, these four environmental factors do not act individually but are instead interdependent as limiting factors.

The evolution of specializations has enabled some plants to thrive in spite of limiting factors. C_4 plants have a system of carbon dioxide fixation that concentrates carbon dioxide at the Calvin cycle. As a result, C_4 plants photosynthesize more efficiently than C_3 plants in conditions that favor photorespiration. Thus, it appears the evolution of C_4 photosynthesis overcame the effects of photorespiration. In CAM plants, the stomates open at night and close during the day, greatly reducing transpiration. Both C_4 and CAM are effective adaptations to hot, dry climates.

Key Concepts

Use the concepts below to build a concept map, linking as many other concepts from the chapter as you can.

light reactions	rubisco
Calvin cycle	chloroplasts
photosynthesis	thylakoids
photorespiration	stroma
C_3	light energy
C_4	chemical energy

Reviewing Ideas

1. During photosynthesis: How is light energy conserved in ATP and NADPH? How are ATP and NADPH used to fix carbon dioxide into sugars? What happens to the sugars made during the Calvin cycle?

2. Several environmental factors influence the rate of photosynthesis. Why must they be considered together and not alone?

3. In what ways is photosynthesis important to humans?

4. What is the relationship between the light reactions and the carbon dioxide fixing reactions of photosynthesis?

5. How does the structure of the C_3 leaf support its function as the photosynthetic organ?

6. How does the special leaf anatomy of the C_4 plant support C_4 photosynthesis?

7. Describe how the structure of the chloroplast relates to its function in photosynthesis.

8. Does the Calvin cycle operate in the dark in C_3 plants? Explain.

9. Compare photosynthesis in C_3 and C_4 plants.

Using Concepts

1. C_4 and CAM mechanisms of photosynthesis have evolved in some plants. What are the selective advantages of each type of mechanism of photosynthesis?

2. Develop a concept map showing how the environment influences the rate of photosynthesis.

3. How does the rate of photosynthesis determine the rate of growth in a plant?

4. The curve in Figure 7.14 shows the effect of temperature increase on the rate of photosynthesis in a typical C_3 plant. Construct and explain a curve showing the response of a C_4 plant to the same increases in temperature.

5. Would you expect the light reactions to occur in mesophyll cells or bundle-sheath cells of C_4 plants? Why? What effect does this localization have on photorespiration?

6. Does the Calvin cycle operate at night in C_4 or CAM plants? Explain.

7. Atmospheric levels of carbon dioxide have increased from 300 ppm to almost 355 ppm in recent years. What will be the effect of this increase on photosynthesis and growth in C_3 plants? In C_4 plants?

Synthesis

Describe the theory that attempts to explain the evolution of eukaryotic chloroplasts.

Extension

You have three plants—one each of a C_3, a C_4, and a CAM type of plant. You also have a pH meter and a microscope. Describe how you could use only your pH meter and microscope (with other necessary supplies that go with each instrument) to identify each plant as C_3, C_4, or CAM.

CONTENTS

Respiration: Harvesting Chemical Energy

*A*ll organisms require energy to carry out their life functions. Nearly all autotrophs use sunlight to produce organic compounds that both they and heterotrophs use as energy sources. The trick is extracting usable energy when the need arises. Evolution has produced a number of biochemical processes that organisms use to obtain the energy stored in nutrients such as carbohydrates, fats, and proteins. The most efficient of those processes is cellular respiration. The respiration reactions in most organisms use atmospheric oxygen to release the maximum amount of energy from food molecules. This chapter discusses the decomposition reactions organisms use to convert the chemical energy stored in nutrients into free energy, which they use for cellular work.

*W*hat problem do birds, in particular, face in winter?

*W*hat mechanisms help them overcome this problem?

◆ *A gray jay*, Perisorius canadensis, *in winter.*

An Overview of Respiration

8.1 Metabolism and Respiration

Recall from Chapter 3 that metabolism includes all chemical reactions in an organism and is composed of two complementary parts. Synthesis consists of the biosynthetic reactions that require energy, and decomposition is the degradation reactions that release energy, some of which is free energy. Biosynthesis uses carbon skeletons and energy to form complex compounds, such as proteins and nucleic acids, for cell growth and maintenance. Decomposition reactions release energy from complex compounds (food) and produce the carbon skeletons used in biosynthesis. The energy harvested from food is used to make ATP, the major energy carrier for most metabolic activities within the cell. By converting the energy in complex compounds to smaller ATP molecules, the cell can maintain a ready supply of free energy in small usable packets. The cell can then use the energy in

FIGURE 8.1 Metabolism includes all decomposition and synthesis reactions in an organism. Respiration is part of decomposition.

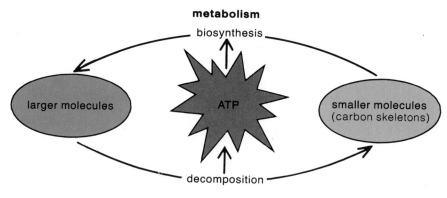

FIGURE 8.2 During respiration, the energy of glucose is transferred to ATP in a stepwise series of reactions. The letters (a) through (h) represent intermediate compounds between glucose and the products carbon dioxide and water.

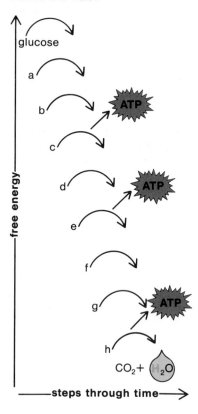

appropriate amounts when needed. Because ATP is made during decomposition and is used during biosynthesis, it links these two processes, as shown in Figure 8.1.

Cellular respiration is a stepwise series of reactions that release energy as they break down complex molecules to carbon dioxide and water. These reactions proceed in a controlled manner, catalyzed by an enzyme at every step. Some of the energy released in the reactions is conserved in ATP (Figure 8.2). In turn, ATP powers most of the cell's life processes by providing the necessary amount of energy. Respiration is the removal of electrons from food molecules and their transfer to carriers. These processes release energy that is used to synthesize ATP. In **aerobic** respiration—occurring in the presence of oxygen—the electrons flow to oxygen. In **anaerobic** respiration—occurring without oxygen—the electrons flow to another acceptor, such as nitrogen or sulphur in bacteria. The discussions in this chapter are limited, for the most part, to cellular respiration in eukaryotes.

The raw materials for aerobic respiration are carbohydrates, fats, and proteins. In animals, an important molecule in respiration is the monosaccharide glucose, $C_6H_{12}O_6$, which is produced by the digestion of carbohydrates or by the breakdown of glycogen in the liver or muscles. During cellular respiration, the energy stored in glucose can be released as the molecule gradually is broken down to six molecules of carbon dioxide. (Plants produce glucose from the breakdown of sucrose and starch.) The overall reaction may be summarized in the following equation:

$$C_6H_{12}O_6 + 6O_2 \xrightarrow{\text{enzymes}} 6CO_2 + 6H_2O + \text{energy}$$

glucose   oxygen   carbon   water
                     dioxide

Glucose contains much more energy than any one reaction needs, however, so glucose is not useful as a direct source of energy. An analogy might be the gas tank in your car. You could perhaps get to the store by dropping a match in the gas tank. The explosion might send some parts of you and the car to the store, but it would be rather inefficient (and foolish). A better way would be to start the engine and allow the carburetor to supply gasoline in small amounts to the engine, where controlled burning would transport you to the store in one piece. The same is true for cells. To

a   b

FIGURE 8.3 A waterfall releases all its energy at once (a). If it is run through several steps, turning turbines at each step, its energy is released in usable amounts (b).

release all the energy in glucose at once would be inefficient and impractical. Instead, the "carburetor"—cellular respiration—provides energy (ATP) to the cell in controlled reactions.

Compare the two waterfalls in Figure 8.3. In (a), the water falls the entire distance, releasing a large amount of energy that does no usable work. In (b), the energy of the falling water does the work of turning the turbines. Thus, the turbines are like the steps of respiration—they efficiently capture and transform energy along the waterfall.

In addition to ATP production, cellular respiration provides the carbon skeletons needed for biosynthesis. These two major functions of cellular respiration are summarized in Figure 8.4.

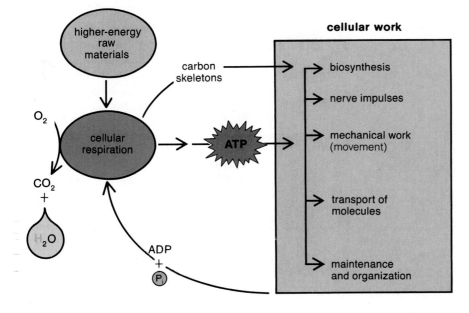

FIGURE 8.4 Respiration supplies carbon skeletons for biosynthesis and ATP for all cellular work.

8.2   The Stages of Aerobic Respiration

The steps involved in the respiration of a simple carbohydrate such as glucose can be divided into three main stages, as shown in Figure 8.5. Refer to the figure as you study each stage. Each stage involves a series of chemical reactions. The first stage is glycolysis (gly KAWL uh sis; *glyco* = sugar, *lysis* = splitting). During several steps, enzymes split glucose into two 3-carbon molecules, and a small amount of ATP forms.

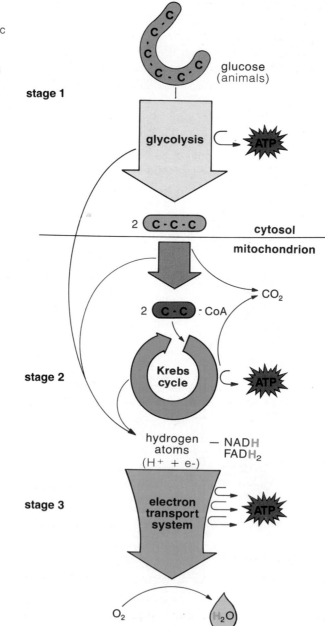

FIGURE 8.5 Aerobic respiration occurs in three stages. In eukaryotic cells, the Krebs cycle and the electron transport system occur in the mitochondria. Glycolysis occurs in the cytosol.

The 3-carbon products of glycolysis enter mitochondria, where enzymes release a molecule of CO_2 from each. The resulting 2-carbon molecules are broken down in the second stage, called the **Krebs cycle**. Additional ATP is formed and more CO_2 is released. Many of the reactions in glycolysis and the Krebs cycle release hydrogen atoms. Special molecules carry the hydrogen atoms to the third stage of respiration, the **electron transport system**, in which most of the ATP is synthesized. In that system, each hydrogen atom is separated into an electron and a proton (H^+). The electrons release energy as they are transferred through many small steps to oxygen, finally forming water.

Because oxygen must accept the electrons at the end of the electron transport system, stages two and three cannot proceed unless oxygen is present. For this reason, cellular respiration often is called aerobic respiration. The term *respiration* commonly refers to breathing—the process of gas exchange (Chapter 21) that supplies cells with oxygen for cellular respiration.

The hydrogen atoms released from reactions in stages one and two combine with **NAD$^+$**—nicotinamide adenine dinucleotide (nik uh TEE nuh myd AD uh neen dy NOO klee oh tyd)—and form the special hydrogen-carrier molecule **NADH**:

$$NAD^+ + 2H \text{ (as } 2e^- + 2H^+) \rightarrow NADH + H^+$$

Recall that in photosynthesis, the hydrogen-carrier molecule is NADPH. NADH and NADPH are structurally identical except for the extra phosphate group in NADPH. NADPH transports hydrogens *from* the light reactions to a biosynthetic cycle (the Calvin cycle); NADH transports hydrogens from a decomposition cycle (the Krebs cycle) *to* an electron transport system.

In one step in the Krebs cycle, a second hydrogen-carrier molecule, **FADH$_2$** (flavin adenine dinucleotide), forms when two hydrogen atoms combine with a molecule of **FAD**:

$$FAD + 2H \rightarrow FADH_2$$

Thus, NADH, NADPH, and $FADH_2$ all serve as hydrogen carriers in cells. Hydrogen carried by NADH and $FADH_2$ is used to synthesize ATP in the electron transport system.

CONNECTIONS

*T*he similarity of these reactions throughout all kingdoms is an example of the unity of pattern in the diversity of living things.

CHECK AND CHALLENGE

1. How are carbon skeletons involved in biosynthesis and degradation reactions?
2. What is the advantage of the stepwise nature of the reactions of cellular respiration?
3. Why is glucose not a direct source of cellular energy?
4. How is harnessing the energy of a waterfall similar to the steps of respiration?
5. Distinguish between respiration and cellular respiration.
6. Distinguish among the three hydrogen carriers and their functions.

FOCUS ON *Respiration in Prokaryotes*

In eukaryotic cells, glycolysis occurs in the cytosol, while the Krebs cycle and the electron transport system are in the mitochondria. Lactate or alcohol fermentation occurs in the cytosol. What about prokaryotes, which lack membrane-enclosed organelles?

In bacteria, plasma membranes contain the enzymes of the electron transport system. Electrons are transported through the system to oxygen in a process similar to that described for eukaryotes. In some bacteria, electrons flow through the system to substances other than oxygen, such as sulfate (SO_4^{2-}) or nitrate (NO_3^-). That process is called anaerobic respiration. The enzymes of glycolysis and the Krebs cycle are suspended in the cytosol of prokaryotes. Fermentation, which does not involve electron transport, also occurs in the cytosol.

The Reactions of Respiration

8.3 Glycolysis

Glucose is the primary raw material for glycolysis in animal cells, as Figure 8.6 illustrates. Four important things happen during these reactions—the carbon chain of glucose breaks into two pieces, some ATP forms, carbon skeletons form, and hydrogen atoms from glucose become available for use in the electron transport system.

FIGURE 8.6 In glycolysis, glucose breaks down in small steps to two 3-carbon molecules of pyruvate. Many of the steps involve rearrangements of carbon skeletons. ATP and NADH form in these reactions. In plant cells, sugars from photosynthesis can enter glycolysis at (a) or (c).

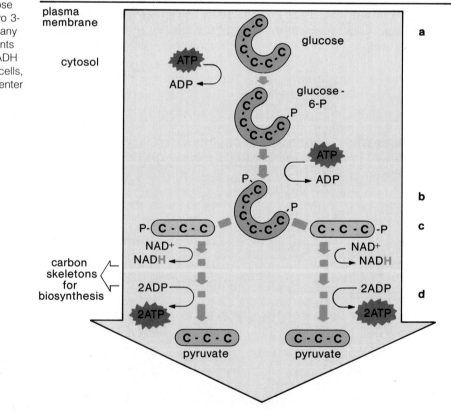

Glycolysis begins when a molecule of glucose enters a cell, and an enzyme quickly converts it to glucose-6-phosphate (Figure 8.6a). A molecule of ATP provides the phosphate and the energy to power the reaction. Another enzyme rearranges the glucose-6-phosphate and a second ATP molecule donates a phosphate group (b). The resulting molecule splits into two 3-carbon phosphates (c), which undergo a series of rearrangements, each catalyzed by a specific enzyme. The result is the formation of four molecules of ATP, two molecules of NADH, and two molecules of the 3-carbon organic acid **pyruvate** (d). Recall that two molecules of ATP were needed to begin glycolysis. Thus, for each molecule of glucose, the net gain from glycolysis is two molecules of ATP. Table 8.1 summarizes the products of glycolysis.

In plant cells, starch and sucrose break down to glucose, which can enter glycolysis in leaf cells directly at (c) in Figure 8.6. In addition to these decomposition reactions, several sugars and organic acids formed during glycolysis can leave the pathway and serve as carbon skeletons for the biosynthesis of macromolecules such as proteins and lipids. Thus, the biological roles of glycolysis are the synthesis of ATP, NADH, and pyruvate, and the formation of carbon skeletons.

At the end of glycolysis, the presence or absence of oxygen in the cell ultimately dictates the fate of pyruvate. Figure 8.7 shows that pyruvate may follow one of two pathways. First, if insufficient oxygen is present, animals cells can convert NADH and pyruvate into NAD^+ and **lactate**, another 3-carbon acid. NAD^+ cycles back to glycolysis, and the pathway continues to provide a small amount of ATP until more oxygen becomes available again in the cell. This anaerobic pathway is known as **lactic acid fermentation**. Evolution has produced many other types of fermentations. For example, yeast and bacteria ferment pyruvate to ethanol and acetic acid (vinegar) respectively.

TABLE 8.1 Products of Glycolysis, per Molecule of Glucose	
Substance	**Molecules Formed**
Pyruvate	2
NADH	2
ATP (net)	2

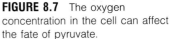

FIGURE 8.7 The oxygen concentration in the cell can affect the fate of pyruvate.

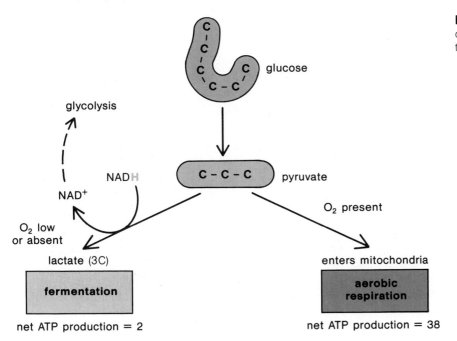

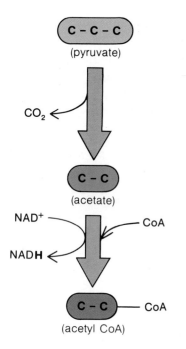

FIGURE 8.8 The conversion of pyruvate to acetyl CoA in a mitochondrion. This step prepares the pyruvate formed during glycolysis for entrance into the Krebs cycle.

If sufficient oxygen is present, however, pyruvate is transported to a mitochondrion. Here a complex enzyme system converts the pyruvate into acetate, a 2-carbon organic acid, plus carbon dioxide. This step also produces a molecule of NADH from NAD^+ (Figure 8.8). A carrier molecule, **coenzyme A** (CoA), picks up the acetate and forms acetyl CoA. Coenzyme A delivers acetate to the Krebs cycle, where respiration continues in stages two and three. Note that glycolysis is the first stage in fermentation as well as in respiration.

8.4 Mitochondria and Respiration

A complex metabolic process such as respiration cannot proceed in a haphazard way. How are the many enzymes and chemical reactions organized and kept apart to prevent interference during respiration? The answer is in the evolution of organelles, the specialized structural compartments that provide efficiency and organization within the eukaryotic cell. Mitochondria (Figure 8.9) are the compartments in which the Krebs cycle and the electron transport system occur. Recall from Chapter 6 that mitochondria are called the powerhouses of the cell because they are the site where most of the cell's ATP is synthesized.

Some cells may have only 10 to 20 mitochondria. Others, such as muscle cells, may have several thousand. A cell's functions and energy requirements directly affect the number of mitochondria present. Each mitochondrion is very small, usually only two or three micrometers (μm) in length and about one micrometer in thickness. When properly stained, larger mitochondria are visible under a compound microscope, but only the electron microscope reveals the detailed structure seen in Figure 8.9a.

A mitochondrion has both an outer and an inner membrane (Figure 8.9b). The two mitochondrial membranes contain lipid and protein molecules organized in a way similar to the fluid-mosaic structure of the plasma membrane discussed in Chapter 6. The inner mitochondrial membrane, however, contains so many enzymes that it is more protein than lipid. The inner membrane forms many projections, or cristae, that extend into the

FIGURE 8.9 (a) Electron micrograph of a mitochondrion in a bat pancreas. (b) A three-dimensional drawing of the mitochondrion shown in (a).

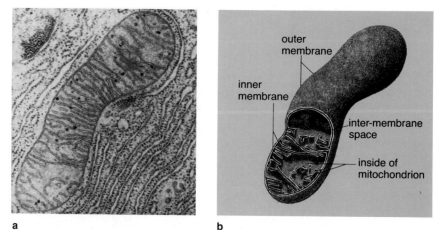

a

b

inside of the mitochondrion. Organized in and on the cristae are all the enzymes of the electron transport system, the enzymes for ATP formation, and some of the enzymes of the Krebs cycle. Most of the enzymes of the Krebs cycle are within the mitochondrion's interior space, or matrix. The outer membrane regulates the movement of molecules into and out of the mitochondrion.

8.5 The Krebs Cycle

Within a single mitochondrion, numerous copies of each enzyme act in harmony to catalyze the steps of the Krebs cycle, which involve the formation and rearrangements of organic acids. Follow Figure 8.10 as you read.

To begin the cycle, at (a), an enzyme combines the acetyl group of acetyl CoA with a 4-carbon acid (oxaloacetate), forming a 6-carbon acid (citrate), and releasing CoA. In several steps (b), other enzymes rearrange the 6-carbon acid and convert it into a 5-carbon acid (ketoglutarate). These reactions release a molecule of carbon dioxide and harvest electrons to form a molecule of NADH from NAD^+. In the next reaction (c), an enzyme

Try Investigation 8B, Rates of Respiration.

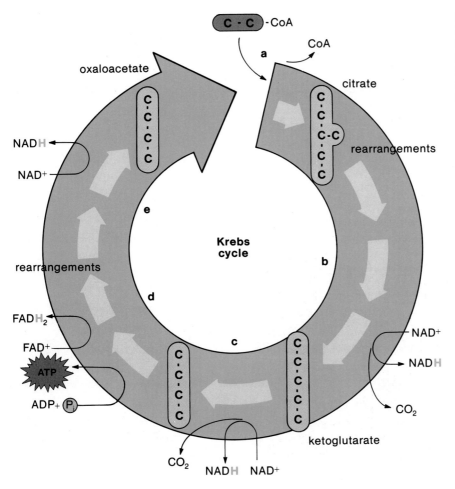

FIGURE 8.10 The reactions of the Krebs cycle complete the breakdown of glucose to carbon dioxide. In addition, ATP, NADH, and $FADH_2$ form in these reactions. Two molecules of acetate enter the Krebs cycle for each molecule of glucose.

FOCUS ON *Fermentation*

Wine makers have long known that the fermentation that produces wine is caused by living yeast. The special feature of fermentation is that it releases energy from sugars without using oxygen. In yeast cells, fermentation of glucose produces ethanol (ethyl alcohol) and carbon dioxide (Figure A). Note that each glucose molecule uses two ATP molecules to start fermentation, and produces four ATP molecules during fermentation (two for each 3-carbon compound). Thus, for each glucose molecule, there is a net gain of two ATP molecules. In addition, two molecules of ethanol (ethyl alcohol) and two molecules of carbon dioxide are produced.

Certain bacteria also can carry out fermentation. In the 1850s, the French wine industry was troubled by spoiled wine. Louis Pasteur discovered that bacteria contaminating the wine were fermenting it. Fermentation by bacteria spoils wine because it produces vinegar (acetic acid) instead of the ethyl alcohol produced by yeast.

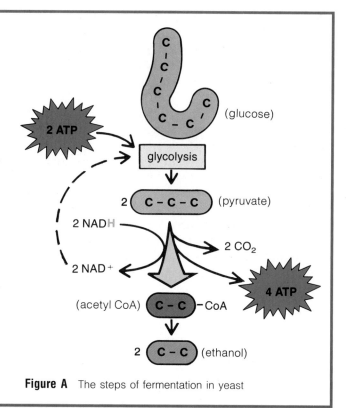

Figure A   The steps of fermentation in yeast

converts the 5-carbon acid into a 4-carbon acid, releases a molecule of carbon dioxide, and forms a second molecule of NADH.

In the reactions at (d), enzymes rearrange the 4-carbon acid two times, forming one molecule each of ATP (from ADP plus P_i) and $FADH_2$ (from FAD). In the final reactions, enzymes convert the rearranged 4-carbon acid into oxaloacetate and form a third molecule of NADH (e). The cycle continues as oxaloacetate enters step (a).

Steps (a) through (e) represent one turn of the Krebs cycle, and result in the products shown in Table 8.2. Because each molecule of glucose produces two molecules of pyruvate in glycolysis, the products shown for

TABLE 8.2
Products of the Krebs Cycle

Reaction	CO_2	NADH	$FADH_2$	ATP
Pyruvate to Acetyl CoA	1	1	0	0
Krebs Cycle	2	3	1	1
Total	3	4	1	1
X2 (1 glucose → 2 pyruvate)	6	8	2	2

the Krebs cycle must be doubled. The complete aerobic respiration of a molecule of glucose to six molecules of carbon dioxide can produce up to 38 molecules of ATP. (See **Appendix 8A**, ATP Synthesis in Animal Cells.) Stage three of respiration, the electron transport system, requires oxygen to produce most of that ATP.

8.6   The Electron Transport System

Glycolysis and the reactions in the mitochondria release hydrogen atoms, which are carried by NADH and $FADH_2$ to the electron transport system. Each electron transport system consists of a series of electron carriers—enzymes and other proteins known as cytochromes—embedded in the cristae membranes of mitochondria. (See Figure 8.11.) Hydrogen atoms are accepted by the system and separated into electrons and protons. The electron carriers transfer the electrons step by step through the system to a terminal cytochrome. The cytochrome combines the electrons with protons and molecular oxygen, forming water. Only this final step of respiration uses oxygen.

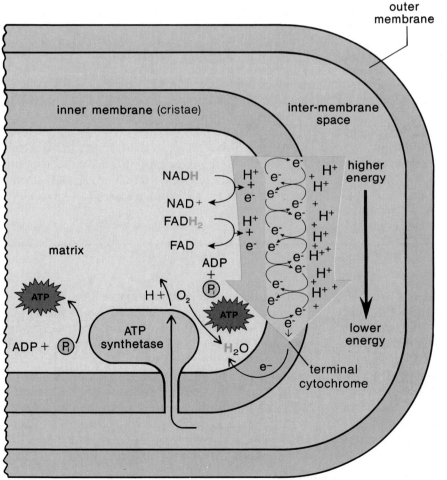

FIGURE 8.11   The electron transport system consists of a series of proteins and enzymes in the cristae membrane through which electrons are transferred. Energy released from electron flow is used to generate a high concentration of protons in the intermembrane space. As protons move down their concentration gradient, they pass through an enzyme complex in the membrane that synthesizes ATP. Most of the cell's ATP is generated in this manner.

At each step the electrons release free energy. Some of the free energy is used by proton pumps to actively transport protons from the matrix across the cristae to the intermembrane space (Figure 8.11). As a result, a relatively high concentration of protons accumulates there. Such an unequal distribution of protons is unstable, and the protons tend to diffuse back to the matrix of the mitochondrion. As the protons move across the membrane and down their concentration gradient, they pass through the ATP synthetase enzyme complex, where ATP is synthesized from ADP + P_i. (See **Appendix 7B**, ATP Synthesis in Chloroplasts and Mitochondria.) Calculations show that electrons from each molecule of NADH can drive the synthesis of up to three molecules of ATP. Each molecule of $FADH_2$ can drive the synthesis of up to two molecules of ATP.

To summarize, the movement of electrons along the transport system provides energy to form a high concentration of protons. The proton concentration gradient, in turn, supplies energy for the synthesis of ATP. Thus, the role of the electron transport system is to synthesize ATP. The ATP can then be transferred out of the mitochondrion and used by the cell. Figure 8.12 is a summary of the entire process of aerobic respiration leading to the synthesis of ATP. Table 8.3 (page 194) shows the number of ATP molecules synthesized from the complete respiration of one molecule of glucose.

8.7 Oxygen, Respiration, and Photosynthesis

With all the importance placed on oxygen in this and previous chapters, does it seem surprising that oxygen becomes involved in only the last single reaction of all the steps of respiration? Keep in mind that oxygen must be present to accept the electrons and protons of hydrogen at the end of the electron transport system. If oxygen is not delivered to the cell, the electron transport system and the Krebs cycle cannot function, and pyruvate begins to accumulate. For animal cells in that situation, lactate quickly forms, and only the two molecules of ATP from glycolysis are available.

FOCUS ON *Aerobics*

What happens in your muscles during exercise in an aerobics class? If you exercise at a moderate pace, the oxygen supply to muscles meets the demand. Such aerobic exercise increases the efficiency of oxygen transport to muscle cells. Aerobic exercise is apparently more beneficial to the heart and general physical fitness than anaerobic exercise.

Most people can exercise at such a fast pace that muscle cells require more oxygen than the blood can deliver, resulting in an "oxygen debt."

When oxygen levels drop, muscle cells begin to form lactate, which causes pain.

The formation of lactate is not an "all-or-none" situation. Muscles may begin to form lactate when oxygen levels become low. Thus, even mild exercise can result in lactate formation and pain. When oxygen becomes available, lactate is transported from the muscle to the liver and converted back to glucose, replenishing supplies. Soreness *after* exercise is more often due to slight tears in the muscle fibers than to lactate accumulation.

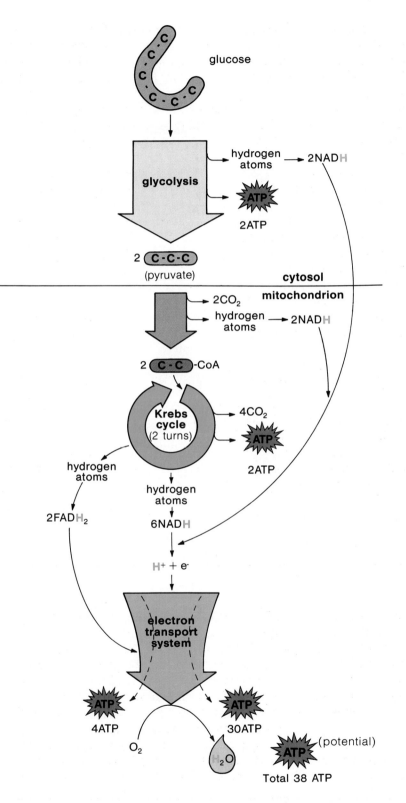

FIGURE 8.12 The release of hydrogen atoms in respiration yields energy for the cell. Hydrogen carriers transfer the hydrogen atoms to the electron transport system. ATP forms as electrons and protons flow through the system. Each molecule of NADH generates three ATP molecules, and each molecule of $FADH_2$ generates two ATP molecules in the transport system.

TABLE 8.3
ATP Synthesis in the Aerobic Respiration of a Molecule of Glucose

Process	Number of Hydrogen Carriers	Direct	ATP Molecules Formed from Hydrogen Carriers in (ETS*)	Potential Total ATP Molecules
Glycolysis	2 NADH	2 ATP**	6 ATP	8 ATP
Pyruvate to acetyl CoA	2 NADH	0	6 ATP	6 ATP
Krebs cycle	6 NADH 2 FADH$_2$	2 ATP	18 ATP 4 ATP	24 ATP

Total per glucose 38 ATP***

*ETS = electron transport system
**Four ATP molecules form, but two are consumed for a net of two ATP molecules.
***See Appendix 8B for an explanation of exceptions to this number of total ATP molecules.

With oxygen present, animals gain all the energy possible from food. In fact, humans and other animals have specialized organs and systems, such as lungs and circulation (Chapters 19, 21), that ensure efficient energy release from food by delivering oxygen to that last step in the electron transport system.

The atmospheric oxygen on which most life today depends is itself a product of life; almost all autotrophs release oxygen to the air during photosynthesis. In general, the products of photosynthesis serve as the raw materials for cellular respiration, and cellular respiration, in turn, provides the raw materials for photosynthesis. Thus, the two processes complement each other. In addition, both processses utilize electron transport systems to form ATP, although the energy sources differ. The Krebs cycle and the Calvin cycle are similar; both involve rearrangements of carbon compounds, and provide carbon skeletons for use in biosynthesis reactions. The Krebs cycle, however, forms ATP, NADH, and FADH$_2$, whereas the Calvin cycle uses ATP and NADH.

CHECK AND CHALLENGE

1. What are the products of each stage of respiration?

2. How does the presence or absence of oxygen determine the fate of pyruvate in cells?

3. Why are the membranes of mitochondria rich in proteins compared to lipids?

4. How many molecules of carbon dioxide result from the breakdown of one molecule of glucose in aerobic respiration?

5. How is oxygen involved in respiration?

6. How many times more ATP does aerobic respiration produce than does fermentation?

Biological Challenges

CREATINE PHOSPHATE, ATP, AND SWIMMING

How can a swimmer supply sufficient ATP in muscle cells to win a 100-meter race? Years ago it was discovered that muscle cells contain little ATP but are packed with a molecule called creatine phosphate. Scientists wondered why so much creatine phosphate and so little ATP were stored in muscles.

It turns out that ATP does not store well or last very long. It is like cash in the pocket that is easily spent. ATP is used quickly by many cell reactions.

Creatine phosphate can be used to make ATP by a simple transfer of phosphate:

$$\text{creatine-}\textcircled{P} + \text{ADP} \underset{\text{enzyme}}{\overset{\text{enzyme}}{\rightleftharpoons}} \text{ATP} + \text{creatine}$$

ATP can be made from creatine phosphate and ADP much more quickly than from respiration. Creatine phosphate is used to make the ATP that powers rapid muscle contractions, reducing the dependence on respiration. It is difficult for a swimmer's blood to supply enough oxygen to the muscle cells for aerobic respiration. Oxygen supply cannot keep up with demand, an oxygen debt develops, lactate begins to form in the muscles, and pain and fatigue result.

When a swimmer dives into the water, creatine phosphate in muscle cells provides a quick way to supply some ATP in the absence of oxygen and to avoid lactate accumulation. But after 30 or 40 meters of fast swimming, lactate begins to build up in muscle cells. By the time the swimmer nears the finish line, there is pain from lactate formation and a feeling of fatigue. Rapid breathing restores oxygen supplies. Lactate diffuses out of the muscles and is carried by the blood to the liver, where liver cells convert lactate to glucose (a process that may require several hours). The glucose is transported to the muscle cells, where it undergoes respiration, resulting in the synthesis of ATP from ADP and P_i. This ATP is used to regenerate the stores of creatine phosphate, and the swimmer is ready for another race.

Figure B Fast swimming is made possible by conversion of creatine phosphate to ATP.

Respiration and Cellular Activities

8.8 The Krebs Cycle in Fat and Protein Metabolism

Biologists originally thought the Krebs cycle explained only the breakdown of carbohydrates in respiration. More recent research has shown that the breakdown and liberation of energy from fats and proteins also involves the Krebs cycle. When cells use the fatty acids of fats for energy, the fatty acids break down to acetyl CoA in the mitochondria. The acetyl portion of acetyl CoA then enters the Krebs cycle and undergoes the reactions described in Section 8.5. Oxygen is necessary to convert the energy in fat into ATP, however. Without oxygen, ATP cannot be synthesized from the NADH and $FADH_2$ produced in the Krebs cycle. Thus, without oxygen, most of the energy in fat (triglycerides) cannot be transferred to ATP.

When cells use proteins in respiration, the digestive system first breaks down the proteins to amino acids. Enzymes in the liver remove the amino groups and convert them into the excretory product urea. The kidneys release urea in urine. The carbon skeletons remaining from some of the amino acids can undergo reactions that form 4- or 5-carbon acids (oxaloacetate or ketoglutarate), which can enter the Krebs cycle. Figure 8.13 summarizes the pathways of carbohydrate, fat, and protein decomposition that supply carbon skeletons used in the Krebs cycle.

The Krebs cycle is a dual-function metabolic system. In addition to serving in the decomposition of carbohydrates, fats, and proteins, the cycle, along with glycolysis, also provides the building blocks for many complex biosynthetic pathways (Figure 8.13). In plants, these pathways, along with

FOCUS ON *The Krebs Cycle*

In the eukaryotic cell, mitochondria and the Krebs cycle are at the center of almost all the chemical reactions of metabolism. The Krebs cycle is like the central interchange of a very elaborate interstate highway system located in the middle of a busy city. Each interstate is a one-way highway that leads to distant points, but connects to most other interstate highways through the central interchange. Traffic leaves the central interchange on a highway going to the destination point. From there, traffic can return to the central interchange via a different highway. Return traffic may travel to a new destination by passing through the interchange and taking the appropriate interstate highway out again. In this analogy, the interstate highways are the metabolic pathways, the traffic is the carbon skeletons, the destination points are the final products of the pathways, the large city is the mitochondrion, and the central interchange is the Krebs cycle. If you can imagine a state with several busy cities, each with several interchanges, you can picture a cell (the state) with several mitochondria (cities) containing multiple Krebs cycles (the interchanges).

Like many interstate systems, the cells' pathways have some roadblocks. For example, the interstate highway from carbohydrate to fat is open, and excess sugar and starch in the diet are converted into fat. In mammals, however, the reverse highway is closed; fat cannot be converted into carbohydrate.

those stemming from photosynthesis, lead to the synthesis of all the organic compounds and macromolecules needed for growth and development of the organism. In animals, these pathways lead to the synthesis of most, but not all, of the necessary organic compounds. Animals must include in their diet the organic compounds they cannot synthesize, such as vitamins, certain amino acids, and certain fatty acids (Chapter 18).

It is important to note that synthesis pathways usually are *not* the reverse of decomposition pathways. For reasons of cellular and enzymatic control and organizational efficiency, synthesis and decomposition systems do not share a common two-way path.

FIGURE 8.13   The reactions of cellular respiration and particularly of the Krebs cycle, serve both in decomposition and biosynthesis of carbohydrates, fats, and proteins. Certain amino acids can be synthesized from the carbon skeletons by adding amino groups (—NH$_2$). Carbon skeletons can be formed from amino acids by removing the amino groups. Fat cannot normally be converted to glucose.

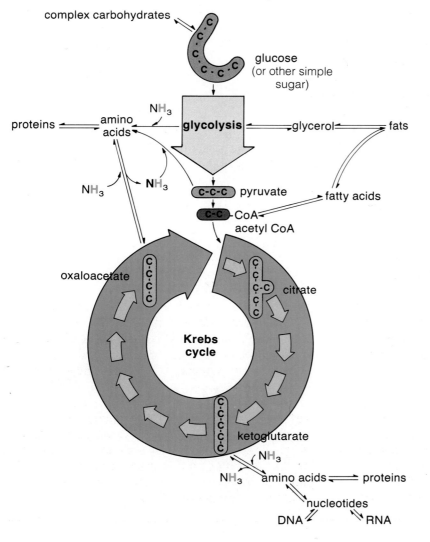

8.9   Respiration and Heat Production

Cellular respiration in animals releases heat, which is important to many organisms in keeping warm. Heat-regulating mechanisms in humans and many other animals keep the body's internal temperature constant within narrow limits. Your own body temperature, for example, stays the same within one or two degrees. It may go up a few degrees when you are ill, but it drops back to normal when you are well.

Mammals born relatively hairless, such as humans, and many hibernating mammals have a tissue called brown fat. Brown fat contains more mitochondria than any other body tissue and is designed for rapid heat production. Respiration of stored fat in brown-fat cells releases most of the energy as heat and produces little ATP. The brown fat, located on the neck and between the shoulders, is especially active at the end of hibernation when the animal must quickly raise its body temperature to normal levels (Figure 8.14a). Why would brown fat be important for human infants?

Respiration in plants also releases heat, and many plants have evolved an alternate pathway of respiration that produces more heat than ATP. The mitochondria of such plants contain an alternate branch of the electron transport system. In this pathway some of the energy of electron flow results in the production of heat and less ATP than in normal respiration. In one group of plants, the heat converts special organic compounds in the flower to gases with an odor of rotting meat. The odor attracts certain flies and beetles. When they land on the flower, pollen sticks to their bodies. As the insects fly from plant to plant, they transfer the pollen to other flowers of the same species. (This process is pollination, discussed in Chapter 11.)

One plant showing the alternate pathway of respiration is aptly named skunk cabbage (Figure 8.14b). In addition to converting organic compounds to odorous gases, the heat from alternate respiration melts snow

CONNECTIONS

These specializations are examples of adaptations that increased survival of the species.

FIGURE 8.14   (a) The arctic ground squirrel, *Citellus undulatus*, spends its summer on the Arctic tundra. In the winter it hibernates in its nest. Brown fat enables the ground squirrel to quickly elevate its body temperature at the end of hibernation. (b) Skunk cabbage, *Symplocarpus foetens*, emerging through snow.

a

b

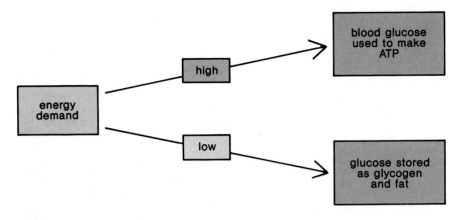

FIGURE 8.15 Supply and demand regulate how glucose and fatty acids are used.

cover over the skunk cabbage. The part of the stem bearing the flower grows through the hole in the snow, allowing pollination to occur while snow still covers the ground.

8.10   Control of Respiration

Cells must control their rate of respiration in order to direct molecules accurately to the pathways and organelles that require energy and chemical building blocks. Control is critical to organization, and cells must be organized to survive.

The mechanisms that control respiration and the fate of molecules—for example, whether glucose is broken down in respiration or used in the pathways of glycogen or fat synthesis—operate by supply and demand (Figure 8.15). If the demand for energy is high, cells use blood glucose to make ATP. If the demand for energy is high and the supply of blood glucose is low, cells break down glycogen to glucose in order to make ATP. On the other hand, if the demand for energy is low, cells do not use excess glucose. Rather, its energy is stored first as glycogen and then as fat. Based on the immediate needs of the cell, key steps in respiration are regulated to determine where molecules are directed.

CONNECTIONS

The control of respiration is an example of how cells regulate their activities to maintain a steady state.

CHECK AND CHALLENGE

1. Why is the Krebs cycle the central factor in metabolism?
2. Why is oxygen necessary for the respiration of fat?
3. Of what adaptive value is the alternate pathway of respiration in plants?
4. How do plants and animals utilize the heat produced in respiration?
5. Discuss the control of glucose flow and ATP production in cells.
6. Describe how fats and proteins are brought into the Krebs cycle. How are their products used by the cell?

Summary

Metabolism consists of all the synthesis and decomposition reactions in an organism. Cellular respiration is an important part of decomposition and involves stepwise reactions that convert carbohydrates, fats, or proteins into smaller molecules with a release of energy that is conserved as ATP. Cellular respiration also provides carbon skeletons for the biosynthesis of macromolecules the cell requires. Supply and demand in the cell determine the direction of flow of carbon to production of ATP, to biosynthesis for energy storage, or to heat.

Most eukaryotic cells carry out aerobic (oxygen-dependent) respiration in three controlled, sequential stages—glycolysis, the Krebs cycle, and the electron transport system. Glycolysis, which occurs in the cytosol, converts glucose and other sugars into pyruvate and produces a net gain of two molecules of ATP and two molecules of NADH. Glycolysis is the beginning stage of both aerobic respiration and fermentation. In fermentation, which occurs in the absence of oxygen, two products of glycolysis, pyruvate and NADH, are converted into lactate or alcohol and NAD^+. The NAD^+ is cycled back to glycolysis. Fermentation results in the net synthesis of only two molecules of ATP per glucose. In the presence of oxygen, aerobic respiration occurs, and pyruvate from glycolysis is transported into a mitochondrion. Enzymes convert the pyruvate into acetyl CoA, release carbon dioxide, and form NADH. The acetyl group enters the Krebs cycle, producing carbon dioxide, ATP, NADH, and $FADH_2$. Hydrogen atoms carried by NADH and $FADH_2$ are used to synthesize ATP as electrons and protons move through the electron transport system to oxygen and form water. The complete aerobic respiration of a molecule of glucose forms 6 molecules of carbon dioxide and a maximum of 38 molecules of ATP.

Key Concepts

Use the concepts below to build a concept map, linking as many other concepts from the chapter as you can.

glycolysis	aerobic respiration
Krebs cycle	energy
electron transport system	carbon skeletons
enzymes	biosynthesis
mitochondrion	ATP
fermentation	

Reviewing Ideas

1. How are membranes involved in respiration?
2. Explain the role of organelles in respiration.
3. What major requirement of organisms cannot be recycled? How is it renewed?

4. What are the biological functions of

    a. respiration?

    b. glycolysis?

    c. the Krebs cycle?

    d. the electron transport system?

5. Discuss the ways in which biosynthesis is dependent on cellular respiration.

6. Compare the functions of glycolysis and the Krebs cycle; of the Krebs cycle and the electron transport system.

Using Concepts

1. If most of the carbon skeletons needed for amino acid and protein synthesis come from the Krebs cycle, how is it possible that strict anaerobic bacteria can grow and survive?

2. Why would you not expect to find mitochondria in anaerobic organisms?

3. Propose a hypothesis to explain why animal cells evolved to produce lactate but not ethanol during fermentation.

4. Do plants contain mitochondria? Why or why not?

5. How is respiration dependent on photosynthesis in plants? in animals?

6. Some active cells at maturity contain no mitochondria. If these cells receive ample glucose, could they use it for energy? Would carbon dioxide be released from active cells? Could these cells use fat as a source of energy? Explain your answers.

7. Propose a hypothesis that explains why aerobic activity is more beneficial than anaerobic activity.

8. Glucose contains about 686 kcal of energy. A molecule of glucose generates a maximum of 38 molecules of ATP in eukaryotic cells. ATP contains about 7.3 kcal of energy. Calculate the efficiency of the ATP energy yield from the complete aerobic respiration of glucose. What happens to the rest of the energy?

9. In human cells, glucose cannot be made from fat. Propose a hypothesis that explains this situation.

Synthesis

1. What is the relationship between the Krebs cycle and the Calvin cycle?

2. The products of photosynthesis, 3-carbon sugar phosphates, enter glycolysis at point (c) of Figure 8.6. How many molecules of ATP can be made from the complete aerobic respiration of one of those sugar phosphates?

Extensions

1. Cyanide is a poisonous chemical that blocks the terminal enzyme of the electron transport system so that electrons do not flow to oxygen. Develop a hypothesis to explain why, as a result of this property, cyanide is lethal to humans.

2. Develop a game or a skit to explain the most important aspects of cellular respiration.

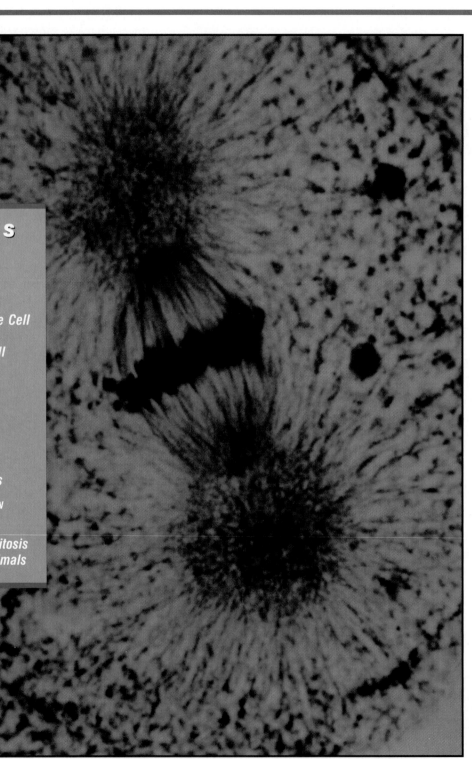

CONTENTS

The Cell Cycle

*T*he cell cycle is a model developed to help us describe and understand the continuous sequence of events in the life of a cell. In previous chapters you read about many of the cell processes that occur during the various phases of the cell cycle. Protein synthesis, which takes place in all phases of the cycle, is presented in detail in Chapter 10. This chapter focuses on the two most distinguishing events of the cell cycle: DNA synthesis and cell reproduction.

As the eukaryotic cell and its complex structures evolved over millions of years, cellular events, especially reproduction, became more complex. A method of cell division evolved that ensured that the chromosomes, with the genetic instructions, were duplicated and divided evenly as the cell reproduced. In eukaryotes, the cycle begins when a new cell forms and lasts until that cell reproduces itself by dividing into two new offspring cells. Each offspring cell then begins the cycle again. Researchers have not studied the cell cycle in prokaryotes as thoroughly.

*W*hat cellular process is illustrated here?

*W*hat phase is shown?

◆ *A whitefish cell magnified 400 times.*

The Life of a Cell

9.1   Cell Division in Eukaryotes

Cell division is a process that produces two cells from one cell. Depending on whether a eukaryotic organism is unicellular or multicellular, cell division has different functions. In unicellular organisms, cell division results in the production of new individuals, or reproduction. In multicellular organisms, cell division is required for growth, repair, and maintenance. For example, many plants grow as their stems and branches extend upward, their roots grow downward, and new leaves develop. All the tissues of a growing plant are made of cells produced through cell division, which takes place in specialized growth regions. Young animals grow as cell division produces new cells, including bone, muscle, skin, nerve, and

FOCUS ON *Cell Division in Prokaryotes*

In prokaryotes, survival of a species is best ensured by rapid growth and division. Usually the nutrient level in the environment is the limiting factor on such growth. Some bacterial cells that are grown in a nutrient-rich laboratory culture can divide as often as every 20 minutes.

The genetic information of prokaryotes is in a single circular chromosome of double-stranded DNA. Although bacteria are smaller and simpler than eukaryotic cells, the replication of their genetic material is still complex. Consider, for example, the chromosome of the bacterium *Escherichia coli.* When the chromosome is fully stretched out, it is about 500 times longer than the bacterium itself. How, then, is the genetic information accurately replicated and the copies equally distributed to the offspring cells?

In the bacteria, the chromosome is attached to a specific region of the plasma membrane and is replicated before cell division, as illustrated in Figure A. Each of the two replicas of the chromosome attaches to the plasma membrane. As division begins, the bacterial cell grows and elongates, moving the chromosomes apart. When the cell volume has approximately doubled, the membrane and cell wall pinch inward and two new cells form, each with an identical single chromosome as illustrated in Figure B. This relatively simple and rapid process of cell division in prokaryotes is known as binary fission.

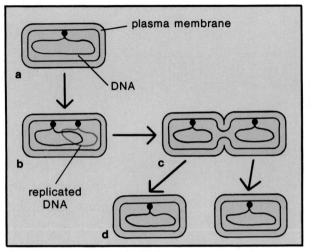

FIGURE A   In prokaryotic cell division, the replicated DNA attaches to the plasma membrane. The membrane grows and pinches inward, dividing the cell in two and separating the DNA into the offspring cells.

FIGURE B   Electron micrograph of a dividing bacterium, X 4500.

blood cells throughout the body. In addition, cell division continually replaces certain cells, such as blood and skin, as they wear out during the life of the animal. Wounded tissues heal as the new cells that are produced by division replace damaged ones.

The examples just described have one important feature of cell division in common. Before eukaryotic cells divide, exact copies of their chromosomes are made in the nucleus. During division, each new offspring cell receives both the same number and type of chromosomes as its parent cell contained. As a result of these events, new cells with complete sets of genetic instructions are produced.

9.2 The Phases of the Cell Cycle

The life of a eukaryotic cell consists of a continuous sequence of events called the cell cycle. You can see in Figure 9.1 that the cell cycle begins with the formation of a new cell and continues until that cell divides into two new offspring cells. Each offspring cell then begins the cycle again. However, as you will read in this chapter, the dramatic events of cell division are just a brief portion of the cell cycle. A cell spends most of its life between divisions in a stage known as **interphase**. During interphase a cell performs all its many normal metabolic activities and carries out the intricate preparations for cell division.

Interphase consists of three main phases—G_1, S, and G_2. Although the main sequence of the phases is fixed, the relative time spent in each phase varies greatly among the cells of different organisms and among different cells within each organism.

The G_1 (Growth 1) phase is the time of cell growth just following cell division. New offspring cells are metabolically active, especially synthesizing RNA and new proteins. In animals, the G_1 phase varies in length from a few hours to several days or more. Although reasons for this variability are not known, research indicates that certain hormones may influence the length of the G_1 phase. Figure 9.1 shows that cells may remain in an extended G_1 phase, often called G_0. Although such cells do not divide, they are usually quite active and serve important functions in the organism. For

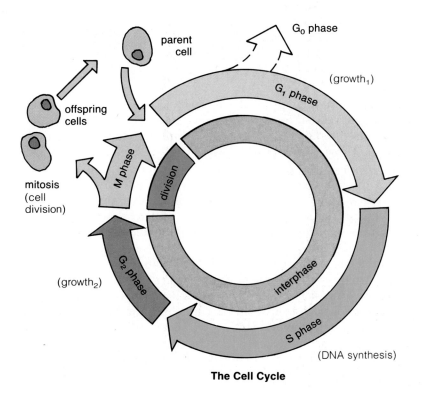

The Cell Cycle

FIGURE 9.1 The cell cycle includes cell division and interphase. Most of a cell's life is spent in interphase.

example, in animals, adult nerve cells remain in a G_0 phase. It is because of this characteristic that damage to nerve tissue, such as the brain or spinal chord, normally cannot be repaired. In plants, the cells that make up most of the roots, stems, leaves, and flowers remain in the G_0 phase. A complete cell cycle occurs only in specialized growth regions usually found at the tips of stems, branches, and roots, and underneath the bark. (For a full discussion of plant growth and development, see Chapter 15.)

In the S (synthesis) phase, an exact copy of the DNA, and therefore the genes, is made, doubling the DNA content of the nucleus. This exact copying, or **replication,** of the DNA ensures that a complete and identical set of genes is available for each new offspring cell following cell division. The length of the S phase does not vary greatly among most cells, usually lasting three to six hours. The S phase begins with the initiation of DNA synthesis and ends with its completion.

G_2 (Growth 2) is the phase of growth and metabolism occurring after the S phase. During this interval, protein, RNA, and other macromolecules are synthesized, but often in smaller amounts than in G_1. Because the DNA replicates in the S phase, a cell in G_2 has twice as much DNA in its nucleus as a cell in G_1. The duration of G_2 is usually short—two to five hours—and is relatively constant among cells.

The M phase (for mitosis) occurs after G_2 and is easily identified because it is the only phase in which the chromosomes are visible with a light microscope. **Mitosis** is nuclear division in which the replicated chromosomes separate to form two nuclei from one. In most cells, mitosis is quickly followed by cell division of the parent cell into two offspring cells—completing the M phase. After the M phase, each offspring cell enters G_1, and the cycle continues.

9.3   Control of the Cell Cycle

Recall that cells from different organisms divide at different rates and that cells within a multicellular organism also divide at different rates. As noted earlier, in animals, certain cells such as nerve, muscle, and red blood cells do not divide. These cells mature in G_1 and may remain in its branch phase, G_0. Other animal cells, such as those of the skin, bone marrow, and the lining of the intestine, divide rapidly and continuously as they pass through all phases of the cell cycle. Cell growth and division may occur as often as every eight hours. What factor(s) control the cell's passage through each phase of the cell cycle or determine whether or not the cell will divide?

When scientists studied rapidly dividing cells, they found that a "trigger" protein determines how quickly a cell matures and when it divides. Animal cells grown in the laboratory accumulate this protein during the G_1 phase. When sufficient trigger protein accumulates, the cell proceeds into the S phase. A variety of factors, such as hormones, cell size, and the cell's position within a tissue, influences the accumulation of the trigger protein and subsequent cell division. Each of these factors may be important in body processes such as healing and tissue replacement.

CONNECTIONS

Homeostasis—the maintenance of a stable internal environment—depends on regulatory mechanisms at the cellular and organismic levels. Control of the cell cycle is one of the most essential of these regulatory mechanisms.

FOCUS ON *Cancer*

On rare occasions, genetic controls over cell division are permanently altered. An affected cell repeatedly divides until its offspring forms a ball of cells, called a tumor, that continues to grow in size. As the tumor grows, it crowds surrounding normal cells and interferes with the functions of the tissue. (Compare Figures C and D.) If cancer cells leave the tumor and invade other tissue, they form additional tumors at distant locations in the body. The spreading cells are called metastases.

Early research on causes of cancer focused on environmental mutagens such as radiation and various chemicals. However, as early as 1910, an American researcher, Peyton Rous, showed that a virus RSV (Rous sarcoma virus) could cause cancer in chickens. Scientists knew that mutagens could cause cancer by altering a cell's controls over its own growth and division. How does a virus initiate cancer?

When researchers compared RSV with a closely related virus, RAY-O, which can not cause cancer, they found the viruses to be identical except for one gene, the *src* gene (for sarcoma) present in RSV. This and other results led to the hypothesis that a specific tumor-

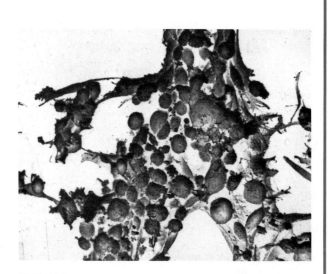

FIGURE D After infection by a virus carrying an oncogene, the cells become round and cluster together.

inducing gene, an *onc* gene, or oncogene (from the Greek word *oncos,* which means cancer), could transform healthy cells into cancerous ones; the *src* gene was one type of oncogene.

In 1977 researchers isolated the *src* protein. Their subsequent investigations showed that it is a type of enzyme that initiates cell division by binding to a specific site on the cell membrane. Scientists were surprised, however, when other experiments showed that the *src* gene was not a viral gene at all. Instead, *src* was found to be a normal growth promoting gene in chickens. Scientists concluded that an ancestral RSV virus had incorporated the normal growth promoting chicken gene into its viral genome. However, once part of the virus, the growth promoting gene was free of its normal cellular controls.

Researchers have now isolated more than 30 viral oncogenes. In each case, they have also discovered a nearly identical gene sequence in the normal DNA of the host—a sequence that codes for a protein used in normal cell activity. When the cell cycle and its control are more completely understood, researchers may find better ways to combat cancers.

FIGURE C Cells are normally flat and stretched out.

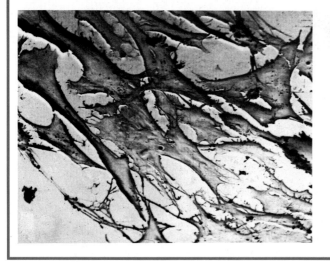

CHECK AND CHALLENGE

1. How does the role of cell division differ in unicellular and multicellular organisms?

2. What is the major event in each of the four phases of the cell cycle?

3. How does binary fission differ from mitotic cell division?

4. What are some factors that might control the cell cycle?

5. Why is DNA replication an essential step in cell division?

Try Investigation 9A, Bacteria, Pneumonia, and DNA.

FIGURE 9.2 A short section of a DNA molecule is shown as it would appear if uncoiled and flattened. Sugar-phosphate bonds connect the nucleotides along each strand. Hydrogen bonds between the nitrogen bases connect the two strands. Notice that the two strands have opposite orientations.

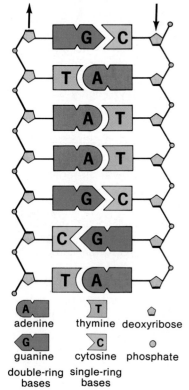

adenine   thymine deoxyribose

guanine   cytosine phosphate

double-ring single-ring
bases   bases

DNA Replication

9.4   DNA Structure

After the discovery of chromosomes, and of DNA as the genetic material, a major problem confronting biologists was to explain how the cell could copy the DNA molecule. It was known that during mitosis each offspring cell received the same type of DNA that the parent cell contained. Also, experiments such as those discussed in Investigation 9A showed that each new cell received instructions from the parent cell on how to function. Biologists found that those instructions were carried in the DNA molecules. From this connection, it was clear that the DNA molecules must be accurately replicated by the parent cell before division.

Refer to Sections 2.11 and 2.12 to review the structure of DNA. The process of replication depends on the molecular shapes of the nitrogen bases, which allow adenine (A) to pair only with thymine (T), and guanine (G) to pair only with cytosine (C). You can use Figure 2.28 to get an idea of how the nucleotides are arranged. Imagine that a small part of the DNA molecule is uncoiled and flattened. Using the symbols introduced in Figure 2.25 to represent the nucleotides, you would have a structure that looks like the one in Figure 9.2. Notice that in the strand on the left the nucleotides do not appear to be arranged in any particular order other than to pair correctly with those on the right. The nucleotides on a single strand can be in any sequence, and many arrangements are possible. Once the sequence of nucleotides on one strand is fixed, however, the sequence on the other strand is determined, because a thymine must pair with an adenine, and a cytosine with a guanine.

9.5   The S Phase

Replication of DNA during the S phase involves a series of events that requires a team of enzymes. First, some of the enzymes unwind a portion of a DNA molecule. Other enzymes break the hydrogen bonds between the paired nucleotides and separate the two strands. Other enzymes can now

Biological Challenges

PACKING THE DNA INTO CHROMOSOMES

The DNA in eukaryotic cells is packed into discrete bodies called chromosomes. Each chromosome may consist of a single DNA molecule containing as many as 10^8 (100 million), perhaps even 3×10^8 (300 million) base pairs. Stretched out, that DNA would be almost 10 cm long. (By comparison, 3×10^8 letters in this book would occupy 100 000 pages.) Nuclei of eukaryotic cells average 5 to 10 μm in diameter and may contain as many as 104 chromosomes. How can all that DNA fit in the nucleus?

The large amount of DNA is packed into the nucleus by means of structures known as nucleosomes. These fundamental packing units are composed of a complex of nuclear proteins around which the DNA is wound, much like the stitching on a baseball (Figure E). The nuclear proteins, called histones, are synthesized along with DNA during the S phase of the cell cycle. Within minutes of its synthesis, new DNA wraps around a histone complex to form a nucleosome. DNA, histones, and other proteins make up chromatin, the material biologists identified as chromosomes when they examined the nuclei of dividing cells through the microscope.

Eight molecules of histone—two each of four different types—combine to make up the nucleosome core, and the DNA strand makes two loops around the core. Nucleosomes are linked by short stretches of DNA bound to a fifth type of histone, giving the appearance of beads on a string. Long strings of nucleosomes then form coils and supercoils, much like those formed when you repeatedly twist a rubber band. Thus, nucleosomes provide a packing structure that enables a large amount of DNA to fit into a small space.

FIGURE E DNA molecules wrap around histones to form nucleosomes, the basic packing unit of chromosomes.

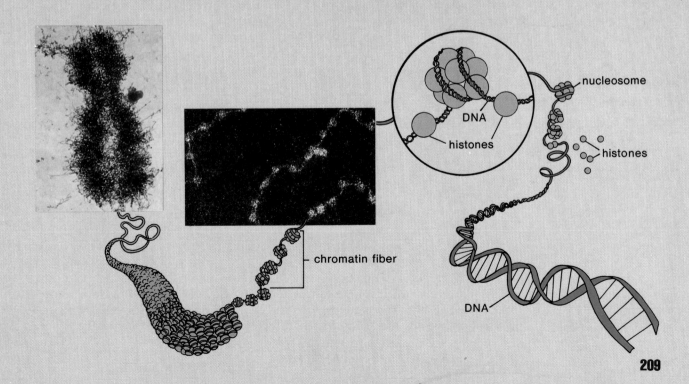

chromatin fiber

nucleosome

DNA

histones

histones

DNA

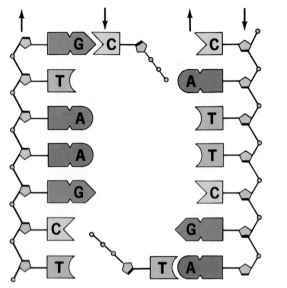

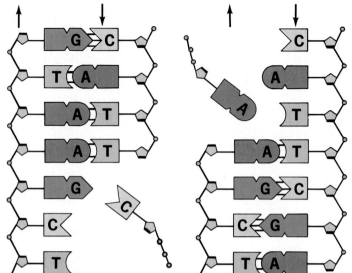

FIGURE 9.3 Two strands of DNA are separated by enzyme action. New nucleotides begin to pair with those of the original strands. Notice that the new nucleotides carry extra phosphates.

FIGURE 9.4 New nucleotides continue to be brought into place. The energy of their extra phosphates is used to bond these new arrivals to the preceding nucleotides.

Try Investigation 9B, DNA Replication.

add new nucleotides to each DNA strand. (Nucleotides synthesized during metabolism are stored in the cell.) In Figure 9.3, a guanine nucleotide in the old strand on the left can pair only with a new cytosine nucleotide. An adenine nucleotide of the old strand on the right can pair only with a new thymine nucleotide, and so on. In this way, each original strand serves as a template, or blueprint, for the synthesis of a new complementary strand.

The arrows in Figure 9.3 indicate that the two strands of a DNA molecule are oriented in opposite directions. However, **DNA polymerases**, the enzymes that carry out DNA synthesis, can work in only one direction. Thus, DNA polymerases must work from opposite ends of the DNA molecule, adding new nucleotides to each strand according to its orientation.

Figure 9.4 shows that the DNA polymerases move along the original strand, adding the proper types of new nucleotides. Then the phosphate of one nucleotide bonds covalently (Chapter 2) to the sugar of the next nucleotide. Soon a new strand is attached to each original strand of DNA, as shown in Figure 9.5. Notice that neither new molecule of DNA is made entirely of all new or all old strands. Instead, as you can see in Figure 9.6, each new molecule of DNA contains one new and one original strand. This method of DNA synthesis is known as semiconservative replication because each of the two new molecules conserves one strand of the original DNA, while adding one strand of new DNA. In contrast, conservative replication would result in one molecule with two old strands and one molecule with two new strands. As a result of replication, each cell formed after the M phase contains a complete set of chromosomes and genes, identical to the parental set and composed of DNA made of one original strand and one new strand of nucleotides.

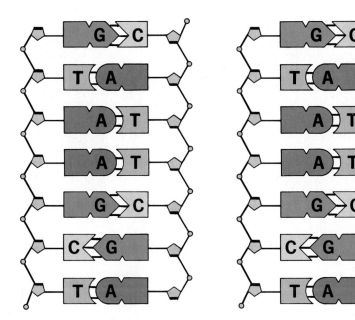

FIGURE 9.5 Two new fragments of double-stranded DNA are completed. Compare them to one another and to the original in Figure 9.2. Has the replication been exact?

9.6 Replication Forks

As scientists experimented with DNA of intact chromosomes, they discovered a puzzling phenomenon. Figures 9.3 through 9.6 show only a short fragment of a DNA molecule. Cells, however, must replicate the very long molecules of DNA that make up chromosomes. If replication progressed from one end of each strand to the other, the process would take a long time. Scientists solved this puzzle when they discovered that replication occurs simultaneously at many sites called replication forks. These forks move along the double-stranded molecule in one direction as new DNA molecules are synthesized.

FIGURE 9.6 In replication, each new DNA molecule produced after the S phase contains one strand of original and one strand of new DNA. The same mechanism produces new DNA in subsequent generations of cells.

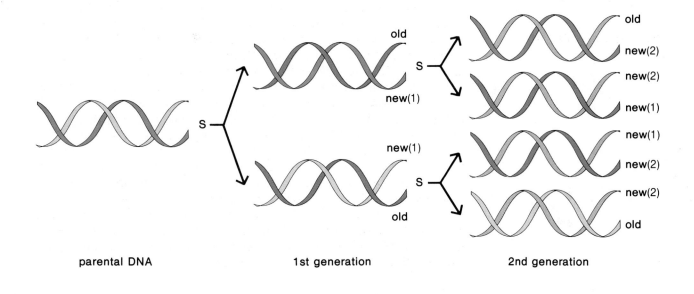

parental DNA   1st generation   2nd generation

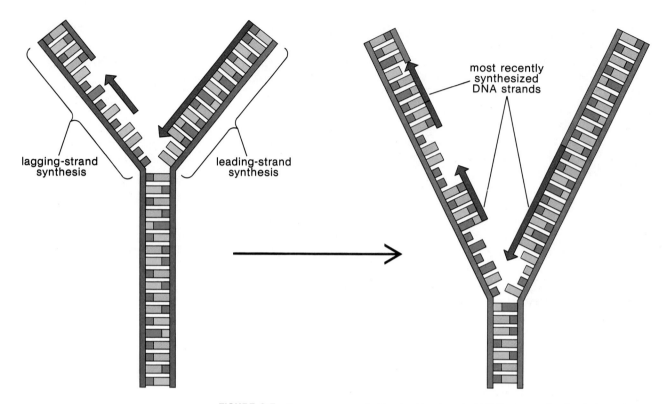

FIGURE 9.7 Enzymes separate the double stranded DNA at a replication fork, and DNA polymerases synthesize new DNA. Numerous replication forks are present along the DNA molecule during the S phase.

This discovery led to another puzzle, though. You have read that the two strands in DNA have opposite orientations. If the DNA polymerases can work only in one direction along each strand, how can synthesis appear to occur in the same direction simultaneously on *both* strands at a replication fork?

Investigators found that replication takes place differently along each strand, as shown in Figure 9.7. On one strand, the leading strand, synthesis at a fork is continuous in one direction. Nucleotides are added one at a time, in order, by the polymerase. On the other DNA strand, the lagging strand, syntheses occurs in the opposite direction. On the lagging strand short, discontinuous segments of DNA are synthesized by DNA polymerases. Then the segments are joined together by other enzymes. The overall effect is synthesis of two new DNA molecules in the same direction behind the replication fork as it moves along the original DNA molecule.

9.7 Correction of Replication Errors

Errors are made during replication. The DNA polymerases may skip a nucleotide, add a nucleotide, or put the wrong nucleotide in place. You might think that surprising until you consider the number of nucleotides copied during synthesis. In addition, environmental factors such as ultraviolet radiation or chemicals may damage nucleotides.

The most surprising thing about replication is its accuracy. The DNA of a typical animal cell contains approximately 3×10^9 (3 billion) nucleotide pairs (therefore 6×10^9 nucleotides), all of which are copied during replication. When a sequence of DNA is synthesized, an error occurs about once in every 1000 nucleotides. In the final DNA strand, however, only about one error remains for each 10^5 to 10^6 nucleotides copied. In many cases, the error rate is closer to one in a billion (10^9). How does such improvement in the final DNA molecule come about?

Figure 9.8 illustrates the elaborate system of enzymes that detects and repairs errors that could harm offspring cells. Specific enzymes serve as proofreaders, identifying and removing incorrect or damaged nucleotides from a DNA strand. Other enzymes synthesize a replacement sequence by complementary base-pairing with the undamaged strand. Still another enzyme (DNA ligase) seals the breaks created by the repair process.

The few errors that may remain in the final DNA molecules are genetic changes called **mutations**, discussed in Chapter 13. Such errors can be harmful or even lethal. Usually, however, because a lethal mutation kills only two cells out of thousands, the organism is never aware of the replication error. Some mutations are damaging but not lethal to offspring cells, so the error remains part of the gene passed to each subsequent offspring cell. This type of mutation may be lethal in another fashion, though. Skin cancer, often caused when sunlight damages skin cell DNA, is an example. Here, the mutation damages skin cells and is passed to the offspring cells, eventually harming or even killing the organism if the cancer remains untreated. Without the DNA repair system, skin cancer would be much more common in humans.

CONNECTIONS

The correction of most replication errors ensures faithful copying of genetic information, hence the genetic continuity of life. At the same time, the errors remaining—mutations—provide variations on which natural selection can act, resulting in evolution.

FIGURE 9.8 DNA repair is carried out by a group of enzymes that identify and remove incorrect or damaged nucleotides, synthesize replacements, and seal the breaks created by the repair process.

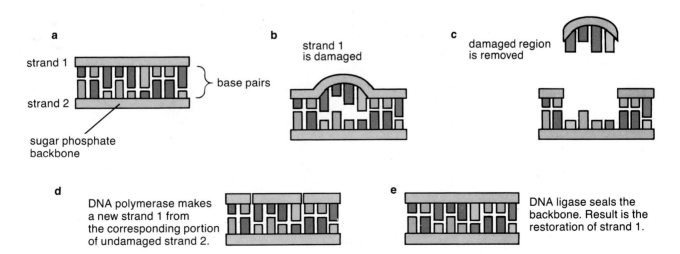

CHECK AND CHALLENGE

1. What are the roles of DNA polymerases in replication?
2. Describe how DNA synthesis can proceed in one direction at a replication fork even though the two strands undergo synthesis in opposite directions.
3. How is the number of replication errors kept to a minimum in cells?
4. What structural characteristic of the DNA molecule is the key factor in its ability to replicate?
5. How are histones involved in the S phase of the cell cycle?

Mitosis and Cell Division

9.8   The M Phase

Once the S phase has ended and the cell nucleus contains two complete sets of DNA, the cell proceeds quickly through the G_2 phase to mitosis. Because mitosis and cell division usually occur together in a continuous series of events, they are often referred to as a single process, mitotic cell division. This process is the M phase of the cell cycle.

During the S phase, the chromosomes are strung out in a fine network of chromatin and are impossible to see with most microscopes. As mitosis begins in eukaryotic cells, however, the replicated chromosomes condense, becoming shorter and thicker. When cells are fixed and stained, the condensed chromosomes are easy to see under the compound microscope. Each chromosome is a double (replicated) structure joined at the **centromere** (SEN troh meer). The two attached replicas of the chromosome are called chromatids (KROH muh tids) until they separate. (See Figure 9.9.)

Although the M phase of the cell cycle is a continuous process, for convenience it is described as a series of stages. Figure 9.10 shows photo-

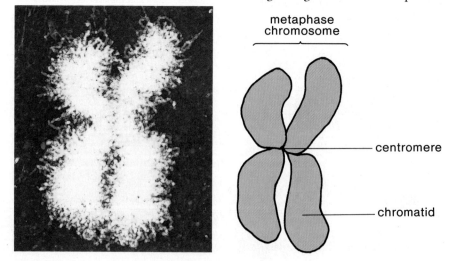

FIGURE 9.9   Compare the scanning electron micrograph of a replicated chromosome with the labeled diagram of the same chromosome.

metaphase chromosome

centromere

chromatid

graphs of stages of mitosis in plant cells. Refer to the figure as you read the paragraphs that follow.

The chromosomes condense during the first stage of mitosis, **prophase** (b, c). Other events also occur during prophase. The nuclear envelope begins to disappear. Microtubules form a diamond-shaped structure called the spindle, which determines the direction of the future cell division. Some of the microtubules attach to the centromeres and later guide the chromosomes to opposite sides of the cell.

During the next stage of mitosis, **metaphase** (d, c), the chromosomes become arranged in a plane across the center of the cell, perpendicular to the spindle. As **anaphase** begins (f, g), the centromeres divide. Microtubules attached to each centromere pull sister chromatids toward opposite

FIGURE 9.10 Stages of mitosis in the blood lily, *Haemanthus:* (a) interphase, (b) prophase, (c) late prophase, showing disintegration of the nuclear envelope, (d) early metaphase, (e) metaphase, (f) early anaphase, (g) late anaphase, (h) early telophase, (i) late telophase showing formation of the cell plate.

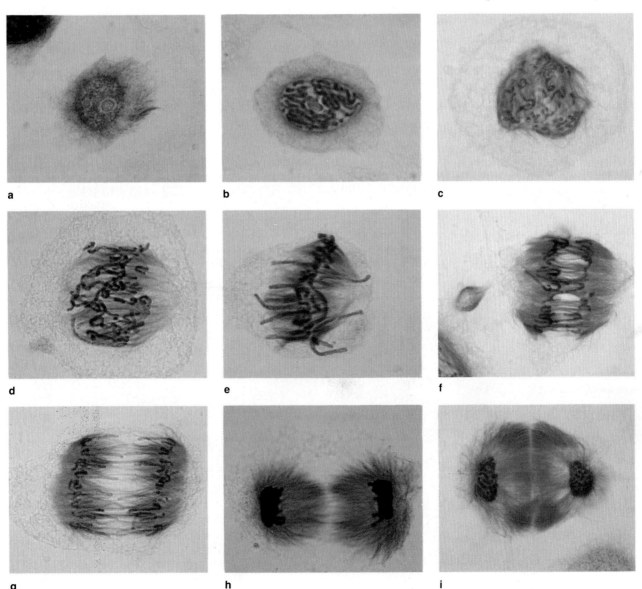

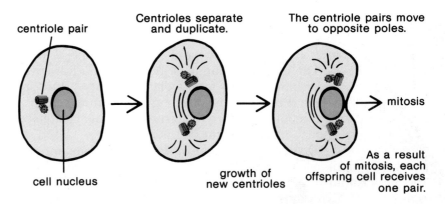

FIGURE 9.11 Before DNA replication, the centrioles duplicate and move to opposite poles of the nucleus. Spindle fibers form between the poles and later guide chromosome movement.

sides of the cell. Notice that this movement results in the separation of chromatids into individual chromosomes located at opposite sides of the cell.

During **telophase** (h, i), the chromosomes gather at opposite sides of the cell. A new nuclear envelope forms around each group of chromosomes. Mitosis ends with the formation of two nuclei, each containing a set of chromosomes identical to those of the parent cell.

Try Investigation 9C, Mitotic Cell Division.

9.9 Comparison of Mitosis in Plants and Animals

In most cells, as mitosis, or nuclear division, comes to an end, cell division occurs, producing two offspring cells. In plant cells, the cell plate (Figure 9.10i) begins to form across the middle of the cell, dividing the cell in two. Each new cell is only about one-half the size of the parent cell but will begin to grow in the G_1 phase. The offspring cells make new material that extends the cell walls and thickens them as the new cells mature.

In animal cells, mitotic cell division is very similar to the process in plants. The major differences are the following:

1. Animal cells contain a pair of centrioles (Figure 6.10e), which duplicate as mitosis begins. One centriole pair gradually moves toward the opposite side of the cell from the other pair (Figure 9.11). The spindle fibers begin to form between these two poles as the nuclear envelope breaks down.

2. A cell plate does not form. Instead the cell constricts (Figure 9.12) across the middle as cell division begins. A new plasma membrane forms across the constricted portion of the cell.

3. Cell division is usually evident earlier during mitosis in animal cells (anaphase) than in plant cells (telophase). The cells in Figure 9.13 are shown in anaphase. A constriction is already evident across the cells. Cell division may even be completed before new nuclear membranes are completed around each nucleus. In both plants and animals new offspring cells resume growth in G_1.

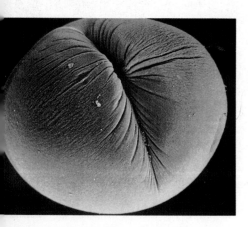

FIGURE 9.12 A scanning electron micrograph of a dividing animal cell, X 42.

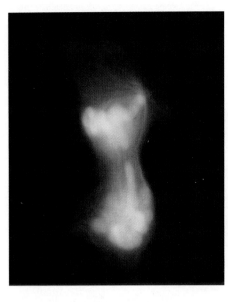

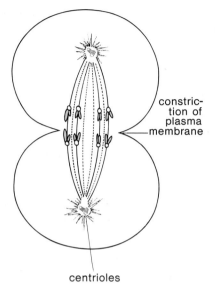

constriction of plasma membrane

centrioles

FIGURE 9.13 The constrictions seen in this anaphase cell indicate the cell is beginning to divide. Animal cells usually begin to divide one stage earlier in mitosis than plant cells do.

CHECK AND CHALLENGE

1. What is the difference between mitosis and mitotic cell division?

2. Differentiate between chromosomes and chromatids in the M phase.

3. Compare and contrast mitotic cell division in plants and animals.

4. Briefly describe the major events of mitosis.

FOCUS ON *The Evolution of Mitosis*

Prokaryotes demonstrate a simple type of cell division in which the DNA attaches to the plasma membrane. Cell division in some primitive protists is similar, except that the chromosomes attach to the nuclear envelope instead of to the plasma membrane. Microtubules form spindle fibers outside the nucleus, which remains intact during division. (See Figure F.) One hypothesis for the evolution of mitosis suggests that microtubules originally helped support the nuclear envelope. Later, the microtubules became attached to the chromosomes themselves. As microtubules assumed a more active role in separating the chromosomes, the nuclear envelope became less important. In more modern plants and animals, the nuclear envelope breaks down during mitosis, and the spindle fibers attach directly to the chromosomes.

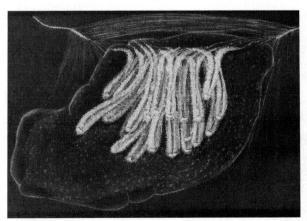

FIGURE F During mitosis in the protist *Trichonympha grandis*, the spindle forms outside the nucleus, and the chromosomes attach to the intact nuclear envelope. Compare with Figure 9.10.

Summary

The eukaryotic cell cycle is a series of events leading to the formation of two offspring cells from a parent cell. There are four phases of the cell cycle: G_1 (growth), S (synthesis), G_2 (growth 2), and M (mitosis). (Interphase consists of G_1, S, and G_2.) During each phase there is considerable metabolic activity in the cell. DNA synthesis in the S phase involves replication of the DNA. The DNA of the parent cell serves as a blueprint for making two identical copies of the chromosomes and genes. Enzymes regulate each part of the process, which includes separating the two original strands, connecting the appropriate new nucleotides to form the new strands, and detecting and correcting errors. One copy of each parental chromosome is passed to each of two offspring cells in the M phase, or mitosis. During the four stages of mitosis, the chromosomes condense and move to opposite sides of the cell, forming new nuclei. Then the parent cell usually divides into two offspring cells.

The phases of the cell cycle always occur in the same order, but the time spent in each phase varies from cell to cell and from organism to organism. Control of the cell cycle is critical to the research and understanding of disorders such as cancer.

Prokaryotes do not divide by mitosis. Instead the bacterial chromosome is replicated and distributed to two offspring cells during binary fission.

Key Concepts

Use the following terms to construct a concept map that includes appropriate linking words. Use additional terms as needed.

cell cycle	G_1
mitosis	G_0
DNA replication	S
telophase	G_2
replicating forks	M
DNA polymerases	

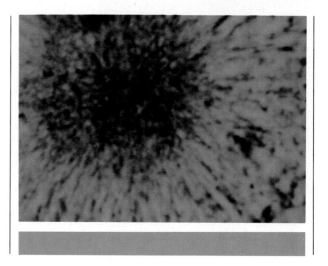

Reviewing Ideas

1. What types of molecules and cell parts would be synthesized during the G_1 phase of the cell cycle?

2. What is the biologic significance of the S phase of the cell cycle? Of the M phase?

3. Describe how errors are corrected in DNA.

4. What is the role of the spindle in mitosis?

5. How are enzymes essential to the replication of DNA?

6. In what respect is mitosis different from the chromosome replication that occurs in prokaryotes before cell division?

7. State how you would recognize a cell in each stage of mitosis.

8. What are replication forks? How do they contribute to the efficiency of DNA replication?

9. What is the difference between the G_1 phase and the G_2 phase of the cell cycle?

10. What is the role of the centromere in mitosis?

Using Concepts

1. A fellow student asks you to look in a microscope and observe the chromosomes in the nucleus of a plant leaf cell. Would you expect to see them? Give two reasons why or why not.

2. Cells can be grown in a laboratory by a process called tissue culture. You have two tissue cultures, one in the G_1 phase and one in the G_2 phase. Unfortunately, the cultures' labels have been misplaced. How would you determine which culture was G_1 and which was G_2?

3. You have animal cells growing in a laboratory tissue culture. You plan to provide the cells with a radioactive nucleotide. Your purpose is to measure incorporation of carbon-14 nucleotide into DNA and determine the rate of DNA synthesis in the cells. Which radioactive nucleotide—A, T, G, C, U—should you use, and why?

4. From the information in this chapter can you predict what organisms would be like if there were no DNA proofreading system in eukaryotic cells? Explain your answer.

5. Before Watson and Crick proposed the double-helix model of DNA structure, another scientist proposed the model shown below. From what you have read in this chapter, explain why this structure is a poor proposal.

6. What could be the consequences of a mutation in a single-celled organism?

7. How does the synthesis of new DNA differ from that of other molecules in the cell?

8. If DNA were only a single-stranded molecule, could it act as the genetic material? Why or why not?

Synthesis

1. You have animal cells growing in a laboratory tissue culture. Radioactive glucose (carbon-14 glucose) is provided to the cells and carbon-14 ends up in the DNA of the chromosomes. Trace the steps of how this happened.

2. What features of the Watson-Crick model of DNA help explain replication?

Extensions

1. Imagine yourself as a single chromosome. Diagram or describe your life as you proceed through an entire cell cycle.

2. Research information about the growth of cancer cells. Write a paragraph describing how their cell cycle differs from that of normal cells.

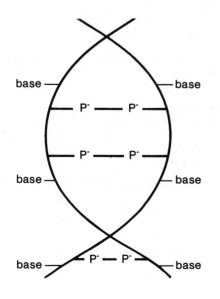

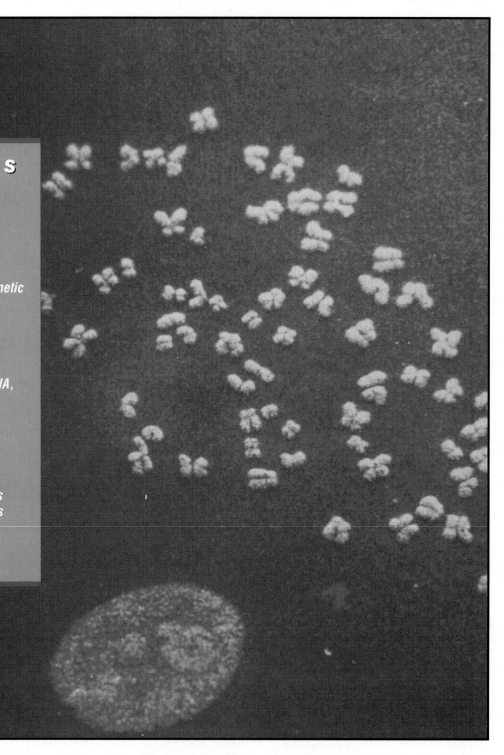

CONTENTS

Information Transfer and Protein Synthesis

*D*espite the differences among the millions of species on Earth, experiments have shown that all known living organisms contain DNA as their genetic material. DNA plays a dual role, storing and transferring the information needed for life processes. Inheritance, or the transfer of genetic information from one generation to the next, is one function of DNA. Recall from Chapter 9 that replication provides the mechanism for transferring the information coded in DNA from parent to offspring. In individual organisms, genetic information also is expressed as specific cell functions. Each function is ultimately the result of the synthesis of a protein, a process directed by information stored in DNA. This second role of DNA, which involves another type of transfer of information, is the topic of this chapter.

An understanding of the genetic code and how it is used to make proteins was one of the biggest breakthroughs in modern biology. Your grasp of the principles of this language of life will help you in your studies of many of the chapters that follow.

*C*an you identify the structures shown?

*H*ow are they important to the cell?

◆ *A scanning electron micrograph of structures from a cell.*

The Genetic Code

10.1 The DNA–RNA Connection

Experiments have repeatedly shown that DNA is the blueprint for the manufacture of hundreds of different types of cellular proteins. By controlling protein synthesis, DNA ultimately controls cell structure and function. Most proteins are enzymes that catalyze chemical reactions in cells. Other proteins are important in the structure and function of cell membranes, the immune system (Chapter 20), and tissues such as muscle, blood, and skin.

Recall from Chapter 2 that the primary structure of a protein—the sequence of amino acids—is responsible for the formation of the functional tertiary (three-dimensional) structure. By directing the primary structure of each protein, DNA, therefore, dictates the function of the protein.

When biochemists investigated protein synthesis, they learned that DNA does not control the process directly. Instead, DNA usually works through RNA, and RNA, in turn, carries out the actual synthesis of the protein. It had long been suspected that RNA was associated with protein synthesis, because cells that were making large amounts of protein always contained large amounts of RNA in the cytoplasm. By using techniques that separated cells into their parts, biochemists found that much of this RNA was contained in the ribosomes.

Other studies using amino acids marked with radioactive isotopes (**Appendix 2B**) showed that ribosomes are the location where new chains of amino acids are formed. A logical conclusion was that the ribosomes must have contained the instructions for assembling the amino acids. How did the instructions get there?

FIGURE 10.1 A summary of the flow of genetic information leading to the synthesis of active proteins

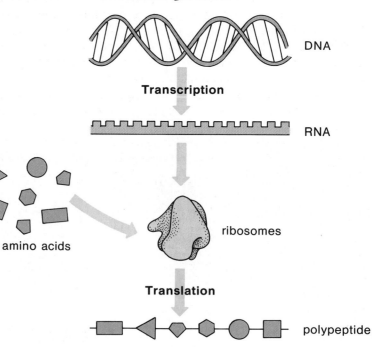

It turned out that the DNA is a sort of master "tape" of instructions that is kept securely locked up in a safe, that is, in the nucleus. From the master DNA tape are made working tapes that carry the genetic instructions to the ribosomes. These working tapes are specific RNA molecules called **messenger RNA** (mRNA). The genetic information carried by much of the DNA is copied onto these RNA molecules.

Messenger RNA strands are synthesized in the nucleus directly alongside the segments of the DNA strand to be copied. This copying must be exact to ensure that the protein molecules will be correctly synthesized. If the mRNA does not contain the proper code, the primary structure of the new protein will be altered. As a result, the protein will have an altered function. Two cellular processes, under the direction of DNA, lead to the formation of the primary structure of proteins: **transcription**, or RNA synthesis, and **translation**, or protein synthesis. Figure 10.1 is an overview of these processes, which form the assembly line of protein manufacture. Refer to the figure as you read the chapter.

10.2   Coding Genetic Information

One of the most exciting chapters in the history of biological investigation has been the work of researchers who cracked the molecular code of life, now known as the **genetic code**. These researchers were able to attach meaning to "words" made from the nucleotide alphabet.

A code is a system of symbols used to store information. Anyone who knows the code can translate the information from one form into another. Written language is one type of code devised by humans. By using just a few symbols, anyone can communicate ideas and experiences to someone else (Figure 10.2). For example, English contains 26 symbols, the letters of its alphabet. With these 26 letters, an unlimited number of code words can be formed, and an unlimited number of books can be written with stored information. Yet, to people who do not know this particular code system, nothing written in English has meaning. They would have to use a dictionary that translates English into their own language to understand the code system. Some codes are simple, using only two or three symbols. The

FIGURE 10.2 A code uses symbols to translate information from one form into another.

a

b

Morse code, for example, represents the English alphabet by using a varying number of dots (·), dashes (−), and precisely controlled spaces.

What are the symbols of the DNA code? Although molecules of DNA may be very long, they are made of varying sequences of only four nucleotides. Thus the nucleotides serve as the four "letters" of the DNA "alphabet." The small size of this alphabet poses a problem. Proteins are large molecules built from smaller units, the amino acids. A genetic code would require at least 20 different messages—one for each amino acid. Each message must be distinct, so that the cell will not confuse one amino acid with another.

How would DNA nucleotides have to be combined to code 20 different messages? If one type of nucleotide were to code a single amino acid, then only four amino acids could be coded with four nucleotides. Obviously, four single letters are not enough. Even two letters in a particular order would provide only 16 combinations, such as AA, AT, AC, AG, TA, TT, and so on. When three nucleotides are grouped at a time, however, 64 triplet combinations, such as CTG, TAC, and ACA, are possible. In fact, using three nucleotides at a time provides extra code messages, so that more than one message can specify the same amino acid. In English, this situation is described as synonyms—different words that code the same meaning (for example, *also* and *too*). Recent experiments indicate that "synonyms" exist in the DNA code as well.

10.3 Cracking the Genetic Code

It was mRNA that provided the clue to the genetic code. An American biochemist, Marshall Nirenberg, working at the National Institute of Health in Bethesda, Maryland, made the first major breakthroughs. He had been studying protein synthesis in an extract of bacterial cells that contained ribosomes. Nirenberg found that adding mRNA isolated from one type of cell increased protein synthesis by the ribosomes from another type of cell. In other words, ribosomes started producing protein molecules even when they received instructions from a "foreign" RNA. This observation suggested an idea for an experiment: testing to see if ribosomes could follow instructions from a synthetic RNA, an RNA made in the laboratory and never before present in a living cell.

To keep matters simple, Nirenberg prepared mRNA molecules that consisted of only one RNA nucleotide, uracil, repeated over and over again. A custom-made chain of uracil nucleotides (U-U-U-U-U-U) was added to each of 20 different test tubes. Each test tube contained ribosomes, enzymes, and other factors needed for protein synthesis. However, each test tube contained a different radioactive amino acid. The results were astonishing. In 19 of the test tubes nothing happened, but in the twentieth test tube, the radioactive amino acid was incorporated into polypeptide chains. The amino acid was phenylalanine. When the polypeptides were analyzed, they were found to consist only of phenylalanine units, one joined to another (Figure 10.3). How would you interpret these data?

Biochemists had previously concluded that a triplet of nucleotides might represent a code word that specifies a particular amino acid to be

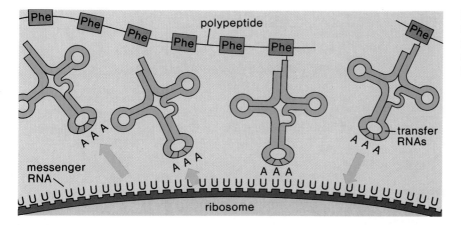

FIGURE 10.3 Each group of three uracil (U) molecules in a synthetic mRNA specifies the addition of one molecule of phenylalanine to a polypeptide chain.

incorporated into a protein. Nirenberg had discovered the first triplet, or **codon**. It was UUU, and it meant: Attach one molecule of the amino acid phenylalanine to the polypeptide chain. Other investigators soon discovered the mRNA codons for the rest of the amino acids. Figure 10.4 shows codons for all the amino acids. Notice the numerous "synonyms" and the "punctuation" codons that mean "start" and "stop." Studies of organisms in all five kingdoms indicate that the genetic code is nearly universal.

FIGURE 10.4 The genetic code is written in mRNA. Each triplet is a codon for an amino acid. For example, UGG codes for the amino acid tryptophan. The codon AUG signals "start," and UAA, UAG, and UGA signal "stop." Several amino acids have more than one codon.

First Letter	Second Letter				Third Letter
	U	**C**	**A**	**G**	
U	phenylalanine	serine	tyrosine	cysteine	U
	phenylalanine	serine	tyrosine	cysteine	C
	leucine	serine	stop	stop	A
	leucine	serine	stop	tryptophan	G
C	leucine	proline	histidine	arginine	U
	leucine	proline	histidine	arginine	C
	leucine	proline	glutamine	arginine	A
	leucine	proline	glutamine	arginine	G
A	isoleucine	threonine	asparagine	serine	U
	isoleucine	threonine	asparagine	serine	C
	isoleucine	threonine	lysine	arginine	A
	(start) methionine	threonine	lysine	arginine	G
G	valine	alanine	aspartate	glycine	U
	valine	alanine	aspartate	glycine	C
	valine	alanine	glutamate	glycine	A
	valine	alanine	glutamate	glycine	G

CONNECTIONS

*T*he almost universal nature of the genetic code is strong evidence for the evolution of all living organisms from a common ancestral life form.

CHECK AND CHALLENGE

1. How does DNA control cell structure and function?
2. Why is a messenger necessary for protein synthesis?
3. Compare and contrast the DNA and RNA codes.
4. Explain the strategy behind Nirenberg's experiment.
5. Use Figure 10.4 to locate and list several code "synonyms."

Transcription

10.4   RNA Synthesis

In eukaryotic cells, DNA does not leave the nucleus to direct the building of proteins in the cytosol. Instead, messenger RNA and two other types, **transfer RNA** (tRNA) and **ribosomal RNA** (rRNA), are assembled in the nucleus according to instructions in the DNA blueprint. The RNA molecules are then modified and moved out of the nucleus to the cytosol, where each carries out a different function in protein synthesis. Figure 10.5 summarizes the formation and function of each type of RNA.

The first step in the expression of a particular gene is the synthesis of RNA on the DNA template. RNA synthesis is known as transcription because the genetic information in DNA is transcribed into the genetic code of RNA.

Like replication, transcription of the three types of RNA on the DNA template requires coordinated enzyme activity. Recall that in replication

Try Investigation 10A, Transcription.

FIGURE 10.5 All three types of RNA are transcribed from the DNA template.

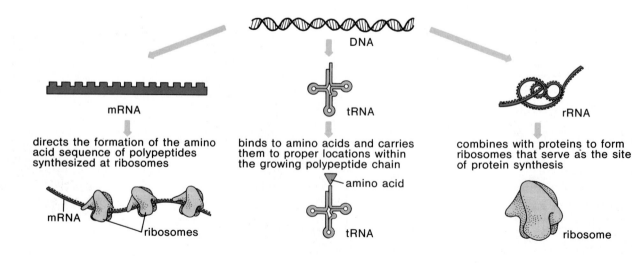

DNA

mRNA

tRNA

rRNA

directs the formation of the amino acid sequence of polypeptides synthesized at ribosomes

binds to amino acids and carries them to proper locations within the growing polypeptide chain

combines with proteins to form ribosomes that serve as the site of protein synthesis

mRNA

ribosomes

amino acid

tRNA

ribosome

Biological Challenges

REVERSE TRANSCRIPTION

Most hereditary material is contained in DNA molecules. These double-helix molecules are transcribed into RNA molecules, which, in turn, are translated into proteins. These processes are almost universal.

An exception is the hereditary material of certain viruses, RNA instead of DNA. RNA stores the same information as DNA, except for introns. The life cycle of RNA viruses, therefore, is similar to that of DNA viruses. Most RNA viruses merely bypass the step in which DNA is transcribed into RNA.

In 1970, scientists noted that an enzyme in certain RNA viruses could build double-stranded DNA

FIGURE A A retrovirus enters a cell and synthesizes double-stranded DNA from its RNA by means of reverse transcriptase. The viral DNA is then inserted into the host cell DNA and is replicated when the host cell DNA replicates.

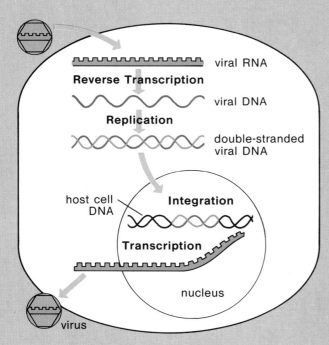

molecules from single-stranded RNA templates. The enzyme is reverse transcriptase, and the viruses that contain it, such as HIV, are called retroviruses.

A retrovirus's first action upon infecting a host cell is to make a DNA replica of its own RNA. The viral DNA then joins the host cell's own DNA and directs the production of new virus particles.

Most vertebrate cells also contain retroviral genes, and certain species, including mice and humans, contain hundreds of copies. The origin of these retroviral genes is unknown, but a few of them give rise to particles associated with reverse transcriptase activity. These particles generate new copies of DNA from RNA and insert them indiscriminately into the host chromosomes. The integration of this new DNA poses a threat to the host cell because mutations often arise at the site of integration. The mutation may disrupt the function of a gene or alter the degree of its expression or activity. In fact, many retroviruses induce tumors when their integration causes an ordinary gene to become a cancer-causing gene, or oncogene.

New research indicates that the products of reverse transcription may account for as much as 10 percent of the genes in a human cell. If reverse transcription does in fact figure so largely in mammalian genes, many questions arise. What is the source of the reverse transcriptase that causes this activity? How often does reverse transcription occur? Why should the process be part of the cell's function?

The last question addresses the most speculative aspect of current research—the search for the evolutionary origins of genetic information. Some biologists believe that RNA was the first molecule of heredity and that DNA is a more recent development. Although RNA stores information and is replicated in a similar manner to DNA, it is less stable. If RNA eventually gave rise to DNA, there must have been a mechanism for transferring information from RNA to DNA. Reverse transcription may have been that mechanism.

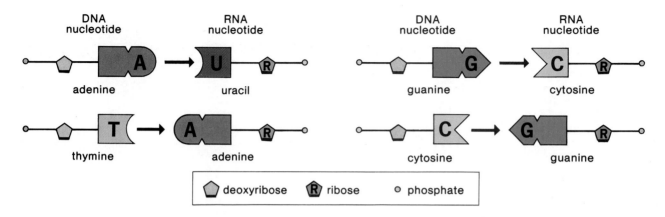

FIGURE 10.6 The letters of the DNA alphabet are transcribed into RNA letters.

both strands of the DNA molecule are copied. In transcription, however, only one strand of the DNA, the coding strand, is used to direct the synthesis of RNA. Recall from Chapter 9 that replication involves the matching of complementary nucleotides—A with T, and G with C. Similarly, in transcription, the sequence of nucleotides in RNA is complementary to the sequence of nucleotides in the coding strand of DNA, except that uracil (U) is substituted for thymine (T), as shown in Figure 10.6.

DNA coding strand nucleotides
A T T C G C A C C T A A
transcription
↓
U A A G C G U G G A U U
RNA nucleotides

Transcription can be divided into three stages, shown in Figure 10.7. Initiation, the first stage, occurs when the transcription enzyme, **RNA polymerase**, attaches to a specific region of the DNA. This site is called the promoter region because it *promotes* transcription. It is located just before the segment of the DNA coding strand that will be transcribed.

In the second stage, elongation, the RNA polymerase leaves the promoter region and moves along the coding strand of the DNA molecule. To RNA polymerase, the sequence of DNA nucleotides is a template of directions that specify the sequence of nucleotides in the RNA chain. As the polymerase "reads" the DNA coding sequence, a single complementary strand of RNA is synthesized. Note in the diagram that the RNA strand is elongated as the polymerase moves along the DNA coding segment. The third stage, termination, occurs when the RNA polymerase reaches the terminator region, or the end of the DNA to be transcribed. The enzyme and the newly synthesized RNA—the primary RNA transcript—are released from the DNA, and transcription ends. This mechanism is thought to occur during the synthesis of all three types of RNA—mRNA, rRNA, and tRNA.

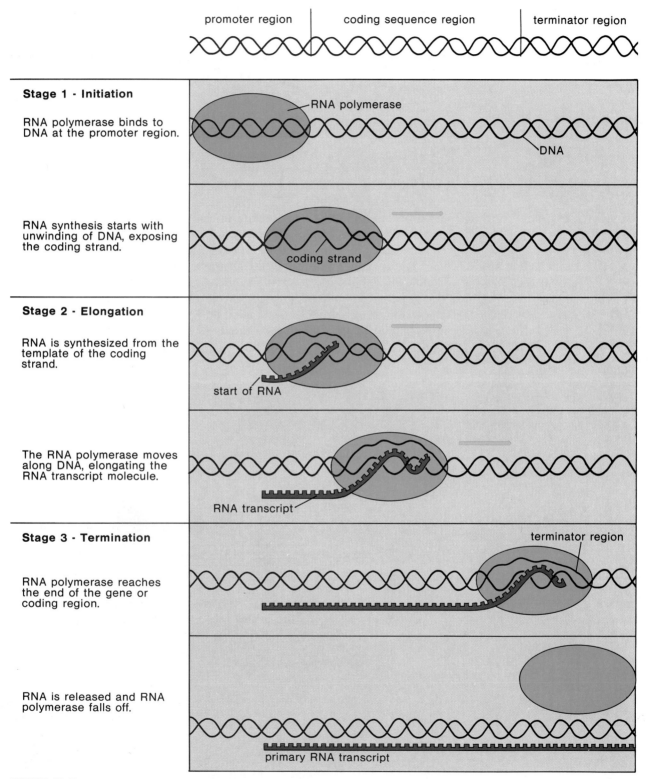

FIGURE 10.7   The three stages of transcription

Transcription is generally less complicated in prokaryotes than in eukaryotes. For example, prokaryotes have one RNA polymerase, whereas a different form of the enzyme is used to transcribe each of the three different types of RNA in the eukaryote nucleus. The overall process, however, is the same in almost all cells. RNA is assembled according to the genetic information in DNA.

10.5   RNA Processing

A primary RNA transcript, copied off the DNA template, may contain as many as 200,000 nucleotides (the average for human cells is 5000). Yet mRNA in the cytosol averages only 1000 nucleotides. What accounts for this difference? Studies have shown that RNA molecules undergo extensive processing before leaving the nucleus. Processing involves addition and chemical modification of certain nucleotides and removal of some segments from the RNA. All three types of RNA are processed in eukaryotes.

Figure 10.8 summarizes the processing of mRNA, which has been studied in detail. First, a cap made of chemically modified guanine nucleotide (methyl-guanine, or mG) is placed on the starting end of the mRNA molecule (a). Then 100 to 200 adenine (A) nucleotides are added to the other end to form what is called a poly-A tail (b). Studies suggest that both

FIGURE 10.8 Processing of a primary RNA transcript to mature mRNA involves the addition of an mG cap (a) and a poly-A tail (b), removal of introns (c), and splicing of exons (d).

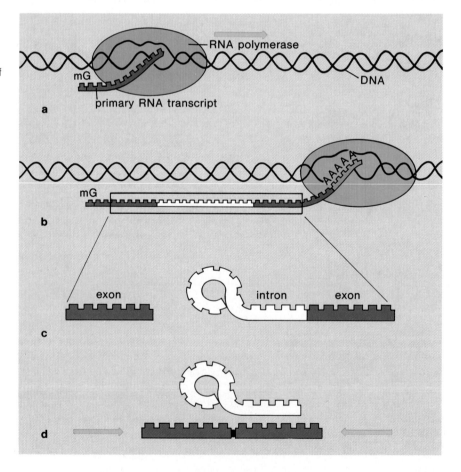

FOCUS ON *Introns*

Why do nearly all eukaryotic genes contain numerous sequences of DNA that appear to have no coding function? Except for the genes for histones (the proteins associated with DNA in chromosomes), all eukaryotic genes studied so far contain introns. Such split genes, so-called because the DNA is split by introns, clearly are not a novelty in nature but, rather, are the rule. In fact, most chromosomal DNA does *not* seem to code for mRNA that directs protein synthesis.

No one knows for certain what introns do. Evidence indicates that RNA, rather than DNA, may have been the first information-storage molecule. Introns may have been present in the first small RNA molecules that formed spontaneously in the primordial seas, and cutting and splicing may have been important processes in precellular evolution. How, then, did DNA evolve?

An enzyme present in all eukaryotic cells can catalyze the reverse transcription of RNA into DNA (see Biological Challenges in this chapter). This process may explain how the information-storage function of RNA was transferred to DNA. The exons and introns present in RNA also would have been preserved in DNA.

Most prokaryotes do not have introns, and translation of RNA follows immediately after transcription. The genes of the earliest prokaryotes probably contained numerous introns, but through countless generations of evolution, they have been deleted as prokaryotes evolved into streamlined protein-making machines. The DNA of eukaryotes has evolved more slowly, and introns remain. If they play a role in the genetic instructions of eukaryotes, it remains to be uncovered.

the cap and the tail protect mRNA from enzymes in the cytosol that degrade nucleic acids. In addition, the tail may aid in transport of the mRNA through the nuclear envelope. The cap apparently helps the mRNA attach to a ribosome and begin translation (Section 10.8).

Next, parts of the primary transcript are cut out and the cut ends joined in a process called **splicing**. The parts removed—**introns**—appear to correspond to noncoding regions of DNA. The parts that remain are **exons**, representing regions of DNA that are expressed as polypeptide chains. Splicing occurs in two steps. First, one end of an intron is cut and joined to a nucleotide near its other end, forming a lariatlike structure (c). Then the two exons are joined, and the intron is released (d). Most splicing involves the precise interaction of several RNA-protein complexes. In some cases, however, RNA itself can catalyze the splicing and therefore act as an enzyme. Once processing is complete, the mature mRNA moves out of the nucleus to the ribosomes in the cytosol, where protein synthesis occurs.

10.6 Formation of tRNA, rRNA, and Ribosomes

Recall that tRNA and rRNA are also processed in the nucleus. Transfer RNA is an adapter molecule that recognizes both an mRNA codon and the amino acid that matches that codon. The primary tRNA transcript is spliced, several nucleotides are chemically modified, and the molecule is folded into a three-dimensional structure. Notice in Figure 10.9a that the tRNA is double-stranded in places where the single strand binds to itself by base pairing, forming stems. The remaining single-stranded regions form loops, so that the molecule resembles a cloverleaf. The cloverleaf is then

FIGURE 10.9 Mature tRNA (a) resembles a cloverleaf, with the amino acid binding site at the end of a stem and the anticodon at the loop on the opposite end. The molecule is folded into a three-dimensional L-shape (b).

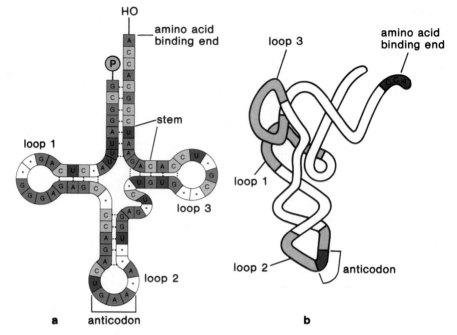

FIGURE 10.10 In the nucleolus, proteins and rRNA combine to form the large and small subunits of a ribosome, which then move into the cytosol. The subunits come together only during translation. Many ribosomes often bind to the same mRNA, forming a polyribosome.

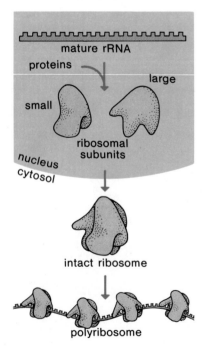

folded into the L-shaped three-dimensional structure shown in Figure 10.9b. Amino acids attach to the stem at one end of the cloverleaf. The loop at the opposite end contains the **anticodon**, a nucleotide triplet that is complementary to a mRNA codon. On the ribosome, base pairing occurs between a codon and anticodon, so that each tRNA delivers the correct amino acid to the ribosome during protein synthesis.

Ribosomal RNA makes up the ribosomes and is not involved in coding. Each ribosome is composed of a large and a small subunit. Ribosomes and rRNA are formed primarily in a chromatin-rich area of the nucleus called the nucleolus. Figure 10.10 illustrates some of the steps involved. The rRNA molecules are transcribed from DNA in the nucleolus. The primary rRNA transcript is spliced and modified to produce mature rRNA molecules. These associate with some 70 proteins (formed in the cytosol) to form the large and small subunits of ribosomes, which are transported through the nuclear envelope to the cytosol. Following further modification, the two mature subunits can join to form an intact ribosome, the site of protein assembly. The intact ribosome contains recognition sites to which tRNA and mRNA can bind during protein synthesis. Often, several ribosomes bind to the same mRNA molecule, forming a polyribosome. Most of the cell's proteins are manufactured on polyribosomes.

CHECK AND CHALLENGE

1. Compare the roles of introns and exons in mRNA production.
2. Distinguish the functions of mRNA, tRNA, and rRNA.
3. What activities occur during transcription of mRNA?
4. How and where are ribosomes formed?

Translation

10.7 Transfer RNA Charging

Protein synthesis is called translation because the codon sequence in mRNA is translated into the amino acid sequence of the protein. The first step in synthesizing proteins is to communicate the necessary instructions from the DNA in the nucleus to the ribosomes in the cytosol. As you have read, mRNA carries these instructions as a transcribed sequence of codons—that is, in genetic code. The second step is to move appropriate amino acids from the cytosol to the ribosome. This step is performed by tRNA molecules, which bind to specific amino acids and move them into place on the ribosome as needed.

Each type of tRNA binds only a single one of the 20 different amino acids used to assemble proteins. There are 20 enzymes that are amino acid-specific in that they can recognize different amino acids and their appropriate tRNAs. Each enzyme can attach one type of amino acid to the end of the matching tRNA molecule. Figure 10.11 illustrates the two-step binding process, called tRNA charging, or activating. First, the enzyme binds a specific amino acid and a molecule of ATP (a). The ATP loses two phosphate groups and joins to the amino acid as AMP (b). Second, the enzyme binds the appropriate tRNA, which displaces the AMP and binds to the amino acid (c). The enzyme then releases the charged tRNA (d). Transfer RNA charging, which depends on enzyme specificity, is the critical step in protein synthesis. Once charging occurs, the accuracy of protein synthesis depends on codon-anticodon base pairing, and that step occurs on the ribosome.

FIGURE 10.11 Charging of tRNA molecules. Each tRNA charging enzyme recognizes one of the 20 amino acids and its appropriate tRNA molecules. Binding of the amino acid to the tRNA occurs in a two-step process on the enzyme.

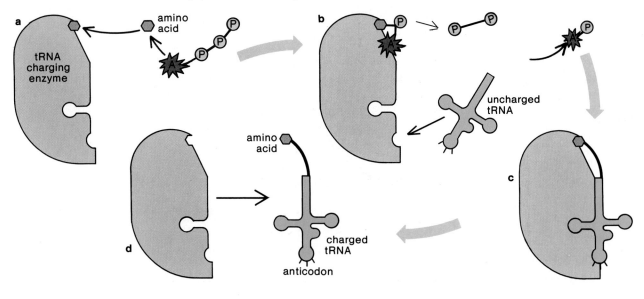

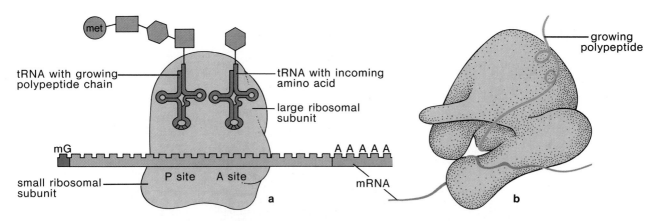

FIGURE 10.12 Diagrams of a ribosome showing (a) the binding sites for mRNA and tRNA, and (b) the groove between the large and small subunits that accommodates mRNA as well as the growing polypeptide chain

10.8 Protein Synthesis

Each ribosome contains two binding sites at which mRNA and tRNA are brought together (Figure 10.12). At these sites, tRNA anticodons base-pair with mRNA codons, and the amino acids they carry are linked to a growing polypeptide chain. Thus, the sequence of codons dictates the amino acid sequence.

One of the binding sites, termed the P site, holds the tRNA carrying the growing polypeptide chain. The other site, called the A site, holds the tRNA carrying the next amino acid to be added to the chain. During translation, the ribosome moves along the mRNA strand one codon at a time, much like a freight car along a railroad track.

Translation involves the same three stages—initiation, elongation, and termination—as transcription. All three stages require enzymes that are part of the ribosome. Initiation and elongation also require energy supplied by GTP, a molecule closely related to ATP. Figures 10.13 through 10.15 show how mRNA, tRNA, and a ribosome work together to synthesize amino acids into a polypeptide chain. Refer to the figures as you read the details about translation.

Try Investigation 10B, Translation.

FIGURE 10.13 Initiation of translation requires the mG cap, various initiation factors, and binding of methionine-charged tRNA at the P site of a ribosome.

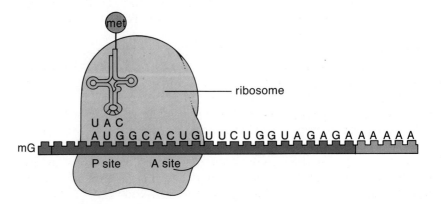

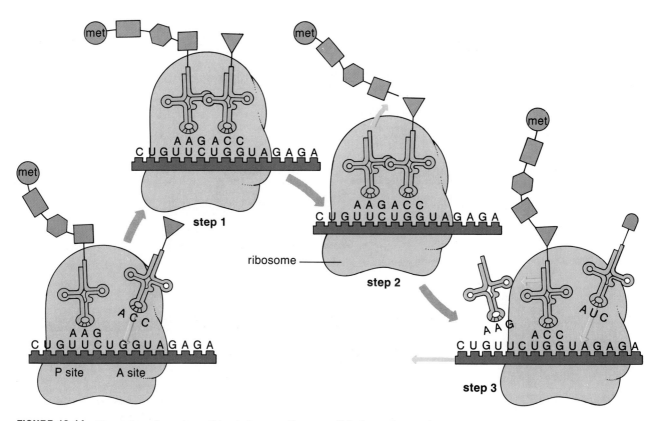

FIGURE 10.14 Elongation of a polypeptide chain on a ribosome. This three-step cycle is repeated until a stop codon is reached. In step 1, a charged tRNA molecule binds to the A site; in step 2, a peptide bond is formed; and in step 3, the ribosome moves one codon along the mRNA so the cycle can be repeated.

The initiation signal for protein synthesis is in two parts. First, the mG cap of mRNA attaches to a ribosome. The cap is followed by several nucleotides that serve to thread the mRNA into a ribosome, much the way the white part of a film is used to thread a movie through a projector. Second, a start codon, AUG, signals the beginning of the sequence of codons to be translated into the amino acid sequence of the protein. AUG, which also codes for the amino acid methionine, is positioned in the P site of the ribosome. Then a methionine-charged tRNA pairs with AUG at the P site, completing initiation (Figure 10.13).

In elongation, illustrated in Figure 10.14, amino acids are added one at a time to the initial amino acid. In the first step of elongation, the mRNA codon in the A site of the ribosome pairs with the anticodon of an incoming tRNA charged with its appropriate amino acid. Next, an enzyme catalyzes the formation of a peptide bond between the polypeptide in the P site and the newly arrived amino acid in the A site. In the process, the polypeptide is transferred from the tRNA in the P site to the amino acid on the tRNA in the A site. The tRNA in the P site now leaves the ribosome, which moves one codon along the mRNA, so that the remaining tRNA is moved from the A site to the P site. During this time the codon and anticodon

CONNECTIONS

Because of its grooved structure, a ribosome is uniquely suited for its function in protein synthesis, an example of the relationship between structure and function.

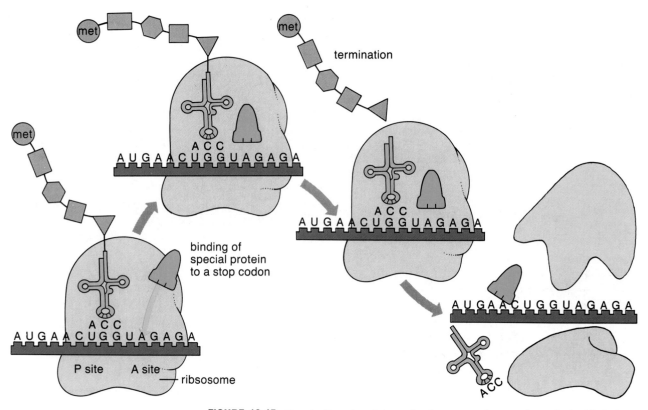

FIGURE 10.15 Termination of protein synthesis occurs when a release factor binds to a stop codon. The completed polypeptide chain is released and the two ribosomal subunits separate.

remain paired. This movement brings into the A site the next codon on the mRNA to be translated, and the process is repeated, adding an amino acid to the chain each time.

The elongation cycle continues until a stop codon reaches the A site of the ribosome. Three codons signal the end of translation: UAA, UAG, and UGA (see Figure 10.4). None of them codes for an amino acid, so instead of a tRNA, a special protein binds to the stop codon in the A site. The completed polypeptide chain then is released from the tRNA in the P site and from the ribosome. The ribosome then separates into its small and large subunits (Figure 10.15).

In summary, genes may be thought of as coding regions of DNA. The coding regions contain specific sequences of DNA nucleotides (exons) that are transcribed onto the complementary sequences of codons in mRNA. The sequences of codons in mature mRNA are then translated into the sequences of amino acids (the primary structure) of proteins. Figure 10.16 is a summary of transcription and translation in eukaryotic cells. Study the diagram and identify each of the steps that have been described in the chapter. Take time to note where and how each component of the process functions.

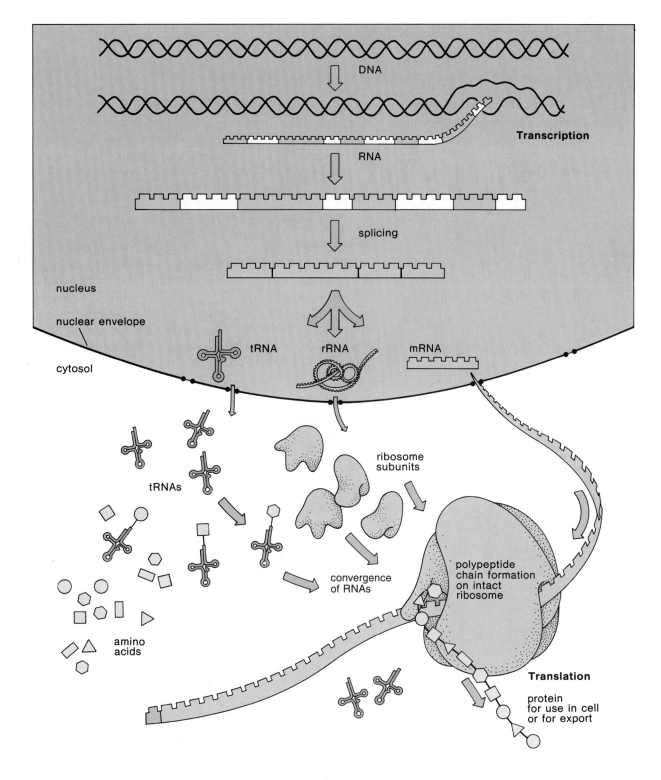

FIGURE 10.16 Summary of transcription and translation in eukaryotes

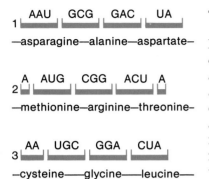

FIGURE 10.17 Three possible reading frames for a segment of mRNA. Each time the reading frame is shifted, a different amino acid sequence results.

10.9 Translation Errors

If the ribosome and tRNA molecules work correctly and the mRNA is coded accurately, the synthesis of the right polypeptide should be almost automatic. Nonetheless, some errors do occur, although most are caught and corrected. The most common error results from misreading the nucleotide sequence. Initiation determines exactly where translation will begin and how the nucleotide sequence will be grouped into codons. The grouping of bases into codons is called the reading frame (Figure 10.17). If the frame is shifted by one or two nucleotides in either direction, the nucleotide sequence will produce a different sequence of amino acids. For example, AAU GCG GAC UA would specify asparagine–alanine–aspartate. If the reading frame were shifted one nucleotide to the right, the message would read methionine–arginine–threonine. What message would be conveyed if the reading frame were shifted two nucleotides to the right?

Some errors can be traced back to the DNA in the cell nucleus. Certain segments of DNA are repeated frequently. Some of the repeated segments may become inverted, coding backwards. Some segments mysteriously jump to a new location on the DNA molecule, resulting in incorrect regions along the DNA strand. Yet the correct strands are needed to transcribe DNA to mRNA properly. Proofreading by enzymes and ribosomes eliminates many errors as proteins are synthesized, but it cannot eliminate them all.

10.10 Transport and Modification of Proteins

Except for the few proteins made in mitochondria and chloroplasts, proteins of eukaryotic cells are made on ribosomes surrounded by cytosol. Most of these proteins eventually end up inside an organelle or in a membrane. How do they get there? Recent research shows that membrane and organelle proteins are synthesized on ribosomes attached to the rough endoplasmic reticulum (rough ER). The ER appears rough in electron micrographs because of the ribosomes attached to the ER membrane (see Figure 6.10). These ribosomes carry out protein synthesis in the manner described in Section 10.8. Next, the ribosome needs to be attached to the ER membrane, and a signal must direct where in the cell the protein to be synthesized will go.

The first few amino acids synthesized on the ribosome provide the directions, or signal sequence, for these activities. After the first few codons of mRNA are translated, the signal sequence extends out of the unattached ribosome and binds to a receptor protein in the rough ER membrane. As translation continues, the growing chain of amino acids is threaded through the membrane and into the space inside the ER. These events are illustrated in Figure 10.18. When the end of the mRNA is reached and the last amino acid is in place, the new protein is released from the ribosome into the inner ER. Often a sugar molecule is added to the protein, forming a glycoprotein that is packaged in the Golgi apparatus and sealed in a vesicle. These proteins may become part of a membrane or an organelle, or they may be exported from the cell as described in Chapter 6.

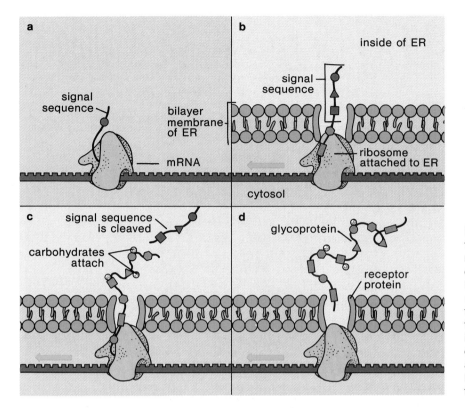

FIGURE 10.18 Synthesis of proteins for secretion or insertion in a membrane. The first few amino acids constitute a signal sequence (a) that binds to a receptor molecule in the rough ER membrane (b) and threads the growing amino acid chain through the membrane and into the inside of the ER as translation continues. Sugar molecules may be added to form glycoproteins (c) before the new protein is released to the inside of the ER (d).

Following translation, the new amino acid chain may be modified before it becomes a functional protein. The chain may be cut into smaller segments, or a piece may be clipped away. Special modification enzymes are responsible for the cutting and clipping activity. For example, in the human stomach and small intestine, two enzymes, pepsin and trypsin, are responsible for the digestion of proteins in the diet. Both of these enzymes are synthesized as much larger, inactive enzymes on the ribosome. They become active when they are clipped at a certain point along the amino acid chain.

CHECK AND CHALLENGE

1. Describe the steps involved in adding amino acids to a polypeptide chain on a ribosome.
2. Why is accurate initiation of protein synthesis important?
3. What is a signal sequence, and what is its significance in protein synthesis?
4. What part do codons and anticodons play in translation?
5. What is a charged tRNA? What is its role in translation?

Summary

Genes, the coding regions of chromosomes, are made of DNA and are expressed as proteins. DNA is a blueprint of instructions that directs the activities of the cell. The instructions in DNA (genes) are like sentences. Each sentence is copied (transcribed) into a message (mRNA) that moves to the print shop (ribosome). The words (codons) of the message are written in three letters (nucleotide triplets) that are translated into action (proteins). Proteins are the structural and functional macromolecules of life.

Transcription is the synthesis of RNA on the DNA template. A coding strand of DNA is transcribed by RNA polymerases into primary RNA transcripts that are processed to tRNA, rRNA or mRNA in the nucleus. Proteins combine with rRNA to form ribosomes, the workbench of protein synthesis. Amino acids are carried by their matching tRNAs to the ribosomes. Protein synthesis is the translation of the sequence of codons in mRNA, the genetic code, into the sequence of amino acids in a protein.

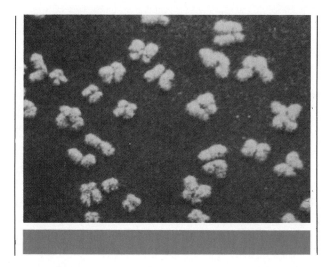

Key Concepts

Below is an incomplete concept map. Use the concepts listed on page 241 and additional concepts from the chapter to build a more complete map.

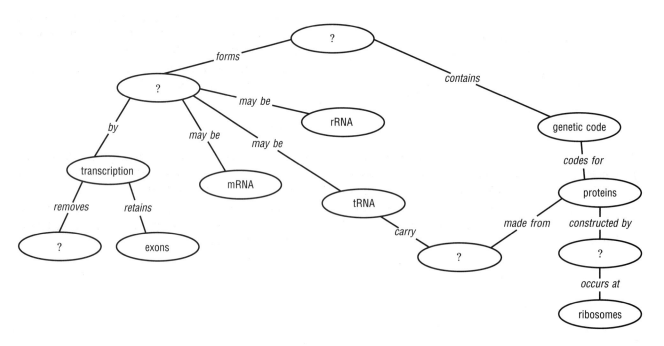

amino acids   introns
anticodons   RNA
codons   translation
DNA

Reviewing Ideas

1. Describe the functions of the three types of RNA in eukaryotic cells.

2. What are the major steps in processing primary RNA transcripts into mRNA, tRNA and rRNA?

3. How did Nirenberg's experiments lead to the cracking of the genetic code?

4. What is the role of the nucleolus?

5. The genetic code is made of triplets. Why are there three nucleotides instead of two or one?

6. Describe the major steps of protein synthesis on the ribosome.

7. What are the possible biological roles of the cap and poly-A tail of mRNA?

8. How is your DNA like that of grasshoppers, paramecia, and pines? How is it different?

9. Describe the mechanism by which proteins that are destined to become part of a membrane or organelle could be packaged and transported after translation.

10. Why is the primary structure of a protein so important in cell function?

11. Explain the difference between transcription and translation.

12. How does tRNA charging take place?

Using Concepts

1. There are three forms of RNA polymerase in eukaryotes. Propose a biological role for each of the three forms—RNA polymerase I, II, and III.

2. Construct an mRNA molecule that is the complement of the following coded sequence of DNA: ATT ACG CGG TCA GTA.

3. You have animal cells growing in a laboratory tissue culture, and your experiment is to measure mRNA synthesis. Which radioactive nucleotide should you provide to the cells to measure RNA synthesis and why?

4. You need to measure protein synthesis in plant cells growing in a tissue culture. You will use a radioactive tracer method, except that you have the radioisotopes of carbon-14, sulphur-35, phosphorus-32, and nitrogen-13. Which isotope should you provide to the cells as a specific measure of protein synthesis? Explain your answer.

5. A polyribosome is several ribosomes attached to a mRNA molecule. Would the proteins manufactured by a polyribosome be different or the same? Explain your answer.

6. How do genes determine whether hair (made of protein) is straight or curly?

7. What would be the end result of translation if the ribosome skipped one or more codons?

8. What would be the end result of translation if the ribosome shifted by only one nucleotide instead of by one codon?

Synthesis

1. What is the relationship between the structure and function of proteins, and what is the role of DNA in that relationship?

2. What are the chief differences between replication and transcription?

Extensions

1. Write a short essay justifying the statement "genes control cellular respiration." Explain in detail how genes do that.

2. Show, as a cartoon or series of cartoons, the sequence of events that occur during translation on the ribosomes.

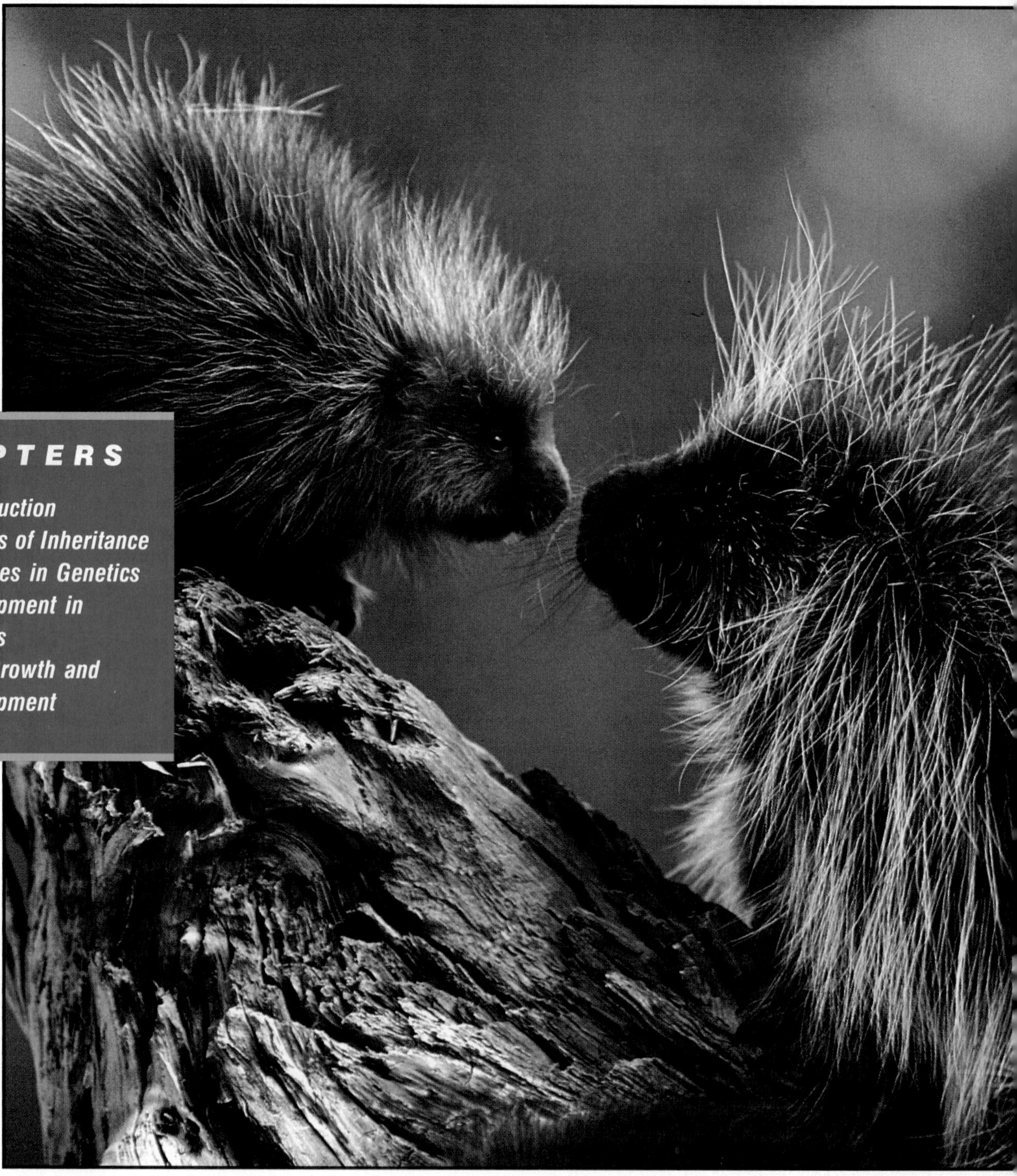

CHAPTERS

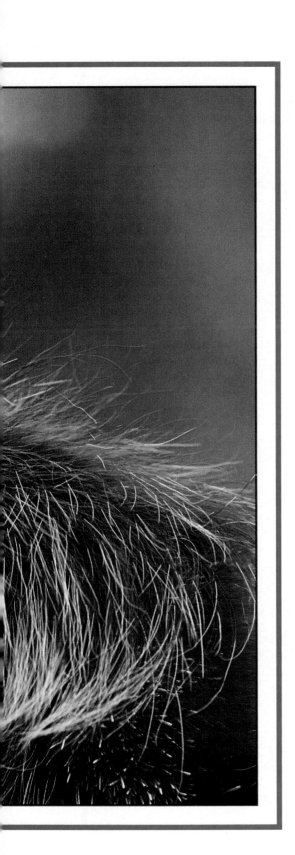

Genetic Continuity

*A*lthough children often resemble their parents in many ways, they also differ from them in many other aspects. Have you noticed similarities and differences in your family? How do we explain why offspring resemble their parents and yet are not completely identical to them?

Genetics is the science of heredity, and genetic continuity is the production of offspring in each generation that are very similar to their parents. The young porcupine shown here eventually will resemble its mother even more closely. The processes responsible for genetic continuity among porcupines operate for all organisms.

*H*ow would you explain the close resemblance between the young porcupine (Erethizon dorsatum) *and its mother?*

*A*side from contributing genetic information, how else might parents influence their offspring?

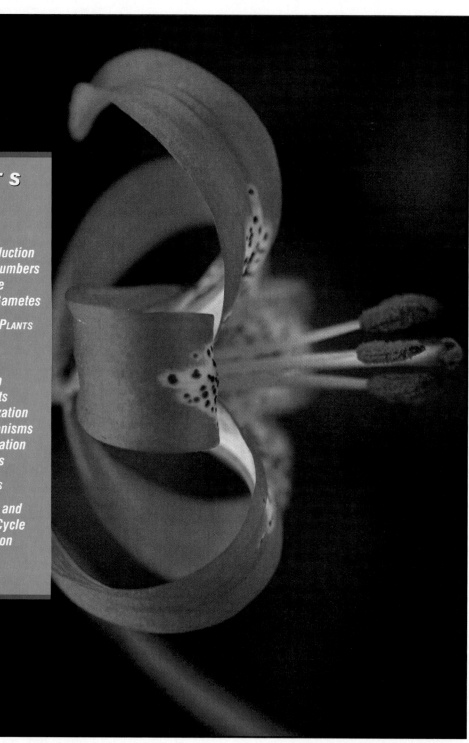

CONTENTS

Reproduction

*W*hat reproductive
structures can you
identify?

*W*hat other
adaptations for
reproduction are
present in this flower?

*R*eproduction is a basic function of living things. However, it is not necessary for the life of an individual organism. Unlike other life functions—eating, sleeping, breathing—reproduction has value only for the survival of a species as a whole. The perpetuation of a species depends on the successful reproduction of its individual members. It is through reproduction that a species passes its unique genetic material to subsequent generations.

What if an individual cannot produce offspring and pass on genetic material? One sixth of the members of your class may face this problem one day. How can knowledge of the cellular and molecular basis of reproduction help? Researchers use such knowledge to help develop technologies that address reproductive problems. For example, in 1978 the development of *in vitro* fertilization technology allowed a woman with blocked Fallopian tubes to give birth to a healthy baby girl. Since then, there have been other significant advances in reproductive technology. However, the same technology that enables the birth of healthy babies raises ethical issues. Knowledge also gives people the information they need to make reproductive decisions that involve values and ethics.

The reproduction and perpetuation of the species is ultimately ensured by evolutionary adaptations. Through more than 3 billion years, species have evolved a variety of ways that ensure their continuity. This chapter also examines some patterns of reproduction that relate to you and the other organisms of the five kingdoms.

◆ *A lily,* Lilium occidentalum.

Cell Division and Reproduction

11.1   Asexual Reproduction

Asexual reproduction requires only one parent to produce an offspring. In every biological kingdom, there are some organisms that reproduce asexually (Figure 11.1). For example, as you read in Chapter 9, prokaryotes reproduce by binary fission. One-celled eukaryotes such as *Paramecium* reproduce by mitotic cell division. Both processes result in two similar-sized offspring cells. Other examples of organisms that reproduce asexually are yeasts and hydras, which reproduce by a process called budding. The buds grow to adult size and detach as new individuals. The flatworm *Planaria* reproduces by fragmentation (breaking into pieces); each piece grows into a new planarian.

Many familiar plants reproduce by vegetative reproduction, a type of asexual reproduction by growth of structures not specialized for reproduction. For example, grasses and strawberries grow new plants along horizontal stems called runners. Potatoes, which are enlarged underground stems, can grow new plants from each "eye." Aspen trees reproduce when new trees sprout from the root system of older trees. If you have ever grown a plant from a cutting, you were taking advantage of vegetative reproduction. Cuttings from a parent plant can be rooted and then grown into mature plants when placed in soil. You can see in Figure 11.2 another less familiar form of vegetative reproduction, in which the parent plant produces new plants along its leaf edges.

In some animals, an unfertilized egg can develop into an individual organism that is genetically identical to its mother. For example, unfertil-

FIGURE 11.1 Methods of asexual reproduction: (a) mitotic cell division in *Paramecium*, (b) budding in *Hydra*, (c) fragmentation in *Planaria*.

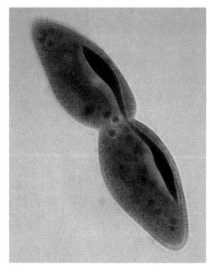
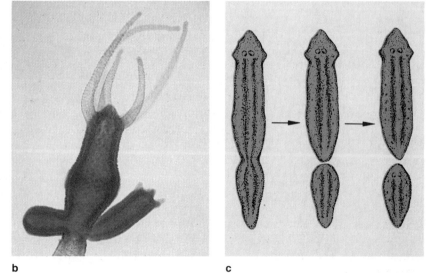

a   b   c

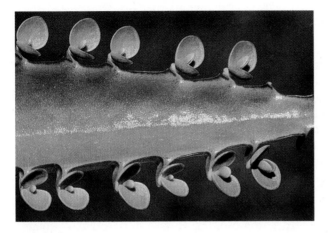

FIGURE 11.2 Leaves of *Bryophyllum* produce little plants, each of which may fall to the ground and grow as a new plant.

FIGURE 11.3 Desert whiptail lizards, *Cnemidophorus neomexicanus*, is a species that consists entirely of females.

ized eggs from queen bees develop into male bees. Some lizards, fish, and amphibians also reproduce by this method. An example is the desert whiptail lizard shown in Figure 11.3. Certain species of this lizard consist entirely of female populations. The females lay eggs that develop into adult females without being fertilized. Seven generations of female lizards have been raised this way in the laboratory.

Asexual reproduction in eukaryotes occurs as a result of mitotic cell division. In the examples of asexual reproduction just described, new organisms develop from one parent whose cells undergo mitosis. Therefore the cells of offspring contain chromosomes identical to those of the parent. The only exception is the occasional occurrence of a mutation (Chapters 9 and 12). Organisms that are genetically identical to their parent are known as clones.

11.2 Chromosome Numbers

Each species has a characteristic number of chromosomes. All humans have 46 chromosomes. House flies have 12 chromosomes, turkeys have 82, and giant redwoods have 22. Like humans, tropical fish called black mollies also have 46 chromosomes. However, the chromosomes of black mollies and of humans are not the same, nor do they have the same genes as those in humans.

Prokaryotes generally have only one chromosome, which may be present as a single circle of DNA, and one or more smaller plasmids. In eukaryotes, chromosomes usually occur in pairs. Thus each species contains an even number of chromosomes. The two chromosomes of a pair are described as **homologous** (ho MOL uh gus). Homologous chromosomes, or homologs, are similar in structure, carry the same types of genes, and have the same evolutionary origin. (An exception is the pair called the sex chromosomes, which determine the sex of the individual. The sex chromosomes may be very different in size and shape and may carry different genes from each other.)

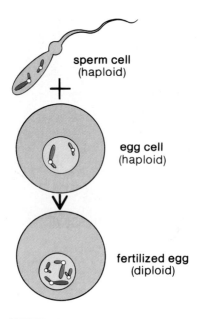

FIGURE 11.4 Gametes unite in the process of fertilization, restoring the diploid number of chromosomes. The new individual has a combination of chromosomes from the two gametes.

Try Investigation 11A, The Yeast Life Cycle

Regardless of whether chromosomes occur singly or in pairs, their numbers from one generation to another remain constant. In asexual reproduction, this constancy is maintained by mitotic cell division. The chromosomes of the single parent duplicate and separate as the offspring's cells form. In sexual reproduction, however, *two* parents contribute chromosomes to offspring.

Each parent produces **gametes** (GAM eets; Greek: "to marry"), or reproductive cells. During fertilization, the nuclei of two gametes—one from each parent—unite and a new individual begins. However, if gametes contained the same number of chromosomes as the body cells of each parent, what would happen to the chromosome number from one generation to the next? The number would double: for humans, the 46 chromosomes from each parent would result in 92 chromosomes in their child. Yet humans normally have 46 chromosomes. How is this constancy maintained? Scientists have found that gametes are different from somatic, or body cells. The reproductive cells have only half the number of chromosomes—*one* chromosome of each homologous pair.

Male gametes are sperm and female gametes are ova (singular ovum), or eggs. Because gametes contain only one chromosome from each homologous pair, they are described as **haploid** (single) cells and are represented by the symbol n. Cells with both chromosomes of each pair are called **diploid** (di = two) and are represented as $2n$. Figure 11.4 shows that the union of two haploid cell nuclei—a sperm and an egg—restores the chromosomes to the diploid number. Note that in the figure, the diploid number is four—two pairs of chromosomes.

A specialized type of cell division known as **meiosis** (my OH sis) halves the number of chromosomes in gametes. In sexual reproduction, meiosis and fertilization are complementary processes: meiosis produces the haploid (n) chromosome number in reproductive cells, and fertilization restores the diploid ($2n$) chromosome number.

11.3 Meiosis and the Production of Gametes

Two hints may help you understand meiosis. First, to determine how many chromosomes are present, count the number of centromeres. Sister chromatids joined at the centromere are considered to be one chromosome, therefore, the number of centromeres equals the number of chromosomes. Second, remember that meiosis consists of one replication of chromosomes followed by two cell divisions. Figure 11.5 illustrates meiosis in a cell with two pairs of chromosomes. Trace the events of meiosis in Figure 11.5 as you read the descriptions that follow.

In a cell about to start meiosis, one chromosome of each homologous pair is called maternal because it came from the organism's female parent; the other is called paternal because it came from the male parent. The chromosomes replicate during the S phase preceding meiosis, as described in Chapter 9. Therefore, as meiosis begins (a), each chromosome is a double structure of two chromatids joined at the centromere. The cells are diploid, because they have two pairs of chromosomes.

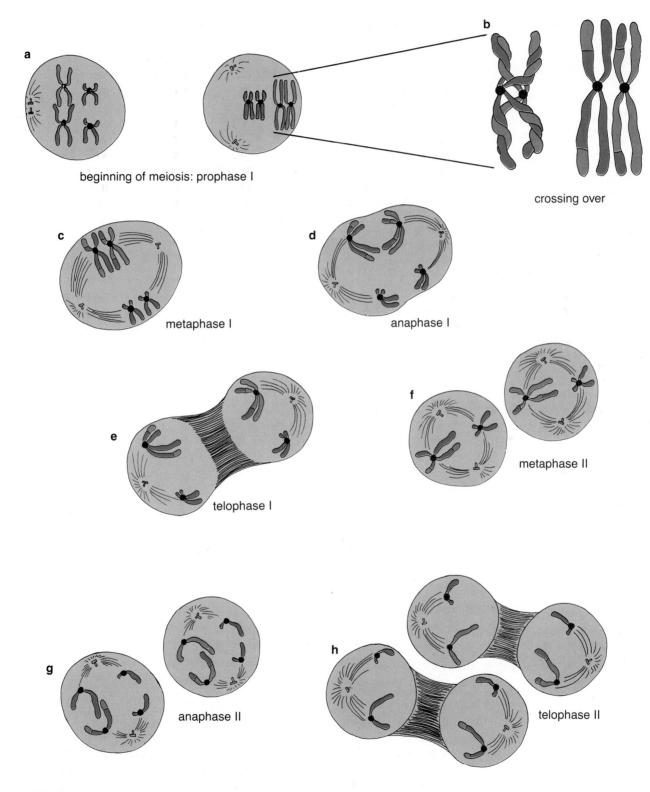

beginning of meiosis: prophase I

crossing over

metaphase I

anaphase I

telophase I

metaphase II

anaphase II

telophase II

FIGURE 11.5 The stages of meiosis

FOCUS ON *Chromosome Position*

In anaphase I, the spindle pulls one chromosome from each homologous pair to one side of the cell and the other homologous chromosome to the opposite side. Eventually, the two new cells that form contain one chromosome from each homologous pair. Each chromosome's alignment on the spindle determines which cell it enters. Look again at the diagram of metaphase I in Figure 11.5c. Notice that the homologous pairs are arranged at the equator of the cell. Each homolog has an equal chance of being on either the right or left side of the equator. Figure A shows the possible combinations of position for the two homologous pairs. Follow one of the two pairs of chromosomes through the entire process of meiosis. Where would that chromosome have gone if it had lined up on the opposite side of the equator in metaphase I? Trace several other chromosomes through the process

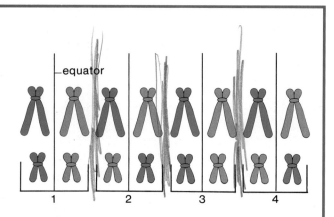

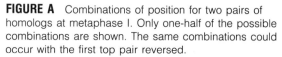

FIGURE A   Combinations of position for two pairs of homologs at metaphase I. Only one-half of the possible combinations are shown. The same combinations could occur with the first top pair reversed.

of meiosis. The significance of this chance assortment of homologous chromosomes will become more apparent as you study the process of heredity in the next two chapters.

In prophase I a unique event occurs. The replicated chromosomes of each homologous pair come close together and may twist around each other (b). In this position, DNA from one chromosome may be exchanged with corresponding DNA from the other homologous chromosome. The process of exchanging DNA between chromatids of homologous chromosomes is called **crossing over.** Note that crossing over occurs between homologs, not replicated sister chromatids. Therefore, after crossing over the chromosomes are no longer identical to the original paternal and maternal chromosomes; they are a mixture of both. In fact, it is no longer appropriate to refer to the chromosomes as maternal and paternal because they are a mixture.

In metaphase I (c), the homologous pairs of chromosomes move to the equator of the cell, and the centromeres attach to the spindle apparatus. In anaphase I (d), the homologs separate as the spindle apparatus pulls the centromeres to opposite sides of the cell. Note that the centromeres do not divide in anaphase I.

In telophase I (e), the homologous chromosomes have separated, and the reproductive cells are dividing. How many chromosomes are now present in each nucleus? Compare them with the original cell at the beginning of meiosis. Counting the centromeres, you should see only two chromosomes in the nucleus of each new cell. The first meiotic division reduces the chromosome number from diploid ($2n$) to haploid (n). However, each chromosome still consists of two chromatids attached at its centromere.

Meiosis continues with a relatively short prophase II, in which no additional crossing over occurs. In metaphase II (f), the chromosomes again move to the equator in each of the two cells. This time, however, there are no homologous chromosome pairs. The chromosomes line up in single file down the equator of each cell, just as in mitosis. The spindle apparatus attaches to the centromere of each chromosome.

In anaphase II (g), the centromeres divide, and the spindle apparatus pulls the chromosomes apart, to opposite sides of the cell. Telophase II (h) completes the second meiotic division. The result is four haploid cells, each containing two *single* chromosomes.

The cytoplasm does not always divide equally among cells formed by meiotic division. Figure 11.6 shows that male animals, including humans, usually produce four equal-sized sperm from each original cell. Females, however, usually produce only one ovum from each original cell. To see how that difference occurs, study Figure 11.7. In the first meiotic division, one complete set of chromosomes is cast off in a polar body. The polar body consists mainly of the single set of chromosomes. Most of the cytoplasm remains in one haploid cell. In the second meiotic division, another polar body with a haploid set of chromosomes is cast off from the larger haploid cell. In most species of animals, the two polar bodies disintegrate. The remaining cell, which becomes the ovum, contains a haploid set of chromosomes. You will read about the evolutionary importance of retaining most of the cytoplasm in the ovum in Chapter 14.

CONNECTIONS

The evolutionary significance of sexual reproduction lies in the genetic variation it produces. Natural selection, acting on genetic variation, leads to the evolution of new adaptations and new species.

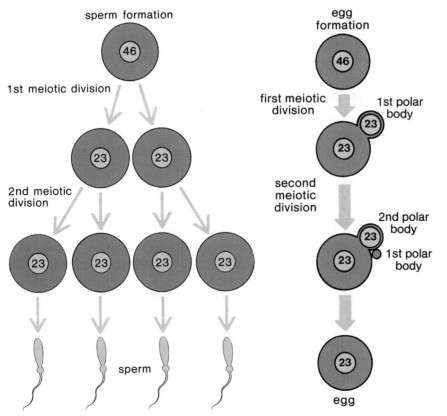

FIGURE 11.6 (*left*) In human males, meiotic division usually results in four equal-sized sperm, each with 23 chromosomes.

FIGURE 11.7 (*right*) Formation of polar bodies

Try Investigation 11B, A Model of Meiosis

You have seen that meiosis produces two important results. One is **genetic recombination,** or the rearrangement of genes and chromosomes. Two sources of recombination are the exchange of genes during crossing over in prophase I and the chance assortment of chromosomes in anaphase I. Genetic recombination is thus a major contributor to variation among individuals of the same species. For example, genetic recombination is the main reason you and your siblings do not look exactly alike (unless you are identical twins). The second important result is the reduction to the haploid chromosome number in telophase I. This change prepares the cells for fertilization, when the diploid number is restored.

CHECK AND CHALLENGE

1. Why does asexual reproduction result in a clone?
2. Describe three different types of vegetative reproduction.
3. Explain how asexual reproduction in animals can result in entire populations of females with no males.
4. Why is the reduction in chromosome number important in sexual reproduction?
5. Why are the chromosome numbers of species even numbers rather than odd numbers?
6. How does sexual reproduction affect genetic variation among individuals of a species?
7. How are meiosis and fertilization complementary processes?

Sexual Reproduction in Plants and Animals

11.4   Life Cycles

In the life cycle of animals, meiotic cell division usually occurs only when gametes are produced. In some plants, however, meiosis produces cells that grow into new, multicellular haploid plants. As these haploid plants mature they produce female and male gametes by mitotic cell division. The fusion of the nuclei of these female and male gametes produces a diploid cell that grows into a diploid plant. Thus, a haploid stage alternates with a diploid stage in the life cycle, which is called alternation of generations.

The haploid stage was the dominant stage in the life cycles of many organisms of the prehistoric past and is the dominant stage among their modern descendants—protists and fungi as well as some plants. For example, the mosses shown in Figure 11.8 produce eggs and sperm at the tips of separate, individual haploid plants. The damp habitats that mosses require provide water that is necessary for the sperm to swim to the tips of female plants, where they fertilize the eggs. Water must be present for fertilization to occur. The fertilized diploid cell grows into a small structure that remains attached to the haploid plant. Meiosis occurs in the diploid struc-

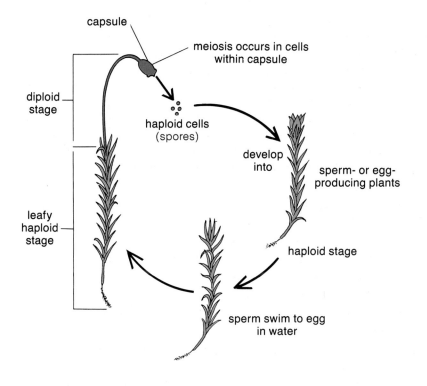

capsule

meiosis occurs in cells
within capsule

diploid
stage

haploid cells
(spores)

develop
into

sperm- or egg-
producing plants

leafy
haploid
stage

haploid stage

sperm swim to egg
in water

FIGURE 11.8 In the life cycle of the
moss, a haploid stage alternates with
a diploid stage. The haploid stage is
the dominant stage.

ture and produces haploid cells called **spores.** When released, spores
develop into new haploid moss plants without fusing with other cells. The
female spores develop into female plants, and the male spores develop into
male plants.

Unlike moss plants, the diploid stage is dominant in the life cycle of
most animal and plant species. In humans, for example, somatic cells have
23 pairs of chromosomes (46 in all). Only the gametes that result from
meiotic cell division are haploid, with 23 unpaired chromosomes. Similarly, an oak tree also is a diploid structure and produces haploid reproductive cells in the spring. In the remainder of this chapter you will read about
the reproductive processes of other plants and animals in which the diploid
stage is dominant and the haploid stage is relatively inconspicuous.

11.5 Reproduction in Flowering Plants

Flowering plants are diploid and produce gametes in specialized organs
located in the flowers. Locate the female organ, or **carpel** (KAR pel) in
Figure 11.9a on the next page. At the base of the carpel is the ovary, which
contains one or more small structures called **ovules** (OHV yoolz), from
which eggs develop. Trace an egg's development in Figure 11.9b. Within
each ovule a specialized cell undergoes meiosis, forming four haploid cells,
three of which disintegrate. The fourth cell undergoes a series of mitotic
divisions to produce seven cells. One of these cells is the ovum, or egg.
Another is a large cell containing two nuclei known as polar nuclei.

**Try Investigation 11C,
Reproduction in Mosses and
Flowering Plants.**

You can trace male pollen grain formation in Figure 11.9c. In the male organs, or **stamens** (STAY menz), cells in the tip—the anther—undergo meiosis, each giving rise to four haploid cells. Each haploid cell divides mitotically to produce a pollen grain containing two cells—a tube cell and a second cell that gives rise to two haploid sperm nuclei.

Pollen is shed by the anther and may be carried to the carpel of the same or of different flowers by wind, water, insects, birds, or other animals. The transfer of pollen from anther to carpel, where fertilization takes place, is called **pollination**. Cross-pollination (pollination between two different

FIGURE 11.9 Reproductive parts of a flower. Gametes in flowering plants form from specialized cells. Meiosis and mitosis both occur during the process.

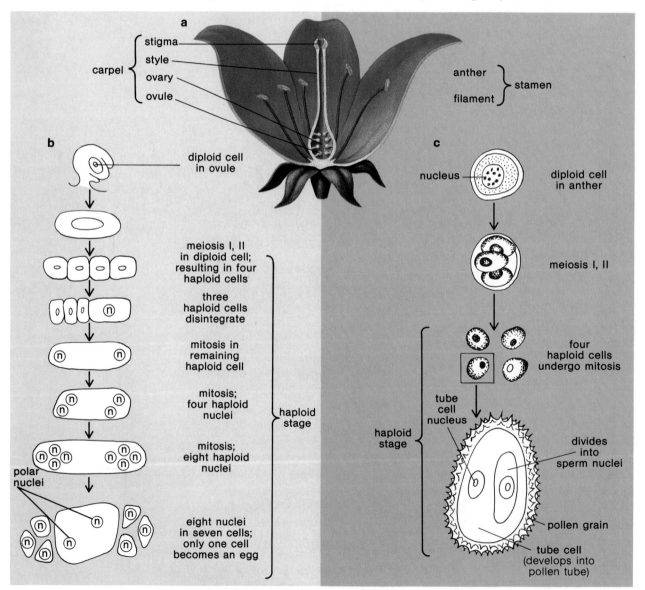

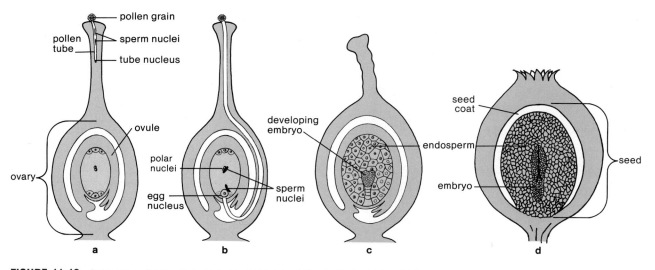

FIGURE 11.10 Pollination, fertilization, and development of the embryo, endosperm, and seed in a flowering plant

plants of the same species) increases genetic variation because the offspring receive a haploid set of chromosomes from each of two different parents. Many intricate mechanisms for pollination have evolved in plants. Some insects and flowering plants have become so completely dependent on each other that neither can reproduce without the other. (See **Appendix 11A**, Pollination by Insects Aids Fertilization.) You will read about how these mechanisms may have evolved in Chapter 16.

When pollen lands on the tip of the carpel, or stigma, the pollen grain germinates and forms a pollen tube that grows toward the ovule, carrying the sperm nuclei. You can follow the path of the pollen tube and sperm nuclei in Figure 11.10. Fertilization occurs when one sperm nucleus fuses with the egg. The resulting diploid cell divides mitotically and eventually develops into a young plant, or **embryo.** The second sperm nucleus fuses with the two polar nuclei, forming a triploid ($3n$) cell that develops into a food storing tissue called the endosperm. This double fertilization signals the end of the short haploid stage in the life cycle of a flowering plant. The ovule then becomes a seed, forming a protective coat that encloses the embryo and endosperm. At about the same time, the ovary enlarges and develops into a fruit. Figure 11.11a on the next page shows the many forms of fruit. The seed's endosperm is rich in energy and nourishes the embryo once a seed germinates and starts to grow. The endosperm of grains such as wheat, oats, corn, and rye, contains stored energy that humans and other animals use as food.

Fruits and seeds are dispersed by a variety of methods, as shown in Figure 11.11b on the next page. A coconut drifting on an ocean current may be transported thousands of miles from one island to another. Many fruits—those of dandelions and maples, for example—are carried by the wind. Others, such as cockleburs, are adapted for sticking to animal fur. Many seeds remain inside fruits, which may be eaten by birds or other

CONNECTIONS

*T*he interdependence of flowering plants and their insect pollinators is an example of coevolution— the parallel development of interacting adaptations.

FIGURE 11.11 (a) Each edible fruit is a mature ovary containing the seeds of the plant. (b) Many seeds have structural adaptations for seed dispersal. Can you describe them?

animals and transported great distances in the animals' digestive tracts. Eventually the animals deposit the undigested seeds along with other organic wastes, which aid the growth of the young plants in their new location.

Figure 11.12 shows that flowering plants are found in widely different environments. Several adaptations contribute much to their success: (1) the dominance of the diploid stage in the life cycle, which allows for the development of complex structures; (2) the evolution of pollen, which allows the transfer of sperm from plant to plant without the need for water; (3) the evolution of the seed, which provides food and protection for the young plant; and (4) a variety of methods for pollen and seed dispersal.

FIGURE 11.12 (a) Pacific rhododendron, *Rhododendron macrophyllum,* in an evergreen forest; (b) ocotillo, *Fouquieria splendens,* in a desert; (c) water lily, *Nymphaea odorata*

a   b   c

11.6   External Fertilization in Aquatic Organisms

Sexual reproduction is the most common method of reproduction among animals. Almost all animals that reproduce sexually have separate organs that produce male and female gametes. These specialized organs are of two types: **ovaries**, which produce ova, and **testes** (TES teez; singular, testis), which produce sperm. Collectively, these organs are known as gonads.

In many species of invertebrate animals, the same individual produces both eggs and sperm. This characteristic is true of hydras, earthworms, some sponges, and a variety of other organisms. Most of these organisms, however, are not usually self-fertilizing. Instead, one individual transfers sperm to the egg or eggs of another individual. Among vertebrates, some species can produce both eggs and sperm, but none are known to produce both types of gametes simultaneously. (Contrast this with the plants, which frequently produce both types of sex cells at the same time.)

The large size of the animal egg is an adaptation that reflects its function as a storehouse for the food, RNA, ribosomes, and mitochondria that support the embryo's early development. This large size makes the egg unable to move by means of a flagella. In contrast, the tiny sperm can move with a swimming motion, which requires a liquid environment. To achieve fertilization, aquatic animals need only release their gametes into the surrounding water, a process known as spawning. Large numbers of gametes are necessary, though, because the water dilutes their numbers, decreasing the likelihood of fertilization. In addition, because most aquatic organisms do not care for their eggs or their young, predators eat most of them. Consider that salmon lay as many as 17 000 eggs at a time, and codfish lay more then 6 000 000. Because of such huge numbers, spawning results in enough fertilized eggs to preserve the species.

Amphibian eggs also are fertilized externally. Amphibians represent an intermediate stage of evolution between aquatic and land-dwelling organisms. Part of their life cycle takes place in the water and part on land. Frogs, for example, can live on land but must lay their eggs in water, as shown in Figure 11.13. The eggs are relatively small, have no shell, and contain only enough stored food for the embryo to develop to the tadpole stage. Amphibians also lay large numbers of eggs, but most of the young that hatch do not survive to become breeding adults.

Because an animal sperm contains little stored nourishment, it cannot live long after being released. If a sperm is to reach an egg, both must be shed at approximately the same time and place. Many patterns of behavior have evolved that help bring this circumstance about. Elaborate movements are "acted out" by reptiles, birds, and other animals as they prepare to mate (Figure 11.14). The movements of one species of animal usually do not attract animals of a different species, so these rituals also serve to maintain breeding within individuals of the same species.

One interesting behavior pattern is the exact timing shown by the grunion, a saltwater fish, in releasing male and female gametes. The grunion swim ashore on the highest waves of the highest night tides of the month. During brief intervals between waves, the female deposits her eggs in the sand, and the male sheds sperm over them. The fertilized eggs hatch in time to be carried out to sea by the highest tides of the next month.

FIGURE 11.13   Southwestern toads, *Bufo microscaphus*, mating. The male deposits sperm over the eggs as the female releases them.

FIGURE 11.14   Many animals have evolved elaborate behavior patterns that result in release of sperm and eggs at approximately the same time.

a. The male fiddler crab attracts attention by waving its one large claw.

b. The male reddish egret adopts this position when courting.

11.7 Internal Fertilization in Land Animals

In all land animals and in some aquatic animals, evolution has produced internal fertilization, an adaptation that further increases the chances of fertilization. During internal fertilization a male releases sperm into the female reproductive tract so that fertilization of the egg occurs within the body of the female. Internal fertilization protects the gametes from the hazards of the outside environment. Liquid necessary for the movement of the sperm is often produced by the male reproductive organs. Therefore, when eggs are released from the ovary of the female, they are likely to be fertilized if sufficient sperm are present.

Because the egg is sheltered within the female's body, animals that have internal fertilization require relatively small numbers of eggs. Nevertheless, for several reasons large numbers of sperm are needed to ensure fertilization. One reason is time. Because sperm contain little stored nutrients, they can live only a short time. For example, the life span of a human sperm is about three days. Furthermore, the human egg usually remains fertile for only about a day. For fertilization to take place, egg and sperm must be released at about the same time.

Another reason large numbers of sperm are needed for fertilization is that the microscopic sperm must swim several centimeters to the egg in the oviduct. In humans the two ovaries alternate in the release of eggs. Therefore, half the sperm swim to an oviduct that has no egg waiting. Relatively few sperm ever reach the egg. Of the 200 million sperm that human males release, the majority die on the way.

A third reason is that the enzyme activity of many sperm is required to break down the membrane and layers of cells that protect the egg. Once one sperm enters the egg, chemical and physical changes immediately take place that make it impossible for other sperm to penetrate the egg. The nucleus of the sperm that is inside the egg unites with the egg's nucleus, and the development of a new individual begins.

In many insects the problem of timing and release of the gametes is solved by storing sperm in a pouch of the female. The female releases sperm as she lays eggs. Bees may store sperm for an entire life span. The way in which this feat is accomplished is not fully understood.

As in animals with external fertilization, in many vertebrates with internal fertilization, elaborate premating rituals have evolved that coordinate the timing of gamete release. For example, newts and salamanders, which are amphibians, have an elaborate display pattern of "dancing" movements and head bobbing prior to gamete release. Once the proper ritual has been performed, the male releases a packet of sperm cells. The female picks up the packet of sperm and deposits it in the opening that leads to her reproductive organs. The sperm fertilize the eggs internally, and then the fertilized eggs are released to develop externally in the water. These amphibians have evolved a type of internal fertilization that is more advanced than the joint release of eggs and sperm into the water. In contrast to other types of internal fertilization, large numbers of eggs are fertilized. However, few of the young survive predation by other organisms to become breeding adults.

FIGURE 11.15 Human sperm penetrating an egg. Scanning electron micrograph, X17 000

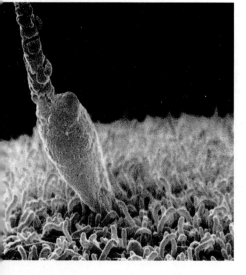

CHECK AND CHALLENGE

1. Distinguish between pollination and fertilization.
2. How does the egg cell develop in a flowering plant?
3. How does a pollen grain form and how does it function in reproduction?
4. Describe the formation and function of the embryo, the endosperm, the seed, and the fruit.
5. In what ways are flowering plants equipped to survive in a wide range of environments?
6. What are the functions of ovaries and testes in animals?
7. How is the number of eggs produced related to the method of fertilization and development?
8. Explain the importance of premating rituals for animals with sexual reproduction.

Reproduction in Humans

11.8   Egg Production and the Menstrual Cycle

In human females, the ovaries are located inside the body cavity (Figure 11.16 on the next page). The ovaries normally release eggs, which are smaller than a pinhead, one at a time. The egg enters one of the two tubular structures called the **oviducts.** They serve as a passageway for the

FOCUS ON *Reproduction in Monotremes and Marsupials*

Reproduction in monotremes (egg-laying mammals) and marsupials (pouched mammals) differs from reproduction in placental mammals, although in all three groups fertilization is internal. The eggs of the duck-billed platypus, a monotreme, are fertilized in the oviduct. As the eggs continue down the oviduct, various glands add albumin and a thin, leathery shell. The platypus lays its eggs in a burrow and incubates them for about 12 days. When the young hatch, they lick milk from the mother's fur. Thus, in the monotremes, there is no period of pregnancy and the developing embryo is nourished by nutrients stored in the egg. As with other mammals, however, monotremes rear their young on milk.

In the red kangaroo, a marsupial, the first pregnancy of the season lasts 33 days. Then the young "joey" is born and crawls unaided to its mother's pouch, where it attaches to a nipple. The mother immediately becomes pregnant again, but the presence of the joey in the pouch arrests the development of the new embryo in the uterus. When the joey leaves the pouch, the embryo in the uterus resumes development and is born about a month later. Again, the mother becomes pregnant, but because the second joey is suckling, the development of the new embryo is arrested. Not all marsupials have this developmental pattern but in all marsupials, the young are born after a very short pregnancy.

FIGURE 11.16 The human female reproductive system. The excretory system is shown in gray for reference.

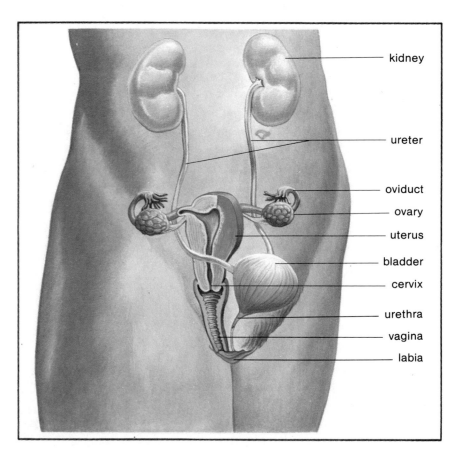

kidney

ureter

oviduct

ovary

uterus

bladder

cervix

urethra

vagina

labia

CONNECTIONS

The interactions that control the menstrual cycle are examples of feedback mechanisms. Such mechanisms enable an organism to function efficiently and are a central part of regulation and homeostasis, the maintenance of a stable internal environment.

egg to move into the **uterus,** a muscular, pear-shaped organ where the fertilized egg develops until birth. At that time, strong muscular contractions push the baby out of the uterus through the **vagina.** The vagina functions in two ways. First, it is a pathway through which a baby passes during birth and through which the menstrual flow passes to the outside of the body. Second, the vagina is where the male deposits sperm during sexual intercourse.

The egg-releasing cycle usually lasts about a month and is called the **menstrual cycle** (*mensis* = Latin for "month"). During the cycle, the inner lining (endometrium) of the uterus builds up in preparation for receiving a fertilized egg. If the egg is not fertilized, the lining, which has a rich blood supply, disintegrates and flows from the uterus through the vagina to the outside of the body. The first day of menstrual flow marks the first day of the menstrual cycle. An "average" length for the menstrual cycle is 28 days, but this varies considerably from one female to another and may vary from cycle to cycle.

The nervous system, several glands and organs, and a variety of hormones interact to regulate the menstrual cycle. Figure 11.17 illustrates the interrelationship of the events of this cycle. The hypothalamus, shown at

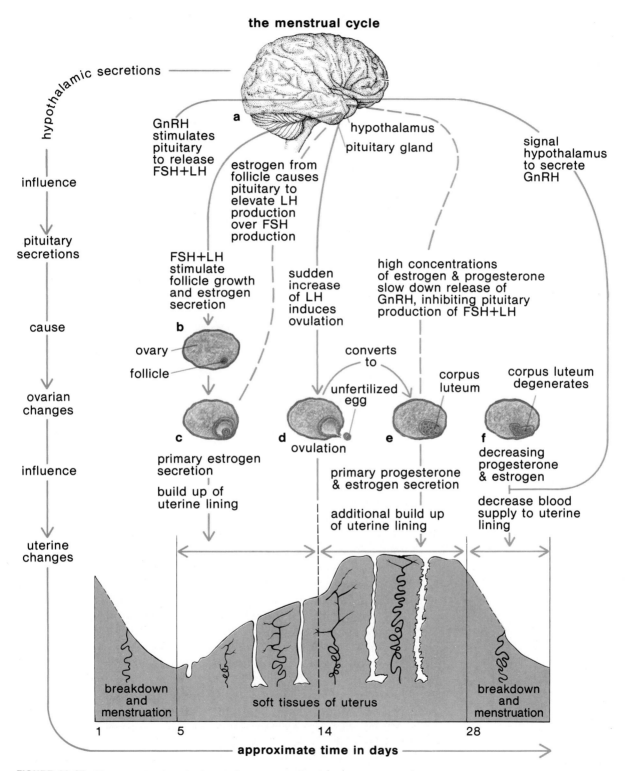

FIGURE 11.17 The menstrual cycle. Interactions among the nervous system and several organs, glands, and hormones regulate the cycle.

(a), acts in the menstrual cycle the way a thermostat acts in a house. A thermostat set at 20°C does not keep the room at exactly that temperature. The room temperature fluctuates slightly as the thermostat causes the furnace to turn on and off. Just as the thermostat monitors and adjusts temperature in a house, the hypothalamus monitors and helps to adjust the level of hormones in the circulatory system.

At the start of the menstrual flow, **estrogen** (ES troh jen) and **progesterone** (proh JES teh rohn), hormones released by the ovaries, are at low levels. These low levels cause the hypothalamus to secrete gonadotropin-releasing hormone (GnRH) into blood vessels that connect directly to the pituitary (pih TOO ih ter ee) gland (a). You can locate the pituitary gland just underneath the brain, next to the hypothalamus. GnRH stimulates the pituitary to release two hormones, follicle-stimulating hormone (FSH) and luteinizing hormone (LH), that act on the ovary. FSH causes an egg to start maturing inside a fluid-filled sac, or follicle (b), in the ovary.

FSH and LH also stimulate the maturing follicle to release the hormone estrogen into the bloodstream. Estrogen affects the uterus, causing an increase in the blood supply and a thickening of the lining. The effects of FSH, LH, and estrogen build up slowly for about 14 days. Just before day 14 of the menstrual cycle, a sudden increase of LH from the pituitary gland causes the follicle to burst and release the egg. This process, shown at (d) is called **ovulation** (ohv yoo LAY shun).

The ruptured follicle becomes the corpus luteum (KOR pus LOOT ee um; Latin for "yellow body"). The corpus luteum (e), inside the ovary, releases estrogen and progesterone. Progesterone adds to the action of estrogen and stimulates additional buildup of the lining of the uterus.

Meanwhile, in the brain, the hypothalamus detects the increased levels of estrogen and progesterone and slows down the release of GnRH. This change causes the pituitary to decrease its release of FSH and LH. Progesterone is now the most highly concentrated hormone in the system. If the egg is not fertilized while traveling down the oviduct toward the uterus, the corpus luteum starts to degenerate (f), and the levels of progesterone and estrogen drop. The drop in estrogen and progesterone levels decreases the blood supply to the lining of the uterus. Menstruation begins as the blood-filled uterine tissues disintegrate and flow through the vagina. The onset of the menstrual flow marks the beginning of another cycle. Notice the approximate timing of the events in the cycle in Figure 11.17.

If the egg is fertilized in the oviduct it undergoes mitotic division on its way to the uterus and becomes an embryo. When the embryo arrives in the uterus, it attaches to the lining, or implants, and begins to form a **placenta** (pluh SENT uh). The placenta is an organ that exchanges nutrients from the mother's blood and waste products from the embryo's blood until birth. The process of implantation is described in more detail in Chapter 14. The placenta begins to release a hormone called human chorionic gonadotropin (HCG). (Many pregnancy tests detect the presence of HCG in the mother's urine.) HCG causes the corpus luteum to continue releasing high levels of progesterone and estrogen. These hormones support the uterine lining in which the embryo develops and indirectly prevent the start of another menstrual cycle, as shown in Figure 11.18a on page 264.

Biological Challenges

INFERTILITY

Despite all we know about human fertility and infertility, many problems cannot be overcome without medical assistance. Some couples can have children only by means of *in vitro* (in glass) fertilization (Figure B). *In vitro* fertilization was originally developed to allow women with blocked oviducts to conceive. If the oviducts are blocked—by malformation or by scarring from infection—sperm cannot reach the ovum to fertilize it. To bypass the blockage, physicians remove several ova directly from the ovaries and fertilize them in a culture dish with the husband's sperm. After fertilization, the embryos are implanted in the mother's uterus.

Usually at least three embryos are placed in the uterus to help ensure that one of them will develop normally. Sometimes additional embryos are removed, frozen, and later thawed for use in case the original embryos do not develop. If it is impossible to use the male's sperm because of an abnormality or genetic disorder, sperm are obtained from an anonymous donor selected by a sperm bank. Donors are checked carefully for possible infectious diseases, and every effort is made to match physical characteristics of the donor with those of the infertile male.

Another alternative for infertile couples is to use the male's sperm to fertilize eggs donated by another woman. In extreme cases, both donor sperm and eggs can be used for implanting embryos.

One interesting case occurred in South Africa. A young woman had to have her uterus removed after the birth of her first child. The couple wanted more children but this was now impossible. The problem was solved when the woman's mother agreed to carry her daughter's embryos for her. Three eggs were removed from the daughter's ovaries, fertilized *in vitro* with the husband's sperm, and implanted in the surrogate mother. The surrogate mother gave birth to triplets that were her own grandchildren.

The possibility of surrogate motherhood raises some difficult questions. Whose baby is it, and which woman has a more substantial claim to motherhood—the surrogate mother or the donor of the eggs? There are no certain or easy answers to these questions. Some people maintain that surrogate motherhood, particularly for payment, should be outlawed. Others see it as a reversal of the progress that has been made in women's rights during the last two decades. These individuals claim that women who become surrogate mothers for money are viewed as worthwhile only because they can produce children.

Progress in dealing with fertility problems is so rapid that it presents us with many new questions we are unprepared to answer. These problems demonstrate both the capabilities and the limitations of science. Knowledge of science tells us what we *can* do, but such knowledge does not tell us what we *should* do.

FIGURE B Ova being fertilized in an embryo culture dish

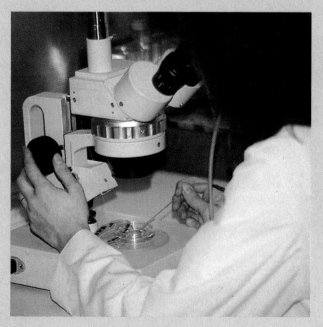

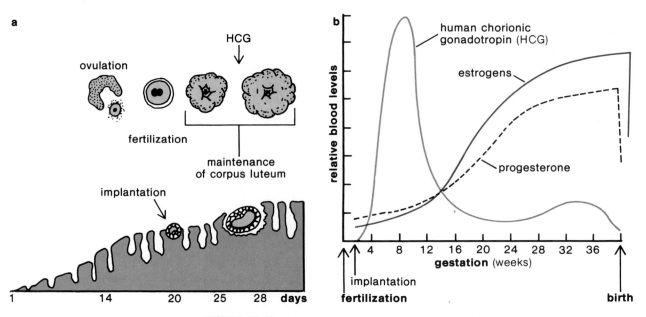

FIGURE 11.18 For the first trimester of pregnancy, HCG secreted by the placenta causes the corpus luteum to produce the estrogen and progesterone necessary to maintain the pregnancy. After that time, the placenta produces these hormones.

The corpus luteum functions for the first three months of gestation, or development of the embryo within the uterus. Figure 11.18b shows that by three months gestation the placenta stops releasing HCG and becomes the main source of estrogen and progesterone. Shortly after birth, the placenta becomes separated from the uterine wall and is expelled as the ''afterbirth.'' Without the placenta, estrogen and progesterone levels drop. The low levels of these hormones signal the hypothalamus to release GnRH, which begins the menstrual cycle again.

Menstruation is a characteristic of female primates. Most other mammals do not menstruate, but they do have estrus, or ''heat,'' cycles when they are receptive to males for reproduction. Animals such as deer and elk enter estrus once a year, and most dogs go into estrus twice a year. In other mammals, such as mice and rabbits, ovulation is stimulated by intercourse. Menstrual cycles, estrus cycles, and ovulation at intercourse are all adaptations that help ensure the continuation of the species.

11.9 Sperm Production

In human males, the testes, which produce sperm, are located in the **scrotum** (SCROH tum), an outpocketing of the body wall. Such a location results in a lower temperature in the scrotum than in the body. Experiments have shown that human sperm need this slightly cooler environment to develop normally. Sperm are produced by meiotic cell division in the highly coiled tubes (seminiferous tubules) of the testes, which are shown in Figure 11.19. Sperm are stored in the epididymis (ep ih DID ih mus), a coiled part of the sperm duct (vas deferens) adjacent to the testes.

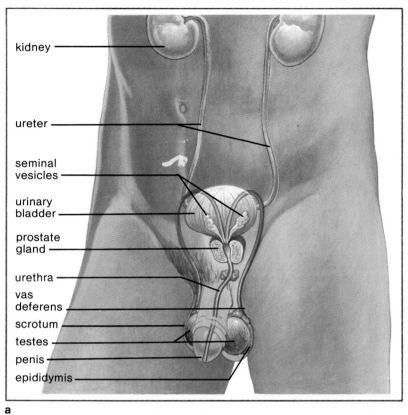

kidney

ureter

seminal
vesicles

urinary
bladder

prostate
gland

urethra

vas
deferens

scrotum

testes

penis

epididymis

a

b

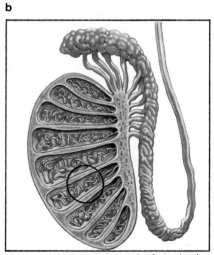

Each testis is composed of packed
coils of tubules in which sperm
develop.

c

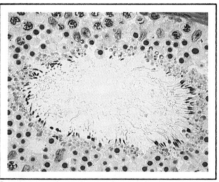

Cross section through a tubule,
×100. Around the edge of the central
canal are the dark heads of the
sperm, with their tails extending into
the canal.

FIGURE 11.19 The human male reproductive system. The excretory system is shown in gray for reference.

Additional structures, the prostate gland and seminal vesicles, produce seminal fluid, which transports sperm. The seminal fluid also contains high levels of fructose, a sugar that provides energy for the sperm. When ejaculation occurs, the sperm and the seminal fluid, together called semen (SEE men), travel through the sperm duct and out of the body through the urethra. If the sperm are not ejaculated, they eventually are reabsorbed by the tissues in the male reproductive tract.

Males and females produce the same regulatory hormones. GnRH from the hypothalamus stimulates the pituitary to release FSH and LH, which stimulate various functions in the testes. LH stimulates cells in the testes to secrete **androgens** (AN droh jenz), a group of male hormones. The major androgen secreted by the testes is **testosterone** (tes TOS ter ohn). FSH stimulates other cells in the testes to produce sperm. There is no evidence that males have a cycle of reproductive hormones similar to that found in the female.

FOCUS ON *Contraception*

Couples may choose to limit the size of their families. Two methods of birth control, or contraception, provide a physical barrier between the egg and sperm. The condom is a sheath that is slipped over the penis prior to intercourse. When used correctly, latex condoms also prevent the spread of AIDS and other sexually transmitted diseases. A diaphragm is a flexible cap that is inserted through the vagina to cover the cervix. Because the cervix differs in size, to be effective, a diaphragm must be fitted by a health-care professional. Both the condom and the diaphragm are quite effective when used properly.

Other methods of contraception prevent ovulation. The Norplant is a progesterone-based device that is surgically implanted in the upper arm. It prevents ovulation for up to five years. Depo-Provera, a progesterone-based injectable drug, suppresses ovulation for 3 months. Similarly, taking pills with carefully regulated doses of estrogen and progesterone inhibits the release of the pituitary hormones that stimulate ovulation. Because all three methods can have serious side effects, they must be prescribed by a physician.

Other contraceptive methods include foams or jellies with spermicides that immobilize the sperm. Foams or jellies are inserted into the vagina before intercourse. They are most effective when used with a diaphragm or condom.

Surgical procedures can provide permanent sterilization. In males, both sperm ducts (vas deferens) may be cut and tied in a process called a vasectomy. In females, the oviducts may be cut and tied in a process called a tubal ligation. Both procedures are difficult to reverse.

Effective contraception requires planning. Once sperm have entered the vagina, there is little chance of preventing some of them from reaching and fertilizing an egg in the oviduct. The only 100 percent reliable method of birth control is abstinence from intercourse.

FIGURE C Contraceptive devices

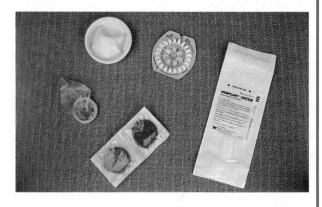

FIGURE 11.20 Some secondary sexual characteristics in animals. Can you think of other instances where the male and female of a species do not closely resemble each other?

11.10 Secondary Sex Characteristics

Although both males and females produce estrogen and androgens, the respective levels vary according to the sex of the individual. The amount of estrogen is high in females and low in males. Estrogen controls the development of secondary sex characteristics in females, causing changes in the breasts, bone structure, and fat deposits under the skin. These changes begin at the onset of **puberty**, which in females begins at about the same time as the first menstrual period. In North America, puberty usually begins in females between the ages of 10 and 12. However, the age at which puberty begins is affected by many factors, such as heredity, percent body fat, and nutrition.

Androgens control the development of secondary sex characteristics in males. Beginning at puberty, the androgens cause changes, for example, in the voice and body hair distribution. Puberty in North American males usually begins around the age of 12, but this varies with the individual. Females usually enter puberty at an earlier age than males.

Throughout the animal kingdom there are often prominent differences in the appearance of males and females within the same species, as Figure 11.20 illustrates. Often the differences can be traced to hormonal differences in the sexes. You will read about the mechanisms of inheritance for many of these characteristics in Chapter 12.

CHECK AND CHALLENGE

1. Develop a concept map that shows the relationship among the following hormones: GnRH, estrogen, progesterone, FSH, and LH.
2. What is the relationship between a follicle and a corpus luteum?
3. What are the effects of FSH and LH in the male reproductive system?
4. Describe the relationship between male and female hormones and the onset of puberty.

Summary

Many organisms reproduce asexually, producing offspring identical to the parent. Prokaryotes reproduce by binary fission. Asexual reproduction in eukaryotes usually involves mitotic cell division. Vegetative reproduction includes budding and fragmentation among animals and numerous examples, such as strawberry runners, among plants. In some animals, an unfertilized egg can develop into an adult organism.

Sexual reproduction requires two gametes and the complementary processes of meiosis and fertilization. Two important events occur in meiosis. First, meiosis reduces the number of chromosomes from diploid to haploid during the production of gametes in most plants and animals. If meiosis did not occur, the number of chromosomes would double in each generation. Second, crossing over, which occurs during the early stages of meiosis, shuffles the genes between homologous pairs of chromosomes. The genetic recombination that results from meiosis and crossing over is important in maintaining genetic variation in species.

Sexual reproduction in flowering plants requires pollination followed by double fertilization, which results in a triploid endosperm and a diploid embryo. Evolution has produced many elaborate schemes through which pollination occurs.

Animals with external fertilization are mainly aquatic and produce large numbers of gametes and young, usually with a high mortality rate. Elaborate behavior patterns have evolved that result in simultaneous release of eggs and sperm into water environments. Animals with internal fertilization usually live on land and produce small numbers of eggs but large numbers of sperm. Premating rituals have evolved that enable fertile females to encounter males capable of mating.

Most mammals have an estrus cycle in which females ovulate and become receptive for mating at specific times during the year. The menstrual cycle of

human females is found only among the primates and is produced by an elaborate interaction among the brain and various glands, organs, and hormones. The end result is a regular release of ova with the coordinated readiness of the uterus to receive a fertilized egg. If the egg is not fertilized, the uterine lining degenerates, resulting in the menstrual flow.

Sperm production in male animals is usually under the control of the same hormones that function in the female system. However, the hormones' target organs and their functions differ from those of females. Sex hormones also cause males and females to exhibit secondary sex characteristics.

Key Concepts

Use the concepts below to build a concept map, linking as many other concepts from the chapter as you can.

meiosis	haploid
gametes	diploid
fertilization	pollination

Reviewing Ideas

1. How is the structure of the ova and sperm related to their function in fertilization?

2. What is the form of the chromatids at prophase I? at telophase II?

3. Describe the differences between metaphase I and metaphasre II in meiosis.

4. Why does moss need a moist environment to reproduce? How might the same conditions prevent flowering plant reproduction?

5. Why is fertilization in plants called double fertilization?

6. Explain how insects help pollination in flowering plants.

7. What adaptations in aquatic animals help ensure that external fertilization will occur?

8. What adaptations in land animals help ensure that internal fertilization will occur?

9. Explain the relationship between the follicle and ovum in a human female.

10. Explain how estrogen and progesterone influence the uterus in the menstrual cycle.

11. What could be concluded from a blood test indicating the presence of human chorionic gonadotropin (HCG) in a human female?

12. What is the action of HCG, and what organ does it affect in human females?

13. Explain how LH and FSH function in human reproduction.

14. Explain the physical changes that occur at puberty in human females and males.

15. What is the relationship between a diploid cell stage and the relative complexity of the organism?

Using Concepts

1. Why is it important to maintain a constant chromosome number within a species?

2. What would prevent the pollen from one plant species from pollinating flowers of another species?

3. Explain how the chromosome number of a species could remain constant if the adults were haploid instead of diploid.

4. Explain why chromosomes cannot be referred to as maternal or paternal after meiosis has occurred.

5. Explain how double fertilization in plants differs from fertilization in humans.

6. Cite as many advantages as you can of having an endosperm inside a seed coat with the plant embryo.

7. What advantages for land animals does internal fertilization have over external fertilization?

8. Explain the difference between estrus (heat) and menstrual cycles.

9. Compare the processes of mitosis and meiosis.

10. How are the organs of the human male and female reproductive tracts adapted for the continuation of the species?

Synthesis

1. Reread "Focus On Species" in Chapter 5. Using your knowledge of the female reproductive system, can you explain why Krause the mule is capable of reproducing?

2. In what way is the first cell division in meiosis unlike cell division associated with mitosis?

Extensions

1. Write a short paper about an imaginary human population that reproduces asexually. Describe how the people look and how they interact with each other.

2. Write a short paper describing a society in which the onset of puberty begins at 25 years of age. Tell how this would affect the society.

3. Draw a one-scene piece of art that depicts the process of meiosis.

4. Write a short paper describing a society where the government allows only certain individuals to reproduce. Describe the feelings of those who can and cannot reproduce.

CONTENTS

Patterns of Inheritance

Look closely at your fellow students. They have characteristics that all humans share, such as eyes, arms, and legs. In that sense, they are all the same. No two of them, however—indeed, no two people on the planet—are exactly alike. There is tremendous variation in the human population and in the rest of the biological world as well. All golden retrievers, for example, have the same basic characteristics, but any dog owner can pick his or her retriever from a group of 10. Each dog has a number of variations that make it unique.

Genetics is the branch of biology that seeks to explain biological variation—the raw material for evolution through natural selection. The search for explanations takes us more deeply into the world of the cell—to chromosomes, genes, and nucleic acids. At the same time, we also find that the external environment plays an important role in shaping variation in living things. Variation is not surprising in itself. Differences in diet during development can have great effects on adult appearance, as can variation in the environments that different individuals experience. Many arctic animals, for example, develop dark feathers or fur when they are exposed to the warm summer months and white feathers or fur during the cold of winter. However, some of the differences that we observe among individuals are inherited and, thus, passed from parent to offspring. Such inherited features are the building blocks of evolution. This chapter examines the nature of genes and chromosomes and the principles by which variations are inherited.

What important biological concept is illustrated here?

What differences do you see?

◆ *A harvest of Heirloom tomatoes.*

Genes and Chromosomes _____

12.1 Genes and Alleles

Genes contain the instructions that guide the development and function of all organisms. Genes transmit these instructions to each new generation and, in so doing, provide an evolutionary link of genetic continuity across thousands and millions of generations. The genetic variation that results from meiosis and mutation supplies the raw material for evolution through natural selection.

Obviously, genes are tremendously important in maintaining and explaining diversity and unity among organisms. But what are genes? The concept of a gene has changed drastically during the past century due to the development of many new methods for studying genes and genetic interactions. Today a gene is defined as a segment of DNA whose sequence of nucleotides codes for a specific functional product. Some of these products are ribosomal and transfer RNA, enzymes, and structural proteins.

Most genes exist in more than one specific sequence of nucleotides. **Alleles** (al LEE uhlz) are alternate forms of a gene that can have different base sequences. A change in the sequence of nucleotides in a gene for a particular protein can result in a different sequence of amino acids in the protein. As a result, the three-dimensional structure and, therefore, the function of the protein may be different. The different kinds of proteins derived from unlike alleles in a population lead to the diversity among individuals on which natural selection can act.

Examples of alleles are found in the characteristics known as cleft chin (dimpled chin) and male pattern baldness. The allele for cleft chin is one form of a gene affecting chin shape. Individuals who have this allele often exhibit the trait—the movie star Kirk Douglas is a well known example. Conversely, individuals who have a different allelic form of the gene will not have cleft chins. Male pattern baldness, in which there is a gradual loss of hair on the top of the head, is another trait determined by one allelic form of a single gene (Figure 12.1). Many traits scientists once thought were determined by single genes, such as hair color, skin color, nose shape, and handedness, actually result from the complex interaction of several genes.

FIGURE 12.1 Male pattern baldness. The expression of the trait is influenced by sex hormones. It is much more common in men, hence its name.

12.2 Organization of Genes on Chromosomes

Chromosomes are gene packages—long molecules of DNA wrapped around nucleosomes (Chapter 9). When the genetic code was first deciphered, biologists assumed that all genes were sequences of nucleotides that translated directly into sequences of amino acids. Since then, research using various new techniques has shown that a chromosome is much more complex than a simple string of functional genes. Some short sequences of bases are repeated thousands of times, and large segments of DNA never become functional mRNA. (Recall from Chapter 10 that introns are removed before translation.) Estimates are that only one percent of the

DNA of a eukaryotic chromosome codes for mRNA that is expressed as protein. Biologists wonder about the evolutionary significance of the uncoded DNA.

The situation is different in prokaryotes. Bacteria have a single circular chromosome with little associated protein. Their genes generally do not have introns, and an estimated 90 percent of their DNA is translated. Many bacteria have plasmids—small circles of DNA that contain additional genes (Figure 12.2, *left*). These plasmids may be transferred from one bacterium to another. Genetic engineers make use of plasmids to introduce modified genetic material into bacterial cells.

12.3 Techniques for Studying Chromosomes

Homologous chromosomes carry genes that code for the same products, although these genes may be present as different alleles. How do biologists identify and distinguish homologous chromosomes from other chromosomes of an organism? Although the size of the chromosome and the location of its centromere provide a preliminary identification, they cannot be used to distinguish all chromosomes with certainty. Stains help because particular stains concentrate in specific regions on chromosomes, creating a characteristic banding pattern. Homologous chromosomes show the same banding pattern, and their pattern is different from those of other homologous chromosomes. Figure 12.2 (*right*) illustrates how two similar-sized chromosomes can be distinguished on the basis of their distinct banding patterns.

Chromosomes are easiest to study in their condensed form and, therefore, must be obtained from dividing cells. White blood cells are used most frequently because they are easily induced to divide and grow in culture. Chemicals are added to stop the cells' growth during prophase and metaphase. The cells are placed on microscope slides and treated so they swell

FIGURE 12.2 *(left)* A scanning electron micrograph of a bacterial plasmid, X79 000 *(right)* Human chromosomes 7 and X. The banding patterns evident in the photographs are shown in the diagrams. These two chromosomes, which have almost the same length and centromere location, can be distinguished by their banding patterns.

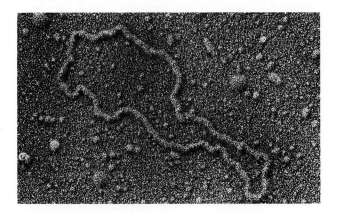

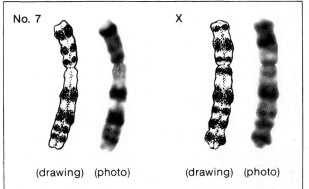

Biological Challenges

THE HUMAN GENOME PROJECT

The primary goal of the human genome project (HGP) is to uncover the genetic information contained in the human chromosomes. For the purpose of the HGP, *genome* means one each of the different chromosomes—22 autosomes (those not involved in the determination of sex), plus an X, a Y, and a mitochondrial chromosome. This genetic material includes approximately 3 billion base pairs of DNA, containing 50 000 to 100 000 genes. Researchers involved in the HGP are first attempting gene mapping—determining the location of genes at specific sites on chromosomes. They then will attempt to determine the DNA sequence of each gene.

The HGP will not provide the DNA sequence from one individual, but rather a collection of sequences from different people. The knowledge and technology that result from the HGP may allow researchers to describe the total genome of humans. In addition to the human genome, researchers are also working on mapping the genes of a bacterium, a yeast, a nematode, a fruit fly, a mouse, and the mouse-ear cress plant. Comparing these genomes to that of humans will help scientists find human genes more easily and will deepen our understanding of how genes function.

The project, which is funded in the United States primarily by the Department of Energy and the National Institutes of Health, will take about 15 years and will cost approximately $3 billion to complete. About six other countries are involved in the HGP. In addition to gene mapping and sequencing, the HGP must develop new data storage systems to handle the enormous amounts of information that will be generated. The HGP also includes specialists to address the social, ethical, and legal implications of genome research.

Geneticists have already identified the genes responsible for cystic fibrosis (CF), Duchenne muscular dystrophy (DMD), and Huntington's disease (HD). By isolating such genes, biologists can learn about the structure of the proteins they code for. This knowledge could lead to better medical management of these diseases.

The HGP may also identify individuals with an increased susceptibility to disorders such as heart disease, cancer, or diabetes. Because these disorders result from complex interactions between genes and the environment, there is no certainty that symptoms will develop in susceptible individuals. However, these individuals might be able to take steps to reduce their chances of developing symptoms. Biologists also are hopeful that the HGP will shed light on basic biological inquiries into human evolution, development, and regulation.

Critics have expressed several concerns about the HGP. One major criticism is that not enough will be learned to justify the high cost. Other critics maintain that funding such a large project takes scarce resources away from other scientific endeavors.

Some critics suggest that the ability to diagnose a genetic disorder such as HD does more harm than good. Because no treatment is available, the diagnosis just creates anxiety and frustration. Other critics worry about unanticipated outcomes. Pointing to the development of atomic weapons, these critics argue that the science that led to their development caused more problems than it resolved.

It is possible that the HGP will allow the determination of personal genetic profiles—individuals' genomes as opposed to the general human genome. There are many unanswered questions about the use of such personal data. Who will have access to the data? Should employers or insurance companies be permitted to use this information to screen against health risks? How can the privacy of this information be ensured?

Some critics believe that the genome project gives too much emphasis to the genetic components of human characteristics while ignoring the environmental components. They worry that society will attribute social problems to "bad" genes while failing to address the environmental factors involved.

and their chromosomes spread apart. Then stains are applied to the resulting chromosome spread, producing the banding patterns seen in Figure 12.3. By such studies, geneticists were able to determine that the correct number of human chromosomes is 46.

Stained chromosomes can be photographed under the microscope. Individual chromosomes then can be cut out of an enlarged photograph and arranged in order by size and shape to form a karyotype. Figure 12.4 shows a karyotype from a human male. Karyotypes made from fetal cells are used to check for possible chromosomal abnormalities in developing fetuses.

12.4   Sex Determination

Do all chromosomes come in matching pairs? Yes, except for the sex chromosomes. Recall from Chapter 11 that one pair of chromosomes may not match in size or shape. (Observe the unmatched pair in the karyotype in Figure 12.4.) The character of this pair of chromosomes determines the sex of the individual. In humans, other mammals, and the fruit fly *Drosophila melanogaster*, the sex chromosomes are labeled *X* and *Y*. Females have two X chromosomes; males have one X chromosome and one Y chromosome. All the eggs produced during meiosis have an X chromosome. Half of the sperm produced by a male contain an X chromosome and the other half have a Y chromosome. Thus, sperm determine the sex of the offspring. If an egg is fertilized by a sperm with an X chromosome, the zygote develops into a female. If the sperm contains a Y chromosome, the offspring is a male. The pairings are diagrammed in Figure 12.5 on the next page.

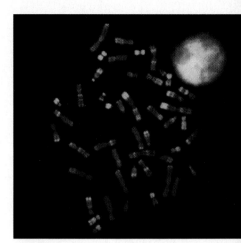

FIGURE 12.3 Human chromosome spread. The banding patterns are the result of differences in absorption of stains by different regions of the chromosomes. Banded chromosomes enable biologists to detect missing or extra chromosome parts more easily than uniformly stained chromosomes do. The banding patterns also have made the mapping of genes on chromosomes more accurate.

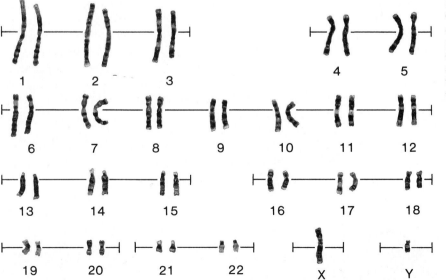

1   2   3   4   5

6   7   8   9   10   11   12

13   14   15   16   17   18

19   20   21   22   X   Y

FIGURE 12.4 A karyotype is a display of human chromosomes arranged as homologous pairs. It is prepared by cutting out individual chromosomes from a photograph and matching them, pair by pair. Is this the karyotype of a male or a female?

FIGURE 12.5 Sex in humans is determined by the sex chromosomes of the egg and the sperm at the moment of fertilization. XX produces a female, XY produces a male. The symbol ♀ represents female; ♂ represents male.

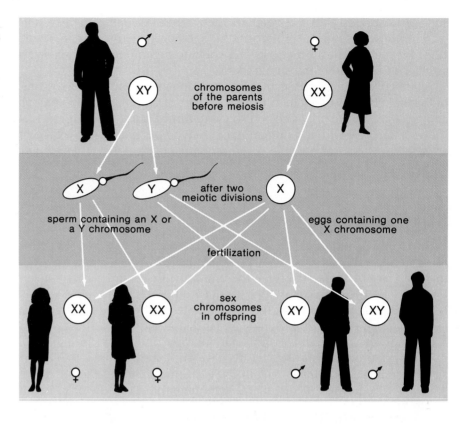

Not all organisms have an X-Y system of sex determination. Some insects, such as grasshoppers, crickets, and roaches, have what is called an X-O system. Females have two X chromosomes, males have one, and there is no Y chromosome. Thus, males have one less chromosome than females. Birds, some fish, and some insects have what is called a Z-W system of sex determination. Here the male has the two matching sex chromosomes (ZZ), whereas the female has one Z chromosome and one W chromosome. Some plants, such as spinach and date palms, have separate female and male plants and have sex chromosomes that follow the X-Y system of sex determination. Most plants and some animals have no sex chromosomes.

CHECK AND CHALLENGE

1. What is the relationship between a gene and an allele? Between genes and chromosomes?

2. Describe several properties that define the term *gene*.

3. How do eukaryotic and prokaryotic chromosomes differ?

4. If a couple has had three daughters in a row, what is the chance their fourth child will be a son?

5. How are the techniques of chromosome staining and matching useful in preparing a karyotype?

Mendelian Inheritance

12.5 Probability and Genetics

The segregation of alleles into gametes and the random recombination of alleles in fertilization demonstrate simple rules of **probability**. Probability is a branch of mathematics that predicts the chances that a certain event will occur. Geneticists use probability to predict the outcomes of crosses.

You are probably familiar with the idea of probability. What are the chances that a flip of a coin will come up heads? What are the chances that you will draw an ace from a deck of cards (Figure 12.6)? Probability is usually expressed as a fraction. The chance of the coin landing heads up is one out of two, or $\frac{1}{2}$. Your chance of drawing an ace is 4 out of 52, or $\frac{1}{13}$. A batting average in baseball also is a statement of probability. A player who has a .250 batting average has about a 25 percent probability ($\frac{1}{4}$, or 1 in 4 chance) of hitting safely when he or she comes to bat.

When working with probabilities, remember that the outcomes of independent events do not influence one another. If you obtain three heads in a row when flipping a coin, the probability that the next toss will land heads up is still $\frac{1}{2}$. The coin does not "remember" the first three tosses—chance events have no memory. You can, however, predict the probability of getting all heads when tossing four coins simultaneously. The chance that two or more independent events will occur together is the multiplication product of their chances of occurring separately. Thus, to determine the chance that all four tosses will land heads up, you multiply $\frac{1}{2} \times \frac{1}{2} \times \frac{1}{2} \times \frac{1}{2}$. The result is a $\frac{1}{16}$ chance.

Geneticists use the principles of probability to predict the genotypes of the offspring of various crosses. These predicted results can be compared with the actual results of breeding experiments. Statistical tests then can be used to decide whether the difference between the observed and predicted results is significant—in other words, whether the difference is due to chance or to some other factor. (See **Appendix 12A**, The Chi-Square Test.) Many genetic disorders in humans are inherited according to Mendel's principles. Genetic counselors use probability to help parents assess the risk of passing on such a genetic disorder to their children.

Remember that genetic ratios are estimates of probability, not estimates of absolute numbers. You do not expect every family to have an equal number of sons and daughters, but you would be surprised if in one year 500 girls and only 100 boys were born in a particular town. The larger the sample size, the less deviation you would expect from predicted ratios.

12.6 Mendel's Work

When families gather, it is common to hear statements such as "Who does the baby look like?" or "She has her mother's eyes and her grandfather's nose." Observations of family resemblances probably led to early theories of inheritance—explanations of the transmission of characteristics from parents to offspring. The domestication and selective breeding of animals

FIGURE 12.6 The chance of drawing one ace is $\frac{1}{13}$. What is the chance of drawing a spade? What is the chance of drawing the ace of spades?

Try Investigation 12A, Probability.

FIGURE 12.7 Gregor Mendel (1822–1884). Experimenting with peas in his monastery garden, Mendel developed the fundamental principles of heredity that became the foundation of modern genetics.

for transportation, labor, or meat production and the development of crop plants with increased yields indicate that our early ancestors had a working knowledge of heredity.

In the 1860s, a monk named Gregor Mendel (Figure 12.7) demonstrated with pea plants that both parents pass on to their offspring separate factors—now called alleles—that retain their individuality generation after generation. Modern genetics, the study of patterns of inheritance and variability, has its foundations in Mendel's work.

Mendel's choice of the garden pea as an experimental organism showed thoughtful planning. Peas are very easy to grow, and Mendel could study many generations during his eight-year experiment. Peas are self-fertilizing; Figure 12.8 shows how fertilization usually occurs in pea plants. When Mendel wanted to cross-fertilize his plants, he cut out the stamens and dusted the stigmas with pollen from a different plant.

Mendel found seven different characteristics of pea plants, shown in Figure 12.8, that he could study in an "either/or" form. Peas could be either smooth or wrinkled; plants were either tall or short; pods were either green or yellow, and so on. Today these "either/or" forms are called **traits**. Mendel worked with his plants for several years to be sure he had true-breeding varieties for each of the traits he selected. True-breeding plants produce offspring identical to themselves generation after generation. Mendel then cross-bred his plants and carefully counted and classified all the offspring. He was able to look for distinctive patterns of inheritance by conducting many breeding experiments and collecting and analyzing the data.

FIGURE 12.8 *(left)* Self-fertilization in a pea flower. The petals of the pea flower (a) completely enclose the reproductive organs. As a result, the pollen from the anthers falls on the stigma of the same flower (b). Pollen tubes grow down through the female reproductive organ to the ovules in the ovary. The ovules develop into seeds, and the ovary wall develops into the pea pod (c). *(right)* The seven characteristics of garden peas studied by Mendel. The dominant trait in each case is shown on top.

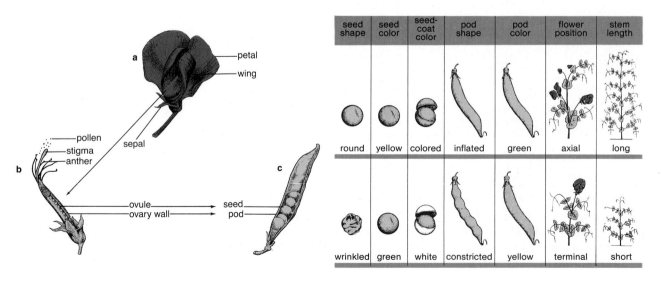

Consider a mating between a plant with green pods and a plant with yellow pods, as shown in Figure 12.9. Would the pods of the offspring plants be greenish-yellow? Would some of the pods be green and others yellow? Mendel found that the next generation of plants produced only green pods. Did the yellow-pod trait disappear completely? In that particular generation, yes. When those plants were allowed to self-fertilize, however, some plants in the next generation produced green pods and other plants produced yellow pods. What conclusions can you draw from these results?

12.7 Principles of Segregation and Independent Assortment

Crosses between parents that differ in only one characteristic, such as pod color, are called monohybrid crosses. In the first cross, which is a cross between plants in the parental (P) generation, Mendel dusted pollen from green-podded plants onto the stigmas of yellow-podded plants. Mendel also performed a reciprocal cross, from yellow-podded plants to green-podded plants. Why was it important to perform the parental cross both ways?

The plants that grew from the seeds of the parental crosses produced all green pea pods. This generation of plants is called the first filial or F_1 generation. Mendel then allowed the F_1 generation plants to self-fertilize. He obtained 428 plants with green pods and 152 plants with yellow pods in this second filial or F_2 generation, an approximately 3:1 ratio. Mendel's results are shown in Figure 12.10 on the next page. (See Table 12B.1 in Investigation 12B.)

For each of the seven characteristics Mendel studied, only one trait was visible in the F_1 generation. He termed this trait the **dominant** trait. The opposing trait, which was not visible in the F_1 generation (but which reappeared unchanged in the F_2 generation), he called the **recessive** trait. In the F_2 generation produced by self-fertilization of F_1 plants, the two traits appeared in a ratio of approximately 3:1, dominant to recessive.

Mendel proposed that each true-breeding plant had two identical copies of the factor for a particular trait. When reproductive cells were formed during meiosis, only one copy of the factor went into each sperm or egg cell. Thus, the F_1 generation received a green-pod factor from one parent and a yellow-pod factor from the other parent. Mendel called this separation of factors the **principle of segregation**. Today, Mendel's factors are considered to be alleles of a gene that codes for a particular characteristic (in this example, pod color).

A simple method for describing genetic crosses makes use of letter symbols. The factor (allele) for the dominant trait is commonly represented by a capital letter (such as G for green pods), and the allele for the recessive trait is represented by the same letter in lower case (such as g for yellow pods). In the F_1 generation, the two alleles, G and g, segregated (separated) during the formation of reproductive cells. Half of the cells received the G allele; the other half received the g allele.

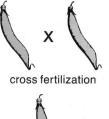

FIGURE 12.9 Results of a mating between plants true-breeding for green pods and yellow pods.

cross fertilization

self-fertilization
ratio: all green-podded

ratio:
3 green-podded:
1 yellow-podded

Try Investigation 12B, Seedling Phenotypes.

FIGURE 12.10 A monohybrid cross that demonstrates Mendel's principle of segregation. Each plant has two factors (alleles) for each trait, which segregate during the formation of gametes. Fertilization restores paired alleles. The Punnett square shows how gametes of the F_1 generation can combine to form the genotypes of the F_2 generation.

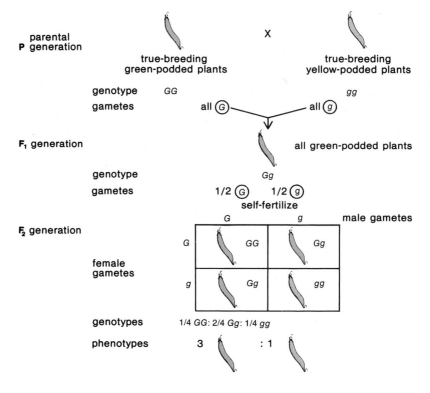

In the cross involving pod color, the **genotype**, or genetic makeup, of the P generation plants would be either *GG* for the plant with green pods or *gg* for the plant with yellow pods. If both alleles are the same, as in the parental generation, the genotype is **homozygous** (*homo* = alike; *zygo* = a pair). If the alleles are different, as in the F_1 individuals, the genotype is **heterozygous** (*hetero* = different). The genotype of the individual is responsible for its **phenotype**—its appearance or observable characteristics. Both the *GG* and the *Gg* genotypes produce a green-podded phenotype.

A Punnett square is a useful tool for visualizing simple crosses. The possible gametes each parent can produce are placed along the two sides, and the square is filled in, like a multiplication table, with the genotypes that would result from the union of those gametes. Figure 12.9 includes a Punnett square for the F_1 cross of heterozygous green-podded pea plants.

What would happen in a cross if the parents differed in two characteristics? To follow the inheritance of two characteristics at once, Mendel made dihybrid crosses. Earlier, he had found that the traits of round seeds and yellow seeds are dominant, and that the traits of wrinkled seeds and green seeds are recessive. Imagine a cross of plants that are true-breeding for round, yellow seeds (*RRYY*) with plants that are true-breeding for wrinkled, green seeds (*rryy*). From what you know about these traits, can you predict the genotype and phenotype of the F_1 generation?

What would the F_2 generation look like? The Punnett square in Figure 12.11 (page 282) shows the four phenotypes Mendel observed. If you

FOCUS ON *The Chromosome Theory of Inheritance*

The connection between chromosomes and Mendel's factors was made independently in 1902 by Theodor Boveri and W. S. Sutton. Boveri showed experimentally that although egg and sperm cells are different, they make equal genetic contributions to the new organism. Mendel had already given evidence for this conclusion by making reciprocal crosses. He found that the ratio of dominant to recessive traits was always the same, regardless of which parent carried the factor for the dominant trait. Mendel concluded that the factors contributed by sperm and egg cells were equally important.

Boveri and Sutton reasoned that if the genetic contributions of sperm and eggs are the same, the genes ought to be located in the same place in the two kinds of gametes. Where

could this be? Sperm cells are composed mostly of a nucleus and just a small amount of cytoplasm. The nucleus of the egg is very similar to the nucleus of the sperm. However, the cytoplasm of the egg is very different from that of the sperm. Because of the similarities of nuclei but differences in cytoplasm, Boveri and Sutton both concluded that the nucleus contains the genes.

Chromosomes are inside the nucleus. Careful observations have shown that they seem to behave much as genes were thought to behave. Table A compares the activity of chromosomes with the behavior of Mendel's factors. The work of Morgan and his students with X-linked traits in *Drosophila* served to verify these ideas, which became known as the chromosome theory of inheritance.

**Table A
Comparison of Genes and Chromosome Behavior**

Hypothesis of Gene Behavior	Observations of Chromosome Behavior
1. Gametes have half the number of genes that body cells have.	1. Gametes have half the number of chromosomes that body cells have.
2. Gene pairs separate during gamete formation.	2. Chromosome pairs separate during gamete formation.
3. In fertilization, gametes unite, restoring the original number of genes.	3. In fertilization, gametes unite, restoring the original number of chromosomes.
4. Individual genes remain unchanged from one generation to the next.	4. Individual chromosomes retain their structure from one generation to the next.
5. The number of possible gene combinations can be calculated.	5. The number of possible chromosome combinations can be calculated.

count the distribution of phenotypes, you will see that their ratio is 9:3:3:1. This ratio is characteristic of the F_2 generation in a dihybrid cross. The genes for seed shape and seed color had separated from each other and were inherited independently. The results of dihybrid crosses formed the basis for Mendel's **principle of independent assortment**: Alleles for one characteristic behave independently of alleles for other characteristics during gamete formation.

Try Investigation 12C, A Dihybrid Cross.

FIGURE 12.11 A dihybrid cross that illustrates the principle of independent assortment. What phenotypes are present in the F₂ generation, and in what ratios? These results demonstrate that the traits for seed shape and seed color assorted separately. (Note that there are 12 round to every 4 wrinkled seeds, and 12 yellow to 4 green seeds. Each trait independently shows the 3:1 ratio typical of a monohybrid cross.) *R* = round seed; *r* = wrinkled seed; *Y* = yellow seed; *y* = green seed.

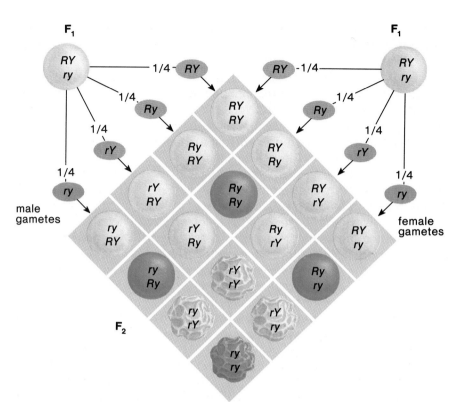

CHECK AND CHALLENGE

1. How do Mendel's two principles of inheritance relate to the behavior of chromosomes during meiosis?

2. What are the chances that a family will have three sons? After two sons, what is the probability that the next child will be a son?

3. Distinguish between genotype and phenotype; between homozygous and heterozygous.

4. Using a Punnett square, work out the probable ratios for the phenotypes of offspring from a cross between a homozygous tall pea plant and a heterozygous tall pea plant.

5. What types of gametes are produced by the following plants: *GGRr* (green pods and round seeds); *TtYy* (tall plants with yellow seeds)?

Other Patterns of Inheritance

12.8 Codominance and Multiple Alleles

Mendel worked with traits that showed clear dominant and recessive inheritance. Complete dominance is not always the case, however. When red snapdragons are crossed with white snapdragons, the F₁ generation is all pink. The offspring do not resemble either parent, but are intermediate in color. When the F₁ plants self-fertilize, the F₂ plants show a 1 red:

2 pink:1 white ratio. Trace the inheritance of flower color in Figure 12.12. When both alleles contribute to the phenotype of a heterozygote, the alleles are said to show **codominance**.

Another example of codominance is seen in the ABO system of human blood types. Blood type is determined by the presence or absence of A or B proteins on the surface of red blood cells. The alleles I^A or I^B code for these proteins. The I^A and I^B alleles show codominance; when a person has the $I^A I^B$ genotype, both types of proteins are produced, and the individual's blood type is AB.

The ABO blood type system also illustrates the existence of **multiple alleles**, genes that have more than two allelic forms. In addition to the I^A and I^B alleles, there is an allele, i, that codes for no surface proteins. An ii genotype produces type O blood. The symbols I^A, I^B, and i are used to show that both codominance and complete dominance operate in the determination of blood types. The genotypes, phenotypes, and surface proteins for the four different blood types are shown in Table 12.1. Note that although there are three alleles for blood type, no individual has more than two of the alleles.

Blood groups are critically important in transfusions. If someone with type A blood is given a transfusion of type B blood, the donated red cells clump, and the clumped cells clog the capillaries. The clumping is caused by **antibodies**, which are proteins found in the blood plasma. Antibodies react when exposed to foreign proteins and are important in protecting the body against disease (Chapter 20). Some of the surface proteins on red blood cells differ among individuals. These differences determine the different blood types. People do not produce antibodies for proteins on their own red blood cells, but do produce antibodies for foreign proteins. Thus, a person with type A blood (who has A surface proteins) cannot produce anti-A antibodies, but can (and does) produce anti-B antibodies. If given a transfusion of type B blood, the anti-B antibodies attack the B surface proteins. Included in Table 12.1 is a list of the antibodies found in individuals of different blood types.

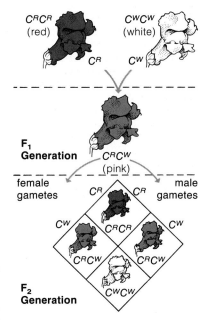

FIGURE 12.12 Codominance of flower color in snapdragons. The phenotype of the F₁ heterozygote is different from that of both true-breeding parents. Both the genotypic and phenotypic ratios of the F₂ generation are 1:2:1.

12.9 Multifactorial Inheritance

There are many cases in which a given trait is controlled by more than one gene. Deviations from the expected Mendelian ratios usually indicate the more complicated mechanism of inheritance in such cases. The blue/brown

TABLE 12.1
Genetics of ABO Blood Types

Phenotype	Genotype	Protein on Red Blood Cells	Antibodies in Plasma
type A	$I^A I^A$ or $I^A i$	A	anti-B
type B	$I^B I^B$ or $I^B i$	B	anti-A
type AB	$I^A I^B$	A and B	neither
type O	ii	neither A nor B	anti-A and anti-B

FIGURE 12.13 Continuous and discontinuous variations. Most human traits are determined by multiple genes and are influenced by the environment. Some traits (usually controlled by single genes) exist in only two forms. Histogram a shows the distribution of the heights of students in a high school biology class. Histogram b shows the distribution of the sexes in the same class. Height is a quantitative or continuous character. Sex is a qualitative or discontinuous character.

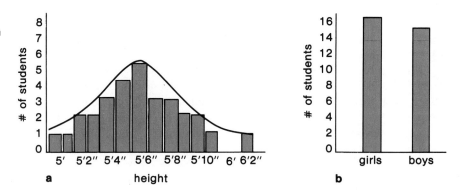

trait for eye color (Section 12.1) is an example of a trait that is controlled by more than a single gene. There are many variations of eye color; several modifier genes are involved in the production and distribution of pigment in eyes. In fact, most human traits are **multifactorial**—their expressions are controlled by at least several genes and also are influenced considerably by the environment.

Most human traits, such as height, weight, intelligence, hair color, skin color, and the control of metabolic processes do not occur as an either/or expression but vary in finely graded steps. Each of these traits is controlled by more than one gene, and each gene contributes to the final expression of the trait. For example, the production of the skin pigment melanin is thought to be controlled by four major genes, none of which demonstrates simple dominance. The independent assortment of the alleles for melanin production results in a continuous variation in skin color among humans. Skin color, however, also is affected by the amount of exposure to sunlight.

Multifactorial traits, such as height or skin coloring, show a continuous distribution in a population. The graph of such a distribution usually resembles a bell-shaped curve, as shown in Figure 12.13a. A discontinuous distribution is typical of characteristics, such as sex, that exist in only two forms (Figure 12.13b). Compare the graphs of the two types of distributions. What type of distribution do most human characteristics show?

12.10   Linked Genes

Because there are far more genes than chromosomes, logic suggests that many genes must be located on a single chromosome. All genes located on the same chromosome are said to be linked. This observation implies that all the genes on a chromosome are inherited together. (As it happened, most of the traits Mendel studied were not determined by linked genes, or he might not have developed the principle of independent assortment.)

Linked genes do not always remain together. Recall from Chapter 11 that homologous chromosomes often exchange fragments when they pair in meiosis (Figure 12.14). That exchange gives rise to genetic recombinations that greatly increase the variability resulting from sexual reproduction. The farther apart two genes are on a chromosome, the more likely a break will occur between them. If two genes are far enough apart on a

FIGURE 12.14 Crossing-over frequently occurs between homologous chromosomes during the early stages of meiosis.

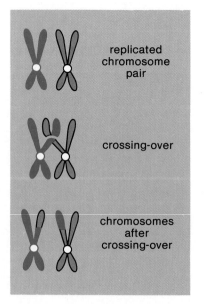

replicated chromosome pair

crossing-over

chromosomes after crossing-over

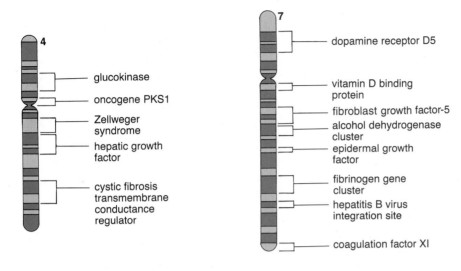

FIGURE 12.15 A few of the genes that have been mapped to the human X chromosome and to autosome 9

chromosome, breaks between them may be so frequent that the principle of independent assortment applies to their inheritance. Some of the genes in Mendel's experiments assorted independently for this reason.

The frequency with which two linked traits become separated provides a measure of the relative distance on the chromosome between the genes for those traits. With this information, geneticists can construct accurate maps showing the sequence of genes on chromosomes. Linkage studies also allow geneticists to localize genes of interest, even when they cannot identify the genes themselves, by using linked markers. Researchers have identified many disease-related genes this way. Figure 12.15 shows maps of two human chromosomes.

12.11 X-Linked Traits

An understanding of linked genes came from studies of fruit flies (Figure 12.16). While working at Columbia University in the 1910s, Thomas Hunt Morgan noted a single white-eyed male fly. When he mated this fly with a normal red-eyed female, all the offspring had red eyes, supporting his assumption that the white-eye trait is recessive. The F_2 generation had the expected 3:1 ratio of red-eyed flies to white-eyed flies, as shown in Figure 12.17a on the next page. Morgan noticed, however, that only males showed the white-eye trait. Although not all males were white-eyed, this trait seemed to be linked to a fly's sex.

Morgan continued breeding his flies and eventually obtained white-eyed females. He then did a reciprocal cross (a white-eyed female with a red-eyed male) and followed the inheritance of white eyes. The F_1 offspring of this reciprocal cross were not all red-eyed. Indeed, only females showed the dominant red-eye trait. All the males had white eyes. The reciprocal cross is diagrammed in Figure 12.17b on the next page.

Morgan's explanation for these unusual results was that the gene for eye color is carried on the X chromosome, whereas there is no corresponding gene on the Y chromosome. Thus, a single allele for the recessive trait,

FIGURE 12.16 An adult fruit fly, *Drosophila melanogaster*

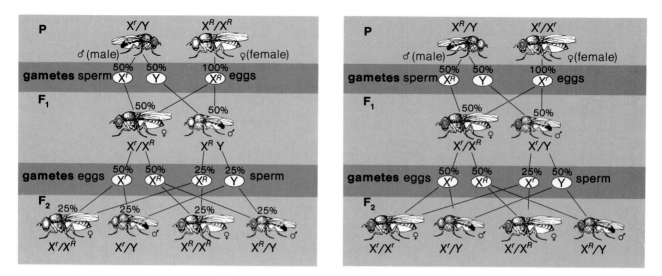

FIGURE 12.17 X-linked inheritance. (a) When Morgan crossed a white-eyed male with a normal red-eyed female, all the F₁ flies had red eyes. The F₂ flies showed the expected 3:1 ratio of red to white eyes, but only male flies showed the recessive trait. (b) A reciprocal cross. All male offspring have white eyes because they inherited their X chromosome from their mother. Compare this cross with the F₁ results of the first cross. The ratio of F₂ flies also is shown.

if on the X chromosome, could result in a white-eyed male. White eye color was the first example of an **X-linked trait**, a trait whose gene is carried on only the X chromosome.

Since then, many other X-linked traits have been found in *Drosophila*, and more than 300 X-linked traits have been identified in humans. Chapter 13 discusses human X-linked traits.

12.12 Nondisjunction

One of the X-linked traits isolated in *Drosophila* was the recessive eye-color trait known as vermilion (bright red). Calvin B. Bridges, a student of Morgan's, made crosses of vermilion-eyed females with normal red-eyed males (Figure 12.18, *left*). Occasionally (about once in every 2000 flies), a vermilion-eyed female or a red-eyed (but sterile) male appeared in the F₁ generation. What could be the explanation for these flies?

For a female in the F₁ generation to show the recessive vermilion trait, she would need two X chromosomes carrying the *v* allele. Clearly, if she had received an X chromosome from her red-eyed father, she would have an allele for the dominant red-eye trait and be red-eyed. How could a vermilion-eyed female be produced? By the same token, how could a red-eyed male appear in the F₁ generation?

Bridges suggested that these unexpected offspring must have developed from gametes produced by abnormal meiosis. If, for some reason, the sex chromosomes failed to separate in meiosis, then the offspring developing from those gametes would have unusual numbers of sex chromosomes. Bridges found that the cells of these exceptional flies did, indeed,

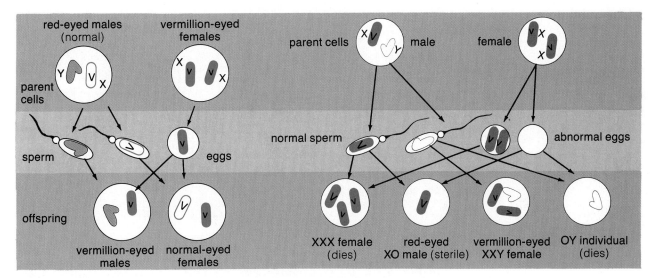

FIGURE 12.18 *(left)* Normal inheritance of an X-linked trait. The gene for eye color is carried on the X chromosome. *V* represents normal eye color; *v* represents vermilion. Males inherit their eye color on the X chromosome they receive from their mothers. *(right)* Nondisjunction of the X chromosome. Bridges explained the rare occurrence of red-eyed sterile males and vermilion-eyed females by suggesting that sometimes the X chromosomes fail to separate during meiosis. When Bridges examined the cells of these exceptional flies, he found his predicted abnormal chromosome number.

have extra or missing sex chromosomes. He called this failure of homologous chromosomes to separate in meiosis **nondisjunction**. Figure 12.18 (*right*) shows the results of a nondisjunction of the X chromosomes in the female parent. Bridges' breeding experiments and chromosome evidence clearly demonstrated that genes are located on chromosomes and firmly established the basis of the modern science of genetics.

Nondisjunction also occurs in the sex chromosomes (and other chromosomes) of humans, and the genotype and phenotype of the individual may be severely affected. Certain syndromes, or combinations of symptoms commonly occurring together, can be associated with abnormal numbers of sex chromosomes. Individuals with only one X chromosome and no Y chromosome (an XO genotype) are usually short, underdeveloped, and sterile females. This condition is known as Turner syndrome. Females with an XXX genotype often have limited fertility and may have slight intellectual impairment. An XXY chromosome combination results in Klinefelter syndrome. These males often are tall, sexually underdeveloped, and may have slight intellectual impairment.

Sex chromosomes are not the only chromosomes that may undergo nondisjunction during meiosis. A condition known as trisomy exists when a chromosome is present in triplicate. Most trisomies of autosomes (all chromosomes other than the sex chromosomes) severely impair development, and the embryo undergoes spontaneous abortion before coming to term. A few autosomal trisomies, however, are viable. Trisomy 21 (Down syndrome) is characterized by limited mental abilities, short stature, characteristic facial features, and heart defects, although the effects vary in

FIGURE 12.19 Chromosomes in Down syndrome (a), and a child showing characteristic facial features of Down syndrome (b)

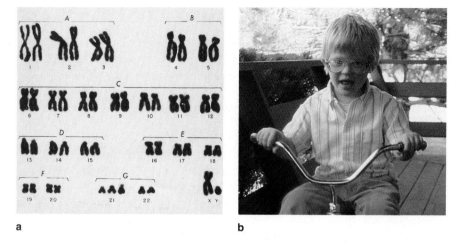

a   b

severity (Figure 12.19). For example, some people with Down syndrome are seriously retarded, others only mildly so. Approximately 95 percent of children with Down syndrome reach adulthood, and of those, 80 percent live into their early 50s. Down syndrome is the most common serious birth defect in the United States, occurring approximately once in every 700 live births. Mothers of age 35 or older have an increased likelihood of giving birth to infants with Down syndrome, and many pregnant women now choose to have the karyotype of the fetus checked for trisomy 21 and other chromosomal abnormalities (see Section 13.6).

12.13   X Inactivation

Why do most trisomies of autosomes result in death of the fetus, whereas trisomies of sex chromosomes do not? Studies of individuals with normal numbers of sex chromosomes provide a possible answer.

In 1961, the British geneticist Mary Lyon suggested that early in the development of a normal female, one X chromosome becomes inactivated in each body cell. Apparently this inactivation is random, so in some cells the X-linked genes inherited from the mother are expressed, whereas in other cells, the X-linked genes inherited from the father are active. Thus, the cells of a female are a genetic mixture of X-linked traits. This mixture of expressed alleles is seen graphically in tortoise-shell cats (Figure 12.20). Usually only female cats show this mottled coloration due to random inactivation of the X-linked color gene.

Lyon proposed X-inactivation as a possible explanation for a darkly staining mass called a Barr body (Figure 12.21) that normally appears in the nucleus of female cells, but not male cells. Females who have XXX syndrome have two Barr bodies, suggesting that all but one X chromosome in a cell become inactivated. One reason trisomies of sex chromosomes may not be as disruptive as autosomal trisomies is that the extra X chromosomes are inactivated and condensed into Barr bodies. Apparently a few genes remain active on the condensed X chromosomes, however, and the expression of these genes results in the abnormalities associated with extra X chromosomes.

FIGURE 12.20 The coloring of this cat is a visual indication of X inactivation. The cat carries two different alleles for coat color on its two X chromosomes. Random X inactivation during embryonic development results in this patchwork coat.

12.14 Genotype-Environment Interaction

Organisms are products of their heredity and of their surroundings. Traits such as height and skin color are influenced by environmental factors—nutrition can affect height, and exposure to sunlight can affect skin color.

A commonly cited example of an environmental effect on phenotype is the coloring of Siamese cats (Figure 12.22). Although these cats have a genotype for dark fur, the enzymes that produce the dark coloring function best at temperatures below the normal body temperature of the cat. Siamese cats are noted for the dark markings on their ears, nose, paws, and tail, all areas that have a low body temperature. If the hair on the cat's belly is shaved and an ice pack is applied, the replacement hair will be dark. Likewise, a shaved tail, kept at higher than normal temperatures, would soon be covered with light-colored fur. These changes are temporary, however, unless the ice pack or heat source is maintained permanently. Because the environment has a strong impact on gene expression, heredity determines only what an organism *may* become, not what it *will* become.

It often is difficult to sort out the effects of genetic inheritance from the effects of the environment, particularly in human genetics. Studies of identical twins provide geneticists with an opportunity to examine the influences of heredity (nature) and environment (nurture). Identical twins develop when the cells arising from a single fertilized egg separate and two complete embryos form. These embryos have exactly the same genetic information. If identical twins exhibit the same expression of a trait, then it would appear that the trait is heavily influenced by genetic factors. If twins differ from one another in the expression of a particular trait, the trait would seem to be heavily influenced by the environment. The message from such studies is that both genes and environment are important. Genes do not function in a vacuum.

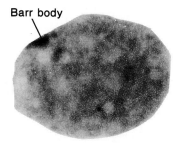

Barr body

FIGURE 12.21 The darkly staining Barr body is the condensed X chromosome. This cell is not dividing, so the chromosomes are uncoiled and visible only as chromatin.

CHECK AND CHALLENGE _____

1. What are multiple alleles? Can a person have more than two alleles for a single gene? Explain.

2. How is a trait that is determined by multiple genes different from one that is determined by multiple alleles?

3. Could a person with type A blood receive a transfusion of type O blood? Why or why not?

4. What offspring would result from a cross of a homozygous red-eyed female fruit fly and a vermilion-eyed male fruit fly? How might vermilion-eyed male offspring be produced?

5. A tall, sexually underdeveloped human male has cells with one Barr body each. What sex chromosomes would you expect to see in a karyotype from this individual?

6. How does crossing-over affect linkage?

7. How does the inheritance of X-linked traits differ from that of other traits?

FIGURE 12.22 Characteristic markings of a Siamese cat. These cats have a genotype that codes for dark fur, but the enzyme produced by the gene functions best at low temperatures. The cat's ears, paws, and tail have temperatures lower than the rest of the animal's body.

Summary

The concept of a gene has changed during the past century as research techniques have allowed more detailed questions to be asked and answered. A gene is defined as a region of DNA that codes for a product. Eukaryotic genes also include introns, which code for regions of mRNA that are later removed. Alleles are alternate forms of a gene that code for altered proteins.

Chromosomes are complex structures containing many genes each. In addition to DNA, chromosomes contain base sequences that are repeated thousands of times and segments of DNA that are never transcribed. Using such techniques as staining to produce banding patterns, homologous chromosomes can be identified. Homologous chromosomes may contain dissimilar alleles.

Mendel's work forms the basis of modern genetics. His principles of segregation and independent assortment can be explained by the behavior of homologous chromosomes during meiosis. Probability can be used to predict the outcome of breeding experiments.

Working with *Drosophila*, Morgan and his students identified many X-linked traits, established the chromosomal basis of inheritance, and explained nondisjunction, crossing-over, and recombination. Studies of twins have helped demonstrate the effects of environment on gene expression.

Key Concepts

Use the following concepts to develop a concept map for this chapter. Include additional concepts as you need them.

alleles	multiple alleles
codominant	nondisjunction
dominant	recessive
genes	trait
multifactorial	X-linked
homologous chromosomes	

Reviewing Ideas

1. How is a karyotype made and used?
2. How does sex determination differ in humans, birds, and grasshoppers?
3. What experimental procedures contributed to Mendel's success as a geneticist?
4. Explain Mendel's two principles of inheritance.
5. What sort of evidence indicates that genes for two traits are linked?
6. What are X-linked traits? What experimental evidence first established their existence?
7. What is the Lyon hypothesis? What observations support this hypothesis?
8. What is meant by "nature vs. nurture"? Distinguish between the contributions of genes and those of the environment.
9. What is meant by nondisjunction? To what sort of conditions can it give rise?

Using Concepts

1. Could you establish a true-breeding variety of pink snapdragons? Why or why not?

2. What are the possible blood types of children in the following families?
   a. Type A mother, Type A father
   b. Type A mother, Type O father
   c. Type B mother, Type AB father
   d. Type AB mother, Type AB father
   e. Type A mother, Type B father

3. In paternity lawsuits, blood typing often is used to provide genetic evidence that the alleged father could not be related to the child. For the following mother-and-child combinations, indicate which blood types could not have been the father's.

Mother	Child	Impossible Blood Types for Father
O	B	
B	A	
AB	B	

4. A brown mouse is crossed with a heterozygous black mouse. If the mother has a litter of four, what are the chances that all of them will be brown?

5. A cross is made between tall, red-flowered plants and short, white-flowered plants. Tall and red are dominant traits. What would the F_1 generation look like? What is the expected phenotypic ratio of the F_2? What is the expected phenotypic ratio of the F_2 generation if red and white are codominant?

6. The storage roots of radishes may be long, round, or oval. In a series of experiments, crosses between radishes with long roots and radishes with oval roots produced 159 plants with long roots and 156 plants with oval roots. Crosses between round and oval produced 199 round and 203 oval. Crosses between long and round produced 576 oval. Crosses between oval and oval produced 121 long, 243 oval, and 119 round. Show how root shape is inherited.

7. In tomatoes, red fruit color is dominant to yellow. Round-shaped fruit is dominant to pear-shaped fruit. Tall vine is dominant to dwarf vine.
   a. If you cross a pure-breeding tall plant bearing red, round fruit with a pure-breeding dwarf plant bearing yellow, pear-shaped fruit, predict the appearance of the F_1 generation.
   b. Assuming that the genes controlling the three traits are located on three different pairs of chromosomes, what are the possible genotypes in the F_2 generation?
   c. What are the expected phenotypic ratios?

8. In which sex would you expect X-linked traits to be found most frequently in the following species: dogs; grasshoppers; robins?

9. What are the goals of the Human Genome project? What issues and questions does this project raise?

10. Often the results of breeding experiments do not follow expected Mendelian ratios. Instead of 3:1 or 9:3:3:1 ratios in F_2 generations, there may be results such as 1:2:1, 9:7, 9:3:4, or 7:1:1:7. What explanations can you develop for such deviations from predicted ratios?

Synthesis

1. Mendel's principles of segregation and independent assortment can be summarized in modern times as follows: alleles segregate, nonalleles assort. Explain this statement as it relates to meiosis.

2. Suppose you examined the cells of a species of plant and found 12 chromosomes: a long straight pair, a short straight pair, a medium-length pair, a long bent pair, a short bent pair, and a medium-length bent pair. You then breed the plants of this species for several generations.
   a. At the end of this time would you expect to find some plants with all the straight chromosomes and none of the bent ones? All bent ones and no straight ones? Explain.
   b. What proportion of the gametes should have 3 straight chromosomes and 3 bent ones? 4 straight and 2 bent? 6 bent?

Extensions

1. Researchers are currently working on a complete gene map for humans. In what ways do you think this information will be useful? In what ways might it be a problem?

2. Imagine an allele for a recessive X-linked trait. Diagram or describe the situations in which it would be evident through five generations, beginning with a heterozygous female.

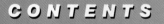

CONTENTS

Advances in Genetics

*W*ould you want to take a test that tells you which diseases you are likely to suffer from later in life? How much would you want to know about your child before it is born? What would you do with the information? Human genetics—the study of variation in humans—and medical genetics—the study of normal and abnormal human genetic variation—have grown rapidly in the last half of the twentieth century. These studies have shown that many human characteristics do not follow Mendelian patterns. That is, there is not a clear-cut, either/or distribution of traits. Unlike the pea plants in Mendel's experiments, humans are not either short or tall, or one color or the other. Rather, we show a large range of variation in height and color. This range of variation implies that more than one gene control such traits. It also suggests that the way genes are expressed may be affected by a number of environmental variables. For example, what are some of the environmental factors that might affect the genes that contribute to height?

New technologies allow us to identify certain genetic variations in humans that cause or predispose an individual to genetic disorders. In this chapter you will read about some human multi-gene disorders, how they are studied, and some of the technology that researchers use to diagnose and treat such disorders.

*W*hat is the function of these structures?

*H*ow are they important in genetic research?

◆ *Bacterial plasmids, magnified 150 000 times.*

Continuity and Variation

13.1   Genetic Links

In both sexual and asexual reproduction, organisms pass genetic information to their offspring, thus maintaining a genetic link between generations (Figure 13.1). Each species has a specific number of chromosomes that carry the genes characteristic of that species. The genes, in turn, may exist as a variety of alleles. This genetic variation within a species provides the basis for evolution by natural selection. Genes link generations, extending back through the history of a species for thousands of years and ensuring the continuity of that species into the future.

Molecular studies of proteins and nucleic acids can reveal the evolutionary links between species. Recall from Chapter 10 that a protein's amino acid sequence is determined by the sequence of bases in an organism's DNA. Therefore, comparison of amino acid sequences of common proteins can help determine whether two organisms share similar genetic information. That comparison, in turn, helps determine the extent of the evolutionary relationship between the two organisms.

Scientists also use DNA sequencing to unravel the genealogies of ancient forms of life. Genes may be altered by mutations over time, but traces of the original gene usually endure. Because every gene that exists today is a modified version of a gene that existed millions of years ago, the sequence of nucleotides in an organism's genes is a record of its evolutionary relationships. When scientists compare genes for the same function in two different organisms, they can correlate the extent of genetic difference to the amount of time that has passed since the two organisms diverged from a common ancestor. Such studies have been useful in determining the evolutionary relationships of various groups of organisms, and they reaffirm the genetic relatedness of all life on Earth.

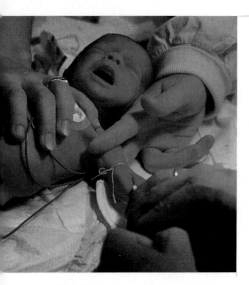

FIGURE 13.1   The genetic information that guided the development of this newborn infant was contained in the nucleus of a single cell, the fertilized egg.

FOCUS ON   *On DNA Sequencing*

With new research methods, the process of DNA sequencing becomes faster and easier. New techniques have reduced procedure times from months to days. In one commonly used method, researchers use gentle heating to separate complementary DNA strands. Then the beginning of the same single strand in each complementary pair is labeled with radioactive phosphate (^{32}P), and the labeled strands are separated into four equal portions. Each portion is treated with an enzyme that cuts the sugar-phosphate backbone adjacent to one of the four DNA nucleotides. However, because the enzymatic treatment is brief, all the bonds before every type of nucleotide are not broken. Thus, the original DNA fragments will be cut into ^{32}P-labeled pieces of varying lengths. The four different fragment mixtures are then separated by electrophoresis. Electrophoresis is a process similar to chromatography but uses an electric field to separate substances by molecular weight—the smaller fragments move faster and travel further across a gel-coated glass plate. Because each fragment is radioactively labeled, researchers can use X-ray film to identify the location of each type of fragment.

13.2 Sexual Reproduction and Genetic Variation

Genetic variation is the raw material for evolution by natural selection. Most of the genetic variation on which natural selection can work is a result of the recombination of parental genes during meiosis and fertilization. During prophase I, crossing-over produces new arrangements of the alleles found on homologous chromosomes. The random assortment of chromosomes during anaphase I increases the variation created by crossing over.

How the chromosomes sort to gametes during anaphase I depends on their orientation during metaphase I of meiosis. Review Focus on Chromosome Position in Chapter 11 to see how this sorting happens. The number of possible combinations can be predicted mathematically. The number is equal to 2^n, where n is the haploid number of chromosomes for that species. For example, if an organism has 6 chromosomes, the number of different gametes is equal to 2^3, or 8. In humans, n is equal to 23, so the number of possible different gametes produced by one individual is 2^{23}, or more than 8 million.

The random union of gametes in sexual reproduction also contributes to genetic variation. For example, because each of your parents could produce 8 million genetically different gametes, there are at least 8 million × 8 million—or 64 trillion—possible combinations of chromosomes among the children in your family. Is it any wonder that you and your sister or brother are not exactly alike? You are indeed a unique individual!

13.3 Mutations and Genetic Variation

Mutations also are a source of genetic variation. Recall from Chapter 9 that a mutation is a change in the DNA of a cell. In organisms that reproduce asexually, such as many plants, a mutation in almost any cell can be passed to the next generation. In organisms that reproduce sexually, such as humans and other animals, mutations can pass to the next generation only if they occur in the chromosomes of a gamete. Mutations occurring in somatic (body) cells, however, may initiate various cancers within an individual. Thus, mutagens (mutation-causing agents) in the environment (Figure 13.2 on the next page) are of concern, not only for their effect on future generations, but also for their impact on your own health.

There are several types of mutations. Point mutations involve a single DNA base pair and may arise when a mispairing occurs spontaneously during replication. Mutagenic chemicals or radiation may also cause the mispairing of bases. Some mutagenic chemicals resemble nucleotide bases. They can be inserted in the forming DNA chain, and then pair with incorrect bases during the next DNA replication. Other chemicals may alter nucleotide bases and cause them to mispair. Proofreader enzymes in the nucleus check for the correct matching of bases during replication and usually replace any mispaired bases. Occasionally, however, a mistake escapes detection.

The change in one base of a sequence may or may not have a large effect on the gene product. Chapter 10 explains that the genetic code is

CONNECTIONS

Genes and the mechanisms that result in genetic variation explain the unity of pattern and diversity of type observed in all organisms. DNA base pairs are the same for all organisms, yet the combination of base pairs is different in each organism.

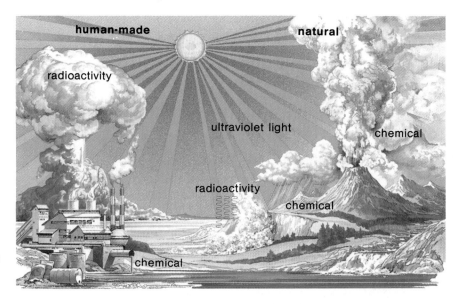

FIGURE 13.2 Known mutagens include several forms of radiation and a variety of chemicals. Mutagens occur both naturally and as a result of human activities.

redundant; several codons may signify the same amino acid. Thus, changes in base sequence may not result in a change in the amino acid sequence of a protein. Occasionally, however, one changed nucleotide by chance forms a stop codon; the resulting polypeptide chain is then terminated prematurely and does not function.

Base additions or deletions are the types of point mutations most likely to disrupt the genetic message. Remember that the genetic code is read as a sequence of three-letter words. Adding or removing some letters from the words can result in what is known as a frame-shift mutation, in which the reading frame of the message is altered. For example, what would happen if the letter *c* were removed from the following sentence?

The cat ate the fat rat.

Does "The ata tet hef atr at" make any sense? Clearly a frame-shift mutation can result in a gene that codes for a completely nonfunctional protein.

You have probably heard about the danger from the ultraviolet (UV) radiation in sunlight. UV light often causes the formation of covalent bonds between two adjacent thymine or cytosine nucleotides. The resulting double nucleotide blocks the replication and transcription of DNA. Usually a cellular UV repair system breaks the double bond or removes the blockage. In skin cells, however, the damage from repeated UV exposure may exceed the cell's repair ability, leading to skin cancer. For this reason, it is wise to use sunscreen during exposure to the sun.

Mutations are not limited to changes in just a few nucleotides. There can be large-scale chromosomal alterations too. Some of these changes can be attributed to damage caused by ionizing radiation, such as X rays or gamma rays. These forms of energy can liberate electrons and create explosively reactive chemicals—called free radicals—that can alter bases in DNA or even tear apart DNA strands. Figure 13.3, *left*, shows that several types

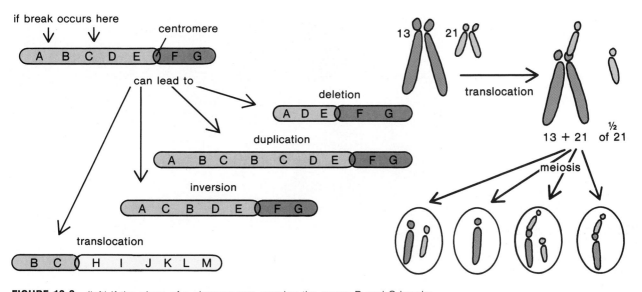

FIGURE 13.3 *(left)* If the piece of a chromosome carrying the genes B and C breaks off, four types of chromosomal mutations can result: deletion, duplication, inversion, or translocation to another chromosome. *(right)* If most of chromosome 21 is translocated to chromosome 13, meiosis can result in gametes with one copy, two copies, or no copies of chromosome 21.

of mutations may result if repair enzymes cannot repair the broken ends or if they incorrectly repair the break. A broken section of chromosome may be lost during the next cell division, resulting in a deletion. The broken section may be reattached in a reversed order, leading to a chromosomal inversion. Should the fragment attach to its homologous chromosome, a duplication is produced because the genes contained in the fragment already exist on the homologous chromosome. Broken pieces may swap positions on different chromosomes, an event called a translocation.

You can see in Figure 13.3, *right,* that a translocation in a developing gamete can result in individuals with too much, not enough, or the right amount of genetic information. For example, suppose the major portion of one chromosome 21 is translocated to chromosome 13. Meiosis would produce some gametes with two copies of chromosome 21, some with no copies, and some with only one copy. Fertilization of those gametes by normal gametes could result in individuals with three, one, or two copies of chromosome 21. (Individuals with only one copy of chromosome 21 do not survive.) In fact, babies with Down syndrome born to young mothers frequently carry this type of translocation.

Many chromosomal alterations cause severe developmental problems. Most human miscarriages are due to abnormalities in chromosome structure or number. Chromosomal abnormalities also appear to be involved in most human cancers. Specific translocations, deletions, or trisomies (Chapter 12) are consistently associated with specific types of tumors.

Some changes in chromosome structure are not due to environmental mutagens or errors in meiosis. Barbara McClintock, working with corn in

FIGURE 13.4 The color patterns of Indian corn, *Zea mays*, are due partly to the action of transposable elements.

the 1940s, proposed that certain genes ''jump around'' on the chromosomes. These transposable elements are fairly common in all organisms. Transposable elements move (or make copies of themselves that move) and insert themselves at various places among the chromosomes of an organism. When they enter the middle of a gene, they act as mutators, disrupting or changing gene function. The insertion of transposable elements can result in deletions, insertions, transpositions, and duplications.

There is much speculation about transposable elements because these jumping sequences bring about major changes in chromosomes. In prokaryotes, jumping sequences apparently can move between organisms, and thus can transmit genes even from one species to another. Retroviruses (Chapter 10) are able to make a DNA copy of their RNA when they enter a cell. This DNA then can insert into the host cell's chromosome, much like a transposable element. This characteristic makes retroviruses a promising tool of genetic engineers, as you will see in the Biological Challenge on gene therapy. HIV, the virus causing AIDS, is a retrovirus. Retroviruses are also linked to several cancers. For these reasons, retroviruses are currently a major focus of scientific research.

CHECK AND CHALLENGE

1. How is DNA sequence comparison a useful technique for studying evolutionary relationships?

2. Create a concept map to help organize your understanding of mutations. Include their effects as well as the various types.

3. What are transposable elements? What effects might they have on genes and chromosomes?

4. Explain how a point mutation can have *no* effect on the amino acid sequence of a protein. Give an example.

5. What aspects of sexual reproduction contribute to species variation?

Human Genetics

13.4 Studying Inheritance in Humans

For several reasons, the study of human genetics is much more difficult than the study of inheritance in garden peas or fruit flies described in Chapter 12. First, the generation time of humans is quite long—approximately 20 years as opposed to the few months or weeks in pea plants and fruit flies. In addition, each set of human parents produces only a few children, unlike the hundreds of offspring of peas and fruit flies. Also, controlled breeding experiments in humans would be ethically unacceptable, as would most experiments that impose different environmental conditions on groups of human subjects. The only tools available for most genetic studies in this country were pedigrees and twin studies.

A **pedigree** is a chart that illustrates a family history of a particular trait, such as eye color or hair color. As you read in Chapter 12, dominant, recessive, or X-linked traits show distinctive patterns of inheritance on pedigrees. Figure 13.5 shows a pedigree for the X-linked disorder hemophilia—a condition in which blood does not clot properly. Can you determine from the chart which females carry the gene for hemophilia? The development of a pedigree is often the first step used in genetic counseling. Through such a pedigree, a genetic counselor can provide prospective parents with information about the probability of transmitting harmful traits to their offspring.

13.5 Genetic Disorders

One reason for interest in human genetics is genetic disorders—diseases, deformities, and handicaps with a genetic basis. (See Focus on Genetic Anticipation.) There are three broad categories of genetic disorders. Researchers have identified approximately 3500 inherited disorders caused by single-gene defects that show Mendelian inheritance. Such disorders are generally apparent early in an individual's life and are expressed regardless of the environment. The second category, chromosomal abnormalities and their association with medical syndromes, is discussed in

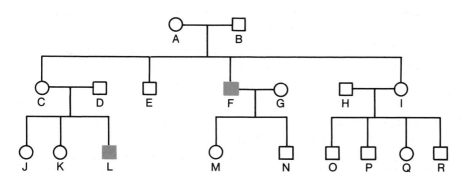

FIGURE 13.5 A pedigree showing the inheritance of hemophilia. Circles = females, squares = males. A horizontal line connects parents, and offspring are drawn below. Shaded symbols indicate individuals who are hemophiliac. The first mother was a carrier because she had a son with hemophilia. Why did his son not inherit the trait? Can you tell which daughter was a carrier? Are you sure the other daughter was not a carrier?

TABLE 13.1	
Frequency of Genetic Disorders in Persons Under 25 Years of Age*	
Type of Disorder	**Frequency/1000 Individuals**
Autosomal dominant	1.4 (0.14%)
Autosomal recessive	1.7 (0.17%)
X-linked recessive	0.5 (0.05%)
Chromosomal abnormalities	1.8 (0.18%)
Multifactorial	46.4 (4.64%)
Unknown genetic origin	1.2 (0.12%)
Total	53.0 (5.30%)

*SOURCE: P.A. Baird *et al.* ''Genetic disorders in children and young adults: A population study.'' *American Journal of Human Genetics.* 42(5):677, 1988.

Section 12.11. Conditions that are multifactorial—controlled by several genes—make up the third category. Individuals with a multifactorial condition may be genetically predisposed to the disorder, but environmental factors influence its onset and severity. This category includes birth defects such as spina bifida (a failure of the vertebrae to close during development) and cleft palate, for which the environmental trigger is not understood. Heart disease, hypertension, certain cancers, and diabetes also are in this third category. They constitute the major health-care burden in developed countries. Table 13.1 lists the frequency of various types of genetic disorders. Note that most genetic disorders are multifactorial, underscoring once again the significance of environmental influences on gene expression.

Studies have shown that one in every 200 newborns has some recognizable chromosomal abnormality. It also is estimated that as many as 70 percent of fertilized eggs are abnormal—most of those eggs are spontaneously aborted. The occurrence of chromosomal abnormalities appears to be sporadic; the causes of most of these events are unknown.

Many genetic disorders are the result of mutant, recessive forms of alleles that follow Mendelian inheritance. The most common lethal genetic disorder in the United States is cystic fibrosis (Figure 13.6). Cystic fibrosis affects about one of every 2000 Caucasians but is much rarer in other races. The disorder is characterized by excessive secretion of mucus, which accumulates and damages the lungs, digestive tract, and other organs. In 1992 researchers identified the gene responsible for cystic fibrosis and are now working to develop gene therapy that will correct the DNA defects. (See the Biological Challenge on gene therapy.) Until that time, improved therapy and medications are enabling people with cystic fibrosis to live longer, more active lives.

Many genetic disorders are caused by a recessive allele that codes for an ineffective or nonfunctional protein product. When that product is an enzyme, the result in a homozygous recessive individual may be a block in

FIGURE 13.6 Children and adults with cystic fibrosis often inhale medicated vapors to help clear the lungs and to treat lung infection.

GENETIC COUNSELOR

Joan A. Scott is a genetic counselor in Sacramento, California. She received her master's degree in genetic counseling from Sarah Lawrence College. Along with other people in the clinic, Joan helps couples make decisions about having children. She finds this position interesting, not only because of the genetics and medicine, but because each family and each situation is different. For Joan, this career is tailor-made.

She counsels four basic groups of people: couples who already have at least one child with a genetic disorder; couples who have a known family genetic disorder yet wish to have children; couples who have a genetic disorder of their own, such as diabetes, and who wish to know the chances of passing on those genes; and couples who are expecting a baby and are of advanced age or have been exposed to a drug or toxin that may cause a genetic disorder in the fetus.

Several steps are followed to equip the couples with the knowledge they need in order to make an intelligent and educated decision. First, the counselor must have a verifiable diagnosis. He or she must be certain that the genetic condition in question exists in the couple or their families. Sometimes this can be very difficult to determine, especially if family photos are the only source of information for the diagnosis.

Second, the counselor must establish whether or not the couple is at risk. Sometimes genetic disorders can be difficult to diagnose, particularly in autosomal dominant disorders, such as neurofibromatosis. This disorder, sometimes called the Elephant Man disease, is widespread. The difficulty lies in the fact that the expression of this disorder is highly variable—sometimes it is only "cafe-au-lait" spots on the skin. In such a case, the person has a fifty-fifty

FIGURE A Joan Scott discusses a couple's karyotypes during genetic counseling.

chance of carrying the genes for the disorder, but no one can determine just how it will be expressed in the child. The degree of expression could be very mild or extremely severe. To date, there is no form of prenatal diagnosis for neurofibromatosis.

Third, the family must weigh the risks against the burden of the disease (a genetic cost-benefit analysis) and keep in mind the worst possible results. Fourth, if they decide to conceive a child, they must also consider the possible development of future techniques that could diagnose the condition. If such techniques are developed and the child is found to have a genetic disorder, what will the couple do then? Should they terminate the pregnancy even though they cannot determine how severe the expression will be? They must also consider the chance that new treatments for disorders may be developed.

Joan finds her work to be very challenging and she is constantly helping couples resolve these questions and problems. Each year, many new families come to the center for counseling, in addition to those families that visit the mobile clinic. One of the most rewarding experiences genetic counselors have is finding out that a couple who decided to begin a family despite the risks now has a healthy child.

FIGURE 13.7 The amino acid phenylalanine is converted to tyrosine in a normal metabolic pathway. Persons having the disorder phenylketonuria (PKU) lack an enzyme needed for this conversion, and phenylalanine or toxic products of its breakdown accumulate in their bodies.

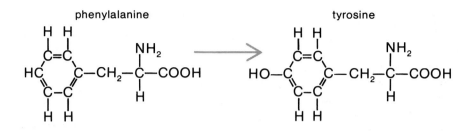

phenylalanine   tyrosine

an essential metabolic pathway. Either the lack of the pathway's product or the substrate's accumulation in the body may account for the symptoms of the disease.

The disorder phenylketonuria (PKU), for example, is caused by a defect in a metabolic enzyme that is needed to convert the amino acid phenylalanine into another amino acid called tyrosine (Figure 13.7). When this pathway is blocked, the buildup of phenylalanine or its abnormal breakdown products causes severe retardation, seizures, and other symptoms. Fortunately, excess phenylalanine can be detected in the blood, and most newborn babies in the United States are tested for its presence. PKU can be treated with a diet low in phenylalanine. Children with PKU may remain on this special diet until their teens.

Not all genetic disorders are caused by defective enzymes. Sickle cell disease is a serious disorder that is caused by a single amino acid substitution in the hemoglobin protein. When the oxygen concentration in the bloodstream decreases, this defective hemoglobin molecule crystallizes and causes red blood cells to become "sickled" in shape (Figure 13.8). These misshapen cells can clog blood vessels and cause severe pain, fever, and even death. Sickle hemoglobin and normal hemoglobin are codominant traits. Heterozygous individuals have what is called sickle cell trait and usually exhibit no symptoms. However, they may experience difficulties under conditions of low oxygen pressure, such as after vigorous exercise or at high altitude. Sickle cell disease affects 1 of every 625 African-Americans in the United States.

Multifactorial disorders are caused by the interaction of several genes with each other and with an individual's environment. For example, heart disease, which is the leading cause of death in the United States, is linked to smoking, diets high in cholesterol and saturated fats, stress, and lack of exercise. One in 500 people in the United States has a dominant trait that results in the accumulation of very high levels of cholesterol in the blood. The environmental factors mentioned above, however, can result in elevated blood cholesterol levels and heart disease in many individuals, even without this trait.

Another multifactorial disorder is hypertension (high blood pressure), which also is associated with heart disease. Hypertension is easy to diagnose and usually can be controlled by diet, exercise, and, if necessary, drug therapy. Awareness of the genetic predisposition to many common, multifactorial disorders and knowledge of your own hereditary history can help you make healthy life-style choices.

FIGURE 13.8 Sickled red blood cells. At low oxgen concentration, molecules of sickle-cell hemoglobin form crystals that distort the plasma membrane.

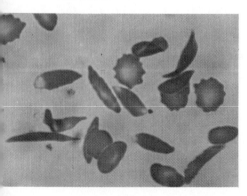

FOCUS ON *Genetic Anticipation*

Scientists working on the Human Genome Project (HGP) have discovered a startling new process that may change the way we think about human inheritance. Called "genetic anticipation," the process is caused by a mutation that increases the likelihood that a mutated piece of DNA will mutate again. In most genes, mutations are passed on to the next generation without further change and with little or no change in the severity of the resulting disorder. In contrast, genes that show genetic anticipation may increase the severity of a disorder in future generations.

Genetic anticipation is the tendency of certain DNA segments to expand to many times their normal length. In the normal alleles for at least five different human disorders, Huntington's disease among them, some short, three nucleotide stretches of DNA are repeated from 5 to almost 50 times. However, when the number of copies of the trinucleotides exceeds certain thresholds, one of the genetic disorders results (Figure B).

When the normal number of copies of the trinucleotide is present, the number of repeats is usually inherited in a stable fashion. That is, there is no change in the number of copies from parent to child. For example, a "normal" allele of the fragile X gene carries at most 50 copies of the CGG trinucleotide. These copies can be inherited without changing for generations. However, when the gene begins to mutate, the number of copies can increase drastically.

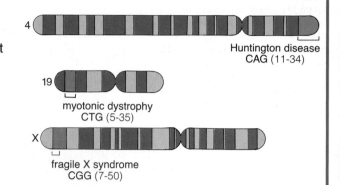

FIGURE B Trinucleotide repeats. Letters show the repeating sequence; numbers show normal size ranges of repeats.

Mutated forms of the gene may contain between 50 and 200 copies of the trinucleotide, although people who carry these copies often are still healthy. Children of such carriers, however, carry fragile X alleles that may have up to 1000 copies and develop the symptoms of fragile X syndrome—primarily mental retardation.

Investigators are not sure why the disorders showing genetic anticipation include neurological or muscular symptoms, or why the trinucleotide repeats are so unstable. Trinucleotide repeats actually are common in the human genome. At least 50 genes are known to contain sections of five or more triplet repeats, and it is likely that other genes have them as well. Discovering why the repeats in some genes are prone to expansion may help explain how the related diseases arise. It also may help clarify how cells normally maintain the stability of genetic material as they transmit it to the next generation.

13.6 Diagnosis and Treatment of Genetic Disorders

The field of genetic counseling has expanded as researchers have developed tests that identify carriers and detect genetic disorders. Individuals often seek genetic counseling if they have a family history of a genetic disorder or after a child is born with a birth defect. The counselor develops a pedigree and may suggest various tests that can help determine the risk of either parent transmitting a genetic disorder to an offspring.

Many tests have also been developed to determine whether a fetus is at risk for a genetic disorder. Figure 13.9 on the next page illustrates amniocentesis (am nee oh sen TEE sus), a procedure that usually is done between

FIGURE 13.9 Prenatal diagnosis of genetic disorders by amniocentesis. Fetal cells from the amniotic fluid are withdrawn and cultured for later chromosomal and biochemical analyses. Biochemical analysis of the fluid also can detect certain abnormalities.

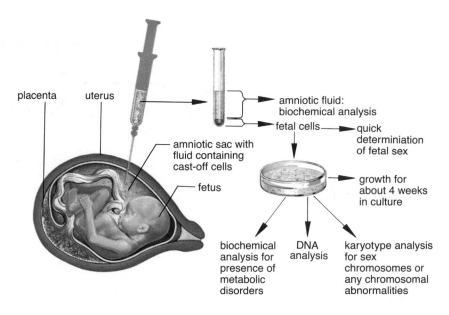

the fourteenth and sixteenth weeks of pregnancy. During amniocentesis, a needle is inserted through the mother's abdomen and uterine wall into the amniotic sac surrounding the fetus, and a small amount of fluid containing fetal cells is withdrawn. Another technique, chorionic villi sampling (CVS), can be done in about the eighth week of pregnancy. In this procedure, an instrument is inserted through the woman's vagina and cervix (or a needle is inserted through the abdomen), and a small amount of fetal tissue from the embryonic membrane, or chorion, is suctioned off. This procedure can provide results sooner than amniocentesis because CVS can be performed earlier in pregnancy, and the cells obtained by CVS are growing rapidly. CVS technology currently is not as widely available as amniocentesis, however, and it poses a somewhat greater risk to the fetus.

Fetal cells obtained by either procedure are cultured, and a karyotype is developed that can show chromosomal abnormalities. Amniotic fluid can be used to diagnose fetal disorders such as spina bifida. An accumulation in the amniotic fluid of a protein called alphafetoprotein signals this defect.

Ultrasound is a common prenatal technique that allows a medical professional to estimate fetal age, identify twins and often fetal sex, and detect several fetal abnormalities, such as enlarged or absent kidneys, hydrocephalus (water on the brain), certain forms of dwarfism, disorders of the brain and spinal chord, and some heart defects. This technique uses high-frequency sound waves in conjunction with a computer to produce an image like the one in Figure 13.10. Ultrasound also is used to locate the fetus during amniocentesis and chorionic villi sampling.

At present, some 600 genetic disorders can be diagnosed prenatally, many through ultrasound. About 100 disorders are diagnosed biochemically, by testing for a gene product. Many others are diagnosed by DNA analysis made possible by the recombinant DNA technology you will read about in Section 13.7.

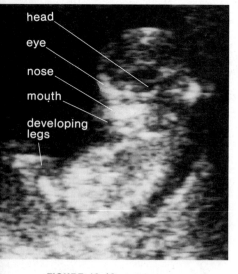

FIGURE 13.10 Ultrasound image of a 12½-week-old fetus.

GENE THERAPY

One result of genetic engineering technology is the ability to correct a genetic disorder through gene therapy. Currently, over 40 gene therapy experiments are underway throughout the world for diseases such as AIDS, cancer, and cystic fibrosis. In 1990, researchers began the first gene therapy trial for ADA (adenosine deaminase) deficiency, a form of severe immunodeficiency disease. Individuals with ADA deficiency lack an enzyme that is essential for the correct functioning of their immune system, and they can live only in controlled environments. In May of 1993, researchers successfully inserted normal ADA genes into bone marrow cells that had been removed from two girls with ADA. Researchers then reinjected the genetically altered cells, which migrated to the girls' bone marrow, developed into immune system cells, and produced ADA.

The most difficult aspect of gene therapy is transporting the "corrected" genes to the defective cells. In the case of ADA deficiency, the researchers used a retrovirus as the delivery vehicle, or vector. Similarly, researchers hope to use the virus that causes the common cold to introduce corrected genetic information into the lung cells of patients with cystic fibrosis. The vector for gene therapy need not always be a virus, however. To treat patients with a lethal type of skin cancer, researchers targeted a type of white blood cell called a tumor infiltrating lymphocyte (TIL). TIL cells normally attack cancerous tumors, but are not strong enough to control tumor growth. In this gene therapy, researchers use a tiny fat bubble, or liposome, as the vector to insert a tumor-fighting gene into TIL cells that have been removed from a cancer patient. The tumor-fighting gene commands the TIL cells to produce a protein that kills tumor cells by preventing them from establishing a blood supply. The genetically enhanced TIL cells are then returned to the patient's bloodstream to attack the tumors. As each genetically altered TIL

FIGURE C   David, born with combined immune deficiency syndrome, lived in a sterile "bubble" to prevent infection.

cell enters a tumor, it becomes a "factory" that makes the tumor-killing protein.

Although some scientists are working on gene therapy involving human cells, others are studying other animals and plants. For example, much AIDS research uses mice whose immune systems contain transplanted human genes. Herds of cows now receive genetically engineered growth hormone, causing them to produce more milk than ordinary cattle. Soon, genetically engineered tomatoes will be commercially available. These tomatoes ripen without becoming too soft for packing and shipping.

So far, researchers have used gene therapy only on human somatic, or body, cells. In somatic-cell gene therapy, an individual's body cells, not their sex cells, contain the altered genetic information. Thus, the effect of the gene therapy is not passed on to new generations. In germ-cell gene therapy, however, the genetic information of the sex cells is altered. Thus, the new information would be passed on to the offspring, generation after generation. Because of the ethical, legal, and social implications of germ-cell gene therapy, clinical trials to treat diseases using germ cells are far in the future.

The results of fetal genetic tests can leave parents with a difficult choice. However, the information gained may help them avoid having a child with a fatal condition, or prepare for the challenges associated with raising a handicapped child. When a positive test indicates a probable genetic abnormality, the genetic counselor will discuss all possible medical options with the couple, including treatments for the abnormality, terminating the pregnancy, and community resources available for caring for an affected infant. Most genetic counseling clinics have social workers, psychologists, and specially trained clergy available to help parents and families make the difficult decisions that often arise in dealing with a genetic disorder.

There are three avenues of treatment for people with genetic disorders: modifying an individual's environment or lifestyle, drug therapy that relieves symptoms or replaces missing enzymes or hormones, and most recently, gene therapy, which actually corrects the defective gene. In the first instance, the environment of the individual with an inherited disorder can be modified to minimize the effect of the disorder. An example is modifying the diet of a child with PKU or of an adult who has a family history of heart disease. As researchers identify genes that predispose individuals to chronic, multifactorial disorders such as heart disease, genetic counselors likely will spend more time discussing environmental variables and lifestyle choices with individuals and families.

Drug therapy can be used to treat genetic disorders that are caused by insufficient levels of hormones, enzymes, or other chemicals. For example, diabetes and pituitary dwarfism can be controlled by the administration of the hormones missing in the affected individuals. Some genetic disorders may require transplanting bone marrow or whole organs. Often environmental modifications, such as diet, are used in combination with drug therapy to treat genetic disorders. Although these approaches control the problem, they do not correct the genetic defect. However gene therapy, the third avenue for the treatment of genetic disorders, actually corrects the genetic defect. (See the Biological Challenges on gene therapy.)

CHECK AND CHALLENGE

1. Why has the study of human inheritance lagged behind the progress made in fruit-fly or corn genetics?

2. Compare the three categories of human genetic disorders.

3. PKU and sickle cell disease are both single-gene disorders. Describe how the abnormal gene causes the disorder in each case.

4. Compare the prenatal genetic tests now available. Amniocentesis and CVS can cause loss of pregnancy in a very small percentage of women (0.5 percent for amniocentesis and 3.9 percent for CVS). Given that information, in what situations would you recommend that prenatal genetic tests be done?

5. Why does germ-cell gene therapy raise more ethical problems than somatic-cell gene therapy?

Genetic Technology

13.7 Genetic Engineering

Chapter 1 describes briefly how, through genetic engineering, bacteria can produce human growth hormone. In this chapter, Section 13.6 described genetic engineering as one source of drugs for the treatment of genetic disorders. What, exactly does genetic engineering mean? Humans have a long history of employing the beneficial characteristics of living organisms to perform practical tasks, as in using bacteria to produce cheese and antibiotics, or yeast to make bread and wine. Charles Darwin pointed out that humans have been practicing the selective breeding of plants and animals for centuries. However, in selective breeding, people could manipulate only those traits that were part of an organism's normal genetic potential. In addition, until recently, the science of genetics relied on breeding experiments that involved the total genetic makeup of organisms. No one could study the action of a single gene in isolation.

FOCUS ON *RFLPs*

Because of inherited variations in DNA, no two people have the same sequence of bases. Person A may have a restriction site (the nucleotide sequence recognized by a specific restriction enzyme) where person B does not. If DNA from both people is cut with the same restriction enzyme, different-sized fragments of DNA result. These fragments are called *r*estriction *f*ragment *l*ength *p*olymorphisms, or RFLPs. They are *fragment lengths* of DNA cut by *restriction* enzymes, and they occur in many forms (lengths), or polymorphisms. The fragments can be separated using gel electrophoresis. In this procedure, molecules are added to a gel through which an electric current is run, causing the molecules to migrate through the gel. The length and charge of the molecules determines how far they move through the gel.

Another type of RFLP occurs in regions where the same DNA sequences repeat frequently. These repeats can vary so much in length among individuals that certain RFLPs occur in as many as 12 different sizes. The number and pattern of these repeats in an individual's DNA is unique; they can be said to form a DNA fingerprint. DNA identification tests have

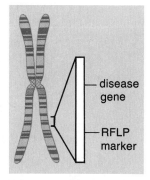

FIGURE D Relationship of a mutant allele and a genetic marker

been used in criminal and paternity cases.

When a RFLP is linked to a mutant allele, it can be used as a reference point, or genetic marker (Figure D), making it possible to detect the presence of the allele and to study its inheritance within a family. As a result, prenatal screening is possible to identify carriers of the gene. The predictive value of a linked marker, however, depends on the tightness of the linkage. Some restriction enzymes provide more powerful markers than others, but good family data are required for linkage analysis.

A few disorders are detectable with a direct gene probe that hybridizes to the mutated gene. In sickle cell disease, the base change responsible for the disorder eliminates a restriction site, creating a longer RFLP that can be detected by gel electrophoresis.

Today, however, techniques developed to study the molecular biology of bacteria and viruses enable the manipulation of individual genes, or genetic engineering. Using genetic engineering, biologists can prepare **recombinant DNA**—DNA whose segments are from different sources. While genetic engineering had its roots in recombinant DNA technology, it now extends beyond recombinant DNA. By using genetic technology, biologists can isolate specific genes, recombine genes from different organisms, and transfer this recombinant DNA into host cells. In cells, the recombinant DNA can be replicated, or cloned, providing multiple copies of the genes for study. Recombinant DNA also can produce proteins, such as human growth hormone or insulin, with a variety of practical applications. What are the basic techniques and uses of genetic engineering?

13.8 Techniques of Genetic Engineering

Try Investigation 13A, Direct Detection of Genetic Disorders.

One of the central techniques of genetic engineering is gene splicing—a process by which DNA from one organism is incorporated into the DNA strand of another organism, producing recombinant DNA. The recombinant DNA then is introduced into a host organism, where the newly incorporated genetic information is expressed. (See Figure 13.11.)

Creating a recombinant organism that produces a desired protein requires several conditions. The first requirement is identifying a specific gene and cutting it from a chromosome. The second is finding a DNA carrier, or vector, that can be inserted into living host cells. Third is a

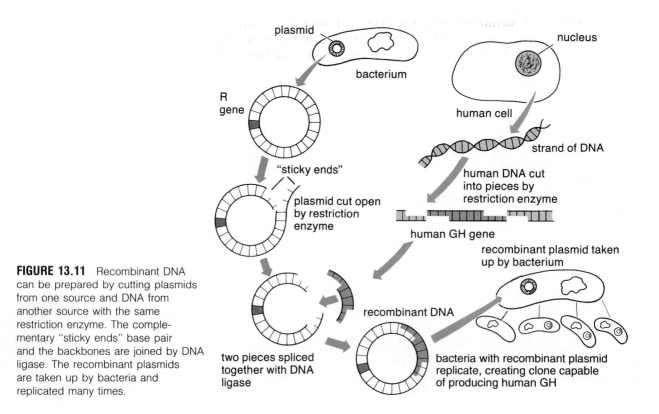

FIGURE 13.11 Recombinant DNA can be prepared by cutting plasmids from one source and DNA from another source with the same restriction enzyme. The complementary "sticky ends" base pair and the backbones are joined by DNA ligase. The recombinant plasmids are taken up by bacteria and replicated many times.

method of joining the gene to the vector DNA to form recombinant DNA. Fourth is a system to introduce the recombinant DNA into a host cell, where it can replicate. Finally a method is needed to detect cells that have replicated the recombinant DNA and that synthesize the desired product.

The gene (DNA segment) of interest first must be identified and isolated. For example, to produce human growth hormone (GH) by genetic engineering, DNA must be obtained from cells that normally produce GH. DNA from GH-producing cells is extracted and cut into segments. The cutting is done by a family of enzymes known as **restriction enzymes** that recognize and cleave specific nucleotide sequences of DNA. You can see in Figure 13.12 that restriction enzymes make a staggered cut through complementary strands of DNA. The process results in two "sticky ends"— unpaired nucleotides at the end of each strand. If the gene of interest and the vector are cut with the same restriction enzyme, their sticky ends tend to pair with each other. The newly paired strands can be joined by another enzyme, DNA ligase, forming recombinant DNA. (DNA ligase, an enzyme essential for DNA replication and repair, is discussed in Chapter 9.)

The most commonly used DNA vectors are plasmids, small circles of DNA found outside the chromosomes of prokaryotes. (See Figure 12.2.) Plasmid DNA is taken directly into bacterial cells (usually *Escherichia coli*) from a culture medium. After entering the host cell, the recombinant DNA replicates along with the host cell's DNA. This process is known as cloning— the reproduction and growth of genetically identical cells or organisms. The product that the recombinant DNA codes for, such as insulin, is synthesized by the genetically engineered host cells. Cloning can also furnish multiple copies of a gene for further research.

One method of identifying bacterial cells that have taken up the recombinant DNA is to use plasmids that carry what is known as a resistance gene. This gene, sometimes called an R gene, confers resistance to

Try Investigation 13B, Recombinant DNA.

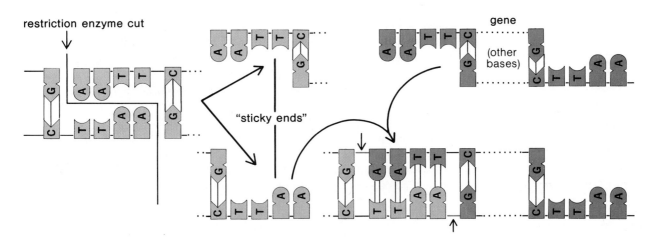

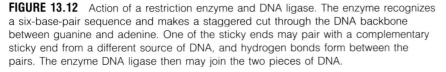

FIGURE 13.12 Action of a restriction enzyme and DNA ligase. The enzyme recognizes a six-base-pair sequence and makes a staggered cut through the DNA backbone between guanine and adenine. One of the sticky ends may pair with a complementary sticky end from a different source of DNA, and hydrogen bonds form between the pairs. The enzyme DNA ligase then may join the two pieces of DNA.

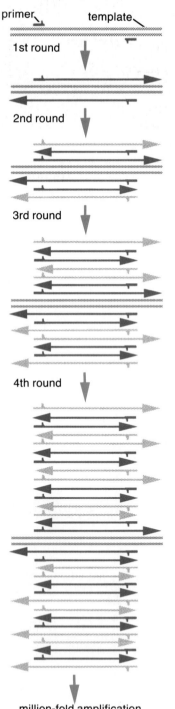

primer template
1st round
2nd round
3rd round
4th round

million-fold amplification
after 20-25 cycles of PCR

various antibiotics. Bacteria containing plasmids with these resistance genes can grow on a culture medium that contains antibiotics, whereas bacteria lacking those plasmids die.

Often, scientists who are studying a particular gene or who are testing for the presence of specific mutations need large amounts of cloned DNA. For example, cystic fibrosis can result when the normal gene mutates at any one of more than 350 sites. Each test for cystic fibrosis requires a certain amount of DNA, which comes from a blood sample. Researchers would need a very large amount of blood to test for each of the 350 or more differences in the CF gene. In addition, while large amounts of DNA for tests such as these can be obtained by recombinant bacterial cloning, this process is very complex, extremely time consuming, and costly.

In 1985, a young chemist named Kary Mullis solved the problem of obtaining large amounts of genetic material quickly and relatively inexpensively. His solution, for which he won the 1993 Nobel Prize in chemistry, is a technique called the DNA polymerase chain reaction, or PCR. In Chapter 10 you read that DNA *polymerase* is an enzyme that can make copies of DNA strands. *Chain reaction* refers to the fact that the polymerase makes many copies, with each copy serving as a template for yet another copy. Figure 13.13 illustrates that at each duplication, or round, the polymerase copies all the existing strands so that there is a doubling in the number of DNA strands. The result is a very rapid increase in the number of DNA molecules. From one or a few original DNA strands, PCR can produce more than enough copies for a large number of screening tests. In addition to making genetic testing less time consuming and expensive, PCR technology has allowed the use of tiny amounts of blood, hair, and other tissue in DNA fingerprinting to solve crimes and to identify missing individuals.

13.9 Ethical, Policy, and Safety Issues

Although genetic technology has great promise in the areas of agriculture and medicine, it is not without controversies. Public interest in the new technology also has raised questions. What are the risks in releasing genetically engineered organisms into the environment? Can we predict how these organisms will interact in the complex ecological balance of nature? Could dangerous new organisms or viruses inadvertently be produced?

Other questions focus on public policy. Should the government regulate genetic technology? Does the public have a right to be informed and to have a voice in decisions about research that might involve moral and ethical, as well as technical issues? Who should make the decisions about what types of research are desirable and what risks are acceptable?

FIGURE 13.13 The polymerase chain reaction (PCR) starts with double-stranded DNA and nucleotide primers that are complementary to sequences at the ends of the fragment to be duplicated. Because of the orientation of the primers, DNA products of previous rounds act as templates in subsequent rounds. At each round the amount of DNA is doubled.

Interesting legal questions have arisen about sharing research techniques and the ownership of genetically engineered organisms. In 1980, the United States Supreme Court ruled that a live, human-made microorganism is patentable, and in 1988, a mouse that was genetically engineered for use in cancer research was, indeed, patented (Figure 13.14). Hundreds of companies have emerged in the potentially lucrative field of genetic engineering. The secrecy and legal protection surrounding product development occasionally conflict with the openness of scientific inquiry.

As the field has grown, both scientists' and nonscientists' initial concerns about safety issues in recombinant technology have decreased. Effective laboratory containment measures have been developed. Microorganisms with highly specific nutritional requirements have been engineered so that they cannot survive outside the laboratory. Regulations prohibit some research, establish levels of containment, and specify the number of acres into which a genetically engineered organism may be released. However, there is some concern that safety precautions such as these will put the United States at a disadvantage in the race with foreign companies to market biotechnology products. There is a general trend, though, toward easing the safety regulations for this research as demonstrations of safety decrease the level of concern.

Many policy and ethical decisions remain, and more will develop as genetic technology grows. If we can insert a gene to correct a genetic disorder in present generations, why not alter the genes of future generations? Is there an ethical difference between somatic-cell gene therapy—manipulating genes in body cells—and germ-cell therapy—inserting and replacing genes in the germ cells that produce gametes? Would germ-cell therapy lead to eugenics—the deliberate effort to "improve" the human genetic condition by selective breeding?

How commercially available should the products of genetic engineering be? Individuals can change their phenotype in many ways ranging from hair dyes to cosmetic surgery. Will hormones and biochemical stimulants be added to the list of "self-improvement" products? If personality traits are genetically determined, will we be able to choose and control human behavior? How much control should we, or other people, have over our genetic potential? Who will decide the answers to these questions? The cure of genetic disorders is a worthy endeavor. We need to look carefully, however, at what we characterize as human "disorders." Future decisions will require an educated, informed electorate that is actively concerned with the issues.

FIGURE 13.14 The "Harvard" mouse is the first genetically engineered animal to be patented.

CHECK AND CHALLENGE

1. What is recombinant DNA technology?
2. Identify the enzymes that genetic engineers use and their actions.
3. What major benefits have come from genetic technology?
4. Describe some safety or ethical concerns about genetic technology.
5. What are two ways genes can be cloned?

Summary

Genes and chromosomes are the genetic link between generations. Independent assortment of chromosomes, crossing-over, and random fertilization of gametes provide the genetic variation that leads to natural selection and evolution. Mutations are changes in DNA structure. They are usually detrimental, but occasionally may produce an advantageous phenotypic trait. Mutations may involve changes in one or several nucleotides, or they may be major chromosomal alterations. Genetic variation increases as a result of mutations.

Knowledge of human genetics has grown substantially during this century. Approximately 2000 genes have been assigned to chromosomes, and many genes for genetic defects have been linked to markers on chromosomes, which allow their detection. Genetic disorders fall into three categories: single-gene disorders that follow Mendelian patterns of inheritance, chromosomal alterations, and conditions that show multifactorial inheritance. The diagnosis and treatment of genetic disorders has improved through the use of genetic engineering. Genetic counseling provides couples with many services, including prenatal diagnosis of some genetic disorders.

Recombinant DNA technology involves the insertion of DNA from a cell of one species into a cell of another species, where the foreign gene(s) may be expressed. Restriction enzymes and DNA ligase are examples of enzymes that genetic engineers use as tools. Genetic engineering is aiding many areas of research. However, the newly acquired ability to manipulate genetic material raises ethical, legal, and public policy questions that are difficult to answer.

Key Concepts

Use the following concepts to develop a concept map. Include additional concepts from the chapter as you need them.

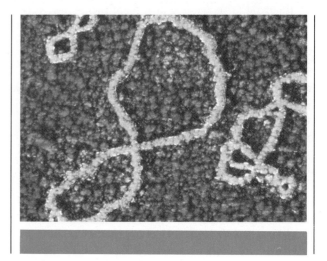

cDNA	mutation
crossing-over	pedigree
enzymes	plasmids
ethics	public policy
gene cloning	recombinant DNA
genetic disorders	technology
genetic recombination	safety
meiosis	variation

Reviewing Ideas

1. What are the major sources of genetic variation in a species?

2. How could a deletion mutation lead to a duplication or to a translocation?

3. What are transposable elements? What role may they have played in evolution?

4. Describe the basic procedure for cloning a gene.

5. Distinguish between somatic-cell therapy and germ-cell gene therapy.

6. What is a genetic disorder? What is the difference between a genetic disorder and an environmentally caused disorder?

7. How are the principles of probability used in genetic counseling?

8. What is multifactorial inheritance? Name some disorders that show this type of inheritance.

9. Humans are not used for controlled breeding. Discuss the scientific and ethical reasons behind this circumstance.

10. How has PCR technology affected research on genetic disorders?

Using Concepts

1. Explain why a frame-shift mutation is usually more disruptive than a base-substitution mutation.

2. How does DNA sequence comparison advance the study of the evolutionary relationship of two species?

3. If a species has a diploid number of 10, how many different combinations of maternal and paternal chromosomes can arise in the gametes?

4. How do geneticists use recombinant DNA technology to diagnose genetic disorders?

5. Explain the relationship between genetic variation and natural selection.

6. A woman whose father is color-blind marries a color-blind man. If they have four daughters and four sons, how many of each sex of their offspring would you expect to exhibit color blindness? Draw a pedigree to illustrate your answer.

7. How is direct detection with an RFLP used to identify the sickle cell gene?

8. How does the distance between a disease-causing gene and a linked RFLP affect the predictive power of the marker?

9. Explain the difference between direct detection of genetic disorders and the use of linked markers for detection.

Synthesis

1. What problems do you foresee in trying to replace a defective gene in a human?

2. Explain how oncogenes may have become part of the human genetic makeup. What are some of their normal functions? How might they cause cancer?

3. Genetic material is described as providing for both genetic continuity and genetic variation. What does that description mean?

4. Some cigarette packages carry the message: "Surgeon General's Warning: Cigarette smoking causes lung cancer." What is the biological explanation for this warning?

5. Based on your knowledge of X inactivation, explain how females may occasionally demonstrate symptoms of X-linked disorders such as hemophilia.

6. Red-green color blindness is a recessive X-linked trait. What are the possible genotypes of the parents of a color-blind man? A color-blind woman? Why is color blindness more common in men than in women?

Extensions

1. The new genetic technology is being used in legal cases. A body has been found, and the medical examiner finds a few hairs under the corpse's fingernails. The prime suspect has a few bloodstains on his shirt, but he claims they are a result of a simple shaving cut. Can this crime be investigated using PCR? Explain.

2. If you were appointed to a federal commission for recombinant DNA research, what regulations would you propose? Should the commission be composed only of scientists? What input should the public have? What limits (if any) would you impose on the questions raised by interested parties?

3. Explain why genetic engineers cannot insert unprocessed (containing introns) eukaryotic DNA into bacteria and have the DNA function "properly."

CONTENTS

Development in Animals

*F*ew events in the biological world are as fascinating as those that result in a newborn baby. Yet it is only recently that biologists could provide much more than a description of a developing animal. The history of developmental biology is a record of imaginative thinking and experimental design that focused on development in a variety of species. Today, new experimental approaches—many of them involving techniques used in molecular genetics—are revealing the underlying mechanisms of embryonic development.

This chapter describes the basic processes and stages of animal development as they are currently understood. Some of the evidence biologists have gathered about how cells become specialized for various functions is examined. In addition, the influence of the egg's cytoplasm on early development and the importance of cell–cell interactions are explored.

---

*W*hat are some obvious differences between an adult bird and its hatchlings?

---

*W*hat biological processes must occur before the flickers will resemble their mother?

◆ *Day-old flickers* (Colaptes auratus cafer) *do not appear very similar to their mother.*

Key Events of Development

14.1 Growth, Cellular Diversity, and Form

The development of a new animal usually begins with fertilization, the union of haploid egg and sperm nuclei to form a single diploid cell called the **zygote** (Chapter 11). Fertilization reestablishes the diploid number of chromosomes. In addition, it activates a series of events that changes the zygote into a complex organism, often consisting of millions or even billions of cells.

Several key features of animal development are illustrated in Figure 14.1 on the following page. As you can see, development includes growth, differentiation, and morphogenesis. First, an embryo starts as a single cell,

FIGURE 14.1 Cells increase in number, differentiate, and undergo morphogenesis during development.

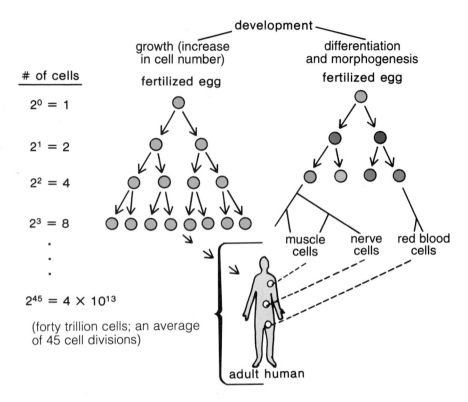

the fertilized egg. Through **growth**, or successive rounds of cell division, the zygote becomes a multicellular organism. Second, as the number of cells in the embryo increases, the cells become increasingly different from one another, both in structure and in function. This process is called **differentiation**. A cell is completely differentiated when it possesses all the features characteristic of a specific cell type. Third, as differentiation proceeds a variety of shaping and patterning processes organize the differentiated cells into tissues and organs. The processes responsible for generating shape and form within an embryo are called **morphogenesis**.

The increase in the number of cells (growth), the appearance of cellular diversity (differentiation), and the organization of cells into tissues and organs (morphogenesis) are critical events in the development of animals. Three types of cells formed during human development—skeletal muscle cells, nerve cells, and red blood cells—are shown in Figure 14.2. Each of these cell types is produced as a result of cell division in the zygote. Yet even a quick glance reveals that each cell type has a different structure. Skeletal muscle cells contain rows of parallel dark lines. Nerve cells have distinct branches that project from the cell body. The human red blood cell is distinguished from other types of cells by its shape and lack of a nucleus.

Each cell type has a unique function as well as a characteristic structure. Muscle cells are specialized for contraction, nerve cells produce chemical stimuli, and red blood cells transport oxygen and carbon dioxide. In an organ—your stomach, for example—each cell type has a specific location, and each performs a specialized and essential role.

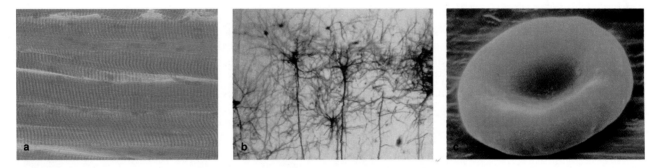

FIGURE 14.2 Three differentiated cell types: (a) skeletal muscle cells (which are fused end to end to form a long fiber with many nuclei), × 140, (b) cerebral cortex nerve cells, × 60, and (c) a red blood cell, × 18 000

Understanding how growth, differentiation, and morphogenesis occur and how they are controlled are the main challenges facing developmental biologists. How, for example, can a variety of cell types result from a single fertilized egg? How are the correct numbers of each cell type produced in the body? How do they perform their unique functions at the appropriate time and location?

One way to answer these questions is to look more closely at the cells involved. For example, Table 14.1 summarizes some characteristics of the three cell types shown in Figure 14.2. Note that each cell type has unique proteins. The banded fibers in muscle contain the protein myosin (MY oh sin), whose molecular properties enable the cells to contract and relax (Chapter 24). Nerve cells contain proteins called neurotransmitters that allow the transmission of nerve impulses from one cell to another (Chapter 22). Ninety percent of the protein content of red blood cells is in the pigment hemoglobin (HEE moh gloh bin), which binds and transports oxygen and carbon dioxide to and from the tissues (Chapter 21).

The hundreds of other specialized cell types in the human body also have unique proteins. In fact, it appears that proteins are the biochemical keys to differentiation in multicellular animals. What causes different cells

TABLE 14.1
Examples of Differentiated Cells

Cell Type	Cell Function	Characteristic Structures	Characteristic Proteins	Protein Function
skeletal muscle	to contract	long, cylindrical shape; banded cell (fiber); more than one nucleus	actin, myosin	contraction
nerve	to produce chemical stimuli	branched extensions of cell body	neurotransmitters such as acetylcholine	transmission of nerve impulses from cell to cell
red blood cell	to transport gas	concave, disk shape; lack of nucleus	hemoglobin	oxygen transport

to produce their characteristic proteins, and to organize in specific patterns at the appropriate time and location? Recall from Chapter 10 that DNA contains the information for synthesizing proteins. How, then, does DNA direct cellular activities so that specific proteins are produced in the appropriate cells? The sections that follow describe some of the research that biologists have conducted in order to answer that question.

14.2 Multiplication of Cells

A logical first step in the effort to understand development is to describe the steps by which it takes place. This was an important goal of many embryologists in the past. Their careful observations have produced a nearly complete account of the basic stages of development.

Figure 14.3 illustrates the events of early development in several animal species. After fertilization, the zygote—typically a large cell with a relatively small nucleus—undergoes multiple rounds of mitosis, eventually producing many small cells. This activity is called **cleavage** because the original mass of the egg is cleaved, or divided, into smaller and smaller cells. Because the volume of cytoplasm does not increase during this period, cleavage generates many cells of a smaller, more adultlike size than the single, relatively large egg cell.

By the end of cleavage the zygote consists of many cells and is organized into a structure called a **blastula**. The number of cells and their

Try Investigation 14A, Development in Polychaete Worms.

FIGURE 14.3 An overview of early development in three organisms. (Not to scale)

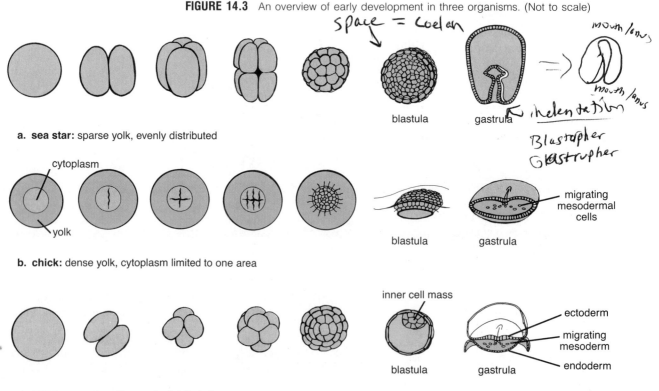

a. **sea star:** sparse yolk, evenly distributed

b. **chick:** dense yolk, cytoplasm limited to one area

c. **mouse:** sparse yolk, evenly distributed

arrangement in the blastula vary, depending on the animal. For example, a sea star zygote (Figure 14.3a) does not have a large amount of yolk to interfere with cleavage. The resulting blastula resembles a hollow ball of cells. However, the dense yolk in a chick egg cell (Figure 14.3b) limits cleavage to the small area of cytoplasm on one side of the egg. Therefore, the chick blastula is a disk of cells lying on a large yolk mass, rather than a sphere of cells.

Although the developmental stages of sea stars, chickens, and mice appear similar (Figure 14.3), the mature organisms are very different. As explained in Chapter 16, such embryonic similarities reflect the evolutionary relationships among animal species. As Charles Darwin noted, comparing embryos suggests two very different ideas. First, the similarities among embryos provide evidence for common descent. Second, the differences among them demonstrate descent "with modification." In other words, the differences reveal how selective pressures have altered development to produce different types of animals adapted to different environments. Thus, embryology—the study of embryos—provides evidence for the evolutionary interrelationships among animals.

14.3 Reorganization of Cells

At a specific time, a series of integrated movements dramatically rearranges the cells of the blastula. In some animals, these movements involve the folding-in of a region of cells, much as the surface of a balloon indents when you poke it with your finger. In other animals these movements involve the spreading of sheets of cells across the surface of the embryo to cover deeper layers. In still other animals, individual cells may migrate to the inside of the embryo, or one layer of cells may split from another to form two parallel cell layers. Regardless of how these changes occur, an embryo in this stage of development is called a **gastrula**. In most animals, gastrulation produces a multilayered embryo composed of three distinct groups of cells. These three cell groups—the ectoderm, the mesoderm, and the endoderm—are the **primary germ layers**. Each layer, shown in Figure 14.4a, will give rise to clearly defined tissues.

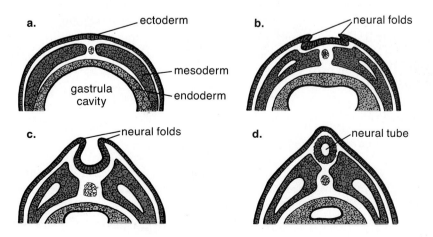

FIGURE 14.4 A vertebrate gastrula (a) undergoing neurulation, development of the neural tube. Note the reorganization of the primary germ layers in the resulting embryo, called a neurula (d).

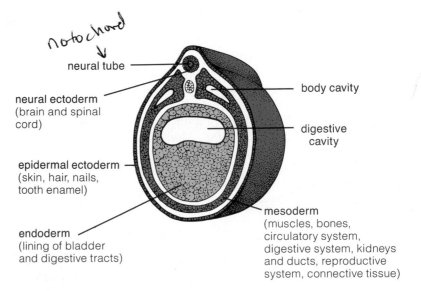

notochord

FIGURE 14.5 Cross section of a vertebrate embryo. Note the approximate locations of the three primary germ layers and the list of some mature tissues and organs into which the layers develop.

Gastrulation results in a radical reorganization of the embryo. Recall that cleavage only subdivides the cytoplasm of the zygote into many smaller cells. As a result, the cytoplasm within most cells of the blastula is in nearly the same position as it was in the fertilized egg. In contrast, the events of gastrulation cause many cells to be located next to new neighboring cells. These shifts in position set the stage for important interactions that will occur between neighboring cells. For example, interactions between the developing nervous system and the overlying cells stimulate the development of the lens of the eye in a vertebrate embryo. (See section 14.9.) In a vertebrate gastrula, earlier interactions between portions of the mesoderm and the overlying ectoderm trigger the formation of the nervous system.

Neurulation, the process by which the nervous system is established during vertebrate development, follows gastrulation. Figure 14.4 shows some of the steps of neurulation that form the neural tube, the foundation of the nervous system, and the resulting embryo, called a neurula. The tissue interactions that establish the neural tube are among the most important in development. This is because the interactions greatly influence the events of morphogenesis—the organization of tissues into organs within a defined body plan. A list of some of these mature tissues—and the primary germ layers in the embryo from which they arise—is shown in Figure 14.5.

14.4   Development in Humans

Despite certain similarities, there are important differences between the development of humans and other mammals, and the development of birds, reptiles, and amphibians. For example, most vertebrate embryos have a relatively large amount of food stored in the egg as yolk. However,

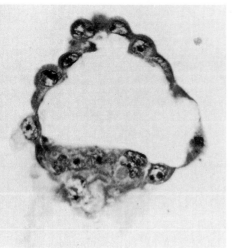

FIGURE 14.6 Section of a human blastocyst. The embryo develops from the inner cell mass, the thicker part on the top.

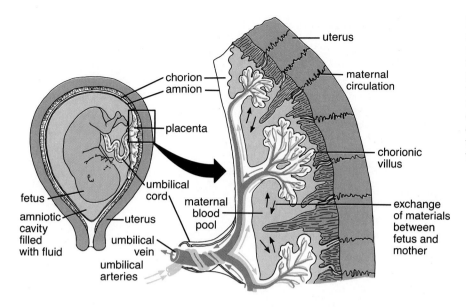

FIGURE 14.7 A cutaway showing a developing human fetus in the uterus, embryonic membranes, and the placental connection. Part of the placenta is enlarged to show both fetal and maternal circulations. The mother's blood does not mix with that of the fetus; exchange of materials occurs across the thin membranes that separate the fetal capillaries from small pools of maternal blood.

mammalian embryos have only a small amount of stored raw material. The mammalian embryo survives despite the small amount of yolk because it embeds in the wall of the uterus and absorbs nutrients provided by the mother's blood. At this stage of development, the human embryo is called a **blastocyst** (BLAS toh sist) and resembles the blastula stage in other vertebrates. As you can see in Figure 14.6, inside the blastocyst is a thick mass of cells; part of this mass develops into the embryo. The other portion of the cell mass develops into membranes that surround, protect, or nourish the embryo—the amnion (AM nee on), the allantois (uh LANT oh wis), and the yolk sac. The thin outer wall of the blastocyst "sphere" becomes the outermost membrane, the chorion (KOR ee on).

The blastocyst develops into a three-layered gastrula. Early in the process, the chorion extends fingerlike projections, or villi, into the inner lining of the mother's uterus. This junction of the chorionic villi and the uterine lining form the placenta, through which the embryo is nourished and cleansed of its waste products by the mother. (See Figure 14.7.) The embryo is connected to the placenta by the flexible umbilical cord that contains the embryo's blood vessels. Wastes pass from the embryo to the maternal blood through the umbilical arteries. Oxygen and nutrients from the mother are carried to the embryo through the umbilical vein. The umbilical arteries and veins are surrounded by a layer of amnion. The rest of the amnion, which surrounds the entire embryo, fills with fluid.

It takes about 39 weeks for a human to develop in the uterus. At the beginning of the eighth week, the embryo is known as a fetus. By the end of three months, or the first trimester, most organs are present in immature form, and the skeleton can be seen on ultrasound images. Figure 14.8 (next page) shows several stages of human development during the first trimester and part of the second. Most of the third and last trimester is a period of rapid growth and maturation of organ systems.

FIGURE 14.8 Stages in the early development of a human embryo and fetus: (a) 4 weeks, (b) 6 weeks, (c) 8 weeks, (d) 12 weeks, (e) 14 weeks, (f) 16 weeks

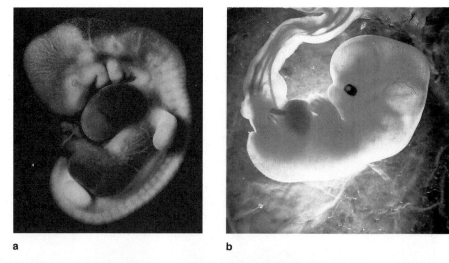

a

b

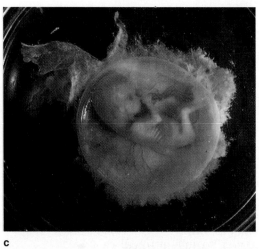

c

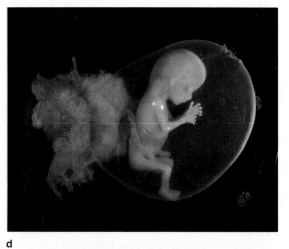

d

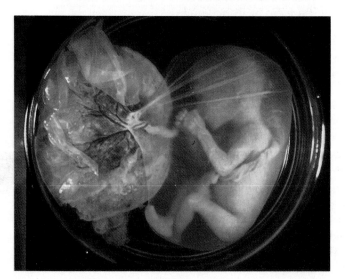

e

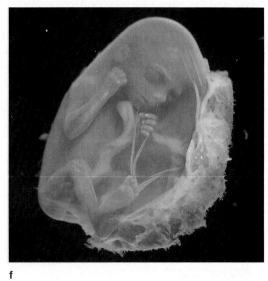

f

The completion of fetal development usually triggers a complex series of hormonal interactions in the mother. The final result is birth (Figure 14.9), when the fetus is pushed from the uterus by strong muscular contractions. The fetus is born through the vagina, which expands to allow the head and body of the fetus to pass through. After birth, the vagina and uterus shrink and become closer to their prepregnancy size and shape.

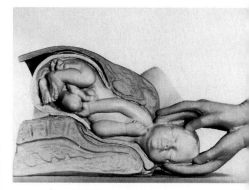

FIGURE 14.9 A model of human birth. As the baby is being born, the head and shoulders appear first; the baby turns so it is face up. After the birth, the placenta and the lining of the uterus are pushed out.

CHECK AND CHALLENGE

1. What is the role of fertilization in development?
2. In your own words, define *differentiation*. Explain your answer using examples of three specialized cell types.
3. What class of molecules is primarily responsible for the specialized structures and functions of differentiated cells? What evidence supports your answer?
4. What is the relationship between DNA and differentiation?
5. Describe what happens to the number of cells during cleavage. What happens to the size of these cells?
6. List two important outcomes of gastrulation.
7. Compare and contrast a sea star gastrula with a human gastrula.

The Genetic Status of Cells

14.5   Exploring the Mechanisms of Differentiation

A description of the stages of development, from zygote to fully formed animal, does not explain the processes involved. What causes these stages to occur in an orderly and predictable fashion? How does the developing embryo generate the many types of cells that make a complete animal? Different types of cells contain different proteins, and these protein differences are partly responsible for the unique functions of each cell type. But what causes these protein differences to arise? What determines the types of proteins each cell will make?

The discovery that DNA directs the synthesis of proteins was an important step in explaining differentiation. The DNA in the nucleus of a fertilized egg contains all of the information used to build each of the thousands of different proteins found in the specialized cells of an animal. As cleavage and differentiation take place, however, what happens to this DNA? It seems possible that each new cell type synthesizes its own set of proteins because each contains a different set of genes. On the other hand, it is possible that all cells contain the same DNA, but that different proteins and cell types result because different genes are expressed in each cell type. Which explanation is correct? What is the genetic status of cells that leads to differentiation?

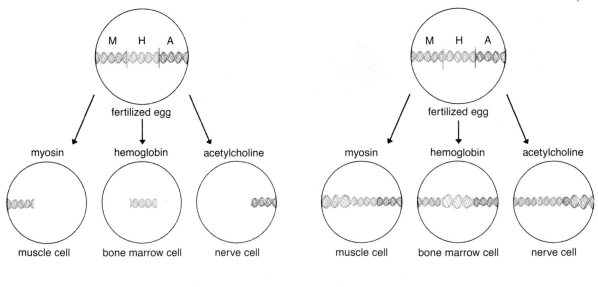

a. selective gene loss hypothesis

b. genetic equivalence hypothesis

FIGURE 14.10 Two possible explanations for differentiation. (a) Selective gene loss: Differential gene activity is due to a selective loss of genes as cells divide during development. Each cell type retains only a specific set of genes. (b) Genetic equivalence: All cells have the same genes, but control mechanisms operate to express only certain genes in certain cells.

Mangold w/ Spemann

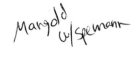

These experiments provide an example of science as inquiry and the development of scientific hypotheses. Each experiment was designed to answer a question about differentiation, leading to other questions that could be tested experimentally.

Lactase
only on when milk is consumed.
NOT on ALWAYS
bc Save Energy

To answer their questions about DNA's role in differentiation, scientists first stated the two explanations as hypotheses. The **selective gene loss hypothesis** (Figure 14.10a) proposed that the different cell types contain different sets of genes. Such a condition might arise if groups of genes were distributed during cleavage somewhat like playing cards dealt at the start of a game. The cards dealt to each player are different; similarly, the genes in each cell type would be different. In contrast, the **genetic equivalence hypothesis** (Figure 14.10b) assumed that all cells contain the same genes, and that different proteins accumulate within each cell as a result of differences in how those genes are expressed.

Scientists then tested the hypotheses using a variety of developing animals. The following experiments illustrate two approaches that biologists have used. Their results can help you decide which hypothesis best explains the genetic mechanism for differentiation.

Approach 1: Nuclear transplantation experiments

How could the scientists develop a decisive test of the selective gene loss hypothesis? In the 1930s, Hans Spemann suggested what he called a "somewhat fantastical" experiment that would demonstrate that differentiation did *not* involve genetic loss. The experiment would determine if a fully differentiated nucleus—for example, a nucleus from a mature skeletal muscle cell—could generate all other types of differentiated

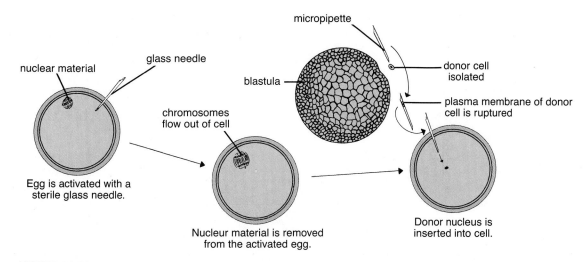

FIGURE 14.11   Procedure to transplant a frog blastula nucleus into a *Rana pipiens* egg, from which the nucleus has been removed. Pricking the egg with a glass needle simulates sperm penetration and activates the egg, causing the nuclear material to move to the cell's edge. The chromosomes are removed with a second needle. A donor cell (nucleus and cytoplasm) from a frog embryo is then inserted into the egg.

cells. Spemann proposed that the nucleus of a differentiated cell be removed and implanted into an egg whose nucleus had been removed. If the nucleus from the differentiated cell was in fact genetically equivalent to the zygote nucleus, this new nucleus would be able to direct the development of a complete, adult animal that was capable of reproducing. Thus, the selective gene loss hypothesis would be disproved.

The techniques needed to perform this experiment, illustrated in Figure 14.11, were later developed by Robert Briggs and Thomas King. In 1952, Briggs and King demonstrated that a nucleus taken from a blastula of the frog *Rana pipiens* and transferred into an egg's cytoplasm could direct the development of a complete tadpole. However, the ability to direct the development of an egg to the tadpole stage decreases significantly as donor nuclei from more mature embryos are used (Figure 14.12 on page 326). Apparently as cells mature and differentiate, they lose the ability to produce all of the cell types of the body.

A few years later, John Gurdon and his colleagues tried a related experiment using the South African clawed frog, *Xenopus laevis*. Gurdon confirmed that nuclei become less able to support complete development as they mature. However, he also showed that the nuclei of skin cells taken from the foot webbing of adult *Xenopus* frogs can direct development from an egg to the swimming tadpole stage. The *Xenopus* tadpoles did not mature to adult frogs. However, Gurdon and his colleagues concluded that completely differentiated nuclei have not been irreversibly changed, and can still give rise to other cell types.

Despite the fact that the nuclear transplantation experiments did not generate fertile adults from fully differentiated nuclei, they demonstrated

FIGURE 14.12 Graph of the percentage of nuclear transplant embryos that develop normally in relationship to the developmental age of the donor nucleus. As cells become more fully differentiated, the ability of their nuclei to direct development to the swimming tadpole stage drops.

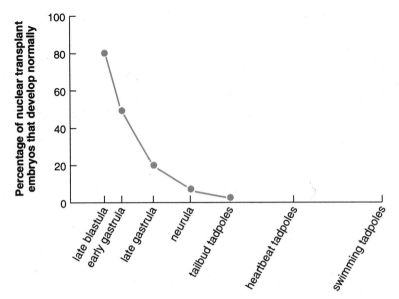

FIGURE 14.13 Molecular hybridization: reassociation of the complementary strands of a nucleic acid. Under certain conditions, double-stranded DNA will "melt," or separate, into single strands. With an appropriate change in conditions, complementary strands reassociate.

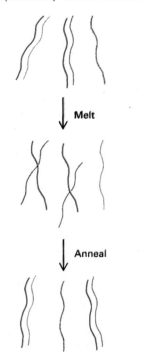

two important points. First, it is clear that the degree of differentiation of a nucleus limits its range of genetic expression. Second, it also is clear that many unused genes in a differentiated nucleus can be reactivated to make proteins normally found only in other cell types. Under the conditions of the Gurdon experiment, a skin cell's nucleus (that had been directing the production of skin-specific proteins) still was able to make the proteins needed to form the nerves, blood, heart, and muscles of a tadpole at the swimming stage of development. These results suggest that while donor nuclei from fully differentiated adult animals may be restricted in their ability to express their genetic potential, they have not *lost* any genes.

Approach 2: Molecular experiments

Nuclear transplantation experiments in amphibians were an attempt to determine if the genes in a fully differentiated cell are the same as those in the fertilized egg. Using modern molecular techniques, scientists can investigate the same question more directly.

The first test of the genetic equivalence hypothesis at the molecular level was a series of experiments performed in the early 1960s. Researchers knew that when DNA is heated gently, it separates into single strands. When cooled, the single strands that contain complementary sequences pair with each other by forming hydrogen bonds, reestablishing the characteristic double-stranded DNA structure. This realignment of complementary strands is called molecular hybridization. (See Figure 17.4.)

Molecular hybridization provides a way to compare the relative similarity of two different samples of DNA. Using this technique, scientists determine the relative number of base pairs formed between single DNA strands that originate from different double-stranded DNA molecules. As Figure 14.13 shows, if the nucleotide sequences on two single strands of

DNA are complementary the single strands will readily hybridize, or reassociate, on cooling. The greater the differences in sequence or number of bases between the two original molecules, the fewer hybridized, double-stranded DNA molecules will be formed.

Scientists found that samples of DNA from a variety of differentiated cells readily hybridized with DNA extracted from zygotes of the same species. This observation is strong evidence that all of the DNA in an animal has similar numbers and sequences of bases, regardless of the animal's age or stage of development. Even if the degree of differentiation limits the expression of DNA, all of the genes present in the zygote appear to be present in fully differentiated cells.

The genetic equivalence hypothesis can also be tested at the molecular level using the technique called cell fusion. When two differentiated cells fuse, their nuclei function in a combined cytoplasm derived from both cells. Under the right conditions, the two nuclei also fuse, creating a hybrid nucleus containing the chromosomes from both parent cells. Fusion of cells occurs naturally in some systems—for example, during the development of skeletal muscle. In the laboratory, fusion can be caused by exposing cells to various external agents. This process can be used to demonstrate the reactivation of unused genes in differentiated cells.

In some ways, the cell fusion experiments represent a molecular version of the nuclear transplantation experiments: If differentiation involves genetic inactivation, *not* genetic loss, then it should be possible to detect the presence of unused genes in differentiated cells by reactivating them. In the mid-1970s, Mary Weiss and her coworkers used cell fusion to test this hypothesis. They fused rat-liver tumor cells and mouse fibroblast cells to create hybrid cells that each contained two sets of rat liver chromosomes to one set of mouse fibroblast chromosomes (Figure 14.14). The hybridized

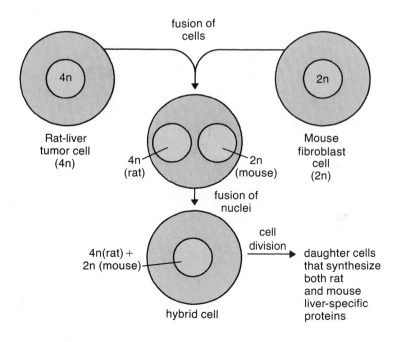

FIGURE 14.14 Fusion experiment using rat-liver tumor cells and mouse fibroblasts. Fusion activates unused genes that code for liver-specific proteins in the mouse fibroblast cell.

cells continued to synthesize liver-specific proteins such as rat albumin and rat aldolase. However, the cells also produced mouse albumin and mouse aldolase—liver-specific proteins that normally would never be made by a mouse fibroblast cell. This finding suggests that the mouse fibroblast cell still had the genes needed to build liver-specific proteins, even though the cell would never use them in the normal course of development.

14.6   Molecular Basis of Differentiation

The nuclear transplantation experiments in amphibians showed that the ability of a nucleus to direct development is restricted during differentiation. Once a nucleus differentiates and begins to direct the production of specific proteins characteristic of its cell type, it is not easily stimulated into again expressing all of the genes required to form a new animal.

The results of the nuclear transplantation experiments, the molecular hybridization experiments, and the cell fusion experiments suggest that even fully differentiated nuclei contain the same genes as the fertilized egg. Thus, it seems clear that the unused genes in differentiated cells are not destroyed or lost—they retain the potential to be expressed again.

The experiments described in section 14.5 provide strong evidence to support the genetic equivalence hypothesis. That is, cellular differentiation during development depends largely on differential gene expression. During the earliest stages of research, differences in gene expression were thought to depend entirely on which genes were used as templates for RNA transcription in a cell. (See Chapter 10.) More recently, however, biologists have shown that gene expression is controlled in many ways. Some means of control include the selection of specific genes for transcription, modification of RNA molecules before they leave the nucleus, alteration of translation, and by control of protein modification and function.

CHECK AND CHALLENGE

1. Compare the main points of the selective gene loss hypothesis to those of the genetic equivalence hypothesis. What does each say? What is the critical difference between these two hypotheses?

2. In your own words, summarize the Gurdon experiment and the Briggs and King experiment. What did each attempt to prove or disprove?

3. What does the Gurdon experiment suggest about the genes in *Xenopus* frog skin cells as compared to the genes in the other cells of a *Xenopus* frog's body?

4. Define the term *molecular hybridization* in your own words. If two single strands of DNA hybridize, what does this suggest about their nucleotide sequence?

5. Describe the process of cell fusion. What is its role in the investigation of differentiation?

Mechanisms of Differentiation _____

14.7 Determination and Differentiation

If differentiation in developing animals results from differences in the expression of genes in specific cells, how do those differences arise? How do some cells express genes that are characteristic of skin, while others express genes characteristic of muscle? When are these developmental "commitments" made?

Scientists were surprised to find that most cells "commit" to a specific cell type long before the changes in gene expression and protein production that characterize differentiation become apparent. Figure 14.15 illustrates one of the earliest experiments demonstrating this point. Notice that when cells that usually form nervous tissue are transplanted from one embryo to a different location in another embryo, they do not form nervous tissue (Figure 14.15a). Instead, they form skin—the tissue normally formed at that location in the second embryo. Because the transplanted cells were not yet "committed" to a cell type, they could take on a structure and function appropriate to their new position in the host embryo.

However, the result is very different when the experiment is repeated in embryos that are only a few hours older. In this case (Figure 14.15b), the transplanted cells form nervous tissue, even though nervous tissue is not normally formed at that location in the host embryo. This observation suggests that the cells transplanted from the older embryo already were "committed" to becoming nervous tissue even though they have not yet

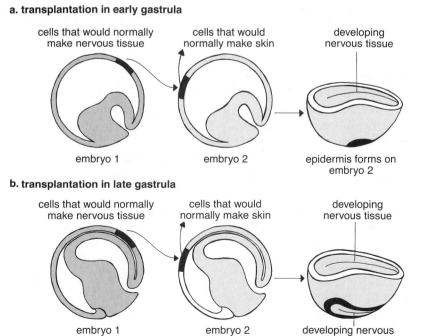

a. transplantation in early gastrula

cells that would normally make nervous tissue   cells that would normally make skin   developing nervous tissue

embryo 1   embryo 2   epidermis forms on embryo 2

b. transplantation in late gastrula

cells that would normally make nervous tissue   cells that would normally make skin   developing nervous tissue

embryo 1   embryo 2   developing nervous tissue on embryo 2

FIGURE 14.15 Determination during newt gastrulation. When the transplant is performed at the beginning of gastrulation (a), the transplanted cells take on an identity characteristic of their new location. When the transplant is performed at the end of gastrulation (b), the cells retain their developmental commitment.

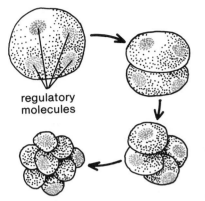

FIGURE 14.16 Regulatory molecules are not uniformly distributed in the cytoplasm of an egg. As the egg divides, different molecules may be incorporated in each offspring cell, resulting in the activation of different genes.

started to show any signs of differentiating. Apparently, that commitment did not change even when the cells were moved to a new location.

Scientists call the process by which cells commit to a particular fate **determination**. Sometimes it is useful to think of determination as the *decision* to become a particular type of cell, whereas differentiation is the *act* of expressing that decision. Determination often takes place long before differentiation.

14.8   Influence of Cytoplasm

Biologists know of two ways by which determination occurs. The first involves the localization, or distribution, of portions of the egg's cytoplasm into individual cells during cleavage. There is considerable evidence that the cytoplasm of an egg is not uniform in composition. In fact, molecules that regulate the expression of different genes are located in particular regions of the cytoplasm. As cleavage proceeds, the newly produced cells inherit only specific regions of the egg's cytoplasm. (See Figure 14.16.) Thus, the regulatory molecules are not equally distributed to all offspring cells. As a result, the interactions between the regulators in the cytoplasm and the nucleus of one cell are quite different from the cytoplasmic-nucleic interactions in a neighboring cell. The proteins synthesized in the two cells are different and contribute to each cell's specialized role.

Consider some of the evidence that supports these findings. The embryos of the marine snail *Ilyanassa* exhibit a peculiarity during cleavage. As mitosis progresses, a region of cytoplasm bulges out from one particular cell to form a lobe (Figure 14.17). A narrow bridge of cytoplasm connects the lobe to the rest of the cell. At each division, the lobe retracts into the cell from which it arose and then bulges out again with the next round of mitosis. This curious occurrence keeps the lobe's cytoplasm within the boundary of one particular cell and makes *Ilyanassa* a good subject for the investigation of cytoplasmic localization.

What is special about the cytoplasm in this lobe? One way of analyzing its significance is obvious—cut off the lobe and observe the effect on the embryo. It turns out that removal of a lobe always results in a defective embryo. The embryo develops into a larva that lacks specific structures, such as certain muscles. This evidence supports the hypothesis that the cytoplasm of the egg varies. Differentiation of particular parts of the embryo results from the localization of regulatory molecules in different parts of the cytoplasm.

FIGURE 14.17   Lobe experiment in a snail embryo. A lobe appears and reappears as part of the same cell during cleavage. Removal of the lobe results in a defective larva, demonstrating that regulatory molecules are unequally distributed in the cytoplasm.

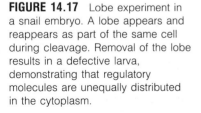

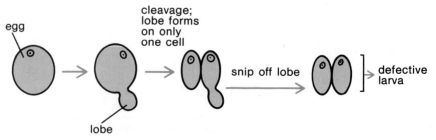

14.9 Cell–Cell Interactions

The second way in which determination occurs is through the interaction of cells and tissues. At key points during development, these interactions may profoundly influence the fates of the cell types involved.

The classic experiments demonstrating such cell–cell interactions were performed in the 1920s by Hans Spemann and Hilde Mangold. These experiments resembled those that led to the discovery of determination, but they involved the portion of the blastula where the first visible signs of gastrulation (infolding) appear. This portion is called the dorsal lip, as shown in Figure 14.18. Recall that most tissue in the very early embryo is not yet determined, and that undetermined tissue transplanted to a different place on the surface of a host embryo will take on a new identity appropriate to its new location. Spemann and Mangold found, however, that when tissue from the dorsal lip is transplanted, it does not take on a new identity. Instead, it triggers a second point of gastrulation in the host embryo (Figure 14.18b), resulting in the formation of two embryos joined at the abdomen (Figure 14.18c). By using genetically different donor and

correct but technology not up to date

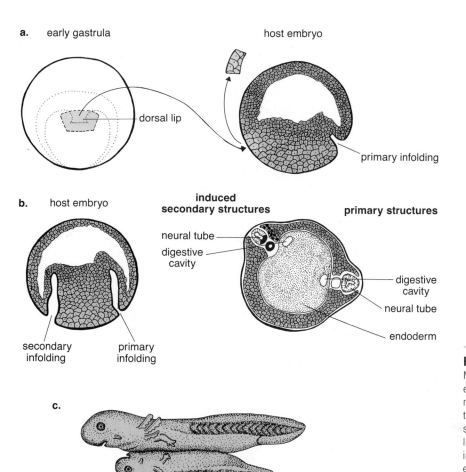

a. early gastrula

host embryo

dorsal lip

primary infolding

b. host embryo

induced secondary structures

primary structures

neural tube

digestive cavity

digestive cavity

neural tube

endoderm

secondary infolding

primary infolding

c.

FIGURE 14.18 The Spemann-Mangold primary organizer experiment. The dorsal lip of an early newt gastrula was removed and transplanted into a host embryo as shown (a). The transplanted dorsal lip caused a second point of infolding to appear in the host embryo (b), producing two embryos joined at the abdomen (c).

FIGURE 14.19 Neural ectoderm (an outpocketing of the forebrain) induces formation of the lens of the eye in the head ectoderm.

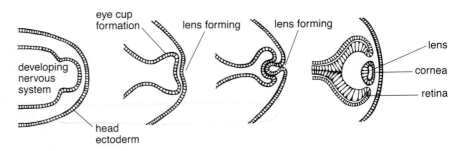

host embryos, Spemann and Mangold were able to show that the small, incomplete, but unmistakable secondary embryo is formed from a combination of host and donor cells. This finding suggests that the transplanted tissue acts as an *organizer* for the surrounding host cells. The host cells in that area of the embryo normally would form belly skin. The transplanted dorsal lip cells, however, induce the host cells to follow a different course of development.

Similar interactions occur during the development of several features of the animal, such as eye development, for example. As Figure 14.19 shows, a group of cells from the growing embryonic nervous system divide and expand outward until they contact the head ectoderm. The ectodermal cells respond to this stimulus by thickening, pushing inward, and pinching off a spherical mass that becomes a lens. The extension of the developing nervous system folds back on itself to form a cuplike structure that becomes the retina (REH tin uh), the light-sensitive part of the eye. Embryonic lens cells then stimulate the ectodermal cells to differentiate into the cornea, the transparent covering of the eye.

As this example illustrates, interactions among embryonic cells commonly occur during development. The exact biochemical mechanisms involved have not yet been determined, but these mechanisms are being actively researched.

CHECK AND CHALLENGE

1. Compare determination with differentiation. Which process occurs first? Which process produces visible changes in the cell?

2. Describe how cytoplasmic localization can explain differentiation in the embryo.

3. What happens to an embryo of the snail *Ilyanassa* when the lobe is experimentally removed?

4. In your own words, summarize the meaning of the phrase *cell–cell interaction*.

5. Draw and label a picture that shows the results of the Spemann and Mangold experiment. Why were their results unexpected?

6. Describe how cell–cell interactions result in the formation of the lens and cornea of the eye.

DEVELOPMENT IN SLIME MOLD

Development in the cellular slime mold, *Dictyostelium discoideum* (Figure A), is an interesting example of cell–cell interactions. In favorable conditions, this organism lives in the soil as individual, haploid, amoebalike cells that feed on bacteria and reproduce by binary fission (page 204, "Focus On"). When the food supply is used up, however, an unusual transformation occurs. Thousands of the individual "amoebas" join in moving streams of cells that converge at a central point (a). Here, the cells form a mound of all the streaming cells. The mound, an aggregate of individual cells, forms the migrating, sluglike grex (b). After migration, the anterior cells of the grex (about 20 percent of the population) form a tubed stalk that lifts the posterior cells (c and d). The stalk cells die, but the elevated posterior cells become spore cells. The spore cells eventually disperse, each becoming an amoebalike haploid individual. In addition to this asexual cycle, *Dictyostelium* may reproduce sexually through fusion. In this process, two cells fuse to form a giant cell that digests the other cells of the aggregate. Then, the fused cell undergoes meiotic and mitotic divisions that eventually result in new haploid individuals.

What causes the cells to aggregate? Researchers found that a soluble substance called cyclic adenosine monophosphate, or cAMP (page 513) guides the cell migration. Aggregation begins when each cell starts the cAMP synthesis that is triggered by nutrient starvation. Cells that receive high levels of cAMP form the posterior of the grex. Cells exposed to low levels of cAMP form the anterior portion.

If all the independent cells that form the grex start out the same, how can some cells become spore cells and others become stalk cells? The answer lies in the observation that not all the original cells *are* the same. The cells that experience starvation early in their cell cycle tend to form the anterior portion of the slug. Those cells that starve towards the end of their cell cycle tend to become the posterior cells. This differentiation into stalk cell or spore reflects a

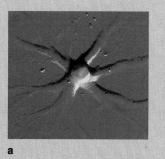

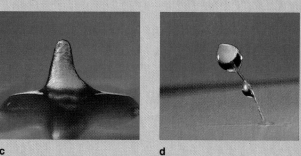

FIGURE A Cell aggregation and differentiation in the slime mold *Dictyostelium discoideum*: (a) aggregation, (b) grex, (c) early stalk formation, (d) stalk and spore case.

major phenomenon of development—the determination of a cell's developmental pathway.

Biologists favor *Dictyostelium* as an experimental organism because cells that are initially identical differentiate into one of two types of cells, spore or stalk. Also, individual cells join to form a cohesive structure of differentiated cell types, a process somewhat similar to the formation of skin in animals. *Dictyostelium* does not form as many cell types as do most animals, and most multicellular organisms do not form from the aggregation of independent cells. Yet the cellular slime mold is useful to researchers because many of its developmental processes are the same as those in the embryos of other phyla. For example, the ability of a cell to sense a chemical gradient—as in a slime mold amoeba's response to cAMP—is important for cell migration and morphogenesis in animal development.

CHAPTER Highlights

Summary

Some general principles governing cellular differentiation have been determined, based on existing experimental data. Proteins are responsible for the variety in structure and function exhibited by the cells of a newborn animal. Control of the types and numbers of proteins synthesized in a particular cell resides in the genes. Typically, the DNA in the nucleus of each embryonic cell is identical. During division, each cell normally inherits a complete set of genes from the fertilized egg. However, the cytoplasm that a cell receives may be quite different from that of its neighboring cells because regulatory molecules that control gene expression are unevenly distributed in the cytoplasm. Interactions between regulators in the cytoplasm and particular nuclei produce regional differences in the embryo. These early developmental differences are amplified as unique cell types begin to interact, exchanging molecular signals that stimulate further specialization of structure and function.

Key Concepts

Use the following concepts to develop a concept map. Add other terms from the chapter as you need them.

differentiation

proteins

genetic equivalence

cytoplasmic localization

cell–cell interactions

determination

Reviewing Ideas

1. How are growth, differentiation, and morphogenesis related to each other? Can any of the three processes occur independently of the others? Explain.

2. The term *morphogenesis* comes from the root *morph*, meaning form, and the root *genesis*, meaning creation. How do these meanings relate to the process of morphogenesis that occurs in development?

3. What are the central challenges of developmental biology?

4. Explain how mammals differ from other vertebrates in their developmental processes.

5. Name two ways in which observations of early embryos relate to the theory of evolution.

6. Which experiments—nuclear transplantation experiments, molecular experiments, or both—demonstrate that nuclei become more restricted in their developmental potential as they differentiate? Which experiment (or experiments) demonstrate that unused genes in differentiated nuclei can still be expressed, given the proper environment? Explain.

7. Describe how regulatory molecules in the cytoplasm might become segregated into different cells during development. How might these regulators affect the subsequent developmental fate of each cell?

Using Concepts

1. List the ways that a zygote differs from a gastrula of the same species. Use information from the chapter, and consider characteristics such as the number and size of cells, the contents of the nucleus and the cytoplasm, and the nuclei's normal capacity for gene expression. Under normal conditions, which cell has more "developmental potential"—the zygote or a cell from a gastrula? Explain your answer.

2. Explain the two alternative hypotheses about the genetic basis for differentiation. Which hypothesis is most strongly supported by the evidence presented in the chapter? Explain.

3. "Housekeeping" proteins are basic to cell survival and so are in almost all of an organism's cells. "Specialized" proteins are required for the specialized functions of specific cell types and so are found only in certain cells. Examine the table below. Name three proteins that might be "housekeeping" proteins, and three possible "specialized" proteins. What might need to occur in a skin cell's nucleus before it could give rise to a daughter cell that would differentiate into a pancreatic cell?

4. When Briggs and King first attempted to test the genetic equivalence hypothesis, they used nuclei from cells lining the intestine of a tadpole. These nuclei supported development all the way to fertile adult frogs. However, some scientists criticized their experiment, arguing that the nuclei used might not have been fully differentiated. These scientists knew that during frog development certain cells migrate through the intestine on their way to the ovaries or testes, and that these cells eventually become eggs or sperm. The scientists thought that Briggs and King could have mistakenly used nuclei from the migrating cells instead of intestinal nuclei. Why would the use of those migrating cells cast doubt on Briggs' and King's conclusions?

5. Considering the results of John Gurdon's *Xenopus* experiments, is the statement below a reasonable conclusion? Explain your answer.
"The processes that restrict gene expression during the embryonic differentiation of skin cells can be reversed."

6. Spemann and Mangold transplanted dorsal lip tissue from one embryo into a *genetically different* host embryo. What did the genetic differences between the host and donor tissue allow them to conclude about the cells that formed the secondary embryo? Why was this conclusion important?

7. Name the two mechanisms by which embryonic cells become committed to particular fates. What is the importance of cleavage to each of these mechanisms? What is the importance of gastrulation?

Synthesis

1. What is the relationship between the processes of reproduction and development? In what way is development part of the process of reproduction? Support your answer.

2. Is there any embryological evidence supporting the theory of evolution? Explain.

3. What is the role of development in the structure and function of an animal?

Extensions

1. Write a short essay about the mechanism by which an egg's cytoplasmic molecules contribute to differentiation of the animal. How might such regulatory molecules function?

2. Research and sketch the development of a specific animal. Some possible choices are a bird, opossum, kangaroo, platypus, butterfly, spider, or sea turtle. What relationship, if any, exists between the animal's environment, its way of life, and its development?

TABLE 14.2
Two Cell Types and Some of Their Proteins

Cell Type	Proteins Synthesized
skin cell	DNA polymerase, phosphoglucokinase, keratin, actin
pancreatic cell	phosphoglucokinase, amylase, typsin, DNA polymerase, actin

CONTENTS

CHAPTER

15

Plant Growth and Development

*I*n the story of Jack and the Beanstalk, Jack's mother threw some bean seeds out of the house in disgust after Jack had traded the family cow for the seeds. During the night, the seeds sprouted and grew high into the sky, finally reaching a place where a giant was living. Although this fairy tale is a bit far-fetched, it illustrates one phenomenon of plant growth and development that is real—some plants undergo extremely rapid growth. Bamboo shoots, for example, can grow more than a meter per day. Other plants, such as the giant sequoia and redwood, can, over a long time, grow extremely tall—almost 100 meters. Certain plant tissues undergo continuous development and growth throughout the life of the plant. Some bristlecone pines are several thousand years old and are still growing.

What is the difference between growth and development? Growth is usually thought of as an increase in size, especially due to an increase in the number of cells present. Development is the process by which the cells of a new organism increase in number and become specialized to perform different functions, thus producing a complete individual. This chapter examines how plants grow and develop and some of the factors that affect these processes.

*H*ow would you design an experiment to learn if this seedling is responding to a source of light?

*W*hat other forces are acting on the growth of this plant?

◆ *A pumpkin seedling,* Cucurbita *sp.,* *emerging from the seed.*

Plant Development

15.1 The Embryo and the Seed

Reproduction in flowering plants begins with two processes—pollination and fertilization—described in Section 11.5. Once the carpel of a flower has been pollinated, the pollen grain sprouts a tube that grows downward to the ovary. Within the ovary are one or more ovules, each containing an egg. Recall that the pollen tube carries two sperm nuclei to the ovule. Fertilization occurs when one of the sperm nuclei fuses with the egg nucleus, producing a zygote. The second sperm nucleus fuses with a pair of nuclei in the ovule (the polar nuclei), forming a triploid nucleus. Because two fusions take place, this event is referred to as double fertilization. The embryo plant and its supporting tissues develop from the products of double fertilization.

The major stages of development of a new plant are shown in Figure 15.1. Mitotic cell divisions of the zygote start the process. The first divisions give rise to a chain of cells that serves to anchor the developing embryo and transfer nutrients to it from the parent plant. At the end of this chain, one cell continues to divide, forming a spherical mass of cells that develops into the embryo.

Differentiation begins as small bumps form on the developing embryo. These bumps become the **cotyledons** (kot uh LEE duns), or ''seed leaves,'' of the embryo. Cotyledons are not true leaves, but in many plants, once above ground, they carry on photosynthesis until the first leaves of the newly sprouted plant develop. In other plants the cotyledons are modified to carry a large amount of food that supports the embryo as it begins to grow.

Next the embryo elongates rapidly. Cells between the cotyledons become the embryonic shoot, which will later give rise to the stem and leaves. At the opposite end of the embryo the embryonic root develops. A

FIGURE 15.1 A plant embryo develops from the zygote and includes one or more cotyledons, a shoot tip and a root tip. Endosperm, a food storage organ, develops from the triploid nucleus.

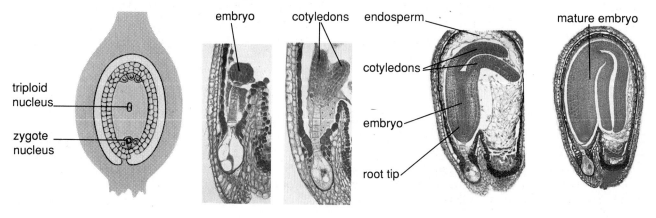

mass of undifferentiated cells remains at the tip, or apex, of both shoot and root. These cells form the **apical meristems** (AY pih kul MER ih stems). After the seed sprouts, meristem cells divide and produce new cells that differentiate into all the specialized tissues of a mature plant. Apical meristems maintain vertical, or primary, growth as long as a plant lives.

Following double fertilization, the triploid nucleus also divides rapidly, producing the endosperm. For the developing embryo, the endosperm is a storehouse of nutrients that sustains growth until the seed sprouts and photosynthesis can begin. The walls of the ovule form a tough **seed coat** enclosing the endosperm and the embryo, which stops growing and remains dormant until the seed sprouts. The maturing seed dries out until its water content is only about 5 to 15 percent of its mass. Dry seeds respire slowly, and can remain alive through dry, cold conditions. The ovary ripens into a fruit, which contains the seed(s), and is dispersed in a variety of ways.

Although plant and animal development are similar in some ways, they show important differences. Recall from Chapter 14, for example, that development of an animal embryo depends on movements of layers of cells. Such movements do not occur in plants, and cells differentiate where they are formed. Thus, the position of an embryonic cell determines its future development. Recall also that the cytoplasm of an egg is not homogeneous. That is true of plants as well. Organelles and molecules that were unevenly distributed in the egg cytoplasm are segregated among the embryonic cells as the zygote divides. The resulting differences in the cytoplasm of the embryonic cells can act as signals to the genes, helping determine how a cell will develop. Development in animals is continuous, however, and does not include a period of dormancy as in plants.

FIGURE 15.2 When a seed germinates, the seed coat fractures, and the embryonic root and shoot emerge.

15.2 Seed Germination

After a variable period of dormancy, **germination**, or sprouting of the seed, occurs. Only if temperatures are suitable and if adequate water and oxygen are available, however, can the seed sprout. Under the appropriate environmental conditions, water and oxygen pass through the seed coat, triggering metabolism in the embryo, which resumes growth and development. Enzymes begin to digest the stored food in the endosperm, and the nutrients are moved to the growing regions of the embryo. The seed coat fractures, and the embryonic root emerges, followed shortly by the shoot, which then breaks through the soil surface. Figure 15.2 shows that in beans and many other dicots (plants that have two cotyledons in their seeds), a hooklike shoot emerges through the soil, pulling the cotyledons and embryonic leaves with it. When light reaches the seedling, the shoot straightens out and begins to elongate, as shown in Figure 15.3a, next page. In monocots (plants with only one cotyledon) such as corn, a protective sheath called the coleoptile encloses the embryonic shoot as it breaks through the soil (Figure 15.3b, next page).

Germination is a critical stage in a plant's life cycle. Intricate mechanisms have evolved that favor germination only at times when survival of

Try Investigation 15A, Seeds and Seedlings.

*T*he different requirements for germination among various species of plants are adaptations to the environment that help ensure survival. These adaptations are examples of evolution through natural selection.

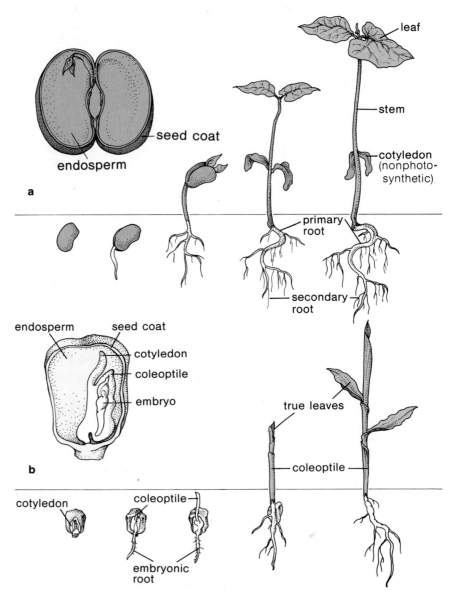

FIGURE 15.3 Germination of a bean seed (a), a dicot, and a corn seed (b), a monocot. Dicots have two cotyledons, monocots have one.

the seedlings is most likely. For example, if the seeds of plants that grow in cold climates (such as pines or apple trees) germinated in the fall, most of the seedlings would die from the harsh winter conditions before reaching a stage of growth that would ensure their survival. The seeds of such plants have become adapted to require freezing temperatures followed by warmer temperatures before they can germinate. Seeds of many desert plants will not germinate unless there has been heavy rainfall, ensuring sufficient ground moisture for survival of the seedlings. Seeds of plants that grow where natural fires are common often require intense heat in order to germinate. Mineral nutrients released from the ash of older plants that

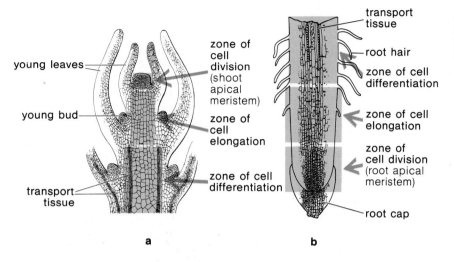

FIGURE 15.4 A longitudinal section of a stem tip (a) and a root tip (b). Notice the correspondence between the zones in the stem and the root.

have burned thus become available for the germinating seeds. Some kinds of seeds must be in total darkness to germinate, whereas many small seeds, such as those of lettuce, require light.

The length of time a seed remains capable of germination varies from a few days to many years, depending on the species and environmental conditions. Most seeds can remain viable several years, until conditions for germination are favorable.

15.3 Primary and Secondary Growth

As germination occurs, the root and then the stem begin their primary growth—growth in length from the apical meristems. The first true leaves develop from the stem just above the cotyledons. Energy reserves in the cotyledons and endosperm support the growing embryo until the first leaves begin to carry on photosynthesis, harvesting energy for the continued growth of the young seedling. The root penetrates the soil, anchoring the plant, and begins to absorb the water and minerals needed for photosynthesis and growth. An unorganized mass of cells called the **root cap** covers and protects the apical meristem as the root grows through the soil. Figure 15.4 illustrates a longitudinal section of a root and a stem. Note the differences and similarities between the tissues in these two parts of the plant.

As they grow in length, the stems and roots of some plants also increase in diameter. This secondary growth comes from the **cambium** (KAM bee um), another type of meristem. Cambium differentiates into two types of transport tissue, shown in Figure 15.5. **Xylem** (ZY lem) is the tissue that transports water and dissolved minerals from the roots throughout the plant. Xylem produced in successive growing seasons of a woody plant supports the plant and results in annual rings that can be used to determine the age of a tree. **Phloem** (FLOH em) is the tissue that transports

FIGURE 15.5 Cross section of a basswood stem, *Tilia americana*, showing annual growth rings

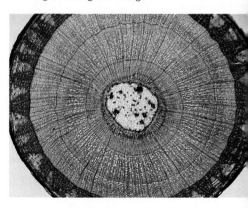

LEAF DEVELOPMENT AND DIFFERENTIATION

The beauty of leaf form has been admired by children, poets, artists, and scientists throughout recorded history. The way in which a leaf actually grows has been poorly understood because when plant parts are studied under a microscope, the specimen is usually dead. Direct observations of the specimen's growth are not possible. Indirect methods, such as computer modeling, often can be used to interpret the processes responsible for the final leaf form. In other cases, computer analysis of a chronological sequence of close-up photos provides the clues. These techniques allow us to study and detail leaf development.

A leaf originates from divisions in a group of cells located on the side of the apical meristem. These cell divisions produce small bumps that give rise to leaf buds (Figure A). The arrangement of these bumps at the shoot apex determines the arrangement of leaves on the mature shoot.

In the immature leaf bud, cells toward the center begin to divide first, producing small fingerlike growths. Then special meristem cells on the sides of the bud begin to grow, and the bud assumes a more flattened appearance. These meristem cells give rise to the future cell layers in the leaf.

The special meristem cells consist of two different types; one forms the surface layers of the leaf, and the other forms the inner tissues. Leaves become broader but not thicker because these cells divide only at right angles to the leaf surface. There is a steady increase in surface area, but the number of layers in the leaf, and thus its thickness, is limited.

Cell division stops at different stages in different layers of the leaf. The cells of the upper epidermis usually stop dividing first. In the tobacco plant, for example, the epidermal cells stop dividing when the leaf is only 6 or 7 cm long—one fifth to one sixth of its mature size. These cells, however, continue to increase in size until the whole leaf stops growing.

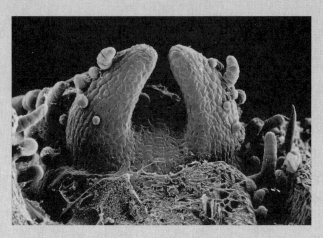

FIGURE A A scanning electron micrograph of a shoot tip of *Coleus*, showing leaf buds developing

The shape of the mature leaf depends on three factors, all of which are genetically determined: the shape of the leaf bud; the number, distribution, and orientation of cell divisions; and the amount and distribution of cell enlargement. Several other factors affect leaf shape. Models based on computer analysis of sequential photos can be used to explain the shapes that different types of leaves attain. The comparative growth rates of the layers and main veins can affect leaf form. For example, if the layers grow at the same rate as the main veins, a leaf with a simple outline, such as an elm, results. On the other hand, if the growth is more vigorous near the veins than in the other regions, a lobed leaf, such as an oak or maple, forms. Leaf shape also may be affected by environmental factors. For example, the submerged leaves of some aquatic plants, such as buttercups, are very different in form from the leaves above water.

Complete development of the leaf, however, requires exposure to light, so that chlorophyll and other photosynthetic pigments can be synthesized. Hormones, especially auxin and cytokinin (see pages 346 and 347), also appear to play an important role in leaf development.

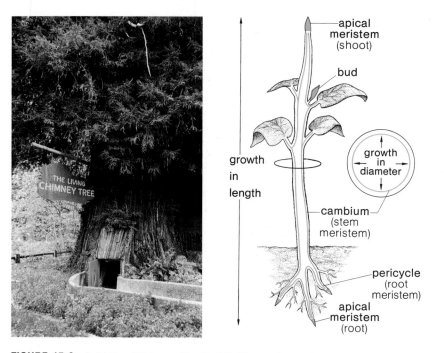

FIGURE 15.6 *(left)* The "Chimney Tree" of California. *(center)* Meristems are the plant tissues responsible for growth. Apical meristems bring about primary growth; cambium is responsible for secondary growth. Meristems in buds produce cells that differentiate into all the tissues of leaves, branches, and flowers. *(right)* A woody twig with buds that will grow into branches, leaves, and flowers

sap containing dissolved sugars and amino acids from the leaves throughout the plant. Chapter 19 describes cambium, xylem, and phloem in more detail.

Some plants develop a secondary layer of cambium, called cork cambium, that produces the bark around the outside of a tree. Bark protects the internal plant tissues from drying out and from physical damage that could interrupt the flow of fluids and dissolved material inside the plant.

The xylem cells at the center of a large tree are dead and contain no cytoplasm. However, the thick, tough walls of its once-living cells usually remain, and make up most of the wood of the tree. Even if these inner, woody tissues are destroyed, the tree often can continue its normal growth because the functioning tissue of a tree trunk is near its bark. The "Chimney Tree" of California (Figure 15.6, *left*) is a giant redwood whose interior was burned out, leaving only the outer shell. You can walk inside the base of the trunk, look straight up through the center of the tree, and see the blue sky above. From the outside, the tree looks normal and continues to grow like other redwood trees.

The locations of the major meristem tissues in plants are illustrated in Figure 15.6, *center*. Note that meristem tissue also is present in buds on the sides of stems. Some buds grow into branches from the main stem (Figure 15.6, *right*); others grow into leaves and flowers. Root branches arise from

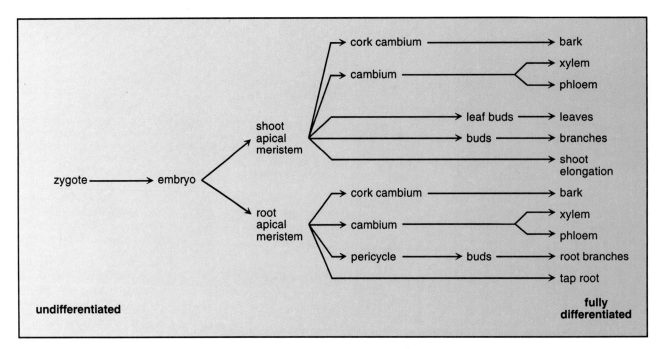

FIGURE 15.7 Stages in plant differentiation. Note the similarities in development between the tissues of the root and the shoot.

buds in the **pericycle**, a cylinder of meristem tissue that surrounds the xylem and phloem in the root. Figure 15.7 summarizes the process of plant differentiation and shows the similarities in development between the tissues of the root and the shoot.

CHECK AND CHALLENGE

1. Describe the development of the plant embryo inside the seed of a flowering plant.

2. What is the role of the endosperm for the developing plant embryo?

3. How do cotyledons function in the growth and development of the young seedling plant?

4. Distinguish between primary growth and secondary growth in plants.

5. What specialized tissues function in primary and secondary growth in plants?

6. What conditions contribute to germination? Describe what happens when a seed germinates.

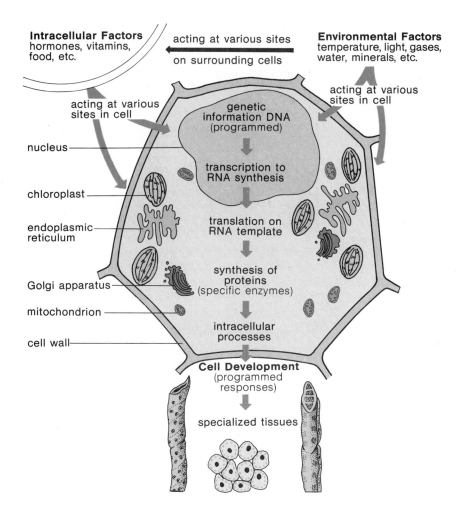

Intracellular Factors
hormones, vitamins,
food, etc.

acting at various sites
on surrounding cells

Environmental Factors
temperature, light, gases,
water, minerals, etc.

acting at various
sites in cell

acting at various
sites in cell

genetic
information DNA
(programmed)

transcription to
RNA synthesis

translation on
RNA template

synthesis of
proteins
(specific enzymes)

intracellular
processes

Cell Development
(programmed
responses)

specialized tissues

nucleus

chloroplast

endoplasmic
reticulum

Golgi apparatus

mitochondrion

cell wall

FIGURE 15.8   Plant development is
regulated by a variety of interacting
internal and external factors.

Control of Plant Growth

15.4   Factors Affecting Plant Growth

After examining some of the events in plant development, a question you
might ask is, "What determines when stems, flowers, branches, leaves, and
other parts of a plant begin to grow?" Genes provide the primary control,
but how do different bits of genetic information direct a cell's growth and
differentiation? A variety of factors apparently act as cues that initiate
expression of different genes at different times. Cues may be signals from
the environment, hormonal signals from other parts of the plant, or activities of neighboring cells or tissues. Other cues are related to nutrition or to
factors that indicate a cell's position within the plant. Figure 15.8 summarizes the interactions of the many internal and external factors that may
affect plant growth and development.

CONNECTIONS

*The difficulties of understand-
ing plant hormones' actions
underscore the inquiry role
of science. The role of auxins, for example, is continuously studied and revised.*

FOCUS ON *Plant Nutrients*

Plants require nutrients for growth and maintenance. The plants obtain carbon as carbon dioxide from the air. The other nutrients enter roots as ions dissolved in water. Roots can take in nitrogen, for example, in the form of ammonium (NH_4^+) or nitrate (NO_3^-) ions. Nutrients that a plant needs in relatively large amounts are known as macronutrients. The most important macronutrients are nitrogen, phosphorus, and potassium. These ingredients are indicated by numbers such as 10-20-10 on commercial fertilizers, indicating percent by weight. Elements such as iron and copper, which are required in extremely small amounts, are called micronutrients. The essential elements have been identified by experiments in which plants were grown in solutions lacking a particular element. The plants illustrated in Figure B show the characteristic signs of nitrogen and magnesium deficien-

FIGURE B Sunflower plants showing characteristic symptoms of nitrogen deficiency *(left)* and magnesium deficiency *(center)*. The plant on the right was supplied with all essential minerals.

cies. **Appendix 15A**, Elements Required by Plants, describes the functions and symptoms of deficiency of these essential nutrients.

Botanists have identified five interacting groups of plant hormones that influence growth. Their production is under genetic control, but environmental cues play critical roles in determining when the hormones are produced, how much is produced, and which cells are sensitive to them. Plant hormones are produced by tissues that have other functions, and they often are produced in one place and transported to different locations within the organism, where they cause specific effects. Plant hormones are produced in minute amounts and are effective in extremely small concentrations.

Plant hormones often interact with each other to produce their effects. The hormones may cause different effects in different parts of the plant, at different times, or in different concentrations. Each hormone may have a primary effect on each cell type, from which a variety of responses can follow. The response depends on poorly understood structural and physiological conditions in the affected cells. These conditions have made it extremely difficult to determine how plant hormones operate.

FIGURE 15.9 This cutting was induced to form roots by the application of auxins.

15.5 Auxins

Auxins (AWK sins) were the first plant hormones to be identified. They are produced in apical meristems and are moved by active transport to other parts of the plant. Experiments suggest that auxins can cause cells in the growing regions of the plant to elongate, but the effects depend on a number of factors, especially the concentration of the auxins. At extremely low concentrations, for example, auxins promote elongation of roots, but at higher concentrations, they inhibit elongation. Auxins present in the apical bud also may inhibit the development and growth of lateral buds. Removal of the apical bud often results in increased branching in a plant.

Auxins can be applied to plant cuttings to stimulate the formation of roots from a place where they do not usually develop. For example, when a stem or a leaf is cut off a plant and placed in water containing an auxin, roots often develop (see Figure 15.9). Auxins also can promote fruit growth. A fruit normally develops only after a flower has been pollinated and its ovules have been fertilized. Scientists found, however, that they could stimulate certain flowers to develop fruit by spraying them with an auxin. The fruit is produced without fertilization, so no seeds develop inside. Seedless tomatoes and cucumbers have been produced this way.

A synthetic auxin called 2,4-D is a herbicide used to kill dicot weeds. At the concentrations generally used, 2,4-D does not affect members of the grass family (monocots), so it can be used to control weeds such as dandelions in lawns and in grain fields (Figure 15.10).

A molecule very similar to 2,4-D is the herbicide 2,4,5-T, which is widely used to kill small woody plants and seeds. This herbicide is a component of the infamous ''Agent Orange'' that was used during the Vietnam conflict to defoliate trees. Dioxin, a by-product of the manufacture of 2,4,5-T that often contaminates the 2,4,5-T, is extremely toxic to people and is considered to be an environmental hazard all over the world.

FIGURE 15.10 Plants sprayed with 2,4-D

15.6 Gibberellins

Gibberellins (jib uh REL ens) were first discovered in the 1920s by the Japanese scientist Kurosawa when a fungal disease infected rice plants, causing them to grow abnormally tall and weak. By working with the fungus *Gibberella*, scientists were able to isolate the chemical that caused the abnormal growth. The newly discovered compound was called gibberellin. More than 60 gibberellins have been discovered in fungi and plants since then, though generally only a few are present in any species.

Gibberellins are synthesized in the apical parts of stems and roots. They can influence stem elongation in mature trees and shrubs and can promote growth in many intact plants. Most dicots and some monocots grow faster when treated with gibberellins. Laboratory experiments suggest the effects of gibberellins can be enhanced if certain concentrations of auxins are present as well. Gibberellins also are involved in stimulating the production of enzymes that break down the stored nutrients in the endosperm of grains. The nutrients then are used by the embryo as it develops.

Plants treated with gibberellins may produce flowers that develop into seedless fruit. Gibberellins also produce larger fruits, such as the grapes shown in Figure 15.11 *left* (next page). Gibberellins also can cause dwarf plants to grow to the height of normal varieties (Figure 15.11 *right*).

15.7 Cytokinins

The **cytokinins** (syt oh KY ninz) are a third group of naturally occurring plant hormones whose main function is to promote cell division and organ

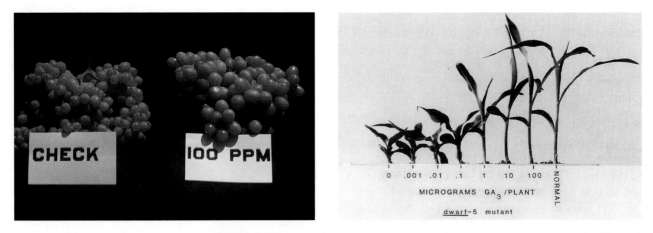

FIGURE 15.11 *(left)* Grapes with and without gibberellic acid treatment *(right)* Effect of gibberellic acid (GA$_3$) on dwarf maize plants. Each dwarf plant was treated with the indicated dosage of GA$_3$ and allowed to continue growing for 7 days. Note the increase in height of the plant with increased dosage. Normal growth is exhibited by plants treated with 10 and 100 μg GA$_3$.

development, such as the growth of lateral buds on stems. Cytokinins usually work in combination with auxins and other hormones to regulate the total growth pattern of the plant. They are found mostly in plant parts with actively dividing cells, such as root tips, germinating seeds, and fruits. Evidence indicates that cytokinins are produced mainly in the roots and then transported throughout the rest of the plant. They also are produced in developing fruits.

Cytokinins are necessary to promote stem and root growth, as well as chloroplast development and chlorophyll synthesis. Cytokinins promote the growth of lateral branches and inhibit the formation of lateral roots. In contrast, auxins inhibit the formation of lateral branches and promote the growth of lateral roots.

15.8 Abscisic Acid and Ethylene

Two naturally occurring plant hormones play important roles in controlling activities within the plant. **Abscisic** (ab SIS ik) **acid** is synthesized mainly in mature green leaves, root caps, and fruits. It is involved in the dormancy of buds and seeds, enabling them to survive extremes of temperature and dryness. Abscisic acid also affects stomate closing and is sometimes called the stress hormone because it may help protect the plant against water loss during unfavorable environmental conditions. Abscisic acid appears to have the opposite effect of cytokinins on plant parts, but the manner in which it functions is not well understood.

Ethylene (ETH ih leen) is a simple gas that occurs as a natural metabolic product in plants. When applied to plants, it can promote fruit ripening and aging of tissues. Through interaction with auxins, cytokinins, and abscisic acid, ethylene apparently plays a major role in causing leaves, flowers, and fruits to drop from a plant (Figure 15.12). This action is often opposite to the effect of auxins, which sometimes promote the growth of

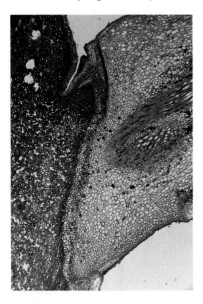

FIGURE 15.12 The vertical band in the micrograph is the abscission layer, which forms at the base of a leaf stem before a leaf falls. A change in the balance of ethylene and auxin may regulate this process.

FOCUS ON *Development of New Plants*

The use of plant hormones has enabled plant physiologists to devise new methods of growing plants. In tissue culture, single cells or groups of cells are placed in sterile containers with minerals, water, and hormones to stimulate growth and development. At equal concentrations of auxins and cytokinins, many cells in culture continue to divide, forming an undifferentiated tissue called a callus. By adjusting the relative concentrations of auxins, cytokinins, and other growth substances, the cells of the callus can be induced to form roots or buds and, in some cases, to grow into a complete plant (Figure C). Plants grown from calluses are clones of the parent plant and thus are genetically identical individuals. Cloning has an important advantage in the development of new plant varieties. There may be only one plant out of thousands that has a particular combination of desired traits, for example, an unusually tasty tomato or a new variety of rose. If that one plant were crossed with another to get seeds, there is no guarantee that the offspring would have the same desired characteristics. Cloning, however, could produce duplicate copies of the desired plant. Most house ferns, for example, are produced by cloning.

Another technique used to develop new and better crops is protoplast fusion, in which cells from two different plants are placed in a special liquid in the same container. Enzymes are used to digest away the cell walls, leaving the living contents, or protoplasts, intact (Figure D). The

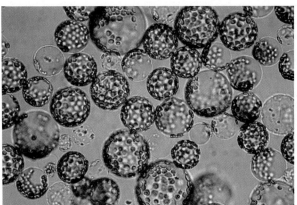

FIGURE D Protoplasts removed from their cell walls in preparation for fusion

protoplasts may fuse, develop a cell wall and begin to grow, forming a hybrid cell. In such hybrid cells, only some of the chromosomes of the original cells survive.

Usually, individuals from two different species cannot form viable offspring. For example, it has not been possible to produce a hybrid offspring between a potato and a tomato by cross fertilization. However, a hybrid cell of these two plants can be formed using protoplast fusion. Results such as these have raised hopes that protoplast fusion could lead to the combining of extremely different plants into "superplants" or "supercrops" that might, for example, be more drought resistant or require smaller amounts of nitrogen.

FIGURE C Interaction of auxins and cytokinins in plant tissue culture. The culture media were supplemented with various levels of the two hormones.

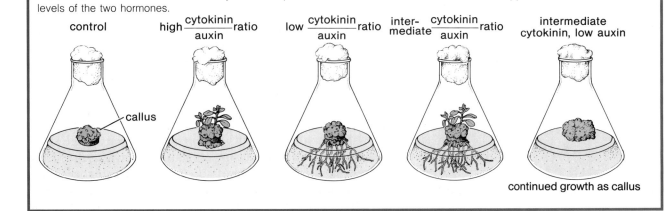

control · high $\frac{\text{cytokinin}}{\text{auxin}}$ ratio · low $\frac{\text{cytokinin}}{\text{auxin}}$ ratio · intermediate $\frac{\text{cytokinin}}{\text{auxin}}$ ratio · intermediate cytokinin, low auxin

callus

continued growth as callus

FIGURE 15.13 Some possible roles and interactions of hormones among the various portions of a plant.

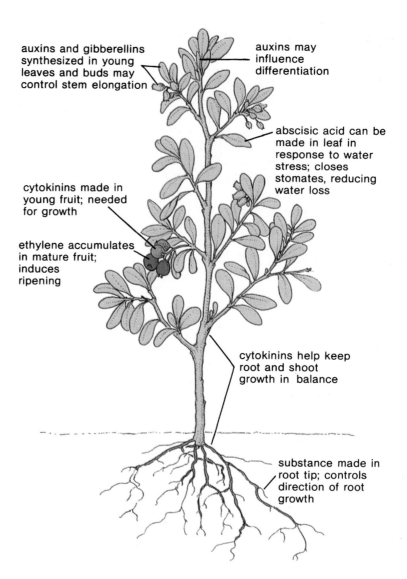

auxins and gibberellins synthesized in young leaves and buds may control stem elongation

auxins may influence differentiation

abscisic acid can be made in leaf in response to water stress; closes stomates, reducing water loss

cytokinins made in young fruit; needed for growth

ethylene accumulates in mature fruit; induces ripening

cytokinins help keep root and shoot growth in balance

substance made in root tip; controls direction of root growth

those structures. Ethylene appears to counteract many effects of auxins in plants. For example, auxins can indirectly suppress the formation of lateral stems by stimulating the production of ethylene around the buds. The ethylene, in turn, suppresses the development of the buds.

Hundreds of years ago, Chinese farmers unknowingly used ethylene when they burned incense (which produces ethylene) to ripen fruit stored in ripening rooms. A more recent observation was that gases produced by ripening oranges would cause bananas to ripen. Taking advantage of this property of ethylene, many farmers pick delicate fruits, such as tomatoes, when they are green and less susceptible to damage. The fruits are shipped in an atmosphere of carbon dioxide, which inhibits ripening. When the tomatoes arrive at their destination, they are treated with ethylene to speed their ripening so they can be sold in stores. Figure 15.13 summarizes the actions of the five groups of plant hormones.

CHECK AND CHALLENGE

1. What are some of the characteristics of plant hormones that have made them particularly difficult to study?

2. Compare the effects of auxins and cytokinins on plant growth. What is the primary effect of each hormone?

3. How can one type of fruit ripening in a room affect how a different kind of fruit ripens in that same room?

4. Gibberellins and auxins both influence elongation of cells. How do their effects differ?

Plant Responses

15.9 Plant Movements

Proper plant growth and development depend, in part, on movements of plants that occur in response to a stimulus. The movements are generally very small and take place so slowly that it is usually necessary to use time-lapse photography to see them. Most plant movements are in response to changes in the environment, and such responses may occur in a particular direction. For example, when any part of the leaf of the sensitive plant, *Mimosa pudica,* is touched, the leaflets droop together suddenly (Figure 15.14). This movement is the result of a sudden loss of water from certain cells at the base of the leaves and leaflets. The significance of this movement is not completely apparent, but the drooping may help prevent further water loss.

Other plant movements are directional, either toward or away from the stimulus. Such directional plant movements are called **tropisms**

Try Investigation 15B, Tropisms.

FIGURE 15.14 Mimosa plant before (a) and after (b) being touched

a

b

FIGURE 15.15 Seedlings bending toward light

(TROH piz umz). Tropisms are the result of differences in growth among cells of a tissue. You probably have observed that most plants grow toward light. Charles Darwin studied this response—called **phototropism**—in which cells on the lighted side of the shoot stop growing, while those on the shaded side continue to elongate (Figure 15.15). This differential growth causes the plant to bend toward the light.

What causes the differential growth? Many experiments designed to answer this question have been carried out on oat coleoptiles, the protective sheaths around monocot seedlings. In uniform lighting or in the dark, oat seedlings grow straight upward. With one-sided lighting, bending occurs.

Evidence from the experiments indicated that the tip of a growing shoot produces a chemical that causes bending. Darwin's experiments showed that if the tip was covered, the shoot would not bend. Other researchers similarly found a substance produced in the tip when it was exposed to light. This chemical, if applied to only one side of the shoot, could cause the shoot to bend even in the dark.

Eventually the chemical was identified as an auxin. It appeared that the auxin was synthesized in the tip of the shoot and transported to the shaded side, where it stimulated elongation of the cells. That hypothesis is now being questioned, however. Improved analytical techniques fail to show any redistribution of auxin within the shoot before bending occurs. At the present time it is not clear how, or even whether, light and auxin interact to produce bending.

Gravitropism (grav ih TROH piz um) is growth toward or away from Earth's gravitational pull. Stems and flower stalks are negatively gravitropic, that is, they grow in a direction away from gravity. If stems are placed in a horizontal position, they bend upward, although this response can be variable. Auxins may play a critical role in gravitropism, as do calcium ions. Roots are positively gravitropic, and the evidence indicates that sensitivity to gravity occurs in the root cap. There, plastids filled with starch grains migrate to the bottom of certain cells (Figure 15.16). Their movement initiates a sequence of events that leads to downward growth. Again, auxins appear to be involved, along with abscisic acid and perhaps other plant hormones.

15.10 Photoperiodism

The changing seasons are an important environmental cue for most organisms. As winter approaches, for example, birds and other animals such as lobsters migrate, insects produce dormant eggs, animals hibernate, and deciduous trees lose their leaves. These activities are triggered by changes in day length. Organisms have mechanisms that are sensitive to the relative amount of light and dark in a 24-hour period, a response called **photoperiodism** (foh toh PIH ree ud iz um).

Many plants show the effects of photoperiodism in flowering. For example, spring-flowering plants, such as daffodils, bloom only when day length exceeds a certain number of hours. Thus they are called long-day plants. Fall-flowering plants, such as asters, on the other hand, can reproduce only when day length is shorter than a certain number of hours, and so are called short-day plants. Many plants flower whenever they become mature, regardless of the day length. They are day-neutral, although temperature may play an important role in their flowering. Florists use knowledge of photoperiod to "force" short-day plants such as chrysanthemums to bloom year-round.

In the 1940s, plant physiologists learned that it is the length of the night rather than the length of the day that controls flowering and other photoperiodic responses. In experiments, they found that a brief period of darkness during the daytime portion of the photoperiod has no effect on flowering. Even a few minutes of light during the dark period, however, prevents flowering, indicating that photoperiodic responses depend on a critical, uninterrupted night length. Long-day plants flower when the night is *shorter* than a critical length; short-day plants flower when the night is *longer* than a critical length.

How does the plant measure the length of darkness in a photoperiod? Plants contain a pigment known as **phytochrome** (FYT oh krohm) that can alternate between two slightly different chemical structures. One form (P_r) absorbs red light; the other form (P_{fr}) absorbs far-red light (a wavelength in the farthest red part of the spectrum—see Figure 7.1). Phytochrome is synthesized as P_r and remains in that form as long as the plant is in the dark. In sunlight, which is richer in red light than in far-red light, the P_r absorbs red light and is converted to P_{fr}. Figure 15.17 summarizes these changes.

After sunset, P_{fr} is gradually converted back to P_r. At sunrise, the level of P_{fr} rapidly increases again as P_r absorbs red light. In this way, the conversion of phytochrome from one form to the other marks the beginning and end of the dark segment of the photoperiod. This conversion also acts as a switching mechanism that controls many events in the life of the plant, such as flowering, seed germination, and opening of the stomates.

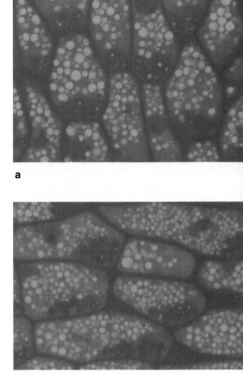

a

b

FIGURE 15.16 Cells in the root cap may detect gravity. When the root is vertical (a), starch-containing plastids (the dark circles) reside at the lower side of the cells. When the root is turned on its side (b), gravity causes the plastids to settle quickly to the new lower side of the cells.

FIGURE 15.17 Phytochrome occurs in two forms: P_r (red absorbing) and P_{fr} (far-red absorbing). Absorption of red light converts P_r to P_{fr}; absorption of far-red light converts P_{fr} to P_r.

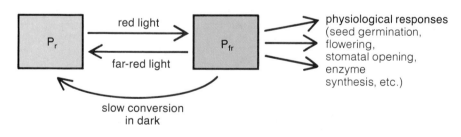

CHECK AND CHALLENGE

1. How do phototropism and gravitropism affect plant growth? Predict the effects on growth if a plant responded abnormally to light and to gravity.
2. Describe how phytochrome acts in plant photoperiodism.
3. Of what importance might time of flowering be to plants?

Summary

Growth is an increase in the number of cells in the plant. Development is the process by which the cells of a new organism grow into a complete individual. A seed contains the embryo with its cotyledons, and a reserve energy supply. When conditions are appropriate the seed germinates. The initial growth of the root tip and then the stem tip use the energy reserves inside the seed. Once the leaves emerge from the buds on the stem, the plant uses photosynthesis to harvest the energy it needs for continued growth, development, and reproduction. Growth occurs at specific areas in the plant called meristems. Primary growth—increase in length—occurs in roots and stems at apical meristems; secondary growth—increase in diameter—occurs at the cambium and, in some plants, at the cork cambium. Leaves and branches arise from the meristem tissue in the buds.

Five groups of plant hormones have been identified—auxins, gibberellins, cytokinins, abscisic acid, and ethylene. These hormones interact in response to environmental cues, such as light and gravity, to produce a variety of effects. Tropisms are variations in plant growth that occur in response to environmental stimuli. Plants also exhibit photoperiodism, a response to relative length of the dark period that involves the pigment phytochrome. Much remains to be learned about the mechanisms by which plant hormones interact with each other and with environmental factors to produce controlled growth and development.

differentiation	leaf formation
embryo	root growth
germination	seed
growth	stem growth

Key Concepts

Following is the beginning of a concept map for plant development. Use the concepts that follow and other concepts from the chapter to build a more complete map.

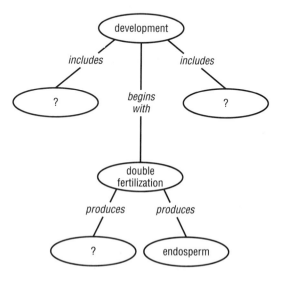

Reviewing Ideas

1. How does the environment act as a selection agent in determining which seeds survive and germinate?

2. Would a seed be able to produce a plant if its endosperm were removed before it germinated? Why or why not?

3. What is the difference between a cotyledon and a true leaf?

4. Why is it advantageous for the root tip to grow from the embryo before the stem tip starts growing?

5. What is the difference between apical meristem and cambium?

6. How are plant hormones used to bring about differentiation and growth of a new plant from a callus?

7. Contrast the action of auxins and cytokinins on the growth of lateral stems and roots.

8. How are xylem and phloem tissues involved in the growth and development of a plant?

Using Concepts

1. What are the advantages for plants of cell division occurring just at meristems and not throughout the entire organism?

2. How would survival of a plant be ensured by a requirement to undergo freezing temperatures followed by warmer temperatures before germination?

3. What are some of the environmental factors that influence plant growth and development? What are their effects?

4. If 2,4-D is a plant growth hormone, how can it kill weeds?

5. What might be some beneficial uses of a plant hormone that functions only in certain species of plants and not in others?

6. How could a short-day plant and a long-day plant growing in the same area flower on the same day of the year?

7. How might day length, phytochrome, and plant hormones interact in the germination of seeds planted just below the soil surface?

8. Deciduous trees lose their leaves in the fall. Describe possible hormonal and environmental stimuli that might bring about this response.

9. Ten years ago, a farmer built a fence 1.5 m high and attached one end of it to a tree that was 7 m high. Now the tree has grown to a height of 14 m. How far above the ground is the attached end of the fence? Explain.

Synthesis

1. Explain how the formation of a plant embryo is similar to and different from the formation of an animal embryo.

2. Genes from plants can be inserted into bacteria and cause the bacteria to produce plant proteins. Explain how this capability supports the theory of evolution by natural selection.

3. Photosynthesis experiments have shown that when plants are grown in an atmosphere without oxygen, they take up carbon dioxide at 1.5 times the rate at which they do so in natural atmosphere, which is about 20 percent oxygen.

   (a) What does this observation indicate about the relationship between photosynthesis and cellular respiration?

   (b) How might this relationship affect the composition of Earth's atmosphere?

4. Plant development appears to be much more closely linked to environmental cues than animal development. Explain how this adaptation would enhance survival of plants.

Extensions

1. Assume auxins have the same effect on humans as they do on plants. Write a short story about how you would use auxins and the effects they would have after you used them.

2. Diagram the life cycle of a plant. Show the hormones likely to be most active at each stage in the cycle.

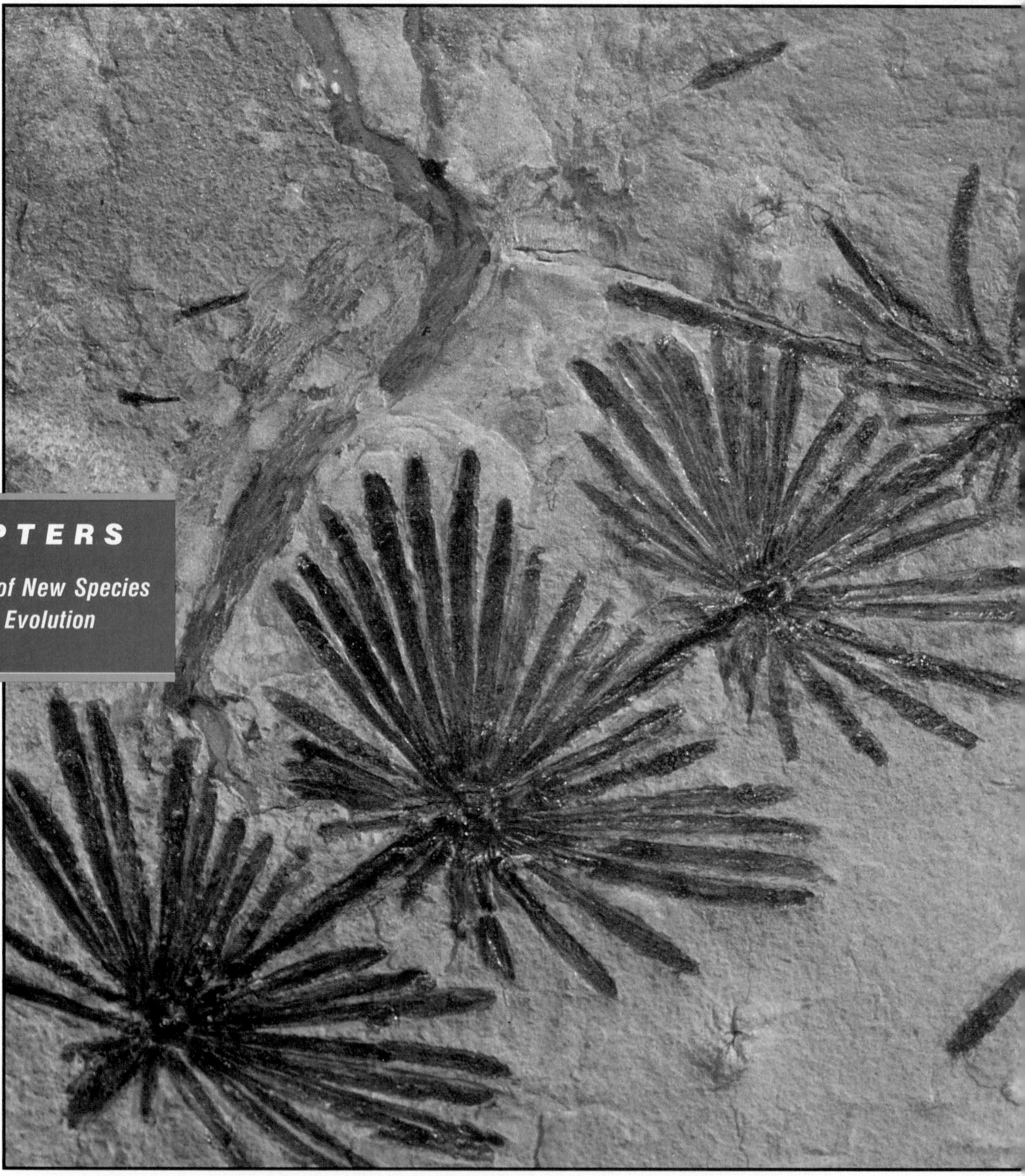

CHAPTERS

Evolution: Change through Time

*T*he world contains a tremendous variety of organisms. Not only is there a great diversity of life today, but evidence from fossils also shows that there were at least as many organisms in the past that have become extinct. How did such diversity come about? Rocks show imprints of organisms that lived millions of years ago and no longer exist. For example, the fossil shown—*Equisetum*, or horsetail— lived during the Carboniferous period, about 360 million years ago.

The chapters in this unit discuss how evolution results in the origin of new species, accounting for the present variety of organisms. These chapters also explain how changes have occurred in populations through time.

*M*odern horsetails closely resemble these fossils. Given that these plants are separated by more than 300 million years, why do they not appear more different from each other?

*H*ow would you explain the similarities?

CONTENTS

Origin of New Species

*T*he history of life is not a story of unchanging species on a static planet. Rather, it is a record of an ancient Earth inhabited by constantly changing populations of organisms. Each species is on a tip of a branching tree of life that extends far back in time. Evolution is the biological process that ties all species together.

In *The Origin of Species,* Charles Darwin made two major points. First, contemporary species result from a succession of ancestors in a process of "descent with modification," or change through time; and second, natural selection is the mechanism of evolution. Natural selection results in organisms that are adapted to the unique characteristics of their environment. Natural selection, though, does not create adaptations. Rather, it affects how frequently certain variations appear in populations. Natural selection is an editing process, whereby inherited variations provide a range of phenotypes, while environmental factors eliminate those phenotypes that are not well suited to that environment.

By the cumulative effects of change through vast periods of time, natural selection produces new species from old species. Evolution is the source of all biological diversity, and it is also the link between the unity and diversity of life. This chapter examines the evidence for evolution and natural selection and the mechanisms by which natural selection operates.

*M*any other organisms are unique to the Galápagos. How would you explain the presence of the many organisms that are unique to these islands?

◆ *A land iguana* (Conolophus subscristat) *from the Galápagos Islands.*

Evidence for Evolution

16.1 The Galápagos Islands

The Galápagos (guh LAH puh guhs) Islands are located on the equator approximately 950 kilometers west of Ecuador (Figure 16.1). The islands originated from volcanic eruptions about 3.3 million years ago and have never been connected to the South American mainland. The organisms found there could have reached the islands only by swimming, flying, or drifting on rafts of vegetation. Today there are only two species of mammals, 7 species of reptiles, and about 20 species of birds inhabiting the islands.

Of the bird species inhabiting the Galápagos Islands, most are finches, known as Darwin's finches. These finches provide an excellent example of the process of natural selection. Look closely at the illustration of these birds in Figure 16.2. Six of the finch groups feed on the ground, six feed in trees, and one feeds in bushes. Although the bodies of the finches are very similar in shape, their beaks are quite different in size and shape. Each beak type is an adaptation to a particular food source.

The different finch species, with their different beaks and diets, likely had a common ancestor that arrived from the west coast of South America about 100 000 years ago. Those ancestral finches, with time and evolution through natural selection, gave rise to the various finch species of the Galápagos Islands.

The newly arrived finches had little or no competition for food or habitat. As the island finch population rapidly expanded, they invaded many ecological **niches** (NIH chez). A *niche* is a way of life, or the "profession" of the organism in its particular environment (Figure 16.3). Evolu-

FIGURE 16.1 This map of the Galápagos Islands shows how many of the 13 species of Darwin's finches are found on each island. None of the islands has all 13 species in permanent residence.

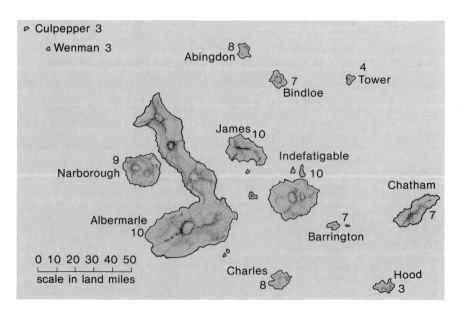

Culpepper 3
Wenman 3
Abingdon 8
7 Bindloe
4 Tower
James 10
Indefatigable 10
9 Narborough
Chatham 7
Albermarle 10
7 Barrington
0 10 20 30 40 50
scale in land miles
Charles 8
Hood 3

FIGURE 16.2 The Galápagos finches were able to adapt to many different food sources, because few species competed with them. Note the variations in the sizes and shapes of the beaks.

tion resulted in finches adapted to the niches in which there was little or no competition from other organisms. For example, finches with short, strong beaks were able to crush the plentiful supply of nuts and seeds. Other populations of finches evolved with beaks adapted for capturing insects under bark and with other adaptations for exploiting different food sources. Natural selection eliminated the finches least able to utilize available resources.

FIGURE 16.3 Birds other than Darwin's finches also are adapted to and occupy different niches. Each type of bird exploits a different portion of the same habitat. By filling different niches, the birds are able to live in close proximity to one another, yet avoid competition for food and nesting sites.

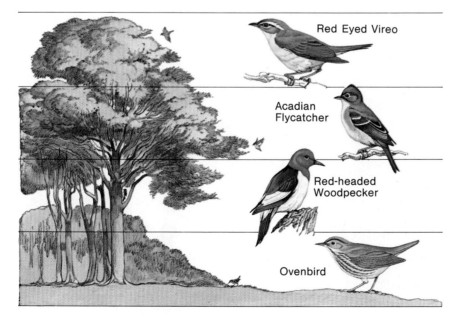

Red Eyed Vireo

Acadian Flycatcher

Red-headed Woodpecker

Ovenbird

CONNECTIONS

The different adaptations of Darwin's finches are examples of the close relationships between organisms and their environment and between structure and function.

During his visit to the Galápagos on the voyage of the *Beagle,* Darwin observed many differences among the organisms, such as the tortoises (Figure 16.4), mockingbirds, and the finches. Initially, he did not attribute those differences to evolution through natural selection. In fact, he failed to notice the dietary differences among the finches and thought they were several varieties of the same species rather than different species. Although Darwin collected specimens of the different types, he did not place great importance on their anatomical differences. Even after the finches had been examined by experts in England and proclaimed to be of different species, Darwin did not attribute their differences to evolution through natural selection. The inference that natural selection was responsible for the different Galápagos finch species was made many years after Darwin observed them.

Instead, Darwin derived his theory of evolution by natural selection mainly from his observations of changes in domestic species. He was particularly intrigued by the work of English breeders who had produced great variation among domestic pigeons. Planned matings of pigeons with different phenotypes led, after several generations, to completely new breeds of pigeons. The new breeds resembled the wild pigeon, or rock dove, yet they were different in many ways, as you can see in Figure 16.5.

Darwin discovered that breeders are able to bring about such unusual variations by **artificial selection**. Artificial selection involves a deliberate choice on the part of the breeder to select particular traits that are desired and to breed individuals with those traits. Darwin observed that humans could produce rapid changes in organisms by artificial selection but that natural selection required much longer periods of time. In modern terms, selection of either type (artificial or natural) is defined as the differential survival and reproduction of genotypes. Those genotypes selected by

FIGURE 16.4 One of the Galápagos tortoises is the saddleback. The elevated portion of its shell allows this tortoise to raise its head higher than other tortoises and thus obtain food the others cannot reach.

FIGURE 16.5 Some examples of the results of selective breeding in pigeons

Pouter

Jacobin

Fantail

Rock dove

humans or not eliminated by nature pass on their genes to the next generation. Organisms that are unsuccessful at reproduction in nature or domestic animals or plants with undesired traits do not pass on their genes to the next generation.

When Charles Darwin set out on the *Beagle,* he held the same convictions as most other nonscientists of his time—life had originated through special creation events and all species were fixed in form. However, due to the large number of fossil discoveries, some scientists had begun to accept the existence of ancient species that were now extinct. Other scholars had begun to consider the inheritability of change and the process of evolution, at least from a philosophical standpoint. (See **Appendix 16A,** Spontaneous Generation.) Darwin eventually accepted that philosophy and, as a result of his observations during the voyage and subsequent observations over the next several years, went on to propose a mechanism by which evolution could occur—the theory of evolution by natural selection.

16.2 Population and Ecological Evidence

Darwin's hypothesis of evolution through natural selection has been supported by the findings of other biologists. A British biologist, E. B. Ford, observed natural selection in action as a result of birds feeding on dark-colored moths on light-colored trees and light-colored moths on dark-colored trees (Figure 16.6). Before the Industrial Revolution, most of the

Try Investigation 16A, Variation in Size of Organisms.

FIGURE 16.6 The basis for natural selection in the peppered moth (*Biston betularia*). Dark and light forms on a tree covered with light-colored lichens (*left*). The two forms of the moth on a tree blackened with soot (*right*). Which moth in each photo is most likely to be eaten by predators?

FIGURE 16.7 The coat color of mice must blend with the background if the mice are to have their best chance for survival.

trees in England had light-colored bark and lichens. Most moths were light-colored. However, as soot began to darken the bark of the trees and kill the lichens, predators could more easily spot the light-colored moths on the dark trunks. As a result, dark-colored moths became much more numerous in the population.

A biologist at the University of Michigan conducted a similar experiment with buff-colored mice and gray mice, colors of soil that matched the two colors of mice, and barn owls. The biologist alternated the color of soil on the floor of an enclosed room each day. An ample supply of sticks was added to give the mice a place to hide. Each day, four mice of each color were released and exposed to the owl for 15 minutes. Depending on the color of soil used, one set of mice was more easily seen against the background than the other set. (See Figure 16.7.) In 44 trials with each soil type, almost twice as many (107 to 65) of the more visible color of mice were caught by the owl.

In other experiments, scientists have demonstrated natural selection with bacteria and antibiotics. Penicillin originally killed many species of bacteria, but there are now strains that are unaffected by penicillin. As nonresistant individuals were killed, penicillin-resistant strains survived to reproduce. Therefore, a greater number of the resistant individuals were born in the next generation.

16.3   Genetic and Molecular Evidence

The sequences of nucleotide bases in DNA make up the genes in your cells. Chapter 10 describes how messenger RNA is transcribed from the DNA in the nuclei of cells. The RNA travels to the cytosol where the codes are translated into a sequence of amino acids that form protein molecules. Biochemical techniques make it possible to examine proteins from different organisms and to determine the exact order of amino acids in each protein. For example, researchers have learned that sickle hemoglobin differs from normal hemoglobin in only one amino acid out of hundreds in the entire molecule. Examining such amino acid similarities and differences helps determine evolutionary relationships. (See Chapter 5.)

Try Investigation 16B, Sickle Cell Disease.

The science of genetics was unknown during Darwin's time. Darwin's major problem in defending his theory of evolution by natural selection was to explain how variations were inherited. Until the laws of inheritance

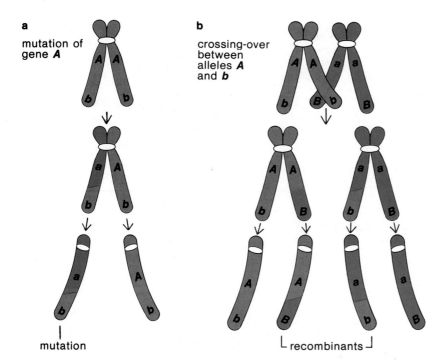

a
mutation of
gene **A**

b
crossing-over
between
alleles **A**
and **b**

mutation

recombinants

FIGURE 16.8 Mutation and crossing over are two sources of genetic variation. Mutations (a) give rise to new alleles, such as when **A** mutates to **a.** Before mutation, only the combination **Ab** was possible. Crossing over (b) provides new combinations of alleles in the gametes. Before meiosis, only the combinations **Ab** and **aB** occur. Crossing over between **A** and **b** results in the recombinants **AB** and **ab.**

became more clearly understood in the twentieth century, the reasons for variation among organisms of the same species were a mystery. The rapid increase in the understanding of genetic principles has allowed scientists to identify two specific sources for variation within species.

One source of variation is mutations, which are changes in the sequence of DNA nucleotides or in the structure of chromosomes (Chapters 9 and 13). Mutations supply the raw material (new alleles) for the variations on which natural selection can act. The second source of variation is the recombination of alleles during meiosis. (See Chapter 11.) Entirely new combinations of genes become possible through crossing over and independent assortment. Figure 16.8 shows how mutations and crossing over can produce variation. As presently understood, mutations and genetic recombination are responsible for all variation within species.

CHECK AND CHALLENGE

1. What evidence did the Galápagos Islands provide in support of evolution by means of natural selection?
2. Compare natural selection and artificial selection.
3. How does a population of bacteria become resistant to antibiotics such as penicillin?
4. Distinguish between mutation and genetic recombination, and explain how they contribute to evolution.
5. How can amino acid sequences in proteins be helpful in classifying animals?

The Origin of New Species _____

16.4 Population Genetics

From the time of Charles Darwin, evolution was defined as change through time. What type of change? The biologists of the early twentieth century would probably say, ''A change in the appearance of organisms through time,'' or ''A change in species through time.'' Modern investigative techniques and the incorporation of mathematics into the field of genetics have made it possible to define evolution in terms of the genetic composition of populations.

Consider Mendel's crosses with pea plants from a modern perspective. Mendel crossed true-breeding (homozygous) purple-flowered plants with true-breeding (homozygous) white-flowered plants. The result was a population of hybrid (heterozygous) purple-flowered plants. Mendel then allowed these hybrids to self-fertilize and produce a second generation of flowers with a phenotypic ratio of 3 purple-flowered plants to 1 white-flowered plant (3:1).

A **gene pool** is described as all of the genes of a population of organisms. If a population consisted entirely of homozygous purple-flowered plants, its gene pool for alleles for flower color would consist of only the allele for purple flowers. The frequency of the allele for purple flowers in that population would be 100 percent, and the frequency of alleles for white flowers would be zero. If the population consisted entirely of white-flowered plants, the frequencies would be reversed—100 percent for white alleles and zero for purple alleles.

Figure 16.9 illustrates Mendel's crosses. In addition, the allele frequencies for each generation are shown. Notice that in the case of the F_1 generation, when all of the flowers were purple but heterozygous, the frequency of alleles for flower color would be 50 percent purple (0.50) and 50 percent white (0.50).

Try Investigation 16C, A Model Gene Pool.

FIGURE 16.9 In this cross of two heterozygous purple flowered plants, what are the allele frequencies in the parental generation? In the offspring generation? What would be the allele frequencies if the parental generation consisted of a homozygous purple-flowered plant and heterozygous purple-flowered plant?

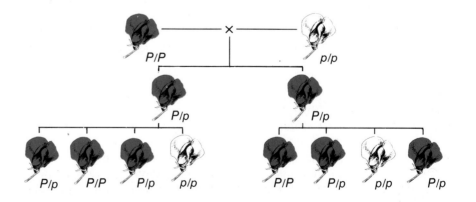

Any condition that alters the frequency of the alleles in the gene pool would change the frequency of the genotypes and phenotypes in the population. If there is a change in the frequency of any of the alleles in the gene pool, the population is said to be undergoing *evolution*. This idea reinforces the definition of natural selection as the differential survival and reproduction of genotypes (Section 16.1). If some genotypes are more successful at reproduction than others, the allele frequency in the gene pool will change because the alleles for the successful trait are passed on and will be more numerous in the next generation. The study of allele frequencies within populations is called **population genetics**.

The important point is that the unit of change in population genetics is the population, not the organism. *Populations* evolve, not organisms within the population. As populations adapt to changing conditions within the environment, some individuals are more successful than others in surviving and reproducing. Those individuals that are more successful in reproduction will contribute more alleles to the gene pool in the next generation.

16.5   Allele Frequencies

The frequency of alleles in a gene pool tends to remain stable, especially in a large population that is well adapted to its environment. Such a gene pool is in a state of equilibrium. Factors that tend to change that equilibrium have less effect if a population is large than if it is small. (See **Appendix 16B**, The Hardy-Weinberg Principle.) Five factors can change the equilibrium of a gene pool. The first is mutation. Introduction of a new allele resulting from a mutation causes an immediate, but small, shift in the equilibrium. Organisms with a short generation time that produce large numbers of offspring are affected more by mutations than populations with long generation times that produce fewer offspring in the same time period.

The second factor is **migration**. Migration is the movement of organisms into or out of the population and, therefore, into or out of the gene pool. If the organisms moving into or out of the population have a genotype different from that of the majority of the population, then a change in equilibrium occurs. If the organisms moving into or out of the population have genotypes that are nearly identical to those of the majority of the population, then the effect on allele frequencies is small. Population geneticists define the movement of genes into and out of a population by migration as **gene flow**.

The third factor that affects genetic equilibrium is a random change in allele frequencies. In small populations particularly, the frequency of a gene may be changed drastically by chance alone, resulting in a population with distinct genetic characteristics. This random change is called **genetic drift**. An example of genetic drift is the Dunker population of West Germany. The Dunker population arose from a group of people that, by chance, had a higher frequency of a particular blood-type allele (and a lower frequency of a second allele) than the surrounding population. The

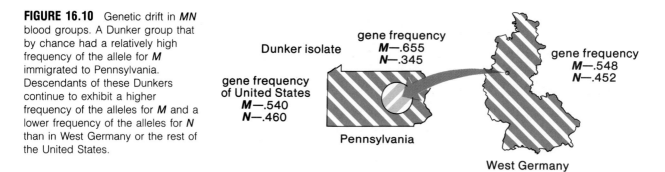

FIGURE 16.10 Genetic drift in *MN* blood groups. A Dunker group that by chance had a relatively high frequency of the allele for *M* immigrated to Pennsylvania. Descendants of these Dunkers continue to exhibit a higher frequency of the alleles for *M* and a lower frequency of the alleles for *N* than in West Germany or the rest of the United States.

Dunkers retained this frequency differential because of religious beliefs against marriage outside the group. Thus, the frequency of those blood-type alleles "drifted" away from the frequency found in the general population (Figure 16.10). Even after migrating to the United States, this differential allele frequency has been maintained because of marriage restrictions adhered to by descendants of the Dunkers. Change of allele frequencies may be due to other chance factors. By chance alone, some organisms may die or be killed by predators, and still others may not be successful in their attempts to reproduce. The allele frequency seems to *drift* one way or another simply by chance.

The fourth factor is selection. Natural or artificial selection can determine which individuals in a population will reproduce and pass their genes to the next generation. If there is strong selection on the population, then the equilibrium of the gene pool will change rapidly. Weak selection on the population results in less change.

The fifth factor that can influence the equilibrium of the gene pool is nonrandom mating. If certain individuals in a population show a prefer-

FIGURE 16.11 Inbreeding can increase recessive genetic disorders. In Japan, first cousins often marry. As a result, the Japanese population is more homozygous than that of the United States, where such marriages often are illegal. Because of the increased homozygosity, recessive alleles are expressed more often in Japan. For five genetic disorders shown, affected children in Japan are much more likely to have parents who are first cousins.

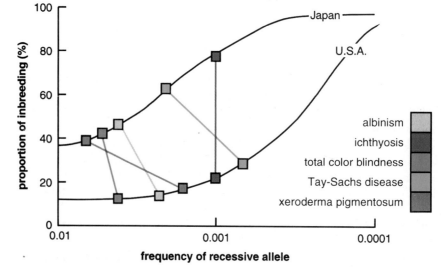

TABLE 16.1
Mechanisms that Affect Gene Pools

Mechanism	Effect on Gene Pool
Genetic drift	Random change in small gene pools
Gene flow	Change in the gene pool resulting from migration of individuals between populations
Mutation	Direct conversion of one allele to another
Nonrandom mating	More homozygous individuals, resulting from mates selected according to specific phenotypes
Natural selection	Increased reproductive success leads to increased allele frequency; poor reproductive success leads to decreased allele frequency

ence for mating with other individuals having the same or different pheno-types, the mating pattern is nonrandom. Nonrandom mating does not change the frequency of the alleles, but rather the proportion of individuals that are homozygous. Inbreeding, which is a type of nonrandom mating, promotes the occurrence of homozygous recessive disorders, such as Tay Sachs disease and albinism (Figure 16.11). Because of this tendency, marriage between relatives is discouraged. Table 16.1 summarizes the mechanisms that produce variations within populations and that provide the raw materials for the evolution of new species.

Two useful terms help summarize the many processes involved in evolution. The first term, **microevolution**, refers to the changes that occur within populations and species. This includes the processes that result in genetic variation, natural selection, genetic drift, and speciation. Evidence of microevolution exists in the form of large quantities of data from many different populations and from many fields within biology, such as genetics, microbiology, molecular biology, and many others. The

FOCUS ON *The Founder Effect*

The divergence of a population in a case like the Galápagos finches is an example of a type of genetic drift called the founder effect. A few individuals may found a new population, away from the original population. The frequencies of the alleles carried by the founding population may be very different from those of the alleles in the original population. Because of the small number of founders, the small number of alleles, and the lack of variation in those alleles, change can occur very rapidly. Why is this so?

Compare the effect of a change in one allele in one bird on two populations—one population with 20 birds and another with 2000 birds. In the 20-bird population, 5 percent of the birds (1 in 20) would be affected. In the 2000-bird population .05 percent (1 in 2000) would be affected. The percentage of offspring with the new trait would be much greater in the small population than in the large population. Thus, change can occur rapidly in small, isolated populations.

FIGURE 16.12 Triticale is an example of a species of grain that was produced by crossing wheat and rye.

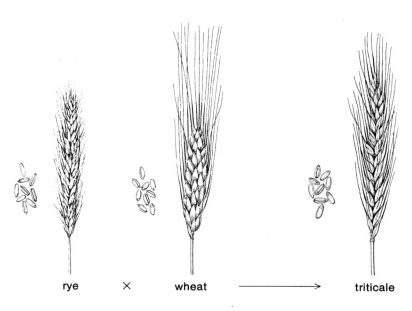

rye   ×   wheat   ——————→   triticale

second term, **macroevolution**, is evolution above the species level. Macroevolution is supported by inferences from the data collected in studying microevolution and by data from the fossil record. Macroevolution includes evolutionary trends, mass extinctions, and those changes that result in new types of organisms.

16.6 Speciation

The evolution of new species through time is called **speciation**. Although speciation occurs gradually in nature, technology has provided ways to accelerate the process. New species of fruit flies have been created by subjecting existing species to the mutation-generating powers of radiation. Triticale (Figure 16.12) is a relatively new species of grain produced by crossing wheat and rye. Genetic engineers routinely alter bacterial DNA to produce new strains.

Of course speciation also occurs naturally. Twelve new species of desert whiptail lizards have arisen as a result of natural crosses between existing species. Since 1969, a new species of saltbush, *Atriplex robusta*, has developed in the alkaline deserts of western Utah. (See Figure 16.13.)

A major factor contributing to speciation is the existence of a small population. As explained earlier, allele frequencies can change much more rapidly in a small population than in a large population. If small populations of organisms are *isolated* in some way from the main group of organisms, evolution proceeds at a much faster rate than with a large population. The most common mechanism that isolates these populations is geographical isolation (Figure 16.14). Organisms that cannot come into contact with one another cannot interbreed. In animal species, geographical isolation can occur when groups are separated by a mountain range or by an impassible canyon, for example. The Grand Canyon separates and isolates two

FIGURE 16.13 A new species of saltbush (*Atriplex*) has evolved in one area since a highway was built in 1969.

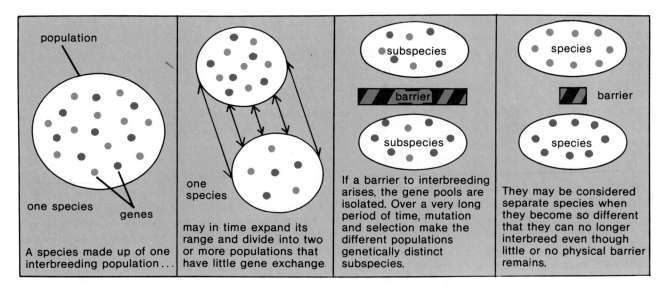

FIGURE 16.14 A simple model of how two populations of a species may become isolated and evolve to produce two species

populations of tufted-ear squirrels. These squirrels have already developed some differing characteristics, shown in Figure 16.15.

Other mechanisms may reproductively isolate speciating populations. Ecological isolation occurs when two populations require different habitats. In Canada, the Traill's Flycatcher was once considered to be one species of bird. Now, however, experts recognize that there are two separate species because their habitats are different and no crossbreeding takes place. The Willow Flycatcher is common on brushy slopes, and the Alder Flycatcher is common in alder swamps (Figure 16.16 next page). The

FIGURE 16.15 The Kaibab (a) and Abert (b) squirrels are related. When they became geographically isolated on opposite rims of the Grand Canyon, they began to develop differences. How many differences can you see?

a

b

FIGURE 16.16 The Alder Flycatcher (a) and the Willow Flycatcher (b) were once considered to be the same species until it was noticed that their habitats are completely different and no crossbreeding takes place.

a   b

FIGURE 16.17 Leopard frogs formerly were considered all one species, *Rana pipiens*. Today, however, biologists consider some of the populations to be separate species. The three frogs pictured are from Massachusetts (top), Oklahoma (middle), and Arizona (bottom).

appearance of the two species is almost identical. A small group of organisms that develops an ecological niche different from that of the main population also can become ecologically isolated from that population.

Not all forms of isolation are the result of physical location. Behavioral isolation can occur among animal populations. As Chapter 11 explains, behavior patterns and physical characteristics related to mating play an important part in the reproductive success of some animals. If the mating pattern of a small group of organisms becomes different from that of the main group, then they can become reproductively isolated. Eventually the groups become separate species. Such a change is happening with the leopard frog, shown in Figure 16.17. If one sex from the northern limits of its range and the opposite sex from the southern limits of its range are brought together, the two will not mate. Subtle differences in premating behavior, together with other events, have isolated these groups of frogs. These frogs are still in the process of speciation, and eventually scientists will group some of them in a new species.

Seasonal isolation occurs in both plants and animals. In plants, the most common example of seasonal isolation is when two closely related species flower at different times. The gametes of two species cannot fuse if one species' pollen is not present when the other species' carpels are ready for pollination. Some of the leopard frog populations are isolated from each other because they mate at slightly different times during the year.

Mechanical isolation results from physical characteristics that keep closely related species from interbreeding. Differences in size of the organisms or in the size or shape of their reproductive organs can prevent mating between the two sexes. Such mechanical isolation prevents mating between the tobacco budworm and the cotton bollworm shown in Chapter

1, Figure 1.11. Prevention of mating can occur in flowers when the reproductive structures are different, but it is most common in insects and other arthropods.

Prevention of gamete fusion is also a type of isolating mechanism. Some species may be so different that the sperm from the male simply are not attracted to the egg of the female. In plants, the pollen tubes of some species may not grow down into the carpel to fertilize the eggs. Sometimes, even though mating (or pollination in plants) has been successful, the gametes do not fuse because of the differences between them.

Another isolating mechanism is failure of the zygote to develop normally. If there are too many differences between the two parents, even though mating and fertilization have occurred, the zygote may not develop normally and will eventually stop growing and die.

Still another isolating mechanism is a failure to become established in nature. Most animal hybrids are sterile (See Focus On Species, Chapter 5.), so they usually are not able to pass on their genes to offspring.

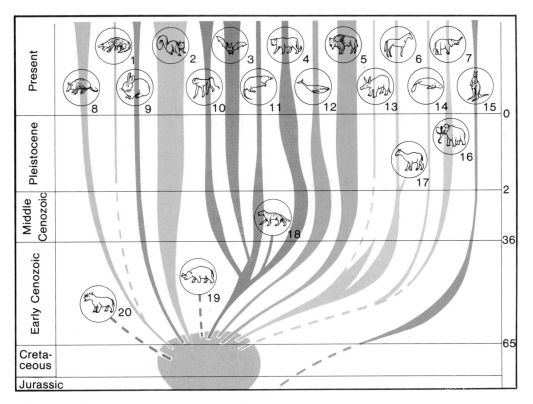

FIGURE 16.18 Adaptive radiation in mammals. As the first mammals dispersed to new areas, they became adapted to the new environmental conditions. Gradually, these adaptations produced different species and, eventually, all the different mammals alive today. Representative animals from the orders included are (1) pangolin, (2) squirrel, (3) bat, (4) lion, (5) buffalo, (6) horse, (7) elephant, (8) armadillo, (9) rabbit, (10) monkey, (11) mole, (12) whale, (13) aardvark, (14) manatee, (15) kangaroo, (16) mastodon, (17) litoptern, (18) creodont, (19) *Brototherium*, (20) *Uintatherium*.

The tendency of a population to disperse into new areas also may lead to speciation. As the parent population grows, offspring populations move off into new areas that offer different opportunities and problems. Each population then gradually adapts to its new environment or dies out. In time, these adaptations render the populations so genotypically different that they do not interbreed even when they inhabit the same area. They have become separate species. This process of dispersal, adaptation, and subsequent speciation is called adaptive radiation (Figure 16.18 page 373).

16.7 Questions about Evolutionary Mechanisms

Based on observations of fossils during his voyage, Darwin predicted that scientists would find fossils of extinct organisms representing an intermediate stage of evolutionary development. In 1861, two years after the publication of *The Origin of Species,* a fossil *Archaeopteryx* was found in Germany. *Archaeopteryx* (See Figure 1.4.) is an organism that is intermediate between birds and reptiles because it had the teeth and tail of a reptile and the wings and feathers of a bird. Since that time, paleontologists—biologists who study fossils—have uncovered and identified millions of fossils representing thousands of different species that are now extinct. Figure 16.19 shows several examples of extinct species.

Most of the fossil record consists of vertebrate animals, whose bones and teeth are most easily fossilized, and invertebrate animals with hard shells. Many plants are in the fossil record, but animals with only soft tissues are not well represented. The lack of these fossils does not mean that those organisms were not present, only that their bodies are not easily fossilized and preserved. Within the past few years, many microfossils have been found. New techniques have enabled paleontologists to discover the fossil remains of microorganisms in Canada, South Africa, and Australia that are almost 3.5 billion years old. (See Figure 4.17.)

Darwin viewed evolution as a slow, gradual change in species through time, but some biologists question whether or not that is the way evolution

FIGURE 16.19 Some representatives of extinct animals: (a) *Eryops,* (b) *Diatryma,* (c) *Syndyoceras,* and (d) *Megatherium*

has proceeded. This question arose because of two characteristics of the fossil record. One characteristic is the apparent stability of different species through millions of years. Often more species appeared *unchanged* than changed during long periods of time. The second characteristic is the disappearance of many of the long-surviving species and the sudden appearance of new species during a short period of time. The fossils of new species increased rapidly in number and then another long period of little change began. These long stable periods followed by short, rapid bursts in the rate of evolution are referred to as **punctuated equilibria** and illustrated in Figure 16.20.

During the periods of greater change, the relatively rapid shift from old to new species left gaps in the fossil record. Is the record incomplete at these points or did evolution jump many of the apparent gaps?

Recent studies of chromosomes from organisms of different taxonomic groups show that chromosomes have changed significantly during evolution. The theory of punctuated equilibria draws upon these studies to explain evolution. Briefly stated, the theory says that chromosomal rearrangements have caused major changes in species in relatively little time. Although the mutation rate may not have increased, the rearrangement of genes on chromosomes would have caused major changes in the effects of many genes. The genes that control the development of organisms would have operated differently, resulting in new types of organisms. All the chromosomal changes could have taken place within a few thousand to tens of thousands of years.

Many features of the theory of punctuated equilibria are attractive. The time periods described in the theory fit the shorter periods of change

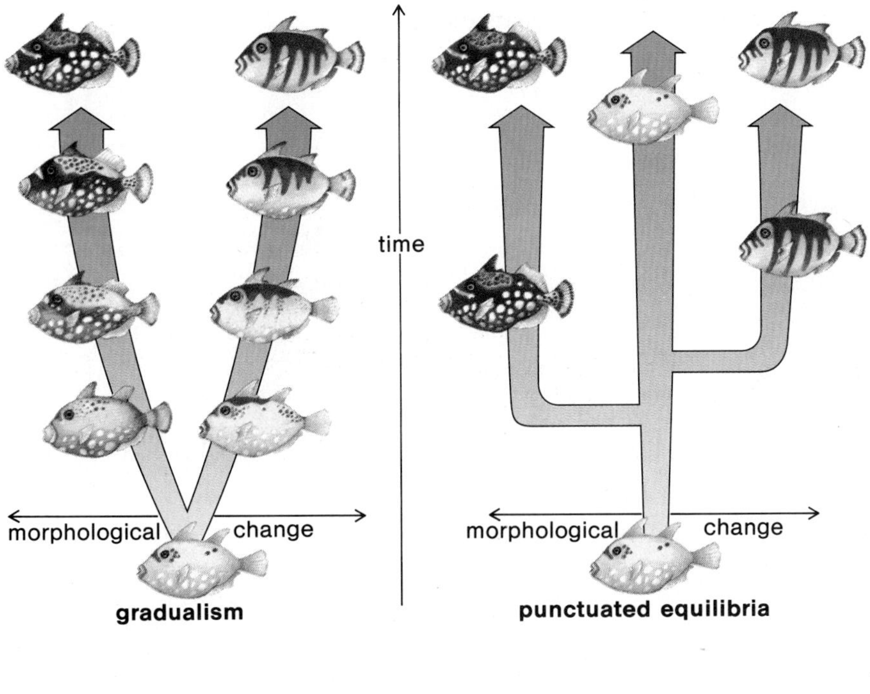

FIGURE 16.20 Two models for the rate of speciation. The traditional model (a) contends that new species branch off the parent species as small populations. Species descended from a common ancestor become more and more unlike as they acquire new adaptations. According to the model of punctuated equilibria (b), a new species changes the most at the time it branches from a parent species and changes little for the rest of its existence.

MASS EXTINCTIONS

A species may become extinct because its habitat has been destroyed or because its environment has changed in a smaller way that is unfavorable to the species. For example, if ocean temperatures fall a few degrees, many species that are otherwise well adapted, may perish. Evolutionary changes that affect one species living in a particular environment may result in changes to other species in that same environment.

The average rate of extinction is usually between two and five families of organisms per million years. However, there have been instances in the history of Earth when global environmental changes have been so rapid and disruptive that a majority of species died out. During these periods of mass extinctions, more than 19 families of organisms may have been destroyed in a million years.

One mass extinction occurred about 65 million years ago. During the late Cretaceous period, more than half of the marine species and many land plant and animal species (including nearly all species of dinosaurs) died. The climate was cooling at that time, and the shallow seas were receding from the continental lowlands.

There also is evidence indicating that at least two asteroids or comets struck Earth while the Cretaceous extinctions were in progress. Sediments deposited between the Mesozoic and Cenozoic eras are composed of a thin layer of clay enriched with iridium, an element very rare on Earth but common in meteorites and other debris that occasionally falls to Earth (Figure A). Luis W. Alvarez and his colleagues have studied the clay, and they believe it to be the fallout from a huge cloud of dust that billowed into the atmosphere when an asteroid hit Earth. The cloud would have blocked sunlight and disturbed the climate for several years.

The evidence for asteroid collisions at the end of the Cretaceous period is credible, but critics of the hypothesis point out that the extinctions, while

FIGURE A   A layer of iridium-rich sediment (the dark band) is located between Mesozoic and Cenozoic sediments. Iridium, an element rare on Earth, is thought to indicate a collision between a large asteroid and Earth. This collision may have caused a mass extinction. The coin near the center of the photograph provides a sense of scale.

rapid on a geologic time scale, were not *that* abrupt. Many geologists and paleontologists believe that changes in climate due to factors other than asteroids are sufficient to account for the mass extinctions. One surprising discovery is that mass extinction events appear to occur regularly every 26 to 28 million years.

Whatever the cause, mass extinctions affect biological diversity, but there is a creative side to the destruction. The species that survive eventually fill many of the niches vacated by the extinctions. The world might be a very different place today if a significant number of dinosaur species had managed to escape the Cretaceous extinctions.

reflected in some parts of the fossil record. Major chromosomal changes could have occurred in these lengths of time. Although natural selection usually operates slowly, it still would have produced its own effects on each change through the period of years involved. Thus, the theory of punctuated equilibria cannot be separated completely from the theory of natural selection. The two views of evolution are closely interrelated.

Scientists are cautious in accepting revisions of theories. The burden of supplying evidence rests with those who propose the changes. The theory of natural selection has been modified by additions in the past. In fact, the concepts of mutations and major chromosomal changes constitute two of those additions. So far, the idea that evolution could occur by *successive* major changes in a brief geologic time has not been firmly established.

The prevailing view is that a species that survives *one* such major change would almost certainly be out of step in some ways with its new genetic and environmental relationships. A long period of natural selection would be required to obtain the best combination of alleles for successful adaptation. Supporters of the theory of punctuated equilibria view natural selection as the ''fine tuning'' of evolution.

Did major changes really occur so close together in geologic time? If so, some biologists predict that punctuated equilibria and natural selection will eventually become two parts of an expanded theory of evolution.

CONNECTIONS

The theory of punctuated equilibria, a proposed alternative to the more gradual process of natural selection, still supports the idea of evolution—the major unifying theme of biology.

CHECK AND CHALLENGE

1. Why did Darwin have difficulty explaining variation within a species?

2. Compare and contrast gene pools and allele frequencies.

3. What factors can change the equilibrium of a gene pool? Explain how they work.

4. What are isolating mechanisms and how do they operate? Give examples.

5. What is the difference between microevolution and macroevolution?

6. Explain the statement, ''Natural selection acts on populations, not individuals.''

Summary

Charles Darwin, while traveling on the *Beagle*, gathered large quantities of data on variation within species and diversity among species. From these and other sources, Darwin formulated his theory of evolution by natural selection. Darwin called the deliberate actions of animal breeders *artificial selection* to distinguish it from *natural selection,* which occurred in nature. Modern studies support Darwin's theory of evolution by natural selection. A modern understanding of variations among individuals in a species explains how they provide the raw material on which natural selection acts.

Population genetics has made it possible to determine the rate at which changes accumulate in populations of organisms. Five factors can influence change in the frequencies of alleles—mutations, gene flow, genetic drift, natural selection, and nonrandom mating.

Microevolution constitutes the genetic changes that occur within populations and species that lead to the development of new species. Macroevolution is evolution above the species level. Microevolution leads to macroevolution.

Isolating mechanisms speed up the process of speciation. Small, isolated populations of organisms evolve much more rapidly than large populations. Geographical, ecological, behavioral, seasonal, and mechanical isolation all occur and function in natural populations. Other types of isolating mechanisms include prevention of gamete fusion, failure of the zygote to develop normally, and failure of the organism to become established in nature.

The theory of punctuated equilibria suggests that long periods of evolutionary stability are interspersed with brief periods of rapid change. Many biologists expect that a record of both a slow, steady rate and of punctuated equilibria will be found as more data become available.

Key Concepts

Use the following concepts to develop a concept map. Include additional terms as you need them.

artificial selection	isolating mechanisms
diversity	mutations
evolution	natural selection
gene pool	extinction
gene flow	speciation
genetic recombination	variations

Reviewing Ideas

1. Explain how adaptations in beak structure could help the finches of the Galápagos Islands survive in their new environment.

2. Describe the founder effect and explain how it functions.

3. What are some similarities and differences between artificial and natural selection?

4. What reptile characteristics does *Archaeopteryx* have? What bird characteristics? Why is the fossil significant?

5. What were the factors affecting moth survival in the study performed in England? In the Michigan mouse-and-owl study?

6. What factors influence natural selection when strains of bacteria become resistant to penicillin?

7. Explain the meaning of the sentence, "Mutations supply the raw material for evolution."

8. What is the difference between genetics and population genetics?

9. How does gene flow differ from genetic drift? How are they similar?

10. Why is macroevolution so difficult to observe?

11. How does the theory of punctuated equilibria differ from the traditional view of evolution? How are these ideas related?

12. What are some of the similarities and differences between the founder effect and adaptive radiation?

13. Explain how different factors affect gene pools.

Using Concepts

1. Why are island populations so important in the study of evolution?

2. Explain the difference between adaptation and natural selection.

3. Explain how radioactive dating methods contribute to the study of evolution.

4. If evolution is defined as change through time, what is changing?

5. Explain why populations evolve although organisms within the population do not.

6. Is today's human gene pool in equilibrium? Why or why not?

7. Where would you go to look for a "living fossil"? Explain your reasoning.

8. Mountain goats live at high altitudes in very rocky terrain. What are some evolutionary mechanisms that operate in such an environment and what might their effects be on the goat population?

Synthesis

1. Review Chapters 1, 12, and 13. Explain how the findings of other scientists influenced both Darwin's theory of evolution by natural selection and the modern explanation of the theory.

2. Relate the forms of isolation presented in this chapter to the problems of maintaining species diversity discussed in Chapter 5. What similarities and differences can you find?

3. Many animals have increased in size throughout their evolutionary history. How would an increase in size improve an animal's chance for survival?

Extensions

1. Write a letter to Charles Darwin, and explain to him how he could strengthen his theory of evolution by natural selection.

2. Write a short story or poem about a pair of parakeets that arrive on an uninhabited island in the Pacific Ocean.

3. Write a short story or poem about a female frog who has a gene mutation that has caused her to ignore the mating calls of the males of her species.

4. Select a favorite organism and make an evolutionary tree indicating its close relatives and major adaptive improvements.

5. Create a new organism in an environment of your choosing, sketch the organism's evolution, and relate its evolution to its geographic movement on a fictitious map. Include as many isolating factors as you can.

CONTENTS

Human Evolution

*W*hat does it mean to be *human*? Who were the first humans? It is impossible to say for sure. Each of us is a new combination of inherited bits and pieces contributed by all our ancestors and shaped by the environment in which we live.

Ten thousand years ago, human ancestors may have been tribal, living in forests and along rivers, perhaps early agriculturists. They may have never touched a piece of metal. A million years before that, they did not even look like us: their brains were smaller, they could not talk as we do, and they may not have known of fire. Perhaps they wore only skins and ate berries, roots, and small animals.

Through an evolutionary approach we can find out how it is that humans have a comparatively larger and more complex brain. Such a brain enables us to read, to write, to build cities, and to fly to the moon. We can learn how it is that humans can walk upright, speak, and speculate about themselves.

This chapter examines how primates are alike and different and how biochemistry helps explain primate relationships. It also discusses how the comparison of primate fossils with bones of modern primates helps establish relationships and a tentative ancestry of humans.

*W*hat different organisms can you identify from these carvings?

*W*hat activity is shown?

◆ *Petroglyphs at Newspaper Rock State Park, Utah.*

FIGURE 17.1 Notice how the thumb and fingers of this batter's hands point in opposite directions.

Determining Relationships

17.1   Primate Patterns

Humans, monkeys, and apes are mammals that are very similar in the details of their anatomy. They are, therefore, classified in the order Primates, along with animals such as lemurs and tarsiers. Most primates are tree climbers, and have structures and behaviors that relate to their way of life.

Chimpanzees and other great apes have the typical primate shoulder structure, although they spend most of their time on the ground. The ape leg and foot structure is adapted to bear a major portion of the individual's weight. The fingers of primates are well developed and flexible, giving the animals a powerful grasp. Most primates also possess an opposable thumb, which can be brought forward and inward until it touches the surface of the palm and the tips of the other fingers, as shown in Figure 17.1. Primate fingers usually have nails, rather than claws, and are extremely sensitive, allowing better tactile control when manipulating objects.

The eyes of primates are directed forward instead of to the side. Both eyes view the same object from slightly different angles. This binocular vision allows the brain to perceive the object in three dimensions and to accurately judge distances. The brains of most primates are exceptionally large and complex compared to those of most other mammals (including whales, dolphins, and porpoises) and allow for highly developed learned behavior. Primates also have a sense of color, something most other mammals lack.

FIGURE 17.2 A juvenile chimpanzee, *Pantroglodytes troglodytes*, exhibiting social behavior by requesting food from its mother.

Primates tend to be **omnivorous**, that is, they eat a wide variety of foods. They gather their food in social groups and have well-established patterns of communication that include elaborate body language and complex vocal signals and calls (Figure 17.2). Primates also share a common birth pattern, that is, they bear generally only one offspring at a time. This pattern provides for extended care and nurturing of the young.

Primates show a unity in all patterns. However, there is a great deal of diversity within the order itself. Figure 17.3 shows some of the different primate species. In what ways are they different?

To answer the question ''What is a human?'' we need to understand the ways in which modern humans differ from other animals, especially other primates. One difference is the presence of a relatively larger and more complex brain. Humans also have other unique physical characteristics. Those that are especially significant include a skeleton adapted for upright, or **bipedal** (by PEE duhl), walking and hands that provide both a powerful grip and permit extremely fine manipulations. Although these features are found to some degree in many primates, they are distinguished in humans by their greater degree of development and use. Controlling and coordinating these characteristics is the human brain that, with additional parts of the body, enables the most distinctively human trait—speech.

FIGURE 17.3 Although primates share many characteristics, there is also great diversity within the group. Weights listed are ranges.

Galago 125-300g

Tarsier 80-165g

Squirrel monkey 0.75-1.1kg

Gibbon 4-8kg

Gorilla 70-275kg

FOCUS ON *The Estrus Cycle*

One of the most important physiological differences between humans and other primates is their reproductive cycle. All primates have an estrus cycle, called the menstrual cycle in humans. Although most cycles fall within approximately a four-week period, humans alone lack the phase of "heat," or estrus, that is common to most mammals. In most primates, this period lasts about three to five days when the female is ovulating. In some monkeys and chimpanzees, the genital region shows pronounced swelling that attracts male sexual attention. Female chimpanzees present themselves for mating only at this time, and a female may mate with all the adult males in the area.

Humans are unique in that they have lost this combination of physiology and behavior associated with ovulation. Women can choose to be sexually active at any time in their cycle. The stage of the cycle cannot be detected through any obvious visual sign.

The loss of the obvious visual signs of estrus may be associated with the development in humans of relatively permanent male-female bonds that do not depend on the female's monthly cycle. Some biologists hypothesize that this bonding helped establish male cooperation in child rearing and protection. Such behaviors may have led to the development of social groups and communities.

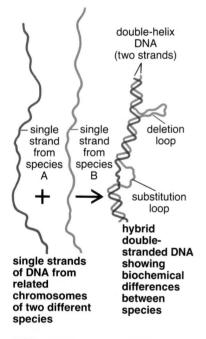

FIGURE 17.4 A single DNA strand from one species and one from the same portion of a related chromosome of another species can be compared. Wherever the two strands are alike they form the typical double helix of a DNA molecule. The more closely they fit together, the more closely they are related.

17.2   Biochemical Comparisons

Only one species of human, **Homo sapiens** (*Homo* = man; *sapiens* = wise), exists today. There are no genetic barriers to mating among modern humans. The genetic differences between human groups are the result of long periods of social and geographic separation.

Most human characteristics have definite genetic roots. Scientists estimate that there are between 50 000 and 100 000 human genes, but only some 6000 have been identified. We know the actual map positions of only about a third of that number. Many characteristics once thought to be determined in a simple manner have been found to be controlled by the complex interaction of many genes. As a result of complex gene interactions and of environmental influences, few traits are determined as simply as the ones Mendel studied in his garden peas.

Human facial features, body size, and body shape are among the physical characteristics that are difficult to investigate. All of these characteristics are determined by several different genes. Moreover, the environment can greatly influence how the genes are expressed and hence the degree to which the traits develop. For example, improved diets throughout much of the world generally have led to increased body size and weight.

Though the current knowledge of human genetics cannot provide a complete understanding of our evolutionary history, geneticists and biochemists have found a means of gathering crucial data. They can analyze the structure of the DNA of human genes and of proteins coded for by these genes. They can then compare those structures with those of the DNA and proteins of other organisms. The comparisons can yield information about human evolution (Figure 17.4).

Biological Challenges

THE MOTHER OF US ALL?

Is it likely that all modern humans descended from one female who lived in Africa about 200 000 years ago? That idea is one possible interpretation of data collected from research on mitochondrial DNA (mtDNA).

Mitochondria have their own DNA. Unlike nuclear DNA, however, mitochondrial DNA does not come from both parents. Although sperm contain mitochondria that provide energy for locomotion, the mitochondria are not contained in the portion of the sperm that penetrates the ovum.

The ovum contains numerous mitochondria, which are replicated in the fertilized egg and passed on to all offspring cells during the development of the fetus. Therefore, all the mitochondria in your cells, whether you are male or female, are derived from your mother.

The maternal transmission of mtDNA in humans has continued since the beginning of the species. In fact, because mtDNA is transmitted only through females, it is theoretically possible to trace the origin of mtDNA to one or to several females who were the first members of a species that was not fully human. How long ago did that species live?

To answer that question, we need to have some indication of the variety of mtDNA among individuals and how frequently mtDNA mutates to produce those changes. Molecular biologists know that mtDNA accumulates mutations five to ten times faster than does nuclear DNA. This characteristic makes mtDNA a good "clock" for measuring short spans in evolutionary time—spans measured in hundreds of thousands of years rather than millions of years.

Molecular biologists at the University of California at Berkeley used restriction enzymes to cut up the mtDNA from 21 geographically and racially diverse individuals. They then measured the amount of variation in the fragments. That data, combined

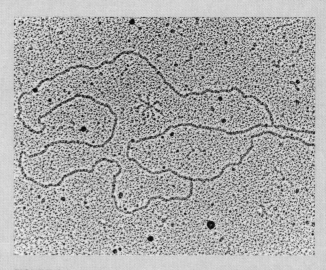

FIGURE A Electron micrograph of mitochondrial DNA

with the information about how fast mtDNA accumulates mutations, led the researchers to conclude that it would have taken between 150 000 and 200 000 years for modern humans to have accumulated that amount of variation from one ancestral female. The biologists also concluded that the ancestors of modern humans originated in Africa.

Other biologists question these data and the conclusions. They contend that mtDNA accumulates mutations more slowly. A slower rate means that it would have taken much longer for the amount of variation in modern mtDNA to accumulate, and that ancestral humans may have lived about 500 000 years ago.

There are still many questions to be answered about a potential "mitochondrial Eve." Most important is the relationship between this hypothetical individual and the evolution of anatomically modern humans. This problem is further complicated in that traits controlled by mtDNA are subjected to the pressure of both natural selection and the interaction of mtDNA with nuclear DNA.

TABLE 17.1 Chimpanzee and Human Protein Differences		
Protein	**Number of Amino Acids**	**Amino Acid Differences**
Hemoglobin	579	1
Myoglobin	153	1
Cytochrome *c*	104	0
Serum albumin	580	7

Biochemical tests of DNA and protein similarities indicate that chimpanzees are the closest living relatives to humans. Indeed, DNA comparisons show that modern humans and chimpanzees are roughly 98 percent genetically the same. Table 17.1 lists several proteins found in both species and indicates how their numbers of amino acids differ. Other tests of gene similarities indicate almost the same closeness of relationship between humans and gorillas. The evolutionary distance between chimpanzees and humans and between humans and gorillas may be less than the distance between foxes and dogs and about the same as that between zebras and horses.

Most of the biochemical data are expressed as percentages of agreement in the amino acid sequences of proteins and in the nucleotide sequences of DNA. Some of the data are based on chromosome banding techniques and comparisons of the banding patterns between different species (Chapter 12).

Unfortunately, most proteins and DNA do not survive in fossils. Otherwise, we could perform biochemical tests of kinship between extinct species and the one living species of *Homo*. Most of the evidence for human evolution, therefore, has come from the study of the physical structure of fossils.

17.3 Skeletal Comparisons

Measures of intelligence and brain size, once thought to indicate evolutionary superiority, are no longer used as criteria in establishing the pattern of human evolution. Many characteristics of "intelligence" are not uniquely ours. Other animals display these characteristics in varying degrees. For example, chimpanzees use twigs as tools to harvest ants and termites (Figure 17.5). Early anthropologists (*anthrop* = man, *logos* = study), scientists who study human evolution and culture, thought that brain volume or size was an indication of intelligence. We now know this is not strictly true. Some human ancestors had average brain sizes larger than ours. The variation among modern humans is so great that measures of size have no significance.

FIGURE 17.5 This chimpanzee is using a twig to pull termites out of the tree.

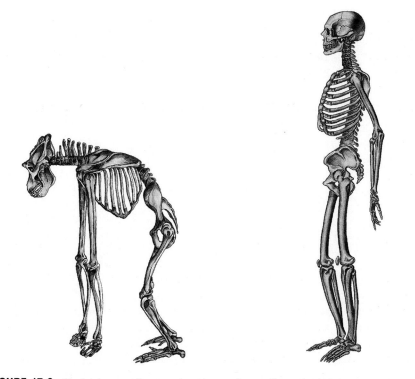

FIGURE 17.6 Skeletal proportions and postures of a gorilla and a human

If biochemical analysis and measurements of brain size cannot help establish the human ancestry, what can? Anthropologists usually concentrate on the morphologic (mor foh LAW jik), or structural, evidence from the fossil record. Fossils tentatively identified as human ancestors are compared with each other and with the skeletons of modern humans and other primates (Figure 17.6). Family trees developed from this method are very similar to ones developed from biochemical studies. Figure 17.7 (on the following page) compares a morphologic family tree with its biochemical counterpart. Notice the different relationships shown for certain animals in the two schemes, especially those among the primates.

To begin to understand who our ancestors were and what they were like, we must study and interpret their fossil remains. Unfortunately, only a small percentage of the bones from all the individuals who ever lived have survived in the fossil record. Few complete fossil skeletons have been found. Anthropologists usually must make their inferences about human ancestry by examining small portions of skulls, a few teeth, and occasionally part of a leg or arm bone.

Fossil **hominids** (HAH mih nidz)—bipedal humanlike animals that belong to the same family as modern humans—have been known and studied for many years. Only within the past few decades, however, have new finds allowed anthropologists to make more concrete inferences about human ancestry. They base their hypotheses on a careful comparison of features of the newly found fossils with other fossils, modern human remains, and the skeletons of other large primates.

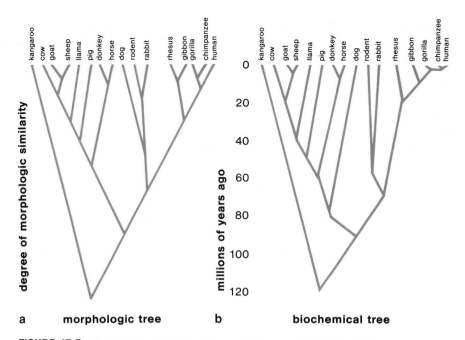

FIGURE 17.7 Family trees based on (a) morphology and (b) biochemistry. Morphologic trees are based on physical characteristics. In this tree, the short distance between the branches leading to humans and chimps indicates that they are morphologically similar. The great distance between the branches leading to humans and kangaroos indicates they are not very similar. Biochemical trees represent the degree of relatedness of organisms based on biochemical data such as amino acid sequences in proteins or base sequences in DNA.

Some of the most important features used in comparing fossils include the skull; the pelvis, or hips; the backbone; and the femur, or thighbone. Important structures of the skull include the jaws and teeth and the cranium, the bones that enclose the brain. Table 17.2 summarizes some of the most common skeletal features anthropologists use to determine the relationship of fossil remains to modern primates. Study the table and the photographs in this chapter. See if you can find examples of the characteristics described.

The shape of the teeth and their wear patterns give anthropologists an idea of the diet of the individual and also provide clues about its behavior (Figure 17.8). If a newly found fossil has teeth similar to those of another fossil, an anthropologist might consider the two to be related. Conversely, a great deal of difference in these features would lead to the conclusion that the two individuals are not closely related.

The amount of curvature and the location of the curves in the backbone can indicate the way in which the individual moved. Likewise, the form of the femur and especially its relationship to the pelvis may indicate whether the individual walked on two legs or on four. (See **Appendix 17A**, Physical Adaptations.) The form of the skull also is used to classify fossil remains and can indicate how much muscle was present. Examine the skulls in Figure 17.9. Which individual probably had more powerful jaws?

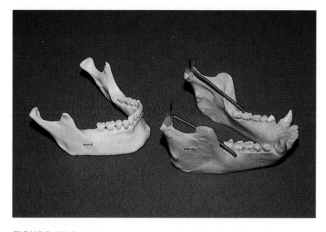

FIGURE 17.8 Differences in tooth size and shape can indicate differences in diet and behavior. Which jaw is human?

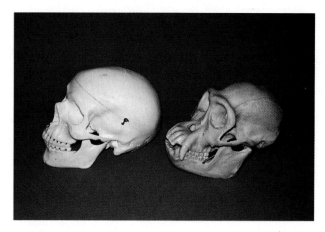

FIGURE 17.9 A human skull and a chimpanzee skull. What differences can you see?

TABLE 17.2
Comparison of Ape and Hominid Characteristics

Characteristic	Ape	Hominid
Posture	bent over or quadrupedal; "knuckle-walking" common	upright or bipedal
Leg and arm length	arms longer than legs; adapted for swinging by arm (brachiation), usually among trees	legs usually longer than arms; adapted for striding
Feet	low arches; opposable big toes for grasping	high arches; big toes in line for walking
Teeth	prominent; large gaps between canines and nearby teeth	reduced; reduced or absent gaps
Skull	bent forward from spinal column; rugged; prominent brow ridges	upright on spinal column; smooth
Face	jaws jut out; very heavy; very wide nasal opening; sloping	vertical profile; more distinct chin; narrow nasal opening, prominent nasal spine
Brain size	280–705 cm^3 (living species)	400–2000 cm^3 (fossil to present)
Age at puberty	usually 10–13 years	usually 13 years or less
Breeding season	estrus at various times	no definite time for modern humans; not known for early hominids

FIGURE 17.10 The stratification of rock layers in this mountainside was exposed when a highway was built. Fossils of different ages are found in different layers.

Try Investigation 17A, Interpretation of Fossils.

17.4 Dating Remains

The fossil record is incomplete, and the remains that do exist are usually only fragmentary. To begin to build a record of human ancestry, we must know how old these bits and pieces of fossils are. Strange shapes and sizes may suggest all sorts of intriguing ideas and hypotheses about our evolutionary history. Yet these hypotheses can be taken seriously only if we have reliable dates for the fossils.

The critical problem of determining the age of fossils can be handled several ways. The first is through the study of the layers of sand, silt, clay, and other types of rock and their relationship to each other. The analysis of these layers—a process called stratigraphy—provides a rough picture of Earth's geological history. From this information we can arrange the fossils in order of age depending on the rock layer in which they were found (Figure 17.10).

The second way to determine fossil age is by studying the fossils themselves. Fossil types are not usually the same in different rock layers. They show evolution through time and thus provide clues to when the organisms lived, particularly if the time sequence of the rocks is worked out. Yet this chronology only provides relative dates—identifying which organisms are older and which are younger. Absolute dates in years are frequently lacking.

A third technique for obtaining dates is provided by atomic physics. Certain radioactive elements discharge energy at constant rates. Once the rate for a specific element is known, a date may be assigned by determining how much of the element is present. One long-lasting radioactive substance, potassium-40, breaks down into the gas argon at a constant and known rate. Another radioactive element is carbon-14, which reverts to the common form of nitrogen, nitrogen-14. (See **Appendix 4A**, Radiometric Dating Methods, for more information.)

Although much more is known now about our fossil ancestors than a hundred years ago, there is still a vast amount we do not know. Every new fossil discovery either supports a generally accepted hypothesis or places that hypothesis in doubt. The second half of this chapter presents some of the common hypotheses regarding human ancestry.

CHECK AND CHALLENGE

1. Describe the characteristics common to most primates.
2. How are biochemical comparisons helpful in determining evolutionary relationships?
3. What advantages do skeletal comparisons have over biochemical comparisons?
4. What are some of the most important skeletal features used to make comparisons?
5. Why is it important to establish dates for human fossils?

Human Origins and Populations _____

17.5   Hominids from Africa

Today anthropologists know that the human lineage began with primate ancestors from whom various hominids evolved. Before then, the hominid lineage and the lineage that led to other modern primates shared a common ancestor. Not all of these organisms were human ancestors, so we only can hypothesize which ones were. Very ancient fossil samples from Africa indicate that Africa may have been the earliest home of the prehominids. Some anthropologists believe that one of these groups may have been the common ancestor of African apes and of the hominids, but so far no concrete fossil evidence has been found.

Variations in the characteristics of prehominid fossil samples make their classification and naming difficult. The variations within this group could indicate distinct species that varied in space and time. It is also possible that the differences are based on sex. Size differences between the sexes are common in many animals. Figure 17.11 shows skulls of a male and a female from a prehistoric human population about 1000 years ago, and of a male and a female gorilla from a single population. As you can see, there

> # CONNECTIONS
>
> *The morphology of an organism—for example, long arms—can be an adaptation to its environment.*

FIGURE 17.11   Variation, the basis for evolutionary change, is present in all species. In most primates, sex differences are a major cause of variability: (a) a human male skull (bottom) and a female skull (top); (b) casts of a male gorilla skull (bottom) and a female gorilla skull (top). What differences can you see between the male and female skulls?

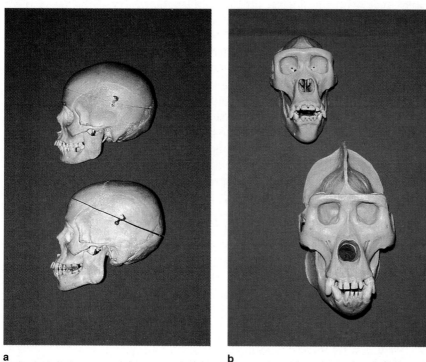

a   b

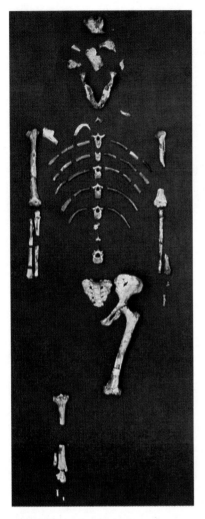

FIGURE 17.12 Lucy is the most complete skeleton known from the genus *Australopithecus*. She stood only slightly more than a meter tall and lived about 3.2 million years ago.

is a great deal of variation between the male and female of each pair. The male human skull is noticeably larger and heavier than the female skull. The male gorilla skull is much bigger and heavier and has much larger teeth than the female gorilla skull, yet they belong to the same species.

The first recognizable hominids appeared between 4 million and 3.75 million years ago in Tanzania and Ethiopia. Mary Leakey and her colleagues uncovered the fossilized footprints of hominids that walked on two legs. The fossils have been firmly dated to 3.75 million years ago. In addition, almost half of a complete skeleton of an individual called "Lucy" (Figure 17.12) as well as other fossil finds have been less firmly dated at between 3 and 4 million years ago. Anthropologists generally agree that these finds represent a distinct group of hominids, and they have classified this group as the **australopithecines** (AH strahl oh PITH uh seenz).

Different forms of australopithecines have been found in East and South Africa and have been dated to different times. *Australopithecus afarensis*, like Lucy, lived in East Africa and is the first definite hominid. *Australopithecus africanus* lived in southern Africa at a slightly later time. There is considerable doubt about the relationship of these groups to each other, as well as to modern humans. However, anthropologists are convinced that all these australopithecines were indeed bipedal. A detailed analysis of the structure of the hip, femur, and foot bones of Lucy and other individuals shows that these hominids were capable of walking upright, though not exactly as modern humans do.

Although these populations shared some traits with humans, there are other characteristics that show how different from us they actually were. Their relatively long arms indicate that perhaps they were more apelike in appearance. Anthropologists do not agree whether the long arms were adaptations to a tree-dwelling life or whether this characteristic was a carryover from an earlier ancestor.

When they are compared with the earlier prehominid fossils, the australopithecines generally have smaller canine teeth—the larger pointed "fangs" you see in the mouths of cats and dogs. The cheek teeth are relatively large and have a thick coating of enamel, possibly an adaptation for eating large quantities of fruit, seeds, tubers, roots, and pods—some of which may have been quite tough. There is no concrete evidence that these hominids used or manufactured tools. If they did use tools, it is possible that they used materials similar to those used by modern primate groups—twigs, sticks, leaves, and unmodified rocks. These types of tools certainly would not survive until today.

At some point between 2.5 and 2 million years ago African hominids underwent adaptive radiation. By the later date, at least two, probably three, and perhaps even more species of hominids were present, although no evidence exists for more than three in any one part of Africa. In eastern Africa, a group of large and robust australopithecines, called *Australopithecus boisei*, lived at the same time as a larger-brained hominid called ***Homo habilis*** (Figure 17.13). Many anthropologists hypothesize that *Homo habilis* was the first member of our own genus *Homo,* but there is still much debate on the subject. In southern Africa, there were two other groups of australopithecines—*Australopithecus robustus* and *Australopithecus africanus*—and possibly *Homo habilis* as well.

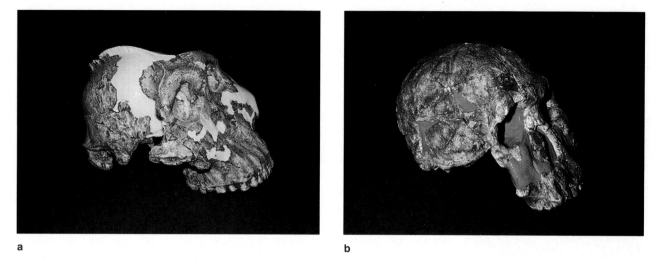

a

b

FIGURE 17.13 (a) An *Australopithecus boisei* skull. (b) *Homo habilis* skull number 1470, named for its index number at the National Museum of Kenya, East Africa. This skull is at least 1.8 million years old. Skull fragments of other individuals have been found, but skull 1470 is the most nearly complete.

17.6 The First Humans

By about 1.50 million years ago, it seems that *Homo habilis* disappeared from Africa and was replaced by an even larger-brained hominid, **Homo erectus**. *Homo erectus* is the first widely distributed hominid. The species appeared earliest in Africa. By one million years ago, the species was present in southeastern and eastern Asia and survived in that area until 300 000 years ago. In that span of time, the physical record shows *Homo erectus* to have remained unchanged.

    Homo erectus resembled later species of *Homo* (excepting modern humans) in both body size and robustness. Larger-brained than *Homo habilis* (about 937 cm³ compared to 640 cm³), the species had front teeth that were generally as big as those of some earlier hominids. The cheek teeth and face, however, were smaller (Figure 17.14). It seems that *Homo*

Try Investigation 17B, Archeological Interpretation.

FIGURE 17.14 Two views of a reconstruction of a *Homo erectus* skull. The original fossil skull fragments were unearthed near Peking, China. More *Homo erectus* fossils have since been discovered in China, Java, East Africa, Europe, and the Middle East. Compare these skulls with those in Figures 17.13, 17.15, and 17.16.

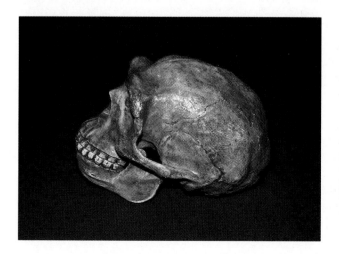

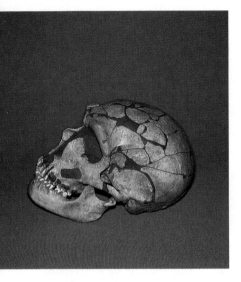

FIGURE 17.15 A fossil archaic *Homo sapiens* skull. The disappearance of these widely distributed archaic people has never been satisfactorily explained. They survived as recently as 40 000 to 50 000 years ago.

erectus groups were manufacturing large, symmetrically flaked stone tools, called hand axes. There is also evidence that some *Homo erectus* populations used fire.

Toward the end of *Homo erectus'* occupation, there is fossil evidence of another group of hominids, archaic *Homo sapiens*, formerly called Neanderthals. Archaic *Homo sapiens* were much more robust, and the muscle attachment sites on their bones indicate they were far stronger than we are (Figure 17.15). Their teeth were larger and more worn. The wear might have resulted from using their teeth as tools—chewing hides to soften them—or from a diet of tough or gritty foods. These archaic humans buried their dead—sometimes with flowers—and perhaps wore jewelry.

Archaic *Homo sapiens* spread out over much of Europe and southwestern Asia, but the fossil evidence for this group disappears about 30 000 years ago. Some anthropologists hypothesize that many, but not all, archaic human populations evolved into modern humans. Other anthropologists infer that all archaic human populations evolved into modern humans. Still others insist that all archaic *Homo sapiens* became extinct and were replaced by modern humans who evolved from unknown genetic stock. One scientist described the problem of trying to determine the genetic relationship between archaic *Homo sapiens* and an early species of modern humans as trying to establish the relationship between cars and buggies based on broken wheels and hubcaps. (See **Appendix 17B**, The Old Man from La Chapelle-aux-Saints.)

A case may be made, however, for the evolution of modern humans from a group of hominids that lived at the same time as archaic humans. These anatomically modern hominids (*Homo sapiens sapiens;* formerly called Cro-Magnon people), also exhibit a great deal of skeletal variation (Figure 17.16). The European fossil record indicates that anatomically modern humans replaced archaic humans in a rather complicated manner. Some early modern humans show primitive skeletal characteristics—large brows and teeth, for example. These traits might have been derived from

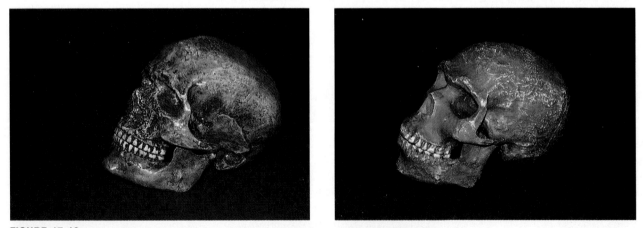

FIGURE 17.16 Two casts of anatomically modern human skulls, possibly representing two somewhat genetically different populations. These peoples, like all people today, have been classified as *Homo sapiens*.

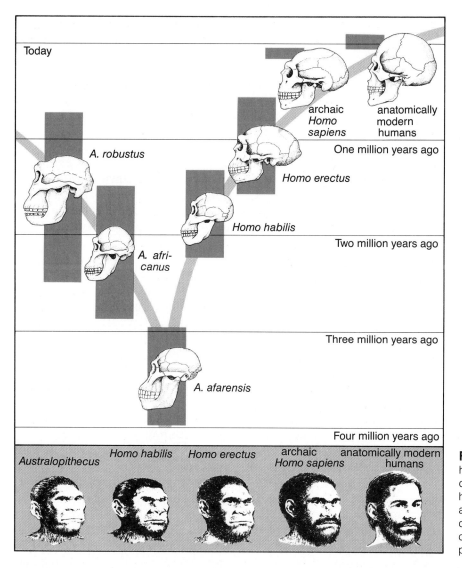

Today

A. robustus

archaic
Homo
sapiens

anatomically
modern
humans

One million years ago

Homo erectus

Homo habilis

A. afri-
canus

Two million years ago

Three million years ago

A. afarensis

Four million years ago

Australopithecus   Homo habilis   Homo erectus   archaic
Homo sapiens   anatomically modern
humans

FIGURE 17.17 One hypothesis of human evolution. It is impossible to define the exact phylogeny of humans because numerous theories are being presented and many debates are taking place. New discoveries have thrown doubt on previously accepted theories.

mating with the archaic population, or they might be relics of more primitive ancestors elsewhere.

The origin of anatomically modern humans seems to lie outside of Europe. The leg-bone proportions of these people appear to resemble those of recent people from tropical and subtropical—rather than cold—environments. Evidence from southwestern Asia suggests that modern people had replaced the archaic populations there by 40 000 years ago. Before then, it is necessary to look to Africa for the origin of the earliest modern humans. Evolutionary events in Africa may have led to the emergence of modern humans, whose later migrations into Europe may have led to the extinction of archaic humans after first coexisting for several thousand years. Figure 17.17 represents one hypothesis of human evolution.

Certainly, modern humans of 30 000 to 35 000 years ago were *Homo sapiens*. They were cave dwellers and were taller than their ancestors.

Many were taller than most people today. Anthropologists also see important behavioral changes in the archaeological record. These changes include a large number of specialized bone and stone tools, shifts in hunting patterns, the use and control of fire, the use of clothing, settlement patterns, population size, ecological range, art, and evidences of ritual activity. All these characteristics point to the emergence of a species possessing modern behavioral capabilities from a *Homo erectus* line.

If peoples who lived as recently as 30 000 to 40 000 years ago can leave behind questions that anthropologists cannot answer, it is easy to see that other questions about still older populations may always exist. The origins of human speech, for example, have not been mentioned because fossil evidence has not helped directly in discovering them. Yet the development of meaningful speech must have had a dramatic effect on the evolution of humans from that point onward. (See **Appendix 17C**, Cultural Evolution.)

17.7 Gene Pools

Much of the genetic variation found in the human population today was present at the beginning of the human lineage. In the past, genetic variation existed between populations of archaic peoples and anatomically modern peoples, and also within each population. At least three distinct modern human cultures existed in Europe at one time. Other cultures—each with a distinctive gene pool—probably lived on other continents. The genetic variation of earlier populations reflected the populations' geographic isolation from one another, as do today's human populations. The gene pools of some smaller human populations have changed significantly in modern times because of increased travel and colonization by groups from other cultures.

The ABO blood groups provide an example of how populations change through crossbreeding. Blood typing for ABO groups was discovered around 1900. About 1920, samples of blood from populations all over the world were analyzed for blood type. Geneticists found that most American Indians, Basques of northern Spain, and Australian Aborigines had no I^B alleles. It now is believed that this gene was absent from these populations until crossbreeding introduced it.

Allele frequencies (such as blood types) can be used to determine genetic relationships between populations. The degree of similarity in the allele frequencies of two or more populations is known as biological distance. The more similar the allele frequencies of two populations, the less biological distance between them and the more genetically related they are. Scientists continue to accumulate more data on blood-group and other allele frequencies. Enough data now exists to draw maps showing the frequencies of alleles in various parts of the world. Study the allele-frequency map of Europe in Figure 17.18. Can you suggest some reasons that might explain the spreading and the different zones of frequency it produced?

Many genetic disorders are restricted to specific populations of people. Eye and hair color, hair texture, skin color, and many other traits also are different for different populations. These variations are evidence of long periods of geographic and partial genetic isolation between populations.

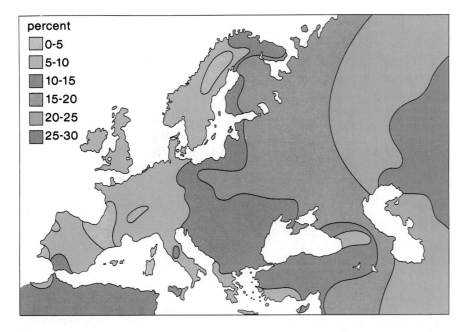

FIGURE 17.18 The distribution of the human blood group allele I^B for type B blood in Europe, western Asia, and northern Africa. The frequencies are expressed as percentages of the population in which the allele is found.

Differences in the gene pools of human populations give geneticists new insights into what formerly were called *races*. Easily visible characteristics such as facial structure, skin color, hair texture, presence or absence of facial hair, eye color, and others once led to racial classification. Research into other genetic traits has not preserved these divisions. In fact, classification by gene pools produces many times the number of human groups represented by traditional races. Nevertheless, all humans share genes that make them *Homo sapiens*. There are fewer genetic differences between any two groups of humans—no matter what their physical differences—than there are between chimpanzees and humans.

The members of different human populations are not as physically isolated as they once were. Travel, migration, and intermarriage have broken barriers. Exceptions are groups such as American Indians, whose populations have remained more isolated.

CHECK AND CHALLENGE _____

1. Name the fossil hominid groups that may have had some role in human evolution.
2. When does *Homo erectus* appear? Describe the physical appearance of this group.
3. How do archaic *Homo sapiens* (Neanderthal) differ from earlier groups?
4. What features are characteristic of anatomically modern hominids?

Summary

Human origins are apparently related to several extinct groups, the australopithecines, and *Homo erectus*. Anthropologists use various dating techniques combined with careful morphological examination of fossils to establish human ancestry. The existence of australopithecines has been traced back 3.75 million years. At some point, members of the australopithecine group coexisted with the first members of the genus *Homo*. Members of both these groups walked erect, may have used tools, and probably reflected a common ancestry long after the ancestors of modern apes branched off into their own lines of descent.

Modern *Homo sapiens* was becoming established as archaic *Homo sapiens* began to disappear and anatomically modern peoples became prominent. Then and now, a variety of different groups of humans existed.

Geneticists use information from modern human groups and primate groups to make inferences concerning relative genetic distance between populations. By studying human gene pools, they have found that there are numerous distinct human groups.

Key Concepts

Use these terms to develop a concept map of human evolution. Add additional terms as you need them.

evolution	fossils
biochemical comparisons	behavior
hominid	bipedal
Homo sapiens	populations
skeletal comparisons	*Homo*

Reviewing Ideas

1. How can genetics and the study of DNA help shed light on the origin of humans? What are the limitations to this method?

2. Why is intelligence no longer used to establish the pattern of human evolution?

3. What are some of the problems associated with studying human evolution through skeletal comparisons?

4. Why is it important to have more than one method for establishing the ages of fossils?

5. How can anthropologists determine if australopithecines were bipedal?

6. How do anatomically modern people differ from earlier populations of *Homo sapiens?*

7. How do modern humans differ from other primate groups?

8. What are five skeletal features used for determining evolutionary relationships?

9. What can an anthropologist infer from the shape of teeth and their wear patterns?

10. Why is stratigraphy important?

11. Who were the first possible hominids and about when did they originate?

12. When did the australopithecines appear and where are their fossils found?

13. How is *Homo erectus* different from earlier populations of hominids?

14. What do anthropologists learn from studying fossils?

Using Concepts

1. The pattern of life on Earth shows both unity and diversity. How are these concepts exhibited in the order Primates?

2. What may account for the diversity among the australopithecines?

3. What is the controversy about archaic *Homo sapiens?* Can you suggest some reasons why they might have disappeared?

4. Does the fossil record indicate physical diversity among the first anatomically modern people? How?

5. What types of mistakes can be made in fossil interpretation?

6. What effects can biochemical comparisons have on determining of evolutionary relationships?

Synthesis

1. How can diversity between populations come about? How does diversity within a population come about?

2. Is anthropology a science? Why or why not?

3. Relate the concept of species to fossil humans and modern human populations. Can the idea of species be applied to fossil humans? Defend your answer.

Extensions

1. The human skeleton is not well-adapted for walking upright, as indicated by the number of foot, knee, back, and neck problems in modern human populations. Design a better system for bipedalism.

2. The discovery of a *Homo habilis* fossil indicates that the individual was about 0.91−1.07 m tall (3 to 3.5 feet tall). Anthropologists estimate most australopithecines to be about 0.9 m (3 feet) tall. *Homo erectus*, on the other hand, is thought to be much taller—almost as tall as modern humans (1.7 m or more). What effect might this new discovery have on hypotheses concerning skeletal versus brain growth in hominid populations? Research the correlation between brain size and stature in fossil populations. Write an essay addressing this question.

Life Processes: Regulation and Homeostasis

*T*he collared lizard shown, *Crotaphytus*, is found in the desert regions of the United States. Because it cannot regulate its internal temperature efficiently, and desert nights can be quite cool, the lizard suns itself to warm up.

Organisms exist in constantly changing environments. In order to stay alive and function properly, all parts of an organism, as well as the organism itself, must maintain a biological balance within the immediate environment. This task is accomplished by a variety of mechanisms that work together to regulate the internal environment of all living things.

*I*n addition to temperature regulation, what other major problem do desert-dwelling organisms face?

*I*dentify some adaptations that allow organisms to survive desert conditions.

CONTENTS

Digestive Systems and Human Nutrition

*W*hat activity is depicted?

*W*hat do the different colors indicate and how would you explain their distribution?

*F*ood is essential for all organisms to survive. Green plants make their own, fungi absorb nutrients, birds eat seeds and insects, and cows eat hay, grass, and grains. Each of these organisms has a system of digestion that is adapted to the type of food the organism obtains.

Humans ingest an amazing variety of foods. Someone spending a Saturday at the mall may have a lunch of a hotdog or a hamburger with fries, several spicy tacos, or a salad, and a soft drink or milk. Dessert might be a candy bar, an ice cream cone, or frozen yogurt. Later in the afternoon, pizza, popcorn, and more soft drinks may be added to the digestive system. How does the human system handle such a diversity of material? Is it any wonder that indigestion and heartburn are not uncommon?

Processed and convenience foods are increasingly replacing more nutritious foods that better supply vitamins and minerals. Many studies have shown that the typical American diet contains too much fat, sugar, and salt. How does what you eat affect your health? What measures can you take to control your intake of potentially harmful substances? Can you have a healthy diet and still enjoy dessert? Can your diet as a teenager affect the quality of your life when you are older? This chapter examines how different organisms obtain and digest food, how the human digestive system operates, and the importance of maintaining a complete and well-balanced diet.

◆ *A computer-generated thermograph.*

Digestion

18.1 Digestion Inside and Outside Cells

You may recall from Chapter 6 that only relatively small molecules can pass through cell membranes. Most food particles that animals ingest are not molecular in size, however. Food that is ingested by animals must be broken down into molecules small enough to enter the cell. The processes that break down food are known collectively as **digestion**.

The breakdown of large pieces of food into smaller ones is the physical part of digestion. In many animals, movements of the digestive cavity help accomplish this task. The gizzard of a bird's digestive system, for example, is specialized to grind up food (Figure 18.1). Some birds swallow sand and small pebbles that aid the grinding action. Many other animals have teeth that cut or grind food into smaller pieces.

The processes of physical digestion, such as chewing, increase the surface area of food, thus enabling the chemical part of digestion to take place more easily. Chemical digestion involves the breaking down of complex food molecules into simpler ones. Enzymes in the various organs of the digestive tract control these chemical reactions. Without chemical digestion, nutrients obtained from large food molecules could not be absorbed and used by the organism.

Most plant digestion takes place inside the cells with foods the plant has made itself. This type of digestion is called **intracellular digestion**. A vacuole forms when a food particle is surrounded by a section of plasma

FIGURE 18.1 In some birds, food is temporarily stored in a crop. Farther along the digestive tract, a specialized part of the stomach—the gizzard—grinds up food to aid digestion. The walls of the gizzard are thick and muscular. Within the gizzard, too, is sand the bird has eaten.

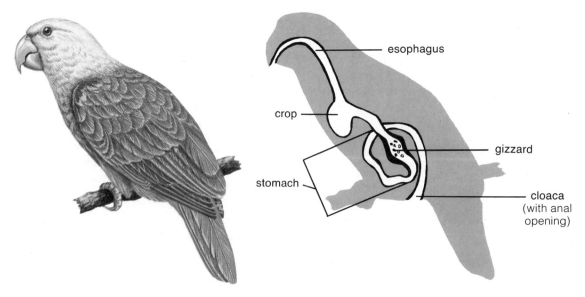

FIGURE 18.2 *(left)* Phase contrast micrograph of *Paramecium caudatum.* Can you identify the vacuoles in this photo?

FIGURE 18.3 *(right)* A Venus's-flytrap in action. As soon as an insect lands on a leaf, the spiked blades start to close. Once trapped, the insect is digested by plant enzymes secreted into special leaf cavities. Such carnivorous plants obtain some of their nitrogen from insect prey and may have evolved in nitrogen-deficient soils.

membrane. A lysosome containing the digestive enzymes fuses with the vacuole, and chemical digestion occurs within that new structure. The small molecules produced by this chemical digestion pass out of the vacuole into the cytosol. Only then can the nutrients be used by the cell. Digestion in unicellular organisms, such as the *Paramecium* shown in Figure 18.2, occurs in the same way.

Most animals rely on **extracellular digestion**—digestion that takes place outside the cells. In this case, enzymes are secreted from cells into a digestive cavity, where chemical digestion yields the simpler molecules that are then absorbed by the cells. In the digestive sac of a sea anemone, for example, certain cells lining the cavity secrete the digestive enzymes. In most animals, however, digestive enzymes are secreted by specialized tissues, or glands. Some herbivorous vertebrates, such as cows, even have special chambers that contain cellulose-digesting microorganisms. They thus are able to utilize plant fibers that normally would not be digested.

Some plants have the ability to capture insects and digest them in special cavities formed by the leaves. Figure 18.3 shows a Venus's-flytrap capturing an insect. After the insect is trapped, the leaf cells secrete enzymes that digest it.

Many organisms produce enzymes that digest food outside the organism itself and then absorb the nutrients into the cells. Fungi, for example, digest materials from dead plants and animals. Bread mold is a fungus that secretes enzymes that diffuse out of the cells to digest bread (Figure 18.4). The molds then absorb the products of digestion into their cells. Amino acids, sugars, minerals, water, and oxygen can diffuse into cells. Large molecules, however, cannot enter a cell by diffusion and are absorbed by other means.

The surface of a cell may fold inward, forming a small pocket. This process is called pinocytosis (PEE noh sy TOH sis). Some of the fluid surrounding the cell and containing the large nutrient molecules flows into the pocket. The edges of the pocket then close, forming a vacuole. Pinocytosis could be called "cell drinking." Many types of cells, including some in

FIGURE 18.4 Enzymes from bread mold diffuse into the bread, digesting complex carbohydrates to their component sugars. The sugars are then absorbed by the mold.

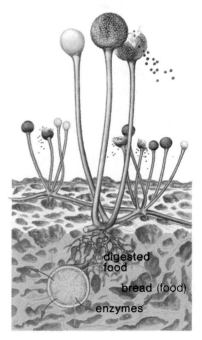

digested food

bread (food)

enzymes

FIGURE 18.5 Pinocytosis. How many infoldings or "pockets" can you count in this electron micrograph of a capillary endothelial cell?

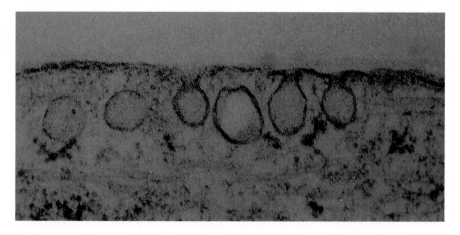

the human stomach and small intestine, take in large molecules by pinocytosis. (See Figure 18.5.)

Some cells take in solid pieces of food simply by surrounding the particles with extensions of the cell body. This process is called phagocytosis (FAYG oh sy TOH sis), or "cell eating." Both pinocytosis and phagocytosis are examples of endocytosis, described in Chapter 6. Figure 18.6 shows an *Amoeba* taking in food by surrounding it with a membrane and forming a vacuole. In the human bloodstream, white blood cells surround and consume bacteria in much the same way. (See Chapter 20.)

Protists such as *Paramecium* have permanent structures for taking in food. The cells lining the internal cavities of simple multicellular animals,

FIGURE 18.6 Phagocytosis. The protist *Amoeba* approaches food (a), begins to surround it (b), and forms a food vacuole (c).

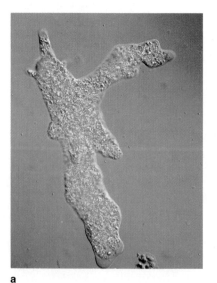

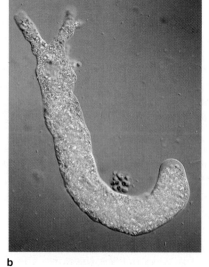

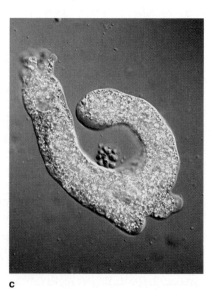

a

b

c

FOCUS ON *Ways to Obtain Nutrients*

Many types of animals live entirely on plant material. Most of these animals do not have enzymes that digest cellulose, the material from which wood and plant fibers are made. How then can these animals make use of cellulose? What modifications do the digestive systems of these animals have? Certain microorganisms that do have enzymes for digestion of cellulose live in the digestive tracts of these animals. The microorganisms are able to produce the enzymes that the animals lack. For example, termites exist on a diet of wood, which is mostly cellulose. Bacteria and protozoa in the termite gut digest the cellulose (Figure A). If these microorganisms are killed, the termite will starve to death. Cows and related mammals have a special digestive pouch called a rumen where these microorganisms live. Such mammals regurgitate and rechew the contents of their rumens ("chewing the cud")—an action that helps them break down the cellulose in their food more thoroughly.

Some organisms absorb food that other organisms have already digested. Therefore, they do not need to digest their own food.

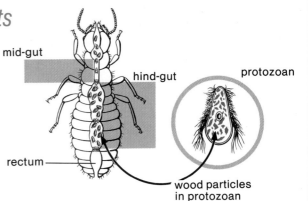

FIGURE A   Microorganisms living in the intestine of the termite produce enzymes that digest the cellulose in wood. Termites without these microorganisms would starve on a diet of wood.

Organisms that obtain food this way are called parasites. For example, mistletoe has rootlike suckers that penetrate the phloem of another plant and absorb the digested food from it. Tapeworms are parasites that live in the intestines of humans and other animals. Tapeworms do not have any digestive organs; they absorb already digested food from the host animal's intestines, usually to the disadvantage of the host.

---

such as sponges and *Hydra*, also take in solid bits of food (Figure 18.7a on the next page).

Multicellular animals digest food in specialized cavities or tubes. The flatworm's digestive cavity is more complex than that of the *Hydra* but also has only one opening (Figure 18.7b). In the flatworm, a muscular organ called the pharynx (FAYR inks) takes in bits of solid food. The food is digested in a branched digestive cavity and absorbed by the body cells. Waste materials are eliminated through the pharynx.

Animals more complex than flatworms ingest larger and more complex nutrient molecules that require considerable processing. Digestion in such animals takes place in digestive tubes with two openings. Food enters the mouth at one end of the tube and material that cannot be digested is passed out of the anus (AY nus) at the other end of the tube. The result is one-way movement of food and waste. The earthworm's digestive system, shown in Figure 18.7c, is an example of such a digestive tube.

The digestive tube of most complex animals is divided into different regions having specialized functions. The specialization may depend on the diet of the animal. Herbivores cannot digest the cellulose in their diet. As a

Try Investigation 18A, Food-Getting Structures.

FIGURE 18.7 Digestive systems of three increasingly complex animals: *Hydra* (a), flatworm (b), and earthworm (c). *Hydra* uses the same opening for both ingesting food and eliminating wastes. Its intracellular and extracellular digestive processes are detailed in the insert. The flatworm's digestive cavity is more specialized than that of *Hydra*, but it too has only one opening. The earthworm's system is an example of a complete digestive tube with two openings—the mouth at one end, through which food is ingested, and the anus at the other end, through which wastes are eliminated. Digestion occurs extracellularly within the tube.

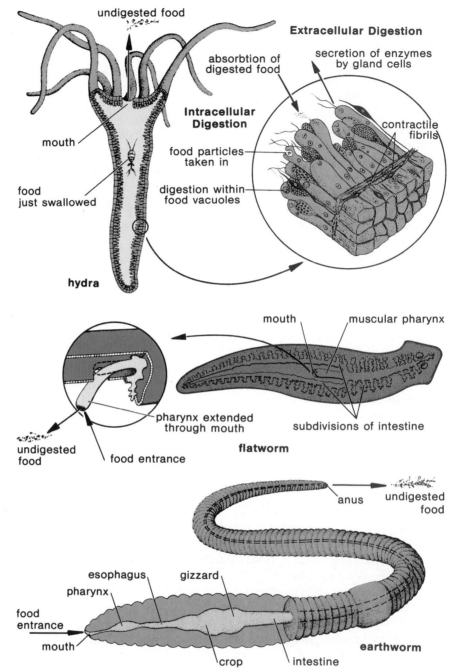

result, they generally have large, long digestive tracts and must consume large amounts of food. Goats and cows have four-chambered stomachs to handle the hard-to-digest food. In the stomachs of horses and rabbits, the digestion of cellulose by microorganisms occurs in a special side pocket. Carnivores consume mostly meat, which is more easily digested than grass. Consequently, a carnivore's digestive tract is relatively short.

18.2   An Overview of Human Digestion

Ingestion is the process of taking food into the digestive tract. In humans, ingestion occurs at the oral cavity, which is bounded by the teeth, tongue, and palate. Here the chewing action of the teeth begins the mechanical breakdown of food. As you chew your food, your highly muscular tongue keeps the food in contact with the teeth and mixes it with saliva—a watery secretion containing digestive enzymes that begin chemical digestion.

Figure 18.8 shows the human digestive system. Refer to the diagram as you read about the events that take place. The esophagus, a tube connecting the oral cavity to the stomach, is made up of two layers of muscles: an

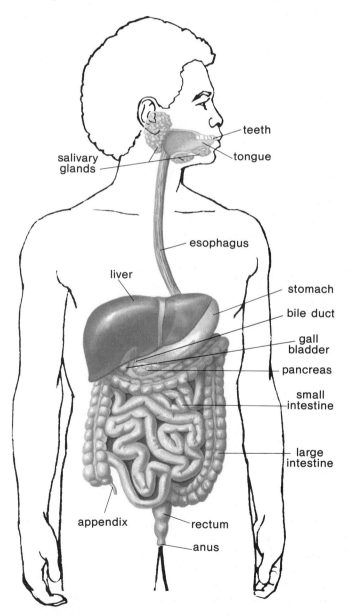

FIGURE 18.8 The human digestive system is a continuous tube with highly specialized organs and tissues along its length. It produces some of its own enzymes and is supplied with other enzymes by nearby glands.

outer layer running the length of the esophagus and an inner circular layer. Together, these muscles move the food to the stomach through a process called peristalsis (per ih STAWL sis). After you swallow, contractions of the circular muscle push food along as the muscle ahead relaxes. Peristalsis proceeds in a wavelike sequence down the length of the esophagus. The same muscle action also moves food at later stages of digestion.

As the food moves along the approximately nine meters of digestive tract, it goes through various sections that function as a disassembly line. The next organ reached is the stomach, an enlargement of the gut between the esophagus and the intestine. A circular muscle, or sphincter (SFINK ter), at either end of the stomach closes the opening to each adjacent organ. Contractions of muscles lining the stomach wall thoroughly break up and mix food with secretions from stomach glands. These secretions, called gastric juices, are composed of enzymes, mucus, and acid. As a result of their action, the contents of the stomach soon become souplike. The partially digested food is held in the stomach by contraction of the pyloric valve, the sphincter between the stomach and the small intestine. From time to time, the pyloric valve relaxes, releasing small amounts of partially digested food into the small intestine. After an average meal, the stomach is usually emptied in approximately four hours.

Food then enters the small intestine, a tube approximately six meters long, where chemical digestion is completed and food molecules are absorbed. The pancreas and liver contribute digestive juices to the small intestine through ducts.

Absorption occurs when the molecules move through the intestinal walls and enter the bloodstream. The blood carries the molecules to the cells, where they are used in metabolism. Any undigested material eventually passes to the large intestine, where numerous bacteria play a part in producing several vitamins, gases, and other compounds. The vitamins are absorbed and used by the body. As the undigested food moves onward, much of the water that was mixed with the food is absorbed through the walls of the large intestine. This absorption partly dries out the wastes, called **feces** (FEE seez). The feces are then eliminated through the anus.

Try Investigation 18B, Starch Digestion.

18.3 Carbohydrate Digestion

Most carbohydrates enter the body as simple or complex sugars and polysaccharides such as starch (Chapter 2). Carbohydrates are the primary energy source in food. Cells cannot use the energy in carbohydrates until the starch and complex sugars are broken down. The digestion of carbohydrates takes place in two regions, the mouth and the small intestine.

Carbohydrate digestion begins in the mouth with the action of an enzyme called salivary amylase. Amylase digests starch to shorter polysaccharides and maltose, or malt sugar. Salivary amylase acts by breaking the chemical bonds in starch molecules and adding water molecules from saliva to the products of this breakdown. The following equation represents the breakdown of starch molecules by amylase.

$$\text{starch} + \text{water} \xrightarrow{\text{salivary amylase}} \text{maltose}$$

In the mouth or elsewhere, enzyme action depends on the pH of the surroundings. Saliva has a pH between 6.0 and 7.4, and salivary amylase functions best at that pH range. The contents of the stomach, however, are very acid (pH 1.0–3.5). This acidic condition inactivates the salivary amylase and, therefore, no carbohydrate digestion takes place in the stomach.

Carbohydrate digestion is completed in the small intestine. The pancreas delivers pancreatic (pan kree AT ik) juices that convert the acidic food mixture to a basic pH again and contribute additional enzymes for further digestion. The maltose produced by salivary amylase is further broken down to glucose by amylases added in the intestine. Most starch is digested in the small intestine. Amylases from the pancreas and other enzymes from the intestine itself work together in this phase of carbohydrate digestion. The final result is usually glucose.

18.4 Protein and Fat Digestion

Protein digestion is a complex process that occurs in the stomach and in the small intestine. The enzymes that break down large protein molecules in the stomach require a strongly acidic environment. This condition is provided by stomach glands that secrete hydrochloric acid. The acid is so concentrated that it could destroy living tissue. The cells of the stomach lining are not harmed, however, because some of them secrete a thick, protective coat of mucus. In addition, the acid is diluted by the food mixture in the stomach. Only when these protective functions fail can stomach cells be attacked by the acid and partly digested by the enzymes. Although damaged cells are rapidly replaced, wounds in the stomach wall called stomach ulcers may result. Recently, scientists discovered that many ulcers are caused by a bacterium, and thus may be treated with antibiotics.

Acid secretion by stomach glands is governed by the presence of food in the stomach. As food enters the stomach, certain cells are stimulated to release a hormone called gastrin (GAS trin), which enters the bloodstream. When gastrin comes in contact with the glands that secrete hydrochloric acid, it acts as a signal that starts secretion. The nervous system is also a factor, so stress and tension can affect stomach acid secretion.

The active protein-digesting enzyme in the stomach is pepsin (PEP sin), which is produced and secreted by stomach gland cells in an inactive form called pepsinogen (pep SIN uh jen). The secretion of pepsinogen is also controlled by the action of gastrin. Hydrochloric acid changes pepsinogen to active pepsin. Pepsin breaks large protein molecules into smaller polypeptides. Each of the polypeptide molecules, however, has a large number of amino acids still bound together. Further digestion occurs in the small intestine. The presence of food in the stomach, the secretion of gastrin, the production of hydrochloric acid, and the conversion of pepsinogen into pepsin are all related. Thus, the entrance of food into the stomach starts a complex sequence of digestive steps.

Food entering the upper part of the small intestine from the stomach is acidic. Yet the food must be basic for the enzymes in the intestine to act. Secretions from the pancreas, which adjust the pH, begin only when there is food in the small intestine. What signals the pancreas to go to work?

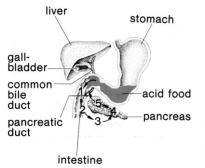

FIGURE 18.9 Acid food enters the small intestine (1) through the pyloric valve and stimulates secretion of the intestinal hormone secretin (2). The secretin enters the bloodstream (3) and circulates to the pancreas (4). In the pancreas, secretin stimulates production of pancreatic juices (5) that flow into the intestine.

When food enters the small intestine, a hormone is secreted by the cells of the small intestine. This hormone, called secretin (seh KREET in), enters the bloodstream and circulates to the pancreas where it stimulates the gland to produce and secrete pancreatic juice. The pancreatic juice enters the intestine through the pancreatic duct and shifts the pH from acidic to basic (Figure 18.9).

Pancreatic juice contains a powerful enzyme called trypsin (TRIP sin) that enters the small intestine in an inactive form, trypsinogen (trip SIN uh jen). Trypsinogen is changed into active trypsin in the intestine by the action of another enzyme secreted only when food is present. Trypsin breaks the peptide bonds of the polypeptides coming into the small intestine from the stomach. Trypsin also acts on any larger protein molecules that were not broken down earlier in the stomach by pepsin. The gland cells lining the small intestine secrete enzymes that also can split peptide bonds. The end products of protein digestion are amino acids.

Fats are digested in the small intestine. Unlike carbohydrates and proteins, fats do not mix with water. Enzymes can digest only the fat molecules on the surface of the fat droplets. Fats are prepared for digestion by bile, a substance secreted by the liver and stored in the gall bladder. Bile salts physically break down fat droplets, increasing the surface area of the droplets available to the fat-digesting pancreatic enzymes. Bile reaches the small intestine through the bile duct (Figure 18.10). Bile does not contain digestive enzymes. However, lipase (LY pays), the fat-digesting enzyme in the pancreatic and intestinal juices, splits fats into fatty acids and glycerol.

18.5   Absorption

Figure 18.10 summarizes the human digestive processes. Note that the end products of digestion of proteins, starch, and fats are amino acids, simple sugars, fatty acids, and glycerol. These end products have two features in common: (1) they are small molecules that can pass through cell membranes, and (2) they are molecules that cells use for energy and as raw materials for building cellular structures.

These small molecules pass through the cells lining the small intestine. The surface area of the intestinal lining is increased tremendously by millions of small fingerlike projections called **villi** (VIL lee; singular *villus*). Each villus contains **capillaries** (KAP ih lair eez)—tiny, thin-walled blood vessels—and a **lymph** (LIMF) vessel (Figure 18.11) that transports tissue fluid. Simple sugars, amino acids, fatty acids and some glycerol, minerals, and vitamins pass through the cells of the villi and enter the capillaries by active transport and diffusion. The products of fat digestion also pass through the cells of the villi, but they enter the lymph vessels instead of the capillaries. Eventually, the lymph vessels conduct the fatty acids and glycerol into the bloodstream.

The blood carries the products of digestion to the cells. Inside the cells the molecules are either broken down further to yield energy or put together again to synthesize the substances the organism needs for growth and repair. Synthesis and decomposition are discussed in Chapter 3. Cellular respiration is discussed in Chapter 8.

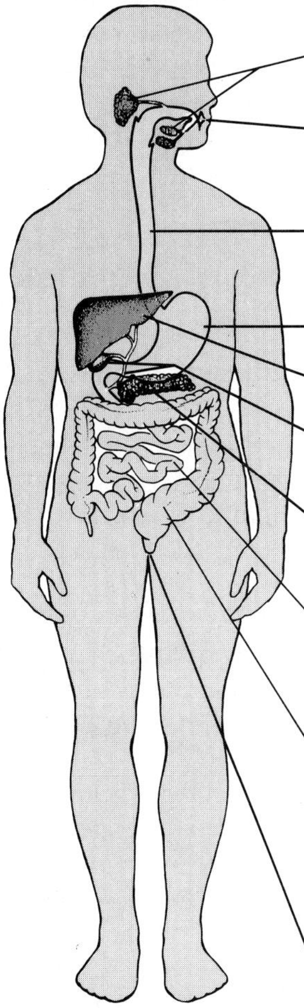

parts of the digestive system		major function	major secretion	source of secretions	substances acted on	product of action
salivary glands		secretion of saliva	salivary amylase	salivary glands	starch	complex sugar (maltose)
mouth and teeth		food entrance; chewing; some starch digestion			large pieces of food	small pieces of food
esophagus		carries food to stomach				
stomach		protein digestion; regulation of HCl and pepsin secretion	HCl pepsinogen (pepsin) gastrin	gland cells of stomach	proteins	polypeptides
liver gallbladder and bile ducts		secretion, storage, and transport of bile	bile salts	liver cells	large fat droplets	small fat droplets
pancreas		secretion of pancreatic juice	trypsinogen (trypsin) lipase amylase	pancreas	polypeptides fats carbohydrates	amino acids fatty acids and glycerol maltose
small intestine		digestion and absorption; regulation of pancreatic secretions	carbohydrases proteinases lipases secretin	pancreas gland cells of small intestine	peptides fats complex sugars	amino acids fatty acids and glycerol glucose
large intestine		reabsorption of water; collection of undigested wastes				
anus		waste exit				

FIGURE 18.10 A summary of the parts and functions of the human digestive system

FIGURE 18.11 A cross section of the small intestine. Intestinal villi are shown enlarged in the micrograph and drawing. Digested foodstuffs enter the blood and the lymph through the villi.

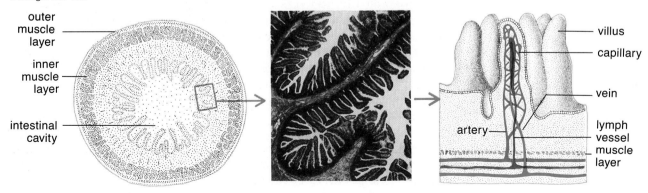

CHECK AND CHALLENGE

1. Trace the movement of food through the human digestive tract.

2. Discuss the digestion of carbohydrates. Be sure to include the regions of the digestive tract where carbohydrate digestion occurs.

3. What is the role of the small intestine in the digestion of proteins and fats?

4. How does acid affect pepsinogen?

5. What is the role of secretin in digestion?

6. Explain how digestive systems in different multicellular animals are adaptive.

7. Compare and contrast phagocytosis and pinocytosis.

Nutrition

18.6 Nutritional Claims

Human nutrition probably enjoys more public concern but suffers from less public understanding than any other area of biology. Every day claims are made about miracle diets to lose weight "effortlessly" or about a "vitamin" that will prolong life or cure a terrible disease. What should you believe? How can you evaluate nutritonal claims intelligently?

There are two things to keep in mind when you analyze nutritional claims: (1) your diet should include a variety of foods eaten in moderation; (2) unless you have an unusual health problem, the food in a normal diet should not be considered extraordinarily harmful or beneficial. Appendix 18A, Dietary Guidelines, is a list of recommendations from the Surgeon General's Report on Nutrition and Health. It provides guidance for developing eating habits and other behaviors that affect good nutrition.

18.7 Carbohydrates

Carbohydrates are the main source of energy in the diet. They supply 4 kilocalories (1 kcal = 4.1833 kjoules) per gram. Sugars such as table sugar (sucrose), dextrose (glucose), and honey (a mixture of glucose, fructose, and sucrose) are added to the diet as sweeteners and preservatives. The ingredient labels on many packaged foods often list one or more of these sugars (Figure 18.12a, on page 416). Because sugars supply only kilocalories and few or no other nutrients, they are called empty-calorie foods. The average American eats 133 pounds a year and reports indicate that three of every five kilocalories ingested by Americans are empty calories from fats and added sugars.

Starch, a complex carbohydrate, often is present with other nutrients in food. For example, potatoes and beans are rich in starch as well as vitamins and minerals. Dietary fibers are indigestible complex carbohydrates, such as cellulose and other plant material, that help move food

EATING DISORDERS

Have you ever tried to take off an extra five pounds that you were unable to lose no matter what measures you took? Recent evidence indicates that each person has a genetic predisposition toward a certain weight. Normally, this predisposition is not a problem, but the current cultural emphasis on being slim and trim has created difficulties, particularly in teenage girls and young women.

Dieting has become almost epidemic in the United States, with millions dieting every day. Unfortunately, in a growing number of cases, dieting becomes an obsession that leads to a potentially fatal eating disorder called anorexia nervosa (Figure B). As a consequence of not eating, anorexics often begin to show signs of severe malnutrition and abnormally low body temperatures and pulse rates. A person suffering from anorexia nervosa literally starves him or herself.

Bulimia is another eating disorder on the rise in the United States. A bulimic individual indulges in eating binges, usually involving large quantities of carbohydrate-rich junk food, and then induces vomiting or uses laxatives in an effort to purge the body of the food so as not to gain weight.

The consequences of frequent purging include a reduction of the body's supply of potassium. Potassium is important in regulating body fluids; its loss may lead to muscle weakness or paralysis, an irregular heartbeat, kidney disease, and death. In addition, repeated vomiting brings into the mouth stomach acids that can erode teeth; it also can severely damage the digestive tract. Both anorexia and bulimia often lead to decreased resistance to infection.

For reasons that are poorly understood, 90 to 95 percent of those individuals suffering from eating disorders are female. Researchers estimate that 5 to 10 percent of the adolescent girls and young women in the United States suffer from eating disorders. As many as one in five female high school and college students may suffer from bulimia.

FIGURE B Although they are extremely underweight, anorexics usually see themselves as overweight.

Anorexia and bulimia are distinct eating disorders, and each has a specific set of diagnostic criteria and medical complications. Some researchers have identified neurological links between eating disorders, depression, and addictive behaviors. Others believe the cause is an inability to cope. The one point researchers agree on, however, is that the disorders are probably influenced by many factors—sociocultural, neurochemical, and psychological—and that treatment requires a multidisciplinary approach. In treatment, it is essential that the shame often associated with the conditions be recognized as a problem and that professional help be promptly sought. Both a psychiatrist or a psychologist and a physician should be involved, and the family as a whole must play a strong, supportive role for the treatment to be effective.

a

b

FIGURE 18.12   (a) Sugar in many forms is present in an amazing variety of foods. It is important to read nutritional labels very carefully. (b) Some high-fiber foods

through the digestive tract by absorbing water. People with constipation often are instructed to include more fiber in their diet because it can counter the effects of an increased consumption of processed and packaged foods—foods notoriously low in fiber. Increased dietary fiber has also been linked with reduced rates of cancer of the colon. Many breakfast cereals are very high in fiber, as are the foods shown in Figure 18.12b. An intake of about 20 to 30 g of fiber a day is desirable. (See **Appendix 18C**, Fiber Values of Common Foods.)

18.8   Fats and Energy

Fats supply 9 kilocalories per gram and are an important source of energy in the diet. Triglycerides (Chapter 2) are the most common dietary form of fat. Recall that saturated fats, those with few or no double bonds between carbon atoms, tend to be solid at room temperature. The saturated, or hard, fats are most often found in meat, fish, poultry, and dairy products. Many reports have shown that people with diets high in saturated fats are more likely to suffer from cardiovascular disease (CVD), the leading cause of death in the United States. Unsaturated fats contain double bonds between carbon atoms and tend to be liquid at room temperature. These fats are often called ''light oils.'' Usually, the more double bonds in the fatty acids, the lighter the oil. The length of the hydrocarbon chain of the fatty acid also affects its state. Longer chains are solid at room temperature. Unsaturated fats are found in plant foods. However, some plant oils, such as coconut oil, contain saturated, hard fats. (See **Appendix 18B**, Fat and Fatty-Acid Content of Some Foods.)

Cholesterol (Chapter 2) is a type of fat found in animal-product foods, but not in fruits and vegetables. This fatty substance, which also is produced by the human body, is in the bloodstream and is essential to life. More than nine-tenths of the body's cholesterol is found in the cell membranes. Elsewhere, cholesterol can serve as the raw material for the synthesis of sex hormones and vitamin D. While traveling in the bloodstream to the cells, however, cholesterol can form deposits in the artery walls, which can lead to CVD. Although medical authorities agree that too much cholesterol in the blood is unhealthy, there is disagreement concerning how much is too much.

Much of the cholesterol and fat is carried in the blood by lipoproteins (complex lipid-protein molecules). One type, called LDL for low-density-lipoprotein, tends to deposit the cholesterol and fats in the arteries. HDL (high-density-lipoprotein) tends to remove them. People with high HDL/LDL ratios and low cholesterol levels are less likely to develop cardiovascular disease. A combination of the following lifestyles lowers blood cholesterol levels in many people: (1) regular exercise; (2) maintenance of proper weight; (3) a diet low in cholesterol—no more than 300 mg/day for men and 225 mg/day for women; and (4) a diet low in saturated fat. These

FOCUS ON *Diet and Cardiovascular Disease*

More than half the deaths each year in the United States are associated with cardiovascular disease. In a disease called atherosclerosis (ATH uh roh skleh ROH sis), layers of cholesterol and fat known as plaque accumulate on the inner lining of the artery walls. Whether the buildup is short-term or long-term, it narrows the openings of the arteries (Figure C). Blood flow is restricted, and blood pressure increases, putting a strain on the heart and further damaging the artery walls. As pressure increases, the wall may expand like a balloon and even burst. If a wall bursts in a major artery such as the aorta, bleeding and usually death occur. If the affected blood vessels are in the brain, there is a stroke and brain cells die.

In addition, plaque creates a surface that can induce the formation of clots. Clots may form in critical arteries, or they may form in less serious vessels, then move to an important area, and block blood flow as plaque does. The same cardiovascular problems mentioned above may occur, causing heart attacks or stroke.

At least three factors are linked to cardiovascular disease: smoking, high blood pressure, and high blood cholesterol. The current advice for reducing cardiovascular risk is rather simple

and applies to people of all ages. Do not smoke. Have your blood pressure checked and regulate it, if necessary, with medical advice. Follow a diet and exercise program that lowers LDL levels in the blood and raises HDL levels. Finally, as with all advice about nutrition and health, try to be aware of new information as it becomes available. New data often result in changed dietary and activity recommendations.

FIGURE C Plaque narrows the opening of an artery in atherosclerosis.

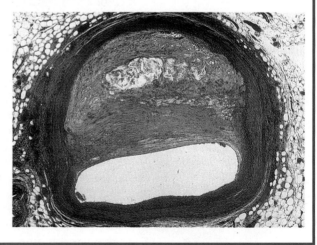

FIGURE 18.13 Cholesterol content of various foods, per 250 mL (1 cup) or 100 g (3 oz) serving

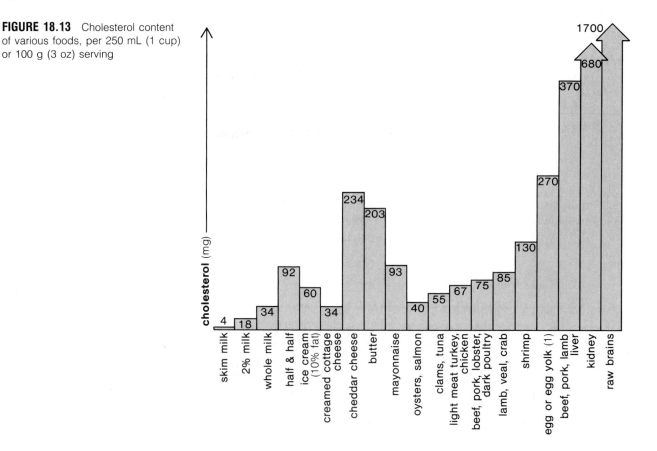

conditions also appear to help raise the amount of HDL compared to LDL in the blood. Figure 18.13 shows the cholesterol content of some common foods.

18.9   Proteins and Amino Acids

Dietary proteins can supply energy at 4 kcal/g. However, they are more important in providing amino acids for synthesizing proteins needed for growth and repair (Figure 18.14). All proteins in the diet are digested to amino acids before they are used in the cells. Humans can use any dietary proteins as starting materials to make roughly one-half of the 20 amino acids needed to build their own proteins. The other required amino acids cannot be synthesized in human cells and must be included in the diet. They are called **essential amino acids**. Table 18.1 is a list of the essential amino acids.

Some forms of dietary protein, primarily from plants, do not contain all of the essential amino acids in adequate amounts. These forms are called incomplete proteins. Complete proteins, such as those from dairy products and meat, supply all the essential amino acids in the correct dietary amounts. People who rely on vegetables for their protein can receive adequate amounts of all essential amino acids in their diet by mixing different vegetables to complement incomplete proteins.

FIGURE 18.14 Foods rich in protein come from a variety of sources.

TABLE 18.1
Average Daily Requirements of Essential Amino Acids

Essential Amino Acids	Daily mg Needed Per kg Body Mass			
	Infants	Toddlers	Children	Adults
Histidine	28	*	*	8–12
Isoleucine	70	31	28	10
Leucine	161	73	44	14
Lysine	103	64	44	12
Methionine & cystine	58	27	22	13
Phenylalanine & tyrosine	125	69	22	14
Threonine	87	37	28	7
Tryptophane	17	12.5	4	3.5
Valine	93	38	25	10

* Amounts have not been determined.

Dietary protein requirements vary with age, sex, and general health, but usually people living in the United States exceed their required amount each day. You can estimate your daily protein requirement by figuring that you need 0.5 g of protein per kilogram of body mass per day. By calculating the number of grams of protein in your food, you can determine whether you meet your daily requirement for protein. Most people in the U.S. can reach their Required Dietary Allowance (RDA) for protein with well-balanced meals.

18.10 Vitamins, Minerals, and RDAs

Vitamins are nutrients required in relatively small amounts in the diet. They do not supply energy. Humans need vitamins for various roles including building bones and tissues, blood clotting, and the regulation of cell chemistry. Several enzymes and several steps in respiration rely on vitamins for proper functioning.

Vitamins are placed in two categories, depending on whether or not they can be dissolved in water. The water-soluble vitamins, which usually are not retained in the body, are the B-complex vitamins and vitamin C. The fat-soluble vitamins, which can be stored in the body, are vitamins A, D, E, and K. Figure 18.15 shows foods rich in the various vitamins. Table 18.2 on the next page provides brief information about the sources, functions, and deficiency symptoms of the vitamins. These 13 compounds are the only known vitamins needed in the human diet.

Minerals are inorganic compounds found in different amounts in different parts of the body. Some minerals, such as iron and zinc, are important in metabolism. Other minerals, such as calcium and phosphorus, are important in metabolism and in building tissue. There is no research evidence to indicate that megadoses of either vitamins or minerals in the diet are of any health benefit. In fact, an overdose of fat-soluble vitamin supplements can be harmful. However, some research suggests that certain vita-

FIGURE 18.15 Examples of some foods high in vitamins

TABLE 18.2
Vitamins Important in Humans

Name	Food Sources	Function	Deficiency Symptoms
A, retinol	Liver, green and yellow vegetables, fruits, egg yolks, butter	Formation of visual pigments; cell growth, especially of epithelial cells	Night blindness, flaky skin, lowered resistance to infection, growth stunting, faulty reproduction
D, calciferol	Fish oils, liver, action of sunlight on lipids in skin	Increases calcium absorption from gut; formation of bones and teeth	Rickets—defective bone formation
E, tocopherol	Oils, whole grains, liver, legumes, green leafy vegetables	Protects red blood cells, plasma membranes, and vitamin A from destruction; important in muscle maintenance	Fragility of red blood cells, muscle wasting
K	Synthesis by intestinal bacteria, green leafy vegetables, cheese, liver	Synthesis of clotting factors by liver	Internal hemorrhaging (deficiency may be caused by oral antibiotics, which kill intestinal bacteria)
C, ascorbic acid	Citrus fruits, tomatoes, green leafy vegetables	Essential to formation of collagen and intercellular substance; protects against infection; maintains strength of blood vessels; increases iron absorption from gut; important in muscle maintenance	Scurvy, failure to form connective tissue, bleeding, slow wound healing
B-Complex Vitamins:			
B$_1$, thiamine	Whole grains, legumes, nuts, liver, heart, kidneys, pork	Carbohydrate metabolism	Beriberi, loss of appetite, indigestion, fatigue, nerve irritability, heart failure
B$_2$, riboflavin	Liver, kidneys, heart, yeast, milk, eggs, whole grains	Forms part of electron carrier in electron transport system	Sore mouth and tongue, cracks at corners of mouth, eye irritation, scaly skin
Pantothenic acid	Yeast, liver, eggs, wheat germ, bran, peanuts, peas	Part of Coenzyme A; essential for energy release and biosynthesis	Fatigue, headache, sleep disturbances, nausea, muscle cramps, loss of antibody production
Niacin	Yeast, liver, kidneys, heart, meat, fish, poultry, legumes, nuts, whole grains	Coenzyme in energy metabolism; part of NAD^+ and NADP	Pellagra, skin lesions, digestive problems, nerve disorders
B$_6$, pyridoxine	Whole grains, potatoes, fish, poultry, red meats, legumes, seeds	Coenzyme for amino acid and fatty acid metabolism	Skin disorders, sore mouth and tongue, nerve disorders, anemia, weight loss, impaired antibody response

Name	Food Sources	Function	Deficiency Symptoms
Biotin	Liver, kidneys, yeast, egg yolks, whole grains, fish, legumes, nuts, meats, dairy products, synthesis by intestinal bacteria	Fatty acid, amino acid, and protein synthesis; energy release from glucose	Skin disorders, appetite loss, depression, sleeplessness, muscle pain
Folacin (folic acid)	Liver, yeast, leafy vegetables	Nucleic acid synthesis, amino acid metabolism	Failure of red blood cells to mature, anemia, intestinal disturbances and diarrhea
B_{12}	Liver and organ meats, muscle meats, fish, eggs, shellfish, milk; synthesis by intestinal bacteria	Nucleic acid synthesis	Pernicious anemia

mins, such as A, C, E, and folic acid, may help prevent cancer and other diseases. Table 18.3 on the next page lists information about the minerals needed for a healthy diet. Use Tables 18.2 and 18.3 for reference as you build your personal nutrition program.

If you examine labels on some food packages or on bottles of vitamins, you will notice a rating system based on RDAs. Recommended Dietary Allowances are nutrient intake guidelines for normal, healthy people living in the United States. RDAs are published by the government based on the best scientific research and analysis. They are recommendations, not requirements or minimums, that include a wide margin of dietary safety for almost all people. (See Appendix 18D, Recommended Dietary Allowances.) By reading labels on packaged foods, you can gain an idea of the nutritional value of the product.

FOCUS ON *Calcium*

Minerals in the diet have received considerable attention over the years, and calcium has been in the limelight. Calcium is important in building and maintaining bone tissue. Scientists have recommended that certain individuals increase the calcium content of their diet. Bone density can only be built up before the age of 35. Therefore, this recommendation is especially important for young people. Older adults with insufficient calcium and bone density tend to develop a bone disease called osteoporosis, which is characterized by porous bones. Osteoporosis results in weak and brittle bones and often leads to fractures, disability, and even death. However, calcium is just one factor in the disease. Other dietary elements and exercise also are very important for building and maintaining strong bones. The reduction of estrogen levels in aging women may be even more influential. Osteoporosis may develop regardless of calcium intake. People should be careful to meet their RDA for calcium through a healthy diet.

TABLE 18.3
Minerals Important in Humans

Name	Food Sources	Function	Deficiency	Excess
Major Minerals				
Calcium (Ca)	Dairy products, green leafy vegetables, eggs, nuts, dried legumes	Development of bones and teeth, muscle contraction, blood clotting, nerve impulse transmission, enzyme activation	Stunted growth, poor quality bones and teeth, rickets, convulsions	Excess blood calcium, loss of appetite, muscle weakness, fever
Chlorine (Cl)	Table salt, most water supplies	Water balance, hydrochloric acid in stomach	Metabolic alkalosis, constipation, failure to gain weight (in infants)	Vomiting; elemental chlorine is a poison used for chemical warfare
Magnesium (Mg)	Whole grains, liver, kidneys, milk, nuts, green leafy vegetables	Component of chlorophyll, bones and teeth; coenzyme in carbohydrate and protein metabolism	Infertility, menstrual disorders	Loss of reflexes, drowsiness, coma, death
Phosphorus (P)	Dairy foods, egg yolk, meat, whole grains	Development of bones and teeth, energy metabolism, pH balance	Bone fractures, disorders of red blood cells, metabolic problems	As phosphorus increases, calcium decreases; muscle spasm, jaw erosion
Potassium (K)	Whole grains, meat, bananas, vegetables	Body water and pH balance, nerve and muscle activity	Muscle and nerve weakness	Abnormalities in heartbeat, muscle weakness, mental confusion, cold and pale skin
Sodium (Na)	Table salt, dairy foods, eggs, baking soda and powder, meat, vegetables	Body water and pH balance, nerve and muscle activity	Weakness, muscle cramps, diarrhea, dehydration	High blood pressure, edema, kidney disease
Sulphur (S)	Dairy products, nuts, legumes	Component of some amino acids, enzyme activator	Related to intake and deficiency of sulfur amino acids	Excess sulfur amino acid intake leads to poor growth
Trace Minerals				
Cobalt (Co)	Common in foods, meat, milk	Component of vitamin B_{12}, essential for red blood cell formation	Rare	Dermatitis, excessive production of red corpuscles
Copper (Cu)	Liver, meat, seafood, whole grains, legumes, nuts	Production of hemoglobin, bone formation, component of electron carriers	Anemia, bone and connective tissue disorders, scurvy-like conditions, an early death	Toxic concentrations in liver and eyes of persons with genetic inability to metabolize

Name	Food Sources	Function	Deficiency	Excess
Fluorine (F)	Most water supplies, seafood	Prevents bacterial tooth decay	Tooth decay, bone weakness	Mottling on teeth, deformed teeth and bones
Iodine (I)	Seafood, iodized salt, dairy products	Component of thyroid hormone, which controls cellular respiration	Inadequate synthesis of thyroid hormone, goiter, cretinism	Antithyroid compounds
Iron (Fe)	Liver, meat, eggs, spinach, enriched bread and cereals	Component of hemoglobin (oxygen and electron transport system)	Iron-deficiency anemia, chronic fatigue, weakness	Accidental poisoning of children, cirrhosis of liver
Manganese (Mn)	Liver, kidneys, legumes, cereals, tea, coffee	Ions necessary in protein and carbohydrate metabolism; Krebs cycle	Infertility, menstrual problems	Brain and nervous system disorders
Molybdenum (Mo)	Organ meats, milk, whole grains, leafy vegetables, legumes	Enzyme component	Edema, lethargy, disorientation, and coma	Weight loss, growth retardation, and changes in connective tissue
Zinc (Zn)	Liver, seafoods, common foods	Essential enzyme component; necessary for normal senses of taste and smell	Slow sexual development, loss of appetite, retarded growth	Nausea, bloating, and cramps, depresses copper absorption

You may wonder why RDAs are guidelines rather than precise values. One answer is that individuals vary in their nutritional needs. Except for identical twins, no two people are exactly alike in their genetic makeup, and nutritional requirements are different. Remember this point when thinking about your own diet, because your nutritional requirements will be different from those of other individuals.

CHECK AND CHALLENGE

1. Why should you be cautious in accepting the nutritional claims made for some products?

2. Explain the importance of dietary fiber.

3. Distinguish between saturated and unsaturated fats. How are these differences important in nutrition?

4. Explain why RDAs are not precise values.

C H A P T E R Highlights

Summary

Digestion is the process of breaking down food into molecules small enough to be absorbed and used by individual cells. Digestive enzymes, which act chemically, break down the food molecules. In intracellular digestion, digestion takes place within the individual cells that will use the food. Most animals accomplish the breakdown of food by extracellular digestion, which takes place within a tube specialized for digestion. The small molecules that are the products of digestion can be used by living cells as a source of energy or as nutrients for growth and repair.

Nutrition is the study of the requirement and use of nutrients—carbohydrates, fats, proteins, vitamins, and minerals. Various nutritional claims are made for new products, and each claim must be evaluated thoroughly in light of sound nutritional knowledge. Carbohydrates and fats are sources of energy in the diet. Protein supplies the amino acids needed for cell and tissue growth, development, and maintenance. Vitamins and minerals are needed in relatively small amounts to build tissue and help regulate metabolism. RDAs are guidelines for nutrient intake but do not specify exact nutrient requirements. Every individual is different and thus requires unique levels of each nutrient. Whenever weight loss or weight gain is desired, the person should make a concerted effort to maintain good, balanced nutrition in order to stay healthy.

Key Concepts

Use the following terms to construct a concept map. You may add additional terms as they are needed.

digestion	ingestion
intracellular digestion	protein
carbohydrate	fat

HDL	stomach
vitamins	evolution
adaptation	RDAs
lipase	bile
secretin	pepsin

Reviewing Ideas

1. Why must most proteins, carbohydrates, and fats be digested?

2. What are the end products of carbohydrate, fat, and protein digestion?

3. Explain how the lining of the stomach is protected from the action of hydrochloric acid and digestive juices.

4. Explain how the pH of the stomach and intestine is regulated and why maintaining a certain pH is necessary.

5. What stimulates or inhibits the secretion of juices by the stomach?

6. What role does the pancreas play in the digestive process?

7. Explain how different organisms obtain food and relate these methods to evolutionary adaptation.

8. What are the dietary functions of carbohydrates, fats, and proteins? How many kilocalories are present in one gram of each of the above nutrients?

9. Compare and contrast intracellular digestion and extracellular digestion.

10. Describe some adaptations in the digestive systems of herbivores.

11. Explain what is meant by essential amino acids. How can a vegetarian be sure of getting all of them?

12. Compare and contrast anorexia nervosa and bulimia. How can they be treated?

13. Where do the amino acids that are used as protein building blocks in the human body come from?

14. Discuss why vitamins and minerals are important in human nutrition.

Using Concepts

1. What advantages, with regard to food types, does extracellular digestion give an animal?

2. In all animals, how is the actual breakdown of large molecules to small molecules accomplished?

3. Birds have no teeth. How do they reduce the size of the pieces of food they ingest?

4. What steps in digestion are started by the entrance of food into the stomach?

5. How is digestion affected by chewing food well as opposed to swallowing large bites?

6. Examine the table of RDA values in Appendix 18D and determine your RDA for each nutrient listed.

7. What is meant by nutritional individuality, and how does it apply to you?

8. Why is a gradual weight-loss program more beneficial than a rapid one?

9. From the graph below, determine the RDA for nutrient X, in mg/day.

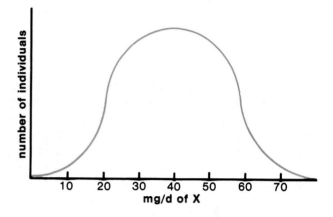

Synthesis

1. From your readings in previous chapters, explain why it is important to include adequate water in the diet. What are the possible consequences of insufficient water?

2. Relate the end products of chemical digestion to the processes of photosynthesis and cellular respiration.

3. Compare your knowledge of today's typical human diet with what you suppose to be a typical early hominid diet. What effects might the differences in diets have on each group?

4. Explain the roles of active and passive transport in the movement of material into the intestinal villi and lymph ducts.

5. Relate what you know about human digestion to stomach and intestinal disorders such as gas and heartburn. What might be the causes? How might antacids work?

Extensions

1. Imagine you are a hamburger. Write an essay about your trip through the human digestive system.

2. You are still a hamburger. Draw a cartoon about the different things that happen to you as you travel through the digestive system.

CONTENTS

Transport Systems

*W*hat process
is responsible
for the movement of
water from the roots
to the leaves
in plants?

Single-celled organisms that live in water obtain nutrients and eliminate wastes by diffusion and active transport. These processes, first discussed in Chapter 6, are sufficient for the needs of both single-celled organisms and organisms composed of a strand of single cells. Multicellular organisms, such as most land plants and the vertebrates, cannot get by that easily.

The chemicals that your cells require must be in solution in order to be absorbed. Yet your cells are not in contact with a watery outside environment containing these chemicals. The chemicals are instead absorbed through a variety of mechanisms. Although we live on land, our cells are in contact with an internal liquid environment. In vertebrates, specialized systems have evolved that maintain the internal environment, provide cells with food and oxygen, remove carbon dioxide, and eliminate the wastes resulting from metabolic processes (Chapter 21). Because of blood and intracellular fluid, control of the chemical and physical properties of the fluid surrounding our cells is possible. By circulating the blood to organs that filter wastes, such as the kidney and liver, the circulatory system plays a central role in maintaining a stable internal environment. Plants have also evolved systems for obtaining and eliminating materials and maintaining a stable internal environment.

The transport system moves needed materials to different parts of the organism and transports wastes for elimination. It is also responsible for surrounding cells with a liquid environment appropriate for the exchange of essential materials. The transport system is a key component in maintaining the internal balance necessary for life.

♦ *The pattern of veins in a yellow poplar leaf,* Liriodendron tulipifera.

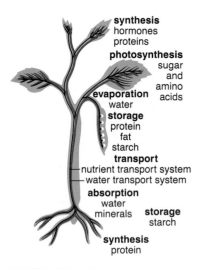

FIGURE 19.1 Different parts of a plant have different activities, all of which involve materials that must be transported where needed. Water is the material needed in greatest amounts. It also serves as the transport fluid, carrying minerals in one type of plant tissue and the products of photosynthesis in another.

Transport Systems in Plants

19.1 Adaptations for Life on Land

The fossil record indicates several major periods of plant evolution. One such period is associated with the origin of land plants from aquatic ancestors during the Paleozoic Era, about 430 million years ago. Most botanists agree that photosynthetic protists similar to certain multicellular green algae probably were the forerunners of today's land plants.

The first adaptations to land included a cuticle (Chapter 7) and a protective covering for the gametes and embryos of the plant. Two distinct groups of early plants emerged during this period. One group had specialized tissue, called **vascular tissue**, consisting of cells joined into tubes that transported water and nutrients throughout the body of the plant. These were the first vascular plants—the ancestors of all plants except mosses and their relatives. The mosses are descendants of the second group, nonvascular plants in which vascular tissues did not evolve.

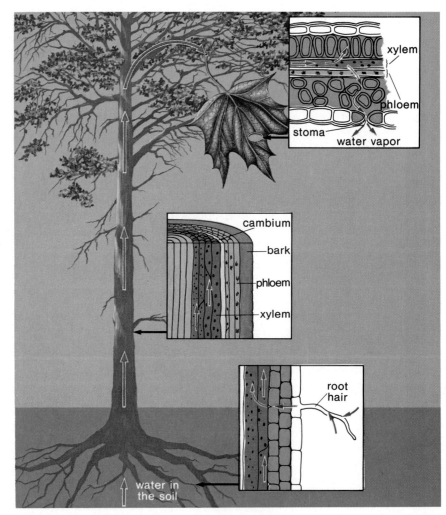

FIGURE 19.2 The arrows identify the principal water-conducting structures of this tree. Trace the path of the water from the root hairs through the xylem tissues to the leaves.

Life on land presented many challenges to which aquatic algae were not adapted. The soil, for example, provides water and minerals, but blocks the light needed for photosynthesis. However, a vascular land plant is differentiated into an underground root system that absorbs water and minerals, and an aerial system of stems and leaves that makes food (Figure 19.1).

The specialization of the plant body into different regions solved certain problems and led to further adaptations. Roots that must absorb water across their surface generally lack the waxy cuticle that limits water evaporation in stems and leaves. Note in the close-up view of the roots in Figure 19.2 that some root cells have long, thin projections. These **root hairs** increase the surface area of the roots in contact with water and thus increase the amount of water that can be absorbed.

Roots anchor, but do not support, the plants. Without the support provided by a water environment, how does a plant shoot stand upright in the air? An important adaptation of vascular plants is **lignin**, a hard material embedded in the cellulose matrix of the cell walls. These lignified walls provide the needed support for a tree or other large vascular plant.

With the increasing specialization of the root system and shoot system came the necessity of transporting vital materials between these distant regions. Water and minerals must be conducted upward from the roots to the leaves. Sugar and other organic products of photosynthesis must be distributed from the leaves to the roots. These tasks are accomplished by an efficient vascular system that is continuous throughout the plant. Tube-shaped cells in the xylem carry water and minerals up from the roots (Figure 19.2). Phloem consists of elongated cells arranged into tubes that distribute organic nutrients throughout the plant. Some nonvascular plants do have types of transport tissues, but neither xylem nor phloem.

FOCUS ON *Mycorrhizae*

In many vascular plants, the root system becomes infected with fungi present in the soil. The relationship between the fungi and the roots causes slight modifications of the roots known as mycorrhizae (my koh RY zee). The fungi either form a sheath around the root or penetrate the root tissue, increasing the surface area of the root through outward extensions (Figure A). The fungi also are good at absorbing minerals, and they secrete an acid that converts the minerals to forms that can be used more readily by the plant. Minerals taken up by the fungi are transferred to the plant, and photosynthetic products from the plant nourish the fungi. In addition to enhancing mineral nutrition, mycorrhizae also absorb water, and the fungi protect the plant against certain disease-causing organisms, or pathogens, in the soil.

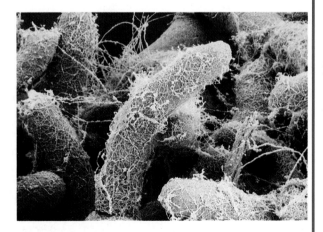

FIGURE A A scanning electron micrograph of mycorrhizae between a *Boletus* mushroom and an aspen, *Populus tremuloides*, X15.

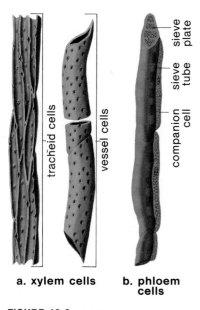

a. xylem cells **b. phloem cells**

FIGURE 19.3 (a) Xylem cells; (b) Phloem cells

Try Investigation 19A, Water Movement in Plants.

19.2 Water Transport

Xylem consists of two types of water-conducting cells: **tracheids** (TRAY kee uds) and **vessels** (Figure 19.3a). Tracheids have pointed ends and thick walls with pits that connect them to nearby cells. Water moves from cell to cell through these pits. Vessels are wider, shorter, thinner-walled, and less tapered. The end walls of vessels are perforated or open, and thus water can flow freely through long chains of xylem vessels.

Tremendous amounts of water evaporate every day through the stomates on the leaf surfaces of most land plants. For example, a typical red maple tree growing in a humid climate may lose as much as 200 liters of water per day. This water must be replaced if the plant is to survive. Water entering through the roots often must be transported upward for great distances to reach the higher stems and leaves. Plants do not have pumping mechanisms like the hearts of animals, so how does the water reach the upper parts of plants?

Scientists suggest the cohesion-tension hypothesis as the likely mechanism for water transport through the xylem. The hypothesis is based on several well-known phenomena—including the molecular properties of water (Chapter 2), and transpiration (Chapter 7). Root pressure also may be a factor, but it cannot completely explain the upward rise of water in plants. The pressure that causes water and other materials to ooze out of a cut plant stem is exerted by the root system—root pressure. However, measurements indicate that root pressure alone would not account for the rise of water in trees taller than 30 meters. The properties of water cannot account completely for water transport either.

Recall that hydrogen bonding is characteristic of water molecules. Cohesion is the result of the attraction of hydrogen bonds between water molecules. In addition, the positive and negative charges of water molecules (which are polar) allow them to cling to other charged molecules—the property called adhesion. The combined effects of adhesion and cohesion cause water to rise up a glass tube placed in a container of water. The smaller the diameter of the tube, the higher the liquid rises above the level of water in the container. However, the rise of water is not very rapid, and the height it can reach is limited by gravity and the diameter of the tube or vessel. This phenomenon—capillary action—does not explain water transport in very tall plants, where water moves rapidly and to great heights.

Transpiration can be thought of as the driving mechanism behind the cohesion-tension hypothesis. During transpiration, water evaporates out of a plant's leaves. Due to cohesion, each water molecule that leaves the plant during transpiration tugs on the one behind it. This tugging spreads from water molecule to water molecule. Molecules in the xylem of leaf veins move to replace those that left the mesophyll cells through the stomates. Replacement molecules are pulled out of the xylem cells in the stem and move into the leaf veins. The result is that a long chain of water molecules is pulled from root to leaf. The column of water inside the xylem is in a state of negative pressure—or tension—because of this pulling action. The water is held in a column because of the tension placed on it in the xylem, and because of the cohesion of the water molecules to each other and their adhesion to the xylem walls.

19.3 Nutrient Transport

In vascular plants, nutrients travel through phloem tissue made of intact, live cells joined end to end (Figure 19.3b). Tiny pores in the walls at the ends of the phloem cells allow the contents of the cells to mix. The porous areas at the ends of these cells resemble tiny strainers or sieves, and so the phloem channels are often called **sieve** (SIHV) **tubes**.

Sugars and amino acids move through the phloem cells from the leaves to the roots and other nonphotosynthetic parts of the plant. Despite their relatively large and numerous sieve pores, phloem cells contain cytoplasm through which water and dissolved sugars pass. Yet the rate at which the fluid moves is thousands of times faster than diffusion alone can account for. What is the possible mechanism of phloem transport?

The best explanation for the movement of sugars through the phloem is the pressure-flow hypothesis (Figure 19.4). According to this hypothesis, water and dissolved sugars are transported through the phloem from sources (areas of higher pressure) to sinks (areas of lower pressure). Sources include cotyledons and endosperm during germination, leaves during spring and summer, and bark tissue and some storage roots in early spring. Sinks are found in many areas of a plant, including food storage areas and growing leaf buds, root tips, flowers, fruits, and seeds.

The process begins at a source such as a leaf, where photosynthesis occurs. There, sucrose is actively transported into the sieve tubes from the mesophyll cells. Companion cells (Figure 19.3b) may also have an important role. The resulting high concentration of sucrose moves water into the phloem from the xylem by osmosis, thus increasing the water pressure in the phloem cells. The higher pressure forces the sucrose to move toward the lower pressure at the sinks. Thus, sucrose molecules move from phloem cell to phloem cell, from source to sink, through the sieve tubes.

At a sink, the sucrose molecules are removed from the phloem—again by active transport—to be used or stored. At this time, water leaves the phloem cells by osmosis; most of it returns to the xylem. Thus, the flow of sucrose and water from the leaves to the root can continue. The entire

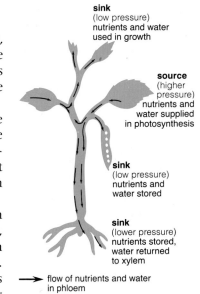

sink
(low pressure)
nutrients and water
used in growth

source
(higher pressure)
nutrients and
water supplied
in photosynthesis

sink
(low pressure)
nutrients and
water stored

sink
(lower pressure)
nutrients stored,
water returned
to xylem

→ flow of nutrients and water
in phloem

FIGURE 19.4 The pressure-flow hypothesis, based on fluid pressure in phloem, for the transport of nutrients and water.

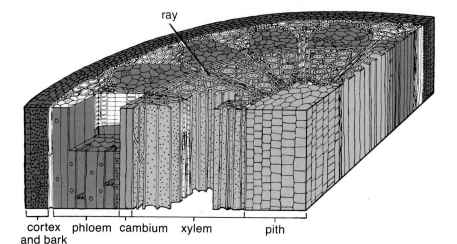

ray

cortex and bark | phloem | cambium | xylem | pith

FIGURE 19.5 Part of a stem in cross section. Note the location of the rays, which contain cells for storage and for transport of materials across the stem. Note also the location of the cambium, the tissue that produces new xylem and phloem cells.

process depends on the uptake of water by phloem cells in the leaves and a loss of water by phloem cells in areas of storage or of rapid growth.

Different materials in solution move up and down a plant through the xylem and the phloem. Water, salts, and other soluble materials move sideways from the xylem to the phloem, or from the phloem to the xylem, through **ray cells** (Figure 19.5). Pits in the walls of the ray cells open channels to pits in both the xylem and the phloem. Water and minerals are supplied to the phloem. Nutrients are supplied to dividing cambium cells as they form plant tissue. Substances also can pass sideways in the plant through the rays, so that all the cells receive the necessary materials.

CHECK AND CHALLENGE

1. Describe some adaptations plants have for living on land.
2. How does a plant benefit from the presence of mycorrhizae?
3. Describe the differences between xylem and phloem tissues.
4. Summarize the cohesion-tension hypothesis.
5. Describe the method by which a plant's cells receive nutrients.

Transport Systems in Animals

19.4　Circulatory Systems

Every organism must exchange materials with its environment. Ultimately, this exchange occurs at the cellular level, with substances passing across the plasma membrane between the cell and its immediate surroundings. Every living cell must be bathed by a watery environment. A protist living in a pond has such an environment, and chemical exchange across the plasma membrane occurs simply by diffusion or active transport. Protists such as the *Paramecium* (Figure 19.6) take in food and form a vacuole that is carried around inside the cell by the movement of the cytosol. A similar strategy works for the simplest multicellular animals. For example, *Hydra* (Figure 19.6) has a saclike body plan and tissues that are only two cell layers thick. Fluid containing food, oxygen, and carbon dioxide moves into and around its body as the *Hydra* moves. A specialized internal transport system is unnecessary. Exchange of materials in planarians and other flatworms occurs through a single opening of an internal cavity. The flatworm's flat body shape and the extent of the cavity keeps its cells in contact with a watery environment.

A single cavity, however, is inadequate for internal transport in animals with many layers of cells, especially if they live out of the water. Many such animals have a **circulatory system**, an organ system that transports materials to and from cells. This transport is typically carried out by a type of pump (heart), and other organs and tissues such as blood vessels and blood. Insects and other arthropods (Figure 19.6) have an open

CONNECTIONS

The structure of an organism's circulatory system reflects adaptation to the demands of its environment.

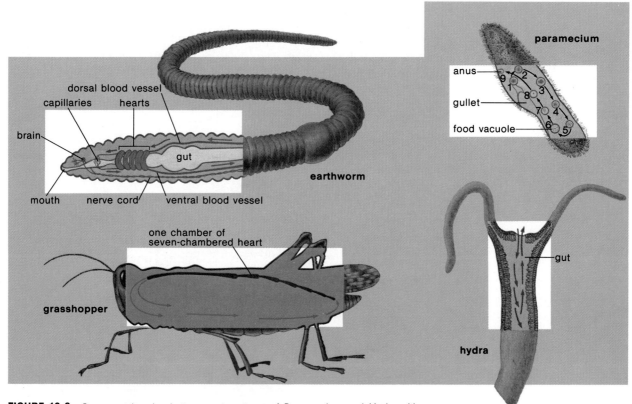

FIGURE 19.6 Compare the simple transport systems of *Paramecium* and *Hydra* with the more complex systems of the earthworm and grasshopper. The grasshopper and earthworm have contractile hearts; which has a continuous system of blood vessels?

circulatory system in which there is no separation between blood and other intercellular fluid. Together these fluids provide the liquid environment that bathes the internal organs. Chemical exchange between the fluid and body cells occurs as the blood oozes through sinuses, or spaces, surrounding the organs. Blood is also circulated by the heart's contraction and body by movements that squeeze the sinuses.

An earthworm has a closed circulatory system, meaning that blood is confined to vessels. Two major vessels branch into smaller vessels that carry blood to or from the various organs. A number of tiny contractile hearts, illustrated in Figure 19.6, pump blood under pressure into a main vessel under the digestive tract and then into the smaller vessels that extend into all the organs. The blood then passes back to a larger vessel running above the digestive tract and returns to the hearts.

Blood travels through a closed circulatory system more rapidly than it flows through an open system. You might expect to find open systems only in animals that move sluggishly, since the circulatory system transports the oxygen needed for cellular respiration. This is not always the case. Insects have open circulatory systems, but can be very active. However they do not transport oxygen long distances in blood. Instead, oxygen is distributed through microscopic air ducts. (See Chapter 21.)

19.5 Circulation in Vertebrates

Internal transport is accomplished in humans and other vertebrates by a closed circulatory system, also called the **cardiovascular system**. Figure 19.7 is a diagram of the human circulatory system. The components of the

FIGURE 19.7 A simplified drawing of the human circulatory system. Blood with a high concentration of oxygen is shown in red. Blood with a low concentration of oxygen is shown in blue. Trace the path of the blood around the body.

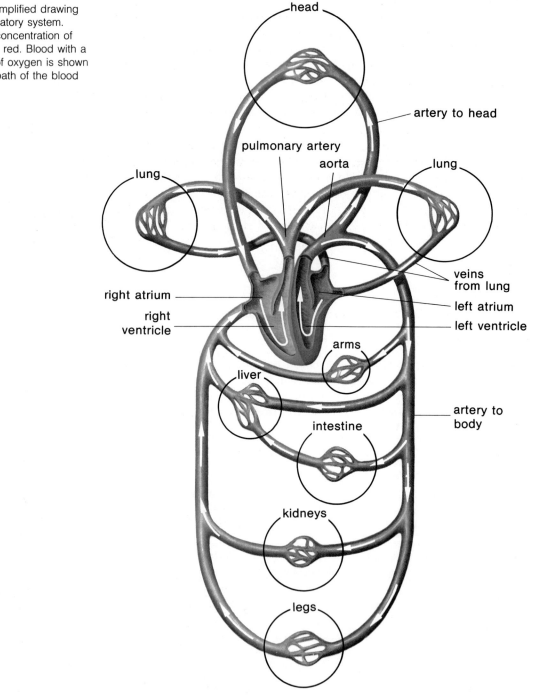

cardiovascular system are the heart, blood vessels, and blood. The vertebrate heart consists of one or more atria (AY tree uh; singular, atrium)—chambers that receive blood returning to the heart—and one or more ventricles—chambers that pump blood out of the heart. There are three types of blood vessels. **Arteries** carry blood away from the heart to organs throughout the body. The major artery leading from the heart and supplying blood to the body is called the aorta. The major arteries that carry blood to the lungs from the heart are the pulmonary arteries. Capillaries form the microscopic network of vessels that infiltrate every tissue. It is across the thin capillary walls that chemicals are exchanged between the blood and the intercellular fluid surrounding the cells. At their "downstream" end, capillaries rejoin to form **veins**, blood vessels that return blood to the heart. The relationship between arteries, veins, and capillaries is illustrated in Figure 19.8. Note that veins and arteries are distinguished by the *direction* of blood flow, not the quality of the blood they carry.

Among the vertebrates, a variety of elaborate closed circulatory systems have evolved. Fish have a two-chambered heart with one atrium and one ventricle. The ventricle pumps blood to the gills, where it picks up oxygen and gives off carbon dioxide, then to the digestive system, where it picks up nutrients, and finally back to the heart. (See Figure 19.9a.) Blood flow slows down in the capillaries because of their small size. The flow of blood to the organs is increased by the whole-body movements the fish makes when it swims.

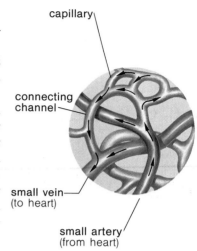

FIGURE 19.8 Arteries and veins connect with capillaries by way of smaller vessels or connecting channels. Blood can pass from arteries to connecting channels to capillaries or directly through the connecting channels to veins.

FIGURE 19.9 Vertebrate circulatory systems. Red represents oxygenated blood and blue represents deoxygenated blood. (a) Fish have a two-chambered heart and a single system for blood flow. (b) Amphibians and most reptiles have three-chambered hearts with only one ventricle and some mixing of oxygenated and deoxygenated blood. (c) Birds, mammals, and crocodilians have four-chambered hearts and double circulation. Oxygenated blood is completely separated from deoxygenated blood.

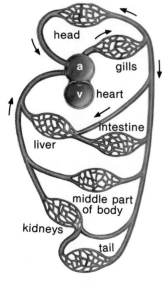

a. fish

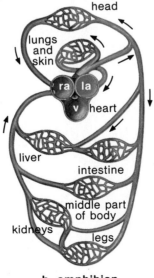

b. amphibian

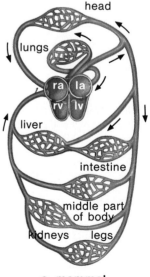

c. mammal

Amphibians and most reptiles have a three-chambered heart with two atria and one ventricle (Figure 19.9b). The ventricle pumps blood into a forked artery that directs the blood into two different circuits. One circuit leads to the lungs and skin where the blood picks up oxygen while flowing through the capillaries. A second circuit leads to all the organs except the lungs and then returns to the heart through veins. This pattern is called double circulation because the blood is pumped a second time after it has lost pressure from its trip through the capillaries. Double circulation ensures a vigorous flow of blood to the brain, muscles, and other organs. The four-chambered heart present in crocodilians, birds, and mammals has two atria and two completely divided ventricles (Figure 19.9c). There is double circulation, but the heart keeps oxygenated blood completely separate from deoxygenated blood. (See **Appendix 19A**, William Harvey Discovers Circulation.)

19.6   The Human Heart

Try Investigation 19B, Exercise and Pulse Rate.

Each heartbeat is a sequence of muscle contraction and relaxation called the cardiac cycle (Figure 19.10). In each cycle, the four chambers of the heart go through phases of contraction, or systole (SIS toh lee), and relaxation, or diastole (dy AS toh lee). The timing of these phases is not the same for all the chambers; the atria contract slightly before the ventricles.

When the atria are relaxed and filling, the ventricles are also relaxed. As pressure rises in the atria, the valves between the atria and ventricles (AV valves) are forced open, and the ventricles start to fill. As the atria contract (atrial systole), additional blood is forced into the ventricles. The ventricles then contract (ventricular systole), causing the AV valves to snap shut, and the pressure inside the ventricles rises sharply. With the increased pressure, the valves leading to the aorta and the pulmonary artery open, and blood flows out of the heart. After the blood has been ejected, the ventricles relax, and the cardiac cycle starts again. The path of the blood through the heart is shown in Figure 19.11 on page 438.

Heartbeats result from rhythmic impulses that come from cells in the heart itself. These impulses arise in the pacemaker, cells of specialized muscle tissue located in the inner wall of the right atrium. This tissue creates electrical impulses through changes in cell membrane properties,

FIGURE 19.10 The cardiac cycle. Blood enters the atria, which contract, forcing blood into the ventricles. Then the atria relax and fill, and the ventricles contract, forcing blood into the pulmonary artery and the aorta. The ventricles relax and the atria contract, repeating the cycle.

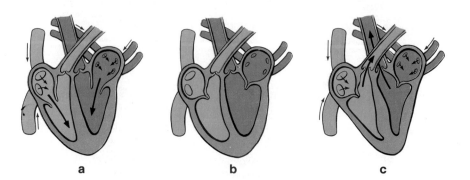

a   b   c

THE EXCIMER LASER

Cardiovascular disease affects an estimated 6 million Americans every year, and it is the leading cause of death. Deposits of plaque (cholesterol and other substances that can stick to the inner walls of blood vessels) reduce the flow of blood through a vessel and may eventually cause heart attacks and death (Chapter 18). Plaque is responsible for almost 90 percent of all cardiovascular disease.

Plaque deposits may be fatty, fibrous, or hard and calcified. Surgeons have been treating plaque deposits with balloon angioplasty, a procedure in which a tiny balloon is inserted into the obstructed blood vessel and then inflated. The pressure of the balloon flattens out the plaque deposits along the artery wall, thus creating more room for blood to pass. Although hundreds of thousands of balloon angioplasty operations are performed every year, the procedure does not work for individuals with fibrous or calcified plaque deposits.

Lasers—concentrated beams of light at a uniform wavelength—are capable of vaporizing even the hardest plaque deposits. By clearing plaque deposits from the artery walls, lasers may allow some patients to avoid bypass surgery. (This type of surgery involves removing a piece of a blood vessel from someplace else in the patient and using it to create a detour around the blocked vessels.) Lasers also are used by surgeons to stop the bleeding of ulcers, repair detached retinas in the eye, and treat a growing list of other medical problems.

Several companies have developed an "excimer" laser (one that produces ultraviolet radiation) for medical use. Excimer lasers have the unique ability to selectively destroy their target without causing significant heat damage to surrounding tissues. These lasers produce powerful, but extremely short, bursts of ultraviolet light that break the chemical bonds holding the organic plaque molecules together. The plaque deposits break apart into tiny

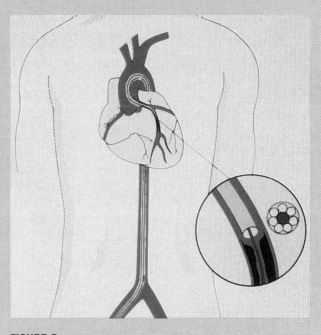

FIGURE B Use of the excimer laser to clear a blocked artery

particles and gases that are carried by the blood to the lungs or the kidneys where they are eliminated with other body wastes.

The laser beam is carried to the target through a flexible fiber-optic tube, or catheter, made of small bundles of glass fibers. The catheter is inserted into the major artery of the thigh and then snaked through the patient's blood vessels until it reaches the site of the blockage (Figure B). Doctors guide and monitor the laser catheter with a fluoroscope—a device similar to an x-ray machine.

Some people are concerned about the potential effect of excimer laser radiation on blood vessel tissue. However, researchers feel the risk to the patient from the blocked vessel is much greater.

FIGURE 19.11 A drawing of a section through a human heart and the blood vessels leading to and from it. Trace the flow of blood into and out of the heart by following the numbers and arrows. How can you account for the wall of the left ventricle being thicker than the wall of the right ventricle?

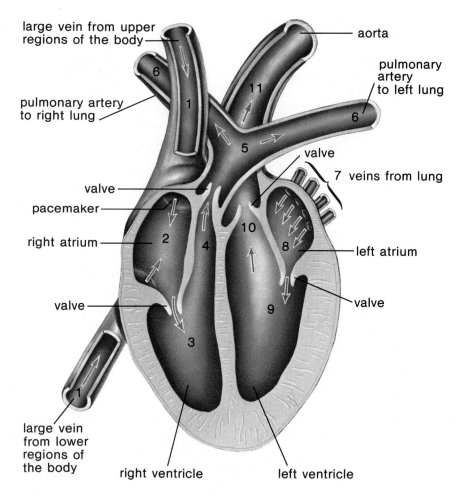

without outside stimulation. The heartbeat impulse spreads from there throughout the heart muscle. Although the heartbeat starts in the heart itself, changes in the rate of the heartbeat are controlled by nerves outside the heart.

Figure 19.12 is a photograph of the valves between the atria and the ventricles in the human heart. These one-way valves prevent blood in the ventricles from backing up into the atria. Leaks in these valves cause the condition known as a heart murmur.

19.7 Blood Vessels

The circulatory system provides a good example of the interrelationship of structure and function. Blood vessels differ in the amounts of muscle and elastic tissue in their walls just as they differ in their functions in the system. For example, the largest arteries have walls made up largely of muscle and other elastic tissue (Figure 19.13). When the heart contracts, it forces blood into these arteries under great pressure, causing the walls of the large arteries to stretch and expand. This expansion allows more space

FIGURE 19.12 Valves of the human heart

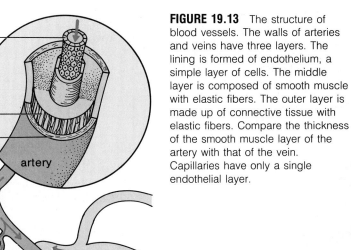

FIGURE 19.13 The structure of blood vessels. The walls of arteries and veins have three layers. The lining is formed of endothelium, a simple layer of cells. The middle layer is composed of smooth muscle with elastic fibers. The outer layer is made up of connective tissue with elastic fibers. Compare the thickness of the smooth muscle layer of the artery with that of the vein. Capillaries have only a single endothelial layer.

FOCUS ON *Blood Pressure*

A healthy blood pressure is maintained through complex interactions among the nervous, endocrine, excretory, and circulatory systems. Nerves from specialized pressure receptors in the aorta and in the artery leading to the head connect directly to cardiac control centers in the brain. Other cardiac centers respond to sensory input, such emotions, and to chemical input, especially the concentration of carbon dioxide. When the blood pressure falls below an individual's normal range, signals sent to the brain result in increased heart rate and constriction of the blood vessels—changes that increase the blood pressure. The opposite adjustment occurs when blood pressure is too high.

Receptors in the hypothalamus (a part of the brain) also help maintain normal blood pressure. These receptors control secretion of hormones in the kidneys and the adrenal glands. If blood pressure falls below normal limits, one group of these hormones acts on the kidneys to return more water to the circulatory system, increasing blood pressure. If blood pressure rises above

normal limits, another group of hormones acts on the kidneys to excrete more water, decreasing the volume of the blood and, hence, lowering blood pressure.

About 20 percent of the adult population in the United States has blood pressure higher than the normal range, a condition called hypertension. Hypertension can cause serious health problems, even death. High blood pressure forces the heart to work harder, which can result in damage to heart muscles; it can damage blood vessels in the brain, which can lead to crippling or fatal strokes (ruptured blood vessels of the brain); and it can contribute to the development of atherosclerosis (Chapter 18), further damaging the circulatory system.

The exact causes of hypertension are not known and it is often undiagnosed until health is seriously affected. However, hypertension can be controlled by medication prescribed by a physician. Regular physical examinations, proper diet, and exercise can help prevent and control the condition.

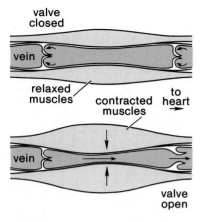

FIGURE 19.14 Movement of blood in veins is brought about by pressure from adjacent muscles. Compression forces blood in both directions, but valves prevent blood from flowing backward and away from the heart.

for the blood to enter and prevents the pressure from increasing greatly. During the relaxed phase of the heartbeat, the stretched elastic walls of the arteries contract and thereby continue to exert pressure on the blood, helping to push it along and maintain blood pressure.

The walls of smaller arteries are made of muscle and elastic tissue. Signals from the nervous system can cause these arteries to contract and expand. Thus, blood pressure and the direction and the amount of blood that flows into different parts of the body may be controlled.

Blood returning to the heart through the veins is under much lower pressure than the blood flowing in the arteries. Veins have thinner walls with less muscle and elastic tissues than arteries. (See Figure 19.13.) Blood flow through the veins is aided by several factors. Valves in the veins prevent the blood from flowing backward. In some parts of the body, contraction of the skeletal muscles around the veins helps to push the blood along (Figure 19.14). Gravity also helps the blood return to the heart, especially from the head region. Astronauts lie flat during blastoff and reentry of their space vehicles to equalize the forces on the blood. This prevents a lack of blood in the brain—and unconsciousness—and excess blood from returning to the heart—which would strain the heart and its vessels.

CHECK AND CHALLENGE

1. How does a vacuole in *Paramecium* serve the same function as a circulatory system in humans?
2. Describe the differences between open and closed circulatory systems.
3. Why is the human heart described as a two-part pump?
4. Explain the differences in the structure of veins and arteries.
5. Why is a pulse taken at an artery and not at a vein?
6. Describe how the heart contracts and moves blood.

Homeostasis: Regulation of the Internal Environment

19.8   Composition of Blood

Blood consists of different types of cells suspended in a fluid. In humans, specialized cells called red blood cells, or **erythrocytes** (ih RITH roh sytz) transport oxygen. Erythrocytes contain an oxygen-carrying red protein, **hemoglobin** (HEE moh gloh bin), that forms a temporary chemical bond with oxygen and transports it to body cells. In other animals, substances of different chemical structure and color combine with oxygen in a similar manner. (See **Appendix 19B**, Oxygen-Transport Pigments in Animals.)

Erythrocytes live only about 120 days, so their numbers must be renewed constantly. New cells are manufactured in the bone marrow of the long bones. As erythrocytes mature, they lose their nuclei, and thus they are unable to reproduce in the bloodstream.

Specialized white blood cells, or **leukocytes** (LOO koh sytz), circulate throughout the body and form the second line of defense against invading organisms such as bacteria. (Your skin and mucus membranes form the first line of defense.) Some types of leukocytes, called macrophages (MAK roh fay jez), surround bacteria and absorb them in much the same way as an amoeba takes in food. When there is an infection in the body, the number of leukocytes increases greatly. They help combat the infection by destroying the bacteria. (Chapter 20 describes how leukocytes and the immune system function together.) Figure 19.15 shows some of the types of cells found in human blood.

The fluid portion of the blood, called **plasma**, is water that contains dissolved proteins, salts (electrolytes), amino acids, sugars, and other substances. Blood absorbs digested food from the intestine, as described in Chapter 18, and carries it in the plasma to all the cells of the body. Unusual variations in the amounts of amino acids, sugars, or fats may sometimes indicate that the organs or glands of the digestive system are not functioning properly. Also contained in the plasma are hormones, such as the reproductive hormones, that are secreted by glands in the body. Upsets in the hormonal system sometimes can be detected by blood analysis.

The concentration of electrolytes, present in the plasma as dissolved ions, is an important factor in maintaining the osmotic balance between the blood and the intercellular fluid. Some of these ions also help maintain normal pH of the blood. The ability of nerves and muscles to function normally depends on the concentration of key ions in the intercellular fluid—a reflection of their concentration in the plasma. The kidneys maintain these plasma electrolytes at precise concentrations.

Some intercellular fluid is recycled into the circulatory system indirectly by the **lymphatic** (lim FAT ik) **system**. The fluid in the lymphatic

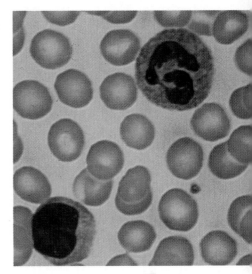

FIGURE 19.15 Human blood smear showing erythrocytes, two types of leukocytes (top right, and bottom left), and a platelet (the small particle, lower right).

FOCUS ON *Wound Healing*

In spite of the many advances in modern medicine, there still is no widespread accepted treatment to promote the healing of wounds. The best approach is to keep them sterile and moist and let nature take its course in the healing process. This old methodology may soon change. Several different companies, using recombinant DNA technology, are producing chemicals that appear to promote healing. These chemicals, called growth factors, occur naturally in our bodies and stimulate cell migration and cell division, both of which are important in wound healing.

Growth factors applied experimentally to incisions in the skin of rats speeded the healing process. Five days after application, treated wounds were healing more than twice as fast as untreated wounds. The tissue-regeneration capabilities of growth factors may be valuable in treating areas that heal slowly, such as the cornea of the eye. Burn victims may also benefit from growth factor research.

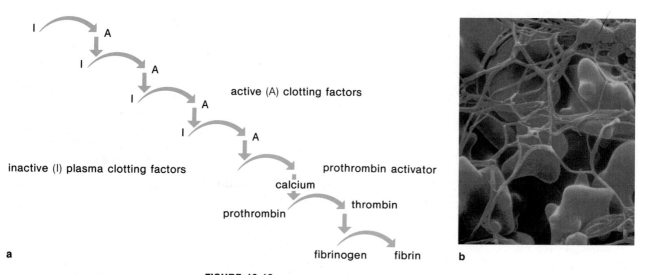

inactive (I) plasma clotting factors

active (A) clotting factors

prothrombin activator

calcium

thrombin

prothrombin

fibrinogen   fibrin

a

b

FIGURE 19.16 A blood clot is the result of a cascade of enzymatic reactions (a) that ends when the soluble protein fibrinogen is converted to insoluble fibrin strands. The fibrin strands provide a network in which platelets are trapped (b), forming a blood clot.

system, which contains certain specialized cells, water, large protein molecules, salts, and other substances, is called lymph (Chapter 18). Lymph picks up intercellular fluid and passes through the walls of small lymph capillaries into larger lymph vessels. Finally, all of the lymph fluid empties from the two largest lymph vessels into the blood stream at veins near the heart. (See Figure 20.6.)

A vital characteristic of blood is its ability to clot, or coagulate (koh AG yoo layt). Like a patch that seals a leaking garden hose, a clot can seal a wound and prevent further loss of blood. Coagulation results from a complex sequence of events involving small cell fragments called platelets (PLAYT lets) that are carried in the blood (Figure 19.15). Coagulation begins when platelets come in contact with a rough surface, such as a torn tissue. The platelets become sticky and attract more platelets, forming a plug that partially seals the wound. The platelets also release substances that, acting with chemicals in the plasma known as clotting factors, begin the chain of reactions diagrammed in Figure 19.16a. As a result of these reactions, a substance called an activator is formed. In the presence of calcium ions (Ca^{2+}), the activator catalyzes the conversion of prothrombin, a plasma protein, to thrombin. Thrombin then acts as an enzyme to convert the soluble plasma protein fibrinogen (fy BRIN oh jen) to its insoluble form, fibrin (FY brin). Fibrin forms a network of threads that trap additional platelets and other materials that form the clot (Figure 19.16b).

A clot may form within a blood vessel, blocking circulation. If the clot blocks one of the arteries supplying blood to the heart, blood flow to that area of the heart is cut off, resulting in a heart attack. A clot blocking an artery in the brain results in one type of stroke. Strokes usually result in temporary or permanent paralysis of part of the body and may result in death.

19.9   The Circulatory System and Homeostasis

Most organisms live in an external environment that is continually changing. Yet the internal environment of living things—the fluids that are transported to the body cells and tissues—must be kept quite steadily balanced. The sum total of the processes by which a steady state is maintained in the internal environment is called **homeostasis** (hoh mee oh STAY sis). An organism's ability to monitor and maintain homeostasis depends on the smooth interactions of the different body systems, linked by the transport system.

Different systems in your body regulate, for example, the amount of hormones that are released, the level of sugar in your blood, and your metabolic rate. The transport system is an essential link with all the other systems because it moves needed materials to different parts of your body, thus helping to maintain homeostasis. Without a dependable system for delivering nutrients and other chemicals and for removing wastes and unwanted materials, your body systems would become unbalanced and eventually shut down.

Many control mechanisms have evolved that detect subtle changes in an organism's external environment and that make necessary adjustments to keep the internal fluid environment constant. For example, when you become overheated, blood vessels just below the skin surface dilate, bringing more blood to your skin where excess heat can be radiated out of the body. Also, chemical messages carried in the blood stimulate the glands in your skin to begin producing and excreting sweat. As sweat evaporates, it removes heat from your body. Both of these responses help you cool down.

The transport, excretory, and gas exchange systems play important roles in the maintenance of homeostasis, but the nervous and endocrine systems are most directly responsible for the overall control in the body. Chapters 21 through 23 discuss many of these homeostatic mechanisms. When you read these later chapters, watch for examples of how the transport system is involved in regulation.

CONNECTIONS

The structures of plant and animal transport systems are diverse, yet they all display unity in their function—the maintenance of homeostasis.

CHECK AND CHALLENGE

1.   What is the difference between blood and erythrocytes?
2.   What is the difference between blood and blood plasma?
3.   Describe the process by which a blood clot forms when the skin is broken.
4.   How do blood and lymph differ?
5.   What two body systems work closely with the circulatory system in the homeostatic control of the internal environment?

Summary

In unicellular aquatic organisms, diffusion supplies materials necessary for life processes. Most multicellular organisms, however, cannot satisfy their needs through diffusion alone. For example, the water and nutrients in soil cannot diffuse directly into a land plant's leaf-cells, meters above the ground. Special structures have evolved in land plants to transport raw materials to all the cells of the plant. Branching root systems, some with the aid of mycorrhizae, obtain and transport water and dissolved minerals from the soil. Xylem, with its tracheids and vessels, serves as the transport channels from roots to leaves. The cohesion-tension hypothesis, as well as capillary action and root pressure, may account for the transport of water to the tops of tall trees. Phloem consists of sieve tubes that transport sucrose and amino acids from the leaves to the rest of the plant. The pressure-flow hypothesis could account for how the food is transported through the phloem.

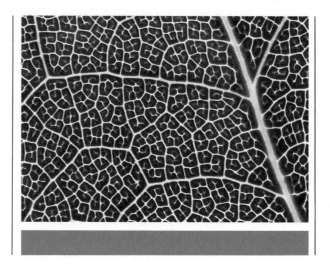

In multicellular animals systems of pumps and vessels evolved, circulatory systems that transport food and oxygen to cells and remove waste products of cellular respiration. Some invertebrates have open circulatory systems in which blood passes through sinuses around the body tissues and then returns to a heart through small vessels. All vertebrates have closed circulatory systems with hearts, arteries, capillaries, and veins.

Arteries have muscular, flexible walls that withstand high blood pressures near the heart. Veins are less muscular and more flexible than arteries, and they are subjected to lower pressure. Exchanges of gases, wastes, and nutrients occur between the blood and the cells through capillaries whose walls are only one cell thick.

Fish have two-chambered hearts, amphibians and most reptiles have three-chambered hearts, and crocodilians, birds, and mammals have four-chambered hearts. A four-chambered heart separates the systems for gas exchange and for circulation.

Blood consists of specialized cells, proteins, and plasma. Human erythrocytes contain the oxygen-carrying protein hemoglobin. Leukocytes provide the second line of defense against invading organisms. Some proteins function with platelets to form clots, which repair injuries and stop blood loss. Some plasma and other tissue fluids are picked up and returned to the circulatory system by the lymphatic system.

The circulatory system plays a major role in maintaining homeostasis. Levels of blood sugar, hormones, and many other chemicals within the circulatory system must be maintained within certain limits or the body's systems will shut down. The circulatory system functions with the nervous, excretory, gas exchange, and endocrine systems in maintaining homeostasis.

Key Concepts

Use the following concepts to develop a concept map. Include additional terms as you need them.

transport systems	water and minerals
animals	nutrients
plants	oxygen
roots	waste products
homeostasis	digestive system
stems	arteries
leaves	veins
xylem	capillaries
phloem	lungs
body	heart

Reviewing Ideas

1. How do root hairs help roots to obtain water?
2. How do mycorrhizae help roots to obtain water and minerals?
3. Explain the function of pits in the tracheids of xylem tissue.
4. What is the function of ray cells in plants?
5. Describe the role of the heart's pacemaker.
6. What is the difference in function between an atrium and a ventricle?
7. Describe the location and function of the different structures of the circulatory system that keep blood flowing in only one direction.
8. Describe the differences in function between erythrocytes and leukocytes.
9. How does the human circulatory system assist the endocrine system in completing its work?
10. How are the products of photosynthesis transported throughout the plant?

Using Concepts

1. Where does active transport function in the conducting tissues of plants?
2. How can transpiration help water reach the top of tall trees?

3. Explain the difference between water movement by capillary action and that explained by the cohesion-tension hypothesis.
4. Explain the pressure-flow hypothesis for food transport in phloem tissue.
5. What might be some advantages of a four-chambered heart over a three-chambered heart?
6. Explain why it would be difficult for gas and waste exchange to occur between cells and blood flowing in arteries.
7. Discuss the similarities and differences between the circulatory system and the lymphatic system.
8. How can some small, multicellular organisms function without closed circulatory systems?

Synthesis

1. Review the process of osmosis described in Chapter 6. Explain how osmosis helps root hairs obtain water from soil.
2. Some modern land plants, such as the giant sequoias, reach tremendous size. Explain how a large size could be advantageous for these plants.
3. Explain how the process of photosynthesis is dependent on leaf structures, xylem, and phloem in a plant.
4. Review the menstrual cycle described in Chapter 11. Explain the role of the circulatory system in the homeostasis of the menstrual cycle.

Extensions

1. Use a stethoscope and listen to your heart for a few minutes. Write a poem expressing your feelings about your heart.
2. A small redwood seedling is growing next to a huge, old redwood tree. Write a short story describing the actions of the seedling roots as they try to find water amid the roots of the large tree.

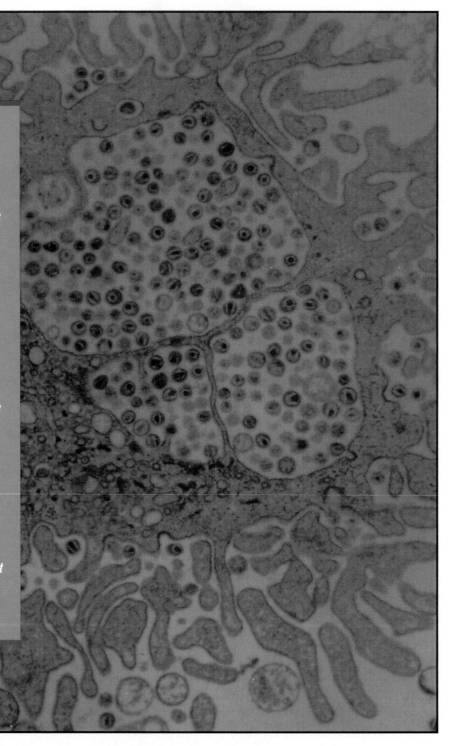

CONTENTS

Immune Systems

*T*he word *immune* literally means "protection." The immune system provides protection from many hazards in the environment. Everyone has had firsthand experience with the immune system. For example, you probably had chicken pox as a child. Because your immune system has specialized cells that "remember" the first chicken pox infection and defend your body against the virus, you do not worry about getting chicken pox again.

In recent years knowledge of the immune system has grown rapidly, and research has begun to answer many of the questions that interested scientists for many years. For example, if you catch a cold, you may feel miserable for a few days, and then recover. However, weeks later, you may catch another cold and go through the same cycle. Why does your immune system not protect you from the second cold as it protected you from a second chicken pox infection? Perhaps you have allergies to pollen, foods, or other substances. What is the relationship between allergies and the immune system? Why does the body often reject transplanted organs, whereas a mother does not reject the foreign cells of a developing fetus? How does the immune system determine that a wide variety of substances, from microorganisms to another individual's cells, are foreign? This chapter examines how the immune system protects against foreign substances, and some diseases that result from immune system disorders.

Protection Against Infection

20.1 Immune System Functions

Foreign substances have special properties enabling them to invade the body and cause disease. Without healthy defenses against infection, you would constantly be ill with various diseases. However, normally your body defenses prevent infections from occurring. The ability to ward off infectious disease through your defenses is called resistance.

---

*W*hat disease is caused by HIV?

*H*ow do HIV and other viruses replicate themselves?

◆ *The HIV in a human cell, magnified 25 000 times.*

Some defenses prevent foreign invaders from ever entering the body; other defenses remove them from the body, and still others fight them if they remain inside. The two basic types of resistance are nonspecific and specific. Nonspecific defenses protect you from *any kind* of foreign substance. Specific defenses, or immunity, protect against a particular type of foreign invader. You will find out more about both types of resistance in the sections that follow.

As multicellular organisms evolved, groups of cells within organisms developed specialized functions. The function of the cells that make up the immune system is to protect the individual organism against threats from cells or molecules that are foreign, or nonself. The primary threat to humans and other animals is **infection**. Infection is an invasion of the body by pathogens—foreign organisms, such as viruses, bacteria, and fungi, that have the potential to cause **disease**. Disease results when cells and tissues have been damaged so much that they can no longer function properly. Without an immune system, humans would certainly die from infectious diseases.

Any foreign material that causes an immune response is called an **antigen** (ANT ih gen—*anti*body *gen*erator). Most antigens are proteins. Because all cells and organisms are composed of many different types of proteins, they contain many antigens. Normally, the immune system discriminates carefully between self molecules and foreign antigens, so that its destructive functions are directed against nonself. A malfunctioning immune system sometimes responds to self molecules as if they were foreign, resulting in destruction of one's own cells and tissues.

20.2   Nonspecific Defenses

Nonspecific defenses are a generalized response to any foreign, nonself material. They do not identify which foreign material or pathogen the nonself material is. Some nonspecific defenses include physical and biochemical barriers. For example, the skin and mucous membranes keep most foreign materials from entering the body. The lining of the respiratory tract is covered with cilia that sweep out dust and microorganisms from the lungs. The low pH of the stomach and the antibacterial enzymes found in saliva, tears, and sweat are biochemical barriers to many microorganisms.

Another way organisms protect themselves is by phagocytosis and the destruction of foreign material. Phagocytic cells, such as the macrophages shown in Figure 20.1, are nonspecific, engulfing and destroying a wide variety of molecules, particles, and organisms. Phagocytic cells are very efficient and engulf not only foreign materials but also self materials such as damaged or dead cells. Phagocytic cells are found in the blood and lymphatic systems, as well as in the skin, lungs, liver, brain, and in most other tissues.

Phagocytosis is an important part of a nonspecific defense process called **inflammation**. Inflammation is a generalized response to tissue damage, such as cuts, and to foreign materials, such as splinters and infectious organisms. During the inflammation response, capillaries in the damaged tissue become permeable to cells and fluid, which leak into the

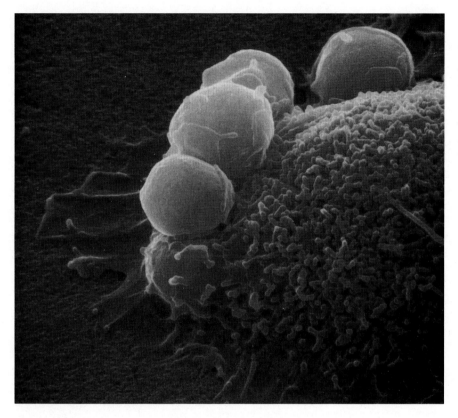

FIGURE 20.1 Macrophages are phagocytic leukocytes (white blood cells). This macrophage (magnified more than 5000 times) was taken from the blood of a mouse. When erythrocytes (red blood cells) from a sheep were introduced, the macrophage began to engulf the foreign cells. One erythrocyte is already surrounded, and four others are about to be engulfed.

inflamed tissue, causing redness, swelling, and warmth. At the site of inflammation, pus forms from the accumulation of millions of phagocytic cells, as well as dead invading organisms and cellular debris. Inflammation is the primary nonspecific protective mechanism in vertebrates.

20.3 Specific Defenses and Immunity

Although nonspecific defenses are very effective, they are not adequate protection against the endless variety of pathogens in our world. Your body's main line of defense is the specific defenses of your immune system. Specialized lymphocytes (white blood cells) called helper T cells trigger the immune system to counteract antigens using a simultaneous, cooperative two-pronged attack—the **cell-mediated response** and the **antibody-mediated response**. In the cell-mediated response, other T cells called killer T cells attack and destroy infected cells and other cells of the body that have become abnormal, such as cancer cells. In the antibody-mediated response, other lymphocytes, called B cells, produce **antibodies**, proteins that bind to antigens and mark them for destruction by the nonspecific defenses. Both the cell-mediated response and the antibody-mediated response are initiated by helper T cells. You will find out more about T cells and B cells as you progress through this chapter.

FIGURE 20.2 A cartoonist of Jenner's day shows the fears that vaccination against small pox aroused.

The immune system not only destroys antigens but also provides long-term resistance, or **immunity**, to pathogens it has destroyed. Once the immune system has encountered a foreign material, it quickly and efficiently responds to subsequent exposures to the same material. Knowledge of this long-term resistence led scientists to discover that immunity could be produced artificially with **vaccines**, suspensions of dead or weakened organisms that induce specific immunity without actually causing disease.

Perhaps the most successful story of immunization is the elimination of the disease smallpox. In ancient China, children developed immunity to smallpox after they inhaled powder made from the scabs of smallpox sores. The Arabs injected matter from smallpox sores under the skin on the point of a needle. In 1717 Lady Mary Wortley Montagu, wife of the British Ambassador to Turkey, introduced the Arabian type of smallpox immunization to England. However, there were problems with these immunizations, such as serious smallpox infections in some patients.

In 1798, the English physician Edward Jenner observed that milkmaids who had recovered from a mild disease called cowpox were protected against smallpox. Jenner inoculated a boy with pus isolated from cowpox sores and subsequently demonstrated that the boy was protected against smallpox. Jenner called the process vaccination, and by 1800 at least 100 000 people had been vaccinated against smallpox (Figure 20.2). Smallpox is now eliminated worldwide—the last two deaths from smallpox occurred in 1978.

Jenner's experiments probably have been responsible for saving more lives than any others in the history of humans. In the nineteenth century, Louis Pasteur developed vaccination procedures for rabies and other diseases. The task of developing effective vaccines is not often easy. Today,

FOCUS ON *Evading the Immune System*

Trypanosomes (Figure A) are microscopic protozoans that spend part of their life cycle in the blood of humans and other mammals. In humans, they cause African sleeping sickness, a fatal disease of the nervous system characterized by fever, lethargy, tremors, and weight loss. The key to the trypanosome's success is its ability to circumvent the human immune system by changing its surface covering. With the initial infection, the host's immune system produces antibodies that bind to antigens in the trypanosome's surface and destroy the organisms. However, during this time some of the trypanosomes change their surface coverings and are not immediately attacked. Eventually the immune system produces antibodies against the new antigens. Meanwhile, some trypanosomes again change their coverings, staying one jump ahead of the immune system. The result is a persistent infection of the host's bloodstream.

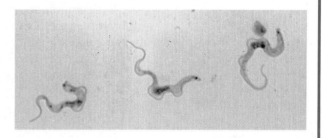

FIGURE A   Trypanosomes that cause African sleeping sickness live in the human bloodstream. They are transmitted by the bite of a certain species of fly.

scientists continue to work on developing vaccines for infectious diseases, such as acquired immune deficiency syndrome (AIDS).

Everyone has had practical experience with immunity. You have probably been vaccinated against polio virus. This vaccination provides long-term, specific immunity against polio. Inoculation with polio vaccine, however, confers no protection against other viruses such as chicken pox. Similarly, because there are hundreds of different viruses that can cause the common cold, immunity to one type of cold virus does not provide resistance to the other types. In addition, many microorganisms, such as flu viruses and certain protozoa, can change their surface proteins. If you become immune to a specific flu virus, a slight alteration of surface proteins allows the virus to evade the immune system and cause disease again.

The many functions of the immune system are extremely complex. No one fully understands how an organism starts, carries to completion, stops, and regulates immune responses. Immunological research has progressed significantly, but there is still much to learn.

CHECK AND CHALLENGE

1. What is the difference between infection and disease?

2. What nonspecific protective mechanisms do humans have?

3. Define the term antigen and provide several examples.

4. What are antibodies?

5. Distinguish between antibody-mediated immunity and cell-mediated immunity.

Components of the Specific Immune Response

20.4 The Cell-mediated Response

The primary cells of the immune system are small white blood cells known as **lymphocytes** (LIM foh syts), and they are responsible for specific immunity. There are approximately two trillion (2×10^{12}) lymphocytes in a mature human, making the immune system comparable to the liver or brain with respect to numbers of cells. Lymphocytes travel individually in the blood and in the lymphatic circulation, and they also collect in specialized lymphoid tissues and organs. Figure 20.3 shows the structures of the human immune system.

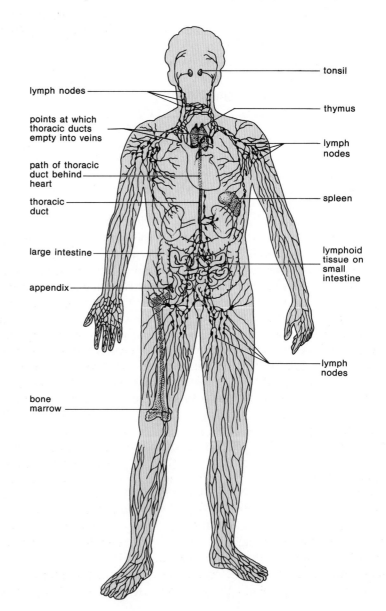

lymph nodes

points at which thoracic ducts empty into veins

path of thoracic duct behind heart

thoracic duct

large intestine

appendix

bone marrow

tonsil

thymus

lymph nodes

spleen

lymphoid tissue on small intestine

lymph nodes

FIGURE 20.3 The human immune system. The primary lymphoid organs are the bone marrow and thymus. Secondary lymphoid organs include the lymph nodes, spleen, and tonsils.

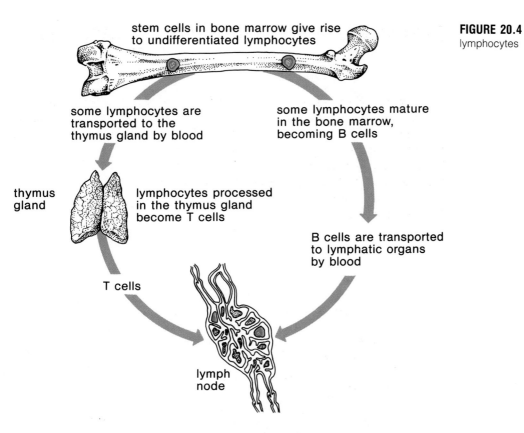

stem cells in bone marrow give rise
to undifferentiated lymphocytes

some lymphocytes are
transported to the
thymus gland by blood

some lymphocytes mature
in the bone marrow,
becoming B cells

thymus
gland

lymphocytes processed
in the thymus gland
become T cells

B cells are transported
to lymphatic organs
by blood

T cells

lymph
node

FIGURE 20.4 The processing of
lymphocytes

In a fetus, lymphocytes, like all other blood cells, are produced in the liver. As a child develops, the bone marrow gradually takes over lymphocyte production, and it continues to produce lymphocytes throughout life (Figure 20.4). In the bone marrow, undifferentiated cells called stem cells are capable of differentiating into all the types of blood cells. Bone marrow is a primary lymphoid organ—some of the lymphocytes produced there are mature and functional when they leave the marrow. Such lymphocytes are called **B cells** (*b*one marrow-derived lymphocytes), and their primary function is to produce antibodies and secrete them into the blood stream. Other cells are produced in the marrow and then travel to the thymus where they continue to divide and mature into *t*hymus-derived lymphocytes, or **T cells**. Thus the thymus is another primary lymphoid organ.

Figure 20.5 (page 454) shows that there are several different types of T cells. Helper T cells activate the increase in number of both T cells and B cells in response to infection. They also stimulate B cells to produce antibodies. As such, they are the key to the entire immune response. Killer T cells—the "foot soldiers" of the cell-mediated response—attack foreign cells and infected host cells directly. Suppressor T cells suppress the responses of both B and T cells, which shuts down the immune response after the infection is overcome. Another type of T cell is involved in delayed hypersensitivity, such as the reactions to poison ivy.

When mature T cells and B cells enter the circulation, many of them lodge in secondary lymphoid tissues, such as the spleen, lymph nodes,

FIGURE 20.5 Major cells of the immune system. *B* cells, when stimulated by an antigen, differentiate and become plasma cells that secrete antibodies. *T* cells are of two types. Killer *T* cells attack infected cells and invading pathogens by secreting toxic chemicals. Helper *T* cells secrete lymphokines—helper molecules that enhance the immune response. Both *B* cells and *T* cells give rise to long-lived memory cells. Macrophages ingest pathogens and display their antigens to *T* cells, triggering the specific immune response.

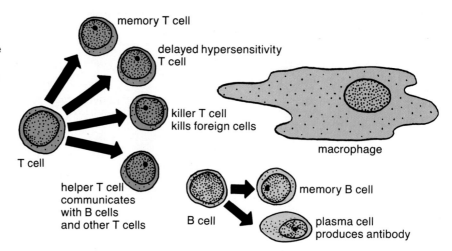

FIGURE 20.6 The lymphatic vessels return lymphocytes and antibody molecules to the circulatory system at the thoracic duct.

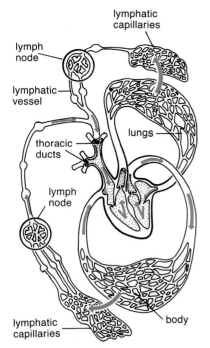

tonsils, appendix, and the lymphoid tissues beneath the skin and in the lining of the intestinal tract. Interaction of T cells and B cells with antigens usually occurs in these tissues. "Swollen glands" are really enlarged lymph nodes in which lymphocytes have multiplied to fight infection.

Unlike red blood cells, lymphocytes travel between the blood and the lymph, entering the lymphatic circulation primarily in the lymph nodes. After passing through numerous lymph nodes, lymphocytes return to the blood by way of the thoracic duct (Figure 20.6). Thus, billions of T cells and B cells are constantly migrating throughout the body.

20.5   The Antibody-mediated Response

Although many antigens that induce an immune response are proteins, almost any large molecule can be an antigen, as long as it is foreign to the individual. The immune system is capable of discriminating among millions of different antigens and between antigens that are nearly identical.

B cells and T cells make proteins that extend across their cell membranes. The protruding ends of these cell surface receptors bind to specific antigens. On the surface of T cells, the proteins are called T-cell receptors. On the surface of B cells, they are called B-cell receptors. Once a B-cell receptor binds to a specific antigen, it begins to divide rapidly. Its offspring cells differentiate into two types of cells, plasma cells and memory cells.

Plasma cells are like tiny factories that produce antibodies identical to the B-cell receptor that bound the original antigen. The antibodies bind to the same type of antigen molecules wherever they are found in the body, marking them for destruction. As you can see in Figure 20.7, antibodies and receptors bind to antigens in a lock and key fashion. The binding sites of the antibodies and the antigens are three-dimensional, complementary images of one another.

Memory cells can also produce antibodies, but whereas plasma cells live only a few days, memory cells continue to circulate for long periods of time—up to a lifetime. The second time the immune system encounters a

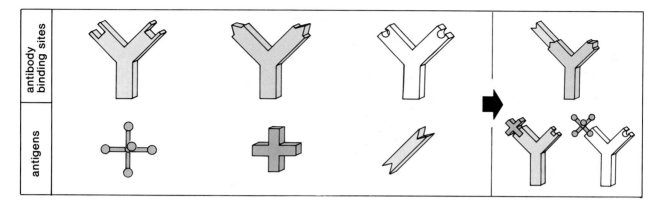

FIGURE 20.7 Antigen-antibody binding

particular pathogen, memory cells can immediately begin the large-scale production of antibodies. Thus memory cells account for immunity to subsequent infections by the same pathogen.

For any single B cell, the thousands of B-cell receptors on its surface are identical. Therefore, that cell can bind to only one specific antigen. The same is true for antigen binding by T cells and their receptors. Because an individual can respond to millions of different antigens, there must be millions of different lymphocytes making different cell surface receptors and antibodies. That leads to a puzzle: There is not enough genetic information in the human genome to code for such a large number of different antibody and receptor proteins. How, then, can the immune system produce such a wide diversity of specific antibody molecules?

20.6 Antibodies as Receptors

The immune system is capable of making antibodies that bind to millions of different antigens. Yet research has shown that there are only a few hundred genes that code for receptors. How then is the great diversity of receptors and antibodies produced?

It is now a generally accepted theory that during embryonic development and throughout life, developing lymphocytes become committed to producing antibody or receptor molecules that specifically bind to a single antigen. This commitment occurs in the absence of any antigens. Once a lymphocyte becomes committed to producing a specific receptor or antibody, all of its descendants will be identical. Such identical descendants are called clones. (See Section 11.1.) Each clone has an antigen-binding capability that is different from that of clones of other lymphocytes. When an antigen appears, antigen binding stimulates specific clones to divide, giving rise to many identical descendants. (See Figure 20.8 on the next page.) The process is known as **clonal selection** because only those clones that are initially capable of antigen binding are selected to divide. The millions of different preexisting lymphocyte clones, with receptors capable of binding to almost any antigen, provide broad protection against a host of pathogens.

FIGURE 20.8 Millions of different B-cell clones with different B-cell receptors are present before an antigen is first encountered. The antigen binds to the best-fitting receptor, and thus selects the clone that will be stimulated to divide, forming thousands of identical descendants.

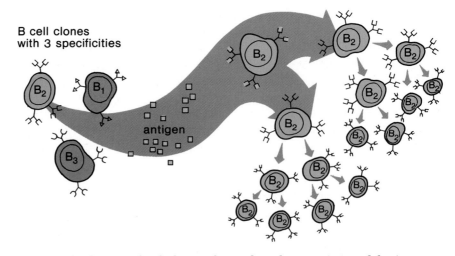

B cell clones with 3 specificities

antigen

Clonal selection also helps explain other characteristics of the immune response. For example, if you were immunized against the measles virus, you did not become immune the day you received the vaccine. It takes 7 to 14 days to reach maximum antibody levels after the initial exposure to an antigen. This is the **primary immune response**, and is shown as the first peak on the graph in Figure 20.9. Prior to antigen exposure, the B cells, with their surface receptors, divide only occasionally. Exposure to a specific antigen stimulates the clones capable of binding to that antigen to divide, producing plasma cells and antibodies—a process that takes several days. Because most foreign materials contain many different antigens, many B-cell clones will be stimulated to produce antibodies.

In addition, during the primary immune response many of the stimulated B cells produce long-lived memory cells, which retain the original specific antigen-binding capability. Memory cells are responsible for the **secondary immune response**, (Figure 20.9). They greatly increase the number of lymphocytes capable of binding to a specific antigen. Reexposure to the same antigen stimulates the memory cells to divide and produce more plasma cells. High levels of antibodies are produced rapidly, within 2 to 6 days.

FIGURE 20.9 Response of the immune system to antigens. In the primary response, it takes 7 to 14 days after the initial exposure to reach a peak concentration of antibody. In the secondary response, subsequent exposure to antigen triggers a much faster response with a much higher concentration of antibodies.

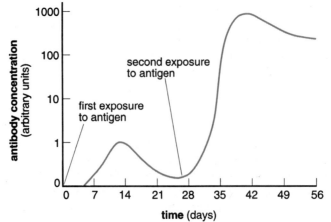
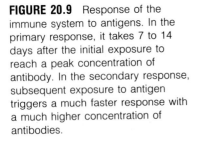

The cell-mediated immune response of T cells also consists of primary and secondary responses. Genes determine which antibodies and T-cell receptors the immune system will make and, thus, which materials the system will recognize as foreign antigens. Without any antigen exposure, however, there is a large library of preexisting antibody and T-cell receptor types. From this library, an antigen "selects" which clones will be stimulated to make antibodies. The puzzle remains: How can a limited amount of genetic material give rise to a large amount of antibody and receptor diversity? The structure of antibody molecules provides some clues.

20.7 A Family of Antibody Proteins

Antibodies are found on the surfaces of B cells as B-cell receptors and circulate in the blood serum and lymph. Antibody molecules serve two important functions. First, they bind to a specific antigen, which means that a given antibody molecule has a unique binding site. Second, after antigen binding, antibody molecules set in motion the nonspecific defense mechanisms, such as phagocytes, that destroy the antigen. Thus antibody molecules are unique with respect to their antigen binding sites, yet similar with respect to their second function—eliminating antigens.

Try Investigation 20A, Antibody Diversity.

If you were to design antibody molecules, how would you do it? One part of the molecule would have to be uniquely tailored to bind to a specific antigen. The second part would have to be similar to all other antibody molecules so that any one of them can activate the nonspecific defenses that destroy the antigen. In short, the antigen-binding end should be highly variable, and the other end should be highly constant.

Figure 20.10 on the next page shows that each antibody molecule consists of four polypeptide chains. There are two identical, smaller "light chains" and two identical, larger "heavy chains." One light chain and one heavy chain combine to make half of an antibody molecule. The two identical half molecules combine to make a complete antibody molecule. In each half, one end of the heavy chain and one end of the light chain together provide one antigen binding site. Thus, each antibody molecule has two antigen binding sites. (See **Appendix 20A**, Antibody Classes.)

Among all antibody molecules, the sequences of amino acids vary greatly at the end that forms the antigen-binding sites. This highly variable region explains how so many different antigens can be bound. At the other end, the sequences of amino acids are very similar among all antibody molecules. This constant region often begins the attack by the nonspecific defense mechanisms that eliminate antigens.

CONNECTIONS

In biology, structure and function are interdependent. The structure of antibodies suits them for their functions: to bind specifically to millions of different antigens.

20.8 Antibody Diversity

As in other proteins, the sequence of amino acids in an antibody determines its shape. In turn, genes determine the sequence of amino acids. However, a different gene cannot code for each antibody molecule. With at least 10^6 different antibodies present in each individual, there are not enough genes present. Biologists estimate there are only about 3 billion

FIGURE 20.10 Two models of antibody structure. (a) is a diagrammatic representation showing the variable and constant regions of the light and heavy chains and the identical halves of the molecule. (b) is based on a computer-generated model that gives a sense of the three-dimensional shape of an antibody molecule. The variable regions of one light and one heavy chain combine to form an antigen-binding site; each antibody molecule has two antigen-binding sites.

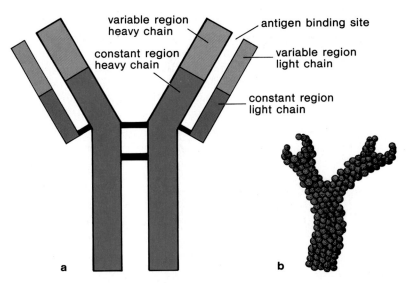

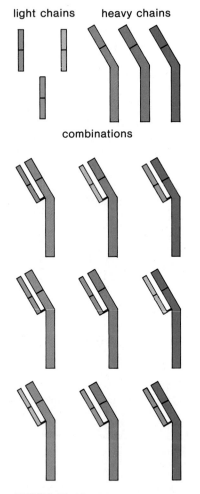

FIGURE 20.11 Three different light chains individually can join with three different heavy chains to form nine different combinations for each antibody half molecule. Two identical halves join to form a complete antibody molecule.

(3×10^9) base pairs and approximately 10^5 genes in the human genome. How, then, can the immune system generate 10^6 different antibodies?

The basis for generating antibody diversity is similar to generating a diversity of lock combinations. If the numbers 0 through 9 are used singly, 10 combinations are possible. Using the 10 numbers two at a time provides 10×10 or 100 different combinations (00 through 99). In the same way, 10 numbers used three at a time yields $10 \times 10 \times 10$ or 1000 different combinations (000 through 999), and so on.

What if there were 1000 genes that coded for the light antibody chains and 1000 genes that coded for the heavy antibody chains? If any light chain could associate with any heavy chain, there would be a million (1000×1000) possible different combinations using only 2000 genes. Figure 20.11 shows the combinations possible with only three different light genes and three different heavy genes.

Using this strategy, the immune system can produce large numbers of different antibody molecules with a relatively small number of genes. (See **Appendix 20B**, Generating Antibody Diversity.) Using a similar strategy but a different set of genes, T cells also make a large number of receptors that recognize specific antigens.

CHECK AND CHALLENGE

1. How do lymphocytes circulate throughout the body?
2. How do antigens and antibodies bind together?
3. Why does the secondary immune response trigger a faster response with more antibodies than the primary response?
4. What does *clonal selection* mean?
5. Where are antibody molecules found? Describe their structure.
6. How is it possible for lymphocytes to make a large number of different antibodies from a limited amount of genetic information?

SUSUMU TONEGAWA—
IMMUNOLOGIST

Until recently, scientists thought the genes in an individual were stable and that mutations were relatively rare. The research of one scientist, Susumu Tonegawa, produced a new picture. In certain cells, the DNA is cut, reshuffled, and assembled in ways that make it possible for the cell to produce billions of different proteins.

Dr. Tonegawa was born in Japan and received his bachelor's degree there. He received his Ph.D. in biology in 1969 from the University of California at San Diego. Then he went to the Basel Institute in Switzerland, where he began investigating the immune system.

The explanation for how the body produces millions of different antibodies was found by Tonegawa and one of his Basel colleagues, Nobumichi Hozumi. Using restriction enzymes (Chapter 13) and DNA hybridization (Chapter 16), Tonegawa and Hozumi mapped the location of the DNA coding for the variable (V) and constant (C) regions of light antibody chains in mice. They found that in embryonic B cells, the C and V region gene segments were located far apart, on separate DNA fragments, separated by a third type of DNA, J (for joining). In mature B cells, however, the V and J regions were close together, on the same fragment. These findings provided a clue that "cutting and pasting" of the DNA might occur. In later experiments they found that genes for heavy chains contain still another type of DNA, D (for diversity).

Tonegawa's studies show that functioning antibody genes are assembled in two stages. First, the V, J, and D portions are moved closer together when enzymes remove the introns that separate the coding regions. Second, the resulting DNA chain is transcribed into RNA, along with RNA representing the C portion of the gene. This RNA is translated into an antibody protein. The combinations are random, and only cells producing antibodies to invading antigens are "selected" to multiply. Because of the randomness of combinations, billions of different antibodies are possible. (See **Appendix 20B**, Generating Antibody Diversity.)

Since 1981, Tonegawa has worked at the Massachusetts Institute of Technology (M.I.T.). His current research concerns T lymphocytes and other aspects of immunity. Tonegawa works with mice, but there are important implications for human medicine. Researchers may eventually learn how to prepare a specific antibody or how to protect a patient from immune reactions to a transplanted organ or to self proteins. The importance of Tonegawa's research was recognized formally in late 1987, when he was awarded the Nobel Prize in Physiology or Medicine.

FIGURE B Susumu Tonegawa

FIGURE 20.12 Antibodies can form bridges between foreign cells or antigens, making aggregates that can be engulfed by phagocytes.

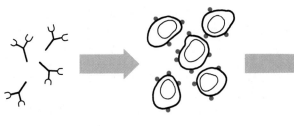

antibodies   foreign cells with   cells cross-linked
                          antigen on surface   by antibodies

The Immune System in Action

20.9   Eliminating Foreign Materials

Try Investigation 20B, Antigen-Antibody Binding.

The immune system acts in various ways to eliminate foreign antigens. In cell-mediated immunity, T cells can bind to antigens on the surface of nonself cells. That binding activates the T cells to destroy such cells directly. T cells also are capable of destroying altered self cells. For example, when certain viruses infect cells, new viral proteins appear on the surfaces of those cells. The T cells recognize the viral proteins as nonself antigens and destroy the infected cells. In a related manner, cancer-causing materials may alter self antigens so that they appear as nonself antigens, leading to destruction of the cell by T cells.

When antibody molecules encounter antigens in antibody-mediated immunity, several outcomes are possible. If the antigen is small, such as a soluble toxic protein about the same size as the antibody, the antibody may bind to it directly. If the antigen is an integral part of a microorganism, antibody binding has little direct effect on the microorganism. Antibody-coated antigens, however, are easier for macrophages to engulf and destroy than noncoated antigens. Because antibody molecules have two binding sites, bridges can form between antigens, forming antibody-antigen clusters that phagocytes can engulf (Figure 20.12).

In addition, antibodies bound to antigens can activate the **complement system**, a complex group of serum proteins that, once activated, can destroy or eliminate antigens (Figure 20.13). Antibody-antigen complexes can activate the first complement factors. These factors in turn activate other complement factors. After a series of step-wise activations, complement factors are activated that eliminate antigens in two ways. First, some of the activated complement proteins can attract phagocytes and greatly enhance phagocytosis and destruction of the antigen. Second, activated complement molecules can aggregate within the plasma membrane of an invading organism, eventually forming holes that cause cells and bacteria to burst. Some complement factors can be activated directly by antigens. That way, certain antigens are destroyed early in the infection's process, before antibodies are formed. Such activated complement factors also stimulate inflammation.

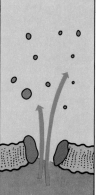

1. An antibody binds to antigen on the surface of a microorganism.

2. Another antibody binds, sending chemical signals that begin the process of activating complement factors.

3. The first activated complement factor binds to the antibodies and activates other complement factors.

4. Activated complement factors gather in sequence on the surface, forming a pore in the membrane.

5. Fluid rushes in through the pore, . . .

6. . . . causing the microorganism to explode. Macrophages then dispose of the microorganism.

FIGURE 20.13 Activation of the complement system. When two antibody molecules bind to adjacent sites on a foreign cell, they can activate the first factor in the complement system, which, in turn, activates other complement factors. Activated complement factors aggregate within the plasma membrane of a microorganism, forming a small pore. Fluid rushes in through the pore, causing the microorganism to explode.

20.10 Regulation of the Immune System

A healthy immune system depends on the coordination of many individual tasks. These tasks include turning on needed responses, producing the components necessary for the response, eliminating the invader, turning off responses that are no longer needed, and regulating the many immune responses that may be occurring at the same time. This complex defense system is a network of specialized cells that constantly interact with one another to discriminate self from nonself.

The immune system determines that an antigen is nonself by comparing the antigen with self proteins. The self proteins that T cells recognize are called **HLA**, which stands for *h*uman *l*eukocyte *a*ntigens. Except for identical twins, each individual has a fairly rare combination of different HLA proteins on the surfaces of all cells except red blood cells. A person's lymphocytes are usually examined to determine their HLA type.

An individual's T cells do not react against self HLA. This nonreaction to self is called **tolerance**. One individual's T cells are not tolerant, however, to HLA proteins from another individual. Therefore, when surgeons transplant tissues or organs between individuals, the recipient's killer T cells begin a cell-mediated immune response against the transplanted cells. If the two individuals happen to have several HLA proteins in common, the immune response is lessened and there is a good chance that the transplant will succeed. A good donor-recipient "match" means that several HLA proteins of the two individuals are identical. The recipient's T cells recognize the shared proteins as self and do not react against them. On the other hand, if there are major differences in the HLA sets, the recipient will reject the transplant. In those cases, patients may be given drugs, such as cyclosporin, that suppress the immune reaction. If the immune system is suppressed too much, however, patients may be unable to defend themselves against infection.

Red blood cells have a different set of cell surface molecules called ABO antigens. (See Chapter 12.) These molecules act as antigens in blood

FIGURE 20.14 Production of antibodies in the specific immune response.

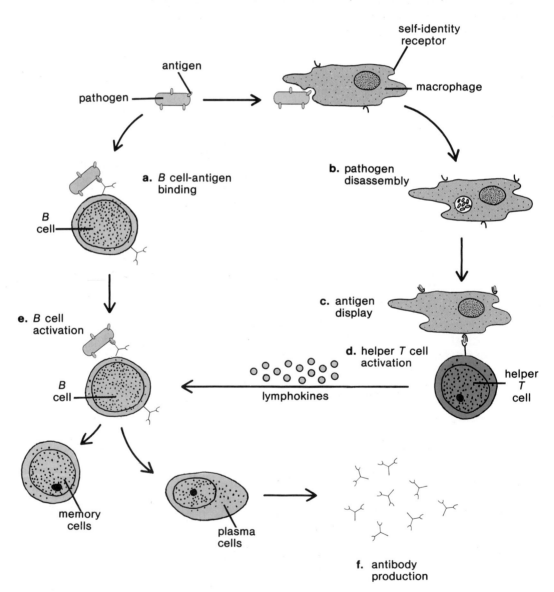

transfusions if the donor and recipient have different blood types. In such cases, the recipient's blood contains antibodies that can eventually destroy the donor's red blood cells.

Most antigens to which you are exposed are not cells from another human. Microorganisms, which consist of many antigens, are the main reason immune responses begin. Figures 20.14 and 20.15 diagram the interactions and regulation of the immune system. Refer to the diagrams as you read the text.

To start an antibody response, macrophages, B cells, and helper T cells must cooperate, as shown in Figure 20.14. When a microorganism enters the body, it may bind to a B cell surface receptor that fits its shape, as shown in (a). At the same time, a macrophage may engulf another microorganism of the same type and disassemble it, as shown in (b). After the microorganism is disassembled, antigens from the microorganism are displayed in self-identity receptors on the macrophage's plasma membrane (c).

FIGURE 20.15   Interactions in the specific immune response.

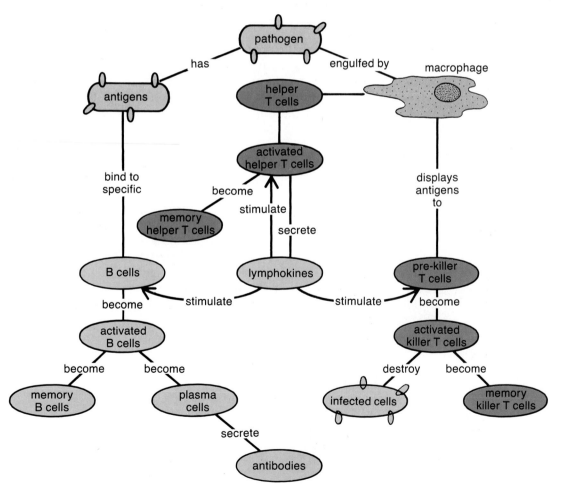

A helper T cell binds to the antigen in these self-identity receptors (d) and becomes activated.

The activated T cell begins to produce molecules known as lymphokines (LIM foh kynz). There are many different lymphokines, including interleukin-2 and interferon. Some lymphokines stimulate microorganism-bound B cells to enlarge and divide rapidly (e), producing a clone of identical plasma cells, which secrete thousands of antibodies into the bloodstream (f). These antibodies are the same as the surface receptors on the original B cell. In the bloodstream, the antibodies bind to the antigens that stimulated their production. Lymphokines also stimulate helper T cells to divide, which produces still more lymphokines and ensures the continued secretion of antibodies.

Once there are sufficient antibody molecules to eliminate the antigens, the immune system must shut down its response. Suppressor T cells apparently are responsible for shutting down the production of antibody molecules by B cells. Thus, helper T cells stimulate B cells to produce antibodies, and suppressor T cells inhibit antibody production.

20.11 The Immune Response Throughout Life

When was the first time the immune response was important to your well-being? Was it when you received your first vaccinations? Or was it when you first got sick with a cold or the flu? Even before you were born, you received antibodies through the placenta. If you were breast-fed, you received antibodies in the milk from your mother. Maternal antibodies provide the newborn with short-term protection against foreign materials to which the mother is immune. Such passive transfer of immunity provides protection until the newborn's immune system can develop and mature to fight its own battles.

Your first important encounter with the immune response, however, occurred about seven days after you were conceived. That is the time when a developing embryo implants in the wall of the uterus. The HLA on cells of the developing embryo are different from the mother's. From the maternal standpoint, the implanting embryo is like a tissue transplant that her immune system should reject. However, the embryo not only escapes rejection, but also establishes intimate contact with maternal tissues. The immune systems of the mother and the fetus are specially modified to allow pregnancy to continue. For example, embryonic cells suppress local immune responses in the uterus. Maternal lymphocytes release substances that block the action of lymphokines. Without lymphokines, the maternal killer T cells do not receive the stimulus necessary to reject the embryo.

Not much is known about the effects of aging on the immune system. The thymus gets smaller, apparently without any drastic effects, although there may be some age-related decrease in T-cell functions. Because the immune system detects and eliminates most cells that may become cancerous, an aging immune system may partially account for the increased incidence of cancer in the elderly. The elderly also are more susceptible to infectious diseases.

20.12 Malfunctions and Disease

There are many reasons for malfunctions in the immune system. How many can you identify? One malfunction you may have experienced is getting sick during times of stress. This phenomenon may be explained by the chemical connections between the brain and the immune system. Certain chemicals the body makes can suppress the immune system. For example, hormones (chemical messengers) made by the adrenal gland in response to stress (Chapter 23) can inhibit the function of T cells. In turn, substances released by the brain and the pituitary gland into the bloodstream control the function of the adrenal gland. Thus, being "stressed-out" can suppress the immune system, causing susceptibility to infection. Also, during times of stress you may not sleep or eat properly. Inadequate intake of vitamins, minerals, and protein may slow down the immune system by interfering with the metabolism of lymphocytes.

FOCUS ON *AIDS*

The virus responsible for AIDS is a retrovirus called *H*uman *I*mmunodeficiency *V*irus, or HIV. HIV primarily affects helper T cells, but it also may infect brain or nerve cells. Helper T cells, brain cells, and nerve cells all have a particular cell-surface molecule called CD4 that serves as the site of attachment for the virus. Inside the host cell, the virus uses an enzyme, reverse transcriptase, to copy its RNA into DNA, which may be incorporated into the host genome. Each infected cell then can serve as a factory for the production of HIV. When the cell eventually ruptures and dies, it releases hundreds of viruses, each able to infect another helper T cell. Reproduction of HIV in helper T cells leads to a gradual decline in the number of helper T cells, weakened function of the immune system, and increased susceptibility to opportunistic infections and cancers, such as pneumonia, tuberculosis, and Kaposi's sarcoma, a rare type of skin cancer. Although HIV can damage organs directly, opportunistic infections account for up to 90 percent of deaths from AIDS.

The incubation period for HIV is two weeks to three months—if infection has occurred, HIV antibodies can be detected in the blood at this time. However, an individual infected with HIV may not develop AIDS symptoms for several months or even as long as 12 years. AIDS is fatal, usually within a few years of diagnosis.

A person is infected with HIV through contact with internal body fluids such as blood and semen. Hemophiliacs and other people requiring blood transfusions have been infected by contaminated blood supplies. Health-care workers exposed to HIV by way of accidental cuts or injections have contracted AIDS. Transmission of the virus also occurs when contaminated needles are used to inject intravenous drugs. During gestation an infected mother can transmit the AIDS virus to her fetus. Infected mothers also can transmit HIV to their babies in their breast milk.

AIDS can be transmitted sexually by both heterosexuals and homosexuals. Abstaining from sexual activity is one way to reduce the risk of infection. Limiting sexual activity to a monagamous relationship in which both partners have repeatedly tested negative for HIV and using condoms with gels containing nonoxynol 9 are two other methods that can reduce the risk of HIV infection by sexual contact. There is no evidence that AIDS can be transmitted through casual contact, such as shaking hands or swimming in the same pool.

a

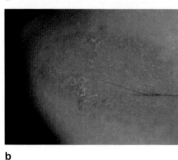

b

FIGURE 20.16 (a) Poison ivy plant; (b) Poison ivy blisters

A variety of external factors can suppress the immune system. Certain medications, such as cortisone, and illegal drugs, such as "angel dust," suppress the function of lymphocytes. Certain infectious agents, such as the AIDS virus, can suppress the immune response. Although your body can mount a good primary and secondary immune response against this virus, the long-term effect is immunodeficiency, or weakening and eventual destruction of the immune response. For example, the AIDS virus selectively infects and destroys lymphocytes, particularly the helper T cell population. The AIDS virus can destroy a previously normal immune system, leading to acquired immunodeficiency syndrome (AIDS). In such severe cases of immunodeficiency, routine infections can cause life-threatening diseases.

A hypersensitive immune system also can result in disease. Hypersensitive responses may be either cell-mediated or antibody-mediated. Contact with poison ivy (Figure 20.16a) can cause a hypersensitive cell-mediated immune response. An organic chemical in poison ivy can combine with your own cell-surface proteins and change their structure. The altered proteins then become foreign to the immune system, and killer T cells attack those cells. The immune destruction of one's own cells leads to inflammation, a rash, and blisters in the tissue that was in contact with the poison ivy (Figure 20.16b). The same type of reaction is sometimes caused by metals released from jewelry such as rings and earrings.

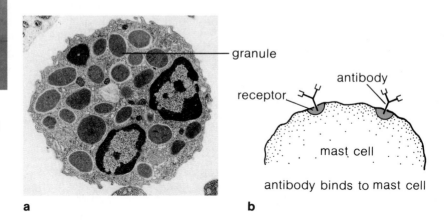

granule

receptor

antibody

mast cell

antibody binds to mast cell

a

b

FIGURE 20.17 Mast cells are involved in allergic reactions. The photos show basophils, which are similar to mast cells. (a) An intact cell, containing numerous cytoplasmic granules. (b) When an antigen binds to antibody molecules attached to the surface, the cell releases the contents of the granules, including histamine (c).

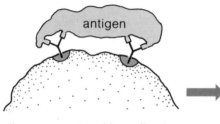

antigen

allergen reacts with antibody bound to receptors on mast cell

c

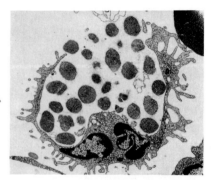

Hypersensitivities also may cause allergies and are responsible for hay fever, asthma, and bee-sting reactions. Antigens in pollen, animal dander, food protein, or insect venom may bind to antibodies attached to mast cells, which are cells found in the blood and tissues. If the antigen is reintroduced (for example, during another pollen season), antigen-antibody binding causes the mast cells to dump their contents into the surrounding tissues (Figure 20.17). Mast cells contain many biologically active substances, including histamine. When released, histamine causes the sneezing, itchiness, and teary eyes associated with hay fever. Histamine also causes smooth muscles to contract and blood vessels to swell. That reaction causes the airways in the lungs to constrict, resulting in the severe breathing difficulty of an asthma attack. Antihistamines are often effective in reducing the effects of such hypersensitivities.

Another malfunction of the immune system is **autoimmunity**. As the name implies, the immune system no longer tolerates self molecules, and it produces an immune response against them. Autoantibodies or killer T cells bind to self molecules and interfere with or destroy their normal function. Diseases such as rheumatoid arthritis, multiple sclerosis, and diabetes have an autoimmune component. Although the exact mechanisms are not understood, it appears that a combination of genetic susceptibility and unknown environmental agents may cause autoimmune diseases.

Often the immune system of individuals with cancer does not function properly. There are several reasons. For example, in leukemia, lymphocytes become cancerous and increase greatly in numbers. The cancerous lymphocytes are nonfunctional and often crowd out the normal lymphocytes in the blood and bone marrow. That change leads to a general decrease in immune functions. Cancers that arise in other tissues, such as lung or breast, often spread to the bone marrow, replace the normal cells, and again cause decreased immune functions. Cancer treatment with chemicals and radiation may also be immunosuppressive because the therapy kills lymphocytes as well as cancer cells.

CHECK AND CHALLENGE

1. How does the immune system eliminate foreign materials?
2. What is the role of the complement system in the immune response?
3. What are HLA molecules and why are they important?
4. What role do lymphokines play in the immune response?
5. What are the roles of the various types of T cells?
6. What is a possible reason a pregnant woman does not reject the embryo?
7. What are two ways the immune system can be weakened?
8. Give an example of a hypersensitivity reaction and explain how it occurs.

CHAPTER Highlights

Summary

Both nonspecific and specific types of immunity provide protection against hazards from the environment, especially infectious agents. Nonspecific protection against foreign materials includes physical and biochemical barriers. Phagocytosis and inflammation are also nonspecific defense mechanisms. Specific immunity is carried out by lymphocytes and antibodies. The immune response distinguishes between self and nonself. Using a limited amount of genetic information, lymphocytes produce an extremely diverse family of antigen-binding molecules known as B cell receptors, antibodies, and T-cell receptors. When foreign material such as a microorganism is detected, the immune system usually eliminates the infectious organism before it can cause disease. If disease does occur and you recover, your immune system then provides long-lasting protection against the original foreign material. The immune system sometimes malfunctions, causing diseases such as allergies rather than providing protection. Certain substances can adversely affect the cells of the immune system, resulting in a nonfunctioning system.

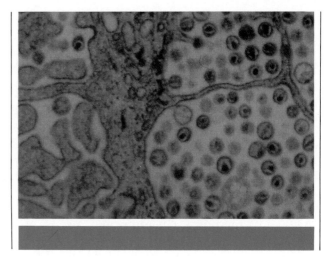

Key Concepts

Use the concepts below to build a concept map, linking as many other concepts from the chapter as you can.

self

nonself

specific

nonspecific

antigen

antibody

T cells

B cells

Reviewing Ideas

1. What is inflammation and how does it differ from specific immunity?

2. What distinguishes primary lymphoid organs from secondary lymphoid organs?

3. Why are antibodies considered to be a family of proteins?

4. Give some examples of nonself.

5. What is the evidence that immunity is specific and long-lasting?

6. How does the structure of an antibody promote its function?

7. Explain the differences between the primary immune response and the secondary immune response.

8. Briefly describe the role of each type of cell involved in a successful immune response.

9. What is meant by ''antibody class'' and why are different antibody classes important?

10. What causes autoimmunity?

11. What is the relationship between stress and the immune system?

12. How are antibodies passed from a mother to her child?

13. What is the cause of poison ivy symptoms?

14. Why are you more likely to get sick at the time of final exams than during summer vacation?

Using Concepts

1. How can a small amount of genetic material give rise to a large number of different antibodies?

2. Explain why vaccination is "artificial infection."

3. How would you make a vaccine against the AIDS virus?

4. What would happen if a person were born without a thymus?

5. Could you survive without a spleen? Why or why not?

6. What is the importance of tolerance? What happens if it is lost?

7. A person is to receive a transplanted kidney. What can be done to increase the chances for a successful transplant?

8. The bacterium *meningococcus* type B causes a serious infection of the brain. Some immunologists think that the membranes of these bacterial cells include structures that are similar to those in the membranes of human brain cells. How might the similarity provide a selective advantage for *meningococcus* type B?

Synthesis

1. What are the advantages of the multiple-reaction steps that activate complement factors in the immune system and clotting in the circulatory system?

2. Humans are born before their immune systems are mature. In what way might that provide a selective advantage?

3. Throughout the 1950s, 1960s, and early 1970s, biologists accumulated evidence that supported the hypothesis of "one gene = one polypeptide." That is, one segment of DNA could code for only one polypeptide. How has knowledge about the production of antibodies revised that hypothesis?

Extensions

1. Investigate the mechanisms by which the immune system can produce allergies. Write a paragraph hypothesizing in what way such a reaction might be helpful.

2. Draw a cartoon of how the cells and molecules of the immune system interact to protect against foreign material.

CONTENTS

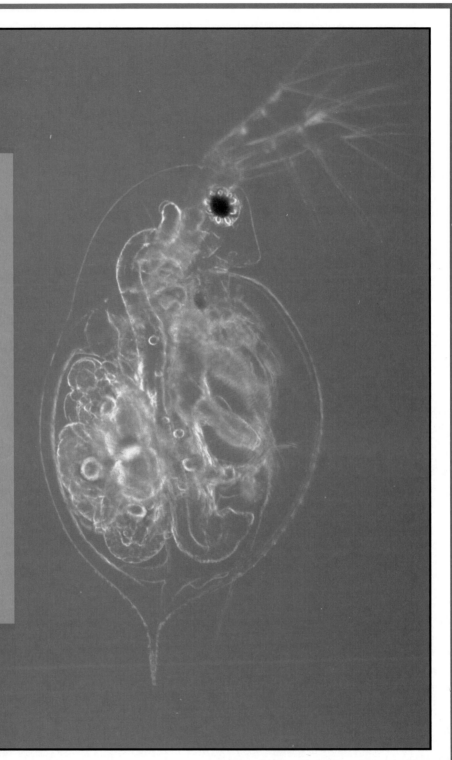

Gas Exchange and Excretory Systems

*W*here are the structures involved in gas exchange located?

*W*hat other structures can you identify?

*E*very time you breathe or eat, you are bringing in materials from your environment. When you take a breath, oxygen and other components of the air around you are brought into your lungs. That hamburger and milk shake you ate last Saturday were digested, absorbed, and metabolized in cellular respiration, which provides energy and building materials for your body. How is the oxygen you breathe into your lungs transported to your cells for cellular respiration? How are the waste materials of metabolism removed?

Systems that maintain and, if disrupted, restore homeostasis must operate constantly. Most organisms have gas exchange and excretory systems that play important roles in this process. These systems are adapted to work efficiently in the environment in which a particular organism lives. Animals that live in hot, dry environments, such as deserts, have systems that help conserve the water in their bodies. In contrast, freshwater fishes must eliminate excess water. The ways in which fishes obtain oxygen are quite different from those of a mouse or human living on land. This chapter discusses how a variety of organisms exchange gases with their environment and eliminate unwanted materials from their bodies, thus maintaining internal homeostasis.

◆ *A crustacean,* Daphnia pulix, *magnified 40 times. Daphnia are aquatic creatures.*

Gas Exchange in Multicellular Organisms _____

21.1 Variation in Gas Exchange Systems

Organs for gas exchange have evolved differently in various organisms, yet they all have a common function: exchanging gas molecules between cells and the external environment. All cells, with the exception of anaerobes, must obtain the oxygen needed for cellular respiration and eliminate the carbon dioxide produced (Chapter 8). Whether free-living microorganisms or the cells of plant or animal tissues, they do this by diffusion through the plasma membrane. In larger organisms, a transport system (Chapter 19) moves oxygen from the external environment to the cells, and carbon dioxide from the cells to the external environment. However, gas exchange ultimately takes place at the cellular level.

Small multicellular animals, such as planarians, obtain oxygen and give off carbon dioxide directly through their body surfaces, as illustrated in Figure 21.1a. These animals do not need highly specialized gas exchange systems because all their cells are in close contact with the external environment. The earthworm also obtains oxygen and gives off carbon dioxide by diffusion through the skin (Figure 21.1b). The outer surface of the earthworm is covered with a film of moist, mucuslike material. Gas molecules dissolve in this moist material and diffuse through it. Notice that the earthworm has a transport system consisting of blood-filled capillaries and larger vessels. The oxygen that diffuses through the skin is picked up by the blood and moved throughout the earthworm's body. Larger and more complex animals need specialized surfaces for the exchange of gases. In general, these surfaces are composed of folds or pockets of tissues that greatly increase the surface area for gas diffusion. The respiratory organs found in many animals that live in water are called **gills**. Gills provide

FIGURE 21.1 Planarians (*a*) and earthworms (*b*) have no special gas exchange organs. Gases are exchanged directly through their skin.

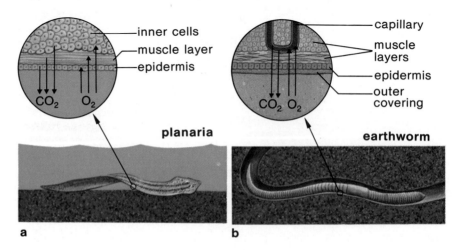

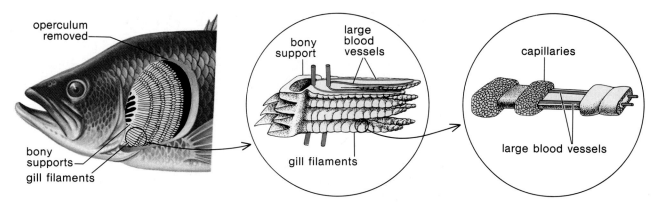

FIGURE 21.2 In fishes, gills are thin filaments supported by bony structures and richly supplied with blood vessels. Each filament is made of disks that contain numerous capillaries. Water flows past these disks in directions opposite (countercurrent) to the flow of blood through the capillaries. A covering over the gills, called the operculum, protects the delicate filaments.

these water dwellers with a large respiratory surface. Because there is little chance of drying out, gills are usually found on or near the outer surface of the animal. Some aquatic worms, crustaceans, and mollusks breathe through gills. The gill of a fish, illustrated in Figure 21.2, is made up of many fine, threadlike filaments. Each filament consists of a thin layer of cells surrounding a network of capillaries. Oxygen and carbon dioxide are exchanged between the blood circulating through these capillaries and the water surrounding the filaments.

Water contains dissolved oxygen, but only in small amounts. To satisfy the need for oxygen in a fish, for example, water must constantly pass over the gill surfaces. Water is taken in through the mouth, forced over the gills, and passed out of the body through an opening in the body cavity that surrounds the delicate gill filaments.

Gills are highly efficient gas exchange organs. By providing a continuous flow of water, the gills of fish maintain a high rate of diffusion. In addition, they are constructed in such a way that they actually maximize the difference in oxygen concentration between the tissues and the environment. The filaments of gills are made up of thin disklike structures lined up parallel with the direction of water movement (Figure 21.2). Water flows over these disks from front to back. Within each disk, the blood circulates in the direction opposite to the movement of the water, from the back of the disk to the front. The concentration difference is maximized because the water flowing over the disks and the blood flowing within the disks run in opposite directions, a process called countercurrent exchange (Figure 21.3). As blood flows through the capillary, it takes up oxygen. At the same time, the blood encounters water that has a higher concentration of oxygen because the water is just beginning its passage over the gills. This arrangement along the entire length of the capillary produces a diffusion gradient favoring the transfer of oxygen from the water into the blood.

FIGURE 21.3 With countercurrent flow, the blood continues to pick up oxygen from the water all along the length of the capillary. More than 80 percent of the dissolved oxygen in the water is transferred to the blood by diffusion.

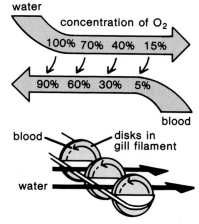

21.2   Gas Exchange in Terrestrial Organisms

When organisms moved onto land, air became the source of their oxygen. Water is relatively poor in oxygen. It contains only about 5 to 10 mL of oxygen per liter of water. Air, in contrast, is rich in oxygen, containing about 210 mL of oxygen per liter of air. Not surprisingly, many members of otherwise aquatic groups (such as whales) utilize atmospheric air as their source of oxygen, as do other vertebrates with a high rate of metabolism and consequently a great need for oxygen. (See **Appendix 21A**, Oxygen Consumption and Temperature Regulation in Animals.)

As organisms became fully adapted to land, an entirely new gas exchange apparatus evolved—one that was based on internal passages rather than gills. If gills are such superb oxygen-capturing mechanisms, why were they not maintained in these land-dwelling organisms?

Two principal reasons may account for the loss of gills. First, air is less buoyant than water. The disks in the filaments of gills lack any great structural strength and must be supported by water to avoid collapsing on one another (as well as to remain moist to function). A fish taken out of water, although awash in oxygen, soon suffocates because its gills collapse. Second, water is lost to the air through evaporation. Atmospheric air is rarely saturated with water vapor, except after a heavy rainstorm. Consequently, organisms that live in air constantly lose water to the atmosphere. Gills would have provided an enormous surface area for water loss.

Two main systems of internal gas exchange evolved among land-dwelling organisms. Both systems sacrifice respiratory efficiency in order to promote water retention. In insects, a system of small, branched air ducts, called tracheae (TRAY kee ee; singular *trachea*) carry oxygen throughout the body. Water loss is prevented by spiracles (SPY rah kuhls) that close the external openings of the tracheae whenever levels of carbon dioxide are below a certain point.

Air enters the insect through the spiracles, located on the side of the body, and passes into air-filled cavities, or sacs. From these sacs, the tracheae branch into smaller and smaller tubes, as shown in Figure 21.4. The

FIGURE 21.4   In insects, gas exchange occurs through branching air tubes called tracheae.

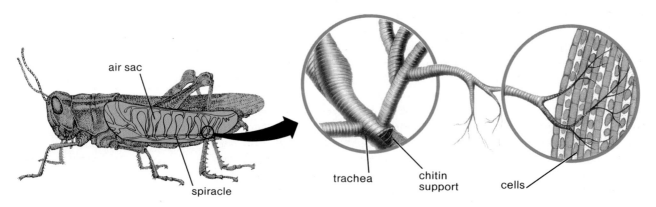

air sac

spiracle

trachea

chitin support

cells

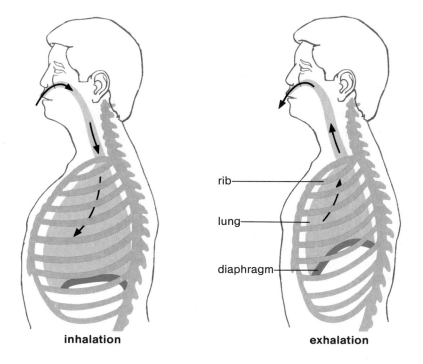

FIGURE 21.5 Movements of breathing in humans

rib

lung

diaphragm

inhalation   **exhalation**

smallest tubes are in direct contact with muscles and other body tissues. Cells can easily receive oxygen and give off carbon dioxide by diffusion through the plasma membrane and the walls of the air tubes. Movements of the insect's body can inflate and deflate the air sacs, but the flow of air within the tracheal tubes is under relatively little pressure. There is no connection between the insect's tracheal system and its circulation. What does this observation suggest about the function of the open circulatory system described in Section 19.4?

In many vertebrates, lungs are the organs of gas exchange. Lungs, which are located deep within the body chest, minimize the effects of drying out by eliminating the one-way flow of oxygen that is so efficient in gills. Air moves into the lungs through a tubular passage and then back out through the same passage. Because the diffusion surfaces of the lungs are exposed to a mixture of oxygen-rich and oxygen-poor air, the concentration difference is not great. Thus, the gas exchange efficiency of lungs is much less than that of gills, but so also is water loss.

Among mammals, including humans, air is taken into and forced out of the lungs through the actions of two groups of muscles, the **diaphragm** (DY uh fram) and the rib muscles. These muscles act together to change the size of the chest cavity, as shown in Figure 21.5. Changes in the size of the chest cavity affect the gas pressure in the lungs. When the chest cavity expands, the pressure within the chest and surrounding the lungs falls. Because of this reduced air pressure, air is forced into the lungs from the outside, where it is under greater atmospheric pressure. When the volume of the chest cavity surrounding the lungs is reduced, the internal pressure becomes greater than the atmospheric pressure, and gas is forced out.

FIGURE 21.6 The human gas exchange system. Two enlargements show clusters of alveoli and their blood supply.

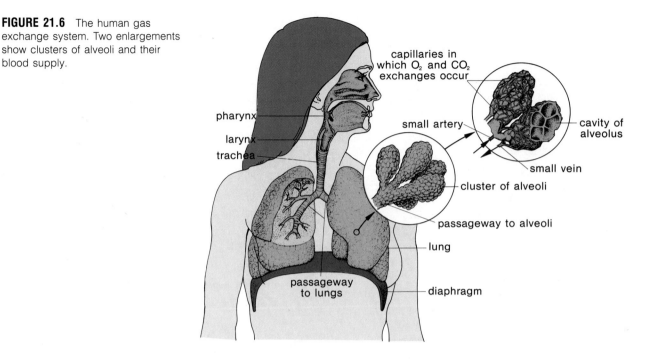

Atmospheric air is usually dry, sometimes cold, and often dirty. The air you breathe passes through your nose, where it is filtered by hairs lining the nasal cavities, moistened, and warmed. It then travels through the pharynx and down the trachea, or windpipe. The trachea branches into passageways, called **bronchial** (BRAWN kee uhl) **tubes**, that enter each lung. The bronchial tubes end in microscopic cavities called **alveoli** (al VEE oh ly). Each lung has millions of alveoli, whose thin walls are richly supplied with capillaries. Figure 21.6 illustrates the human gas exchange system and details of the alveoli. Figure 21.7 is a scanning electron micrograph of alveoli that shows the close association between alveolar walls and blood capillaries. Oxygen and carbon dioxide diffuse across the alveolar walls and the walls of the capillaries. A large volume of gas can be exchanged with the bloodstream in a very short time because the numerous alveoli of the lungs provide an enormous amount of surface area. If all the alveoli in an average person's lungs were spread out flat, they would cover an area of about 60 square meters (about the size of two large parking spaces).

FIGURE 21.7 Scanning electron micrograph of alveoli, X1300. Capillaries in the alveolar walls provide a close relationship between blood and air.

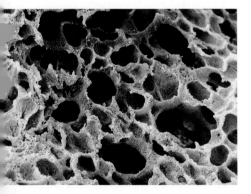

21.3   Oxygen Transport

Recall from Chapter 19 that human blood consists of cells suspended in a watery fluid called plasma. Blood has a great capacity to carry both oxygen and carbon dioxide. Oxygen, however, is not very soluble in water (or plasma) under normal atmospheric conditions. It is the cells in the plasma that are responsible for transporting oxygen. How do the cells carry the oxygen?

FOCUS ON *Gas Exchange in Birds*

There is a limit to the improvement in gas exchange that can result from increasing the total lung surface area for diffusion. With the evolution of birds, flying introduced gas exchange demands that exceeded the capacities of saclike lungs. Many birds, such as hummingbirds, beat their wings rapidly for prolonged periods of time. Such fast wing movement uses energy very quickly because it depends on rapid contractions of the wing muscles. Flying birds must carry out intensive cellular respiration to replenish the ATP used in flight muscles. Thus, they require a great deal of oxygen—more than a lung with a large surface area can deliver.

What system of gas exchange has evolved in birds? A bird's lung works like a two-cycle pump (Figure A). When the bird inhales, the air passes directly into a set of chambers called the posterior air sacs. When the bird exhales, the air passes into the lungs. On the following inhalation, the air passes from the lungs to a second set of air sacs, called the anterior air sacs. Finally, on the second exhalation, the air flows from the anterior air sacs out of the body. What is the advantage of this complicated system? Air passes through the lungs in a single direction. Thus, there is no mixing of oxygen-rich and oxygen-poor air as in the human lung—the air passing through the lung of a bird is always

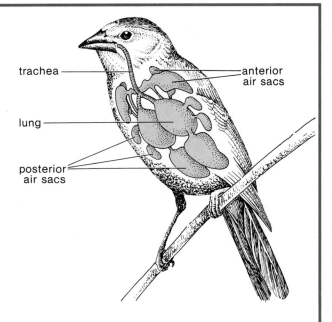

trachea

anterior air sacs

lung

posterior air sacs

FIGURE A   The air sacs in birds function to ventilate the lungs where gas exchange occurs. Two cycles of inhalation and exhalation are required for the air to pass all the way through the system. Inhaled air travels directly to the posterior air sacs, then to the lungs, then to the anterior air sacs, and out to the external environment.

oxygen-rich. As in the gills of fish, the flow of blood past the bird lung runs in the direction opposite to the air flow in the lung (countercurrent flow). Thus, bird lungs are very efficient at picking up oxygen from the air.

Erythrocytes contain large quantities of hemoglobin—a transport pigment. (See **Appendix 19B**.) Hemoglobin is a protein composed of four polypeptide subunits. Each polypeptide is combined with an atom of iron in such a way that oxygen can bind to it temporarily. Recall from Chapter 6 that molecules diffuse from a region of higher concentration to a region of lower concentration. The air entering the alveoli of the lungs has a relatively high concentration of oxygen, so oxygen diffuses from the alveoli into the blood. As the iron atoms in the hemoglobin molecules combine with oxygen, the hemoglobin becomes bright red and is called oxyhemoglobin. Oxyhemoglobin is transported to the tissues. When the concentration of oxygen in the intercellular spaces is low, oxygen is released from its weak chemical combination with hemoglobin, leaves the erythrocytes, and diffuses into the tissues. The hemoglobin then becomes darker red in color. The ease with which oxygen passes into and out of erythrocytes makes the

FIGURE 21.8 Oxygen and carbon dioxide transport. Oxygen from the alveolus enters erythrocytes and combines with hemoglobin (Hb) to form oxyhemoglobin (HbO_2). The oxygen is carried in this form to body cells where it is released (see lower left side of illustration). Carbon dioxide diffuses from body cells into the erythrocytes. There it combines with water to form carbonic acid (H_2CO_3), which ionizes to bicarbonate (HCO_3^-) and hydrogen ions (H^+). The bicarbonate diffuses into the plasma. The hydrogen ions combine with hemoglobin (H—Hb). Some of the carbon dioxide combines directly with hemoglobin ($HbCO_2$). In the lung capillary, the reverse reactions occur. Bicarbonate ions from the plasma are converted to carbon dioxide and diffuse into the alveolus.

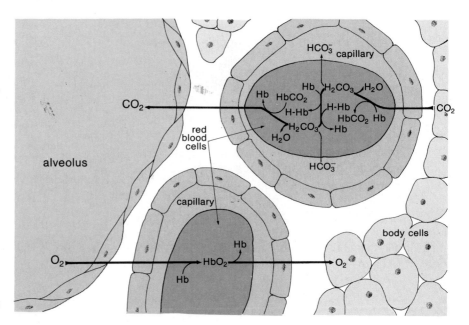

oxygen-exchange system in the human body quick and efficient. The bottom part of Figure 21.8 summarizes the reactions of hemoglobin and oxygen in the lungs and body tissues.

21.4 Carbon Dioxide Transport

Blood returning to the lungs from the tissues contains more carbon dioxide than does the air in the alveolar spaces. Carbon dioxide diffuses from the capillaries to the alveolar spaces. The top part of Figure 21.8 illustrates the diffusion of carbon dioxide from the tissue spaces into the capillaries and then into the air spaces of the lungs. Only about ten percent of the carbon dioxide entering the capillaries dissolves in the plasma; the rest enters the erythrocytes. There, some of the carbon dioxide combines with hemoglobin. Most, however, reacts with water to form carbonic acid (H_2CO_3), which quickly breaks down into hydrogen ions and bicarbonate ions. (See Figure 21.8.) The formation of carbonic acid and bicarbonate ions are reversible reactions:

$$CO_2 + H_2O \rightleftharpoons H_2CO_3 \rightleftharpoons H^+ + HCO_3^-$$

| carbon dioxide | water | carbonic acid | hydrogen ion | bicarbonate ion |

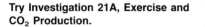
Try Investigation 21A, Exercise and CO_2 Production.

The bicarbonate ions diffuse out of the erythrocytes into the plasma and are carried to the lungs where they reenter the erythrocytes. Here the equation reverses itself. The bicarbonate ions combine with hydrogen ions to form carbonic acid, which then breaks down into carbon dioxide and water. The hemoglobin releases its carbon dioxide. The carbon dioxide from both sources diffuses into the alveolar spaces and is exhaled to the external environment. Some water exits in the form of water vapor. The processes of oxygen and carbon dioxide transport are another example of how complex, interrelated body functions maintain homeostasis.

FOCUS ON *Control of Breathing Rate*

The muscles in the diaphragm and between the ribs that function in breathing are controlled directly by nerves from at least two respiratory centers in the brain. These respiratory centers continue to regulate your breathing rate even when you are unconscious or asleep. Other nerves connect the respiratory centers with receptors in the arch of the aorta (Figure 19.18), in the arteries leading to the brain, and in the brain itself.

If the level of carbon dioxide in the blood rises, for example during exercise when the rate of cellular respiration increases, there is an increase in the level of hydrogen ions (H^+), which lowers the pH of the blood. (See the equation on page 478.) The three receptors detect the increase in hydrogen ions and send a message to the respiratory centers in the brain. Then, the respiratory centers send messages that stimulate the diaphragm and rib muscles to contract

more rapidly. This change increases the breathing rate, bringing more oxygen into the blood and transferring carbon dioxide out of the blood. As the level of carbon dioxide declines, the drop is detected by the receptors and relayed to the brain, which signals the diaphragm and rib muscles to slow down.

You can exert some control over your breathing rate, but only within limits. For example, it would be possible, but not advisable, to hold your breath until you faint from lack of oxygen to the brain. As soon as you faint, however, the respiratory centers within the brain resume their control over the breathing muscles, and normal breathing returns. You also can breathe very rapidly (hyperventilate) and increase the level of oxygen coming into your body, but you cannot maintain such control for long. After a short time, your body resumes normal control of your breathing rate.

CHECK AND CHALLENGE

1. In mammals, where does diffusion occur in the removal of respiratory waste products?

2. Why are gills efficient organs for gas exchange in water-dwelling organisms?

3. Explain how oxygen is transported in human blood.

4. How is carbon dioxide transported in human blood?

5. Why does oxygen diffuse into the capillaries around the alveoli?

6. How do the air sacs of birds make possible the high rate of cellular respiration that flying demands?

Homeostasis and Materials Exchange

21.5   Balance with External Environments

All organisms must exchange materials with the environment to live. Both essential and unnecessary materials may pass into an organism from its surroundings. In turn, some needed materials are lost to the environment. Transport mechanisms that selectively regulate the passage of materials through plasma membranes (Section 6.7) help to retain needed materials, while keeping unwanted substances out.

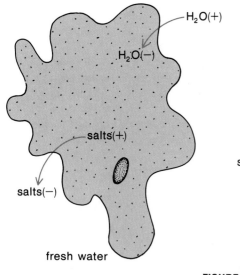

fresh water

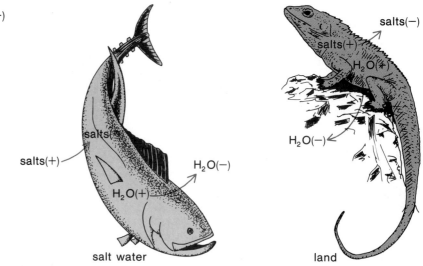

salt water

land

FIGURE 21.9 Water-salt balance problems differ in each environment. Freshwater organisms tend to gain water and lose salts; saltwater organisms tend to lose water and gain salts; and land organisms tend to lose both. Excretory systems that cope with the problems have evolved in each environment. **+ and − indicate higher and lower concentrations.**

Freshwater organisms, like all other organisms, require water in their bodies. Excess water from the environment, however, constantly enters these organisms by osmosis. To maintain homeostasis, freshwater organisms must eliminate the excess water without losing significant quantities of soluble body salts, or electrolytes.

Saltwater fishes and some marine invertebrates have a problem almost opposite that of freshwater organisms. In these organisms, the salt concentration is lower inside the body than in the surrounding water. Therefore, the organism tends to lose water by osmosis to the surroundings. Replacing the lost water with salt water requires elimination of excess salts from the replacement water. For these organisms, homeostasis means retaining body water while excreting salts from water taken in to offset water loss.

In balancing water and salt to maintain homeostasis, land-dwelling organisms and salt water organisms are somewhat similar. Water must be retained and salt excreted by land-dwelling animals, including humans. Figure 21.9 summarizes the water-balance problems of organisms in each environment.

21.6 Nitrogenous Wastes

Metabolism produces toxic by-products. Perhaps the most troublesome by-product is the nitrogen-containing waste from the metabolism of proteins and nucleic acids. Nitrogen is removed from these nutrients when they are converted to carbohydrates or fats. Amino groups removed from amino acids immediately become **ammonia** (NH_3) with the addition of a third hydrogen, a reaction that requires little energy. Some animals excrete ammonia directly, but it is very toxic to body tissues, so this form of nitrog-

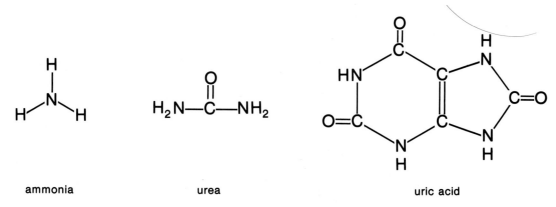

FIGURE 21.10   The structural formulas of ammonia, urea, and uric acid

enous waste can be used only if the organism lives in an environment where sufficient water is available to flush it from the body. The high solubility of ammonia makes it a safe excretory product in freshwater and saltwater protists and animals. *Paramecium* and other protists, as well as planarians and many other invertebrates, excrete ammonia directly through their plasma membranes or body coverings. Ammonia also is the chief nitrogenous waste of some vertebrates—the ocean fishes.

Some organisms convert their nitrogenous wastes to urea, which is much less toxic than ammonia. Urea can be excreted safely when diluted in a moderate amount of water, allowing body water to be conserved, an important advantage for land-dwelling animals. Humans and other mammals, some fishes, and amphibians excrete nitrogenous wastes chiefly as urea.

The third major type of nitrogenous waste is uric acid. Uric acid is not toxic because it is almost insoluble. Uric acid excretion has evolved as an adaptation of land animals, especially desert-dwelling ones, because little loss of water is involved. Grasshoppers and other insects, reptiles, birds, and many mammals excrete nitrogenous wastes as uric acid crystals. Humans and other mammals excrete uric acid, although in small amounts compared to urea.

The different forms of nitrogenous wastes show important evolutionary patterns. Animals that have evolved in water and land environments show differences in nitrogenous wastes related to the abundance or scarcity of water. Urea is less toxic than ammonia, but it requires more water than uric acid for its excretion. The structural formulas for ammonia, urea, and uric acid are shown in Figure 21.10.

21.7   Materials Balance and Excretion

What organs remove nitrogenous wastes, ions, and water—the products of metabolism—from the internal environment? Protists living in fresh water utilize diffusion and osmosis for the exchange of these materials. Structures called contractile vacuoles function in the removal of excess water. Water collects in the vacuoles, and contractions of the vacuoles squeeze the water

FIGURE 21.11 Contractile vacuoles in *Paramecium* rid the animal of excess water. The vacuoles expand as water fills them through radiating canals. The vacuoles then contract and eject the water from the organism.

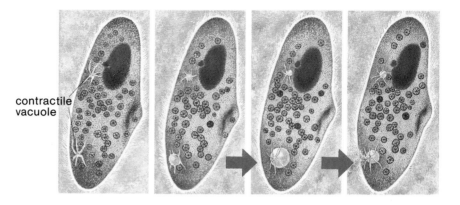

FIGURE 21.12 The excretory system of a planarian. A flame cell and an excretory pore are shown enlarged. Wastes and excess water removed by flame cells are eliminated through pores in the body wall.

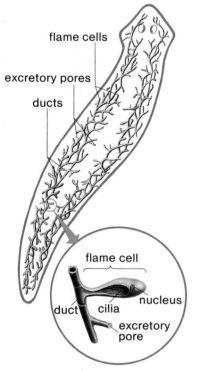

out of the cell. Figure 21.11 shows how contractile vacuoles function in *Paramecium*. Other freshwater protists have similar contractile vacuoles.

Sponges and *Hydra* excrete wastes from each cell directly through the external surface. In animals larger and more complex than these, however, not enough of the body cells are in contact with the external environment for each cell to dispose of its own wastes. Special organs have evolved for excretion and maintaining water balance.

Planarians are freshwater organisms and have an overabundance of water entering their bodies. Water is removed constantly from the body by a system of ducts, or tubes, illustrated in Figure 21.12. Flame cells, so named because the beating of their cilia resembles the flickering of a flame, create a current in the tubular system. Water is moved through the ducts and eliminated through pores opening out of the body wall. Carbon dioxide and nitrogenous wastes in the form of ammonia diffuse through the body wall. (See Figure 21.1.)

The land-dwelling grasshopper has a different problem of water balance from that of a planarian—it must avoid large losses of water. The excretory organs excrete wastes in an almost insoluble form, as crystals of uric acid. The grasshopper has specialized excretory tubes called Malpighian (mal PIH jee uhn) tubules that extend into the body sinuses where the blood circulates, as illustrated in Figure 21.13. Wastes from the blood pass into the tubules, and nitrogenous wastes are converted into uric acid crystals. The tubules empty into the digestive tract, from which fluids are reabsorbed into the sinuses. The uric acid crystals are excreted through the anus along with undigested food remnants. Carbon dioxide is excreted by the grasshopper through its tracheae. (See Figure 21.4.)

In fishes, the excretion of carbon dioxide takes place in the gills (Figure 21.2), the same organs through which the supply of oxygen is obtained. Nitrogenous wastes are excreted chiefly as ammonia—once again as the blood circulates through the gills. Hence the gills are the chief excretory organs of fishes. In saltwater fishes, special cells in the gills also excrete salt, thus helping maintain the body's water-salt balance.

Sea turtles and marine birds excrete salt through special glands in their heads (Figure 21.14). Like other air-breathing animals with lungs, they excrete carbon dioxide from the blood as it passes through the lungs.

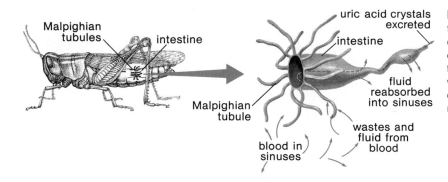

FIGURE 21.13 Wastes and fluid from the blood of the grasshopper enter Malpighian tubules. The tubules empty into the digestive tract where the fluids are reabsorbed. The wastes are excreted as uric acid crystals along with undigested food remnants from the digestive system.

CHECK AND CHALLENGE

1. Describe the excretory function of gills in fishes.
2. Compare the problems of osmosis encountered by freshwater and saltwater fishes.
3. Compare the excretion of nitrogenous wastes in protists, planarians, and grasshoppers.
4. Why is ammonia an advantageous excretory product for aquatic organisms?

FIGURE 21.14 Salt glands in birds. (*a*) Many marine birds excrete excess salt through nasal glands. A salt gland (*b*) has numerous lobes that contain tubules radiating from a central duct. Each tubule is surrounded by capillaries where the blood flows opposite to the flow of salt secretion. Special cells lining the tubules pump sodium ions from the blood into the tubules (*c*). Negatively charged chloride ions follow the sodium ions.

Human Urinary System

21.8 Structure of the Urinary System

Rather than being scattered throughout the body like the Malpighian tubules of insects, the excretory tubules of humans, called **nephrons** (NEF rahnz), are collected into compact organs, the **kidneys**. The kidneys are the major organs in humans (as well as other mammals) responsible for processing the waste products of metabolism. Blood is cycled through the kidneys, and nitrogenous wastes are removed. The removal of these wastes serves to regulate the water balance by adjusting the concentrations of various salts in the blood. The kidneys, the blood vessels that serve them, and the plumbing that carries fluid formed in the kidneys out of the body compose the **urinary system**, illustrated in Figure 21.15 on the next page. Blood to be filtered enters the kidneys through the renal artery and leaves via the renal vein. The kidneys process the entire blood supply of the human body about once every five minutes. The waste fluid, **urine**, leaves the kidneys through a duct called the **ureter** (YOOR eh ter). The ureter drains into a "holding tank," the **urinary bladder**. The urinary bladder is periodically drained by passing the urine through a tube called the **ure-thra** (yoo REE thruh) during urination.

Humans have two kidneys, one on each side of the body just above waist height, against the back wall of the body cavity. The nephrons are closely packed tubules that extend from the kidney's cortex (outer part)

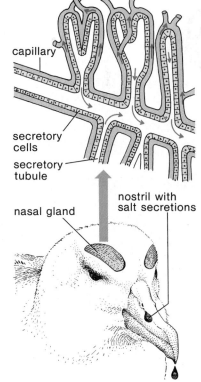

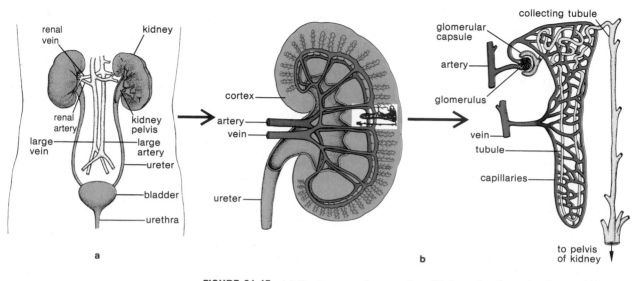

FIGURE 21.15 (a) The human urinary system (b) A section through a human kidney and an enlarged view of one nephron with its surrounding capillaries.

into the medulla (inner part). Each kidney contains approximately one million nephrons.

A nephron (Figure 21.15) is a long, coiled structure with one end fashioned as a cup that fits over a mass of capillaries. The other end of the nephron opens into a duct that collects urine. The tubular portions of the nephron are closely associated with a network of capillaries along the entire length.

The cup of the nephron is called the **glomerular** (glah MER yoo lehr) **capsule**, or Bowman's capsule. The ball of capillaries within the cup is called a **glomerulus** (glah MER yoo lus). A glomerulus is shown clearly in the scanning electron micrograph in Figure 21.16. The glomerular capsule and the glomerulus are located in the cortex of the kidney. The wall of the tubules is never more than a single cell thick and is often in direct contact with the capillary walls (also one cell thick). In some places along the tubules, the capillary and tubule walls appear to be merged into one undivided structure. Each tubule has a U-shaped section, the **nephron loop** (Loop of Henle), that descends from the cortex into the medulla and ascends back to the cortex. After the nephron loop, the tubule of a nephron leads out into a collecting duct, which in turn leads to a larger duct. Collecting ducts from all the nephrons eventually empty into the ureter.

21.9 Function of the Human Nephron

Nephrons have three functions: filtration, reabsorption, and secretion. These processes are summarized in Figure 21.17. Filtration occurs in the glomerulus, where the fluid portion of the blood is forced into the glomerular capsule. Blood cells and most of the plasma proteins are retained in the capillaries of the glomerulus. The filtrate includes the blood plasma,

FIGURE 21.16 Scanning electron micrograph of a glomerulus with the glomerular capsule removed, X1180.

nitrogenous wastes from cells, urea, salts, ions, glucose, and amino acids. Approximately 180 L of fluid enter the nephrons each day, yet only about 1.5 L of urine is eliminated from the bladder. That difference means that more than 99 percent of the fluid arriving in the glomerular capsule is returned to the blood.

Reabsorption and secretion take place in the tubule of the nephron. Cells of the tubule walls reabsorb substances needed by the body from the filtrate and return them to the blood. Approximately 65 percent of the salt and water in the tubule is reabsorbed into the capillaries before the filtrate reaches the nephron loop. An additional 20 percent is reabsorbed at the nephron loop. The water is returned by osmosis, but active transport is necessary for the reabsorption of the sodium and potassium ions. Glucose, amino acids, and some urea also are reabsorbed by active transport before they reach the nephron loop.

Secretion occurs as the filtrate moves through the tubule. Cells of the tubule wall selectively remove substances from the surrounding capillaries that were left in the plasma after filtration or returned by reabsorption. The cells then secrete these substances into the filtrate. Excess potassium ions are excreted in this manner.

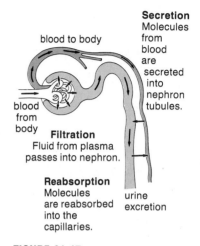

FIGURE 21.17 Major steps in the formation of urine

21.10 Control of Nephron Function

Reabsorption accounts for 85 percent of the salt, water, and other substances processed by the kidney. The remaining 15 percent is regulated by endocrine or nervous system controls. Excretion of sodium and potassium is regulated by **aldosterone** (al DAH steh rohn), a hormone secreted by the adrenal gland (Chapter 23). The presence of aldosterone stimulates the secretion of potassium from the blood into the tubule near the collecting duct (Figure 21.18) and enhances the reabsorption of sodium. Aldosterone is secreted in response to a rise in blood potassium levels. Aldosterone also functions in control of the blood pH by promoting secretion of excess hydrogen ions into the tubules. The urinary system is assisted in controlling the level of blood pH by the gas exchange system, which eliminates carbon dioxide.

The filtrate coming from the glomerulus becomes more concentrated as it passes through the tubules. The final concentration of substances in the urine is regulated in the collecting duct, which is permeable to water, but not to salts. Water is lost by osmosis to the surrounding tissues, but the amount of this loss is under the control of **ADH**, or antidiuretic hormone, which is released from the pituitary gland (Chapter 23). If a person becomes dehydrated, the water volume of the blood decreases. Receptors in a part of the brain called the hypothalamus (Chapter 22) detect the change, stimulating the pituitary gland to release more ADH into the bloodstream. The ADH causes the plasma membranes of collecting duct cells to become more permeable to water. Water passes from the collecting duct to the circulatory system, and the proper volume of water in the blood is restored. Receptors in the hypothalamus detect the increased volume of the blood and decrease the levels of ADH, which, in turn, decreases the permeability

FIGURE 21.18 All of the potassium ions in the filtrate are reabsorbed into the blood by the time the filtrate passes the nephron loop. Under the influence of aldosterone, potassium ions are secreted back into the filtrate near the collecting duct.

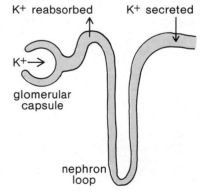

MEDICAL TECHNOLOGIST

When someone draws blood from you, where does it go? It probably goes to the laboratory where a medical technologist (MT), such as Susan Yost, runs the tests that your doctor requests.

Sue is a chief technician at the Penrose Hospital in Colorado Springs, Colorado. She supervises about 25 other technicians in the Special Chemistry and Radioimmunoassay Departments of the chemistry laboratory. As a supervisor, her primary responsibilities include overseeing the other employees, maintaining the equipment, and ensuring the accuracy of test results.

Sue attended the University of Nebraska Medical Center in Omaha, where she obtained a bachelor's degree in medical technology. After graduating, Sue worked in a small hospital in Alabama where MTs performed a wide range of duties, such as drawing blood and running electrocardiograms.

When her family moved to Colorado, Sue joined Penrose Hospital, where she is still working 18 years later. Sue enjoys her job because, even though the stress level is high, the wide range of tests she performs ensures that there is never a dull moment. Usually, most of the tests involve the analysis of blood or other body fluids to determine various levels of gases, hormones, toxins, bacteria, clotting factors, and other substances. The levels of different substances may indicate a particular condition or a problem with medication. For instance, a doctor may order a blood profile on a patient. This profile is actually a battery of 13 different tests. The results of each of these tests may indicate that further, more specific tests should be run to pinpoint the problem area, such as renal (kidney) malfunction.

Patients undergoing open heart surgery have their blood gases analyzed as the surgery is actually performed. The pH of the blood, the levels of carbon dioxide and oxygen in the blood, and the patient's temperature all are critical. If too much carbon diox-

FIGURE B Susan Yost operates an automatic analyzer that can run 35 tests at one time.

ide is present or the blood pH is too high, for example, the mixture of air being delivered to the patient is adjusted to bring these levels into line.

Sue enjoys maintaining the instruments in the laboratory, many of which are costly. Among the high-tech equipment is an automatic analyzer that can run up to 35 different tests at one time, and a machine that does blood cell counts by itself. There are also pieces of equipment that are more familiar—microscopes, centrifuges, and machines that stain slides.

All of this equipment requires a trained medical technologist to run it. Sue says there is great demand for MTs in hospitals and, in fact, Penrose Hospital operates its own training course, as do many large hospitals. She says, however, that after you take the courses and graduate, the training does not stop. Because changes are always occurring, MTs need to take additional classes and attend lectures and seminars to stay current with the new technology in medicine.

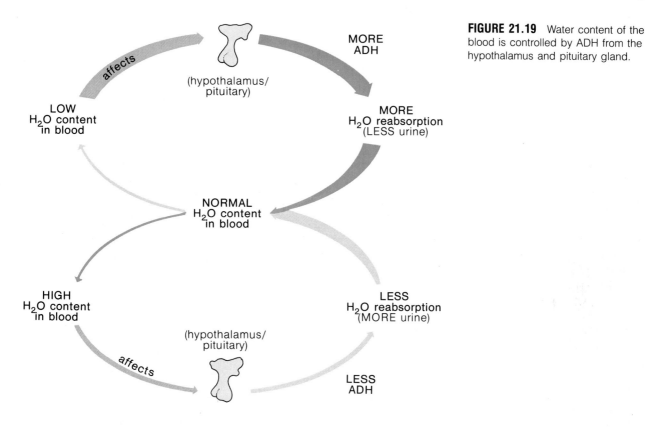

FIGURE 21.19 Water content of the blood is controlled by ADH from the hypothalamus and pituitary gland.

of the collecting duct to water. Figure 21.19 illustrates this regulating mechanism, which is similar to the one in the female reproductive system described in Chapter 11.

Excess salt also can be removed from the body by the kidneys, but only in small amounts. When humans eat or drink substances (such as sea water) that have high salt concentrations, their bodies actually lose water because, while trying to eliminate the excess salt, the body excretes more water than was taken in. That is why shipwrecked people can easily perish from dehydration if they drink sea water.

As a net result of the kidney's activities of filtration, reabsorption, secretion, and excretion, nitrogenous wastes are removed from the blood as urea; blood pressure is partially regulated; water-salt balance and blood pH are regulated; blood glucose is conserved; and excess salt, within limits, is excreted.

Try Investigation 21B, The Kidney and Homeostasis.

CHECK AND CHALLENGE _____

1. Describe the structure of a nephron and how it functions.
2. Distinguish among filtration, reabsorption, and secretion.
3. Describe the function of aldosterone in the human nephron.
4. How does ADH act to regulate water balance?

Summary

Single-celled organisms and many small animals obtain oxygen and carbon dioxide by diffusion through the plasma membrane. Larger organisms have self-contained gas exchange systems. Organisms larger than most insects require the interaction of the circulatory system with the gas exchange system to remove carbon dioxide.

Hemoglobin is one of several compounds in the blood of animals specialized for oxygen transport. In humans, oxygen is transported by hemoglobin in the erythrocytes. Carbon dioxide is transported mainly as bicarbonate ions in the plasma. Oxygen and carbon dioxide are exchanged by diffusion through the capillaries in the alveoli of the lungs.

Freshwater and saltwater organisms face different problems in maintaining a homeostatic water and salt balance with their external environment. Land-dwelling organisms face problems similar to those of saltwater organisms—they must conserve water and excrete excess salts.

Ammonia, urea, and uric acid are compounds by which organisms excrete nitrogenous wastes. Many aquatic organisms excrete ammonia which, though toxic, can be diluted in the water from the environment. Urea, which is less toxic than ammonia and requires dilution with only moderate amounts of water, is the main excretory product of mammals. Many land-dwelling organisms, especially those in desert environments, convert nitrogenous wastes to uric acid, which can be excreted as solid crystals without a loss of water.

Contractile vacuoles, flame cells, Malpighian tubules, and nephrons in kidneys are all involved in the excretion of waste products. The human kidney has several other functions in addition to that of nitrogenous waste excretion, such as regulation of blood pressure and water-salt balance.

The nephron is the functional unit of the kidney. Filtration of the blood occurs in the glomerulus and glomerular capsule. Reabsorption of plasma and many salts occurs in the nephron tubule near the glomerular capsule. The final regulation of water and salt balance occurs in the most distant parts of the nephron and in the collecting ducts that lead to the ureter. Aldosterone, a hormone of the adrenal gland, functions with the nephron in regulating the secretion and reabsorption of potassium and sodium ions in the blood. Antidiuretic hormone from the pituitary gland functions with the collecting ducts in regulating the reabsorption of water.

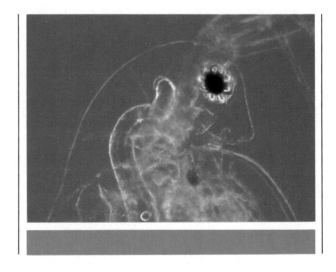

Key Concepts

Use the following concepts to develop a concept map about excretion in humans. Include additional terms as you need them.

ADH	kidneys
aldosterone	lungs
alveoli	Na^+ and K^+ concentration
capillaries	nephrons
diffusion	nitrogenous wastes
filtration	reabsorption
gas exchange	secretion
hemoglobin	water balance
homeostasis	

Reviewing Ideas

1. What processes do organisms use to obtain the materials they need from the environment?

2. Describe the different homeostatic problems encountered by freshwater and saltwater fishes.

3. Why would it be a problem for land-dwelling organisms to excrete their wastes as liquid ammonia?

4. Explain in what way flame cells are more complex than contractile vacuoles for water and waste excretion.

5. Describe how the Malpighian tubules function with the open circulatory system of the grasshopper in excretion.

6. What organs, in addition to the kidneys, function in excretion in humans?

7. Describe how the kidney functions in excretion in humans.

8. Distinguish between the structure and function of a glomerular capsule and a glomerulus.

9. How does secretion function in homeostatic regulation in humans?

10. How does a desert-dwelling mammal keep gas exchange surfaces wet enough for gas exchange to occur?

11. Why is uric acid an advantageous excretory product for desert organisms?

12. What is the difference between hemoglobin and oxyhemoglobin?

13. Compare oxygen transport mechanisms in vertebrates and insects.

14. Describe how gills work.

Using Concepts

1. Why is the differential excretion of urea, ammonia, and uric acid considered to be an adaptation?

2. Why is it more useful for protists to utilize contractile vacuoles instead of kidneys for water excretion?

3. Describe the similarities between gills and lungs in terms of gas exchange and excretion.

4. Describe how the nephron functions in helping to regulate blood pressure.

5. Compare the structural variations that increase the surface area of lungs and gills.

6. Describe how the breathing rate affects the pH of the blood.

7. Carbon monoxide is attracted more strongly to hemoglobin than is oxygen. What problem could this pose for people?

8. A person participating in a heavy workout loses materials needed by the body. What should this person eat or drink to replace what has been lost?

9. Why would it be unlikely for aquatic organisms to excrete uric acid crystals?

Synthesis

1. Review Chapters 3, 18, and 19. How do the cellular processes described in Chapter 3 relate to the digestive, transport, and excretory systems?

2. If you had to eliminate one system from your body—either the digestive, transport, or excretory system—which one would you choose? Explain how you might overcome the problems caused by the elimination of that system.

3. What advantage does a closed circulatory system have over an open circulatory system in its function with the excretory system?

Extensions

1. Write a story about a molecule of oxygen and what happens to it from the time it enters the nasal passages of a human until it leaves the body again.

2. Take a trip to a local wastewater treatment facility. Are any human wastes recycled? Are any other organisms involved in the treatment? Would you be willing to drink the water that comes from the treatment plant? Why or why not? Write a short paper on the importance of wastewater treatment.

3. Some limestone caves are being damaged by exposure to carbon dioxide exhaled by humans. Write a short report on the damage and the chemistry involved.

CONTENTS

signals go to muscles or glands, called effectors. **Sensory neurons** receive information from the internal and external environments and transmit impulses toward the brain or spinal cord, which together compose the **central nervous system**. **Interneurons** transmit signals from one neuron to another within the central nervous system. Interneurons are the most abundant type of neuron in vertebrate nervous systems. Figure 22.3 shows the structure of sensory neurons and interneurons. Motor neurons and sensory neurons form the **peripheral nervous system**, which functions as a communication network between the central nervous system and the rest of the body.

CONNECTIONS

The nervous system is integral to the maintenance of homeostasis and influences an organism's behavior. It coordinates the reception of stimuli with appropriate responses.

FOCUS ON *The Eye*

The human eye is sensitive to almost 7 million shades of color and about 10 million variations of light intensity. What makes this sensitivity possible? Light waves that enter the eye through the cornea [Figure A(a)] are bent toward the lens. The iris (colored part of the eye) consists of muscles that can contract and relax, changing the size of the pupil, thus regulating the amount of light that enters the eye. The waves pass through the lens and are focused on the retina, which has several different layers of tissue [Figure A(b)]. The rods and cones receive stimuli caused by the incoming light waves. **Rods** are responsible for peripheral vision (the edges of the field of vision) and respond to dim light for black-and-white vision. **Cones** are responsible for daylight color vision.

Nerve impulses from the rods and cones are transmitted through the optic nerves (one from each eye) to the brain. The forward position of the eyes allows the brain to perceive vision in three dimensions and to perceive depth.

Most invertebrates detect light with receptors that contain light-absorbing pigments. One of the simplest light receptors is the eye cup of planarians. It detects light intensity and direction without forming an image. Two major types of image-forming eyes have evolved in invertebrates. One type is the compound eye of arthropods. This eye consists of several thousand light detectors, each with its own lenses and receptor cell [Figure A(c)]. Although the resolution is not as sharp as with a human eye, the compound eye is good at detecting movement. Insects also have excellent color vision, and some can see ultraviolet light. The second type of invertebrate eye is the camera eye, like that of the octopus. This eye has a single lens that focuses light onto the retina. Humans and other vertebrates also have the camera-type eye.

FIGURE A A cross section diagram of a mammalian eye (a); rods and cones in the retina detect light (b); a section of a compound eye (c).

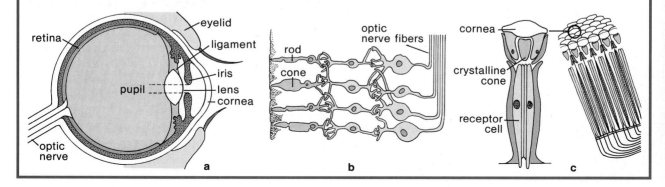

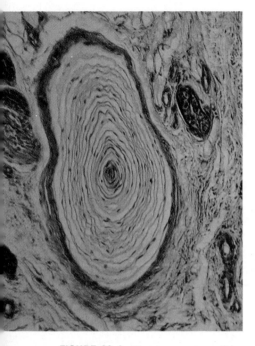

FIGURE 22.4 Touch receptor cell in the finger, ×100

Try Investigation 22A, Sensory Receptors.

22.2 Response to Stimuli

A change in the environment that causes an organism to respond is called a **stimulus**. The response can be an internal change within the organism or an external change in behavior. Stimuli are received through **sensory receptors** such as those in Figure 22.4. Sensory receptors are the brain's windows to the outside world. These specialized structures at the dendrite ends of sensory neurons collect and transmit information about all sorts of environmental stimuli, including heat, light, pressure, and chemicals. They vary from single, naked neuron endings to complex organs such as eyes and ears that integrate information from thousands of receptor cells. The stimuli that receptors respond to are all different forms of energy. The role of receptor cells is to convert the energy of the stimuli into the type of energy that can be understood by the rest of the nervous system.

22.3 Transmission of Impulses

How are stimuli converted to energy that the rest of the nervous system can interpret? Generally, plasma membranes are electrically charged, or polarized, because ions are distributed unequally on the outside and inside of the cell. (See Figure 22.5.) A change in **polarization**, or electrical charge, of the membrane results in the transmission of information as nerve impulses through neurons and muscle and gland cells.

The unequal distribution is due to two major factors. First, the membrane is very permeable to potassium ions (K^+) and only slightly permeable to sodium ions (Na^+). This permeability is related to the transport proteins in the membrane. (See section 6.7. Some transport proteins form channels through which specific ions diffuse. Other proteins act as carriers for active transport.) Both diffusion and active transport help establish and maintain polarization of the plasma membrane. Second, there are relatively high concentrations of potassium ions in the cytosol and of sodium ions in the extracellular fluid (Figure 22.5). In addition, the cytosol contains a relatively high concentration of negatively charged ions or molecules such as organic phosphates and proteins, that cannot diffuse through the plasma membrane.

As a result of the differential membrane permeability and the ionic imbalance, potassium ions tend to diffuse freely out of the cell, and sodium ions tend to diffuse in—but much more slowly. At the same time, active transport moves sodium ions out of the cell and potassium ions in. The net effect is that more positively charged ions leave the cell than enter it, and the outside of the membrane becomes positively charged with respect to the inside. The difference in charge is called an electric potential.

Stimulation of a neuron causes a local, sudden change in permeability. Channels in the membrane that are highly selective for sodium ions open, and sodium ions quickly diffuse into the neuron. As a result, the membrane loses its electrical potential and becomes depolarized (Figure 22.6b). Potassium channels then open and potassium ions diffuse out, restoring the positive charge of the outside of the membrane. The membrane is thus temporarily repolarized and can transmit another impulse.

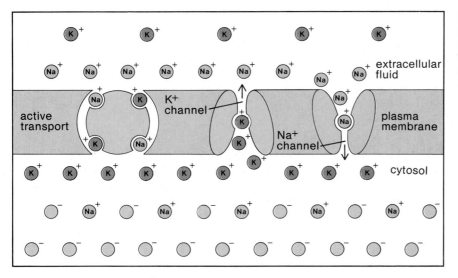

FIGURE 22.5 Polarization of a plasma membrane is due to the membrane's differential permeability to sodium and potassium ions and to an ionic imbalance maintained by active transport.

Depolarization at one point in a neuron membrane sets up an electric current that flows to adjacent portions of the membrane. The current spreads rapidly along the axon. This wave of depolarization traveling along a neuron is called a **nerve impulse**, illustrated in Figure 22.6. The nerve impulse moves in one direction along an axon. This is because Na^+ channels on the axon behind the area of depolarization become temporarily closed. The impulse therefore moves away from the point of stimulation.

Neurons need time to recover before they can receive a new stimulus. Recovery time is directly related to how long it takes potassium ions to diffuse outside the membrane and reestablish the electric potential. If a second stimulus is received before repolarization, there will not be an impulse. In some neurons, the recovery time after an impulse is as brief as one thousandth of a second. After impulses have stopped, the original polarization is restored by active transport of sodium ions to the outside of the membrane.

In the case of myelinated neurons, which are insulated by a myelin sheath, the wave of depolarization does not travel down the axons as it does in unmyelinated neurons. In myelinated neurons, the impulse actually jumps from one node of Ranvier to the next. This jumping of depolarization and repolarization speeds up the transmission of the nerve impulse. Many of the neurons that control your muscles are myelinated, allowing for speedy reaction times to stimuli received from the environment.

Neurons obey an ''all-or-none'' law in transmitting impulses. A stimulus must reach a critical level to cause the impulse to begin traveling down the neuron. The level at which the impulse is triggered is called the **threshold**. Stimuli that do not reach the threshold do not cause the neuron to fire, or depolarize. A stimulus above the threshold causes the same impulse as a stimulus that just barely surpasses the threshold. How then can a person distinguish between weak and strong stimuli? Usually, strong stimuli cause more neurons to fire. The more neurons that fire, the stronger the stimulus perceived in the brain.

FIGURE 22.6 (a) The plasma membrane of a polarized neuron is more positive on the outside than on the inside. A stimulus changes membrane permeability, Na^+ rushes in, and the membrane is locally depolarized (b). K^+ diffuses out (c), repolarizing the membrane. The impulse moves as a wave of such changes in electrical charges (d,e,f).

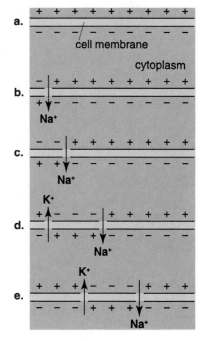

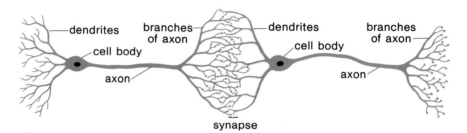

FIGURE 22.7 Trace the path of an impulse across the synapse. In which direction does the impulse travel from neuron to neuron?

22.4 Synapses

A **synapse** (SIH naps) is a junction between a neuron and a second cell, which may be a muscle cell, a gland cell, or another neuron (Figure 22.7). The impulse cannot travel directly across the synapse because there is a small space between the axon of one neuron and the dendrites of the second neuron. Figure 22.8 shows a highly magnified picture of the ends of an axon at the synapse. How does the impulse cross this gap?

Chemical messengers called **neurotransmitters** are released into the synapse when a nerve impulse reaches the end of the axon. The neurotransmitters quickly diffuse across the synapse and stimulate the dendrite to trigger an impulse in the second neuron. In muscle cells, neurotransmitters cause contractions to occur, and in gland cells, they cause secretions to be released.

If neurotransmitters cause the impulses to be transmitted, why aren't impulses transmitted continuously to the second neuron, muscle, or gland? The dendrites of neurons and specialized cells in the muscles and glands secrete an enzyme that quickly breaks down the neurotransmitter, preventing continuous stimulation. If nerve impulses were transmitted continuously, there would be no way to regulate or interpret the activity of the nervous system.

Recently, a large number of polypeptide chains have been recognized as important neurotransmitters. Some of these substances were first identified as hormones and later associated with neurotransmission. Endorphins (en DOR finz) and enkephalins (en KEH fah linz) are among the most interesting neurotransmitters. These neurotransmitters are produced by neurons in the brain and mimic the effects of opiates such as morphine and heroin. They are sometimes called the body's "natural opiates." The discovery of receptors for morphine and heroin in the nervous system was quite puzzling. It seemed odd that humans would have molecular receptors for chemicals from a poppy plant. Subsequently, however, scientists recognized that the human body produces both substances, which act like derivatives of the opium poppy. In addition to reducing pain, these neurotransmitters decrease urine output by affecting ADH secretion (section 21.10), depress breathing (gas exchange), produce euphoria, and have other emotional effects through specific pathways in parts of the brain.

FIGURE 22.8 An electron micrograph of part of a synapse, showing terminal knobs on the ends of the branches of the axons. An impulse coming to the ends of the axon stimulates the synaptic knobs to secrete a chemical messenger, or neurotransmitter. The chemical crosses the gap and stimulates the dendrites of neighboring neurons, reinitiating the impulse in them.

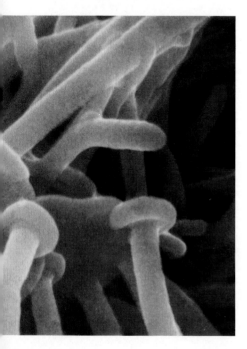

22.5 Drugs and the Brain

Understanding the function of neurotransmitters (and the enzymes that break them down) helps us understand how drugs affect the nervous system. Broadly speaking, a drug is any chemical substance that has no nutritional value and is introduced into the body to elicit some effect on physiological processes. Psychoactive drugs are those that affect parts of the central nervous system concerned with consciousness and behavior. Many of these drugs alter synaptic transmission, for example, by modifying or blocking the synthesis, release, or uptake of transmitter substances. Most psychoactive drugs are addictive—that is, they cause a strong physical, and sometimes psychological, need for the drug. In addition, psychoactive drugs produce some degree of tolerance with chronic use or abuse. Because the human body has the ability to adapt to the drug and its effects, this tolerance results in the requirement of increased doses of the drug to produce the same effects that smaller doses used to produce.

Depressants such as alcohol and barbiturates lower the activity in certain parts of the brain and nervous system and thus reduce activity throughout the body. Some depressants inhibit synaptic transmission. Alcohol does not act at synapses, rather it acts directly on plasma membranes to alter cell function.

Caffeine, nicotine, amphetamines, and cocaine are stimulants. Stimulants initially increase alertness and activity but they eventually lead to a period of depression. Caffeine apparently plays a role in the breakdown of glycogen into glucose and lowers the threshold at certain synapses so the neurons are more easily excited. Nicotine has powerful effects on both the central and peripheral nervous systems. It chemically mimics a neurotransmitter and can directly stimulate a number of sensory receptors. Amphetamines and cocaine apparently mimic or enhance the effect of the neurotransmitter norepinephrine, which underlies the fight-or-flight responses. (See section 23.13.) Figure 22.9 shows the effect of amphetamines on the web-building ability of a spider.

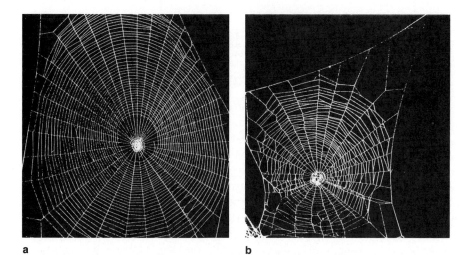

a   b

FIGURE 22.9 Many of the complex behavior patterns of animals can be disturbed by chemical substances. A female spider builds webs in the characteristic regular form (a). Several hours after feeding on sugar water containing a small dose of amphetamine, the spider built an unusually small, irregular web (b). Although we cannot compare directly the behavior patterns of invertebrates and humans, experiments such as this provide important information about the effects of chemical substances on brain function.

Hallucinogens are drugs that alter sensory perception, particularly visual and auditory perception. Some hallucinogens alter acetylcholine or norepinephrine activity. Others, such as LSD, affect the activity of the neurotransmitters serotonin and dopamine. These neurotransmitters affect sleep, mood, attention, and learning. An imbalance in these neurotransmitters is associated with psychological disorders and mental illness. LSD and mescaline mimic the structure and function of these neurotransmitters in the brain. (See **Appendix 22A**, Sources, Uses, and Effects of Some Psychoactive Drugs, for more detailed information.)

Understanding the function of neurotransmitters also has enabled researchers to identify the cause of some diseases that affect the nervous system. For example, investigators found that victims of Alzheimer's disease, which is characterized by a loss of memory and mental abilities, do not produce as much of the neurotransmitter acetylcholine as other people. Parkinson's disease—characterized by slow movements, lack of control over muscle actions, and tremors—is caused by a lack of dopamine. Myasthenia gravis is characterized by weak muscles due to the secretion of antibodies by the immune system that block the acetylcholine receptors of affected persons.

CHECK AND CHALLENGE

1. Describe the similarities and differences among sensory, motor, and interneurons.
2. What is the function of Schwann cells?
3. How is an impulse transmitted along a neuron?
4. How are impulses transmitted between two neurons?
5. What would happen if neurotransmitters did not break down quickly in synapses?
6. Describe the relationship between neurotransmitters and drugs.

Structure and Function of Nervous Systems

22.6 Evolution of Nervous Systems

Neurons are arranged in circuits or groups that interconnect and carry information along specific pathways. Nerve cell bodies are not uniformly distributed within the nervous system but are arranged in functional groups called **ganglia**. These clusters of nerve cells allow parts of the nervous system to coordinate activities without involving the entire system. This centralization of nervous system coordination is one of the key features of the evolution of nervous systems in animals.

Though there is a tremendous uniformity in how nerve cells function throughout the animal kingdom, there is great diversity in how nervous systems are organized. A *Hydra* (Figure 22.10a), for example, has a nervous

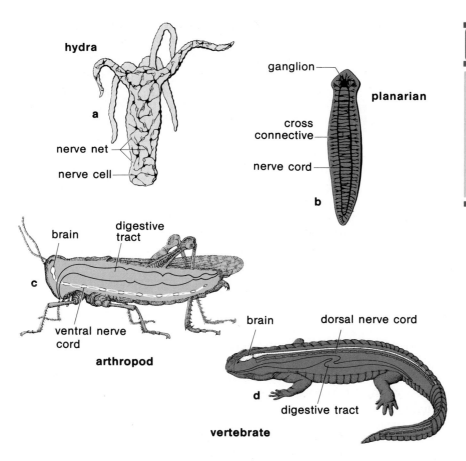

FIGURE 22.10 A *Hydra* (a) has a nerve net made up of nerve cells that are all alike. A planarian (b) has a nervous system with two nerve cords, many nerve cells, and a small brain (ganglion) in the head region. In insects (c) the nerve cord is ventral, beneath the digestive tract. In vertebrates (d) it is dorsal, above the digestive tract.

system made only of nerve cells evenly distributed throughout the animal. Such a system is called a nerve net. Most of the synapses in a nerve net are electrical rather than chemical and, therefore, impulses are carried in both directions. When a stimulus is applied at any point on a *Hydra*, the resulting impulse eventually spreads along the nerve net in all directions throughout the organism. For the effect to spread very far, however, the stimulus must be strong and last a long time. The nerve net carries signals more slowly than does a more specialized, centralized nervous system.

Some animals have both a nerve net and a more organized nervous system. Animals with active life-styles tend to have sense organs and nerve centers located at the anterior, or head, end of their bodies. The planarian, for example, has a small brain that sends information along two parallel nerve cords on each side of its body (Figure 22.10b). Many versions of this basic type of nervous system are found in the animal kingdom. An insect's nervous system and that of a vertebrate are illustrated in Figure 22.10c and d.

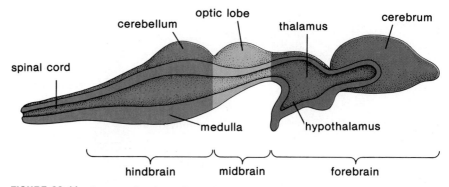

FIGURE 22.11 A generalized vertebrate brain

The vertebrate brain evolved from a series of three bulges at the anterior end of the spinal (nerve) cord. These three regions, the hindbrain, midbrain, and forebrain (Figure 22.11), are all present in vertebrates. In more complex brains, they become further subdivided, providing for the integration of more complex activities. The hindbrain in mammals is a knobby extension of the spinal cord, called the brainstem. The human brainstem is illustrated in Figure 22.14. The brainstem contains clusters of nerve cell bodies that are involved with certain reflexes. For example, the centers of the brainstem control heartbeat and breathing, among other functions—the reason why a blow to the base of the skull is so dangerous. The brainstem also contains all the nerve fibers that pass between the spinal cord and other brain centers. In less complex vertebrates, a major portion of the midbrain is made up of the optic lobes. In mammals, the analysis of visual information is a function of the forebrain, and the midbrain serves primarily as a relay and reflex center.

Three trends characterize vertebrate brain evolution. First, the relative size of the brain increases in certain evolutionary lines. Brain size is a fairly constant reflection of body size in amphibians, fishes, and reptiles. In birds and mammals, however, brain size relative to body size increases dramatically. A mouse weighing 100 g has a much larger brain than a lizard weighing 100 g. The brain of a 100-g lizard and a 100-g fish, however, are about the same.

A second evolutionary trend is increased specialization of function. The three major brain regions still remain, but they become subdivided into areas that have specific functions. In the hindbrain, for example, a region known as the **cerebellum** (seh reh BEL um) becomes the major structure for coordinating movement. The forebrain is subdivided into the cerebrum, the thalamus, and the hypothalamus. The thalamus acts as a relay station that analyzes and transmits sensory input. The hypothalamus regulates many homeostatic mechanisms and serves as a link between the nervous and endocrine systems. The **cerebrum** (seh REE brum) is the part of the brain most important in learning and memory. As these specific structures become more complex, the original divisions between the three bulges become blurred.

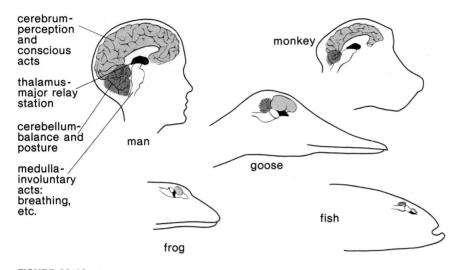

cerebrum-
perception
and
conscious
acts

thalamus-
major relay
station

cerebellum-
balance and
posture

medulla-
involuntary
acts:
breathing,
etc.

man

monkey

goose

frog

fish

FIGURE 22.12 Compare these five vertebrate brains. Notice the relative sizes of the various parts in the different animals.

The third trend in vertebrate brain evolution is the increasing sophistication and complexity of the forebrain. The appearance of more complex behaviors parallels the evolution of the cerebrum. Among mammals, in particular, complex behavior is associated with the relative size of the cerebrum and the presence of folds, or convolutions, that increase the surface area of the brain. Because the cell bodies of the cerebrum are in the cortex, or outer layer, the surface area of the brain is more important in determining performance than is the overall brain volume. Although the human cerebral cortex is less than 5 mm thick, it covers such a large surface area that it occupies more than 80 percent of the total brain mass. Primates and porpoises have dramatically larger and more complex cerebral cortices than any other vertebrates. In fact, the cerebral cortex of the porpoise is second in surface area (relative to body size) only to that of humans. Figure 22.12 compares the brains of five vertebrates.

22.7 The Central Nervous System

The central nervous system (CNS) consists of the brain and the spinal cord and forms the bridge between the sensory and motor functions of the peripheral nervous system. The CNS is specialized to interpret nerve impulses, and functions with the endocrine system to coordinate the activities of all of the other body systems. The CNS also can store experiences in memory and learn by establishing patterns of responses based on prior experiences.

The brain and spinal cord are covered by protective membranes called the meninges (meh NIN jeez) and are further cushioned from shock by cerebrospinal fluid, which circulates around the brain and the spinal cord. The entire central nervous system is encased in and protected by bone. The

Try Investigation 22B, Reaction Time.

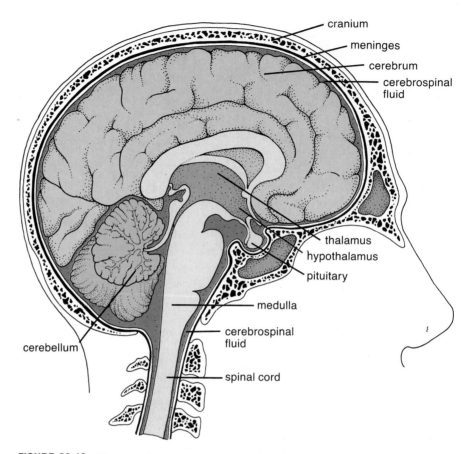

FIGURE 22.13   The central nervous system consists of the brain and spinal cord, both of which are covered with meninges and bathed in cerebrospinal fluid.

skull surrounds the brain and the backbone, or spine, surrounds the spinal cord. Examine Figure 22.13. The spine is made up of many separate bones that permit flexibility. Nerves run through openings in the bones of the spine, connecting the CNS to the PNS, the peripheral nervous system. (See section 22.8.)

The spinal cord has two principal functions. It integrates simple responses to certain types of stimuli, and it carries information to and from the brain. Spinal integration is normally in the form of a reflex. Most reflexes are fairly complex and sometimes involve many interneurons between the sensory and motor neurons.

The brain of an adult human weighs about 1.5 kg and is composed of an estimated 100 billion neurons. Neurons of the brain communicate with each other by means of specialized neurotransmitters (as described in section 22.4).

The senses of seeing, hearing, tasting, smelling, and feeling are experienced in the cerebrum. Much of the information about the cerebrum has been gained by studying people whose brains have been damaged in accidents. By determining the parts of the brain that have been injured and

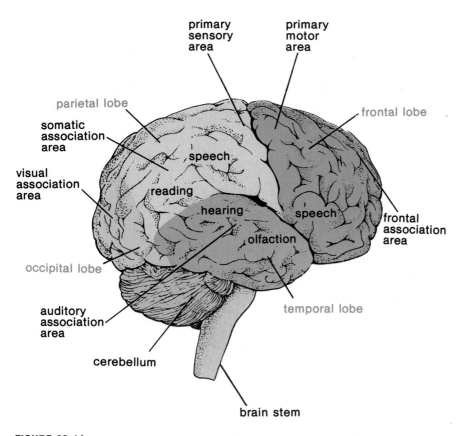

primary
sensory
area

primary
motor
area

parietal lobe

frontal lobe

somatic
association
area

speech

visual
association
area

reading

hearing

speech

frontal
association
area

olfaction

occipital lobe

temporal lobe

auditory
association
area

cerebellum

brain stem

FIGURE 22.14 The major functional areas of the cerebrum are associated with specific senses and abilities.

studying the affected body functions in the injured person, specific functions of areas have been identified. Figure 22.14 shows the major functional areas of the human brain.

The cerebrum is divided into a left and a right hemisphere, each having very different functions. The left hemisphere is generally associated with verbal and analytical skills such as reading, speech, writing, mathematics, and logic. The right hemisphere controls functions on the left side of the body. Conversely, the left hemisphere controls functions on the right side of the body. The surface of each of the two hemispheres is divided into four lobes, identified in Figure 22.14.

The cerebellum functions mainly in coordinating contractions of the skeletal muscles. Walking and running are under the influence of this part of the brain.

The **medulla** (meh DUL lah) regulates "automatic" reflex, vital activities, such as the heart rate, contractions of the blood vessels, and the depth and rate of breathing. Other functions include the control of coughing, sneezing, swallowing, and vomiting. The medulla keeps your body's vital functions operating properly without any intervention from the conscious mind.

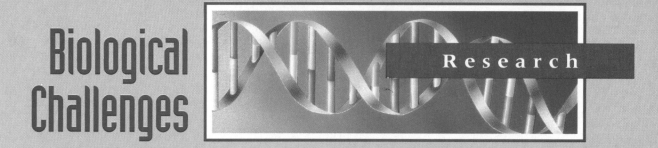

Biological Challenges

RETICULAR ACTIVATING SYSTEM

Why is it possible to sleep through the noise made by the carpenters next door, yet awaken when someone turns the knob on the door to your room? Similarly, why are you unaware of the contents of a dimly overheard conversation until something familiar, your name for instance, is mentioned? Researchers believe that a portion of the human brain, called the reticular formation, is responsible. The reticular formation is a collection of neurons within the brain stem that functions as the reticular activating system (RAS). The RAS extends from the medulla to the thalamus and functions as a filter that selects which sensory information reaches the cerebral cortex (Figure B). The RAS is involved with wakefulness and that hard-to-define state we know as consciousness. The more input the cortex receives, the more alert and aware the person is.

When sensory impulses reach the RAS, it responds by signaling the cerebral cortex, activating it into a state of wakefulness. Without this arousal, the cortex remains unaware of stimulation and cannot interpret sensory information or carry on thought processes. Sleep, the opposite condition of wakefulness, results from decreased activity in the RAS.

The RAS also acts as a filter for incoming sensory impulses. Those impulses that it judges to be important, such as those originating in pain receptors, are passed on to the cerebral cortex, while other impulses are disregarded. This selective action of the RAS frees the cerebral cortex from what would otherwise be a bombardment of sensory stimulation and allows the cortex to concentrate on more significant information. The cerebral cortex also can activate the RAS, so that intense cerebral activity tends to keep an individual awake. For example, despite being tired, you may be unable to sleep after having a particularly stimulating day.

The RAS also plays a role in regulating various motor activities so that the coordinated movements of muscles are smooth. It exerts an influence on spinal reflexes so that some movements are inhibited and others are enhanced.

Are people always fully alert? Do they always respond correctly to all impulses their brains receive? Many things, drugs for example, can interfere with the proper function of the RAS. The RAS is a major relay center in your brain. A depressant, such as alcohol, depresses the activity of the RAS, resulting in diminished or nonexistent ability of the system to perform its functions. If alcohol interferes with the ability of the system to efficiently filter and direct incoming stimuli and direct motor functions, what might the results be? Slurred speech, distorted perception, imbalance, impaired motor function, inattention, drowsiness, the inability to feel cold or pain, and unconsciousness all may result from the interference of alcohol with the performance of the reticular activating system.

FIGURE B The reticular activating system

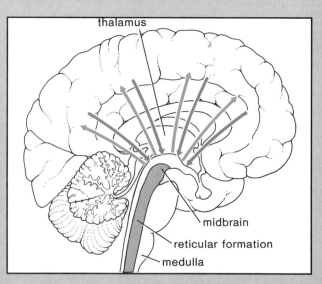

22.8 The Peripheral Nervous System

Because the vertebrate nervous system is complex, it is convenient to divide it into parts that differ in function, illustrated in Figure 22.15. As described earlier, the primary division is between the central nervous system and the peripheral nervous system. The peripheral nervous system is composed of two different groups of cells. Sensory neurons bring information *to* the central nervous system from sensory receptors. The motor neurons carry signals *away* from the central nervous system to various organs.

The human peripheral nervous system consists of 12 pairs of cranial nerves that originate in the brain and stimulate organs in the head and upper body. There are also 31 pairs of spinal nerves that stimulate the entire body. Most of the cranial nerves and all of the spinal nerves contain both sensory and motor neurons.

Nervous systems have two basic functions: to control responses to the external environment and to coordinate the functions of internal organs and thereby maintain homeostasis. The sensory division does both—bringing in stimuli from the external environment and monitoring the status of the internal environment. The motor division has two separate systems that deal with these functions. The motor neurons of the **somatic nervous system** carry signals to skeletal muscles in response to external stimuli. The somatic nervous system is often considered "voluntary" because it is under conscious control, though a large proportion of skeletal muscle movement is actually determined by reflexes. The **autonomic nervous system** coordinates the functions of organs and helps to maintain homeostasis.

The autonomic nervous system consists of two subdivisions that are anatomically, physiologically, and chemically distinguishable. These two subdivisions are the **sympathetic** and **parasympathetic** systems. Most

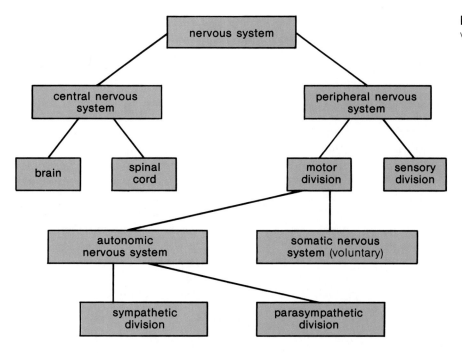

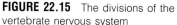

FIGURE 22.15 The divisions of the vertebrate nervous system

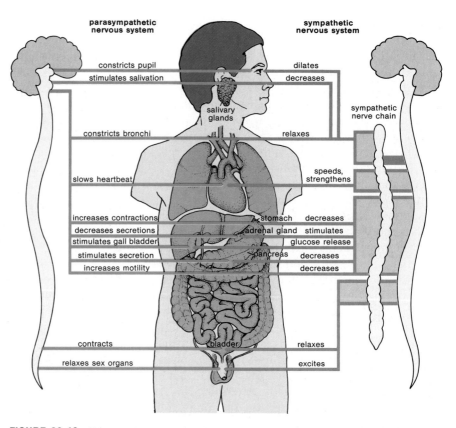

parasympathetic nervous system

sympathetic nervous system

constricts pupil — dilates
stimulates salivation — decreases

salivary glands

sympathetic nerve chain

constricts bronchi — relaxes

slows heartbeat — speeds, strengthens

increases contractions — stomach — decreases
decreases secretions — adrenal gland — stimulates
stimulates gall bladder — glucose release
stimulates secretion — pancreas — decreases
increases motility — decreases

contracts — bladder — relaxes
relaxes sex organs — excites

FIGURE 22.16 The two divisions of the autonomic nervous system. The parasympathetic nervous system generally acts to maintain normal body function. The sympathetic nervous system acts to prepare the body for emergency. The two divisions have opposing effects on a variety of organs and body functions.

internal organs are connected to both systems, as shown in Figure 22.16. When sympathetic and parasympathetic nerves stimulate the same organ, they often (but not always) have opposite effects and act much like a "brake pedal" and an "accelerator." If one system stimulates a particular organ, the other inhibits the organ. For example, the sympathetic nervous system speeds up the heart rate in emergencies and the parasympathetic system slows it down again. In general, the sympathetic system serves as a stimulator, and is often called the fight-or-flight system because of its role in preparing an organism to respond to emergency situations. The parasympathetic system has more of a nurturing role in maintaining homeostasis. The parasympathetic system also is responsible for moving food through the digestive tract.

The somatic and autonomic nervous systems are not entirely opposed. In response to a drop in temperature, for example, the hypothalamus signals the autonomic nervous system to constrict surface blood vessels to reduce heat loss, at the same time signaling the somatic nervous system to cause shivering. The autonomic nervous system acts in conjunction with hormones from the endocrine system to regulate many body functions. Chapter 23 describes these interactions more fully.

FOCUS ON *Reflex Arcs*

Reflex arcs involve both the peripheral and central nervous systems. A **reflex arc** is an automatic, involuntary response to a stimulus. Because it occurs before the stimulus is received and interpreted by the brain, a reflex arc decreases the reaction time to potentially life-threatening situations. The simplest type of reflex arc involves a receptor, a sensory neuron, a motor neuron, and the organ or muscle to which the motor neuron is connected.

You probably have had a physical examination in which the doctor strikes your leg just below the knee to check your reflexes. The impact of the rubber hammer triggers a receptor on the dendrites of a sensory neuron. The impulse travels along the sensory neuron to a motor neuron in the spinal cord, and continues to the muscles in your leg, which then contract and jerk your leg and foot upward. Figure C(a) shows the pathway of this reflex arc. Meanwhile, another impulse travels through an interneuron and up the nerves of your spinal cord to the brain where the sensation of the hammer's impact is received and interpreted. Neurons in reflex arcs are myelinated, enabling them to conduct impulses very rapidly.

The pain receptors in your fingertips are involved in a slightly more complicated reflex arc, illustrated in Figure C(b). A stimulus causes an impulse to travel up a sensory neuron toward the spinal cord. Before reaching the spinal cord, however, the sensory neuron transmits the impulse to an interneuron. The impulse travels through the interneuron to a motor neuron and on to the muscles of your arm. Your arm immediately jerks away from the stimulus. As in the case of the knee-jerk response, all of this happens automatically while the stimulus is traveling up the spinal cord toward the brain, where it is received and interpreted as pain.

FIGURE C (a) A simple two-neuron reflex arc involving a sensory neuron and a motor neuron; (b) getting jabbed with a pin initiates a three-neuron reflex. Most reflexes involve at least three neurons.

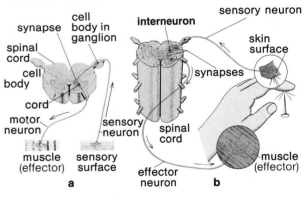

CHECK AND CHALLENGE

1. Describe the trends in vertebrate brain evolution.

2. What is the difference between a stimulus and an impulse?

3. How is the human cerebrum unique in the animal kingdom?

4. Compare the function of an interneuron in the two types of reflex arcs.

5. Compare and contrast the functions of the central, autonomic, and peripheral nervous systems.

Summary

Neurons are the structural and functional units of an animal's nervous system. Sensory neurons conduct impulses from the body toward the central nervous system; motor neurons conduct impulses from the central nervous system toward a muscle or gland. Interneurons are inside the spinal cord and connect some sensory neurons with motor neurons. Sensory neurons may have sensory receptors at the ends of their dendrites. Dendrites receive stimuli and conduct impulses toward the cell body of a neuron. Axons, with or without myelin, carry impulses away from the cell body. Neurons respond to stimuli, conduct impulses through depolarization and repolarization of their membranes, and release chemical regulators.

A stimulus is any change in the environment that causes an organism to respond. Sensory receptors can be grouped together in receptor organs, such as in the eye or ear. Impulses from sensory receptors are transmitted along neurons as a wave of depolarization. Both diffusion and active transport of sodium and potassium ions function in the transmission of the impulse and in the restoration of the neuron to its resting state. Impulses are transmitted across synapses by chemicals called neurotransmitters. Many drugs mimic neurotransmitters or interfere with their action.

Evolution has produced an increase in the complexity of nervous systems within the animal kingdom. In humans, the central nervous system consists of the spinal cord and the brain. The peripheral nervous system connects the central nervous system to all parts of the body and includes the cranial nerves and spinal nerves. The autonomic nervous system includes parts of both the central and peripheral nervous systems and controls many involuntary functions of the body. It is divided into two opposite-acting systems—the sympathetic and parasympathetic divisions. Reflex arcs involve both the peripheral and the central nervous systems.

Key Concepts

Use the following concepts to develop a concept map. You may add additional terms as you need them.

neuron	neurotransmitter	dendrite
cell body	axon	stimulus
cerebrum	receptors	cerebellum
medulla	autonomic	sympathetic
parasympathetic	nerve	synapse

Reviewing Ideas

1. Describe the similarities and differences between axons and dendrites.
2. What are the three major functions of neurons?
3. Describe the difference between depolarization and a nerve impulse.
4. Describe the function of the threshold in the transmission of nerve impulses.

5. How do neurotransmitters function?

6. What are the main functions of the central nervous system?

7. Compare the functions of the rods and cones in the human eye.

8. Describe the different functions of the left and right hemispheres of the human brain.

9. What are the differences between the cranial and spinal nerves?

10. Compare the functions of the sympathetic and parasympathetic divisions of the autonomic nervous system.

11. How does knowledge about the actions of neurotransmitters influence medicine?

12. What is the relationship between morphine and endorphins?

13. Describe the differences between a nerve net and the nervous system of mammals.

Using Concepts

1. Most motor neurons are covered with a myelin sheath instead of being unmyelinated. Discuss the adaptive advantages of myelin sheaths.

2. Describe the relationships among a receptor, a stimulus, and a motor neuron.

3. Explain why it is impossible for a neuron to continually transmit impulses, one after the other, without resting.

4. What is the role of active transport in transmitting impulses along neurons?

5. Describe specific responses of the sympathetic nervous system that you might experience before a difficult exam. How might those responses affect your performance?

6. What difficulties would a person experience if some neurotransmitters ceased to function?

Synthesis

1. Describe how the nervous system and the gas exchange system function together in regulating breathing rate.

2. Describe how the nervous system and the circulatory system function together in regulating blood pressure.

Extensions

1. Write a short story about the life and times of a sodium ion (Na^+). Describe how it got into the body, where it might be located, and some of the body functions with which it is associated on a day-to-day basis.

2. Visit a local organization or treatment center that deals with persons who are trying to overcome physical addictions to alcohol or some psychoactive drug. Give a report to your class on your findings.

3. Prepare a bulletin board display on psychoactive drugs and their effects on humans.

4. With the help of your teacher, invite a doctor or other professional into your class to discuss and answer questions about drug abuse.

5. Conduct a survey about drug abuse among a group of people of your choice. What drugs do they consider harmful? How much factual information do they have about drugs? Write a short paper on what you would do to help eliminate drug abuse.

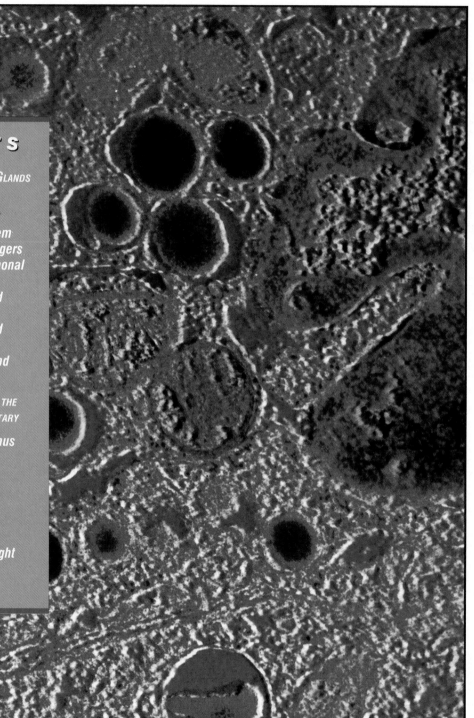

CONTENTS

Endocrine Systems

*T*he endocrine system exerts tremendous control over the human body. Your growth and development, the regulation of your blood sugar level, the calcium level in your bones and blood, and the rate at which you metabolize food are but a few examples of the endocrine system at work.

The endocrine system also controls the changes that occur to make reproduction possible. These changes, which occur during puberty, are some of the most dramatic examples of the endocrine system in action. For example, the deepening of the voice and the growth of facial hair in males, the breast and hip enlargement of females, and the growth of underarm and pubic hair in both sexes are a direct result of the action of hormones. Puberty also marks the beginning of ovulation in females and of sperm production in males.

A delicate balance exists in your body, so that conditions are constantly monitored and adjusted to maintain an internal environment that keeps your cells healthy and functioning. From the time you were born, endocrine glands and hormones have played a crucial role in maintaining homeostasis in your body. This chapter discusses the hormonal interactions that coordinate body functions to maintain homeostasis.

*W*hat two major hormones are produced by the pancreas?

*W*hat role do these hormones play in metabolism?

◆ *A transmission electron micrograph of cells in a human pancreatic islet, the endocrine component of the pancreas (X17 500).*

Function of Endocrine Glands and Hormones

23.1 The Human Endocrine System

Chapter 18 describes glands of the digestive system that release their secretions through ducts that lead to the site of action. Such glands—for example, the salivary glands—are called **exocrine** (EK suh krin) **glands**. In

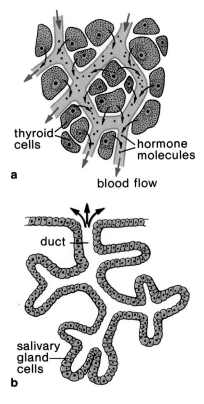

thyroid cells

hormone molecules

a

blood flow

duct

salivary gland cells

b

FIGURE 23.1 Endocrine glands, such as the thyroid gland (a), release hormones into the bloodstream. Exocrine glands, such as the salivary glands (b), release their secretions into ducts.

contrast, **endocrine** (EN duh krin) **glands** secrete their biologically active chemicals, called hormones, directly into the bloodstream. Figure 23.1 shows an illustration of each type of gland. Some glands are entirely endocrine and all their secretions enter directly into the bloodstream. Other glands are both endocrine and exocrine—some secretions enter directly into the bloodstream, and others move through ducts. The stomach and small intestine contain both exocrine and endocrine gland cells. Their exocrine secretions are the digestive enzymes that are delivered through ducts to the areas where they are used. Their endocrine secretions are the hormones gastrin and secretin, which are released directly into the circulatory system and cause additional secretions of digestive enzymes by other organs.

Endocrine glands are located throughout the main portion of the body—the head, neck, and torso. These glands do not constitute a system comparable to the circulatory or digestive systems. However, they are grouped together because they all function in a similar manner and because they interact with each other. Figure 23.2 shows the location of the major endocrine glands in humans.

Hormones are carried throughout the body by the circulatory system. However, they produce their effects only on specific **target organs**, such as the ovaries or testes of the reproductive system, as discussed in Chapter 11. The length of time a hormone is effective can be as short as 2 minutes, or as long as several hours. Hormones are constantly being removed from the blood by the target organs, excreted by the kidneys, or broken down to simpler compounds by the liver.

FIGURE 23.2 The major endocrine glands in the human body. The dotted lines show organs such as the stomach and kidneys.

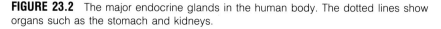

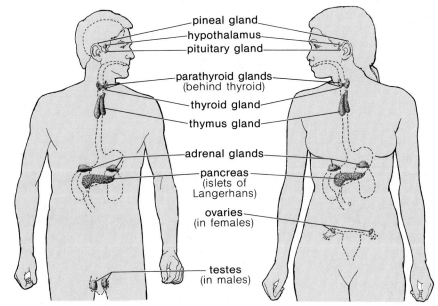

pineal gland
hypothalamus
pituitary gland
parathyroid glands (behind thyroid)
thyroid gland
thymus gland
adrenal glands
pancreas (islets of Langerhans)
ovaries (in females)
testes (in males)

The mechanism by which hormones work is similar to that of antibodies, which recognize and bind to antigens in the immune system. Recall from Chapter 20 that receptors on the antibodies have a shape that exactly fits the shape of the antigens. In the case of the endocrine system, receptors on or in the cells of the target organs have shapes that fit the shapes of the hormones in the blood. When hormone molecules reach the cells of their target organ, they bind to the receptors and, through various mechanisms discussed in Section 23.2, cause the target organ to perform specific actions.

The effect of a hormone on the cells of its target organ depends to a great degree on the concentration of the hormone in the blood. Homeostatic mechanisms maintain the levels of most hormones within a normal low-to-high range. When some hormones occur in abnormally high concentrations (such as when they are taken as drugs), the results can be very different from the standard action on the target organ. This is the case with anabolic steroid hormones that are taken by athletes in an attempt to produce more muscle mass and increase strength. Some of the side effects of these large doses can be dangerous and occasionally even fatal.

23.2 Second Messengers

Biologists have only recently begun to understand how hormones affect the functions of cells in the target organs. Some hormones act directly when they arrive at the surfaces of the cells of the target organ. Other hormones cannot enter the cells and, instead, produce their effect by what are called "second messengers." If you think of a hormone as a messenger from an endocrine gland to a target organ, then the name "second messenger" takes on more meaning. It applies to the intracellular chemicals that carry a message from a hormone on the plasma membrane to the interior of the cell.

The first "second messenger" to be identified was cAMP (cyclic adenosine monophosphate). Its actions are more clearly understood than those of other second messengers. Glucagon, a hormone from the pancreas that promotes the breakdown of glycogen into glucose, produces its effect through cAMP. Figure 23.3 illustrates the events that occur when glucagon binds to a receptor on the surface of a liver or muscle cell. The binding stimulates the enzyme adenyl cyclase (*a*) to begin the breakdown of ATP into cAMP and two free phosphate groups (*b*). The cAMP molecule then activates an enzyme in the cytosol called protein kinase (*c*), which transfers the two phosphate groups to other enzymes (*d*). In the case of glucagon, the phosphates activate enzymes in the plasma membrane that promote the breakdown of glycogen into glucose. After activating protein kinase, cAMP is "recycled" back to ATP by the reattachment of two phosphates.

Two other second messengers have been identified in the human endocrine system. They are cGMP (cyclic guanosine monophosphate) and calcium ions (Ca^{2+}). The cGMP molecule acts in almost the same way as cAMP. Ca^{2+} enters a cell when specific hormones attach to receptors on the outside of the plasma membrane, changing its permeability to Ca^{2+}. Once inside the cytosol, Ca^{2+} stimulates other molecules to react.

FIGURE 23.3 The second-messenger model of cyclic AMP

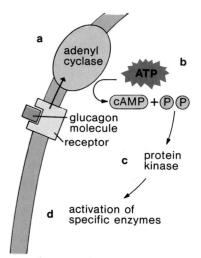

CONNECTIONS

The endocrine system is responsible for the overall regulation and coordination of body systems. Homeostasis results from interactions of the endocrine hormones and from their effects on all other body systems.

23.3 Control of Hormonal Secretions

Hormones are potent substances that, in minute concentrations, direct metabolic processes. Therefore, the amount of a hormone released by an endocrine gland must be regulated closely. One mechanism that serves to control secretions is a **feedback system**. A feedback system operates as a cycle in which the last step affects the first step. Hormone-secreting tissue continuously receives information, or feedback, in the form of chemical signals about the cellular process it controls. If conditions change, the tissue reacts and adjusts its rate of secretion.

Usually the control of hormonal secretions involves a *negative* feedback system. In such a system, an endocrine gland *decreases* its activity in response to an *increased* concentration of the substance it regulates. The increased concentration inhibits the endocrine gland (a negative effect), and hormonal secretion decreases. As the concentration of the hormone drops, the concentration of the regulated substance also drops, and the inhibition of the gland subsides. When the gland is no longer inhibited, it begins secretion of its hormone again. (See Figure 23.4.) Several examples of negative feedback systems are described in this chapter.

A *positive* feedback system operates when an endocrine gland increases its rate of hormonal secretion in response to a rising concentration of the substance the hormone regulates. The increased concentration stimulates the gland (a positive effect). Consequently, still more product forms, and then more hormone is secreted (Figure 23.5). Such a system is unstable because it tends to produce extreme changes in conditions (as occurs with luteinizing hormone in the female reproductive system). Positive feedback systems are rare in organisms.

FIGURE 23.4 A negative feedback system—gland A secretes a hormone that stimulates gland B to release another hormone. (The secretion may affect a different target organ as well.) Gland B then secretes a hormone that inhibits the action of gland A, and that also may affect another target organ.

FIGURE 23.5 A positive feedback system. How does this system differ from that of a negative feedback system shown in Figure 23.4?

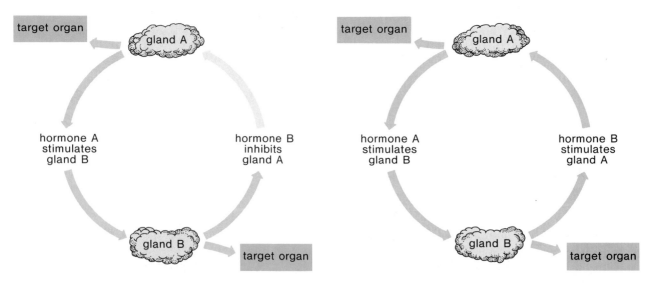

23.4 Control of Blood Glucose

The pancreas is one of several endocrine glands, such as the stomach and small intestine, that is both endocrine and exocrine in function. One of its endocrine functions is the release of the hormone glucagon, mentioned in Section 23.2.

    The endocrine cells of the pancreas are found in scattered locations throughout the organ. These scattered endocrine cells are called the **pancreatic islets**, or the Islets of Langerhans (Figure 23.6), after the German scientist who first discovered them. When the level of blood glucose is low, the pancreas secretes glucagon. The glucagon causes an increased rate of conversion of glycogen to glucose in the muscles and liver. The resulting rise in the blood glucose level has a negative feedback effect on the pancreas, and glucagon secretion is inhibited. (See Figure 23.7.)

    A second pancreatic hormone, insulin, is secreted in response to high levels of blood glucose. The effect of insulin is opposite to that of glucagon—it enhances the uptake of glucose by muscle and liver cells and, hence,

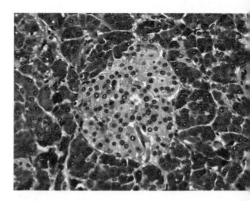

FIGURE 23.6 The hormone-secreting cells of the pancreas are arranged in clusters, or islets, called pancreatic islets (Islets of Langerhans). These islets are surrounded by cells that secrete digestive enzymes.

Try Investigation 23A, A Bike Trip.

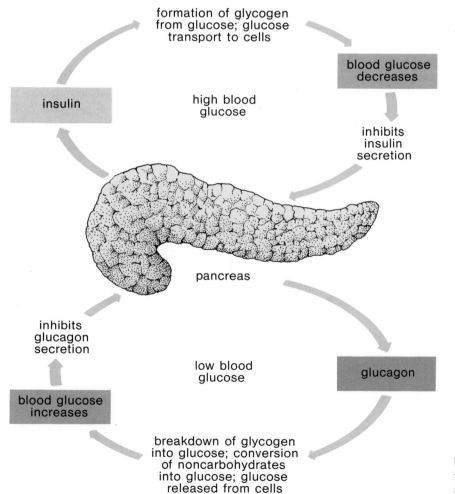

formation of glycogen from glucose; glucose transport to cells

blood glucose decreases

insulin

high blood glucose

inhibits insulin secretion

pancreas

inhibits glucagon secretion

low blood glucose

glucagon

blood glucose increases

breakdown of glycogen into glucose; conversion of noncarbohydrates into glucose; glucose released from cells

FIGURE 23.7 Insulin and glucagon function together to maintain a fairly stable level of blood glucose.

removes glucose from the blood. Like glucagon, insulin is regulated by a negative feedback system. As the level of blood glucose returns to normal, the secretion of insulin decreases. Insulin and glucagon are antagonistic because their effects are opposite each other in the homeostatic control of the blood glucose level. Figure 23.7 summarizes these control mechanisms.

At least three other hormones function in the homeostatic control of the level of blood glucose. Growth hormone from the pituitary, corticotropic hormones from the adrenal cortex, and epinephrine (often called adrenaline) from the adrenal medulla all act to increase the level of blood glucose. Other functions of these hormones are discussed in more detail in the following sections.

FOCUS ON *Diabetes*

There are several forms of diabetes. All of them result from a malfunction either of one of the endocrine glands or in the mechanisms involving the hormones. Diabetes insipidus (in SIH pih dus) is caused by insufficient secretion of ADH (antidiuretic hormone) from the posterior pituitary. Because of the lack of ADH, the permeability to water of the collecting ducts in the kidneys decreases. As a result, less water is reabsorbed by the kidneys, and large volumes of dilute urine are produced. The resulting dehydration produces intense thirst, but individuals with this illness have difficulty drinking enough water to make up for what is lost in the urine. Regular injections of ADH can bring diabetes insipidus under control.

Diabetes mellitus (MEL luh tus) can result from a lack of insulin secretion by the pancreatic islets, resulting in high blood glucose levels. Complications resulting from the high blood glucose levels may include circulatory and vision problems that can lead to blindness. The lack of insulin prevents glucose from entering body cells, which then metabolize fats and proteins

instead. Thus, one of the symptoms of diabetes is an abnormally high blood glucose level. Products of fat and protein metabolism enter the blood and lower the pH, interfering with many body functions.

The active transport systems of the kidneys become overloaded with glucose and cannot remove all of it from the filtrate. The excess glucose interferes with the concentration gradient of the filtrate, and less water is removed from the collecting ducts. As a result, the volume of urine (and amount of water loss) increases. Glucose in the urine and thirst are both symptoms of this disorder. There are two major forms of diabetes mellitus, both inherited—juvenile diabetes, which is an autoimmune disorder, and adult-onset diabetes.

Many adult-onset diabetics have sufficient or even surplus amounts of insulin in the blood. For these individuals diabetes does not arise from a shortage of insulin, but probably from a loss of receptors for insulin on the surface of target cells. Adult-onset diabetes is referred to as noninsulin-dependent diabetes.

23.5   Control of Blood Calcium

Each person usually has four **parathyroid glands**, which are located on the surface of the thyroid. These tiny glands (each only about 5 mm in length) secrete **parathyroid hormone** (PTH), which regulates the level of calcium in the blood. A negative feedback system controls PTH levels. As the level of blood calcium rises, less PTH is secreted by the parathyroid glands; as the level of blood calcium drops, more PTH is secreted.

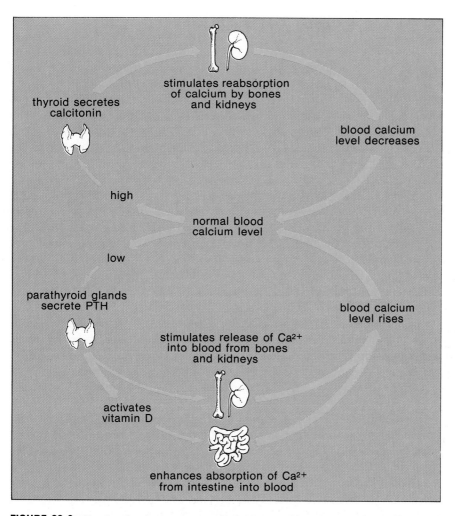

FIGURE 23.8 The feedback system controlling blood calcium. Homeostasis is maintained by balancing two antagonistic hormones—PTH and calcitonin.

PTH stimulates the release of calcium from the bones and the conservation of calcium by the kidneys. It also causes the activation of vitamin D, a chemical manufactured from cholesterol in the skin when ultraviolet rays from sunlight strike the skin. This form of vitamin D (and the vitamin D in pills and food additives) is inactive. It is modified once by the liver and a second time by the kidneys. (The chemical modification in the kidneys also is controlled by PTH.) Once activated, vitamin D indirectly functions as a hormone, increasing the absorption of calcium from the intestines into the bloodstream.

Calcitonin, a hormone of the **thyroid gland**, functions in an opposite manner to regulate the calcium level in the blood and body tissues. Calcitonin promotes a lowering of the blood calcium level by stimulating the uptake of calcium by the bone cells and by inhibiting the release of calcium by the kidneys. Calcitonin also inhibits the uptake of calcium in the intestines. Figure 23.8 summarizes the mechanisms that control blood calcium.

23.6 Other Glands and Hormones

Not much is known about the **pineal gland** in humans except that it gets smaller in size beginning at about age 7. In an adult, the pineal gland appears as a thickened strand of fibrous tissue. The only known hormone of the pineal gland is **melatonin**, whose exact function in humans is not clear. Its secretion is inhibited by light and is most abundant at night. The secretion of melatonin reaches its lowest level after the onset of puberty. This observation that has led some researchers to conclude that the secretion of melatonin somehow inhibits the hormones that influence sexual development.

In other animals, the pineal gland functions in annual reproductive cycles. Nerves from the eyes stimulate the pineal gland, and when a specific amount of continuous daylight is present, the pineal secretions prepare the animals for their annual mating period. The amount of daylight needed varies from one animal to another. There is some evidence that the pineal gland in some animals may interact with the pituitary gland and help to control the release of the hormones that stimulate the testes and ovaries.

In humans, the **thymus gland** functions in the maturation of T cells in the immune system (Chapter 20). Like the pineal gland, the thymus is larger in young children than in adults and diminishes in size after puberty, when the immune system is well established.

Prostaglandins (PRAHS tuh GLAN dihnz) are fatty acids that are produced by most body tissues and some white blood cells. Prostaglandins help regulate blood vessel diameter, blood clotting, inflammation reactions, ovulation, and uterine contractions during labor. An additional effect of prostaglandins is the enhanced perception of pain. They are also suspected of causing menstrual cramps.

Bradykinins (BRAD ee KIH nihnz) are polypeptides that, like prostaglandins, are secreted by various tissues throughout the body. When secreted by the sweat glands, bradykinins cause the nearby surface blood vessels to dilate, and thus help to radiate excess heat from the body. Bradykinins also function in dissolving blood clots and in countering the effects of prostaglandins.

CHECK AND CHALLENGE

1. Describe two differences between endocrine and exocrine glands.

2. What is the role of a second messenger?

3. Compare the functions of insulin and glucagon in the control of blood glucose.

4. Compare and contrast the function of calcitonin with the functions of parathyroid hormone (PTH) and vitamin D in regulating the blood calcium level.

5. Describe the function of prostaglandins and how their effects are controlled by bradykinins.

6. Compare and contrast negative and positive feedback systems.

Functions Regulated by the Hypothalamus and Pituitary

23.7 The Hypothalamus and Pituitary

The hypothalamus, described previously in Chapters 11 and 22, is technically part of the nervous system. However, this gland also plays a key role in many of the homeostatic functions of the endocrine system through its interaction with the pituitary gland. The pituitary gland is pea-shaped and about 1.5 cm in diameter, and is attached to the underside of the hypothalamus (Figure 23.9). The pituitary is divided structurally and functionally into two parts—the anterior, or front, lobe and the posterior, or rear, lobe. The anterior pituitary secretes six hormones and the posterior pituitary stores and releases two hormones that are produced by the hypothalamus. Table 23.1 names these hormones and summarizes their functions.

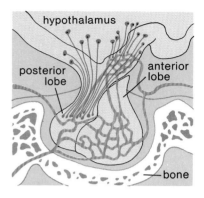

FIGURE 23.9 The pituitary gland and hypothalamus. The pituitary gland is located beneath the brain.

TABLE 23.1
Major Hormones Secreted or Stored by the Pituitary

Anterior Lobe Hormone	Target Tissue	Stimulates	Regulation of Secretion
ACTH (adrenocorticotropic hormone)	Adrenal cortex	Secretion of glucocorticoids	Stimulated by CRH (corticotropin-releasing hormone); inhibited by glucocorticoids
TSH (thyroid-stimulating hormone)	Thyroid gland	Secretion of thyroid hormones	Stimulated by TRH (thyrotropin-releasing hormone); inhibited by thyroid hormones
GH (growth hormone)	Most tissue	Protein synthesis and growth; breakdown of fats and increased blood glucose	Stimulated by growth-hormone-releasing hormone; inhibited by somatostatin
FSH (follicle-stimulating hormone)	Gonads	Gamete production and sex hormone secretion	Stimulated by GnRH (gonadotropin-releasing hormone); inhibited by sex hormones
Prolactin	Mammary glands and other sex organs	Milk production; actions in other organs unclear	Inhibited by PIH (prolactin-inhibiting hormone)
LH (luteinizing hormone)	Gonads	Sex hormone secretion; ovulation and formation of corpus luteum	Stimulated by GnRH; inhibited by sex hormones
Posterior Lobe (Stored hypothalamic hormones)			**(Regulation of Hormone Release)**
ADH (antidiuretic hormone)	Kidneys	Water retention; constriction of blood vessels	Stimulated by nerve impulses from hypothalamus
Oxytocin	Mammary glands and uterus	Mammary gland and uterine contraction	Stimulated by nerve impulses from hypothalamus

TABLE 23.2 Hormones from the Hypothalamus that Affect the Anterior Pituitary	
Hormone	**Effect on Anterior Pituitary**
Corticotropin-releasing hormone (CRH)	Stimulates secretion of adrenocorticotropic hormone (ACTH)
Gonadotropin-releasing hormone (GnRH)	Stimulates secretion of follicle-stimulating hormone (FSH) and luteinizing hormone (LH)
Prolactin-inhibiting hormone (PIH)	Inhibits prolactin secretion
Somatostatin	Inhibits secretion of growth hormone
Thyrotropin-releasing hormone (TRH)	Stimulates secretion of thyroid-stimulating hormone (TSH)

Before the function of the hypothalamus was understood, the pituitary gland was called the "master gland" because it seemed to control the functions of several other endocrine glands. Now, many of the functions of the pituitary gland are understood to be regulated by the hypothalamus. Neurons in the hypothalamus secrete releasing and inhibiting hormones into blood vessels that go directly to the anterior lobe of the pituitary gland. These hypothalamic hormones control the release of other hormones from the anterior pituitary. Table 23.2 summarizes the hypothalamic hormones and their effect on the anterior pituitary.

Neurons in another part of the hypothalamus secrete two other hormones—ADH and oxytocin—directly into the posterior lobe of the pituitary, where they are stored. Nerve impulses from the hypothalamus stimulate the posterior pituitary to reIease these stored hormones into the bloodstream. The secretions of the hypothalamus and the pituitary are regulated by feedback mechanisms among these two glands and their target tissues.

23.8 Growth

Although the total growth you attain during your lifetime is under the control of your genes and is influenced by your environment, the rate at which you grow is determined by a hormone from the pituitary gland. Growth hormone (GH) generally stimulates body cells to increase in size and to divide more rapidly than usual. It also enhances the movement of amino acids through the plasma membranes and increases the rate at which cells convert these amino acids into proteins. GH also decreases the rate at which cells utilize carbohydrates and increases the rate at which they use fats. Growth hormone is unique among the anterior pituitary hormones because its release is controlled by two hypothalamic hormones.

These are **growth-hormone-releasing hormone** (GHRH), and **somatostatin**. GHRH stimulates the release of GH, and somatostatin, a hypothalamic inhibiting hormone, slows the secretion of GH. The response of the pituitary gland in secreting GH appears to depend, in part, on the relative amounts of these two hormones. An interesting point about growth hormone is that it is released in greater amounts during sleep. Why this occurs is not understood.

23.9 Metabolism

The rate at which you metabolize food is controlled by the hormone **thyroxine** (thy ROK sin) from the thyroid gland. Most young people have a high metabolic rate and burn up food rapidly. During the aging process, however, the metabolic rate slows down, and many people find that they cannot continue to eat the quantities of food they consumed as a teenager without gaining weight.

The thyroid gland contains two lobes that are located on the right and left sides of the trachea, just below the larynx. The production and release of thyroxine from the thyroid is controlled by hormones from the pituitary and the hypothalamus. **Thyroid-stimulating hormone** (TSH) from the anterior pituitary stimulates the thyroid to secrete thyroxin. The release of TSH by the anterior pituitary is controlled by **thyroid-releasing hormone** (TRH) from the hypothalamus.

Two separate, negative feedback mechanisms control thyroxine secretion. First, as the level of thyroxine increases in the blood, the response of the anterior pituitary to hypothalamic TRH is inhibited, making the pituitary less sensitive to TRH. Second, the increasing level of thyroxine also slows the release of TRH from the hypothalamus. As the thyroxine level decreases in the blood, both actions are reversed—the anterior pituitary becomes more sensitive to TRH, and TRH secretion increases from the hypothalamus. In turn, the increasing secretion of TSH stimulates an increase in production and secretion of thyroxine. Figure 23.10 (next page) shows these feedback mechanisms.

Most thyroxine in the blood is attached to specialized carrier molecules. Only about 0.04 percent of the thyroxine is free in the blood, and only this free thyroxine can cross the plasma membrane of the target cells. Once inside the cell, thyroxine attaches to receptor proteins on the nuclear membrane and activates genes on the chromosomes. The activated genes produce the new messenger RNA and new proteins needed for the increased rate of cell metabolism. As free thyroxine is used up in the blood, additional thyroxine is released from the carrier molecules, which serve as a storage reservoir for the hormone.

Thyroxine is the major secretion of the thyroid gland, and iodine is constantly needed by the gland to manufacture the hormone. If insufficient iodine is present in the diet, the level of thyroxine decreases. As a result, TRH secretion from the hypothalamus increases, causing an increased level of TSH from the pituitary. The TSH stimulates the thyroid cells to produce and secrete thyroxine, but it is impossible to make thyroxine without iodine. This continued stimulation of the thyroid by TSH results in the

FIGURE 23.10 The feedback mechanism between the pituitary, hypothalamus, and the thyroid glands. This mechanism controls the level of thyroxine in the blood.

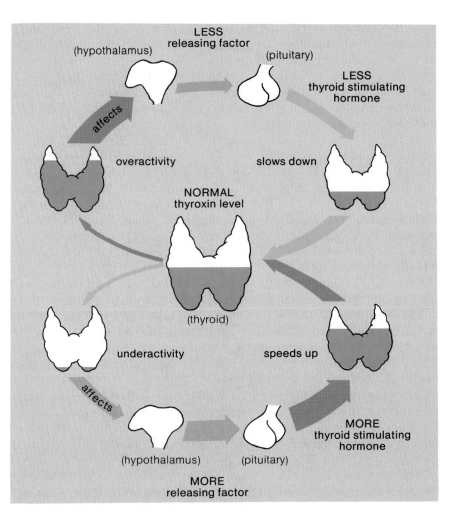

FIGURE 23.11 Goiter (an enlarged thyroid) is due to a deficiency of iodine. The incidence of this condition in the United States and Europe has been dramatically decreased due to the addition of iodine to table salt.

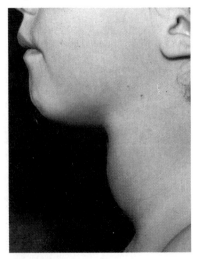

enlargement of the thyroid gland, a condition known as a goiter. (See Figure 23.11.) An increase of iodine in the diet usually relieves the problem.

Overproduction of thyroxine results in hyperthyroidism, a condition characterized by a high metabolic rate, sweating, weight loss, muscular weakness, diarrhea, nervousness, hyperactivity, and bulging eyes. The most direct treatment for hyperthyroidism is the surgical removal of the thyroid gland after the individual has been treated with medicine to return the metabolic rate to normal. Some cases are treated with an injection of radioactive iodine, which is absorbed by the thyroid and destroys some secretory cells. After a few weeks, if the thyroid is still overproductive, repeated doses of radioactive iodine are administered until thyroid activity returns to normal.

Secretion of too little thyroxine results in hypothyroidism, with symptoms that are generally opposite to those of hyperthyroidism. Hypothyroidism can be treated by administration of the deficient hormone. As long as drug therapy continues, recovery from hypothyroidism is generally complete.

In addition to regulating metabolism, thyroxine also influences several adrenal hormones and their target organs. The increased metabolic rate caused by high thyroxine levels leads to blood vessel dilation, increased blood volume, and increased heart rate and blood pressure. Other effects of excess thyroxine include increased secretions of digestive enzymes and intestinal contractions, sleeplessness, and interference with normal sexual functions.

23.10   Milk Production

Newborn babies have very special nutritional and immunological requirements that are best met by a diet of mother's milk. Studies comparing the overall health of breast-fed children with that of bottle-fed children conclude that breast-feeding is more beneficial for infants. Additional studies also indicate that breast-feeding appears to favorably affect the emotional well-being of the infant.

Milk production is under the control of the nervous and endocrine systems. Three hormones are known to be involved—**prolactin** (proh LAK tin) from the anterior pituitary, **oxytocin** (ahk see TOH sin) produced by the hypothalamus and secreted by the posterior pituitary, and **prolactin-inhibiting hormone** (PIH) from the hypothalamus. Prolactin is secreted by both males and females. However, its function in females— to stimulate the production of milk in the mammary glands after the birth of a child—is better understood.

The regulation of prolactin secretion involves PIH. Secretion of PIH, in turn, is controlled in two ways. First, high levels of estrogen during pregnancy stimulate the production of PIH, which inhibits the release of prolactin. After the birth of the baby, declining levels of estrogen inhibit the release of PIH. The lower level of PIH, in turn, stimulates the anterior pituitary to release prolactin. In the second mechanism, the suckling of the baby stimulates nerve endings in the breasts that relay impulses to the hypothalamus. The hypothalamus, in turn, inhibits the release of PIH, again causing increased secretion of prolactin. As the level of prolactin rises, it stimulates milk production in the mammary glands. The effects of prolactin on other organs is unclear.

Oxytocin is also under the control of the nervous system and is also secreted in both males and females. Its role in males is not clear. However, in females, when the stimulus of a baby's suckling is relayed to the hypothalamus, the hypothalamus stimulates the posterior pituitary to release stored oxytocin into the bloodstream. The oxytocin in turn stimulates the contraction of milk-producing ducts in the mammary glands, thus initiating lactation, or milk ejection.

Prolactin initiates the process of milk production in the mammary glands. Oxytocin causes the milk-producing glands to contract and expel the milk into the area of the nipple where the suckling action of the baby removes it. Figure 23.12 summarizes the effects of prolactin and oxytocin on lactation. Oxytocin has an additional function in females—it stimulates contractions of the uterus during labor to help in the birth process.

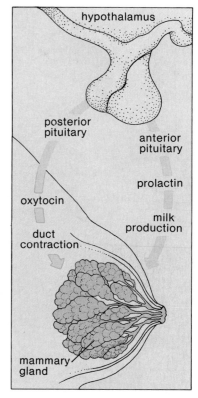

FIGURE 23.12 The anterior and posterior lobes of the pituitary release their hormones for the production and ejection of milk in response to signals received from the hypothalamus.

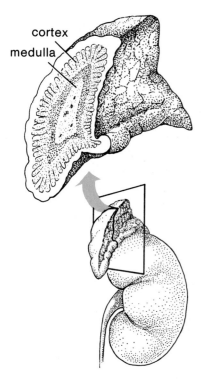

cortex
medulla

FIGURE 23.13 The structure of the adrenal gland showing the cortex and the medulla

23.11 Adrenal Cortex Hormones

There are two adrenal glands, one on top of each kidney. Each adrenal gland has two parts that function as separate endocrine glands—the outer **adrenal cortex** and the inner **adrenal medulla** (Figure 23.13). The adrenal cortex makes up most of the mass of the adrenal glands and secretes a group of steroid hormones called **corticosteroids**. Table 23.3 reviews the adrenal cortex hormones.

There are three general categories of corticosteroid hormones. Gonadocorticoids (sex steroids) are a combination of androgens (male hormones) and estrogens (female hormones) that supplement the action of the sex hormones secreted by the gonads. Mineralocorticoids, such as aldosterone, help regulate ion balance. Glucocorticoids fight inflammation and help regulate the metabolism of proteins, fats, and carbohydrates.

The release of glucocorticoids is controlled by hormones from the hypothalamus and the pituitary. **Corticotropin-releasing hormone** (CRH) from the hypothalamus stimulates the anterior pituitary to produce **adrenocorticotropic hormone** (ACTH). ACTH, in turn, stimulates the adrenal cortex to produce and secrete glucocorticoids. The release of ACTH is regulated by negative feedback. A rise in the level of glucocorticoids inhibits the release of ACTH. ACTH secretion also is affected by stress, which influences the hypothalamus and the release of CRH.

Glucocorticoids are widely used in sports medicine and in organ transplants to suppress inflammation and to inhibit the response of the immune system. Athletes with joint injuries, patients with severe arthritis and allergies, and organ transplant patients are some of the more common recipients of glucocorticoids. These hormones, however, have side effects that can cause problems. Cortisol, one of the frequently used glucocorticoids, inhibits the regeneration of some injured tissue in joints. Thus, although cortisol reduces inflammation around the injury, it also slows the recovery of the tissue that has been damaged. Because of their side effects, glucocorticoids should be used only under competent medical supervision.

TABLE 23.3
Hormones of the Adrenal Cortex

Hormone	Effects	Regulated by
Glucocorticoids	Regulate metabolism of carbohydrates, fats, and proteins; constrict blood vessels; fight inflammation	ACTH released by pituitary gland in response to stress
Gonadocorticoids	Supplement the action of sex hormones produced by the gonads	
Mineralocorticoids	Regulate levels of electrolytes (sodium and potassium) in intercellular fluids	Electrolyte concentration in the blood

23.12   The Fight-or-Flight Response

The adrenal medulla secretes two major hormones, **epinephrine** (also known as adrenaline) and **norepinephrine**. Both hormones produce effects similar to, but longer lasting than, those of the sympathetic nervous system. Epinephrine and norepinephrine help increase mental alertness, increase heartbeat rate, dilate coronary blood vessels, increase the respiratory rate, and speed up the rate of metabolism for the entire body.

In combination, the endocrine and nervous systems enable the body to respond almost instantaneously to emergencies, a phenomenon known as the "fight-or-flight" response. Neurons of the sympathetic nervous system that originate in the hypothalamus connect to the adrenal medulla. An emergency situation leads to stimulation of the sympathetic nervous system, which also stimulates the adrenal medulla to release its hormones. The hormones supplement the immediate response of the sympathetic nervous system and prepare the body to withstand the physical demands of coping with an emergency. The hormones sustain physical performance for a longer time than can the sympathetic nervous system alone.

CONNECTIONS

Hormones and the actions of the endocrine system are responsible for many aspects of behavior. The physical expression of emotions, including rage and fright, are results of a functioning endocrine system.

23.13   Stress

Stress is a general term for the body's response to any disruption of homeostasis that is not promptly resolved. Subsequent changes that occur in the body are a direct result of physical or emotional factors that trigger impulses from the nervous system, especially the hypothalamus. Physical causes of stress may include exposure to extreme heat or cold, infections, injuries, prolonged heavy exercise, and loud sounds. Emotional causes of stress may include thoughts about real or imagined dangers, personal losses, or unpleasant social interactions (or conversely, a lack of social interactions). Stress can even result from pleasant stimuli, such as feelings of joy or happiness. The hypothalamic impulses generated by stress influence the adrenal cortex, the adrenal medulla, and other tissues throughout the body. Figure 23.14, on the next page, summarizes the effects of stress on the human body.

Stressors, the factors that cause stress, stimulate the release of pituitary and adrenal hormones, resulting in increased secretion of ACTH and corticosteroids. There are three general stages of response to stress. First, stimulations from the nervous system and the endocrine system can activate the body's fight-or-flight response. The adrenal medulla secretes epinephrine and norepinephrine, which causes the reactions described in Figure 23.14. Second, stimulation of the adrenal cortex results in increased secretions of corticosteroids, which can interfere with the actions of the immune system. Prolonged exposure to stressors can result in an increased susceptibility to disease. Third, the body attempts to adjust to the increased levels of pituitary and adrenal hormones. If the body is unable to adjust completely, exhaustion occurs as a result of depletion of the body's energy reserves. If exhaustion continues for long periods of time, sickness follows, and in extreme cases, death. Because of the increasing pressures of the modern world, stress management has become a frequent topic for research.

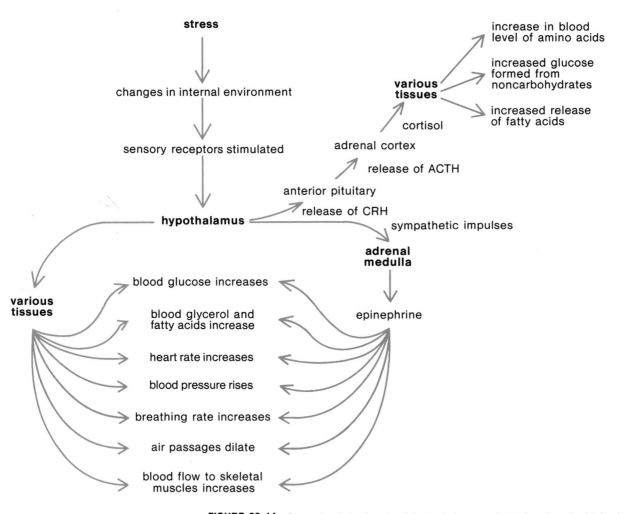

FIGURE 23.14   Stress leads to the physiological changes that take place in the body to prepare it for a fight-or-flight response. These changes are initiated by 1) impulses arising from the hypothalamus that directly affect body tissues, 2) impulses directed toward the adrenal medulla that cause it to release epinephrine and norepinephrine (which affect the same target tissues), and 3) impulses directed toward the anterior pituitary that initiate events resulting in the release of corticosteroids.

CHECK AND CHALLENGE

1. Describe the structures, relationships, and interactions of the hypothalamus and the pituitary gland.

2. Describe, in your own words, two different feedback mechanisms that you have read about in this chapter.

3. Describe how prolactin and oxytocin function together in the control of milk production.

4. Why could the adrenal gland be called two separate glands?

5. What are stressors and how can they affect the body?

Biological Challenges

STRESS MANAGEMENT

When a person is under stress, nearly the entire body is involved. However, stress is not all bad. The activation of your fight-or-flight mechanism can help you escape from dangerous situations, win a ball game, or stay alert so you can pass an important examination. This type of stress lasts only as long as it takes to deal with the specific situation.

Conversely, stress that lasts for a long time can cause considerable damage to your body. Continued high levels of stress create a situation of anxiety, which can lead to depression without any apparent cause. Research shows that people under stress have increased levels of epinephrine and cortisol in their blood and urine. The increased secretion of cortisol may depress the activity of the lymphatic system and, in turn, may lower the number of leukocytes in the blood. Because leukocytes help defend the body against infection, a person who is under stress may have a lowered resistance to infectious diseases. In addition, excessive amounts of cortisol can promote high blood pressure, atherosclerosis, and ulcers in the stomach and intestines. It is helpful and healthful to learn how to reduce this type of long-term stress. The American Heart Association makes the following recommendations:

1. Don't take on too much. The most frequent cause of stress is being overextended—trying to do too much with the time and mental and physical resources you have.

2. Balance your time. Make sure you have time to work and to play. Learn to work effectively, but also teach yourself how to relax—through hobbies and/or exercise. The word *recreation* is just that—a "re-creation" of energies for your mind and body. It breaks the cycle of strain.

3. Get enough rest, sleep, and exercise. Take time to allow your mind and body to renew.

FIGURE A Long-term stress, either physiological or psychological, can be extremely harmful to the body.

4. "Work off" the stress. If you recognize that you are under stress for hours and days at a time, take a break, blow off steam. Do it constructively through playing tennis, biking, swimming, fishing, or other forms of exercise.

5. Avoid self-medication. Drugs, alcohol, or tobacco often can provide *temporary* relief to tension, but they do not cure the causes, and they have harmful side effects.

6. Talk to your doctor, nurse, or another health professional. Make sure there is no medical cause for your stressful feelings, and get advice on how you can avoid stress.

Each individual handles stress in a different way. Some people enjoy jogging or aerobic exercise; some a pickup game of basketball. Others enjoy reading a book or swimming; still others can just relax and watch a video or a movie on television. The important thing is to recognize what is causing stress in your life and then to find the best outlet to diffuse the effects of the stress.

Summary

Endocrine glands secrete hormones directly into the bloodstream, which carries them to their target organs. Hormones recognize and bind to receptors on the surface of the target organs, where they exert their influence, either directly or indirectly through second messengers such as cAMP. Most hormone secretions are controlled through negative feedback mechanisms involving a particular gland and the associated secretions from the target organs. In the case of blood glucose levels, control results from the antagonistic action of two pancreatic hormones—insulin and glucagon.

The hypothalamus secretes hormones and controls the secretions of the pituitary and other endocrine glands mostly through negative feedback mechanisms. Releasing hormones from the hypothalamus control the secretion of several anterior pituitary hormones, which in turn influence the activity of other glands. The posterior pituitary is a storage organ for two hormones secreted by the hypothalamus. Based on messages from sensory receptors throughout the body, the hypothalamus exerts direct influence over a variety of body functions and is especially important in regulating the "fight-or-flight" response.

The adrenal cortex releases several stress-related hormones under the control of a feedback mechanism involving the hypothalamus and the anterior pituitary. Stress can have both beneficial and harmful effects on the body. The major harmful effects occur if the body is subjected to long periods of sustained stress.

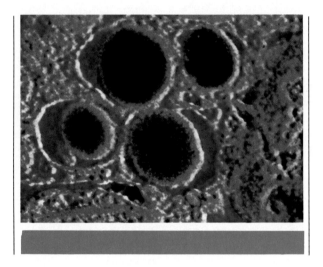

Key Concepts

Use the following concepts to develop a concept map. Add other terms from the chapter as you need them.

hypothalamus	thyroid gland
TSH	cell metabolic rate
feedback	TRH
anterior pituitary	thyroxine

Reviewing Ideas

1. If endocrine hormones are transported throughout the body in the circulatory system, how are they able to act on a specific target organ?

2. If glucagon cannot enter liver or muscle cells, how does it regulate the production of glycogen from glucose within those cells?

3. Describe how cAMP cycles inside the cell in its role as a second messenger.

4. Why are insulin and glucagon characterized as antagonists in the control of blood glucose?

5. What is the function of the thymus gland?

6. How do parathyroid hormone and calcitonin act in the control of the blood calcium level?

7. Compare the functions of prostaglandins and bradykinins.

8. How does the function of the posterior pituitary differ from that of the anterior pituitary?

9. How does the hypothalamus function in milk production in humans?

10. What is the relationship between TSH, iodine availability, and thyroxine secretion by the thyroid gland?

11. Describe how pleasant stimuli can produce stress.

12. How can a high level of blood glucose cause a high degree of thirst in a diabetic person?

13. Why is the hypothalamus—which is part of the central nervous system—considered to be part of the endocrine system?

Using Concepts

1. Select one endocrine gland and describe how a negative feedback loop involving the gland, the hypothalamus, and the pituitary gland works.

2. What is the difference between positive and negative feedback?

3. If the pineal gland functions in annual reproductive cycles in other animals, what evidence would indicate that this is not its function in humans?

4. How do prostaglandins and bradykinins differ from most hormones of the endocrine system?

5. What roles do growth hormone, corticotropic hormones, and epinephrine play in the homeostatic control of blood glucose?

6. If cortisol is administered to a person to counteract the inflammation produced by asthma, how could this treatment lead to a shutdown of the adrenal cortex secretions?

7. Why would the effects of secretions from the adrenal medulla last longer than the effects of the sympathetic nervous system in the fight-or-flight response?

8. How does being able to express your feelings to someone help relieve symptoms of stress?

9. Explain how having a hobby can help reduce the effects of stress.

10. Why is it possible to use insulin from cattle, sheep, or pigs to control human diabetes?

Synthesis

1. Describe how the circulatory, endocrine, and urinary systems function together to produce the symptoms of diabetes mellitus.

2. Describe how the nervous system and the endocrine system function together in the fight-or-flight response.

3. During the evolution of animals, what advantage would the development of a fight-or-flight response give an organism?

Extensions

1. Through genetic engineering, bacteria can be used to produce human growth hormone. Should potential athletes have the opportunity of receiving injections of growth hormone to help them achieve larger and more muscular bodies than they would normally have? Take a position on this question and write a short paper defending your decision.

2. Bacteria can be used to produce human insulin, but some people are afraid of products that have been produced by bacteria. Write a letter to an insulin-dependent diabetic to reassure the person about the use of bacteria-produced human insulin and to describe the benefits of using it instead of cattle insulin.

3. Write a poem or song about how epinephrine acts on the cells of the body.

CONTENTS

Locomotion Systems

What enables this sidewinder rattlesnake to move across the sand?

What would it be like if you did not have bones and muscles? How would you move around? How would you feed yourself? Movement of some kind is essential. An animal must either move through its environment or make objects in the environment move toward it. Sea anemones, for example, do not move from place to place. However, they wave tentacles that generate water currents; the water currents draw small food particles and prey toward them. Their tentacles can then trap the prey.

Unlike sea anemones, most animals are mobile and spend much of their time and energy actively searching for food, escaping from predators, and looking for mates. The methods they employ, however, can be very different. The form of locomotion an organism uses is closely related to its way of life. The structures associated with locomotion are related to their particular function. This chapter examines the different methods of locomotion, the structures that make movement possible, and the cellular basis of muscle contractions.

Movement Systems

24.1 Movement in Single Cells

How do the cells of the immune system move about in your body? How do sperm travel through the oviduct to fertilize eggs? Single cells generally move in one of two ways (and sometimes both). In amoeboid movement, a cell moves by continually extending and retracting portions of itself. The temporary projections are called pseudopods (SOO doh pahdz), and they

◆ *A sidewinder,* Crotalus ceraster, *traveling across a sand dune.*

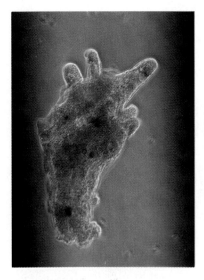

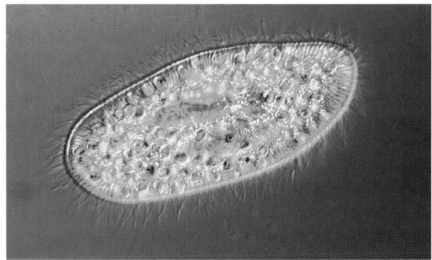

FIGURE 24.1 A giant amoeba, *Pelomyxa carolinensis*, extending its pseudopodia, X100

FIGURE 24.2 *Paramecium*, a predatory ciliate, X300. Notice the wavelike pattern created by the cilia.

FIGURE 24.3 Human sperm on an egg, X1 000

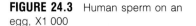

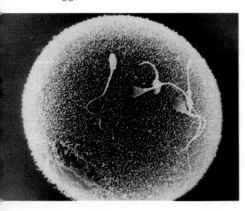

appear to support the cell like tiny feet (Figure 24.1). Beneath the plasma membrane is a thin layer of microfilaments. These filaments assemble to extend the pseudopod and disassemble to retract the pseudopod, thus making movement possible. Amoeboid movement is characteristic of amoebas and other protozoa, but it also occurs in wandering cells, such as white blood cells, that are present in many animals.

Ciliary movement occurs by means of cilia, tiny hairlike structures that extend from the surface of many types of cells. Fields of cilia move in coordinated waves (Figure 24.2). Each cilium (singular for *cilia*) moves like a tiny whip. The movements of the nearby cilia are not quite synchronized, and the small delay produces undulating patterns.

Cilia may move materials over the surface of a layer of cells, such as the cells lining the air passages in the lungs. They may also propel single cells through a liquid. Protozoa use cilia for the collection of food as well as for locomotion.

The single flagellum of a sperm cell (Figure 24.3) and of many protozoa is usually longer than a cilium but moves in a similar manner. For most purposes, the terms *cilia* and *flagella* can be used synonymously in eukaryotes. Bacterial flagella, however, are much different. Bacteria rotate their flagella in either a clockwise or counterclockwise direction, and the organisms appear to tumble.

Ciliary and amoeboid movement are suitable methods of locomotion for cells and very small organisms. These organisms have no need for additional supportive structures, such as muscles and skeletons, because they have little mass to move. In addition, most cells and organisms that employ these methods live in a liquid environment. In contrast, think about how much energy it takes you to swim two lengths of a pool. Would the way a human swims be a very efficient method of locomotion for organisms that *live* in water?

FIGURE 24.4 Each segment of the earthworm is filled with fluid. When the animal contracts its muscles, the fluid in one segment exerts pressure on the next, and so on down its length. In this way, the earthworm appears to expand and contract.

24.2 Invertebrate Systems

Generally, both vertebrates and invertebrates use muscular movement to move. This requires the combination of a skeleton and a system of muscles. Two general types of skeletons combine with muscles to form the basis of the motor systems in invertebrates. In motor systems with **hydrostatic skeletons**, movement depends on fluid and muscles. In motor systems with **exoskeletons**, movements depend on the interaction of a hard covering, or exoskeleton, and muscles.

In a hydrostatic skeleton, fluid is held within the body in a compartment that cannot compress—somewhat like a hydraulic brake system in a car. For example, earthworms have a body cavity that is divided into a series of segments, each with a flexible wall surrounding a fluid-filled chamber (Figure 24.4). Each segment has a set of longitudinal and circular muscles. When the circular muscles contract, the force of contraction is applied against the fluid-filled interior. The fluid resists compression, so it is squeezed along the axis of the body, much like toothpaste being squeezed down a tube.

Insects, crabs, and other invertebrates also have segmented bodies (Figure 24.5). Each segment has a hard covering that forms an external

CONNECTIONS

The method of locomotion employed by an organism is a product of evolution. Different methods of locomotion reflect adaptations to different environments and ways of life.

FIGURE 24.5 The exoskeleton of the sowbug, *Oniscus*, clearly shows the segmented body.

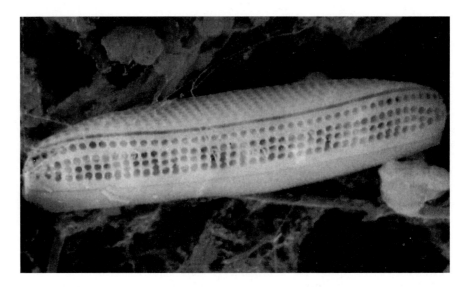

FIGURE 24.6 Scanning electron micrograph of a diatom, *Navicula*, X2 000, showing the silica shell

FIGURE 24.7 A cicada (*right*) sheds its exoskeleton (*left*), and a new, larger exoskeleton is made by the secretion of chitin.

skeleton, or exoskeleton. In addition to covering the segments, the exoskeleton covers the muscles that bridge the gaps between segments. It also serves as the site for muscle attachment. The exoskeleton remains pliable at these gaps. When the muscles cause movement in different directions, it acts like a set of hinges.

Exoskeletons are made of a variety of materials. For example, the single-celled diatoms, shown in Figure 24.6, have exoskeletons made largely of silicon, the same material from which glass is made. Other organisms, such as grasshoppers and lobsters, have exoskeletons made of chitin. Chitin is an organic material that is secreted by a layer of cells just underneath the exoskeleton. Regardless of their composition, exoskeletons protect, support, and aid in the movement of the organism. Sometimes, exoskeletons grow as the organisms grow. In a snail or clam, for example, the exoskeleton grows as more material is secreted. Other times the exoskeleton is shed as the animal grows (Figure 24.7).

Exoskeletons are generally found in organisms larger than single cells. They provide some protection for the internal organs, but cannot provide maximum support. Imagine the effect of gravity on your internal organs if you had an exoskeleton. The lack of support for body tissues is one major reason that exoskeletons are not found in very large animals.

24.3 Vertebrate Systems

Humans and other vertebrates have motor systems with an **endoskeleton**, or internal skeleton. In most vertebrates, bone is the main skeletal material and forms the joints. **Cartilage** is an elastic tissue that usually connects bones or covers the ends of bones at the joints. (Sharks and rays, on the other hand, have endoskeletons composed entirely of cartilage.) The interactions of bones and muscles provide support and protection for other parts of the body, and they enable the animal to move around in its environment. The muscles of vertebrates are connected to specific bones of the endoskeleton and serve specific motor functions.

The design of endoskeletons is closely related to their function. This close relationship can be seen in the skeletons of birds. One of the major adaptations that allows a bird to fly is its light skeleton (Figure 24.8). The skeleton of a frigate bird with a 2-meter (6-foot) wingspan weighs only about 114 grams (4 ounces)—less than the weight of all its feathers. Although a bird's bones are incredibly lightweight, delicate, and laced with air cavities, they are very strong.

The backbone of birds is highly specialized for flight, and its most distinctive feature is its rigidity. Most of the vertebrae, except those in the neck, are fused. With the pelvis, they form a stiff yet light framework to

Try Investigation 24A, Observing Movement.

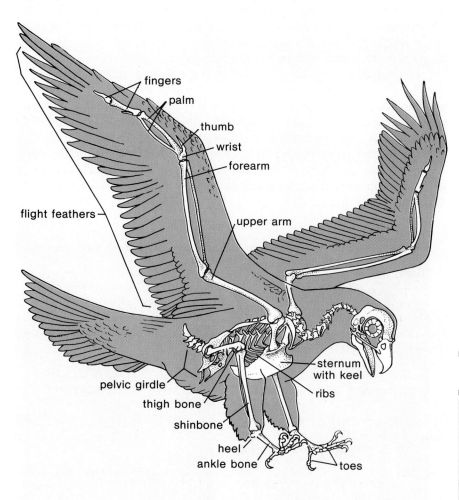

FIGURE 24.8 Bird skeletons are highly adapted for flight. They are incredibly lightweight yet stable.

CONNECTIONS

The three major types of locomotion are quite different, yet within each type, the structure and function of the systems exhibit a remarkable unity in pattern.

FIGURE 24.9 The slug, *Ariolimax columbianus*, leaves a slime trail in its wake.

FIGURE 24.10 Different types of coverings all serve the same basic functions—protection and insulation. (a) scales on a western diamondback rattlesnake, *Crotalus atrox;* (b) feathers of the eastern rosella, *Platycercus eximus;* (c) fur on a short-tailed weasel, *Mustela erminea*

support the legs and provide rigidity for flight. The ribs are mostly fused with the vertebrae, the shoulder bones, and the breastbone. The broad and deep breastbone provides ample room for the attachment of powerful flight muscles. The bones of the forelimb also have become modified for flight. They are hollow, and several of the bones are fused. The design of the legs varies, depending on whether the bird swims, perches, or walks.

Skeletons of other vertebrates are adapted for other forms of movement, such as running, crawling, or walking. Review the description in Chapter 17 of how humans are adapted for bipedal motion, for example.

24.4 Protective Coverings

Endoskeletons provide support for animals and make movement possible. Except for the skull, rib cage, backbone, and hips, however, they do not protect the soft parts of the body from injury, and bones do not keep the tissues from drying out. These functions are carried out by a softer, more flexible layer of cells called the epidermis, commonly referred to as skin. The epidermis provides an outer covering that protects all soft-bodied creatures, whether or not they have an endoskeleton. Sometimes the epidermis secretes a protective substance, such as mucus (Figure 24.9) or nail.

Invertebrates have an epidermis that is only one cell layer thick, but vertebrates have evolved more complex coverings. The body of a vertebrate is covered by a skin made of two layers, an outer epidermis and an inner **dermis**. In land vertebrates, the epidermis itself is several layers thick. The outer layer is composed of hardened dead cells, such as you find on reptiles, birds, and mammals. As these outer cells rub off, cells from the growing epidermal layer beneath replace them. This type of skin helps conserve body moisture and also helps to minimize the seriousness of many injuries, such as bruises and scrapes.

a

b

c

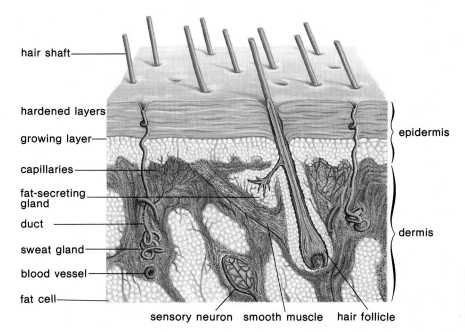

hair shaft

hardened layers

growing layer

epidermis

capillaries

fat-secreting gland

duct

dermis

sweat gland

blood vessel

fat cell

sensory neuron   smooth muscle   hair follicle

FIGURE 24.11   A drawing of a section through human skin. The skin of other mammals is similar but has many more hair follicles and hairs.

Nonliving features of the epidermis include the scales of reptiles, the feathers of birds, and the hair of mammals, all shown in Figure 24.10. All these features provide physical protection and insulation against temperature changes, and all can be periodically lost and replaced.

Human skin is similar to the skin of other mammals. Figure 24.11 shows a cross section through the epidermis and dermis. The epidermis is only 0.07 mm thick, and the dermis is from 2.5 to 5.0 mm thick. The cells of the dermis contain blood vessels, nerves, pigment, oil glands, and fibrous connective tissue. Humans have less body hair for insulation than most other mammals, but sweat glands in the dermis provide a means for lowering the body temperature. As the moisture given off by the sweat glands evaporates, heat energy is given off, and the skin is cooled.

CHECK AND CHALLENGE

1. Compare and contrast amoeboid, ciliary, and muscular movement. Give examples of each.

2. How is the method of locomotion related to the life-style of the organism?

3. Explain why movement of some type is necessary for most organisms.

4. Compare and contrast hydrostatic skeletons, exoskeletons, and endoskeletons.

5. Describe the composition and function of human skin.

FOCUS ON *Feathers*

A feather is very lightweight, yet it is incredibly tough. It is one of the most remarkable vertebrate adaptations. Feathers are made of keratin, the same protein that forms your fingernails and hair and the scales of reptiles. In fact, feathers evolved from reptilian scales. Only birds have feathers, and the presence of feathers is enough to classify an animal as a bird.

A feather (Figure A) consists of a central hollow shaft, or rachis, from which the vanes radiate. The vanes are composed of barbs, which in turn have even smaller branches called barbules. Birds have two types of feathers: contour feathers that are stiff and shape the wings and body, and downy feathers that trap air and provide excellent insulation. If you examine a contour feather under the microscope, you may find as many as 600 barbules on each side of a barb—more than 1 000 000 barbules on the entire feather. The barbules of neighboring barbs overlap in a herringbone pattern and are held together by tiny hooks. If two adjoining barbs are separated, the bird instantly zips them together again by drawing the feather through its beak, an action called preening.

When fully grown, a feather is a dead structure. Except in penguins, which molt all at once, the molting, or shedding, of feathers occurs gradually. Tail feathers and flight feathers—those on the wings used for flying—are lost in exact pairs, one from each side, so that the bird maintains balance.

The replacements emerge before the next pair is lost, and most birds fly unhampered during the molting period. Nearly all birds molt at least once a year, usually in late summer after the nesting season. Many birds also undergo a second partial or complete molt just before breeding season, and this equips them with the breeding finery needed for courtship displays. (See Chapter 25.)

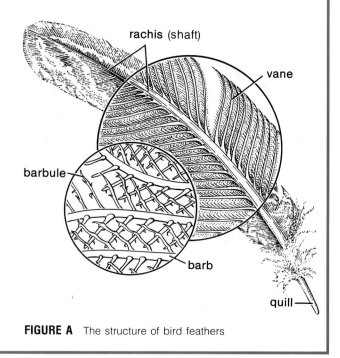

FIGURE A The structure of bird feathers

Human Systems

24.5 Human Bones

The human skeleton is composed of cartilage and numerous different bones. The bones of the human skeleton are similar in structure, function, and the way they develop. However, they vary greatly in size and shape (Figure 24.12), and are classified according to their shape. Long bones, such as those of the arms and legs, are relatively slender and have expanded ends. Short bones are similar to long bones, but they are smaller and have less prominent ends. These bones include the wrist and ankle bones. Flat bones are platelike and have broad surfaces, such as the bones of the skull and ribs. Irregular bones come in a variety of shapes and are usually connected to several other bones. Irregular bones include the vertebrae and the bones of the face.

The structure of each bone is closely related to its function. Bony projections provide a site for the attachment of connecting tissues. Grooves and openings in the bone are passageways for blood vessels and nerves. In the diagram of a longitudinal section of bone in Figure 24.13, note that the

FIGURE 24.12 The human skeletal system

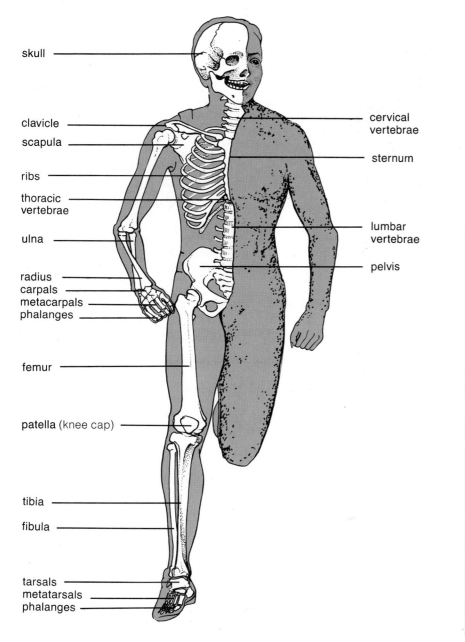

- skull
- clavicle
- scapula
- ribs
- thoracic vertebrae
- ulna
- radius
- carpals
- metacarpals
- phalanges
- femur
- patella (knee cap)
- tibia
- fibula
- tarsals
- metatarsals
- phalanges
- cervical vertebrae
- sternum
- lumbar vertebrae
- pelvis

FIGURE 24.13 The structure of a single bone varies greatly according to its function. Compact bone is dense and heavy, whereas cancellous bone, with its honeycomb construction, provides strength in areas subjected to stress.

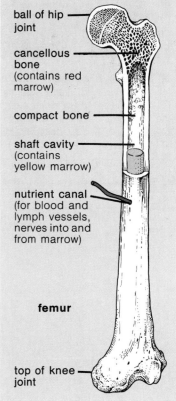

- ball of hip joint
- cancellous bone (contains red marrow)
- compact bone
- shaft cavity (contains yellow marrow)
- nutrient canal (for blood and lymph vessels, nerves into and from marrow)
- **femur**
- top of knee joint

FOCUS ON *Bone Structure*

The microscopic structure of compact bone consists of repeating units called Haversian systems (Figure B). Through these systems, living bone cells, or osteocytes, receive nourishment and hormones by way of blood vessels (Figure C). The osteocytes reside in spaces in the bone tissue called lacunae (lah COO nee). Small tunnels connect neighboring lacunae. Each system has circular layers of mineralized matrix deposited around the central canal, which contains the blood vessels and nerves servicing the bone. This matrix, a mixture of calcium phosphate and the protein collagen, is deposited by the osteocytes.

The combination of flexible collagen and hard mineral makes the bony material sturdy yet flexible without being brittle. There are two types of osteocytes—one that builds bone (osteoblasts) and one that destroys bone (osteoclasts). These cells constantly replace the bony material in your body and keep the bones in good repair.

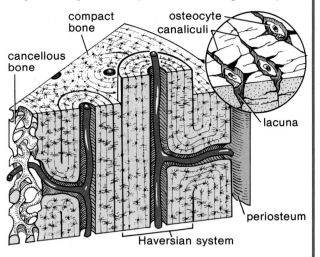

FIGURE B A cross section through compact bone showing Haversian systems. These systems provide the pathway for the nourishment of bone tissue. Compare this photograph to the structures diagrammed in Figure C.

FIGURE C A diagram of a longitudinal cross section through bone illustrates the various structures found in compact bone. Note the blood vessels in the Haversian system.

structure of bone varies from place to place. The length of a long bone, for example, is composed of very dense compact bone. This type of bone is solid, strong, and resistant to bending. The ends of the bone are composed of spongy, or **cancellous bone**, covered by a thin layer of compact bone. Cancellous bone consists of numerous bony plates separated by spaces. This type of construction reduces the weight of the bone and provides strength in areas such as the hip joint that are subjected to a great deal of stress and compression.

Both compact and cancellous tissues are usually present in every bone. The hollow tubes in long bone shafts and the spaces in cancellous bone contain specialized connective tissue called **marrow**. Red marrow (in cancellous bone spaces) produces red blood cells. The yellow marrow (in long bone shafts) serves as fat storage tissue.

Biological Challenges

PIEZOELECTRICITY

One of the more unusual properties of bone is that it generates electricity when it becomes deformed. This phenomenon is called piezo (PEET zoh) electricity. Apparently, the crystalline structures that compose bone produce electricity when they are subjected to pressure. The pressure, which causes the bone to become deformed, separates negative and positive ions, thus producing an electric current.

The true significance of this effect is not known, but researchers suggest that piezoelectricity is a mechanism for remodeling bone in response to stress. Bone samples subjected to compression generate negative charges, whereas bone samples subjected to tension generate positive charges (Figure D). In experiments with animals, the negative charges stimulate the building of new bone. Though the precise mechanism is not known, the effect is to thicken and strengthen the bone being compressed. On the other hand, the positive charges generated by tension do not have the opposite effect of stimulating the breakdown of bone. From an evolutionary standpoint, the distinction is significant. Muscle contraction produces tension at the insertion site on the bone, and the breakdown of bony material at such points would not be adaptive.

If the natural electrical activity of bone is related to bone growth or remodeling, there may be a clinical application for the discovery. Artificially produced electrical activity could be used to stimulate the repair of fractures. This application could be especially beneficial for elderly patients. It is not uncommon for older people to fall and suffer a fracture, for example, at the hip. Their bones do not heal quickly or well, and they are often bedridden for many months. This inactivity encourages pneumonia and other respiratory ailments that can lead to death.

Experiments in which electrodes were attached to fractured bones showed that healing and new bone growth were somewhat accelerated at the negative electrode. Although the precise way in which piezoelectricity works is unknown and the general usefulness of this application is unclear, researchers are continuing to study the phenomenon.

Additional experiments utilizing electricity have been performed on salamanders. Normally, salamanders—as well as humans—do not regenerate bone or muscle tissue. The application of electricity, however, appeared to stimulate a primitive regenerative process. If further research and refinement of techniques result in an increased ability of salamanders to regenerate lost limbs, the consequences could be enormous. Suppose a method is developed that encourages a marked increase in bone growth in humans. What would be the implications? Could this technology lead to the ability to regenerate lost fingers? Or even arms and legs?

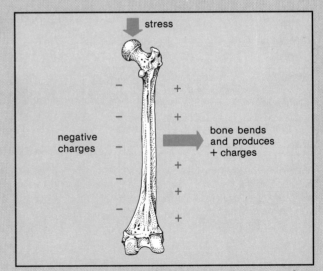

FIGURE D In the femur, for example, the application of pressure to the head causes the bone to bow outwards. In response to this stress, negative charges are produced on the inward side of the bone, and positive charges are produced on the outward side.

24.6 Bone Composition and Formation

The chemical composition of human bone differs from that of soft body tissues. Only 25 percent of the bone tissue of a young adult is water, whereas the other tissues may be 60 to 90 percent water. About 45 percent of bone consists of calcium combined with either phosphate or carbonate. These minerals give bone its rigidity and hardness.

The minerals in bone are not fixed in place as are the minerals in a rock. Instead, there is a continual exchange between bone and other parts of the body. In an individual suffering from starvation, the bones may give up as much as a third of their content to the blood and body tissues. This loss leaves bones soft, brittle, and easily broken. During pregnancy, the mother's body supplies the fetus with material to build its skeleton, and minerals may be withdrawn from the mother's skeleton. In order to keep herself and her fetus healthy, a pregnant woman must supplement her diet with vitamins and minerals to avoid possible deficiencies.

The balanced exchange of materials between bone and other body tissues is maintained by hormones that interact with minerals and vitamins supplied by the diet. Several endocrine glands produce hormones that directly affect bone formation and growth. The thyroid and parathyroid glands, for example, produce calcitonin and parathyroid hormone (PTH) respectively. These hormones help control the calcium and phosphate levels in the blood and bone. (See Chapter 23.) Estrogen and testosterone, hormones produced by the gonads, help regulate bone growth.

A growth hormone produced in the pituitary gland governs the overall growth of the skeleton. (See Section 1.3.) When the hypothalamus and the pituitary gland do not function together normally, the pituitary may secrete too much or too little growth hormone. If the disorders occur during childhood, the individual may become either extremely tall or exceptionally short. If the disorders occur later in life, the size of the hands, feet, and jaws may be affected (Figure 24.14).

FIGURE 24.14 Acromegaly is a result of the excessive secretion of growth hormone as an adult. With this disorder, a person does not grow taller because the long bones have fused to the cartilage end plates. The soft tissue, however, may continue to enlarge, and the bones may become thicker. As a result, an individual may develop abnormally large hands and feet, a massive jaw, and a large tongue and nose.

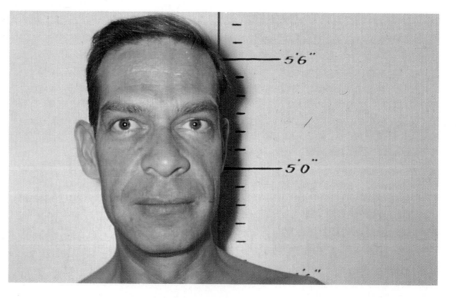

24.7   Bone Growth and Development

How do human bones develop? Some bones form directly in the connective tissue in the embryo. The flat bones of the skull are an example. Cartilage models serve as the starting point for other bones in the embryo, as shown in Figure 24.15. For example, when a long bone develops, cartilage inside the shaft of the model calcifies and is invaded by blood vessels and cells known as osteoblasts and osteoclasts. Osteoclasts release enzymes that dissolve the calcified cartilage and bone tissue. The osteoblasts then start to deposit material that will form bone tissue along the shaft walls. This same activity occurs at the knobby ends of long bones. As development continues, cartilage remains as a covering for the bone in the joints at both ends of the shaft. There it forms plates that extend across the width of the bone.

Growth in length occurs at the ends of the bone. Underneath the cartilage end plates, calcified cartilage is removed, and bone tissue is deposited. At the same time, long bones grow wider as new bone tissue is deposited under the dense connecting tissue surrounding the outside of the bone. When growth in length is completed, the cartilage end plates disappear. Marrow fills the shaft cavities of the long bones and the inner spaces of cancellous bones almost as soon as they develop. Red marrow, a major site of red blood cell production, is found in the vertebrae, ribs, breastbone, and pelvis. Yellow marrow is present at other locations and contains blood vessels, nerve cells, and fat cells. When a great deal of blood is lost, this tissue assists the red marrow in producing additional red blood cells.

FIGURE 24.15   The stages in the development of long bones

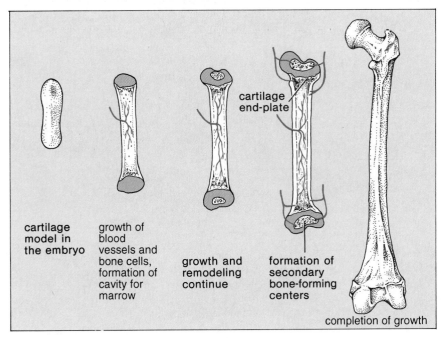

cartilage end-plate

cartilage model in the embryo

growth of blood vessels and bone cells, formation of cavity for marrow

growth and remodeling continue

formation of secondary bone-forming centers

completion of growth

24.8   Joints

Joints are points of contact or near contact between bones or between cartilage and bone. Structurally, there are three types of joints, as illustrated in Figure 24.16.

Immovable joints basically have no gap between the bones and hardly move at all. The joints between the bones of the skull and of the face are examples. Slightly movable joints have a small gap between the bones, which are held together by cartilage. These joints permit limited movement. The disks between the vertebrae are an example. These disks form strong joints that allow some movement along the spinal column. They also absorb shocks, such as when you jump to the ground and land on your feet. Freely movable joints are the most common. Bones at these joints are separated by a cavity and are held together by flexible connective tissues called **ligaments**. Ligaments attach bones to bones, whereas **tendons** (another group of connective tissues) attach muscles to bones or muscles to muscles. Cartilage covers the surface of the bone ends in the joint itself. Freely movable joints, such as the knee, may be twisted or strained by repeated impact, resulting in damage to the joint.

FIGURE 24.16   (a) The joints between the bones of the skull are immovable. The bones are separated by a thin layer of connecting tissue. (b) The vertebrae of the spinal column are slightly movable joints. (c) The generalized structure of a freely movable joint is seen in hinge, ball-and-socket, and gliding joints.

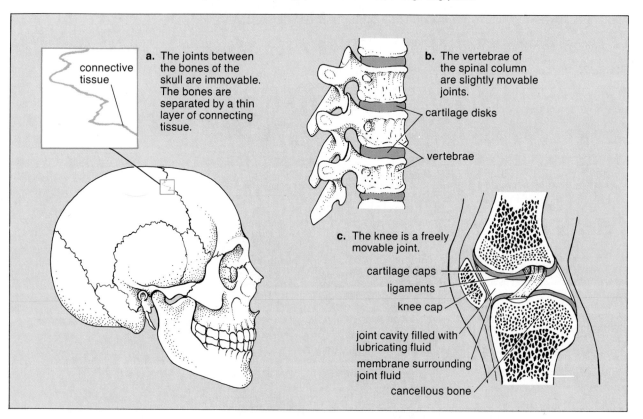

Freely movable joints are subject to wear and tear through time. In osteoarthritis, the cartilage in the joint simply wears out, and deposits of calcium form. Rheumatoid arthritis is a degenerative disorder that has a genetic basis. A membrane in the joint thickens and becomes inflamed to the degree that the joint becomes stiff and painful.

Freely movable joints come in three basic "styles": hinge, ball-and-socket, and gliding. Knees and elbows are called hinge joints because the movement of the joint is limited, much like the hinge on a door. You can open a door in one direction, but not the other. The shoulder and hip joints are examples of the ball-and-socket style. These joints move fairly freely and are capable of a circular rotation. The wrist is called a gliding joint because the numerous bones of the wrist "glide" past one another during movement.

24.9   Muscles

Muscles that move bones are called **skeletal muscles**. In order to move a bone, a muscle must be attached at one end to the bone it is to move and at the opposite end to an anchoring bone or bones. As shown in Figure 24.17, tendons attach muscles to bones. The attachment to the anchoring bone is called the origin of the muscle. The attachment of the muscle to the bone it moves is called the insertion. Without such attachment points the muscle could produce only a fraction of its effect in moving a part of the body. Imagine that the muscles in your arm are not attached to the bones. How well do you think you could move your arm?

The skeleton, along with its muscles, is like a system of levers in which rods (bones) move at certain points (the joints). When a typical muscle

Try Investigation 24B, Muscles and Muscle Fatigue.

FIGURE 24.17   A flexor-extensor muscle pair in the human arm. Flexors bend a limb at a skeletal joint; extensors straighten the limb again.

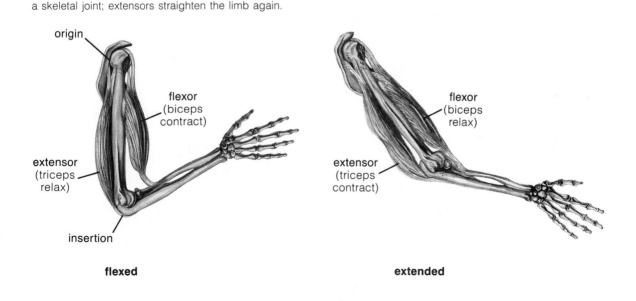

flexed   **extended**

contracts, the origin remains stationary and the insertion moves. Most insertions are close to the joints. This arrangement means that the muscle has to contract just a small distance to produce a large body movement.

An arm or a leg can be rotated because of arrangements between pairs or groups of muscles. Skeletal muscles usually act in opposing, or antagonistic, pairs. Figure 24.17 illustrates a good example of such a pair in the combination of a **flexor** muscle and an **extensor** muscle in the upper arm. When one of the muscle pair contracts, the elbow joint flexes. As the muscle relaxes, its partner contracts, and the limb straightens out again.

24.10   Muscle Structure

In addition to skeletal muscles, there are two other types of muscle: **cardiac muscle** and **smooth muscle**. Cardiac muscle (Figure 24.18) is found only in the heart. Other organs of the body and the walls of arteries and veins contain smooth muscle. Each type of muscle tissue is structurally different.

Smooth muscle cells are named for their appearance (Figure 24.19). They are shaped like slender rods tapered at each end. A smooth muscle cell is a few tenths of a millimeter in length and contains a single nucleus located in the center portion of the cell. If a smooth muscle cell is viewed under a microscope, tiny fibers can be seen running along its length. These fibers produce the muscular contraction in smooth muscle. The contractions of smooth muscle are slow and rhythmic. They are involuntary: That is, the contractions are not controlled by the conscious part of the brain. The contraction of the intestinal muscles that move food through your digestive tract is an example of involuntary muscle action.

Cardiac muscle is structurally similar to skeletal muscle (described in the following paragraphs) in that it has small cross stripes, or striations, when viewed under the microscope. The contractions of cardiac muscle, however, are involuntary, similar to smooth muscle. Cardiac muscle constantly contracts and relaxes in a continuing rhythmic pattern. During the entire life of an individual, the only time that cardiac muscle rests is during a momentary pause before each contraction.

FIGURE 24.18 Cardiac muscle

FIGURE 24.19 Smooth muscle structure

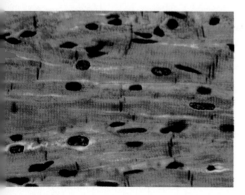

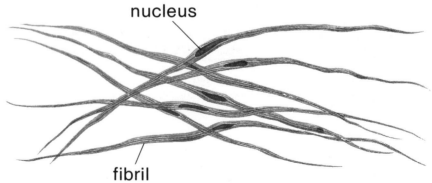

nucleus

fibril

Skeletal muscle (Figure 24.20) is often called striated muscle because of the presence of small cross stripes. Clearly defined individual cells, however, cannot be seen in skeletal muscle. The tissue consists of long, continuous fibers without clear separations between the cells. Skeletal muscle contracts more rapidly than cardiac or smooth muscle, and contractions are under voluntary control. Conscious messages from the brain can bring about an increase or decrease in the rate and degree of muscular contraction. Thus, when you hear the signal for the start of a race, you begin running. How rapidly you run depends on the number of messages sent by your brain to your leg muscles.

Figure 24.21 illustrates the structure of skeletal muscle, which is composed of many muscle fibers that are bundled together inside a sheath of connective tissue (a). Each fiber consists of fine, threadlike structures called **myofibrils** (b). Each myofibril, in turn, consists of filaments of the proteins actin and myosin (c). An actin filament looks like two beaded chains twisted around one another (d). The "beads" are molecules of actin.

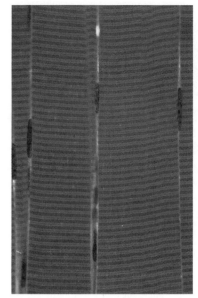

FIGURE 24.20 (*above*) A skeletal muscle showing the characteristic stripes or banded pattern

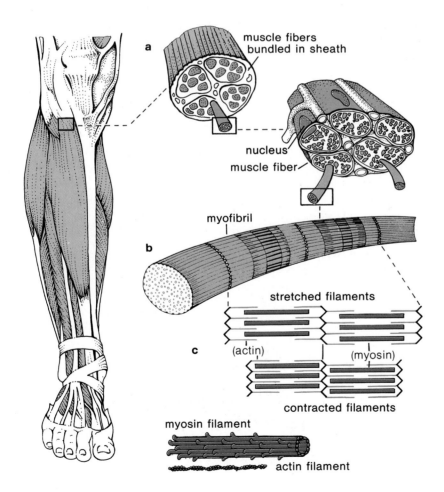

FIGURE 24.21 The structure of skeletal muscle. See text for details.

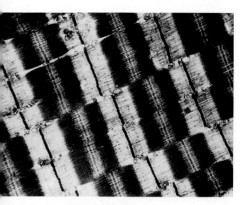

FIGURE 24.22 Under high magnification (X 24 000), this rabbit muscle tissue shows individual fibrils within a fiber and filaments within the fibrils.

Myosin filaments are actually 200 to 400 rod-shaped myosin molecules lined up parallel to one another. The actin and myosin filaments are arranged in alternating bands. This banding pattern gives skeletal and cardiac muscles their striped or striated appearance. The pattern is interrupted at regular intervals by thin, dark lines, called Z lines, which are the anchors for actin filaments. The lines define the **sarcomere**, the smallest unit of muscle contraction (Figure 24.22). Sarcomeres either contract completely, or not at all.

24.11 Mechanism of Muscle Contraction

The only way that skeletal muscles can bring about the movement of body parts is to shorten. When a skeletal muscle shortens, its muscle fibers are shortening. When a muscle fiber shortens, its sarcomeres are shortening. The combined decrease in length of the individual sarcomeres accounts for the contraction of the whole muscle.

How does a sarcomere alternately contract and relax? The sliding-filament model represents the most reasonable explanation of currently available data. According to this model, actin filaments physically slide over the myosin filaments as diagrammed in Figure 24.23. They move toward the center of the sarcomere during contraction and away from the

FIGURE 24.23 A simplified diagram of the sliding filament model of muscle contraction

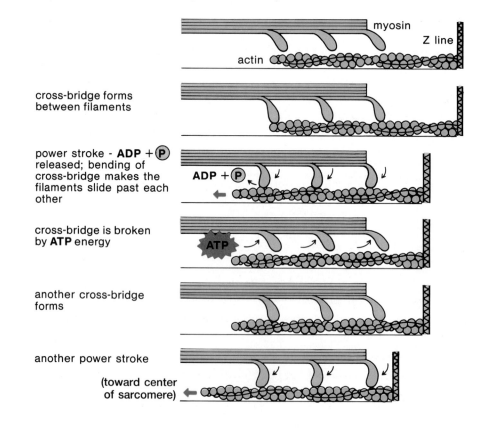

cross-bridge forms between filaments

power stroke - **ADP** + (P) released; bending of cross-bridge makes the filaments slide past each other

cross-bridge is broken by **ATP** energy

another cross-bridge forms

another power stroke

(toward center of sarcomere)

center when the sarcomere relaxes. For the sliding to occur, "heads" on the myosin filaments must attach to binding sites on the actin molecules. When they are attached, the myosin heads form links, or cross bridges, between the two types of filaments. When these cross bridges are activated, the myosin heads tilt inward toward the center of the sarcomere in a short, powerful stroke. Because the heads are attached to the actin filaments, these filaments also move slightly inward. The myosin heads then detach and reattach at the next binding site in line, moving the actin filaments a bit more. A single contraction of the sarcomere requires a whole series of these power strokes. The energy needed for these contractions comes from splitting ATP into ADP and phosphate.

In the absence of ATP, the myosin heads never detach. The muscle becomes rigid, a condition known as rigor. Following death, ATP production stops. The myosin heads remain locked in place and all skeletal muscles in the body become rigid. This condition, known as *rigor mortis*, lasts up to 60 hours after death.

How do your muscles know when to contract? Muscle contraction is governed by the nervous system. Each muscle fiber is connected to a fiber from a nerve cell. This nerve fiber is part of a motor neuron that is ultimately connected to the brain or spinal cord. Usually a muscle fiber contracts only when it is stimulated by the action of a motor neuron. The end of the motor neuron fiber is branched, and the ends of these branches extend into the muscle fibers (Figure 24.24). The cytosol at the ends of neuron fibers is rich in mitochondria and contains numerous vesicles that store chemicals called neurotransmitters. When a nerve impulse traveling from the brain or spinal cord reaches the end of a motor neuron fiber, some of the vesicles release neurotransmitters. These chemicals stimulate the muscle fiber to contract. Together, a motor neuron and the muscle fibers that it controls constitute a motor unit. The number of muscle fibers in a motor unit varies. Motor units containing few muscle fibers produce finer movements than those containing many fibers. Compare, for example, the range of delicate movement in your fingers with the limited movements of your toes. Although much is known about the action of muscles, more research must be done before the precise mechanisms of muscular contractions are fully understood.

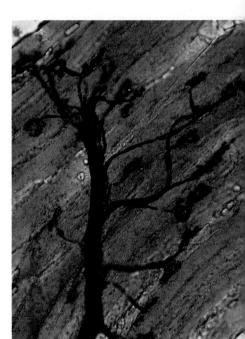

FIGURE 24.24 Nerve endings on striated muscle fibers. Nerve impulses stimulate the nerve endings to secrete their chemical messengers, initiating the events that result in contraction of the muscle fibers.

CHECK AND CHALLENGE

1. Describe the composition of the human skeleton.
2. How is the structure of bone related to its function?
3. Explain the process by which long bones grow, beginning with the cartilage model.
4. How do muscles move bones?
5. Describe the structure and action of the different types of muscle.
6. How does a muscle contract and how is contraction controlled?

C H A P T E R Highlights

Summary

Each animal uses a system of locomotion that is tailored to its way of life. Vertebrates and most invertebrates use muscular movement. These systems are composed of a skeletal structure, either an endoskeleton or exoskeleton, and muscles. Other invertebrates, such as worms, have hydrostatic skeletons. Single cells and microscopic organisms employ either amoeboid or ciliary movement.

The bones of endoskeletons are composed of two general types of tissue: cancellous bone or compact bone. The particular type of tissue present in a given area of a bone is related to the amount of stress and compression to which that area is subject. Four general classes of bones constitute the human skeleton: long, short, flat, and irregular. Although bones provide support for body tissues, few provide much protection. The epidermis is primarily responsible for protecting body tissues from injury and drying. The epidermis also provides insulation from extreme temperatures.

Muscle contraction is governed by the nervous system through a network of neuron fibers. In response to chemical messages received from the brain or spinal cord, muscle fibers contract. The sarcomere is the basic unit of contraction. Numerous power strokes by myosin filaments result in movement of actin filaments and, thus, contraction of the entire muscle fiber. Sarcomeres contract all the way or not at all. The degree of muscle movement that results is dependent upon the number of muscle fibers involved.

Movement in humans (and other vertebrates) is accomplished through the use of muscles that move parts of the skeleton. Of the three general types of muscle tissue—cardiac, smooth, and skeletal—only skeletal muscle is used for locomotion.

Key Concepts

Use the following terms to construct a concept map. Add additional terms as you need them.

evolution	amoeboid movement
structure	ciliary movement
function	myosin
hydrostatic skeletons	actin
exoskeletal skeletons	flexors
epidermis	cardiac muscle
muscles	skeletal muscle
joints	smooth muscle
compact bone	neurotransmitters
cancellous bone	osteocytes

Reviewing Ideas

1. Explain the difference between exoskeletons and endoskeletons.

2. What is a hydrostatic skeleton and how does it work?

3. How does an exoskeleton accommodate the growth of the organism?

4. How do the different shapes of bones relate to their functions?

5. What is compact bone and where is it found?

6. What is cancellous bone and where is it found?

7. What functions does skin serve?

8. How do long bones grow?

9. Describe the two types of movement occurring at the cellular level in animals.

10. Compare and contrast flexors and extensors.

11. What are the roles of myosin and actin in muscle contraction?

12. What structures are involved in muscle contraction?

13. What is cartilage, where is it found, and what function does it serve?

14. What is the sliding-filament hypothesis, and how does it work?

Using Concepts

1. Why might a skeleton composed mostly of cartilage be adaptive for an animal such as a shark?

2. What is the adaptive value for humans of two layers of skin?

3. What might be the reason for having different types of muscle tissue?

4. Suggest some reasons why there are three general methods of locomotion. Relate your answer to the life-style of the organisms.

5. What might be the adaptive value of feathers for birds and scales for reptiles?

6. Explain how the human skeletal system is adaptive.

Synthesis

1. In what ways does animal movement differ from plant movement?

2. Relate your knowledge of the endocrine system to human bone growth and development.

3. Relate cellular respiration to muscle contraction.

4. How do the different methods of locomotion reflect adaptation and natural selection? Give specific examples.

Extensions

1. Design an organism with a method of locomotion different from any discussed in this chapter. You either may describe this system or sketch it. Be sure to relate the method of movement to the organism's environment.

2. Imagine you are a macrophage. Write an essay describing, in detail, how you move through the immune system and attack an invading virus.

CHAPTERS

Organisms and Their Environment

*O*rganisms live in almost every conceivable environment, from the top of the highest mountain to the bottom of the deepest ocean trench. There are algae that grow only in melting snow. Many plants and animals spend their lives in lightless caves. Some bacteria live in hot springs, where temperatures are near the boiling point.

Knowledge of an organism's environment is very important to our understanding of that particular organism. Organisms also are part of each other's environment and thus interact in complex ways. Consider some of ways in which organisms in this alpine environment interact.

*W*hat environmental factors affect the organisms that live in this alpine pond?

*W*hat factors affect those living in the surrounding area?

CONTENTS

Animal Interactions

*E*very day each of us engages in some type of complex activity. We may go to school or work, dance, participate in sports, drive cars, and sometimes become involved in conflicts. We also perform other, less complex activities such as eating and sleeping. Our nervous system determines the complexity of activities that we are able to perform. Animals with nervous systems similar to a worm's cannot play soccer, much less chess.

Why are some activities, such as food-getting and mating, common to all organisms whereas other activities, such as nest-building, are limited to certain species? Why do some animals live in groups and others live alone? Why are some animals, including humans, capable of extreme aggression toward their own kind? Questions such as these are the focus of the study of **behavior**. In its simplest form, behavior is the conduct of an organism—the way it acts. Behavior is the most immediate means through which an organism interacts with its environment.

Animal behavior is actually the result of genes selected by the environment. It is a biological process with a genetic basis that is shaped by evolution. If an individual organism is to survive and reproduce, its behavior must be adaptive to new situations. If most members of a species behave in a similar adaptive manner, the species will likely survive.

This chapter introduces some concepts in the study of behavior. Studying different aspects of behavior, both simple and complex, leads to an understanding of why different animals act the way they do.

◆ *Walruses,* Odobaenus rosmarus, *sunning themselves.*

FIGURE 25.1 An example of how camouflage and behavior can help a species to survive. Motionless during the daylight hours, the tiny frog looks like a bird dropping.

*M*any behaviors—activities that aid in temperature regulation, for example— are closely related to an organism's homeostasis.

Evolution and Behavior

25.1 Behavior and Adaptation

The internal organ systems of multicellular organisms are coordinated to produce unified outward expressions. These outward expressions are the behavior of the organisms. Behavior is a reaction to the environment, both internal and external. For example, when you are cold, you may stamp your feet, rub your arms, or put on a coat. When you are tired, you yawn. Successful behavior occurs when an animal reacts to its particular environment in a way that helps it to survive.

Behavior mostly affects the ability of the individual organism to survive, but it also plays a part in preserving the species. If the behavior of individuals is successful, they may live to produce many offspring. The number of descendants affects the survival of the species as a whole. Therefore, the behavior of each member of a species helps to determine whether the species continues to reproduce and thrive.

For example, the tiny tropical frog pictured in Figure 25.1 remains totally still during the daylight hours. Would-be predators probably view it as a bird dropping instead of a meal. The frog's behavior patterns include night activity and long, motionless hours during the day. Thus, it continues to survive. Because behavior helps an organism survive, it is closely related to the evolution of the species. Can you think of some ways in which you are behaviorally adapted to your environment?

Behavior is only one aspect of adaptation. Adaptation is a combination of inherited and learned characteristics that improve an organism's chances to survive and reproduce. Species that exist today are adapted to the conditions in which they live, and they may eventually give rise to new species. Poorly adapted organisms do not usually survive, and their species even may become extinct. Those adaptations that help an organism live successfully in its environment—that is, to survive long enough to reproduce—are an important part of the study of both evolution and behavior.

25.2 Innate and Learned Behaviors

Generally, behavior is considered to be either **innate** or **learned**. Innate, or inborn, behavior is not dependent on experience. Sometimes it is a behavioral pattern that occurs as soon as the organism is hatched or born, such as sucking or crying. (See **Appendix 25A**, Innate Behavior.)

It has long been known that some animals are born with certain established behaviors. Dogs that have spent their entire lives indoors will attempt to bury a bone by scratching on the carpet as if they were digging. Captive raccoons go through the motions of dunking and washing their food in water, even if that food is already clean or wet and whether or not water is available. Such patterns of behavior, which are innate and characteristic of a given species, are called fixed action patterns. An animal may not possess all its fixed action patterns when it is very young. Many patterns develop as the animal matures. For example, wing flapping and other

*I*nnate behaviors are characteristic of a species and as such are a product of heredity.

patterns associated with flight in birds typically appear shortly before the bird is ready to fly. A baby mouse may flail its leg vigorously in thin air; later it will apply the motion to scratch an itch.

Environmental influences may trigger innate behavior but do not explain it, nor does learning explain it because no previous experience is involved. For example, the kitten in Figure 25.2 is standing on a checkerboard surface while looking down a visual cliff, or drop. The drop is visual, not actual, because a plate of glass covers it. The kitten will not venture out onto the glass, even though it has had no experience with heights or falling. This reaction can be classified as an innate behavior in response to the visual stimulus. A complex innate behavior is called an **instinct**.

Learned behavior, on the other hand, consists of all those responses an organism develops as a result of environmental experiences. Most animals can learn to behave in new ways. Learned behavior ranges from simple changes that modify innate behavior to the type of complex learned behavior you would use to drive a car. Other examples include dogs learning to bark or sit on command and parrots learning to imitate speech.

A series of experiments with the southern toad indicates how experience may change an innate behavior (Figure 25.3). The toad is a natural predator of the robber fly, some of which resemble bumblebees in size and shape. A toad's instinct is to capture and eat these robber flies. If it mistakenly eats a real bumblebee and is stung on the tongue, the toad does not try to eat either the robber flies or real bumblebees after recovering from its unpleasant experience. It continues to eat other insects. The toad has changed its innate behavior.

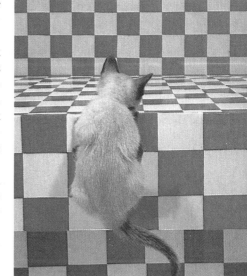

FIGURE 25.2 This Siamese kitten has never fallen or been dropped. It has had no experience with high places. The drop you see here is only visual; a plate of glass gives the kitten firm underfooting. Yet the kitten hesitates. Such experiments are used to help determine when behavior is innate and when it is learned.

FIGURE 25.3 The toad is eating a bumblebee, which stings it on the tongue (a). Although initially appearing interested in a mimic of a bumblebee, a harmless robber fly (b), the toad does not attempt to capture it (c).

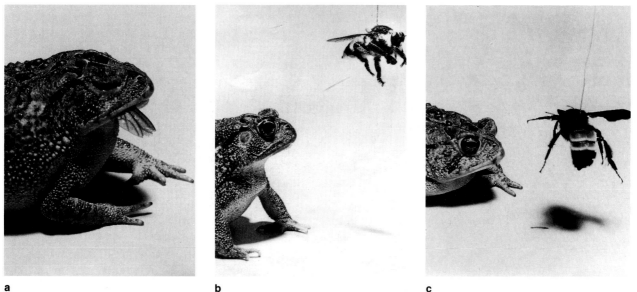

a   b   c

For many years, researchers have argued as to whether or not many types of behavior are innate or learned. Most scientists agree today that many behaviors are neither exclusively innate nor exclusively learned.

25.3 Types of Learned Behavior

There are several forms of learned behavior. One unique type of learning is called **imprinting** (Figure 25.4). As soon as a newly hatched gosling or duckling is strong enough to walk, it follows its mother away from the nest. After it has followed its mother for a while, it will no longer follow any other animal. If the eggs are hatched away from the mother, the young will follow the first moving object they see. As they grow, they prefer the artificial mother to anything else, including their true mother. They are said to be imprinted on the artificial mother. This type of learning is unique because it has a sensitive period, or genetically determined time, in which the learning occurs and requires little or no practice.

A type of simple learning is **habituation**. If an animal is exposed to a stimulus over and over again, it may slowly lose its response to the stimulus. For example, a dog responds to the sound of an airplane passing overhead by turning its head. If airplanes continue to fly overhead, the dog may learn to disregard the sound. Such a reaction can be thought of as learning *not* to respond to stimuli that are of little importance to the animal.

A more complex type of learning is **conditioning**. Conditioning occurs when the patterns of an innate behavior are changed. In the early 1900s, the Russian physiologist Ivan Pavlov investigated classical conditioning (Figure 25.5). Pavlov's most famous experiments involved the innate reflex of the flow of saliva in a dog when presented with food.

FIGURE 25.4 Imprinting occurs in many species of birds, such as these common mergansers, *Mergus merganser*. The young follow their mother as a result of imprinting.

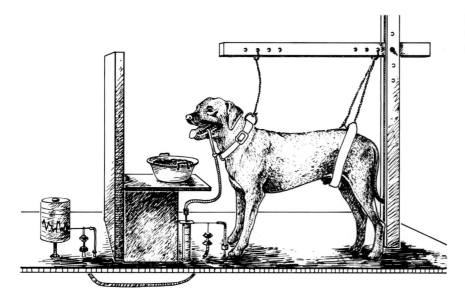

FIGURE 25.5 Pavlov's apparatus, used in his experiments on conditioning.

Pavlov first showed that when a bell was rung the dog did not produce a flow of saliva. Then the bell was rung as meat was presented to the dog. The dog secreted saliva. The acts of ringing the bell and presenting the meat were repeated together many times. Eventually the dog secreted saliva on hearing the bell, even when no food was present. Pavlov reasoned that a new reflex had been set up. A change had occurred in the neuron pathway between the dog's ears, brain, and salivary glands.

Conditioned responses have been developed in many types of animals. One of the most interesting experiments was performed on planarians. In the early 1950s, two biologists developed a conditioned response in planarians (Figure 25.6). First, the biologists shined a strong light (stimulus) on a planarian. Several seconds later, they administered a mild electric shock (another stimulus). The planarian's normal response to the light was to stretch. Its normal response to the shock was to contract or turn its head. This sequence, in which the light was followed by the shock, was repeated about 100 times. Soon the response to the light alone was about the same as though the electric shock had been given also. A "trained" planarian would show a shock response 23 out of 25 times when the light was

Try Investigation 25A, A Lesson in Conditioning.

FIGURE 25.6 A conditioned-reflex experiment with a planarian. As a result of the conditioning, the planarian eventually responds to light as it would to an electric shock.

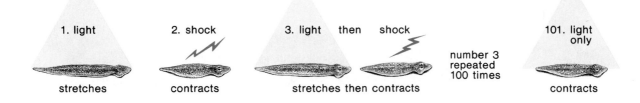

1. light — stretches

2. shock — contracts

3. light then shock — stretches then contracts

number 3 repeated 100 times

101. light only — contracts

Try Investigation 25B, Trial-and-Error Learning.

turned on. However, the animal soon forgot its lesson unless it was retrained periodically.

A somewhat higher level of learning is trial-and-error learning, sometimes called trial-and-success learning. An animal faced with two or more responses may eventually be taught the preferred one when a reward is given for this response. Other responses may result in punishment. Many organisms learn, after many trials, to make the ''correct'' response.

25.4   Determining Behavior Patterns

There are probably elements of both heredity and learning in many behavior patterns that were once thought to be only learned or only innate. For example, the process by which a squirrel opens a nut has been shown to be a combination of innate and learned behavior.

Humans are capable of the most complex types of learned behavior, such as developing concepts, dealing with abstract matters, and solving problems involving new situations. Do animals other than humans have this same ability? To what degree are their actions the result of innate or learned behavior, or a combination of both? How can different types of behavior in animals be measured?

Researchers have studied the ability of other animals to solve problems by using ''detour'' problems. In such a problem, an animal must follow an indirect path to get a desired object. Animals used in these types of studies range from microorganisms to primates.

Chimpanzees and monkeys show the ability to solve difficult problems. A classic demonstration of reasoning ability made use of some bananas that were hung out of the reach of a chimpanzee. Boxes lying on the floor would provide access to the bananas if they were stacked. Figure 25.7 shows the chimpanzee's response.

FIGURE 25.7 Three stills from a motion picture film of a chimpanzee, a bunch of bananas too high to reach, and some empty boxes. The chimp sized up the situation (*left*), stacked the boxes (*center*), and obtained the bananas (*right*).

In any behavior experiment, it is not always easy to determine how the problem was solved. Was it by reasoning or by application of some previous experience? How are reasoning, trial and error, and experience to be distinguished in each experiment? Determining the specific cause of certain behaviors makes behavioral science a challenging field to study.

FOCUS ON *A Detour Problem*

In detour experiments, the important question is whether the animal used reason or simply trial-and-error learning to solve the problem. It is a difficult question to answer. Figure A compares the responses of a dog and a squirrel to the detour problem. Dogs are not good at such tasks—a dog strains at its leash, whines, and runs about wildly. It may even fall asleep. Then it starts again. By luck alone, it might find itself on the far side of the post and rush toward the food. By contrast, tree squirrels are uncommonly good at solving this problem. After first failing to reach the food, the animals try an alternate path around the post and to the food. Can you think of a reason for this difference?

This type of result can be puzzling unless evolution is taken into account. Although dogs have a larger and more complex brain than squirrels, they live almost exclusively in a horizontal, two-dimensional world. They see food on their level, and they take the most direct path to it. Squirrels, on the other hand, live in trees. In their three-dimensional world (vertical, as well as horizontal), a squirrel moving from tree to tree has a choice. It can climb down the tree, go along the ground, and then climb the next tree; or it can remain in the treetops and try to jump from one tree to the next. The first choice would expose the squirrel to ground-dwelling predators. The second choice would be safer. Yet the second choice may require the squirrel initially to go away from the goal (the food) to reach it eventually. In other words, the ancestors of the squirrels that were relatively more adept at solving such problems were better nourished, more likely to survive, and more likely to leave more offspring than those who were not so adept.

Thus the ability to conduct successful detours was favored by natural selection. Each population of squirrels became composed of individuals who were good at moving away from goals in order to reach them. Is this behavior a product of reasoning or trial-and-error learning? Is it an innate behavior?

FIGURE A   A detour problem. The dog strains at the leash to get to the food. The squirrel, however, backs up and goes around the post to the food.

dog   squirrel

CHECK AND CHALLENGE _____

1. How does an organism's behavior relate to the species as a whole?

2. Why is behavior considered adaptive? Give specific examples.

3. Compare and contrast innate behavior and learned behavior.

4. Explain how the environment influences innate behavior.

5. Discuss imprinting, habituation, and conditioning. How are they similar and different?

The Biological Roots of Behavior _____

25.5 Effects of External and Internal Stimuli

CONNECTIONS

An organism's behavior is closely related to the environment in which the organism lives.

An animal behaves in context with the world around it. For example, you do not put on a heavy coat unless you are cold or you anticipate being cold in the near future. To understand why animals behave as they do, it is necessary to study them in their natural surroundings and also in the laboratory where conditions can be controlled. Both internal and external stimuli, such as hormones, enzymes, temperature, and light are almost always at work, shaping the way in which an organism behaves. Sometimes behaviorists change external or internal stimuli, thus affecting the animal they are studying.

The study of how the American silkworm, the Cecropia moth, constructs its cocoon reveals how both external and internal stimuli interact to determine an organism's behavior. The larva, or caterpillar, spins a cocoon at the end of summer. The adult moth comes out of the cocoon the following spring (Figure 25.8). The Cecropia cocoon consists of two baglike structures, one inside the other. A small opening on the upper end of each bag serves as the escape route for the adult moth. The two thick layers provided by the inner and outer bags protect the developing moth.

Because the silkworm larvae do not have an opportunity to learn how to spin a cocoon, this behavior must be innate—a product of their genetic makeup. What starts and controls the silkworm's spinning behavior? In investigations, biologists found that a pair of glands in the insect's head helps control cocoon-spinning. When these glands are surgically removed early in the life of the caterpillar, it does not spin the structures it normally would. Thus, it appears that there is an internal stimulus for the caterpillar's cocoon-spinning behavior.

Scientists also have studied external, or environmental, influences on this caterpillar's behavior. Consider what happens if the caterpillar and cocoon are turned upside down after the animal spins the outer bag, but before it has started to spin the inner bag (Figure 25.9). In actual experiments, the caterpillars built the inner bag of the cocoon with the opening upward despite the fact that the outer bag's opening now pointed down.

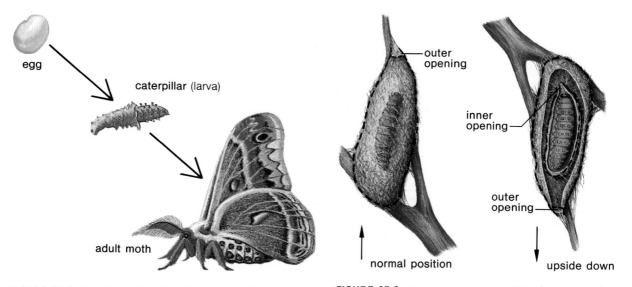

FIGURE 25.8 The life cycle of the Cecropia moth, or American silkworm. An egg develops into a small caterpillar in 10 days. The caterpillar, or larva, eats leaves, molts four times, and grows to as much as 10 centimeters in length in several weeks. It then spins a cocoon, and the larva, now called a pupa, develops within the cocoon. The adult moth emerges in the spring.

FIGURE 25.9 The normal cocoon of the Cecropia moth has an inner and outer bag with the entrances to both facing upward. In an experiment, the cocoon was turned upside down after only the outer bag (*left*) was spun. Although the entrance to the outer bag was on the bottom, the caterpillar built the inner bag with its opening on the top (*right*).

You might conclude from these observations that the caterpillar orients its spinning based on gravity.

Studies such as these, with different animals, have shown the importance of internal and external stimuli in animal behavior. The experiments show that behavior not only is a reaction to stimuli from the external environment, such as gravity, but also is controlled by internal stimuli such as hormones and enzymes.

Complex innate, or instinctive, behavior often depends on the animal's physiology. For example, the courting and reproductive behavior of birds and fishes depends on the levels of certain hormones. The levels of hormones, in turn, may be due to external factors, such as the length of day.

The courting and reproductive behavior of the three-spined stickleback fish has been widely studied as one example of the interaction of internal and external stimuli (Figure 25.10 on the next page). In early spring, reproductive hormones cause changes in both the appearance and behavior of the stickleback. The male moves to the warm, shallow edge of the pond to select a breeding area, or territory. Physical change, such as the red color of the male's belly, becomes an external stimulus affecting the behavior of the females and other males.

Experiments have shown that specific stimuli cause a certain type of behavior by the stickleback. For example, the male stickleback defends its territory against other males of the same species. The male defends its nest even against a dummy fish of any shape in the same territory, as long as the dummy has a red belly. On the other hand, if a model of a male stickleback

CONNECTIONS

Complex instinctive behavior may be affected by hormones. These behaviors then, are a part of the organism's regulatory systems.

FIGURE 25.10 At breeding time a male stickleback has a red belly. The male attracts a female with dancelike swimming motions and leads her to the nest he has built. The female lays eggs, then leaves. The male enters the nest, fertilizes the eggs, and thereafter guards the nest from intruders.

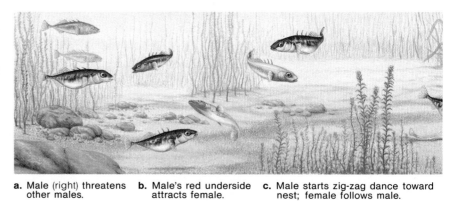

a. Male (right) threatens other males.   **b.** Male's red underside attracts female.   **c.** Male starts zig-zag dance toward nest; female follows male.

d. Male guides female into nest.   **e.** Male taps female near tail; female lays eggs.   **f.** Male bites female; female leaves nest; male enters nest and fertilizes eggs.

without a red underside is presented, the male stickleback does not display fighting behavior (Figure 25.11). The red underside seems to be the stimulus that starts the male's defense behavior.

The effect of external and internal stimuli on the innate behavior of some vertebrates is of tremendous interest to biologists. Innate behavior, although unlearned and characteristic of a specific species, is not as rigid and unchanging as once was thought—changes sometimes are observed. For example, both the external stimuli and the internal condition of the animal affect the nature and strength of its responses.

FIGURE 25.11 Aggression in the male stickleback (a) is triggered by a simple external stimulus. The realistic model (b) without the red belly produces no response at all. All the other models (c) produce a strong response because they have the necessary red underside.

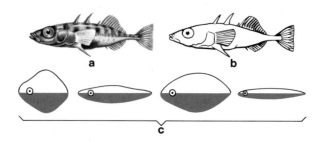

Biological Challenges

MIGRATION

One of the most remarkable aspects of animal behavior is that animals have what might be termed a sense of place. Foraging animals may move great distances from their homes and still find their way back. Other animals demonstrate a more impressive ability to find their way back, even after traveling several hundreds or thousands of kilometers away during migration.

Many common birds migrate across large portions of a continent or even from one continent to another. The arctic tern probably travels the greatest distance of any migrant. In autumn, the terns that nest in the arctic regions of North America migrate across the Atlantic and travel south along the coasts of Europe and Africa until they reach the tip of South Africa. They then cross the South Atlantic to Antarctica, where they spend the summer. This journey covers roughly 18 000 kilometers.

Many other bird migrations are spectacular because of the great endurance they require. A flock of blue geese and snow geese flew from James Bay, Canada, to Louisiana, apparently without stopping. They traveled 2700 kilometers in 60 hours.

How do birds find their way on these journeys? Some species of birds (and other animals) use celestial navigation—orienting by the sun and the stars. The Indigo Bunting, for example, fixes on the North Star. Starlings orient by the sun and can compensate for the sun's apparent movement. If an experimental "sun" is held in a constant position, starlings change their orientation steadily at a rate of about 15° per hour.

If birds can use the sun and stars for navigation, why do the migratory flights of birds not stop when the sky is overcast? In early migration studies, some researchers suggested that birds could sense the Earth's magnetic field and use it for navigation. Others dismissed this idea because they assumed animals could not detect the low energy levels of the Earth's magnetic field.

FIGURE B Transmission electron micrograph of *Aquaspirillum magnetotacticum*, a bacterium containing magnetite particles. This magnetite chain acts as a miniature compass.

Finally, during the 1970s, the idea that animals sense the Earth's magnetic field and can use it to orient and navigate became widely accepted. Some of the most convincing data came from homing pigeons. Homing pigeons were released some distance from their loft. Observers recorded the direction in which they began to fly. Even in cloudy weather, the pigeons oriented themselves in the direction of their home loft. Further experiments involved attaching small bar magnets to pigeon's backs. The birds became disoriented, but only on cloudy days. Thus, it appears that a magnetic compass for orientation is a backup to a celestial compass.

How do organisms actually perceive magnetic fields? This question has been only partially answered. Some organisms possess magnetite (Fe_3O_4), an iron-bearing mineral, in their bodies. For example, bacteria that show orientation in magnetic fields contain chains of magnetite particles (Figure B). These particles also have been reported in a number of other animals, such as tuna, dolphins, whales, and pigeons. It is apparent that organisms can respond to relatively weak magnetic fields. It is now important to determine how organisms respond to those fields, and to investigate the adaptive significance of those responses.

FIGURE 25.12 Body language is frequently an involuntary form of behavior.

25.6 Human Behavior

In animals with very complex nervous systems, behavior becomes more complicated, and therefore more difficult to study. Innate behaviors make up fewer of the total acts observed, and the environmental influences on learning increase. Human subjects often claim that they determine their own behavior. Does this opinion mean that humans are free of their evolutionary and genetic heritage? Are you *always* in control of what you do?

We are not separate from our evolutionary past. Much of the human body is controlled and coordinated involuntarily (Figure 25.12). We usually blink, blush, breathe, digest a meal, and get goose bumps without thinking about these activities. Although learning plays a greater role in humans than in other animals, there is no evidence that human behavior is free of evolutionary and genetic influences.

Survival value is easy to identify as an explanation for some human behaviors. Holding your hands in the air when a robber is pointing a gun at you will probably allow you to live longer than if you attempt to take the gun away, for example. Yet humans, the most behaviorally complicated species, are also the most puzzling. Our behavior is full of inconsistencies. For example, numerous individuals have placed their own lives in jeopardy to save the life of someone unknown and unrelated to them. On the other hand, some citizens living in large cities have completely ignored pleas for help from people who had been assaulted.

We humans also are able to contemplate our species' past and future. Awareness that our activities can negatively affect our descendants in the future should be of survival value to our species. Yet consider that population numbers, energy consumption, and environmental damage are increasing. Many established negative behaviors and activities—those with known injurious results—continue, possibly endangering the survival of our species. How is survival an issue for our species in these circumstances? If we learn more about the basis of behavior in ourselves and other animals, we may be able to better understand our behavior. We can then develop models to predict how our current behavior will affect our species in the future, eliminate negative behaviors, and develop positive behaviors.

CHECK AND CHALLENGE

1. Identify examples of how internal and external stimuli affect the behavior of an organism.
2. Does human behavior have survival value? Explain your answer.
3. Do humans always determine their own behavior? Why or why not?
4. What are some examples of innate human behavior?
5. How is an organism's physiology related to its innate behavior?
6. What types of human behaviors might need to be changed for the species to survive?

Populations and Organization _____

25.7 Populations and Behavior

It can be said that all living things are interdependent, since the world population consists of all living organisms, not merely almost six billion humans. Experimentally, however, a **population** is defined as all the organisms of a single species that live at the same time in the same area. The group that makes up a population can be further divided into the adult and juvenile populations or the male and female populations. Unless such a division is specified, however, a population is all the individuals of that species living in that place—regardless of their age or gender.

Many animal populations are considered a group only because they share a common habitat. They are not organized in any way, as humans are in neighborhoods or other familiar groups. For example, you may not think of all the earthworms in your garden or all the trout in a specific stream as populations. For these animals, the gene pool and gene flow (Chapter 16) are almost the only common population characteristics. Populations of this type often include animals that produce many fertilized eggs and then abandon them. What animals fit this description?

Activities within many animal populations are organized through complex, genetically-transmitted behavioral patterns. Some types of ants, for example, have job specialization in their colony and also maintain herds of aphids. The ants place the aphids on succulent plant leaves and "milk" the aphids to obtain some of the colony's food (Figure 25.13). Other genetically-influenced behaviors within a population include the recognition of prey and predators, the physical distribution of individuals, types of communication, and the competition for food, territory, and mates. Of course, such behaviors also are influenced by the environment—learning, planning, or reasoning can change such behaviors, especially in humans.

How much do you know of the populations of insects, birds, and other creatures you frequently see on your way to and from school? Are these individuals' activities solitary or part of an organized whole?

FIGURE 25.13 An ant tending aphids

Try Investigation 25C, A Field Study of Animal Behavior.

25.8 Social Behavior

The presence in a population of leaders, followers, job specialists, and coordinators is evidence of organized and usually cooperative behavior. Populations that exhibit such patterns are identified as **animal societies**.

Societies may be loose-knit or highly organized. Dogs in a relatively stable neighborhood have a fairly well-organized society consisting of a "top dog" that is dominant over all the others; each dog has its own social standing. There is no constant, serious fighting, although there are "skirmishes" during which an "underdog" tries to improve its social position or by which a more dominant dog maintains its status. You can easily observe the nonviolent behavioral acts that acknowledge which dog has the higher place in the society. (See **Appendix 25B**, Aggression.) However, a new

FOCUS ON *Caste Systems*

Social insects, such as termites and bees, have a caste system. The division of labor is indicated by body types that are adapted for special jobs. The honeybee society has three castes: queen, drone, and worker (Figure C). A drone supplies the sperm, and the queen supplies the eggs. The workers carry out all other activities of the hive. What differences can you see among the queen, the worker, and the drone?

The different body structures are determined by diet and by heredity. The workers and queens develop from female larvae, and the drones from male larvae. During development, the workers and queens are fed "royal jelly" for the first three days. After that only the few larvae that become queens are fed royal jelly. When the queens emerge, they fight until a lone survivor becomes the hive's queen.

Neither the queen nor the drones gather or produce food. Their role in the hive is to reproduce. A drone must catch a flying queen to mate. Drones with the more highly developed sensory organs, longer wings, and longer antennae are most successful in mating.

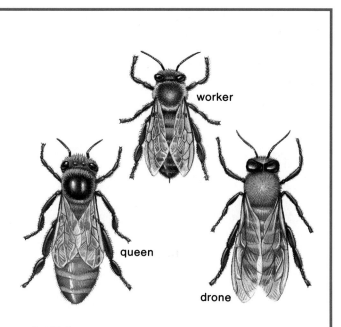

FIGURE C The three castes of honeybees

The workers gather the food, produce wax, rear and protect the brood, and carry on all the work of the hive. Their special body adaptations increase the work efficiency of the hive and thereby the chance of the society's survival.

FIGURE 25.14 A prairie dog's bark can warn other animals in the general area, as well as members of the immediate population.

dog will be quickly challenged by the neighborhood dogs. The new dog either submits immediately and accepts a lower, less dominant position, bluffs the challenger into submitting, or fights. The outcome of the fight determines the new dog's social position. Such behaviors, similar to those seen in wolves, reveal **dominance hierarchies**, levels in a society where individuals fit.

Many animal societies are so highly organized that the population's survival depends on each type of individual doing its job. These types of societies have **caste systems**. In some cases each caste is so specialized that the bodies of the members are actually different. The physical characteristics of ants belonging to the soldier caste differ markedly from those of ants in the worker caste, even though they are the same species.

25.9 Social Behavior and Communication

Living in societies may benefit a species in many ways. One advantage of social organization is defense from predators. Musk oxen form a defensive circle when threatened by wolves and thus are less vulnerable than an individual facing predators alone. Similarly, the members of a prairie dog town cooperate by warning each other of danger with a special bark (Figure 25.14). Thus, each individual in the social organization benefits from the senses of all the group members. Large numbers of prey grouped together also may distract or even frighten away predators.

Social behavior also can benefit reproduction. Living in a group can synchronize reproductive behavior through mutual stimulation. For example, a bird's mating calls and displays can start prereproductive endocrine changes in fellow colony members. Due to higher levels of social stimulation, large colonies of gulls produce more young per nest than do small gull colonies.

Other benefits of social behavior include increased care of the young through social networks and cooperation in obtaining food. There also are increased opportunities for reproduction (especially for dominant individuals), for division of labor, and for the distribution of useful information.

If social living is so advantageous, why do species with solitary life styles exist? The answer is that living alone also offers advantages. For example, species that avoid predators by camouflage are more likely to survive if spread out in their environment. There is no overriding adaptive advantage to social behavior that selects against a solitary way of life. A species' life style is closely linked to its ecological role and environment.

Communication is the way one animal influences the behavior of another. Imagine you see a dog eating a bone. You walk to the dog and reach out as if to take the bone away. You would probably notice several changes in the dog's behavior and appearance. The hair on its back may rise, its lips may curl back to expose its teeth, and it may utter peculiar, guttural noises. It is communicating with you. You would find out the meaning of the message, if you were unwise enough to grab the bone.

Many animals communicate by sound. The hunting wolf gives a characteristic combination of a short bark and howl when closing in for the kill. A human may yell a warning when someone is about to get hit by a baseball. All these sounds tell something specific to the listener, and the listener reacts by fleeing or ducking, depending on the sound.

Different animals also communicate by sight, smell, touch, and taste. The pronghorns of the western United States (Figure 25.15), give a visual

FIGURE 25.15 *(left)* Pronghorns, an antelopelike animal. The rump patch of white hairs usually lies flat. When muscles cause these hairs to stand up, nearby pronghorns are warned of an intruder or other danger.

FIGURE 25.16 *(right)* Male prairie chickens, *Tympanuchus cupido*, inflate colored neck sacks and produce loud, booming calls during their mating season.

alarm by flashing the white hair of their rump patch. Visual signals may be part of a display. Courtship displays are common in bird populations (Figure 25.16 on page 569). Such displays can establish cooperation between males and females, and help ensure mating or care of the young.

Like many animals, female silkworm moths produce a chemical substance, called a **pheromone**, that alters the behavior of members of its species. The female's pheromone acts as a sex attractant that the male moths smell with their antennae. Small amounts of this chemical are carried downwind from the female. When a few molecules reach the male's antennae, he is stimulated to find the female and mate. Natural selection favors males with receptors sensitive enough to detect the chemical at great distances. Males with less well-developed sensory systems fail to locate a female and thus are reproductively eliminated from the population.

Honeybees communicate the location of food through dance (Figure 25.17). A honeybee that finds nectar returns to the hive, gives the nectar to the other bees, and begins a dance. A round dance tells the others to search for food nearby. A figure eight means the food is far away. The orientation of this dance reveals the nectar's location in relation to the sun.

Studies in communication and behavior have revealed that wild chimpanzees communicate in various ways. When they play, they use a panting laughter. When young chimpanzees are frightened or lonely, they whimper. When chimpanzees meet after a separation they appear to greet each other much as humans do. They also use a sound to show rage or anger.

Physical contact among chimpanzees seems to extend their vocal communication. They pat each other on the back, embrace, and even hold hands. Grooming is an important social activity. Do chimpanzees feel love,

FIGURE 25.17 (a) Round dance, (b) waggle dance. The direction of the waggle dance apparently tells observing bees where the food is in relation to the sun. For example, in (c), the food is in a straight line from the hive to the sun; in (d) the food is on the opposite side of the hive from the sun; and in (e), the food is 60 degrees to the left of the sun.

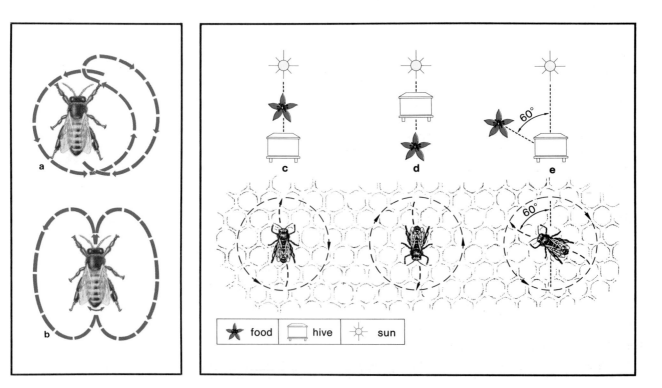

FIGURE 25.18 This young chimp is using sign language to communicate.

anger, acceptance, rejection, and friendship? Evidence from field studies indicates they do. Using sign language (Figure 25.18), chimpanzees also can learn to communicate facts and feelings (or judgments) to humans.

Humans have the most highly organized societies of all. Our societies are made possible by the most abstract and complex system of communication in the animal kingdom. In human societies all sorts of information, general and specific, are passed among individuals and from generation to generation by various means. Many of us have been taught the same nursery rhymes and fairy stories. To communicate, humans use a wide variety of written and vocal symbols and other signals. We can write poetry and novels for others to read, and we can compose, paint, sculpt, and build to convey thoughts and feelings. We smile at one another when we are happy and cry when we are sad. We often engage in physical contact such as holding hands and hugging, and we commonly use the other senses and instruments that are extensions of these senses. Our elaborate systems of communication are unique in the living world.

CHECK AND CHALLENGE

1. How do dominance hierarchies help organize a population?
2. Explain how a caste system differs from a dominance hierarchy.
3. How is social behavior advantageous for individuals? Populations?
4. Describe how an individual can influence the behavior of another.
5. Why is communication necessary for a cooperative society?
6. How do displays promote cooperation?
7. How is the use of pheromones an example of natural selection?

Summary

An organism's behavior is adapted to the demands of the environment in which the organism lives. Behavior is the result of evolution and, as with other characteristics of an organism, can be investigated by science.

There are two general types of behavior, innate and learned. Both forms of behavior are influenced by internal and external stimuli. Innate behavior is not dependent on environmental experience and can be easily overlooked in studying populations. Learned behavior consists of the responses an organism develops as a result of environmental experiences. Innate behavior can be changed by learning.

Learned behavior can be difficult to determine. Whether an animal uses trial and error, experience, or reasoning to solve a problem is hard to determine. Generally, simple learning occurs either through habituation or conditioning.

Societies exhibit cooperative behavior. Different societies may have different social structure, such as a dominance hierarchy or a caste system. This cooperative behavior may confer many advantages to the members of the society. These advantages can include protection and increased successful reproduction.

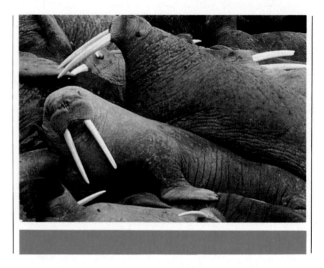

Social animals must be able to communicate with each other. This communication can be chemical, visual, acoustical, or physical. Human societies are the most complex and employ a wide variety of signals to communicate.

Key Concepts

1. Complete and extend the following concept map using concept words and linking words of your choice.

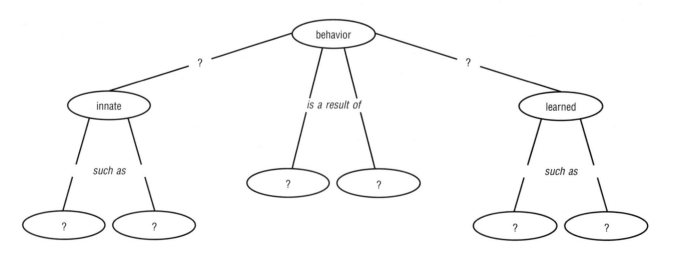

Reviewing Ideas

1. What are some environmental stimuli that might bring about responses in organisms?

2. How is behavior related to the survival of individual organisms? The survival of a population?

3. How is the study of animal behavior useful in approaching the study of human behavior?

4. Explain how societies differ from populations.

5. How does the form of a group affect the life of its members?

6. How do castes solve the problems of conflict versus cooperation?

7. How does innate behavior affect the formation of societies?

8. How may learning be related to social behavior?

Using Concepts

1. Have human societies evolved castes like the bees and the ants? Explain.

2. How would you determine if a dominance hierarchy existed in one of the following groups? What evidence would you seek?
   a. a group of your friends
   b. a group of children on a playground
   c. one of your classes at school
   d. your family

3. How would you determine if walking is innate or learned?

4. Explain how individual survival and species survival in humans may correspond in some behavioral situations yet conflict in others.

5. How would you plan an experiment to test imprinting in baby chicks? What useful background information might be obtained from a commercial hatchery?

6. People may respond to a human behavioral study with improved performance that is unre-lated to the study itself. The human subjects try harder. How could you design a control for this unwanted effect on the study?

7. Ants spread scent trails from the anthill to food. How would you find out whether the ants require the scent trails to find their way back to the anthill?

8. Compare the scent trails of ants with the dancing of honeybees. Are the two functions similar? Are *both* forms of communication? Explain.

9. Which is more efficient, a society organized by conscious cooperation or by innate behavior? Defend your reasoning with examples.

10. It was suggested in this chapter that societies are a product of evolution. What type of evidence supports this idea?

Synthesis

1. Do plants respond in ways similar to animals to internal and external stimuli? Give examples.

2. Would you call these plant responses "behavior"? Why or why not? Defend your position.

Extensions

1. Go to a park, shopping mall, or bank. Observe the ways in which people behave toward one another in various circumstances. Write a report detailing what you observed.

2. Go to the zoo. Pick a group of animals—for example, gorillas. Spend several hours observing their behavior and write a report about what you saw. Be sure to highlight the similarities and differences between their behavior and human behavior.

3. Choose an extinct species and research that species in the library. Write an essay on how the behavior of that species might have influenced their ability to survive. Possible topics could be the passenger pigeon or the Carolina parakeet.

CONTENTS

Interrelationships

*L*ife on Earth is extremely diverse. Each organism is unique, yet also similar to other organisms. No organism can live entirely alone, and no population can live without interacting with other populations and with the environment. The distribution of organisms on Earth is a result of the nature of the environment and the ways in which the organisms interact with it. The actions of the organisms affect the environment, and the environment in turn influences the actions of the organisms. Thus, the environment and the organisms that live within it complement one another. This complementarity is a product of evolution through natural selection, and it causes continuous changes.

This chapter discusses how the environment influences the types of organisms that live in it, their special adaptations to that environment, and how all organisms are dependent upon each other. It also explains how the flow of energy and the cycling of matter support the diversity of life on Earth.

*B*ased on the vegetation you see, what inferences can you make about the climate here?

CONNECTIONS

*O*rganisms and the environment in which they live are complementary in that they constantly influence one another.

◆ *The Garden of the Gods, Colorado.*

The Character of Ecosystems _____

26.1 Abiotic Factors

The biosphere is composed of all Earth's ecosystems. It is a patchwork of habitats (Section 3.3) that differ in abiotic factors such as temperature range and amount of rainfall and sunlight received. These environmental conditions may be limiting factors because of their effect on the distribution and variety of living organisms (Figure 26.1 on the next page).

Special adaptations allow some organisms to live at extreme temperatures. For example, some bacteria can live only in hot springs because their enzymes have evolved to function best at high temperatures. Other aquatic organisms—certain Antarctic fish, for example—have "antifreeze" molecules in their blood that allow them to tolerate the extremely cold temperatures of their environment.

Water is essential for life, but often there may be too little or too much. Both plants and animals have adaptations that permit survival in the face

FIGURE 26.1 What abiotic factors affect these tundra plants?

of the extreme variations present on Earth. Aquatic organisms live in an abundance of water, yet they still face problems with water balance. Marine fish must resist being "pickled" by salty sea water, and freshwater fish must keep their tissues from being diluted. Water balance is maintained either by excreting salts out of the animal into the sea (marine fish) or by pumping water out of the tissues into the surrounding water (freshwater fish). Terrestrial, or land, organisms face the threat of drying up. They must conserve both water *and* salts, and have appropriate adaptations for both. Desert organisms are especially vulnerable to water loss. Cacti, for example, have waxy surfaces that minimize water loss through transpiration. Small desert mammals are nocturnal, avoiding the hot, dry air of the day. (See Chapter 21.)

Most ecosystems are powered primarily by sunlight. Photosynthetic organisms use sunlight to manufacture molecules that store the energy and carbon needed by all organisms. In terrestrial environments, light is usually not a limiting factor. In ponds, lakes, and oceans, however, the intensity and quality of light decreases with depth. This decrease in light limits the downward distribution and numbers of photosynthetic organisms. As a result, most photosynthesis in aquatic environments occurs near the surface of the water.

Other abiotic factors also affect terrestrial organisms. The physical structure, pH, and mineral composition of soil are all important limiting factors in the distribution of plants and, hence, of the animals that feed on

FOCUS ON *Plants and Salt Tolerance*

A common and important stress on plants in coastal areas and poorly drained deserts is high salt levels in the soil. In such an area, plants face two problems: 1) obtaining enough water from the soil, and 2) dealing with potentially toxic levels of sodium, chloride, and carbonate. Some crop plants, such as beets and tomatoes, are more salt-tolerant than others, such as onions and peas. Some plants can live where salt levels in the soil are very high. One plant, saltbush, is tolerant of high salt levels because it concentrates the sodium and chloride in its outer tissues. Saltbush accumulates salt in epidermal bladders on its surface, keeping internal levels low (Figure A). Salt from the leaf tissues is transferred through a small stalk into the bladder. As the leaf ages, the salt concentration in the bladders increases. Eventually the bladders burst, releasing salt to the outside of the leaf.

FIGURE A Scanning electron micrograph of salt bladders on the leaf of the saltbush, *Atriplex spongiosa*, X450.

FIGURE 26.2 Most of the branches on these trees point in one direction. From which direction does the wind blow?

them. For example, clay soils with their tiny particles dry out quickly at the surface. Only deeply rooted plants do well in such conditions. Too much salt in the soil makes it difficult for plants to absorb water.

Wind—air set in motion by heat from sunlight—may increase cooling and drying by carrying heat and water away from the organism. Wind increases water loss by speeding up evaporation in animals and transpiration in plants. Wind also can affect the form and structure of plants. Figure 26.2 shows the effect of wind on the growth of tree limbs.

Fires, floods, avalanches, and other catastrophes may remove organisms from an area temporarily. Sooner or later, however, the area is repopulated by survivors or recolonized by organisms from outside. For example, many of the shrubs in coastal California, where fires are common, store food in fire-resistant root crowns, enabling these plants to resprout after a cool fire.

Organisms survive and reproduce successfully nearly everywhere in the biosphere, tolerating extreme variations in the physical environment. Usually, however, there is a trade-off involved: adaptation to one environment generally means restriction from another. For example, saltbush cannot compete with other shrub species on moist soils, light-tolerant trees such as oaks cannot survive in the shade, trout are pickled in sea water, and marine fish such as tuna will drown in a freshwater lake.

26.2 Succession

The survival and reproduction of species adapted to stable environments is one matter, but what happens to organisms when environments change? The gradual process by which one type of community replaces another is called **succession**. Succession can begin even on a bare lifeless substrate, such as rocks. Lichens usually grow first, forming small pockets of soil and breaking down the stone. Mosses then may colonize, eventually followed by ferns and the seedlings of flowering plants. After many thousands of years, the rocks may be completely broken down, and the vegetation like that of the surrounding forest or grassland. (See Figure 26.3.)

Lakes and ponds, as well as bare rock or disturbed areas, are subject to succession. Plants standing along the edge of a lake, such as cattails and rushes, those that are submerged, such as pond weeds, and other organisms may all contribute to the formation of rich organic soil (Figure 26.4). As this process continues, the lake may gradually fill with vegetation. Eventually, the area where the lake once stood may become indistinguishable from the surrounding landscape.

Wherever succession begins, the early stages are generally dominated by plants that disperse easily, grow rapidly, and have adaptations that favor colonization. Most of these colonizers are small annuals that grow close to the ground and produce many seeds, as opposed to perennials with well-developed roots, stems, and leaves. Common colonizers can tolerate a wide range of adverse environmental conditions such as poor soil, high temperatures, and low precipitation. In later stages of succession,

FIGURE 26.3 Possible successional stages and animals in a coniferous forest

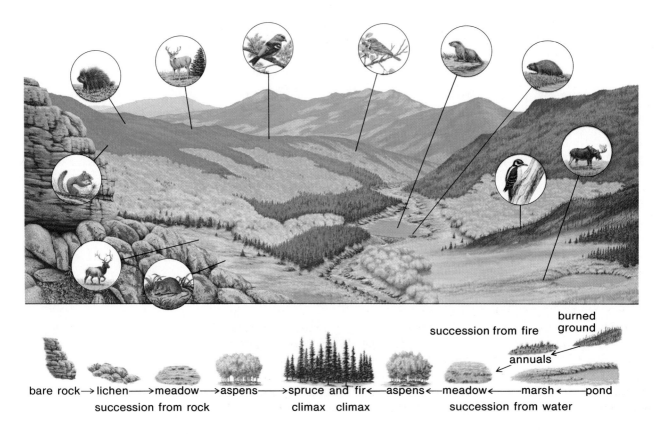

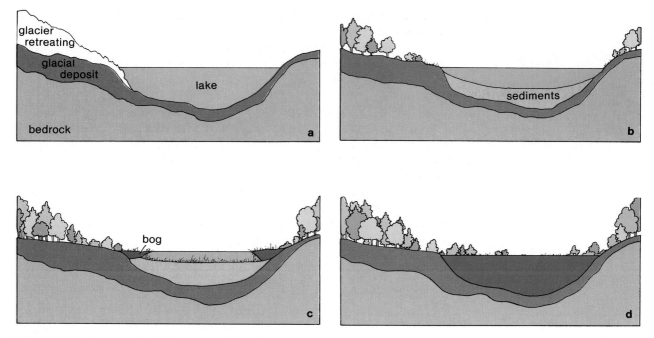

FIGURE 26.4   An example of lake succession

the dominant species tend to be longer-living—with large roots, stems, and leaves—and able to endure increased competition and increased shade.

Interactions between animals, such as predation and competition, become more complex and extensive as succession progresses, thus opening new niches and increasing the diversity of animals that live in the community. Eventually, the web of interaction may become so intricate that no additional species can fit into the community unless niches become available through localized extinction. Such a community is considered to be a climax community. Unlike the other communities in the succession process, a climax community is not replaced by another community unless a disturbance or change in the climate occurs. For example, if a single spruce dies, the space it leaves behind is too shaded by neighboring spruces for a sun-loving tree such as an aspen to grow. A young spruce, tolerant of shade, will probably take the place of the old one, thus maintaining the community. However, the climate is always changing, the process of succession is often slow, and human activities may affect a region's vegetation. As a result, succession does not always lead to a climax community.

Most communities are in a constant state of flux. The types and numbers of species change throughout all the stages of succession, even at the climax stage. The course of succession varies, depending on the species that colonize an area in the early stages, and on the type of disturbances causing further changes. Periodic fires, floods, hurricanes, and even unseasonable temperatures can prevent a community from ever reaching a state of equilibrium. When disturbances are severe and frequent, community membership may be restricted to organisms that are good colonizers. If

FIGURE 26.5 An area of Mount St. Helens colonized by *Penstemon*

disturbances are rare and mild, the species that are the most competitive may make up the community. Species diversity, therefore, may be greatest when disturbances are *intermediate* in frequency and severity, because then organisms of many different successional stages make up the community.

The recovery of the Mt. St. Helens area after the volcanic eruption in 1980 provided an interesting study in succession. (See Figure 26.5.) Scientists were divided on their predictions of how the recovery would progress. One group expected an orderly progression beginning with pioneer plants and eventually ending in a mature forest. Others thought recovery would begin as a matter of chance—a seed would arrive, perhaps blown by the wind, take root, and then play a role in influencing the other plants that would grow nearby. To the surprise of both groups, recovery is occurring both ways. Seeds of alpine lupine, a pioneer plant, began to grow in areas that were nearly sterile. After they died, their stalks and dead leaves collected sand and dust particles, allowing middle-stage plants to root. This pattern of recovery supports the orderly succession idea. At the same time, however, individual trees, mostly alder, quickly became established in the middle of desolate areas, without the benefit of earlier pioneer plants.

CHECK AND CHALLENGE

1. How do aquatic and terrestrial organisms differ in their problems of water and salt balance?
2. How do abiotic factors influence the adaptations of organisms?
3. Why is succession not always a steady progression from bare rock to a climax community?
4. Can the different limiting factors, such as water and light, influence one another? Explain your answer, and give an example.

Types of Ecosystems

The process of evolution through natural selection has produced organisms with adaptations that allow them to survive and reproduce under extreme conditions in different biomes.

26.3 Terrestrial Biomes

Regions of the world with similar physical environments usually have similar vegetation. These areas are called **biomes** (BY ohmz). Biomes are defined by the most conspicuous types of vegetation—those plants that are the largest or most numerous and convert the most energy from the sun. The main climatic factors affecting the growth of vegetation, and thus the geographic distribution of biomes, are the temperature and rainfall at different altitudes and latitudes. The boundaries of biomes are usually indistinct because changes in climate from place to place are gradual. The major biomes of the world are shown in Figure 26.6. Refer to the figure as you read about the different biomes in the descriptions that follow.

Tropical rain forests are found on lowlands near the equator, where temperature and day length show little seasonal variation (Figure 26.7, left, on the next page). Rainfall in equatorial areas, however, depends on elevation and the effect of mountains on moisture-laden winds. Very little light reaches the ground because the tall dense canopy of foliage blocks the light. The low light intensity on the forest floor limits the growth of vegetation and, hence, the animal species that live there. Figure 26.7 (right) on the next page shows the typical vegetation layers in a tropical rain forest. These forests are the most complex of all communities and support more species of plants and animals than any other biome.

Many of the world's rain forests have been cleared for lumber, farming, mining, or cattle ranching (Figure 26.8 on page 583). Beef is a major product of such Latin American countries as Costa Rica. The demand for beef in the United States, especially from fast-food restaurant chains, has encouraged the removal of a tremendous amount of rain forest to make pasture for grazing. Soil in the rain forest is poor and erodes easily once the vegetation is removed. As a result, totally cleared land recovers slowly, if

FIGURE 26.6 Major biomes of Earth. Many parts of Earth have not been thoroughly studied, and even where observations are plentiful, ecologists sometimes disagree about the correct interpretation.

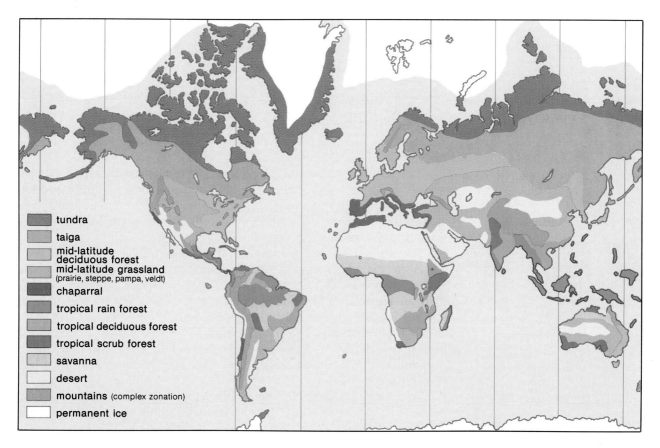

- tundra
- taiga
- mid-latitude deciduous forest
- mid-latitude grassland (prairie, steppe, pampa, veldt)
- chaparral
- tropical rain forest
- tropical deciduous forest
- tropical scrub forest
- savanna
- desert
- mountains (complex zonation)
- permanent ice

FIGURE 26.7 (*left*) Rain forest in Hawaii. (*right*) The layering effect in a tropical rain forest. Virtually no sunlight reaches the rain forest floor, and few organisms are able to live on the ground as compared to in the trees.

ever. Usually the land degrades. Much of the world's tropical rain forest is already gone, and some scientists predict that the remainder will be gone entirely by the end of this century. Loss of the rain forests will cause changes in the local weather and perhaps in the world climate. An inevitable result is a large-scale reduction in the variety and abundance of many plant and animal species.

The savanna is a tropical or subtropical grassland with a few scattered trees (Figure 26.9). Grasslands are usually found in areas with low precipitation, generally in the interior of continents. There are three distinct seasons in the savanna: cool and dry, hot and dry, and warm and wet. Most savanna soils are rather poor.

The savanna is home to some of the world's largest herbivores—organisms that eat plant material. These include elephants, giraffes, rhinos, and kangaroos, as well as many types of grazers, such as antelope. Because there are few trees or other tall plants in the grasslands, most animals' nests and shelters are on or under the ground.

Deserts often have severely hot and dry climates, in which temperatures may reach 54° C. There are also cool deserts, where winter temperatures are very cold. Both types are characterized by a lack of precipitation. (See Figure 26.10a, b.)

The driest deserts have almost no perennial vegetation. In less arid areas, the predominant plants are usually scattered shrubs, interspersed

FIGURE 26.8 The clearing of rain forests could have major effects on the world's weather and climate.

FIGURE 26.9 Elephants, *Loxodonta africana*, and zebras, *Equus burchelli*, share a water hole on the savanna in Kenya.

with cacti or other succulents. Growth and reproduction in the desert are stimulated by brief, heavy rains, which result in spectacular blooms of plants. Desert plants have physiological and structural adaptations to extreme drought and temperatures. For example, cacti and other succulents store water, thus avoiding dehydration. (See Figure 26.11 on page 584.) Other adaptations, such as those of CAM (crassulacean acid metabolism) plants, are discussed in Section 7.11.

Seed-eating animals, such as ants, birds, and rodents, are common in deserts. Lizards and snakes are important predators. Like the desert plants,

FIGURE 26.10 (*a*) Hot desert. (*b*) Cool desert. How do the plants of the cool desert differ from those of the hot desert?

a

b

FIGURE 26.11 The pleated structure of the trunk of the saguaro cactus, *Cereus gigantea*, allows the plant to expand or contract as it gains or loses water.

many of these animals are adapted to living where there are low amounts of available water and extreme temperatures. Many desert animals live in burrows and are active only at night. Others are light colored, thereby reflecting light. Some animals have adaptations that enable them to conserve water. The kangaroo rat, which lives in the American Southwest, can survive without drinking any water (Figure 26.12). What adaptations do you think might enable the kangaroo rat to survive in this manner?

Mid-latitude areas along coasts where cool ocean currents circulate are characterized by mild, rainy winters and long, hot, dry summers. These areas, such as the California coast, are dominated by chaparral (shap uh RAL), or brushland, communities. These biomes are composed of dense, spiny shrubs with tough evergreen leaves, often coated with a waxy material that inhibits moisture loss but increases the plants' flammability. Chaparral vegetation is also found along the coastlines of Chile, southwestern Africa, southwestern Australia, and the region around the Mediterranean Sea. Plants from these regions are unrelated, but they resemble one another in form and function and show the same types of adaptations. Annual plants are also common in the chaparral during winter and early spring when rainfall is most abundant. Figure 26.13 shows the vegetation of a typical chaparral.

The organisms of the chaparral are adapted to, and maintained by, periodic fires. Many of the shrubs have deep and extensive root systems that permit quick regeneration. The fires burn all the plant structures above the ground, thus releasing the minerals in them. The minerals are then available for use by the new plant shoots. In addition, many chaparral

FIGURE 26.12 The kangaroo rat, a desert dweller, can survive without drinking any water.

FIGURE 26.13 A chaparral in California

a   b   c

FIGURE 26.14 (a) Tall-grass prairie; (b) mixed-grass prairie; (c) short-grass prairie

species produce seeds that germinate only after a hot fire, whereas others reproduce by cloning. Deer, fruit-eating birds, rodents, lizards, and snakes are characteristic chaparral animals.

Temperate grasslands, such as the prairies of North America, have most of the same characteristics as savannas, except that trees are limited to areas near streams. Grasslands typically receive 25 to 28 inches of annual precipitation, have low winter temperatures, and may be relatively high in elevation. Drought and periodic fires keep woody shrubs and trees from invading the environment.

The grasslands expanded in size when warmer and drier climates prevailed after the last retreat of the glaciers. Coupled with that expansion was the diversification of grazing animals, such as the bison and pronghorns of North America. Because of the openness of the grasslands, speed and endurance are important adaptations that enable many organisms to escape predators. Small mammals seek shelter below ground, and grassland birds and reptiles escape detection because of protectively colored skins. Three distinct types of grasslands are native to North America: the tall-grass prairie in the northern Midwest, the short-grass prairie in the area east of the Rocky Mountains to about Kansas, and the mixed-grass prairie in the central Great Plains. Figure 26.14 shows these typical grasslands. The geographic distribution of these grasses is due mostly to the proximity to the Rocky Mountains and the rain shadow the mountains produce. The boundaries of the grasslands are indistinct. They have many animal and plant species in common.

Temperate forests develop throughout the mid-latitude regions where there is enough moisture to support the growth of large trees. Temperatures range from cold in the winter ($-30°$ C) to hot in the summer ($+35°$ C), with a five- to six-month growing season. Rain and snowfall are abundant, humidity tends to be high, growth and decomposition rates are

FIGURE 26.15 Animals of the temperate forest: (a) southern flying squirrel, *Glaucomys volans;* (b) white-tailed deer, *Odocoileus virginianus*

a
          b

FIGURE 26.16 The northern coniferous forests and high-altitude coniferous forests of all continents make up the taiga biome in which ponds, lakes, and bogs are abundant.

high, and the soil is thick and rich. Although they are more open and not as tall as tropical forests, temperate forests also have several layers of vegetation, usually short herbs, intermediate shrubs, and tall trees.

The temperate forest supports a diversity of animal life (Figure 26.15). A large variety of organisms, such as beetles, sow bugs, and leaf hoppers, live in the soil and leaf litter or feed on the leaves of trees and shrubs. The forest is home for many species of birds and small mammals. In some forests, such larger predators as wolves and mountain lions can still be found.

The taiga (TY guh), known as coniferous or boreal forest, extends across North America, Europe, and Asia. Taiga is also found at higher elevations, such as the mountainous region of western North America (Figure 26.16). It is characterized by harsh winters and short, cool summers. Snow is the major form of precipitation, but this water is not available to plants until the spring thaw.

The taiga vegetation consists primarily of conifers, or evergreens, and is generally very dense. Because these woody plants keep out the sunlight, only mosses, lichens, and a few shrubs can grow near the ground. Most food production, therefore, takes place in the upper parts of the trees. Conifers, including spruce, fir, pine, and hemlock, grow in a variety of combinations with deciduous trees, such as willow, alder, and aspen. However, usually only the conifers are conspicuous.

Taiga animals include squirrels, jays, moose, elk, hares, beavers, and porcupines. Predators of the taiga include grizzly bears, wolves, lynxes, wolverines, mountain lions, and owls. What adaptations to the cold might these predators have?

Beyond the northern limit of tree growth or at very high altitudes is the tundra (TUN druh), where plants are compact, shrubby, and matlike (Figure 26.17). The arctic tundra (determined by latitude) is characterized by permafrost, continuously frozen ground that prevents plant roots from penetrating very far into the soil. Spring comes in mid-May; only plants remaining near the sun-warmed ground can grow, flower, and produce seeds before the advent of fall in August. During the brief, warm summers, daylight lasts for almost 24 hours. Most plant reproduction and growth occur during this period. The tundra may receive less precipitation than many deserts, yet the combination of permafrost, low temperatures, and low evaporation leaves the soil saturated. These conditions also restrict the species that grow there. Dwarf perennial shrubs, sedges, grasses, mosses, and lichens are the dominant forms of vegetation.

Alpine tundra (determined by altitude) is found above the tree line on high mountains. Because of the similarity in conditions, many of the plant and animal species found in the arctic tundra are also found in the alpine tundra. Alpine tundra occurs at all latitudes if the elevation is high enough (Figure 26.18). In contrast to the arctic tundra, day length in the summer is shorter. Brief and intense periods of productivity occur daily in summer, but freezes may happen any night. The long winters, characterized by heavy snowfall and gale winds, cause very short growing seasons.

Many animals of the tundra withstand the cold by living in burrows, having a large body size, or having good body insulation that retains heat. Other species, especially birds, are migratory and leave the area during the harshest part of the winter. Large animals of the tundra include musk oxen and caribou in North America and the reindeer of Europe and Asia. Smaller animals include lemmings, marmots, pikas, white foxes, and snowy owls. (See Figure 26.19 on the next page.)

FIGURE 26.17 What environmental conditions limit the growth of these tundra plants?

FIGURE 26.18 Types of vegetation and animal life are affected by both altitude and latitude.

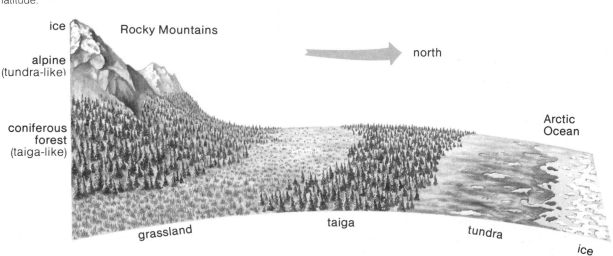

a

b

FIGURE 26.19 Animals of the arctic tundra: (a) snowy owl, *Nyctea scandiaca*, (b) musk ox, *Ovibos moschatus*.

26.4 Aquatic Communities

The largest part of the biosphere is occupied by aquatic habitats. Although the term *biome* is not used to describe the major types of aquatic communities, similar division into several types of environments can be made.

Rivers and streams change significantly from the source, or headwaters, to the point where they empty into an ocean or lake (Figure 26.20). At the source, the water is usually cold, clear, and rapidly moving, has a low salt content, and contains few nutrients. Downstream, the water increases in turbidity, or cloudiness, as well as in its nutrient and salt content. In general, the speed of the current also decreases.

The physical and chemical changes of a river flowing downstream are reflected in the communities of its organisms. Upstream, the communities are relatively simple and include fish such as trout that thrive in water with high levels of dissolved oxygen and low temperatures. Downstream, as pools form, the communities become more complex. Photosynthesis is limited to areas near the banks. As oxygen levels decrease and the temperature increases, species such as carp, catfish, and bass replace the trout.

Rivers and streams usually end in lakes or ponds, standing bodies of water ranging from a few square meters to thousands of square kilometers (Figure 26.21). As a river or stream enters a lake, the speed of the current decreases and suspended particles begin to settle to the bottom. The amount of material that remains suspended in the water and the amount of light scattered by these particles determine the depth to which photosynthesis can occur. Phytoplankton (FYT oh PLANK tun) are microscopic aquatic organisms that carry on photosynthesis.

The waters of lakes and ponds have layers with different physical and chemical features. Phytoplankton and zooplankton (ZOH oh PLANK tun)—

FIGURE 26.20 A mountain brook. What evidence can you see that this aquatic ecosystem has few producers?

FIGURE 26.21 A natural pond. It is easy to see the relationship between the forest and aquatic ecosystems.

heterotrophic, swimming microorganisms—are found in the upper stratus. Photosynthesis takes place in this first layer where sunlight is able to penetrate the water. Nutrients such as phosphorus and nitrogen are the limiting factors in the growth of plankton populations.

Many small fish and aquatic insects feed on plankton. These animals are, in turn, fed on by larger fish, snakes, frogs, toads, and salamanders. Larger predators include raccoons, kingfishers, and osprey.

Marine, or ocean, ecosystems can be described several different ways. Figure 26.22 diagrams the regional labels that are used to distinguish the ecosystems. Refer to the figure as you read the discussion that follows.

The distribution of marine organisms is dependent on the penetration of light, which varies with the depth and clarity of the water. The photic

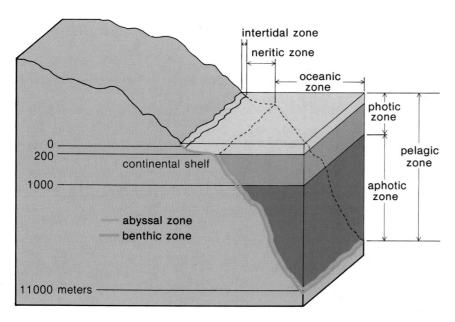

FIGURE 26.22 Marine ecosystems are three-dimensional in nature. Zones depend on depth, light penetration, and distance from the shoreline.

a   b   c

FIGURE 26.23 Littoral zone animals (a) include the sea star, *Linckia multifora*, and cupcoral sponges, *Tubastarea coccinea*. The blue striped grunts, *Haemulon sciurus* (b), are benthic zone animals that live among corals and sponges. This unidentified anemone (c) lives in the abyssal zone.

(FOH tik) zone is the narrow top layer of the ocean where enough light penetrates for photosynthesis to occur. Almost all the energy that sustains marine communities comes from the photosynthesis of phytoplankton in this zone. Underneath the photic zone is the aphotic (AY foh tik) zone where there is insufficient light for photosynthesis. Organisms that live in this zone obtain their energy by consuming living or dead organic material produced in the photic zone.

Marine communities are also described according to depth. The shallow zone where the land meets the water is called the intertidal, or littoral, zone. This area is bounded by the high tide and low tide marks. Barnacles, mussels, sponges, clams, algae, and worms are some of the organisms that inhabit this zone. (See Figure 26.23a.) The second zone, beyond the littoral zone, is called the neritic zone. The neritic zone is the shallow water over the continental shelf. Past the shelf is the third zone, the open ocean, or oceanic zone.

In all these zones, the open water not associated with the sea floor is called the pelagic zone. The sea floor is called the benthic zone. The benthic community consists of bacteria, sponges, worms, sea stars, crustaceans, fish, and other organisms. (See Figure 26.23b.) The area of the benthic zone where light does not penetrate is called the abyssal zone. The few organisms living there are adapted to continuous darkness, cold temperatures, and extreme pressure. (See Figure 26.23c.) Most animals in the abyssal zone are dependent on waste matter from the photic zone above. Many of the bacteria there are chemosynthetic—they obtain their energy from inorganic materials. (See **Appendix 26A**, Vent Ecosystems.)

CHECK AND CHALLENGE

1. What are the major terrestrial biomes of the world and how do they differ from each other?

2. What special adaptations do some of the plants and animals have that allow them to live in their biomes?

3. In what ways are river and stream communities similar to lake and pond communities? How are they different? What accounts for these differences?

4. Relate light, the major limiting factor of marine ecosystems, to the structure of those ecosystems.

5. Discuss the character of the tropical rain forest biome. What is the major limiting factor, and how does it affect the plant and animal life found there?

6. Discuss the three-dimensional character of marine zones and explain what the limiting factors might be for each of the zones.

Energy Flow and Chemical Cycling

26.5 Energy in Ecosystems

All organisms convert energy for use in growth, maintenance, reproduction, and, in many species, locomotion. Producers use light energy to synthesize organic molecules, which can be used to form ATP. (See Chapters 3 and 7.) Consumers acquire their energy second-, third-, or fourth-hand through food chains—simplified food webs (Chapter 3). Ultimately, photosynthesis determines the amount of energy available for most systems.

How is this energy passed through an ecosystem? Each ecosystem has a **trophic** (TROH fik) **structure**, which is determined by the method in which organisms in the ecosystem obtain their energy. This organization, in turn, determines the route of energy flow and the pattern of chemical cycling within the ecosystem. The trophic level supporting all other levels consists of autotrophs that utilize nonliving energy sources, such as light, soil, or the air. The organic compounds they produce are used as fuel for cellular respiration and as building materials for growth. All the other organisms—heterotrophs—are either directly or indirectly dependent on the output of the autotrophs. Herbivores (organisms that eat plants or algae) are the primary consumers. At the next trophic level are secondary consumers—carnivores that eat herbivores. These carnivores may, in turn, be eaten by other carnivores that are tertiary consumers. Some ecosystems have even higher levels of consumers. Decomposers derive their energy from the organic wastes and dead organisms from all trophic levels.

The main producers in terrestrial ecosystems are plants. In most aquatic ecosystems, the primary producers are photosynthetic protists (algae) and cyanobacteria. What are some primary and secondary consumers in terrestrial and aquatic ecosystems?

FIGURE 26.24 In this idealized energy pyramid, 10 percent of the energy available at each trophic level is available at the next level. In actual ecosystems the productivity varies somewhat with organisms involved in the food chains.

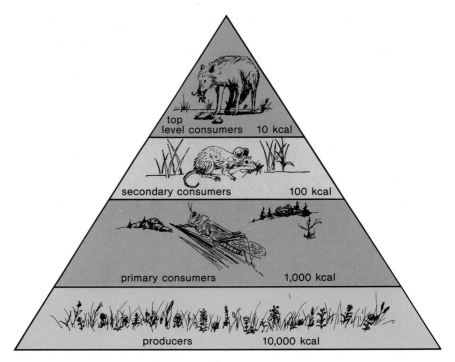

top level consumers   10 kcal

secondary consumers   100 kcal

primary consumers   1,000 kcal

producers   10,000 kcal

Try Investigation 26A, Producers in an Ecosystem.

In most ecosystems, bacteria and fungi are the primary decomposers. They secrete acids and enzymes that digest complex organic compounds, such as cellulose, and then they absorb the smaller digested products. Earthworms and scavengers such as cockroaches also are decomposers.

The transfer of food from one trophic level to another, beginning with the producers, is known as a food chain. However, few ecosystems are so simple that they have only a single food chain. Several different primary consumers may feed on the same plant, and one species of primary consumer may feed on several different plants. Such a branching of food chains occurs at other trophic levels as well. Omnivores, such as humans, eat a variety of producers as well as consumers from different levels. Thus, the feeding relationships in an ecosystem are usually woven into elaborate food webs.

The loss of energy from a food chain can be represented by an energy pyramid (Figure 26.24). The trophic levels are stacked in blocks proportional in size to the kilocalories of energy acquired from the level below. The primary producers are the foundation. In general, each level is one-tenth of the equivalent of the level below it. This concept is often referred to as the 10 percent rule in that only 10 percent of the energy at any given level is available for use (consumption) by the next higher level. Most organisms use or release most of their energy; only a fraction is passed on in a food chain. The important implication in the steplike decline of energy in a food chain is that the number of top-level carnivores that can be sustained in an ecosystem is substantially smaller than the number of low-level consumers and producers. Only about one one-thousandth of the chemical energy fixed by the producers can flow all the way through a three-consumer food chain to a top predator, such as a hawk.

The concept of an energy pyramid also has implications for humans. Eating meat is an inefficient way to obtain the energy fixed by photosynthesis. A human can obtain far more of the original energy by eating grain directly as a primary consumer instead of passing that grain through another trophic level by eating grain-fed beef.

26.6 Chemical Cycles

Chemical elements in ecosystems are limited, and those essential for life must be recycled. Some substances, such as carbon, oxygen, and nitrogen, move through large-scale global cycles. Less-mobile elements, such as phosphorus and sulfur, do not move far from where they originated. The soil is the main abiotic reservoir for those elements.

Photosynthesis and cellular respiration are the means by which carbon cycles through the biosphere. Plants absorb carbon dioxide from the atmosphere and use the carbon to form other plant molecules. Consumers eat the plants and break down the carbon-containing molecules into smaller molecules and energy. Some of the carbon is incorporated in the body of the consumer. The rest may be exhaled back into the air as carbon dioxide. Decomposers return carbon dioxide to the air in the same way. When fossil fuels, such as oil, coal, and gas, are burned, they also release carbon into the air as carbon dioxide. Figure 26.25 summarizes the carbon cycle.

Most organisms cannot use nitrogen gas. Only certain prokaryotes can convert the nitrogen (N_2) in the atmosphere to ammonia (NH_3), a process called nitrogen fixation. Other bacteria convert the ammonia to nitrite (NO_2^-) or nitrate (NO_3^-). Plants can absorb either ammonia or nitrates from the soil and use them to synthesize nitrogen-containing compounds,

Try Investigation 26B, Relationships Between a Plant and an Animal.

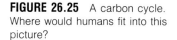

FIGURE 26.25 A carbon cycle. Where would humans fit into this picture?

FIGURE 26.26 A nitrogen cycle. In addition, calcium, phosphorus, oxygen, carbon dioxide, and other materials necessary for life are recycled.

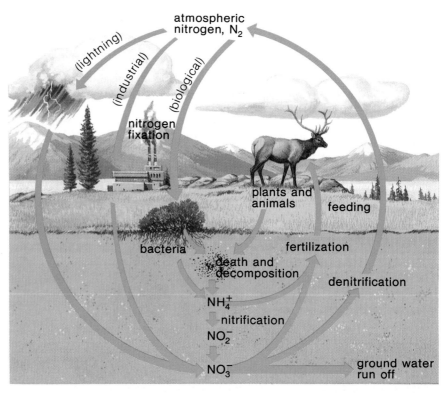

such as amino acids. This process is called *nitrification*. Animals must obtain their nitrogen by consuming plants or other animals. Denitrifying bacteria convert nitrate (NO_3^-) to nitrogen gas (N_2), thus completing the cycle. Figure 26.26 summarizes the nitrogen cycle.

Figure 26.27 shows the water cycle in an ecosystem. Plants absorb water from the soil. Land animals absorb water from their food, or they

FIGURE 26.27 A water cycle. Water is the most plentiful material in the tissues of organisms. The decomposition of water in photosynthesis is offset by its reappearance as a by-product of cellular respiration

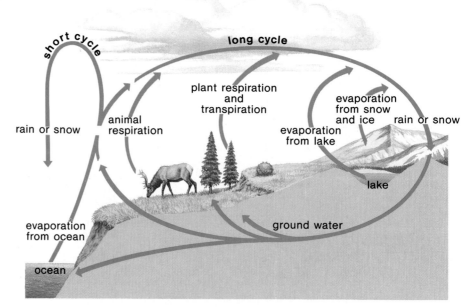

Biological Challenges

BIODIVERSITY IN DANGER

All organisms on Earth, including humans, are dependent on each other in some way. The interplay between biotic and abiotic factors makes possible the diversity of organisms that exists today.

Natural ecosystems have a vast genetic library, yet researchers have strong evidence that ecosystems are in the opening stages of an extinction episode. There is a sudden and pronounced decline in the worldwide abundance and diversity of ecologically different groups of organisms, particularly in tropical rain forests. Such a rate of extinction is the most extreme in the past 65 million years. Some researchers estimate that at the current rate, at least one million species will become extinct by the end of this century.

The primary cause of this decay in diversity is not direct human exploitation, but the indirect habitat destruction that results from the expansion of human populations and activities. As the human population grows, it places greater demands on the ecosystem for space and goods. As a result, land is cleared for cultivation and living space, destroying the habitats of many organisms.

Organisms require appropriate habitats if they are to survive. Just as humans cannot live in an atmosphere with too little oxygen, trout cannot breed in water that is too warm or too acidic. Red-eyed vireos, scarlet tanagers, and other birds must have mature tropical forests in which to spend the winters. Black-footed ferrets (Figure B) require a prairie that still supports prairie dogs, their major source of food.

Many organisms provide humans with crops, domesticated animals, a variety of industrial products, and many important medicines. However, the roles that microorganisms, plants, and animals play within the natural ecosystem are more important. All these organisms exchange gases with their environments and thus help to maintain the mix of gases in the atmosphere. Changes in that mix, such as

FIGURE B A black-footed ferret. Attempts are being made to breed these endangered animals in captivity so they can be reintroduced in the wild.

increases in carbon dioxide, nitrogen oxides, and methane, may lead to rapid climatic change and, in turn, agricultural disaster. Destroying forests may lead to timber shortages, water shortages, and increased danger of flooding. Destruction of some insects may lead to the failure of crops that depend on insect pollination. Extermination of the enemies of insect pests may lead to severe pest outbreaks. The extermination of soil organisms may destroy the fertility of the soil.

Researchers are currently attempting to determine the extent to which humans have devastated the diversity of organisms and the effect these changes will have on the ecosystems of the world. Solutions to this problem are even more difficult to determine. Some solutions require a massive change in life-style. Others involve the use of new genetic techniques to perpetuate diversity, such as embryo transplants between an endangered species and a domestic species. Whether or not some of these solutions work is yet to be seen.

FIGURE 26.28 Trees exposed to acid rain eventually die.

Try Investigation 26C, Water Quality Assessment.

drink it directly. Aquatic organisms are constantly bathed in water. Water is returned to the atmosphere through transpiration and cellular respiration. Most atmospheric water evaporates from the oceans. Eventually, much of the atmospheric water vapor condenses and returns to the system as rain or snow.

The burning of fossil fuels adds large amounts of sulfur and nitrogen oxides to the atmosphere. There, these oxides react with water and are transformed into sulfuric and nitric acids, which fall to Earth as acid rain. Normal rain has a pH of 5.6. The pH of acid rain ranges from 5.5 to as low as 2.4. In general, the precipitation in much of the world is now 30 times more acid than normal.

The soils supporting forests watered with acid rain can no longer counteract the acid precipitation, which leaches minerals out of the soils. That leaching deprives the trees of mineral salts needed for plant growth. Consequently, the trees weaken and die. Whole forest ecosystems are threatened by acid rain. The forests of the eastern United States, Canada, and Europe have so far experienced the greatest destruction (Figure 26.28).

26.7 Unwanted Materials

The environment contains more types of materials than those necessary for life. A whole new source of environmental materials has resulted from human activity. More than 100 000 types of mined or manufactured materials are produced and processed each year. Waste gases and other lightweight materials are vented into the atmosphere through chimneys, smokestacks, and exhaust systems. The heavier materials accumulate on the land and in streams, lakes, and oceans. You might think that we can select only the materials we need from the environment and reject those we do not want. Such choice is not possible at the molecular level. We often take in high levels of unanticipated materials with the air we breathe and the food we eat.

The food pyramid can demonstrate the effects of these materials. Consider an insecticide absorbed by plants, which are at the bottom level of the pyramid. When plants absorb such substances, which they can neither use nor eliminate, these substances are trapped. As the plants are eaten, the unneeded materials move into the next level of the pyramid. Each herbivore eats many plants and thus accumulates many times the concentration of the insecticide present in the plants. A carnivore that is a second-order consumer then eats many of the insecticide-laden herbivores and may end up with 100 times the concentration of the chemical that was in the original individual plants. This concentrating effect continues upward through the pyramid's trophic levels, usually increased at each level by another factor of 10. This phenomenon is the biological reason behind the idea that there are no "low" or "safe" levels for the use of toxic substances.

The insecticide DDT provides another example. DDT and its toxic breakdown products remain in the environment for a long time. The effects of the concentration phenomenon became well known during the 1980s. The concentration of DDT in the tissues of organisms increases nearly ten

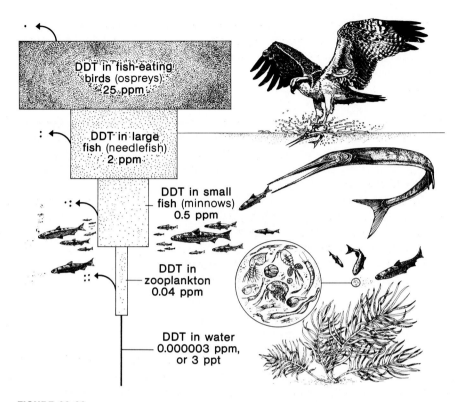

DDT in fish-eating
birds (ospreys)
25 ppm

DDT in large
fish (needlefish)
2 ppm

DDT in small
fish (minnows)
0.5 ppm

DDT in
zooplankton
0.04 ppm

DDT in water
0.000003 ppm,
or 3 ppt

FIGURE 26.29   As DDT is passed from organism to organism in a food chain, the concentration is magnified about 10 million times. Dots represent DDT, and arrows show small amounts lost in the daily activities of the organisms.

million times as it moves up the food chain from algae to clams and minnows to ospreys (Figure 26.29). The high concentration of DDT in the ospreys affects their ability to produce eggs with shells strong enough to survive in the nest and hatch. As a result, the osprey population is endangered. Although people are attempting to help, it is too late to remove the DDT from the food chain. It will continue to plague living systems for many years to come.

CHECK AND CHALLENGE

1. Describe the concept behind an energy pyramid.
2. What implication does the energy pyramid have for humans?
3. How is carbon cycled through the biosphere?
4. Compare the long and short cycles of the water cycle. What abiotic factors in an ecosystem might affect precipitation patterns?
5. How do food pyramids and toxic substances relate?

Summary

Plants and animals have adapted to abiotic factors that shape their ecosystem. Temperature, light energy, and water are the most important factors in determining the character of an ecosystem. The success of the organisms in surviving to reproduce depends directly on their tolerance of the prevailing abiotic factors.

Biomes are determined by the climate and characterized by the predominant energy-fixing vegetation growing there. Both latitude and altitude affect the climate and, hence, the vegetation. Aquatic ecosystems are different from terrestrial ecosystems. The predominant limiting factors for rivers and streams are temperature, turbidity, chemistry, and current. Ponds, lakes, and oceans are three-dimensional. The organisms that live in the different zones have adapted to differences in the temperature, pressure, and amount of light available for photosynthesis.

No ecosystem is permanent. Natural and human-made catastrophes can change the character of an ecosystem. As a result, a succession of communities may occur, often ending in a relatively stable climax community. Succession occurs in both aquatic and terrestrial ecosystems.

Energy flows and chemicals cycle through ecosystems. Producers capture light energy. Only about 10 percent of that incoming energy is passed from one trophic level to the next, so a very small percent of the light energy is available for higher level consumers. Water and compounds of nitrogen, carbon, and other essential elements are all cycled through an ecosystem. The chemicals may change form during the cycle, but ultimately they are returned to the atmosphere or the soil to begin the cycle again.

Unwanted materials such as pesticides also cycle through an ecosystem. Once they have been introduced, they remain in the system to cycle and concentrate again.

Key Concepts

Construct two concept maps, one for the cycling of matter and one illustrating relationships among the different biomes. Try to find a way to link the two together.

Reviewing Ideas

1. Describe how abiotic factors affect biotic factors in an ecosystem. Give examples.
2. What are the autotrophs found in the food pyramid? The heterotrophs?
3. What are decomposers, and how do they affect the recycling of materials in an ecosystem?
4. What abiotic factors affect the character of marine ecosystems?
5. How does depth affect organisms that live in marine ecosystems?
6. Explain how climate affects the adaptations of terrestrial animals to ecosystems. Give examples.

7. Why are there no "safe" levels for the use of toxic substances that can enter the food pyramid? Give some examples.

8. Compare and contrast food chains and food webs.

9. What is meant by a climax community? Does this type of community ever change? How?

10. Explain how succession on land differs from succession in a lake or pond.

11. What is a limiting factor?

12. What is the 10 percent rule and how does it affect productivity? What are implications of this rule for human population?

Using Concepts

1. Describe some relationships between populations and communities in a grassland ecosystem.

2. Many bacteria and some algae can take nitrogen from the air and make ammonia and nitrates. Crop plants require ammonia or nitrates for their nitrogen source. Describe the gene-splicing experiment that these data suggest.

3. Why do different ecosystems have different plants and animals?

4. Why is energy said to *flow* through an ecosystem, whereas chemicals *cycle?*

5. Describe the relationship between ecosystems and biomes.

6. Describe the biome your community is in. How is it similar to or different from those described in this chapter?

7. What would be the limiting factors for each of the following: a desert, the tundra, a tropical rain forest, the open ocean?

8. Discuss how the devastation of the North American grasslands has affected herds of grazing animals such as bison.

9. Explain why trade-offs are involved in an organism's ability to tolerate extreme environments. Give some examples.

Synthesis

1. Explain how evolution through natural selection affects the plants and animals in different biomes.

2. What might be the major limiting factor for the human population? Defend your answer.

3. Discuss environmental tolerance in relation to the human population. Are humans subject to the same pressures as other organisms?

Extensions

1. Much of the tropical rain forest in Latin American countries is being clearcut for cattle ranching. Beef raised in these countries is an important economic resource for them. The beef is being sold to fast-food restaurant chains in the United States, an important economic resource of ours. The rain forest, once the vegetation has been removed, will likely never recover. This condition will lead to widespread climatic change. Which issue has the most impact on the most people: the destruction of the rain forest, or the effect on Third World and United States economies if the clearcutting is stopped? Choose a position and write an essay defending your position.

2. Sketch a food web for a specific biome. Be sure to include as many decomposers, producers, and different-level consumers as you can. If you would like to draw the organisms of the biome, photos obtained from library reference books will provide helpful models.

3. Describe a new biome with particular limiting factors. Create and sketch an organism that has particular adaptations to that biome.

Investigations

Introduction to Laboratory Work

The laboratory is a scientist's workshop—the place where ideas are tested. In the laboratory portion of this course, you will see evidence that supports major biological concepts. To pursue your investigations effectively, you need to learn certain basic techniques, including safe laboratory practices, record keeping, report writing, and measurement. The information on the following pages will help you learn these skills and techniques.

Laboratory Safety

The laboratory has the potential to be either a safe place or a dangerous place. The difference depends on your knowledge of and adherence to safe laboratory practices. It is important that you read the information here and learn how to recognize and avoid potentially hazardous situations. Basic rules for working safely in the laboratory include the following:

1. Be prepared. Study the assigned investigation before you come to class. Be prepared to ask questions about the procedures you do not understand before you begin to work.

2. Be organized. Arrange the materials needed for the investigation in an orderly fashion.

3. Maintain a clean, open work area, free of everything except those materials necessary for the assigned investigation. Store books, backpacks, and purses out of the way. Keep laboratory materials away from the edge of the work surface.

4. Tie back long hair and remove dangling jewelry. Roll up long sleeves and tuck long neckties into your shirt. Do not wear loose-fitting sleeves or open-toed shoes in the laboratory.

5. Wear a lab apron and safety goggles whenever working with chemicals, hot liquids, lab burners, hot plates, or apparatus that could break or shatter. Wear protective gloves when working with preserved specimens, toxic or corrosive chemicals, or when otherwise directed.

6. Never wear contact lenses while conducting any experiment involving the use of chemicals. If you must wear them (by a physician's order), inform your teacher *prior* to conducting any experiment involving chemicals.

7. Never use direct or reflected sunlight to illuminate your microscope or any other optical device. Direct or reflected sunlight can cause serious damage to your retina.

8. Keep your hands away from the sharp or pointed ends of equipment such as scalpels, dissecting needles, or scissors.

9. Observe all cautions in the procedural steps of the investigation. **CAUTION, WARNING,** and **DANGER** are signal words used in the text and on labeled chemicals or reagents that tell you about the potential for harm and/or injury. They remind you to observe specific practices. *Always read and follow these statements.* They are meant to help keep you and your fellow students safe.

   CAUTION statements advise you that the material or procedure has *some potential risk* of harm or injury if directions are not followed.

   WARNING statements advise you that the material or procedure has a *moderate risk* of harm or injury if directions are not followed.

   DANGER statements advise you that the material or procedure has a *high risk* of harm or injury if directions are not followed.

10. Become familiar with caution symbols identified in Figure A.

11. Never put anything into your mouth and never touch or taste substances in the laboratory unless specifically instructed to by your teacher.

12. Never smell substances in the laboratory without specific instructions. Even then, do not inhale fumes directly; wave the air above the substance toward your nose and sniff carefully.

13. Never eat, drink, chew gum, or apply cosmetics in the laboratory. Do not store food or beverages in the lab area.

14. Know the location of all safety equipment and learn how to use each piece of equipment.

15. If you witness an unsafe incident, an accident, or a chemical spill, report it to your teacher immediately.

16. Use materials only from containers labeled with the name of the chemical and the precautions to be used. Become familiar with the safety precautions for each chemical by reading the label before use.

17. When diluting acid with water, *always add acid to water*.

18. Never return unused chemicals to the stock bottles. Do not put any object into a chemical bottle, except the dropper with which it may be equipped.

19. Clean up thoroughly. Dispose of chemicals and wash used glassware and instruments according to the teacher's instructions. Clean tables and sinks. Put away all equipment and supplies. Make sure all water, gas jets, burners, and electrical appliances are turned off. Return all laboratory equipment and supplies to their proper places.

20. Wash your hands thoroughly after handling any living organisms or hazardous materials and before leaving the laboratory.

safety goggles

Safety goggles are for eye protection. Wear goggles whenever you see this symbol. If you wear glasses, be sure the goggles fit comfortably over them. In case of splashes into the eye, flush the eye (including under the lid) at an eyewash station for 15 to 20 minutes. If you wear contact lenses, remove them *immediately* and flush the eye as directed. Call your teacher.

lab apron

A lab apron is intended to protect your clothing. Whenever you see this symbol, put on your lab apron and tie it securely behind you. If you spill any substance on your clothing, call your teacher.

gloves

Wear gloves when you see this symbol or whenever your teacher directs you to do so. Wear them when using **any** chemical or reagent solution. Do not wear your gloves for an extended period of time.

sharp object

Sharp objects can cause injury, either as a cut or a puncture. Handle all sharp objects with caution and use them only as your teacher instructs you. **Do not** use them for any purpose other than the intended one. If you do get a cut or puncture, call your teacher and get first aid.

irritant

An irritant is any substance that, on contact, can cause reddening of living tissue. Wear safety goggles, lab apron, and protective gloves when handling any irritating chemical. In case of contact, flush the affected area with soap and water for at least 15 minutes and call your teacher. Remove contaminated clothing.

reactive

These chemicals are capable of reacting with any other substance, including water, and can cause a violent reaction. **Do not** mix a reactive chemical with any other substance, including water, unless directed to do so by your teacher. Wear your safety goggles, lab apron, and protective gloves.

corrosive

A corrosive substance injures or destroys body tissue on contact by direct chemical action. When handling any corrosive substance, wear safety goggles, lab apron, and protective gloves. In case of contact with a corrosive material, *immediately* flush the affected area with water and call your teacher.

flammable

A flammable substance is any material capable of igniting under certain conditions. Do not bring flammable materials into contact with open flames or near heat sources unless instructed to do so by your teacher. Remember that flammable liquids give off vapors that can be ignited by a nearby heat source. Should a fire occur, *do not* attempt to extinguish it yourself. Call your teacher. Wear safety goggles, lab apron, and protective gloves whenever handling a flammable substance.

poison

Poisons can cause injury by direct action within a body system through direct contact (skin), inhalation, ingestion, or penetration. **Always** wear safety goggles, lab apron, and protective gloves when handling any material with this label. Before handling any poison, inform your teacher if you have preexisting injuries to your skin. In case of contact, call your teacher *immediately*.

biohazard

Any biological substance that can cause infection through exposure is a biohazard. Before handling any material so labeled, review your teacher's specific instructions. **Do not** handle in any manner other than as instructed. Wear safety goggles, lab apron, and protective gloves. Any contact with a biohazard should be reported to your teacher immediately.

NO FOOD OR DRINKS SHOULD BE PRESENT IN THE LAB AT ANY TIME.

FIGURE A Caution symbols

21. Never perform unauthorized experiments. Do only those experiments assigned by your teacher.

22. Never work alone in the laboratory, and never work without the teacher's supervision.

23. Approach laboratory work with maturity. Never run, push, or engage in horseplay or practical jokes of any type in the laboratory. Use laboratory materials and equipment only as directed.

In addition to observing these general safety precautions, you need to know about some specific categories of safety. Before you do any laboratory work, familiarize yourself with the following precautions.

Heat

1. Use only the source of heat specified in the investigation.

2. Never allow flammable materials, such as alcohol, near a flame or any other source of ignition.

3. When heating a substance in a test tube, point the mouth of the tube away from other students and yourself.

4. Never leave a lighted lab burner, hot plate, or any other hot object unattended.

5. Never reach over an exposed flame or other heat source.

6. Use tongs, test-tube clamps, insulated gloves, or pot holders to handle hot equipment.

Glassware

1. Never use cracked or chipped glassware.

2. Use caution and proper equipment when handling hot glassware; remember that hot glass looks the same as cool glass.

3. Make sure glassware is clean before you use it and clean when you store it.

4. When putting glass tubing into a rubber stopper, use a lubricant such as glycerine or vaseline on both the stopper and the glass tubing. When putting glass tubing into or removing it from a rubber stopper, protect your hands with heavy cloth. Never force or twist the tubing.

5. Broken glassware should be swept up immediately (never picked up with your fingers) and discarded in a special, labeled container for broken glass.

Electrical Equipment and Other Apparatus

1. Before you begin any work, always be sure you learn how to use each piece of apparatus safely and correctly to obtain accurate scientific information.

2. Never use equipment with frayed insulation or with loose or broken wires.

3. Make sure the area under and around electrical equipment is dry and free of flammable materials. Never touch electrical equipment with wet hands.

4. Turn off all power switches before plugging an appliance into an outlet. Never jerk wires from outlets or pull appliance plugs out by the wire.

Living and Preserved Specimens

1. Specimens for dissection should be properly mounted and supported. Do not cut a specimen while holding it in your hand.

2. Wash down your work surface with a disinfectant solution both before and after using live microorganisms.

3. Always wash your hands with soap and water after working with live or preserved specimens.

4. Animals must be cared for humanely. General rules are as follows:
   a. Always carefully follow the teacher's instructions concerning the care of laboratory animals.
   b. Provide a suitable escape-proof container in a location where the animal will not be constantly disturbed.
   c. Keep the container clean. Cages of small birds and mammals should be cleaned daily. Provide proper ventilation, light, and temperature.
   d. Provide water at all times.
   e. Feed regularly, depending on the animal's needs.
   f. Treat laboratory animals gently and with kindness in all situations.
   g. If you are reponsible for the regular care of any animals, be sure to make arrangements for weekends, holidays, and vacations.
   h. When animals must be disposed of or released, your teacher will provide a suitable method.

5. Many plants or plant parts are poisonous. Work only with the plants specified by your teacher. Never put any plant or plant parts in your mouth.

6. Handle plants carefully and gently. Most plants must have light, soil, and water, although requirements differ.

Accident Procedures

1. Report *all* incidents, accidents, injuries, and all breakage and spills, no matter how minor, to the teacher.

2. If a chemical spills on your skin or clothing, wash it off immediately with plenty of water and notify the teacher.

3. If a chemical gets into your eyes or on your face, wash immediately at the eyewash fountain with plenty of water. Wash for at least 15 minutes, flushing the eyes—including under each eyelid. Have a classmate notify the teacher.

4. If a chemical spills on the floor or work surface, do not clean it up yourself. Notify your teacher immediately.

5. If a thermometer breaks, do not touch the broken pieces with your bare hands. Notify the teacher immediately.

6. Smother small fires with a wet towel. Use a blanket or the safety shower to extinguish clothing fires. Always notify the teacher.

7. All cuts and abrasions received in the laboratory, no matter how small, should be reported to your teacher.

Chemical Safety

All chemicals are hazardous in some way. A hazardous chemical is defined as a substance that is likely to cause injury. Chemicals can be placed in four hazard categories: flammable, corrosive, toxic, and reactive.

In the laboratory investigations for this course, every effort is made to minimize the use of dangerous materials. However, many "less hazardous" chemicals can cause injury if not handled properly. The following information will help you become aware of the types of chemical hazards that exist and of how you can reduce the risk of injury when using chemicals. Be sure also to review safety rules 1 through 23 described earlier before you work with any chemical.

Flammable/Combustible substances. Flammable/combustible substances are solids, liquids, or gases that will sustain burning. The process of burning involves three interrelated components—fuel (any substance capable of burning), oxidizer (often air or a specific chemical), and ignition source (a spark, flame, or heat). The three components are represented in the diagram of a fire triangle in Figure B. For burning to occur, all three components (sides) of the fire triangle must be present. To control fire hazard, one must remove, or otherwise make inaccessible, at least one side of the fire triangle. Flammable chemicals should not be used in the presence of ignition sources such as lab burners, hot plates, and sparks from electrical equipment or static electricity. Containers of flammables should be closed when not in use. Sufficient ventilation in the laboratory will help to keep the concentration of flammable vapors to a minimum. Wearing safety goggles, lab aprons, and protective gloves are important precautionary measures when using flammable/combustible materials.

FIGURE B The fire triangle

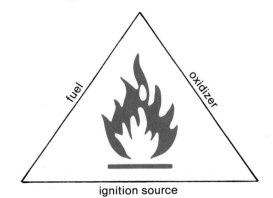

ignition source

Toxic substances. Most of the chemicals in a laboratory are toxic, or poisonous to life. The degree of toxicity depends on the properties of the specific substance, its concentration, the type of exposure, and other variables. The effects of a toxic substance can range from minor discomfort to serious illness or death. Exposure to toxic substances can occur through ingestion, skin contact, or through inhaling toxic vapors. Wearing a lab apron, safety goggles, and protective gloves are important precautions when using toxic chemicals. A clean work area, prompt spill cleanup, and good ventilation also are important.

Corrosive substances. Corrosive chemicals are solids, liquids, or gases that by direct chemical action either destroy living tissue or cause permanent change in the tissue. Corrosive substances can destroy eye and respiratory-tract tissues, causing impaired sight or permanent blindness, severe disfigurement, permanent severe breathing difficulties, and even death. Lab aprons, safety goggles, and protective gloves should be worn when handling corrosive chemicals to prevent contact with the skin or eyes. Splashes on the skin or in the eye should be washed off immediately while a classmate notifies the teacher.

Reactive substances. Reactive chemicals promote violent reactions under certain conditions. A chemical may explode spontaneously or when mechanically disturbed. Reactive chemicals also include those that react rapidly when mixed with another chemical, releasing a large amount of energy. Keep chemicals separate from each other unless they are being combined according to specific instructions in an investigation. Heed any other cautions your teacher may give you. Always wear your lab apron, safety goggles, and protective gloves when handling reactive chemicals.

Record Keeping

Science deals with verifiable observations. No one—not even the original observer—can trust the accuracy of a confusing, indefinite, or incomplete observation. Scientific record keeping requires clear and accurate records made *at the time of observation.*

The best method of keeping records is to jot them down in a data book. It should be a hardcover book, permanently bound (not loose-leaf), and preferably with square grid (graph-paper type) pages.

Keep records in diary form, recording the date first. Keep observations of two or more investigations separate. Data recorded in words should be notes that are brief but to the point. Complete sentences are not necessary, but single words are seldom descriptive enough to represent accurately what you have observed.

You may choose to sketch your observations. A drawing often records an observation more easily, completely, and accurately than words can. Your sketches need not be works of art. Their success depends on your ability to observe, not on your artistic talent. Keep the drawings simple, use a hard pencil, and include clearly written labels.

Data recorded numerically as counts or measurements should include the units in which the measurements are made. Often numerical data are most easily recorded in the form of a table.

Do not record your data on other papers, to be copied into the data book later. Doing so might increase neatness, but it will decrease accuracy. Your data book is *your* record, regardless of the blots and stains that are a normal circumstance of field and laboratory work.

You will do much of your laboratory work as a member of a team. Your data book, therefore, will sometimes contain data contributed by other members of your team. Keep track of the source of observations by circling (or recording in a different color) the data reported by others.

Writing Laboratory Reports

Discoveries become a part of science only when they are made known to others. Communication, therefore, is an important part of science. In writing, scientists must express themselves so clearly that another person can repeat their procedures exactly. The reader must know what material was used (in biology this includes the species of organism) and must understand every detail of the work. Scientific reports frequently are written in a standard form as follows:

1. Title
2. Introduction: a statement of how the problem arose, often including a summary of past work
3. Materials and equipment: usually a list of all equipment, chemicals, specimens, and other materials
4. Procedure: a complete and exact account of the methods used in gathering data
5. Results: data obtained from the procedure, often in the form of tables and graphs
6. Discussion: a section that demonstrates the relationship between the data and the purpose of the work
7. Conclusion: a summary of the meaning of the results, often suggesting further work that might be done
8. References: published scientific reports and papers that you have mentioned specifically.

Your teacher will tell you what form your laboratory reports should take for this course. Part of your work may include written answers to the Analysis questions at the end of each investigation. In any event, the material in your data book is the basis for your reports.

Measurement

Measurement in science is made using the *Systèm International d'Unités* (the International System of Units), more commonly referred to as "SI." A modification of the older metric system, it was used first in France and now is the common system of measurement throughout the world.

Among the basic units of SI measurement are the meter (length), the kilogram (mass), the kelvin (temperature), and the second (time). All other SI units are derived from these four. Units of temperature that you will use in this course are degrees Celsius, which are equal to kelvins.

SI units for volume are based on meters cubed. In addition, you will use units based on the liter for measuring volumes of liquids. Although not officially part of SI, liter measure is used commonly. Like meters cubed, the liter is metric (1 L = 0.001 m³).

Some of the SI units derived from the basic units for length, mass, volume, and temperature follow. Note, especially, those units described as most common to your laboratory work.

Length

1 kilometer (km) = 1000 meters

1 hectometer (hm) = 100 meters

1 dekameter (dkm) = 10 meters

1 meter (m)

1 decimeter (dm) = 0.1 meter

1 centimeter (cm) = 0.01 meter

1 millimeter (mm) = 0.001 meter

1 micrometer (μm) = 0.000001 meter

1 nanometer (nm) = 0.000000001 meter

Measurements under microscopes often are made in micrometers. Still smaller measurements, as for wavelengths of light used by plants in photosynthesis, are made in nanometers. The units of length you will use most frequently in the laboratory are centimeters (cm).

Units of area are derived from units of length by multiplication. One hectometer squared is a measure often used for ecological studies; it is commonly called a hectare and equals 10 000 m². Measurements of area made in the laboratory most frequently will be in centimeters squared (cm²).

Units of volume are also derived from units of length by multiplication. One meter cubed (m³) is the standard, but it is too large for practical use in the laboratory. Centimeters cubed (cm³) are the more common units you will see. For the conditions you will encounter in these laboratory investigations, 1 cm³ measures a volume equal to 1 mL.

Mass

1 kilogram (kg) = 1000 grams

1 hectogram (hg) = 100 grams

1 dekagram (dkg) = 10 grams

1 gram (g)

1 decigram (dg) = 0.1 gram

1 centigram (cg) = 0.01 gram

1 milligram (mg) = 0.001 gram

1 microgram (μg) = 0.000001 gram

1 nanogram (ng) = 0.000000001 gram

   Measurements of mass in your biology laboratory usually will be made in kilograms, grams, centigrams, and milligrams.

Volume

1 kiloliter (kL) = 1000 liters

1 hectoliter (hL) = 100 liters

1 dekaliter (dkL) = 10 liters

1 liter (L)

1 deciliter (dL) = 0.1 liter

1 centiliter (cL) = 0.01 liter

1 milliliter (mL) = 0.001 liter

   Your measurements in the laboratory will usually be made in glassware marked for milliliters and liters.

Temperature

On the Celsius scale, 0°C is commonly known as the freezing point of water, and 100°C is the boiling point of water. (Atmospheric pressure affects both of these temperatures.) Figure C illustrates the Celsius scale alongside the Fahrenheit scale, which is still used in the United States. On the Fahrenheit scale, 32°F is the freezing point of water, and 212°F is the boiling point of water. The figure is useful in converting from one scale to the other.

   Another type of measurement you will encounter in this course is molarity (labeled with the letter M). Molarity measures the concentration of a dissolved substance in a solution. A high molarity indicates a high concentration. The solutions you will use in the investigations frequently will be identified by their molarity.

   If you wish to learn more about SI measure, write to the United States Department of Commerce, National Institute of Standards and Technology (NIST), Washington, DC 20234.

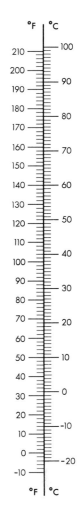

FIGURE C Temperature-conversion scale

Investigations for Chapter 1
Biology and You

Investigation 1A • Analyzing Ethical Issues

Biological Challenges in Chapter 1 explains that ethical analysis ''is a process of critical inquiry.'' There are various models for conducting such inquiries; this investigation introduces you to one such model, which focuses on goals, rights, and duties. You will apply this model to a case study that involves the use of biosynthetic human growth hormone (GH).

Materials (per person)

paper and pen

Procedure

1. Read the following case study:

   Sharon has just completed ninth grade at Deerfield Junior High School in Iowa. She has attended summer basketball camp for the past three years and already is one of the best players in the state. Deerfield's girls basketball team has won two district championships, and Sharon—a forward—has been the leading scorer. It is clear she has great potential both as a high school and college player.

   Sharon and her coaches, however, are concerned about her height. She is only 5 feet 7 inches (170 cm) tall. Sharon's coaches want to develop her skills through high school and would like her to attain as much height as possible. She is not likely to gain much more height naturally. Sharon and her parents have discussed her problem with an endocrinologist and asked that he provide her with biosynthetic GH. Thus far, he has refused, saying that GH is used only to treat children who are abnormally short. The doctor maintains that Sharon is not handicapped and should not risk the possible side effects of GH when she does not need the hormone for a legitimate medical reason. The potential side effects, which are irreversible, include developing diabetes and heart problems,

   and elongation of the facial bones, hands, and feet.

   Sharon has told the doctor that she can get GH on the black market and will do so if he does not prescribe it for her. She prefers to have the hormone administered under the doctor's supervision because the hormone will be pure and he can monitor her progress. What should the doctor do?

2. Read the following information about goals, rights, and duties.

   Goals: One way to judge the morality of an action is by looking at what it intends to accomplish. If this view is the basis for determining whether an action is morally correct, then a ''good'' outcome may be judged morally correct no matter how the outcome was achieved. Assume, for example, that a given physician's primary goal is the preservation of life. She might then refuse to disconnect a respirator that is keeping a terminally ill patient alive, even if the patient or the patient's family wishes her to do so. In her view, going against the rights of the patient is justified by her goal of the preservation of life.

   Rights: Moral arguments based on rights are familiar to all of us. Our Constitution, for example, guarantees the right to free speech, the right to religious freedom, and the right to trial by a jury of one's peers. Most physicians agree that a patient has a right to know all of the relevant information about a given treatment and the right to refuse that treatment. Consider a situation in which the physician knows that a patient will refuse lifesaving treatment if the patient knows all of the potential side effects. Should the physician violate the patient's *right* to the information to further the physician's *goal* of the preservation of life?

   Duties: Some moral arguments are based on the obligation, or duty, to act in a certain way. For example, we generally have a duty to tell the truth, keep a promise, or help a friend. The justification for a duty often is based on the achievement of a worthy goal or on the basis of someone's right. Duties, therefore, can be derived from goals or rights, but they can also be in conflict with goals or rights. Suppose, for example, that a dying man asks a physician not to prolong his life. Does the physician have a *duty* to respect the man's *right* to die? Or does the physician have a *duty* to pursue his own *goal* of the preservation of life?

3. Work in teams of three or four to discuss the case study of Sharon and her desire to use GH to increase her height. List the goals, rights, and duties for Sharon, the doctor, Sharon's parents, and the basketball coaches in this situation. When you have completed your discussion, your teacher will compile a list of the responses from each group so you can discuss the Analysis questions as a class.

Analysis

1. Where are the major conflicts in the goals, rights, and duties for Sharon, the doctor, Sharon's parents, and the basketball coaches?

2. Should the doctor prescribe GH for Sharon?

3. What are the most important justifications for the position you have chosen?

4. Two United States companies now produce GH for distribution through prescription and under a physician's supervision. What are the goals, rights, and duties of these companies with respect to production and distribution of GH?

5. Is Sharon handicapped?

Investigation 1B • Scientific Observation

Careful observation is important in any science. The results you obtain from an experiment must be replicable. Detailed observations and notes not only help to identify possible areas of error, but also allow others to duplicate, and thus verify, your work. This investigation is an exercise in observation.

Materials (per person)

balance

metric ruler

10-cm piece of string

unshelled peanuts (one bowl for each group of 4 or 5)

FIGURE 1B.1   What observations best describe a peanut?

Procedure

1. Your team will be given a bowl of unshelled peanuts. Without looking in the bowl, remove a peanut. If it is cracked or broken, set it aside and remove another. When you have found a peanut that is not discolored or broken, proceed to step 2.

2. Observe the peanut carefully and record all of your observations in your data book. Decribe the shape of the peanut shell (or sketch it), measure it, and determine its mass. Do anything else necessary to help identify the shell except mark or crack it.

3. When you have recorded as many observations as you can, return the peanut to its original bowl. Mix up the peanuts and use your notes to find your peanut again.

4. If you had any difficulty locating your peanut, start over with another peanut. This time compare your methods with those of some other students. Work more on your observations and measurements so that you will not have difficulty finding the peanut again.

5. When you have recorded your observations and measurements as completely and as accurately as possible, your teacher will give you instructions for one more part to this exercise. It will be a realistic test of how careful you were in your observations and note-taking.

Analysis

1. What were the different ways you found to distinguish one peanut from another?

2. What proved to be the most helpful information in finding a specific peanut?

3. What percent of your class could locate their own peanut?

4. What percent of your class could locate someone else's peanut based on the other person's data?

5. Account for the differences in percent between questions 3 and 4.

6. What steps could be taken to improve both percentages?

7. How important were your notes of your observations and measurements in locating the peanut? If your memory was a better guide, what does that say about your notes?

8. People often confuse observations with inferences. Observations are collected on the scene, using your senses. Inferences are ideas or conclusions based on what you observe or already know. Based on this distinction, which of the following statements are observations and which are inferences?

The shell will crack easily.
The shell has a rough surface.
The shell is uniformly colored.
The shell has two lobes and is smaller in diameter between them.
The peanuts have a skin around them.
There are two peanuts in the shell.
The peanuts are roasted.
The surface markings on the shell are in rows, running lengthwise.
The shell has 13 rows of surface markings.

9. Now look at your notes and label any inferences that you included.

Investigation 1C • The Compound Microscope

The human eye cannot distinguish objects much smaller than 0.1 mm in size. The microscope is a biological tool that extends vision and allows observation of much smaller objects. The most commonly used compound microscope (Figure 1C.1) is monocular (one eyepiece). Light reaches the eye after being passed through the objects to be examined.

In this investigation, you will learn how to use and care for a microscope.

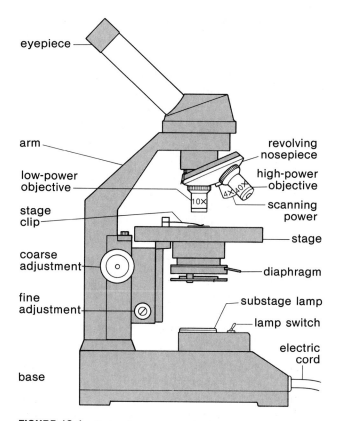

FIGURE 1C.1 Parts of a compound microscope

Materials (per person or team of 2)

3 cover slips

dropping pipet

3 microscope slides

compound microscope

newspaper

scissors

transparent metric ruler

Procedure

PART A   Care of the Microscope

1. The microscope is a precision instrument that requires proper care. Always carry the microscope with both hands, one hand under its base, the other on its arm.

2. When setting the microscope on a table, keep it away from the edge. If a lamp is attached to the

microscope, keep its wire out of the way. Keep everything not needed for microscope studies off your lab table.

3. Avoid tilting the microscope when using temporary slides made with water.

4. The lenses of the microscope cost almost as much as all the other parts put together. Never clean lenses with anything other than the lens paper designed for this task.

5. Before putting away the microscope, *always* return it to the low-power setting. The high-power objective reaches too near the stage to be left in place safely.

PART B Setting Up the Microscope

6. Rotate the low-power objective into place if it is not already there. When you change from one objective to another you will hear a click as the objective sets into position.

7. Move the mirror so that even illumination is obtained through the opening in the stage, or turn on the substage lamp. Most microscopes are equipped with a diaphragm for regulating light. Some materials are best viewed in dim light, others in bright light. Remember that direct sunlight can damage eyes. If you use natural light as your light source, do not reflect direct sunlight through the diaphragm.

8. Make sure that the lenses are dry and free of fingerprints and debris. Wipe lenses with lens paper only.

TABLE 1C.1 Microscopic Observations

Object being viewed	Observations and comments
letter *o*	
letter *c*	
etc.	
mm ruler	

PART C Using the Microscope

9. In your data book, prepare a table similar to Table 1C.1.

10. Cut a lowercase *o* from a piece of newspaper. Place it right side up on a clean slide. With a dropping pipet, place one drop of water on the letter. This type of slide is called a wet mount.
    CAUTION: Scissors are sharp. Handle with care.

11. Wait until the paper is soaked before adding a cover slip. Hold the cover slip at about a 45° angle to the slide and then slowly lower it. Figure 1C.2 shows these first steps.

12. Place the slide on the microscope stage and clamp it down. Move the slide so the letter is in the middle of the hole in the stage. Use the coarse-adjustment knob to lower the low-power objective to the lowest position.

FIGURE 1C.2 Preparing a wet mount with a microscope slide and coverslip

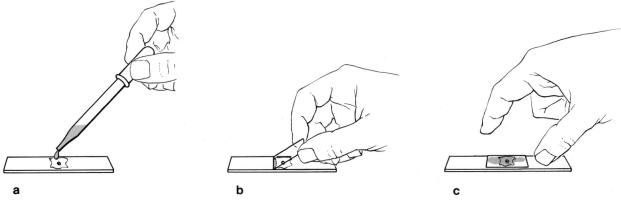

a   b   c

13. Look through the eyepiece and use the coarse-adjustment knob to raise the objective slowly, until the letter *o* is in view. Use the fine-adjustment knob to sharpen the focus. Position the diaphragm for the best light. Compare the way the letter looks through the microscope with the way it looks to the naked eye.

14. To determine how greatly magnified the view is, multiply the number inscribed on the eyepiece by the number on the objective being used. For example, eyepiece (10X) X objective (10X) = total (100X).

15. Follow the same procedure with a lowercase letter *c*. In your data book, describe how the letter appears when viewed through a microscope.

16. Make a wet mount of the letter *e* or the letter *r*. Describe how the letter appears when viewed through the microscope. What new information (not revealed by the letter *c*) is revealed by the *e* or *r*?

17. Look through the eyepiece at the letter as you use your thumbs and forefingers to move the slide slowly *away* from you. Which way does your view of the letter move? Move the slide to the right. In which direction does the image move?

18. Make a pencil sketch of the letter as you see it under the microscope. Label the changes in image and movement that occur under the microscope.

19. Make a wet mount of two different-colored hairs, one light and one dark. Cross one hair over the other. Position the slide so that the hairs cross in the center of the field. Sketch the hairs under low power, then go to Part D.

PART D   Using High Power

20. With the crossed hairs centered under low power, adjust the diaphragm for the best light.

21. Turn the high-power objective into viewing position. Do *not* change the focus.

22. Sharpen the focus with the *fine-adjustment knob only. Do not focus under high power with the coarse-adjustment knob.*

23. Readjust the diaphragm to get the best light. If you are not successful in finding the object

under high power the first time, return to step 20 and repeat the whole procedure carefully.

24. Using the fine-adjustment knob, focus on the hairs at the point where they cross. Can you see both hairs sharply at the same focus level? How can you use the fine-adjustment knob to determine which hair is crossed over the other? Sketch the hairs under high power.

PART E   Measuring with a Microscope

25. Because objects examined with a microscope usually are small, biologists use units of length smaller than centimeters or millimeters for microscopic measurement. One such unit is the micrometer, which is one thousandth of a millimeter. The symbol for micrometer is μm, the Greek letter μ (called mu) followed by m.

26. You can estimate the size of a microscopic object by comparing it with the size of the circular field of view. To determine the size of the field, place a plastic mm rule on the stage. Use the low-power objective to obtain a clear image of the divisions on the rule. Carefully move the rule until its marked edge passes through the exact center of the field of view. Now, count the number of divisions that you can see in the field of view. The marks on the rule will appear quite wide; 1 mm is the distance from the center of one mark to the center of the next. Record the diameter, in millimeters, of the low-power field of your microscope.

27. Remove the plastic rule and replace it with the wet mount of the letter *e*. (If the wet mount has dried, lift the cover slip and add water.) Using low power, compare the height of the letter with the diameter of the field of view. Estimate as accurately as possible the actual height of the letter in millimeters.

Analysis

1. Summarize the differences between an image viewed through a microscope and the same image viewed with the naked eye.

2. When viewing an object through the high-power objective, not all of the object may be in focus. Explain.

3. What is the relationship between magnification and the diameter of the field of view?

4. What is the diameter in micrometers of the low-power field of view of your microscope?

5. Calculate the diameter in micrometers of your high-power field. Use the following equations:

$$\frac{\text{magnification number of high-power objective}}{\text{magnification number of low-power objective}} = A$$

$$\frac{\text{diameter of low-power field of view}}{A} = \frac{\text{diameter of high-power field of view}}{}$$

For example, if the magnification of your low-power objective is 12X and that of your high-power is 48X, A = 4. If the diameter of the low-power field of view is 1600 μm, the diameter of the high-power field of view is $\frac{1600}{4}$, or 400 μm.

Investigation 1D • Developing Concept Maps

As you study biology, you will be exposed to many new ideas and processes. At times the amount of information and the number of new words can seem overwhelming. There is, however, a method you can use to manage this new information. Concept maps are tools that can help you organize and review ideas in a way that emphasizes the relationships among ideas. Ideas are much easier to learn and remember once you understand how they are related to one another.

Concept maps are constructed using ideas, objects, processes, or actions as the *concept words*. Other words that explain the relationship between two concepts are the *linking words*. For example, look at the simple concept map (*above right*) of the information about AIDS presented in Section 1.2.

The words that appear in the ovals are the concepts. *Notice that the concepts become increasingly specific*

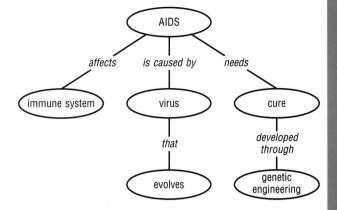

as you travel downward through the map. The relationships between the concepts are shown by the connecting lines. The words that appear with the lines are the linking words that describe the relationships among the concepts.

Examine a second concept map of the AIDS discussion. Notice that this map makes different connections between concepts.

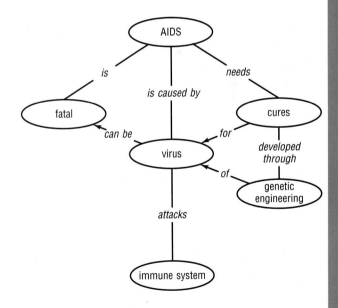

There is no single, correct concept map for a body of information. Each map may be different and may emphasize different concepts. In the second map, notice also that some of the connecting lines do not follow the downward trend. These lines are cross linkages. They describe additional, and perhaps more complex, relationships. You can follow a few simple steps that will help you build your own concept maps:

1. Identify and list the major concepts you want to map.

2. Decide which idea is the main concept. Group similar remaining concepts together and rank them within each group from the more general to the more specific.

3. Choose linking words that identify the relationships between the concepts. Be sure that the linking words are not concepts themselves.

4. Begin constructing your map by branching one or two concepts from your major concept. Add the remaining, more specific concepts as you progress. Be sure to look for opportunities to establish cross-linkages.

Materials (per team of 3)

pictures of laboratory equipment
scissors

PART A   Laboratory Equipment

Procedure

You will work in cooperative teams during this investigation, which means you must share your information to build a complete concept map. Each of you have received only part of a complete set of pictures. You will need to build a map of your set of pictures, and then work with your teammates to construct a team map for all the pictures.

1. Cut out each individual picture of equipment from the sheet you receive.

2. Group together the pieces of equipment that are somehow similar.

3. Subdivide the groups according to more specific characteristics. For example, the microscope is larger than the slides, and the slides are larger than the cover slips.

4. Using *laboratory equipment* as your main concept, arrange the pictures on a sheet of paper in the groupings you have determined.

5. Link the pictures together with linking words. For example, laboratory equipment *may be* glass or *may be* metal.

6. Try to establish some cross-linkages in your map. For example, glass items *can be used with* metal items.

7. Once you have completed your own map, work with your teammates to construct a team map of all the items, still using *laboratory equipment* as your major concept. Your teacher will assign you a job to do during the construction of the team map: The checker will make sure all concepts have been included and determine whether or not all team members agree on the structure of the map; the recorder will draw the map and make changes and corrections suggested by the team; and the arranger will make sure linking words are accurate and that cross-linkages have been identified.

8. Once you have completed your map, your teacher will randomly select one member of your team to explain your map to the class. Any teammate may be called on, so all members must be able to explain the teams' work.

Analysis

1. Compare your map with your classmates' maps. How is your concept map different?

2. Which concept map is easiest for you to understand?

3. What did members of your team do that worked well? What did not work well? What problems did you encounter? How did you solve those problems?

4. What would you do differently next time you work in a group?

PART B   Evolution

Procedure

9. Working with your teammates, use the concepts and linking words listed here to complete the following concept map for *evolution* based on Sections 1.5 and 1.6. (linking words can be used more than once.) Add other concepts to the map if you wish.

Concept Words

evolution

natural selection

observations

predictions

acquired characteristics

Darwin

Lamarck

theory

diversity

variation

Linking Words

is a

developed by

made

based on

lead to

accounts for

about

does not account for

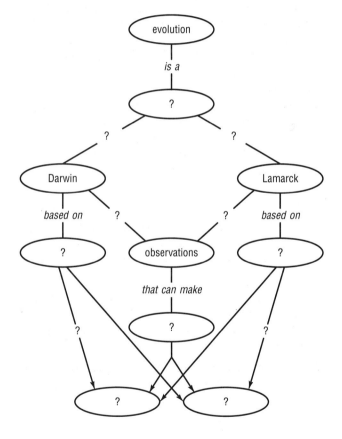

Analysis

1. Compare the concept maps you drew in Parts A and B. Do their characteristics differ? If so, how?

2. Compare your own concept map for Part B with the maps of other teams. How are the maps different? How are they the same?

PART C Science and Pseudoscience

Procedure

10. Construct a concept map dealing with science and pseudoscience based on Section 1.8 in the text.

11. Use the following concepts and linking words. You may add additional concepts and linking words as you need them.

Concept Words

theory

hypothesis

data

observation

experimentation

faith

science

pseudoscience

Linking Words

may be

based on

may include/includes

such as

from

affects

results in

Analysis

1. Compare your concept map for Part C with the maps of other teams. How are they similar? How are they different?

Investigations for Chapter 2
The Chemistry of Life

Investigation 2A • Organisms and pH

Individual organisms and cells must maintain a relatively stable internal environment, but many factors can affect that stability—for example, the relative concentrations of hydrogen ions (H^+) and hydroxide ions (OH^-). The biochemical activities of living tissues frequently affect pH, yet life depends on maintaining a pH range that is normal for each tissue or system. Using a pH probe and the LEAP-System™, or a pH meter or wide-range pH paper if the LEAP-System is not available, you can compare the responses of several materials to the addition of an acid and a base. Instructions for the use of the

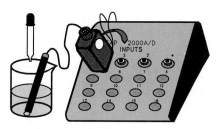

FIGURE 2A.1 The LEAP-System with pH probe.

LEAP-System are provided in the LEAP-System BSCS Biology Lab Pac 2.

Hypothesis: Before you begin, study the investigation and develop a hypothesis that addresses the question ''How do organisms survive and function despite metabolic activities that tend to shift pH toward either acidic or basic ends of the scale?''

Materials (per team of 4)

4 pairs of safety goggles

4 lab aprons

50-mL beaker or small jar

50-mL graduated cylinder

3 colored pencils

Apple IIe, Apple IIGS, Macintosh, or IBM computer

LEAP-System™

printer

pH probe

pH meter or wide-range pH paper (optional)

forceps

tap water

HCl (0.1*M*) in dropping bottle

NaOH (0.1*M*) in dropping bottle

sodium phosphate pH 7 buffer solution

liver homogenate

potato homogenate

egg white (diluted 1:5 with water)

warm gelatin suspension (2% solution)

> **SAFETY** Put on your safety goggles and lab apron. Tie back long hair.

Procedure

1. In your data book, prepare a table similar to Table 2A.1 or tape in the table provided by your teacher.

2. Pour 25 mL of tap water into a 50-mL beaker.

3. Record the initial pH by using a pH probe with the LEAP-System (Figure 2A.1), a pH meter, or by dipping small strips of pH paper into the water and comparing the color change to a standard color chart.

4. Add 0.1 *M* HCl a drop at a time. Gently swirl the mixture after each drop. Determine the pH after

TABLE 2A.1   Testing pH

Solution Tested	Tests with 0.1*M* HCl pH after addition of							Tests with 0.1*M* NaOH pH after addition of						
	0	5	10	15	20	25	30 drops	0	5	10	15	20	25	30 drops
Tap water														
Liver														
Potato														
Egg white														
Gelatin														
Buffer														

5 drops have been added. Repeat this procedure until 30 drops have been used. Record the pH measurements in your table.

> ⚠ **CAUTION: 0.1 *M* HCl is a mild *irritant*. Avoid skin/eye contact; do not ingest. If contact occurs, flush affected area with water for 15 minutes; rinse mouth with water; call the teacher.**

5. Rinse the beaker thoroughly and pour into it another 25 mL of tap water. Record the initial pH of the water and add 0.1 *M* NaOH drop by drop, recording the pH changes in exactly the same way as for the 0.1 *M* HCl.

> ⚠ **CAUTION: 0.1 NaOH is a mild *irritant*. Avoid skin/eye contact; do not ingest. If contact occurs, flush affected area with water for 15 minutes; rinse mouth with water; call the teacher.**

6. Using the biological material assigned by your teacher, repeat Steps 2–5. Record the data in your table.

7. Test the buffer solution (a nonliving chemical solution) using the same method outlined in Steps 2–5. Record the data in your table.

8. Wash your hands thoroughly before leaving the laboratory.

Analysis

1. Summarize the effects of HCl and NaOH on tap water.

2. What was the total pH change for the 30 drops of HCl added to the biological material? For the 30 drops of NaOH added? How do these data compare with the changes in tap water?

3. Run strip charts to obtain individual graphs of the data. In your data book, prepare a simple graph of pH versus the number of drops of acid and base solutions added to tap water. Plot two lines—a solid line for changes with acid and a dashed line for changes with base. Using different colored solid and dashed lines, add the results for your biological material. Compare your graph to the graphs of teams who used a different biological material. What patterns do the graphs indicate for biological materials?

4. How do biological materials respond to changes in pH?

5. Use different colored solid and dashed lines to plot the reaction of the buffer solution on the same graph. How does the buffer system respond to the HCl and NaOH?

6. Is the pH response of the buffer system more like that of water or of the biological material?

7. How does the reaction of the buffer solution serve as a model for the response of biological materials to pH changes?

8. Would buffers aid or hinder the maintenance of a relatively stable environment within a living cell in a changing external environment?

9. What does the model suggest about a mechanism for regulating pH in an organism?

Investigation 2B • Compounds in Living Organisms

The compounds your body needs for energy and growth are carbohydrates, proteins, fats, vitamins, and other nutrients. These compounds are present in the plants and animals you use as food. In this investigation, you will observe tests for specific compounds and then use those tests to determine which compounds are found in ordinary foods.

Materials (per team of 4)

4 pairs of safety goggles

4 lab aprons

4 pairs of plastic gloves

250-mL beaker

10-mL graduated cylinder

6 18-mm × 150-mm test tubes

test-tube clamp

hot plate

Benedict's solution in dropping bottle

Biuret solution in dropping bottle

indophenol solution in dropping bottle

Lugol's iodine solution in dropping bottle

silver nitrate (1%) in dropping bottle

isopropyl alcohol (99%) in screw-top jar

brown wrapping paper

apple, egg white, liver, onion, orange, potato, or other foods of your choice

SAFETY   Put on your safety goggles, lab apron, and gloves. Tie back long hair.

Procedure

PART A   Test Demonstration

1. In your data book, prepare a table similar to Table 2B.1.

2. Reagents are chemical solutions that scientists use to detect the presence of certain compounds. Observe the six reagent tests your teacher performs. In your table, describe the results of each test.

PART B   Compounds in Foods

3. In your data book, prepare a table similar to Table 2B.2. Then, record the presence (+) or absence (−) of each chemical substance in the foods you test.

    WARNING: The reagents you will use in this procedure may be corrosive, poisonous, and/or irritants, and they may damage clothing. Avoid skin and eye contact; do not ingest. If contact occurs, flush the area with water for 15 minutes; rinse mouth with water; call the teacher immediately.

4. Predict the substances you will find in each sample your teacher assigns to you. Then, test the samples as your teacher demonstrated or as described in steps 5–10. Record the result of each test in your data book, using a + or −.

5. Protein test: Place 5 mL of the assigned food in a test tube. Add 10 drops of biuret solution.

6. Glucose test: Add 3 mL of Benedict's solution to 5 mL of the assigned food. Place the test tube in a beaker of boiling water and heat for five minutes.

    WARNING: Use test-tube clamps to hold hot test tubes. Boiling water will scald, causing second-degree burns. Do not touch the beaker or allow boiling water to

contact your skin. Avoid vigorous boiling. If a burn occurs, *immediately* place burned area under *cold* running water; *then* call the teacher.

7. Starch test: Add 5 drops of Lugol's iodine solution to 5 mL of the assigned food.

8. Vitamin C test: Add 8 drops of indophenol to 5 mL of the assigned food.

9. Chloride test: Add 5 drops of silver nitrate solution to 5 mL of the assigned food.

10. Fat test: Rub the assigned food on a piece of brown wrapping paper. Hold the paper up to the light. When food contains only a small amount of fat, the fat may not be detected by this method. If no fat has been detected, place the assigned food in 10 mL of a fat solvent such as isopropyl alcohol (99%). Allow the food to dissolve in the solvent for about five minutes. Then, pour the solvent on brown paper. The spot should dry in about ten minutes. Check the paper.

    WARNING: Isopropyl alcohol is *flammable* and is a *poison*. Do not expose the liquid or its vapors to heat, sparks, open flame, or other ignition sources. Do not ingest; avoid skin/eye contact. If contact occurs, flush

TABLE 2B.1 Reagent Tests of Known Food Substances

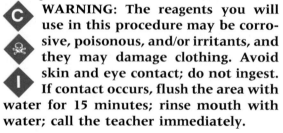

Food substance	Reagent test	Results
Gelatin	Biuret reagent	
Glucose	Benedict's solution	
Starch	Lugol's iodine solution	
Vitamin C	Indophenol solution (0.1%)	
Sodium chloride	Silver nitrate solution (1%)	
Butter or vegetable oil	Brown paper	

TABLE 2B.2 Analysis of Compounds in Common Foods

Substance		Protein	Glucose	Starch	Vitamin C	Chloride	Lipid
Egg	Prediction						
	Test results						
Potato	Prediction						
	Test results						
Etc.	Prediction						
	Test results						

affected area with water for 15 minutes; rinse mouth with water. If a spill occurs, flood spill area with water; *then* call the teacher.

11. Wash your hands thoroughly before leaving the laboratory.

Analysis

1. How did your predictions compare with the test results?

2. Which of your predictions was totally correct?

3. Which foods contained all the compounds for which you tested?

4. On the basis of your tests, which food could be used as source of protein? glucose? starch? vitamin C? fat?

5. How might the original colors of the test materials affect the results?

Investigation 2C • Enzyme Activity

In this investigation, you will study several factors that affect the activity of enzymes. The enzyme you will use is catalase, which is present in most cells and found in high concentrations in liver and blood cells. You will use liver homogenate as the source of catalase. Catalase promotes the decomposition of hydrogen peroxide (H_2O_2) in the following reaction:

$$2H_2O_2 \xrightarrow{\text{catalase}} 2H_2O + O_2$$

Hydrogen peroxide is formed as a by-product of chemical reactions in cells. It is toxic and soon would kill cells if not immediately removed or broken down. (Hydrogen peroxide is also used as an antiseptic. However, it is not a good antiseptic for open wounds, as it quickly is broken down by the enzyme catalase, which is present in human cells.)

Materials (per team of 3)

3 pairs of safety goggles

3 lab aprons

50-mL beaker

2 250-mL beakers

10-mL and 50-mL graduated cylinders

reaction chamber

6 18-mm × 150-mm test tubes

forceps

square or rectangular pan

test-tube rack

nonmercury thermometer

filter-paper discs

ice

water bath at 37°C

buffer solution: pH 5, pH 6, pH 7, pH 8

catalase solution

fresh H_2O_2 (3%)

	SAFETY Put on your safety goggles and lab apron. Tie back long hair.

Procedure

In all experiments, make certain that your reaction chamber is scrupulously clean. Catalase is a potent enzyme. If the chamber is not washed thoroughly, the enzyme will adhere to the sides and make subsequent tests inaccurate. Measure all substances carefully. Results depend on comparisons between experiments, so the amounts measured must be equal or your comparisons will be valueless. Before you do the experiment, read through the instructions completely. Make sure that you have all required materials on hand, that you understand the sequence of steps, and that each member of your team knows his or her assigned function.

PART A The Time Course of Enzyme Activity

1. Prepare a table in your data book similar to Table 2C.1

2. Obtain a small amount of stock catalase solution in a 50-mL beaker.

3. Obtain a reaction chamber and a number of filter-paper discs.

4. Place 4 catalase-soaked filter-paper discs on *one* interior sidewall of the reaction chamber. (They will stick to the sidewall.) Prepare a disc for use in the reaction chamber by holding it by its edge with a pair of forceps and dipping it into the stock catalase solution for a few seconds. Drain excess solution from the disc by holding it against the side of the beaker before you transfer it to the reaction chamber.

5. Stand the reaction chamber upright and carefully add 10 mL of 3% hydrogen peroxide (H_2O_2) solution. *Do not allow the peroxide to touch the filter-paper discs.*

CAUTION: H_2O_2 is reactive. Avoid contact between H_2O_2 and other chemicals unless instructed. Avoid skin/eye contact; do not ingest. If contact occurs, flush affected area with water for 15 minutes; rinse mouth with water; call the teacher immediately.

6. Tightly stopper the chamber.

7. Fill a pan almost full with water.

8. Lay the 50-mL graduated cylinder on its side in the pan so that it fills with water completely. If any air bubbles are present, carefully work these out by tilting the cylinder slightly. Turn the cylinder upside down into an upright position, keeping its mouth underwater at all times.

9. Making certain the side with the discs is at the top, carefully place the reaction chamber and its contents on its side in the pan of water.

10. Move the graduated cylinder into a position such that its mouth comes to lie directly over the tip of the dropping pipet extending from the reaction chamber, as shown in Figure 2C.1. One member of the team should hold it in this position for the duration of the experiment.

11. Rotate the reaction chamber 180° on its side so that the hydrogen peroxide solution comes into contact with the soaked disks.

12. Measure the gas levels in the graduated cylinder at 30-second intervals for 10 minutes. Record the levels in your data table.

PART B The Effect of Enzyme Concentration on Enzyme Activity

13. Test 3/4, 1/2, and 1/4 concentrations of enzyme solution, using the procedure for Part A with the following changes:

TABLE 2C.1 Catalase Activity Under Various Conditions

Experiment	mL O_2 evolved/30 sec																			
Full concentration	1	2	3	4	5	6	7	8	9	10	11	12	13	14	15	16	17	18	19	20
3/4 concentration																				
etc.																				

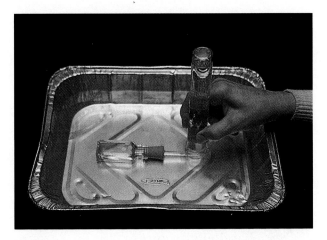

FIGURE 2C.1 Apparatus for measuring O₂ production in a reaction between catalase and hydrogen peroxide.

3/4 concentration: Use 3 catalase-soaked disks instead of 4.

1/2 concentration: Use 2 catalase-soaked disks and a 10-mL graduated cylinder.

1/4 concentration: Use 1 catalase-soaked disk and a 10-mL graduated cylinder.

14. Record all data in your data table.

PART C   The Effect of Temperature on Enzyme Activity

15. Add 10 mL of 3% H_2O_2 to each of two test tubes. Place one tube in a beaker of ice water and the other in a beaker with water maintained at 37°C.

16. When the temperature of the contents of the chilled H_2O_2 reaches approximately 10°C, repeat Part A with the following changes:

    a. In Step 5, use 10 mL of chilled 3% H_2O_2.
    b. In Step 7, add ice to the pan to chill the water to approximately 10°C.

17. When the temperature of the warmed H_2O_2 reaches approximately 37°C, repeat Part A with the following changes:

    a. In Step 5, use 10 mL of warmed 3% H_2O_2.
    b. In Step 7, fill the pan with water warmed to approximately 37°C.

18. Record the data in your data table.

PART D   The Effect of pH on Enzyme Activity

19. Label 4 test tubes as follows: *pH 5, pH 6, pH 7,* and *pH 8,* respectively. Add to each of these 8 mL of 3% H_2O_2.

20. Add 4 mL of pH 5 buffer solution to the *pH 5* test tube, shaking well to ensure mixing. To each of the other three test tubes, add 4 mL of pH 6, pH 7, and pH 8 buffer solutions, respectively, shaking each test tube well.

21. Repeat the procedure of Part A for each pH value, substituting the buffered 3% H_2O_2 solutions in step 5.

22. Record the results in your data table.

23. Wash your hands thoroughly before leaving the laboratory.

Analysis

1. In your data book, plot the data from Part A on a graph. Label the horizontal axis *Time (sec)*, and the vertical axis *mL O₂ Evolved*. Does the action of catalase change through time?

2. Plot the data from Part B on the grid used for Part A and label the enzyme concentrations on the graph. Based on these data, how does enzyme activity vary with concentration?

3. Copy the graph for Part A and plot the data from Part C on it. Based on these data, how does temperature affect enzyme action?

4. Plot the results for all four runs of Part D on a third graph. How does pH affect the activity of enzymes?

5. What is a buffer? Would the results of Parts A, B, and C have been different if buffers also had been used in those experiments? If so, how?

6. Summarize the general conditions necessary for effective enzyme action. Are these conditions the same for each enzyme? Why?

7. How would you design an experiment to show how much faster H_2O_2 decomposes in the presence of catalase than it does without the enzyme?

8. Explain how the enzyme catalase was still active, even though the liver cells from which you obtained the enzyme were no longer living.

Investigations for Chapter 3
Life, Energy, and the Biosphere

Investigation 3A • Are Corn Seeds Alive?

Observe a corn seed carefully. Can you tell whether or not the seed is alive? How could you determine if it is? If a seed is alive, it is said to be viable—capable of growing and developing. There are two ways to investigate whether or not a seed is viable. One way is to perform a tetrazolium (tet ruh ZOH lee um) test. Tetrazolium is a colorless chemical that turns pink or red in the presence of hydrogen, which is released by all living organisms as they carry on their daily chemical activities. The second way is to do a germination test. You will do both these tests using corn seeds from two different batches, labeled I and II. Keep the two groups separated.

Materials (per team of 4)

4 pairs of safety goggles

4 lab aprons

4 pairs of plastic gloves

10-mL graduated cylinder

2 jars or paper cups

2 petri dish halves

forceps

glass-marking pencil

paper towels

rubber bands

scalpel

wax paper

20 mL tetrazolium reagent (1%)

soaked corn seeds (50 Type I and 50 Type II)

SAFETY Put on your safety goggles, lab apron, and gloves.

Procedure
PART A Tetrazolium Test

1. Mark the outside bottom of one petri dish half *Type I* and the outside bottom of the other petri dish half *Type II*.

2. Obtain 25 corn seeds of Type I. Using the scalpel, cut each kernel lengthwise down the middle, as shown in Figure 3A.1 (*left*). The seeds may have been treated with a pesticide. Do not handle them without your gloves. You should be able to see the miniature plant (the embryo) inside the seed after it is cut.

   CAUTION: Scalpels are sharp; handle with care.

3. Discard one half of each seed and place the other half in the teams' petri dish with the cut surface down.

4. Cover the seed halves with 10 mL of tetrazolium reagent.

   WARNING: Tetrazolium is a contact irritant and poison. Avoid skin/eye contact; do not ingest. If contact occurs, flush affected area with water for 15 minutes; rinse mouth with water; call the teacher immediately.

5. Repeat steps 2, 3, and 4 with 25 seeds of Type II.

6. After 25 minutes, use gloves and forceps to remove the seeds. Examine the cut surface of each seed for a color change. A red or pink color indicates a living substance.

7. Copy Table 3A.1 in your data book and record your results there.

PART B Germination Test

8. Place a wet paper towel on a sheet of wax paper (see Figure 3A.1 [*right*]).

9. Place 25 Type I corn seeds in 5 rows of 5 across the wet paper towel. Place the seeds so the pointed end is toward the top of the towel.

10. Cover the seeds with another wet paper towel.

11. Fold the left side of the wax paper over the edge of the wet paper towels. Roll the wax paper, wet paper towels, and corn seeds from the left side toward the right side of the paper. Make the roll tight.

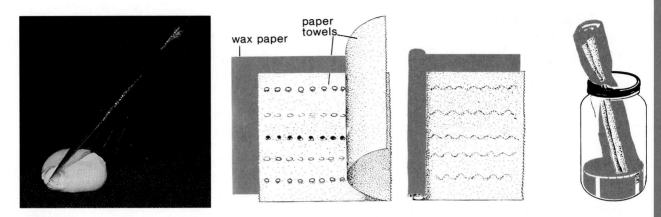

FIGURE 3A.1 (*left*) Procedure for cutting corn seed for tetrazolium test; (*right*) technique for preparing seeds for germination in a moist paper roll

12. Secure the roll with a rubber band so it will stay rolled up and place it upright in a jar of water (see Figure 3A.1 [*right*]).

13. Repeat Steps 8 through 12 with 25 Type II corn seeds.

14. Label each jar either *Type I* or *Type II*. Place the jars in a dark area designated by your teacher.

15. Wash your hands thoroughly before leaving the laboratory.

16. After three days, determine the total number of seeds in each jar that have begun to germinate (grow). Record the data in the table.

Analysis

1. For each treatment done per team and per class, calculate the percent viability as follows and enter the percentages in the table.

$$\frac{\text{Number of seeds showing viability}}{\text{Total number of seeds per treatment}} \times 100 = \% \text{ viability}$$

2. In Part A, if a color change indicates activity in living things, what can you conclude about the Type I and Type II seeds?

TABLE 3A.1 Results of Tetrazolium Test and Germination Test on Corn Seeds

| | Tetrazolium test | | | | Germination test | | | |
| | Type I seeds | | Type II seeds | | Type I seeds | | Type II seeds | |
	Team	Class	Team	Class	Team	Class	Team	Class
Number of seeds used								
Number of seeds viable or germinated								
Percentage of seeds viable or germinated								

3. What evidence have you found that the Type I seeds are alive? Not alive?

4. What evidence have you found that the Type II seeds are alive? Not alive?

5. Discuss in class the results of both experiments. Does the information provided by your teacher change any of your conclusions? Explain.

6. How does the percentage of viability, as determined from the tetrazolium test, compare with the percentage from the germination test?

7. Are the two percentages the same? If not, can you suggest a reason for the difference?

8. Is it possible to tell if seeds are alive by just looking at them? Why or why not?

9. What is the advantage of combining data from several teams in the class?

Investigation 3B • Food Energy

All foods contain energy, but the amount varies greatly from one food to another. You can use a calorimeter (Figure 3B.1) to measure the amount of energy, in calories, in some foods. A calorie is the amount of heat required to raise the temperature of 1 g (1 mL) of water 1°C. Calorie values of foods on diet charts are given in kilocalories (1000 calories) or kcals. (The kilocalorie is also referred to as the large Calorie.) Your teacher will provide tables listing caloric values for common foods.

Using a thermistor, you can measure the change in temperature (ΔT) of a known volume of water. The temperature change is caused by absorption of the heat given off by burning a known mass of food. Based on the change in temperature, you can calculate the amount of energy in the food. Instructions for use of the LEAP-System™ are provided in the LEAP-System BSCS Biology Lab Pac 2.

Materials (per team of 3)

3 pairs of safety goggles

3 lab aprons

100-mL graduated cylinder

250-mL Erlenmeyer flask

Apple IIe, Apple IIGS, Macintosh, or IBM computer

LEAP-System™

printer

thermistor

extension cable for thermistor

15-cm nonroll nonmercury thermometer (optional)

balance

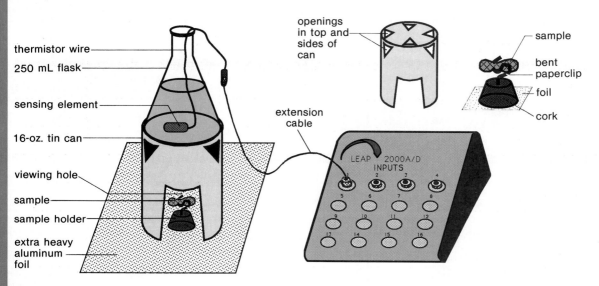

FIGURE 3B.1 The calorimeter setup

forceps

16 oz. tin can (with cutout air and viewing holes)

cork with sample holder

kitchen matches

20-cm × 30-cm piece of heavy duty aluminum foil

2 pot holders

small container of water

3 whole peanuts

3 walnut halves

SAFETY Put on your safety goggles and lab apron. Tie back long hair and roll up long, loose sleeves.

Procedure

1. Decide who in your team will be the experimenter, who will be the recorder/computer operator, and who will be the safety monitor to assure correct safety procedures are followed.

2. Copy Table 3B.1 in your data book or tape in the table your teacher provides.

3. Using the balance, determine the mass to the nearest 0.1 g of each peanut and each walnut half. Record the mass in the table.

4. Obtain a 250-mL flask, a tin can, a cork with sample holder, and a piece of extra heavy aluminum foil. This equipment may be used to make a calorimeter like the one shown in Figure 3B.1. Practice assembling and disassembling the equipment.

5. With the calorimeter disassembled, measure 100 mL of tap water and pour it into the flask.

6. Bend the thermistor wire at a right angle about 3 cm from the tip of the sensing element. Insert the thermistor into the flask so the sensing element is fully submerged in the eater and not touching the glass. Bend the thermistor wire at the top of the flask to hold the sensing element in position. If not using the thermistor, set the thermometer in the flask.

7. Measure the temperature of the water and record it in the table.

TABLE 3B.1 **Energy Content of Nut Samples**

		Temperature of water, °C			Food energy		
	Mass of sample	Before burning	After burning	Change	calories	kcal	kcal per gram
Walnut sample 1							
Walnut sample 2							
Walnut sample 3							
Average							
Peanut sample 1							
Peanut sample 2							
Peanut sample 3							
Average							

8. Place a peanut in the wire holder anchored in the cork. Then, place the cork on the piece of aluminum foil.

9. Carefully set fire to the peanut. This may require several matches. Discard burned matches in the container of water.

    WARNING: Matches are *flammable* solids. In case of burns, *immediately* place burned area under *cold* running water; *then* call the teacher.

10. Place the tin can over the burning sample with the viewing hole facing you. Place the flask of water on top of the tin can.

11. Begin recording data. Continue recording, even when the peanut has burned completely, until the water temperature begins to decrease. (The temperature will continue to rise after the sample has burned out as the water absorbs heat from the tin can.) Record the maximum water temperature from the numerical data displayed near the graph on the computer screen. If using a thermometer, take readings as soon as the sample has burned out and then at 30-second intervals.

12. Allow the calorimeter to cool about 2 minutes before disassembling.
    WARNING: Use pot holders to handle hot flasks. Boiling water will scald, causing second-degree burns. Do not touch the flask or allow boiling water to contact your skin. Avoid vigorous boiling. If a burn occurs, *immediately* place burned area under *cold* running water; *then* call the teacher.

13. Repeat Steps 7 through 12 until you have data for three samples each of a peanut and walnut half. Change the water in the flask each time.

14. Wash your hands thoroughly before leaving the laboratory.

Analysis

1. Print stripcharts or screen prints to obtain graphs of the data. Determine the average change in temperature for each sample. Calculate the number of kcals produced per gram. To do this, multiply the increase in water tempera-ture (average change) by 100 (the number of mL of water used). This step will give you the number of calories. To convert to kcals, divide by 1000 calories/kcal. To calculate kcals produced per gram of food, divide this number by the number of grams of food burned. Enter all data in the table.

2. How do your data (adjusted for 100 g) compare with the values for 100 g of the same or similar food listed by your teacher? (The kcals listed in most diet charts are per 100 g, per ounce, per cup, or per serving. To compare your results, you may need to convert to common units.)

3. How do you account for any differences?

4. If the same amount of food you tested were completely burned in the cells of the human body, would you expect the energy release to be greater or less than your results? Greater or less than published charts of the caloric content of foods?

5. Which of the two foods tested seems to be the better energy source?

6. Why might some foods with fewer kcals be better energy sources than other foods with more kcals?

7. What was the original source of energy in all the foods tested?

Investigations for Chapter 4
The Origin of Life

Investigation 4A • Coacervates

Under certain conditions, the proteins, carbohydrates, and other materials in a solution may group together into organized droplets called coacervates. Because coacervates have some properties that resemble those of living things, droplets like them might have been an important step in the origin of life. In this investigation, you can produce coacervates and study the conditions under which they form. You also can compare the appearance of coacervates with the appearance of the one-celled organisms, amoebas.

Materials (per team of 2)

2 pairs of safety goggles

2 lab aprons

cover slips

dropping pipet

10-mL graduated cylinder

microscope slides

test tubes with stoppers

compound microscope

wide-range pH test paper

gelatin suspension (1%)

gum arabic suspension (1%)

HCl (0.1*M*)

amoebas, living or prepared slides (optional)

> **SAFETY**   Put on your safety goggles and lab apron.

Procedure

1. Mix together 5 mL of the gelatin suspension and 3 mL of the gum arabic solution in a test tube. Gelatin is a protein. Gum arabic is a carbohydrate and is related to sugars and starches. Measure and record in your data book the pH of this mixture.

2. Place a drop of the gelatin-gum arabic mixture on a slide and observe it under the low power of the microscope.

3. Slowly add dilute hydrochloric acid (0.1*M* HCl) to the test tube, one drop at a time. After the addition of each drop, mix well and then wait a few seconds to see if the mixture becomes uniformly cloudy. If the liquid in the tube remains clear, add another drop of acid. Continue adding acid one drop at a time until the mixture remains uniformly cloudy.

CAUTION: 0.1*M* HCl is a mild irritant. Avoid skin /eye contact; do not ingest. If contact occurs, flush affected area with water for 15 minutes; rinse mouth with water; call the teacher.

4. When the material turns cloudy, take another pH reading. At this point, carefully observe a drop of liquid under the microscope. Look for coacervates, structures resembling those in Figure 4.12. If you cannot see them, try adjusting the light and using high power. Add another drop of acid to the test tube, mix, and observe again. If you still do not observe coacervates, repeat the procedure from the beginning, for you may have added acid too rapidly. When you are successful, record your observations and make sketches of the coacervate droplets.

5. Examine a wet-mount preparation of living amoebas or a prepared slide and compare their structure and organization with the larger coacervates.

6. When you have finished your observation of the coacervates, add more dilute acid to the test tube, a drop at a time. Mix after adding each drop and measure the pH after every third drop. Continue until the solution becomes clear again. When the liquid becomes clear again, examine a drop under the microscope and measure the new pH.

7. Wash your hands before leaving the laboratory.

Analysis

1. How do the materials you used to make coacervates compare with those that might have been present in the ancient ocean?

2. In what pH range did the coacervate droplets form?

3. Did the pH change as expected as a result of adding more acid to the solution between coacervate formation and clearing?

4. When dilute hydrochloric acid was added beyond a certain point, the coacervates disappeared. What might you add to the test tube to make the coacervates reappear?

5. How might the coacervate droplets be made more visible under the microscope?

Investigations for Chapter 5
Diversity and Variation

Investigation 5A • Classifying Flowering Plants

Flowering plants are divided into two classes: monocotyledons and dicotyledons (see Figure 15.3 on page 340). A cotyledon is a structure in seeds that provides food for the plant embryo. Monocotyledons have only one such structure and dicotyledons have two of these structures. To classify these plants you need to become familiar with the structure of flowers and the use of a classification key. You will examine both of these in this investigation. You will be able to identify selected flowering plants to the family level.

Materials (per team of 2)

hand lens or dissecting microscope

dissecting needles

forceps

scalpel

scissors

representatives of common families of flowering plants

Procedure

1. Select a flowering plant and determine whether it is a monocotyledon or a dicotyledon, using the definitions that follow the procedural steps and Figure 5A.1.

2. Use forceps, scissors, scalpel, dissecting needles, and hand lens or microscope to reveal key characteristics of the plant's flowers.

    CAUTION: Scalpel blades, scissors, and dissecting needles are sharp; handle with care. Replace cork on needle tip after use. Some plants or plant parts may be poisonous. Never taste any plant material you are studying.

3. Match the flower characteristics to the definitions that follow and to the illustrations in Figure 5A.1.

4. Use this information and Table 5A.1 or 5A.2 on the following pages to classify the plant.

5. Repeat Steps 1–4 for other selected plants.

6. Wash your hands thoroughly before leaving the laboratory.

Definitions (illustrated in Figure 5A.1)

Calyx: entire group of sepals and their bases (e)

Carpel: female reproductive organ in flowering plant (a)

Dicotyledons: flower parts in fours and fives or multiples of fours and fives; leaf veins in a network (i)

Head: many small flowers, with no stalks, tightly clustered in a group (g)

Inferior ovary: ovary below the bases of petals and sepals (b)

Irregular flower: one or more sepals, petals, stamens, etc. unlike others (c)

Monocotyledons: flower parts in threes or multiples of threes; leaf veins usually parallel (k)

Ovary: enlarged base of carpel in which the ova develop (a)

Ray flower: in the sunflower family, a petal-like flower, one of the many individual flowers that make up the head (g)

Receptacle: stem enlargement at flower base (a, g)

Regular flower: flower parts of each kind (sepals, petals, stamens, etc.) all alike (d)

Separate petals: petals distinct from one another beginning at their bases (f)

Sheath: specialized portion of a leaf that encloses the stem (k)

Stamen: male reproductive organ in flowering plant (a)

Stigma: receptive portion of style to which pollen sticks (a)

Stipules: small paired structures sometimes present at the base of a leaf stalk (j)

Style: slender column of tissue arising from the ovary (a)

(Definitions continue on page 636.)

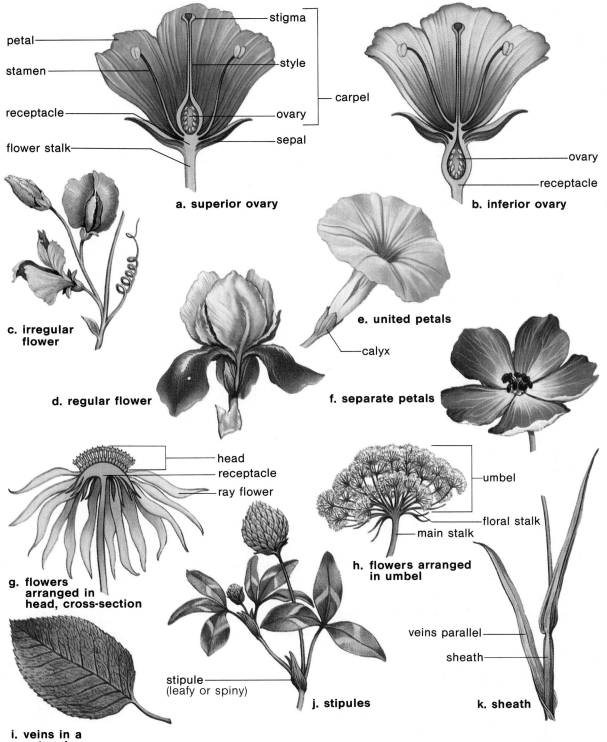

FIGURE 5A.1   Some flower characteristics used in classifying flowering plants.

TABLE 5A.1 Classification Key for Families of Monocotyledons

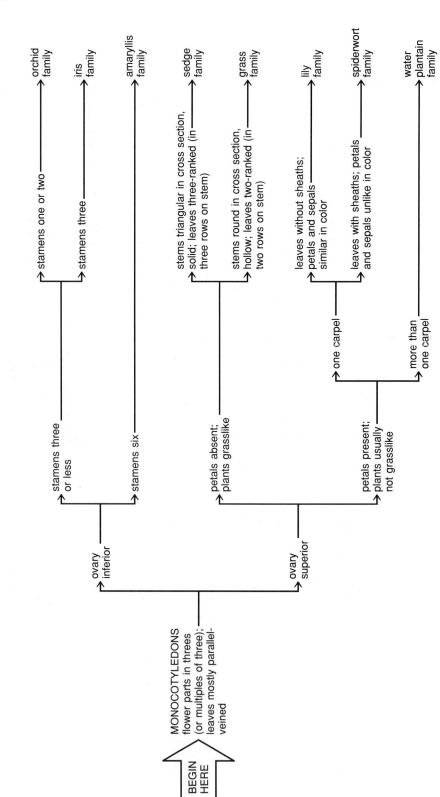

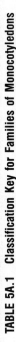

TABLE 5A.2 Classification Key for Families of Dicotyledons

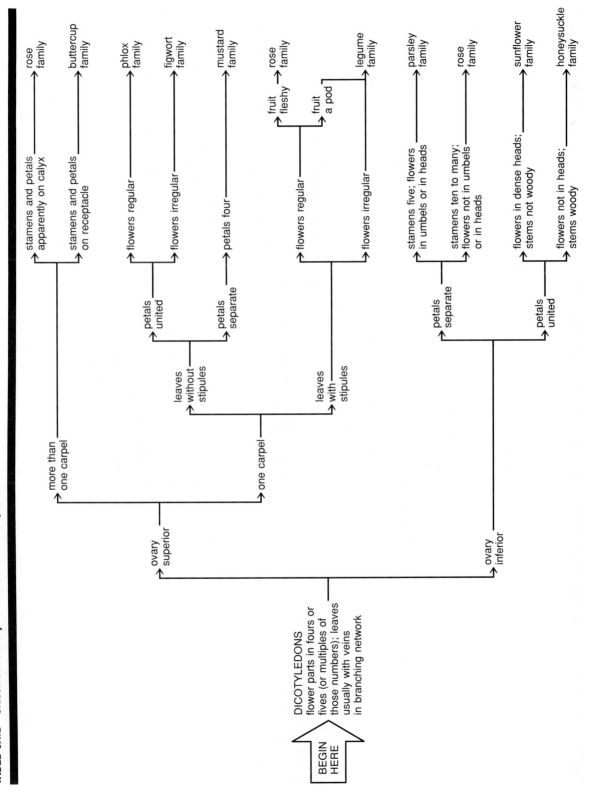

Superior ovary: ovary above the bases of petals and sepals (a)

Umbel: many small flowers, with stalks, loosely clustered in a group (h)

United petals: petals continuous or attached to each other, at least at base (e)

Analysis

1. Look up the term *dichotomous* and describe how it applies to the key you have used.

2. Which characteristics seem most important in identifying families of flowering plants?

3. Are size and color helpful when classifying plants? Explain your answer.

Investigation 5B • Structural Characteristics of Animals

In this investigation you will observe selected external characteristics of animals, and you will use these characteristics to classify the animals. Careful observation and note-taking are required. Two questions may help guide your observations: "How are these animals similar?" and "How are they different?"

This investigation will be a field trip. Your teacher will describe the objectives, schedule, and place or places to be visited. Make careful observations of the animals you see, and attempt to work out a classification scheme based on your observations.

Materials (per student)

charts of animal characteristics to be observed and recorded

data book

pen

textbook

Procedure

1. Before the field trip, study Figure 5.9 and the illustrations of Kingdom Animalia in "A Brief Summary of Organisms." Make a mental note of types of characteristics that could help in organizing and recording your data.

2. On the field trip, observe an animal carefully before you record any data. Note those features that can be used to distinguish it from other animals. Also note the more general characteristics that can be used to group the animal with others that appear related to it.

3. Record your observations on charts similar to those shown in Tables 5B.1 and 5B.2 (pages 637–638) or use other charts as directed by your teacher. Try to identify the phylum or class to which the animal belongs.

4. Make additional notes beyond the observations you record on the charts. Save these notes for discussion after the field trip.

5. Repeat steps 2, 3, and 4 for each animal to be observed. If you have questions, try to ask them before making entries in the charts.

Analysis

1. Which of the external characteristics you observed were of the greatest value in grouping animals together?

2. What features were of greatest value in distinguishing one species from another?

3. Which of the animals you observed seemed most closely related to one another?

4. Which of the animals you observed seemed least closely related to one another?

5. On the basis of your observations, write a short paragraph that distinguishes animals from organisms in other kingdoms.

6. Based on the animals you observed, what changes, if any, would you make in the classification charts you used?

7. What advantages and what disadvantages did you find in studying living animals rather than preserved specimens or illustrations in magazines and books?

8. What types of characteristics that you were unable to observe would have proved helpful in distinguishing between species of some of the animals you saw?

9. What roles did type of food and characteristics of feeding play in your classification of similar and different groups of animals?

TABLE 5B.1   Classification Chart for Invertebrates

		Name of animal							
Exoskeleton[1]	Present								
	Absent								
Body symmetry	Radial[2]								
	Bilateral[3]								
	Part bilateral, part spiral								
Jointed walking legs	3 pairs present								
	4 pairs present								
	More than 4 pairs present								
	Absent								
Body segmentation[4]	Present								
	Absent								
Tentacles[5]	More than 4 present								
	4 or fewer present								
	Absent								
Antennae[6]	2 or more pairs present								
	1 pair present								
	Absent								
		Phylum	Phylum	Phylum	Phylum	Phylum	Phylum	Phylum	

[1]Exoskeleton: a skeleton on the outer surface of an animal, enclosing the animal.
[2]Radial symmetry: body parts arranged in a circular manner around a central point or region, as in a bicycle wheel.
[3]Bilateral symmetry: matching body parts along the right and left sides of a line running from one end of the animal to the other, as in the body of a bus.
[4]Body segmentation: a structural pattern in which the body is divided into a series of more or less similar sections, the boundaries of which are usually indicated by grooves encircling the body.
[5]Tentacles: slender, flexible structures that can be lengthened or shortened; usually attached near the mouth.
[6]Antennae: slender structures that can be waved about but cannot be changed in length; usually attached to the head.

TABLE 5B.2 Classification Chart for Vertebrates

		Name of animal							
Skin structures	Hair present								
	Feathers present								
	Scales present								
	None of above present								
Appendages	Wings present								
	Legs present								
	Fins present								
	None of above present								
Skeleton	Bony[1]								
	Cartilaginous[2]								
Teeth	Present								
	Absent								
		Class	Class	Class	Class	Class	Class	Class	

[1]Bony skeleton: a skeleton in which most of the parts are hard and relatively rigid, because of the hard mineral matter they contain.
[2]Cartilaginous skeleton: a skeleton in which all the parts are tough but flexible because they are composed of cartilage—a substance that does not contain significant deposits of hard minerals.

Investigations for Chapter 6
Organization of Cells

Investigation 6A • Cell Structure

In this investigation you will examine some cells from multicellular and unicellular organisms.

Materials (per team of 2)

2 pairs of safety goggles

2 lab aprons

3 cover slips

dropping pipet

3 microscope slides

compound microscope

fine-pointed forceps

paper towel

Detain™ in dropping bottle (slowing agent)

Lugol's iodine solution in dropping bottle

pond water culture

salt solution in dropping bottle (5%)

onion

elodea leaf (*Anacharis*)

prepared slides of stained human cheek cells

Procedure

1. Separate one layer from an onion quarter and hold it so that the concave (curved inward) surface faces you. Snap it backwards (see Figure 6A.1 *left*) to separate the transparent, paper-thin layer of cells from the outer curve of the scale.

2. Use forceps to peel off a small section of the thin layer and lay it flat on a microscope slide. Discard the rest of the onion piece. Trim the piece with a scalpel if necessary and smooth any wrinkles.

   CAUTION: Scalpel blades are sharp; handle with care.

3. Add 1 or 2 drops of Lugol's iodine solution and a cover slip.

   WARNING: Lugol's iodine solution is a *poison* if ingested, a *strong irritant*, and can stain clothing. Avoid skin/ eye contact; do not ingest. If contact occurs, flush affected area with water for 15 minutes; rinse mouth with water; call the teacher immediately.

4. Examine the slide first with low power and then with high power.

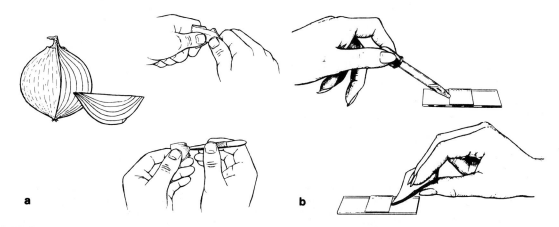

FIGURE 6A.1 Removing the thin layer of cells from a section of onion *(left)* and adding sugar or salt solution under a cover slip *(right)*.

5. Sketch a few cells as they appear under high power. How many dimensions do the cells appear to have when viewed through high power? Sketch a single cell as it would appear if you could see three dimensions. Using the procedure from Investigation 1C, estimate and record cell size.

6. Identify the cell wall, nucleus, and cytosol. Sketch each in a diagram. You may be able to see a nucleolus within a nucleus. If so, sketch it also. Add a drop of salt solution at one edge of the cover slip. Touch the tip of a piece of paper towel to the opposite edge of the cover slip (Figure 6A.1 *right*). The paper will act as a wick, pulling the salt solution across the slide and into contact with the cells. Continue observing the cells until the cytosol appears to pull away from the cell walls. The boundary of the cytosol is the plasma membrane.

7. Prepare a wet mount of an elodea leaf and observe it with low power and then with high power. Sketch a few cells as they appear under high power. Add a drop of Lugol's iodine solution at one edge of the cover slip and pull it into contact with the leaf as in Step 5. Are there structures now visible that you could not see without the iodine? Add these structures to your sketch. Estimate and record cell size.

8. Obtain a prepared slide of stained human cheek cells. Examine the cells with the low and then the high power of the microscope. Find a field where the cells are separate and distinct, and sketch a few under high power. Estimate and record cell size. Label the structures you can identify.

9. Place 1 or 2 drops of the pond water culture on a slide, add a cover slip, and examine under low power with your microscope.

10. Try making some observations through the high-power lens, keeping in mind that most of the organisms are transparent or almost transparent. Decrease the amount of light by adjusting the diaphragm. Many of the organisms move rapidly and are hard to find under high power. The cover slip will slow down some of them, but you also can add a drop of Detain, a slowing agent.

11. Use the keys available in the laboratory to identify some of the organisms. Roundworms, daphnia, cyclops, rotifers, and immature forms (larvae) of insects are among the multicellular creatures that could be in your pond water.

12. Estimate the size of some of the organisms.

13. Wash your hands thoroughly before leaving the laboratory.

Analysis

1. Construct a summary table comparing the common organelles of plant and animal cells. What part of the cell did you find in your samples of plant cells that you did not find around the cheek cells?

2. Are the plasma membranes of plant cells difficult to see? Explain your answer.

3. Did the Lugol's iodine solution aid in your observation of cells? Why do biologists use stains to study cells?

4. How many different organisms did you observe in the pond water? Describe some of the differences among them.

Investigation 6B • Cells and Movement of Materials

To survive, all organisms need to balance their internal environment despite constantly changing conditions. Multicellular organisms have complex systems of organs that maintain this balance, but a single cell must rely on a solitary structure. The contents of a cell are surrounded by a thin membrane—the plasma membrane. Anything entering or leaving the cell must pass through this membrane. Certain materials can pass into the cell, whereas others cannot. Similarly, some materials pass out of the cell, while others that are vital to the cell's existence remain inside.

In this investigation, you will explore the movement of substances through membranes—both living plasma membranes and nonliving material that models plasma membranes. This nonliving material—called dialysis tubing—separates larger molecules from smaller molecules. The size of the pores in the tubing determines which molecules may pass through it.

Materials (per team of 2)

2 pairs of safety goggles

2 lab aprons

2 250-mL beakers

3 cover slips

2 dropping pipets

3 microscope slides

2 test tubes

glass-marking pencil

compound microscope

2 15-cm pieces of dialysis tubing

hot plate

paper towel

4 10-cm pieces of string

test-tube clamp

test-tube rack

urine glucose test strips

brilliant cresyl blue solution in dropping bottle (0.5%)

distilled water

15 mL glucose solution

salt solution (5%)

15 mL soluble-starch solution

Lugol's iodine solution in dropping bottle

yeast suspension

elodea leaf (*Anacharis*)

SAFETY Put on your safety goggles and lab apron; tie back long hair.

PART A Diffusion Through a Membrane

Procedure

1. Twist one end of a piece of dialysis tubing. Fold the twisted end over and tie it tightly with a piece of string. Prepare the other piece the same way.

2. Pour soluble-starch solution to within 15 cm of the top of one piece of tubing. Twist and tie the end as in Step 1. Rinse the tubing under running water to remove any starch from the outside.

Lugol's iodine solution

dialysis tubing containing starch solution

water in beaker

FIGURE 6B.1 Setup for diffusion

3. Place the tubing in a beaker of water labeled *A* (see Figure 6B.1). Add enough Lugol's iodine to give the water a distinct yellowish color.

> ☠ ⓵ **WARNING: Lugol's iodine solution is a *poison* if ingested, a *strong irritant*, and can stain clothing. Avoid skin/ eye contact; do not ingest. If contact occurs, flush affected area with water for 15 minutes; rinse mouth with water; call the teacher immediately.**

4. Repeat Step 2 with the second piece of dialysis tubing, using glucose solution instead of the soluble starch. Place this tubing in a beaker of water labeled *B*.

5. Allow the pieces of tubing to stand for about 20 minutes. Dip a urine glucose test strip into the water in beaker B. Record the color on the strip.

6. Observe the tubing in beaker A. Record any changes, including color, that you see in either the tubing or the water in the beaker.

7. Let beakers A and B stand overnight. Record any changes observed the next day.

8. Wash your hands thoroughly before leaving the laboratory.

Analysis

1. On the basis of the results from steps 3 and 6, what must have happened to the iodine molecules in beaker A?

2. On the basis of the chemical test for glucose (step 5), what must have happened to the glucose molecules in beaker B?

3. From the evidence obtained after the beakers stood overnight, what other substances passed through the membrane in beaker B?

4. Which substance did not pass through a membrane? Explain your answer.

5. Physicists can show that all the molecules of a given substance are about the same size, but that molecules of different substances are different in size. Measurements show that iodine molecules and water molecules are very small, glucose molecules are considerably larger, and starch molecules are very large. On the basis of this information, suggest a hypothesis to account for your observations.

6. What assumption did you make about the structure of the dialysis tubing?

PART B   Osmosis and the Living Cell

Procedure

7. Place a leaf from the growing tip of an elodea plant in a drop of water on a clean slide. Add a cover slip and examine under low power. Position the slide so that the cells along one edge of the leaf are near the center.

8. Switch to high power and focus sharply on a few cells near the edge of a leaf. Place a small piece of absorbent paper at the edge of the cover slip opposite the side of the leaf you are observing, as shown in Figure 6A.1 (*right*). (Remember, directions are reversed when you look through a microscope.) Have your lab partner place several drops of glucose solution at the cover slip edge nearest the part of the leaf being observed. Use the fine adjustment to adjust the focus while the water is being replaced. Continue observing the cells until you see changes in them.

9. Make simple sketches showing cells both before and after the glucose solution was added.

10. Remove the glucose solution and replace it with distilled water. Use a new piece of absorbent paper and allow 2 or 3 drops of distilled water to flow across the slide into the paper to make sure that most of the glucose solution is washed away. Make observations while this is being done.

11. Exchange places with your lab partner. Repeat steps 7 through 10.

12. Repeat steps 7 through 10 with salt solution in place of the glucose solution.

Analysis

1. Did water move into or out of the cells while the leaf was surrounded by the glucose solution? By the salt solution? What evidence do you have to support your answer?

2. In which direction did water move through the plasma membrane when the cell was surrounded by the distilled water?

3. What do you think would happen to elodea cells if they were left in the glucose solution for several hours? Could elodea from a freshwater lake be expected to survive if transplanted into the ocean? (Assume that the salt concentration of the ocean is about the same as the salt solution used in this experiment.)

4. An effective way to kill plants is to pour salt on the ground around them. Using principles discovered in this investigation, explain why the plants die.

5. Bacteria cause food to spoil and meat to rot. Explain why salted pork, strawberry preserves, and sweet pickles do not spoil even though they are exposed to bacteria. Name other foods preserved in the same manner.

PART C   Membranes in Living and Dead Cells

Procedure

13. Place one drop of yeast suspension on a slide, add a cover slip, and observe the yeast cells under low and then high power. Describe what you see and make sketches of two or three cells to show their general appearance.

14. Place about 1 mL of yeast suspension in each of two small test tubes. Label one tube "boiled" and the other "unboiled." Heat one of the test tubes in a beaker of boiling water until the contents have boiled for at least 2 minutes. This action will kill the yeast cells. Allow the test tube and its contents to cool for a few minutes.

WARNING: Use test tube clamps to hold hot test tubes. Boiling water will scald, causing second-degree burns. Do not touch the beaker or allow boiling water to contact your skin. Avoid vigorous boiling. If a burn occurs, *immediately,* **place the burned area under** *cold* **running water;** *then* **call the teacher.**

15. Add 5 drops of brilliant cresyl blue solution to the boiled yeast suspension and 5 drops to the unheated yeast suspension.

    CAUTION: Brilliant cresyl blue solution is a mild *irritant.* **Avoid skin/eye contact; do not ingest. If contact occurs, flush affected area with water for 15 minutes; rinse mouth with water; call the teacher.**

16. Label one microscope slide "boiled" and another "unboiled." Prepare a slide from each test tube and examine under high power. Record any differences between the yeast cells in the two suspensions.

17. Wash your hands thoroughly before leaving the laboratory.

Analysis

1. What effect does heat seem to have on the yeast plasma membrane?

2. In a preparation of unheated yeast solution and brilliant cresyl blue, a few blue yeast cells are usually visible. What assumption can you make concerning these cells?

3. Which passes more easily through membranes of living cells, brilliant cresyl blue molecules or water molecules? Develop a hypothesis to account for your observation and answer.

Investigation 6C • Diffusion and Cell Size

Does diffusion proceed rapidly enough to supply a cell efficiently with some of its materials? The same question can be asked about removing cell wastes. In this investigation you will discover how the rate of diffusion and the size of a cell are related.

Materials (per team of 2)

2 pairs of safety goggles

2 lab aprons

2 pairs of plastic gloves

250-mL beaker

metric ruler

paper towel

plastic knife

plastic spoon

3 cm × 3 cm × 6 cm cube of phenolphthalein agar

150 mL HCl (0.1%)

SAFETY   Put on your safety goggles, lab apron, and gloves.

Procedure

1. Using a plastic knife, trim the agar block to make three cubes—3 cm, 2 cm, and 1 cm on a side, respectively.

2. Place the cubes in the beaker and add 0.1% HCl until the cubes are submerged. Record the time. Use the plastic spoon to turn the cubes frequently for the next 10 minutes.

    CAUTION: 0.1% HCl is a mild *irritant.* **Avoid skin/eye contact; do not ingest. If contact occurs, flush affected area with water for 15 minutes; rinse mouth with water, call the teacher.**

3. Prepare a table similar to Table 6C.1 (page 644) and do the calculations necessary to complete it. The surface area-to-volume ratio is calculated as follows:

$$\text{Ratio of surface area to volume} = \frac{\text{surface area}}{\text{volume}}$$

This ratio also may be written as "surface area:volume." The ratio should be expressed in its simplest form (for example, 3:1 rather than 24:8).

4. Wear gloves and use the plastic spoon to remove the agar cubes from the HCl after 10 minutes.

Blot them dry. Avoid handling the cubes until they are blotted dry. Use the plastic knife to slice each cube in half. Rinse and dry the knife between cuts. Record your observations of the sliced surface. Measure the depth of diffusion of the HCl in each of the three cubes.

TABLE 6C.1 Comparison of Agar Cubes

Cube dimension	Surface area (cm²)	Volume (cm³)	Simplest ratio
3 cm			
2 cm			
1 cm			
0.01 cm			

Analysis

1. List the agar cubes in order of size, from largest to smallest. List them in order of the ratios of surface area to volume, from the largest to the smallest ratio. How do the lists compare?

2. Calculate the surface area-to-volume ratio for a cube 0.01 cm on a side.

3. Which has the greater surface area, a cube 3 cm on a side or a microscopic cube the size of an onion skin cell? (Assume the cell to be 0.01 cm on a side.) Which has the greater surface area *in proportion* to its volume?

4. What evidence is there that HCl diffuses into an agar cube? What evidence is there that the rate of diffusion is about the same for each cube? Explain.

5. What happens to the surface area-to-volume ratio of cubes as they increase in size?

6. Most cells and microorganisms measure less than 0.01 cm on a side. What is the relationship between rate of diffusion and cell size?

7. Propose a hypothesis to explain one reason why large organisms have developed from *more* cells rather than *larger* cells.

Investigations for Chapter 7
Photosynthesis: Harvesting Light Energy

Investigation 7A • Leaf Structure and Stomates

Leaves have structural adaptations that enable them to perform their specific functions efficiently. In this investigation you will examine those structures and try to identify the functions for which they are adapted.

Materials (per team of 2)

cover slip

dropping pipet

iris scissors

microscope slide

forceps

compound microscope

prepared cross section of a leaf

several types of fresh leaves

variety of mature plants

PART A Leaf Structure and Function

Procedure

1. Examine the various plants, the different types of leaves, and the arrangement of leaves on the stems. Record your observations.

2. Examine a prepared cross section of a leaf under the high power of your microscope. Compare your slide with Figure 7.2 to become familiar with the various regions of the leaf. Consider its structures in relation to the functions of light absorption, water supply, and carbon dioxide absorption.

3. Locate chloroplasts in the leaf cells. Note their shape and abundance in the various leaf cells.

4. Locate a cross section of a small vein in the center tissues of the leaf. The vein is surrounded by a sheath of cells that also are photosynthetic.

Notice some of the empty cells with thick walls in the upper part of the sectioned leaf.

5. Examine the covering layers of the leaf—the upper epidermis and the lower epidermis. These single layers of cells are covered by cuticle, which may have been removed when the slide was made.

6. Locate a stomate and its guard cells. Locate the spongy tissue just below the lower epidermis. Note how the stomates are located in relation to the spongy tissue.

Analysis

1. What might be the advantage of a flat, thin leaf blade to the photosynthetic capacity of the plant?

2. How does the arrangement of leaves on a stem relate to the photosynthetic capacity of a plant?

3. On the basis of your observations of chloroplast location in the leaf, which cells are the main photosynthetic cells?

4. How might the location of chloroplasts in these cells be advantageous to the plant?

5. Suggest a function for the thick-walled, empty cells in a leaf vein.

6. Explain how the cuticle may affect the efficiency of photosynthesis.

7. Compare the structure of the spongy tissue to that of the other leaf tissues.

8. Explain how the location of stomates in spongy tissue is related to the function of the spongy layer.

9. Write a short paragraph summarizing how the leaf structures you observed are adapted for leaf functions.

PART B   Number of Stomates

Procedure

7. While holding the lower surface of a leaf upward, tear the leaf at an angle. The tearing action should peel off a portion of the lower epidermis. It will appear as a narrow, colorless zone extending beyond the green part of the leaf.

8. Lay the epidermis in a drop of water on a slide and use the scissors to cut off a small piece. Add a cover slip. Do not allow the epidermis to dry out.

   CAUTION: Scissors are sharp; handle with care.

9. Using the low-power objective of your microscope, locate some stomates. Then switch to the high-power objective. Make a sketch to show the shape of a stomate, its guard cells, and a few adjacent cells in the epidermis.

10. Count the number of stomates in the high-power field for 10 different areas of the epidermis. Record your observations.

11. In the same manner, count the stomates on the upper epidermis of the same leaf. Examine as many other types of leaves as possible. Compare the number of stomates per mm² on the upper and lower surfaces of each type of leaf.

12. Wash your hands thoroughly before leaving the laboratory.

Analysis

1. Calculate the average number of stomates per mm² of the leaf's surface. (Refer to Investigation 1C to calculate the diameter of the high-power field. Use the diameter to calculate the area of the leaf observed under the microscope.)

2. How did the number of stomates per mm² in different areas of the same side of a piece of leaf epidermis compare? On opposite sides?

3. Did the stomates vary in the amount they were open? How can you explain your findings?

4. What would you do to assure a reliable comparison of the number of stomates per mm² for two species of plants?

5. What do your data suggest about the distribution of stomates in leaves of your species of plant? What assumption must you make in drawing this conclusion?

Investigation 7B • Photosynthesis

Section 7.5 of your text developed the following equation to represent the materials and products of photosynthesis:

$$3CO_2 + 3H_2O \xrightarrow[\text{light}]{\text{plants}} C_3H_6O_3 + 3O_2$$

carbon   water   sugar   oxygen
dioxide

This equation raises several questions, which can serve as a basis for experiments that will help you understand the process of photosynthesis.

A. Does a green plant use carbon dioxide in the light?

B. Is light necessary in order for this reaction to take place?

C. Are the materials shown in the equation involved in any plant process other than photosynthesis?

D. Do plants release the oxygen produced in photosynthesis?

In this investigation, you are asked to design experiments to answer the questions above. There are several factors you will need to consider before starting work.

1. What type of plant could best serve your purpose, a water plant or a land plant?

2. What factor affecting photosynthesis could best be used to start and stop the process?

3. What type of detector can be used to show that photosynthesis has or has not occurred?

4. How can you identify the substances that are produced or given off during photosynthesis?

5. What type of controls are necessary?

Materials (per team of 2)

2 lab aprons

2 pairs of safety goggles

15-mm x 125-mm test tubes

wrapped drinking straws

stoppers to fit test tubes

carbonated water

bromothymol blue solution

elodea (*Anacharis*)

SAFETY   Put on your safety goggles and lab apron. Tie back long hair.

Procedure

PART A   Use of CO$_2$ in Light

1. Add enough bromothymol blue solution to a test tube to give a light blue color, and using a drinking straw, gently bubble your breath through it until you see a color change.
   CAUTION: Do not suck any liquid through the straw.
   Discard the straw after use.

2. Add a few drops of carbonated water to a small amount of bromothymol blue in a test tube and observe any color change. What do carbonated water and your breath have in common that might be responsible for the similar result? What action would be necessary to restore the original color of the bromothymol blue?

3. Using elodea, bromothymol blue solution, and test tubes, set up an experiment to answer Question A. (Hint: Bromothymol blue solution is not poisonous to elodea.)

4. Using Table 7B.1 as a guide, prepare a table listing the test tubes in your experiment. Show what you added to each tube, what change you expected in the bromothymol blue solution, and what change actually occurred. Explain the change. Fill in the first three columns of the table on the day the experiments are set up, and fill in the last two columns the next day.

5. Wash your hands before leaving the laboratory.

PART B   Light and Photosynthesis

6. Using the same types of materials as in Part A, set up an experiment to answer Question B. Use as many plants and test tubes as necessary to be sure of your answer.

7. Prepare and complete a data table as in Part A.

PART C   CO$_2$ in Other Plant Processes

8. Using the same types of materials as in Part A, set up an experiment to answer Question C for CO$_2$.

9. Prepare and complete a data table as in Part A.

TABLE 7B.1   Form for Data Table

Test Tube	Material Added (procedure)	Expected Indicator Change (hypothesis)	Actual Indicator Change (data)	What the Change Shows (interpretation)
1	Bromothymol blue solution, elodea, CO_2 and light	Yellow bromothymol blue solution will turn blue.		

PART D   Oxygen and Photosynthesis

10. Your teacher or a selected group of students can set up a demonstration experiment to answer Question D (page 646). What observations in Parts A, B, or C indicate that the elodea in light was giving off a gas? How might some of this gas be collected and tested to determine its identity?

Analysis

1. Do you have evidence from Procedure A that light alone does not change the color of the bromothymol blue solution? Explain.

2. What test tubes show that light is necessary for a plant to carry on photosynthesis?

3. How is CO_2 used by a plant that is not carrying on photosynthesis? What test tubes show CO_2's role? What biological process accounts for your findings?

4. Determine where your expected changes disagree with the actual changes. Are the differences, if any, due to experimental error or a wrong hypothesis? Explain.

Investigation 7C • Rate of Photosynthesis

There are several ways to measure the rate of photosynthesis. In this investigation, you will use elodea and pH probes with the LEAP-System™, or narrow-range pH paper. The rate of photosynthesis is determined indirectly be measuring the amount of carbon dioxide removed from water by elodea. Carbon dioxide is added by bubbling breath into the water, which absorbs the carbon dioxide. The carbon diox-

ide combines with water to produce carbonic acid ($H_2O + CO_2 \rightleftharpoons H_2CO_3$), a reversible reaction. As carbon dioxide is used by elodea in photosynthesis, less carbonic acid is present and the pH of the water increases. The LEAP-System BSCS Biology Lab Pac 2 includes instructions for the use of the system.

Hypothesis: After reading the procedure, develop hypotheses that predict the effects of light intensity and color on the rate of photosynthesis.

Materials (per team of 4)

4 pairs of safety goggles

2-L beaker

100-mL beaker or small jar

250-mL flask

2 1-mL pipets (optional)

2 25-mm x 200-mm test tubes

2 wrapped drinking straws

lamp with 100-watt spotlight

Apple IIe, Apple GS, Macintosh, or IBM computer

LEAP-System™

printer

2 pH probes

thermistor

narrow-range pH paper (optional)

nonmercury thermometer (optional)

red, blue, and green cellophane

distilled water

tap water at 25°C and 10°C

2 15-cm sprigs of young elodea

SAFETY   Put on your safety goggles.

FIGURE 7C.1 LEAP-System setup

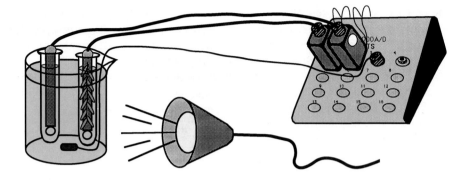

Procedure

PART A   Equipment Assembly

1. In your data book, prepare a table similar to Table 7C.1, or tape in the table your teacher provides.

2. Place 125 mL of distilled water into the flask. Blow through a small straw into the water for 2 minutes.
   CAUTION: Be careful not to suck any liquid through the straw.
   Discard the straw after use as your teacher directs. What is the purpose of blowing into the water in the flask?

3. Place two sprigs of elodea, cut end up, into one of the test tubes (experimental tube).

4. Fill both test tubes 3/4 full with the water you blew into. What is the purpose of the second test tube?

5. Remove the plastic cap from the tip of the pH probe. Insert the pH probe from input 1 into the experimental test tube and the pH probe from input 2 into the other test tube, as shown in Figure 7C.1.

6. Stand the test tubes in a 2-L beaker; add 25°C tap water to the beaker until it is about 2/3 full.

7. Insert the thermistor (or a thermometer) into the water in the 2-L beaker. Determine the temperature in the beaker and maintain this temperature throughout the experiment. (Use the small beaker to add ice water and/or to remove water from the 2-L beaker.)

TABLE 7C.1 Rate of Photosynthesis

| | Experimental Condition | | | | | | | | | | | | | | | | | |
| | 30 cm | | | 10 cm | | | 50 cm | | | Red | | | Blue | | | Green | | |
Reading #	pH 1	pH 2	°C	pH 1	pH 2	°C	pH 1	pH 2	°C	pH 1	pH 2	°C	pH 1	pH 2	°C	pH 1	pH 2	°C
1																		
2																		
3																		
4																		
5																		
6																		

8. Let the entire assembly stand for about 5 minutes to permit the temperature to become uniform throughout the system. Note the initial pH in the test tubes and record both readings in the data table. (If the LEAP-System is not available, use the 1-mL pipets to transfer a drop of water from halfway down each test tube to a piece of narrow-range pH paper and read the pH from the comparison chart on the strip.)

PART B   Basic Photosynthetic Rate

9. Place the lamp with the 100-watt spotlight 30 cm from the beaker and illuminate the two test tubes.

10. Take pH and temperature readings every 5 minutes, for a total of 30 minutes. Record the readings in the data table.

11. Wash your hands thoroughly before leaving the laboratory.

PART C   Effects of Light Intensity on Photosynthetic Rate

12. Repeat Steps 2–10 with the light source first 10 cm and then 50 cm away from the test-tube assembly.

PART D   Effects of Light Color on Photosynthetic Rate

13. Repeat Steps 2–10 using first red, then blue, and then green cellophane over the beaker.

14. Wash your hands thoroughly before leaving the laboratory.

Analysis

1. What chemical change occurred in the water you blew into?

2. What happens during photosynthesis that causes the pH to increase in the test tubes?

3. What two environmental factors are being controlled by the test tube without the elodea?

4. How much did the pH change during the 30-minute period for each condition tested?

5. How would you use any change in pH in the test tube without elodea to correct the data for the experimental test tube?

6. Run stripcharts to produce graphs for each part of the investigation. What variables are on the horizontal and vertical axes of the graphs? (If using pH paper, prepare graphs showing pH every 5 minutes under the various conditions being tested.)

7. Use the change in pH that occurs at the three light intensities you tested to determine the effect of light intensity on the rate of photosynthesis. Do your data support your hypothesis?

8. Use the change in pH with the three colors (red, blue, and green) to determine the effect of light color on the rate of photosynthesis. Do your data support the hypothesis you constructed?

Investigations for Chapter 8
Harvesting Chemical Energy

Investigation 8A • How Does Oxygen Affect Cells?

Oxygen is very important in the release of energy from food. Most organisms, including plants and humans, cannot live without a constant supply of oxygen. Some organisms, however, can get energy from food without oxygen. Additionally, there are a few kinds of microorganisms that use oxygen if it is available, but still can get energy from food if oxygen is not available. These microorganisms that are both aerobic and anaerobic are called facultative anaerobes. The bacterium *Aerobacter aerogenes* (AIR oh back ter air AH jih neez) is an example of a facultative anaerobe.

This investigation provides data from an experiment with *Aerobacter aerogenes*. The bacteria were allowed to grow in test tubes containing distilled water to which only a few salts and various concentrations of glucose were added. Some of the tubes were sealed so that no air was available to the cells. Other tubes had a stream of air bubbling through the growth solution. You will work with and interpret the data and develop a hypothesis to explain the findings.

Materials (per student)

graph paper
pencil

Procedure

1. Graph the data shown in Table 8A.1. Label the vertical axis *millions of cells per mL* and the horizontal axis *glucose (mg/100 mL)*. Plot the data from series A (test tubes without air). Label the line *Growth without air*.

2. On the same graph, plot the data from series B (test tubes with air). Label the second line *Growth with air*.

3. Use your graphs to help you answer Analysis questions 1 through 8.

Analysis

1. What are the two most obvious differences between the graph curves for series A and B?

2. Look at Table 8A.1 and compare test tubes 4A and 4B. How many times greater was the growth when air was present?

3. Compare the other test tubes in the A and B series at the various glucose concentrations. How much greater is the growth in air for each

TABLE 8A.1 Effects of Different Glucose Concentrations on Growth of Bacteria

Concentration of Glucose (mg per 100 mL of H$_2$O)	Number of Bacteria at Maximum Growth (millions per mL)			
	Series A		Series B	
	Tube no.	Tubes without air	Tube no.	Tubes with air
18	1A	50	1B	200
36	2A	90	2B	500
54	3A	170	3B	800
72	4A	220	4B	1100
162	5A	450	5B	2100
288	6A	650	6B	
360	7A	675	7B	
432	8A	675	8B	
540	9A	670	9B	

pair of test tubes from 1A and 1B through 5A and 5B?

4. Notice that the number of bacteria are not given for test tubes 6B, 7B, 8B, and 9B. How many bacteria would you predict in test tube 6B? In 7B? These numbers were omitted from the table because the bacteria are too numerous to count.

5. After each test tube reached maximum growth, the solution was tested for the presence of glucose. In all the test tubes from 1A to 6A and from 1B to 9B, there was no glucose. (Test tubes 7A, 8A, and 9A contained some glucose even after maximum growth had been reached.) Compare test tubes 4A and 4B. How many bacteria were produced per milligram of glucose in each case?

6. Develop a hypothesis that explains the numbers you calculated for question 5. Why are there many more bacteria per milligram of glucose in the B test tubes than in the A test tubes?

7. Each milligram of glucose has the same amount of energy available to do work. The series B test tubes produced more bacteria per milligram of glucose than did the series A test tubes. Assuming that each bacterium produced requires a certain amount of energy, which test tubes should contain some products of glucose that still contain some "unused" energy?

8. In additional tests, it also was determined that alcohol accumulates in the A test tubes. How does this information relate to your answer concerning "unused" energy in question 7?

Investigation 8B • Comparing Rates of Respiration

Precise measurement of the rate of respiration requires elaborate equipment. Reasonably accurate measurements can be obtained by placing living material in a closed system and measuring the amount of oxygen consumed within the system or the amount of carbon dioxide produced over a period of time. In this investigation, you will use a simple volumeter to measure the amount of oxygen taken up by germinating seeds.

Hypothesis: After reading the procedure, develop a hypothesis to explain the movement of the colored drops in the capillary tubes.

Materials (per team of 3)

3 pairs safety goggles

3 lab aprons

volumeter jar with spacers and screw-on lid

3 volumeters

100-mL graduated cylinder

3 250-mL beakers

Pasteur pipet

2 jars or paper cups

glass or plastic beads or washed gravel

non-mercury thermometer

nonabsorbent cotton

8½" x 11" piece of cardboard

8½" x 11" piece of white paper

forceps

ring stand with support ring

paper towels

masking tape

rubber bands

wax paper

soda lime packets

colored water

45 Alaska pea seeds

45 Yellow Dent corn seeds

water at room temperature (25°C)

Procedure

In this investigation you will use three volumeters inserted into a jar with spacers and a screw-on lid (Figure 8B.1). Each volumeter consists of a 25-mm x 200-mm test tube, a 30-cm glass capillary tube calibrated at 1-cm intervals, and a stopper assembly. The stopper assembly includes a two-hole rubber stopper, two glass tubes with latex tubing attached, and a 5-mL syringe.

All the test tubes must contain equal volumes of material to ensure that an equal volume of air is present in each tube. A small drop of colored water is inserted into each capillary tube at its outer end. If the volume of gas changes in the tube, the drop of colored water moves, and the direction of water

FIGURE 8B.1 Volumeter setup

movement depends on whether the volume of gas in the system increases or decreases.

When measuring respiration with the volumeter, consider not only that oxygen enters the living material (and thus leaves the environment of the test tube), but also that carbon dioxide leaves the living material (and enters the test tube environment). To measure the oxygen uptake by the respiring material, a substance is added to absorb the carbon dioxide as it evolves so it is not added to the volume of gas in the tube.

Day 1

1. Germinate the pea and corn seeds according to the procedure used in Investigation 3A, Part B. Label the jars with your team, class, experiment, and date.

   ☠ **CAUTION: Wash your hands immediately after handling the seeds. They may be treated with a fungicide.**

   As the seeds begin to germinate, what biochemical process increases?

Day 2

2. Select 40 pea seeds from the germination jar. Discard the 5 extra seeds. Determine the volume of the 40 soaked seeds by adding them to a measured volume of water in a graduated cylinder and reading the volume of displaced water. Record the volume of the seeds. Return the 40 seeds to the germination jar.

3. Repeat step 2 using the corn seeds.

4. Wash your hands thoroughly after handling the seeds.

Day 3

> **SAFETY   Put on your safety goggles and lab apron.**

5. The volume in the test tubes of the corn and pea seeds must be equal. Measure the volumes of both types of seeds again and add beads or gravel to the seeds that have the smaller total volume until the volume is equal to that of the test tube with the other seeds. What change occurred in the volume of the seeds after 48 hours in the germination jar?

6. Measure an amount of beads or gravel to equal the volume determined for the seeds.

7. Fill the volumeter jar about two-thirds full with room-temperature water. Screw on the lid. Why is water added to the volumeter jar?

8. Clip a piece of white paper to the cardboard and place it on the ring stand support ring.

9. Remove the stopper assemblies from each of the three test tubes. Add the peas (and beads or gravel, if any) to one test tube; add the corn seeds (and beads or gravel, if any) to another. In the third test tube, place the equal volume of beads or gravel you measured in step 6. This third tube is a thermobarometer, which is used to determine any changes in the system. What two variables will the thermobarometer help you measure?

10. Place a 2-cm plug of *dry* nonabsorbent cotton about 1 cm above the seeds or beads in each test tube (Figure 8B.2). Use forceps to place a small packet of soda lime wrapped in gauze on top of the plug.

   C CAUTION: Soda lime is a corrosive solid. Do not touch; do not ingest. If it gets on skin or clothing, or in the mouth, rinse thoroughly with water; if in eyes, wash gently but thoroughly for 15 minutes. Call your teacher.

11. Gently, but firmly, press a stopper assembly into each test tube. Insert the test tubes through the lid into the volumeter jar.

12. Insert the thermometer into the jar through the thermometer hole in the lid. Record the temperature of the water in the volumeter jar and maintain this temperature throughout the experiment.

13. With a Pasteur pipet, insert a small drop of colored water into the calibrated end of each *dry* capillary tube. Rotate each tube until the drop is correctly positioned. The drop of colored water in the thermobarometer should be positioned at about the middle of the calibrations and the other drops should be positioned at the outermost calibration.

14. Carefully attach each capillary tube (by its *un*calibrated end) to the longer glass tube in a stopper assembly. Support the tubes in a level, horizontal position on the paper prepared in step 8.

FIGURE 8B.2   Volumeter tubes after preparation

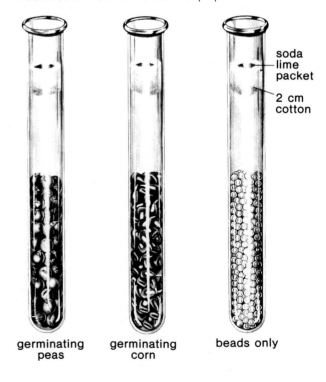

germinating peas   germinating corn   beads only

soda lime packet

2 cm cotton

TABLE 8B.1   Distance Colored Drop Moves in a Closed System

Time	Thermobarometer Readings (mm)	Germinating Pea Readings (mm)		Germinating Corn Readings (mm)	
		Uncorrected	Corrected	Uncorrected	Corrected

15. Use the syringe to reposition the drop in the capillary tube, if necessary. Tape the tubes in place on the paper.

16. Allow the apparatus to stand for about 5 minutes to permit the temperature to become uniform throughout the system.

17. Prepare a table in your data book similar to Table 8B.1, above. On the paper beneath the capillary tubes, mark the position of one end of each drop.

18. Record the position of each drop every 5 minutes for 20 minutes. If respiration is rapid, you may need to reposition the colored drop as you did in step 13 or 14. If you do this, be sure to add both measurements of the distance moved by the drop to calculate the total change during the experiment.

19. Wash your hands thoroughly before leaving the laboratory.

Analysis

1. What is the effect of moisture on the respiration rate of pea and corn seeds?

2. Would adding more water to the soaked seeds result in an increased rate of respiration?

3. What if the CO_2 absorbent (soda lime) were not used? Use the equation

$$C_6H_{12}O_2 + 6O_2 \longrightarrow 6H_2O + 6CO_2$$

to calculate how much, if any, the volume within the volumeter would change if the CO_2 were not removed. Do you think the six water molecules that are released per molecule of sugar should be considered? Why or why not?

4. Use any changes in the thermobarometer to determine the corrected distance moved by the drops in the volumeters containing the pea and corn seeds.

5. Calculate the total volume of O_2 used by the pea seeds and by the corn seeds. Each 1-cm mark on the capillary tube equals 0.063 mL of O_2 by volume. Determine the rate of respiration for both types of seeds by calculating O_2 consumed per minute.

6. Is the rate of respiration for the pea and corn seeds different?

7. What control would be desirable for this experiment? If your class set up a control, compare the respiration rates of the control seeds with those of the germinating seeds. What is the significance of this difference as far as the seeds' ability to survive in nature is concerned?

8. Make a linear graph comparing the rates of respiration of the different seeds.

Investigations for Chapter 9
The Cell Cycle

Investigation 9A • Bacteria, Pneumonia, and DNA

Nucleic acids were known for 75 years before their importance in living cells was fully realized. The mystery of how DNA acts was first explored in bacteria. Research biologists focused their attention on the role of DNA in a particular species of bacterium, *Streptococcus pneumoniae*, formerly known as *Diplococcus*. As its name indicates, this is a bacterium that causes the disease pneumonia.

There are two main types of *S. pneumoniae*, as shown in Figure 9A.1. In one type, each pair of bacterial cells is surrounded by a capsule of sugarlike substance. The other type has no capsule around the cells. When cells with capsules divide, they form new cells with capsules. Likewise, cells without capsules form new cells without capsules. *S. pneumoniae* cells with capsules cause pneumonia and subsequent death when they are injected into mice.

S. pneumoniae cells without capsules do not cause pneumonia when they are injected into mice.

Materials

None

PART A

Procedure

Because of the dangers involved in handling *S. pneumoniae*, it is not possible for you to carry out any experiments using these disease-causing bacteria. Instead, you will work with data that is already available.

The following paragraphs describe a number of experiments that already have been performed. Read about the experiments, analyze the results, and propose hypotheses about the results of these experiments, as directed in the Analysis questions.

Experiment 1 Healthy mice were injected with a few *S. pneumoniae* cells *without* capsules, as illustrated in Figure 9A.1a. The mice remained healthy.

Experiment 2 Healthy mice were injected with a few *S. pneumoniae* cells *with* capsules (Figure

FIGURE 9A.1 Experiments with two strains of *S. pneumoniae* on mice

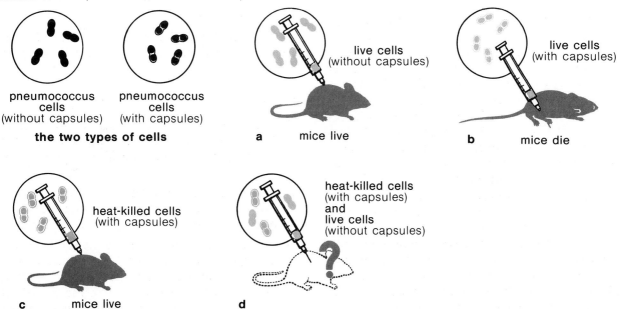

pneumococcus cells (without capsules) pneumococcus cells (with capsules)

the two types of cells

live cells (without capsules)

a mice live

live cells (with capsules)

b mice die

heat-killed cells (with capsules)

c mice live

heat-killed cells (with capsules) and live cells (without capsules)

d

9A.1b). The mice died. Autopsies showed that death was caused by pneumonia.

Experiment 3 *S. pneumoniae* cells with capsules were killed by heat. These dead cells were injected into healthy mice (Figure 9A.1c). The mice remained healthy.

Experiment 4 Healthy mice were injected with a mixture of living *S. pneumoniae* cells *without* capsules and a few heat-killed *S. pneumoniae* cells *with* capsules (Figure 9A.1d).

Analysis

1. Based on the results of Experiments 1, 2, and 3, write a sentence that predicts what will happen to the mice in Experiment 4. Give a reason for your prediction.

2. If you assume that the mice in Experiment 4 died of pneumonia, what could account for their having the disease? Give at least two hypotheses.

PART B

Procedure

Read the following information.

Experiment 5 In an actual experiment like the one described in Experiment 4, the mice did get pneumonia and die. The scientists proposed a hypothesis to explain this. Perhaps somehow the *S. pneumoniae* cells without capsules gained the ability to produce capsules and could pass this ability to their offspring. (Remember that the capsule must be present for the cells to cause pneumonia.) To test this hypothesis, the scientists prepared a culture medium—a mixture of nutrients in which *S. pneumoniae* cells could grow outside the body of a living organism. The experimenters could grow the *S. pneumoniae* cells in a culture medium in petri dishes and observe them with microscopes to see whether or not capsules were formed.

The experimenters first grew large numbers of *S. pneumoniae* cells with capsules. Then they killed these cells, ground them up, and dissolved them in a solution. The resulting extract contained the materials ordinarily found within the cell membranes.

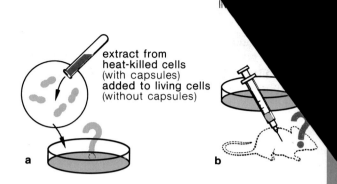

FIGURE 9A.2 Further experiments with *S. pneumoniae*

The extract from heat-killed cells with capsules was mixed with living cells without capsules. This mixture was added to a culture medium and allowed to grow, as in Figure 9A.2a.

Analysis

3. According to the actual results of Experiment 4, predict the type or types of bacteria that will be found growing on the culture medium of Experiment 5.

PART C

Procedure

Read the following information and answer the analysis questions.

Experiment 6 Some of the cells from Experiment 5 were injected into healthy mice, as in Figure 9A.2b.

Analysis

4. The mice in Experiment 6 died of pneumonia. What conclusion could be made about the cells growing on the culture medium of Experiment 5?

5. Could these cells have caused pneumonia before they were grown on the special culture medium of Experiment 5? Explain your reasoning.

6. Microscopic examination of the bacteria grown in Experiment 5 showed the presence of live cells with capsules. These cells could reproduce to form more bacteria with capsules. When these were injected into mice, they caused

...ad the following information. Using this information along with the previous readings, answer the Analysis questions.

Experiment 7 At the Rockefeller University in New York City, Oswald Avery, Colin McLeod, and Maclyn McCarty worked to find the part of the extract from the dead cells that caused the change in hereditary material. They wanted to find out what made cells without capsules able to produce cells with capsules. They performed careful experiments in which each part of the extract was tested. They hypothesized that a molecule in the extract was being taken up by the living cells and that this molecule was responsible for the new hereditary information. The molecule was finally identified as DNA. *S. pneumoniae* characteristics had been changed as a result of the incorporation of DNA molecules from the extract.

Analysis

7. What apparently happens to the DNA of the *S. pneumoniae* cells before they divide to form new cells?

8. Using what you now know about DNA molecules, form a conclusion that explains the results of Experiment 4.

Investigation 9B • DNA Replication

DNA replication is the process by which exact copies are made of the DNA in prokaryotes and in the chromosomes of eukaryotes. During replication, the genetic code contained within a sequence of nucleotide bases in DNA is preserved. How does replication take place? This investigation will give you an opportunity to observe some of the basic steps involved in the process of replication.

Materials (per team of 2)

pop-it beads: 40 black, 40 white, 32 red, 32 green

pen

string or twist ties

4 tags with string

Procedure

PART A   Building the DNA Molecule

You will build a double-stranded segment of DNA using colored pop-it beads and the following key for the nucleotide bases:

black = adenine (A)	white = thymine (T)
green = guanine (G)	red = cytosine (C)

1. Construct the first DNA strand by linking the colored pop-it beads together to represent the following sequence of nucleotide bases:

   A A A G G T C T C C T C T A A T T G G T C T C C T T A G G T C T C C T T

2. Attach a tag to the AAA end of the strand, and label the strand Roman numeral *I* by marking the tag.

3. Now construct the complementary strand of DNA that would pair with strand I. Remember that thymine (T) bonds with adenine (A), and guanine (G) bonds with cytosine (C).

4. Attach a tag to the TTT end of the complementary strand, and label the strand Roman numeral *II* by marking the tag.

5. Place strand II beside strand I and check to make certain that you have constructed the proper sequence of nucleotide bases in strand II. Green pop-it beads should be opposite red pop-it beads and black pop-it beads should be opposite white pop-it beads. Make any necessary corrections in strand II in order to have the proper sequence of base pairs.

6. Tie a simple overhand knot with a short piece of string, or use a twist-tie to join the first pop-it beads in strand I and strand II, as shown in Figure 9B.1 *(top)*.

7. Repeat step 6 for the pop-it beads on the other end of strands I and II.

FIGURE 9B.1 *(top)* An overhand knot with string holds the ends of the two strands together; *(bottom)* the knot at the 22nd pop-it bead represents the temporary end point of DNA replication.

PART B   DNA Replication

8. Place your double-stranded DNA molecule on your table so that both strands are in horizontal straight lines and the AAA end of strand I is on your left. (Do not unfasten the ends.)

9. Beginning at the AAA end of strand I, count 22 pop-it beads from left to right. Tie the strands together between the 22nd and 23rd pairs of beads as shown in Figure 9B.1 *(bottom)*.

10. Untie the string holding the two strands together at the AAA end of strand I. Separate strand I and strand II so they form a "Y."

11. DNA replication on strand I begins with the action of DNA polymerase at the AAA end and proceeds toward the replication fork (the point at which the nucleotide bases are joined at the 22nd base pair). Construct the new complementary strand for strand I beginning at the AAA end and working toward the replication fork. When you have finished, tie another overhand knot at the AAA end of strand I to join it to its new complementary strand.

12. Replication of strand II begins with the action of DNA polymerase at the replication fork and works outward toward the TTT end (this is the lagging strand of DNA). Build the complementary DNA strand for strand II, proceeding from right to left, and then tie the two strands together at the TTT end.

13. Now untie the overhand knots that join strands I and II at the 22nd base pair and at the right-hand end of the original double strand.

14. Continue the replication of strand I from left to right until you complete the new complementary strand. Tie another overhand knot to join strand I and its complement at the right-hand end of the molecule.

15. Continue the replication of strand II from the right-hand end to the left. When you reach the 22nd base pair, use another knot to join the two segments of the newly formed strand (the complement of strand II).

16. Tie another overhand knot in the right-hand end of strand II to join it to its new complementary strand.

ble-stranded mole-
ed. How are they
lecule containing
different?

a replication fork.

nces in the way strands I and
icated.

Describe how DNA replication makes it possible
to produce two identical cells from one parent.

Investigation 9C • Mitotic Cell Division

To study mitosis you will examine groups of cells
that have been preserved and then stained. Their
nuclear structures are visible with the ordinary
compound microscope. Some of the cells you will
see are at very early stages of mitosis, some at later
stages, and others may be in interphase—a term
used for G_1, S, and G_2 collectively. Biologists have
been able to trace, from such slides as these, the steps
a cell goes through during mitotic division. It is very
difficult to tell from slides just which stages come
first and which come later. Keep this in mind as you
try to reconstruct the process for yourself.

Materials (per team of 2)

compound microscope

modeling clay

prepared slide of animal embryo cells (*Ascaris* or
whitefish)

prepared slide of onion root tip cells

Procedure

1. Place the slide of root tip cells on the microscope
stage and examine it under low power. Scan the
entire section. Observe that cells far from the tip
and cells right at the tip are not actively dividing.
Locate the region of active mitosis between
these two regions.

2. Change to the high-power objective. As you
observe the cells, focus up and down slowly
with the fine-adjustment knob to bring different
structures into sharp focus. Find cells at various
stages of mitosis. When the slide was prepared,
the cells were killed at different stages of a continuous process. The cells can be compared to
scrambled, single frames of film. Figure out how
you would piece the frames of the film together.
Refer to Figure 9.11 for help. Make sketches
from the slide of cells in *interphase*, *prophase*,
metaphase, *anaphase*, and *telophase* as described
in Section 9.8. Identify each by stage.

3. Examine a slide of developing *Ascaris*. Find a cell
in which the chromosomes are long and threadlike. Try to count the number of individual chromosomes.

4. Find a cell in which the chromosomes are at the
equator of the spindle. Compare the poles of this
spindle with those of the spindles in the dividing
plant cells you have studied in Steps 1 and 2.

5. Find a cell in which the chromosomes are separating and the cell is beginning to pinch together
in the middle. Compare this method of cytoplasmic division with the method you observed in
plants.

6. With clay and four large sketches of a plant cell,
model each stage of mitosis, from prophase to
telophase, for a plant cell with three pairs of
chromosomes. Make each pair of chromosomes
a different length or color.

Analysis

1. How is the process of mitosis in plant and
animal cells similar?

2. How does mitosis in plant and animal cells
differ?

3. Refer to Figure 9C.1 on the next page and study
cells numbered 2, 7, 9, 11, 12, 13, 16, and 33.
Rewrite the order of these cells to reflect the
sequence of stages if you were watching one cell
undergo mitosis.

4. Compare the number and types of chromosomes in the two new nuclei of the clay model
with the number and types from the original
parent nucleus.

5. If mitosis occurs in a cell but cell division does
not occur, what is the result?

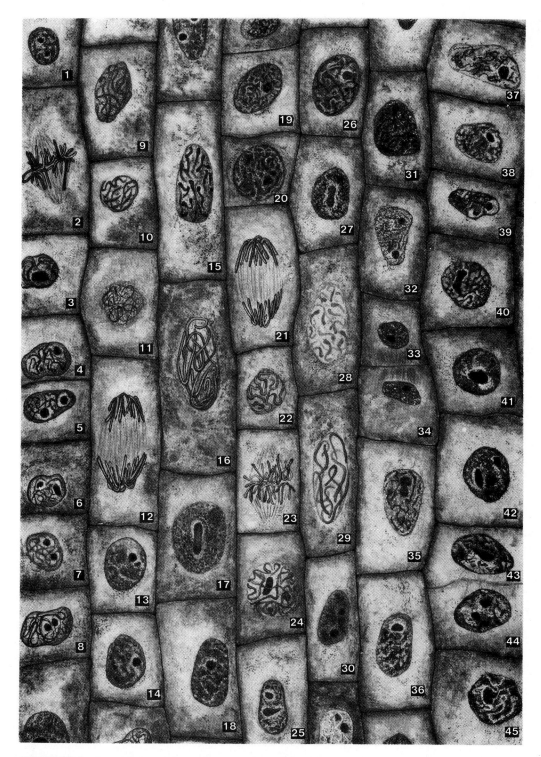

FIGURE 9C.1 Drawing of dividing cells in an onion root as seen through a compound microscope. Arrange cells 2, 7, 9, 11, 12, 13, 16, and 33 in the correct order, demonstrating stages in mitosis.

apter 10
otein

10A • Transcription

is the molecule in which all of the genetic information for the cell is stored. The information is encoded as a triplet code in which each sequence of three nucleotide bases codes for a specific piece of information. The DNA is contained within the nucleus, but the cellular processes take place in the cytosol. How does the information from the DNA get into the cytosol where it can be used? This investigation will help you understand that process.

Materials (per team of 2)

masking tape

pop-it beads: 40 black, 40 white, 32 green, 32 red, 20 pink

string

tags

Procedure

PART A DNA Transcription

You will build a double-stranded segment of DNA and a single-stranded segment of messenger RNA (mRNA) using colored pop-it beads and the following color code for the nucleotide bases:

black = adenine (A)   white = thymine (T)
green = guanine (G)   red = cytosine (C)
pink = uracil (U)

1. Construct DNA strand I, as you did in Investigation 9B, by linking the colored pop-it beads together to represent the following sequence of nucleotide bases:

A A A G G T C T C C T C T A A T T G G T C
T C C T T A G G T C T C C T T

2. Attach a tag labeled Roman numeral I to the AAA end of strand I.

3. Now construct the complementary strand of DNA that would pair with strand I. Remember that thymine (T) bonds with adenine (A), and guanine (G) bonds with cytosine (C).

4. Attach a tag labeled Roman numeral II to the TTT end of the complementary strand.

5. Place strand II beside strand I and check to make certain that you have constructed the proper sequence of nucleotide bases in strand II. Green pop-it beads should be opposite red pop-it beads, and black pop-it beads should be opposite white pop-it beads. Make any corrections necessary to have the proper sequence of base pairs.

6. Position the strands on your work surface so that the AAA end of strand I is to your left. Using two pieces of string, tie together nucleotide bases 22 and also the right end of the double strands with an overhand knot as you did in Investigation 9B.

7. Open the left-hand side of the DNA molecule to form the replication fork. Assume that a molecule of RNA polymerase has just attached to the left-hand end of strand I, and that a molecule of DNA polymerase has just attached to strand II at the replication fork.

8. Strand I will produce a single-stranded molecule of mRNA instead of a new double-stranded molecule of DNA. RNA is produced by the process of transcription from strand I. The rules for forming mRNA are the same as for DNA except that uracil (pink) is used in place of thymine (white). Beginning at the AAA end of strand I, construct the mRNA molecule according to the sequence of bases in strand I. Continue moving toward the replication fork.

9. Untie the overhand knot at base pair 22. Continue the mRNA transcription on strand I, moving from left to right toward the right-hand end of the molecule. When you have finished, attach a tag labeled *mRNA* at the left-hand end of the mRNA molecule.

PART B DNA Replication

10. Complete the DNA replication of strand II by moving to the right-hand end of the molecule and working back to the left. Join the two seg-

ments of the complementary strand to complete the new DNA molecule. Tie together both ends of the double-stranded DNA molecule with string and set it aside.

11. Check the sequence of nucleotide bases on the mRNA molecule against strand I of the DNA. Remember that uracil (pink) is substituted for thymine (white) in RNA. The mRNA molecule is now ready to move from the nucleus into the cytosol where its message will be translated. Save your mRNA molecule ant the double-stranded DNA molecule to use in Investigation 10B.

Analysis

1. Compare the sequence of nucleotide bases in the mRNA molecule with the sequence of nucleotide bases in strand II. How are they the same? How are they different?

2. Compare the mRNA molecule with the DNA molecule that you have set aside for use in Investigation 10B. How are they the same? How are they different?

3. Why do you think mRNA can leave the nucleus and DNA cannot?

Investigation 10B • Translation

You have seen how DNA is replicated and how messenger RNA is formed from a DNA template. The messenger RNA is able to leave the nucleus and move into the cytosol where the message it carries from the DNA can be translated into a sequence of amino acids in the formation of a protein. In this investigation, you will study another type of RNA, transfer RNA (tRNA), and the important role it plays in translation.

Materials (per team of 2)

DNA molecule from Investigation 10A
masking tape
modeling clay
mRNA molecule from Investigation 10A
pen

pop-it beads: 7 black, 10 red, 6 green
tags

Procedure

Throughout this investigation, refer to Figure 10B which shows what amino acids are coded for b each DNA triplet. The DNA triplets are in black type and the mRNA complementary codons are in blue type.

The tRNA anticodons pair with the mRNA codons in the same way the mRNA complementary codons pair with DNA codons, except for the substitution of uracil for thymine in tRNA. If you have difficulties decoding the tRNA codons, ask your teacher for help. Use the same color code for the pop-it beads that you used in Investigation 10A:

black = adenine (A)   white = thymine (T)
green = guanine (G)   red = cytosine (C)
pink = uracil (U)

1. Place the double-stranded DNA molecule and the mRNA molecule across your work surface so that the mRNA lies next to Strand I of the DNA, and their complementary codons are side by side. Beginning at the AAA end, record the letters representing the first three nucleotide bases (the first codon) in strand I of your DNA molecule. Next, record the letters representing the first three bases (the first complementary codon) in your messenger RNA molecule. In the same way, record the letters representing the bases of the remaining 11 codons in the DNA and mRNA molecules.

2. Use Figure 10B.1 (page 662) to determine which amino acid is coded for by each mRNA codon. (The DNA triplet and the mRNA complementary codon are adjacent in the figure.) List the appropriate amino acid opposite each mRNA codon.

3. Write the name of the first amino acid on a tag. Label a tag for each of the 11 other amino acids indicated by the codons in the mRNA strand.

4. Determine the anticodon sequence for the transfer RNA that would pair with the mRNA codon. Build the tRNA anticodon from pop-it beads using the code given above. Tie the tag showing

	Second Base			Third Base
	G or C	**T or A**	**C or G**	
	GA *UCU* ⎫ GG *UCC* T *UCA* ⎬ serine *UCG* ⎭	ATA *UAU* ⎱ tyrosine ATG *UAC* ⎰ ATT *UAA* ⎱ stop ATC *UAG* ⎰	ACA *UGU* ⎱ cysteine ACG *UGC* ⎰ ACT *UGA* ⎱ stop ACC *UGG* ⎰ tryptophan	A or *U* G or *C* T or *A* C or *G*
	GA *CCU* ⎫ GGG *CCC* GGT *CCA* ⎬ proline GGC *CCG* ⎭	GTA *CAU* ⎱ histidine GTG *CAC* ⎰ GTT *CAA* ⎱ glutamine GTC *CAG* ⎰	GCA *CGU* ⎫ GCG *CGC* GCT *CGA* ⎬ arginine GCC *CGG* ⎭	A or *U* G or *C* T or *A* C or *G*
A	AA *AUU* ⎫ TAG *AUC* ⎬ isoleucine TAT *AUA* ⎭ TAC *AUG* ⎬ methionine	TGA *ACU* ⎫ TGG *ACC* TGT *ACA* ⎬ threonine TGC *ACG* ⎭	TTA *AAU* ⎱ asparagine TTG *AAC* ⎰ TTT *AAA* ⎱ lysine TTC *AAG* ⎰	TCA *AGU* ⎱ serine TCG *AGC* ⎰ TCT *AGA* ⎱ arginine TCC *AGG* ⎰	A or *U* G or *C* T or *A* C or *G*
C or G	CAA *GUU* ⎫ CAG *GUC* CAT *GUA* ⎬ valine CAC *GUG* ⎭	CGA *GCU* ⎫ CGG *GCC* CGT *GCA* ⎬ alanine CGC *GCG* ⎭	CTA *GAU* ⎱ aspartic CTG *GAC* ⎰ acid CTT *GAA* ⎱ glutamic CTC *GAG* ⎰ acid	CCA *GGU* ⎫ CCG *GGC* CCT *GGA* ⎬ glycine CCC *GGG* ⎭	A or *U* G or *C* T or *A* C or *G*

FIGURE 10B.1 The genetic code. The DNA codons appear in black type; the complementary RNA codons are in blue. A = adenine, C = cytosine, G = guanine, T = thymine, U = uracil. "Stop" = chain termination or "nonsense" codon.

the name of the appropriate amino acid near the middle pop-it bead as shown in Figure 10B.2 (*left*). This model represents the tRNA anticodon with its attached amino acid that will take part in protein synthesis.

5. Repeat step 4 to build tRNA's for each of the remaining 11 triplet codons in the mRNA.

6. To represent the large subunit of a ribosome, use one color of modeling clay to make a large oval the length of six pop-it beads. To represent the smaller subunit of a ribosome, make a narrower oval of a different color of modeling clay, also the length of six pop-it beads. Push the long sides of the two ovals together so their edges are joined and the smaller subunit lies on top of the larger subunit, as shown in Figure 10B.2 (*right*). These two ovals represent a functional ribosome.
When you finish you should have the following:
a. 1 double-stranded DNA molecule
b. 1 single-stranded mRNA molecule
c. 12 tRNA molecules with amino acids attached
d. 1 ribosome

7. Mark a small piece of masking tape *A site* and another piece *P site*. Press the A-site tape into

the smaller ribosome subunit near the right side and the P-site tape near the left side of the smaller subunit.

8. Place the first codon of the mRNA molecule on the A site of the smaller subunit of the ribosome and lightly press the three pop-it beads of the codon into the clay.

9. Select the tRNA anticodon that will pair with the mRNA codon. Place the tRNA on the larger subunit of the ribosome so that the amino acid

FIGURE 10B.2 Amino acid tag attached to the middle pop-it bead of a tRNA (*left*); the two parts of a ribosome as simulated with modeling clay (*right*)

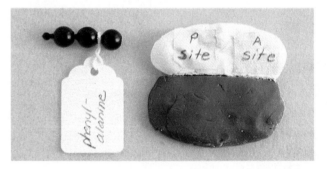

points away from the mRNA molecule. Figure 10B.3 (*top*) shows these positions.

10. Next, move the mRNA molecule to the left so that the first codon is on the P site and the second codon is on the A site. Move the first tRNA anticodon to keep it paired with its mRNA codon.

11. Select the correct tRNA molecule to pair with the second mRNA codon that is now on the A site of the ribosome. Press both the mRNA and the tRNA molecules lightly into the clay.

12. Remove the tag representing the first amino acid from its tRNA anticodon and tape it to the tag representing the second amino acid, as shown in Figure 10B.4 (*top*) on the next page. You have just formed a peptide bond.

13. Move the mRNA molecule to the left by one codon, so that the first codon with its tRNA anticodon is no longer on the ribosome. Put the first tRNA anticodon off to the side.

14. Select the appropriate tRNA anticodon to pair with the third mRNA codon, which is now on the A site of the ribosome, as shown in Figure 10B.4 (*bottom*). Attach the dipeptide formed in step 12 to this third amino acid.

15. Continue moving the mRNA molecule across the ribosome and pairing the tRNA anticodons with the mRNA codons. After each tRNA anticodon with its amino acid has arrived at the ribosome, the amino acid should be removed and attached to the growing chain of amino acids.

FIGURE 10B.4 Two amino acids joined to form a dipeptide on the A site (*top*); mRNA and tRNA transposed to the P site and a third tRNA on the A site (*bottom*)

16. When all 12 amino acids have been joined together, remove the chain of amino acids from the tRNA and the ribosome. This model represents part of a protein molecule.

Analysis

1. Compare the first DNA triplet with the first tRNA anticodon that you built.

2. What role does the ribosome play in protein synthesis?

3. What role does tRNA play in protein synthesis?

4. What role does mRNA play in protein synthesis?

5. Write a short paragraph that summarizes transcription and translation in protein synthesis.

FIGURE 10B.3 mRNA and tRNA positioned on the ribosome to line up the first (*top*) and second (*bottom*) amino acids

Investigations for Chapter 11
Reproduction

Investigation 11A • The Yeast Life Cycle

Baker's yeast (*Saccharomyces cerevisiae*) is a unicellular organism that reproduces both sexually and asexually. Because the cells have a characteristic shape at each stage, it is possible to distinguish all the major stages of the life cycle under the microscope.

Yeast cells may be either haploid or diploid. Haploid cells occur in two mating types ("sexes"): mating-type **a** (HAR) and mating-type **α** (HBT). When **a** and **α** cells come in contact, they secrete hormonelike substances called mating pheromones (FER uh mohnz), which cause them to develop into gametes. The **a** and **α** gametes pair and then fuse, forming a diploid zygote. The fusion of **a** and **α** gametes is similar to fertilization in animals, except that both parents contribute cytoplasm and nuclei. Yeast zygotes reproduce asexually by budding. When cultured on a solid growth medium, a yeast zygote may grow into a visible colony that contains up to 100 million cells.

Diploid yeast do not mate, but in times of stress, such as during a period in which they have an unbalanced food supply, the diploid cells may sporulate, or form spores. The spores remain together, looking like ball bearings, in a transparent saclike structure called an ascus (ASK us).

In this investigation, you will start with two haploid yeast strains of opposite mating types, mate them to form a diploid strain, and try to complete an entire yeast life cycle.

Materials (per team of 2)

microscope slide

cover slip

dropping pipet

glass-marking pencil

compound microscope

container of clean, flat toothpicks

bottle of water

6 self-sealing plastic bags labeled *waste* (1 for each day)

3 YED medium agar plates

1 MV medium agar plate

1 "unknown" medium agar plate

agar slant cultures of HAR and HBT yeast strains

Procedure

Day 0

1. Prepare fresh cultures of both mating types. Colonies of the HAR strain of mating-type **a** are red; those of the HBT strain of mating-type **α** are cream colored. Touch the flat end of a clean toothpick to the HAR strain, then gently drag it across the surface of a YED medium agar plate to make a streak about 1 cm long and 1 cm from the edge. (See Figure 11A.1.) Discard the toothpick in the self-sealing plastic waste bag, being careful not to touch anything with it. Use a glass-marking pencil to label the bottom of the

FIGURE 11A.1 Procedure for making a mating mixture from HAR and HBT yeast strains (a), for subculturing the mating mixture (b), and for inoculating the "unknown" medium plate (c).

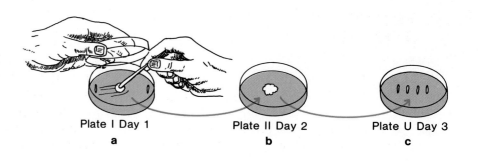

Plate I Day 1
a

Plate II Day 2
b

Plate U Day 3
c

plate near the streak with an *a*. Use a new, clean toothpick to put a streak of the HBT strain near the opposite side of the agar on the same plate, and label it *α*. *Use a new, clean toothpick from the container for each thing you do. Be careful not to touch the ends of the toothpicks to anything except yeast or the sterile agar. Discard used toothpicks in the plastic waste bag. Keep the lid on the agar plate except when transferring yeast.* Label this plate *I* and add the date and your names. Incubate upside down for 1 day, or 2 days if your room is very cool.

2. Wash your hands thoroughly before leaving the laboratory.

Day 1

3. Use a microscope to examine some yeast cells of either mating type. To prepare a slide, touch a toothpick to the streak of either the **a** mating type *or* the *α* mating type in plate I, mix it with a small drop of water on the slide, and place a cover slip over the drop. Discard the toothpick in the waste bag. Examine the cells with the high power lens. In your data book, sketch the cells.

4. Use a clean toothpick to transfer a small amount of the **a** mating type from the streak in plate I to the middle of the agar. Use another clean toothpick to transfer an equal amount of the *α* mating type to the same place. Being careful not to tear the agar surface, thoroughly mix these two dots of yeast to make a mating mixture. Discard used toothpicks in the waste bag. Invert and incubate plate I at room temperature for 3 or 4 hours, then refrigerate until the next lab period. (Or, refrigerate immediately, and then incubate at room temperature for 3 or 4 hours before the next step.)

5. Wash your hands thoroughly before leaving the laboratory.

Day 2

6. Remove plate I from the refrigerator. What color is the mating mixture colony? Use the microscope to examine the mating mixture, as in Step 3. Discard used toothpicks in the waste bag.

Sketch what you see and compare with your earlier drawings. Describe any differences in the types of cells you see. When haploid cells of opposite mating types (**a** and *α*) are mixed, they develop into pear-shaped, haploid gametes. Do you see any gametes? A diploid zygote is formed when two gametes fuse. Growing diploid cells are slightly larger and more oval than haploid cells. Do you see any evidence that gametes may be fusing into zygotes? Compared to Day 1, are there more or fewer diploid cells?

7. Make a subculture by transferring some of the mating mixture with a clean toothpick to an MV agar plate. Discard used toothpicks in the waste bag. Label this plate *II*. Invert and incubate at least overnight, but not more than 2 nights.

8. Wash your hands thoroughly before leaving the laboratory.

Day 3

9. Use the microscope to examine the freshly grown subculture in plate II. Discard used toothpicks in the waste bag. What types of cells are present? Sketch each type. If any of the types seen in Step 6 have disappeared, explain what happened to them.

10. On a plate of "unknown" medium, make several thick streaks of the freshly grown subculture. Discard used toothpicks in the waste bag. Label this plate *U*. Invert and incubate at room temperature at least 4 days.

11. Wash your hands thoroughly before leaving the laboratory.

Day 7

12. Use the microscope to examine yeast from plate U. Discard used toothpicks in the waste bag. You may need to use the fine adjustment on the microscope to distinguish cells at different levels. What cell types are present today that were not present before? Sketch these cell types, and compare them with the cell types you saw at other stages.

13. Refer to the introduction. How do you think the "unknown" medium differs from the YED medium? If the cells in the sacks are most fre-

quently found in groups of four, do you think they were formed by meiosis or mitosis? Explain. Are the cells in the sacks haploid or diploid? Explain. What part of the life cycle seen on Day 1 do these cells most resemble?

14. Transfer some yeast from plate U to a fresh YED medium agar plate. Discard used toothpicks in the waste bag. Label this plate *III*, invert and incubate at room temperature for about 5 hours, and then refrigerate until the next lab period. (Or, refrigerate immediately and then incubate at room temperature for 5 hours before the next step.)

15. Wash your hands thoroughly before leaving the laboratory.

Day 8

16. Use the microscope to examine the growth from plate III. Discard used toothpicks in the waste bag. What life-cycle stages are present? Sketch the cells and compare them with the stages you observed before. What evidence is there that a new life cycle has started?

17. Discard used culture plates as directed by your teacher, and wash your hands thoroughly before leaving the laboratory.

Analysis

1. In this investigation, you have observed the major events of a sexual life cycle. You could readily observe these events in yeast because it is a unicellular organism. In plants and animals, including humans, similar cellular events occur, but they are difficult to see. Although the changes were occurring too slowly for you to see, your sketches provide a record of the sequences. Think of them as ''pauses'' in a tape of a continually changing process. Notice in particular how the cycle repeats. Draw a life cycle diagram on one page, showing the different shapes of cells you observed in the order in which they appeared. Indicate where you first saw each type and when it disappeared if it did.

2. Compare your sketches with the life cycle diagram in Figure 11A.2, and try to identify each of the forms you saw.

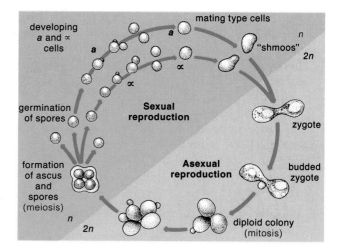

FIGURE 11A.2 Yeast life cycle, showing both asexual and sexual reproduction.

3. For each of the cell forms you observed, indicate whether it was haploid or diploid.

4. Mark the points in your diagram where cells changed from haploid to diploid and from diploid to haploid.

5. Why do you think the two different mating types are not called ''female'' and ''male''?

6. Can you think of a good argument for calling any particular point in the cycle the ''beginning'' or the ''end''? Why or why not?

7. What would you expect to happen if you allowed the yeast in Step 14 to grow for another day and then put them on the ''unknown'' medium again?

8. Table 11A.1 summarizes the similarities between stages in the yeast life cycle and the events in sexual reproduction in animals. For each change you observed in the yeast life cycle, indicate the step in the human sexual reproduction cycle that is most similar.

Investigation 11B • A Model of Meiosis

Many biological events are easier to understand when they are modeled. In this investigation, you will use a model to simulate the events of meiosis.

TABLE 11A.1 Comparison of the Yeast Life Cycle and Sexual Reproduction in Animals

Yeast	Animals
Mating pheromones	Sex hormones
Mating type **a** and α gametes	Gametes (ova and sperm)
Fusion	Fertilization
Zygote	Zygote
Asexually reproducing diploid cells	Diploid body cells
Meiosis and formation of spores	Meiosis and formation of gametes

Materials (per team of 2)

modeling clay, red and blue

4 2-cm pieces of pipe cleaner

large piece of paper

PART A   Basic Meiosis

Procedure

1. Use the clay to form two blue and two red chromatids, each 6 cm long and about as thick as a pencil.

2. Place the pairs of similar chromatids side by side. Use pipe cleaners to represent centromeres. Press a piece of pipe cleaner across the centers of the two red, 6-cm chromatids. This represents a chromosome that has replicated itself at the start of meiosis. Do the same for the blue replicated chromosomes (see Figure 11B.1).

3. Form four more chromatids, two of each color, 10 cm long. Again, press a piece of pipe cleaner across the centers of the two pairs of red and blue chromatids.

4. On a sheet of paper, draw a spindle large enough to contain the chromosomes you have made. Assume that the spindle and chromatids have been formed, and the nuclear membrane has disappeared.

5. Pair the two 6-cm chromosomes so that the centromeres touch. Pair the two 10-cm chromosomes. Assume that the red chromosome of

each pair came from the female parent. Its matching chromosome, the blue one, came from the male parent.

6. Arrange the two chromosome pairs along the equator (middle) of the spindle so that the red chromosomes are on one side and the blue on the other.

7. Holding on to the centromeres, pull the chromosomes of each matching pair toward opposite poles of the spindle. Once the chromosomes have been moved to the two poles, you have modeled the first meiotic division.

8. Draw two more spindles on the paper. These new spindles should be centered on each of the

FIGURE 11B.1 Chromosome models.

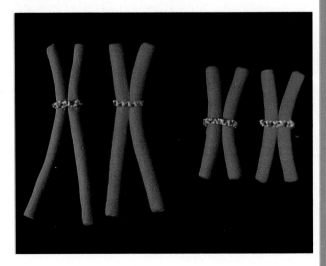

poles of the first meiotic division. Both spindles should be perpendicular to the first spindle. Your model cells are now ready for the second division of meiosis.

9. Place the chromosomes from each pole along the equator of each of the two new spindles. Unfasten the centromere of each chromosome. Grasp each chromatid at the point where the centromere was attached. Pull the chromatids to opposite poles of their spindles. Try to move each spindle's chromatids simultaneously, as occurs in a living cell. Draw a circle around each group of chromosomes that you have.

Analysis

1. How many cells were there at the start of meiosis? How many cells are formed at the end of meiosis?

2. How many chromosomes were in the cell at the beginning of meiosis? How many chromosomes were in each of the cells formed by meiosis?

3. What types of cells does meiosis produce?

4. How many of your cells at the end of meiosis had only red chromosomes in them? How many had only blue chromosomes in them?

PART B Effects of Chromosome Position on Sorting

Procedure

10. A real cell is three-dimensional. Although the red chromosomes (from the female) may be on one side of the equator and the blue (from the male) may be on the other when they line up on the spindle, there is an equal chance that one red and one blue chromosome will be on the same side. Attach the chromatids as they were at the beginning of the investigation. Go back to Step 6 and arrange the chromosomes so that one blue and one red chromosome are on each side of the equator. Complete meiosis I and II.

Analysis

1. How do these gametes compare with those you made earlier?

2. What difference does this change in position make in terms of genetic variation in the offspring?

3. How many different types of gametes could be made if there were three sets of chromosomes instead of just two?

PART C Effects of Crossing-Over

Procedure

11. Reassemble your chromosome models. To show crossing-over (Figure 11.5), exchange a small part of the clay from a chromatid making up one chromosome with an equal part from a chromatid of its homologous pair. The colors make the exchange visible throughout the rest of the investigation.

12. Place your chromosome pairs along the equator of the spindle as in Step 6 and complete meiosis I and II.

Analysis

1. How many different types of gametes did you form? Did you form any gametes different from those formed by others in your class?

2. In general, how do you think crossing-over affects the number of different types of gametes that are formed?

3. In crossing-over, what actually is exchanged between the chromatids?

4. What are some of the advantages of using a model to visualize a process?

5. How did this model improve your understanding of the process of meiosis?

6. What are some disadvantages of this model?

Investigation 11C • Reproduction in Mosses and Flowering Plants

Although their reproductive organs differ as much as the environments in which they live and reproduce, the basic principles of sexual reproduction are the same in a moss, a flower, a bee, and a human. In this investigation you will learn how the structures of a moss and a flower serve reproductive functions in their respective environments.

Mosses form mats on logs and on the forest floor, growing best in damp, shaded environments. Sporophytes, or diploid spore-producing structures, grow out of the tops of haploid gamete-producing structures, called gametophytes. Sporophytes often look like browish-colored hairs growing out of the mat of moss. Mosses cannot reproduce unless they are moist. Flowering plants, on the other hand, are found in many different environments and climates. They need water to live but not to reproduce.

Materials (per team of 2)

2 microscope slides

2 cover slips

dissecting needle

scalpel

forceps

compound microscope

stereomicroscope or 10X hand lens

modeling clay

prepared slide of filamentous stage of moss

prepared slide of moss male and female reproductive organs

15% sucrose solution

moss plant with sporophyte

fresh moss

gladiolus flower

other simple flowers for comparison

fresh bean or pea pods

Procedure

PART A   Moss

1. Examine a moss plant with a sporophyte attached. The sporophyte consists of a smooth, brownish stalk terminated by a small capsule. Separate the two generations by pulling the sporophyte stalk out of the leafy gametophyte shoot.

2. Using a dissecting needle, break open the sporophyte capsule into a drop of water on a slide.

 CAUTION: Needles are sharp. Handle with care.

Add a cover slip and examine under the lower power of a compound microscope. What are the structures you observe? How are these structures dispersed in nature? How are they adapted for life on land?

3. Most moss spores germinate on damp soil and produce a filamentous stage that looks like a branching green alga. Examine a prepared slide of this stage.

4. The filamentous stage gives rise to the leafy shoot of the gametophyte. Using forceps, carefully remove a leafy shoot from the fresh moss. How does this shoot obtain water for growth?

5. The reproductive organs of the gametophyte are at the upper end of the leafy shoot. Examine a prepared slide of these organs under the low power of a compound microscope. The male sex organs are saclike structures that produce large numbers of sperm cells. The female sex organs are flask-shaped and have long, twisted necks. An egg forms within the base of the female organ. How does a sperm reach the egg? Would you expect to find moss plants growing where there was little or no water? Explain. The union of the egg and sperm results in a cell called the zygote. Where is the zygote formed? What grows from the zygote?

PART B   Flowers

6. Examine the outside parts of a gladiolus flower. The outermost whorl of floral parts may be green and leaflike. These green sepals protected the flower bud when it was young. In some flowers, such as lilies, the sepals look like an outer whorl of petals. Petals are usually large and colorful and lie just inside the sepals. Both sepals and petals are attached to the enlarged end of a branch. These parts of the flower are not directly involved in sexual reproduction. What functions might petals have?

7. Strip away the sepals and petals to examine the reproductive structures. Around a central stalk-like body are 5 to 10 delicate stalks, each ending in a small sac, or anther. These are the male reproductive organs, or stamens. Thousands of

pollen grains are produced in the anther. The number of stamens varies according to the type of flower. How many stamens are present in the flower you are using? How may pollen be carried from the anthers to the female part of the flower?

8. If the anthers are mature, shake some of the pollen into a drop of 15% sucrose solution on a clean slide. Add a cover slip and examine with the lower power of a compound microscope. What is the appearance of the pollen? How is the pollen adapted for dispersal?

9. Make another pollen preparation on a clean cover slip. Use modeling clay to make a 5-mm-high chamber, slightly smaller than the cover slip, on a clean slide. Add a small drop of water to the chamber and invert the pollen preparation over it. Examine after 15 minutes and again at the end of the lab period. What, if any, changes have occurred? (If no changes have occurred, store the slide in a covered petri dish containing a piece of cotton moistened with water and examine it the next day.)

10. The central stalk surrounded by the stamens is the female reproductive organ, or carpel. It is composed of a large basal part, the ovary, above which is an elongated part, the style, ending in a stigma. How is the stigma adapted to trap the pollen grains and to provide a place for them to grow?

11. Use a scalpel to cut the ovary lengthwise.

    CAUTION: Scalpels are sharp; handle with care.

    Using a hand lens or stereomicroscope, look at the cut surface. How many ovules can you see? Each ovule contains one egg. To what stage of the moss life cycle is the ovule comparable? Where is the pollen grain deposited? How does the sperm in the pollen grain reach the egg? To what stage of the moss life cycle is a pollen grain comparable?

12. The union of egg and sperm causes extensive changes in the female reproductive parts. Fertilization of the egg stimulates the growth of the ovary and the enclosed ovules. Carefully examine a fresh bean or pea pod. Open the pod to find the seeds. Which of the female reproductive structures is the pod of a bean or pea? What is the origin of a seed? If you plant ripe bean or pea seeds and water them, what will they produce? What can you conclude develops within a seed as a result of fertilization?

13. If time permits, examine other types of flowers. Compare the numbers of various parts and the ways the parts are arranged with respect to each other.

14. Wash your hands thoroughly before leaving the laboratory.

Analysis

1. In alternation of generations in a moss, which is the predominant, independent generation? Which is the less conspicuous generation?

2. Compare the life cycle of a moss (with alternation of generations) with your life cycle (with no alternation of generations).

3. Would you expect more variation in flowering plants or in those that reproduce asexually? Explain.

4. Compare and contrast the sporophyte and gametophyte stages of a moss to those of a flowering plant.

5. Do flowering plants demonstrate more or less adaptation to a land environment than mosses? Explain your reasoning.

Investigations for Chapter 12
Patterns of Inheritance

Investigation 12A • Probability

The probability of a chance event can be calculated mathematically using the following formula:

$$\text{probability} = \frac{\text{number of events of choice}}{\text{number of possible events}}$$

What is the probability that you will draw a spade from a shuffled deck of cards like that shown in Figure 12.6? There are 52 cards in the deck (52 possible events). Of these, 13 cards are spades (13 events of choice). Therefore, the probability of choosing a spade from this deck is 13/52 (or 1/4 or 0.25 or 25%). To determine the probability that you will draw the ace of diamonds, you again have 52 possible events, but this time there is only one event of choice. The probability is 1/52 or 2%. In this investigation, you will determine the probability for the results of a coin toss.

Materials (per team of 2)

2 pennies (1 shiny, 1 dull)
cardboard box

Procedure

1. Work in teams of two. One person will be student A and the other will be student B.

2. Student A will prepare a score sheet with two columns—one labeled *H* (heads), and the other *T* (tails). Student B will toss a penny 10 times. Toss it into a cardboard box to prevent the coin from rolling away.

3. Student A will use a slash mark (/) to indicate the result of each toss. Tally the tosses in the appropriate column on the score sheet. After 10 tosses, draw a line across the two columns and pass the sheet to student B. Student A then will make 10 tosses, and student B will tally the results.

4. Continue reversing roles until the results of 100 (10 series of 10) tosses have been tallied.

5. Prepare a score sheet with four columns labeled *H/H*, *Dull H/Shiny T*, *Dull T/Shiny H*, and *T/T* (*H* = heads; *T* = tails). Obtain 2 pennies—1 dull and 1 shiny. Toss both pennies together 20 times, while your partner tallies each result in the appropriate column of the score sheet.

6. Reverse roles once so that you have a total of 40 tosses.

Analysis

1. How many heads are probable in a series of 10 tosses? How many did you actually observe in the first 10 tosses?

2. Deviation is a measure of the difference between the expected and observed results. It is not the difference itself. It is the ratio of the sum of the differences between expected and observed results to the total number of observations.

   Thus:

   $$\text{deviation} = \frac{\begin{array}{c}\text{difference between heads expected}\\ \text{and heads observed}\\ +\\ \text{difference between tails expected}\\ \text{and tails observed}\end{array}}{\text{number of tosses}}$$

   Calculate the deviation for each of the 10 sets of tosses.

3. Calculate the deviation for your team's total (100 tosses).

4. Add the data of all teams in your class. Calculate the class deviation.

5. If your school has more than one biology class, combine the data of all classes. Calculate the deviation for all classes.

6. How does increasing the number of tosses affect the average size of the deviation? These results demonstrate an important principle of probability. State what it is.

7. On the chalkboard, record the data for tossing two pennies together. Add each column of the chart. In how many columns do data concerning heads of a dull penny appear?

8. In what fraction of the total number of tosses did heads of dull pennies occur?

9. In how many columns do data concerning heads of a shiny penny occur?

10. In what fraction of the total number of tosses did heads of the shiny pennies occur?

11. In how many columns do heads of both dull and shiny pennies appear?

12. In what fraction of the total number of tosses did heads of both of the pennies appear at the same time?

13. To which of the following is this fraction closest: the sum, the difference, or the product of the two fractions for heads of one penny at a time?

14. Your answer suggests a second important principle of probability that concerns the relationship between the probabilities of separate events and the probability of a combination of events. State this relationship.

15. When you toss two coins together, there are only three possibilities—H/H, T/T, or H/T. These three combinations will occur 100% of the time. The rules of probability predict that H/H and T/T each will occur 25% of the time. What is the expected probability for the combination of heads on one coin and tails on the other?

16. When you toss a dull penny and a shiny penny together, what is the probability that heads will occur on the dull penny? What is the probability that tails will occur on the shiny penny? Calculate the probability that the dull penny will be "heads" and the shiny penny will be "tails" if you toss the two pennies together. Compare this answer to the answer in question 15. How do you account for the different answers? Are there other ways than *Dull H/Shiny T* to get the *H/T* combination?

17. How many different ways can you get the *H/T* combination on two coins tossed together? What is the probability of each of those different ways occurring? Is the probability of getting heads and tails in any combination of pennies closest to the sum, the difference, or the product of the probabilities for getting heads and tails in each of the different ways?

18. Your answer suggests a third important principle of probability that concerns the relationship between (a) the probability of either one of two mutually exclusive events occurring and (b) the individual probabilities of those events. State this relationship.

Investigation 12B • Seedling Phenotypes

Albinism is a rare condition found in both plants and animals. The cells of albino animals or plants lack certain pigments. Albino plants, for example, have no chlorophyll. In this investigation you will observe the influence of both heredity and environment on a plant's ability to produce chlorophyll.

Materials (per team of 2)

petri dish

filter or blotting paper to fit petri dish

lightproof box or aluminum foil to fit over petri dish

about 50 tobacco seeds

Procedure

1. Evenly sprinkle tobacco seeds over moistened filter paper in the bottom of a petri dish. The seeds should be separated by at least twice their length.

    CAUTION: Wash hands after handling tobacco seeds. They may be treated with a fungicide.

2. Put the cover over the dish. Put the dish in a lighted area for about 4 days. Record observations daily in your data book.

3. After 4 or 5 days, wrap the dish in foil or cover it with a lightproof box. Put the setup in a dark place where it will not be disturbed for 3 or 4 more days. Be sure the paper is moist at all times, and add water if necessary. Do not expose the seeds to light when checking them.

4. After the seeds have germinated, usually in about a week to 10 days, remove the lightproof cover and examine the seedlings. Observe especially the color of the tiny leaves. Record your observations.

5. Replace the cover on the petri dish and put it in a well-lighted place for a few days. Be sure the paper is moist at all times. Observe the seedlings each day as they are exposed to the light.

6. After being in the light for a few days, count the number of plants of each color. Record your observations and the numbers of each type of plant in your data book.

TABLE 12B.1
Mendel's Results from Crossing Pea Plants with Single Contrasting Traits

P$_1$ cross	F$_1$ plants	F$_1$ plants (self-pollinated)	F$_2$ plants	Actual ratio
round × wrinkled seeds	all round	round × round	5474 round 1850 wrinkled 7324 total	2.96:1
yellow × green seed (cotyledons)	all yellow	yellow × yellow	6022 yellow 2001 green 8023 total	3.01:1
green × yellow pods	all green	green × green	428 green 152 yellow 580 total	2.82:1
long × short stems	all long	long × long	787 long 277 1064 total	2.84:1

7. Wash your hands thoroughly before leaving the laboratory.

Analysis

1. What was the color of the tobacco plants while they were growing in the dark?

2. Did light have the same effect on all of the plants? Explain.

3. The seeds used in this investigation came from a specially bred tobacco plant. Do you suppose the parent plants were both green, one green and one albino, or both albino? (Hint: Consider the role of chlorophyll in the life of a plant.) Give reasons for your answer.

4. Does light have any effect on a tobacco plant's ability to produce chlorophyll? Explain.

5. Is light the only factor required for a tobacco plant to produce chlorophyll? Explain.

6. Which seedlings showed the influence of heredity on chlorophyll development? Explain.

7. What was the approximate ratio of green to albino plants that appeared when seedlings were grown in the light for several days? Compare this ratio with Mendel's data for crossing garden peas shown in Table 12B.1.

Investigation 12C • A Dihybrid Cross

Sexually reproducing organisms have haploid and diploid stages. In flowering plants and animals, only the gametes are haploid, and traits (the phenotype) can be observed only in the diploid stage. When Mendel made dihybrid crosses to study the inheritance of two different traits, such as seed shape and seed color, he could observe the traits only in the diploid cells of the parents and their offspring. He had to use probability to calculate the most likely genotypes of the gametes.

In the yeast *Saccharomyces cerevisiae*, however, phenotypes of some traits can be seen in the haploid cell colonies. In Investigation 11A, for example, you could observe the color trait red or cream, in both haploid and diploid stages of the yeast life cycle. Not all yeast traits are visible, however, so geneticists use the methods Beadle and Tatum devised for studying mutations. That is, they isolate mutants that cannot make some essential substance. The inability of the mutant strain to make the substance and the ability of the normal strain to make it are two different forms of a trait.

In this yeast dihybrid cross, you will follow two forms of each of two traits: red versus cream color, and tryptophan-dependent (requiring this amino

TABLE 12C.1 Growth of Yeast on Two Media

Haploid	Diploid	On COMP medium	On MIN medium
RT	*R/R T/T* *R/R T/t* *R/r T/T* *R/r T/t*	growth, cream	growth, cream
Rt	*R/R t/t* *R/r t/t*	growth, cream	no growth, (cream?)
rT	*r/r T/T* *r/r T/t*	growth, red	growth, red
rt	*r/r t/t*	growth, red	no growth, (red?)

acid to grow) versus tryptophan-independent (not requiring this amino acid). In Investigation 11A, a red strain of yeast of one mating type is crossed with a cream-colored strain of the other type. The diploid strain is cream colored. If there is a single gene for this trait, then there must be one allele that determines cream color in the haploid strain and another allele that determines red color. In the diploid strain, then, there must be one of each of these alleles. Which form of the color trait is dominant?

By observing the color of a colony that a haploid strain forms, you can predict with certainty which allele it carries. In the case of a cream-colored diploid, however, you cannot be sure of the genotype. It could carry either one allele for cream color and one for red, or two alleles for cream color. The trait defined by tryptophan-dependence or independence works in much the same way. A tryptophan-dependent haploid must carry the allele for tryptophan-dependence (a defective form of the gene) and a tryptophan-independent haploid must carry the allele for tryptophan-independence (the functional form of the gene), but a tryptophan-independent diploid could be either homozygous or heterozygous for the functional allele.

Using symbols for the traits, the allele for the dominant cream form is *R* and the recessive red form is *r*; the normal, tryptophan-independent form of that gene is *T* and the tryptophan-dependent form is *t*. Whereas the color trait is visible, determining tryptophan dependence or independence requires a simple growth test.

Table 12C.1 shows how all possible combinations of these two traits can be determined by testing the yeast on two types of growth medium: a nutritionally complete medium (COMP), and a medium lacking tryptophan (MIN).

Materials (per team of 2)

PART C

container of clean flat toothpicks

glass-marking pencil

2 paper templates for streaking strains

3 self-sealing plastic bags labeled waste (1 for each day) biohazard bag

complete growth medium agar plate (COMP)
minimal + adenine growth medium agar plate (MIN)

COMP plate with 24-hr. cultures of yeast strains HAO, HAR, HAT, HART, HBO, HBR, HBT, and HBRT

Procedure

PART A Predicting the Gametes of the Parents

The diploid parents of this dihybrid cross would have been *r/r T/T* and *R/R t/t*. To predict the F$_2$ offspring, it is necessary to predict the different types and relative numbers of gametes that can be produced. The simplest way to make this prediction is to

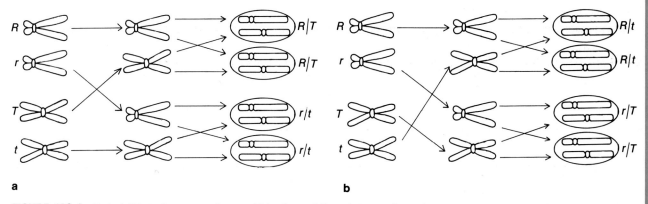

FIGURE 12C.1 Probabilities of gametes that could be formed by yeast organisms that are homozygous for two traits.

diagram how the chromosomes separate at meiosis. Figure 12C.1a shows the gametes predicted from the pure-breeding diploid red parent (*r/r T/T*).

Two pairs of chromosomes are represented, one carrying the gene for color (in this case red, *r*) and the other carrying the gene for the ability to make tryptophan (in this case tryptophan-independent, *T*). At the first meiotic division (M$_I$), chromosome pairs segregate (separate). At the second meiotic division (M$_{II}$), the two chromatids of each chromosome segregate into the nuclei of the gametes. In this case, segregation can occur in only one way because only one allele of each gene is represented. All the gametes from a pure-breeding diploid are the same (*rT*). The probability of this parent producing a gamete with the genotype of *rT* is 1/1, or 100%.

1. In your data book, copy the diagram shown above in Figure 12C.1b (or use the diagram your teacher provides) for the cream, tryptophan-dependent parent (*R/R t/t*). Fill in the missing symbols. Each chromatid should have one letter.

2. Use the symbols given to describe for each parent strain the genotypes and phenotypes of all the possible gametes and the relative probabilities of their occurrence.

3. The haploid gametes produced from these two pure-breeding parents mate to form the diploid zygotes of the F$_1$ generation. Use the symbols to describe the genotype and phenotype of the diploid zygotes that could be formed from the fusion of these gametes. At this point your dia-

grams should show that they all will have the dihybrid genotype *R/r T/t*.

PART B Predicting the Gametes of the F$_1$ Diploids

Because there are two equally probable ways that the alleles of the two genes can separate at M$_I$, the chromosome diagram for the segregation of the *R*, *r*, *T*, and *t* alleles is more complicated. These are shown in Figures 12C.2a and 12C.2b (page 676). Since these two patterns of segregation are equally probable, the two diagrams together illustrate the relative numbers of all possible genotypes.

4. Copy the diagrams in Figure 12C.2 (page 676) in your data book, or use the diagrams your teacher provides. Fill in the missing symbols. Each chromatid should have a symbol.

5. What is the total number of different gametes represented in the diagram?

6. How many different genotypes are represented? Give their symbols.

7. How many times is each genotype represented?

8. What is the probability of occurrence of each genotype among the total number of gametes shown? Compare this prediction with the gametes in Figure 12.11 on page 281.

9. Draw a checkerboard diagram for all the possible crosses among these gametes. This diagram should illustrate the 16 different combinations predicted. Instead of male and female gametes, use mating-type **a** and mating-type α haploid

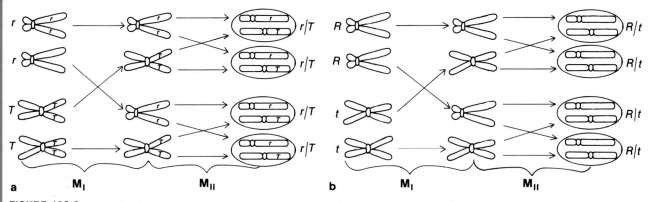

a M_I M_{II} **b** M_I M_{II}

FIGURE 12C.2 Gametes that could be formed by yeast organisms heterozygous for two traits.

strains. In each square of the diagram construct the diploid genotype that would result from the fusion of the corresponding gametes. How many different genotypes are there? How many different phenotypes? Does this diagram predict a 9:3:3:1 ratio? What specific phenotypes would be represented in these ratios?

PART C Testing the Predicted Phenotypes

Day 0

10. Make two templates for setting up crosses. Copy the pattern shown in Figure 12C.3 onto a piece of paper twice, so that each fits the bottom of a petri plate (or use the templates your teacher provides).

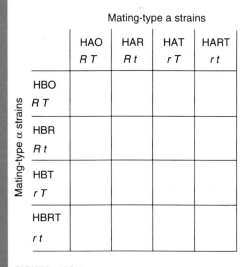

Mating-type a strains

	HAO R T	HAR R t	HAT r T	HART r t
HBO R T				
HBR R t				
HBT r T				
HBRT r t				

Mating-type α strains

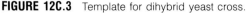

FIGURE 12C.3 Template for dihybrid yeast cross.

11. Tape one template to the bottom of a plate of complete growth medium (COMP) so that you can read it through the agar.

12. Transfer a small sample of each strain onto the agar directly over its corresponding label. To do this, touch the flat end of a clean toothpick to strain HAO on the plate your teacher provides. Then, gently drag the toothpick along the box labeled HAO on the COMP agar plate to make a streak about one cm long. Discard the toothpick in the self-closing waste bag, being careful not to touch anything with it. Repeat this procedure for all eight strains, using a new toothpick for each transfer. Be careful not to touch the ends of the toothpicks to anything except yeast or the sterile agar. Discard used toothpicks in the self-closing plastic waste bag. Keep the lid on the plate at all times except when transferring yeast.

13. Invert and incubate at room temperature.

14. Wash your hands before leaving the laboratory.

Day 1

15. On the same COMP plate, make a mating mixture for each of the mating-type **a** strains with each of the mating-type α strains. To do this, use the flat end of a clean toothpick to transfer a dot of the HAO strain of freshly grown cells to each of the boxes below it on the template. Discard the toothpick in the waste bag. Repeat this procedure for HAR, HAT, and HART, using a new toothpick for each strain. Using the same procedure, transfer a dot of the freshly grown cells of each HB strain to each of the boxes to the right of the strain on the template. Place these dots side-by-

side, but not touching, as shown in the first box in Figure 12C.3. Use a clean toothpick to mix each pair of spots together. Be sure to use a clean toothpick each time you mix pairs together. Discard all toothpicks in the waste bag.

16. Invert and incubate at room temperature.

17. Wash your hands before leaving the laboratory.

Day 2

18. Test each mating mixture and parent strain for its ability to grow on MIN agar. To keep track of the tests, tape a copy of the template to the bottom of the MIN plate. Then, use the flat end of a clean toothpick to transfer a small amount of each strain and mixture from the COMP plate to the corresponding position on the MIN plate. Be sure to use a clean toothpick each time you change strains and mixtures. Discard all toothpicks in the waste bag.

19. Invert and incubate both plates until the next day.

20. Wash your hands before leaving the laboratory.

Day 3

21. Copy the score sheet in Figure 12C.4 in your data book (or tape in the copy your teacher provides). Record the color and growth phenotypes of each parent haploid strain and F_2 diploid on the score sheet for both plates.

22. Tabulate the different phenotypes observed among the F_2 diploids and the number of times each one occurred among the 16 crosses.

23. Compare the F_2 phenotypes with the predictions you made in Part A. Explain how your actual results either support or contradict your predictions.

24. Discard all plates in the biohazard bag.

25. Wash your hands before leaving the laboratory.

Analysis

Because yeast exhibit most of the same traits in the haploid stage (gametes) and the diploid stage, you knew the precise genotypes of the gametes (haploid strains) that you mated to produce the F_2 diploids. This removed the element of chance at this step. In Part B, however, you had to deal with the role of

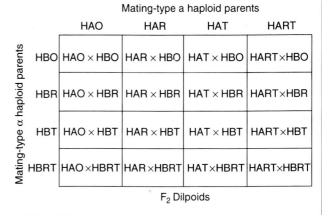

FIGURE 12C.4 Score sheet for dihybrid yeast cross.

chance to predict the numbers and genotypes of the gametes from the F_1 diploids. Throughout the entire process, beginning with the parental cross (P) and going through to the F_2 offspring, there are some steps at which chance plays a role, so the results can only be expressed as a probability. In other steps, chance is not a factor, so you can predict the outcome exactly.

1. List the steps in which chance is a factor.

2. List the steps in which chance is not a factor.

3. Explain why the outcome of some steps involves chance, whereas the outcome of others does not.

Investigations for Chapter 13
Advances in Genetics

Investigation 13A • Direct Detection of Genetic Disorders

About 1 in 625 African-American children in the United States is born each year with sickle cell disease. It is caused by an abnormality in hemoglobin, the protein in red blood cells that carries oxygen to the cells. As a result of the abnormal hemoglobin, the blood cells take on a sickled shape, as shown in Figure 13.8. People with the disorder have pain in their long bones and joints and are susceptible to infections. Although some individuals do not live beyond childhood, others can live reasonably normal lives into adulthood with proper care.

Individuals with sickle cell disease have two abnormal genes, one from each parent. About 1 in 10 people in the African-American population is heterozygous, with one gene for sickle hemoglobin and one for normal hemoglobin. They are said to be carriers and to have sickle cell trait. They have no health problems, but if they have children with another carrier, there is a 25 percent chance that each child will have sickle cell disease.

Sickle hemoglobin results from a mutation in the DNA that changes the amino acid glutamate in normal hemoglobin to the amino acid valine. That change gives the red blood cells a different shape. The mutation also eliminates a restriction enzyme recognition site, creating RFLPs different from those in the DNA that codes for normal hemoglobin. As a result, RFLPs provide an accurate prenatal test to determine whether a developing fetus has sickle cell disease, sickle cell trait, or normal hemoglobin. In this investigation, you will simulate that test.

Materials (per team of 2)

pop-it beads: 6 black, 30 white, 12 green, 22 red

Procedure

1. The following codons are part of the DNA sequences for normal hemoglobin and sickle hemoglobin:

	Codon	Amino acids
Normal hemoglobin DNA	GGT CTC CTC	
Sickle hemoglobin DNA	GGT CAC CTC	

Copy the table above in your data book. Use the genetic code in Figure 10B.1 to determine the amino acids that these codons signal. Describe the difference in the genetic code between the two types of hemoglobin and the result of that difference.

2. Strands I and II in Figure 13A.1 represent two single strands of DNA. Using the pop-it beads, one team member will make a model of strand I, and the other team member will make a model of strand II. Key: black = adenine (A); white = thymine (T); green = guanine (G); red = cytosine (C). What is the difference between strand I and strand II? Based on that difference, what can you predict about an individual who has strand I in her genetic make-up? Strand II?

3. The restriction enzyme MstII recognizes the DNA sequence GGTCTCC and cuts the DNA between the first T and the first C of that sequence, reading from left to right. Locate the places on strand I where cuts can be made by MstII and break the strand at those points. Do the same for strand II.

Analysis

1. What will be the length of the fragments (how many bases) if strand I is cut with MstII? What will be the length of the fragments (how many bases) if strand II is cut with MstII?

2. How could you use MstII to distinguish sickle-cell DNA from DNA that codes for normal hemoglobin?

3. Three couples undergo prenatal testing, and are shown the results of DNA tests performed on the fetal cells. In each case, give the diagnosis for the developing fetus: (a) fragment sizes = 5, 14, 10, 6; (b) fragment sizes = 5, 14, 10, 24, 6; (c) fragment sizes = 5, 24, 6.

4. You have just used RFLPs to test for the presence of sickle-cell DNA. RFLP stands for *restriction fragment length polymorphism*. Use your knowledge of restriction enzymes and variations in DNA sequences to write a paragraph that

FIGURE 13A.1 Building double-stranded DNA.

Strand I

1	2	3	4	5	6	7	8	9	10	11	12	13	14	15	16	17	18	19	20	21	22	23	24	25	26	27	28	29	30	31	32	33	34	35
A	A	G	G	T	C	T	C	C	T	C	T	T	T	T	T	G	G	T	C	T	C	C	T	C	A	G	G	T	C	T	C	C	T	T

Strand II

1	2	3	4	5	6	7	8	9	10	11	12	13	14	15	16	17	18	19	20	21	22	23	24	25	26	27	28	29	30	31	32	33	34	35
A	A	G	G	T	C	T	C	C	T	C	T	T	T	T	T	G	G	T	C	A	C	C	T	C	A	G	G	T	C	T	C	C	T	T

explains the name restriction fragment length polymorphisms.

5. What type of tissues could be used to make this diagnosis?

6. How would different mutations causing the same disorder affect a diagnosis made on the basis of RFLPs?

Investigation 13B • Recombinant DNA

Among the most significant developments in biology during the last 20 years is genetic engineering—the ability to manipulate DNA. Scientists can manipulate genetic material to produce substances such as insulin, human growth hormone, interferon, and hepatitis B vaccine. The technology to produce these substances is called recombinant DNA technology. In this investigation, you will model the procedures used in recombinant DNA technology to produce insulin. Figure 13B.1 summarizes the steps involved in the production of the insulin gene.

Materials (per team of 3)

PART A

pop-it beads: 30 black, 18 white, 30 green, 27 red, 10 pink

string

PART B

pop-it beads: 12 black, 12 white, 18 green, 18 red

masking tape

Procedure

PART A Preparing the Insulin Gene

1. This is a portion of messenger RNA (mRNA) for insulin isolated from cells in the pancreas:

1	2	3	4	5	6	7	8	9	10	11	12	13	14	15	16	17	18
C	C	U	A	G	G	A	C	C	U	A	U	A	G	U	C	G	A

19	20	21	22	23	24	25	26	27	28	29	30	31	32	33	34
G	G	G	U	A	A	U	G	A	A	U	U	C	G	A	A

35	36	37	38	39	40	41	42	43
G	U	C	C	C	U	A	G	G

Use the following key and pop-it beads to construct the mRNA strand.

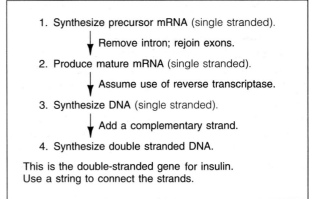

1. Synthesize precursor mRNA (single stranded).
   ↓ Remove intron; rejoin exons.
2. Produce mature mRNA (single stranded).
   ↓ Assume use of reverse transcriptase.
3. Synthesize DNA (single stranded).
   ↓ Add a complementary strand.
4. Synthesize double stranded DNA.

This is the double-stranded gene for insulin. Use a string to connect the strands.

FIGURE 13B.1 Flow chart for production of the insulin gene

black = adenine (A)   red = cytosine (C)
white = thymine (T)   pink = uracil (U)
green = guanine (G)

2. Human DNA—from which mRNA is made—contains base sequences, called introns, that do not contain information used in the production of protein. The portions of the gene that code for the amino-acids of a protein are called exons. The mRNA with introns is called precursor mRNA. Eubacteria lack the enzymes that remove introns. Therefore, before mRNA can be inserted into eubacteria, the introns must be removed to form mature, functional mRNA. First you must locate the intron in the human mRNA you constructed. The amino acid sequence for the piece of the insulin gene you are working with is as follows:

proline—arginine—threonine—tyrosine—serine—arginine—glutamate—phenylalanine—glutamate—valine—proline—arginine

Use the genetic code in Figure 10B.1 to identify and locate the intron in the precursor mRNA you formed. For example, the first codon in the mRNA is CCU, for proline, the first amino acid in insulin. The second codon is AGG, for arginine—the second amino acid. Compare codons and amino acids until you reach bases that do not contain the proper information for insulin production. These bases make up the intron. What are the numbers of the bases?

3. Clip out the intron by removing the intron bases from the mRNA. Reconnect the exons. You now

FIGURE 13B.2 Building double-stranded DNA.

have mature, functional mRNA containing only exons. What must happen next, before the insulin gene can be placed into a eubacterium?

4. Scientists use the enzyme reverse transcriptase to copy an mRNA molecule into a DNA molecule. (It reverses the transcription process, which normally proceeds from DNA to RNA.) Use pop-it beads to construct a DNA strand complementary to your mature mRNA strand. Remember adenine is complementary to uracil.

5. To make the DNA molecule double-stranded, use pop-it beads to construct a second, complementary strand of DNA. Use a string to connect the complementary strands (Figure 13B.2). You have now constructed an insulin gene. What is the next step in the recombinant DNA process?

PART B   Forming Recombinant Plasmids

6. Figure 13B.3 summarizes the steps you will follow to insert the insulin gene into the genetic system of a bacterium. Some bacterial DNA exists in small circular pieces called plasmids.

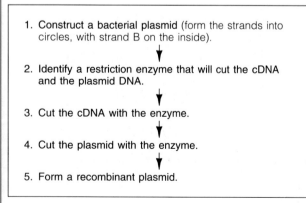

1. Construct a bacterial plasmid (form the strands into circles, with strand B on the inside).

2. Identify a restriction enzyme that will cut the cDNA and the plasmid DNA.

3. Cut the cDNA with the enzyme.

4. Cut the plasmid with the enzyme.

5. Form a recombinant plasmid.

FIGURE 13B.3 Flow chart for formation of a recombinant plasmid.

Genetic engineers use plasmids to introduce new genes into bacteria. Use pop-it beads and the following DNA sequence to build a double-stranded DNA sequence that will become the plasmid. (Use the same color key as in Part A.)

Strand A

1	2	3	4	5	6	7	8	9	10	11	12	13	14	15	16	17	18
G	G	A	T	C	C	T	G	A	C	A	C	C	G	G	A	A	C

19	20	21	22	23	24	25	26	27	28	29	30
G	T	C	A	A	G	G	T	T	C	C	C

Strand B

1	2	3	4	5	6	7	8	9	10	11	12	13	14	15	16	17	18
C	C	T	A	G	G	A	C	T	G	T	G	G	C	C	T	T	G

19	20	21	22	23	24	25	26	27	28	29	30
C	A	G	T	T	C	G	A	A	G	G	G

7. To represent the circular plasmids, connect the two ends of each strand, and mark the beginning of strand A with a small piece of masking tape. Tie the strands together with 2 pieces of string. What is the next step in the process?

8. Genetic engineers use restriction enzymes as "scissors" to cut DNA sequences at specific locations. Each restriction enzyme recognizes a specific sequence of bases, and cuts within that sequence. When the DNA is cut, the ends become "sticky." They can bond to other sticky ends that have been cut with the same restriction enzyme and, therefore, have complementary nucleotide sequences. Table 13B.1 lists three restriction enzymes, their recognition sites, and the sticky ends they create. Imagine that the insulin gene you constructed in Part A is only a portion of a long DNA molecule. To cut this gene from the DNA molecule, you must use a restriction enzyme that will yield sticky ends in the insulin gene that can bind with complementary sticky ends in the plasmid. Examine the model of the insulin gene you constructed in Part A. Which restriction enzyme in Table 13B.1 can you use to remove the insulin gene from the complete DNA molecule? Examine your plasmid and locate a similar DNA sequence cutting site. Which restriction enzyme can you use to

TABLE 13B.1   Examples of restriction enzymes

Enzyme Name	DNA Recognition Sequence and Cutting Site	"Sticky Ends"
Bam H1	—G⌐GATC C—	GATCC
	—C CTAG⌐G—	CCTAG
HindIII	—A⌐AGCT T—	AGCTT
	—T TCGA⌐A—	TTCGA
HpaII	—C⌐CG G—	CGG
	—G GC⌐C—	GGC

cut open both the gene and the plasmid so they have complementary sticky ends?

9. Cut the insulin gene at the proper site. What sticky ends have you made in the insulin gene?

10. Acting as the restriction enzyme, cut open the plasmid. What sticky ends have you made in the plasmid? Compare the sticky ends of the insulin gene and the plasmid. What do you observe?

11. Complementary sticky ends of a gene and a plasmid are joined by enzymes called ligases. Perform the function of a ligase by connecting the sticky ends of your gene and your plasmid. Use small pieces of tape to identify the connections (called splices). You now have produced a model of a recombinant plasmid.

Analysis

1. What is the difference between precursor mRNA and functional mRNA? Why is this difference significant in recombinant DNA techniques?

2. How did you check your work at each step of the "genetic engineering" procedure?

3. What would you look for to determine whether your gene insertion into the plasmid is correct?

4. What is the next step in producing recombinant DNA?

5. Briefly describe the genetic engineering procedures you used to produce an insulin "factory."

6. What would have resulted if the insulin gene was cut near the middle rather than at the ends?

Investigations for Chapter 14
Development in Animals

Investigation 14A • Development in Polychaete Worms

The marine polychaete worm, *Chaetopterus variopedatus,* lives in the sand near the low tide level inside a leathery, U-shaped tube (Figure 14A.1). The sperm or eggs are visible inside the parapodia (leg-like extensions from the body) near the posterior end of the worm. The sperm appear ivory-white and give the parapodia a smooth, white appearance. The ovaries are in yellow coils and contain eggs that give the female parapodia a grainy appearance. You will observe the worm, remove eggs and sperm, fertilize the eggs, and observe the development of the embryos. The initial stages of development that you will observe appear the same for nearly all sexually reproducing organisms.

Materials (per team of 2)

microscope slides
cover slips
dropping pipet
finger bowls
compound microscope

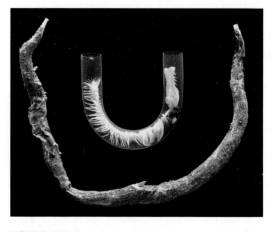

FIGURE 14A.1   Polychaete worm in a glass tube (top) and the worm's natural tube (bottom).

forceps

dissecting scissors

dissecting needle

cheesecloth

paper towels

sea water

male and female parapodia of *Chaetopterus*

SAFETY Spilled water can cause slippery footing and falls. Wipe up any spilled water immediately. Handle dissecting tools with care; immediately report any injuries to your teacher.

Procedure

1. Rinse a small double-thickness piece of cheesecloth in fresh water, and then rinse it in sea water. Place the wet cheesecloth in the bottom of a finger bowl.

2. Using forceps and dissecting scissors, remove one parapodium with eggs from the female worm and place it on the wet cheesecloth in the finger bowl. Use the pipet to remove any eggs that spilled out of the parapodium, and squeeze the sea water and eggs out of the pipet onto the cheesecloth. Cut open the parapodium and with the dissecting needle and forceps, tear the parapodium apart and release the eggs.

   CAUTION: Dissecting tools are sharp; handle with care.

3. Lift the cheesecloth and pour about 1 cm of sea water into the finger bowl. Pick up the cheesecloth by the four corners and gently dip it up and down in the water and move it around slowly. The movement should allow most of the eggs to filter into the sea water while sand and other debris stay behind. The eggs are tiny yellow or yellow-orange dots. Note the time in your data book. Discard the cheesecloth in a container designated by your teacher.

4. *You must wait 15 minutes from the time you put the eggs in sea water before you add sperm.* While you wait, you can obtain and study the sperm. Add 10 mL of fresh sea water to another finger bowl. Remove a parapodium with sperm from the male worm and quickly place the parapodium into the fresh sea water. With a dropping pipet, pick up any sperm that were released in the bowl with the worm. The sperm will appear as a small cloud in the water. Add these sperm to those already in the 10 mL of water.

5. Place one drop of the sperm and sea water mixture on a clean microscope slide and add a cover slip. Examine the sperm with low power of a microscope. They will appear as small dots moving around. Switch to high power and observe the sperm. If you do not have many moving sperm, take another sample from the 10 mL of sea water. If moving sperm still are not evident, repeat steps 4 and 5.

6. After the eggs have been in the sea water for 15 minutes, add one drop of the sperm and sea water mixture to the eggs. The eggs should all be fertilized within 30 minutes. After 30 minutes, remove the eggs from the finger bowl and place them in another finger bowl with fresh sea water. The development of the embryos will take place in this bowl.

7. While you are waiting for the 30 minutes to pass, obtain fertilized eggs from bowls designated by your teacher and examine them under the microscope. Look for embryos at the 4-, 8-, and 16-cell stages and note any other developmental stages you observe.

8. Wash your hands before leaving the laboratory.

Analysis

1. Examine the photo of human sperm in Figure 24.3. How do the sperm of the polychaete worm compare with the picture of human sperm? Describe any similarities or differences you observe.

2. Describe the development process you observed in the polychaete worm embryos.

3. The polychaete worm larvae usually develop within 24 hours after fertilization. Based on what you observed and your knowledge of cleavage and cell division, approximately how many cell divisions have occurred between the one-cell stage and the swimming larvae?

4. Describe any similarities between the development of the polychaete worm embryos and the development of human embryos.

Investigations for Chapter 15
Plant Growth and Development

Investigation 15A • Seeds and Seedlings

A seed is a packaged plant—a complete set of instructions for growing a plant such as a maple tree or a geranium. The seed contains everything needed to produce a young plant. How does the change from seed to plant occur? What are the functions of the structures of the seed and the growing plant? What changes can you observe? In this investigation you will have an opportunity to find out.

Hypothesis: After reading the procedures, construct a hypothesis that predicts how petri dishes C and D will differ.

Materials (per team of 2)

2 pairs of safety goggles

2 lab aprons

10X hand lens

scalpel

petri dish with starch agar—dish A

petri dish with plain agar—dish B

petri dish with starch agar and germinating corn grains—dish C

petri dish with starch agar and boiled corn grains—dish D

Lugol's iodine solution in dropping bottle

soaked germinating corn grains

soaked bean seeds

bean seeds germinated 1, 2, 3, and 10 days

> **SAFETY** Put on your safety goggles and lab apron.

PART A The Seed

Procedure

1. Examine the external features of a bean seed. Notice that the seed is covered by a tough, leathery coat. Look along the concave, inner edge of the seed and find a scar. This scar marks the place where the seed was attached to the pod.

2. Remove the seed coat and examine the two fleshy halves, the cotyledons, which are part of the embryo.

3. Using a scalpel, cut a small sliver from one of the cotyledons.

> **CAUTION: Scalpels are sharp; handle with care.**

Test the sliver with a drop of Lugol's iodine solution. Record the results in your data book.

> **WARNING: Lugol's iodine solution is a *poison* if ingested; a *strong irritant*, and can stain clothing. Avoid skin/eye contact; do not ingest. If contact occurs, immediately flush affected area with water for 15 minutes; rinse mouth with water. If a spill occurs, call your teacher; *then* flood spill area with water.**

4. Separate the two cotyledons and find the little plant attached to one end of one of the cotyledons. Use a hand lens to examine the plant. You will see that this part of the embryo has two miniature leaves and a root. The small leaves and a tiny tip make up the epicotyl (*epi* = above; above the cotyledon) of the embryo. The root portion is the hypoctyl (*hypo* = below; below the cotyledon).

Analysis

1. Based on your observations, what do you think is the function of the seed coat? Explain your reasoning.

2. What do you think is the function of a connection between a parent plant and a developing seed?

3. Based on your observations, what do you conclude is the primary function of the cotyledons? Explain your reasoning.

4. What was the original source of the matter that makes up the cotyledons?

PART B The Seedling

Procedure

5. Examine bean seedlings that are 1, 2, and 3 days old.

6. Compare the 10-day-old seedling with the 3-day-old seedling.

Analysis

1. What part of the plant becomes established first?

2. Where are the first true leaves of the 3-day-old seedling?

3. What has happened to the cotyledons in the 10-day-old seedling?

4. Where is the seed coat in this plant?

5. Which part or parts of the embryo developed into the stem?

6. How are the first two tiny true leaves arranged on the stem?

PART C   Corn Seeds

Procedure

7. Cut a soaked, germinated corn grain lengthwise with the scalpel.

8. Test the cut surfaces with a few drops of Lugol's iodine solution. Record your observations and conclusion.

9. The starch agar and plain agar in petri dishes A and B were tested with Lugol's iodine solution as a demonstration. Observe the dishes. Record your observations and conclusion in your data book.

10. On petri dish C, 2 or 3 corn grains have started to germinate on starch agar. Each grain was cut lengthwise, and the cut surfaces were placed on the starch agar for about 2 days. Petri dish D contains starch agar and boiled corn grains.

11. Cover the surface of the starch agar in petri dishes C and D with Lugol's iodine solution.

12. After a few seconds, pour off the excess.

13. Wash your hands thoroughly before leaving the laboratory.

Analysis

1. When you tested the cut surface of corn grains, what food was present?

2. What other nutrients might be present in the corn that were not demonstrated by the test of the cut surfaces?

3. What difference did you observe when you tested the agars in petri dishes A and B?

4. What difference did you observe when you tested petri dishes C and D? Suggest hypotheses that might account for what you observed.

5. What food substance would you expect to find in the areas where the germinating corn grains were?

Investigation 15B • Tropisms

This investigation allows you to observe tropisms. One-half of each team will conduct either Part A or Part B of the investigation. Observe all your team's work so you can discuss all the results as a class.

Hypothesis: After reading the procedures, construct two hypotheses—one predicting how the germinating corn grains will be affected and the other predicting the patterns of growth of the radish seeds.

PART A

Materials   (per team of 4; one-half of each team performing Part A or Part B)

petri dish

scissors

glass-marking pencil

nonabsorbent cotton

heavy blotting paper

transparent tape

modeling clay

4 soaked corn grains

PART B

Materials

4 flowerpots, about 8 cm in diameter

4 cardboard boxes, at least 5 cm higher than the
   flowerpots

red, blue and clear cellophane

scissors

transparent tape

40 radish seeds

soil

PART A Orientation of Shoots and Roots in Germinating Corn

Procedure

1. Place 4 soaked corn grains in the bottom half of a petri dish. Arrange them cotyledon side down, as shown in Figure 15B.1.

2. Fill the spaces between the corn grains with wads of nonabsorbent cotton to a depth slightly greater than the thickness of the grains.

3. Cut a piece of blotting paper slightly larger than the bottom of the petri dish, wet it thoroughly, and fit it snugly over the grains and the cotton.
   CAUTION: Scissors are sharp; handle with care.

4. Hold the dish on its edge and observe the grains through the bottom. If they do not stay in place, pack them with more cotton.

5. When the grains are secure in the dish, seal the two halves of the petri dish together with tape.

6. Rotate the dish until one of the grains is at the top. With the glass-marking pencil, write an A on the petri dish beside the topmost grain. Then, proceeding clockwise, label the other grains B, C, and D. Also label the petri dish with a team symbol.

7. Use modeling clay to support the dish on edge, as shown in Figure 15B.1, and place it in dim light.

8. When the grains begin to germinate, make sketches every day for 5 days, showing the direction in which the root and the shoot grow from each grain.

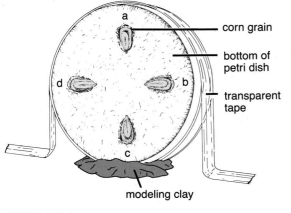

a — corn grain

— bottom of petri dish

— transparent tape

d   b

c

modeling clay

FIGURE 15B.1 Petri dish setup

9. Wash your hands thoroughly before leaving the laboratory.

Analysis

1. From which end of the corn grains did the roots grow? From which end of the grains did the shoots grow?

2. Did the roots eventually turn toward one direction? If so, what direction?

3. Did the shoots eventually turn toward one direction? If so, what direction?

4. To what stimulus did the roots and shoots seem to be responding?

5. In each case, were the responses positive (toward the stimulus) or negative (away from the stimulus)?

6. Why was it important to have the seeds oriented in four different directions?

PART B Orientation of Radish Seedlings

Procedure

10. Turn the four cardboard boxes upside down. Number them 1 to 4. Label each box with your team symbol.

11. Cut a rectangular hole in one side of boxes 1, 2, and 3. (Use the dimensions shown in Figure 15B.2.) Do not cut a hole in box 4.

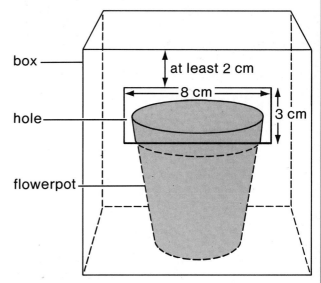

box —

at least 2 cm

— 8 cm —

hole —

3 cm

flowerpot —

FIGURE 15B.2 Flowerpot setup

12. Tape a piece of red cellophane over the hole in box 1, blue cellophane over the hole in box 2, and clear cellophane over the hole in box 3.

13. Number four flowerpots 1 to 4. Label each with your team symbol. Fill the pots to 1 cm below the top with soil.

14. In each pot, plant 10 radish seeds about 0.5 cm deep and 2 cm apart. Press the soil down firmly over the seeds and water them gently. Place the pots in a location that receives strong light but not direct sunlight.

15. Cover each pot with the box labeled with its number. Turn the boxes so the sides with holes face the light.

16. Once each day remove the boxes and water the soil. (Do not move the pots; replace the boxes in their original positions.)

17. When most of the radish seedlings have been above the ground for 2 or 3 days, record the height (length) of each seedling and calculate an average seedling height for each pot. Record the direction of stem growth in each pot—upright, curved slightly, or curved greatly. If curved, record in what direction with respect to the hole in the box.

18. Wash your hands thoroughly before leaving the laboratory.

Analysis

1. Construct a data table to organize your observations. Include box number, average seedling height, direction of curving, and amount of curving.

2. In which flowerpot were the radish stems most nearly upright?

3. In which pot were the radish stems most curved? In what direction were they curved? Were the stems curved in any of the other pots? Which ones and in what direction did they curve?

4. To what stimulus do you think the radish stems responded?

5. What effect, if any, did the red and blue cellophane have on the direction of the radish stem growth?

Investigations for Chapter 16
Origin of New Species

Investigation 16A • Variation in Size of Organisms

Within a population of organisms, small or large variations make each individual different from the others. Variations among familiar organisms are fairly obvious. For example, you are very aware of differences among humans, but all bluebirds may look alike to you. In this investigation, you will collect data on individual variations in size among members of a sample population, and graph and interpret the data.

Materials (per team of 3)

metric ruler

graph paper

50 objects of one type—dried beans, unshelled peanuts, leaves from the same type of tree

SAFETY   Do not eat any of the materials. Wash your hands immediately after handling beans or seeds. They may be treated with a fungicide.

PART A   Line Graph

Procedure

1. Choose one object and measure its length in millimeters. How "typical" do you think this object is in terms of its length? Estimate how many millimeters longer the longest object will be. Then, estimate how much smaller the smallest object will be. Record the object's length and your two estimates in your data book. **CAUTION: Wash your hands immediately after handling seeds. They may be treated with a fungicide.**

2. Choose two team members to measure the objects while a third member records the data.

Use a metric ruler to measure the length of the other 49 objects to the nearest millimeter. (If an object measures 11.5 mm, for example, round up to 12.0 mm.) Record the measurements in your data book with your first measurement.

3. Construct a line graph of your data. Label the *x* (horizontal) axis *Length*. Label the *y* (vertical) axis *Number of Objects*. Divide this axis into 20 equal intervals and label each *1,2,3,* and so on.

4. Plot your data by counting the number of objects of each length and marking this number on the graph.

5. Connect all of the points with one continuous line.

Analysis

1. Is there variation within your population of objects? What is the shape of your line? Does it resemble those of your classmates?

2. What would be the shape of the line if you pooled all of the data in the class?

3. How close were your estimates of the largest and smallest objects? Do you think that using a small sample is a good way to infer the characteristics of a large population? Explain your reasoning.

PART B   Frequency Distribution Table and Histogram

Procedure

6. Using your data from Part A, construct a frequency distribution table as follows:
   a. Determine the range of length in the sample by finding the difference between the largest and smallest objects.
   b. Divide the range into 8 to 10 intervals, selecting a convenient size. For example, if the range of the sample is 23 (the smallest, 16 mm; the largest, 39 mm), it could be divided into 8 intervals of 3 mm each, as follows: 16–18, 19–21, 22–24, 25–27, 28–30, 31–33, 34–36, and 37–39.
   c. Assemble your data in a frequency distribution table with the intervals listed in the *x* column and the number of individuals falling

TABLE 16A.1

x	f
16–18	2
19–21	7
22–24	4
25–27	9
28–30	14
etc.	etc.

into each interval (frequency) listed in the *f* column, as shown in Table 16A.1.

7. Construct a histogram similar to Figure 16A.1 from your frequency distribution table. A histogram is simply a bar graph with intervals representing classes of variables on the horizontal axis and frequency on the vertical axis.

8. Calculate the mean (average) of your data. The mean is the sum of all measurements divided by the number of individuals measured.

9. What is the mode, or value occurring most frequently, on the histogram? The numerical value of the mode usually is given as the midpoint of the interval having the greatest frequency. For example, if the greatest value falls in the 16 to 18 range for example, 17 is the mode. In Figure 16A.1, the mode is 29.

10. Find the median, which is the value of the middle number of the sample, when the values

FIGURE 16A.1   A sample histogram

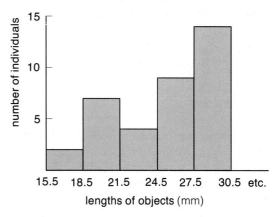

(lengths) are arranged in numerical order. For example, if a series of measurements is 2, 2, 3, 4, 7, 8, 9, 9, and 11, the median would be 7.

Analysis

1. Using the data and your histogram, identify the difference in length between the longest and the shortest objects in your sample.

2. Given the overall size of the objects, do you think this difference is significant? What might be the advantage or disadvantage of being smaller or larger than average?

3. How does measuring the objects affect collecting the data? Would you have noticed the differences in length if you had not measured the objects?

4. Do you think there would be a size difference if the examples studied were of different ages or from different plants?

5. For what type of data is a histogram more useful than a line graph? When is a line graph a more useful way to represent data?

Investigation 16B • A Model Gene Pool

In 1908, Godfrey Hardy, an English mathematician, wrote to the editor of *Science* with regard to some remarks of a Mr. Yule:

> Mr. Yule is reported to have suggested, as a criticism of the Mendelian position, that if brachydactyly is dominant, "in the course of time one would expect, in the absence of counteracting factors, to get three brachydactylous persons to one normal."
>
> It is not difficult to prove, however, that such an expectation would be quite groundless [using] . . . a little mathematics of the multiplication-table type.

The letter addresses an early and common criticism of Gregor Mendel's work on inheritance. Many scientists thought that Mendel's explanations of dominance and recessiveness suggested that recessive traits ultimately would be eliminated from the population and only dominant traits would remain. This investigation allows you to explore the validity of that assumption, using brachydactyly as an example.

Brachydactyly is a dominant disorder of the hands in which the fingers are shortened because of shortening of the bones. The actual frequency of occurrence is about one in 1 million births. You will use smaller numbers in setting up a model of a gene pool from which to randomly select pairs of alleles that represent individuals of a new generation.

Materials (per team of 3)

2 containers with lids, one labeled *male* and one labeled *female*

38 white beans

82 red beans

 SAFETY Do not eat the beans. Wash your hands immediately after handling the beans or seeds. They may be treated with a fungicide.

Procedure

1. In this activity, you will set up a model of a human population by using red beans to represent the allele (*B*) for the dominant trait—brachydactyly—and white beans to represent the allele (*b*) for the recessive trait—normal hands. Before you begin, review the Hardy-Weinberg principle in *Appendix 16B*. List the five assumptions made by the Hardy-Weinberg principle for a population that maintains a genetic equilibrium.

2. Place 19 white beans in the container labeled *male* and 19 white beans in the container labeled *female*. Add 41 red beans to each of the containers. Place the lid on each container and shake the beans. What do the beans in each container represent?

3. To represent fertilization and the resulting possible allele combinations that make up the genotype of a new individual (F_1 generation), you will select one bean from each container. What genotypes are possible?

4. In your data book, prepare a table similar to Table 16B.1.

5. Remove the lid and, without looking, select one bean from each container. Use tally marks to record the results of this first selection in the table. Return the beans to their respective containers, cover, and shake the containers again.

TABLE 16B.1   Genotypes for Two Generations

Genotype	F₁ Generation				F₂ Generation	
	Tally Marks	Total	Male	Female	Tally Marks	Total
BB						
Bb						
bb						

Make a total of 60 selections for the F_1 generation, returning the beans to the containers each time. In the table, total the number of each genotype in the F_1 generation. Why should you return the beans to their respective containers after each selection?

6. Examine the data in your table for the F_1 generation. Each pair of beans represents an individual of the F_1 generation having a certain genotype. Assume that half of the bean pairs of one genotype represent the males of the population, and the other half of the bean pairs of that genotype represent the females. For example, if you have 18 pairs of red-red (BB) combinations, nine pairs are males and nine pairs are females. Determine how many of each type (BB, Bb, bb) should be male and how many female. Record the numbers in your table.

7. Use the information in your table to determine how many red beans (B) and how many white beans (b) should be in each container to represent the parents of the next generation. Correct the bean counts in each container. Mix the beans thoroughly.

8. Make 60 more selections from the containers of beans as you did in step 5. This will be the F_2 generation. Tally and record the totals for the numbers of each genotype.

9. Wash your hands before leaving the laboratory.

Analysis

1. What is the total population of individuals in the F_1 generation?

2. In genetics, frequency refers to the probability that a particular event will occur in a population, or

$$\frac{\text{number of individuals of one genotype}}{\text{number of individuals of all genotypes}} = \text{frequency}$$

Determine the frequency of homozygous recessive individuals (bb) for the F_1 generation.

3. According to the Hardy-Weinberg principle, the frequency of homozygous recessive individuals (bb) in a population is expressed as q^2. Therefore, the frequency of the b allele $= \sqrt{q^2}$, or q. What is the frequency of the b allele for the F_1 population?

4. The Hardy-Weinberg principle states that the frequencies for two alleles of a trait add up to 1, or 100%. The frequency of the allele for the dominant trait (in this case, B) is represented by p. Therefore, $p + q = 1$, or 100% of alleles for the trait in the population. To calculate the frequency of the allele for the dominant trait, use the following formula:

$$p = 1 - q \text{ (remember, } p = B \text{ and } q = b)$$

Calculate the frequency of the B allele for the F_1 population.

5. Prepare a population gene analysis table like the one shown in Appendix 16B to show the expected frequency of each genotype in the next generation (F_2). Cross two heterozygous individuals and show the frequencies you have determined for each allele. Multiply to show the frequency of each F_2 genotype.

6. Review Analysis question 2. To determine the number of individuals of a particular genotype, you can multiply the frequency of the genotype by the number of individuals of all genotypes in

the population. Predict the number of each genotype (*BB, Bb, bb*) that would occur in an F₂ generation of 60 individuals.

7. How do the results of your bean selections for the F₂ generation compare with your predictions from Analysis question 5?

8. Based on this model, respond to Mr. Yule's 1908 critique of Mendelian genetics.

9. Suppose the *BB* and *Bb* genotypes represented a lethal condition in the population you have been studying. Can the Hardy-Weinberg principle still be applied in this situation? Explain your reasoning.

10. Hardy made the following statement in his 1908 paper: "There is not the slightest foundation for the idea that a dominant character should show a tendency to spread over a whole population, or that a recessive should tend to die out." Do your results support this statement?

11. What was the primary mistake in Mr. Yule's suggestion?

Investigation 16C • Sickle Cell Disease

What is the significance of the variations we see from one individual to another? Does each variation provide some special advantage? Biologists assume that most variations within a species have survival value. Could this assumption include variations that cause diseases? For example, geneticists have described hundreds of variations in the structure of the hemoglobin molecule inside human red blood cells. Some of these variations cause disease and others do not. Could a variation in hemoglobin structure that causes disease have survival value to a population? If so, under what circumstances?

Sickle cell disease is a disorder in which the abnormal hemoglobin molecules inside red blood cells combine with each other when the oxygen supply is low, causing the cells to lose their flexibility and assume an abnormal, sickle, shape. The sickle cells clump together and block small blood vessels, stopping the flow of nutrients and oxygen. Vital organs may be damaged and the individual may die. In this investigation, you will examine the conditions that influence the inheritance of sickle cell disease.

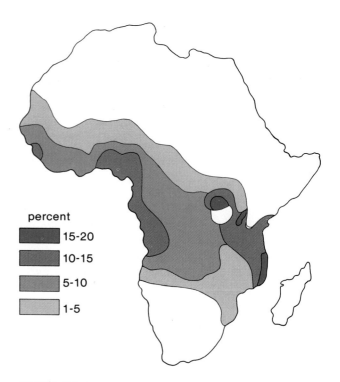

percent
15-20
10-15
5-10
1-5

FIGURE 16C.1 Frequency of the gene that causes sickle cell disease plotted as percentages of the population gene pool in parts of Africa

Materials (per team of 3)

paper and pencil

PART A

Procedure

Read the following information about sickle cell disease and answer the Analysis questions.

Sickle cell disease is due to the homozygous presence of the sickle cell allele (symbol: Hb^S). Heterozygous ($Hb^S Hb^A$) individuals have sickle cell trait and can be identified by a blood test. About one quarter of one percent (0.25%) of African-Americans are homozygous ($Hb^S Hb^S$) and have sickle cell disease. In certain parts of Africa, about 4 percent of black Africans have sickle cell disease.

The Hardy-Weinberg principle (Appendix 16B) enables us to predict when the allele frequencies in a population will remain constant. Because people with sickle cell disease frequently die in childhood, though, the frequency of the allele causing this disease should not remain constant. Each death removes a pair of the sickle cell-causing alleles from the population.

Figure 16C.1 shows the locations in Africa where the allele frequency of the Hb^S form is highest. These locations are also the areas where a fatal form of malaria is found. Studies reveal that people homozygous for the normal allele ($Hb^A Hb^A$) often die of malaria. However, people with the heterozygous genotype do not contract the fatal form of malaria.

Analysis

1. What are the three possible genotypes involving the sickle cell allele and its normal allele? (Hb^A represents the allele for normal hemoglobin.)

2. What are the phenotypes that would be associated with each genotype?

3. Based on the Hardy-Weinberg principle described in Appendix 16B, what percent of the African-American population has the genotype $Hb^S Hb^A$?

4. In some areas of Africa, the frequency of the Hb^S allele is very high. What percentage of the black African population in these areas has the genotype $Hb^S Hb^A$?

5. The relatively high frequency of the Hb^S allele has tended to remain constant in these areas of Africa. Under usual conditions, would you expect the frequency of a harmful allele to remain constant? Explain your reasoning.

6. Propose three possible explanations for the observation that the frequency of the Hb^S allele remains high in these areas, despite its lethal effect in the homozygous condition.

7. What are the advantages and disadvantages of having each of the three genotypes you determined in question 1? Which genotype(s) would tend to survive?

8. What would be the allele frequencies of Hb^S and Hb^A in a population made up of the surviving genotype(s)?

9. The allele frequencies in the African population under discussion are not 0.5 for each form. Considering that fact, do you think the assumption in question 8 is reasonable? Which genotype do you think is less likely to be fatal? Give reasons for your answer.

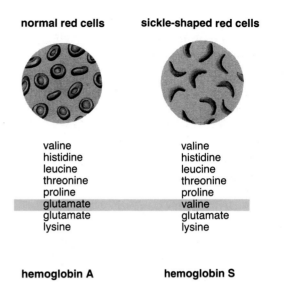

normal red cells	sickle-shaped red cells
valine	valine
histidine	histidine
leucine	leucine
threonine	threonine
proline	proline
glutamate	valine
glutamate	glutamate
lysine	lysine

hemoglobin A   hemoglobin S

FIGURE 16C.2 A comparison of the amino acid sequences for the polypeptide affected in normal and sickle hemoglobin

10. How can you explain the lower frequency of the allele causing sickle cell disease among African-Americans?

PART B

Procedure

Read the following information about the differing chemical structures of normal hemoglobin and sickle cell hemoglobin and answer the Analysis questions.

The sickle-shaped red blood cell is caused by a mutation that affects the hemoglobin molecule in the cells. Hemoglobin is a protein substance and is, therefore, made of amino acids. Scientists have been able to compare the chemical structure of normal hemoglobin, called hemoglobin A, with the hemoglobin found in sickle cells, called hemoglobin S. They found that both types of hemoglobin molecules contain 560 amino acids of 19 different types. Figure 16C.2 shows that the two molecules are identical except for one amino acid.

Analysis

1. What is the significant molecular difference between hemoglobin A and hemoglobin S?

2. What are the nucleotide codes for the two amino acids that are different in hemoglobin A and hemoglobin S? Consult the genetic code in Figure 10.4. What is the simplest error in coding that could have occurred to cause the mutation?

3. Write a few paragraphs to summarize sickle cell disease. Emphasize the ideas of mutation, selection, survival value, and evolution.

Investigations for Chapter 17
Human Evolution

Investigation 17A • Interpretation of Fossils

How do anthropologists learn about evolution? Fossil remains form a record of the evolution of early humans, hominids, and other primates. Even though humans and other primates share many similar features, humans did not evolve from apes. Although primate brains have increased in both size and complexity during the course of evolution, the relationships between modern humans and other primates and fossil hominids cannot be determined only by an examination of braincase, or cranial, casts. Anthropologists often compare the skulls, jaws and teeth, pelvises, and femurs of fossil hominids and apes with those of modern primates.

This investigation simulates some of the comparisons anthropologists make when studying fossil hominid remains. The activities include examination of several hominid cranial casts and comparison of some skeletal measurements for a human, an early hominid, and a gorilla.

Materials (per team of 2)

paper and pencils

metric ruler

protractor

graph paper

PART A   Comparison of Cranial Casts

Procedure

1. Examine the five cranial casts shown in Figure 17A.1. What is the volume of each? Which

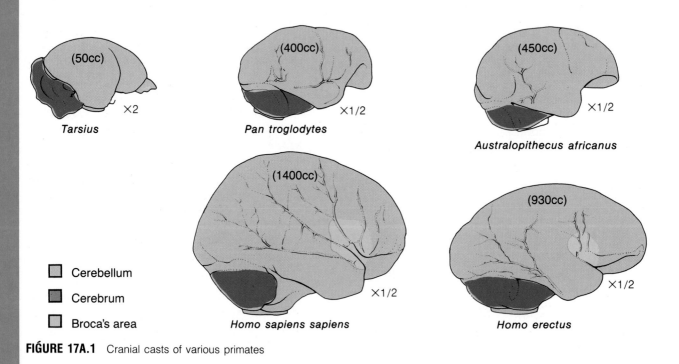

(50cc)

Tarsius ×2

(400cc)

Pan troglodytes ×1/2

(450cc)

Australopithecus africanus ×1/2

(1400cc)

☐ Cerebellum
■ Cerebrum
☐ Broca's area

Homo sapiens sapiens ×1/2

(930cc)

Homo erectus ×1/2

FIGURE 17A.1   Cranial casts of various primates

TABLE 17A.1   Body Weight of Selected Species

Species	Average Body Mass (grams)
Tarsius (tarsier)	900
Australopithecus	22 700
Homo erectus	41 300
Pan troglodytes (chimpanzee)	45 360
Homo sapiens	63 500

TABLE 17A.2   Brain-Mass-to-Body-Mass Ratios

Mammal	Brain-Mass-to-Body-Mass Ratio
Tree shrew	1:40
Macaque	1:170
Blue whale	1:10 000
Human	1:45
Squirrel monkey	1:12
House mouse	1:40
Elephant	1:600
Porpoise	1:38
Gorilla	1:200

species do you predict to have the largest brain volume compared with body weight?

2. Using the information in Table 17A.1 and a sheet of graph paper, plot the brain-volume-to-body-mass ratio for each of the five species.

3. In Figure 17.A.1, which species have Broca's area? On the *Homo sapiens* cranial cast you can see that Broca's area is an enlargement of part of the cerebrum. Broca's area and two other areas of the brain are important in language and speech. Broca's area sends signals to a part of the brain that controls the muscles of the face, jaw, tongue, and upper part of the throat. If a person is injured in Broca's area, normal speech is impossible. What might the presence of Broca's area indicate?

4. Convert the ratios of brain mass to body mass shown in Table 17A.2 to decimal fractions. Draw a bar graph of the fractions. On your graph, the x-axis should represent the five species, and the y-axis the brain-mass-to-body-mass ratio.

Analysis

1. Based on your first graph, what could you infer is the relationship between evolution in primates and the ratio of brain mass to body mass?

2. What major portion of the brain has become most noticeably enlarged during the course of primate evolution?

3. Do you think the cranial cast of *Australopithecus* indicates that this hominid could have had a Broca's area in its brain? Explain.

4. Does the presence or absence of Broca's area alone determine the language capabilities of a hominid? Explain.

5. How does your bar graph affect your answer to Question 1? Are brain size and brain-mass-to-body-mass ratios reliable indicators of the course of primate evolution? Why or why not?

PART B   Skeletal Comparisons

Procedure

5. Examine the three primate skulls in Figure 17A.2 and the drawings of lower jaws and the pelvises in Figure 17A.3 (page 694). Imagine you are an anthropologist and these fossils have been placed before you for identification. Complete this hypothesis in your data book: "If the skulls, jaws, and pelvises are significantly different, then. . . . "

6. In your data book, prepare a table similar to Table 17A.3 (page 695) or tape in the table your teacher provides. Your task is to determine which skull, jaw, and pelvis belong to a human, which belong to an early hominid, and which belong to a gorilla. Record all observations and measurements in your table.

7. Cranial volume: The straight line drawn on each skull represents the brain volume for each primate. Measure in centimeters the distance from point A to point B for each skull. Multiply by 175 to approximate the cranial volume in cm^3.

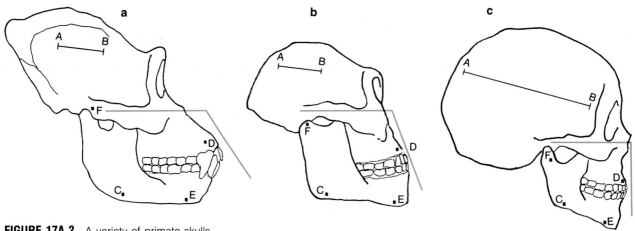

FIGURE 17A.2 A variety of primate skulls

8. Facial area: Measure in centimeters from points C to D and from E to F on each skull. Multiply the measurements of each skull to determine the approximate area of the lower face. What might you infer about how the size of the facial area has changed through primate evolution?

9. Facial projection: Use a protractor to determine the angle created by the colored lines. What can you infer from this measurement?

10. Brow ridge: This is the bony ridge above the eye sockets. Record the presence or absence of this feature for each skull. Also note the relative sizes.

11. Teeth: Study the drawings of the jaws that are shown in Figure 17A.3. Record the number of teeth and the number of each type of tooth. Also look at the relative sizes of the different types of teeth.

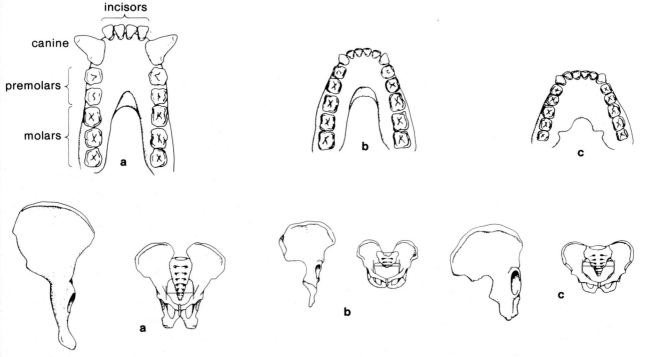

FIGURE 17A.3 Primate lower jaws and pelvises

12. Pelvis: Study the drawings of the pelvises in Figure 17A.3. Notice their relative sizes and whether the flange, or lower portion, projects to the rear. Measure in millimeters the diameter of the pelvic opening at the widest point.

13. Read these additional data:
    a. A larger cranial volume is characteristic of humans.
    b. A smaller lower facial area is characteristic of humans.
    c. A facial projection of about 90° is characteristic of humans.
    d. Modern humans have lost most of the brow ridge.
    e. All primates have the same number of teeth and the same number of each type.
    f. Humans and other hominids have smaller canine teeth than do gorillas.
    g. A smaller pelvis, with a broad blade, a flange extending the rear, and a wider opening are characteristics of primates that walk on two feet.
    h. As brain size increased, the width of the pelvic opening increased to accommodate the birth of offspring with a larger head-to-body ratio.

Analysis

1. Compare the data you have assembled for each specimen. Which ones are hominid? Which characteristics are similar in all three primates? Which characteristics are similar in A and B?

2. Compare your data with the additional data. On the basis of your observations and measurements and the additional data, which fossil remains would you say are human, which are gorilla, and which are early hominid?

3. What might an anthropologist infer from the size of the pelvic opening?

4. Write a few paragraphs discussing the methods anthropologists use to determine human ancestry. Which of the characteristics you examined were most helpful? Which were least helpful? List any other additional observations or measurements that could be made for these specimens. Would having a more complete skeleton be helpful? Why?

TABLE 17A.3 Comparison of Primate Characteristics

Characteristic	Fossil A	Fossil B	Fossil C
Cranial volume			
Facial area			
Facial projection			
Brow ridge			
Number of teeth (lower jaw)			
Number of each type of teeth (lower jaw)			
Relative size of teeth (lower jaw)			
Relative size of pelvis			
Direction of flange			
Width of pelvic opening			

Investigation 17B • Archaeological Interpretation

Because we cannot travel through time to see how people worked and lived thousands of years ago, we can never be sure that we understand the details of earlier cultures. Archaeologists search for clues among the remains of ancient peoples and civilizations. When they have found, dated, and studied the evidence, they formulate hypotheses to explain their findings. What emerges is a picture of life in a particular place hundreds or thousands of years ago. It is impossible to create a complete, detailed picture, but many reasonable and logical conclusions can be drawn. Some findings, however, can be interpreted in a variety of ways, and archaeologists may disagree about which interpretation is correct.

This investigation requires the analysis of data found in archaeological digs. In nearly every case, several interpretations are possible. Think of as many interpretations as you can. Remember that your interpretations should account for all, not just some, of the existing data. In the final section of this investigation, you will predict how archaeologists far in the future might interpret evidence of today's cultures and lifestyles.

Materials (per team of 3)

paper and pencils

PART A   A Native American Cemetery in Newfoundland

Procedure

1. Read the following paragraphs:

     One scientist investigated a Native American burial site located near Port aux Choix, a small village on the west coast of Newfoundland (Figure 17B.1, *left*). The burial ground appeared to have been used between 4000 and 5000 years ago. The graves were located in strips of very fine sand and were often covered with boulders or slabs of rock. One of the sandy strips was almost 1.6 km long, varying from about 9 to 22 m in width. It lay about 6 m above and parallel to the present high water mark of the ocean shore. The ages of the skeletons found at the site were estimated as shown in Table 17B.1. What do these data suggest about the lives of the Native Americans?

     The teeth of many of the adults were worn; often the sensitive inner nerve was exposed. Some skeletons also had teeth missing, but there was no evidence of tooth decay.

     Figure 17B.1 (*right* a, b, c, d), shows some artifacts that were found in the graves. A great number of woodworking tools were also found.

Analysis

Answer the following questions. Give reasonable answers that are supported by the evidence found at the site, or from your own knowledge and past experience.

1. What type of area might the Newfoundland burial site have been at the time the Native Americans lived there (for example, forest, mountains, beach)? Explain.

2. List some possible reasons why the sandy strip was chosen as a burial site.

3. Boulders or slabs of rock covered many graves. Why might that practice have been common?

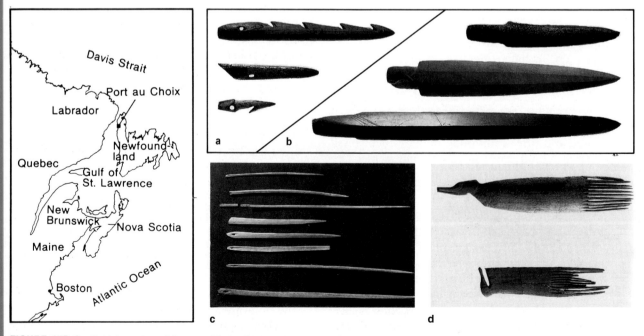

FIGURE 17B.1   (*left*) Location of Port au Choix; (*right a, b, c, and d*) objects found at Port au Choix excavation

TABLE 17B.1 Port au Choix Skeletal Ages

Age at Time of Death	Number of Skeletons
newborn infants	12
under 2 years	15
2–6 years old	2
6–18	15
18–21	1
21–50	36
50+	7

4. From the data on teeth, what can you infer about Native American diet and lifestyle?

5. What do you think the objects shown in Figure 17B.1a were used for? What purpose might the holes have served?

6. What might the objects in Figures 17B.1b and 17B.1c have been used for?

7. What modern implement do the objects in Figure 17B.1d resemble? What might their function have been?

8. Considering the location of the site and its objects, what might the Native Americans have built from wood?

PART B Ancient People of Greece

Procedure

2. Read the following paragraphs:

Stone Age people inhabited Greece long before the dawn of Classical Greek civilization. Until recently, little was known about the culture of these people who lived between 5000 and 20 000 years ago—3000 B.C. to 18 000 B.C. Excavations in and around a particular cave on the east coast of Greece began in 1967. Since then, archaeologists have gathered much evidence of the changes that occurred in the culture and lifestyles of Stone Age Greeks living there.

The oldest remains (20 000 years old) in the cave primarily are the bones of a single species of horse and some tools made from flint (rock that forms sharp edges when it breaks). What might explain the presence of the horse bones mixed with flint tools?

Newer remains (10 000 years old) include bones of red deer, bison, horses, and a species of wild goat as well as remains of wild plants such as vetch and lentils (pealike plants), shells of land snails, marine mollusks, and some small fish bones. These newer remains date from the time when a great ice age had come to an end. In still later finds, from about 9250 years ago, very large fish bones were found—the fish might have been 100 kg or more. At about the same time, tools made of obsidian, a type of volcanic glass, were found. The nearest source of obsidian is 150 km away from the excavation site and across a body of water. The site also yielded the oldest complete human skeleton found in Greece. A male of about 25 years of age was buried in a shallow grave covered with stones. Certain bone abnormalities indicated that he may have suffered from malaria, a tropical disease spread by mosquitoes.

Remains dated about 8000 years old are dominated by the bones of goats and sheep found in and around the cave. These bones were very different from the goat and sheep bones found away from the cave. Evidence of wheat and barley seeds also was found. Among the tools found were axes and millstones. Only a few of the human graves at the site contained objects such as tools or jewelry. A 40-year-old woman, who probably died about 6500 years ago, was buried with some bone tools and some obsidian blades. One infant was found near a marble vessel and a broken clay pot.

Analysis

1. In what ways did the diet of the cave's inhabitants change over the centuries? Explain your answer.

2. What does the evidence from about 9250 years ago suggest about a change in the people's lifestyle?

3. How do you think the ancient people obtained the obsidian?

4. From the 8000-year-old remains, what can you infer about the cave inhabitants' lifestyle?

5. What might be the significance of finding items buried along with people?

PART C Excavating the Present

Procedure

3. Imagine that you are an archaeologist living in the year 4000 A.D. A catastrophe has destroyed the records of the past. You have only the remains that have survived the last 2000 years as clues to what life was like in the 1990s. Imagine furthermore, that you are excavating a site that was a school 2000 years ago—your own school.

Analysis

1. What objects do you think you would find at the site? Make drawings of or list descriptions of the objects. Exchange them with your teammates.

2. For each object, suggest several interpretations. (Remember, you know nothing about the time when the objects were left—the only clues are the objects themselves.)

3. Some materials can last thousands of years. Other materials decay rapidly. What important things—of value to you or to society—would be absent in the archaeological dig that once was your school? What ideas about our society might you miss because the clues were not preserved?

4. Consider questions 1 through 3 again. This time, imagine you are excavating a different site, such as a mall or business park, a residence, a farm, or an industrial area. How would your findings and interpretations differ?

5. Suppose you wanted to build a time capsule to tell people in the distant future about our lives today. How would you construct your capsule? What would you put inside it? Explain your answer.

Investigations for Chapter 18
Digestive Systems and Human Nutrition

Investigation 18A • Food-Getting Structures

One-celled organisms take in food directly from their environment, but it is difficult for cells of multicellular organisms to do the same. By examining several organisms, you can compare their methods of foodgathering.

Materials (per team of 2)

2 pairs safety goggles

2 lab aprons

slides

cover slips

dropping pipet

watch glasses or finger bowls

flat toothpicks

compound microscope

hand lens or dissecting microscope

Detain™

yeast-brilliant cresyl blue preparation

Paramecium culture

Hydra culture

Daphnia culture

Planaria (flatworms)

> **SAFETY** Put on your safety goggles and lab apron.

PART A *Paramecium*

Procedure

1. Place one drop of Detain on a slide and add one drop of *Paramecium* culture; mix together. Add a small drop of yeast-brilliant cresyl blue preparation and gently mix with a toothpick. Cover with a cover slip and observe under low power and then high power.

CAUTION: Brilliant cresyl blue solution is an irritant. Avoid skin/eye contact; do not ingest. Flush spills and splashes with water for 15 minutes; rinse mouth with water. Call your teacher.

2. Under high power, locate a single organism. Continue to watch it for some time. Try to observe how *Paramecium* takes in food, what structures it uses, and where the food is contained in the cell after ingestion. Look for any movements of food in the cell.

3. Make a sketch of the organism indicating the general shape, structure, and location of its food-getting parts. Show by arrows any pattern of movement within the cell.

Analysis

1. Does *Paramecium* have a special place for food to enter?

2. Describe the specific structures of *Paramecium* for food-getting.

3. Describe the general pattern of food movement while digestion is taking place.

4. How does *Hydra* take in food?

PART B *Hydra*

Procedure

4. Place two or three *Hydras* in a watch glass or finger bowl half full of water. Observe them through a hand lens or a dissecting microscope until they become extended and relaxed.

5. Using the dropping pipet, add several living *Daphnia* to the water. Observe any food-getting activities for several minutes.

6. Make sketches of the *Hydras* before, during, and after the food-getting process.

7. Store the containers with the *Hydras* and observe them the following day.

8. Wash your hands before leaving the laboratory.

Analysis

1. Describe the specific structures of *Hydra* that are involved in getting food.

2. What happens to items taken in by *Hydra* that cannot be digested?

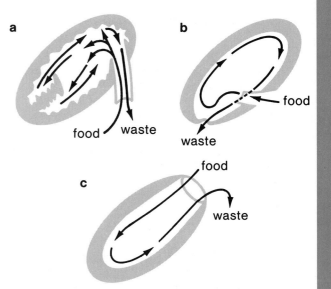

FIGURE 18A.1 Three diagrams of digestive pathways

3. How does a *Planarian* (flatworm) take in food?

PART C *Planarian*

Procedure

9. Place a *Planarian* (flatworm) in a watch glass or finger bowl half full of water. Observe with a hand lens or dissecting microscope, but do not use strong light. With a toothpick, gently turn the *Planarian* over and observe its underside. Sketch both body surfaces.

10. Obtain another *Planarian* recently fed raw liver. Again observe both body surfaces. Add any new observations to your sketch.

11. Wash your hands before leaving the laboratory.

Analysis

1. Based on your observations, which appears to have a more advanced digestive apparatus— *Hydra* or *Planaria*?

2. Match *Paramecium*, *Hydra*, and *Planaria* to the digestive pathways in Figure 18A.1.

Investigation 18B • Starch Digestion

How do you obtain the energy you need for performing activities? Starch makes up a large part of the food of many organisms and is a major source of energy for them. Human saliva contains an enzyme, amylase, that begins the breakdown of starch into the sugar molecules that can be absorbed into the bloodstream and taken up by cells. In this investigation, you will explore the action of amylase on starch and identify some sources of this enzyme.

To determine if the results you observe are caused by amylase or by some other factor, such as elapsed time, you will set up controls. In an experiment, all the factors that might cause the observed results are referred to as variables. When scientists test a particular factor, they must control all the other factors, or variables, so that they know what causes the results. One way to do this is to set up additional tests, called controls, to rule out the other variables. For example, when starch and amylase are dissolved in water, a change in the starch is observed. To be sure that this change is caused by the amylase rather than by the water, you could set up one test with starch and amylase and another with starch and water. The starch and water become the control for the test of the effect of amylase on starch.

Scientists use special chemical solutions called indicators to detect the presence of certain substances. For example, as you did in Chapter 6, they use Lugol's iodine solution to detect the presence of starch.

Materials (per team of 4)

4 pairs of safety goggles

4 lab aprons

7 dropping pipets

6 18-mm × 150-mm test tubes

10-mL graduated cylinder

spot plate

test-tube rack

6 rubber stoppers to fit test tubes

glass-marking pencil

funnel

scissors

mortar and pestle

cheesecloth (several layers)

pinch of sand

10 mL 5% starch suspension

10 mL 0.1% starch suspension

10 mL 1% amylase solution

25 mL distilled water

Lugol's iodine solution in dropping bottle

7 glucose test strips

5 g fresh spinach

SAFETY   Put on your safety goggles and lab apron; tie back long hair.

Procedure

PART A   Designing a Controlled Experiment

Participate in the discussion/demonstration that your teacher leads, keeping notes in your data book.

PART B   Starch Digestion in Animals (Half of the teams will conduct this part of the activity.)

Day 1

1. Read through the procedure for Day 1 and prepare a data table in which to record predictions, observations, and results of any tests.

2. Place 5 mL of starch suspension and 5 mL of amylase solution into a test tube labeled *starch/amylase*.

3. What factors (variables) might affect your results in step 2? Set up controls for those variables in additional test tubes. Label the controls appropriately and record the contents of each control in your data table.

4. Stopper each of the tubes and store them in a dark place for 24 hours.

5. Based on the introduction to this activity, predict what substances will be present in each tube after 24 hours, recording your predictions in your data table.

6. Wash your hands before leaving the laboratory.

Day 2

7. Observe the tubes that you set up the previous day and record your observations in the table.

8. What indicator tests should you use to determine what has occurred in each tube? Perform those tests, recording the results in your data table and in the class data table that your teacher has set up.

Use dropping pipets to remove samples, a spot plate for the tests, and the test indicators you observed in Part A.

> ⚠️☠️ **WARNING: Lugol's iodine solution is a *poison* if ingested, a *strong irritant*, and can stain clothing. Avoid skin/ eye contact; do not ingest. If contact occurs, flush affected area with water for 15 minutes; rinse mouth with water; call the teacher immediately.**

9. Wash your hands thoroughly before leaving the laboratory.

PART C   Starch Digestion in Plants (The other half of the teams will conduct this part of the activity.)

Day 1

1. Using scissors, cut up about 5 g of fresh spinach leaves into small pieces.

2. Put the pieces into a mortar with 10 mL of distilled water and a pinch of sand. Grind them thoroughly with a pestle.

3. Line the funnel with several layers of cheesecloth and set it in a test tube labeled *filtrate*. Filter the crushed plant material through the funnel. Save the resulting filtrate (plant juice).

4. Prepare a data table in which to record predictions, observations, and results of any tests.

5. Using the indicators that you observed in Part A, can you tell what substances probably are present in the filtrate? Perform appropriate tests to find out. Record your results in your data table.
Use a dropping pipet to remove samples, a spot plate for the tests, and the test indicators you observed in Part A.

> ⚠️☠️ **WARNING: Lugol's iodine solution is a *poison* if ingested, a *strong irritant*, and can stain clothing. Avoid skin/ eye contact; do not ingest. If contact occurs, flush affected area with water for 15 minutes; rinse mouth with water; call the teacher immediately.**

6. Into a test tube labeled *filtrate/starch*, place 5 mL of filtrate and 5 mL of starch suspension, swirling to mix the solutions.

7. What factors (variables) might affect your results in step 6? Set up controls for those variables in additional test tubes. Label the controls appropriately and record the contents of each control in your data table.

8. Stopper each of the tubes and store them in a dark place for 24 hours.

9. Based on the results from step 5, predict what substances will be present in each tube after 24 hours. Record your predictions in your data table.

10. Wash your hands thoroughly before leaving the laboratory.

Day 2

11. Using the procedures of step 5, test the contents of the tubes that you set up in steps 6 and 7. Record the results in your data table and in the class data table that your teacher has set up.

12. Wash your hands before leaving the laboratory.

Analysis

1. From the results of Part B, what can you conclude about the effect of amylase on starch?

2. From the results of Part C, what can you conclude about a plant's ability to digest starch?

3. If you had not controlled the variables in this experiment, what conclusions could you have drawn?

4. Of what value to an organism is the ability to digest starch?

5. Animals have special glands for the production of enzymes that break large food molecules into smaller ones. What, if any, evidence from the results of this experiment indicates that plant cells possess similar enzymes?

6. Describe the processes responsible for food breakdown in the major compartments of the digestive system and the role of each.

7. Why do doctors give glucose rather than starch as intravenous injections to patients whose digestive systems are not functioning properly?

Investigations for Chapter 19
Transport Systems

Investigation 19A • Water Movement in Plants

The normal pathway of moving water in a living plant is first into the roots, then through the stem, and finally into the leaves. Environmental influences, the chemical properties of water, and structures in the plant are involved in the movement. This laboratory investigation deals with the following questions:

1. What plant structures—roots, stems, or leaves—are most important in the movement of water?

2. What are the types of cells that transport water in a plant? What are their characteristics?

3. Is all the water that is delivered to the leaves used, or is some lost?

4. How would you describe the source and direction of the force that moves water upward in a plant, against the force of gravity?

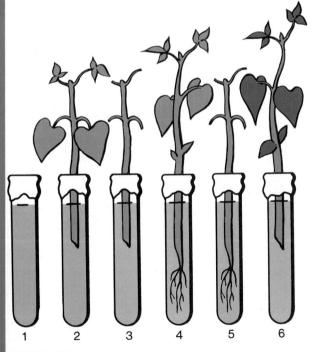

FIGURE 19A.1 Setup of test tubes and plants for the water-uptake experiment

Hypothesis: Before beginning the investigation, read the procedure for Part A. Write a prediction that describes what you think will happen to each test tube.

Materials (per team of 3)

3 pairs safety goggles

6 18-mm × 150-mm test tubes

test-tube rack

glass-marking pencil

aluminum foil

scalpel

petroleum jelly

cotton swab

compound microscope

prepared slide of woody stem cross section

prepared slide of leaf cross section

prepared slide of leaf epidermis

6 bean or sunflower seedlings

radish or grass seedlings in a petri dish

 **SAFETY   Put on your safety goggles.**

PART A.   Measuring Water Uptake

Procedure

1. Fill six test tubes with water to within 2 cm of the top, and cover the tops with aluminum foil. Label the test tubes 1 through 6. Treat each test tube as follows, using Figure 19A.1 as a guide.

   Tube 1: Mark the water line.

   Tube 2: With a scalpel remove the roots of one bean or sunflower seedling, 6 cm below the cotyledons. Pierce the aluminum foil with a pencil point and ease the plant through the hole into the water. Mark the water line after the plant is in place.

   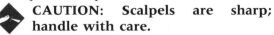 **CAUTION: Scalpels are sharp; handle with care.**

   Tube 3: Remove all leaf blades from another seedling, leaving only the leaf stems. Then repeat the procedure for test tube 2.

Tube 4: Remove the aluminum foil from the test tube. Sink an intact plant's roots into the water. Mark the water line. Mold the aluminum foil to the rim of the test tube so that it seals the tube and supports the plant stem.

Tube 5: Remove the leaf blades from another seedling. Only the leaf stems should remain. Then repeat the procedure described for test tube 4 for this leafless plant.

Tube 6: Brush petroleum jelly on the upper and lower surfaces of the leaves with a cotton swab. Repeat the procedure for test tube 2.

2. Allow the rack of treated plants to stand in indirect light overnight. After 24 hours, observe the test tubes for any changes. Record your observations and any measurements you take.

Analysis

1. What is the purpose of the first test tube?

2. Identify variables in this experiment and how they were controlled.

3. Do the results of the investigation support or disprove your prediction? Explain.

4. Based on your results, what do you predict would happen if:
   a. you used seedlings that had twice the number of leaves as those you actually used for test tubes 2, 4, and 6? Explain.
   b. the seedling in test tube 5 had twice the number of roots as the one you actually used? Explain.
   c. you put petroleum jelly on the stem cut of the plant in test tube 6, as well as on the leaves? Explain.

5. Based on your observations alone, which of the following statements is most likely correct? Explain the reasons for your choice.
   a. Water is pushed upward in a plant by a force created in the lower parts of the plant.
   b. Water is pulled upward in a plant by a force created in the upper parts of the plant.

6. Account for your observations and results regarding any changes that occur in the experimental set-up.

7. Do the results of this experiment support or disprove the cohesion-tension hypothesis? Explain.

8. Using your experimental results and your readings, describe the path of a water molecule through a seedling. Where does it begin? Where does it end up?

9. Describe an experiment that would trace the path of water molecules through a plant. How would you track the water molecules? How would you set up the experiment? How would you control variables? (Hint: See **Appendix 2B**, Radioisotopes and Research in Biology.)

PART B.   Transport Structures in Plants

Procedure

3. Study the cross section of a leaf with first low power and then high power of the microscope. Identify the following structures using Figure 19A.2 (page 704) as a reference.

   Upper epidermis: Thick-walled, flat cells without chloroplasts, covered with a waxy layer

   Palisade cells: Tightly packed and column-shaped cells containing many chloroplasts

   Spongy cells: Rounded cells containing chloroplasts, with air spaces between them

   Veins: Transport tissue composed of thick-walled *xylem* cells and *phloem* cells

   Lower epidermis: Thick-walled, flat cells without chloroplasts but with openings at intervals

   Stomates: Openings in the lower epidermis

   Guard cells: Two small cells surrounding each stomate and containing chloroplasts

4. Observe a slide showing the lower epidermis of a leaf under high power. Locate the guard cells enclosing a small slit, the stomate. Sketch the stomate and guard cells.

5. Study a cross section of a woody stem under low power. Identify the regions of the *pith, vascular bundles, cambium,* and *bark*. Turn to high power and observe a vascular bundle in more detail. Identify the *xylem*, heavy-walled cells toward the center area of the stem, and the *phloem*, small thin-walled cells toward the outside area of the stem. Xylem and phloem cells are separated by a layer of living cells called *cambium*.

6. Carefully place a radish or grass seedling in a drop of water on a microscope slide and observe

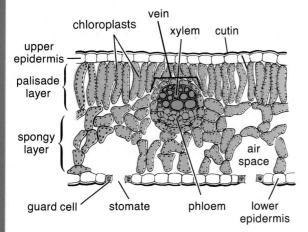

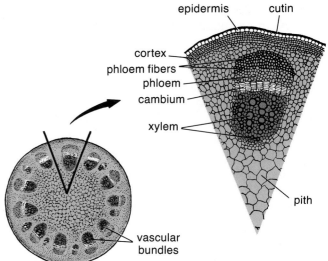

FIGURE 19A.2 Cross section of a leaf (*left*) and a young woody stem (*right*)

with low power. Notice the extent of absorptive area provided by the root hairs. The young root's darker, denser center region includes developing vascular bundles, also composed of xylem, phloem, and cambium cells.

7. Wash your hands before leaving the laboratory.

Analysis

1. Which adaptations of the leaf for the prevention of water loss did you observe? Describe them. In what ways may water loss by leaves help the plant? In what ways might it harm the plant?

2. Describe the adaptations to absorb water from the soil that you observed.

3. How does water enter the root hairs and epidermal cells?

4. What structure in the stem connects the water-conducting vessels of the roots and the veins of the leaf? Describe the structure.

5. Illustrate a pathway showing the route followed by water molecules as they move from the soil,

through a plant, and into the atmosphere. Include the specific structures of the root, stem, and leaf that are involved. Use the information and observations you gathered during this investigation to create your illustrations.

Investigation 19B • Exercise and Pulse Rate

You probably have experienced the sensation of your heart beating strongly inside your chest when you participated in a physical activity such as running, aerobic exercise, or athletic competition. The heartbeat rate increases in response to signals from the nervous and endocrine systems, which are monitoring the entire body. Pulse rate, as measured by using a pulse probe with the LEAP-System™, or by taking the pulse rate manually at the wrist if a LEAP-System is not available, is a measure of how fast the heart is beating. The LEAP-System BSCS Biology Lab Pac 2 includes instructions for use.

Read the Analysis questions and develop a hypothesis about how exercise (mild or vigorous)

FIGURE 19B.1 Taking a pulse with (a) the pulse probe and the LEAP-System or by (b) the wrist method

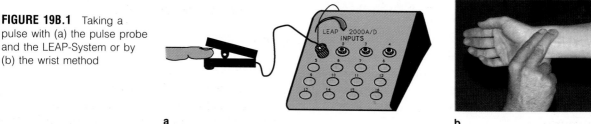

a

b

affects heart rate and recovery time. Recovery time is the length of time it takes for the heartbeat to return to the resting rate. Design an experiment to test your hypothesis using the materials listed below.

Materials (per team of 2)

Apple IIe, Apple IIGS, Macintosh, or IBM computer
LEAP-System™
pulse probe
watch (or clock) with second hand (optional)

Safety

Keep in mind that you must have plenty of room to safely perform your pulse-raising activity; avoid bumping into other persons or objects. Be certain that the electrical cords and leads for the LEAP-System do not create a tripping hazard. Keep away from water.

Procedure

Use the LEAP-System with a pulse probe (Figure 19B.1a) to carry out the experiment you designed and that your teacher has approved. In your data book, record the pulse rate from the screen. Organize your data in a table, and print or construct the graphs at the end of the experiment to display the data. If a LEAP-System is not available, use the wrist method. (See Figure 19B.1b.) Count the pulse directly, organize your data in a table, and construct graphs to display the data.

Analysis

1. What was the control in your experiment?

2. What label did you put on the *y* axis of your graph? On the *x* axis?

3. Are there any differences in heartbeat rates and recovery times for the different types of exercise among the students in your class? Explain.

4. Describe the effect of varying degrees of exercise—mild, moderate, and strenuous—on heartbeat.

5. Are there any differences in heartbeat rates and recovery times between males and females in your class?

6. Note any other conclusions you can make based on your data.

Investigations for Chapter 20
Immune Systems

Investigation 20A • Antibody Diversity

We live in a microbe-filled world. There are numerous pathogens, or antigens, that have the potential to make us sick or even kill us. As you have read in Chapter 20, the immune system generally keeps these infectious agents in check through an organized set of responses.

One of the mechanisms the immune system uses to control infection and disease is the production of antibody proteins in response to the presence of antigens. Immunologists estimate that humans have the potential to produce approximately 10^6 specific antibody proteins.

As Chapter 10 explains, proteins are gene products. Therefore, the human genome (the complete complement of an organism's genes) must contain enough genetic information to code for the production of 10^6 antibody proteins in addition to all the other information an organism needs. But, consider that there are approximately 3×10^9 base pairs in the human genome. Assuming that each gene is about 3×10^4 base pairs long on average, there are about 10^5 genes in the human genome. Clearly, this number is not large enough to account for one gene devoted to the production of only one antibody. This investigation will help you explore the genetic rearrangement mechanism, discovered by Tonegawa and others, by which the human genome encodes information for such an incredible amount of antibody diversity. (See Biological Challenges: Careers in Chapter 20.)

Materials (per team of 2)

pop-it beads: 1 red, 1 pink, 1 orange, 1 yellow, 1 blue, 1 green, 1 white, 1 black, 15 lilac

PART A

Procedure

1. Assume that your body has been invaded by 12 different pathogens and must produce a different antibody light chain against each one. The

FIGURE 20A.1 Pop-it bead sequence.

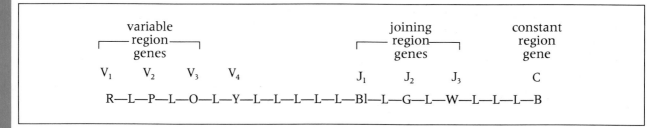

complete gene for a light chain includes three classes of smaller genes: variable (V); joining (J); and constant (C).

2. Working as a team, use your pop-it beads to construct a DNA sequence that will code for the production of an antibody light chain. Each colored pop-it bead represents a gene segment. Snap the beads together in the sequence indicated in Figure 20A.1, using the following key: R (red), P (pink), O (orange), Y (yellow), Bl (blue), G (green), W (white), B (black), L (lilac).

   The gene segments are labeled V_1-V_4 for the variable region genes and J_1-J_3 for the joining region genes. There is only one C gene. The lilac pop-it beads represent introns. If necessary, review the section on exons and introns in Chapter 10.

3. Each complete light chain gene is coded for by *one* V gene, *one* J gene, and the C gene. Construct a gene sequence that codes for a light chain by combining V_1 (red), J_1 (blue), and C (black).

4. Return V_1, J_1, and C to the original DNA strand. Now combine V_2, J_2, and C.

Analysis

1. How do the chains constructed in steps 3 and 4 differ?

2. Is there enough genetic information present in these two sequences (V_1-J_1-C and V_2-J_2-C) to produce 10 different light chains? How many chains are possible?

3. How many light chains could you produce using V_1 and each of the J genes?

PART B

Procedure

5. Assume that any V gene can combine with any J gene (and C) to produce a complete gene coding for an antibody light chain. Use the pop-it beads to construct complete genes that will code for 10 distinct light chains. Record the sequences. You have already completed two:

| 1 | R | Bl | B | V_1 | J_1 | C |
| 2 | P | G | B | V_2 | J_2 | C |

Analysis

1. How many complete light chains could you produce using the genetic information in the original strand?

2. If there were approximately 250 V genes, 5 J genes, and 1 C gene for the antibody light chain of the Kappa type, how many different light chains could this information code for?

3. Using the symbols V, J, and C, write an equation for the number of light chains that can be produced by any given segment of DNA.

4. Chapter 12 defines a gene as a sequence of nucleotides that codes for a functional product, such as tRNA, an enzyme, a structural protein, or a pigment. Does the model for production of antibodies support that definition? Explain.

5. The classical definition of a gene is "a hereditary unit that occupies a specific position (locus) within the genome or chromosome."* Does the model for production of antibodies support that definition? Why or why not?

*King, R.C. and W. Stansfield, *A Dictionary of Genetics*. New York, Oxford University Press, 1985.

Investigation 20B • Antigen-Antibody Reactions

One of the body's most important defense mechanisms against infection is the production of antibodies, or immunoglobulins. These proteins circulate in the bloodstream, where they make up a part of the gamma globulin (IgG) fraction of blood plasma. (See Appendix 20A, Antibody Classes.) The production of antibodies can be stimulated by the antigens of an infecting agent such as a bacterium or virus. An antibody binds to an antigen in a reaction that is highly specific—each type of antibody binds to a particular type of antigen and no other.

There are many laboratory procedures designed to detect the presence of antibodies and the interactions between antibodies and antigens. One such test is called ELISA—*E*nzyme-*L*inked *I*mmuno*s*orbent *A*ssay—an immunological technique used to detect and quantify specific serum antibodies. (Serum is blood plasma without the clotting factors.)

In ELISA, serum to be tested is allowed to react with specific antigens. Serum antibodies that combine with the antigens are detected by treating the test system with a conjugate—another antibody linked to an enzyme. This second antibody binds to the antigen-antibody complex that formed earlier. The enzyme serves as a marker. When a substrate for the enzyme is added, a reaction between the substrate and the conjugate is indicated by a color change. (If no serum antibodies are present to bind with the conjugate, no color change will occur during the time of observation.) These reactions are diagrammed in Figure 20B.1. ELISA is used rou-

tinely in the screening of blood donors for antibody to HIV.

In this investigation, you will perform ELISAs to observe a specific antigen-antibody reaction and to determine the amount of antibody present. You will make use of a microwell plate—a piece of plastic molded to form many small wells, somewhat like a miniature egg carton. Once applied, the antigen is absorbed onto the surface of the wells and can react with serum antibodies added later.

The test will span three days and will include the following steps:

Day 1—application of antigens, block unbound sites
Day 2—addition of primary antibodies
Day 3—addition of secondary antibodies with conjugate, addition of substrate, check for color

Materials (per team of 5)

5 pairs safety goggles

5 lab aprons

15 pairs disposable gloves

paper towels

white index card

glass-marking pencil

incubator

3 sheets of parafilm

96-well polyvinyl microwell plate

4 1-mL transfer pipets

10 1.5-mL microfuge tubes

distilled water

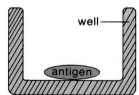 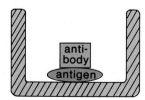 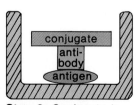 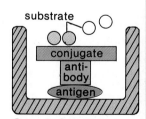

Step 1: Antigen is added and binds to the well.

Step 2: Antibody is added and binds to the antigen.

Step 3: Conjugate is added and binds to the antibody-antigen complex.

Step 4: Substrate is added for the enzyme in the conjugate. A change from colorless to color indicates antigen-antibody reaction.

FIGURE 20B.1 Steps in ELISA

FIGURE 20B.2 Diagram of microwell plate for recording data

Shared Materials

antigen 1 (bovine serum albumin; BSA) at antigen station 1

antigen 2 (bovine serum tranferrin) at antigen station 1

10X PBS-Tween at washing station 7

10X phosphate buffer saline (PBS) at washing station 7

1 mg gelatin mixed with distilled water at station 2

1 mL of antibody 1 at station 3

1 bottle of antibody 2 at station 4

1 bottle of antibody 3 at station 5

substrate (ABTS) at station 6

> **SAFETY** Put on your safety goggles, lab apron and gloves

Procedure

Day 1

1. In your data book, prepare a grid like the diagram in Figure 20B.2. The numbers identify the rows in the microwell plate and the letters identify the wells. Along the sides and top of the grid, record what you add to each well as you follow the procedures. (On day 3, you will record ELISA results in each square of the grid.)

   CAUTION: The chemicals you will be working with are irritants.

Avoid skin/eye contact; do not ingest. Flush spills and splashes with water for 15 minutes. Call your teacher.

2. With a clean 1-mL transfer pipet, add 1 drop of antigen 1 (from station 1) to all 12 wells in rows A–D (top of plate).

3. With a clean 1-mL transfer pipet, add 1 drop of antigen 2 (from station 1) to all 12 wells in row E (bottom of plate).

4. Write your names on a piece of parafilm and cover the plate with the parafilm. Place the plate in the 37°C incubator for 30 minutes.

5. Move your plate from the incubator to washing station 7 and remove the parafilm. Spray PBS-Tween across the plate and recover it with the same parafilm. Gently shake the plate back and forth, but be careful not to spill the contents.

6. Remove the parafilm and empty the plate into the sink. Spray PBS (at washing station 7) across the plate and recover with the same parafilm. Gently shake the plate back and forth, but be careful not to spill the contents. Empty the contents into the sink.

7. With a clean 1-mL transfer pipet, add 1 drop of gelatin (from station 2) to every well (to block the unbound sites). Use the same piece of parafilm to recover your plate and place it in the refrigerator.

8. Wash your hands before leaving the laboratory.

Day 2

> **SAFETY** Put on your safety goggles, lab apron, and gloves

9. Remove your plate from the refrigerator and place it in the incubator for 5 minutes.

10. Take your plate to the washing station and remove the parafilm. Spray PBS across the plate and recover the plate with the same parafilm. Gently shake the plate back and forth, but be careful not to spill the contents.

11. Go to station 3 and get 10 1.5-mL microfuge tubes. Label five tubes *BSA 1*, *BSA 2*, *BSA 3*, *BSA 4*, and *BSA 5*.

12. With a clean 1-mL transfer pipet, add 1 mL of antibody 1 to the tube labeled BSA 1. From tube BSA 1, use the transfer pipet to remove $500\mu L$ (one-half of a mL) and place this in tube BSA 2. With a clean transfer pipet, add $500\mu L$ of distilled water to tube BSA 2.

From tube BSA 2, remove $500\mu L$ and place this in tube BSA 3. With a clean transfer pipet, add $500\mu L$ of distilled water. What is your dilution in tube BSA 3?

From tube BSA 3, remove $500\mu L$ and place this in tube BSA 4. With a clean transfer pipet, add $500\mu L$ of distilled water.

From tube BSA 4, remove $500\mu L$ and place this in tube BSA 5. With a clean transfer pipet, add $500\mu L$ of distilled water.

13. Add BSA 1 to all the wells in row 2.
Add BSA 2 to all the wells in row 3.
Add BSA 3 to all the wells in row 4.
Add BSA 4 to all the wells in row 5.
Add BSA 5 to all the wells in row 6.

14. Go to station 3 and get 10 1.5-mL microfuge tubes. Label five tubes *T* (transferrin) *1, T2, T3, T4,* and *T5.*

15. With a clean transfer pipet, add 1 mL of antibody 1 to tube T1. Remove $500\mu L$ and place it in tube T2. With a clean transfer pipet, add $500\mu L$ of distilled water to tube T2.

From tube T2, remove $500\mu L$ and place it in tube T3. With a clean transfer pipet, add $500\mu L$ of distilled water to tube T3.

From tube T3, remove $500\mu L$ and place it in tube T4. With a clean transfer pipet, add $500\mu L$ of distilled water to tube T4.

From tube T4, remove $500\mu L$ and place it in tube T5. With a clean transfer pipet, add $500\mu L$ of distilled water to tube T5.

16. Add T1 to all wells in row 8.
Add T2 to all wells in row 9.
Add T3 to all wells in row 10.
Add T4 to all wells in row 11.
Add T5 to all wells in row 12.

17. Get a new piece of parafilm and write your names on it. Place it on the plate. Put your plate in the incubator for 30 minutes. Then place your plate in the refrigerator overnight.

18. Wash your hands thoroughly before leaving the laboratory.

Day 3

> SAFETY   Put on your safety goggles, lab apron, and gloves

19. Remove your plate from the refrigerator and take it to the washing station. Remove the parafilm and spray PBS-Tween across the plate and recover it with the same parafilm. Shake the plate gently back and forth, but be careful not to spill the contents of the plate.

20. Remove the parafilm and empty the plate into the sink. Spray PBS across the plate and recover it with the parafilm. Gently shake the plate back and forth, but be careful not to spill the contents of the plate. Remove the parafilm and empty the plate into the sink.

21. Go to station 5 and with a clean 1 mL transfer pipet, add 1 drop of antibody 3 to each well. Cover the plate with a new piece of parafilm and place the plate in the incubator for 30 minutes.

22. Take the plate to the washing station and remove the parafilm. Spray PBS-Tween across the plate and recover it with the parafilm. Gently shake the plate back and forth, but be careful not to spill the contents.

23. Remove the parafilm and empty the plate into the sink. Spray PBS across the plate and recover it with the parafilm. Gently shake the plate back and forth, but be careful not to spill the contents. Empty the plate into the sink.

24. Go to station 6 and with a clean 1 mL transfer pipet, add 1 drop of substrate (ABTS) to each well.

25. In your data book, or on a 3 × 5 card, use a plus sign (+) to record which wells have a color change. Put three plus signs in the darkest blocks, two plus signs in the moderately changed blocks, and one plus sign for the lightest blocks.

26. Wash your hands before leaving the laboratory.

Analysis

1. Antigen 1 is bovine serum albumin (BSA)—a protein from cattle blood. Antigen 2 is bovine serum transferrin, another protein from cattle blood. What effect would these proteins have if they were injected into a different animal?

2. If the starting dilution of tube BSA 1 is 1:1000, what are the final dilutions for tubes BSA 2, 3, 4, and 5? If the starting dilution of tube T1 is 1:1000, are the end dilutions of tubes T2, T3, T4, and T5 the same as for the BSA tubes?

3. Rabbit antibody 1 is from a rabbit that was previously injected with antigen from cattle (BSA). What should the rabbit serum contain as a result of that injection?

4. Rabbit antibody 2 is from a rabbit that was injected previously with antigen from cattle (transferrin). What should the rabbit serum contain as a result of that injection? How are these antibodies different?

5. Predict the ELISA results by completing the following hypotheses:

   A. If rabbit antiserum BSA is added to wells containing BSA, then . . .

   B. If rabbit antiserum BSA is added to wells containing transferrin, then . . .

   C. If rabbit antiserum BSA is added to wells containing nothing, then . . .

   D. If rabbit antiserum transferrin is added to wells containing BSA, then . . .

   E. If rabbit antiserum transferrin is added to wells containing transferrin, then . . .

   F. If rabbit antiserum transferrin is added to wells containing nothing, then . . .

6. The secondary antibody is goat anti-rabbit with a conjugate HRP (horse radish peroxides). How is this antibody made?

7. Why is antibody added to the wells?

8. Based on your results, which wells demonstrated an antigen-antibody reaction? Did these results confirm your hypotheses in question 5?

9. What is the highest dilution that gave a positive result? How does the serial dilution enable you to determine how much antibody is present?

10. Identify the controls used in this investigation and explain the specific purpose of each.

11. Based on the steps in this investigation, describe how ELISA can be used to detect antibodies to HIV.

12. Does a positive ELISA test for the antibodies against HIV indicate that the individual has AIDS? Explain.

13. ELISA also is the basis for the pregnancy test kits that can be purchased at a pharmacy. How might ELISA work in a pregnancy test? (Hint: What substances might be present in the blood or urine of a woman only during pregnancy?)

Investigations for Chapter 21
Gas Exchange and Excretory Systems

Investigation 21A • Exercise and Carbon Dioxide Production

When you exercise, you breathe faster than when you are at rest. Does exercise also affect the concentration of carbon dioxide in the air you exhale? You can test for the presence of carbon dioxide by bubbling your breath through water. Carbon dioxide in your breath combines with water to form carbonic acid ($CO_2 + H_2O \longleftrightarrow H_2CO_3$), which lowers the pH of the solution. Using a pH probe and the LEAP-System™, or a pH meter or wide-range pH paper if the LEAP-System is not available, you can measure the amount of carbon dioxide in the water by detecting a change in pH. The LEAP-System BSCS Biology Lab Pac 2 includes instructions for use of the system. **Hypothesis:** Read the procedure for the investigation and complete this statement: If carbon dioxide is a waste product of cellular respiration, then . . .

Materials (per team of 2)

100-mL graduated cylinder

2 250-mL flasks

Apple IIe, Apple IIGS, Macintosh, or IBM computer

LEAP-System™

printer

2 pH probes

pH meter or wide-range pH paper (optional)

forceps (optional)

2 wrapped drinking straws

watch or clock with a second hand

distilled water

Procedure

Each member of the team should do the investigation. One person should be responsible for the computer while the other keeps track of his or her own time breathing into the flask. Then switch responsibilities.

1. In your data book, prepare a table similar to Table 21A.1.

2. Label two flasks *A* and *B*.

3. Place 100 mL of tap water in each flask.

4. Record the initial pH in both flasks by using two pH probes with the LEAP-System (Figure 21A.1), a pH meter, or by dipping small strips of pH paper into the water and comparing the color to a standard color chart.

5. Put a drinking straw in the water in Flask B. Sit quietly for 1 minute and then gently blow air from your lungs through the straw into the water for 1 minute. Do not suck any material through the straw. Swirl the flask.

6. Determine the pH in both flasks and record the readings in the table.

7. Discard the water in both flasks. Rinse the flasks and the straw with distilled water.

8. Repeat steps 3–7, but this time, before blowing through the straw, exercise for 1 minute by walking in place.

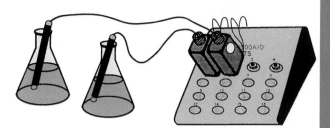

FIGURE 21A.1 LEAP-System setup for measuring production

9. Repeat steps 3–7, but this time exercise more vigorously for 1 minute. (Run in place, dance, or do jumping jacks.) Discard the straw.

10. Wash your hands thoroughly before leaving the laboratory.

Analysis

1. Run stripcharts to obtain graphs of the data. Under which condition was the decrease in pH in Flask B greatest? Smallest? Explain.

2. If the pH changed in Flask A, how would you use that information to interpret the results in Flask B?

3. How is the production of carbon dioxide related to activity?

4. What factors other than exercise might play a part in determining the amount of carbon dioxide given off?

5. Compare your results with those of other students in your class. Try to explain any differences.

6. What is the source of carbon dioxide in your breath?

7. What was the purpose of Flask A?

Investigation 21B • The Kidney and Homeostasis

The cells of the human body are surrounded by liquid that is remarkably constant in its properties. The continuous regulation of the many dissolved compounds and ions in this internal environment is referred to as homeostasis.

The kidneys play an important role in homeostasis by regulating blood composition and by regulating the levels of many important chemicals and

TABLE 21A.1 pH Readings

Experimental Condition	pH Readings			
	Flask A		Flask B	
	Initial	Final	Initial	Final
At rest				
Mild exercise				
Vigorous exercise				

TABLE 21B.1 Comparison of Substances in Blood and Urine

	% in Blood as it Enters Kidney	% in Urine as it Leaves Kidney
Water	91.5	96.0
Protein	7.0	0.0
Glucose	0.1	0.0
Sodium	0.33	0.29
Potassium	0.02	0.24
Urea	0.03	2.70

ions. The production of urine and its elimination from the body are critical functions of the kidneys and the urinary system.

Materials (per team of 3)

pencil and paper

PART A Blood versus Urine

Procedure

1. The relationship of structure and function in the kidney is illustrated in Figure 21.15 in Chapter

21. Use this illustration and the data in Table 21B.1 to answer the Analysis questions.

Analysis

1. What do the data for water indicate?

2. Protein molecules are not normally found in the urine. Explain why.

3. The information for glucose is similar to that for protein. Can you explain these data?

4. Based on what the sodium data indicate, what do you think may happen to the sodium content in the urine of a person who increases his or her intake of sodium chloride?

5. How do the data for potassium differ from those for sodium?

6. How would you interpret the data for urea?

7. Summarize the functions that take place between blood and urine and identify the structures where these functions occur.

PART B Filtration, Reabsorption, and Secretion

Procedure

2. The micropuncture method was used in a second study of the six materials listed in Table 21B.1. Under a microscope, a very fine pipet

TABLE 21B.2 Proportions of Substances at Four Points Along the Nephron*

	In Blood Entering Glomerulus	In Tubule from Glomerulus	In Urine Leaving Nephron	In Blood Leaving Nephron†
Water	100	30	1	99
Protein	100	0	0	100
Glucose	100	20	0	100
Sodium	100	30	1	99
Potassium	100	23	12	88
Urea	100	50	90	10

*The numbers in this table represent proportions, not actual numbers of molecules or ions. For example, for every 100 molecules of water in the blood, 30 will be found in the tubule.

†The numbers in this column were obtained by subtracting the proportionate number of molecules of the substance in the urine from the proportionate number of molecules of the substance originally in the blood (100).

was used to withdraw samples of fluid at four points along the nephron. Study Table 21B.2 on the previous page, which shows the data that were collected using this technique. Use the data to answer the Analysis questions.

Analysis

1. Which function, secretion or reabsorption, involves the movement of a greater amount of water in the kidney? Explain.

2. Proteins are involved in which of the three kidney functions?

3. Compare the protein data with the glucose data. What is the difference? Explain the difference.

4. In some samples, glucose is found in the urine. What might cause this condition?

5. Why are excess glucose molecules in the blood excreted?

6. The data tell us that the concentration of sodium in the blood is greater than in the urine, yet most of the sodium ions in the urine move back into the blood. What process makes this movement possible?

7. Urea is a by-product of amino acid metabolism. Next to water, urea is the most abundant material found in urine. If urea were allowed to accumulate in the blood, what might happen?

8. Homeostasis is the maintenance of a relatively stable internal environment in an organism. Summarize how the kidney functions as a homeostatic organ.

Investigations for Chapter 22
Nervous Systems

Investigation 22A • Sensory Receptors

How do you know and learn about the world in which you live? Information is received through receptor cells that function as part of the nervous system. Specialized receptors make possible the senses of touch, sight, hearing, smell, and taste. In this investigation you will test some touch receptors.

Materials (per team of 2)

non-mercury thermometer

2 round toothpicks

2 10d nails with blunt points

pen with water-soluble ink

paper towels

large container of hot water

large container of lukewarm water

large container of ice water

Procedure

PART A   Skin and Temperature Sensations

1. Check the hot water with a thermometer to make sure it is more than comfortably warm (45° to 50°C), but not hot enough to burn your hand.
   CAUTION: Hot water can cause serious burns. Do not let the water temperature exceed 50°C.

2. Put one of your hands in the hot water and the other in ice water. Leave them there one minute.

3. After one minute, remove your hands from the hot water and ice water. Immediately sink both hands in the lukewarm water.

4. Record in your data book how the lukewarm water felt to each hand.

PART B   Sensory Receptors in Skin

5. Work in pairs for this part of the investigation. Determine who will be the experimenter and who will be the subject. Place one of the 10d nails in the ice water container; place the other 10d nail in the hot water container.

6. Experimenter: Make a 5 × 7 cm grid of small points of ink on the inside of the subject's wrist with the points 5 mm apart. (See Figure 22A.1 on page 714.) Then make a larger copy of the grid in the data book. Make it large enough to mark an ''H'' (hot) and a ''C'' (cold) by each grid point. If the sensation is felt by the subject, circle the letter. If it is not felt, put a line through the letter. This will allow you to test each grid

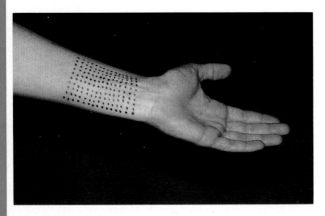

FIGURE 22A.1 Grid on wrist

point with a hot and cold probe and keep track of which points have been tested.

Subject: Sit so your arm is resting comfortably on top of the desk with the wrist up. Look away from the experimenter.

7. Experimenter: Test hot and cold receptors on the subject's wrist by allowing the blunted point of a nail taken from the hot or cold water to touch each grid spot. Dry the nail quickly with the paper towel before touching the grid points. Alternate the hot and cold nails randomly.

    CAUTION: Do not push the nails into the skin or in any way break the surface of the skin with the nails. Call your teacher in case of abrasion or cut. Do not put nails near your, or another's, face.

Subject: Tell the experimenter whether a hot or cold sensation is experienced.

Experimenter: Record the results of each touch by marking the appropriate letter in your data book.

8. Reverse roles with your partner and repeat the experiment.

PART C Distance between Receptors

9. Subject: Close your eyes and turn your head away from the experimenter.

Experimenter: Gently touch the end of the subject's index finger with the points of two toothpicks. Start with the points relatively far apart (1 cm), and then move them slowly together for each subsequent contact.

    CAUTION: Do not push the toothpicks into the skin or in any way break the surface of the skin. Call your teacher in case of abrasion or cut. Do not put toothpicks near your, or another's, face.

Subject: Tell the experimenter whether you sense one or two toothpick points.

Experimenter: If the subject senses two points, lift the toothpicks and move them slowly together for the next test. Continue testing the subject until only one toothpick point is sensed.

10. Experimenter: Trace the outline of the subject's finger in the data book. Use two pencil dots to represent the closest points where the subject sensed both toothpick points.

11. Measure the distance, in millimeters, between the dots on the diagram. Measure the width of the finger in millimeters. Express these two measurements as the ratio *width of finger* (mm)/ *minimum distance* (mm). Reduce the fraction to a small whole number.

12. Repeat steps 9 through 11 using the back of the hand. Start the touching technique with the points at least 6 cm apart. Record your results as a ratio and reduce as in step 11.

13. Switch roles and repeat the experiment.

Analysis

1. List the ratios you obtained for the fingertip and the back of the hand on the chalkboard under the correct heading, *male* or *female*. How similar are the ratios for the people in your class? Are there any differences between the ratios for males and females?

2. Feeling the forehead is a common way to find out whether body temperature is above normal. On the basis of what you learned in Part A of this investigation, explain how a person with a slightly raised temperature of 40° C could feel cool to the touch.

3. Are the sensitive areas that are stimulated by cold the same sensitive areas that are stimulated by heat? Explain.

4. If a person heard a crackling fire and people talking about heat, and then suddenly was touched with a piece of ice on the back of the

neck, what sensation might he or she first experience? Explain.

5. How does the distance between touch receptors on the fingers and those on the back of the hand compare? Explain the significance of the difference.

6. Develop a hypothesis that could account for the fact that, when two toothpicks touch the skin, sometimes only one is felt.

Investigation 22B • Reaction Time

Various sensory organs receive stimuli from the environment and send signals to the brain where they are interpreted. Other messages sent back to muscles and glands cause specific reactions to occur. How fast can you react to sound stimuli? How fast can you react to visual stimuli? Are your reactions any faster if you use both sound and visual stimuli? Are your fingers faster than your arms in reacting to stimuli? This investigation will give you a chance to answer those questions.

Materials (per team of 2)

meter stick

metric ruler

Procedure

PART A   Finger Muscles

1. Copy Table 22B.1 in your data book to help organize your data collection.

2. Work in pairs for this experiment. Determine who will be the experimenter and who will be the subject.
   Subject: Sit down with an arm resting on the desk so that your hand extends past the edge of the desk. Your thumb and forefinger should be parallel to the ground and 4 cm apart. Use the metric ruler to keep the fingers about 4 cm apart. If the distance between the fingers varies too much, the results will be affected.

3. Experimenter: Stand and hold a meter stick vertically between the thumb and forefinger of the subject so that the lowest number on the meter stick is between the subject's thumb and forefinger.

4. Without warning, drop the stick.

TABLE 22B.1   Summary of Reaction Times

Method	Average Distance Meter Stick Travels (cm)		
	Sight Only	Sound Only	Sight and Sound
Finger muscles			
Arm muscles			
Difference			

5. Subject: Try to catch the meter stick with just your thumb and forefinger.

6. Experimenter: Look at the meter stick and note the number of centimeters the stick dropped before the subject caught it. Record the distance in your data book, but do not enter it into your table at this time.

7. Repeat the test four times, recording each distance the stick dropped. Determine the average for the five trials. Record the average in the data table under the heading *Sight Only*.

8. Repeat the investigation with the subject's eyes closed. The experimenter will snap his or her fingers or otherwise signal aloud when the stick is released. Calculate the average for five trials and enter the figure in the data table under *Sound Only*.

9. Repeat the investigation with the subject's eyes open. The experimenter will use the same signal used in step 8 when the stick is released. Calculate the average for five trials and enter the figure in the data table under *Sight and Sound*.

PART B   Arm Muscles

10. Subject: Stand an arm's length away from a classroom or hall wall and place the palm of your hand, fingers up, flat against the wall. Next, lean slightly backward, or move slightly backward, so the palm of the hand is 4 cm away from the wall.

11. Experimenter: Stand and hold a meter stick against the wall so that the base of the subject's hand is even with the lowest number on the meter stick.

12. Without warning, drop the stick.

13. Subject: Try to catch the stick by pinning it to the wall with the flat of your hand.

14. Experimenter: Look at the meter stick and find the number of centimeters the stick dropped before the subject caught it (measure from the base of the hand). Record the distance in your data book, but do not enter it into your table at this time.

15. Repeat the test four times, recording each distance the stick dropped. Determine the average for the five trials. Record the average in the data table under the heading *Sight Only*.

16. Repeat the investigation with the subject's eyes closed. The experimenter will snap his or her fingers or otherwise signal aloud when the stick is released. Calculate the average for five trials and enter the figure in the data table under *Sound Only*.

17. Repeat the investigation with the subject's eyes open. The experimenter will use the same signal used in step 16 when the stick is released. Calculate the average for five trials and enter the figure in the data table under *Sight and Sound*.

18. Calculate the differences in the distances dropped by the meter stick for the two methods of catching it. Record the differences.

Analysis

1. In the sight-only test, what parts of your body are involved in catching the meter stick with your fingers? Which parts are involved when you catch the meter stick with your hand? Explain.

2. In the sight-only test, what receptors are involved in both methods of catching the stick?

3. How do the results of the sound-only test compare with the results of the sight-only test?

4. Are there any differences between the reaction times of the finger muscles and those of the arm muscles? Explain this difference.

5. Compare the results of the sight-and-sound test with the sound-only and sight-only tests.

6. What can you conclude about your reactions to different stimuli?

7. What can you conclude about your reactions with different muscle groups?

Investigations for Chapter 23
Endocrine Systems

Investigation 23A • A Bike Trip

During summer, an all-day bike trip can be fun, but it needs planning. In this computer simulation, planning is especially necessary for rider 1, an insulin-dependent diabetic. Among factors to be considered are conditioning, diet, pretrip meals, breathing rate, heart rate, and the levels of liver glycogen, blood glucose, body fluid, and blood lactic acid. These internal conditions are regulated by homeostatic mechanisms and vary from one person to another. This simulation considers only a few of these factors.

Figure 23A.1 shows the conditions of the trip as they appear on the computer screen. The trip starts and ends at home; midway is a forest park where you can stop as long as you like. The temperature will rise to 95°F by midafternoon, and the trip covers hills as well as level stretches. The left bar on the screen shows the grade of the road at each point of the trip. Uphill is a positive percentage, with a maximum grade of 6 percent. Downhill is a negative percentage; a flat road shows as 0 percent. You control the speed of travel by using the dial to change the bicycle gears. This simulation assumes a constant rate of pedaling. The bikes can cover more distance in tenth gear but climb hills more easily in lower gears. You must watch the demand and level of glucose and fluid. If either level drops too low, you will "crash." If a rider crashes, the other(s) must stop.

Cooperation is essential as you develop strategies and test your hypotheses about how to complete the bike trip, beginning with the pretrip selections—insulin dose for the diabetic rider, breakfast for all riders, and the food and drinks to pack in the saddlebags. Cooperate with your team in planning the best strategy for the trip. This is not a race—the goal is to complete the trip and return home.

Materials (per team of 7 or 8)

Apple IIe, Apple IIGS, Macintosh, or IBM computer LEAP-System™

2 dials

FIGURE 23A.1 Appearance of computer screen for the bike trip with two riders, one across the top, the other across the bottom. From left to right, the bars show grade percentage, glucose demand, blood glucose, fluid demand, and body fluid level. The box to the left of the bars shows the gear that is controlled by the dial.

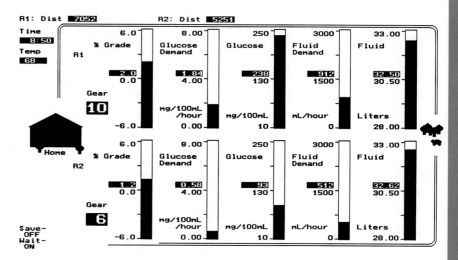

Procedure

PART A   Practice Trip

1. In each team, a group of three controls each rider, and one team member is the keyboard operator. Decide which group will control rider 1 (diabetic) and which rider 2. Each group includes one gear shift dial operator and two advisers—one to watch glucose demand and level, and one to watch fluid demand and level. Designate one of the advisers to be a recorder also. The dial operator changes gears according to the grade and input from the advisers. Each group must cooperate to enable its rider to complete the bicycle trip. Each group also must cooperate with the other rider's group, because if either rider crashes, both riders stop and you must start again with another strategy.

2. In your data book, prepare a pretrip selection record like Table 23A.1 and a trip selection record like Table 23A.2 (page 718), or tape in the tables your teacher provides.

3. For this practice trip, the team should work with the diabetic rider only. Use the LEAP-System "run" procedure to select **BIKETRP1.SPU** for one rider. The menu shown in Figure 23A.2 (next page) will appear on the screen.

4. Follow the prompts at the bottom of the screen to make pretrip decisions about insulin dose, breakfast, and what to pack in the saddlebags. Each rider is allowed 2500 g. As you make

selections, the computer displays total grams in the **BIKETRIP** box. If you overload the saddlebags, the computer will beep. Record all selections in Table 23A.1.

5. Follow the prompt on the screen to start the bike trip. To stop for a snack or a meal, press your rider number. A window will appear showing the items and the quantity of each remaining in the saddlebags. Follow the prompts to select items for your rider. Use Table 23A.2 (page 718) to record for each stop the rider number, stop number, distance covered, time from the screen, the snack/drink taken by the rider, and the resulting changes in glucose and/or fluid levels.

6. Watch the changing levels of glucose and fluid on the screen as the bike trip proceeds. Use the LEAP-System "reinitialize" procedure to restart the trip. The menu will reappear.

7. Experiment with different doses of insulin, with different breakfasts, and with different selections of food and drinks for the saddlebags. In your data book, record what problems you encounter and what steps you can take to overcome them.

8. Repeat the trip as often as time permits, recording the selections for each run.

PART B   Planning the Trip

9. As a class, discuss the relationships between glucose, insulin, and exercise, and the effects of exercise on body fluid and fluid demand.

TABLE 23A.1 Pretrip Selection Record

Menu: Biketrip			Rider Startup Information	
	Trip No. 1	2	Trip No.	
Saddle bag weight allowed (grams)	___	___	R1 Insulin dose:	___
Current saddle bag weight (grams)	___	___	R1 Breakfast:	___
			R2 Breakfast:	___
			R3 Breakfast:	___

Meals/Drinks			Snacks	
	Trip No.			Trip No.
Peanut butter & jelly sandwich (120g)	___	___	Hard boiled egg (60g)	___
Ham & cheese sandwich (9g)	___		Granola bar (30g)	___
Tuna fish sandwich (90g)	___		Chocolate bar (45g)	___
Pizza slice (120g)	___		Potato chips (30g)	___
Hot dog in bun (90g)	___		Carrot sticks (30g)	___
Water (250g)	___		Apple (120g)	___
Sport drink (250g)	___		Orange (120g)	___
Orange juice (250g)	___		Peanuts (30g)	___
Milk (240g)	___		M & M's (45g)	___
Diet soda pop (360g)	___		Canned pudding (120g)	___
Soda pop (360g)	___		Cheese (30g)	___
Vegetable juice (180g)	___	___		

TABLE 23A.2 Trip Selection Record

Trip No. _____

Rider No.	Stop No.	Distance Covered	Computer Time	Meals/Drinks/ Snacks Taken	Consequences/ Conclusions

10. Decide on several trip strategies that account for all the variables you encountered in your practice trips. This could include not only what to eat for breakfast and what foods to take along but when to stop for food and/or drink. What assumptions are you making in your strategy? Record these assumptions in your data book. For example, if you stop for orange juice, what are you assuming about the effect of the orange juice on your ability to continue?

11. In your data book, write if/then hypotheses that include the strategies and assumptions from step 10. The "if" part of each hypothesis should contain the conditions specified in the strategies. The "then" part of each hypothesis should contain the predicted outcome, assuming your conditions are met. For example, "If breakfast is skipped, then the rider will need to stop for a snack at 9:00 a.m."

Menu: BIKETRIP
Saddle Bag Weight Allowed (grams) 5000
Current Saddle Bag Weight (grams) 1935

RIDER STARTUP INFORMATION	
R1 Insulin Dose:	Low
R1 Breakfast:	Bacon and Eggs
R2 Breakfast:	Captain Krunch
R3 Breakfast:	Not going today

MEALS/DRINKS	
Peanut Butter Jelly Sandwich (120g)	2
Ham & Cheese Sandwich (90g)	0
Tuna Fish Sandwich (90g)	0
Pizza Slice (120g)	0
Hot Dog in Bun (90g)	0
Water (250g)	2
Gatorade (250g)	2
Orange Juice (250g)	2
Milk (240g)	0
Diet Soda Pop (360g)	0
Soda Pop (360g)	0
Vegetable Juice [V8] (180g)	0

SNACKS	
Hard Boiled Egg (60g)	0
Granola Bar (30g)	1
Chocolate Bar (45g)	0
Potato Chips (30g)	0
Carrot Sticks (30g)	0
Apple (120g)	1
Orange (120g)	0
Peanuts (30g)	0
M & M's (45g)	1
Canned Pudding (120g)	0
Cheese (30g)	0

F10-Exit Menu ↑ ↔ ↓ Select Ret-Enter Box

FIGURE 23A.2 Menu screen for the bike trip.

PART C   The Trip

12. Start the trip as you did in step 3, but select **BIKETRP2.SPU** for two riders or **BIKETRP3.SPU** for three riders. (All riders share the same saddlebags.) Follow your strategies carefully. Record any changes in strategies made during the trip. Record snacks/meals for all riders in the trip selection record.

13. Revise your strategies, if necessary. Develop a new hypothesis about how the trip will be completed, including insulin dosage, breakfast, and saddlebag contents. Record your hypothesis in your data book.

14. Use your new strategies and rerun the bike trip.

Analysis

1. Compare the results of your strategies. Were the prediction parts of your hypotheses correct? What changes did you make in the second trip?

2. Compare your strategies with those of other teams in the class. How were they similar? How were they different? Which strategies resulted in successful completion of the bike trip?

3. Describe the trip strategy that produced the most successful result in the bike trip. Tell why it was better than another strategy used.

4. What effect did the insulin dose have on rider 1's performance in the trip?

5. What effect did the food you selected for breakfast have on the outcome of the trip?

6. What effect did the type of food and drink you packed in the saddlebags have on the outcome of the trip? What effect did the time at which you stopped to eat or drink have?

7. Describe how cooperation between riders influences the outcome of the trip.

8. What effect does temperature have on the outcome of the trip? What body functions are influenced by temperature?

9. Now that you know the effects of selecting the proper food and drink for a bike trip, describe how the foods you eat and drink can be important in your everyday activities.

10. How does the diet of an insulin-dependent diabetic differ from the diet of another bike rider on the trip?

11. Write a short paragraph describing what you have learned about the type of activities in which an insulin-dependent diabetic can participate and what limitations diabetes does and does not place on a person's life.

Investigations for Chapter 24
Locomotion Systems

Investigation 24A • Observing Movement

Different organisms employ different methods of locomotion that are suited to the organism's environment and life-style. In this investigation, you will observe and compare the movement of a *Paramecium*, an amoeba, and an earthworm.

Materials (per team of 2)

2 pairs safety goggles

2 lab aprons

microscope slides

cover slips

dropping pipet

compound microscope

dissecting pan

cotton fibers

damp paper toweling

moist garden soil

Detain™

India ink solution

Paramecium culture

amoeba culture

living earthworm

SAFETY   Put on your safety goggles and lab apron.

PART A   Paramecium

Procedure

1. Place a drop of Detain™ (protozoa slowing agent) on a clean slide. Add a drop of *Paramecium* culture and cover with a cover slip.

2. Before the slowing agent has diffused into the water, the organisms will move very rapidly. When they begin to slow down, switch to high power to observe movement in detail. In your data book, record which end of *Paramecium* is usually in front as the animal moves.

3. The front end of an organism is referred to as *anterior*. The back end is referred to as *posterior*. Sketch one organism and label what you believe to be the anterior and posterior ends.

4. Diagram the motion of *Paramecium* as it moves in one direction. Use arrows to show the directions of the motions of the body.

5. Gently raise the cover slip on your slide and add a few cotton fibers to the *Paramecium* culture. Replace the cover slip and observe with low power. Describe what happens when an organism bumps into one of the fibers. In your data book, sketch a line to indicate a cotton fiber. Add arrows to show the direction of movement of an organism that has just bumped into a fiber.

6. Add a small drop of India ink solution to the drop of *Paramecium* culture on the slide. Under high power, observe the surface of one of the organisms. The hairlike structures you see are cilia. Notice carefully what happens to India ink particles that touch an organism. Adjust the light until you can see individual cilia.

Analysis

1. How do the cilia function?

2. What evidence did you see that *Paramecium* is not enclosed by a stiff wall?

3. What do the reactions of *Paramecium* to an obstacle in its path suggest about its behavior?

4. What does the pattern of movement of the India ink particles tell you about the activities of the cilia?

5. Based on your observations, what is *Paramecium*'s method of locomotion?

6. How might *Paramecium*'s method of locomotion be related to the nature of its environment?

7. What characteristic of movement in *Paramecium* is common to locomotion of animals in general?

PART B   Amoeba

Procedure

7. Place a drop of amoeba culture on a clean slide. Carefully place a cover slip over the culture and examine under low power.

8. In your data book, make three drawings of the locomotion of an amoeba at 30-second intervals. Carefully observe the flow of the cytoplasm in the cell. Use arrows to indicate the direction in which it flows.

9. Label all identifiable parts of the amoeba.

Analysis

1. Did the cytoplasm stream faster in any portion of the cell? Explain your observation.

2. Did the amoeba form more than one pseudopod in one direction?

3. Did the amoeba engulf food? If so, describe what happened.

PART C   Earthworm

Procedure

10. Dampen a piece of paper toweling and place it in the bottom of a dissecting pan. Put the earthworm on the paper and observe its movements.

11. Sketch the worm. Use arrows to show how the earthworm moves and describe the movement.

12. Place a small mound of moist garden soil in one end of your dissecting pan.

13. Put the earthworm on top of the soil and record its behavior.

14. Wash your hands thoroughly before leaving the laboratory.

Analysis

1. In terms of what you know about its muscles, explain how the earthworm moves.

2. What might be the advantage of segmentation in the earthworm?

3. How might the method of locomotion used by the earthworm be related to its environment and life-style?

4. Compare and contrast the different methods of locomotion used by each organism. What are some advantages and disadvantages of each?

Investigation 24B • Muscles and Muscle Fatigue

How do muscles move bones? Do muscles always work efficiently and at the same rate, or do they suffer from fatigue? In this investigation, you will observe the relationship between muscle movement, exercise, and muscle fatigue.

Materials (per team of 2)

PART A

sheet of thin cardboard

scissors

string

brass brad

tape

metric ruler

PART B

watch or clock with a second hand

PART A   Muscles and Movement

Procedure

1. Using the materials provided and Figure 24.17 in your text as a guide, construct a working model of the upper and lower arm that shows the attachment of the biceps and triceps. Use cardboard for bones, string for muscles, tape for tendons, and a brad for the elbow joint. (Hint: When cutting the string for the biceps and triceps muscles, be sure you have enough to compensate for the movement of the joint.)

2. Place the model on the table. Grasp the biceps string just below the upper arm attachment site.

Gently pull the string. What do you observe? Release the string, but do not reposition the lower arm.

3. Now grasp the triceps string just below its upper attachment site and gently pull. What do you observe? How does this movement differ from that in step 2?

Analysis

1. Many muscles in the body work in pairs. Some of the paired muscles are called flexors and extensors. How do such muscle pairs result in movement of a body part?

2. Is the biceps a flexor or an extensor? Is the triceps a flexor or an extensor?

3. What other joints of the body are moved by such muscle pairs?

4. Would movement of body parts be possible without flexors? Without extensors? Explain your answer.

5. How do animals with external skeletons, such as lobsters and beetles, move?

PART B   Exercise and Muscle Fatigue

Procedure

4. Rest your forearm on the table, palm up, and grasp your upper arm with your other hand. Have your partner rest his or her forearm on the table with the hand over your hand and wrist and grasp his or her own upper arm with the free hand.

5. Try to bend your arm up as your partner exerts pressure to keep your hand on the table. Describe what happens in your arm.

6. Switch roles with your partner and repeat steps 4 and 5. Record any differences.

7. Make a tight fist with one hand, and then extend the fingers as far as you can. Do this as fast as possible for 30 seconds. Keep track of the elapsed time on a watch or clock with a second hand while your partner counts the number of times you make a fist. Record the data. Do you feel any muscle fatigue? Where?

8. Rest one minute and repeat step 7.

9. Repeat steps 7 and 8 using your left hand. Compare the performance of your left and right hands. Is there any difference?

Analysis

1. How many times were you able to make a fist the first time? After the rest period?

2. What differences did you notice between when you started and when you finished? What might have caused those differences?

3. Account for any performance differences between your right and left hands.

Investigations for Chapter 25
Animal Interactions

Investigation 25A • A Lesson in Conditioning

Conditioning occurs when the patterns of innate behavior or reflexes are changed. In this investigation, you will determine if it is possible to condition

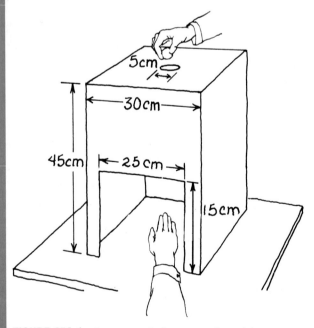

FIGURE 25A.1 Screen made from a cardboard box. Dimensions are approximate.

a classmate to jerk his or her hand away when you make a noise.

Materials (per team of 2)

small rubber ball

scissors

cardboard box (book-box size)

noisemaker, such as an electric buzzer, a metal "cricket," or anything else that makes a similar noise

Procedure

1. Cut a hole near the bottom of one side of a cardboard box, similar to the one shown in Figure 25A.1. In the center of the top side of the box, cut a small circular hole through which the ball can easily pass.
   CAUTION: Scissors are sharp. Handle with care.

2. Determine which person will be the experimenter and which person will be the subject. *The subject should not read any further directions.* In your data book, prepare a table similar to Table 25A.1. Be sure you have room to record how the subject reacted and what combination of stimuli you used.

3. Place the subject in front of the box with his or her hand inserted through the hole, directly underneath the circular hole on the top. Make sure that the subject's hand is mostly out of his or her sight.

4. Inform the subject that he or she will be attempting to keep the hand from being hit by the ball as it drops. Be sure the subject understands that the hand must remain in position at all times unless he or she removes it to keep from being hit by the ball.

5. Stand behind the box with your noisemaker hidden from the subject's view. Now drop the ball through the hole *at the same time* you make a noise with your noisemaker. Do this several times in a row. The subject probably will not be hit more than once or twice. Record the subject's reaction and the stimulus used for each trial.

6. On the next trial, instead of dropping the ball, just make the noise. Record your results.

TABLE 25A.1   Results of Conditioning Trials

Trial number	Type of Stimulus			Subject's Reaction	
	Noise	Dropped ball	Both	Hand in	Hand out
1					
2					
etc.					

7. After this, randomly change the order of the stimuli used. Try some with both, several with just the noise alone, and several with just the ball. Again, record the results.

8. Wash your hands before leaving the laboratory.

Analysis

1. Compare your results with those from the rest of the class. Do you observe a pattern in the subjects' reactions?

2. Are there any differences in the results? If so, can you suggest any reasons why?

3. Do you think another stimulus besides noise would work the same way? Why or why not?

Investigation 25B • Trial-and-Error Learning

This investigation will allow you to experience how trial-and-error learning operates. You will be asked to do something differently from the way you are used to doing it, and to examine the learning process that occurs.

Materials (per team of 2)

small mirror

watch, stopwatch, or clock with a second hand

20 star diagrams

4 pieces of graph paper

2 pencils

2 pieces of notebook paper

4 to 6 books (enough to make the screen in Figure 25B.2 on the next page)

Procedure

1. Decide who will begin as the experimenter and who will be the subject. You will change roles later.

2. Divide the 20 star diagrams into two sets of 10. Number each set from 1 through 10. On each diagram, choose one of the star points and label it "start." (See Figure 25B.1.) Do this for all 20 figures.

3. Construct a screen using the books. Make two piles of books and lay the last book across the top of the two piles. (See Figure 25B.2 on the next page.) Leave enough room for your arm to fit through the space between the two piles of books.

4. In your data book, prepare a table with three headings: *Trial Number*, *Number of Errors*, and *Time in Seconds*.

FIGURE 25B.1   Star diagram with start position labeled

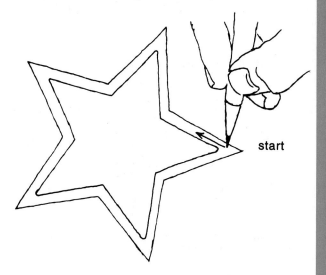

start

FIGURE 25B.2 Outlining a star reflected in a mirror

5. The subject will sit with his or her arm between the piles of books and will be asked to outline the star on the diagram without looking directly at the paper. The experimenter will hold a mirror in which the subject will be able to see the reflected star diagram. The experimenter will time how long it takes the subject to outline the star.

6. The subject should begin at the point on the diagram labeled "start" and draw a line all the way around the star, trying to stay within the lines. The subject should look *only* at the reflec-

tion of the star diagram in the mirror held by the experimenter.

7. The experimenter should record, in seconds, how long it takes the subject to complete the outline of the star.

8. Repeat this procedure for the other nine figures. For each diagram, record the time to completion.

9. Change roles with your partner. The experimenter should now be the subject and the subject becomes the experimenter. Repeat steps 6 through 8.

10. When you and your partner have completed all 20 trials, count the number of errors in each of the 20 trials. An error is counted every time the subject's pencil line went outside the lines of the star diagram and returned. See Figure 25B.3 for an illustration of an error.

11. After you have counted the errors for each of the 20 trials, graph the results for the 10 trials you completed as the subject. Your partner will do the same for the other 10 trials. Label the horizontal axis *time* and the vertical axis *number of errors*.

Analysis

1. Examine the number of errors for each of your 10 trials and compare those with the time it took you to complete the outline. What, if any, evidence indicates that learning occurred?

2. Compare your graph with those of your partner and with the other teams. Is there any pattern in the data? Explain.

3. Summarize the results of this investigation in terms of trial-and-error learning. Use your data to support your conclusions.

Investigation 25C • A Field Study of Animal Behavior

The study of an organism's behaviors in an ecosystem is called ethology. These behaviors include its responses to the abiotic environment, to other species, and to other members of its own species. You can learn a great deal about an organism by observing it under natural conditions where its behavior is

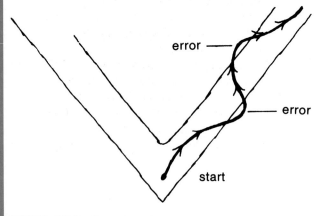

FIGURE 25B.3 Illustration of errors

likely to be typical of the species. In this investigation, you will develop a systematic field study of an organism in its natural habitat and then relate its behaviors to its basic needs. Be careful not to attribute human values and emotions to the organism.

Materials (per person)

data book

pen

Procedure

1. Select a nondomesticated animal that is available for observation. Some of the following animals would make good subjects: insects and spiders; birds such as robins, blue jays, pigeons, sparrows, ducks, and geese; mammals such as deer, squirrels, chipmunks, muskrats, and raccoons; snails, slugs, and fish.

2. Most of these organisms live in fields, ponds, parks, or forests. Even an aquarium, though not the same as a natural habitat, provides a suitable environment for observation. The best times to observe are just before sunset and just after sunrise. Many animals feed at these times. You do not need to study the same individual each time because the behaviors you observe should be typical of the species.

3. Some behaviors on which to focus include:
   a. Orientation to external stimuli, such as wind, sun, and moisture
   b. Communication with other members of the species or with other species
   c. Feeding
   d. Courtship and mating
   e. Interaction with other members of the species or with members from other species, including protective measures for itself or its young
   f. Reactions to the presence of other species, including humans

4. Once you have selected an organism to study, devise a procedure for your study and submit it to your teacher for approval. Your plan should include:
   a. The scientific and common names of your organism
   b. Where and when you will make your observations (If possible, the organism should be observed several different times.)
   c. The question you plan to investigate
   d. A hypothesis related to your question

5. Conduct your observations. Your results will more accurately reflect natural behaviors if your subject is not aware of your presence.
   CAUTION: Avoid any type of physical contact with wild animals. In natural settings, be aware of your surroundings; avoid contact with poisonous plants and biting or stinging insects. Your procedure must be approved by your teacher; inform an adult of your whereabouts and your schedule.

6. Record your observations accurately and comprehensively in your data book. You will use your data to prepare your report.

Analysis

1. Write a report relating the behaviors you observed to the organism's basic needs. Remember not to attribute human motives to the animal. Your report should include:
   a. Title, your name, and date
   b. The procedure approved by your teacher
   c. The actual procedure you followed if it differed from your proposal
   d. Your question and hypothesis
   e. The data you collected: Organize your notes by quantifying as much data as possible (how many, how much, how often, and so on) using tables, charts, or graphs.
   f. Conclusions: Interpretations or explanations of the behaviors observed in light of the basic needs of the animal
   g. Evaluation of your hypothesis: Did the data support or refute your hypothesis?
   h. Recommendations for further study: What would you suggest if someone else were going to do the same study, or what would you do differently if you did the study again?

Investigations for Chapter 26
Interrelationships

Investigation 26A • Producers in an Ecosystem

In this investigation, you will study the producers in a small piece of the biosphere. It need not be a very large piece—only large enough to contain several types of producers that show interrelationships. Different schools have different opportunities for outdoor studies. Therefore, the study procedures used by you and your class will have to be designed to fit the piece of biosphere that is to be used by your school. Read the following sections carefully to get an overview of what you might do.

Selecting a study area. A forest is a complex environment, providing opportunities to collect abundant data, but it is difficult to picture as a whole. A prairie is almost as complex, but is somewhat easier to study. Cultivated areas, such as cornfields and pastures, are relatively simple to study. They are as important as forests and prairies, since they now cover a large portion of the land in the world.

Suitable areas also can be found in cities. Many schools have lawns with trees and shrubs. Here there are many fewer types of organisms than outside the city, but you can be more thorough in your study. You also can study vacant lots and spaces between buildings. Even such small places as cracks in the pavement, gutters, and the areas around trees often contain a surprising number of organisms.

Organizing the work. Teamwork will be necessary for this study. Plan the work carefully, divide responsibilities, and take extensive notes.

Organizing the data. It is convenient to divide producers into three groups for study: trees, shrubs, and saplings; herbaceous plants; and seedlings. In addition, organic litter, such as fallen leaves, or ground cover, such as lichen and mosses, may be present. Trees may be classified as either deciduous or coniferous. Canopy trees are at the top of the forest and receive direct sunlight. The trees below this top layer form the subcanopy. Shrubs are low woody plants between 0.5 and 3 m tall. A sapling is a young tree that is 2.5 to 4 cm in diameter and

about 1.3 m high. Herbaceous plants are nonwoody plants that die down to the ground in the autumn. These include grasses, grains, and small flowering plants. A seedling is a very young tree with a stem less than 1 cm in diameter.

Materials (per team of 8)

The materials required depend on the methods used, but the following list is minimal for the field.

strong twine, over 100 m long

4 stakes

compass, magnetic

15-centimeter ruler

data book and pen

graph paper

2 meter sticks

hoop with area of 1 m^2

plastic bags

tin can, 5-cm diameter

plastic gloves

Procedure

1. Choose your site.
   a. In a forest, study areas should be approximately 10 m square and broken down into smaller areas, as shown in Figure 26A.1a.
   b. In unforested areas, study areas should be 2 to 4 m on a side without internal divisions.
   c. In vacant city lots, cultivated fields, and pastures, use smaller areas, about 1 m^2. (An area the size of a hula hoop works well.)

2. Each team should develop a hypothesis concerning the type of ecosystem of their site and what vegetation they expect to find.

3. Within the chosen site, measure a study area of appropriate size. Drive stakes into the ground at the corner points and connect the stakes with string. The study area should be as square as possible. You may want to subdivide the area to make counting organisms easier.

4. Stand back and look at your study area. Walk around the outer boundary. Use symbols like the ones shown in Figure 26A.1b to sketch a profile of the ecosystem as you see it.

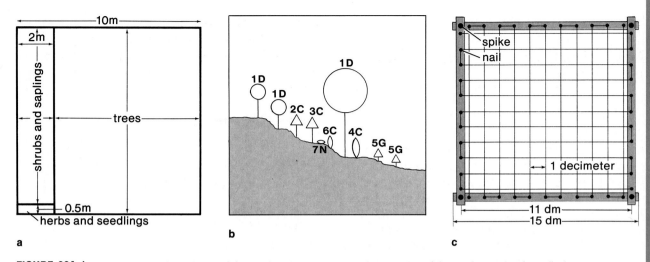

FIGURE 26A.1 *(a)* Study plot for a forest; *(b)* a profile showing layers of vegetation; *(c)* area for study of small plants

5. Indicate with numbers the various plant types that are recognizably different. For example, in Figure 26A.1b, the first plant observed was a deciduous (D) canopy tree 1D. Three of these were found on the study area. The second species observed (labeled 2) was a conifer (C) subcanopy species. Species 3 also was a subcanopy conifer species, but different from species 2.

6. Once the profile of your study area is made, you are ready for a closer look at its vegetation. Different teams can gather data on trees, shrubs, and saplings, herbaceous plants and seedlings; and litter, so that the class as a whole gains a detailed picture of the vegetation.

7. Abundance refers to the number of individuals of one kind within a given area. Count the number of each type of producer in your study area. For example, count the number of each type of tree in the forest canopy and subcanopy layers in the main study area. Count shrubs and saplings in one of the smaller subdivided areas. Also count the herbaceous plants and seedlings in an even smaller area. Special problems may arise. In a lawn, for example, there is no need to count blades of grass. However, a count of the weeds might be worthwhile, especially if comparisons will be made between well-trodden areas and protected ones. A frame (Figure 26A.1c) may be useful for this work.

8. Make a table to record your counts. Across the top, list the types of plants in your subdivided area. For example, if you are counting shrubs and seedlings you may list evergreen shrubs, rosebushes, raspberry bushes, and so on. Under these headings, record your count of each type of plant. You may wish to gather a sample or characteristic part of the plant, such as a leaf, and place it in a plastic bag. Do not collect the whole plant and be sure to wear plastic gloves.

CAUTION: Do not collect any plants you cannot identify as harmless.
Some plants are rare or endangered species. Be sure to record where you collected the sample.

9. Teams that study organic litter and ground cover should collect samples in plastic bags (wear gloves). Take samples from the ground around trees, shrubs, and small plants in a small subdivided area. Secure the bag with a rubber band or twist tie and mark it to indicate where it was gathered. You will study these samples later in the laboratory. At the study site, examine a 15-cm^2 sample of litter in place. Carefully pick the sample apart. Record the layers and composition of each layer. Also try to determine its physical condition. These observations should include the state of decay, the moisture level, odor, the amount of shade at the location, and nearness to large plants.

Analysis

1. Calculate the number of each type of plant to determine its abundance. If several teams had study areas near one another, average the data for plants of the same type. List all of the plants on the study site in order of their abundance.

2. To determine density, divide the total number of individuals of each type by the area of the study site in square meters:

$$\text{Density} = \frac{\text{Total number of each species}}{\text{Total sample area (in m}^2\text{)}}$$

3. List the plants in order of their densities. The teams analyzing the litter and ground cover also should calculate the abundance and density of each species in the samples from the study area.

4. With your classmates, make a summary of the important features of the plants in the ecosystems you studied. Include such factors as profile, abundance, density, and litter. Record this information in your data book.

5. Ecosystems are usually named for the most obvious or important species of plants. For example, a deciduous forest might be called a beach-maple forest if those trees are dominant. After you have analyzed the data, determine the one or two species that appear to be the most abundant in the area you studied. What would you name this ecosystem? How does the data support or refute your hypothesis concerning the type of vegetation you expected to find?

6. How many layers of vegetation did you find in the entire study area? List the important species in each of these layers.

7. Some of the plants are in a layer because they are limited genetically to that maximum height. Others are young individuals that will some day grow higher. Review your data to determine how many of these young individuals were among the plants in each layer.

Investigation 26B • Relationships Between a Plant and an Animal

Plants and animals interact in a variety of ways. By setting up closed systems with an aquatic plant and an aquatic animal, you can study an interaction related to the carbon cycle. Carbon dioxide dissolves in water and forms a weak acid, which lowers the pH. This drop in pH indicates an increase in the concentration of carbon dioxide. Conversely, an increase in pH indicates a decrease in the concentration of carbon dioxide. Thus, you can measure any changes that occur in the systems by measuring indirectly the concentration of carbon dioxide using pH probes with the LEAP-System™, or a pH meter or wide-range pH paper if the LEAP-System™ is not available. The LEAP-System™ BSCS Biology Lab Pac 2 provides instructions for use of the system.

Before beginning the experiment, read through the procedure and develop hypotheses that predict the changes that will occur in each test tube in the light and in the dark.

Materials (per team of 4)

4 25-mm × 200-mm test tubes

test-tube rack

aluminum foil

light source

LEAP-System™

Apple IIe, Apple IIGS, Macintosh, or IBM computer

2 pH probes with interface modules

pH meter or wide-range pH paper (optional)

forceps (optional)

200 mL dechlorinated water

2 15-cm pieces of elodea

2 1- to 1½-cm fresh water snails

Procedure

Day 1

1. Record all data in your data book, or use the table your teacher provides.

2. Label the test tubes 1 through 4 and place them in the test-tube rack.

3. Pour dechlorinated water into each test tube to approximately 4 cm from the top. (Tap water becomes dechlorinated by standing for 24 hours—the chlorine escapes into the air).

4. Add nothing more to test tube 1. To test tube 2 add a snail and a leafy stem of elodea, to test

tube 3 add only a snail, and to test tube 4, add only a leafy stem of elodea.

5. Determine the initial pH of each tube by using a pH probe with the LEAP-System™ (Figure 26B.1), a pH meter, or by dipping small strips of pH paper held with forceps into the test tubes and comparing the color change to a standard color chart. For the LEAP-System™, remove the cap from the tip of each pH probe. Insert the pH probe from Input 1 into test tube 1 and the pH probe from Input 2 into test tube 2.

6. When the readings have stabilized, record the current pH readings for test tubes 1 and 2 from the numerical data displayed near the graph, or record your readings from the pH paper and color chart.

7. To determine the initial pH readings of test tubes 3 and 4, remove the pH probe from test tube 2, rinse with dechlorinated water, and insert into test tube 3. When the readings have stabilized, record the current pH for test tube 3. Then remove the pH probe from test tube 3, rinse, and insert into test tube 4, and record the current pH for test tube 4. Rinse the pH probe and replace in test tube 2.

8. Seal the top of each test tube with a double layer of aluminum foil. Press the foil tightly to the sides of the test tube and around the wire from the pH probe. Place the test tubes in strong artificial light.

9. Repeat steps 5 through 7 every 10 minutes until the end of the period. Record all readings in the data table.

10. Remove the pH probes and rinse with tap water. Half fill the caps with tap water and replace on the probes for storage.

11. Seal the test tubes and leave in the light overnight.

12. Wash your hands thoroughly before leaving the laboratory.

Day 2

13. Observe the test tubes and take pH readings as in steps 6 and 7. In the data table, record the pH readings and the condition of the organisms in each test tube.

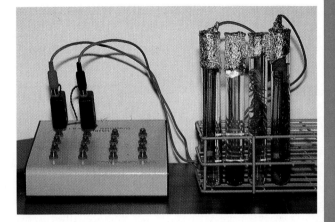

FIGURE 26B.1 LEAP-System setup for measuring pH

14. Store the pH probes as in step 10. Seal the test tubes and wrap each one in aluminum foil to keep dark.

15. Wash your hands thoroughly before leaving the laboratory.

Day 3

16. Repeat steps 13 and 14, but this time remove the aluminum foil and place the test tubes in the light.

17. Wash your hands before leaving the laboratory.

Day 4

18. Observe the test tubes again, record pH data, and stop the experiment.

19. Wash your hands thoroughly before leaving the laboratory.

Analysis

1. Construct graphs from your data, using a different color for each test tube.

2. Use information about photosynthesis, cellular respiration, and the carbon cycle to write a paragraph that explains the data.

3. What was the purpose of test tube 1?

4. Did the pH change in test tube 1? If so, how might you explain this change?

5. What effect would a pH change in test tube 1 have on the data for the other three test tubes?

6. What results might you expect if all the test tubes were kept in total darkness for the duration of the experiment?

7. Do the experimental data support your hypotheses? Explain. If not, try to devise a general hypothesis that is consistent with all of your observations.

8. Suppose a snail were kept by itself in a sealed test tube for a week. Predict what is likely to happen and provide an explanation.

Investigation 26C • Water Quality Assessment

How clean is the water in a lake, pond, or stream near your school? Technical tests can determine exact types and amounts of water pollution, but a simple survey of algae and cyanobacteria can serve as a reliable index of water quality. Clean water usually has many different species of algae and cyanobacteria, and no single species predominates. Polluted water has fewer species and high numbers of each. This investigation consists of three parts: identifying key genera of algae and cyanobacteria; testing known samples of clean, intermediate, and polluted water; and testing a local water source.

Materials (per team of 2)

3 microscope slides

3 cover slips (22 mm x 22 mm)

dropping pipet

1 L beaker

plankton net

compound microscope

protist/cyanobacteria key

2-cm^2 piece of graph paper with 1-mm squares

4 flat toothpicks

pocket calculator (optional)

Detain™ in a squeeze bottle

water sample with algae and cyanobacteria

water samples—clean, intermediate, and polluted

Procedure

PART A Field of View Calculations

1. Place the 2-cm^2 piece of graph paper on a microscope slide and add a cover slip. Examine the slide with the low power (100X) of your microscope. Align the squares so one edge of a square just touches the bottom edge of the field of view. Count the number of squares from the bottom to the top of the field. (See Figure 26C.1, *top*.) The number of squares equals the diameter of the field of view in millimeters. Record the results and the low-power magnification.

2. Repeat step 1 with the high power (400X) of your microscope. (Do not use the oil immersion lens.) The field of view will be less than one millimeter in diameter.

3. You will count individual organisms on a slide made from your water samples. To do so, you will move the slide across the microscope stage,

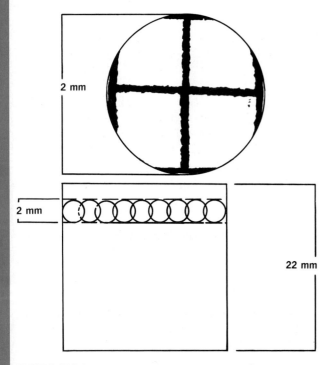

FIGURE 26C.1 *(top)* Microscopic view of 1 mm^2 graph paper at 100X. Field diameter = 2 mm; *(bottom)* The area of a strip = the length of the coverslip (22 mm) × diameter of the microscope field.

the width of one field of view at a time, as illustrated in Figure 26C.1 (*bottom*). The area of the strip of fields of view equals the diameter of the field of view multiplied by the width of the cover slip (22 mm). Practice moving the slide one field of view at a time, going from one side of the cover slip to the other.

PART B   Algae Identification

4. Place a drop of Detain™ (protist slowing agent) on a clean microscope slide. Using a dropping pipet, add one drop (0.1 mL) of a sample, and use a toothpick to mix the two drops. Carefully add a cover slip.

5. Practice locating and identifying different organisms using the protist/cyanobacteria key. Locate organisms under low power and then use high power to make a positive identification.

6. Move the slide, one field of view at a time, going from one side of the cover slip to the other. In each strip, count the numbers of individuals for each genus you can identify. Ask your teacher for help if you cannot identify some of the organisms.

7. Wash your hands thoroughly before leaving the laboratory.

PART C   Identification of Water Samples

8. Table 26C.1 above lists the pollution index of each genus used to determine water quality with the Palmer method. You will use this information to determine the pollution index of several samples of water.

TABLE 26C.1 Algal Genera Pollution Index (Palmer 1969)

Genera	Pollution Index
Anacystis	1
Ankistrodesmus	2
Chlamydomonas	4
Chlorella	3
Closterium	1
Cyclotella	1
Euglena	5
Gomphonema	1
Lepocinclis	1
Melosira	1
Micractinium	1
Navicula	3
Nitzschia	3
Oscillatoria	5
Pandorina	1
Phacus	2
Phormidium	1
Scenedesmus	4
Stigeoclonium	2
Synedra	2

9. For each of the three water samples, you will count the number of organisms in each genus in three strips of fields of view. Then you will compute the pollution index for each sample in order to decide which sample is clean, which is intermediate, and which is polluted. In your data book, prepare four worksheets with the headings in Table 26C.2 or tape in the worksheets your teacher provides. Use the worksheets for your calculations.

TABLE 26C.2 Work Sheet for Determining Water Quality

Algal Genus	Number of Cells or Units			A total	B Area of sample	C Strip area	D Number of strips	E Volume of sample	F A × B / C × D × E	G Sample volume	H Lake water filtered	I F × G / H	Palmer Score
	strip 1	strip 2	strip 3										
(Example) Oscill.	++++ ++++ ++++	++++ ++++ 0.2	++++ ++++ iii	38.2	484 mm²	44 mm²	3	0.1 mL	1400/mL	100 mL	1000 mL	140/mL	5

10. Put one drop of Detain™ and one drop (0.1 mL) Sample 1 on a slide. Mix with a clean toothpick. Add a cover slip. In your worksheet, note the sample number.

11. Count and record in the table the number of individuals from each genus present in a strip of fields of view. Count *units* (colonies or filaments are counted as one unit). Large filaments and colonies only partly lying in the strip should be counted as fractions. For example, if a filament of *Stigeoclonium* is only half in your field of view, record 0.5 instead of 1.

12. Repeat steps 10 and 11 two more times.

13. The calculations for the Palmer score assume the sample from which you extracted the organisms was 1 L (1000 mL) of water that was filtered and concentrated in 100 mL of water. Study the example in Table 26C.2. The first calculation (column F) determines the number of individuals from each genus in your 0.1-mL concentrated sample. The second calculation (column I) calculates the number of units per mL in the original 1-L sample. *You must obtain at least 50 units per mL for the 1-L sample or you cannot enter a Palmer score for that genus.*

14. After obtaining the final count for each genus with a frequency of at least 50 units per mL, look up the pollution index for that genus and enter it in your worksheet. (Only the genera included in the Palmer list are scored as indicator organisms.) A total score (the sum of the Palmer scores for all species in a sample) of 20 or more for a sample is evidence for high organic pollution. Scores between 15 and 19 indicate moderate pollution, and scores less than 15 indicate absence of pollution.

15. Repeat steps 10 through 14 for Samples 2 and 3.

16. Check with your teacher to determine whether your total Palmer scores correctly identify the water quality of the three samples.

PART D   Investigation of Local Water Source

17. Using water from a local pond or lake, filter 1 L through a plankton net to trap the organisms. Rinse the organisms from the net into the 1-L beaker and add clean water to total 100 mL. Repeat steps 10 through 14 to determine the pollution index.

18. Wash your hands thoroughly before leaving the laboratory.

Analysis

1. Which algal genera can tolerate the highest levels of organic pollution?

2. If a genus has a Palmer score of 1, what does that indicate?

3. If your local water source has a moderate or high pollution level, what might be the source of pollution?

4. How can algae and cyanobacteria be helpful in polluted water?

5. How can algae and cyanobacteria be harmful in polluted water?

Appendices

Appendix 1A
Ideas behind Natural Selection

The major result of Darwin's voyage on the *Beagle*, the theory of evolution by natural selection, did not appear in print until more than 20 years after his return to England in 1836. In 1838, Darwin happened to read an essay on populations by Reverend T. R. Malthus (1766–1834). Malthus stated that animal and plant populations, including human populations, tend to increase beyond the capacity of the environment to support them. He pointed out that populations increase in a geometric progression, whereas the food supply increases in an arithmetic progression (see Figure 1A.1). If humans, for example, continued to reproduce at the same rate, they would eventually outstrip their food supply. Malthus' essay provided Darwin with one important idea: The reproductive potential of animals is high, but not all animals survive long enough to reproduce, and this difference in survival among members of populations has kept those populations in check. After reading Malthus' article, Darwin realized that a process of selection in nature, in essence a struggle for existence because of overpopulation, could be a powerful force for the evolution of species.

Darwin allowed this idea to develop until 1844, when he wrote an essay that he did not publish. Finally, in 1856, he began to pull together his data into a work on the origin of species by natural selection. Darwin had no hard proof for his idea. There was no experimental evidence for the inheritance of the variations that formed the core of his theory. The entire field of heredity and genetics was then unknown. He was, therefore, reluctant to present his theory without being able to explain the mechanism by which the process of natural selection worked.

In 1858, Darwin received a manuscript from Alfred Russel Wallace (1823–1913). He was stunned to find that, in a few pages, Wallace summarized the main points of the theory that Darwin had been working on for nearly 20 years. Darwin asked that Wallace's paper be presented to the Linnaean Society of London first. He thought that would be the proper thing to do under the circumstances. Instead, Darwin was persuaded by two

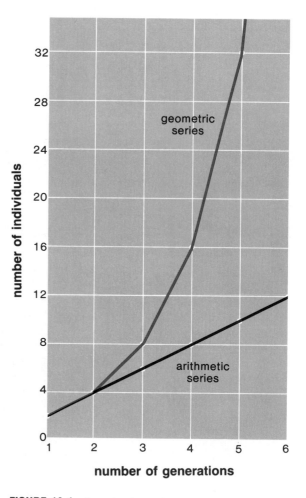

FIGURE 1A.1 A comparison of rates of increase

friends, the geologist Lyell and the botanist Hooker, to publish his views in a short paper that would appear together with Wallace's paper in the *Journal of the Linnaean Society*. Portions of both papers were read in front of an unimpressed audience on July 1, 1858.

Appendix 2A
The Periodic Table of the Elements

The periodic table of the elements shows the name and symbol for each element, as well as its atomic number and atomic mass. Atomic number is the

PERIODIC TABLE OF THE ELEMENTS

(based on $^{12}_{6}C = 12.0000$)

Legend:
- Atomic number
- Symbol
- Name
- Atomic mass (parentheses indicate the mass number of the isotope of longest half-life for that element)

Example:
14 — Si — Silicon — 28.086

TRANSITION METALS

Group	Z	Symbol	Name	Atomic mass
1	1	H	Hydrogen	1.008
18	2	He	Helium	4.003
1	3	Li	Lithium	6.941
2	4	Be	Beryllium	9.012
13	5	B	Boron	10.811
14	6	C	Carbon	12.011
15	7	N	Nitrogen	14.007
16	8	O	Oxygen	15.999
17	9	F	Fluorine	18.998
18	10	Ne	Neon	20.180
1	11	Na	Sodium	22.990
2	12	Mg	Magnesium	24.305
13	13	Al	Aluminum	26.982
14	14	Si	Silicon	28.086
15	15	P	Phosphorus	30.974
16	16	S	Sulfur	32.066
17	17	Cl	Chlorine	35.453
18	18	Ar	Argon	39.948
1	19	K	Potassium	39.098
2	20	Ca	Calcium	40.078
3	21	Sc	Scandium	44.956
4	22	Ti	Titanium	47.88
5	23	V	Vanadium	50.942
6	24	Cr	Chromium	51.996
7	25	Mn	Manganese	54.938
8	26	Fe	Iron	55.847
9	27	Co	Cobalt	58.933
10	28	Ni	Nickel	58.693
11	29	Cu	Copper	63.546
12	30	Zn	Zinc	65.39
13	31	Ga	Gallium	69.723
14	32	Ge	Germanium	72.61
15	33	As	Arsenic	74.922
16	34	Se	Selenium	78.96
17	35	Br	Bromine	79.904
18	36	Kr	Krypton	83.80
1	37	Rb	Rubidium	85.468
2	38	Sr	Strontium	87.62
3	39	Y	Yttrium	88.906
4	40	Zr	Zirconium	91.224
5	41	Nb	Niobium	92.906
6	42	Mo	Molybdenum	95.94
7	43	Tc	Technetium	(98)
8	44	Ru	Ruthenium	101.07
9	45	Rh	Rhodium	102.906
10	46	Pd	Palladium	106.42
11	47	Ag	Silver	107.868
12	48	Cd	Cadmium	112.411
13	49	In	Indium	114.82
14	50	Sn	Tin	118.710
15	51	Sb	Antimony	121.757
16	52	Te	Tellurium	127.60
17	53	I	Iodine	126.904
18	54	Xe	Xenon	131.29
1	55	Cs	Cesium	132.905
2	56	Ba	Barium	137.327
3	57	La	Lanthanum	138.906
4	72	Hf	Hafnium	178.49
5	73	Ta	Tantalum	180.948
6	74	W	Tungsten	183.85
7	75	Re	Rhenium	186.207
8	76	Os	Osmium	190.2
9	77	Ir	Iridium	192.22
10	78	Pt	Platinum	195.08
11	79	Au	Gold	196.967
12	80	Hg	Mercury	200.59
13	81	Tl	Thallium	204.383
14	82	Pb	Lead	207.2
15	83	Bi	Bismuth	208.980
16	84	Po	Polonium	(209)
17	85	At	Astatine	(210)
18	86	Rn	Radon	(222)
1	87	Fr	Francium	(223)
2	88	Ra	Radium	(226.025)
3	89	Ac	Actinium	227.028
4	104	Unq	Unnilquadium	(261)
5	105	Unp	Unnilpentium	(262)
6	106	Unh	Unnilhexium	(263)
7	107	Uns	Unnilseptium	(262)
8	108	Uno	Unniloctium	(265)
9	109	Une	Unnilennium	(266)

INNER TRANSITION METALS

Lanthanide series:

Z	Symbol	Name	Atomic mass
58	Ce	Cerium	140.115
59	Pr	Praseodymium	140.908
60	Nd	Neodymium	144.24
61	Pm	Promethium	(145)
62	Sm	Samarium	150.36
63	Eu	Europium	151.96
64	Gd	Gadolinium	157.25
65	Tb	Terbium	158.925
66	Dy	Dysprosium	162.50
67	Ho	Holmium	164.930
68	Er	Erbium	167.26
69	Tm	Thulium	168.934
70	Yb	Ytterbium	173.04
71	Lu	Lutetium	174.967

Actinide series:

Z	Symbol	Name	Atomic mass
90	Th	Thorium	232.038
91	Pa	Protactinium	231.036
92	U	Uranium	238.029
93	Np	Neptunium	237.048
94	Pu	Plutonium	(244)
95	Am	Americium	(243)
96	Cm	Curium	(247)
97	Bk	Berkelium	(247)
98	Cf	Californium	(251)
99	Es	Einsteinium	(252)
100	Fm	Fermium	(257)
101	Md	Mendelevium	(258)
102	No	Nobelium	(259)
103	Lr	Lawrencium	(260)

number of positive charges, or protons, for an element. Atomic mass is the mass of one atom of the element, as compared to a standard. The accepted standard is a form (isotope) of carbon with a mass of 12.0000. One atomic mass unit is then defined as $\frac{1}{12}$ the mass of the standard. All atomic masses are measured as some number of atomic mass units (amu). For example, hydrogen has an atomic mass of 1 amu, oxygen's atomic mass is 16 amu, and nitrogen's atomic mass is 14 amu.

The periodic table is organized to provide information about the characteristics of elements. For example, elements in group 1, at the left of the table, have one electron in the outer energy levels of their atoms. They are highly reactive and tend to lose one electron and become positively charged ions (each forms a +1 ion). Atoms of elements in group 2 tend to lose two electrons. Atoms of elements at the right of the table, such as oxygen and chlorine, tend to gain electrons, becoming negatively charged ions. (See Figure 2.5.) The behavior of elements such as carbon, nitrogen, and phosphorus is more difficult to predict. Those elements react differently depending on the other elements present for a reaction.

Appendix 2B
Radioisotopes and Research in Biology

Radioactive tracers and labels are valuable research tools in biology. Use of radioactive isotopes made possible many important discoveries about cells and their functions.

Radioactive isotopes are elements that have unstable atomic nuclei. For example, the common form of the element carbon is carbon-12 (with six protons and six neutrons). Carbon-14 (with two extra neutrons) is a radioactive isotope. Over time, the nuclei of unstable radioactive isotopes give off subatomic particles and energy as they break down to a more stable atomic form. The decay of radioactive isotopes occurs at a constant rate known as the half-life. The decay of carbon-14 is very slow. It takes 5730 years for half of the carbon-14 in any specific sample to decay to nitrogen-14. This steady and predictable rate of decay can be used in radioactive dating of

fossils and minerals (Appendix 4A). Other radioactive isotopes decay much more quickly and reach a stable condition in days or weeks.

Radioactive isotopes can be introduced into living systems and cells as molecular tracers or labels. Special decay-counting instruments such as a Geiger counter can detect the energy given off by the isotopes as they decay. Thus, the pathway of the isotopes in chemical reactions can be followed. For example, Melvin Calvin and his co-workers introduced carbon dioxide containing radioactive carbon-14 into photosynthetic algae. Then they traced the path of carbon-14 as the algae produced sugars in photosynthesis. Radioactive nucleotides can be used to study the synthesis and fate of DNA and RNA in cells.

Appendix 4A
Radiometric Dating Methods

Accurate dating of rocks and fossils provides important information about the history of Earth and of organisms. Dating methods use the decay of radioisotopes (Appendix 2B) such as carbon-to-nitrogen, potassium-to-argon, and uranium-to-lead. Researchers used radiometric dating methods to determine the age of the oldest fossils at approximately 3.5 billion years.

The most important direct method of dating young fossils, or other organic matgerial, is through the decay of radiocarbon, carbon-14. In the upper atmosphere, bombardment by cosmic rays transforms nitrogen into carbon-14, an unstable form of carbon (Figure 4A.1a). The carbon-14 reacts with oxygen to form carbon dioxide molecules, and filters down into the lower atmosphere where all living things absorb it (Figure 4A.1b). When an organism dies, however, it absorbs no new carbon, and the carbon-14 slowly decays into nitrogen-14 (Figure 4A.1c). Assuming the production of carbon-14 in the atmosphere is constant, the proportion of carbon-14 to nitrogen-14 in once-living material indicates how long it has been since the organism died. There are, however, two limitations to this technique. One is that the half-life of carbon-14 is

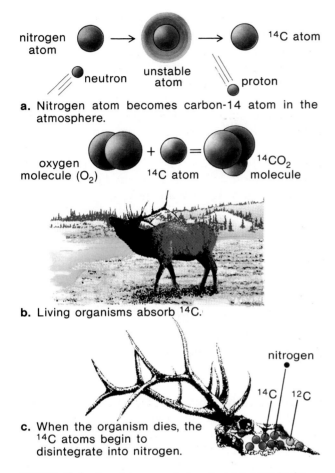

a. Nitrogen atom becomes carbon-14 atom in the atmosphere.

b. Living organisms absorb ^{14}C.

c. When the organism dies, the ^{14}C atoms begin to disintegrate into nitrogen.

FIGURE 4A.1 A certain amount of carbon-14 exists in the atmosphere as carbon dioxide, and plants incorporate it into their tissues. Animals absorb the carbon-14 by eating plants. When an organism dies, the carbon-14 decays at a known rate. The amount of carbon-14 remaining can be measured to determine the approximate age of the organism's remains.

only 5730 years. If a specimen is 57 300 years old, 10 half-lives have elapsed. As a result, so little of the original carbon-14 remains that it is difficult to measure accurately. The other disadvantage is that fossils and other organic material do not have much carbon-14 to begin with.

An indirect radiometric technique that has been in use since the 1960s is the potassium-40 method of dating. This dating method is the one commonly used for nonorganic material, and it indicates the age of sedimentary rocks that contain fossils. Potassium-40 isotopes decay into inert argon gas. In many types of rocks, the argon gas can accumulate as the potassium decays. In uncontaminated samples, the ratio of potassium-40 to argon-40 will tell how long it has been since the argon began to accumulate. Some event must link the deposit with the beginning of argon accumulation. The most common possibility is a volcanic eruption. The technique is useful where there are volcanic eruptions, and has provided the first dates for many ancient fossils. It is useful in other circumstances and was the technique NASA scientists used to determine the age of moon craters. Unlike carbon-14, potassium-40 has a long half-life (1.3 billion years), but it takes a long time for potassium-40 to decay into argon. We cannot use carbon-14 to date deposits that are very old, and we cannot use potassium-40 to date deposits that are relatively young. Though many researchers have claimed recent dates using potassium-40, these dates do not seem to be accurate on deposits younger than between 400 000 and 500 000 years.

Another radioactive "clock" depends on the decay of uranium into lead. When magma (molten rock) solidifies, uranium usually forms and the radioactive clock starts. As time passes, uranium-238 decays into lead-206, and uranium-235 decays into lead-207. Under favorable conditions both isotopes of lead remain locked in the rock. In the laboratory, it is possible to measure the amount of lead isotopes. Radiometric dating of rocks more than 2 billion years old has a probable error of less than 1 percent using the uranium-to-lead method.

There are many uncertainties in radioactive dating techniques, and the methods require sophisticated equipment and exacting methodology. If two or more methods provide similar data, the age is usually accepted as reliable.

Appendix 5A
Early Classification Schemes

The Greek philosopher and naturalist Aristotle, who lived about 384–322 B.C., knew of only a few hundred types of animals and plants. Yet Aristotle faced the same problems of classification as biologists today. The major problem was, and still is, whether the common characteristics of a group should be emphasized, or whether each type of animal or plant should be treated separately.

Aristotle and one of his pupils tried to classify the small number of species they knew. They classified the plants as herbs, shrubs, or trees. On the other hand, they grouped animals according to where they lived: air, land, or water. Another philosopher developed a system that divided animals into the useful ones, the harmful ones, and the unnecessary ones. Many other systems were used by other people, but each system was based only upon limited, and often subjective, observation.

The Swedish naturalist, Carolus Linnaeus, felt that the major goal of science is to find order in nature. He believed each organism had its special place in the pattern of life. It was his ambition to classify every species according to its proper place in this pattern. Linnaeus spent his life changing and adding to his work of classifying animals and plants. The present-day classification system can be traced back to Linnaeus' major work, *Systema Naturae* (10th edition, 1758).

Linnaeus grouped organisms according to their physical characteristics. He based his system on two assumptions: (1) that each species has an ideal type, a standard specimen to which each individual organism can be compared, and (2) that the number and type of each species is fixed and unchanging. Linnaeus' method grouped each organism with the ideal type that it most resembled. The fact that organisms often differed from the standard type as much as they resembled it was a problem Linnaeus' system did not try to solve. Though his classification scheme seemed to work better than any earlier one, it did not explain variation among organisms within a single species.

Appendix 6A
Preparing Cells for Study

Cells are very small and complex. It is difficult to directly observe their structure and discover their composition. It is even more difficult to find out how their various components function. For more than 300 years scientists have worked to develop a variety of techniques to study cells. The strength and limitations of each technique have largely determined our concept of the structure and function of the cell.

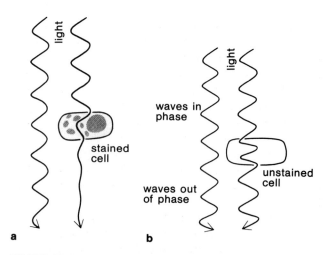

FIGURE 6A.1 The stained portions of the cell in (*a*) bend certain light waves more than others as light passes through the cell. The resulting differences in color make cell structures more visible than in an unstained cell (*b*), which scarcely bends the light waves. Certain changes do occur in the light passing through an unstained cell, however. These changes are utilized to produce a high-contrast image in phase-contrast and differential-interference-contrast microscopy.

Except for water, most cell contents do not interfere with the passage of light through the cell. (See Figure 6A.1.) Therefore, untreated cells are almost invisible when viewed through an ordinary light microscope. One way to make them more visible is to stain them.

The use of stains for preparing tissue samples was a direct outgrowth of the demand for dyes in the nineteenth-century textile industry. Some of the dyes were found to stain tissues and also unexpectedly showed an affinity for particular parts of the cell, such as the nucleus or membrane. This differential staining allowed the internal structure of the cell to be seen clearly. Today, many of the organic dyes available bind specifically to particular cellular components. For example, methylene blue binds to proteins, and fuschin (FYOO shin) binds to DNA. The chemical basis for the affinity of some dyes, however, is not known.

Techniques for observing the components of cells that are even more specific than organic dyes are available. For example, certain enzymes can be located in cells by exposing them to substrates that produce a visible product. Antibodies against specific macromolecules can be covalently bonded to a fluorescent dye and then used to mark the distribution of that macromolecule in the cell.

Before they can be stained, most tissues must be fixed. Fixation makes the cells permeable to stains and stabilizes their macromolecules. Some of the earliest fixation techniques involved brief immersion in acid, or organic solvents such as methanol. Current procedures usually include exposure of the cell to compounds that form covalent bonds with free amino groups of proteins, thereby linking adjacent molecules.

Most tissues are too thick for their cells to be examined without further preparation and must first be cut into thin slices or sections. The tissues are cut with a microtome, a machine that operates somewhat like a meat slicer. Then the sectioned tissue is placed on a glass microscope slide and stained.

Tissues are generally too soft to be cut directly into thin sections. After fixation, they are embedded in a liquid wax or plastic resin that surrounds and permeates the cell. This preparation is hardened to a solid block and then sectioned by the microtome. Frozen tissue can be cut by a special microtome kept in a cold chamber. Frozen sections produced in this way represent a more original form of the tissue, but they are difficult to prepare and the presence of ice crystals can cause many details to be lost.

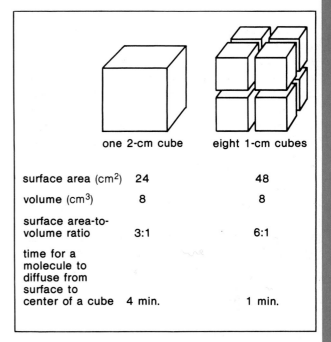

	one 2-cm cube	eight 1-cm cubes
surface area (cm^2)	24	48
volume (cm^3)	8	8
surface area-to-volume ratio	3:1	6:1
time for a molecule to diffuse from surface to center of a cube	4 min.	1 min.

FIGURE 6B.1 The single 2-cm cube and the eight 1-cm cubes all have the same total volume. As the volume is divided into smaller units, the amount of surface area increases. The single cube represents a large, unicellular organism that must exchange materials at the surface and move materials to the center. In a multicellular organism, represented by the eight cubes, transport problems are reduced by the larger surface area available for material exchange.

Appendix 6B
Constraints on Cell Size

Eukaryotic cells generally are much larger than prokaryotic cells. Yet in most multicellular organisms, cells are minute compared to the size of the entire organism. With a few exceptions, cells of large organisms are only 5 to 20 μm in diameter.

In general, small cell size is dictated by the relative inefficiency and slowness of diffusion. Problems that result from the changing ratio of surface area-to-volume with increasing size also limit cell size.

Diffusion is often demonstrated by dropping a dye into water. In organisms, the extracellular matrix and intracellular fluid are much thicker, and diffusion is comparatively slow. Moreover, the rate of diffusion is proportional to the distance of diffusion squared (distance^2). Thus, if a distance is doubled, it takes four times, not two times, longer for a molecule to diffuse across that distance.

Surface area is a measure of how much of the surface of the plasma membrane is exposed to the external environment. Exposure is necessary for the exchange of materials discussed in sections 6.6 and 6.7. Materials passing through the membrane must diffuse throughout the cell. If cells were larger, they would have more internal volume than could be accommodated by the surface area (Figure 6B.1). If a cell were doubled in size, the surface area would only increase fourfold, but the internal volume would increase eightfold. The difference of surface area-to-volume ratio becomes even more pronounced as cells become larger. At some point, the size would be too large to provide sufficient surface area on the plasma membrane to service the volume of cytoplasm. It would be physically impossible for enough material to move through the relatively small surface area of membrane to nourish the relatively large volume of cell contents.

Thus, the larger the cell, the less the amount of material that can be moved into the cell per unit of cell volume, and the more time it takes to move the material to the center of the cell. Small cells, in comparison to large cells, are much more efficient. Small cells have an optimum surface area-to-volume ratio for efficient exchange of materials between the cell and its environment. Large organisms are composed of millions of small cells that are more efficient for materials exchange, fed by transport systems (section 6.10 and Chapter 19).

Appendix 7A
The Mechanisms of Stomate Opening

Stomates in leaves open because the guard cells absorb water and swell. It would first appear that this swelling would cause the guard cells to close rather than open. The best current model of stomatal opening is based on the presence of special submicroscopic cellulose fibers called micelles in the walls of the guard cells. These fibers radiate from the area near the center of the two guard cells, much like the spokes of a wheel. (See Figure 7A.1.) When the guard cells absorb water, their diameter does not increase because the micelles do not stretch very much. Gaps between the micelles, however, allow the guard cells to increase in length. The guard cells are attached to one another at each end. The attachments and the radial orientation of the micelles cause the guard cells to bend outward when they absorb water. As a result, the stomate opens.

How are these changes in swelling brought about? Changes in several external factors can trigger stomate opening and closing: light, water, carbon dioxide, and temperature. Light generally causes opening, and darkness causes closing. Wilting (a lack of water in the leaves) or an increase in carbon dioxide around the leaves may cause closure. In addition, a change in temperature frequently causes stomates to open or close.

If such widely different environmental changes can result in the opening or closing of stomates, what precisely causes this action? The opening of stomates in light appears to be correlated with the

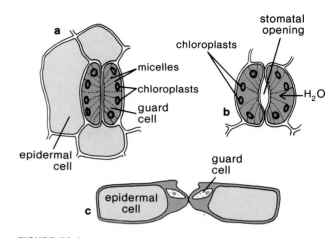

FIGURE 7A.1 A pair of guard cells controls the opening and closing of a stomate; (*a*) closed stomate, bottom view; (*b*) open stomate; (*c*) closed stomate, side view.

accumulation of potassium ions in the guard cells. A decrease in the level of carbon dioxide in the intercellular spaces and in the guard cells induces the guard cells to accumulate potassium ions by active transport. Potassium accumulation is followed by water absorption and stomate opening. Low levels of carbon dioxide may occur when the stomates are closed or only partly open and light strikes the leaf, activating photosynthesis. The reactions apparently require cellular energy supplied by ATP produced in the normal processes of photosynthesis and cellular respiration.

Appendix 7B
ATP Synthesis in Chloroplasts and Mitochondria

In 1961, British biochemist Peter Mitchell proposed a hypothesis to explain the synthesis of ATP in chloroplasts and mitochondria. The process links chemical reactions and transport. Mitchell called the process chemiosmosis, from the Greek *osmos*, to push. He won the Nobel Prize in 1978 for his work.

The chemiosmotic model of ATP synthesis is an example of the relationship between structure and function. Most ATP is made by enzymes called ATP synthetases that are inserted in membranes. The

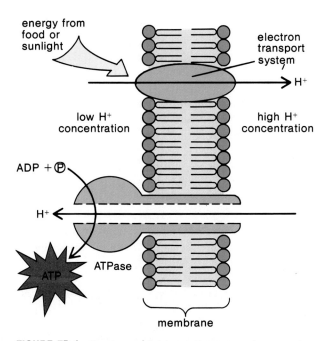

FIGURE 7B.1 Food or sunlight supplies energy to generate a proton gradient by way of an electron transport system. ATP forms as protons diffuse down a concentration gradient through the membrane enzyme ATP synthetase (ATPase).

enzymes use a concentration gradient of protons as an energy source to make ATP. The Mitchell hypothesis proposes that the energy to establish the proton gradient comes from the flow of electrons through electron transport systems in membranes. As electrons flow through the thylakoids of chloroplasts or the cristae of mitochondria, they release energy that is used to "pump," or expel, protons (H^+ ions) to one side of the membrane.

A proton gradient results, with a higher concentration of protons in the solution on one side of the membrane than on the other side. The relatively high concentration of protons is highly organized and can store energy. ATP synthetase uses that stored energy to form ATP from ADP and phosphate as the protons diffuse down the concentration gradient and through the enzyme (Figure 7B.1). Thus, the energy from electron flow is used to concentrate protons and ultimately to synthesize ATP. In chloroplasts, light supplies the energy to drive the electron flow. In mitochondria, the original energy for electron flow comes from the sugars, fats, or proteins used in respiration.

Appendix 8A
ATP Synthesis in Animal Cells

NADH produced in the cytosol during glycolysis cannot directly enter a mitochondrion. Instead, the hydrogen atoms from NADH are passed to other molecules that "shuttle" them across the mitochondrial membrane. In liver, kidney, and heart cells, hydrogen atoms are shuttled from NADH in the cytosol to NAD^+ in the mitochondrion, again forming NADH. Each NADH gives rise to three molecules of ATP in the electron transport system; thus, a total of 38 ATP can be synthesized from each molecule of glucose respired to carbon dioxide in these cells. (Review Table 8.3 for sources of ATP molecules.)

In skeletal muscle and brain cells, however, the hydrogen atoms from NADH formed during glycolysis are shuttled through the mitochondrial mem-

FIGURE 8A.1 The two hydrogen shuttles in animal cells

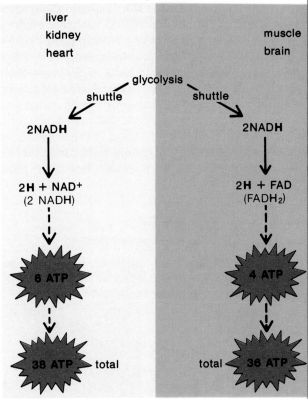

brane to FAD instead of to NAD^+. Each resulting molecule of $FADH_2$ gives rise to only two molecules of ATP in the electron transport system (instead of the three ATP for NADH). For each glucose molecule respired in these animal cells, two molecules of $FADH_2$ are substituted for two NADH molecules in the mitochondrion. As a result, the total number of ATP molecules produced per molecule of glucose is only 36. Figure 8A.1 on the previous page compares the two shuttle systems.

Appendix 11A
Pollination by Insects Aids Fertilization

Although the flowers of many plants have both male and female organs, most species have some means of cross-pollination. This adaptation provides for more genetic variety than self-pollination and thus has been selected for as flowering plants have evolved.

Insects are often the agents that carry pollen from one plant to another. The fossil record indicates that flowering plants and insects probably evolved together; evidence for this relationship is their parallel successes once both groups appeared on land. The most striking characteristics of flowers—their colors, scents, and unusual shapes—are adaptations that attract insects. Pollination by insects makes fertilization more likely. In some cases, the adaptation of plant and insect is intertwined. A single species of insect may be totally or mainly responsible for the pollination of a single plant species. One of the most

extraordinary examples of such a relationship is that of the yucca plant and the pronuba moth of the southwestern United States (Figure 11A.1).

When the yucca flowers open up, several small pronuba moths, apparently attracted by the fragrance, fly into the blossoms and mate there. The female moth then collects pollen from the anthers of that flower and rolls it into a ball. Then she flies to another yucca flower, bores into its ovary, and deposits a fertilized egg into the opening she has made. Afterwards, she carries the ball of pollen to the stigma above the ovary that will serve as a hatching place for the egg. She presses the pollen into the sticky stigma, increasing the chances of pollen tube formation. This behavior is repeated until several eggs are in the ovary and several balls of pollen dot the stigma of the same blossom. Somewhat later, the moth eggs hatch into larvae that feed on a few, but by no means all, of the seeds that have begun to mature within the ovary of the yucca blossom.

Both the yucca and the pronuba moth benefit from this remarkable relationship. Neither organism can complete its full life cycle without the other. In an area where pronuba moths were accidentally destroyed, yucca blossoms were not pollinated and, of course, no seeds later developed. This circumstance illustrates the interdependence of these two organisms. Other insects that are attracted to a yucca blossom may derive benefit for themselves but are unlikely to pollinate the flowers.

Appendix 12A
The Chi-Square Test

Suppose that in studying a test-cross between two types of tomato plants, a scientist expects half the offspring to have green leaves and half to have yellow. In the actual experiment, however, 671 out of 1240 seedlings turn out to have green leaves, and 569 out of the 1240 have yellow leaves. Is this a minor difference due to chance, or is it a relatively significant deviation from the expected numbers?

Scientists have devised a method to determine whether or not a deviation from expected experimental results is large enough to be significant. This

FIGURE 11A.1 A yucca, *Yucca glauca* (*left*), and a Pronuba moth (*right*) on the carpel of a yucca flower

TABLE 12A.1   Values for Chi-Square Test

Number of Classes	χ^2 Values							
2	0.0002	0.004	0.455	1.074	1.642	2.706	3.841	6.635
3	0.020	0.103	1.386	2.408	3.219	4.605	5.991	9.210
4	0.115	0.352	2.366	3.665	4.642	6.251	7.815	11.345
Number of times per hundred that chance alone would produce a deviation as large or larger	99	95	50	30	20	10	5	1

method is called the chi-square test. It consists of two steps: (1) calculating the chi-square (χ^2) value for the data in question, and (2) determining how often a chi-square value of that size is likely to result from chance alone.

The chi-square value is a measure of the deviation between observed and expected experimental results. In mathematical shorthand, this value can be expressed as follows:

$$\chi^2 = \Sum \frac{\left(\begin{matrix}\text{observed} \\ \text{number}\end{matrix} - \begin{matrix}\text{expected} \\ \text{number}\end{matrix}\right)^2}{\text{expected number}}$$

where χ is the Greek letter "chi" and Σ is the Greek letter "sigma," standing for "sum" and meaning here "the sum of all." See how this formula is used to find the chi-square value for the experiment described above. In that experiment, 620 green-leaved plants and 620 yellow-leaved plants were expected, but the numbers observed were 671 and 569 respectively. Therefore,

$$\chi^2 = \frac{(671 - 620)^2}{620} + \frac{(569 - 620)^2}{620}$$

$$= \frac{(51)^2}{620} + \frac{(-51)^2}{620} = \frac{2601 + 2601}{620}$$

$$= \frac{5202}{620} = 8.4$$

Thus, the value of chi-square for this experiment is 8.4. What does the value mean? How do you know if this value is significant?

Mathematicians have compiled tables to provide a basis for judging how likely any chi-square value is of having arisen by chance alone. By consulting Table 12A.1, you will see that a chi-square value of 8.4 for just two classes (green-leaved plants and

yellow-leaved plants) is larger than any of the values listed. This value means that the probability that this deviation is the result of chance alone is less than 1 in 100. By custom, when the probability that a deviation would occur by chance alone is as low as (or less than) 5 in 100, the deviation is said to result from other causes. Such a deviation is said to be statistically significant, that is, the results differ from those that were expected. In the case of the green- and yellow-leaved tomato plants, for example, subsequent studies showed that fewer of the yellow-leaved plants germinated and survived; they were less hardy than the green-leaved ones.

How is the chi-square test applied to experimental results involving more than two classes of objects or events? Suppose, for example, that a scientist has crossed pink-flowered four-o'clocks and obtained 236 offspring. From Mendel's laws, the offspring are expected to be red-, pink-, and white-flowered in the ratio of 1:2:1. For the 236 offspring, this ratio would mean 59 red, 118 pink, and 59 white. But the actual results are 66 red, 115 pink, and 55 white. The chi-square test is applied as follows:

$$\chi^2 = \frac{(66 - 59)^2}{59} + \frac{(115 - 118)^2}{118} + \frac{(55 - 59)^2}{59}$$

$$= \frac{49}{59} + \frac{9}{118} + \frac{16}{59} = \frac{98 + 9 + 32}{118}$$

$$= \frac{139}{118} = 1.18$$

By consulting the table, you will see that a chi-square value of 1.18 for three classes is really quite small. Between 50 and 95 times in 100 a value this large or larger might be produced by chance alone. The experimenter therefore concludes that the observed results agree with those predicted.

Appendix 12B
Gene Mapping

Linked genes are inherited together unless recombination occurs betwene their chromosome sites. In 1971, A. H. Sturtevant, one of Thomas Morgan's students, suggested that recombination frequencies are proportional to the distance separating two genes on a chromosome. He defined a *map unit* as a 1 percent recombination frequency. With this standard of measurement, the mutant genes for black body and vestial wings in *Drosophila*, for example, are described as 17 map units apart; thus, they have a recombination frequency of nearly 17 percent. By determining recombination frequencies in many different crosses, Sturtevant and his co-workers were able to determine the linkage groups and linear arrangement of the known *Drosophila* genes.

In human genetics, determining linkage and map distance of genes has been more difficult. Two genes must be located on the same chromosome and close enough to reveal their linkage; at least one parent must be heterozygous for both genes; how the genes were inherited from the grandparent generation must be known; and recombination of the genes must be obvious in offspring.

These criteria may be met more easily for X-linked genes than for autosomal genes because the phenotype of a grandfather and his grandsons is determined by single copies of these genes. If a mother has a mutant allele for both color blindness (*c*) and hemophilia (*h*) on one X chromosome and normal alleles for these genes (*C, H*) on the other, her sons would be expected to be either color-blind and hemophiliac or normal for both traits. The percentage of times that either a color-blind, nonhemophiliac son, or a normal-sighted, hemophiliac son is born reveals the map distance between these two genes. Recombination has been found to occur between these genes 10 percent of the time. Therefore, the eggs this mother produces would be 45 percent *CH*, 45 percent *ch*, 5 percent *Ch*, and 5 percent *cH*. Given the low frequencies of these mutant alleles in the population, and the few children produced in most families, you can see why the task of mapping human genes has proceeded slowly.

How have technological advances accelerated the mapping of human chromosomes? In 1960, molecular biologists learned to fuse cells from different organisms. The nuclei of these hybrid cells contained the chromosomes from both cells. Human skin cells and mouse cells were fused, and as the hybrid cells divided in culture, many of the human chromosomes were lost. Often one chromosome or only a piece of a human chromosome was left in a stabilized cell line. Any human protein produced by such hybrid cells had to come from a gene located on the remaining chromosome. With this technique, many genes were mapped to specific chromosomes and roughly located along the chromosomes.

Recombinant DNA technology has provided new tools for mapping genes. Restriction fragment length polymorphisms (RFLPs) are used as reference points, or genetic markers, along the chromosomes. When individuals of a family with a genetic disorder also share an unusual RFLP, that RFLP may serve as a marker of the disorder. The frequency with which the disorder and the marker are inherited together indicates the distance between the two locations. The closer a disease-causing gene and a linked RFLP are, the more often they will be inherited together and the more reliable the marker.

Humans have 3 billion DNA nucleotides distributed over their 23 pairs of chromosomes. A distance of approximately 1.5 million nucleotides between markers (approximately one map unit) means that the markers will recombine only 1 percent of the time. A gene may be only 10 000 nucleotides long. Thus there may be many genes between two RFLP sites, but the sites still can be linked closely enough to allow 99 percent accuracy in predicting the presence of one RFLP from the presence of the other.

Researchers are working to develop a complete human gene map. The DNA from large families (three generations with many children) is cut up with restriction enzymes and analyzed for RFLP polymorphisms. This DNA is being shared with scientists worldwide; their findings are collected in computerized data banks. Potential benefits from this effort include the ability to locate and study the genes responsible for the more than 4000 recognized genetic disorders and the combinations of genes that appear to cause illnesses such as hypertension, heart disease, and certain cancers. The identification, isolation, and cloning of human genes will enable scientists to study how genes function at the molecular level. Determining the products of these genes may lead to new methods of preventing and treating genetic disorders.

Many people support the Human Genome Project (HGP), which may develop a complete human gene map. Yet some researchers are concerned that this multibillion-dollar, 15-year project would take needed funds from other areas of scientific research. Even if a complete human gene map were developed, they say, it would not yield immediate understanding of how the DNA sequence is translated. For example, the map would not explain how nerve cells become connected in the complex structure of the brain, nor provide answers to how individuals differ.

What use should be made of the new genetic information? Among the most important questions are those about personal freedom, privacy, and societal rights versus individual rights of access to genetic information. For example, could such information be used to deny employment? What would be the impact of discovering that, genetically, humans are less equal than we now suppose? These and other questions must be considered in any policy decisions about the human gene map.

Appendix 15A
Elements Required by Plants

Element	Function	Deficiency
Macronutrients		
Calcium	Component of cell walls; enzyme cofactor; involved in cell membrane permeability; encourages root development	Characterized by death of the growing points
Magnesium	Part of the chlorophyll molecule; many enzymes	Development of pale, sickly foliage, an unhealthy condition known as chlorosis
Nitrogen	Component of amino acids, chlorophyll, coenzymes, and proteins. An excess causes vigorous vegetative growth and suppresses food storage and fruit and seed development	Early symptom is yellowing of leaves, followed by a stunting in the growth of all parts of the plant.
Phosphorus	Promotes root growth and hastens maturity, particularly of cereal grains	Underdeveloped root system; all parts of plant stunted
Potassium	Enzyme activator; production of chlorophyll	Pale, sickly foliage
Sulfur	Component of some amino acids	Chlorosis; poor root system
Micronutrients		
Boron	Pollen germination; regulation of carbohydrate metabolism	Darker leaves; abnormal growth; malformations
Chlorine	Production of oxygen during photosynthesis	Small leaves; slow growth
Copper	Component of some enzymes	Lowered protein synthesis
Iron	Needed for chlorophyll production	Chlorosis, appearing first in youngest leaves
Manganese	Activates Krebs cycle enzymes	Mottled leaves
Molybdenum	Part of enzymes needed for nitrate reduction	Severe stunting of older leaves
Zinc	Component of some enzymes; stem elongation	Small leaves; short distances between leaves

Appendix 16A
Spontaneous Generation

Early Greek philosophers observed events in nature but did not carry out experiments to verify their observations. For example, they observed that pond life seems to disappear when ponds dry up, and reappear when the ponds fill with rain. All the animals and other organisms that reappeared were not observed in the raindrops, so the Greeks assumed that the organisms formed from the mud on the bottom of the ponds. These and similar events were carefully described and recorded with the observation: "Life can be renewed by Earth itself."

The eggs of most pond organisms are small and difficult to observe. Microscopes were unknown, as were laboratory methods of collecting organisms and observing their reproduction and development. The Greek observers knew that organisms reproduced, yet they had no reason to believe that this was the only method by which organisms could arise. To them, reproduction explained neither life's origin (as it does not today) nor its reappearance following fires, drought, or other natural occurrences. The belief in the spontaneous generation of life from Earth or from other materials appeared to be a straightforward observation that anyone could make.

From the fourth century B.C. to the seventeenth century A.D., spontaneous generation was a widely accepted idea. As experimentation was introduced to biology, however, some biologists openly expressed skepticism. Yet even as they designed experiments to test some of the accepted observations, new examples of spontaneous generation were reported. As late as 1652, an experiment by a Belgian physician described the spontaneous generation of mice. Baby mice appeared in 21 days, the report stated, in a pot containing only a sweaty shirt and kernels of wheat. The sweat in the shirt was cited as the important ingredient.

Spontaneous generation of maggots on decaying meat was one of the widely observed examples supporting this belief. In an experiment in which meat was kept covered (and, therefore, inaccessible to flies), no maggots appeared. Disproof of spontaneous generation was not this simple, however. Critics of the experiment claimed that the cover over the meat kept out a needed ingredient in the air. The experiment was repeated with a finely meshed cloth that effectively kept all flies away from the meat but permitted air to circulate freely. No maggots appeared.

Even with this and other careful investigations, the possibility of spontaneous generation for some organisms was difficult to exclude. One by one the examples yielded—until only microorganisms remained in question. From the standpoint of the spontaneous generation controversy, microorganisms were discovered just in time to add another century or more to the dispute.

Once discovered—by the newly invented microscope—microorganisms were found everywhere. Wrapping or sealing foodstuffs was of no use against them. In many experiments, investigators even boiled liquid preparations in an effort to kill any microorganisms present. Table 16A.1 shows why this procedure did not always work. The dispute concerning spontaneous generation raged as microorganisms continued to appear in supposedly sterile liquids.

It was not until the nineteenth century that Louis Pasteur, working with yeast cells, was able to prove that microorganisms cannot arise from non-living matter. Pasteur prepared and boiled four yeast infusions in flasks for which he made long S-curved necks (Figure 16A.1 on the next page). Condensed water in the curved necks served as a trap for particles entering the open end. Pasteur left the flasks open, yet all remained sterile indefinitely. No microorganisms grew in the sterilized yeast infusions

TABLE 16A.1 Average Survival Time of Microorganisms in Boiling Water

Organisms	Survival Time (in minutes)
Protists	0
Bacteria	
most species	0
Bacillus subtilis	14
Clostridium perfringens	20
Clostridium botulinum	360

FIGURE 16A.1 Louis Pasteur at work in his laboratory

because air, without its impurities, did not affect the infusions. When methods similar to Pasteur's were used, spontaneous generation was no longer reported in experiments with microorganisms. Biologists at last united in accepting the idea that all organisms arise only from others of their type. They described this principle as *biogenesis*.

Appendix 16B
Hardy–Weinberg Principle

Early in the twentieth century the mathematician G. H. Hardy and the physician W. Weinberg recognized a mathematical relationship in the allele frequencies within a single population. According to this relationship, the frequencies would stay the same from generation to generation, unless acted on by natural selection, mating preferences, chance, or other factors.

There will be no frequency changes *only* if numerous conditions are met.

1. The population size must be large enough to offset the effects of probability on the frequencies of different alleles.

2. Natural selection must already have produced stability in the population. Natural selection must not act in such a way as to change the existing allele frequencies.

3. New mutations must not occur.

4. Mating effects should be random. If mating preferences do occur, the pattern must have the same effect overall as random mating.

5. Organisms with a different frequency of alleles or entirely different alleles do not migrate into the population.

6. Organisms with allele frequencies different from the population as a whole do not migrate out of the population.

No population meets all or even most of these conditions. Many populations, however, have stable frequencies for alleles that are studied. In fact, many large populations are found to maintain the same allele frequencies when studied over a number of generations.

In the Hardy–Weinberg Principle, the frequencies of two alleles are represented by the letters p and q. The allele for a dominant trait is represented by p. The allele for a recessive trait is represented by q. Figure 16B.1 represents a cross between two individuals. The cross is described using generalized algebraic numbers. This format is used for population gene analysis.

Figure 16B.2 on the next page reproduces information about the frequencies of two alleles for hair type in a population. In this example, S represents the allele for the dominant trait (straight hair), and corresponds to p. The symbol s represents the allele for the recessive trait (curly hair) and corresponds to q.

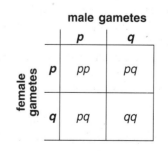

	male gametes	
	p	q
p	pp	pq
q	pq	qq

female gametes

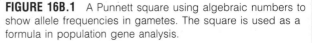

FIGURE 16B.1 A Punnett square using algebraic numbers to show allele frequencies in gametes. The square is used as a formula in population gene analysis.

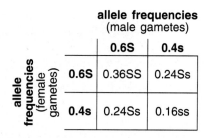

		allele frequencies (male gametes)	
		0.6S	**0.4s**
allele frequencies (female gametes)	**0.6S**	0.36SS	0.24Ss
	0.4s	0.24Ss	0.16ss

FIGURE 16B.2 Population gene analysis with data, showing frequencies in a population of two alleles for hair type.

Just as $0.6S$ plus $0.4s$ add up to 1, or 100 percent of the population, so do p and q always add up to 1, no matter how the two frequencies differ individually. Hence, $p + q = 1$ is one of two statements in the Hardy–Weinberg principle.

The other statement is: $p^2 + 2pq + q^2 = 1$. Using Figure 16B.2, you can see that for the population this mathematical statement becomes:

$$(0.60)^2 + 2(0.60)(0.40) + (0.40)^2 = 1$$

You can work out this equation to verify that the proportions of the population having straight hair or curly hair are those found in the data table.

The Hardy–Weinberg principle is useful for many population genetics problems. For example, about 0.040 percent of the population in the United States has cystic fibrosis. Cystic fibrosis is a recessive disorder, so only people with a pair of alleles for this disorder are affected. How can the proportion of people who do not carry even one such allele be determined?

In this case, $q^2 = 0.0004$ (0.040 percent of the population). Thus, q, the square root of q^2, is 0.020. This figure is the proportion of gametes with the defective allele. Since $p + q = 1$, $p = 0.980$. The proportion of people who are free of the allele is p^2, which is $(0.980)^2$, or 0.9604. Using the Hardy–Weinberg equation to represent the population yields the following:

p^2	+	$2pq$	+	q^2
0.96040		0.03920		0.00040
				(cystic fibrosis)

Roughly 96 percent of the U.S. population is free of the allele. Almost 4 percent (0.03920) are carriers (people with one defective allele).

It can be expected that about 0.040 percent of the population in the next generation will again have cystic fibrosis. This number assumes, of course, that no new mutations occur and that people with different alleles or allele frequencies do not move into or out of the population. This expected percentage also does not reflect any natural selection against cystic fibrosis victims, which would affect their contribution to the gene pool.

Appendix 17A
Physical Adaptations

In becoming a stable bipedal animal, the human ancestor underwent evolutionary changes in the shape and proportions of the foot, leg, and pelvic bones and also in the muscles of the legs and buttocks. A chimpanzee can walk rather comfortably on its hind legs, but not for long. It also can run surprisingly fast. Nonetheless, the chimpanzee's body is not adapted for efficient bipedal walking and running. Its feet are better adapted for gripping than for upright walking (Figure 17A.1b), as its big toes stick out to the side like thumbs instead of forward to provide spring in the stride. Its legs are too short and,

FIGURE 17A.1 A human foot (a) is adapted for bipedal walking. The different structure and function of a chimpanzee foot (b) makes prolonged bipedalism difficult.

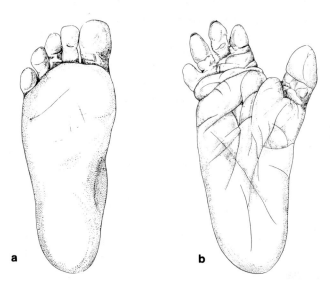

a   b

due to the small size and location of the buttock muscles, propulsion is limited. The muscles that the chimpanzee can use for bipedalism are attached to the bones in a way that supplies inefficient leverage for a vigorous stride. The chimpanzee walks upright in a waddle or rolling gait because it must shift its body weight at each step.

A more efficient method of walking erect is to have the legs straighter and closer together. This arrangement is possible in humans because of marked evolutionary changes in the shape and proportion of bones in the leg, foot, and particularly in the pelvis. Over time, there has been a twisting and flattening of the two large pelvic blades. The modern human pelvis helps place the torso more vertically over the legs and also provides better anchorage and leverage for the three sets of buttock muscles used in walking.

Appendix 17B
The Old Man from La Chapelle-aux-Saints

Fossils of archaic *Homo sapiens* from southwestern France were discovered in the first decade of the twentieth century. Among them was the skeleton of an old man from a cave near the village of La Chapelle-aux-Saints. This fossil was selected for reconstruction as a typical archaic specimen. The task of rebuilding the old man fell to a French paleontologist, Marcellin Boule.

Although there were abundant and well-preserved materials, Boule proceeded to commit an astonishing number of errors that were not recognized and corrected for decades. Boule misinterpreted the bones and made the individual appear much like an ape. He arranged the foot bones so that the big toe diverged from the other toes like an opposable thumb, thus forcing the man to walk on the outside of his feet. The knee joint could not be entirely extended, resulting in a bent-kneed gait. The spine lacked the curves that allow modern humans to stand upright, and the head was thrust so far forward that it appeared as if Boule's archaic human

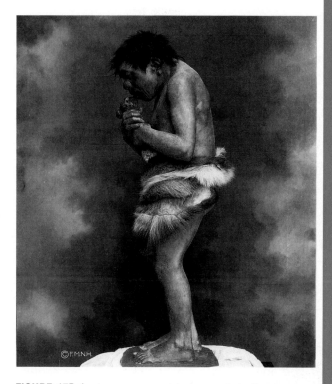

FIGURE 17B.1 A museum model of an archaic *Homo sapiens* based on an incorrect skeletal reconstruction

would have to use his arms to keep from falling on his face. In addition, Boule completely ignored the large cranial capacity (1600 cm^3) of the old man. Instead, Boule stated that there was not much room for the frontal portion of the brain, which was then incorrectly thought to be the center of higher intelligence. Boule ranked the archaic human's brainpower somewhere between that of apes and modern humans, but closer to the apes. The full reconstructions of archaic individuals were even more misleading (Figure 17B.1). The hunched shoulders and apelike posture were quite incorrect; worse still was the dull expression. Actually, archaic humans were probably of considerable intelligence.

The discovery of additional archaic *Homo sapiens* fossils slowly led to a contradiction of Boule's reconstruction of the old man from La Chapelle-aux-Saints. What had Boule done wrong? He had overlooked the effects of arthritis when he reconstructed the skeleton and allowed his biases to influence his interpretation. That oversight led him to incorrectly assume that all archaic people walked with a stooped gait and bent knees.

Appendix 17C
Cultural Evolution

Normally, the brains of mammalian fetuses grow rapidly, but usually the growth slows down and ceases shortly after birth. A prolonged growth period of the human skull, longer than for any other primate, allowed for a larger human brain. The extended developmental period lengthened the time parents were required to care for their offspring and subsequently extended the child's learning period. This learning is the basis of human culture—the transmission of accumulated knowledge through time by means of written or spoken language.

The first, very long stage in human cultural evolution probably began with hunters and gatherers of the African grasslands who later spread to other parts of the Old World. They made tools, divided labor, and probably organized communal activities. The second and much more recent stage came with the agricultural revolution in Eurasia and the Americas about 10 000 to 15 000 years ago. Along with agriculture came permanent settlements and eventually the first cities. The third major stage in human cultural evolution was the Industrial Revolution that began in the eighteenth century. Since then, new technology has grown exponentially. Through all of this recent cultural evolution, humans have not changed biologically in any significant way. We are probably no more intelligent than earlier modern humans. The know-how to build microcomputers or produce recombinant DNA is not stored in the human genes but is, instead, a product of hundreds of generations of human experience and the capacity for intelligence—which is inherited.

Evolution of the human brain may have been anatomically simpler than the change to walking upright, yet the consequences are enormous. Cultural evolution has made *Homo sapiens* a species that can modify its own environment. We do not have to wait to adapt to a new environment. Instead, we use artificial "adaptations"—clothing, irrigation, heated or cooled buildings, for example—or otherwise change the environment to suit our needs. Humans are the most numerous and widespread of all large animals. Everywhere we go we bring change, faster than many other species can adapt to. Of the many upheavals in the history of Earth, the emergence of humans is the latest and perhaps one of the greatest.

Appendix 18A
Dietary Guidelines

In 1992, the United States Department of Agriculture issued its *Daily Food Guide* in response to the public's increased interest in healthy eating. The *Daily Food Guide* differs from traditional plans by separating vegetables from fruits, resulting in six food groups—breads and cereals, vegetables, fruits, meats and their alternatives, milk and milk products, and the fats, oils, and sweets. (See Figure 18A.1.) The USDA recommends that the bulk of a healthy diet consist of foods from the lower three groups.

The topmost group contains fats and oils (lipids) and sweets (simple carbohydrates) that can be unhealthy when eaten too often or in large amounts. Excluding all lipids from a diet also can be unhealthy, particularly for infants and young children. However, as Figure 18A.1 illustrates, lipids and sugars occur throughout the other groups of the pyramid, and so are eaten in sufficient amounts in a

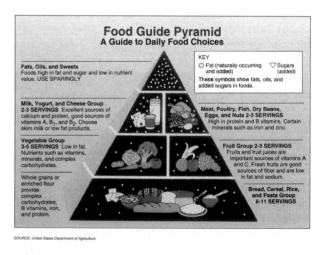

SOURCE: United States Department of Agriculture

FIGURE 18A.1 The USDA's Food Guide Pyramid, used to guide daily food choices. The relative size of the sections indicates that a healthy diet consists of more grains, then vegetables and fruits, less meats and dairy products, and very little fats, oils, and sweets.

healthy diet without frequent use of foods from the fats, oils, and sweets group.

Bread, cereal, rice, and pasta group: These foods are good sources of complex carbohydrates, riboflavin, thiamin, niacin, iron, protein, magnesium, and fiber; they also contain small amounts of fats and sugars. Foods in this category include whole grains (wheat, rice, barley, oats, sorghum, pearl millet) and their products, including enriched breads, tabouli, tortillas, some hot and cold cereals, pasta, and plain air-popped popcorn. Allow 6−11 servings per day.

Vegetable group: Vegetables and similar foods contribute substantial amounts of vitamin A, vitamin C, potassium, magnesium, and fiber to a healthy diet. Most are low in or lack fat and cholesterol. Examples include bean sprouts, cabbages, lettuces, broccoli, okra, squash, cucumber, tomato, sweet peas, corn on the cob, carrots, mushrooms, and potatoes. Allow 3−5 servings per day.

Fruit group: Fruits are characterized by significant amounts of vitamin A, vitamin C, potassium, and fiber. Most are low in or lack sodium, fat, and cholesterol. This category includes melons, citrus fruit (oranges, grapefruits), mangos, apples, carambolas (star fruit), bananas, fruit juices, and dried fruit. Allow 2−4 servings per day.

Meat, poultry, fish, dry beans, eggs, and nuts group: Some foods in this category have high lipid levels, but the group provides essential protein, phosphorus, vitamin B_6, vitamin B_{12}, zinc, magnesium, iron, niacin, and thiamin. Representative foods are poultry (chicken, turkey), fish, lean meats (beef, lamb, pork, veal), low-fat luncheon meats, legumes (soybeans, peanuts, lentils), tofu, eggs, and nuts. Allow 2−3 servings per day.

Milk, cheese, and yogurt group: This group supplies calcium, riboflavin, protein, vitamin B_{12}, and, when fortified, vitamin A and vitamin D. Some foods in this group can be high in lipids and added sugars, such as sour cream and ice cream. Examples of healthier choices include low-fat milks and cheeses, buttermilk, cottage cheese, and plain yogurt. Adults should allow 2 servings per day. Teens, young adults, pregnant or lactating women, and women past menopause should allow 3 servings per day. Pregnant or lactating teens should allow 4 servings per day.

Fats, oils, and sweets: Foods in this group contain substantial amounts of lipids—unsaturated fats, saturated fats, or cholesterol—and simple sugars. They provide very few nutrients and may also be high in salt. Examples include oils, salad dressings, mayonnaise, butter, cream cheese, gravy, potato chips, soft drinks, pastries, candy, jelly, and syrup. Alcoholic beverages also are part of this group; they provide calories, but very few vitamins and minerals.

The Department of Health and Human Services also urges most people to heed the following general recommendations.*

Fats and cholesterol: Reduce consumption of fat (especially saturated fat) and cholesterol. Choose foods relatively low in these substances, such as vegetables, fruits, whole grain foods, fish, poultry, lean meats, and low-fat dairy products. Use food preparation methods that add little or no fat.

Energy and weight control: Consult your physician to identify, achieve, and maintain a desirable body weight. To do so, choose a dietary pattern in which energy (caloric) intake is consistent with energy expenditure. To reduce energy intake, limit consumption of foods relatively high in calories, fats, and sugars, and minimize alcohol consumption. Increase energy expenditure through regular and sustained physical activity.

Complex carbohydrates and fiber: Increase consumption of whole grain foods (like bread) and cereal products, vegetables (including dried beans and peas), and fruits.

Sodium: Reduce intake of sodium by choosing foods relatively low in sodium content and limiting the amount of salt added during food preparation and at the table.

Alcohol: To reduce the risk for chronic disease, take alcohol only in moderation (no more than two drinks a day), if at all. Avoid drinking any alcohol before or while driving, operating machinery, taking medications, or engaging in any other activity requiring judgment. Avoid drinking alcohol while pregnant.

*from *The Surgeon General's Report on Nutrition and Health*, U.S. Department of Health and Human Services, DHHS Publication No. 88-50211, Washington, DC 20402: U.S. Government Printing Office, 1988.

Other Issues

Fluoride: Community water systems should contain fluoride at optimal levels for prevention of tooth decay. If such water is not available, use other appropriate sources of fluoride.

Calcium: Adolescent girls and adult women should increase consumption of foods high in calcium, including low-fat dairy products.

Iron: Children, adolescents, and women of child-bearing age should be sure to consume foods that are good sources of iron, such as lean meats, fish, certain beans, and iron-enriched cereals and whole grain products. This issue is of special concern for low-income families.

Sugars: Those who are particularly vulnerable to dental caries (cavities), especially children, should limit their consumption and frequency of use of foods high in sugars.

Appendix 18B
Fat and Fatty Acid Content of Some Foods

Food	Total Fat (% by Mass)	Fatty Acids (% of Fat) Saturated	Fatty Acids (% of Fat) Unsaturated
Cooking and Salad oils			
Safflower	100	9	74
Sunflower	100	10	66
Wheat germ	100	19	62
Corn	100	13	59
Soybean	100	14	58
Sesame	100	14	42
Peanut	100	17	32
Olive	100	14	8
Coconut	100	86	2
Vegetable shortening	100	25–30	12–26
Margarines			
Safflower oil	80	14	60
Corn oil	80	18	48
Corn or soy	80	20	28
Butter	81	62	4
Walnuts	64	11	62
Peanuts	51	18	27
Almonds	54	8	17
Avocado	17	19	12
Chicken or turkey	5–20	30	20
Pork	20–35	39	11
Beef or lamb	10–40	50	4
Salmon or trout	9	17	51
Tuna	2	41	30
Mayonnaise	79	15	52
Egg yolk	33	30	13

Appendix 18C
Fiber Values of Common Food

Food	Kcal per 100g	Total CHO*	Crude Fiber
Breads			
Whole wheat	243	47.8	17.4
White	270	47.8	**
Bran, raisin	308	56.7	10.4
Fruits (raw)			
Apple	58	14.5	1.0
Banana	85	22.2	0.5
Blackberries	58	12.9	4.1
Orange	49	12.2	0.5
Pear	61	15.3	1.4
Strawberries	37	8.4	1.3
Watermelon	26	6.4	0.3
Vegetables (raw)			
Asparagus	26	5.0	0.7
Beans, pinto	349	63.7	4.3
Beans, snap	32	7.1	1.0
Beet greens	24	4.6	1.3
Broccoli	32	5.9	1.5
Cabbage	24	5.4	0.8
Celery	17	3.9	0.6
Collards	40	7.2	0.9
Corn, sweet	96	22.1	0.7
Kale	38	6.0	1.3
Lettuce	14	2.5	0.5
Peas, green	84	14.4	2.0
Potatoes, white	76	17.1	0.5
Potatoes, sweet	114	26.3	0.7
Soybeans, mature	403	33.5	4.9
Spinach	26	4.3	0.6
Squash, summer	19	4.2	0.6
Tomatoes, ripe	22	4.7	0.5
Turnip, white root	30	6.6	0.9

*carbohydrates   **trace

Appendix 18D
Recommended Dietary Allowances (RDA), 1989*

	Age (yr)	Mass (kg)	Height (cm)	Energy (kcal)	Protein (g)	Vitamin A (µg)	Vitamin D (µg)	Vitamin E (mg)	Vitamin K (µg)	Vitamin C (mg)	Thiamin (mg)	Riboflavin (mg)	Niacin (mg)	Vitamin B$_6$ (mg)	Folate (µg)	Vitamin B$_{12}$ (µg)	Calcium (mg)	Phosphorus (mg)	Magnesium (mg)	Iron (mg)	Zinc (mg)	Iodine (µg)
Infants																						
	0.0–0.5	6	60	650	13	375	7.5	3	5	30	0.3	0.4	5	0.3	25	0.3	400	300	40	6	5	40
	0.5–1.0	9	71	850	14	375	10	4	10	35	0.4	0.5	6	0.6	35	0.5	600	500	60	10	5	50
Children																						
	1–3	13	90	1300	16	400	10	6	15	40	0.7	0.8	9	1.0	50	0.7	800	800	80	10	10	70
	4–6	20	112	1800	24	500	10	7	20	45	0.9	1.1	12	1.1	75	1.0	800	800	120	10	10	90
	7–10	28	132	2000	28	700	10	7	30	45	1.0	1.2	13	1.4	100	1.4	800	800	170	10	10	120
Males																						
	11–14	45	157	2500	45	1000	10	10	45	50	1.3	1.5	17	1.7	150	2.0	1200	1200	270	12	15	150
	15–18	66	176	3000	59	1000	10	10	65	60	1.5	1.8	20	2.0	200	2.0	1200	1200	400	12	15	150
	19–24	72	177	2900	58	1000	10	10	70	60	1.5	1.7	19	2.0	200	2.0	1200	1200	350	10	15	150
	25–50	79	176	2900	63	1000	5	10	80	60	1.5	1.7	19	2.0	200	2.0	800	800	350	10	15	150
	51+	77	173	2300	63	1000	5	10	80	60	1.2	1.4	15	2.0	200	2.0	800	800	350	10	15	150
Females																						
	11–14	46	157	2200	46	800	10	8	45	50	1.1	1.3	15	1.4	150	2.0	1200	1200	280	15	12	150
	15–18	55	163	2200	44	800	10	8	55	60	1.1	1.3	15	1.5	180	2.0	1200	1200	300	15	12	150
	19–24	58	164	2200	46	800	10	8	60	60	1.1	1.3	15	1.6	180	2.0	1200	1200	280	15	12	150
	25–50	63	163	2200	50	800	5	8	65	60	1.1	1.3	15	1.6	180	2.0	800	800	280	15	12	150
	51+	65	160	1900	50	800	5	8	65	60	1.0	1.2	13	1.6	180	2.0	800	800	280	10	12	150
Pregnant			+300	60	800	10	10	65	70	1.5	1.6	17	2.2	400	2.2	1200	1200	320	30	15	175	
Lactating																						
1st 6 months			+500	65	1300	10	12	65	95	1.6	1.8	20	2.1	280	2.6	1200	1200	355	15	19	200	
2nd 6 months			+500	62	1200	10	11	65	90	1.6	1.7	20	2.1	260	2.6	1200	1200	340	15	16	200	

Note: The Committee on Dietary Allowances has published a separate table showing estimated safe and adequate daily dietary intakes for selected vitamins and minerals. These tables appear in Appendix I. The FDA has published a special table of selected values for use on food labels; these appear on the opposite page.

Source: Recommended Dietary Allowances, 10th edition. © 1989 by the National Academy of Sciences, National Academy Press, Washington, D.C.

Appendix 19A
William Harvey Discovers Circulation

William Harvey was trained as a physician and scientist in England in the seventeenth century. At that time, no one knew that blood constantly circulates throughout the body. In medical school, Harvey was taught that blood flowed to and from the head over the same route and through the same vessels, much like the ebb and flow of the tides along the seashore.

One day, Harvey's anatomy teacher showed a group of students some tiny flaplike structures discovered in the heart and in certain blood vessels of humans and some lower animals. Harvey's curiosity about the function of these structures led him to investigate the transport system.

During the years after his graduation from medical school, Harvey operated on many live animals to observe their heartbeats and the flow of their blood. After many years of careful observation and experimentation, Harvey presented the idea to his colleagues that blood circulates around the body like a

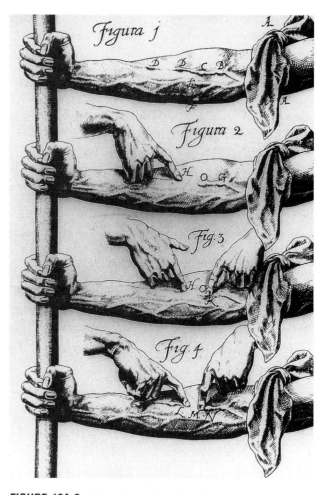

FIGURE 19A.1 The valves in veins operate something like the locks in a canal, opening and closing to regulate the flow of blood toward the heart. Note that the back pressure of blood tends to keep the valve closed until added pressure of blood on the other side of the valve opens it.

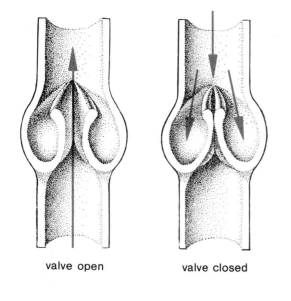

valve open   valve closed

FIGURE 19A.2 Harvey's explanation of the function of valves: "Let an arm be tied above the elbow as (A,A, Fig.1). In the course of the veins certain large knots or elevations (B,C,D,E,F) will be perceived, and this not only at the places where a branch is received (E,F) but also where none enters (C,D): These are all formed by valves. If you press the blood from the space above one of the valves, from H to O (Fig. 2), you will see no influx of blood from above; yet will the vessel continue sufficiently distended above that valve (O,G). If you now apply a finger of the other hand upon the distended part of the vein above the valve O (Fig. 3), and press downwards, you will find that you cannot force the blood through or beyond the valve. If you press at one part in the course of a vein with the point of a finger (L, Fig. 4), and then with another finger streak the blood upwards beyond the next valve (N), you will perceive that this portion of the vein continues empty (L,N). That the blood in the veins therefore proceeds from inferior to superior parts of the heart appears most obviously."

"river with no end." One of the arguments used to support this idea was an explanation of the flaplike structures Harvey had seen as a student. What were these tiny structures? A small probing instrument inserted into a blood vessel would go in one direction but not in the other. Harvey reasoned that the structures were valves and that if they prevented a probe from moving in both directions, they also would prevent the blood from flowing backward (Figure 19A.1). Therefore, the blood could not "ebb" back into the heart by the same vessels through which it had come. Rather, Harvey concluded, the blood must circulate from the heart through one set of vessels (arteries) and back to the heart through another set (veins). It was in the veins that the tiny valves had been observed.

Figure 19A.2 illustrates Harvey's demonstration of the effect produced by valves in the veins of the arm. In the caption, Harvey's own words describe what happens.

One piece of evidence was lacking in Harvey's demonstration of the circulation of the blood. He could not describe how the blood moved from the arteries to the veins. Several years later, Marcello Malpighi (Mal PEE jee), an Italian scientist, used a crude microscope to examine the lung of a frog. Malpighi observed that the blood flowed from the smallest arteries into tiny connecting vessels (capillaries) and then flowed from these tiny vessels into veins. With the discovery of capillaries, the circulation of the blood was established beyond reasonable doubt.

Appendix 19B
Oxygen-Transport Pigments in Animals

A pigment is a substance that gives color to other materials. The oxygen-transporting pigment that gives your blood its characteristic color is the protein hemoglobin. However, a number of different types of pigments capable of combining with oxygen are found throughout the animal kingdom. Table 19B.1 lists these pigments and some of their characteristics. Once bound to one of these pigments, oxygen is transported to the cells. Sometimes these pigments are contained in blood cells, as they are in mammals. In other cases, the pigments are dissolved in the plasma, or fluid portion of the blood, as they are in some mollusks. These pigments differ in their ability to carry oxygen.

TABLE 19B.1 Some Characteristics of Various Oxygen-Transporting Pigments

Pigment	Color	Element	Location	Animal	Holding Capacity (mL/O_2/100 mL Blood)
Hemoglobin	red	iron	erythrocytes	mammals	15–30
				birds	10–25
				reptiles	7–12
				amphibians	6–13
				fishes	1–16
			plasma	annelids	5–15
				mollusks	1–6
Hemocyanin	blue	copper	plasma	mollusks	1–5
Chlorocruorin	green	iron	plasma	annelids	9
Hemoerythrin	red	iron	erythrocytes	annelids	2

Appendix 20A
Antibody Classes

The more constant regions of the heavy chains of antibody molecules, that is, the ends that do not bind to antigens, determine antibody class. There are five major classes of antibodies, or immunoglobulins (Igs), termed IgM, IgD, IgG, IgA, and IgE. The antibody class determines certain biological activities of the molecules. For instance, IgM can form ''superantibody'' molecules (5 antibody molecules hooked together to make a molecule with 10 identical binding sites). IgM is the predominant antibody of the primary immune response. The predominant antibody of the secondary immune response is IgG. It is the most abundant antibody in the circulation, and, because it is smaller than IgM, it can pass from the mother to the fetus. IgA molecules often form doublets that are found in body secretions such as breast milk and saliva. IgE appears to be important in fighting parasitic infections, and also is responsible for allergic reactions such as asthma. Although IgD is present on young lymphocytes, its function is unknown. The structures and functions of the immunoglobulins are summarized in Table 20A.1

TABLE 20A.1 Antibody Classes

Ig Class	Structure	Where Found	Function
M		blood	protects blood, primary immune response
A		mucus secretions	makes secretions more protective forms the first line of defense against infection
D		on young lymphocytes	may have a role in differentiation
G		blood and extracellular fluid	secondary immune response
E		blood and extracellular fluid	allergic reactions, combats parasitic infections

The constant regions of light chains, again the ends that are not involved in antigen binding, determine the light chain type. The two light chain types, kappa and lambda, have no known biological functions.

Appendix 20B
Generating Antibody Diversity

The enormous diversity in antibodies likely evolved in vertebrates as a protective mechanism against the numerous environmental antigens and against malignant cells within the body itself. The discovery of the mechanisms that generate antibody diversity was among the first research benefits of recombinant DNA technology.

Large numbers of different antibody molecules can be made using different combinations of a limited number of light and heavy chains. Even greater numbers of different antibody molecules are made by combining several smaller genes to make a larger gene that codes for one polypeptide chain. Three different genes code for each light chain: C for the constant region, V for the variable region, and J for the joining region. Four different genes code for each heavy chain: C, V, and J, plus an additional D (diversity) gene. Figure 20B.1 shows how V, J, and C genes might combine to produce the larger gene that codes for one light chain of the kappa type. Frequent somatic mutations in the V region also increase antibody diversity.

Thousands of combinations are possible. For example, if there were three sets of 10 genes coding for the light chain polypeptides, recombination of genes would produce $10 \times 10 \times 10$ or 1000 different polypeptides. Although the exact number of genes in each gene family (kappa, lambda, and heavy chain) is not known, there appear to be enough genes to recombine and ultimately code for millions of different antibody molecules. For example, in mice there are approximately 350 V genes, 5 J genes, and 1 C gene that can recombine to form one light chain of the kappa type.

Exactly when and how this genetic recombination takes place in the B cells is not known. Presumably, every possible combination of genes is produced. Once the combination of genes has occurred in a particular B cell, the final step has been completed in determining what binding site will be expressed by that cell and all of its descendants.

FIGURE 20B.1 Light chain gene recombination (kappa). During B-cell differentiation, a V gene recombines with a J gene to form a VJ recombination. The B cell transcribes a segment of DNA into a primary RNA transcript with a long intervening sequence of introns and additional J segments. Introns are removed and exons spliced together to form mRNA, which is translated into kappa light chains. The rearrangement illustrated is only one of thousands that are possible.

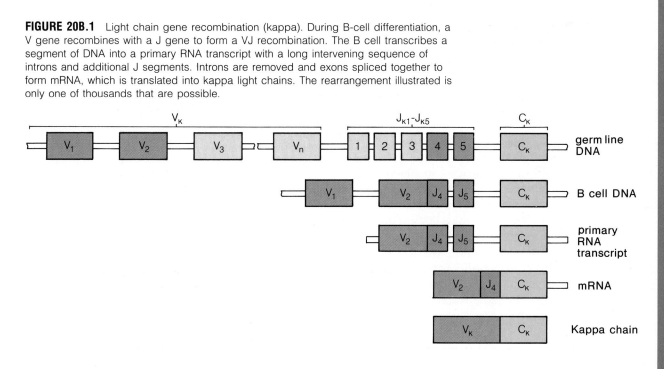

Appendix 21A
Oxygen Consumption and Temperature Regulation in Animals

Oxygen is used by cells in the series of chemical reactions called cell respiration (Chapter 8). Like all chemical reactions, the rate of cell respiration depends on the temperature of the organism. If an animal's body temperature is low, cell respiration is slower and less oxygen is used.

In many animals the body temperature is not constant, but varies with the temperature of the surrounding air or water. Animals whose body temperature varies in this way are called ectothermic (EK toh THER mik). Fishes, amphibians, and reptiles are ectothermic vertebrates. Many ectothermic animals have temperature-regulating processes, but these processes can compensate only for moderate changes in environmental temperature. In extreme cold, the animals become sluggish or almost totally inactive. When their surroundings are warmer, their body temperature increases and they become more active. Oxygen consumption also changes with temperature. More oxygen is needed by those animals in warm environments.

No animal can live if its temperature rises beyond or falls below certain limits. To remain alive, an ectothermic animal must avoid extremes of temperature. For example, on chilly days snakes and lizards often bask on a sunny rock and can become quite warm. In the desert, during the hot days, ectothermic animals stay in shaded spots or underground. Ectothermic animals seek changes in their environment to maintain a suitable metabolic rate.

Birds and mammals are called endothermic (EN doh THER mik) animals, for they can maintain a constant internal temperature even when the temperature of the environment changes. Whether they are in a warm or a cold place, their body temperature remains almost the same. When some endothermic animals are too warm, they sweat. The surface of their bodies is cooled as the water evaporates. Other endothermic animals have different means of cooling their bodies. Some salivate (camels), and others pant (dogs, birds). Some desert mammals do not use evaporative cooling at all. Endothermic animals use a great deal of energy in maintaining body temperature and thus require a large amount of food. However, animals that can internally regulate body temperature are able to occupy a greater range of habitats than ectothermic animals.

When the air is very cold, shivering increases body activity, increasing the metabolic rate and warming the body. The increased metabolic rate requires more oxygen. Therefore, an endothermic animal actually uses more oxygen when the surroundings get colder. These temperature-regulating mechanisms make it possible for an endothermic animal to remain active even in extremely cold temperatures. An ectothermic animal tends to become inactive in the cold. The difference in oxygen consumption between ectothermic and endothermic animals is thus most apparent in cold temperatures.

Many endothermic and ectothermic animals have a special reaction to extreme cold. They go into a period of dormancy called hibernation (hy ber NA shun). Their metabolism slows to a point ordinarily considered near death. The heart beats slowly, the blood circulates very sluggishly, the body temperature drops, and they may breathe as slowly as once every five minutes. By slowing their metabolic rate, they are able to exist for a long period of time on stored body fat. Animals that hibernate, such as chipmunks and some kinds of bats, cannot wake up from this dormant period as quickly as they would from normal sleep. They must warm up slowly and gradually increase the rate of their body processes. Some animals, such as bears, sleep through the winter, but their body processes merely slow down. This is not considered hibernation, for their metabolic rate is only a little less than their normal rate. On warm winter days they may even awaken and leave their dens in search of food.

Hibernation causes a massive change in the respiration, metabolism, and whole functioning of the animal. What initiates this great change? How and why do certain animals in warm climates go into estivation, or summer hibernation? These tropical animals seem to be reacting to changes in the environment, particularly changes in the length of day. Scientists are studying the proces of hibernation, hoping to discover why and how an animal can change its whole metabolism so drastically.

Appendix 22A
Sources, Uses, and Effects of Some Psychoactive Drugs

Name	Source and Use	Effect
Depressants		
Alcohol—ethyl alcohol; in wine, beer, ale, spirits, liquors, mixed drinks	Synthesized or produced naturally by fermentation of fruits, vegetables, or grains. Used as beverages, in cooking and as part of some nonprescription medications such as cold remedies, sleep aids, and cough syrups.	Affects brain in proportion to amount in bloodstream. Small dose produces euphoria, drowsiness, dizziness, flushing, and release of inhibitions and tensions. Slurred speech, staggering, and double vision may result from large dose. Impairs driving in any dose and exaggerates effects of other drugs. Liver damage and brain damage can occur with excessive use. Use of 3 oz or more per day during pregnancy may result in underweight babies with physical, mental, and behavioral abnormalities. May produce tolerance and addiction. Most common of all forms of drug abuse today.
Tranquilizers—Valium, Librium, Miltown	Synthetic chemicals. Used to treat anxiety, nervousness, tension, and muscle spasm.	Produces mildly impaired coordination and balance, reduced alertness and emotional reactions, loss of inhibition. Produces calm without sleepiness. May produce sleep disturbances or depression. Use during pregnancy may cause congenital malformations. Use with alcohol or while driving is very dangerous. Tolerance-inducing and addictive.
Opiates—opium, morphine, codeine, heroin; also called dope, horse, smack, skag	Seed capsules of the opium poppy (*Papaver somniferum*) produce a milky juice. From this juice, many drugs can be prepared, including morphine and codeine. Heroin is formed from morphine by chemical synthesis. Taken by smoking, by mouth, or by injection. Used as narcotic pain killers.	Injection produces surge of pleasure, state of gratification and stupor. Sensations of pain, hunger, and sexual desire are lost. Physical effects include nausea, vomiting, insensitivity to pain, constipation, sweating, slowed breathing. Long-term effects include severe constipation, moodiness, menstrual irregularities, liver and brain damage. Use with alcohol very dangerous. Tolerance-inducing and highly addictive.
Barbiturates—pentobarbital, seconbarbital; also called goofballs, downers, yellow jackets, red devils	Many compounds; developed to suppress pain, treat sleeplessness, anxiety, tension, high blood pressure, convulsions, and to induce anesthesia. Taken by mouth or injected into muscles.	Effects similar to alcohol: release from tension and inhibition, followed by interference with mental function, depression, and hostility. Overdoses cause unconsciousness, coma, and death. Extremely dangerous in combination with alcohol. Long-term effects include liver damage and chronic intoxication. Addictive.

Name	Source and Use	Effect
Stimulants		
Caffeine	White, bitter, crystalline substance in coffee beans, tea leaves, cocoa leaves, kola nuts. Ingredient in stimulant mixtures, beverages such as tea, coffee, and some soft drinks, and some pain relievers and cold remedies.	Increases metabolic rate, blood pressure, urination, and temperature; impairs sleep, appetite, and coordination. Long-term or heavy use can cause insomnia, anxiety, depression, or birth problems. Regular consumption of 4 cups of coffee a day can lead to physical dependence.
Nicotine—in various forms of tobacco; cigarettes, cigars, pipe tobacco, chewing tobacco, snuff	Highly toxic oil with a strong odor and bitter burning taste; in shredded, dried leaves of tobacco plant. Enters body when tobacco is sniffed, chewed, or smoked. Smokers also exposed to tar and cancer-causing substances, carbon monoxide, and 2000 different chemical compounds.	Constricts blood vessels, increases heart rate and blood pressure, reduces blood flow to extremities. Can cause vomiting, clammy skin, diarrhea, confusion, dizziness, and convulsions. Causes psychological and physical dependence. Carbon monoxide displaces oxygen in the blood. Tars collect in the lungs, hinder normal breathing, and cause lung cancer. Long-term tobacco use can cause cancers of lung, mouth, or throat, blocked blood vessels, respiratory disease, stomach ulcers, and reduced immunity. Smoking during pregnancy increases risk of miscarriage, and of low birth weight and developmental problems in newborns.
Amphetamines—benzadrine, dexedrine, methedrine; also called speed, splash, uppers, bennies, dexies, crystal	Synthetic drugs taken by mouth or injected into veins.	Increased alertness and energy, rapid heart rate and breathing, increased blood pressure. Restlessness or hostility common. Very large doses can produce irregular heartbeat, hallucinations, or heart failure. Long-term use can produce mental illness, kidney damage, or lung problems. Psychological and physical dependence.
Cocaine—also called coke, snow, nose candy, crack	Comes from the leaves of the coca plant. Sniffed, ingested, injected, or smoked as freebase.	Effects similar to amphetamines but of shorter duration. Toxic; large doses can cause hallucinations, muscle spasms, convulsions, and death. Long-term use produces restlessness, insomnia, hallucinations. Psychological and physical dependence.
Hallucinogens		
THC—delta-9 tetrahydrocannabinol; the active ingredient in marijuana and hashish, which are also called pot, grass, weed, reefer, joint, hash	Flowers, leaves, oils, or resin of the Indian hemp plant *Cannabis sativa*. Smoked in pipe or hand-rolled cigarette, or ingested by mouth.	Impairs concentration, short-term memory, coordination, and motor skills. Enhances sensory perception and feelings of relaxation. Distorts space-time sense. Long-term effects include loss of motivation, interest, memory, and concentration. The smoke can cause chronic lung disease and lung cancer. Psychological dependence common.

Name	Source and Use	Effect
LSD—Lysergic acid diethylamide; also called acid	Can be derived chemically from the ergot fungus that infects certain grains. Also an artificial chemical compound first developed in the 1940s. Usually taken by mouth.	Physical effects include: dilated pupils; increased heart rate, blood pressure, body temperature, salivation, and perspiration; muscle twitches; nausea. Psychological effects include: hallucinations; extreme mood swings; distortion of senses and perceptions of time, distance, and own body; impaired memory; flashbacks. Overdose can cause: panic; long periods of mental confusion resembling severe mental illness. No physical addiction but tolerance may develop, and psychological dependence does occur.
Mescaline—also called the street drugs DOM, STP, TMA, and MMDA	A natural product of the top or "button" of the peyote cactus. Eaten during religious practices and ceremonies of some Native Americans. Also an artificially produced chemical usually taken by mouth.	Resembles that of LSD. May cause nausea and vomiting. Psychological dependence is possible—regular users may become unproductive and disinterested in life.
Psilocybin—also called 'shrooms	In certain species of mushrooms. Usually taken by mouth. Has been used in religious ceremonies by Native Americans of the United States and Mexico.	Resembles that of LSD and mescaline; often causes nausea and vomiting.

Appendix 25A
Innate Behavior

There are many different types of innate behavior. One primitive behavior is called a taxis (plural, *taxes*). A taxis is a change in the direction of movement caused by some stimulation in the environment. For example, shining a light head-on to a planarian will cause it to change direction. Random movements are not taxes. The movement must be in response to a definite stimulus. Taxes are innate behavior because they usually are fixed and unchanging for the species—the organism always reacts in the same way to the same stimulus.

Another form of innate behavior is a simple reflex. The human knee-jerk reflex is an example. When the tendon below the knee is struck, the leg responds with a jerking movement. Simple reflex behavior is innate because it can be characteristic of the species. In general, innate reflexes protect an organism from harm or help it maintain normal conditions. Other reflexes involving more complicated nervous system responses can be innate or learned.

Many automatic human behavioral responses are learned reflexes. For example, normal posture is maintained by constant muscle adjustment. This adjustment is stimulated by slight changes in the environment. In any normal movement, such as taking a step, coordination of muscles also depends on a series of reflex acts. These acts involve many muscles, nerves, and sensory receptors located in different parts of the body.

The most complex patterns of innate behavior are those called instincts. Instinct is an inherited form of behavior that usually involves a whole series of actions. For example, the nest-building instinct in birds includes all of the activities of searching for good nesting sites and building materials, bringing the materials to the site, and making a particular type of nest from them. The migratory behavior of certain fish and birds is another example.

Sometimes the species of an animal can be recognized by the observation of the animal's behavior pattern. An expert can tell the species of spider by examining its web. Clues to the evolution of certain spiders may be gathered by analyzing the behavior patterns recorded in their webs. Similarities in webs may show genetic relationships between groups of spiders.

Appendix 25B
Aggression

Many animal species are social because of the benefits that social behavior offers. Being social requires cooperation, yet at the same time, animals, like governments, tend to look after their own interests. In short, they are in competition with each other for the limited resources available. Animals may compete for food, mates, water, shelter, or other resources when they are in short supply.

Much of what animals do to resolve this competition is called aggression. Aggression is an offensive physical act or threat that forces another individual to abandon something it wants or owns.

Contrary to the widely held notion that aggressive behavior involves the defeat or destruction of the opponent, many of these encounters consist of

FIGURE 25B.1 Ritualized displays, such as this contest for mates between two male bighorn sheep, rarely result in injury.

more threat than actual combat. Many species have dangerous teeth, beaks, claws, or horns that easily may inflict serious injury or even kill an opponent. Usually such well-armed animals do not use their "weapons" to kill members of their own species, yet they use them in killing prey or defending against attack from another species. Overcrowding in a population and the resulting stresses caused by increased competition for living space, food, and mates may be a factor in aggression-caused injuries and deaths.

Animal aggression within many healthy populations seldom results in death because the species have evolved symbolic aggressive displays that carry mutually understood meanings. Fights between bighorn rams are spectacular to watch, and the sound of clashing horns may be heard for several hundred yards (Figure 25B.1). The ritual battles almost always consist of head-on encounters. The brain is so well protected by the skull and massive horns, however, that injury occurs only by accident, and death is almost unheard of.

The loser in such encounters may either run away or signal his submission. If it is apparent that the individual is going to lose anyway, the loser is usually better off communicating submission as soon as possible. These submissive displays are almost the opposite of threat displays. A defeated wolf or dog presents its neck to the victor as a sign of complete submission. The display of submission usually inhibits the further display of aggression on the part of the winner. It is not difficult to see how natural selection would favor genes that induce aggressive restraint. Inappropriate aggression is not adaptive. For example, continuing to threaten the six-foot, 200-pound school bully is likely to prove disastrous.

The winner of an aggressive competition is dominant to the loser. The winner has enhanced access to food, mates, territory, and so on. In a social species, dominance interactions often take the form of a dominance hierarchy. Life for the subordinates in any social order is likely to be difficult. Subordinates almost never get a chance to reproduce, and when times are difficult, they are the first to die. During times of food scarcity, the death of the weaker members helps to protect the resources for the stronger members. For the species, it is better for the weaker members to starve before the resources dwindle to crisis levels, thus risking the ultimate starvation of the entire population.

Appendix 26A
Vent Ecosystems

Nearly all life on Earth depends on radiant energy from the sun that is converted by photosynthetic organisms to chemical energy. This energy provides the basis for life. Not all organisms, however, are dependent on photosynthesis or photosynthetic organisms for their chemical energy.

A different type of ecosystem has been discovered—one based on chemosynthesis. It was discovered by the *Alvin*, a deep-ocean research vessel, and its crew of scientists from Woods Hole Oceanographic Institution. The place was the Galapagos rift, a boundary between tectonic plates. Sea water seeps into the fissures in the volcanic rocks that are erupting along this boundary, becomes heated, and rises again. As a result, oases of warmth are created in the normally near-freezing waters 2.5 kilometers below the surface. More important, the water reacts with the rocks deep in the crust. The chemical reactions take place under extreme heat and pressure. The crucial reaction is the conversion of sulfate (SO_4^{2-}) in the sea water to sulfide (S^{2-}). Heat supplies the energy necessary for the reaction. Chemosynthetic bacteria obtain energy by converting the sulfide back to sulfate. The bacteria use the energy to extract carbon from carbon dioxide in the sea water and fix it in organic molecules, thereby becoming the primary producers in the ecosystem.

Numerous such oases have been located, each with a somewhat different animal community. Among the most spectacular inhabitants are clams measuring some 20 centimeters in diameter. Other permanent inhabitants include crabs and mussels. The clams and mussels feed on the bacteria and are, in turn, fed on by the crustaceans.

One oasis, known as the Garden of Eden, is dominated by huge tube worms (Figure 26A.1). The tube worms lack mouths and digestive tracts. Apparently, they utilize organic carbon synthesized by

FIGURE 26A.1 Among the animals that live in vent ecosystems are giant tube worms, *Riftia pachyptila*, many more than a meter long. They obtain their nutrients from chemosynthetic bacteria that live within the worms.

chemosynthetic bacteria living within the worms. These organisms demonstrate that although almost all life on Earth is based on radiant energy from the sun, alternatives clearly exist. Their discovery also has implications for the possibility of life on other planets, where conditions may be more extreme than those on Earth.

Glossary

GLOSSARY

Numbers in parentheses indicate the page where a glossary term is introduced and defined within the text.

A site: in protein synthesis, the binding site on a ribosome that holds the tRNA carrying the next amino acid to be added to the chain (234)

abiotic (AY by ah tik) **factor:** a physical or nonliving component of an ecosystem (52)

abscisic (ab SIS ik) **acid:** a plant hormone that protects a plant in an unfavorable environment by promoting dormancy in buds and seeds and closing of stomates (348)

abyssal (uh BIS uhl) **zone:** the portion of the ocean floor where light does not penetrate, temperatures are cold, and pressure is extreme (590)

acidic: having a pH of less than 7, reflecting more dissolved hydrogen ions than hydroxide ions (29)

Acquired Immune Deficiency Syndrome: See AIDS.

ACTH: adrenocorticotropic hormone; a hormone secreted by the pituitary that stimulates the adrenal cortex to secrete corticosteroid hormones (524)

actin: a protein in muscle fiber that, together with myosin, is responsible for muscle contraction and relaxation (547)

activation energy: the energy necessary to start a chemical reaction (26)

active site: the specific portion of an enzyme that attaches to the substrate through weak chemical bonds (36)

active transport: the movement of a substance across a biological membrane against its concentration gradient with the help of energy input and specific transport proteins (146)

adaptation: in natural selection, a hereditary characteristic of some organisms in a population that improves their chances for survival and reproduction, compared with other organisms in the population (11)

adaptive radiation: the emergence of numerous species from a common ancestor introduced to an environment presenting a diversity of conditions (374)

adenosine diphosphate: See ADP.

adenosine triphosphate: See ATP.

ADH: antidiuretic hormone; a hormone released from the posterior lobe of the pituitary that enhances conservation of water by the kidneys (485)

ADP: adenosine diphosphate (uh DEN oh seen dy FOS fayt); the compound that remains when a phosphate group is transferred from ATP to a cell reaction site requiring energy input (63)

adrenal cortex: the outer portion of the adrenal gland (524)

adrenal gland: an endocrine gland located on the top of the kidney, that secretes a number of hormones (524)

adrenal medulla: the central portion of the adrenal gland that secretes epinephrine (524)

adrenocorticotropic hormone: See ACTH.

aerobic (ehr ROH bik): occurring or living in the presence of free or dissolved oxygen (182, 192)

AIDS: acquired immune deficiency syndrome; a condition caused by a virus that attacks and kills certain cells of the immune system so that the system is unable to protect the organism against disease (3, 465)

aldosterone (al DOH stoh rohn): a hormone secreted by the adrenal cortex that helps regulate sodium and potassium concentrations and water balance (485)

alkaline: basic; having a pH greater than 7, reflecting more dissolved hydroxide ions than hydrogen ions (29)

allantois (AL an TOH is): one of the embryonic membranes of reptiles, birds, and mammals; in birds and reptiles it may serve a respiratory and waste-collecting function (321)

allele (uh LEEL): one of two or more possible forms of a gene, each affecting the hereditary trait somewhat differently (272)

alveoli (al VEE oh ly): air sacs in a lung (476)

amino (uh MEE noh) **acid:** an organic compound composed of a central carbon atom to which are bonded a hydrogen atom, an amino group (—NH₂), an acid group (—COOH), and one of a variety of other atoms or groups of atoms; the building block of polypeptides and proteins (34)

ammonia: a toxic nitrogenous waste excreted primarily by aquatic organisms; also, a gas in Earth's early atmosphere (480)

amniocentesis (AM nee oh sen TEE sis): a technique used to detect genetic abnormalities in a fetus through the presence of certain chemicals or defects in fetal cells in the amniotic fluid; the fluid is obtained through a needle inserted into the amniotic sac (303)

amnion (AM nee ahn): a sac or membrane, filled with fluid, that encloses the embryo of a reptile, bird, or mammal (321)

amoeboid (uh MEE boyd) **movement:** locomotion resulting from streaming of the cytosol; characteristic of *Amoeba* and other protists, as well as some individual cells, such as white blood cells (531)

anaerobic (an ehr ROH bik): occurring or living in conditions without free or dissolved oxygen (82, 182)

anaphase (AN uh fayz): the stage in mitosis in which chromosomes on the spindle separate and are pulled toward opposite ends of the cell (215)

anatomically modern hominids: *Homo sapiens*; broadly refers to all modern humans, including the first modern humans (40 000 to 100 000 years ago); formerly called Cro-Magnon (394)

androgen (AN droh jen): a male sex hormone, such as testosterone (266)

animal society: an organized population showing cooperative behavior (567)

Animalia (an uh MAYL yuh): the animal kingdom (105)

anorexia nervosa (an oh REX ee uh ner VOH suh): a condition characterized by abnormal loss of appetite and induced self-starvation to reduce body weight (415)

anthropologist (an thruh PAH loh jist): a scientist who studies humans—human evolution, variability, and both past and present cultures and behavior (386)

antibody: a blood protein produced in response to an antigen, with which it combines specifically (283, 449)

antibody-mediated response: immune response in which B cells produce antibodies to bind with and mark antigens for destruction by nonspecific defenses; initiated by helper T cells (449)

anticodon (an tee COH dahn): three-nucleotide sequence at the end of a tRNA molecule that is complementary to, and base pairs with, a specific amino acid codon in mRNA (232)

antidiuretic hormone: See ADH.

antigen: any material, usually a protein, that is recognized as foreign and elicits an immune response (448)

anus (AY nus): the outlet of the digestive tube (407)

aorta (ay OHR tuh): the major artery of the heart that carries blood from the left ventricle to all parts of the body (435)

aphotic (AY foh tik) **zone:** the part of the ocean beneath the photic zone, where light does not penetrate enough for photosynthesis (590)

apical meristem (AY pih kuhl MAYR uh stem): embryonic plant tissue in the tips of roots and shoots that supplies cells for growth in length (339)

archaebacteria: the more ancient of the two major lineages of prokaryotes represented today by a few groups of bacteria inhabiting extreme environments (101)

archaic *Homo sapiens***:** broadly refers to those humans who lived in Europe, Africa, and Asia from about 100 000 to 35 000 years ago (formerly called Neanderthals); their relationship to modern humans is debated (394)

artery (AHR tehr ee): a vessel that transports blood away from the heart (435)

artificial selection: the selective breeding of domesticated plants and animals to encourage the occurrence of desirable traits (362)

asexual reproduction: any method of reproduction that requires only one parent or one parent cell (101, 246)

atom: the smallest particle of an element; in turn, an atom is made of smaller particles that do not separately have the properties of the element (22)

atomic theory: the theory that all matter is made of particles called atoms, different for each element, with the differences accounting for chemical and physical properties (22)

ATP: adenosine triphosphate (uh DEN oh seen try FOS fayt); a compound that has three phosphate groups and is used by cells to store energy (62)

ATP synthetase: an enzyme complex in the inner membrane of a mitochondrion and the thylakoid membrane of a chloroplast, through which protons flow; the formation site of ATP from ADP and Pi during phosphorylation (167)

atrium (AY tree um; plural *atria*): a chamber of the heart that receives blood from the veins (435)

australopithecine (AH stral oh PITH uh seen): any of the earliest known hominids that walked erect and had humanlike teeth, but whose skull, jaw, and brain capacity were more apelike; may include several species (392)

Australopithecus (AH stral oh PITH uh kus): genus of several species of australopithecines, including *A. afarensis, A. africanus, A. boisei,* and *A. robustus* (392)

autoimmunity: a disorder in which antibodies are produced against some of the body's own cells (467)

autonomic nervous system: a division of the nervous system that controls involuntary activities of the body such as blood pressure, body temperature, and other functions necessary to the maintenance of homeostasis (505)

autotroph (AWT oh trohf): an organism able to make and store food, using sunlight or another abiotic energy source (50)

auxins (AWK sinz): a group of plant hormones produced in an actively growing region of a plant and transported to another part of the plant, resulting in a growth effect (346)

axon: a structure that extends out from a neuron and conducts impulses away from the cell body (492)

AZT: azido-deoxythymidine; a drug used to treat some individuals who have AIDS (3)

B

B cell: a lymphocyte that matures in the bone marrow and later produces and secretes antibodies into the blood stream (453)

Barr body: a dense object that lies along the inside of the nuclear envelope in cells of female mammals, representing one inactivated X chromosome (288)

basic: alkaline; having a pH greater than 7, reflecting more dissolved hydroxide ions than hydrogen ions (29)

behavior: the way an organism acts; the actions and interactions of organisms with each other and with their environment (555)

behavioral isolation: the division or separation of a single breeding population by a behavioral barrier, such as courtship differences (372)

benthic zone: the bottom surfaces of the ocean (590)

bile: a secretion of the liver, stored in the gall bladder and released through a duct to the small intestine; breaks large fat droplets into smaller ones that enzymes can act on more efficiently (412)

binocular vision: vision that uses both eyes at once; produces an appearance of solidity or depth because of the slightly different angle from which each eye views an object (382)

binomial nomenclature (by NOH mee yul NOH men klay cher): the two-word naming system used in systematics or taxonomy (98)

biodiversity: the number and variety of living organisms in an area (89)

bioenergetics: the study of energy flow and energy transformations among living systems (47)

bioethics: the consideration of right and wrong with respect to issues raised by biological knowledge or technology (5)

biological evolution: changes that have occurred in life forms, from the origination of the first cell to the many diverse forms that exist today (76)

biome: the distinctive plant cover and the rest of the community of organisms associated with a particular physical environment; often named for its plant cover (580)

biosphere: the outer portion of Earth—air, water, and soil—where life is found (53)

biosynthesis: the process of putting together or building up the large molecules characteristic of a particular type of cell or tissue (59)

biotic (by OT ik) **factor:** an organism, or its remains, in an ecosystem (52)

bipedal (by PEE dul): capable of walking erect on the hind limbs, freeing the hands for other uses (383)

blastocyst (BLAS toh sist): the mammalian embryonic stage that corresponds to the blastula of other animals (321)

blastula (BLAS tyoo lah): an animal embryo after the cleavage stage, when cell movements toward the outside of the ball of cells result in a fluid-filled cavity inside (318)

bradykinins: several polypeptides in blood and tissue fluid that cause dilation of blood vessels and increase capillary permeability (518)

brainstem: that part of the brain that connects the spinal cord to the forebrain and cerebrum (500)

bronchial tubes: small branches of a trachea that end in alveoli (476)

bulimia (buh LEE mee uh): an abnormal craving for food beyond the body's needs; frequently expressed as gorging followed by forced vomiting (415)

bundle sheath: tightly packed cells surrounding veins in the leaves of C_4 plants that receive a rearranged 4-carbon acid in the first stage of C_4 photosynthesis; within the bundle sheath cells, carbon dioxide is released and reincorporated by rubisco into PGA (175)

C_3 plants: plants that incorporate carbon dioxide into 3-carbon compounds before beginning the Calvin cycle (169)

C_4 plants: plants that incorporate carbon dioxide into 4-carbon compounds before beginning the Calvin cycle (175)

calcitonin (cal sih TOH nin): a hormone, secreted by the thyroid gland, that helps regulate the level of blood calcium (517)

callus: a mass of dividing, undifferentiated cells at the cut end of a shoot or in a tissue culture, from which adventitious roots develop (349)

calorie: the amount of heat required to raise the temperature of one gram of water 1°C (50)

Calvin cycle: the cycle (named for its discoverer) that involves the enzyme rubisco and that causes carbon dioxide to be incorporated, or fixed, in sugars during photosynthesis; uses chemical energy previously converted from light energy (164)

CAM: crassulacean (kras yoo LAY see un) acid metabolism; an adaptation for photosynthesis in arid conditions, in which carbon dioxide entering open stomates at night is converted into organic acids that release carbon dioxide during the day when the stomates are closed (176)

cambium (KAM bee um): a layer of meristem tissue in the stems and roots of plants that produces all growth in diameter, including new xylem and phloem cells (341)

cAMP: See cyclic adenosine monophosphate.

cancellous (KAN sel us) **bone:** bone tissue with numerous bony plates separated by spaces; spongy bone (540)

cancer: malignancy arising from cells that are characterized by profound abnormalities in the plasma membrane and in the cytosol, and by abnormal growth and division (207)

capillary (KAP il ayr ee): a microscopic blood vessel penetrating the tissues and consisting of a single layer of cells that allows exchange between the blood and tissue fluids (412, 435)

capillary action: a way in which liquid can be raised to a limited height in very small diameter tubes by the attraction of the liquid molecules to the inside walls of the tube (430)

carbohydrate (KAR boh HY drayt): an organic compound made of carbon, hydrogen, and oxygen, with the hydrogen and oxygen atoms in a 2:1 ratio; examples are sugars, starches, glycogen, and cellulose (30)

carbon-14 dating: a technique to date fossils that uses the known disintegration rate of radioactive carbon; the amount of carbon-14 remaining in fossils indicates their age (390)

carbon cycle: the biogeochemical cycle in which carbon compounds made by some organisms are digested and decomposed by others, releasing the carbon in small inorganic molecules that can be used again by more organisms to synthesize carbon compounds (593)

carbon skeleton: the long carbon-atom chain that forms the backbone of macromolecules (30)

cardiac muscle: a specialized type of muscle tissue found only in the heart (546)

cardiovascular disease: CVD; a disease of the heart and/or blood vessels, such as atherosclerosis (416, 417)

cardiovascular system: the body's circulatory system composed of the heart and blood vessels (434)

carpel (KAR pul): the female reproductive organ of a flower, consisting of the stigma, style, and ovary (253)

carrier: a transport protein, involved in facilitated diffusion, that possesses a binding site for a specific substance (147)

cartilage: a tough, elastic connective tissue that makes up the skeleton of cartilaginous fish, but that in other vertebrates is mostly replaced by bone as the animal matures (534)

caste system: a highly organized society in which each member has a specific task (568)

catalyst (KAT uh list): a chemical that promotes a reaction between other chemicals and may take part in the reaction but emerges in its original form (36)

cell: the basic living unit (130)

cell body: the enlarged portion of a neuron that contains the nucleus (492)

cell fusion: a technique in which the cytoplasm of cells, and sometimes their nuclei, are combined (327)

cell-mediated response: immune response in which highly specialized lymphocytes circulate in the blood and lymphoid tissue and attack and destroy infected or abnormal cells (449)

cell theory: the theory that organisms are composed of cells and their products, and that these cells are all derived from preexisting cells (131)

cell wall: a nonliving covering around the plasma membrane of certain cells, as in plants, many algae, and some prokaryotes; in plants the cell wall is constructed of cellulose and other materials (137)

cellular respiration: the series of chemical reactions by which a living cell breaks down food molecules and obtains energy from them (51)

cellulose (SEL yoo lohs): a polysaccharide (carbohydrate) found in cell walls (31)

central nervous system: the brain and spinal cord in vertebrates (493)

centriole (SEN tree ohl): one of two structures in animal cells, composed of cylinders of nine triplet microtubules in a ring; centrioles help organize microtubule assembly during cell division (140)

centromere (SEN troh meer): the specialized region of a chromosome that holds two replicated chromosomal strands together and that attaches to the spindle in mitosis (214)

cerebellum (seh reh BEL um): the part of the brain in vertebrates that is associated with regulating muscular coordination, balance, and similar functions (500)

cerebrospinal fluid: a serumlike fluid that bathes the brain and spinal cord (501)

cerebrum (seh REE brum): the largest portion of the brain in humans and many other animals; controls the higher mental functions such as learning (500)

chaparral (SHAP uh RAL): a scrubland biome of dense, spiny evergreen shrubs found at mid-latitudes along the coast where cold ocean currents circulate offshore; characterized by mild, rainy winters and long, hot, dry summers (584)

chemical bond: the attraction between two atoms resulting from the sharing or transfer of outer electrons from one atom to another (25)

chemical energy: energy stored in the structure of molecules, particularly organic molecules (50)

chemical evolution: a gradual increase in the complexity of chemical compounds that may have brought about the origination of the first cells (72)

chemical reaction: a process of change in chemical bonds that produces one or more new substances (25)

chitin (KYT in): a hard organic substance secreted by insects and certain other invertebrates as the supporting material in their exoskeletons (100)

chlorophyll (KLOR uh fil): the green pigments of plants and many microorganisms; converts light energy (via changes involving electrons) to chemical energy that is used in biological reactions (161)

chloroplast (KLOR uh plast): an organelle found in plants and photosynthetic protists; contains chlorophyll that absorbs light energy used to drive photosynthesis (140)

cholesterol (koh LES ter ol): a lipid associated particularly with animal plasma membranes and linked to deposits in blood vessels and corresponding heart disorders; important as a precursor of hormones and other organic compounds (33)

chorion (KOR ee ahn): an embryonic membrane that surrounds all the other embryonic membranes in reptiles, birds, and mammals (321)

chorionic villi sampling: CVS; a procedure by which a small piece of membrane surrounding a fetus is removed and analyzed to detect genetic defects (304)

chromatid (KROH muh tid): one of two strands of a replicated chromosome before their separation during mitosis or meiosis (214)

chromatin (KROH muh tin): the chromosomal material as it ordinarily appears in a cell's nucleus, with individual chromosomes indistinct (209)

chromosome: a long, threadlike group of genes found in the nucleus of all eukaryotic cells and most visible during mitosis and meiosis; chromosomes consist of DNA and protein (137)

cilia (SIL ee uh; singular *cilium*): short, hairlike cell appendages specialized for locomotion and formed from a core of nine outer doublet microtubules and two inner single microtubules (141)

ciliary movement: movement characteristic of ciliates and flagellates in which locomotion is accomplished through the rotation or whipping of hairlike appendages (532)

circulatory system: an organ system consisting of a muscular pump (heart), blood vessels, and blood itself; the means by which materials are transported to and from cells; in many animals, also helps stabilize body temperature and pH (432)

class: the third largest grouping, after kingdom and phylum or division, in the biological classification system (97)

cleavage: the process of cell division in animal cells, characterized by the pinching of the plasma membrane; the rapid cell divisions, without growth, that take place during early embryonic development (318)

climax community: a stable, self-perpetuating community established by succession and considered semipermanent; persists until interrupted or destroyed by environmental change (579)

clonal selection: a process in the immune system through which only antibodies capable of binding to specific antigens are selected to divide (455)

clone: a lineage of genetically identical individuals (247)

closed circulatory system: a type of internal transport in which blood is confined to vessels (432)

coacervate (koh AS er vayt): a cluster of proteinlike substances held together in a small droplet within a surrounding liquid; used as a model for a precell to investigate the formation of the first life on Earth (76)

coagulate: clot (442)

coding strand: the one DNA strand, during transcription, that directs the synthesis of RNA (228)

codominance: the condition in which both alleles in a heterozygous organism are expressed (283)

codon (KOH dahn): the basic unit of the genetic code; a sequence of three adjacent nucleotides in DNA or mRNA (225)

coenzyme A: a coenzyme present in all cells and necessary for cellular respiration and for fatty acid metabolism (188)

cohesion-tension hypothesis: the hypothesis that water is raised upward in an unbroken column in the xylem of plants by the force holding together the water molecules and by the continuing evaporation of water from the top of the column, in leaves (430)

coleoptile (KOH lee OP tyl): the structure that covers the embryonic shoot in germinating monocot seeds (339)

collagen: a tough, fibrous protein that is the main constituent of connective tissue in vertebrates (540)

communication: the process of exchanging information through sound, scent, actions, or other visual signals (569)

compact bone: a type of bony tissue that is very dense and hard, composing the shafts of long bones and the outer layer of all bones (540)

complement system: a complex group of serum proteins that can destroy antigens (460)

compound: a substance formed by chemical bonds between atoms of two or more different elements (23)

concentration gradient: a difference in the concentration of certain molecules over a distance (144)

conditioning: training that associates a response with a stimulus different from the stimulus that causes the response by innate behavior (558)

cone: a color receptor located in the retina of the eye (493)

consumer: a heterotroph; an organism that feeds on other organisms or on their organic wastes (51)

contractile vacuole: a cell structure primarily for the elimination of excess water, in single-celled and certain other organisms (481)

corpus luteum (KOR pus LOOT ee um): the structure that forms from the tissues of a ruptured ovarian follicle and secretes female hormones (262)

corticosteroids (kor ti coh STEER oydz): hormones secreted by the adrenal cortex that help regulate protein and carbohydrate metabolism in the body (524)

corticotropin-releasing hormone: a hormone, produced by the hypothalamus and released by the anterior pituitary, that controls ACTH secretion (524)

cotyledon (KOT ih LEE don): the single (monocot) or double (dicot) seed leaf of a flowering plant embryo (338)

countercurrent exchange: the opposite flow of adjacent fluids that maximizes transfer rates; for example, the blood in gills flows opposite to the direction in which water passes over the gills, thus maximizing oxygen uptake and carbon dioxide loss (473)

covalent (koh VAY lent) **bond:** a chemical bond formed by the sharing of a pair of electrons between two atoms (27)

cranium (KRAY nee um): the skull (without the jaw) (388)

crassulacean acid metabolism: See CAM.

creatine phosphate (KREE uh tin FOS fayt): an energy-storage compound used by muscle cells of vertebrates to replenish ATP supplies; replenished by the breakdown of glycogen (195)

CRH: See corticotropin-releasing hormone.

cristae (KRIS tee): in mitochondria, the foldings of the inner mitochondrial membrane that form a series of "shelves" containing the electron transport systems involved in ATP formation (188)

crossing over: during prophase I of meiosis, the breakage and exchange of corresponding segments of homologous chromosomes at one or more sites along their length, resulting in genetic recombination (250)

cuticle (KYOO tih kul): in plants, a noncellular, waxy outer layer covering certain leaves and fruits (160)

CVD: See cardiovascular disease.

CVS: See chorionic villi sampling.

cyanobacteria (sy AN oh bak TEER ee uh): the blue-green bacteria, which carry on oxygen-producing photosynthesis much like plants, but without membrane-enclosed chloroplasts to isolate their chlorophyll (81, 111)

cyclic adenosine monophosphate (uh DEN oh seen mon oh FOS fayt): cAMP; a small, ring-shaped molecule that acts as a chemical second messenger in vertebrate endocrine systems (513)

cytochrome (SY toh krohm): a respiratory pigment in cell respiratory chains; cytochrome *c* is the most abundant in different organisms (191)

cytokinins (SY toh KY ninz): a group of plant hormones that promotes cell division, stem and root growth, chlorophyll synthesis, and chloroplast development (347)

cytoplasm (SY toh plazm): the entire contents of the cell, except the nucleus, bounded by the plasma membrane (137)

cytoskeleton: a network of microtubules, microfilaments, and intermediate filaments that run throughout the cytoplasm and serve a variety of mechanical and transport functions (141)

cytosol (SYT oh sol): the gelatinlike portion of the cytoplasm that bathes the organelles of the cell (137)

D

data: (singular *datum*) observations and experimental evidence bearing on a question or problem (6)

decomposer: an organism that lives on decaying organic material, from which it obtains energy and its own raw materials for life (51)

decomposition: the process of taking molecules apart; heat and chemicals are the chief agents (59)

deletion: the loss of a piece of a chromosome and the genes it carries (297)

dendrite: a structure that extends out from a neuron and transmits impulses toward the cell body (492)

deoxyribonucleic (dee OK sih ry boh noo KLEE ik) **acid:** DNA; the hereditary material of most organisms; composed of nucleic acids containing deoxyribose, a phosphate group and one of four nitrogen bases; DNA composes the genes (38)

deoxyribose: a sugar used in the structure of DNA; it contains one less oxygen atom than does ribose (38)

depolarized: the condition of a membrane when it has lost its electrical potential (494)

depressant: a drug that slows the functioning of the central nervous system (497)

dermis: the thick layer of the skin beneath the epidermis, or outer covering (536)

desert: a biome characterized by lack of precipitation and by extreme temperature variation; there are both hot and cold deserts (582)

desmosome: a type of intercellular junction in animal cells, functioning as a ''spot weld'' (151)

determination: the process wherein a cell commits to a particular fate (330)

diabetes: a disease that results from insufficient insulin secretion or from impairment of insulin receptors on cells of the body; characterized by abnormal absorption and use of glucose (516)

diaphragm: the sheet of muscle that separates the chest and abdominal cavities in mammals, and, along with rib muscles, functions in breathing; also, a caplike rubber device inserted in the vagina and used as a contraceptive (475)

diastole (dy AS tuh lee): the stage of the cardiac cycle in which the heart muscle is relaxed, allowing the chambers to fill with blood (436)

dicot: a flowering plant that has two embryonic seed leaves, or cotyledons (339)

differentiation: specialization, as with cells during development that become ordered into certain tissues and organs (316)

diffusion: the movement of a substance down its concentration gradient from a more concentrated area to a less concentrated area (144)

digestion: the process by which larger food molecules are broken down into smaller molecules that can be absorbed (404)

dihybrid cross: a genetic cross between individuals differing in two traits (280)

diploid (DIH ployd): a cell containing two sets of homologous chromosomes (2*n*), one set inherited from each parent (248)

disaccharide (DY SAK uh ryd): a double sugar, composed of two chemically bonded simple sugars (31)

disease: an abnormal condition of an organism as a consequence of infection, inherent weakness, or environmental stress, that impairs normal physiological functions (448)

division: the second largest grouping, after kingdom, in the biological classification system for plants (98)

DNA: See deoxyribonucleic acid.

DNA polymerase (pol ih mer AYS): an enzyme that catalyzes the synthesis of a new DNA strand, using one of the original strands as a template (210)

dominance hierarchy: a linear peck order of animals in which position dictates characteristic social behaviors (568)

dominant: a trait that is expressed in a heterozygous organism (279)

dorsal lip: in a blastula, the area in which the first signs of gastrulation appear (331)

double circulation: circulation with separate pulmonary and systemic circuits, which ensures vigorous blood flow to all organs (436)

duplication: the presence of more than one copy of a particular chromosomal segment in a chromosome set (297)

E

ecological isolation: the division or separation of a single breeding population by an ecological barrier, such as occupying different habitats (371)

ecosystem: a biological community in its abiotic environment (53)

ectoderm (EK tuh derm): the outer layer of cells in the gastrula stage of an animal embryo (319)

ectothermic (EK toh THER mik): using environmental energy and behavioral adaptations to regulate body temperature; reptiles, fishes, and amphibians are ectothermic (758)

electron: a negatively charged particle that occurs in varying numbers in the electron clouds surrounding the nuclei of atoms (24)

electron transport system: the process in which electrons are transferred from one carrier molecule to another in photosynthesis and in cellular respiration; results in storage of some of the energy in ATP molecules (185)

element: a substance composed of atoms that are chemically identical—alike in their proton and electron numbers (23)

embryo: an organism in its earliest stages of development (255)

embryology: the science dealing with formation, early growth, and development of organisms (319)

endocrine (EN doh krin) **gland:** a ductless gland that secretes one or more hormones into the bloodstream (512)

endocytosis (EN doh sy TOH sis): the cellular uptake of materials (147)

endoderm (EN doh derm): an inner layer of cells, as in an embryo (319)

endoplasmic reticulum (en doh PLAZ mik reh TIK yoo lum): an extensive membranous network in eukaryotic cells composed of ribosome-studded (rough) and ribosome-free (smooth) regions (137)

endorphin (en DOR fin): any of several neuropeptides produced in the brain that have pain-supressing action (496)

endoskeleton: a hard skeleton buried in the soft tissues of an animal; such as the spicules of sponges and bony skeletons of vertebrates (534)

endosperm: a nutrient-rich structure formed by the union of a sperm cell with two polar nuclei during double fertilization; provides nourishment to the developing embryo in seeds of flowering plants (255)

endothelium (EN doh THEE lee um): the innermost layer of cells lining blood vessels and the only constituent of capillaries (439)

endothermic (EN doh THER mik): using metabolic energy to maintain a constant body temperature; birds and mammals are endothermic (758)

enkephalin (en KEH fah lin): a hormone produced in the brain and spinal cord that inhibits pain reception by imitating the effects of morphine on the nervous system (496)

entropy (EN truh pee): a measure of the degree of disorganization of a system, that is, how much energy in a system has become so dispersed that it is no longer available to do work (56)

enzyme (EN ZYM): a protein or part-protein molecule made by an organism and used as a catalyst in a specific biochemical reaction (34)

enzyme-substrate complex: an enzyme molecule together with the molecules on which it acts, correctly arranged at the active site of the enzyme (36)

epidermis: the outer covering of animals and the dermal tissue system in plants (149, 536)

epididymis (ep ih DID ih mus): the highly coiled tubule that leads from the seminiferous tubules of the testis to the vas deferens (264)

epinephrine (ep ih NEF rin): an adrenal hormone, also called adrenaline, that speeds up heart rate and raises blood sugar level and blood pressure; the "fight-or-flight" hormone secreted during a sudden fright or emergency (525)

epithelial tissue: a thin layer of cells that covers the internal and external surfaces of the body, such as the lining of the lungs or skin (151)

ER: See endoplasmic reticulum.

erythrocyte (ih RITH roh syt): a red blood cell; a type of cell in vertebrates that carries hemoglobin and certain other blood proteins with highly specialized functions (440)

esophagus (ih SOF ah gus): the tubular portion of the digestive tract that leads from the pharynx to the stomach (409)

essential amino acid: an amino acid required for health and that cannot be synthesized in adequate amounts by body cells (418)

estivation (es tuh VAY shun): a physiological state, characterized by metabolism and inactivity, that permits survival during long periods of elevated temperature and diminished water supplies (758)

estrogen (ES troh jen): a hormone that stimulates the development of female secondary sexual characteristics (262)

estrus (ES trus) **cycle:** a cycle of changes governed by the endocrine system; includes a limited period of heat, or sexual receptivity, called estrus, that occurs around ovulation in female mammals, except higher primates (264, 384)

ethylene (ETH ih leen): a gaseous plant hormone that promotes fruit ripening while inhibiting further plant growth in roots and stems (348)

eubacteria: bacterial group including the cyanobacteria, but not the archaebacteria; sometimes called the "true bacteria," they differ from archaebacteria in their rRNA, tRNA, and in other ways (101)

eukaryote (yoo KAIR ee oht): an organism whose cells have a membrane-enclosed nucleus and organelles; a protist, fungus, plant, or animal (83)

evolution: change through time that results from natural selection acting on genetic variations present among individuals of a species; evolution results in the development of new species (7, Chapter 16)

exocrine (EK soh krin) **gland:** any gland that delivers its secretion through a tube or duct; for example, a tear gland or a sweat gland (511)

exocytosis (EK soh sy TOH sis): the secretion of macromolecules from a cell by the fusion of vesicles with the plasma membrane (147)

exon (EX ahn): a segment of DNA that is transcribed into RNA and translated into protein, specifying the amino acid sequence of a polypeptide; characteristic of eukaryotes and some prokaryotes (231)

exoskeleton: a hard encasement deposited on the surface of an animal, such as the shells of mollusks, that provides protection and points of attachment for muscles (533)

extensor: a muscle that extends a limb or skeletal part (546)

extracellular digestion: the breakdown of nutrient molecules occurring outside of cells (405)

extracellular matrix: the substance that surrounds cells (151)

F$_1$ generation: the first filial, or hybrid, offspring in a genetic cross-fertilization (279)

F$_2$ generation: offspring resulting from interbreeding of the hybrid F$_1$ generation (279)

facilitated diffusion: the spontaneous passage of molecules and/or ions, bound to specific carrier proteins, across a biological membrane down their concentration gradients (147)

FAD: flavin adenine dinucleotide; combines with two hydrogen molecules during cellular respiration to form FADH$_2$ (185)

FADH$_2$: flavin adenine dinucleotide; in cellular respiration, a hydrogen-carrying form of FAD (185)

family: the fifth largest grouping, after kingdom, phylum or division, class, and order, in the biological classification system; a group of related genera (96)

fatty acid: a long, unbranched hydrocarbon with a —COOH group at the end (32)

feces (FEE seez): the waste material expelled from the digestive tract (410)

feedback system: a relationship in which one activity of an organism affects another activity, which in turn affects the first, yielding a regulatory balance (514)

femur (FEE muhr): the thighbone (388)

fermentation: the incomplete breakdown of food molecules, especially sugars, in the absence of oxygen (187)

fertilization: the union of an egg nucleus and a sperm nucleus (248)

fibrin (FY brin): an insoluble, fibrous protein that forms a network of fibers around which a blood clot develops (442)

fibrinogen (fy BRIN oh jen): a soluble blood protein that is changed into its insoluble form, fibrin, during the blood-clotting process (442)

first filial generation: See F$_1$ generation.

first law of bioenergetics: states that the energy present in living organisms cannot be created or destroyed, only changed in form; derived from the law of conservation of energy and matter (54)

fixed action pattern: a highly stereotyped behavior that is innate and must be carried to completion once it is initiated (556)

flagella (fluh JEL uh; singular *flagellum*): the long cellular appendages specialized for locomotion and formed from a core of nine outer doublet microtubules and two single inner microtubules; many protists and certain animal cells have flagella (141)

flame cell: in planarians, a cell with cilia in a network connected by tubules; absorbs fluid and wastes and moves fluid through the tubules to eliminate excess water (482)

flavin adenine dinucleotide: See FAD.

flexor: a muscle that bends a joint (546)

follicle: in mammals, any of several different structures—an ovarian sac from which an egg is released; a thyroid tissue that produces and stores a hormone; and a tiny skin cavity from which a hair grows (262)

follicle-stimulating hormone: FSH; a substance secreted by the anterior lobe of the pituitary that stimulates the development of an ovarian follicle in a female or the production of sperm in a male (262)

food chain: the transfer of food from one trophic level to another, beginning with producers (592)

food web: food chains in an ecosystem taken collectively, showing partial overlapping and competition for many food organisms (51)

frame-shift mutation: the insertion or deletion of a nucleotide pair causing disruption of the reading frame (296)

free energy: the available energy used by living organisms to do work (50)

freely movable joint: a type of joint in vertebrate skeletons that allows for fairly free movement, such as in the knee, hip, and shoulder joints (544)

FSH: See follicle-stimulating hormone.

Fungi (FUN jee): a kingdom of heterotrophic organisms that develop spores; many are decomposers; some are parasites of other organisms (106)

fungus: a heterotrophic organism that takes in food by absorption (106)

G

G$_0$ phase: an extended G$_1$ phase of the cell cycle (205)

G$_1$ phase: the first growth phase of the cell cycle, starting just after offspring cells form (205)

G$_2$ phase: the second growth phase of the cell cycle, beginning after DNA synthesis (206)

gamete (GAM eet): a sex cell, either an egg or a sperm, formed by meiosis (248)

ganglia (singular *ganglion*): clusters of nerve cell bodies (498)

gap junction: a type of intercellular junction in animal cells that allows passage of material or current from cell to cell (151)

gastric juices: in digestion, secretions of stomach glands composed of enzymes, mucus, and acid (410)

gastrin: a hormone secreted by the stomach lining that stimulates the secretion of fluid by gastric glands in the stomach (411)

gastrula (GAS troo lah): the two-layered, cup-shaped embryonic stage (319)

gene: the fundamental physical unit of heredity, which transmits a set of specifications from one generation to the next; a segment of DNA that codes for a specific product (40)

gene flow: the loss or gain of alleles in a population due to the emigration or immigration of fertile individuals (367)

gene pool: the total aggregate of genes in a population at any one time (366)

gene therapy: the use of biotechnology to treat genetic disorders and illnesses (305, 306)

genetic anticipation: the phenomenon in which the severity of symptoms associated with a genetic disorder increases (or the symptoms appear at an earlier age) in successive generations (303)

genetic code: the "language" of the genes dictating the correspondence between nucleotide sequence in DNA (in triplets, or codons) and amino acid sequence in proteins (223)

genetic counseling: the process of identifying parents at risk for producing children with genetic defects and of assessing the genetic state of early embryos (303)

genetic drift: changes in the gene pool of a small population due to chance (367)

genetic engineering: a collective term for the techniques of transferring genes from one type of organism to another and multiplying them (3)

genetic equivalence hypothesis: in development, the hypothesis that assumes all cells contain the same genes (324)

genetic map: a diagram showing the relative positions of genes on a chromosome (285)

genetic recombination: presence of new combinations of alleles in a DNA molecule as the result of crossing over at meiosis, chromosomal alterations, or gene mutations (252)

genome: the total genetic content or complement of a haploid cell from any given species (274)

genotype (JEE noh typ): the genetic makeup of an organism (280)

genus: the next largest grouping after kingdom, phylum or division, class, order, and family in the biological classification system; a group of related species (96)

geographical isolation: the division or separation of a single breeding population by a physical barrier, such as a mountain range (370)

germination: the sprouting of a seed (339)

GH: See growth hormone.

GHRH: See growth-hormone-releasing hormone.

gibberellins (JIB ur EL inz): a group of plant hormones that stimulate elongation of the stems and leaves, trigger the germination of seeds, and, with auxins, stimulate fruit development (347)

gill: the gas exchange organ of aquatic organisms such as fish; the chief excretory organ in many ocean fish (472)

glomerular (glah MER yoo lahr) **capsule:** the cup of a nephron, containing a ball of blood capillaries; also called Bowman's capsule (484)

glomerulus (glah MER yoo lus): a ball of capillaries surrounded by a capsule in the nephron and serving as the site of filtration in the kidneys (484)

glucagon: a pancreatic hormone that acts to raise the blood glucose level (513)

glucose: a common 6-carbon sugar (31)

glycerol: a 3-carbon alcohol molecule that combines with fatty acids to form fats and oils (32)

glycogen (GLY koh jen): the chief carbohydrate used by animals for energy storage (31)

glycolysis (gly KAWL uh sis): the initial breakdown of a carbohydrate, usually glucose, into smaller molecules at the beginning of cellular respiration (184)

GnRH: See gonadotropin-releasing hormone.

Golgi (GOHL jee) **apparatus:** an organelle in eukaryotic cells consisting of stacked membranes that modifies and packages materials for export from the cell (137)

gonadotropin-releasing hormone: GnRH; a hormone released by the hypothalamus that stimulates the secretion of gonadotropin by the anterior pituitary (262)

grana (GRAY na; singular *granum*): stacks of thylakoids within a chloroplast (161)

gravitropism (GRAV ih TROH piz um): a positive or negative response of a plant or animal in relationship to gravity (352)

greenhouse effect: the warming of Earth due to the atmospheric accumulation of carbon dioxide, which absorbs infrared radiation and slows its escape (77)

growth: in development, the successive rounds of cell division that produce a multicellular organism (316)

growth hormone: GH; a hormone, released by the anterior lobe of the pituitary, that promotes growth (4)

growth-hormone-releasing hormone: GHRH; a hormone, released by the hypothalamus, that stimulates the secretion of growth hormone by the anterior pituitary (521)

guard cells: a pair of cells that surround a stomate in a plant leaf's epidermis; turgor pressure in the guard cell regulates the opening and closing of a stomate (160)

habitat: place where an organism lives; even in the same ecosystem, different organisms differ in their habitats (53)

habituation: a simple type of learning that involves the loss of sensitivity to unimportant stimuli (558)

hallucinogen: a drug that causes the user to see, feel, or hear things that are not there (498)

haploid (HAH ployd): a cell containing only one set of homologous chromosomes (*n*) (248)

Hardy-Weinberg equilibrium: the presence in a population of three genotypes, *AA*, *Aa*, and *aa* in the frequencies of p^2, $2pq$, and q^2, respectively (where *p* and *q* are the frequencies of the alleles *A* and *a*); at these genotype frequencies, there is no change from one generation to the next (747)

Haversian system: a group of bone cells and the canal that they surround; the basic unit of structure in bone (540)

HCG: See human chorionic gonadotropin.

HDL: See high density lipoprotein.

helper T cell: a type of T cell required for some B cells to make antibodies or that help other T cells to respond to antigens or to secrete lymphokines (453)

hemoglobin (HEE moh gloh bin): the pigment of red blood cells responsible for the transport of oxygen (317, 440, 477)

heterotroph: an organism that obtains carbon and all metabolic energy from organic molecules previously assembled by autotrophs; a consumer (50)

heterotroph hypothesis: the hypothesis that the first life forms used the supply of naturally occurring organic compounds for food (73)

heterozygous (HET er oh ZY gus): having two different alleles for a given trait (280)

hibernation (hy ber NAY shun): a physiological state that permits survival during long periods of cold and diminished food, in which metabolism decreases, the heart and respiratory system slow down, and body temperature is maintained at a lower level than normal (758)

high density lipoprotein: HDL; a complex lipid-protein molecule that does not deposit cholesterol in blood vessels (417)

HIV: *H*uman *I*mmunodeficiency *V*irus; the virus that causes AIDS (3)

histone (HIS tohn): a small protein, with a high proportion of positively charged amino acids, that binds to the negatively charged DNA and plays a key role in its folding into chromatin (209)

HLA: human leukocyte antigens; the self-proteins that T cells recognize (461)

homeostasis (hoh mee oh STAY sis): the tendency for an organism, or a population of organisms, to remain relatively stable under the range of conditions to which it is subjected (443)

hominid (HAH mih nid): a primate of the family Hominidae, which includes modern humans, earlier subspecies, and australopithecines (387)

Homo erectus (HOH moh ee REK tus): an extinct tool-using human species that lived from 1.6 million to 300 000 years ago; the first undisputed human species (393)

Homo habilis (HOH moh HAB ul is): a fossil hominid, larger than an australopithecine, thought to be between 1.6 and 2 million years old (392)

Homo sapiens (HOH moh SAY pee enz): the human species, including modern humans and archaic humans (384)

Homo sapiens sapiens (HOH moh SAY pee enz SAY pee enz): a subspecies of anatomically modern humans comprised of present-day human groups; formerly called Cro-Magnon people (394)

homologies (hoh MOL uh jees): likeness in form, as a result of evolution from the same ancestors (95)

homologous (hoh MOL uh gus) **chromosomes:** chromosome pairs of the same length, centromere position, and staining pattern, that possess alleles for the same traits at corresponding locations (247)

homozygous (HOH moh ZY gus): having two identical alleles for a given trait (280)

hormone: a substance, secreted by cells or glands, that has a regulatory effect on cells and organs elsewhere in the body; a chemical messenger (512, Chapter 23)

human chorionic gonadotropin: HCG; a hormone released by the placenta that causes the corpus luteum to release high levels of progesterone and estrogen (262)

human immunodeficiency virus: See HIV.

human leukocyte antigens: See HLA.

hybrid: having different alleles, one inherited from each parent, for a trait in a pair of alleles; heterozygous (278)

hydrogen bond: a weak attraction between hydrogen atoms and oxygen, nitrogen, or fluorine atoms; hydrogen bonds hold together the two strands of DNA in their double helix (28)

hydrostatic skeleton: a mass of fluid enclosed within a muscular wall to provide the support necessary for antagonistic muscle action (533)

hypertension: high blood pressure (439)

hypothesis: a statement suggesting an explanation for an observation or an answer to a scientific problem (8)

immovable joint: a type of joint in the vertebrate skeleton that does not allow movement, such as the joint between the bones of the skull and of the face (544)

immune system: a body system composed of cells and their products that interact to protect the individual against threats from foreign cells or materials (447)

immunity: resistance to disease, usually specific for one disease or pathogen (450)

imprinting: a type of learned behavior with a significant innate component, acquired during a limited period early in life (558)

induced fit: the change in shape of the active site of an enzyme so that it binds more snugly to the substrate (37)

infection: an invasion of the body by pathogens, disease-causing organisms (448)

inflammation: a generalized response of the body to tissue damage or foreign materials in which capillaries near an injury become more permeable, causing redness and swelling (448)

initiation: a two-step process in protein synthesis that signals the beginning of transcription (228, 234)

innate behavior: a behavior that is genetically determined, as in the organization of an ant society; also called instinctive behavior (556)

insertion: the end of a muscle that is attached to a movable skeletal part (545)

instinct: the capacity of an animal to complete a fairly complex, stereotyped response to a key stimulus without having prior experience (557)

interneuron: association neuron; a neuron located between a sensory neuron and a motor neuron (493)

interphase: a normal interval between successive cell divisions when the only evidence of future divisions is that chromosomes begin to be replicated; a cell at work, rather than a cell dividing (205)

intertidal zone: the shallow zone of the ocean where land meets water; also called the littoral zone (590)

intracellular digestion: the breakdown of nutrient particles within the cell (404)

intron (IN tron): a segment of DNA that is transcribed into precursor mRNA but then removed before the mRNA leaves the nucleus (227, 231)

inversion: a sequence of genes reversed from their normal order in a segment of a chromosome, often as a result of looping, breakage, and repair (297)

invertebrate: an animal lacking a backbone (105)

ion: an atom or molecule that has either gained or lost one or more electrons, giving it a positive or negative charge (26)

ionic bond: a chemical bond formed by the attraction between oppositely charged ions (27)

ionization: the conversion of a substance into ions, as by chemical reaction, radiation damage, or solution in water (28)

isolating mechanism: some aspect of structure, function, or behavior that prevents interbreeding between populations that are undergoing or have undergone speciation (373)

isotope: a form of atom having the same atomic number but a different atomic mass (25)

karyotype (KAYR ee oh TYP): a method of organizing the chromosomes of a cell in relation to number, size, and type (275)

kidney: an organ that regulates water and salt levels; composed of nephron and capillary units that filter and selec-

tively reabsorb water and other noncellular components of blood (483)

killer T cell: a type of T cell of the cell-mediated response that directly attacks foreign cells and infected host cells (453)

kilocalorie: a measure of food energy equal to 1000 calories (50)

kingdom: the largest grouping in the biological classification system (98)

Krebs cycle: the cycle in cellular respiration that completes the breakdown of the intermediate products of glycolysis, releasing energy; also, a source of carbon skeletons for use in biosynthesis reactions (185)

lactate: a 3-carbon acid formed from NADH and pyruvate at the end of glycolysis when little oxygen is available (187)

lactic acid fermentation: the anaerobic pathway at the end of glycolysis that recycles NAD^+ and provides a small amount of ATP until oxygen becomes available (187)

lacunae (lah KOO nee; singular *lacuna*): the hollow cavities usually found in bone (540)

LDL: See low density lipoprotein.

learned behavior: behavior developed as a result of experience (556)

leukocyte (LOO koh syt): a white blood cell; any of the nucleated cells in the blood plasma that are the first line of defense against invading microorganisms; examples include lymphocytes (B cells, T cells) and macrophages (441)

LH: See luteinizing hormone.

lichen (LY kin): an alga and a fungus that live in symbiosis, forming a distinctive structure, or thallus, that may be low and crusty, leafy, or bushy; lichens are pioneers on rock or other surfaces (106)

ligament: a cord or sheet of connective tissue by which two or more bones are bound together at a joint (544)

light reactions: the energy-capturing reactions in photosynthesis; also, reactions in the human skin leading to the production of vitamin D (164)

lignin: a hard substance embedded in the cellulose of plant cell walls, that provides support (429)

limiting factor: an environmental condition such as food, temperature, water, or sunlight that restricts the types of organisms and population numbers that an environment can support (172)

linked genes: genes that are located on the same chromosome (284)

lipase (LIH pays): a fat-digesting enzyme (412)

lipid (LIP id): a fat, oil, or fatlike compound that usually has fatty acids in its molecular structure; an important component of the plasma membrane (32)

lipoprotein (LIH poh PROH teen): a complex of lipid and protein (417)

littoral zone: the shallow zone of the ocean where land meets water; the intertidal zone (590)

low density lipoprotein: LDL; a complex lipid-protein molecule that tends to deposit cholesterol in the blood vessels (417)

luteinizing hormone: LH; a hormone, secreted by the anterior lobe of the pituitary, that controls the formation of the corpus luteum in females and the secretion of testosterone in males (262)

lymph (LIMF): the fluid transported by the lymphatic vessels (412)

lymphatic (lim FAT ik) **system:** a system of vessels through which body lymph flows, eventually entering the bloodstream where the largest lymph duct joins a vein (441)

lymphocyte (LIMF oh syt): a type of small leukocyte (white blood cell) important in the immune response; examples include B cells and T cells (452)

lymphokines: a class of molecules produced by activated T cells that stimulates production of plasma cells by B cells and division of helper T cells (464)

lysosome (LY soh sohm): a cell vesicle that contains digestive enzymes (140)

lysozyme (LY soh zym): an enzyme produced by mucous-secreting cells in tear ducts; destroys bacteria (140)

M

M phase: the mitotic phase of the cell cycle (206, 214)

macroevolution: evolutionary change on a large scale, including evolutionary trends, adaptive radiation, and mass extinction (370)

macromolecule: a large, complex molecule with a backbone formed from long carbon chains (30)

macrophage (MAK roh fayj): a type of large, phagocytic white blood cell (441)

Malpighian (mal PIG ee un) **tubules:** the excretory organs of insects (482)

marrow: the connective tissue that occupies the spaces within bones (540)

marsupial: one of a group of mammals, such as koalas, kangaroos, and opossums, whose young complete their embryonic development inside a maternal pouch called a marsupium (259)

matrix: in mitochondria, the inside area where the enzymes of the Krebs cycle are found; also, the intercellular substance of a tissue (189)

mechanical isolation: the separation or division of a single breeding population by a mechanical barrier, such as incompatible sex organs (372)

medulla: the inner portion of an organ, such as the kidney; also, the most posterior region of the vertebrate brain, the hindbrain (503)

meiosis (my OH sis): two successive nuclear divisions (with corresponding cell divisions) that produce gametes (in animals) or sexual spores (in plants) having half of the genetic material of the original cell (248)

melatonin: a hormone thought to be secreted by the pineal gland (518)

memory cell: a B- or T-lymphocyte produced in response to a primary immune response; remains dormant and can respond rapidly if the same antigen is encountered again (454)

meninges (meh NIN jeez): a group of three membranes that covers the brain and spinal cord (501)

menstrual cycle: the female reproductive cycle that is characterized by regularly recurring changes in the uterine lining (260)

mesoderm: in most animal embryos, a tissue layer between the ectoderm and endoderm (319)

mesophyll (MEZ oh fil): the green leaf cells between the upper and lower epidermis of a leaf; the primary site of photosynthesis in leaves (160)

mesosome: an infolding of the plasma membrane in prokaryote cells (135)

messenger RNA: mRNA; the RNA complementary to one strand of DNA; transcribed from genes and translated by ribosomes into protein (223)

metabolism: the sum of all the chemical changes taking place in an organism (59)

metaphase: the stage in mitosis in which replicated chromosomes move to the center of the spindle and become attached to it (215)

metastasis: the spread of cancer cells to other parts of the body, forming new tumors at distant sites (207)

methanogen (meth AN uh jen): a methane-producing bacterium (82)

mG cap: in RNA processing, a cap of methylguanine that is placed on the starting end of the mRNA molecule (230)

microevolution: a change in the gene pool of a population over a succession of generations (369)

microfilament: a tiny rod of protein that occurs in the cytosol of almost all eukaryotic cells, making up part of the cytoskeleton and involved in cell contraction (141)

microtubule: a hollow rod of protein found in the cytosol of all eukaryotic cells, making up part of the cytoskeleton and involved in cell contraction (141)

migration: the movement of a population to a different environment during certain seasons of the year; or in population genetics, the arrival or departure of individuals, which causes a change in the gene pool (367)

mineral: any inorganic nutrient necessary for proper functioning of the body (419)

mineralocorticoid: any one of a group of hormones secreted by the adrenal cortex that influences the concentrations of electrolytes in body fluids (524)

mitochondria (my toh KON dree uh; singular *mitochon-*

drion): the organelles in eukaryotic cells that carry on cellular respiration; the site of ATP synthesis and of the Krebs cycle (83)

mitosis (my TOH sis): the continuous events that lead to the production of two nuclei in one cell; usually followed by cell division (206)

model: a tentative description of a system or hypothesis that accounts for all its known properties (22)

molecular hybridization: the realignment of complementary strands of DNA after gently heating double-stranded DNA (326, 384)

molecule (MOL uh KYOOL): the smallest naturally occurring particle of elements or compounds whose atoms are covalently bonded to one another (22)

Monera (moh NEHR uh): a kingdom of bacteria and related microscopic organisms whose one-celled or acellular bodies have no clearly defined cell nuclei or many of the other structures found in cells of complex organisms; prokaryotes (101)

monocot: a flowering plant that has one embryonic seed leaf, or cotyledon (339)

monohybrid cross: a genetic cross between individuals differing in one trait (279)

monosaccharide (MON oh SAK uh ryd): a simple sugar with three to seven carbon atoms in its carbon skeleton (30)

monotreme: one of a group of egg-laying mammals represented by the platypus and the echidna (259)

morphogenesis: the embryological development of the structure of an organism (316)

morphologic (mor foh LAH jik): describes form, structure, or aspect (387)

motile: capable of movement from place to place; a characteristic of most animals (105)

motor neuron: a neuron that receives impulses from a sensory neuron or interneuron and transmits them to a muscle or gland (492)

mRNA: See messenger RNA.

multicellular: composed of many cells (101)

multifactorial: when the expression of a trait is controlled by several genes and also influenced by the environment (284)

multiple alleles: the existence of several known alleles for a gene (283)

muscular movement: movement requiring the interaction of some form of skeletal system and a system of muscles (533)

mutagen: a substance or form of energy that is capable of increasing the mutation rate (295)

mutation: a chemical change in a gene, resulting in a new allele; or, a change in the portion of a chromosome that regulates the gene (213)

mycorrhizae (my koh RY zee; singular *mycorrhiza*): root structures that result from mutualistic associations of plant roots and fungi (429)

myelin sheath: a fatty layer surrounding the long axons of motor neurons in the peripheral nervous system of vertebrates; composed of the membranes of Schwann cells (492)

myofibril: a contractile fiber found within muscle cells (547)

myosin: a protein that, together with actin, is responsible for muscular contraction and relaxation (317, 547)

NAD+: nicotinamide adenine dinucleotide; an electron and hydrogen carrier in cellular respiration (185)

NADH: the hydrogen-carrying form of NAD$^+$ (185)

NADP+: nicotinamide adenine dinucleotide phosphate; a hydrogen-carrier molecule that forms NADPH in the light reactions of photosynthesis (166)

NADPH: the reduced form of NADP (166)

natural selection: a mechanism of evolution whereby members of a population with the most successful adaptations to their environment are most likely to survive and reproduce (10)

Neanderthal: See archaic *Homo sapiens*.

negative feedback system: a homeostatic mechanism whereby a change in a physiological variable triggers a response that counteracts the initial change (514)

nephron (NEF ron): the functional unit of a kidney, consisting of a convoluted tubule surrounded by capillaries (483)

nephron loop: loop of Henle; a section of tubule between the ends in a nephron (484)

neritic (neh RIH tik) **zone:** the shallow regions of the ocean overlying the continental shelves (590)

nerve: a bundle of nerve fibers (492)

nerve impulse: a wave of chemical and electrical changes that passes along a nerve fiber in response to a stimulus (495)

neuron (NYOO rahn): a nerve cell; a name usually reserved for nerve cells in animals that have a complex brain and specialized associative, motor, and sensory nerves (491)

neurotransmitter: a chemical messenger, often a hormone, that diffuses across a nerve synapse and transmits an impulse from one neuron to another (496)

neural tube: the foundation of the nervous system that forms in an embryo after gastrulation (320)

neurula: the stage of embryological development in which the neural tube forms (320)

neutral: a condition characterized by equal numbers of negative and positive charges or by no charge (29)

neutron (NOO tron): an atomic particle carrying no electrical charge (24)

niche (NICH): the total of an organism's utilization of the biotic and abiotic resources of its environment (360)

nicotinamide adenine dinucleotide: See NAD$^+$.

nicotinamide adenine dinucleotide phosphate: See NADP$^+$.

nodes of Ranvier: constrictions in the myelin sheath of a neuron between Schwann cells   (492)

nondisjunction: failure of a pair of chromosomes to separate during meiosis   (287)

nonpolar covalent bond: a chemical bond resulting from the equal sharing of electrons between atoms   (27)

nonrandom mating: a mating pattern in which individuals in a population exhibit a preference for mates of a particular phenotype   (368)

norepinephrine: a neurotransmitter released from the axon ends of some nerve fibers; also, a hormone secreted by the adrenal medulla   (525)

nuclear envelope: the membrane in eukaryotes that encloses the genetic material, separating it from the cytosol   (137)

nucleic (noo KLEE ik) **acids:** DNA or RNA; organic compounds (macromolecules) composed of nucleotides and important in coding instructions for cell processes   (38)

nucleoid (NOO klee oyd): a region in a prokaryotic cell consisting of a concentrated mass of DNA   (136)

nucleolus (noo KLEE oh lus): a structure, in the nucleus of a eukaryotic cell, associated with the production of ribosomes   (232)

nucleotide (NOO klee oh tyd): a subunit of DNA or RNA, composed of a 5-carbon sugar, a nitrogen base, and a phosphate group   (38)

nucleus (NOO klee us): in atoms, the central core, containing protons and neutrons; in eukaryotic cells, the membranous organelle that houses the chromosomal DNA   (137)

nutrient: a substance that supports the growth and maintenance of an organism   (50)

omnivorous (ahm NIH vuh rus): capable of eating both plant and animal material   (383)

oncogene: a gene found in viruses or as part of the normal genome that triggers cancerous characteristics   (207)

open circulatory system: a system in which the blood does not travel through the body completely enclosed in vessels   (432)

oral cavity: the inside of the mouth, bounded by the palate, teeth, and tongue   (409)

order: the fourth largest grouping, after kingdom, phylum or division, and class, in the biological classification system; a group of related families   (97)

organ: an organized group of tissues that carries on a specialized function in a multicellular organism   (150)

organelle (or guh NEL): an organized structure within a cell, with a specific function   (83)

organic compound: a carbon compound in which carbon is chemically combined with hydrogen, usually oxygen, and often one or more of the elements nitrogen, phosphorus, and sulfur   (30)

origin: the end of a muscle that is attached to a relatively immovable skeletal part   (545)

osmosis (os MOH sis): the movement of water across a selectively permeable membrane   (144)

osteoblast: a bone-forming cell   (540, 543)

osteoclast: a cell that causes the erosion of bone   (540, 543)

osteocyte: a mature bone cell developed from an osteoblast   (540)

osteoporosis: a bone disease characterized by porous bones associated, in part, with calcium deficiency   (421)

ovum (OH vuhm): a mature egg cell; a female gamete, haploid (n) in chromosome number   (248)

ovaries (singular *ovary*): the primary reproductive organs of a female; egg-cell-producing organs   (257)

oviduct: a tube that leads from an ovary to the uterus   (259)

ovulation (ohv yoo LAY shun): the release of an egg cell from a mature ovarian follicle   (262)

ovule (OHV yool): a structure that develops in a plant ovary and contains the egg   (253)

oxyhemoglobin (ok see HEE moh gloh bin): the compound formed when oxygen combines with hemoglobin   (477)

oxytocin (ok see TOH sin): a hormone, produced by the hypothalamus and secreted by the posterior pituitary, that causes contraction of smooth muscles in the uterus and mammary glands   (523)

P generation: the parental organisms in a genetic cross-fertilization   (279)

P site: in protein synthesis, the site holding the tRNA that carries the growing polypeptide chain   (234)

pacemaker: a mass of specialized muscle tissue that controls the rhythm of the heartbeat; also, a mechanical device implanted in the chest that controls the heartbeat rhythm   (436)

pancreatic islets: islets of Langerhans; the islandlike clusters of tissues in the pancreas that secrete the hormone insulin   (515)

pancreatic juice: digestive fluid secreted by the pancreas   (411)

parasympathetic nervous system: in vertebrates, one of two subdivisions of the autonomic nervous system; stimulates resting activities, such as digestion, and restores the body to normal after emergencies   (505)

parathyroid glands: small endocrine glands embedded in the posterior portion of the thyroid gland   (516)

parathyroid hormone: PTH; a hormone secreted by the parathyroid glands that helps regulate the level of blood calcium and phosphate   (516)

plasma cell: antibody-producing cell that formed as a result of the proliferation of sensitized B lymphocytes (454)

plasma membrane: the membrane at the boundary of every cell, which serves as a selective barrier to the passage of ions and molecules (135)

plasmid (PLAZ mid): a small ring of DNA in bacteria that carries genes separate from those of the chromosome (100)

plasmodesmata (PLAZ moh dez MAH tuh): open channels in the cell wall of plants through which strands of cytoplasm connect from adjacent cells (151)

plastid (PLAS tid): a plant organelle that functions in photosynthesis or food storage (83)

platelet (PLAYT let): a small plate-shaped blood factor that contributes to blood clotting at the site of a wound; platelets release substances that begin formation of a clot (442)

point mutation: a change in a chromosome at a single nucleotide within a gene (295)

polar body: small, nonfunctioning cell produced as a result of meiosis during egg cell formation (251)

polar covalent bond: a chemical bond formed when two atoms share electrons unequally (27)

polar nuclei: in flowering plants, two nuclei that fuse with a sperm nucleus to form the 3n endosperm nucleus (253)

polarization: the process by which a plasma membrane gains an electrical potential due to the unequal distribution of ions on either side of the membrane (494)

pollination: the placement of pollen by wind or animal vectors onto the stigma of a carpel; a prerequisite to fertilization (254)

poly-A tail: in protein synthesis, the 100 to 200 adenine nucleotides that are added to the end of the mRNA molecule (230)

polymerase chain reaction: PCR; a technique that uses double-stranded DNA and two primers as templates for numerous duplications; at the end of each round of duplication, the amount of DNA product doubles (310)

polymorphism: the coexistence of two or more distinct forms of individuals in the same population (90)

polypeptide: a long chain of chemically bonded amino acids (35)

polysaccharide (POL ee SAK uh ryd): a complex carbohydrate composed of many simple sugars (monosaccharides) chemically bonded in a chain; for example, starch, glycogen, and cellulose (31)

population: all the organisms of a particular species that live in the same area at the same time (567)

population genetics: the study of the genetics of a group of individuals in order to determine gene frequencies, the frequencies of particular genotypes and mutations, and patterns of stability or change (367)

positive feedback system: a homeostatic mechanism whereby a change in a physiological variable triggers a response that reinforces the initial change (514)

pressure-flow hypothesis: the concept that food is transported through the phloem as a result of differences in pressure (431)

primary germ layers: in animals, the three cells groups—endoderm, ectoderm, and mesoderm—that give rise to all the tissues of the body (319)

primary growth: growth in the length of a plant's roots and stems (341)

primary immune response: the initial immune response to an antigen; appears after a lag of several days (456)

primary RNA transcript: newly synthesized RNA, the final product of transcription (228)

principle of independent assortment: states that the inheritance of alleles residing on one pair of chromosomes does not affect the inheritance of alleles on a different pair of chromosomes (281)

principle of segregation: states that during meiosis, homologous chromosomes, with the genes they carry, separate into different gametes such that the two alleles for a given trait will appear each in a different gamete (279)

probability: the chance that any given event will occur (277)

producer: an autotroph; any organism that produces its own food (51)

progesterone (proh JES teh rohn): a female hormone, secreted by the corpus luteum and the placenta, that prepares the uterus for pregnancy and the breasts for lactation (262)

prokaryote (proh kayr ee oht): an organism whose cells do not have membrane-enclosed nuclei or organelles; a moneran (bacteria) (82)

prolactin (proh LAK tin): a hormone, secreted by the anterior pituitary, that stimulates the production of milk from the mammary glands (523)

prolactin-inhibiting hormone: PIH; a hormone secreted by the hypothalamus that regulates the release of prolactin by the anterior pituitary (523)

promoter region: the region of a chromosome containing a specific nucleotide sequence to which RNA polymerase attaches to initiate transcription of mRNA (228)

prophase: the stage in mitosis during which replicated strands of chromosomes condense, the nuclear envelope begins to disappear, and a spindle forms (215)

prostaglandins (PRAH stuh GLAN dihnz): chemicals, secreted by virtually all tissues, that serve a variety of functions as messengers and mediate hormonal action (518)

prostate (PROS tayt) **gland:** a gland, located around the male urethra below the urinary bladder, that adds its secretions to seminal fluid during ejaculation (266)

protein (PROH teen): an organic compound composed of one or more polypeptide chains of amino acids; most structural materials and enzymes in a cell are proteins (34)

prothrombin (proh THROM bin): a plasma protein that functions in the formation of blood clots (442)

protist: a member of the kingdom Protista (106)

Protista (proh TIST uh): a kingdom of mostly aquatic,

parental generation: See P generation.

passive transport: the diffusion of a substance across a biological membrane (146)

pathogen: a foreign organism, such as a virus, bacterium, or fungus, that has the potential to cause disease (448)

PCR: See polymerase chain reaction.

pedigree: a record of the heredity of a particular trait through many generations of a family (299)

pelagic (puh LAY jik) **zone:** the area of the ocean past the continental shelf; open water often reaching to great depths (590)

pelvis: the bony structure forming a basinlike ring of bone with which the legs articulate at the base of the vertebral column (388)

pepsin: a protein-splitting enzyme secreted by the gastric glands of the stomach (411)

pepsinogen (pep SIN oh jen): the inactive form of pepsin (411)

peptide bond: a covalent chemical bond formed between two amino acids; bonds the amino group of one amino acid to the acid group of the next (35)

pericycle: in plants, a layer of cells around the vascular tissues from which branch roots grow (344)

peripheral nervous system: the sensory and motor neurons that connect to the central nervous system (493)

peristalsis (payr ih STAHL sis): the rhythmic waves of contraction of the smooth muscle that pushes food along the digestive tract (410)

permafrost: the frozen sublayers of soil that remain frozen through the summer thaw in the tundra of northern latitudes (587)

permeable: open to passage or penetration (146)

PGA: phosphoglyceric (fos foh gly SER ik) acid; an intermediate compound in the fermentation of glucose and in the synthesis of PGAL in the Calvin cycle of photosynthesis (168)

PGAL: phosphoglyceraldehyde (fos foh glis uh RAL deh hyd); a 3-carbon sugar phosphate formed in the Calvin cycle of photosynthesis (168)

pH scale: a scale from 0 to 14 reflecting the concentration of hydrogen ions in solution; the lower numbers denote acidic conditions and the upper numbers denote basic, or alkaline, conditions (29)

phagocytosis (FAY goh sy TOH sis): the process by which cells engulf material and enclose it within a vacuole in the cytosol (406, 448)

pharynx (FAYR inks): an area in the throat of vertebrates where the air and food passages cross; also, in flatworms, the muscular tube that protrudes from the bottom side of the worm and ends in the mouth (407)

phenotype (FEE noh typ): the expression of a genotype in the appearance or function of an organism; the observed trait (280)

pheromone (FER uh mohn): a small chemical signal between animals; acts much like hormones to influence physiology and behavior (570)

phloem (FLOH um): a portion of the vascular system in plants, consisting of living cells arranged into elongated tubes that transport sugar and other organic nutrients throughout the plant (341)

phosphate group: an atom of phosphorus and three atoms of oxygen that bond to the carbon skeleton of biologically important molecules; usually indicated by the symbol ⓟ (31)

phosphoglyceraldehyde: See PGAL.

phosphoglyceric acid: See PGA.

phospholipid: a lipid formed from two fatty acids and a phosphate group; one component of cellular membranes (33)

photic (FOH tik) **zone:** the narrow top portion of the ocean where light penetrates sufficiently for photosynthesis (590)

photoperiodism: a physiological response to day length, such as in flowering plants (352)

photorespiration: a metabolic pathway in plants that uses oxygen, produces carbon dioxide, generates no ATP, and slows photosynthetic output; generally occurs on hot, dry, bright days, when stomates close and the oxygen concentration in the leaf exceeds that of carbon dioxide (173)

photosynthesis (foh toh SIN thuh sis): the process by which cells use light energy to make organic compounds from inorganic materials (51)

phototropism: movement or growth curvature toward light (352)

phylum (FY lum): the second largest grouping, after kingdom, in the biological classification system, for all organisms except plants, which are classified in divisions (98)

phytochrome: a pigment involved in many responses of plants to light (353)

phytoplankton (FYT oh PLANK tun): small, floating aquatic organisms, many microscopic, that carry on photosynthesis (588)

PIH: See prolactin-inhibiting hormone.

pineal gland: a small structure located in the central part of the brain; may play a role in regulating certain physiological cycles (518)

pinocytosis (PEE noh sy TOH sis): the pinching-in process of a plasma membrane by which liquids and very small particles are taken into the cell (405)

pituitary gland: endocrine gland attached to the base of the brain, consisting of anterior and posterior lobes (262)

placenta (pluh SEN tuh): a structure in the pregnant uterus for exchange of materials between a fetus and the mother's blood supply; formed from the uterine lining and embryonic membranes (262, 321)

Plantae (PLAN tee): the plant kingdom (105)

plasma (PLAZ muh): the liquid portion of the blood in which the cells are suspended (441)

mostly microscopic organisms whose cells are eukaryotic (106)

proton (PROH ton): a particle bearing a positive electrical charge, found in the nuclei of all atoms (24)

protoplast: a plant cell with the cell wall removed (349)

pseudopod (SOO doh pahd): literally, a false foot; a term used to describe an amoebalike extension of a cell; used in locomotion and obtaining food, or, as in white blood cells, in engulfing bacteria and foreign particles (531)

pseudoscience: false science; research that does not meet the criteria of science (15)

psychoactive drug: a drug that affects the mind or mental processes (497)

PTH: See parathyroid hormone.

puberty: the stage of development in which the reproductive organs become functional (267)

public policy: a set of action guidelines or rules that result from the actions or lack of actions of governmental agencies (5)

punctuated equilibria: a theory of evolution advocating spurts of relatively rapid change followed by long periods of stability (375)

pyruvate: the 3-carbon compound that is the end product of glycolysis (187)

quaternary structure: the particular shape of a complex protein defined by the characteristic three-dimensional arrangement of its subunits, each a polypeptide (35)

R

rachis: the main shaft of a feather (538)

RAS: See reticular activating system.

rate: the amount of change measured over a period of time (170)

ray cell: any of the cells in the stems of woody plants that form a channel allowing the passage of material laterally (432)

reactant: a substance that takes part in a chemical reaction (36)

reaction center: a special chlorophyll *a* molecule to which other chlorophylls and pigments transfer light energy during photosynthesis (166)

reading frame: the grouping of bases into codons (238)

recessive: a trait whose expression is masked in a heterozygous organism (279)

recombinant DNA: whole molecules or fragments that incorporate parts of different parent DNA molecules, as formed by natural recombination mechanisms or by recombinant DNA technology (308)

recombinant DNA technology: a set of techniques for recombining genes from different sources and transferring the product DNA into cells where it is expressed (308)

red blood cell: See erythrocyte.

reflex arc: a nerve pathway, consisting of a sensory neuron, interneuron, and motor neuron, that forms the structural and functional basis for a reflex (507)

regulatory genes: genes that are involved in turning on or off the transcription of genes that code for amino acid sequences (330)

replication (rep lih KAY shun): the process of making a copy of the DNA in a cell nucleus and in certain organelles outside the nucleus—particularly chloroplasts and mitochondria (206)

replication fork: a site on DNA molecules at which replication, performed by DNA polymerases, takes place (211)

repolarized: the condition of a plasma membrane that has reestablished its electrical potential (494)

restriction enzyme: an enzyme that recognizes specific nucleotide sequences in DNA and breaks the DNA chain at those points; used in genetic engineering (309)

reticular activating system: RAS; a complex network of nerve fibers within the brainstem that functions in arousing the cerebrum (504)

retina: the photosensitive layer of the vertebrate eye that contains several layers of neurons and light receptors (rods and cones); receives the image formed by the lens and transmits it to the brain via the optic nerve (493)

retrovirus: a virus whose genetic material is RNA; enters host cells where the viral RNA is transcribed into DNA, which then is replicated by the host cell; associated with many human diseases, including cancer and AIDS (227)

reverse transcriptase: an enzyme that transcribes RNA into DNA; found in association with retroviruses (227)

reverse transcription: the process by which viral RNA (in retroviruses) is transcribed into DNA (227)

ribonucleic (ry boh noo KLEE ik) **acid:** RNA; a single-stranded nucleic acid similar to DNA but having the sugar ribose rather than deoxyribose, and uracil rather than thymine as one of the bases; the material coded by DNA to carry out specific genetic functions (38)

ribose: a 5-carbon sugar found in RNA molecules (38)

ribosomal RNA: rRNA; a class of RNA molecules found, together with characteristic proteins, in ribosomes (226)

ribosome: a cell organelle constructed in the nucleus, consisting of two subunits and functioning as the site of protein synthesis in the cytoplasm (137)

ribulose bisphosphate: See RuBP.

rigor: a state of rigidity in living tissues or organs that prevents response to stimuli (549)

RNA: See ribonucleic acid.

RNA polymerase: an enzyme that catalyzes the assembly of an RNA molecule (228)

RNA processing: the addition and chemical modification of certain nucleotides and the removal of some segments from all three types of RNA (in eukaryotes) (230)

rod: a light-sensitive nerve cell found in the vertebrate retina; sensitive to very dim light and responsible for "night vision" (493)

root cap: a layer of protective cells that covers the growing tip of a plant root (341)

root hair: a fine extension of an epidermal cell of a plant root; absorbs water and minerals (429)

root pressure: the upward push of water within the central core of vascular plants, caused by active pumping of minerals into the xylem by root cells (430)

rRNA: See ribosomal RNA.

rubisco (roo BIS koh): an enzyme that catalyzes the initial incorporation of carbon dioxide in the Calvin cycle; ribulose bisphosphate carboxylase (RY byoo lose BIS fos fayt kar BOX uh lays) (169)

RuBP: ribulose bisphosphate (RY byoo lose BIS fos fayt); a 5-carbon sugar that combines with carbon dioxide in the first stage of the Calvin cycle, called carbon dioxide fixation (168)

S phase: the synthesis phase of the cell cycle during which DNA is replicated (206)

salivary amylase: an enzyme in saliva that begins digestion of starch; converts starch to disaccharides (410)

sarcomere (SAR koh meer): the structural and functional contractile unit of a muscle cell (548)

saturated fat: a fat containing fatty acids in which carbon atoms are joined by single bonds; usually solid at room temperature, as in butter or lard (33)

saturated fatty acid: a fatty acid in which carbon atoms are joined by single bonds (32)

savanna: a tropical grassland biome with scattered individual trees and large herbivores; water is the major limiting factor (582)

Schwann cell: a cell that surrounds a fiber of a peripheral nerve and forms the myelin sheath (492)

scientific name: name of a specific organism consisting of the genus and species classification, according to binomial nomenclature (99)

scrotum (SCROH tum): a pouch of skin that encloses the testes (264)

seasonal isolation: the separation or division of a single breeding population caused by a seasonal barrier, such as different estrus cycles or mating times (372)

second filial generation: See F_2 generation.

second law of bioenergetics: states that natural processes tend to proceed toward increased entropy, or disorder (56)

second messenger: a chemical signal, such as cyclic AMP, that relays a hormonal message from the cell's surface to its interior (513)

secondary growth: the growth in girth or diameter of plant and root (341)

secondary immune response: occurs when an animal encounters the same antigen at a later time; more rapid, of greater magnitude, and of longer duration than the primary immune response (456)

secretin (see KREE tin): a hormone secreted by the small intestine that stimulates the release of pancreatic juice (412)

seed coat: the tough, protective outer covering of a seed (339)

selective gene loss hypothesis: in development, the hypothesis that proposes that the different types of cells in the body contain different sets of genes (324)

selectively permeable: a property of biological membranes that allows some substances to cross and prevents others from crossing (146)

semen (SEE men): the thick fluid in which sperm are transported in mammalian males (266)

seminal vesicle: a part of the male reproductive tract that stores sperm in invertebrates and produces semen in vertebrates (266)

seminiferous tubules: highly coiled tubules in the testes that produce sperm (264)

sensory neuron: a neuron that receives impulses from a sensory organ or receptor and transmits them toward the central nervous system (493)

sensory receptor: a specialized sensory structure or organ that receives stimuli (494)

sexual reproduction: reproduction involving the contribution of genetic material from two parents (101, 248)

sieve tube: a column of phloem cells in a plant (431)

signal sequence: the directions provided by the first few amino acids synthesized on the ribosomes for the transport of proteins to different parts of the cell (238)

skeletal muscle: muscle tissue found attached to skeletal parts and responsible for voluntary movement (545)

slightly movable joint: a type of joint in the vertebrate skeleton that allows a minute amount of movement, such as the disks between vertebrae (544)

smooth muscle: muscle tissue found in the walls of hollow internal organs (546)

somatic (soh MAT ik) **nervous system:** those nerves leading from the central nervous system to skeletal muscles (505)

somatostatin: a human growth hormone (521)

speciation: the origin of new species in evolution (370)

species (SPEE sheez): all individuals and populations of a particular type of organism that breed mostly with their kind (90)

sperm: male gametes, each haploid (n) in chromosome number (248)

sphincter (SFINK ter): a circular muscle that closes an opening of a tubular structure (410)

spiracle (SPY ra kuhl): an opening into a trachea in insects (474)

splicing: the process by which portions of the primary RNA transcript (introns) are cut out and the ends are rejoined (231)

spongy bone: cancellous bone; consists of plates separated by spaces (540)

spore: a one-celled reproductive body that is usually resistant to harsh environmental conditions and may remain dormant for long periods; asexual in some organisms and may initiate growth of a new organism under favorable conditions; sexual in other organisms and must unite with another before producing a new organism (253)

stamen (STAY men): the pollen-producing male reproductive organ of a flower; consists of an anther and filament (254)

starch: a plant polysaccharide composed of glucose (31)

stimulant: a drug that increases the activity of the central nervous system (497)

stimulus (STIM yoo lus): a change or signal in the internal or external environment that causes an adjustment or reaction by an organism (494)

stomate (STOH mayt): the opening between two guard cells in the epidermis of a plant leaf through which gases are exchanged with the air (160)

stratigraphy: the sequence of geologic strata, or layers, formed by materials dropped by water or wind; also, the study of this sequence (390)

stress: a condition produced by factors causing disruptive or potentially life-threatening changes in the body's internal environment (525)

stressors: factors capable of stimulating a stress response (525)

stroma (STROH muh): the pale, semiliquid substance in a chloroplast in which the grana and the enzymes of the Calvin cycle occur (161)

stromatolite (stroh MAT uh lyt): a rock made of banded domes of sediment in which are found evidence of prokaryotes dating back as far as 3.5 billion years (81)

substrate: a molecule on which enzymes act (36)

succession: the replacement of one community by another in a progression to a climax community (577)

suppressor T cell: a type of T cell that suppresses the response of both B and T cells, shutting down the immune response (453)

sympathetic nervous system: a subdivision of the autonomic nervous system of vertebrates that functions in an alarm response; increases heart rate and dilates blood vessels while putting the body's everyday functions, such as digestion, on hold; mobilizes the body for rapid response to stress, danger, or excitement (505)

synapse (SIH naps): an open junction between neurons, across which an impulse is transmitted by a chemical messenger, or neurotransmitter (496)

synaptic knob: one of many swollen bulbs at the end of an axon, in which neurotransmitters are stored and released (496)

syndrome: a group of symptoms that almost always occur together, reflecting the same or a related cause (287)

synthesis: the process of putting together or building up; applicable to ideas, chemical compounds, and so on (59)

system: a group of interacting, interrelated, or interdependent elements forming a complex whole (152)

systole (SIS toh lee): the stage of the cardiac cycle in which the heart muscle contracts and the chambers pump blood (436)

T cells: a class of lymphocytes that is produced in the bone marrow and matures in the thymus; involved in the cell-mediated response; examples include helper T cells, killer T cells, and suppressor T cells (453)

taiga (TY guh): the coniferous or boreal forest biome, characterized by considerable snow, harsh winters, short summers, and evergreen trees (586)

target organ: a specific organ on which a hormone acts (512)

taxonomy (tak SAHN uh mee): the study of species and their classification by genus, family, order, class, phylum or division, and kingdom (90)

telophase (TEL oh fayz): the final stage in mitosis; characterized by two new cell nuclei forming at opposite ends of the cell; frequently followed by cell division (216)

temperate forest: a biome located throughout the midlatitude regions where there is sufficient moisture to support the growth of large trees, mostly deciduous (585)

temperate grassland: a biome similar to savanna, characterized by low precipitation and lack of trees, except along stream courses, such as the prairies of North America (585)

tendon: a cordlike mass of white fibrous connective tissue that connects muscle to bone (544)

termination: stage of protein synthesis in which the completed polypeptide chain is released, and the two ribosomal subunits separate (234)

terminator region: the end of the DNA to be transcribed (228)

testes (TES teez; singular *testis*): the primary reproductive organs of a male; sperm-cell producing organs (257)

testosterone (tes TOS ter ohn): a male sex hormone secreted by the testes (266)

theory: in scientific usage, a suggested explanation or conjecture; in science, a well-tested hypothesis that organizes knowledge in a field, fits existing data, explains how events or processes are thought to occur, and successfully predicts future discoveries and events (7)

threshold: the strength of stimulus below which no nerve impulse will be initiated (495)

thrombin (THROM bin): a blood protein important in the clotting process   (442)

thylakoid (THY luh koid): a flattened sac in a chloroplast; arranged in stacks known as grana; contains the pigments and enzymes for the light reactions of photosynthesis   (161)

thymus gland: a two-lobed glandular organ located behind the breastbone and between the lungs; functions in the immune system   (518)

thyroid gland: an endocrine gland in the neck region of most vertebrates that controls the rate of cell metabolism in the body through one of its hormones, thyroxine   (517)

thyroid-releasing hormone: TRH; a hormone produced in the hypothalamus that acts on the pituitary causing it to secrete thyroid-stimulating hormone (TSH) into the bloodstream   (521)

thyroid-stimulating hormone: TSH; a hormone, secreted by the anterior pituitary that stimulates the thyroid to secrete hormones   (521)

thyroxine (thy ROK sin): a principal hormone of the thyroid that regulates the rate of cell metabolism   (521)

tight junction: a type of intercellular junction that prevents the leakage of material between animal cells   (151)

tissue: a group of cells with a common function and structure   (150)

tolerance: the ability to withstand or survive a particular environmental condition; in the immune system, the failure of an individual's T cells to react against self HLA   (461)

trachea (TRAY kee uh; plural *tracheae*): in insects, one of the tubes in the tracheal system used in obtaining oxygen from the air; in air-breathing vertebrates, the airway connecting the pharynx with the lungs   (474)

tracheid (TRAY kee ud): a water-conducting and supportive element of xylem composed of long, thin cells with tapered ends and hardened walls   (430)

trait: a characteristic of an organism, genetically determined or environmentally determined, or both   (278)

transcription: the enzyme-catalyzed assembly of an RNA molecule complementary to a strand of DNA; may be either mRNA, tRNA, or rRNA   (223)

transfer RNA: tRNA; a class of small RNA molecules with two functional sites—one for attachment of a specific amino acid, the other carrying the nucleotide triplet (anticodon) for that amino acid; each type of tRNA transfers a specific amino acid to a growing polypeptide chain   (226)

translation: the assembly of a protein on the ribosomes, using mRNA to direct the order of amino acids   (223)

translocation: in vascular plants, the transport of soluble food molecules from one plant organ to another by way of the phloem tissue; in genetics, the relocation of a chromosomal segment   (297)

transpiration (trans pih RAY shun): the loss of water to the atmosphere by a plant, through the stomates in its leaves   (160)

transport protein: a specific protein that plays either an active or passive role in the movement of substances across plasma membranes   (146)

transposable element: a "jumping gene"; mobile segment of DNA that serves as the agent of genetic change   (298)

TRH: See thyroid-releasing hormone.

triglyceride (try GLIS uh ryd): a simple fat formed of three fatty acids and one glycerol molecule   (32)

trinucleotide repeat: base sequence composed of three nucleotides that are repeated over and over again without interruption along a segment of chromosome   (303)

triplet: the three nucleotide pairs that comprise a codon   (225)

trisomy: the presence of three homologous chromosomes instead of a pair, usually caused by nondisjunction in the egg or sperm   (287)

tRNA: See transfer RNA.

tRNA charging: a two-step process in which an enzyme binds a specific amino acid with a molecule of ATP and then binds the appropriate tRNA to the amino acid, displacing AMP   (233)

trophic structure: the different feeding levels of an ecosystem that determine the path of energy flow and pattern of chemical cycling   (591)

tropical rain forest: the most complex of all communities, located near the equator where rainfall is abundant; harbors more species of plants and animals than any other biome in the world; light is the major limiting factor   (581)

tropism (TROH piz um): a change in the orientation of a plant, or part of a plant, in response to light, gravity, or other environmental factors   (351)

true-breeding: organisms that produce offspring identical to themselves, generation after generation   (278)

trypsin: an enzyme in pancreatic juice that breaks down protein molecules   (412)

trypsinogen (trip SIN uh jen): the inactive form of trypsin   (412)

TSH: See thyroid-stimulating hormone.

tubal ligation: in females, a form of contraception in which the oviducts are cut and tied   (266)

tundra: a biome at the northernmost limits of plant growth and at high altitudes, where plant forms are limited to low, shrubby, or matlike vegetation   (587)

ultrasound: high-frequency sound waves; a method used to determine some fetal abnormalities   (304)

unicellular: one-celled   (101)

unsaturated fatty acid: a fatty acid in which some carbon atoms are joined by double bonds; component of unsaturated fats, which are usually liquid at room temperatures, such as oil   (32)

urea: a nonprotein, nitrogenous substance produced as a result of protein metabolism   (481)

ureter (yer EE ter): a muscular tube that carries urine from the kidney to the urinary bladder (483)

urethra: the tube through which urine is carried from the bladder to the outside of the body in vertebrates (483)

uric acid: the insoluble nitrogenous waste excreted by land snails, insects, birds, and some reptiles (481)

urinary bladder: an organ that stores urine before it is discharged from the body through the urethra (483)

urinary system: an organ system that regulates levels of water and dissolved substances in the body (483)

urine: the form in which urea is excreted from the kidney in vertebrates (483)

uterus: a hollow muscular organ, located in the female pelvis, in which a fetus develops (260)

vaccine: a substance, often a suspension of a dead or weakened pathogen, that contains antigens and is used to stimulate the production of antibodies without causing disease (450)

vacuole (VAK yoo ohl): a membrane-enclosed structure in the cytoplasm of a cell; different types serve different functions (140)

vagina: a tubular organ that leads from the uterus to the opening of the female reproductive tract (260)

vane: the flattened weblike part of a feather, consisting of a series of barbs on either side of the rachis, or shaft (538)

variations: small differences among individuals within a population or species that provide the raw material for evolution (11)

vas deferens (vas DEF er enz): a tube that leads from the epididymis to the urethra of the male reproductive tract (264, 266)

vascular plant: a plant with specialized conducting tissue; all modern species except the mosses and their relatives (428)

vascular tissue: plant tissues specialized for the transport of food, water, and minerals; also, for support (428)

vasectomy: in males, a form of contraception in which the sperm ducts are cut and tied (266)

vegetative reproduction: asexual reproduction by plants that also may produce sexually; for example, potato plants from "eyes" and grass plants from runners (246)

vein (VAYN): a vessel that carries blood toward the heart (435)

ventricle (VEN trih kul): a chamber of the heart that pumps blood out of the heart (435)

vertebrate: a chordate animal with a backbone; mammals, birds, reptiles, amphibians, and various classes of fishes (105)

vesicle: a small, intracellular, membrane-enclosed sac in which various substances are transported or stored (140)

vessel: a type of water-conducting xylem cell (430)

villi (VIHL ee): fingerlike projections of the small intestine that increase surface area for absorption of digested food (412)

virus: lifelike particles that carry on activity outside a living cell, but reproduce only inside a living cell; composed of DNA and protein, or RNA and protein (3, 79)

vitamin: an organic substance other than a carbohydrate, lipid, or protein that is needed for normal metabolism but cannot be synthesized in adequate amounts by the body (419)

white blood cell: See leukocyte.

X chromosome: the chromosome in many animals that is associated with the female sex or, paired with a Y chromosome, with the male sex (275)

X inactivation: the random "turning off" of one X chromosome early in the development of a female, resulting in the expression of some X-linked genes from the mother and some X-linked genes from the father (288)

X-linked trait: a trait determined by a gene carried on the X chromosome (286)

xylem (ZY lem): the tube-shaped nonliving portion of the vascular system in plants that carries water and minerals from the roots to the rest of the plant (341)

Y chromosome: the chromosome in many animals that is associated with the male sex; usually shorter than the X chromosome and carrying no alleles for many of the genes on the X chromosome (275)

yolk sac: in fishes, sharks, reptiles, birds, and some mammals, a membranous sac attached to the embryo that provides early nourishment; also functions as a part of the circulatory system in human embryos prior to the initiation of circulation by the pumping of the heart (321)

zooplankton (ZOH oh PLANK tun): very small, feebly swimming aquatic organisms that are herbivorous, carnivorous, or both (589)

zygote: the diploid product of the union of haploid gametes in conception; a fertilized egg (315)

Index

Illustrations and tables are referenced by page numbers in italics.

E

cells, 642–643; selective permeability of, 146; structure of, 33, *33*, 142–143, *143*; transfer of materials across, 144–148, 640–642, 739; *See also* Plasma membrane.

Memory, 500–501

Memory cells, 454–456, *454*

Mendel, Gregor, 277–279, *278–279*, 366, *366*, 674

Mendelian inheritance, 277–282

Meninges, 501, *502*

Menstrual cycle, 259–264, *261*, 384

Merganser, *558*

Mergus merganser, 558

Meristem, 342; apical, 339, 341–342, *343*

Mescaline, 498, *760*

Mesoderm, 319–320, *319–320*

Mesophyll cells, 160, 175, *175*

Mesosome, 135

Messenger RNA (mRNA), 223–224; functions of, 226, *226*; mG cap of, 230–231, *230*, 235; poly-A tail of, *230*, 231; processing of, 230–231, *230*; splicing of, *230*, 231; synthesis of, 226, *226*, 660; translation of, 233–237, 661–663, *662–663*

Metabolic rate, 521–523

Metabolism, 59–60; cellular respiration and, 181–183, *182*; concept map for, *61*; energy transfer and, 59–63; hormonal control of, 521–523, *522*; pH and, 619–621, *621*

Metaphase, meiosis I, *249–250*, 250; meiosis II, *249*, 251; mitotic, 215, *215*

Metastasis, 207

Meteorite, 69; organic material in, 74–75, *75*, 79; role in mass extinctions, 376

Methane gas, 103

Methanogen, 82, 103

Methylene blue, 738

Microevolution, 369

Microfilament, 141, 532

Microfossil, 81–83, *81–82*, 176, 374

Micronutrient, 346, *745*

Microorganism, immune response to, 463–464

Microscope, 131, *131*, 746, 755; care of, 614–615; compound, 614–617, *614*; Hooke's, *133*; measurements under, 610, 616; observing cell structure, 639–640; preparing cells for study, 738–739; procedure for use of, 615–616; scanning tunneling, 42, *42*; using high power, 616

Microscope slide, 615–616, *615*

Microtome, 739

Microtubule, *140–141*, 141, 215, 217

Midbrain, 500, *500*

Migration, 367–368; of birds, 565, 761

Milk, production of, 523, *523*

Milk sugar, *See* Lactose.

Miller, Stanley, 73–74, *74*

Mimosa pudica, 351, *352*

Mineral, 419–423; deficiency symptoms, *422–423*; excess of, *422–423*; food sources of, *422–423*; functions of, *422–423*

Mineralocorticoid, 524, *524*

Miracle cure, 16

Miscarriage, 297

Misreading, 238

Mistletoe, 407

Mitchell, Peter, 740–741

Mitochondria, 83, 140, 185; ATP production in, 740–741; DNA of, 385, *385*; evolution of, 83–84, *84*; respiration and, 188–189; structure of, 188, *188*

Mitochondrial Eve, 385

Mitosis, 206, 214–217, *217*, 658, *659*; evolution of, 217, *217*

MN blood group, *368*

Molarity, 611

Mold, 106

Molecular clock hypothesis, 109, 385

Molecular hybridization, 326–328, *327*

Molecular model, 22

Molecule, 21–24

Mollusk, 473

Molybdenum, *423;* in plants, *745*

Monera, 101, *102, 104,* 135–136, *135*

Monkey, 382, 384, 560

Monocotyledon, 339, *340,* 632, *634*

Monohybrid cross, 279, *280*

Monosaccharide, 30–31, *32*

Monotreme, 259

Montagu, Lady Mary Wortley, 450

Moon, 69

Moose, 586

Morgan, Thomas Hunt, 281, 285–286, *286*

Morph, 90–91

Morphine, 496, *759*

Morphogenesis, 315–317, *316*

Morphologic family tree, 387, *388*

Moss, *104,* 105, 578, 586–587; hairy cap, *156*; life cycle of, 252–253, *253*; reproduction in, 668–670

Moth, Cecropia, 562–563, *563*; peppered, *91,* 363–364, *363*; pronuba, 742, *742*

Motor neuron, 492–493, *492*, 505, 507, 549, *549*

Motor unit, 549, *549*

Mountain lion, *10,* 586

Mt. St. Helens, 580, *580*

Mouse, coat color in, 364, *364*; development in, *318,* 319; Harvard, 311, *311*; piñon, 98, 99; white-footed, 98, 99

Mouth, 407, *408,* 409–411

Movement, 48; amoeboid, 531–532, *532*, 721; ciliary, 532, *532*; observation of, 719–722; of *Paramecium,* 720; of plants, 351–352, *351–352*; in single cells, 531–533

Movement system, of invertebrates, 533–534; of vertebrates, 534–536, *535*

M phase, 206, 214–216, *214–215*

mRNA, *See* Messenger RNA.

Mucous membrane, 448

Mucus, 411, 536, *536*

Mule, 93–94, *94*

Root cap, 341, 352, *353*
Root pressure, 430
Rose, 172, *635*
Rosella, eastern, *536*
Round dance, 570, *570*
Rous, Peyton, 207
Rous sarcoma virus, 207
Royal jelly, 568
rRNA, *See* Ribosomal RNA.
Rubisco, *168*, 169, 173–176
Rumen, 407
Runner (plant), 246
Rush, 578
Rust (plant fungus), *106*
Rye, 255

S

Saber-toothed cat, 7
Saccharomyces, *106*
Safety, of genetic engineering, 310–311; laboratory, 602–608
Safety goggles, *604*
Salamander, 258, 541, 589
Saliva, 409, 411, 448, 700
Salivary gland, 511, *512*
Salmon, 257
Salt balance, 480, *480*, 482, *483*
Saltbush, 370, *370*, 576–577, *576*
Salt gland, 482, *483*
Salt-tolerant plant, 576, *576*
Saltwater organism, *See* Marine organism.
Sandburg, Carl, 14
Sand lily, *104*
Sap, 343
Sarcoma, Kaposi's, 465
Sarcomere, 548–549
Saturated fatty acid, 32–33
Savanna, 582, *583*
Scale, of reptile, 536, *536*
Scanning electron microscope, *131*, 220
Scanning tunneling microscope,

42, *42*
Schleiden, M.J., 133
Schopf, J.B., 81
Schwann, Theodor, 133
Schwann cells, 492, *492*
Science, definition of, 13
Scientific method, 6
Scientific name, 99–100, *99*
Scott, Joan A., 301, *301*
Scrotum, 264
Scurvy, *420*
Sea anemone, 405
Seasonal isolation, 372
Sea star, *105*; development in, 318, *319*
Sea turtle, 482, *483*
Seawater, pH of, 29, *29*
Sebastes pinnager, *105*
Secondary sexual characteristics, 267, *267*
Second filial generation, 279–280, *280*, 282
Second messenger, 513, *513*
Secretin, 412, *412*, 512
Secretion, by nephron, 484–485, *485*, 712–713, *712*; of proteins, 238–239, *239*
Sedge, 587, *634*
Seed, 56–57, *56*, 255, *255–256*, 338–339, *338*, 683–686; dispersal of, 255–256; germination of, 339–341, *339–340*, 626–628, *627*, 650–653, *651–653*, 684–685, *685*; structure of, 683; tetrazolium test, 626–628, *627*; viability of, 341, 626–628
Seed coat, 339, *339*, 683
Seedling, *336*, 683–684; orientation of, 685–686; phenotype of, 673, *673*
Segmentation, body, 637
Segregation, principle of, 279–282, *280*
Selective breeding, 307
Selective gene loss hypothesis, 324–325, *324*
Self-fertilization, 278, *278*
Self-replication, 78, 85
Self-reproduction, 76

Semen, 266
Semiconservative replication, 210
Seminal vesicle, 266
Seminiferous tubule, 264–266
Sensitive plant, 351, *352*
Sensory neuron, 493–494, 505, 507
Sensory receptor, 494, *494*, 713–715; distance between, 714–715; in skin, 713–714, *714*
Sepal, 669
Serotonin, 498
Serum albumin, *386*
Sex attractant, 570
Sex chromosome, 247, 275–276, *276*, 287
Sex determination, 275–276, *276*
Sex hormone, 33, *33*
Sexual intercourse, 260
Sexually transmitted disease, 266
Sexual reproduction, 101, 252–259, *667*; in humans, 259–267; in plants, 253–256, *254*; variation and, 295
Shark, 534
Sharp object, *604*
Sheath, leaf, 632, *633*
Sheep, bighorn, 762, *762*; variation in, *91*
Shivering, 758
Shoot, embryonic, 338–339, *339*; orientation of, 685, *685*
Shoulder, *544*, 545
Sickle cell disease, 302, 307, 677–679, 690–692, *690–691*
Sickle cell trait, 302, 690
Sidewinder, *530*
Sieve tube, 431
Signal sequence, 238, *239*
Silicon, 534
Silkworm, 562–563, *563*, 570
Silver nitrate, 621–623, *622*
Single-gene defect, 299
SI units, 609–611
Size, variation among organisms, 686–688, *687*

ation stage of, 234–235, *234*, 238; termination stage of, 234, 236, *236*

Translocation, chromosomal, 297, *297*

Transmission electron micro-scope, *131*

Transpiration, 160, 430, 596

Transport, 50, 144–148

Transport system, 427, 702–705; in animals, 432–440; in humans, 703–704; in *Hydra*, 432, *433–434*; in multicellular organisms, 152–153, *152*; in plants, 428–432, *431*, 703–704; in unicellular organisms, 432, *433–434*

Transposable element, 298, *298*

Tree ring, 341, *341*

TRH, *See* Thyrotropin-releasing hormone.

Trial-and-error learning, 560–561, 723–724, *723–724*

Trichonympha, *141*, *217*

Trigger protein, 206

Triglyceride, 32, 416–418

Trinucleotide repeat, 303, *303*

Triple bond, 28

Triploid nucleus, 338–339, *338*

Trisomy, 287, 297

Trisomy 21, 287–288, *288*, 297

Triticale, 370, *370*

tRNA, *See* Transfer RNA.

Trophic structure, 591

Tropical rain forest, *16*, 581–582, *582*, 595

Tropism, 351–352, *351–352*, 684–686, *685*

Trout, 577, 588

True-breeding trait, 279–280

Trypanosome, 451, *451*

Trypsin, 239, 412

Trypsinogen, 412

TSH, *See* Thyroid-stimulating hormone.

Tubal ligation, 266

Tube worm, 763, *763*

Tubifera ferruginosa, *107*

Tumor infiltrating lymphocytes, 305

Tuna, 565, 577

Tundra, *198*, 587, *587*; alpine, 587; arctic, 587, *588*

Turkey, 247

Turner syndrome, 287

Turtle, gopher, *96*

Twins, identical, 289

Twin studies, 289, 299

Tyrosine, 302

U

Ulcer, 411, 527

Ultrasound imaging, prenatal, 304

Ultraviolet radiation, 159, 296; on primitive Earth, 71–72

Umbel, 632, *633*

Umbilical artery, 321

Umbilical vein, 321

Unicellular organism, 130, *130*, 135–136, 148; cell division in, 203; cell structure in, 639–640; digestion in, 405, *405*; movement in, 531–533; transport system in, 432, *433–434*

Universe, origin of, 67–71

Unsaturated fatty acid, 32–33, 416

Unwanted material, 596–597, *597*

Uracil, 43, *43*

Uranium-to-lead dating, 737

Urea, 196, 481, *481*

Uredinales, *106*

Ureter, 483–484

Urethra, 483

Urey, Harold, 73–74, *74*

Uric acid, 481–482, *481*, 483

Urinary bladder, 483

Urinary system, of humans, 483–487, *484*; structure of, 483–484, *484*

Urine, 483, 485, *485*, 711–712; concentration of, 485; pH of, *29*

Ursus arctos horribilis, *92*

Ursus maritimus, *92*

Uterus, 260, 262; contraction of, 323, *323*

V

Vaccine, 3, 450–451, *450*, 456

Vaccinia **virus,** 3

Vacuole, 140; contractile, 481–482, *482*; food, 406, *406*, 432

Vagina, 260, 323, *323*

Valve, in heart, 436, 438, *438*; in veins, 440, 754–755, *754*

Variation, 11–12, *11*, 89–100, 252, 271, 294; advantageous and disadvantageous, 11–12; continuous, 284, *284*; discontinuous, 284, *284*; genetic, 294–298; geographic, 90–91, *91*; in hominids, 391–392; in humans, 396–397, *397*; individual, 90–91, *91*; mutation and, 295–298; sex differences in primates, 391–392, *391*; sexual reproduction and, 294–295; in size of organisms, 686–688, *687*; sources for, 365

Vascular bundle, 703–704

Vascular tissue, of plant, 428

Vas deferens, 266

Vasectomy, 266

Vector, for gene therapy, 305; in genetic engineering, 309

Vegetative reproduction, 246

Vein, 435, *435*, 439, 754–755, *754*; of leaf, 159–160, *426*, 703; movement of blood through, 440, *440*

Vent ecosystem, 762–763, *763*

Ventricle (heart), 435

Venus's flytrap, 405, *405*

Vertebrate, 105; brain of, 500, *501*; circulatory system of, 434–436, *434–435*; classification chart for, *638*; forelimbs of, 95, *95*; movement system of, 534–536, *535*; nervous system of, *499–500*, 500

Vesicle, 140

Vessel, xylem, 430, *430*

Viking **lander,** 49, *49*

ILLUSTRATION ACKNOWLEDGMENTS

UNIT 1 INTRODUCTION OCHRE STARS ON TIDAL ROCKS, CANNON BEACH, OREGON/Gary Brassch

Chapter 1: Introduction and Chapter Highlights David M. Dennis/TOM STACK & ASSOC; **1.1** (*up*) David C. London/TOM STACK & ASSOC; **1.1** (*left*) Jon Feingersh/TOM STACK & ASSOC; **1.1** (*right*) C. Allan Morgan; **1.3** Nathaniel S. Butler/NBA Photos; **1.4** (*a*) BSCS by Carlye Calvin; **1.4** (*b*) Neg./Trans. no. 34711 Courtesy Department of Library Services American Museum of Natural History; **1.4** (*c*) Carl Lilliequist; **1.5** (*a*) BSCS by Doug Sokell; **1.5** (*b*) Barbara Fleischaker; **1.6** (*left*) The Natural History Museum; **1.6** (*right*) BSCS Art; **1.7** (*left*) David M. Dennis/TOM STACK & ASSOC; **1.7** (*right*) ©John D. Cunningham/VISUALS UNLIMITED; **1.8** (*left*) Brian Parker/TOM STACK & ASSOC; **1.8** (*right*) Rod Allin/TOM STACK & ASSOC; **1.9** C. Allan Morgan; **1.10** G. C. Kelley/TOM STACK & ASSOC; **1.11** (*a*) U. S. Dept. of Agriculture; **1.11** (*b*) U. S. Dept. of Agriculture; **1.12** The Bettman Archive; **1.13** Mark Newman/TOM STACK & ASSOC; **A** BSCS by Jacqueline Ott-Rogers

Chapter 2: Introduction and Chapter Highlights Jeff Foott; **2.26** (*a,b*) UPI/Bettman Newsphotos; **2.26** (*c*) *The Double Helix*, by James D. Watson, Atheneum, NY 1968; **2.26** (*d*) UPI/Bettman Newsphotos; **C** M. Amrein *et al., Science*, vol. 240, April 22, 1988, © 1988 by the American Association for the Advancement of Science

Chapter 3: Introduction and Chapter Highlights Ron Sanford; **3.1** (*a*) BSCS by Doug Sokell; **3.1**(*b*) Carolyn Noble; **3.6** Richard P. Smith/TOM STACK & ASSOC; **3.8** *From Living in the Environment, Third Edition,* by G. Tyler Miller, Jr. ©1982 by Wadsworth, Inc. Used by permission.; **3.9** (a-c) BSCS by Doug Sokell; **A** NASA

Chapter 4: Introduction and Chapter Highlights Greg Vaughn/TOM STACK & ASSOC; **4.1** BSCS by Doug Sokell; **4.2** National Optical Astronomy Observatories; **4.3** National Optical Astronomy Observatories; **4.6** ©Greg Vaughn; **4.10** BSCS by Doug Sokell; **4.11** Stock Imagery, Inc.; **4.14** The University of Wyoming Research Corporation, a.k.a. Western Research Institute; **4.15** (*a*) M. Wurtz; **4.16** University of California at Berkeley, Virus Laboratory; **4.17** BPS/S.M. Awramik, University of California/TOM STACK & ASSOC; **4.18** (*a,b*) S.M. Awramik, University of California; **4.19** J. G. Zeikus; **4.20** Dr. Gonzalo Vidal, Lund University; **4.21** (*left*) Paulette Brunner/TOM STACK & ASSOC; (*right*) BPS/S.C. Holt, University of Texas Health Science Center, San Antonio/TOM STACK & ASSOC; **A** @ K. G. Murti/VISUALS UNLIMITED; **Ch 4 Biological Challenge text:** An RNA World Adapted from Gerald F. Joyce, "The RNA World: Life Before DNA and Protein," in *Extraterrestrials: Where Are They?* (M. Hart, B. Zuckerman, eds.) "Reprinted with the permission of Cambridge University Press

Chapter 5: Introduction and Chapter Highlights Nancy Sefton **5.2** (*a*) BSCS by Carlye Calvin; **5.2** (*b*) BSCS by Carlye Calvin; **5.2** (*c*) BSCS by Carlye Calvin; **5.2** (*d*) BSCS by Carlye Calvin; **5.3** (*a*) BSCS by Carlye Calvin; **5.3** (*b*) BSCS by Carlye Calvin; **5.4** (*a*) BSCS by Nathan W. Cohen; **5.4** (*b*) Larry Brock/TOM STACK ASSOC; **5.5** (*a*) Thomas Kitchin/TOM STACK & ASSOC; **5.5** (*b*) W. Perry Conway/TOM STACK & ASSOC; **5.6** (*a,b*) BSCS by Doug Sokell; **5.11** (*a, b*) John & Gloria Tveten; **5.12** (*a*) BSCS by Doug Sokell; **5.12** (*b*) Feldman Corn North Carolina Forest Service; **5.15** (*a*) Professor K. O. Stetter; **5.15** (*b*) Ed Reschke; **5.15** (*c*) J. G. Zeikus; **5.16** (*a*) BSCS by Carlye Calvin; **5.16** (*b-d*) BSCS by Doug Sokell; **5.17** (*a*) BSCS by Bert Kempers; (**5.17** *b*) Dr. Werner W. Schulz **5.17** (*c*) Gary Milburn/TOM STACK & ASSOC; **5.17** (*d*) D. C. Gordon; **5.18** (*a*) BSCS by Doug Sokell; **5.18** (*b*) Nathan W. Cohen; **5.18** (*c*) BSCS by Richard Tolman; **5.19** (*a*) BSCS by Doug Sokell; **5.19** (*b*) ©T. E. Adams/VISUALS UNLIMITED; **5.19** (*c*) Robert C. Simpson/TOM STACK & ASSOC; **A** (*a*) Kaylene Silvester, Walnut Creek, CA; **B** ©David M. Phillips/VISUALS UNLIMITED; **C** BSCS by Doug Sokell; **D** BSCS by Doug Sokell; **E** Robert C. Simpson/TOM STACK & ASSOC

UNIT 2 INTRODUCTION ©David M. Phillips/VISUALS UNLIMITED

Chapter 6: Introduction and Chapter Highlights @ M. Abbey/VISUALS UNLIMITED; **6.1** (*a*) Ed Reschke; **6.1** (*b*) BIODISC, INC.; **6.1** (*c*) ©Dwight R. Kuhn; **6.1** (*d*) Tom Stack/TOM STACK & ASSOC; **6.2** (*a*) BSCS by Doug Sokell; **6.2** (*b*) BSCS; **6.4** Tony Brain/SPL/Photo Researchers; **6.7** BPS/J. Robert Waaland, Department of Botany, University of Washington, Seattle/TOM STACK & ASSOC; **6.8** BPS/Barry King, University of California, Davis/TOM STACK & ASSOC; **6.9** BPS/W. Rosenberg, Iona College/TOM STACK & ASSOC; **6.11** (*a*) ©David M. Phillips/VISUALS UNLIMITED; **6.11** (*b*) ©K.G. Murti/VISUALS UNLIMITED; **6.12** ©David M. Phillips/VISUALS UNLIMITED **6.13** (*a*) Ron Hathaway; **6.13** (*b*) BPS/T.J. Beveridge, Department of Microbiology, University of Guelph, Guelph, Ontario/TOM STACK & ASSOC; **6.14** ©Harold H. Edwards/VISUALS UNLIMITED; **6.16** (*a,b,c*) BSCS by Doug Sokell; **6.22** (*c*) ©Dwight R. Kuhn; **6.23** (*a*) ©Dwight R. Kuhn; **6.24** (*a,b*) Ed Reschke; **A** Trustees of the Science Museum (London); **C** (*d*) BPS/E.H. Newcomb and W.P. Wergin, University of Wisconsin-Madison/TOM STACK & ASSOC; **C** (*e*) BPS/W.L. Dentler, Center for Biomedical Research, University of Kansas, Lawrence/TOM STACK & ASSOC

Chapter 7: Introduction and Chapter Highlights ©Gary Braasch; **7.3** (*a,b*) J.H. Troughton and K.A. Card, Physics and Engineering Laboratory, Department of Scientific and Industrial Research, Lower Hutt, New Zealand; **7.4** Dr. Lewis K. Shumway, College of Eastern Utah; **7.7** BSCS by Carlye Calvin; **7.21** BSCS by Doug Sokell

Chapter 8: Introduction and Chapter Highlights ©Joe McDonald/VISUALS UNLIMITED; **8.9** (*a*) K. R. Porter; **8.14** (*a*) John Shaw/TOM STACK & ASSOC; **8.14** (*b*) Robert C. Simpson/TOM STACK & ASSOC; **B** Swimmer BSCS by Carlye Calvin

Chapter 9: Introduction and Chapter Highlights John D. Cunningham/VISUALS UNLIMITED; **9.9** (*a*) Electron Micrograph by G. F. Bahr; **9.10** (*a-i*) Dr. Andrew S. Bajer, Department of Biology, University of Oregon, Eugene; **9.12** ©David M. Phillips/VISUALS UNLIMITED; **9.13** (*a*) Mark S. Ladinsky and J. Richard McIntosh, University of Colorado, Boulder; **B** David Chase; **C** Jerry Guyden and G. Steven Martin; **D** Jerry Guyden and G. Steven Martin; **E** (*left*) Electron Micrograph by G. F. Bahr; (*right*) BPS/A.L. Olins, University of Tennessee/TOM STACK & ASSOC

UNIT THREE INTRODUCTION BSCS by Carlye Calvin

Chapter 10: Introduction and Chapter Highlights ©K.G. Murti/VISUALS UNLIMITED; **10.2** (*a,b*) BSCS by Jacqueline Ott-Rogers

Chapter 11: Introduction and Chapter Highlights ©Gary Braasch; **11.1** (*a,b*) Ed Reschke; **11.2** Dr. Werner W. Schulz; **11.3** Bob McKeever/TOM STACK & ASSOC; **11.11** (*a*) BSCS by Doug Sokell; **11.12** (*a*) Doug Sokell/TOM STACK & ASSOC; **11.12**(*b,c*) Doug Sokell; **11.13** Ed Reschke; **11.15** David M. Phillips/VISUALS UNLIMITED; **11.19** (*c*) Ed Reschke; **B** Courtesy of Jonathan and Cathy Van Blerkon; **C** BSCS by Carlye Calvin

Chapter 12: Introduction and Chapter Highlights @D. Cavgnaro/VISUALS UNLIMITED; **12.1** ©K. Murakami/TOM STACK & ASSOC; **12.2** (*left*) Stanley N. Cohen, Stanford University; **12.2** (*right*) David C. Peakman, Reproductive Genetics Center, Denver, CO; **12.3** Dr. Ram S. Verna; **12.4** David C. Peakman, Reproductive Genetics Center, Denver, CO; **12.6** BSCS by Doug Sokell; **12.7** M. Hofer; **12.16** BPS/P.J. Bryant, University of California, Irvine/TOM STACK & ASSOC; **12.19** (*a*) Margery W. Shaw, M.D., University of Texas Health Science Center at Houston; **12.19** (*b*) March of Dimes Birth Defects Foundation; **12.20** ©CHIMA/VISUALS UNLIMITED; **12.21** Carolyn Trunca, Ph.D.; **12.22** BSCS by Doug Sokell

Chapter 13: Introduction and Chapter Highlights K.G. Murti/VISUALS UNLIMITED; **13.1** Dwain Patton, Stock Imagery, Inc.; **13.4** BSCS by Doug Sokell; **13.6** Cystic Fibrosis Foundation; **13.8** Ed Reschke; **13.10** Penrose Hospital, Colorado Springs, CO; **13.14** AFP PHOTO/Vin Catania; **A** BSCS by Doug Sokell; **C** Baylor College of Medicine/Peter Arnold, Inc.

Chapter 14: Introduction and Chapter Highlights ©Dwight R. Kuhn; **14.2** (*a*) ©John D. Cunningham/VISUALS UNLIMITED; (*b*) ©John D.Cunningham/VISUALS UNLIMITED; (*c*) ©Stanley Flegler/VISUALS UNLIMITED; **14.3** From Cleveland P. Hickman, Jr. and Larry S. Roberts, *Biology of Animals*, 6th edition, Copyright © 1994 Wm. C. Brown

Communications, Inc. Dubuque, Iowa. All Rights Reserved. Reprinted by permission; **14.6** Carnegie Institution of Washington, Department of Embryology, Davis Division; **14.8** (*a*) Carnegie Institute of Washington, Department of Embryology, Davis Division; **14.8** (*b*) Lennart Nilsson, *A Child Is Born*, Dell Publishing Co., Inc.; **14.8** (*c-e*) *From Conception to Birth*, by Robert Rugh, et al., Harper and Row, Inc.; **14.8** (*f*) Lennart Nilsson, *A Child Is Born*, Dell Publishing Co., Inc.; **14.9** Reprinted from the *Birth Atlas*, Maternity Center Association, New York, NY; **14.11** Adapted from *Cloning: Nuclear Transplation in Amphibia,* by R.G. McKinnel. Copyright 1978 by the University of Minnesota. Published by the University of Minnesota Press; **14.12** Adapted from *Developmental Biology*, Third Edition, 1991, by Scott F. Gilbert with permission of Sinauer Associates, Inc.; **14.13** From: MOL-ECULAR CELL BIOLOGY by Darnell, Lodish and Baltimore. Copyright (*c*) 1990 by Scientific American Books. Reprinted with permission of W.H. Freeman and Company; **14.15** Adapted from *Developmental Biology*, Third Edition, 1991, by Scott F. Gilbert with permission of Sinauer Associates, Inc.; **14.18** Adapted from *Developmental Biology*, Third Edition, 1991, by Scott F. Gilbert with permission of Sinauer Associates, Inc.

Chapter 15: Introduction and Chapter Highlights ©Dwight R. Kuhn; **15.1** Ripon Microslides, Inc.; **15.2** @David Newman/VISUALS UNLIMITED; **15.5** Biodisc, Inc.; **15.6** (*left*) FVN Corporation; **15.6** (*right*) BSCS by Doug Sokell; **15.9** BSCS by Doug Sokell; **15.10** @David Newman/VISUALS UNLIMITED; **15.11** (*left*) Don Luvisi, University of California Cooperative Extension; **15.11** (*right*) B.O. Phinney; **15.12** Ed Reschke; **15.14** (*a,b*) BSCS by Carlye Calvin; **15.15** @ David Newman/VISUALS UNLIMITED; **15.16** (*a,b*) Randy Moore; **A** Courtesy of Roland R. Dute, Auburn University, and Ann E. Rushing, Baylor University; **B** BSCS by Doug Sokell; **D** Dean Engler, Ph.D.

UNIT FOUR INTRODUCTION John Cancalosi/TOM STACK & ASSOC

Chapter 16: Introduction and Chapter Highlights Joe McDonald/TOM STACK & ASSOC; **16.4** Photograph by C.P. Hickman, Jr.; **16.6** (*a,b*) J.A. Bishop, University of Liverpool; **16.11** Mosby Year Book, Inc.; **16.13** Howard C. Stutz, Brigham Young University; **16.15** (*a*) Jeff Foott/TOM STACK & ASSOC; **16.15** (*b*) W. Perry Conway/TOM STACK & ASSOC; **16.16** (*a*) Robert C. Simpson/TOM STACK & ASSOC; **16.16** (*b*) ©Stephen J. Lang/VISUALS UNLIMITED; **16.17** John A. Moore; **A** Lawrence Berkeley Laboratory

Chapter 17: Introduction and Chapter Highlights ©Doug Sokell/VISUALS UNLIMITED **17.1** BSCS by Doug Sokell; **17.2** Geza Teleki; **17.5** Warren and Genny Garst/TOM STACK & ASSOCIATES; **17.8** BSCS by Doug Sokell; **17.9** BSCS by Doug Sokell; **17.10** BSCS by Carlye Calvin; **17.11** (*a, b*) BSCS by Doug Sokell; **17.12** Institute of Human Origins; **17.13** (*a, b*) BSCS by Doug Sokell; **17.14** (*a, b*) BSCS by Doug Sokell; **17.15** BSCS by Doug Sokell; **17.16** by Doug Sokell; **17.17** BSCS by Doug Sokell; **A** David R. Wolstenholme, Katsuro Koike, and Patricia Cochran-Fouts. (Cold Springs Harbor Symposium on Quantitative Biology Vol. 38: 267-280, (1974)

UNIT FIVE INTRODUCTION Ed Reschke

Chapter 18: Introduction and Chapter Highlights SPL/Photo Researchers **18.2** Ron Hathaway; **18.3** ©Kerry T. Givens/TOM STACK & ASSOC; **18.5** ©M. Schliwa/VISUALS UNLIMITED; **18.6** (*a,b,c*) ©M. Abbey/VISUALS UNLIMITED; **18.11** (*middle*) Carl Struwe, Monkmeyer Press Photo; **18.12** (*a,b*) BSCS by Doug Sokell; **18.14** BSCS by Doug Sokell; **18.15** BSCS by Doug Sokell; **C** Ripon Microslides, Inc.

Chapter 19: Introduction and Chapter Highlights John Shaw/TOM STACK & ASSOC; **19.12** C. Yokochi and J.W. Rohen, Photographic Anatomy of the Human Body, 2nd ed., 1978; **19.15** Ed Reschke; **19.16** (*b*) ©David M. Phillips/VISUALS UNLIMITED; **A** ©Stanley L. Flegler/VISUALS UNLIMITED **B** Courtesy Spectranetics Corporation

Chapter 20: Introduction and Chapter Highlights ©Hans Gelderblom/VISUALS UNLIMITED; **20.1** Drs. Jan M. Orenstein and Emma Shelton; **20.2** BBC-Hulton Picture Library/The Bettman Archive; **20.16** (*a*) John Cancalosi/TOM STACK & ASSOC; **20.16** (*b*) © Jim W. Grace/Photo Researchers; **20.17** (*a,c*) Courtesy Dr. Ann M. Dvorak; **A** Ron Hathaway; **B** Allan Green/Photo Researchers

Chapter 21: Introduction and Chapter Highlights ©T.E. Adams/VISUALS UNLIMITED; **21.7** ©David M. Phillips/VISUALS UNLIMITED; **21.16** BPS/Dr. John R. Kennedy, Department of Zoology, University of Tennessee, Knoxville/TOM STACK & ASSOC; **B** BSCS by Doug Sokell

Chapter 22: Introduction and Chapter Highlights C. Allan Morgan; **22.2** ©C.S. Raines/VISUALS UNLIMITED; **22.4** ©S. Elems/VISUALS UNLIMITED; **22.8** E.R. Lewis, T.E. Everhart, and Y.Y. Zeevi; **22.9** (*a,b*) Peter N. Witt, M.D., Raleigh, N.C.

Chapter 23: Introduction and Chapter Highlights Secchi-Lecaque/Roosel-Oclar/CNRI/SPL/Photo Researchers; **23.6** Ed Reschke; **23.11** Lester V. Bergman, NY; **A** BSCS by Carlye Calvin

Chapter 24: Introduction and Chapter Highlights Jeff Foott; **24.1** Brian Parker/TOM STACK & ASSOC; **24.2** ©M. Abbey/VISUALS UNLIMITED; **24.3** ©David M.Phillips/VISUALS UNLIMITED; **24.4** BSCS by Doug Sokell; **24.5** Dwight R. Kuhn; **24.6** ©Stanley Flegler/VISUALS UNLIMITED; **24.7** ©John Serrao/VISUALS UNLIMITED; **24.9** Jack D. Swenson/TOM STACK & ASSOC; **24.10** (*a*) Brian Parker/TOM STACK & ASSOC; **24.10** (*b*) Gary Milburn/TOM STACK & ASSOC; **24.10** (*c*) Dwight R. Kuhn; **24.14** Lester V. Bergman, NY; **24.18** ©John D. Cunningham/VISUALS UNLIMITED; **24.20** Ed Reschke; **24.22** Dr. H.E. Huxley; **24.24** ©John D. Cunningham/VISUALS UNLIMITED; **B** Ed Reschke

UNIT SIX INTRODUCTION Rich Buzzelli

Chapter 25: Introduction and Chapter Highlights ©Tom J. Ulrich/VISUALS UNLIMITED; **25.2** William Vandivert; **25.3** (*a,b,c*) Lee Boltin; **25.4** ©Tom J. Ulrich/VISUALS UNLIMITED; **25.7** Three Lions; **25.12** BSCS; **25.13** ©Dwight R. Kuhn; **25.14** Nancy Adams; **25.15** © William J. Weber/VISUALS UNLIMITED; **25.18** H.S. Terrace/Anthro-Photo; **B** R. Blakemore

Chapter 26: Introduction and Chapter Highlights Rich Buzzelli **26.1** BSCS by Doug Sokell; **26.2** Doug Sokell; **26.5** Gary Braasch; **26.7** (*left*) Brian Parker/TOM STACK & ASSOC; **26.8** ©G. Prance/VISUALS UNLIMITED; **26.9** ©David L.Pearson/VISUALS UNLIMITED; **26.10** (*a*) BSCS by Carlye Calvin; **26.10** (*b*) Doug Sokell; **26.11** Doug Sokell; **26.12** Jeff Foott/TOM STACK & ASSOC; **26.13** ©Frank T. Awbery/VISUALS UNLIMITED; **26.14** (*a*) Kenneth A. Pals; **26.14** (*b*) Brian Parker/TOM STACK & ASSOC; **26.14** (*c*) BSCS; **26.15** (*a*) ©Steve Maslowski/VISUALS UNLIMITED; **26.15** (*b*) Thomas Kitchin/TOM STACK & ASSOC; **26.16** BSCS by Doug Sokell; **26.17** Doug Sokell; **26.19** (*a*) Thomas Kitchin/TOM STACK & ASSOC; **26.19** (*b*) Joe McDonald/TOM STACK & ASSOC; **26.20** BSCS by Carlye Calvin; **26.21** Paul McIver; **26.23** (*a*) Brian Parker/TOM STACK & ASSOC; **26.23** (*b*) Nancy Sefton; **26.23** (*c*) J. Frederick Grassle, Woods Hole Oceanographic Institution; **26.28** ©John D. Cunningham/VISUALS UNLIMITED; **A** J. Troughton and L.A. Donaldson, Physics and Engineering Laboratory, DSIR, New Zealand; **B** Jeff Foott/TOM STACK & ASSOC

Investigations: Introduction BSCS by Doug Sokell; **A,B** Courtesy of Ward's Natural Science Establishment; **2A.1, 2C.1, 3A.1, 7C.1, 7C.2, 8B.1, 9B.1, 10B.2, 10B.3, 10B.4, 11B.1, 17C.1** (*c-e*) **19B.1, 21A.1, 22A.1, 26B.2** BSCS by Doug Sokell; **14A.1** Courtesy Ward's Natural Science; **17B.2** (*a-e*) James A. Tuck Memorial University of Newfoundland; **17C.1** (*d-e*) BSCS

Appendices: Introduction BSCS by Doug Sokell; **11A.1** (*left*), BSCS by Carlye Calvin; **11A.1** (*right*) C. Allan Morgan; **16A.1** Parke-Davis, Division of Warner-Lambert Company, Morris Plains, NJ; **17B.1** Courtesy, The Field Museum, Neg #66830, Chicago; **19A.2** Linda Hall Library; **25B.1** W. Perry Conway/TOM STACK & ASSOC; **26A.1** J. Frederick Grassle, Woods Hole Oceanographic Institution